CLYMER®

BMW

R850, R1100, R1150 AND R1200C • 1993-2004

The world's finest publisher of mechanical how-to manuals

PRIMEDIA
Business Magazines & Media

P.O. Box 12901, Overland Park, Kansas 66282-2901

FIRST EDITION
First Printing July, 2004

Printed in U.S.A.

CLYMER and colophon are registered trademarks of PRIMEDIA Business Magazines & Media Inc.

ISBN: 0-89287-899-1

Library of Congress: 2004107045

AUTHOR: Ed Scott.

TECHNICAL PHOTOGRAPHY: Ed Scott with assistance from Curt Jordan of Jordan Engineering, Oceanside, CA. Special thanks to Brattin Motors, San Diego, CA for their assistance.

TECHNICAL ILLUSTRATIONS: Errol McCarthy.

WIRING DIAGRAMS: Bob Meyer and Lee Buell.

EDITOR: James Grooms. Special thanks to Gary Smith at BMWON (www.bmwmoa.org).

PRODUCTION: Greg Araujo.

TOOLS AND EQUIPMENT: K&L Supply Co. at www.klsupply.com.

COVER: Mark Clifford Photography at www.markclifford.com.

General Information 1

Troubleshooting 2

Lubrication, Maintenance and Tune-Up 3

Engine Top End 4

Engine Lower End 5

Clutch 6

Five Speed Transmission and Gearshift Mechanisms 7

Six Speed Transmission and Gearshift Mechanisms 8

Fuel, Emission Control and Exhaust Systems 9

Electrical System 10

Wheels, Hubs and Tires 11

Front Suspension and Steering 12

Rear Suspension and Final Drive 13

Brakes 14

Body and Frame 15

Index 16

Wiring Diagrams 17

CLYMER®

Publisher Shawn Etheridge

EDITORIAL

Managing Editor
James Grooms

Associate Editor
Lee Buell

Technical Writers
Jay Bogart
Michael Morlan
George Parise
Mark Rolling
Ed Scott
Ron Wright

Editorial Production Manager
Dylan Goodwin

Senior Production Editor
Greg Araujo

Production Editors
Holly Messinger
Darin Watson

Associate Production Editor
Susan Hartington
Julie Jantzer
Justin Marciniak

Technical Illustrators
Steve Amos
Errol McCarthy
Mitzi McCarthy
Bob Meyer

MARKETING/SALES AND ADMINISTRATION

Advertising & Promotions Manager
Elda Starke

Advertising & Promotions Coordinators
Melissa Abbott
Wendy Stringfellow

Art Director
Chris Paxton

Sales Managers
Ted Metzger, Manuals
Dutch Sadler, Marine
Matt Tusken, Motorcycles

Business Manager
Ron Rogers

Customer Service Manager
Terri Cannon

Customer Service Representatives
Shawna Davis
Courtney Hollars
Susan Kohlmeyer
April LeBlond
Jennifer Lassiter
Ernesto Suarez

Warehouse & Inventory Manager
Leah Hicks

PRIMEDIA
Business Magazines & Media
P.O. Box 12901, Overland Park, KS 66282-2901 • 800-262-1954 • 913-967-1719

The following books and guides are published by PRIMEDIA Business Directories & Books.

More information available at *primediabooks.com*

Table of Contents

QUICK REFERENCE DATA XI

CHAPTER ONE
GENERAL INFORMATION 1

Manual Organization
Warnings, Cautions, and Notes
Safety
Serial Numbers
Fasteners
Shop Supplies
Basic Tools
Precision Measuring Tools
Electrical Fundamentals
Basic Service Methods
Storage

CHAPTER TWO
TROUBLESHOOTING 30

Operating Requirements
Starting The Engine
Starting Difficulties
Engine Performance
Engine Noises
Engine Lubrication
Cylinder Leakdown Test
Clutch
Transmission
Final Drive
Electrical Testing
Lighting System
Starting System
Charging System
Ignition System
Front Suspension and Steering
Brake System

CHAPTER THREE

LUBRICATION, MAINTENANCE AND TUNE-UP **47**

Fuel Type
Pre-Ride Check List
Tires and Wheels
Battery
Engine Oil and Filter
Transmission
Final Drive
Control Cable Service
Rear Brake Pedal Pivot Shaft Bolt and Bushing Lubrication
Shift LeverCleaning and Lubrication
Sidestand
Windshield Adjust Shaft (RS Models)
Air Filter
Brake System
Clutch
Fuel Filter Replacement
Fuel Hose Inspection
Crankcase Breather Inspection
Evaporative Emission Control System
Exhaust System
Handlebars
Handlebar Grips
Front Suspension Inspection
Rear Suspension Inspection
Rear Frame Inspection
Fastener Inspection
Tune-Up Precedures
Cylinder Head Fasteners
Valve Clearance
Ignition Timing
Engine Compression Test
Spark Plugs (Single Plug Ignition System)
Spark Plugs (Dual-Plug Ignition System)
Spark Plug Inspection
Throttle And Choke Cable Adjustment (All Models Except R850C and 1200C Models)
Throttle Cable Adjustment (1993-1995 R850C and R1200C Models)
Throttle Body Synchronization and Idle Speed Adjustment
Alternator Drive Belt Adjustment

CHAPTER FOUR

ENGINE TOP END **102**

Engine Service Notes
Cylinder Head Cover
Cylinder Head
Valve Gear Holder
Valves and Valve Components
Cylinder and Piston
Piston and Piston Rings

CHAPTER FIVE

ENGINE LOWER END **151**

Engine Service Notes
Servicing The Engine In Frame
Engine (GS, R, RS and RT Models)
Engine (R1100S Models)
Engine (R850C and R1200C Models)
Alternator Support Cover
Auxiliary Drive Shaft Mechanism
Oil Pump
Crankcase
Rear Main Seal Replacement
Auxiliary Drive Shaft, Camshaft Chains and Tensioner Assemblies
Crankshaft
Connecting Rods
Oil Coolers and Hoses
Engine Break-In

CHAPTER SIX

CLUTCH **208**

Clutch
Clutch Release Mechanism (Cable Operated Models)
Clutch Cable
Clutch Master Cylinder
Clutch Release Cylinder
Clutch System Hydraulic

CHAPTER SEVEN
FIVE SPEED TRANSMISSION AND GEARSHIFT MECHANISMS 225
Transmission Case
Neutral Switch and Gear Position Switch
Transmission Housing Cover
Transmission Shafts and Gearshift Mechanism
Transmission Shafts
Gearshift Mechanism
Transmission Cover and Housing
Bearings and Seals

CHAPTER EIGHT
SIX SPEED TRANSMISSION AND GEARSHIFT MECHANISMS. 261
Transmission Case
Neutral/Gear Position Switch
Transmission Housing
Transmission Shafts and Gearshift Mechanism
Transmision Housing and Cover
Transmission Shafts
Gearshift Mechanism
Transmission Cover and Housing Oil Seals

CHAPTER NINE
FUEL, EMISSION CONTROL AND EXHAUST SYSTEMS. 303
Motronic System
Fuel Injection System Components
Depressurizing The Fuel System
Fuel Injection System Precautions
Fuel Injectors
Throttle Body
Pressure Regulator
Motronic Control Unit
Throttle Position Sensor
Air Filter Assembly
Throttle Cables
Increase Idle (Choke)
Cable Replacement
(All Models Except R850C and R1200C)
Fuel Tank
Rollover Valve (All R1150 Models)
Fuel Filter Replacement
Fuel Pump
Fuel Pump Pressure Test
Fuel Level Sending Unit
Crankcase Breather System (U.S. Models Only)
Evaporative Emission Control System
(California Models Only)
Exhaust System

CHAPTER TEN
ELECTRICAL SYSTEM. 369
Electrical Component Replacement
Charging System
Alternator
Ignition System
Hall Sensor Unit
Main Ignition Coil
Direct Ignition Coils
Spark Plug Secondary Wires
Spark Plug Primary Wires (Dual-Plug Models)
Starting System
Starter
Starter Relay
Lighting System
Headlight
Taillight/Brake Light And
License Plate Light
Turn Signals
Switches
Rider Information Display
(1993-1998 GS, RS and RT Models)
Instrument Panel
Central Electrical Equipment Box or Modules
Relays
Fuses
Battery Case
Horn
Wiring Diagrams

CHAPTER ELEVEN
WHEELS, HUBS AND TIRES 447

Front Wheel
Rear Wheel
Front Hub
Wheel Runout And Balance
Spoke Wheel Service
Tire Changing
Tire Repairs

CHAPTER TWELVE
FRONT SUSPENSION AND STEERING 468

Handlebar
Handlebar Controls
Handlebar Lever
Clearance Adjustment (R1100S and All R1150 Models)
Upper Fork Bridge
Lower Fork Bridge
Front Fork (GS, R, RS and RT)
Front Fork (R1100S)
Front Fork (R850C and R1200C)
Front Fork Overhaul (All Models)
Front Strut Adjustments
Front Strut
Front Suspension A-Arm
Steering Damper (R1100R Models)

CHAPTER THIRTEEN
REAR SUSPENSION AND FINAL DRIVE 514

Shock Absorber
Swing Arm and Drive Shaft (Paralever Models)
Final Drive Unit (Paralever Models)
Swing Arm and Drive Shaft (Monolever Models)
Final Drive Unit (Monolever Models)
Final Drive Overhaul (All Models)
Pinion Gear-To-Ring Gear Adjustment (All Models)
Tapered Roller Bearing Preload

CHAPTER FOURTEEN
BRAKES 556

Brake Service
Evo and Integral Brakes
Brake Pad Replacement Interval
Front Brake Pad Replacement
Front Master Cylinder
Front Caliper
Rear Brake Pad Replacement
Rear Master Cylinder
And Remote Reservoir
Rear Caliper
Brake Hose and Line Replacement (Non-ABS Models)
Brake Disc
ABS Brake System
Brake Hose and Line Replacement
(ABS Equipped Models Without Integral Brakes)
Brake Hose and Line Replacement
(ABS Equipped Models With Integral Brakes)
ABS Unit (Without Integral Brakes)
Abs Pressure Modulator (With Integral Brakes)
Trigger Sensors
Bleeding The System (All Models Without ABS)
Brake Bleeding (ABS Models)
Rear Brake Pedal

CHAPTER FIFTEEN
BODY AND FRAME

BODY AND FRAME 644

Seat
Seat Backrest (R850C and R1200C Models)
Front Fender and Mud Guard
Rear Fender and Mud Guard
Body Side Panels (R Models)
Windshield (GS Models)
Body Panels (RS Models)
Body Panels (RT Models)
Body Panels (R1100S Models)
Luggage And Luggage Carrier
Windshield Cleaning (All Models)
Sidestand
Centerstand
Footrests (R1100GS, R1100R and R1100RS Models)
Footrests (R1150R and R1150RS Models)
Footrests (R1150GS Models)
Footrest (RT Models)
Footrests (R1100S Models)
Footrests (R850C and R1200C Models)
Front Safety Bars
Handle (RT Models)
Engine Guard
Main Frame (R1100S Models)
Front Frame (R850C and R1200C Models)
Rear Frame
Raising Rear Frame

INDEX 731

WIRING DIAGRAMS 736

QUICK REFERENCE DATA

MODEL:______________________________YEAR:______________________________

VIN NUMBER:______________________________

ENGINE SERIAL NUMBER:______________________________

CARBURETOR SERIAL NUMBER OR I.D. MARK:______________________________

TIRE INFLATION PRESSURE (COLD)*

Item	kPa	psi
Front (1993-1998 R850, R1100 models [except R1100S]		
Solo	213	31
Rider and passenger	269	39
Rider, passenger and luggage	283	41
Front (1999-on R850, R1100S, R1150 models)		
Solo	213	31
Rider and passenger	248	36
Rider, passenger and luggage	248	36
Rear (all models)		
Solo	248	36
Rider and passenger	269	39
Rider, passenger and luggage	286	42

*Tire inflation pressure is for original equipment tires. Aftermarket tires may require different inflation pressure. The use of tires other than those specified by BMW may cause instability.

MAINTENANCE AND TUNE-UP SPECIFICATIONS

Item	Specifications
Brake pedal height	Rider preference
Clutch (cable operated models)	
Free play	5-7 mm (0.19-0.27 in.)
Locknut-to-adjuster clearance	12 mm (0.47 in.)
Cold start (choke) free play	Minimum 1 mm (0.04 in.)
Engine compression	
Good	Above 1000 kPa (145 psi)
Normal	862-1000 1000 kPa (125-145 psi)
Poor	Less than 862 kPa (125 psi)
Idle speed	
1993-1998	1000-1150 rpm
1999-on	1050-1150 rpm
Ignition timing	Non-adjustable
Rocker arm end float	
Minimum	0.05 mm (0.002 in.)
Maximum	0.40 mm (0.016 in.)

(continued)

MAINTENANCE AND TUNE-UP SPECIFICATIONS (continued)

Item	Specifications
Spark plug type and gap (single-plug ignition)	
R850, R1100 (except R1100S), R1200C models	
Type	Bosch FR 6 DDC
Specified gap	0.8 mm (0.031 in.)
Gap limit	1.0 mm (0.04 in.)
Spark plug type and gap (single-spark ignition)	
R1150	
Type	NGK BKR 7 EKC
Specified gap	0.8 mm (0.031 in.)
Gap limit	1.0 mm (0.04 in.)
Spark plug type and gap (dual-plug ignition)	
R1100, R1150, R1200 models	
Primary spark plug	
Type	NGK BKR 7 EKC
Specified gap	0.8 mm (0.031 in.)
Gap limit	1.0 mm (0.04 in.)
Spark plug type and gap (dual-plug ignition)	
R1100, R1150, R1200 models (continued)	
Secondary spark plug	
Type	NGK DCPR 8 EKC or Bosch YR 6 LDE
Specified gap	0.8 mm (0.031 in.)
Gap limit	1.0 mm (0.04 in.)
Throttle cable free play	
1993-1995	Minimum 0.5 mm (0.02 in.)
1996-on	Minimum 2 mm (0.08 in.)
Throttle synchronization*	
Maximum allowable difference in BMW Synchronizer bars	5 mm (0.19 in.)
Valve clearance (cold)	
Intake	0.17-0.23 mm (0.007-0.009 in.)
Exhaust	0.25-0.31 mm (0.010-0.012 in.)

* All R850C, R1100, R1150 and R1200C models must be adjusted using the BMW MoDiTec diagnostic unit.

RECOMMENDED LUBRICANTS AND CAPACITIES

Battery water (conventional batteries)	Distilled or purified water	
Brake fluid	–	DOT4
Clutch fluid	–	DOT4
Engine oil type		
1993-1998 R850, R1100 models (except R1100S)	HD oil API SE, SF or SG	
1999-on R850, R1100S, R1150 models	HD oil API SF, SG or SH; the suffixes CD or CE are acceptable; or HD oil CCMC G4 or G5; the suffix PD2 is acceptable	
Engine oil change		
Oil change only	3.5 L (3.7 U.S. qts.)	
Oil and filter	3.75 L (4.0 U.S. qts.)	
Difference between MIN and MAX marks	0.50 L (0.53 U.S. qt.)	
Final drive unit		Hypoid gear oil GL5
Above 5° C (41° F)	SAE 90	
Below 5° C (41° F)	SAE 80	
Alternative	SAE 80W/90W	
R850C, R1200C models		
Oil change	0.18 L (0.19 U.S. qt.)	
Rebuild	0.20 L (0.21 U.S. qt.)	
All models except R850C, R1200C models		
Oil change	0.23 L (0.24 U.S. qt.)	
Rebuild	0.25 L (0.26 U.S. qt.)	
Front fork oil	0.47 L (0.50 U.S. qt)	BMW fork oil 5W or 10W

(continued)

RECOMMENDED LUBRICANTS AND CAPACITIES (continued)

Grease		
Clutch splines	–	Optimoly MP3 or Microlube GL261or BelRay Total Performance Lube
Assembly paste	–	Optimoly TA
Roller bearings, final drive and drive shaft splines, chassis components	–	Retinax EP2 or Kluberplex BEM 34-132
Fuel grade		
Models with catalytic converter		Premium unleaded fuel with a minimum Octane rating of 95 (RON) or 85 (MON), AKI 91 premium
Models without catalytic converter		Premium leaded fuel with a minimum Octane rating of 95 (RON) or 85 (MON)
Transmission oil		Hypoid gear oil GL5
Above 5° C (41° F)	SAE 90	
Below 5° C (41° F)	SAE 80	
Oil change	0.81 L (0.86 U.S. qt.)	
Rebuild	1.0 L (1.06 U.S. qts.)	

MAINTENANCE AND TUNE UP TORQUE SPECIFICATIONS

Item	N•m	in.-lb.	ft.-lb.
Alternator drive belt bolt	8	70	–
Cylinder head			
10 mm Torx bolt	40	–	29
Nuts			
Preliminary	20	–	15
Final	an additional 180°		
Final drive unit			
Drain plug	23	–	17
Oil filler cap	23	–	17
Handlebar			
R1100S models			
Locating bolt	9	80	–
Pinch bolt	25	–	18
All models except R1100S			
Mounting bolt	21	–	15
Engine oil drain plug	32	–	23
Oil filter cartridge	11	97	–
Transmission			
1999-on R850C, R1200C, R1100S models			
Drain plug	55	–	40
Oil filler cap	23	–	17
1150 cc models			
Drain plug	30	–	22
Oil filler cap	30	–	22
Transmission (continued)			
All models except 1999-on R850C, R1200C, R1100S, 1150 cc models			
Drain plug	23	–	17
Oil filler cap	23	–	17
Valve adjuster locknut	8	70	–

CHAPTER ONE

GENERAL INFORMATION

This detailed and comprehensive manual covers the BMW R850-1200 series from 1993-2004.

The text provides complete information on maintenance, tune-up, repair and overhaul. Hundreds of original photographs and illustrations created during the complete disassembly of the motorcycle guide the reader through every job. All procedures are in step-by-step form and designed for the reader who may be working on the motorcycle for the first time.

MANUAL ORGANIZATION

A shop manual is a tool and as in all Clymer manuals, the chapters are thumb tabbed for easy reference. Main headings are listed in the table of contents and the index. Frequently used specifications and capacities from the tables at the end of the chapters are listed in the *Quick Reference Data* section at the front of the manual. Specifications and capacities are expressed in metric and U.S. standard units of measurement.

During some of the procedures there will be references to headings in other chapters or sections of the manual. When a specific heading is called out in the step it will be *italicized* as it appears in the manual. If a sub-heading is indicated as being "in this section" it is located within the same main heading. For example, the sub-heading *Handling Gasoline Safely* is located within the main heading *Safety.*

This chapter provides general information on shop safety, tool use, service fundamentals and shop supplies. **Tables 1-5**, at the end of this chapter, list the following:

Table 1 lists general torque specifications.

Table 2 lists conversion formulas.

Table 3 lists technical abbreviations.

Table 4 lists metric tap and drill sizes.

Table 5 lists metric, inch and fractional equivalents.

Chapter Two provides methods for quick and accurate diagnosis of problems. Troubleshooting procedures present typical symptoms and logical methods to pinpoint and repair the problem.

Chapter Three explains all routine maintenance necessary to keep the motorcycle running well. Chapter Three also includes recommended tune-up procedures, eliminating the need to constantly consult the chapters on the various assemblies.

Subsequent chapters describe specific systems such as engine, transmission, clutch, drive system, fuel and exhaust systems, suspension and brakes. Each disassembly, repair and assembly procedure is discussed in step-by-step form.

WARNINGS, CAUTIONS, AND NOTES

The terms WARNING, CAUTION, and NOTE have specific meanings in this manual.

A WARNING emphasizes areas where injury or even death could result from negligence. Mechanical damage may also occur. WARNINGS *are to be taken seriously.*

A CAUTION emphasizes areas where equipment damage could result. Disregarding a CAUTION could cause permanent mechanical damage, though injury is unlikely.

A NOTE provides additional information to make a step or procedure easier or clearer. Disregarding a NOTE could cause inconvenience, but would not cause equipment damage or personal injury.

SAFETY

Professional mechanics can work for years and never sustain a serious injury or mishap. Follow these guidelines and practice common sense to safely service the motorcycle.

1. Do not operate the motorcycle in an enclosed area. The exhaust gasses contain carbon monoxide, an odorless, colorless, and tasteless poisonous gas. Carbon monoxide levels build quickly in small enclosed areas and can cause unconsciousness and death in a short time. Make sure the work area is properly ventilated or operate the motorcycle outside.
2. *Never* use gasoline or any extremely flammable liquid to clean parts. Refer to *Cleaning Parts* and *Handling Gasoline Safely* in this section.
3. *Never* smoke or use a torch in the vicinity of flammable liquids, such as gasoline or cleaning solvent.
4. If welding or brazing on the motorcycle, remove the fuel tankto a safe distance at least 50 ft. (15 m) away.
5. Use the correct type and size of tools to avoid damaging fasteners.
6. Keep tools clean and in good condition. Replace or repair worn or damaged equipment.
7. When loosening a tight fastener, be guided by what would happen if the tool slips.
8. When replacing fasteners, make sure the new fasteners are of the same size and strength as the original ones.
9. Keep the work area clean and organized.

10. Wear eye protection *anytime* the safety of the eyes is in question. This includes procedures involving drilling, grinding, hammering, compressed air and chemicals.
11. Wear the correct clothing for the job. Tie up or cover long hair so it can not get caught in moving equipment.
12. Do not carry sharp tools in clothing pockets.
13. Always have an approved fire extinguisher available. Make sure it is rated for gasoline (Class B) and electrical (Class C) fires.
14. Do not use compressed air to clean clothes, the motorcycle or the work area. Debris may be blown into the eyes or skin. *Never* direct compressed air at anyone. Do not allow children to use or play with any compressed air equipment.
15. When using compressed air to dry rotating parts, hold the part so it can not rotate. Do not allow the force of the air to spin the part. The air jet is capable of rotating parts at extreme speed. The part may be damaged or disintegrate, causing serious injury.
16. Do not inhale the dust created by brake pad and clutch wear. These particles may contain asbestos. In addition, some types of insulating materials and gaskets may contain asbestos. Inhaling asbestos particles is hazardous to health.
17. Never work on the motorcycle while someone is working under it.
18. When placing the motorcycle on a stand, make sure it is secure before walking away.

Handling Gasoline Safely

Gasoline is a volatile flammable liquid and is one of the most dangerous items in the shop. Because gasoline is used so often, many people forget that it is hazardous. Only use gasoline as fuel for gasoline internal combustion engines. Keep in mind, when working on a motorcycle, gasoline is always present in the fuel tank, fuel line and carburetor. To avoid a disastrous accident when working

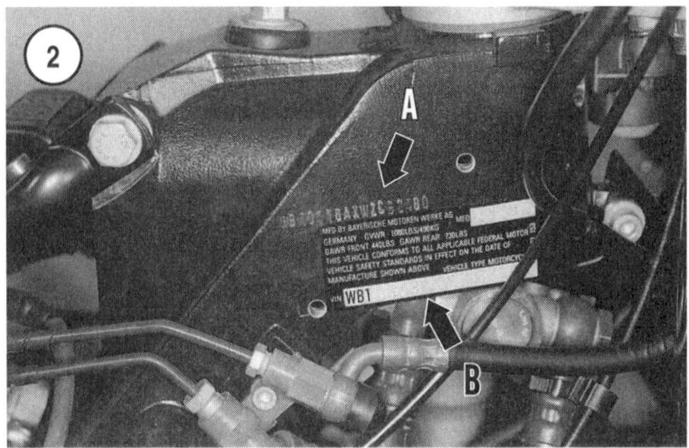

around the fuel system, carefully observe the following precautions:

1. *Never* use gasoline to clean parts. Refer to *Cleaning Parts* in this section.
2. When working on the fuel system, work outside or in a well-ventilated area.
3. Do not add fuel to the fuel tank or service the fuel system while the motorcycle is near open flames, sparks or where someone is smoking. Gasoline vapor is heavier than air, it collects in low areas and is more easily ignited than liquid gasoline.
4. Allow the engine to cool completely before working on any fuel system component.
5. On carburetted models, when draining the carburetor, catch the fuel in a plastic container and then pour it into an approved gasoline storage container.
6. Do not store gasoline in glass containers. If the glass breaks, a serious explosion or fire may occur.
7. Immediately wipe up spilled gasoline with rags. Store the rags in a metal container with a lid until they can be properly disposed of, or place them outside in a safe place for the fuel to evaporate.
8. Do not pour water onto a gasoline fire. Water spreads the fire and makes it more difficult to put out. Use a class B, BC or ABC fire extinguisher to extinguish the fire.
9. Always turn off the engine before refueling. Do not spill fuel onto the engine or exhaust system. Do not overfill the fuel tank. Leave an air space at the top of the tank to allow room for the fuel to expand due to temperature fluctuations.

Cleaning Parts

Cleaning parts is one of the more tedious and difficult service jobs performed in the home garage. There are many types of chemical cleaners and solvents available for shop use. Most are poisonous and extremely flammable. To prevent chemical exposure, vapor buildup, fire and serious injury, observe each product warning label and note the following:

1. Read and observe the entire product label before using any chemical. Always know what type of chemical is being used and whether it is poisonous and/or flammable.
2. Do not use more than one type of cleaning solvent at a time. If mixing chemicals is called for, measure the proper amounts according to the manufacturer.
3. Work in a well-ventilated area.
4. Wear chemical-resistant gloves.
5. Wear safety glasses.
6. Wear a vapor respirator if the instructions call for it.
7. Wash hands and arms thoroughly after cleaning parts.
8. Keep chemical products away from children and pets.
9. Thoroughly clean all oil, grease and cleaner residue from any part that must be heated.
10. Use a nylon brush when cleaning parts. Metal brushes may cause a spark.
11. When using a parts washer, only use the solvent recommended by the manufacturer. Make sure the parts washer is equipped with a metal lid that will lower in case of fire.

Warning Labels

Most manufacturers attach information and warning labels to the motorcycle. These labels contain instructions that are important to personal safety when operating, servicing, transporting and storing the motorcycle Refer to the owner's manual for the description and location of labels. Order replacement labels from the manufacturer if they are missing or damaged.

SERIAL NUMBERS

Serial numbers are stamped on various locations on the frame, engine, transmission and carburetor. Record these numbers in the *Quick Reference Data* section in the front of the book. Have these numbers available when ordering parts.

The engine serial number (**Figure 1**) is stamped on a pad on the right-hand side of the crankcase below the cylinder.

The frame serial number (A, **Figure 2**) is stamped on the right-hand side of the front frame next to the steering stem.

The VIN label plate (B, **Figure 2**) is attached to the right-hand side of the front frame below the frame stamped serial number.

The body color label (**Figure 3**) is located at various locations on top of the rear frame under the rider's seat.

FASTENERS

Proper fastener selection and installation is important to ensure that the motorcycle operates as designed and can be serviced efficiently. The choice of original equipment fasteners is not arrived at by chance. Make sure that replacement fasteners meet all the same requirements as the originals.

Threaded Fasteners

Threaded fasteners secure most of the components on the motorcycle. Most are tightened by turning them clockwise (right-hand threads). If the normal rotation of the component being tightened would loosen the fastener, it may have left-hand threads. If a left-hand threaded fastener is used, it is noted in the text.

Two dimensions are required to match the size of the fastener: the number of threads in a given distance and the outside diameter of the threads.

Two systems are currently used to specify threaded fastener dimensions: the U.S. standard system and the metric system (**Figure 4**). Pay particular attention when working with unidentified fasteners; mismatching thread types can damage threads.

CAUTION
To ensure that the fastener threads are not mismatched or cross-threaded, start all fasteners by hand. If a fastener is hard to start or turn, determine the cause before tightening with a wrench.

The length (L, **Figure 5**), diameter (D) and distance between thread crests (pitch) (T) classify metric screws and bolts. A typical bolt may be identified by the numbers, 8—1.25 × 130. This indicates the bolt has diameter of 8 mm, the distance between thread crests is 1.25 mm and the length is 130 mm. Always measure bolt length as shown in L, **Figure 5** to avoid purchasing replacements of the wrong length.

The numbers located on the top of the fastener (**Figure 5**) indicate the strength of metric screws and bolts. The higher the number, the stronger the fastener is. Generally, unnumbered fasteners are the weakest.

Many screws, bolts and studs are combined with nuts to secure particular components. To indicate the size of a nut, manufacturers specify the internal diameter and the thread pitch.

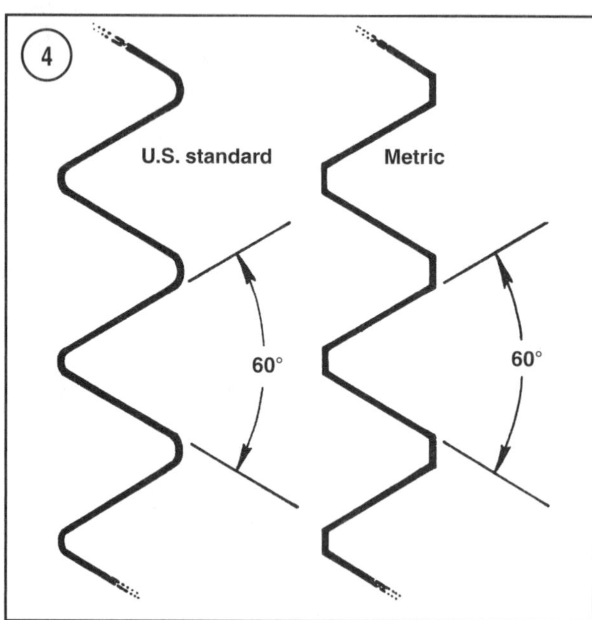

The measurement across two flats on a nut or bolt indicates the wrench size.

WARNING
Do not install fasteners with a strength classification lower than what was originally installed by the manufacturer. Doing so may cause equipment failure and/or damage.

Torque Specifications

The materials used in the manufacture of the motorcycle may be subjected to uneven stresses if the fasteners of the various subassemblies are not installed and tightened correctly. Fasteners that are improperly installed or work loose can cause extensive damage. It is essential to use an

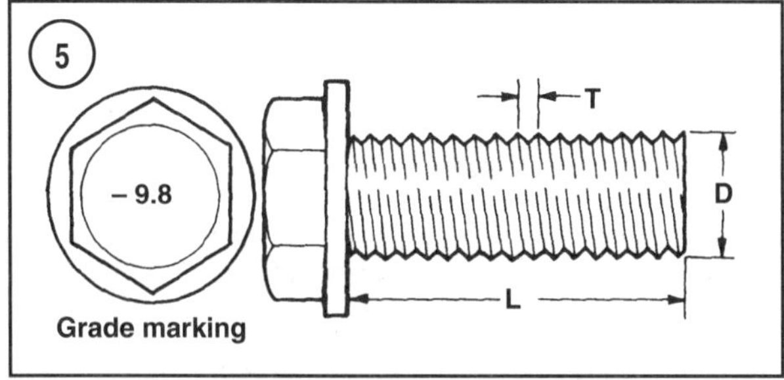

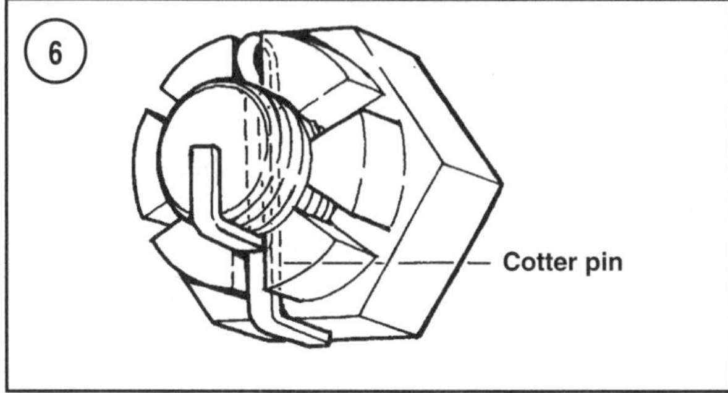

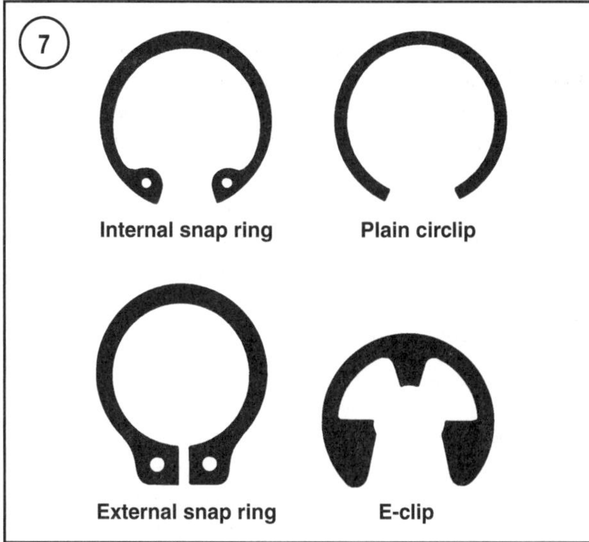

accurate torque wrench, described in this chapter, with the torque specifications in this manual.

Specifications for torque are provided in Newton-meters (N•m), foot-pounds (ft.-lb.) and inch- pounds (in.-lb.). Refer to **Table 1** for general torque specifications. To use the table, first determine the size of the fastener as described in this section. Torque specifications for specific components are at the end of the appropriate chapters. Torque wrenches are covered in *Basic Tools*.

Self-Locking Fasteners

Several types of bolts, screws and nuts incorporate a system that creates interference between the two fasteners. Interference is achieved in various ways. The most common type is the nylon insert nut and a dry adhesive coating on the threads of a bolt.

Self-locking fasteners offer greater holding strength than standard fasteners, which improves their resistance to vibration. Self-locking fasteners cannot be reused. The materials used to form the lock become distorted after the initial installation and removal. It is a good practice to discard and replace self-locking fasteners after their removal. Do not replace self-locking fasteners with standard fasteners.

Washers

There are two basic types of washers: flat washers and lockwashers. Flat washers are simple discs with a hole to fit a screw or bolt. Lockwashers are used to prevent a fastener from working loose. Washers can be used as spacers and seals, or to help distribute fastener load and to prevent the fastener from damaging the component.

As with fasteners, when replacing washers make sure the replacement washers are of the same design and quality.

Cotter Pins

A cotter pin is a split metal pin inserted into a hole or slot to prevent a fastener from loosening. In certain applications, such as the rear axle on an ATV or motorcycle, the fastener must be secured in this way. For these applications, a cotter pin and castellated (slotted) nut is used.

To use a cotter pin, first make sure the diameter is correct for the hole in the fastener. After correctly tightening the fastener and aligning the holes, insert the cotter pin through the hole and bend the ends over the fastener (**Figure 6**). Unless instructed to do so, never loosen a tightened fastener to align the holes. If the holes do not align, tighten the fastener just enough to achieve alignment.

Cotter pins are available in various diameters and lengths. Measure length from the bottom of the head to the tip of the shortest pin.

Snap Rings and E-clips

Snap rings (**Figure 7**) are circular-shaped metal retaining clips. They are required to secure parts and gears in place on parts such as shafts, pins or rods. External type snap rings are used to retain items on shafts. Internal type snap rings secure parts within housing bores. In some applications, in addition to securing the component(s), snap rings of varying thickness also determine endplay. These are usually called selective snap rings.

Two basic types of snap rings are used: machined and stamped snap rings. Machined snap rings (**Figure 8**) can be installed in either direction, since both faces have sharp edges. Stamped snap rings (**Figure 9**) are manufactured with a sharp edge and a round edge. When installing a stamped snap ring in a thrust application, install the sharp edge facing away from the part producing the thrust.

E-clips are used when it is not practical to use a snap ring. Remove E-clips with a flat blade screwdriver by prying between the shaft and E-clip. To install an E-clip, center it over the shaft groove and push or tap it into place.

Observe the following when installing snap rings:

1. Remove and install snap rings with snap ring pliers. Refer to *Snap Ring Pliers* in this chapter.
2. In some applications, it may be necessary to replace snap rings after removing them.
3. Compress or expand snap rings only enough to install them. If overly expanded, they lose their retaining ability.
4. After installing a snap ring, make sure it seats completely.
5. Wear eye protection when removing and installing snap rings.

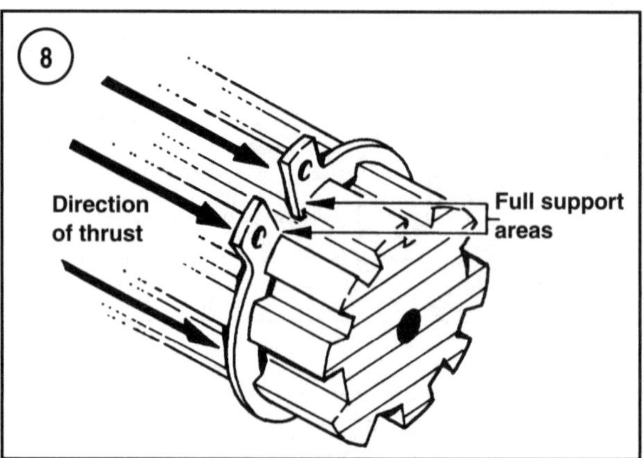

SHOP SUPPLIES

Lubricants and Fluids

Periodic lubrication helps ensure a long service life for any type of equipment. Using the correct type of lubricant is as important as performing the lubrication service, although in an emergency the wrong type is better than not using one. The following section describes the types of lubricants most often required. Make sure to follow the manufacturer's recommendations for lubricant types.

Engine oils

Engine oil is classified by two standards: the American Petroleum Institute (API) service classification and the Society of Automotive Engineers (SAE) viscosity rating. This information is on the oil container label. Two letters indicate the API service classification. The number or sequence of numbers and letter (10W-40 for example) is the oil's viscosity rating. The API service classification and the SAE viscosity index are not indications of oil quality.

The service classification indicates that the oil meets specific lubrication standards. The first letter in the classification *S* indicates that the oil is for gasoline engines. The second letter indicates the standard the oil satisfies.

Always use an oil with a classification recommended by the manufacturer. Using an oil with a different classification can cause engine damage.

Viscosity is an indication of the oil's thickness. Thin oils have a lower number while thick oils have a higher number. Engine oils fall into the 5- to 50-weight range for single-grade oils.

Most manufacturers recommend multi-grade oil. These oils perform efficiently across a wide range of operating conditions. Multi-grade oils are identified by a *W* after the first number, which indicates the low-temperature viscosity.

Engine oils are most commonly mineral (petroleum) based; however, synthetic and semi-synthetic types are used more frequently. When selecting engine oil, follow the manufacturer's recommendation for type, classification and viscosity when selecting engine oil.

Greases

Grease is lubricating oil with thickening agents added to it. The National Lubricating Grease Institute (NLGI) grades grease. Grades range from No. 000 to No. 6, with No. 6 being the thickest. Typical multipurpose grease is NLGI No. 2. For specific applications, manufacturers may recommend water-resistant type grease or one with an additive such as molybdenum disulfide (MoS_2).

BMW recommends two unique lubricants for the various components as follows:

1. Optimoly MP3 or Microlube GL261: Recommended for the clutch splines. If these specific lubricants are not available an alternative is Bel Rey Total Performance Lube (part No. 950004301).
2. Shell Retinax EP2 or Kluberplex BEM 34-132: Recommended for the drive shaft splines, final drive unit

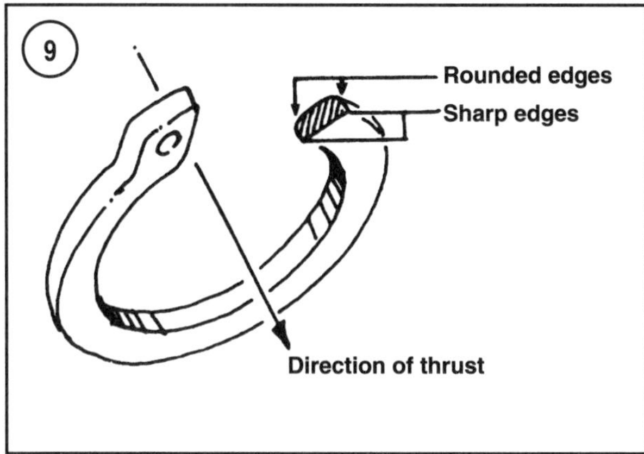

splines and bearings, swing arm bearings, steering head bearings, wheel bearings and chassis components. If these specific lubricants are not available, use anti-friction bearing grease with high corrosion protection and good resistance to water and oxidation, similar to Shell Retinax EP2.

3. Optimoly TA: Assembly paste.

Brake fluid

Brake fluid is the hydraulic fluid used to transmit hydraulic pressure (force) to the wheel brakes. Brake fluid is also used in the hydraulic clutch system on later models.

Brake fluid is classified by the Department of Transportation (DOT). Current designations for brake fluid are DOT 3, DOT 4 and DOT 5. This classification appears on the fluid container.

Each type of brake fluid has its own definite characteristics. Do not intermix DOT 3 or DOT 4 with DOT 5 brake fluid as this may cause brake, or clutch, system failure since the DOT 5 brake fluid is not compatible with other brake fluids. When adding brake fluid, *only* use the fluid recommended by the manufacturer.

Brake fluid will damage any plastic, painted or plated surface it contacts. Use extreme care when working with brake fluid and remove any spills immediately with soap and water.

Hydraulic brake and clutch systems require clean and moisture free brake fluid. Never reuse brake fluid. Keep containers and reservoirs properly sealed.

WARNING

Never put a mineral-based (petroleum) oil into the brake system. Mineral oil will cause rubber parts in the system to swell and break apart, resulting in complete brake failure.

Cleaners, Degreasers and Solvents

Many chemicals are available to remove oil, grease and other residue from the motorcycle. Before using cleaning solvents, consider how they will be used and disposed of, particularly if they are not water-soluble. Local ordinances may require special procedures for the disposal of many types of cleaning chemicals. Refer to *Safety* and *Parts Cleaning Parts* in this chapter for more information on their use.

To clean brake system components, use brake parts cleaner. Petroleum-based products will damage brake and clutch system seals. Brake parts cleaner leaves no residue. Use electrical contact cleaner to clean electrical connections and components without leaving any residue.

Generally, degreasers are strong cleaners used to remove heavy accumulations of grease from engine and frame components.

Most solvents are designed to be used in a parts washing cabinet for individual component cleaning. For safety, use only nonflammable or high flash point solvents.

Gasket Sealant

Sealants are used in combination with a gasket or seal and are occasionally alone. Follow the manufacturer's recommendation when using sealants. Use extreme care when choosing a sealant different from the type originally recommended. Choose sealants based on their resistance to heat, various fluids and their sealing capabilities.

One of the most common sealants is RTV, or room temperature vulcanizing sealant. This sealant cures at room temperature over a specific time period. This allows the repositioning of components without damaging gaskets.

Moisture in the air causes the RTV sealant to cure. Always install the tube cap as soon as possible after applying RTV sealant. RTV sealant has a limited shelf life and will not cure properly if the shelf life has expired. Keep partial tubes sealed and discard them if they have surpassed the expiration date.

Applying RTV sealant

Clean all old gasket residue from the mating surfaces. Remove all gasket material from blind threaded holes; it can cause inaccurate bolt torque. Spray the mating surfaces with aerosol parts cleaner and then wipe with a lint-free cloth. The area must be clean for the sealant to adhere.

Apply RTV sealant in a continuous bead 2-3 mm (0.08-0.12 in.) thick. Circle all the fastener holes unless otherwise specified. Do not allow any sealant to enter these holes. Assemble and tighten the fasteners to the specified torque within the time frame recommended by the RTV sealant manufacturer.

Gasket Remover

Aerosol gasket remover can help remove stubborn gaskets. This product can speed up the removal process and prevent damage to the mating surface that may be caused by using a scraping tool. Most of these types of products are very caustic. Follow the gasket remover manufacturer's instructions for use.

Threadlocking Compound

A threadlocking compound is a fluid applied to the threads of fasteners. After tightening the fastener, the fluid dries and becomes a solid filler between the threads. This makes it difficult for the fastener to work loose from vibration, or heat expansion and contraction. Some threadlocking compounds also provide a seal against fluid leakage.

Before applying threadlocking compound, remove any old compound from both thread areas and clean them with aerosol parts cleaner. Use the compound sparingly. Excess fluid can run into adjoining parts.

Threadlocking compounds are available in different strengths. Follow the particular manufacturer's recommendations regarding compound selection. A number of manufacturers offer a wide range of threadlocking compounds for various strength, temperature and repair applications.

BASIC TOOLS

Most of the procedures in this manual can be carried out with simple hand tools and test equipment familiar to the home mechanic. Always use the correct tools for the job at hand. Keep tools organized and clean. Store them in a tool chest with related tools organized together.

Some of the procedures in this manual specify special tools. In most cases, the tool is illustrated in use. Well-equipped mechanics may be able to substitute similar tools or fabricate a suitable replacement. In some cases, specialized equipment or experience may make it impractical for the home mechanic to attempt the procedure. Such operations are identified in the text with the recommendation to have a dealership or specialist perform the task. It may be less expensive to have a professional perform these jobs, especially when considering the cost of the equipment.

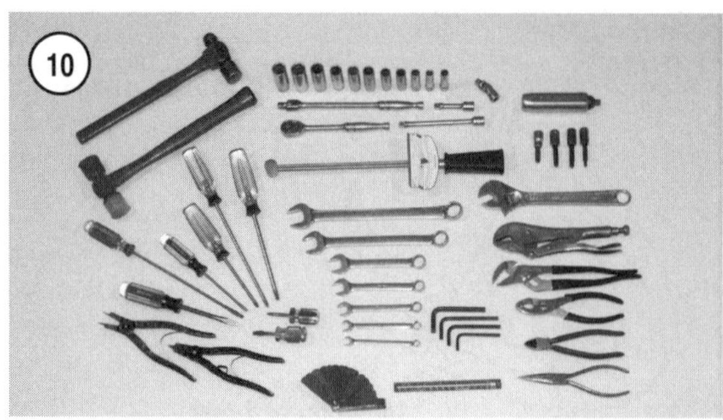

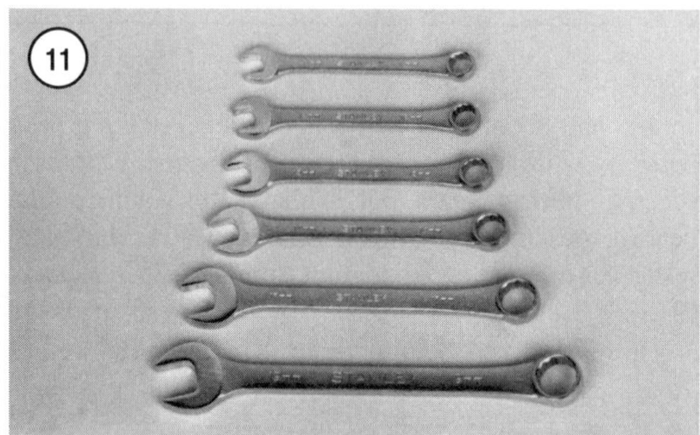

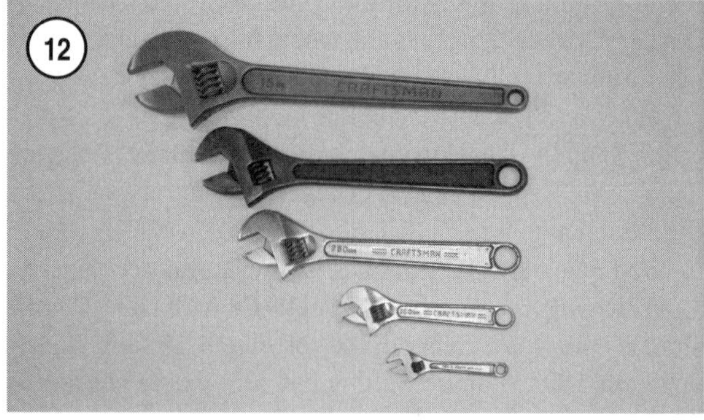

Quality tools are essential. The best are constructed of high-strength alloy steel. These tools are light, easy to use and resistant to wear. Their working surface is devoid of sharp edges and the tool is carefully polished. They have an easy-to-clean finish and are comfortable to use. Quality tools are a good investment.

When purchasing tools to perform the procedures covered in this manual, consider the tool's potential frequency of use. If a tool kit is just now being started, consider purchasing a basic tool set (**Figure 10**) from a quality tool supplier. These sets are available in many tool combinations and offer substantial savings when compared to individually purchased tools. As work experi-

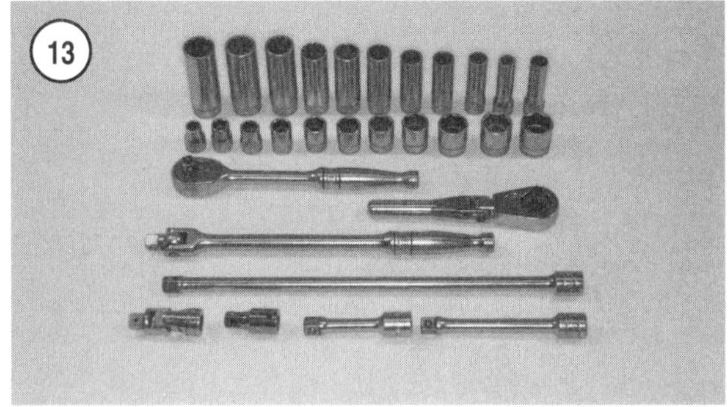

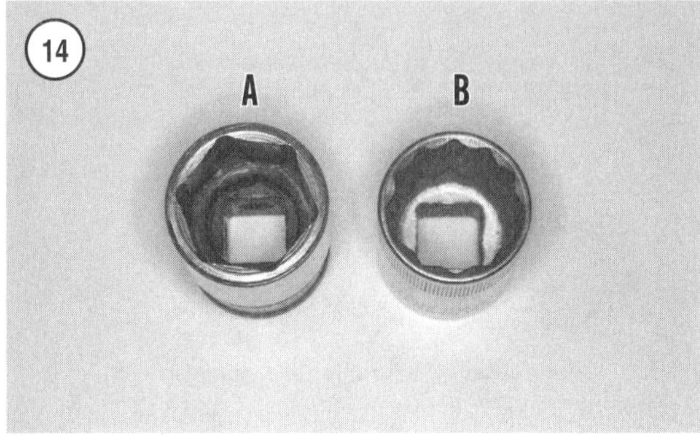

ence grows and tasks become more complicated, specialized tools can be added.

Screwdrivers

Screwdrivers of various lengths and types are mandatory for the simplest tool kit. The two basic types are the slotted tip (flat blade) and the Phillips tip. These are available in sets that often include an assortment of tip sizes and shaft lengths.

As with all tools, use a screwdriver designed for the job. Make sure the size of the tip conforms to the size and shape of the fastener. Use them only for driving screws. Never use a screwdriver for prying or chiseling metal. Repair or replace worn or damaged screwdrivers. A worn tip may damage the fastener, making it difficult to remove.

Torx Drivers

Many components are secured with internal Torx fasteners. These fasteners require specific Torx drivers for removal and installation. These fasteners reduce cam-out and fastener damage, and allow high torque transmission due to the complete enclosure of the driver within the fastener.

Torx screwdrivers in individual sizes, or screwdrivers that accept various bit sizes are available. However, the most practical application is a Torx bit set that accepts various drive types and sizes. A typical set contains T-10 through T40 bits that accept 1/4 and 3/8 in. drive attachments.

Wrenches

Open-end, box-end, and combination wrenches (**Figure 11**) are available in a variety of types and sizes.

The number stamped on the wrench refers to the distance between the work areas. This size must match the size of the fastener head.

The box-end wrench is an excellent tool because it grips the fastener on all sides. This reduces the chance of the tool slipping. The box-end wrench is designed with either a 6 or 12-point opening. For stubborn or damaged fasteners, the 6-point provides superior holding ability by contacting the fastener across a wider area at all six edges. For general use, the 12-point works well. It allows the wrench to be removed and reinstalled without moving the handle over such a wide arc.

An open-end wrench is fast and works best in areas with limited overhead access. It contacts the fastener at only two points, and is subject to slipping under heavy force, or if the tool or fastener is worn. A box-end wrench is preferred in most instances, especially when breaking loose and applying the final tightness to a fastener.

The combination wrench has a box-end on one end, and an open-end on the other. This combination makes it a very convenient tool.

Adjustable Wrenches

An adjustable wrench or Crescent wrench (**Figure 12**) can fit nearly any nut or bolt head that has clear access around its entire perimeter. Adjustable wrenches are best used as a backup wrench to keep a large nut or bolt from turning while the other end is being loosened or tightened with a box-end or socket wrench.

Adjustable wrenches contact the fastener at only two points, which makes them more subject to slipping off the fastener. The fact that one jaw is adjustable and may loosen only aggravates this shortcoming. Make certain the solid jaw is the one transmitting the force.

Socket Wrenches, Ratchets and Handles

Sockets that attach to a ratchet handle (**Figure 13**) are available with 6-point (A, **Figure 14**) or 12-point (B) openings and different drive sizes. The drive size indi-

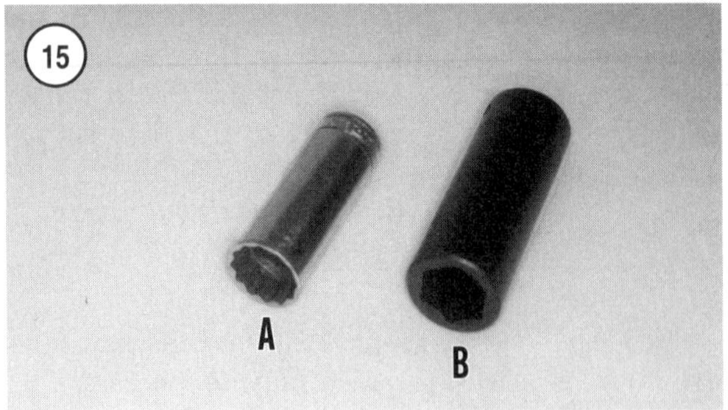

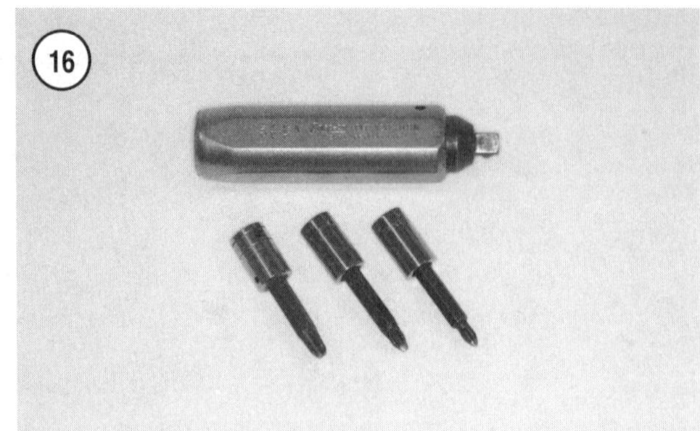

cates the size of the square hole that accepts the ratchet handle. The number stamped on the socket is the size of the work area and must match the fastener head.

As with wrenches, a 6-point socket provides superior-holding ability, while a 12-point socket needs to be moved only half as far to reposition it on the fastener.

Sockets are designated for either hand or impact use. Impact sockets are made of thicker material for more durability. Compare the size and wall thickness of a 19-mm hand socket (A, **Figure 15**) and the 19-mm impact socket (B). Use impact sockets when using an impact driver or air tools. Use hand sockets with hand-driven attachments.

WARNING
Do not use hand sockets with air or impact tools, as they may shatter and cause injury. Always wear eye protection when using impact or air tools.

Various handles are available for sockets. The speed handle is used for fast operation. Flexible ratchet heads in varying lengths allow the socket to be turned with varying force, and at odd angles. Extension bars allow the socket setup to reach difficult areas. The ratchet is the most versatile. It allows the user to install or remove the nut without removing the socket.

Sockets combined with any number of drivers make them undoubtedly the fastest, safest and most convenient tool for fastener removal and installation.

Impact Driver

An impact driver provides extra force for removing fasteners, by converting the impact of a hammer into a turning motion. This makes it possible to remove stubborn fasteners without damaging them. Impact drivers and interchangeable bits (**Figure 16**) are available from most tool suppliers. When using a socket with an impact driver make sure the socket is designed for impact use. Refer to *Socket Wrenches, Ratchets and Handles* in this section.

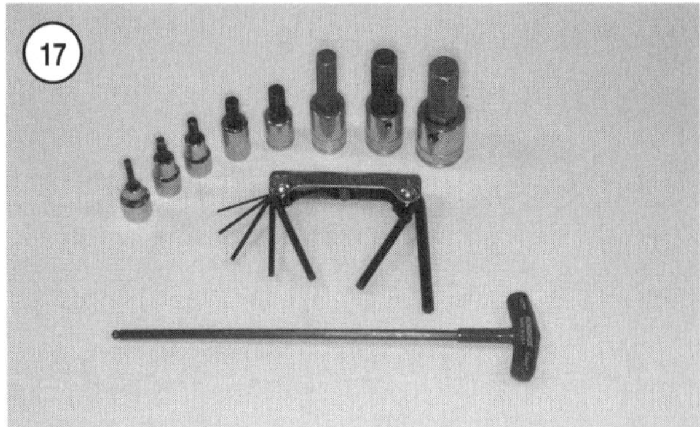

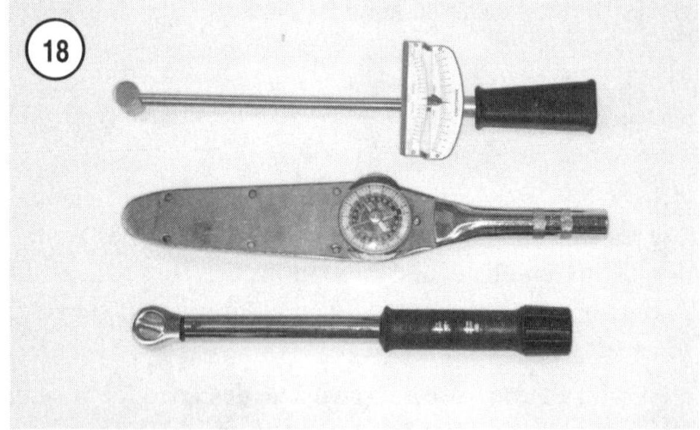

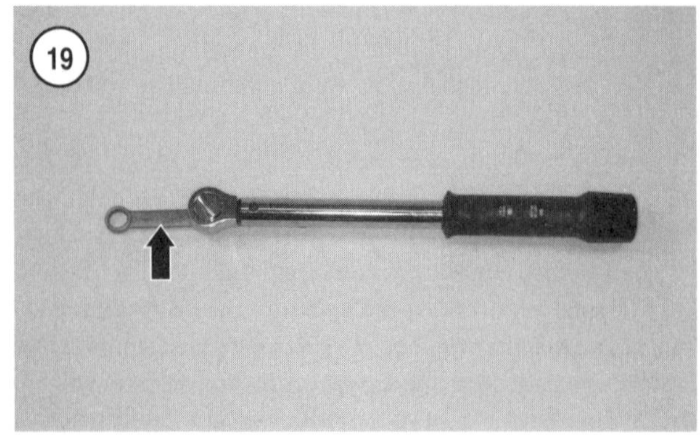

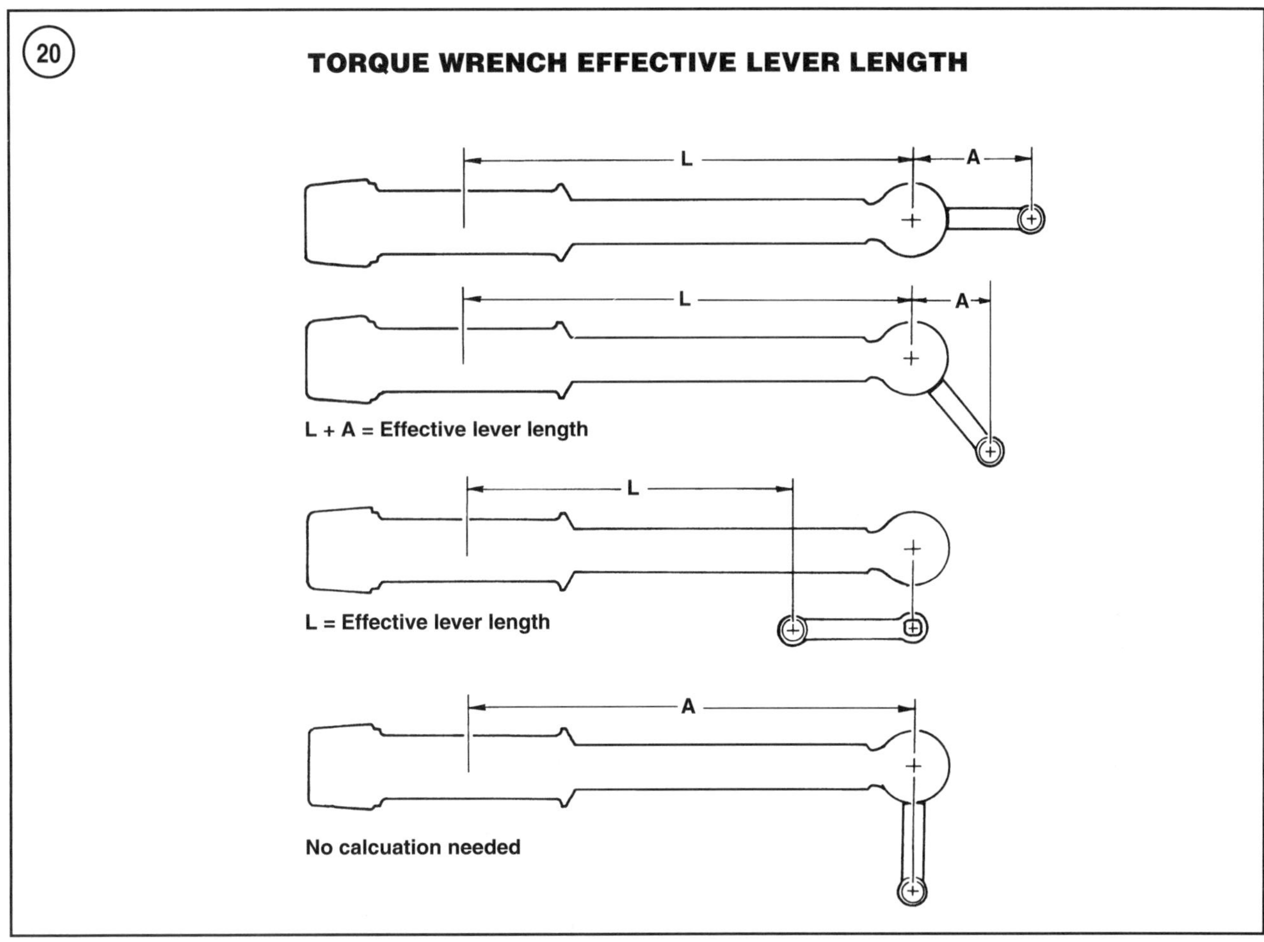

WARNING
Do not use hand sockets with air or impact tools as they may shatter and cause injury. Always wear eye protection when using impact or air tools.

Allen Wrenches

Allen or setscrew wrenches (**Figure 17**) are used on fasteners with hexagonal recesses in the fastener head. These wrenches are available in L-shaped bar, socket and T-handle types. A metric set is required when working on most motorcycles. Allen bolts are sometimes called socket bolts.

Torque Wrenches

A torque wrench (**Figure 18**) is used with a socket, torque adapter or similar extension to tighten a fastener to a measured torque. Torque wrenches come in several drive sizes (1/4, 3/8, 1/2 and 3/4) and have various methods of reading the torque value. The drive size indicates the size of the square drive that accepts the socket, adapter or extension. Common methods of reading the torque value are the deflecting beam, the dial indicator and the audible click. When choosing a torque wrench, consider the torque range, drive size and accuracy. The torque specifications in this manual provide an indication of the range required. A torque wrench is a precision tool that must be properly cared for to remain accurate. Store torque wrenches in cases or separate padded drawers within the toolbox. Follow the manufacturer's instructions for their care and calibration.

Torque Adapters

Torque adapters or extensions extend or reduce the reach of a torque wrench. The torque adapter shown in **Figure 19** is used to tighten a fastener that cannot be reached due to the size of the torque wrench head, drive, and socket. If a torque adapter changes the effective lever length (**Figure 20**), the torque reading on the wrench will not equal the actual torque applied to the fastener. It is necessary to recalibrate the torque setting on the wrench to compensate for the change in effective lever length. When a torque adapter is used at a right angle to the drive head, calibration is not required, since the effective lever length has not changed.

To recalculate a torque reading when using a torque adapter, use the following formula, and refer to **Figure 20**.

$$TW = \frac{TA \times L}{L + A}$$

TW is the torque setting or dial reading on the wrench.

TA is the torque specification and the actual amount of torque that will be applied to the fastener.

A is the amount that the adapter increases (or in some cases reduces) the effective lever length as measured along the centerline of the torque wrench.

L is the lever length of the wrench as measured from the center of the drive to the center of the grip.

The effective length is the sum of L and A.

Example:

TA = 20 ft.-lb.

A = 3 in.

L = 14 in.

$$TW = \frac{20 \times 14}{14 + 3} = \frac{280}{17} = 16.5 \text{ ft. lb.}$$

In this example, the torque wrench would be set to the recalculated torque value (TW = 16.5 ft.-lb.). When using a beam-type wrench, tighten the fastener until the pointer aligns with 16.5 ft.-lb. In this example, although the torque wrench is pre set to 16.5 ft.-lb., the actual torque is 20 ft.-lb.

Pliers

Pliers come in a wide range of types and sizes. Pliers are useful for holding, cutting, bending, and crimping. Do not use them to turn fasteners. **Figure 21** shows several types of useful pliers. Each design has a specialized function. Slip-joint pliers are general-purpose pliers used for gripping and bending. Diagonal cutting pliers are needed to cut wire and can be used to remove cotter pins. Needlenose pliers are used to hold or bend small objects. Locking pliers (**Figure 22**), sometimes called ViseGrips, are used to hold objects very tightly. They have many uses ranging from holding two parts together, to gripping the end of a broken stud. Use caution when using locking pliers, as the sharp jaws will damage the objects they hold.

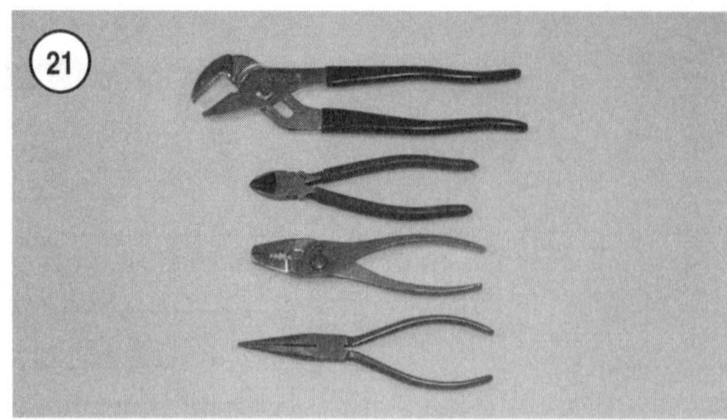

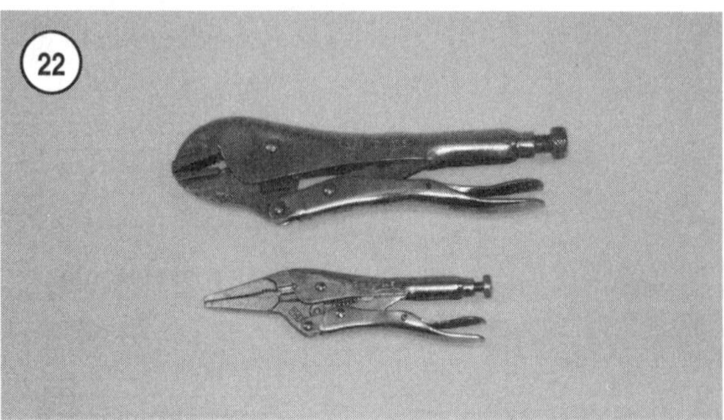

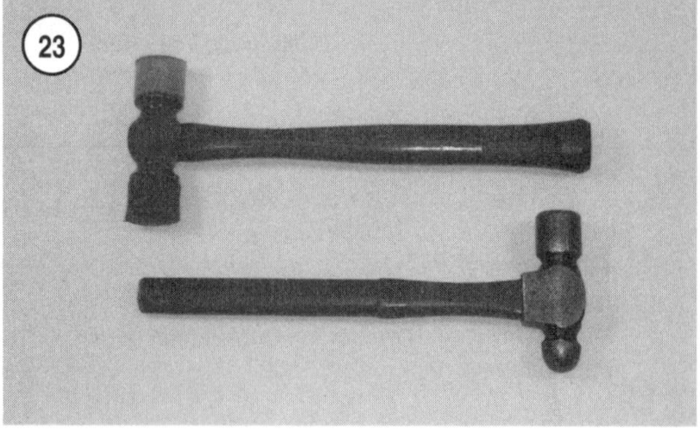

Snap Ring Pliers

Snap ring pliers are specialized pliers with tips that fit into the ends of snap rings to remove and install them.

Snap ring pliers are available with a fixed action (either internal or external) or convertible (one tool works on both internal and external snap rings). They may have fixed tips or interchangeable ones of various sizes and angles. For general use, select a convertible type of pliers with interchangeable tips.

WARNING

Snap rings can slip and fly off when removing and installing them. Also, the snap ring

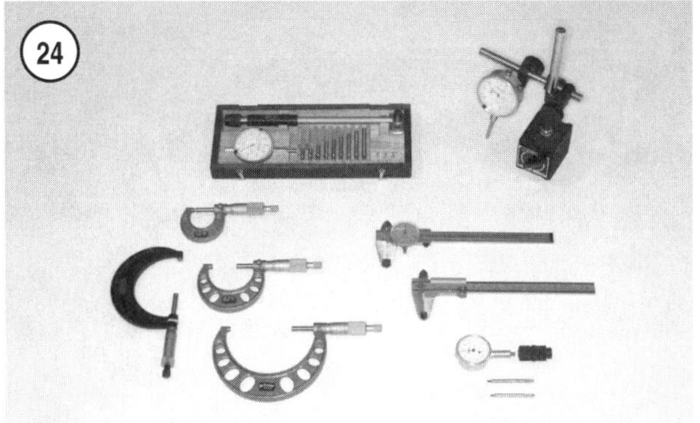
24

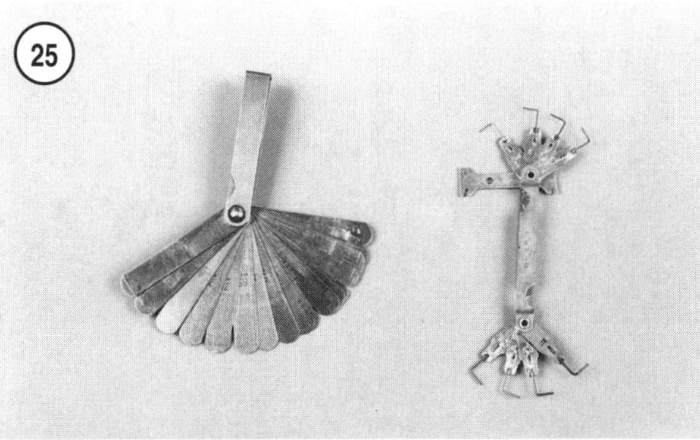
25

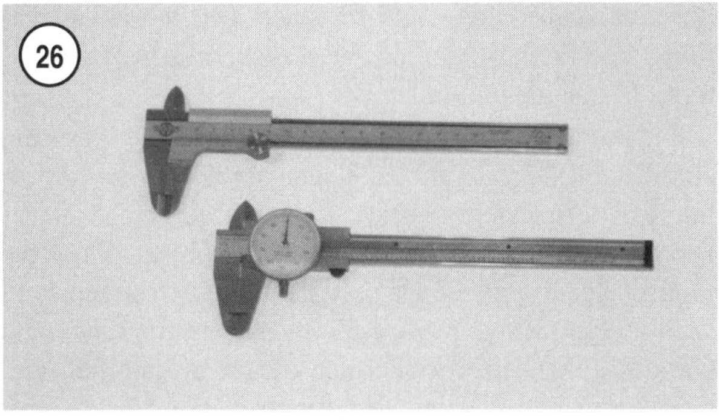
26

pliers' tips may break. Always wear eye protection when using snap ring pliers.

Hammers

Various types of hammers (**Figure 23**) are available to fit a number of applications. A ball-peen hammer is used to strike another tool, such as a punch or chisel. Soft-faced hammers are required when a metal object must be struck without damaging it. *Never* use a metal-faced hammer on engine and suspension components, as damage will occur in most cases.

Always wear eye protection when using hammers. Make sure the hammer face is in good condition and the handle is not cracked. Select the correct hammer for the job and make sure to strike the object squarely. Do not use the handle or the side of the hammer to strike an object.

PRECISION MEASURING TOOLS

The ability to accurately measure components is essential to successfully rebuild an engine. Equipment is manufactured to close tolerances, and obtaining consistently accurate measurements is essential to determining which components require replacement or further service.

Each type of measuring instrument is designed to measure a dimension with a certain degree of accuracy and within a certain range. When selecting the measuring tool, make sure it is applicable to the task. Refer to **Figure 24** for a typical measuring set.

As with all tools, measuring tools provide the best results if cared for properly. Improper use can damage the tool and result in inaccurate results. If any measurement is questionable, verify the measurement using another tool. A standard gauge is usually provided with measuring tools to check accuracy and calibrate the tool if necessary.

Precision measurements can vary according to the experience of the person performing the procedure. Accurate results are only possible if the mechanic possesses a feel for using the tool. Heavy-handed use of measuring tools will produce less accurate results. Hold the tool gently by the fingertips so the point at which the tool contacts the object is easily felt. This feel for the equipment will produce more accurate measurements and reduce the risk of damaging the tool or component. Refer to the following sections for specific measuring tools.

Feeler Gauge

The feeler or thickness gauge (**Figure 25**) is used for measuring the distance between two surfaces.

A feeler gauge set consists of an assortment of steel strips of graduated thickness. Each blade is marked with its thickness. Blades can be of various lengths and angles for different procedures.

A common use for a feeler gauge is to measure valve clearance. Wire (round) type gauges are used to measure spark plug gap.

Calipers

Calipers (**Figure 26**) are excellent tools for obtaining inside, outside and depth measurements. Although not as precise as a micrometer, they typically allow measurement to within 0.05 mm (0.001 in.). Most calipers have a range up to 150 mm (6 in.).

Calipers are available in dial, vernier or digital versions. Dial calipers have a dial readout that provides convenient reading. Vernier calipers have marked scales that must be compared to determine the measurement. The digital caliper uses a LCD to show the measurement.

Properly maintain the measuring surfaces of the caliper. There must not be any dirt or burrs between the tool and the object being measured. Never force the caliper closed around an object; close the caliper around the highest point so it can be removed with a slight drag. Some calipers require calibration. Always refer to the manufacturer's instructions when using a new or unfamiliar caliper.

To read a vernier caliper, refer to **Figure 27** and the metric scale. The fixed scale is marked in 1 mm increments. Ten individual lines on the fixed scale equal 1 cm. The moveable scale is marked in 0.05 mm (hundredth) increments. To obtain a reading, establish the first number by the location of the 0 line on the movable scale in relation to the first line to the left on the fixed scale. In this example, the number is 10 mm. To determine the next number, note which of the lines on the movable scale align with a mark on the fixed scale. A number of lines will seem close, but only one will align exactly. In this case, 0.50 mm is the reading to add to the first number. The result of adding 10 mm and 0.50 mm is a measurement of 10.50 mm.

Micrometers

A micrometer is a precision instrument designed for linear measurement using the decimal divisions of the inch or meter (**Figure 28**). They must be used maintained with great care.While there are many types and styles of micrometers, most of the procedures in this manual call for an outside micrometer. The outside micrometer is used to measure the outside diameter of cylindrical forms and the thickness of materials.

A micrometer's size indicates the minimum and maximum size of a part that it can measure. The usual sizes (**Figure 29**) are 0-1 in. (0-25 mm), 1-2 in. (25-50 mm), 2-3 in. (50-75 mm) and 3-4 in. (75-100 mm).

Micrometers that cover a wider range of measurements are available. These use a large frame with interchangeable anvils of various lengths. This type of micrometer offers a cost savings; however, its overall size may make it less convenient.

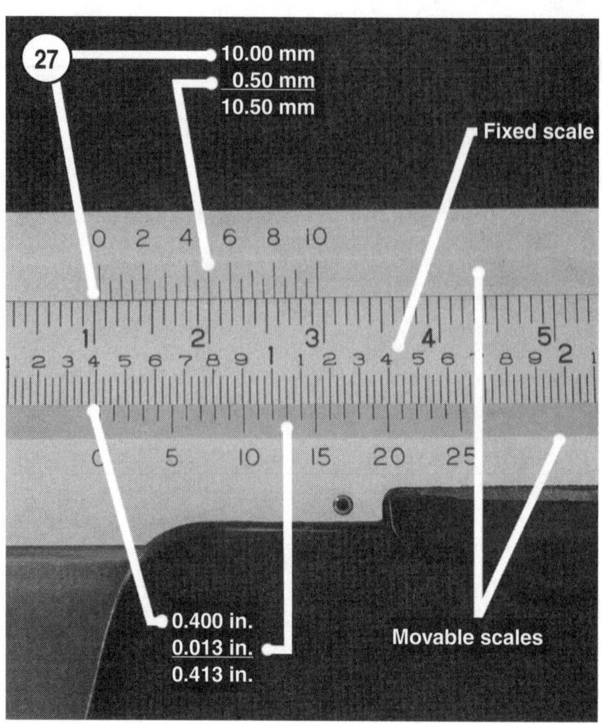

Reading a Metric micrometer

When reading a micrometer, numbers are taken from different scales and added together. The following sections describe how to read the measurements of various types of outside micrometers.

For accurate results, properly maintain the measuring surfaces of the micrometer. There can not be any dirt or burrs between the tool and the measured object. Never force the micrometer closed around an object. Close the micrometer around the highest point so it can be removed with a slight drag. **Figure 30** shows the markings and parts of a standard metric micrometer. Be familiar with these terms before using a micrometer in the follow sections.

The standard metric micrometer is accurate to one one-hundredth of a millimeter (0.01-mm). The sleeve line is graduated in millimeter and half millimeter increments. The marks on the upper half of the sleeve line equal 1.00 mm. Each fifth mark above the sleeve line is identified with a number. The number sequence depends on the size of the micrometer. A 0-25 mm micrometer, for example, will have sleeve marks numbered 0 through 25 in 5 mm increments. This numbering sequence continues with larger micrometers. On all metric micrometers, each mark on the lower half of the sleeve equals 0.50 mm.

The tapered end of the thimble has fifty lines marked around it. Each mark equals 0.01 mm. One complete turn

DECIMAL PLACE VALUES*

0.1	Indicates 1/10 (one tenth of an inch or millimeter)
0.010	Indicates 1/100 (one one-hundreth of an inch or millimeter)
0.001	Indicates 1/1,000 (one one-thousandth of an inch or millimeter)

*This chart represents the values of figures placed to the right of the decimal point. Use it when reading decimals from one-tenth to one one-thousandth of an inch or millimeter. It is not a conversion chart (for example: 0.001 in. is not equal to 0.001 mm).

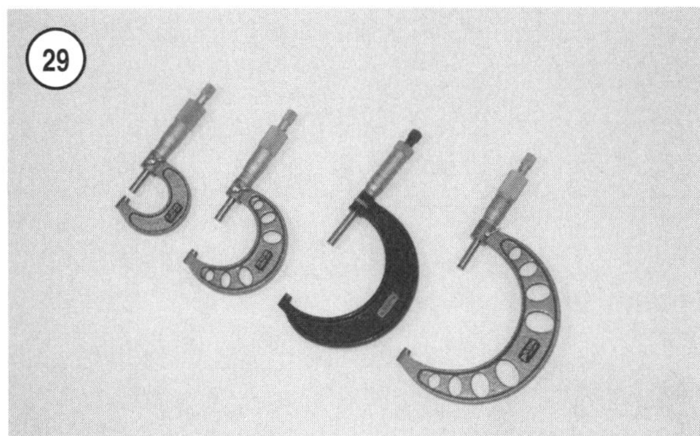

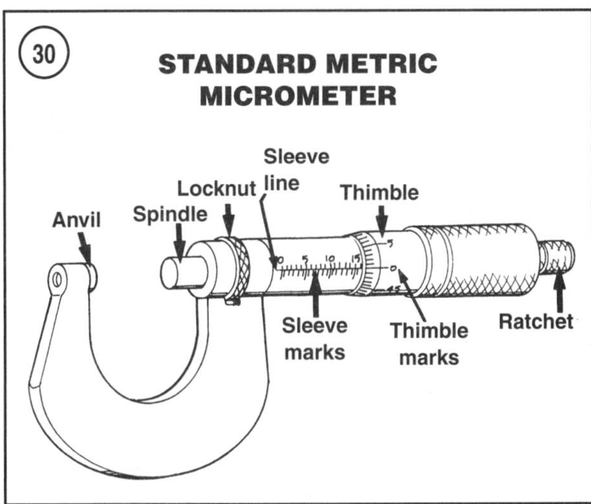

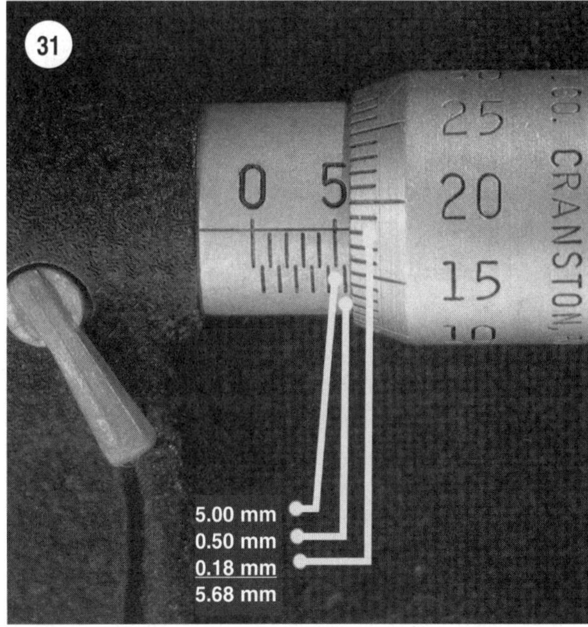

of the thimble aligns its 0 mark with the first line on the lower half of the sleeve line or 0.50 mm.

When reading a metric micrometer, add the number of millimeters and half-millimeters on the sleeve line to the number of one one-hundredth millimeters on the thimble. Perform the following steps while referring to **Figure 31**.

1. Read the upper half of the sleeve line and count the number of lines visible. Each upper line equals 1 mm.

2. See if the half-millimeter line is visible on the lower sleeve line. If so, add 0.50 mm to the reading in Step 1.

3. Read the thimble mark that aligns with the sleeve line. Each thimble mark equals 0.01 mm.

NOTE

If a thimble mark does not align exactly with the sleeve line, estimate the amount between the lines. For accurate readings in two-thou-

sandths of a millimeter (0.002 mm), use a metric vernier micrometer.

4. Add the readings from Steps 1-3.

Adjustment/care

Before using a micrometer, check its adjustment as follows.

1. Clean the anvil and spindle faces.

2A. To check a 0-1 in. or 0-25 mm micrometer:
   a. Turn the thimble until the spindle contacts the anvil. If the micrometer has a ratchet stop, use it to ensure that the proper amount of pressure is applied.
   b. If the adjustment is correct, the 0 mark on the thimble will align exactly with the 0 mark on the sleeve line. If the marks do not align, the micrometer is out of adjustment.
   c. Follow the manufacturer's instructions to adjust the micrometer.

2B. To check a micrometer larger than 1 in. or 25 mm use the standard gauge supplied by the manufacturer. A standard gauge is a steel block, disc or rod that is machined to an exact size.
   a. Place the standard gauge between the spindle and anvil, and measure its outside diameter or length. If the micrometer has a ratchet stop, use it to ensure that the proper amount of pressure is applied.
   b. If the adjustment is correct, the 0 mark on the thimble will align exactly with the 0 mark on the sleeve line. If the marks do not align, the micrometer is out of adjustment.
   c. Follow the manufacturer's instructions to adjust the micrometer.

3. Store micrometers in protective cases or separate padded drawers in a toolbox.
4. When in storage, make sure the spindle and anvil faces do not contact each other or another object. If they do, temperature changes and corrosion may damage the contact faces.
5. Do not clean a micrometer with compressed air. Dirt forced into the tool will cause wear.
6. Lubricate micrometers with WD-40 to prevent corrosion.

Telescoping and Small Bore Gauges

Use telescoping gauges (**Figure 32**) and small bore gauges (**Figure 33**) to measure bores. Neither gauge has a scale for direct readings. An outside micrometer must be used to determine the reading.

32

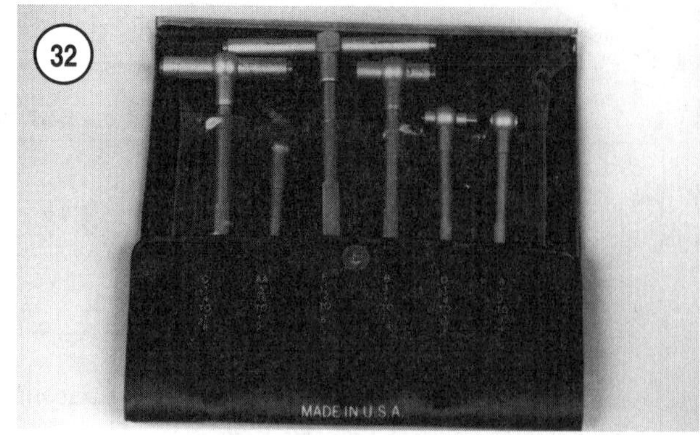

33

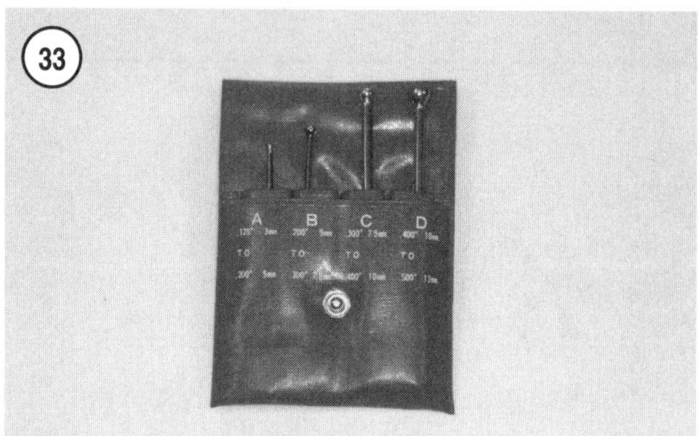

34

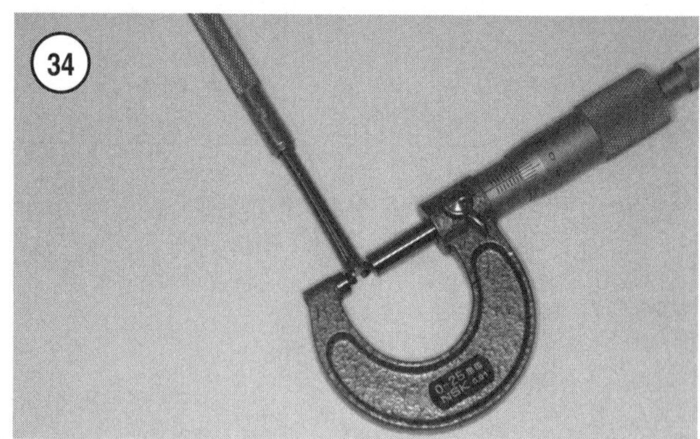

35

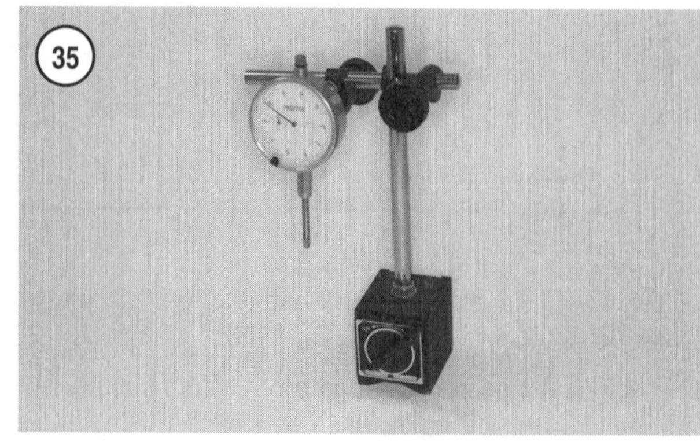

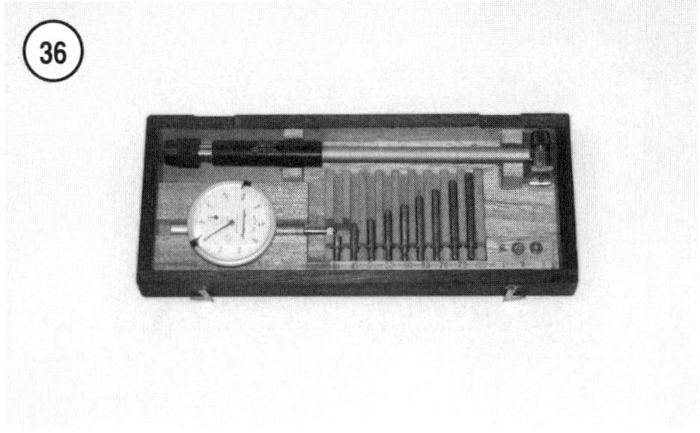
36

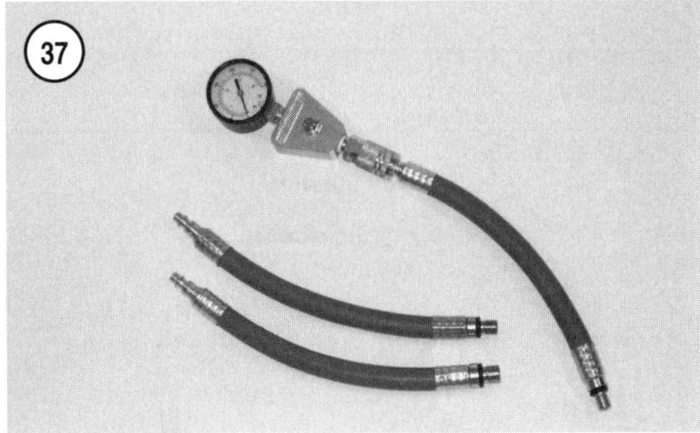
37

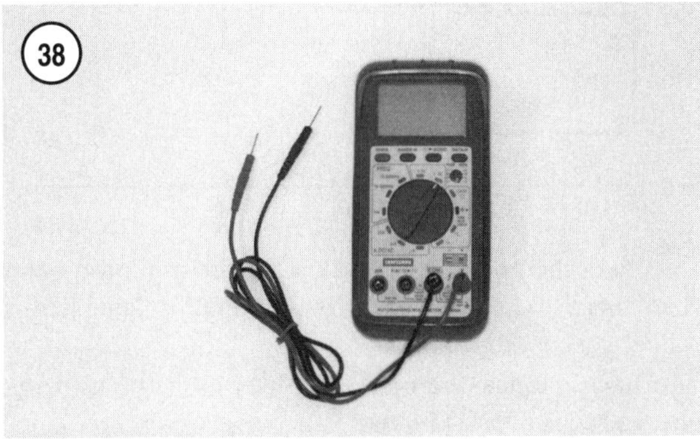
38

To use a telescoping gauge, select the correct size gauge for the bore. Compress the movable post and carefully insert the gauge into the bore. Carefully move the gauge in the bore to make sure it is centered. Tighten the knurled end of the gauge to hold the movable post in position. Remove the gauge and measure the length of the posts. Telescoping gauges are typically used to measure cylinder bores.

To use a small-bore gauge, select the correct size gauge for the bore. Carefully insert the gauge into the bore. Tighten the knurled end of the gauge to carefully expand the gauge fingers to the limit within the bore. Do not overtighten the gauge, as there is no built-in release. Excessive tightening can damage the bore surface and damage the tool. Remove the gauge and measure the outside dimension (**Figure 34**). Small bore gauges are typically used to measure valve guides.

Dial Indicator

A dial indicator (**Figure 35**) is a gauge with a dial face and needle used to measure variations in dimensions and movements. Measuring brake rotor runout is a typical use for a dial indicator.

Dial indicators are available in various ranges and graduations and with three basic types of mounting bases: magnetic, clamp or screw-in stud. When purchasing a dial indicator, select the magnetic stand type with a continuous dial.

Cylinder Bore Gauge

A cylinder bore gauge is similar to a dial indicator. The gauge set shown in **Figure 36** consists of a dial indicator, handle, and different length adapters (anvils) to fit the gauge to various bore sizes. The bore gauge is used to measure bore size, taper and out-of-round. When using a bore gauge, follow the manufacturer's instructions.

Compression Gauge

A compression gauge (**Figure 37**) measures combustion chamber (cylinder) pressure, usually in psi or kg/cm^2. The gauge adapter is either inserted or screwed into the spark plug hole to obtain the reading. Disable the engine so it will not start and hold the throttle in the wide-open position when performing a compression test. An engine that does not have adequate compression cannot be properly tuned. See Chapter Three.

Multimeter

A multimeter (**Figure 38**) is an essential tool for electrical system diagnosis. The voltage function indicates the voltage applied or available to various electrical components. The ohmmeter function tests circuits for continuity, or lack of continuity, and measures the resistance of a circuit.

Some manufacturers' specifications for electrical components are based on results using a specific test meter. Results may vary if using a meter not recommend by the manufacturer is used. Such requirements are noted when applicable.

Ohmmeter (analog) calibration

Each time an analog ohmmeter is used or if the scale is changed, the ohmmeter must be calibrated.

Digital ohmmeters do not require calibration.

1. Make sure the meter battery is in good condition.
2. Make sure the meter probes are in good condition.
3. Touch the two probes together and observe the needle location on the ohms scale. The needle must align with the 0 mark to obtain accurate measurements.
4. If necessary, rotate the meter ohms adjust knob until the needle and 0 mark align.

ELECTRICAL FUNDAMENTALS

A thorough study of the many types of electrical systems used in today's motorcycles is beyond the scope of this manual. However, a basic understanding of electrical basics is necessary to perform simple diagnostic tests.

Voltage

Voltage is the electrical potential or pressure in an electrical circuit and is expressed in volts. The more pressure (voltage) in a circuit, the more work that can be performed.

Direct current (DC) voltage means the electricity flows in one direction. All circuits powered by a battery are DC circuits.

Alternating current (AC) means that the electricity flows in one direction momentarily then switches to the opposite direction. Alternator output is an example of AC voltage. This voltage must be changed or rectified to direct current to operate in a battery powered system.

Measuring voltage

Unless otherwise specified, perform all voltage tests with the electrical connectors attached. When measuring voltage, select the meter range that is one scale higher than the expected voltage of the circuit to prevent damage to the meter. To determine the actual voltage in a circuit, use a voltmeter. To simply check if voltage is present, use a test light.

NOTE

When using a test light, either lead can be attached to ground.

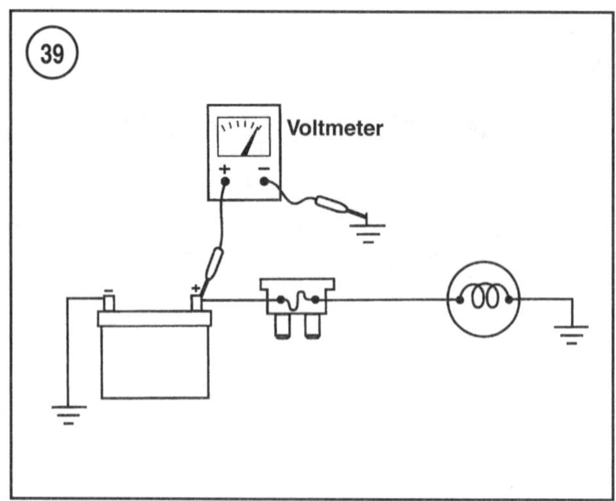

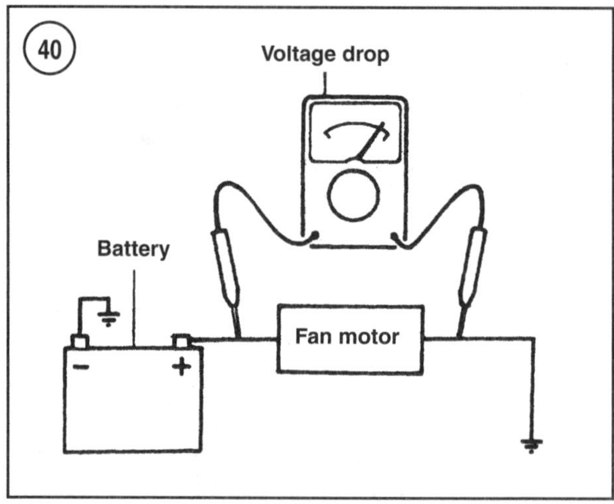

1. Attach the negative meter test lead to a good ground (bare metal). Make sure the ground is not insulated with a rubber gasket or grommet.
2. Attach the positive meter test lead to the point being checked for voltage (**Figure 39**).
3. Turn on the ignition switch. The test light should light or the meter should display a reading. The reading should be within one volt of battery voltage. If the voltage is less, there is a problem in the circuit.

Voltage drop test

Resistance causes voltage to drop. This resistance can be measured in an active circuit by using a voltmeter to perform a voltage drop test. A voltage drop test compares the difference between the voltage available at the start of a circuit to the voltage at the end of the circuit while the circuit is operational. If the circuit has no resistance, there

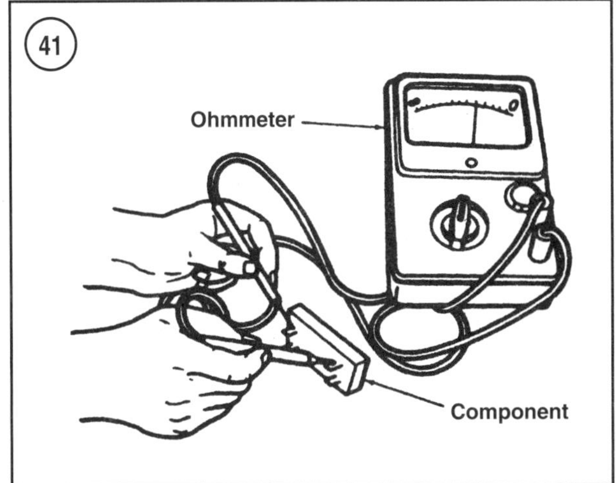

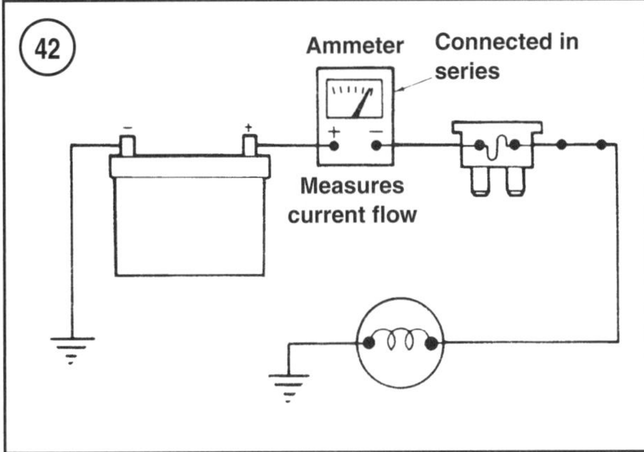

will be no voltage drop. The greater the resistance, the greater the voltage drop will be. A voltage drop of one volt or more indicates excessive resistance in the circuit.

1. Connect the positive meter test lead to the electrical source (where electricity is coming from).
2. Connect the negative meter test lead to the electrical load (where electricity is going). See **Figure 40**.
3. If necessary, activate the component(s) in the circuit.
4. A voltage reading of 1 volt or more indicates excessive resistance in the circuit. A reading equal to battery voltage indicates an open circuit.

Resistance

Resistance is the opposition to the flow of electricity within a circuit or component and is measured in ohms. Resistance causes a reduction in available current and voltage.

Resistance is measured in an inactive circuit with an ohmmeter. The ohmmeter sends a small amount of current into the circuit and measures how difficult it is to push the current through the circuit.

An ohmmeter, although useful, is not always a good indicator of a circuit's actual ability under operating conditions. This is due to the low voltage (6-9 volts) that the meter uses to test the circuit. The voltage in the ignition coil secondary winding can be several thousand volts. Such high voltage can cause the coil to malfunction, even though it tests acceptable during a resistance test.

Resistance generally increases with temperature. Perform all testing with the component or circuit at room temperature. Resistance tests performed at high temperatures may indicate high resistance readings and result in the unnecessary replacement of a component.

Measuring resistance and continuity testing

CAUTION

*Only use an ohmmeter on a circuit that has no voltage present. The meter will be damaged if it is connected to a live circuit. An analog meter must be calibrated each time it is used or the scale is changed. Refer to **Multimeter** in this chapter.*

A continuity test can determine if the circuit is complete. This test is performed with an ohmmeter or a self-powered test lamp.

1. Disconnect the negative battery cable.
2. Attach one test lead (ohmmeter or test light) to one end of the component or circuit.
3. Attach the other test lead to the opposite end of the component or circuit (**Figure 41**).
4. A self-powered test light will come on if the circuit has continuity or is complete. An ohmmeter will indicate either low or no resistance if the circuit has continuity. An open circuit is indicated if the meter displays infinite resistance.

Amperage

Amperage is the unit of measure for the amount of current within a circuit. Current is the actual flow of electricity. The higher the current, the more work that can be performed up to a given point. If the current flow exceeds the circuit or component capacity, the system will be damaged.

Measuring amps

An ammeter measures the current flow or amps of a circuit (**Figure 42**). Amperage measurement requires that the circuit be disconnected and the ammeter be connected in series to the circuit. Always use an ammeter that can read higher than the anticipated current flow to prevent damage to the meter. Connect the red test lead to the electrical source and the black test lead to the electrical load.

BASIC SERVICE METHODS

Most of the procedures in this manual are straightforward and can be performed by anyone reasonably competent with tools. However, consider personal capabilities carefully before attempting any operation involving major disassembly of the engine.

1. Front, in this manual, refers to the front of the motorcycle. The front of any component is the end closest to the front of the motorcycle. The left and right sides refer to the position of the parts as viewed by the rider sitting on the seat facing forward.
2. Whenever servicing an engine or suspension component, secure the motorcycle in a safe manner.
3. Tag all similar parts for location and mark all mating parts for position. Record the number and thickness of any shims as they are removed. Identify parts by placing them in sealed and labeled plastic sandwich bags.
4. Tag disconnected wires and connectors with masking tape and a marking pen. Do not rely on memory alone.
5. Protect finished surfaces from physical damage or corrosion. Keep gasoline and other chemicals off painted surfaces.
6. Use penetrating oil on frozen or tight bolts. Avoid using heat where possible. Heat can warp, melt or affect the temper of parts. Heat also damages the finish of paint and plastics.
7. When a part is a press fit or requires a special tool for removal, the information or type of tool is identified in the text. Otherwise, if a part is difficult to remove or install, determine the cause before proceeding.
8. To prevent objects or debris from falling into the engine, cover all openings.
9. Read each procedure thoroughly and compare the illustrations to the actual components before starting the procedure. Perform the procedure in sequence.
10. Recommendations are occasionally made to refer service to a dealership or specialist. In these cases, the work can be performed more economically by the specialist, than by the home mechanic.
11. The term *replace* means to discard a defective part and replace it with a new part. *Overhaul* means to remove, disassemble, inspect, measure, repair and/or replace parts as required to recondition an assembly.
12. Some operations require the use of a hydraulic press. If a press is not available, have these operations performed by a shop equipped with the necessary equipment. Do not use makeshift equipment that may damage the motorcycle.

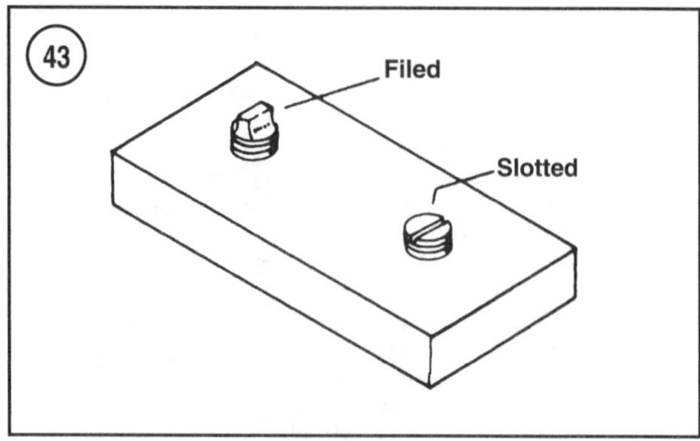

13. Repairs are much faster and easier if the motorcycle is clean before starting work. Degrease the motorcycle with a commercial degreaser; follow the directions on the container for the best results. Clean all parts with cleaning solvent as they are removed.

CAUTION

Do not direct high-pressure water at steering bearings, carburetor hoses, wheel bearings, suspension and electrical components. The water will force the grease out of the bearings and possibly damage the seals.

14. If special tools are required, have them available before starting the procedure. When special tools are required, they will be described at the beginning of the procedure.
15. Make diagrams of similar-appearing parts. For instance, crankcase bolts are often not the same lengths. Do not rely on memory alone. It is possible that carefully laid out parts will become disturbed, making it difficult to reassemble the components correctly without a diagram.
16. Make sure all shims and washers are reinstalled in the same location and position.
17. Whenever rotating parts contact a stationary part, look for a shim or washer.
18. Use new gaskets if there is any doubt about the condition of old ones.
19. If self-locking fasteners are used, replace them with new ones. Do not install standard fasteners in place of self-locking ones.
20. Use grease to hold small parts in place if they tend to fall out during assembly. Do not apply grease to electrical or brake components.

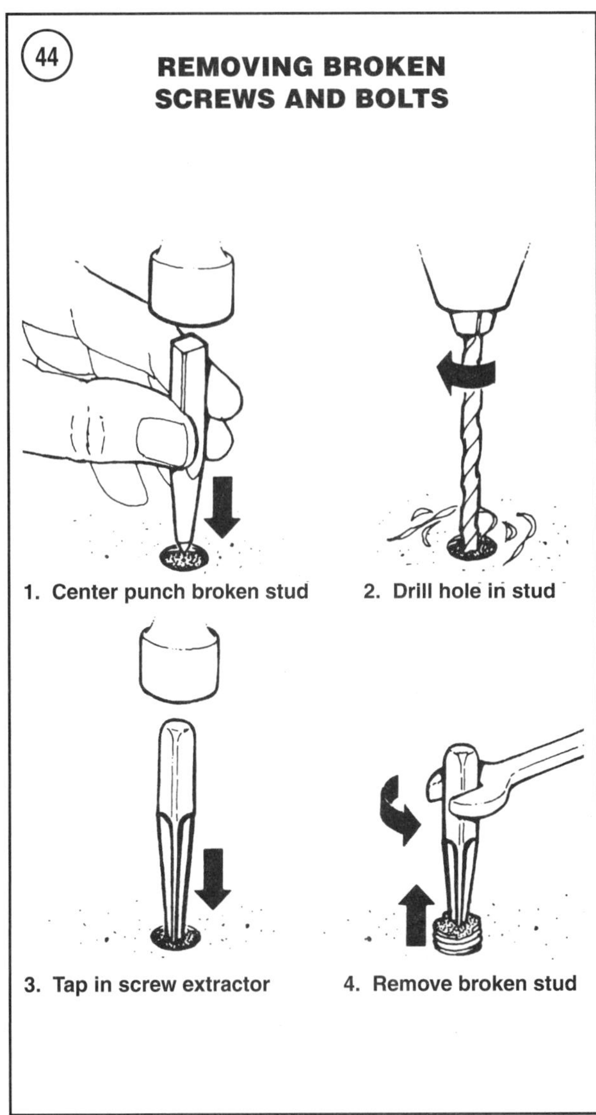

Removing Frozen Fasteners

If a fastener cannot be removed, several methods may be used to loosen it. First, apply penetrating oil such as Liquid Wrench or WD-40. Apply it liberally and let it penetrate for 10-15 minutes. Rap the fastener several times with a small hammer. Do not hit it hard enough to cause damage. Reapply the penetrating oil if necessary.

For frozen screws, apply penetrating oil as described, then insert a screwdriver in the slot and rap the top of the screwdriver with a hammer. This loosens the rust so the screw can be removed in the normal way. If the screw head is too damaged to use this method, grip the head with locking pliers and twist the screw out.

Avoid applying heat unless specifically instructed, as it may melt, warp or remove the temper from parts.

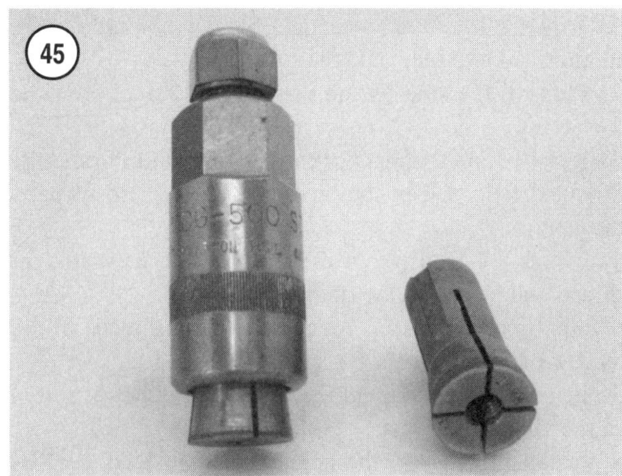

Removing Broken Fasteners

If the head breaks off of a screw or bolt, several methods are available for removing the remaining portion. If a large portion of the remainder projects out, try gripping it with locking pliers. If the projecting portion is too small, file it to fit a wrench or cut a slot in it to fit a screwdriver (**Figure 43**).

If the head breaks off flush, use a screw extractor. To do this, centerpunch the exact center of the remaining portion of the screw or bolt. Drill a small hole in the screw and tap the extractor into the hole. Back the screw out with a wrench on the extractor (**Figure 44**).

Repairing Damaged Threads

Occasionally, threads are stripped through carelessness or impact damage. Often the threads can be repaired by running a tap (for internal threads on nuts) or die (for external threads on bolts) through the threads. To clean or repair spark plug threads, use a spark plug tap.

If an internal thread is damaged, it may be necessary to install a Helicoil or some other type of thread insert. Follow the manufacturer's instructions when installing their insert.

If it is necessary to drill and tap a hole, refer to **Table 4** for metric tap and drill sizes.

Stud Removal/Installation

A stud removal tool (**Figure 45**) is available from most tool suppliers. This tool makes the removal and installation of studs easier. If one is not available, thread two nuts onto the stud and tighten them against each other. Remove the stud by turning the lower nut.

1. Measure the height of the stud above the surface.

2. Thread the stud removal tool onto the stud and tighten it, or thread two nuts onto the stud.
3. Remove the stud by turning the stud remover or the lower nut.
4. Remove any threadlocking compound from the threaded hole. Clean the threads with an aerosol parts cleaner.
5. Install the stud removal tool onto the new stud or thread two nuts onto the stud.
6. Apply threadlocking compound to the threads of the stud.
7. Install the stud and tighten with the stud removal tool or the top nut.
8. Install the stud to the height noted in Step 1 or its torque specification.
9. Remove the stud removal tool or the two nuts.

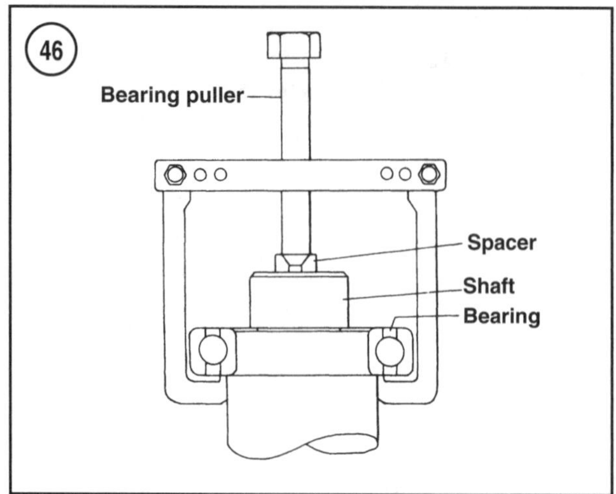

Removing Hoses

When removing stubborn hoses, do not exert excessive force on the hose or fitting. Remove the hose clamp and carefully insert a small screwdriver or pick tool between the fitting and hose. Apply a spray lubricant under the hose and carefully twist the hose off the fitting. Clean the fitting of any corrosion or rubber hose material with a wire brush. Clean the inside of the hose thoroughly. Do not use any lubricant when installing the hose (new or old). The lubricant may allow the hose to come off the fitting, even with the clamp secure.

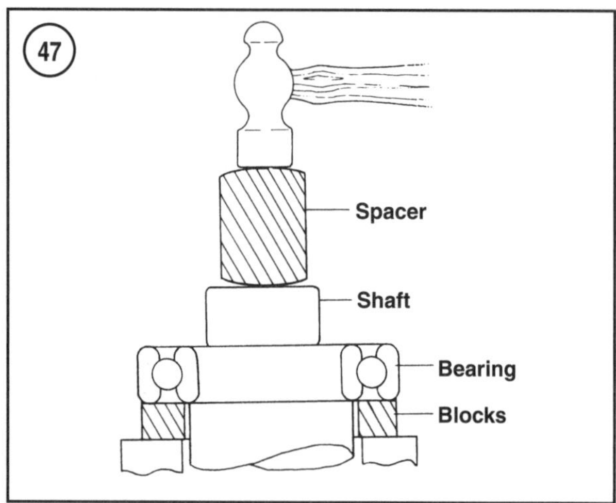

Bearings

Bearings are used in the engine and transmission assembly to reduce power loss, heat and noise resulting from friction. Because bearings are precision parts, they must be maintained with proper lubrication and maintenance. If a bearing is damaged, replace it immediately. When installing a new bearing, take care to prevent damaging it. Bearing replacement procedures are included in the individual chapters where applicable; however, use the following sections as a guideline.

NOTE
Unless otherwise specified, install bearings with the manufacturer's mark or number facing outward.

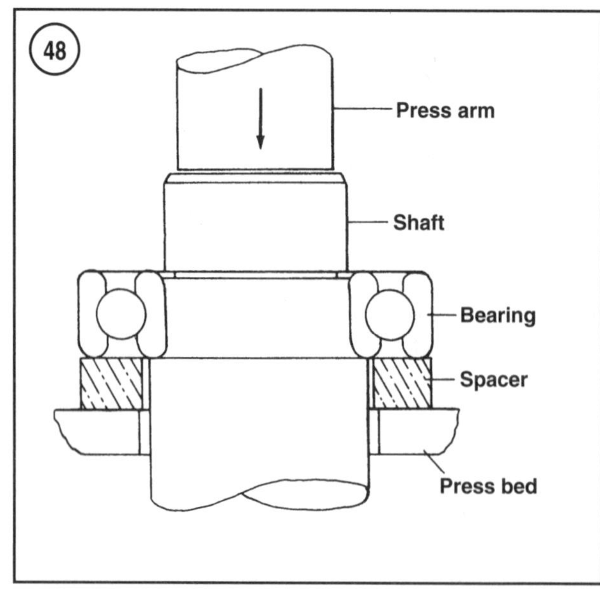

Removal

While bearings are normally removed only when damaged, there may be times when it is necessary to remove a bearing that is in good condition. However, improper

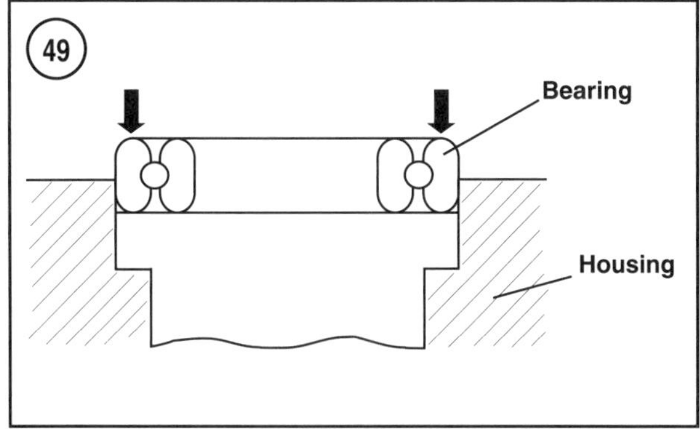

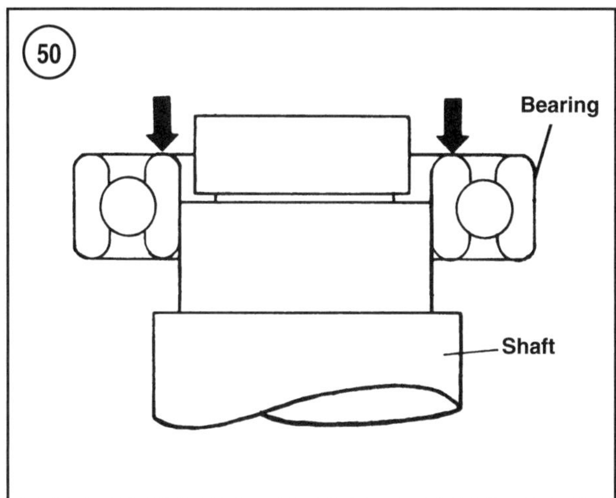

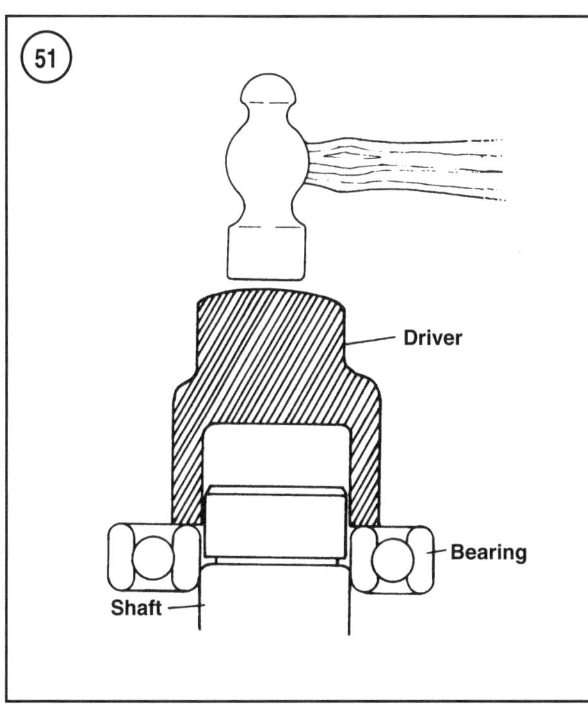

bearing removal will damage the bearing and maybe the shaft or case half. Note the following when removing bearings.

1. When using a puller to remove a bearing from a shaft, take care that the shaft is not damaged. Always place a piece of metal between the end of the shaft and the puller screw. In addition, place the puller arms next to the inner bearing race. See **Figure 46**.

2. When using a hammer to remove a bearing from a shaft, do not strike the hammer directly against the shaft. Instead, use a brass or aluminum rod between the hammer and shaft (**Figure 47**) and make sure to support both bearing races with wooden blocks as shown.

3. The ideal method of bearing removal is with a hydraulic press. Note the following when using a press:

   a. Always support the inner and outer bearing races with a suitable size wooden or aluminum ring (**Figure 48**). If only the outer race is supported, pressure applied against the balls and/or the inner race will damage them.

   b. Always make sure the press arm (**Figure 48**) aligns with the center of the shaft. If the arm is not centered, it may damage the bearing and/or shaft.

   c. The moment the shaft is free of the bearing, it will drop to the floor. Secure or hold the shaft to prevent it from falling.

Installation

1. When installing a bearing in a housing, apply pressure to the *outer* bearing race (**Figure 49**). When installing a bearing on a shaft, apply pressure to the *inner* bearing race (**Figure 50**).

2. When installing a bearing as described in Step 1, some type of driver is required. Never strike the bearing directly with a hammer or the bearing will be damaged. When installing a bearing, use a piece of pipe or a driver with a diameter that matches the bearing inner race. **Figure 51** shows the correct way to use a driver and hammer to install a bearing.

3. Step 1 describes how to install a bearing in a case half or over a shaft. However, when installing a bearing over a shaft and into the housing at the same time, a tight fit will be required for both outer and inner bearing races. In this situation, install a spacer underneath the driver tool so that pressure is applied evenly across both races. If the outer race is not supported as shown in **Figure 52**, the balls will push against the outer bearing race and damage it.

Interference fit

1. Follow this procedure when installing a bearing over a shaft. When a tight fit is required, the bearing inside diameter will be smaller than the shaft. In this case, driving the bearing on the shaft using normal methods may cause bearing damage. Instead, heat the bearing before installation. Note the following:

a. Secure the shaft so it is ready for bearing installation.
b. Clean all residues from the bearing surface of the shaft. Remove burrs with a file or sandpaper.
c. Fill a suitable pot or beaker with clean mineral oil. Place a thermometer rated above 120° C (248° F) in the oil. Support the thermometer so that it does not rest on the bottom or side of the pot.
d. Remove the bearing from its wrapper and secure it with a piece of heavy wire bent to hold it in the pot. Hang the bearing in the pot so it does not touch the bottom or sides of the pot.
e. Turn the heat on and monitor the thermometer. When the oil temperature rises to approximately 120° C (248° F), remove the bearing from the pot and quickly install it. If necessary, place a socket on the inner bearing race and tap the bearing into place. As the bearing chills, it will tighten on the shaft, so installation must be done quickly. Make sure the bearing is installed completely.

2. Follow this step when installing a bearing in a housing. Bearings are generally installed in a housing with a slight interference fit. Driving the bearing into the housing using normal methods may damage the housing or cause bearing damage. Instead, heat the housing before the bearing is installed. Note the following:

CAUTION
Before heating the housing in this procedure, wash the housing thoroughly with detergent and water. Rinse and rewash the cases as required to remove all traces of oil and other chemical deposits.

a. Heat the housing to approximately 100° C (212° F) in an oven or on a hot plate. An easy way to check that it is the proper temperature is to place tiny drops of water on the housing; if they sizzle and evaporate immediately, the temperature is correct. Heat only one housing at a time.

CAUTION
Do not heat the housing with a propane or acetylene torch. Never bring a flame into contact with the bearing or housing. The direct heat will destroy the case hardening of the bearing and will likely warp the housing.

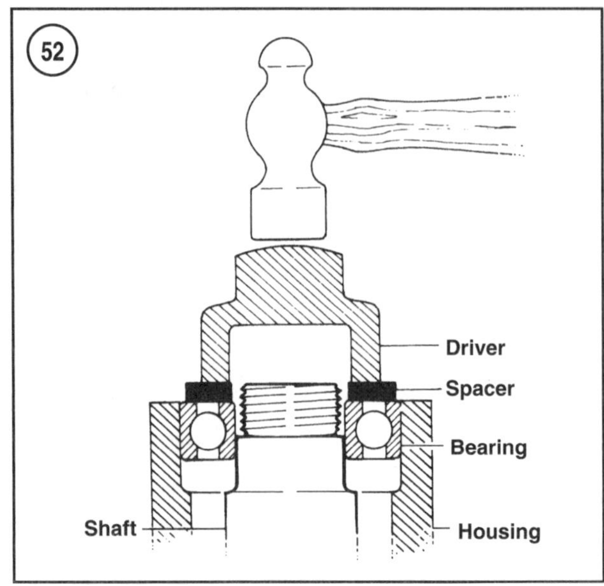

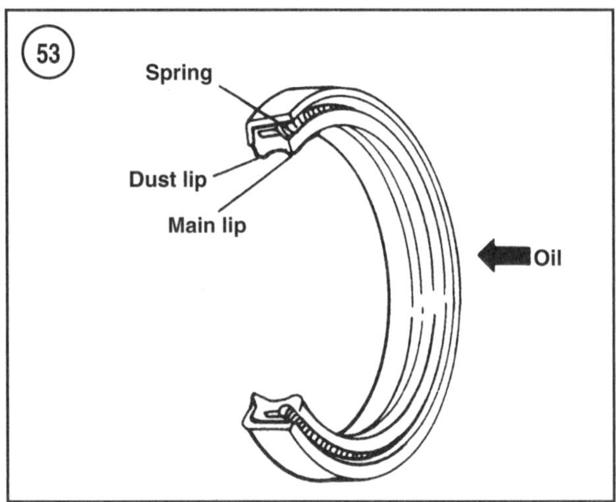

b. Remove the housing from the oven or hot plate, and hold onto the housing with a kitchen potholder, heavy gloves or heavy shop cloth. It is hot!

NOTE
Remove and install the bearings with a suitable size socket and extension.

c. Hold the housing with the bearing side down and tap the bearing out. Repeat for all bearings in the housing.
d. Before heating the bearing housing, place the new bearing in a freezer if possible. Chilling a bearing

54

55

56

slightly reduces its outside diameter while the heated bearing housing assembly is slightly larger due to heat expansion. This will make bearing installation easier.

NOTE
Always install bearings with the manufacturer's mark or number facing outward.

e. While the housing is still hot, install the new bearing(s) into the housing. Install the bearings by hand, if possible. If necessary, lightly tap the bearing(s) into the housing with a socket placed on the outer bearing race. Do not install new bearings by driving on the inner-bearing race. Install the bearing(s) until it seats completely.

Seal Replacement

Seals (**Figure 53**) are used to contain oil, water, grease or combustion gasses in a housing or shaft. Improper removal of a seal can damage the housing or shaft. Improper installation of the seal can damage the seal. Note the following:

1. Prying is generally the easiest and most effective method of removing a seal from the housing. However, always place a rag, or piece of wood (**Figure 54**), underneath the pry tool to prevent damage to the housing.
2. Pack waterproof grease in the seal lips before the seal is installed.
3. In most cases, install seals with the manufacturer's numbers or marks face out.
4. Install seals with a socket placed on the outside of the seal as shown in **Figure 55**. Drive the seal squarely into the housing until it is flush (**Figure 56**). Never install a seal by hitting against the top of the seal with a hammer.

STORAGE

Several months of non-use can cause a general deterioration of the motorcycle. This is especially true in areas of extreme temperature variations. This deterioration can be minimized with careful preparation for storage. A properly stored motorcycle will be much easier to return to service.

Storage Area Selection

When selecting a storage area, consider the following:

1. The storage area must be dry. A heated area is best, but not necessary. It should be insulated to minimize extreme temperature variations.
2. If the building has large window areas, mask them to keep sunlight off the motorcycle.
3. Avoid buildings in industrial areas where corrosive emissions may be present. Avoid areas close to saltwater.
4. Consider the area's risk of fire, theft or vandalism. Check with an insurer regarding motorcycle coverage while in storage.

Preparing the Motorcycle for Storage

The amount of preparation a motorcycle should undergo before storage depends on the expected length of non-use, storage area conditions and personal preference. Consider the following list the minimum requirement:

1. Wash the motorcycle thoroughly. Make sure all dirt, mud and road debris are removed.
2. Start the engine and allow it to reach operating temperature. Drain the engine oil and transmission oil, regardless of the riding time since the last service. Fill the engine and transmission with the recommended type of oil.
3. Fill the fuel tank completely. There is no need to try to empty the fuel delivery or return lines since they are not vented to the atmosphere.
4. Remove the spark plugs and pour a teaspoon of engine oil into the cylinders. Place a rag over the openings and slowly turn the engine over to distribute the oil. Reinstall the spark plugs.
5. Remove the battery. Store the battery in a cool and dry location.
6. Cover the exhaust and intake openings.
7. Reduce the normal tire pressure by 20%.
8. Apply a protective substance to the plastic and rubber components, including the tires. Make sure to follow the manufacturer's instructions for each type of product being used.
9. Place the motorcycle on a stand or wooden blocks, so the wheels are off the ground. If this is not possible, place a piece of plywood between the tires and the ground. Inflate the tires to the recommended pressure if the motorcycle can not be elevated.
10. Cover the motorcycle with old bed sheets or something similar. Do not cover it with any plastic material that will trap moisture.

Returning the Motorcycle to Service

The amount of service required when returning a motorcycle to service after storage depends on the length of non-use and storage conditions. In addition to performing the reverse of the above procedure, make sure the brakes, clutch, throttle and engine stop switch work properly before operating the motorcycle. Refer to Chapter Three and evaluate the service intervals to determine which areas require service.

Table 1 GENERAL TORQUE SPECIFICATIONS

Thread diameter	N•m	ft.-lb.
5 mm		
Bolt and nut	5	4
Screw	4	3
6 mm		
Bolt and nut	10	8
Screw	9	7
6 mm flange bolt and nut	12	9
6 mm bolt with 8 mm head	9	7
8 mm		
Bolt and nut	22	16
Flange bolt and nut	27	20
10 mm		
Bolt and nut	35	25
Flange bolt and nut	40	29
12 mm		
Bolt and nut	55	40

*Use the torque specifications in this table for tightening non-critical fasteners. Always refer to the specified torque table listed at the end of of the respective chapter(s) for critical applications. If a torque specification is not included in the table, use the general specifications in this table.

Table 2 CONVERSION FORMULAS

Multiply:	By:	To get the equivalent of:
Length		
Inches	25.4	Millimeter
Inches	2.54	Centimeter
Miles	1.609	Kilometer
Feet	0.3048	Meter
Millimeter	0.03937	Inches
Centimeter	0.3937	Inches
Kilometer	0.6214	Mile
Meter	0.0006214	Mile
Fluid volume		
U.S. quarts	0.9463	Liters
U.S. gallons	3.785	Liters
U.S. ounces	29.573529	Milliliters
Imperial gallons	4.54609	Liters
Imperial quarts	1.1365	Liters
Liters	0.2641721	U.S. gallons
Liters	1.0566882	U.S. quarts
Liters	33.814023	U.S. ounces
Liters	0.22	Imperial gallons
Liters	0.8799	Imperial quarts
Milliliters	0.033814	U.S. ounces
Milliliters	1.0	Cubic centimeters
Milliliters	0.001	Liters
Torque		
Foot-pounds	1.3558	Newton-meters
Foot-pounds	0.138255	Meters-kilograms
Inch-pounds	0.11299	Newton-meters
Newton-meters	0.7375622	Foot-pounds
Newton-meters	8.8507	Inch-pounds
Meters-kilograms	7.2330139	Foot-pounds
Volume		
Cubic inches	16.387064	Cubic centimeters
Cubic centimeters	0.0610237	Cubic inches
emperature		
Fahrenheit	(F – 32°) × 0.556	Centigrade
Centigrade	(C × 1.8) + 32°	Fahrenheit
Weight		
Ounces	28.3495	Grams
Pounds	0.4535924	Kilograms
Grams	0.035274	Ounces
Kilograms	2.2046224	Pounds
Pressure		
Pounds per square inch	0.070307	Kilograms per square centimeter
Kilograms per square centimeter	14.223343	Pounds per square inch
Kilopascals	0.1450	Pounds per square inch
Pounds per square inch	6.895	Kilopascals
Speed		
Miles per hour	1.609344	Kilometers per hour
Kilometers per hour	0.6213712	Miles per hour

Table 3 TECHNICAL ABBREVIATIONS

ABDC	After bottom dead center
ATDC	After top dead center
BBDC	Before bottom dead center
BDC	Bottom dead center
BTDC	Before top dead center
C	Celsius (Centigrade)
cc	Cubic centimeters
cid	Cubic inch displacement
CDI	Capacitor discharge ignition
cu. in.	Cubic inches
EVO	Evolution brake system
F	Fahrenheit
ft.	Feet
ft.-lb.	Foot-pounds
gal.	Gallons
H/A	High altitude
hp	Horsepower
in.	Inches
in.-lb.	Inch-pounds
I.D.	Inside diameter
kg	Kilograms
kgm	Kilogram meters
km	Kilometer
kPa	Kilopascals
L	Liter
m	Meter
MAG	Magneto
ml	Milliliter
mm	Millimeter
N•m	Newton-meters
O.D.	Outside diameter
oz.	Ounces
psi	Pounds per square inch
PTO	Power take off
pt.	Pint
qt.	Quart
rpm	Revolutions per minute
SOHC	Single overhead cam

Table 4 METRIC TAP AND DRILL SIZE

Metric size	Drill equivalent	Decimal fraction	Nearest fraction
3 × 0.50	No. 39	0.0995	3/32
3 × 0.60	3/32	0.0937	3/32
4 × 0.70	No. 30	0.1285	1/8
4 × 0.75	1/8	0.125	1/8
5 × 0.80	No. 19	0.166	11/64
5 × 0.90	No. 20	0.161	5/32
6 × 1.00	No. 9	0.196	13/64
7 × 1.00	16/64	0.234	15/64
8 × 1.00	J	0.277	9/32
8 × 1.25	17/64	0.265	17/64
9 × 1.00	5/16	0.3125	5/16
9 × 1.25	5/16	0.3125	5/16
10 × 1.25	11/32	0.3437	11/32
10 × 1.50	R	0.339	11/32
11 × 1.50	3/8	0.375	3/8
12 × 1.50	13/32	0.406	13/32
12 × 1.75	13/32	0.406	13/32

Table 5 METRIC, INCH AND FRACTIONAL EQUIVALENTS

mm	in.	Nearest fraction	mm	in.	Nearest fraction
1	0.0394	1/32	26	1.0236	1 1/32
2	0.0787	3/32	27	1.0630	1 1/16
3	0.1181	1/8	28	1.1024	1 3/32
4	0.1575	5/32	29	1.1417	1 5/32
5	0.1969	3/16	30	1.1811	1 3/16
6	0.2362	1/4	31	1.2205	1 7/32
7	0.2756	9/32	32	1.2598	1 1/4
8	0.3150	5/16	33	1.2992	1 5/16
9	0.3543	11/32	34	1.3386	1 11/32
10	0.3937	13/32	35	1.3780	1 3/8
11	0.4331	7/16	36	1.4173	1 13/32
12	0.4724	15/32	37	1.4567	1 15/32
13	0.5118	1/2	38	1.4961	1 1/2
14	0.5512	9/16	39	1.5354	1 17/32
15	0.5906	19/32	40	1.5748	1 9/16
16	0.6299	5/8	41	1.6142	1 5/8
17	0.6693	21/32	42	1.6535	1 21/32
18	0.7087	23/32	43	1.6929	1 11/16
19	0.7480	3/4	44	1.7323	1 23/32
20	0.7874	25/32	45	1.7717	1 25/32
21	0.8268	13/16	46	1.8110	1 13/16
22	0.8661	7/8	47	1.8504	1 27/32
23	0.9055	29/32	48	1.8898	1 7/8
24	0.9449	15/16	49	1.9291	1 15/16
25	0.9843	31/32	50	1.9685	1 31/32

CHAPTER TWO

TROUBLESHOOTING

The troubleshooting procedures described in this chapter provide typical symptoms and logical methods for isolating the cause(s). There may be several ways to solve a problem, but only a systematic approach will be successful in avoiding wasted time and possibly unnecessary parts replacement.

Gather as much information as possible to aid in diagnosis. Never assume anything and do not overlook the obvious. Make sure the stop switch is in the run position and there is fuel in the tank. Learning to recognize symptoms will make troubleshooting easier. In most cases, expensive and complicated test equipment is not needed to determine whether repairs can be performed at home. On the other hand, be realistic and do not start procedures that are beyond the experience and equipment available. Many service departments will not take work that involves the reassembly of damaged or abused equipment; if they do, expect the cost to be high. If the motorcycle does require the attention of a professional, describe symptoms and conditions accurately and fully. The more information a technician has available, the easier it will be to diagnose the problem.

Proper lubrication and maintenance reduces the chance that problems will occur. However, even with the best of care, the motorcycle may require troubleshooting.

OPERATING REQUIREMENTS

An engine needs three basics to run properly: correct air/fuel mixture, compression and spark at the right time. If one basic requirement is missing, the engine will not run. Four-stroke engine operating principles are shown in **Figure 1**.

If the motorcycle has not been used for any length of time and refuses to start, check and clean the spark plugs. If the plugs are not fouled, inspect the fuel system. This includes the fuel tank, fuel and vacuum hoses, fuel pump, and the fuel injection system. Gasoline tends to lose its potency after standing for long periods; as it evaporates, the mixture becomes richer. Condensation may contaminate gasoline with water. Drain the old gas and try starting with a fresh tankful.

STARTING THE ENGINE

When experiencing engine-starting troubles, it is easy to work out of sequence and forget basic starting procedures. The following section describes the recommended starting procedures.

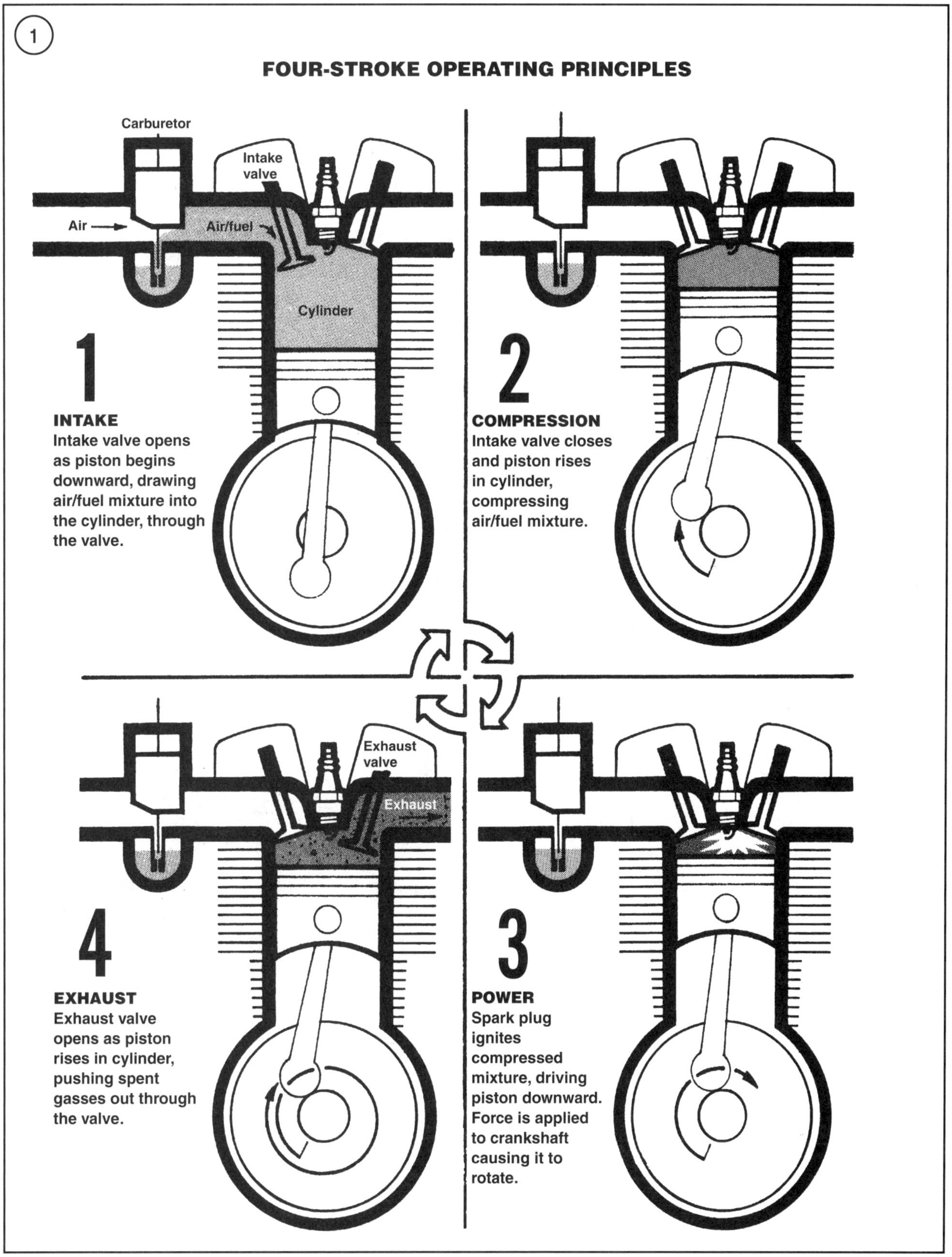

(1)

FOUR-STROKE OPERATING PRINCIPLES

Carburetor
Intake valve
Air
Air/fuel
Cylinder

1

INTAKE
Intake valve opens as piston begins downward, drawing air/fuel mixture into the cylinder, through the valve.

2

COMPRESSION
Intake valve closes and piston rises in cylinder, compressing air/fuel mixture.

Exhaust valve
Exhaust

4

EXHAUST
Exhaust valve opens as piston rises in cylinder, pushing spent gasses out through the valve.

3

POWER
Spark plug ignites compressed mixture, driving piston downward. Force is applied to crankshaft causing it to rotate.

Starting Procedure

1. All models are equipped with a sidestand ignition cut-off system. The position of the sidestand will affect engine starting. Note the following:
   - a. The engine cannot start when the sidestand is down and the transmission is in gear.
   - b. The engine can start when the sidestand is down and the transmission is in neutral. The engine will stop if the transmission is put in gear with the sidestand down.
   - c. The engine can be started when the sidestand is up and the transmission is in neutral or in gear with the clutch lever pulled in.
2. Before starting the engine, shift the transmission into neutral and confirm that the engine stop switch is in the RUN position (**Figure 2**).
3. Turn the ignition switch on and confirm that the following warning lights are on:
   - a. The neutral indicator light (when the transmission is in neutral).
   - b. The oil pressure warning light.
   - c. ABS warning light (models so equipped).
   - d. Engine trouble warning light.
4. The warning lights should go off a few seconds after the engine starts. If any light stays on, turn the engine off and determine the cause.
5. The engine is now ready to start as follows:

CAUTION

Once the engine starts, the oil pressure warning light should go off in a few seconds. If the light stays on longer than a few seconds, stop the engine immediately. Check the oil level as described in Chapter Three. If the oil level is good, the oil filter or oil cooler(s) may be plugged, the oil pressure may be too low, or the oil pressure switch may be shorted. Check the lubrication system and correct the problem before restarting the engine. If the oil pressure switch is good, some type of stoppage has occurred in the lubrication system and oil is not being delivered to engine components. Severe engine damage will occur if the engine is run with low oil pressure. Refer to ***Engine Lubrication*** *in this chapter.*

   - a. On models so equipped, move the choke lever to the UP position (**Figure 3**) for a cold start or DOWN position (**Figure 4**) when engine is at operating temperature.

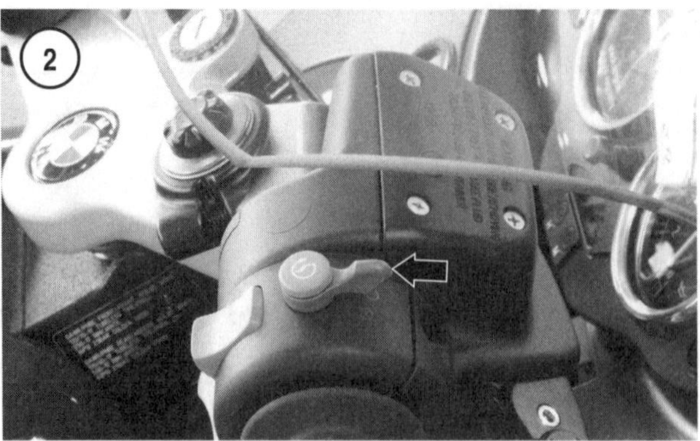

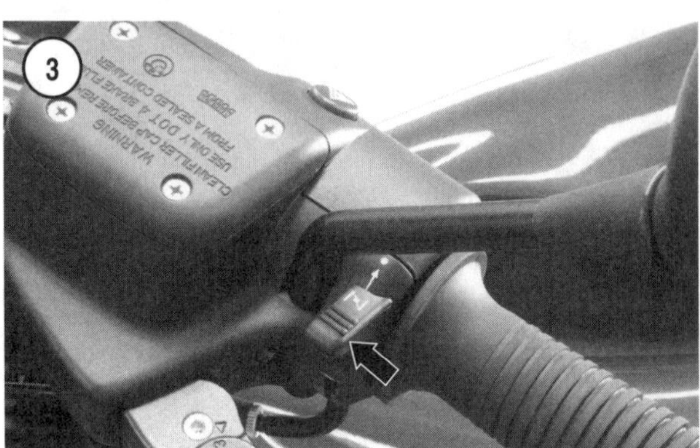

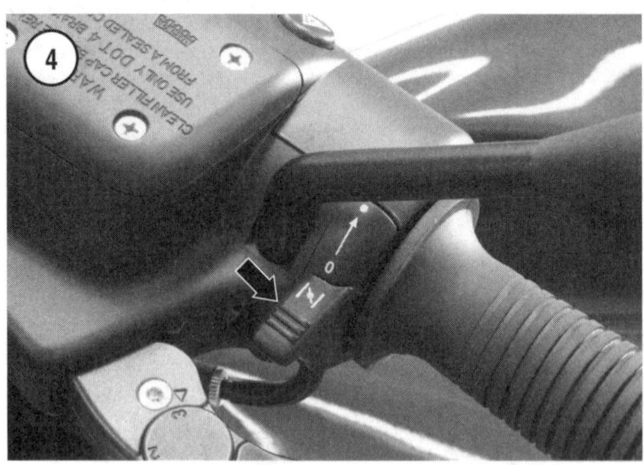

NOTE

Do not twist the throttle when pressing the start button.

   - b. Press the start button (**Figure 5**).
   - c. Rotate the throttle twist grip carefully to increase engine idle speed.
   - d. Move the choke lever to the down position (**Figure 4**) after the engine runs smoothly.

5

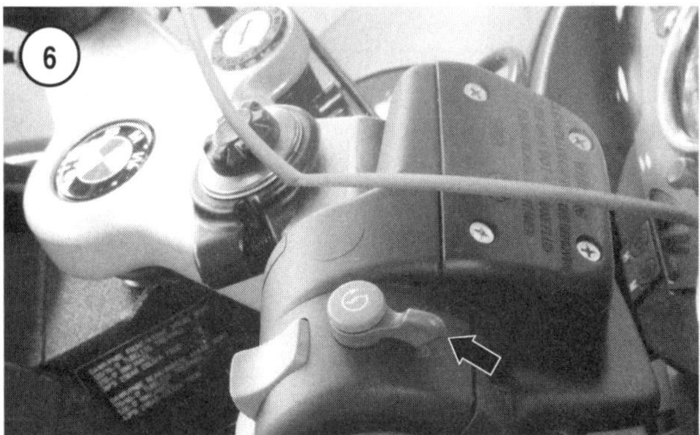

6

7

8

Engine is flooded

If the engine will not start after a few attempts, it may be flooded. If a gasoline smell is present after attempting to start the engine, the engine is probably flooded. To start a flooded engine:

1. Turn the engine stop switch off (**Figure 6**).
2. Open the throttle fully.
3. Turn the ignition switch on and operate the starter button for five seconds.
4. Follow the *Starting Procedure*. Note the following:
   a. If the engine starts but idles roughly, vary the throttle position slightly until the engine idles and responds smoothly.
   b. If the engine does not start, turn the ignition switch off and wait approximately ten seconds. Then repeat Steps 2-4. If the engine still will not start, refer to *Starting Difficulties* in this chapter.

STARTING DIFFICULTIES

If the engine does not start, perform the following procedure in sequence while remembering the *Operating Requirements* described in this chapter. If the engine fails to start after performing these checks, refer to the troubleshooting procedures indicated in the steps.

1. Refer to *Starting the Engine* in this chapter to make sure all switches and starting procedures are correct.
2. If the starter does not operate, refer to *Starting System* in this chapter.
3. If the starter operates, and the engine seems flooded, refer to *Engine is flooded* in this chapter. If the engine is not flooded, continue with Step 4.
4. Turn the ignition switch on and check the fuel level. If the fuel level warning light is on, the fuel level in the tank is low.
5. If there is sufficient fuel in the fuel tank, remove one of the spark plugs immediately after attempting to start the engine. The plug's insulator should be wet, indicating that fuel is reaching the engine. If the plug tip is dry, fuel is not reaching the engine. Confirm this condition by checking another spark plug. A faulty fuel pump, a clogged fuel filter or strainer can cause this condition. Refer to *Fuel System* in this chapter. If there is fuel on the spark plug and the engine will not start, the engine may not have adequate spark. Continue with Step 6.
6. Make sure each spark plug wire is secure. Remove the cover (**Figure 7**), push both wires and boots (**Figure 8**) on and slightly rotate them to clean the electrical connector between the spark plug and the connector. If the engine does not start, continue with Step 7.

7. Perform the *Spark Test* described in this section. If there is a strong spark, perform Step 8. If there is no spark or if the spark is very weak, refer to *Ignition System* in Chapter Ten.
8. Check cylinder compression as described in Chapter Three.

Spark Test

Perform a spark test to determine if the ignition system is producing adequate spark. This test can be performed with a spark plug or a spark tester (**Figure 9**). A spark tester is used as a substitute for the spark plug and allows the spark to be more easily observed between the adjustable air gap. The tool shown is available from Motion Pro (part No. 08-0122). If a spark tester is not available, always use a *new* spark plug.

This test can be performed on both sets of spark plugs on dual-plug ignition systems.

WARNING
Step 1 must be performed to disable the fuel system. Otherwise, fuel will enter into the cylinders when the engine is turned over during the spark test, flooding the cylinders and creating explosive fuel vapors.

1. Refer to *Fuses* in Chapter Ten and disconnect the fuel pump fuse.
2. Remove the spark plugs as described in Chapter Three.
3. Connect each spark plug wire and connector to a new spark plug or tester, and touch each spark plug base or tester to a good engine ground. Position the spark plugs or tester so the electrodes are visible.

WARNING
Mount the spark plugs, or spark tester, away from the spark plug holes in the cylinder head so the spark plugs or tester cannot ignite the gasoline vapors in the cylinder. If the engine is flooded, do not perform this test. The firing of the spark plugs or spark tester can ignite fuel that is ejected through the spark plug holes.

4. Shift the transmission to neutral, turn the ignition switch on and place the engine stop switch in the RUN position (**Figure 2**).

WARNING
Do not hold the spark plugs, tester, wire or connector, or a serious electrical shock may result.

9

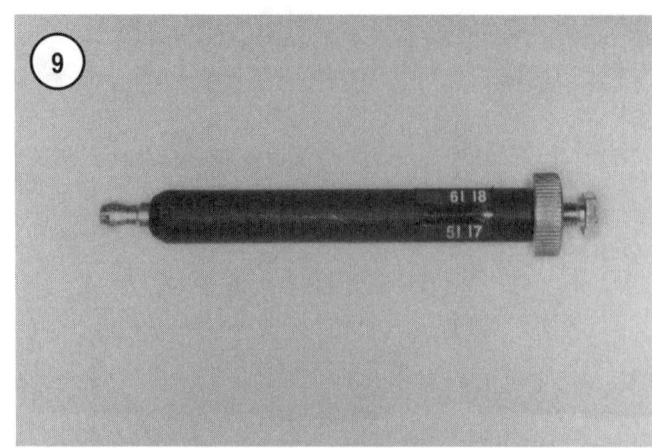

5. Operate the starter button to turn the engine over. A fat blue spark must be evident across the spark plug electrodes or between the tester terminals. Repeat for each cylinder.
6. If the spark is good at each spark plug, the ignition system is functioning properly. Check for one or more of the following possible malfunctions:
   a. Faulty fuel system component. Refer to *Fuel System* in this chapter.
   b. Engine damage (low compression).
   c. Engine flooded.
7. If the spark was weak or if there was no spark at either plug, refer to *Engine is Difficult to Start* in this section.

NOTE
If the engine backfires when starting the engine, the ignition timing may be incorrect. The Hall sensor mounting plate may be loose or a defective ignition component could have changed the ignition timing. Refer to ***Ignition System*** *in this chapter.*

Engine is Difficult to Start

1. After attempting to start the engine, remove one of the spark plugs as described in Chapter Three and check for the presence of fuel on the plug tip. Note the following:
   a. If there is no fuel visible on the plug, remove the remaining spark plug. If there is no fuel on this plug, perform Step 2.
   b. If there is fuel present on the plug tip, go to Step 4.
   c. If there is an excessive amount of fuel on the plug, check for a clogged or plugged air filter, incorrect choke operation and adjustment or incorrect throttle valve operation (stuck open).

2. Perform the *Fuel Pump Pressure Check* in Chapter Nine. Note the following:
   a. If the fuel pump operation is correct, go to Step 4.
   b. If the fuel pump operation is faulty, replace the fuel pump and retest the fuel system.
3. Inspect the fuel injectors as described in Chapter Nine.
4. Perform the *Spark Test* as described in this section. Note the following:
   a. If the spark is weak or if there is no spark, go to Step 5.
   b. If the spark is good, go to Step 6.
5. If the spark is weak or if there is no spark, check the following:
   a. Fouled spark plug(s).
   b. Damaged spark plug(s).
   c. Loose or damaged spark plug wire(s).
   d. Loose or damaged spark plug cap(s).
   e. Damaged Motronic unitor Hall sensor unit.
   f. Damaged ignition coil(s).
   g. Damaged engine stop switch.
   h. Damaged ignition switch.
   i. Dirty or loose-fitting terminals.
6. If the engine turns over but does not start, the engine compression may be low. Check for the following possible malfunctions:
   a. Leaking cylinder head gasket(s).
   b. Valve clearance too tight.
   c. Bent or stuck valve(s).
   d. Incorrect valve timing. Worn cylinders and/or pistons rings.
7. If the spark is good, try starting the engine by following normal starting procedures. If the engine starts but then stops, check for the following conditions:
   a. Incorrect choke operation.
   b. Leaking or damaged flexible inlet hose(s) between the air filter housing and the throttle body.
   c. Contaminated fuel.
   d. Incorrect ignition timing due to a damaged ignition coil(s) or Hall sensor alignment.

Engine Will Not Crank

If the engine will not turn over, check for one or more of the following possible malfunctions:

1. Blown main fuse.
2. Discharged battery.
3. Defective starter or starter relay switch.
4. Seized piston(s).
5. Seized crankshaft bearings.
6. Broken connecting rod(s).
7. Locked-up transmission or clutch assembly.
8. Defective starter clutch.

ENGINE PERFORMANCE

If the engine runs, but performance is unsatisfactory, refer to the following procedure(s) that best describes the symptom(s).

Engine Will Not Idle

1. Clogged air filter element.
2. Poor fuel flow.
3. Fouled or improperly gapped spark plug(s).
4. Leaking head gasket or vacuum leak.
5. Leaking or damaged flexible inlet hose(s) between the air filter housing and the throttle body.
6. Incorrect ignition timing due to a damaged ignition coil(s) or Hall sensor alignment.
7. Obstructed or defective fuel injector(s).
8. Low engine compression.

Poor Overall Performance

1. Support the motorcycle with the rear wheel off the ground, then rotate the rear wheel by hand. If the wheel rotates freely, perform Step 2. If the wheel does not rotate freely, check for the following conditions:
   a. Dragging rear brake.
   b. Damaged final drive unit or drive shaft assembly.
2. Check the clutch adjustment (cable-operated models) and operation. If the clutch slips, refer to *Clutch* in this chapter.
3. Test ride the motorcycle and accelerate lightly. If the engine speed increased according to throttle position, perform Step 4. If the engine speed did not increase, check for one or more of the following problems:
   a. Clogged air filter.
   b. Restricted fuel flow.
   c. Pinched fuel tank breather hose.
   d. Clogged or damaged muffler(s).
4. Check for one or more of the following problems:
   a. Low engine compression.
   b. Worn spark plugs.
   c. Fouled spark plug(s).
   d. Incorrect spark plug heat range.
   e. Clogged or defective fuel injector(s).
   f. Incorrect ignition timing due to a damaged ignition coil or Hall sensor alignment.
   g. Incorrect oil level (too high or too low).
   h. Contaminated oil.
   i. Worn or damaged valve train assembly.
   j. Engine overheating. Refer to *Engine Overheating* in this section.

5. If the engine knocks when it is accelerated or when running at high speed, check for one or more of the following possible malfunctions:
   a. Incorrect type of fuel.
   b. Lean fuel mixture.
   c. Incorrect ignition timing due to a damaged ignition coil or Hall sensor alignment.
   d. Excessive carbon buildup in combustion chamber.
   e. Worn pistons and/or cylinder bores.

Poor Idle or Low Speed Performance

1. Check for damaged flexible inlet hose(s) between the air filter housing and the throttle body.
2. Check the fuel flow to the fuel injectors (Chapter Nine).
3. Perform the *Spark Test* described in this section. Note the following:
   a. If the spark is good, go to Step 4.
   b. If the spark is weak, test the ignition system as described in this chapter.
4. Check the ignition timing as described in Chapter Three. Note the following:
   a. If the ignition is incorrect, check for a damaged ignition coil or Hall sensor mis-alignment.
   b. If the ignition timing is correct, recheck the fuel system.

Poor High Speed Performance

1. Check the fuel injectors (Chapter Nine).
2. Check ignition timing as described in Chapter Three. If ignition timing is correct, perform Step 3.
3. If the timing is incorrect, test the following ignition system components as described in Chapter Ten:
   a. Hall sensor assembly.
   b. Ignition coil.
4. Check the valve clearance as described in Chapter Three. Note the following:
   a. If the valve clearance is correct, perform Step 5.
   b. If the clearance is incorrect, readjust the valves.
5. Incorrect valve timing and worn or damaged valve springs can cause poor high-speed performance. If the camshafts were timed just prior to the motorcycle experiencing this type of problem, the cam timing may be incorrect. If the cam timing was not set or changed, and all of the other inspection procedures in this section failed to locate the problem, remove the cylinder heads and inspect the camshafts and valve assembly.

Engine Overheating

Engine overheating can quickly cause engine seizure and damage. The following section groups six main systems with probable causes that can lead to engine overheating.

1. Ignition system:
   a. Incorrect spark plug gap.
   b. Incorrect spark plug heat range; see Chapter Three.
   c. Faulty ignition system component.
2. Engine compression system:
   a. Cylinder head gasket(s) leakage.
   b. Heavy carbon buildup in combustion chamber(s).
3. Engine lubrication system:
   a. Incorrect oil level.
   b. Incorrect oil viscosity.
   c. Faulty oil pump.
   d. Plugged oil filter.
   e. Oil not circulating properly.
   f. Clogged oil cooler(s).
4. Fuel system:
   a. Clogged air filter element.
   b. Leaking or damaged throttle body-to-air filter housing air boot(s).
   c. Incorrect air fuel mixture.
   d. Defective fuel pump.
5. Engine load:
   a. Dragging brake(s).
   b. Damaged drive train components.
   c. Slipping clutch.
   d. Engine oil level too high.
6. Engine cooling system:
   a. Clogged or dirty cooling fins on cylinder head cover, cylinder head and cylinder block.
   b. Clogged or dirty cooling fins on lower portion of crankcase.
   c. Clogged oil cooler(s).

ENGINE NOISES

Unusual noises are often the first indication of a developing problem. Investigate any new noises as soon as possible. Something that may be a minor problem, if corrected, could prevent the possibility of more extensive damage.

Use a mechanic's stethoscope or a small section of hose held near the ear (not directly on the ear) with the other end close to the source of the noise to isolate the location. Determining the exact cause of a noise can be difficult. If this is the case, consult with a professional mechanic to determine the cause. Do not disassemble major components until all other possibilities have been eliminated.

Consider the following when troubleshooting engine noises:

1. Knocking or pinging during acceleration caused by using a lower octane fuel than recommended. May also be caused by poor fuel. Pinging can also be caused by an incorrect spark plug heat range or carbon build-up in the combustion chamber. Refer to *Spark Plug Inspection* and *Engine Compression Test* in Chapter Three.

2. Slapping or rattling noises at low speed or during acceleration may be caused by excessive piston-to-cylinder wall clearance (piston slap).

NOTE

Piston slap is easier to detect when the engine is cold and before the pistons have expanded. Once the engine has warmed up, piston expansion reduces piston-to-cylinder clearance.

3. Knocking or rapping while decelerating usually caused by excessive rod bearing clearance.

4. Persistent knocking and vibration occurring every crankshaft rotation usually caused by worn rod or main bearing(s). Can also be caused by broken piston rings or damaged piston pins.

5. Rapid on-off squeal by compression leak around cylinder head gaskets or spark plug(s).

6. Valve train noise, check for the following:
   a. Valve clearance excessive.
   b. Worn or damaged camshaft(s).
   c. Damaged camshaft, camshaft drive chain and guides.
   d. Worn or damaged push rods, rocker arms and/or tappets.
   e. Damaged tappet bore(s).
   f. Valve sticking in guide(s).
   g. Broken valve spring(s).
   h. Low oil pressure.
   i. Clogged cylinder oil hole or oil passage.

ENGINE LUBRICATION

An improperly operating engine lubrication system will quickly lead to engine seizure. Check the engine oil level before each ride, and top off as described in Chapter Three. Oil pump service is described in Chapter Five.

High Oil Consumption or Excessive Exhaust Smoke

1. Worn valve guides.
2. Worn or damaged piston rings.

Oil Leaks

1. Clogged air filter housing breather hose.
2. Loose engine parts.
3. Damaged gasket sealing surfaces.

High Oil Pressure

1. Clogged oil filter.
2. Clogged oil cooler(s).
3. Clogged oil gallery or metering orifices.
4. Incorrect type of engine oil.

Low Oil Pressure

1. Low oil level.
2. Worn or damaged oil pump.
3. Clogged oil strainer screen.
4. Clogged oil filter.
5. Clogged oil cooler(s).
6. Internal oil leakage.
7. Incorrect type of engine oil.

No Oil Pressure

1. Damaged oil pump.
2. Low oil level.
3. Damaged oil pump drive shaft.
4. Damaged oil pump drive sprocket.
5. Incorrect oil pump installation.

Oil Pressure Warning Light Stays On

1. Low oil level.
2. Damaged oil pressure switch.
3. Short circuit in warning light circuit.

Oil Level Too Low

1. Oil level not maintained at correct level.
2. Worn piston rings.
3. Worn cylinder(s).
4. Worn valve guides.
5. Worn valve stem seals.

6. Piston rings incorrectly installed during engine overhaul.
7. External oil leakage.

Oil Contamination

Oil and filter not changed at specified intervals or when operating conditions demand more frequent changes.

CYLINDER LEAKDOWN TEST

A cylinder leakdown test can locate engine problems from leaking valves, blown head gasket or broken, worn or stuck piston rings. To perform this test, apply compressed air to the cylinder and then measuring the percent of leakage. Use a cylinder leakdown tester (**Figure 10**) and an air compressor to perform this test.

Follow the manufacturer's directions along with the following information when performing a cylinder leakdown test.

1. Start and run the engine until it is warm. Turn off the engine.
2. Set the piston for the cylinder to be tested to TDC on its compression stroke as described under *Valve Clearance* in Chapter Three.
3. Remove the spark plug for the cylinder to be tested as described in Chapter Three.

WARNING
The crankshaft may rotate when compressed air is applied to the cylinder. To prevent the engine from turning over as compressed air is applied to the cylinder, shift the transmission into top gear and then have an assistant apply the rear brake.

4. Install the leak down tester following the manufacturer's instructions.
5. Apply compressed air to the leakdown tester and make a cylinder leakdown test following the manufacturer's instructions. Read the percent of leakage on the gauge, following the manufacturer's instructions. Note the following:
   a. For a new or rebuilt engine, a leakage rate of 0 to 5% per cylinder is desired. A leakage rate of 6 to 14% is acceptable and means the engine is in good condition.
   b. When testing a used engine, the critical rate is not the percent of leakage for each cylinder, but instead, the difference between the cylinders. On a used engine, a leakage rate of 10% or less between cylinders is satisfactory.

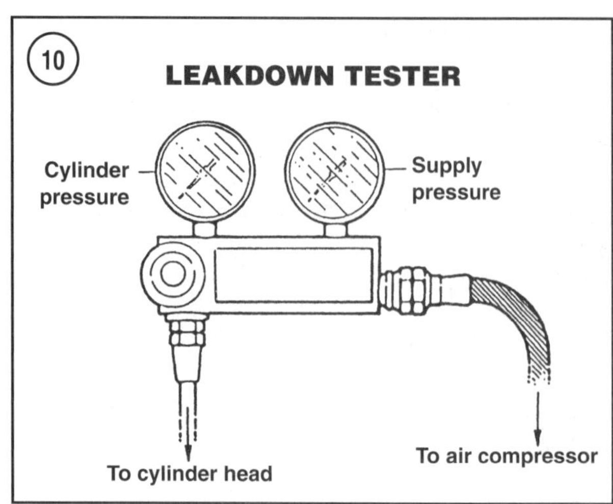

   c. A leakage rate exceeding 10% between cylinders points to an engine that is in poor condition and requires further inspection and possible repair.
6. After checking the percent of leakage, and with air pressure still applied to the combustion chamber, listen for air escaping from the following areas. If necessary, use a mechanic's stethoscope to pinpoint the source.
   a. Air leaking through the exhaust pipe indicates a leaking exhaust valve.
   b. Air leaking through the throttle body indicates a leaking intake valve.
   c. Air leaking through the crankcase breather tube indicates worn piston rings or a worn cylinder bore.
   d. Air leaking around the cylinder head. When this condition is indicated, check for a damaged cylinder head gasket and warped cylinder head or cylinder surfaces.
7. Remove the leakdown tester and repeat these steps for the remaining cylinder.
8. Install the spark plugs as described in Chapter Three.

CLUTCH

Excessive Clutch Lever Operation

If the clutch lever is hard to pull in, check the following:

1A. On cable operated models, dry and/or dirty clutch cable or kinked or damaged clutch cable.

1B. On hydraulically operated clutch, low clutch hydraulic fluid level.

2. Damaged clutch diaphragm spring.

Clutch Slip

If the engine speed increases without an increase in motorcycle speed, the clutch is probably slipping. The main causes of clutch slippage are:

1. Worn clutch friction plate.
2. Weak clutch diaphragm plate.
3. Warped clutch friction plate.
4. Incorrectly assembled clutch components.
5. Clutch friction plate and/or pressure place contaminated by leaking engine oil.

Clutch Drag

If the clutch will not disengage or if the motorcycle creeps with the transmission in gear and the clutch disengaged, the clutch is dragging. Some main causes of clutch drag are:

1. Excessive clutch lever free play (cable operated models).
2. Weak or damaged clutch diaphragm spring.
3. Worn clutch friction plate.
4. Warped clutch friction plate.
5. Incorrectly assembled clutch components.

TRANSMISSION

Transmission symptoms can be hard to distinguish from clutch symptoms. Be sure that the clutch is not causing the trouble before working on the transmission.

Typical transmission malfunctions include difficult shifting or gears popping out of mesh.

Difficult Shifting

If the gearshift selector shaft does not move smoothly from one gear to the next, check the following:

1. Selector shaft:
   a. Incorrectly installed selector shaft.
   b. Stripped shift lever-to-gearshift selector shaft splines.
   c. Damaged pawls where they engage the shift drum.
2. Stopper lever:
   a. Seized or damaged stopper lever roller.
   b. Broken stopper lever spring.
   c. Loose stopper lever mounting bolt.
3. Shift drum and shift forks:
   a. Bent shift fork(s).
   b. Damaged shift fork guide pin(s).
   c. Seized shift fork (on shaft).
   d. Broken shift fork or shift fork shaft.
   e. Damaged shift drum groove(s).
   f. Damaged shift drum bearing.

Gears Pop Out Of Mesh

If the transmission shifts into gear but then slips or pops out, check the following:

1. Shift shaft:
   a. Incorrect shift lever position/adjustment.
   b. Stopper lever fails to move or set properly.
2. Shift drum:
   a. Incorrect thrust play.
   b. Worn or damaged shift drum groove(s).
3. Bent shift fork.
4. Transmission:
   a. Worn or damaged gear dogs.
   b. Excessive gear thrust play.
   c. Worn or damaged shaft snap rings or thrust washers.

Transmission Over Shifts

If the transmission over shifts when shifting up or down, check for a weak or broken shift mechanism arm spring or a weak or broken shift drum positioning lever.

FINAL DRIVE

Excessive Final Drive Noise

1. Low oil level.
2. Worn or damaged pinion and ring gears.
3. Excessive pinion to ring gear backlash.
4. Worn or damaged drive pinion and splines.
5. Scored driven flange and wheel hub.
6. Scored or worn ring gear shaft and driven flange.

Oil Leaks

1. Loose or missing cover bolts.
2. Damaged final drive seals.
3. Clogged breather.
4. Oil level too high.

Rear Wheel Does Not Rotate Freely

1. Bent drive shaft.
2. Damaged ring gear and pinion bearing in final drive unit.
3. Stuck pinion and ring gear in final drive unit.
4. Worn or damaged universal joint(s) in final drive units.

ELECTRICAL TESTING

This section describes basic electrical troubleshooting and test equipment use.

The keys to successful electrical troubleshooting are to understand how the circuit should work and to have a systematic plan. Refer to the wiring diagrams at the end of the manual for component and connector identification. Use the wiring diagrams to help determine how the circuit works by tracing the current paths from the power source through the circuit components to ground. Also check any circuits that share the same fuse, ground or switch. If the other circuits work properly and the shared wiring is in good condition, the cause must be in the wiring used only by the suspect circuit. If all related circuits are faulty at the same time, the probable cause is a poor ground connection or a blown fuse(s).

As with all troubleshooting procedures, analyze typical symptoms in a systematic process. Never assume anything and do not overlook the obvious like a blown fuse or an electrical connector that has separated. Test the simplest and most obvious cause first and try to make tests at easily accessible points on the motorcycle.

Electrical Component Replacement

Most motorcycle dealerships and parts suppliers will not accept the return of any electrical part. If you cannot determine the *exact* cause of any electrical system malfunction, have a BMW dealership retest that specific system to verify your test results. If you purchase a new electrical component(s), install it, and then find that the system still does not work properly, you will probably be unable to return the unit for a refund.

Electrical testing on the models covered in this manual is limited due to the Motronic system and the need to use BMW MoDiTec diagnostic equipment. Refer to Chapter Nine.

Consider any test results carefully before replacing a component that tests only *slightly* out of specification, especially resistance. A number of variables can affect test results dramatically. These include: the testing meter's internal circuitry, ambient temperature and conditions under which the machine has been operated. All instructions and specifications have been checked for accuracy; however, successful test results depend to a great degree upon individual accuracy.

Preliminary Checks and Precautions

Prior to starting any electrical troubleshooting procedure, perform the following:

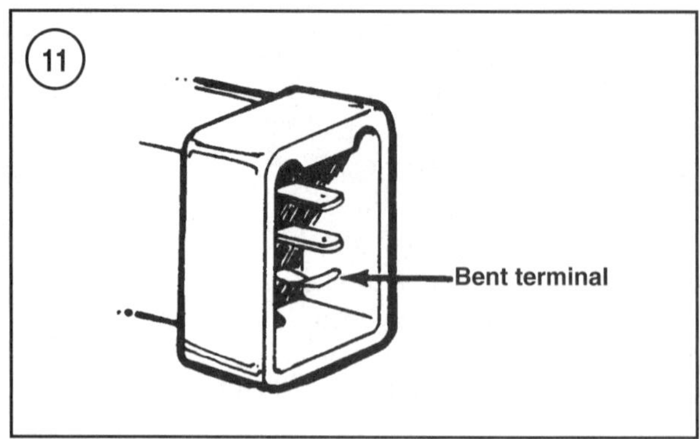

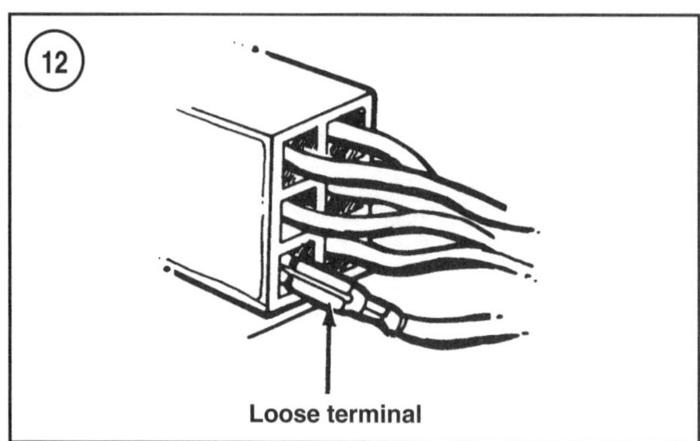

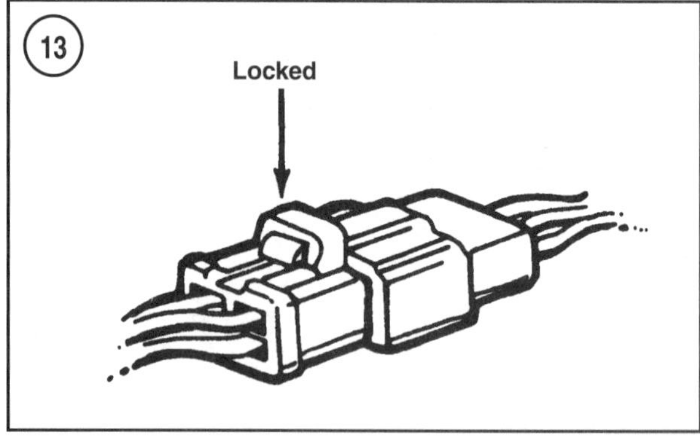

1. Check the individual fuses mounted in the fuse box (Chapter Ten). Remove the suspected fuse and replace if blown.

2. Inspect the battery. Make sure it is fully charged, and that the battery leads are clean and securely attached to the battery terminals. Refer to *Battery* in Chapter Three.

NOTE

Always consider electrical connectors the weak link in the electrical system. Dirty, loose fitting and corroded connectors cause numerous electrical related problems, espe-

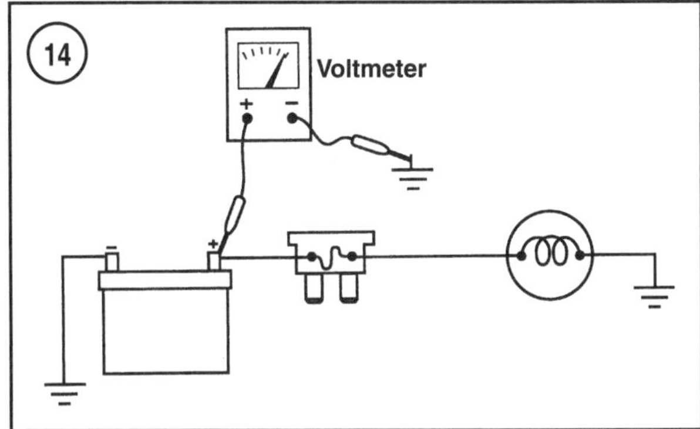

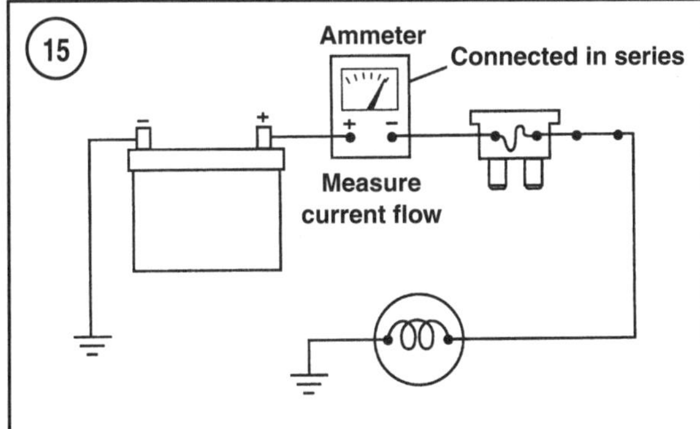

cially on high-mileage motorcycles. When troubleshooting an electrical problem, carefully inspect the connectors and wiring harness.

3. Disconnect each electrical connector in the suspect circuit and check that there are no bent terminals (**Figure 11**) inside the connectors. Bent terminals will not connect, causing an open circuit.
4. Make sure the terminals (**Figure 12**) are pushed all the way into the plastic connector. If not, carefully push them in with a narrow blade screwdriver.
5. Check the wires where they enter the connectors for damage.
6. Make sure each terminal is clean and free of corrosion. Clean, if necessary, and pack the connectors with dielectric grease.

NOTE
Dielectric grease is used as an insulator on electrical components such as connectors and battery connections. Dielectric grease can be purchased at automotive part stores.

7. Push the connectors together and make sure they are fully engaged and locked together (**Figure 13**).
8. Never pull on the electrical wires when disconnecting an electrical connector. Pull only on the connector plastic housing.
9. Never use a self-powered test light on circuits that contain solid-state devices. The solid-state devices may be damaged.

Test Light or Voltmeter

A test light can be constructed from a 12-volt light bulb with a pair of test leads carefully soldered to the bulb. To check for battery voltage in a circuit, attach one lead to ground and the other lead to various points along the circuit. Where battery voltage is present, the light bulb will light.

A voltmeter is used in the same manner as the test light to determine if battery voltage is present in any given circuit. The voltmeter, unlike the test light, will also indicate how much voltage is present at each test point. When using a voltmeter, attach the positive lead to the component or wire to be checked and the negative lead to a good ground (**Figure 14**).

Ammeter

An ammeter measures the flow of current (amps) in a circuit (**Figure 15**). When connected in series in the circuit, the ammeter determines whether current is flowing in the circuit, and whether the current flow is excessive because of a short in the circuit. This current flow is usually referred to as current draw. Comparing actual current draw in the circuit or component to the manufacturer's specified current draw rating provides useful diagnostic information.

Self-Powered Test Light

A self-powered test light can be constructed of a 12-volt light bulb, a pair of test leads and a 12-volt battery. When the test leads are touched together, the light bulb illuminates.

Use a self-powered test light as follows:

1. Touch the test leads together to make sure the light bulb goes on. If not, correct the problem prior to using it in a test procedure.
2. Disconnect the motorcycle's battery or remove the fuse(s) that protects the circuit to be tested. Refer to Chapter Ten.
3. Select two points within the circuit that should have continuity.

4. Attach one lead of the self-powered test light to each point.
5. If there is continuity, the self-powered test light bulb will come on.
6. If there is no continuity, the self-powered test light bulb will not come on. This indicates an open circuit.

Ohmmeter

The ohmmeter reads resistance in ohms. Like the self-powered test light, an ohmmeter contains its own power source and should not be connected to a live circuit.

Ohmmeters may be an analog type (needle scale) or a digital type (LCD or LED readout). Both types of ohmmeters have a switch that allows the selection of different ranges of resistance for accurate readings. The analog ohmmeter also has a set-adjust control that is used to zero or calibrate the meter needle for accurate adjustments. Digital ohmmeters do not require calibration.

An ohmmeter is used by connecting its test leads to the terminals or leads of the circuit or component being tested (**Figure 16**). If an analog meter is used, it should be calibrated by crossing the test leads and adjusting the meter needle until it reads zero. When the leads are uncrossed, the needle should move to the other end of the scale, indicating infinite resistance.

The infinite reading indicates an open in the circuit or component; a reading of zero indicates continuity. If the meter needle falls between these two points on the scale, it indicates the actual resistance to current flow that is present. To determine the resistance, multiply the meter reading by the ohmmeter scale. For example, a meter reading of 5 ohms multiplied by the R × 1000 scale is 5000 ohms of resistance.

CAUTION
Never connect an ohmmeter to a circuit that has power applied to it. Always disconnect the negative battery cable before using the ohmmeter.

Jumper Wire

When using a jumper wire, always install an inline fuse/fuse holder (available at most auto supply stores or electronic supply stores) to the jumper wire. Never place a jumper wire across any load (a component that is connected and turned on). This would result in a direct short and will blow the fuse(s).

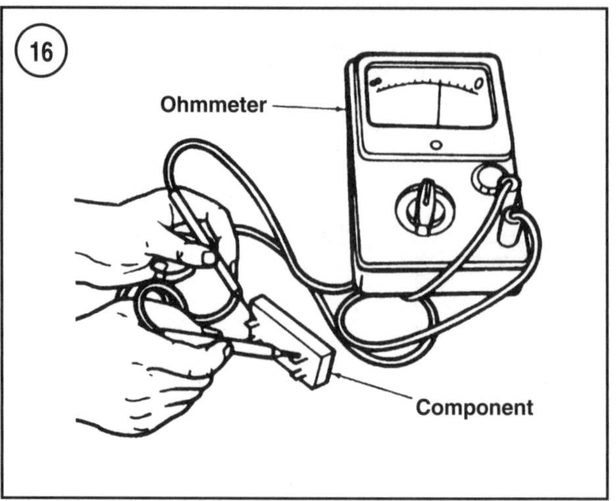

Voltage Testing

Unless otherwise specified, all voltage tests are made with the electrical connectors still connected. Insert the test leads into the backside of the connector. Make sure the test lead touches the wire or metal terminal within the connector. If the test lead only touches the wire insulation, a false reading will result.

Always check both sides of the connector, as one side may be loose or corroded. This prevents electrical flow through the connector. This type of test can be performed with a test light or a voltmeter. A voltmeter gives the best results.

NOTE
If using a test lamp, it does not make any difference which test lead is attached to ground.

1. Attach the negative test lead (if using a voltmeter) to a good ground (bare metal). Make sure the part used for ground is not insulated with a rubber gasket or rubber grommet.
2. Attach the positive test lead (if using a voltmeter) to the point being checked.
3. Turn the ignition switch on. If using a test light, the test light will come on if voltage is present. If using a voltmeter, note the voltage reading. The reading should be within 1 volt of battery voltage. If the voltage is less, there is a problem in the circuit.

Voltage Drop Test

Resistance causes voltage to drop. This resistance can be measured in an active circuit by using a voltmeter to perform a voltage drop test. A voltage drop test compares

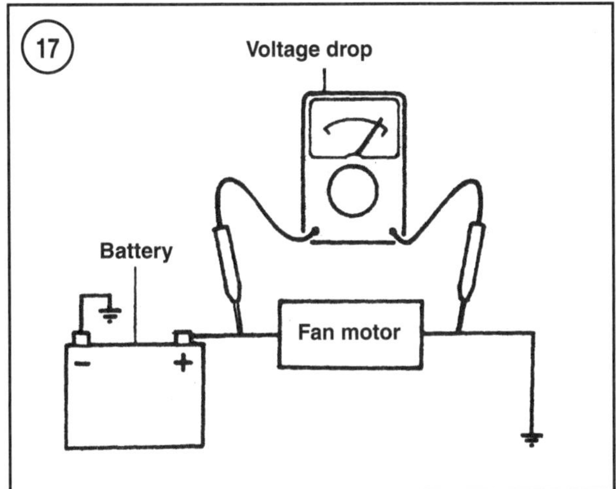

the difference between the voltage available from the start of a circuit to the voltage at the end of the circuit while the circuit is operational. If the circuit has no resistance, there will be no voltage drop. The greater the resistance, the greater the voltage drop will be. A voltage drop of one volt or more indicates excessive resistance in the circuit. It is important to remember that a 0 reading on a voltage drop test is good; a battery voltage reading indicates an open circuit. A voltage drop test is an excellent way to check the condition of relays, battery cables and other high-current electrical loads.

1. Connect the positive meter test lead to the electrical source (where electricity is coming from).
2. Connect the negative meter test lead to the electrical load (where electricity is going). See **Figure 17**.
3. If necessary, activate the component(s) in the circuit.
4. A voltage reading of 1 volt or more indicates excessive resistance in the circuit. A reading equal to battery voltage indicates an open circuit.

Continuity Test

A continuity test is made to determine if the circuit is complete with no opens in either the electrical wires or components within that circuit.

Unless otherwise specified, all continuity tests are made with the electrical connector still connected. Insert the test leads into the backside of the connector. Make sure the test lead touches the wire or metal terminal within the connector. If the test lead only touches the wire insulation, a false reading will result. Always check both sides of the connectors as one side may be loose or corroded. This prevents electrical flow through the connector.

This type of test can be performed with a self-powered test light or an ohmmeter. An ohmmeter will give the best results. If using an analog ohmmeter, calibrate the meter by touching the leads together and turning the ohm calibration knob until the meter reads zero.

1. Disconnect the negative battery cable.
2. Attach one test lead, the test light or ohmmeter, to one end of the part of the circuit to be tested.
3. Attach the other test lead to the other end of the part of the circuit to be tested.
4. If the circuit has continuity, a self-powered test lamp will illuminate and an ohmmeter will indicate low or no resistance. If the circuit is open, a self-powered test lamp will not illuminate and an ohmmeter will indicate infinite resistance.

Testing for a Short With a Self-Powered Test Light or Ohmmeter

This test can be performed with either a self-powered test light or an ohmmeter.

1. Disconnect the battery negative lead from the battery.
2. Remove the blown fuse from the fuse panel.
3. Connect one test lead of the test light or ohmmeter to the load side or battery side of the fuse terminal in the fuse panel.
4. Connect the other test lead to a good ground (bare metal). Make sure the part used for a ground is not insulated with a rubber gasket or rubber grommet.
5. With the self-powered test light or ohmmeter attached to the fuse terminal and ground, wiggle the wiring harness relating to the suspect circuit at 15.2 cm (6 in.) intervals. Start next to the fuse panel and work away from the fuse panel. Watch the self-powered test light or ohmmeter while moving along the harness.
6. If the test light blinks or the needle on the ohmmeter moves, there is a short-to-ground at that point in the harness.

Testing For a Short with a Test Light or Voltmeter

1. Remove the blown fuse from the fuse panel.
2. Connect the test light or voltmeter across the fuse terminals in the fuse panel. Turn the ignition switch on and check for battery voltage.
3. With the test light or voltmeter attached to the fuse terminals, wiggle the wiring harness relating to the suspect circuit at 15.2 cm (6 in.) intervals. Start next to the fuse panel and work away from the fuse panel. Watch the test light or voltmeter while moving along the harness.
4. If the test light blinks or the needle on the voltmeter moves, there is a short-to-ground at that point in the harness.

LIGHTING SYSTEM

If bulbs burn out frequently, the cause may be excessive vibration, loose connections that permit sudden current surges or the installation of the wrong type of bulb. Most light and ignition problems are caused by loose or corroded ground connections. Check these prior to replacing a bulb or electrical component.

STARTING SYSTEM

The starter is mounted horizontally on the left side of the crankcase.

The starting system requires a fully charged battery to provide the large amount of current required to run the starter.

The starter relay, located in the electrical component box under the rider's seat, carries the heavy electrical current to the starter. Depressing the START button energizes the starter relay coil causing the starter relay contacts to close and allow current to flow from the battery through the starter relay to the starter.

CAUTION
Do not operate the starter continuously for more than 5 seconds. Allow the starter to cool for at least 15 seconds between attempts to start the engine.

If the starter does not operate, perform the following. After completing each test, reconnect all connectors before beginning the next test.

1. Check the main fuse mounted in the electrical component box under the rider's seat.
2. Refer to *Fuses* in Chapter Ten and disconnect the fuse for the starter. If the fuse is blown (**Figure 18**); replace the fuse. If the fuse is good, reinstall it, then go to the next step.
3. Test the battery as described under *Battery* in Chapter Three. If the battery voltage is not within the specified range, clean and charge the battery as described. Replace a damaged battery.
4. Battery cables are the proper size and length. Replace cables that are undersize or damaged.
5. Make sure the battery cables are securely attached to the battery terminals and that both are clean and in good condition.
6. Check the wiring system for dirty or loose-fitting terminals or damaged wires; clean and repair as required. If all the connectors and wires are in good condition, the starter is probably faulty. Repair or replace the starter as described under *Starter* in Chapter Ten. Also refer to Chapter Ten for additional testing instructions.

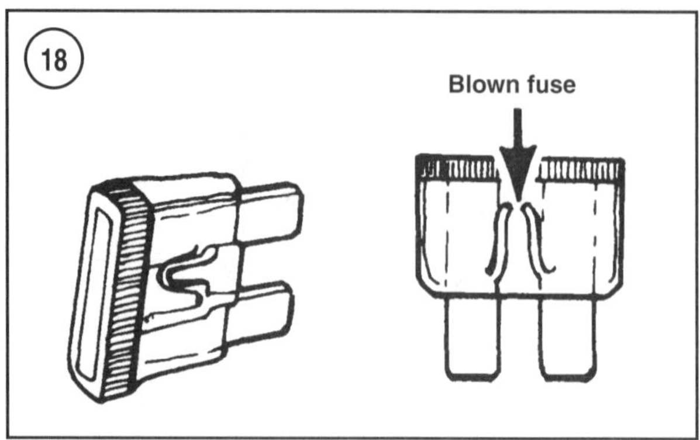

7. Make sure all connectors disassembled during this procedure are free of corrosion and are reconnected properly.

CHARGING SYSTEM

A malfunction in the charging system generally causes the battery to remain undercharged.

Before testing the charging system, visually check the following:

1. Check the battery connections at the battery. If polarity is reversed, check for a damaged regulator/rectifier.
2. Remove the rider's seat as described in Chapter Fifteen.
3. Inspect all wiring between the battery and alternator stator for worn or cracked insulation or loose connections. Replace wiring or clean and tighten connections as required.
4. Check battery condition. Clean and charge as required. Refer to *Battery* in Chapter Three.
5. Perform the *Charging System Output Test* listed under *Charging System* in Chapter Ten.

IGNITION SYSTEM

Refer to Chapter Ten.

FRONT SUSPENSION AND STEERING

Steering is Sluggish

1. Damaged steering head bearings.
2. Tire pressure too low.

Motorcycle Steers to One Side

1. Bent axle.
2. Worn or damaged wheel bearings.

3. Worn or damaged swing arm pivot bearings.
4. Damaged steering head bearings.
5. Damaged swing arm.
6. Incorrectly installed wheels.
7. Front and rear wheels are not aligned.
8. Front fork legs positioned unevenly in steering stem.

Front Suspension Noise

1. Loose mounting fasteners.
2. Damaged fork(s) or front shock absorber.
3. Low fork oil capacity.
4. Loose or damaged fairing mounts (models so equipped).

Front Wheel Wobble/Vibration

1. Loose front wheel axle.
2. Loose or damaged wheel bearing(s).
3. Damaged wheel rim.
4. Damaged tire.
5. Unbalanced tire and wheel assembly.

Hard Suspension (Front Fork)

1. Excessive tire pressure.
2. Damaged steering head bearings.
3. Bent fork tube(s).
4. Binding slider(s).

Hard Suspension (Rear Shock Absorber)

1. Incorrectly adjuster rear shock.
2. Excessive rear tire pressure.
3. Shock incorrectly adjusted.
4. Damaged shock absorber collar(s).

Soft Suspension (Front Fork)

1. Insufficient tire pressure.
2. Incorrect adjusted front shock absorber.

Soft Suspension (Rear Shock Absorber)

1. Insufficient rear tire pressure.
2. Weak or damaged shock absorber spring.
3. Damaged shock absorber.
4. Incorrect shock absorber adjustment.
5. Leaking damper unit.

BRAKE SYSTEM

The brake system is critical to riding performance and safety. Inspect the front and rear brakes frequently; repair any problem immediately. When replacing or refilling the brake fluid, use only DOT 4 brake fluid from a closed container. Refer to Chapter Fourteen for additional information on brake fluid selection and disc brake service.

When checking brake pad wear, check that the brake pads in each caliper contact the disc squarely. If one of the brake pads is wearing unevenly, suspect a warped or bent brake disc or damaged caliper.

Always check the brake operation before riding the motorcycle.

Soft or Spongy Brake Lever or Pedal

When the front brake lever or rear brake pedal travel increases, the brake system is not capable of producing sufficient brake force. When an increase in lever/pedal travel is noticed or when the brake feels soft or spongy, check the following possible causes:

1. Air in brake system.

NOTE

If the brake level in the reservoir drops too low, air can enter the hydraulic system through the master cylinder. Air can also enter the system from loose or damaged hose fittings. Air in the hydraulic system results in a soft or spongy brake lever or pedal action. This condition is noticeable and reduces brake performance. When it is suspected that air has entered the hydraulic system, flush the brake system and bleed the brakes as described in Chapter Fourteen.

2. Low brake fluid level.

NOTE

As the brake pads wear, the brake fluid level in the master cylinder reservoir drops. Whenever adding brake fluid to the reservoirs, visually check the brake pads for wear. If there does not appear to be an increase in pad wear, check the brake hoses and banjo bolts for leaks and brake lines for loose fittings.

3. Leak in the brake system.
4. Contaminated brake fluid.
5. Plugged brake fluid passages.
6. Damaged brake lever or pedal assembly.
7. Worn or damaged brake pads.
8. Worn or damaged brake disc.

9. Warped brake disc.
10. Contaminated brake pads and disc.

NOTE
A leaking fork seal can allow oil to contaminate the brake pads and disc.

11. Worn or damaged master cylinder cups and/or cylinder bore.
12. Worn or damaged brake caliper piston seals.
13. Contaminated master cylinder assembly.
14. Contaminated brake caliper assembly.
15. Brake caliper not sliding correctly on slide pins.
16. Sticking master cylinder piston assembly.
17. Sticking brake caliper pistons.

Brake Drag

When the brakes drag, the brake pads are not capable of moving away from the brake disc when the brake lever or pedal is released. Any of the following causes, if they occur, would prevent correct brake pad movement and cause brake drag.

1. Warped or damaged brake disc.
2. Brake caliper not sliding correctly on slide pins.
3. Sticking or damaged brake caliper pistons.
4. Contaminated brake pads and disc.
5. Plugged master cylinder port.
6. Contaminated brake fluid and hydraulic passages.
7. Restricted brake hose and/or line joint.
8. Loose brake disc mounting bolts.
9. Damaged or misaligned wheel.
10. Incorrect wheel alignment.
11. Incorrectly installed brake caliper.

Hard Brake Lever or Pedal Operation

When the brakes are applied and there is sufficient brake performance but the operation of the brake lever or pedal feels excessively hard, check for the following possible causes:

1. Clogged brake hydraulic system.
2. Sticking caliper piston.
3. Sticking master cylinder piston.
4. Glazed or worn brake pads.
5. Mismatched brake pads.
6. Damaged front brake lever.
7. Damaged rear brake pedal.
8. Brake caliper not sliding correctly on slide pins.
9. Worn or damaged brake caliper seals.

Brakes Grab

1. Damaged brake pad pin bolt. Look for steps or cracks along the pad pin bolt surface.
2. Contaminated brake pads and disc.
3. Incorrect wheel alignment.
4. Warped brake disc.
5. Loose brake disc mounting bolts.
6. Brake caliper not sliding correctly on slide pins.
7. Mismatched brake pads.
8. Damaged wheel bearings.

Brake Squeal or Chatter

1. Contaminated brake pads and disc.
2. Incorrectly installed brake caliper.
3. Warped brake disc.
4. Incorrect wheel alignment.
5. Mismatched brake pads.
6. Incorrectly installed brake pads.

Leaking Brake Caliper

1. Damaged dust and piston seals.
2. Damaged cylinder bore.
3. Loose caliper body bolts.
4. Loose banjo bolt.
5. Damaged banjo bolt washers.
6. Damaged banjo bolt threads in caliper body.

Leaking Master Cylinder

1. Damaged piston secondary seal.
2. Damaged piston snap ring/snap ring groove.
3. Worn or damaged master cylinder bore.
4. Loose banjo bolt or brake line fittings.
5. Damaged banjo bolt washers.
6. Damaged banjo bolt threads in master cylinder body.
7. Loose or damaged reservoir cap.

CHAPTER THREE

LUBRICATION, MAINTENANCE AND TUNE-UP

This chapter describes lubrication, maintenance and tune-up procedures.

To maximize the service life of the motorcycle and gain the utmost in safety and performance, it is necessary to perform periodic inspections and maintenance. Minor problems found during routine service can be corrected before they develop into major ones.

Table 1 lists the recommended lubrication, maintenance and tune-up intervals. If the motorcycle is operated in extreme conditions, it may be appropriate to reduce the time interval between some maintenance items.

For convenience, most of the services listed in **Table 1** are described in this chapter. Procedures that require more than minor disassembly or adjustment are covered in the appropriate chapter.

Record the service you perform in the maintenance log at the end of the manual.

Before servicing the motorcycle, make sure the procedures and the required skills are thoroughly understood. If your experience and equipment are limited, start by performing basic procedures, perform more involved tasks as further experience is gained and the necessary tools have been acquired.

Tables 1-7 are located at the end of this chapter.

FUEL TYPE

All models require gasoline with a specific pump octane number (**Table 5**). Using a gasoline with a lower octane number can cause pinging or spark knock, and lead to engine damage.

When choosing gasoline and filling the fuel tank, note the following:

1. When filling the tank, do not overfill it. There should be no fuel in the filler neck (tube located between the fuel cap and tank).
2. Because oxygenated fuels can damage plastic and paint, make sure not to spill fuel onto the fuel tank during filling.
3. An ethanol (ethyl or grain alcohol) gasoline that contains more than 10% ethanol by volume may cause engine starting and performance related problems.

4. A methanol (methyl or wood alcohol) gasoline that contains more than 5% methanol by volume may cause engine starting and performance related problems. Gasoline that contains methanol must have corrosion inhibitors to protect the metal, plastic and rubber parts in the fuel system from damage.

PRE-RIDE CHECK LIST

Perform the following pre-ride inspection.

1. Check the engine oil level on the level inspection window (**Figure 1**) located on the left side of the crankcase. The oil level must be between the upper and lower lines.
2. Turn the handlebar from side to side and check for steering play. Confirm that the control cables are properly routed and do not interfere with the handlebar or the handlebar controls.
3. Check the throttle operation. Open the throttle all of the way and release it. The throttle should close quickly with no binding or roughness. Repeat this step with the handlebar facing straight ahead and sitting in left and right full lock positions.
4. Confirm that the clutch and the brake levers operate properly with no binding. Replace any broken levers. Check the lever housings for damage.

WARNING

When checking the brake and clutch levers, check the ball on the end of the lever. If it is broken off, replace the lever immediately. The lever balls help prevent the lever from puncturing your hand or arm during a fall or crash.

5. Inspect the front and rear suspension. Make sure they have a good solid feel with no looseness.
6. Check both wheels and tires for wear and damage.
7. Check tire pressure as listed in **Table 2**.
8. Check the exhaust system for looseness or damage.
9. Make sure the fuel tank is full of fresh gasoline.
10. Inspect the fuel lines and fittings for leakage.
11. Check the brake fluid level in both front and rear brake reservoirs.
12. On models so equipped, check the fluid level in the clutch master cylinder reservoir.

TIRES AND WHEELS

Tire Pressure

Check and adjust the tire pressure to maintain the tire profile (**Figure 2**), good traction, handling and to get the maximum mileage from the tire. Check tire pressure (**Table 2**) when the tires are cold. Never release air pressure from a warm or hot tire to adjust the pressure; doing so causes the tire to be under-inflated.

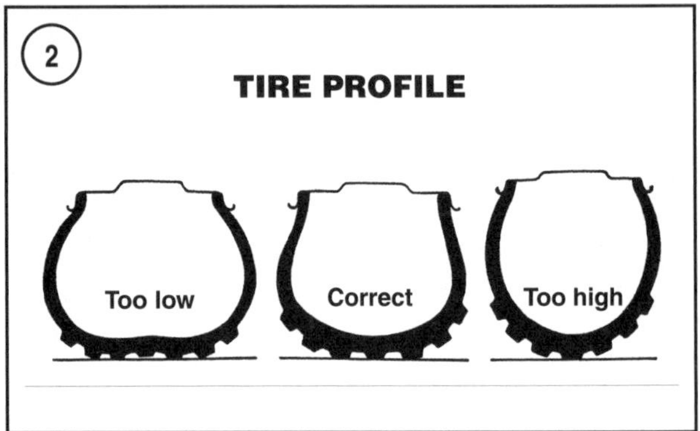

NOTE

A loss of air pressure may be due to a loose or damaged valve core. Put a few drops of water on the top of the valve core. If the water bubbles, tighten the valve core and recheck. If air is still leaking from the valve after tightening it, replace the valve.

Tire Inspection

Inspect the tires periodically for wear and damage. Inspect the tires for the following:

1. Deep cuts and imbedded objects. If a nail or other object is in a tire, mark its location with a crayon prior to removing it. Refer to Chapter Eleven for tire changing and repair information.
2. Flat spots.
3. Cracks.
4. Separating plies.
5. Sidewall damage.

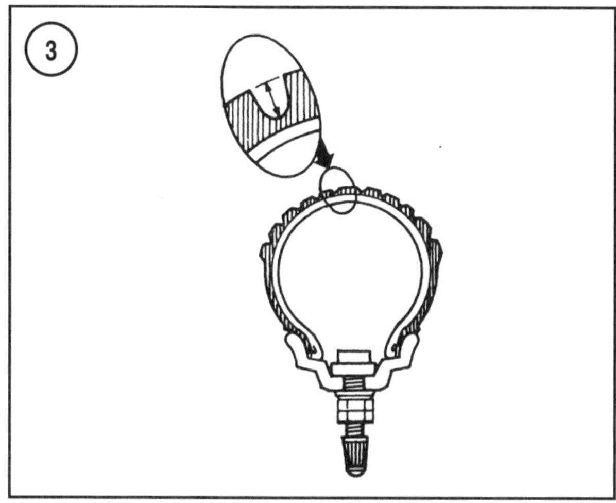

WARNING
If a small object has punctured the tire, air loss may be very slow due to the tendency of tubeless tire to self-seal when punctured. Check the tires carefully.

Tire Wear Analysis

Analyze tire wear to determine the cause. Common causes are:

1. Incorrect tire pressure. Check the tire pressure and examine the tire tread. Compare the wear in the center of the contact patch with the wear at the edge of the contact patch. Note the following:
   a. If the tire shows excessive wear at the edge of the contact patch, but the wear at the center of the contact patch is normal, the tire has been under inflated. Under inflated tires result in higher tire temperatures, hard or imprecise steering and abnormal wear.
   b. If the tire shows excessive wear in the center of the contact patch, but wear at the edge of the contact patch in normal, the tire has been over inflated. Over inflated tires result in a hard ride and abnormal wear.
2. Overloading.
3. Incorrect wheel alignment.
4. Incorrect wheel balance.
5. Worn or damaged wheel bearings.

Tread Depth

Measure the tread depth (**Figure 3**) in the center of the tire using a small ruler or a tread depth gauge.

The tires are also designed with tread wear indicators that appear when the tires are worn out. When these are visible, the tires are no longer safe and must be replaced.

Wheel Inspection and Runout

Frequently inspect wheels for cracks, warp or dents.

Wheel runout is the amount of wobble a wheel shows as it rotates. Check runout with the wheel on the motorcycle by supporting the motorcycle with the wheel off the ground. Slowly turn the wheel while holding a pointer solidly against a fork leg or the swing arm with the other end against the wheel rim.

To obtain a precise measurement refer to Chapter Eleven.

The maximum allowable runout with the tire installed on the rim is as follows:

1. Cast alloy wheels:
   a. Front wheel axial and radial runout is 0.5 mm (0.02 in.).
   b. Rear wheel axial and radial runout is 0.3 mm (0.012 in.).
2. Wire wheels: Front and rear wheel axial and radial runout is 1.3 mm (0.05 in.).

If the wire wheel runout is excessive, adjust the spokes or replace the wheel. If the rim portion of an alloy wheel is damaged, the wheel must be replaced.

BATTERY

The battery is an important component in the motorcycle's electrical system, yet most electrical system prolems are due to an undercharged battery. Clean and inspect the battery at periodic intervals.

The battery on these models must be maintained at a *full charge* at all times. If the battery is allowed to fall below a maximum charge, the ignition, fuel injection and the ABS systems may not operate correctly. Check the condition of the battery when troubleshooting.

Negative Cable

1999-on R850C, R1100S, all R1150 and R1200C

The negative battery cable is ground and the battery negative terminal is located on the left side of the motorcycle.

Many procedures covered in this manual require disconnecting the negative battery cable from the battery. It is not necessary to remove the battery.

On these models, disconnecting the battery negative cable deletes all stored Motronic data. This includes any fault codes that may have been set. The loss of Motronic memory can temporarily alter the operational characteristics when the engine is restarted if Step 4 is not performed.

1. Perform Steps 1-10 of *Removal and Installation* in this section and disconnect the negative cable from the battery.
2. Wrap the negative cable end with a shop towel and move it away from the battery. Secure it so it will not accidentally contact the battery terminal.
3. Reconnect the negative cable to the battery.

WARNING
Step 4 must be performed to maintain the safe riding operation of the motorcycle. If any fault codes were set prior to disconnecting the battery, they will be re-set as soon as the motorcycle has been ridden a short distance.

4. Do not start the engine. Turn the ignition switch on and then *fully* open the throttle once or twice to enable the Motronic control unit to register the throttle-valve positions.
5. Install all components removed.
6. Start the engine and test ride the motorcycle *slowly* at first to make sure all systems are operating correctly.

All models except 1999-on R850C, R1100S, all R1150 and R1200C

1. Perform Steps 1-10 of *Removal and Installation* in this section and disconnect the negative cable from the battery.
2. Wrap the negative cable end with a shop towel and move it away from the battery. Secure it so it will not accidentally contact the battery terminal or the frame.
3. Reconnect the negative cable to the battery.
4. Install all components removed.

Cable Service

To ensure good electrical contact between the battery and the electrical cables, the cables must be clean and free of corrosion.

1. If the electrical cable terminals are badly corroded, disconnect them from the motorcycle's electrical system.
2. Thoroughly clean each connector with a small brush and then with a baking soda solution. Rinse thoroughly with clean water and wipe dry with a clean cloth.

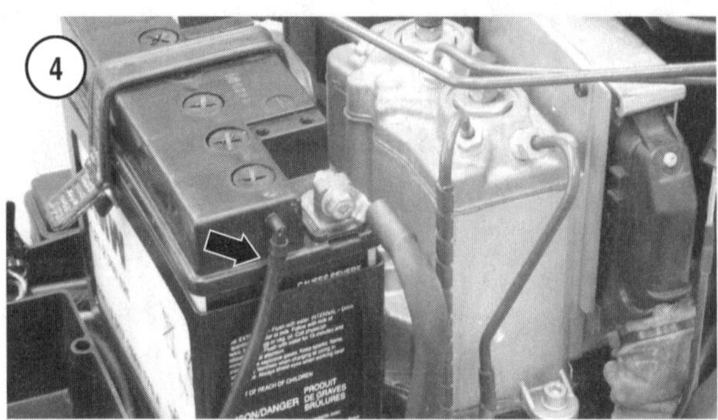

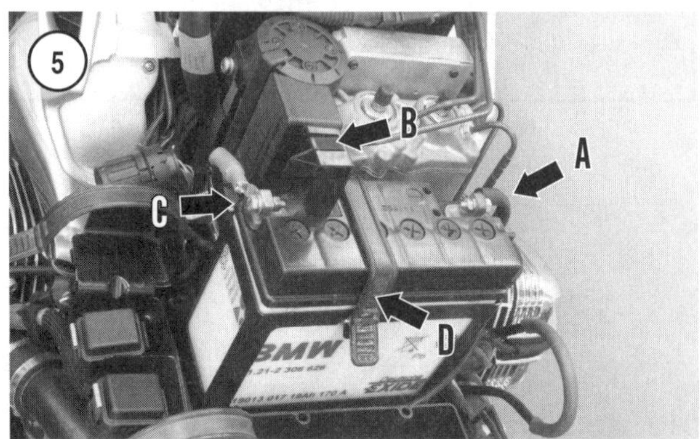

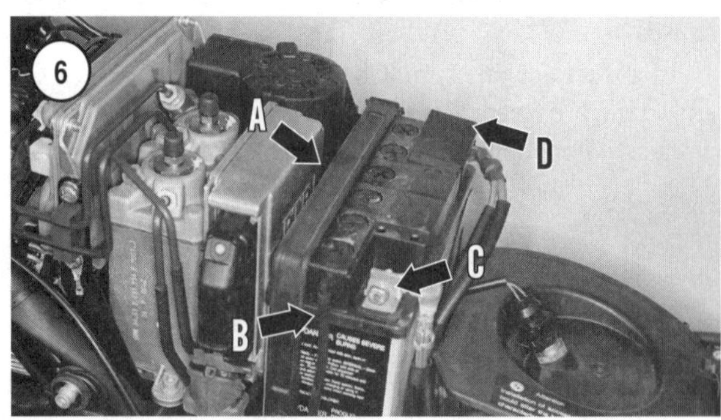

3. After cleaning, apply a thin layer of dielectric grease to the battery terminals before reattaching the cables.
4. If disconnected, attach the electrical cables to the motorcycle's electrical system.
5. After connecting the electrical cables, apply a light coat of dielectric grease to the terminals to retard corrosion and decomposition of the terminals.

Removal and Installation

1. Place the motorcycle on the sidestand.
2. Remove the rider's seat as described in Chapter Fifteen.

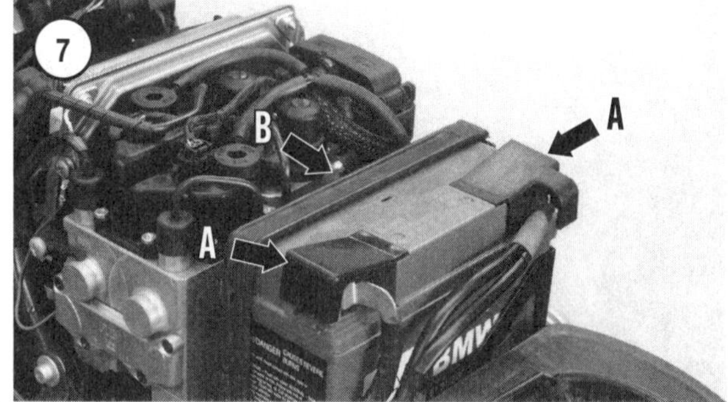

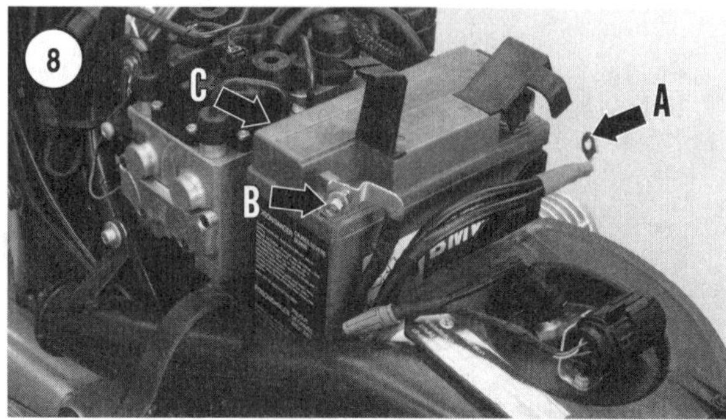

3. Remove the fuel tank as described in Chapter Nine.
4. On RS, RT and S models, remove both side fairing panels as described in Chapter Fifteen.
5A. On R850C and R1200C models, perform the following:
   a. On the right side, disconnect the vent tube (**Figure 4**) from the battery and leave it routed through the frame.
   b. Disconnect the negative (black) battery cable from the battery (A, **Figure 5**).
   c. Move the negative battery cable out of the way to ensure it will not accidentally contact with the battery terminal or the frame.
   d. Move the protective cap (B, **Figure 5**) off of the positive (red) terminal.
   e. Disconnect the positive battery cable from the battery (C, **Figure 5**).
   f. Unhook and remove the retaining strap (D, **Figure 5**).
   g. Carefully pull the battery straight up and out of the holder.

5B. On all models except R850C and R1200C with a *conventional* battery, perform the following:
   a. Unhook and remove the retaining strap (A, **Figure 6**).
   b. On the left side, disconnect the vent tube (B, **Figure 6**) from the battery, leave it in routed through the frame.
   c. Disconnect the negative (black) battery cable from the battery (C, **Figure 6**).
   d. Move the negative battery cable out of the way to ensure it will not accidentally contact with the battery terminal or the frame.
   e. Move the protective cap (D, **Figure 6**) off of the positive (red) terminal.
   f. Disconnect the positive battery cable from the battery.
   g. Carefully pull the battery straight up and out of the holder.

5C. On all models except R850C and R1200C models with a *maintenance-free* battery, perform the following:
   a. Move the protective cap (A, **Figure 7**) off both battery terminals.
   b. Unhook and remove the battery retaining strap (B, **Figure 7**).
   c. Disconnect the negative (black) battery cable from the battery (A, **Figure 8**).
   d. Move the negative battery cable out of the way to ensure it will not accidentally contact with the battery terminal or the frame.
   e. Disconnect the positive battery cable from the battery (B, **Figure 8**).
   f. Carefully pull the battery (C, **Figure 8**) straight up and out of the holder.

CAUTION

Be sure the battery cables are connected to their proper terminals. Reversing the battery polarity will damage the rectifier and ignition components.

6. First install and tighten the negative battery cable then install and tighten the positive battery cable. Tighten the bolts securely.
7. Coat the battery connections with dielectric grease to retard corrosion. Move the protective cap(s) onto the terminal(s) and make sure it seats properly.
8. On conventional batteries, reconnect the battery vent hose to the battery fitting. Make sure it is correctly connected.

WARNING

On conventional batteries, after installing the battery, make sure the vent hose is not pinched. A pinched or kinked hose allows pressure to accumulate in the battery and may cause the battery case to expand and crack, allowing electrolyte to drain out onto the frame. If the vent hose is damaged, replace it.

9. Make sure the battery seats correctly in its holder, then install the retaining strap.

10. On RS, RT and S models, install the side fairing panels as described in Chapter Fifteen.

11. Install the fuel tank as described in Chapter Nine.

12. Install the rider's seat as described in Chapter Fifteen.

CAUTION

Step 13 must be performed to maintain the safe riding operation of the motorcycle.

13. On 1999-on R850C, R1100S, all R1150 and R1200C, perform the following:

a. Do not start the engine. Turn the ignition switch on.

b. Fully open the throttle once or twice so that the Motronic control unit can register the throttle-valve positions.

c. Start the engine and test ride the motorcycle slowly at first to make sure all systems are operating correctly.

Conventional Battery Service

Electrolyte level check

1. Place the motorcycle on the sidestand.

2. Remove the rider's seat as described in Chapter Fifteen.

3. Maintain the electrolyte level between the two marks on the battery case (**Figure 9**).

4. If the water must be added, remove the battery from the frame as described in the next procedure to avoid spilling water/electrolyte.

5. Make sure the cell caps are secure.

6. If the electrolyte level is correct, reinstall the seat.

Cleaning, inspection and adding water

1. Remove the battery (**Figure 10**) as described in this section and set it on newspapers or shop rags to protect the surface of the workbench.

2. Inspect the battery holder (**Figure 11**) in the frame for contamination or damage. Clean with a solution of baking soda and water.

3. Check the battery case (A, **Figure 12**) for cracks or other damage. If the battery case is warped, discolored or has a raised top, the battery has been overcharged or overheated.

4. Check the battery terminal bolts (B, **Figure 12**), spacers and nuts for corrosion, deterioration or damage. Clean all parts thoroughly with a solution of baking soda and water. Replace severely corroded or damaged parts.

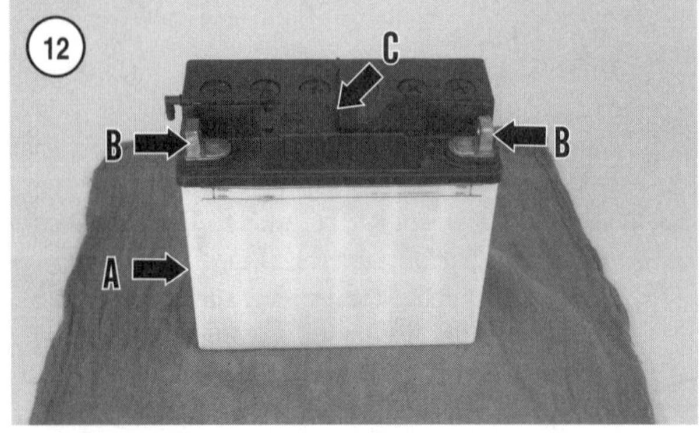

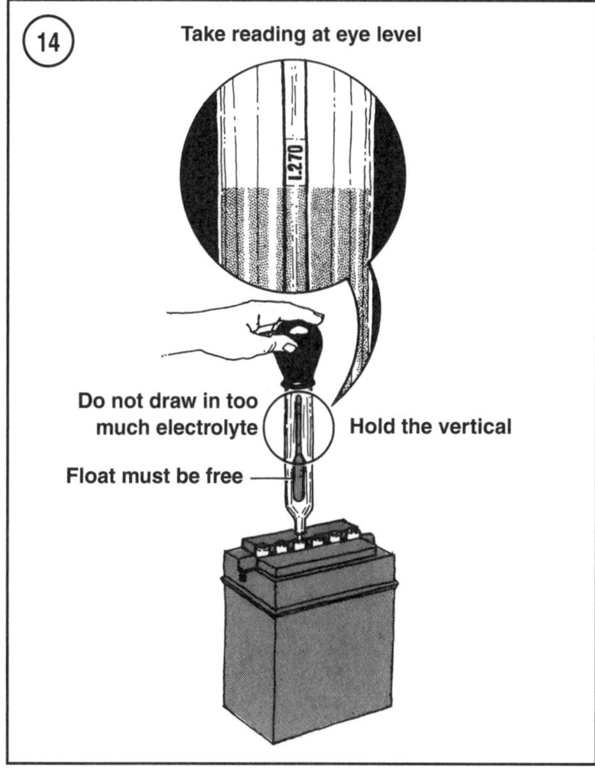

CAUTION
Keep cleaning solution out of the battery cells or the battery will be damaged.

5. Clean the top of the battery (C, **Figure 12**) with a stiff bristle brush using the baking soda and water solution. Thoroughly rinse off all baking soda solution with freshwater.

6. Check the battery cable ends for corrosion and damage. If corrosion is minor, clean the battery cable clamps with a stiff wire brush. Replace severely worn or damaged cables.

CAUTION
Do not overfill the battery in Step 7. The electrolyte expands due to heat from charging and will overflow if the level is above the upper level line.

7. Remove the fill caps (**Figure 13**) from the battery cells and check the electrolyte level in each cell. Add distilled water, if necessary, to bring the level within the upper and lower level lines on the battery case. Never add electrolyte (acid) to correct the level. Install the caps and tighten securely.

3

CAUTION
Adding distilled water to the battery cells will dilute the electrolyte and raise the freezing point of the electrolyte. Therefore, if adding water to the battery in freezing or near-freezing temperature, charge the battery for at least 30 minutes to convert the water to electrolyte (sulfuric acid) and maintain its freezing point at an acceptable level.

Testing

WARNING
Electrolyte splashed into the eyes is extremely harmful. Always wear safety glasses while working with a battery. If electrolyte gets into the eyes, call a physician immediately and force the eyes open and flood them with cool, clean water for approximately 15 minutes.

NOTE
Adding distilled water to the battery will lower the specific gravity (density) of the electrolyte. After adding water, charge the battery for 15-20 minutes at a high rate to mix the water with the electrolyte.

Check the specific gravity of the battery electrolyte to check the state of charge of the battery. The specific gravity is the density of the electrolyte as compared to pure water.

1. To check the specific gravity, refer to **Figure 14** and use a hydrometer with numbered graduations from 1.100 to 1.300 as follows:
   a. Squeeze the rubber ball, insert the tip into the cell and release the ball.
   b. Draw enough electrolyte to raise the weighted float inside the hydrometer. When using a temperature-compensated hydrometer, release the electrolyte and repeat this process several times to make sure the thermometer is adjusted to the electrolyte temperature before taking the reading.
   c. Hold the hydrometer vertically and note the number aligned with the surface of the electrolyte. This is the

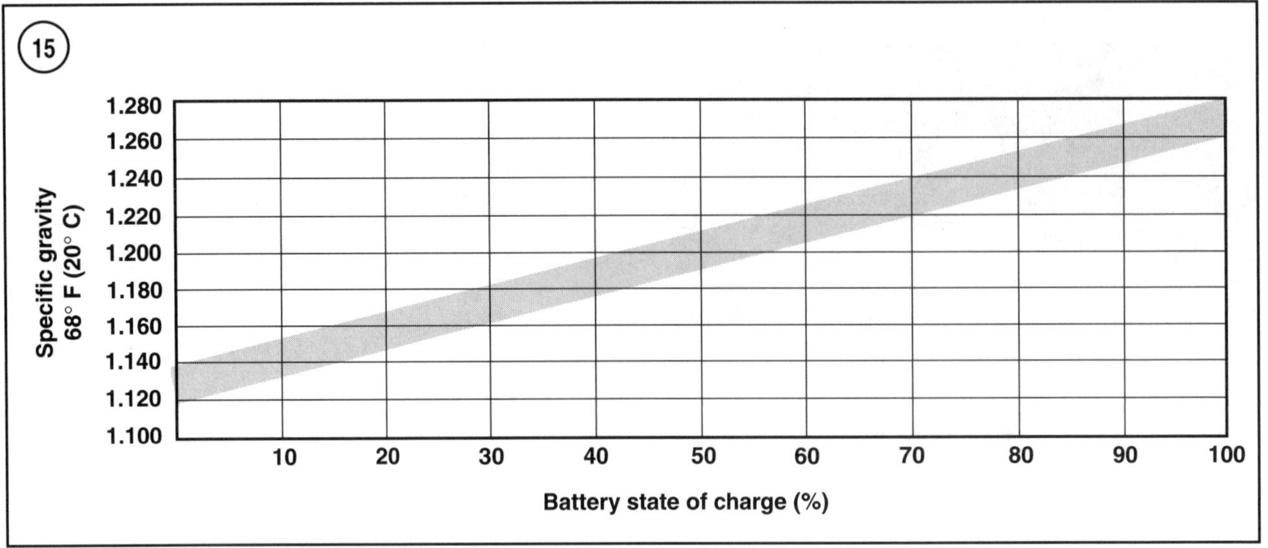

specific gravity for this cell. Return the electrolyte to the cell from which it came.

2. Refer to **Figure 15**. A fully charged cell will read 1.260-1.280 points specific gravity while a cell in good condition will read from 1.230-1.250 and anything below 1.120 is discharged. Charging is also necessary if the specific gravity varies more than 0.050 points from cell to cell.

NOTE

If a temperature-compensated hydrometer is not used, add 0.004 to the specific gravity reading for every 10° above 25° C (80° F). For every 10° below 25° C (80° F), subtract 0.004.

Charging

The battery should only self-discharge approximately 1% of its given capacity each day. If a battery not in use, without any load connected, loses its charge within a week of being fully charged, the battery is defective.

If the motorcycle is not used for long periods of time, an automatic charger with variable voltage and amperage outputs is recommended for optimum battery service life.

WARNING

During charging, highly explosive hydrogen gas is released from the battery. Charge the battery in a well-ventilated area absent from open flames, including pilot lights on gas appliances. Do not allow smoking in the area. Never check the charge of the battery by arcing across the terminals; the resulting spark can ignite the hydrogen gas.

CAUTION

Always remove the battery from the motorcycle before connecting charging equipment.

1. Remove the battery as described in this section.
2. Set the battery on newspapers or shop cloths to protect the surface of the workbench.
3. Make sure the charger is turned off prior to attaching the charger leads to the battery.
4. Connect the positive charger lead to the positive battery terminal and the negative charger lead to the negative battery terminal.
5. Remove all fill caps (**Figure 13**) from the battery. Set the charger to 12 volts, and switch it on. Normally, a battery should be charged at a slow charge rate of 1/10 its given capacity.
   a. As the battery charges, the electrolyte will begin to bubble (gassing). If one cell does not bubble, it is usually an indication that it is defective. Refer to *Testing* in this section.
   b. The charging time depends on the state of discharged condition of the battery. Normally, a battery should be charged at a slow rate of 1/10 its given capacity.

CAUTION

Maintain the electrolyte level at the upper level during the charging cycle. Check and refill with distilled water as necessary.

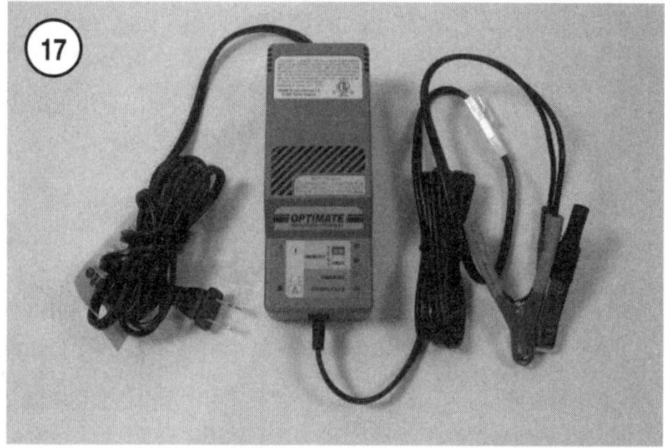

6. Disconnect the leads and check the specific gravity. It should be within the limits in **Figure 15**. If it is, and remains stable for one hour, the battery is charged.

Maintenance-Free Battery Service

Inspection and testing

The battery electrolyte level cannot be serviced in a maintenance-free battery. *Never* attempt to remove the sealing bar cap from the top of the battery. The battery does not require periodic electrolyte inspection or water refilling. Refer to the label on the battery.

Even though the battery is a sealed type, protect eyes, skin and clothing. The corrosive electrolyte may have spilled out and can cause injury. The battery case may be cracked and leaking electrolyte. If any electrolyte is spilled or splashed on clothing or skin, immediately neutralize with a solution of baking soda and water, then flush with an abundance of clean water.

WARNING

Electrolyte splashed into the eyes is extremely harmful. Always wear safety glasses while working with a battery. If electrolyte gets into the eyes, call a physician immediately and force the eyes open and flood them with cool, clean water for approximately 15 minutes.

1. Remove the battery as described in this chapter. Do not clean the battery while it is mounted in the frame.
2. Set the battery on newspapers or shop cloths to protect the surface of the workbench.
3. Check the battery case (A, **Figure 16**) for cracks or other damage. If the battery case is warped, discolored or has a raised top, the battery has been overcharged and overheated.
4. Check the battery terminal bolts, spacers and nuts (B, **Figure 16**) for corrosion or damage. Clean parts thoroughly with a solution of baking soda and water. Replace corroded or damaged parts.
5. If corroded, clean the top of the battery with a stiff bristle brush using the baking soda and water solution.
6. Check the battery cable ends for corrosion and damage. If corrosion is minor, clean the battery cable ends with a stiff wire brush. Replace worn or damaged cables.
7. Connect a digital voltmeter between the battery negative and positive leads. Note the following:
   a. If the battery voltage is 12.8 volts (at 20° C [68° F]), or greater, the battery is fully charged
   b. If the battery voltage is 12.0 to 12.5 volts (at 20° C [68° F]), or lower, the battery is undercharged and requires charging.
8. If the battery is undercharged, recharge it as described in this section. If necessary, test the charging system as described in Chapter Ten.
9. Inspect the battery holder in the frame for contamination or damage. Clean with a solution of baking soda and water.
10. Install the battery as described in this chapter.

Charging

Refer to *Initialization* in this section if the battery is new.

If recharging is required on a maintenance-free battery, a digital voltmeter and a charger (**Figure 17**) with an adjustable amperage output are required. If this equipment is not available, it is recommended that battery charging be entrusted to a BMW dealership or shop with the proper equipment. Excessive voltage and amperage (6 amps max.) from an unregulated charger can damage the battery and shorten service life.

The battery should only self-discharge approximately 1% each day. If a battery not in use, without any loads connected, loses its charge within a week after charging, the battery is defective.

If the motorcycle is not used for long periods of time, an automatic battery charger with variable voltage and amperage outputs is recommended for optimum battery service life.

WARNING
During charging, highly explosive hydrogen gas is released from the battery. Charge the battery in a well-ventilated area away from open flames, including pilot lights on gas appliances. Do not allow any smoking in the area. Never check the charge of the battery by arcing across the terminals; the resulting spark can ignite the hydrogen gas.

CAUTION
Always disconnect the battery cables from the battery. If the cables are left connected during the charging procedure, the charger may damage electrical system components.

1. Remove the battery from the motorcycle as described in this chapter.
2. Set the battery on a stack of newspapers or shop cloths to protect the surface of the workbench.
3. Make sure the battery charger is turned off prior to attaching the charger leads to the battery.
4. Connect the positive charger lead to the positive battery terminal and the negative charger lead to the negative battery terminal.
5. Set the charger at 12 volts. If the output of the charger is variable, select the low setting.
6. The charging time depends on the discharged condition of the battery. Refer to **Table 4** for the suggested charging time. Normally, a battery should be charged at 1/10th its given capacity.

CAUTION
If the battery emits an excessive amount of gas during the charging cycle, decrease the charge rate. If the battery becomes hotter than 43° C (110° F) during the charging cycle, turn the charger off and allow the battery to cool. After cooling down, continue with a reduced charging rate and continue to monitor the battery temperature.

7. Turn the charger on.
8. After the battery has been charged for the pre-determined time, turn the charger off, disconnect the leads and measure the battery voltage. Refer to the following:

a. If the battery voltage is 12.8 volts (at 20° C [68° F]), or greater, the battery is fully charged

b. If the battery voltage is 12.5 volts (at 20° C [68° F]), or lower, the battery is undercharged and requires additional charging time.

9. If the battery remains stable for one hour, the battery is charged.

10. Install the battery as described in this section.

Initialization

A new battery must be fully charged before installation. Failure to do so reduces the life of the battery. Using a new battery without an initial charge will cause permanent battery damage. That is, the battery will never be able to hold more than an 80% charge. Charging a new battery after it is used will not bring its charge to 100%. When purchasing a new battery from a dealership or parts store, verify its charge status. If necessary, have them perform the initial or booster charge before accepting the battery.

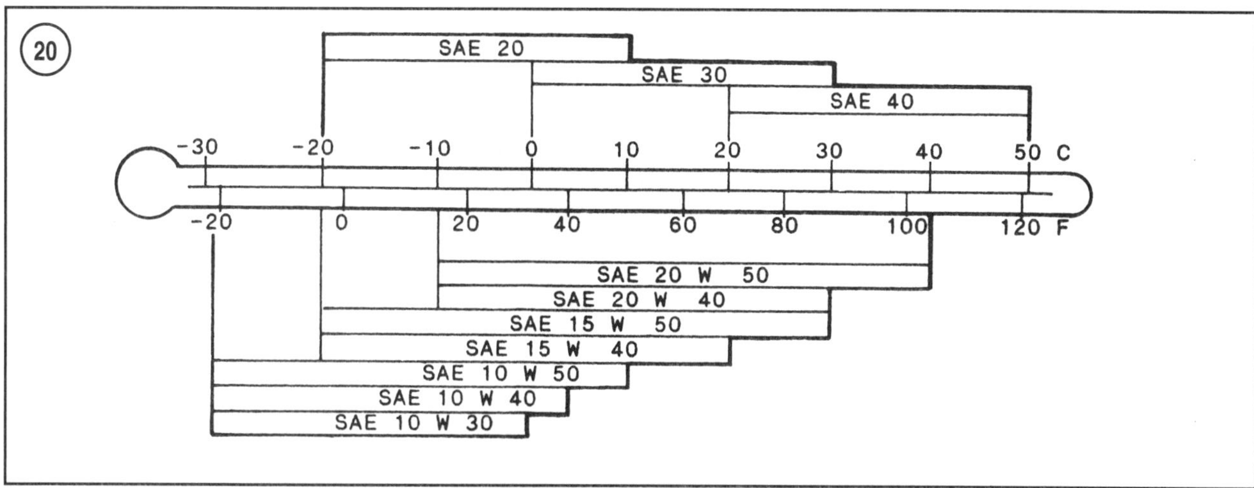

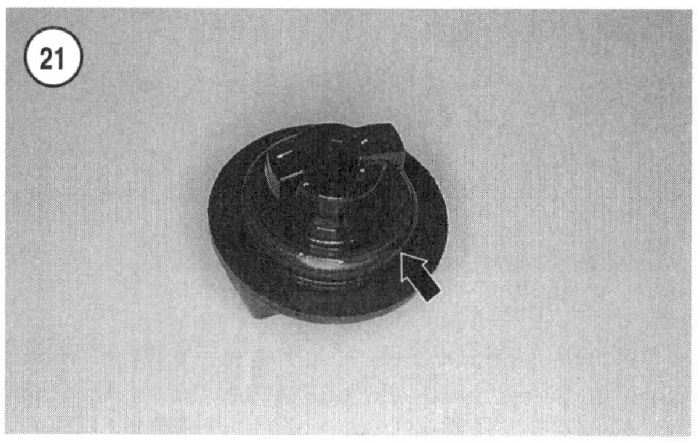

ENGINE OIL AND FILTER

Engine Oil Level Check

Check the engine oil level at the oil level inspection window, located at the left side of the engine.

1A. On models so equipped, place the motorcycle on the centerstand with the front wheel off of the ground.

1B. On models without a centerstand, place a suitable size jack under the engine to support the motorcycle with the front wheel off the ground.

2. Start the engine and let it idle for 2-3 minutes.

3. Shut off the engine and let the oil settle for 1-2 minutes.

4. On the front left side of the crankcase, look at the oil level inspection window (**Figure 18**). The oil level should be between the upper (MAX) and lower (MIN) marks.

CAUTION
Never exceed the MAX mark on the oil level inspection window.

5. If the oil level is below the lower mark, remove the oil fill cap (**Figure 19**) and add the recommended oil until the level is even with the upper mark. Refer to **Figure 20** for the viscocity and **Table 6** for the service classification. Approximately 0.6 L (1 pt.) of oil will raise the level from the lower mark (MIN) to the upper mark (MAX).

6. Inspect the oil fill cap O-ring (**Figure 21**) for hardness, cracking or deterioration. Replace the O-ring if necessary.

7. Install the fill cap and tighten it securely.

Engine Oil and Oil Filter Change

The recommended oil and filter change interval is listed in **Table 1**. If the motorcycle is operated under dusty conditions, the oil will get dirty more quickly and should be changed more frequently than recommended.

Use a mineral or synthetic based oil with an API classification specified in **Table 6**. Try to use the same brand of oil at each change. Refer to **Figure 20** for the oil viscosity to use under anticipated ambient temperatures (not engine oil temperature).

NOTE
Never dispose of engine oil in the trash, on the ground or down a storm drain. Many service stations and oil retailers will accept used oil for recycling. Do not combine other fluids with engine oil to be recycled. To locate a recycler, contact the American Petroleum Institute (API) at www.recycleoil.org.

NOTE
Warming the engine allows the oil to heat up; thus it flows freely and carries more contamination and sludge out with it.

1. Start the engine and let it reach operating temperature; 15-20 minutes of stop-and-go riding is usually sufficient.
2. Turn the engine off and place the motorcycle on level ground on the sidestand.
3A. On GS models, remove the skid plate assembly as described in Chapter Fifteen.
3B. On RT models, remove the spoiler from the lower fairing sections as described in Chapter Fifteen.

WARNING
During the next step, hot oil will drain quickly from the drain plug opening. Protect yourself accordingly.

4. Place a drain pan under the engine and remove the drain plug (**Figure 22**). Allow the oil to drain for at least 15-20 minutes.
5. Unscrew the oil fill cap (**Figure 19**) located on the top of the left cylinder head cover; this will hasten the flow of oil.
6. Remove and discard the sealing washer on the oil pan drain plug. Replace the sealing washer every time the drain plug is removed.
7. Install the oil drain plug and new sealing washer. Tighten the drain plug to 32 N•m (24 ft.-lb.).
8. Prior to removing the oil filter, thoroughly clean off all dirt and oil around it to prevent dirt from entering the crankcase.

NOTE
Make sure the oil drain pan is still positioned correctly as some residual oil will run out after the oil filter is removed.

WARNING
The exterior of the oil filter is hot—protect hands accordingly.

9. Using the oil filter wrench (BMW part No. 11-4-650) (**Figure 23**) and ratchet, unscrew the oil filter from the crankcase (**Figure 24**) .
10. Remove the oil filter wrench from the filter and drain the residual oil into the drain pan. Place the filter in a heavy plastic bag to contain any remaining oil. Seal the bag to prevent oil from draining.
11. Clean the inner surface of the oil filter cavity in the crankcase with a shop rag and cleaning solvent. Wipe it dry with a clean cloth.

WARNING
The inner receptacle in the crankcase where the oil filter fits is sharp. Protect hands and fingers while installing the new oil filter.

12. Apply a light coat of clean engine oil to the rubber seal on the new filter.

13. Screw on the new oil filter by hand until the rubber ring just touches the crankcase surface. At this point there will be a very slight resistance when turning the filter.
14. Using the oil filter wrench and torque wrench, tighten the oil filter to 11 N•m (97 in.-lb.).
15. Insert a funnel into the oil fill hole in the cylinder head cover and fill the engine with the correct quantity and classification of oil. Refer to **Table 5**.
16. Inspect the oil fill cap O-ring seal (**Figure 21**) for hardness or deterioration and replace it if necessary.
17. Install the oil fill cap and tighten securely. Thoroughly clean any spilled oil off of the cylinder head with an aerosol parts cleaner.
18. Start the engine, let it run at idle speed and check for leaks.
19. Turn the engine off and check the oil level; adjust as necessary.

WARNING
Prolonged contact with oil may cause skin cancer. Wash hands thoroughly with soap and water after handling engine oil.

20A. On GS models, install the skid plate assembly as described in Chapter Fifteen.
20B. On RT models, install the spoiler onto the lower fairing sections as described in Chapter Fifteen.

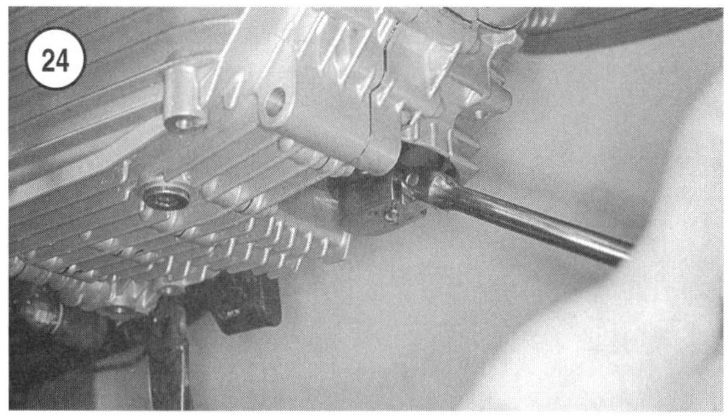

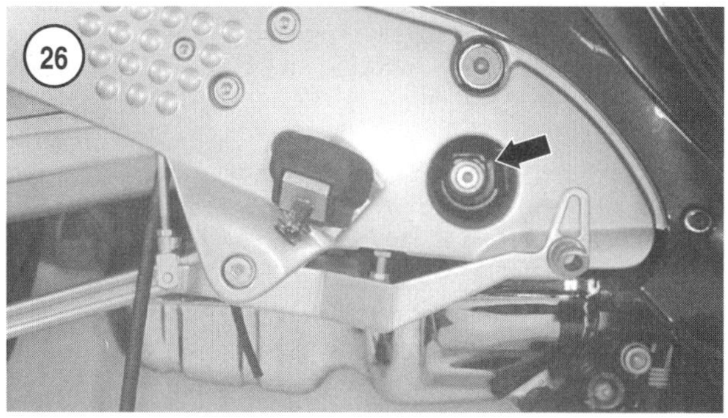

TRANSMISSION

Oil Level Check

Inspect the transmission oil level at the intervals listed in **Table 1**. If the motorcycle has been running, allow it to cool (a minimum of 10 minutes), then check the transmission oil level. When checking the transmission oil level, do not allow any debris to enter the case opening.

1. Place the motorcycle on the sidestand, or auxiliary stand, on level ground.

2. Clean all debris from around the oil filler cap. Use an Allen wrench and unscrew the oil fill cap and sealing washer (A, **Figure 25**).

3. The oil level is correct if the oil is even with the lower edge of the fill cap hole.

NOTE

Add only enough oil to bring the oil level up to the lower edge of the fill cap hole. Do not over fill the transmission.

4. If the oil level is low, add the recommended type of oil listed in **Table 5**.

5. Inspect the sealing washer on the oil fill cap and replace if necessary.

6. Install the sealing washer and the oil fill cap and tighten to 23 N•m (17 ft.-lb.) on all models except R1150. On R1150 models, tighten to 30 N•m (22 ft.-lb.).

7. Wipe any spilled oil from the transmission case.

Oil Change

Replace the transmission oil at the intervals listed in **Table 1**.

1. Ride the motorcycle until the transmission oil reaches normal operating temperature. Usually 10-15 minutes of stop and go riding is sufficient. Shut the engine off.

2A. On models so equipped, place the motorcycle on the centerstand with the front wheel off of the ground.

2B. On models without a centerstand, place a suitable size jack under the engine to support the motorcycle with the front wheel off the ground.

NOTE

Prior to removing the drain plug, loosen the oil fill cap. If the oil fill cap cannot be loosened, do not remove the oil drain plug until the oil fill cap can be removed.

3. Wipe the area around the oil fill cap clean.

4. On RT models, install the oil drain pipe (BMW part No. 23-4-680) through the opening in the right footrest assembly and into the oil drain plug area of the transmission (**Figure 26**). Turn the oil drain pipe clockwise and lock it in place.

5. Unscrew the oil fill cap and sealing washer (A, **Figure 25**) to speed the flow of oil.

6A. On all models except R850C, R1100S and R1200C, perform the following:

   a. Place aluminum foil over the right side of the exhaust system directly below the oil drain hole. Then place a shop rag over the foil to catch any oil that will drain onto it.
   b. Place a drain pan under the transmission drain plug.

3

WARNING
During the next step, hot oil will drain quickly from the drain plug opening. Protect yourself accordingly.

c. Remove the drain plug and sealing (B, **Figure 25**). Allow the oil to drain for at least 15-20 minutes.

NOTE
***Figure 27** is shown with the transmission case removed to better illustrate the procedure.*

6B. On R850C, R1100S and R1200C models, on the bottom surface of the transmission case, remove the drain plug and sealing washer (**Figure 27**). Allow the oil to drain for at least 15-20 minutes.

7. Remove and discard the sealing washer from the transmission oil drain plug. Replace the sealing washer every time the drain plug is removed.

8A. On all models except R850C, R1100S and R1200C, install the drain plug and new sealing washer and tighten to 23 N•m (17 ft.-lb.).

8B. On R850C, R1100S models and R1200C, install the drain plug and new sealing washer and tighten to 55 N•m (40 ft.-lb.).

8C. On R1150 models, install the drain plug and new sealing washer and tighten to 30 N•m (22 ft.-lb.)

9. On RT models, turn the oil drain pipe counterclockwise and remove it from the transmission and the opening in the right footrest assembly.

10. Insert a funnel into the oil fill hole and fill the transmission with the correct viscosity and quantity of oil. Refer to **Table 5**.

11. On all models except R1150, install the oil fill cap and tighten to 23 N•m (17 ft.-lb.). On R1150 models, tighten to 30 N•m (22 ft.-lb.).

12. Remove the shop cloth and aluminum foil from the exhaust system. If any oil found its way onto the exhaust system, wipe it clean then finish cleaning with an aerosol parts cleaner.

13. Thoroughly clean all oil from the exterior of the transmission case.

14. Discard the used oil as outlined under *Engine Oil and Filter Change* in this chapter.

15. Ride the motorcycle until the transmission oil reaches normal operating temperature. Usually 10-15 minutes of stop and go riding is sufficient. Shut the engine off.

16. Check the transmission oil level as described in this chapter and readjust if necessary.

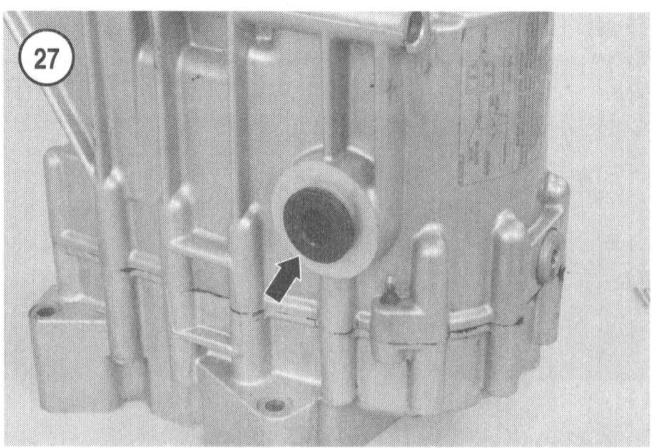

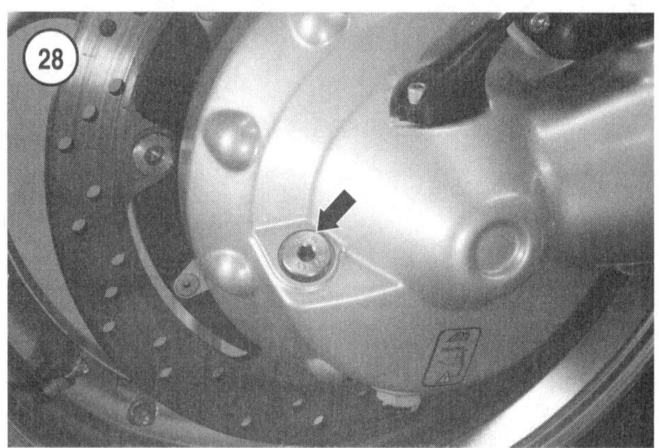

FINAL DRIVE

Oil Level Check

Inspect the final drive oil level at the intervals listed in **Table 1**. If the motorcycle has been running, allow it to cool (a minimum of 10 minutes) before checking the oil level. When checking the final drive oil level, do not allow any debris to enter the case opening.

1. Place the motorcycle on the sidestand on level ground.
2. Wipe the area around the oil fill cap clean.
3. Use a 6–mm Allen wrench and unscrew the oil fill cap (**Figure 28**).
4. The oil level is correct if it is even with the lower edge of the fill cap hole.
5. If the oil level is low, add the recommended type of oil listed in **Table 5**.
6. Inspect the sealing washer on the oil fill cap, replacing it if necessary.
7. Install the sealing washer and the oil fill cap and tighten it to 23 N•m (17 ft.-lb.).
8. Wipe any spilled oil from the final drive case.

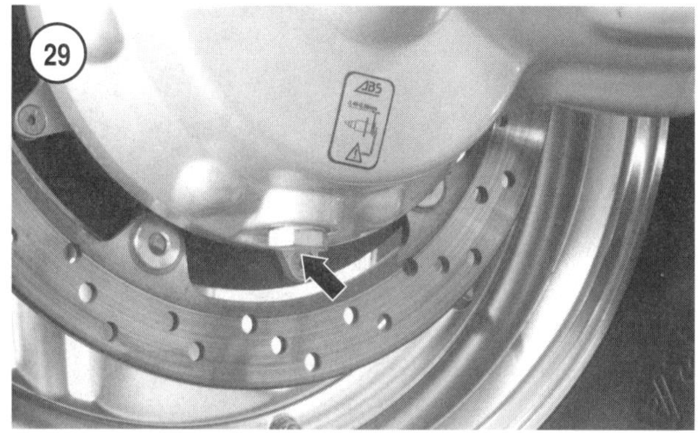

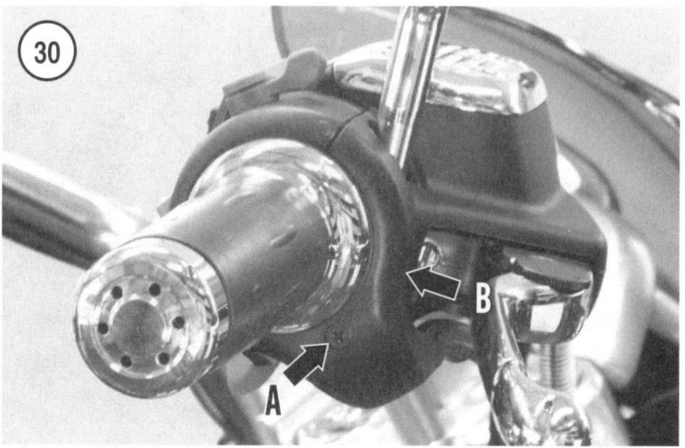

Oil Change

Replace the final drive oil at the intervals listed in **Table 1**.

1. Ride the motorcycle until the final drive oil reaches normal operating temperature. Usually 10-15 minutes of stop and go riding is sufficient. Shut the engine off.
2. Place the motorcycle on the sidestand, or auxiliary stand, on level ground.

NOTE
Prior to removing the drain plug, loosen the oil fill cap. If the oil fill cap cannot be loosened, do not remove the oil drain plug until the oil fill cap can be removed.

3. Wipe the area around the oil fill cap clean and unscrew the oil fill cap (**Figure 28**) to speed the flow of oil.
4. Place a drain pan under the drain plug.

WARNING
During the next step, hot oil will spurt from the drain plug hole. Be ready to move your hand away quickly once the drain plug is removed so hot oil will not run on your hand and down your arm.

5A. On R1100S models, use the offset Allen socket tool (BMW part No. 23-4 690) or an equivalent, to access the drain plug. Remove the drain plug.

5B. On all models except R1100S, remove the drain plug (**Figure 29**) with a 19 mm box wrench. Allow the oil to drain for at least 15-20 minutes.

6. Remove and discard the sealing washer from the drain plug. Replace the sealing washer every time the drain plug is removed.
7. Install the drain plug and a new sealing washer.

8A. On R1100S models use offset Allen socket, tighten the drain plug to 23 N•m (17 ft.-lb.).

8B. On all models except R1100S, tighten the drain plug to 23 N•m (17 ft.-lb.).

9. Insert a funnel into the oil fill hole and fill the transmission with the correct viscosity and quantity of oil. Refer to **Table 5**.
10. Install the oil fill cap and sealing washer and tighten to 23 N•m (17 ft.-lb.).
11. Discard the used oil as outlined under *Engine Oil and Filter Change* in this chapter.
12. Ride the motorcycle until the transmission oil reaches normal operating temperature. Usually 10-15 minutes of stop and go riding is sufficient. Shut the engine off.
13. Check the final drive units oil level as described in this chapter and readjust if necessary.

CONTROL CABLE SERVICE

The original equipment (OE) control cables in most applications are nylon-lined. Nylon lined cables do not require periodic cable lubrication. Lubrication of the nylon liner may cause it to swell and damage the cable.

The following procedures outline lubrication for non-nylon cables. If the OE cables have been replaced with this type, refer to the entire procedure. Also included are steps to lubricate the cable ends, which would apply to either type of cable.

Inspect the cables for fraying and check the sheath for chafing during service. Replace any defective cables.

CAUTION
When servicing nylon-lined and other aftermarket cables, follow the cable manufacturer's instructions.

Throttle Cable

1. Remove the screw (A, **Figure 30**) securing the throttle cable cover and remove the cover (B).

3

2. On models so equipped, remove the screw (A, **Figure 31**) securing the throttle cable guide and remove the guide (B).
3. Disconnect the throttle cable end (**Figure 32**) from the grip assembly.
4. Disconnect the throttle cable from the throttle grip assembly.
5. Attach a cable lubricator to the end of the throttle cable following the manufacturer's instructions.
6. Place a shop cloth at the throttle body linkage end of the cable to catch the lubricant as it runs out.
7. Attach the cable lubricator to the cable following the manufacture's instructions.
8. Insert the nozzle of the lubricant, press the button on the can and hold it down until the lubricant begins to flow out of the other end of the cable. If the lubricant flows out from the cable lubricator, the lubricant is not installed properly onto the end of the cable. The lubricator may have to be installed a few times to get it to seal properly. Place a shop cloth at the throttle body linkage end of the cable to catch the lubricant as it runs out.

NOTE
If the lubricant does not flow out of the end of the cable, check the entire cable for fraying, bending or other damage.

9. Remove the lubricator and wipe off all excessive lubricant from the cable.
10. Place a dab of grease onto the cable barrel before reconnecting it.
11. Connect the throttle cable to the throttle grip assembly and make sure it seats correctly in the cable receptacle (**Figure 32**).
12. On models so equipped, install the throttle cable guide (B, **Figure 31**) and screw (A). Tighten the screw securely.
13. Install the throttle cable cover (B, **Figure 30**) and screw (A) and tighten securely.
14. After lubricating the throttle cable, operate the throttle grip at the handlebar. It should open and close smoothly with no binding.
15. Adjust the throttle cable as described in this chapter.

Cold-start (Choke) Cable

NOTE
The R850C and R1200C models are not equipped with a cold-start (choke) cable.

1. On RT models, remove the right front fairing panel as described in Chapter Fifteen.

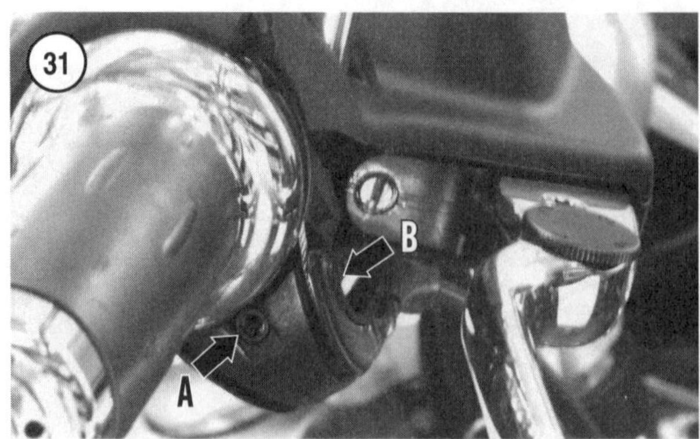

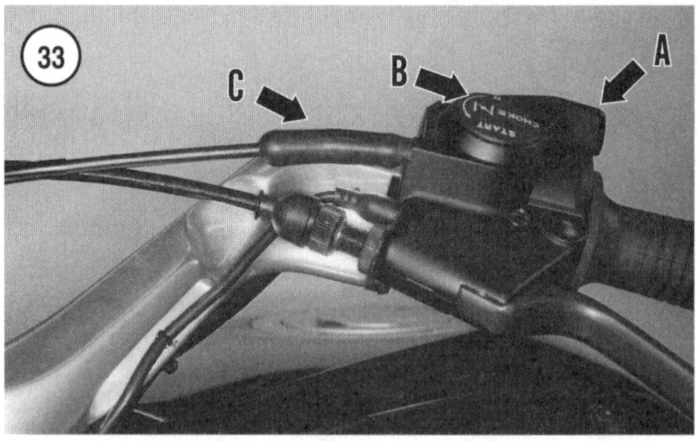

NOTE
On later models, the choke cable is and integral part of the lever assembly. It cannot be disconnected to attached a lubricator.

2. On early models, perform the following:
   a. Carefully remove the trim cap (A, **Figure 33**) from the cold-start lever.
   b. Remove the screw and washer, located under the trim cap, securing the cold-start lever (B, **Figure 33**).
   c. Pull the lever up and out of the left switch assembly.

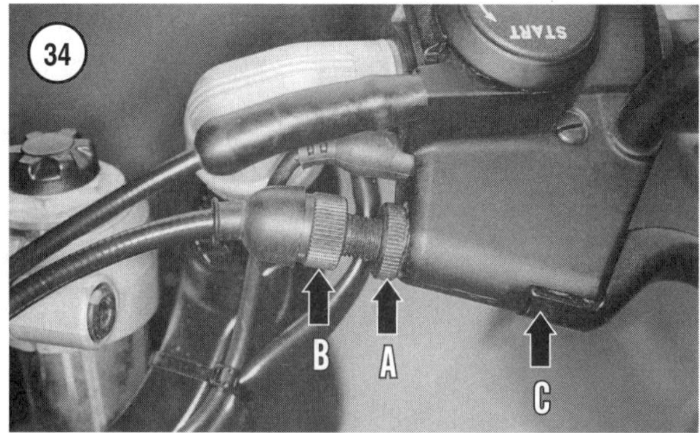

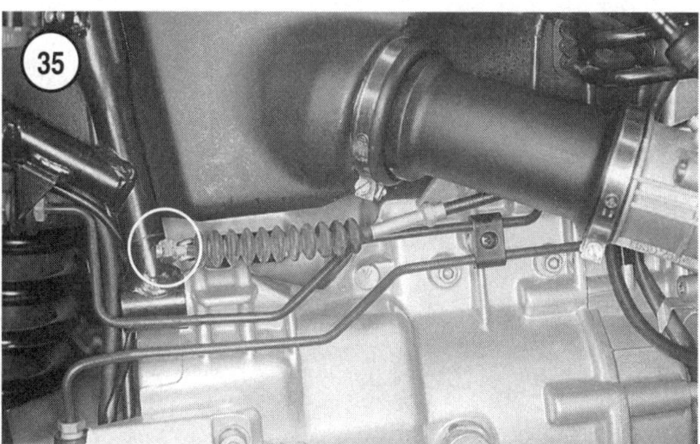

d. Disconnect the cold-start cable end (C, **Figure 33**) from the lever.

3. Attach a cable lubricator to the end of the choke cable following the manufacturer's instructions.
4. Place a shop cloth at the throttle body linkage end of the cable to catch the lubricant as it runs out.
5. Attach the cable lubricator to the cable following the manufacture's instructions.
6. Insert the nozzle of the lubricant, press the button on the can and hold it down until the lubricant begins to flow out of the other end of the cable. If the lubricant flows out from the cable lubricator, the lubricant is not installed properly onto the end of the cable. The lubricator may have to be installed a few times to get it to seal properly. Place a shop cloth at the throttle body linkage end of the cable to catch the lubricant as it runs out.

NOTE
If the lubricant does not flow out of the end of the cable, check the entire cable for fraying, bending or other damage.

7. Remove the lubricator and wipe off all excessive lubricant from the cable.
8. Place a dab of grease onto the cable barrel before reconnecting it.
9. On early models, perform the following:
   a. Connect the cold-start cable to the end of the lever.
   b. Align the cable with the cutout in the switch assembly and carefully push the lever down into the switch assembly.
   c. Install the screw and washer and tighten securely. Install the trim cap and push it down until it seats.
10. After lubricating the cold-start cable, operate the lever at the handlebar. It should open and close smoothly with no binding.
11. On RT models, install the right front fairing panel as described in Chapter Fifteen.

3

Clutch Cable

1. Loosen the locknut (A, **Figure 34**) and turn the adjuster (B) in all the way. This will allow slack in the clutch cable.
2. Disconnect the clutch cable from the underside of the clutch lever. Remove the clutch cable from the lever (C, **Figure 34**).
3. Attach a cable lubricator to the end of the throttle cable following the manufacturer's instructions.
4. Place a shop cloth at the clutch cable release lever on the upper right side of the transmission case to catch the lubricant as it runs out.
5. Attach the cable lubricator to the cable following the manufacture's instructions.
6. Insert the nozzle of the lubricant, press the button on the can and hold it down until the lubricant begins to flow out of the other end of the cable. If the lubricant flows out from the cable lubricator, the lubricant is not installed properly onto the end of the cable. The lubricator may have to be installed a few times to get it to seal properly. Place a shop cloth at the throttle body linkage end of the cable to catch the lubricant as it runs out.

NOTE
If the lubricant does not flow out of the end of the cable, check the entire cable for fraying, bending or other damage.

7. Remove the lubricator and wipe off all excessive lubricant from the cable.
8. Apply a small amount of Shell Retinax A grease to the clutch cable nipple at the handlebar lever and at the release lever (**Figure 35**) on the upper right side of the transmission case.
9. Connect the clutch cable onto the under side of the clutch lever.
10. Tighten the adjuster (B, **Figure 34**) to take up any slack in the cable.

11. Adjust the clutch as described in this chapter.

Speedometer Cable

NOTE
The R850C and R1200C models are not equipped with a speedometer cable. These models use a speed sensor, mounted on the final drive unit.

1. Remove the mounting screw (A, **Figure 36**) and disconnect the speedometer cable end piece (B) from the speedometer drive gear at the front wheel.
2. Remove the cable from the sheath.
3. Thoroughly clean off the old grease if it is contaminated. Wipe the cable with a cloth dipped in solvent, then thoroughly dry with a lint-free cloth.
4. Thoroughly coat the cable with a good grade of multipurpose grease and reinstall it in the sheath.
5. Slowly rotate the cable until it is engaged correctly with the speedometer unit.
6. Insert the cable into the speedometer drive gear and slowly rotate the front wheel until the cable end indexes into the drive gear. Tighten the mounting screw (A, **Figure 36**).

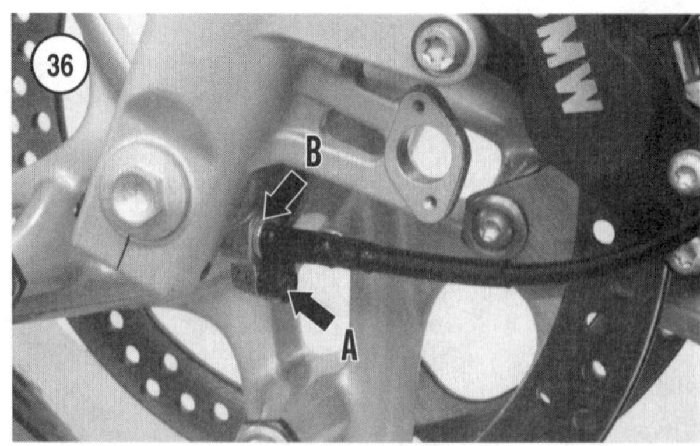

REAR BRAKE PEDAL PIVOT SHAFT BOLT AND BUSHING LUBRICATION

Remove the rear brake pedal and lubricate the pivot shaft (**Figure 37**, typical) and bushings with water-resistant grease as described in Chapter Fourteen. Inspect the pedal return spring for weakness or damage and replace it if necessary.

SHIFT LEVER CLEANING AND LUBRICATION

1. Remove the shift lever as described in Chapter Seven or Chapter Eight.
2. Lubricate the shift lever pivot bolt area and the shift lever pivot area.
3. Install the shift lever as described in Chapter Seven or Chapter Eight.

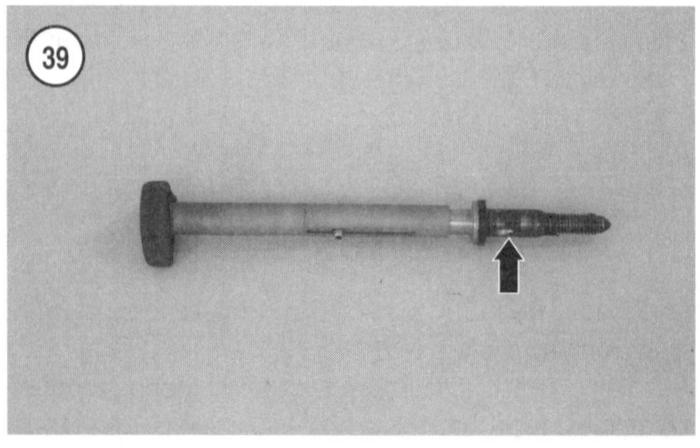

SIDESTAND LUBRICATION

On the left side, apply waterproof grease or equivalent to the fittings until the grease starts to flow from the bearings.

WINDSHIELD ADJUST SHAFT (RS MODELS)

Completely unscrew the windshield adjust shaft (**Figure 38**) from between the meters. Apply a small amount of Shell Retinax A grease to the threads and lower portion of the shaft (**Figure 39**), then reinstall the adjust shaft.

AIR FILTER

The air filter removes dust and abrasive particles from the air before the air enters the fuel injection system and the engine. A clogged air filter element will decrease the efficiency and life of the engine. With a damaged air filter, dirt could enter the engine and cause rapid wear of the piston rings, cylinders and bearings. Replace the air filter element at the intervals listed in **Table 1**. Replace the air filter more often if dusty areas are frequently encountered. Cleaning the air filter element is not recommended. If contaminated, replace it.

Replacement

All models except R850C, R1100S and R1200C

1. Place the motorcycle on the sidestand.
2. Remove the fuel tank as described in Chapter Nine.

3A. On early models, perform the following:
   a. Unhook the rear spring clamps (**Figure 40**) securing the cover.
   b. Disconnect the electrical connector (A, **Figure 41**) from the sensor.
   c. Remove the cover (B, **Figure 41**).

3B. On later models, perform the following:
   a. Remove the screws (**Figure 42**) securing the cover.
   b. Carefully pivot the cover (**Figure 43**) up and release the locating tabs from the slots in the air box. Do not pull on the cover until the tabs are released, otherwise the tabs will break off.
   c. Remove the cover and set it aside.

4. Remove the element (A, **Figure 44**) from the air box.
5. Wipe out the interior of the air box with a shop rag dampened with cleaning solvent.
6. Inspect the new element to make sure it is in good condition. Make sure it is not torn or defective.
7. Apply a light coat of multipurpose grease to the sealing edges (**Figure 45**) of the air filter element. This will ensure an air-tight fitting of the element to the air filter case.

8A. On early models, perform the following:

a. Install the air filter into the air box and press it down.

b. Secure the upper case to the lower case with the spring clamps. Make sure the spring clamps are snapped over-center and are holding tight.

c. Reconnect the electrical connector (A, **Figure 41**) onto the sensor.

8B. On later models, perform the following:

a. Insert the cover locating tabs into the air box slots (B, **Figure 44**). Make sure they are correctly inserted, then slowly pivot the cover (**Figure 43**) down.

b. Push the rear of the cover down and make sure it seats correctly all the way around the perimeter.

c. Install the cover screws (**Figure 42**) and tighten securely. Do not overtighten as the they will strip out the air box receptacles.

9. Install the fuel tank as described in Chapter Nine.

R1100S models

1. Place the motorcycle on the sidestand.
2. Remove the fuel tank rear mounting hardware as described in Chapter Nine. Raise the rear of the fuel tank and securely support it in the raised position.
3. Remove the front fairing side panels as described in Chapter Fifteen.
4. Remove the screws securing the air filter housing top cover and remove it.
5. Remove the element from the air box.
6. Wipe out the interior of the air box with a shop rag dampened with cleaning solvent.
7. Inspect the new element to make sure it is in good condition. Make sure it is not torn or defective in any area.
8. Apply a light coat of multipurpose grease to the sealing edges of the air filter element. This will ensure an air-tight fitting of the element to the air filter case.
9. Install the air filter into the air box and press it down to make sure it seats correctly. Make sure the sealing surface is tight against the air box surfaces.
10. Install the top cover onto the lower case and make sure it correctly seats all the way around the perimeter. Install the screws and tighten securely.
11. Lower the fuel tank and attach and tighten the rear mounting hardware.

R850C and R1200C models

1. Place the motorcycle on the sidestand.

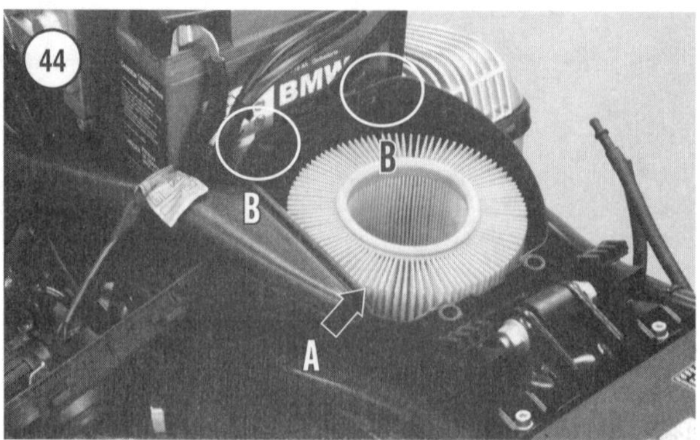

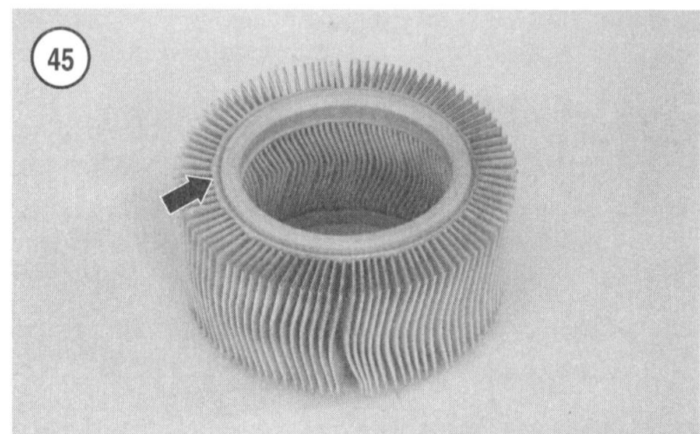

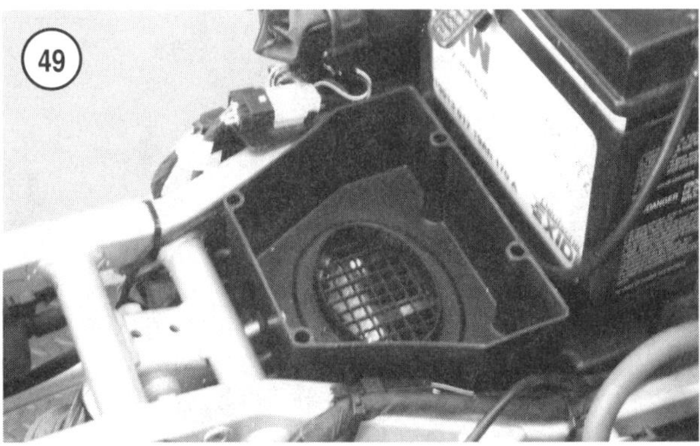

2. Remove the fuel tank as described in Chapter Nine.
3. Disconnect the electrical connector (**Figure 46**) from the sensor.
4. Remove the screws securing the air filter housing top cover (**Figure 47**) and remove it.
5. Remove the element (**Figure 48**) from the air box.
6. Wipe out the interior of the air box (**Figure 49**) with a shop rag dampened with cleaning solvent.
7. Inspect the element to make sure it is in good condition. Make sure it is not torn or defective.
8. Apply a light coat of multipurpose grease to the sealing edges (**Figure 45**) of the air filter element. This will ensure an air-tight fitting of the element to the air filter case.
9. Inspect the top cover perimeter seal (**Figure 50**) for damage.
10. Install the air filter into the air box and press it down to make sure it seats correctly. Make sure the sealing surface is tight against the air box surfaces.
11. Install the top cover (**Figure 47**) onto the lower case and make sure it correctly seats all the way around the perimeter. Install the screws and tighten securely.
12. Reconnect the electrical connector (**Figure 46**) onto the sensor.
13. Install the fuel tank as described in Chapter Nine.

BRAKE SYSTEM

Front Brake Fluid Level Inspection

All models except R850C, R1100S, all R1150 and R1200C

1. Place the motorcycle on level ground on the sidestand. Position the handlebars so the front master cylinder reservoir is level.
2. The fluid level must be between the MAX and MIN marks on the reservoir (**Figure 51**). If the brake fluid level is at or below the lower level mark, continue to Step 3.

NOTE

If the master cylinder is empty, air has probably entered the brake system. On non-ABS models, bleed the front brake system as described in Chapter Fourteen. On ABS models, have the brake system bled by a BMW dealership.

3. Clean any dirt from the area around the cover prior to removing the cover.
4. Remove the screws securing the cover (**Figure 52**). Remove the cover and the diaphragm.

5. Add fresh DOT 4 brake fluid to fill the reservoir to the upper level mark in the reservoir.
6. Reinstall the diaphragm and cover. Tighten the screws securely.
7. If the brake fluid level was low, check the brake pads for excessive wear as described in this section.

NOTE
A low brake fluid level usually indicates brake pad wear. As the pads wear and become thinner, the brake caliper pistons automatically extend farther out of their bores. As the caliper pistons move outward, the brake fluid level drops in the system. However, if the brake fluid level is low and the brake pads are not worn excessively, check all of the brake hoses for leaks.

R850, R1100S, all R1150 and R1200 models

1. Place the motorcycle on level ground on the sidestand.
2A. On R850C and R1200C models, move the handlebars to the straight-ahead position.
2B. On all other models, move the handlebars to the full left side position.
3. The fluid level must be above the center marking ring on the master cylinder reservoir. If the brake fluid level is at or below the lower level mark, continue to Step 3.

NOTE
If the master cylinder is empty, air has probably entered the brake system. Have the brake system bled by a BMW dealership.

4. Clean any dirt from the area around the cover prior to removing the cover.
5. Remove the screws securing the cover (**Figure 53**). Remove the cover and the diaphragm.
6. Add fresh DOT 4 brake fluid to fill the reservoir until the level is above the minimum level marking ring on the master cylinder reservoir. Refer to **Figure 54-56**.
7. Reinstall the diaphragm and cover. Tighten the screws securely.
8. If the brake fluid level was low, check the brake pads for excessive wear as described in this section.

NOTE
A low brake fluid level usually indicates brake pad wear. As the pads wear and become thinner, the brake caliper pistons automatically extend farther out of their bores.

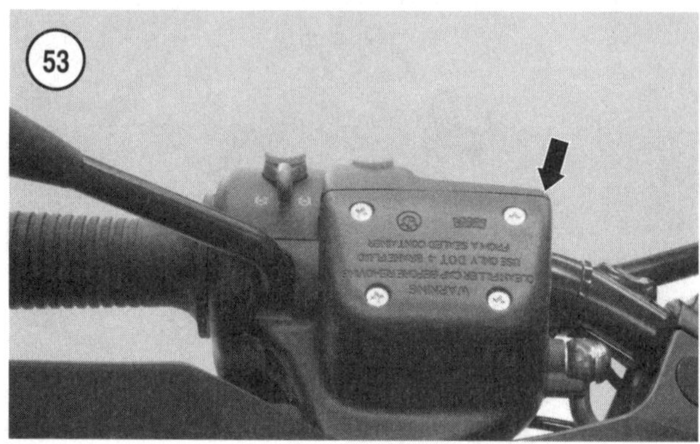

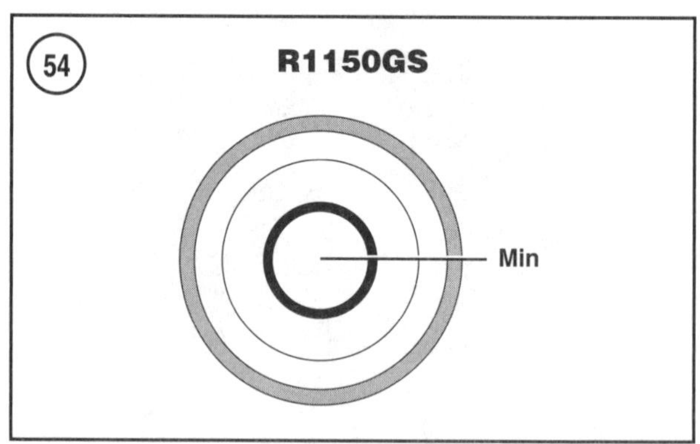

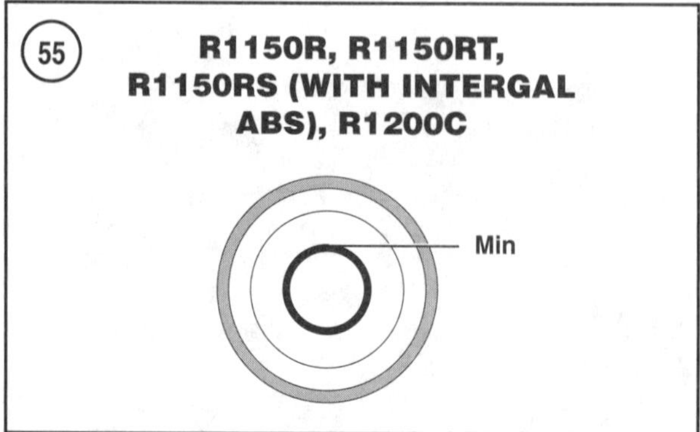

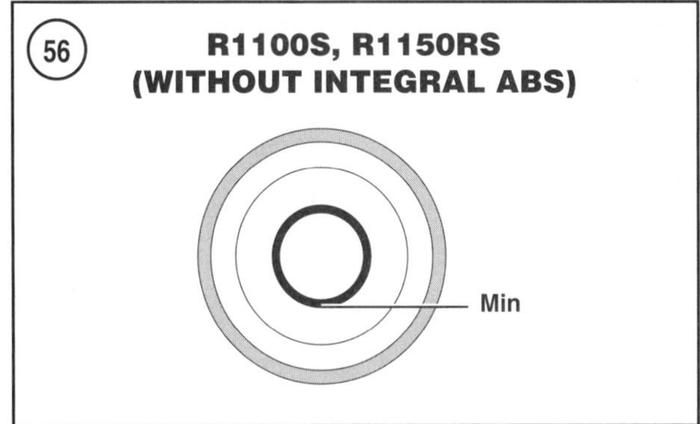

As the caliper pistons move outward, the brake fluid level drops in the system. However, if the brake fluid level is low and the brake pads are not worn excessively, check all of the brake hoses for leaks.

Rear Brake Fluid Level Inspection

1. Place the motorcycle on level ground so the rear master cylinder reservoir is level.

2. Remove the right fairing panel as described in Chapter Fifteen.

3A. On R850C and R1200C models, the fluid level must be between the MAX and MIN marks on the reservoir (A, **Figure 57**). If the brake fluid level is at or below the lower level mark, continue to Step 4.

3B. On all models except R850C and R1200C models, the fluid level must be between the MAX and MIN marks on the reservoir (A, **Figure 58**). If the brake fluid level is at or below the lower level mark, continue to Step 4.

4. Clean any dirt from the area around the cover prior to removing the cover.

NOTE

If the master cylinder is empty, air has probably entered the brake system. On non-ABS models, bleed the front brake system as described in Chapter Fourteen. On ABS models, have the brake system bled by a BMW dealership.

5A. On R850C and R1200C models, unscrew and remove the cover (B, **Figure 57**) and the diaphragm.

5B. On all models except R850C and R1200C models, unscrew and remove the cover (B, **Figure 58**) and the diaphragm.

6. Add brake fluid until the level is even with the upper level line on the master cylinder reservoir.

7. Reinstall the diaphragm and cover. Tighten the screws securely.

8. If the brake fluid level was low, check the brake pads for excessive wear as described in this section.

NOTE

A low brake fluid level usually indicates brake pad wear. As the pads wear and become thinner, the brake caliper pistons automatically extend farther out of their bores. As the caliper pistons move outward, the brake fluid level drops in the system. However, if the brake fluid level is low and the brake pads are not worn excessively, check all of the brake hoses for leaks.

9. Install the right fairing panel as described in Chapter Fifteen.

Brake Lines and Hose

Check the brake lines and hoses between the master cylinders, the brake calipers and ABS unit, or ABS pressure module, on models equipped with ABS. If there is any leakage, tighten the connections and bleed the brakes as described under *Bleeding the System* in Chapter Fourteen. If this does not stop the leak or if a brake line is obviously damaged, cracked or chafed, replace the brake line and bleed the system as described in Chapter Fourteen. The system must be bled using BMW special tools if the motorcycle is equipped with ABS (antilock brake system). Refer this procedure to a BMW dealership.

Brake Pad Wear

Inspect the brake pads for excessive or uneven wear.

1. Remove the caliper as described in Chapter Fourteen.
2. Look down into the caliper assembly and check the pad thickness (**Figure 59**).
3. Replace both pads if they are worn to 1.0 mm (0.039 in.) as described in Chapter Fourteen.
4. Install the caliper assembly as described in Chapter Fourteen.

Brake Fluid Change (Non-ABS Models)

NOTE
On models equipped with the ABS system, the brake fluid change must be performed at a BMW dealership since a power bleeder is required to bleed the brake system.

Every time the reservoir cap is removed, a small amount of dirt and moisture enters the brake fluid. The same thing happens if a leak occurs or any part of the hydraulic system is loosened or disconnected. Dirt can clog the system and cause unnecessary wear. Water in the brake fluid vaporizes at a high temperature, impairing the hydraulic action and reducing the brake's stopping ability. To maintain peak performance, change the brake fluid at the interval indicated in **Table 1**, or whenever the caliper or master cylinder is removed. Refer to the brake bleeding procedure in Chapter Fourteen.

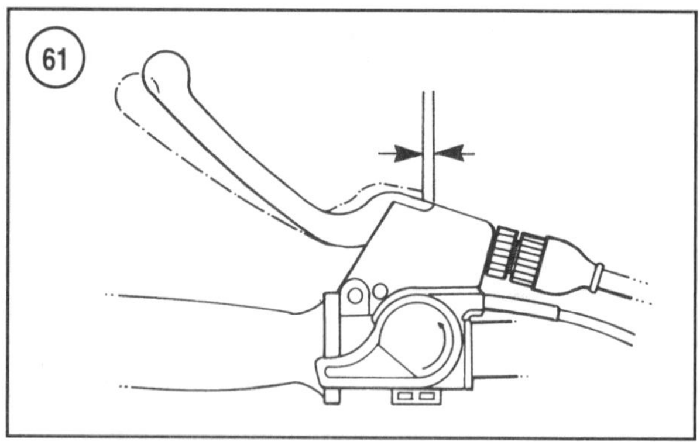

Rear Brake Pedal Height Adjustment (All Models Except R850C and R1200C)

Adjust the rear brake pedal height for the individual rider's preference. Position the top of the brake pedal so it is close to the base of the rider's boot in the normal riding position.

NOTE
The rear brake pedal height cannot be adjusted on the R850C and R1200C models.

To adjust the brake pedal height, perform the following:

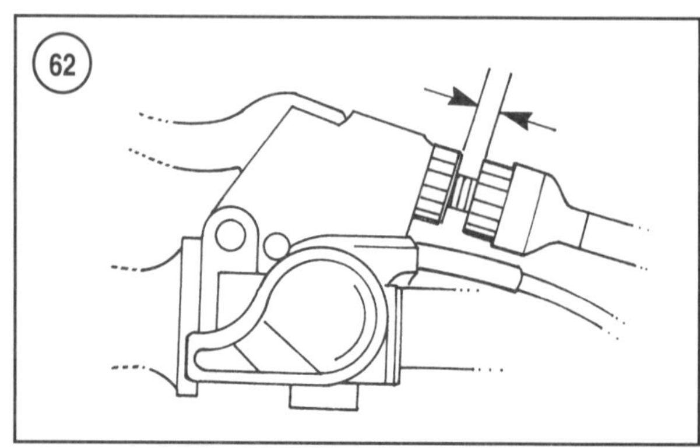

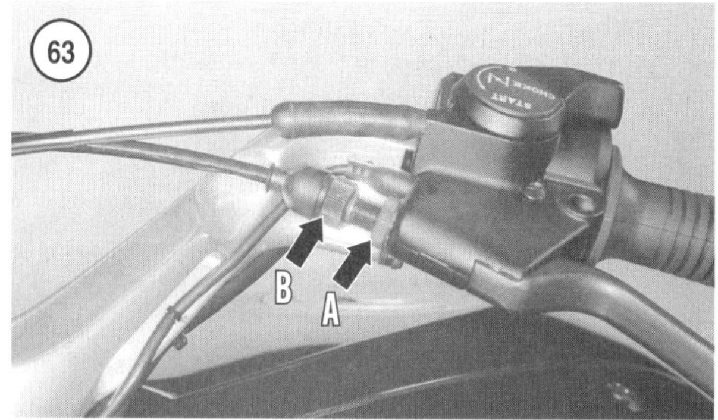

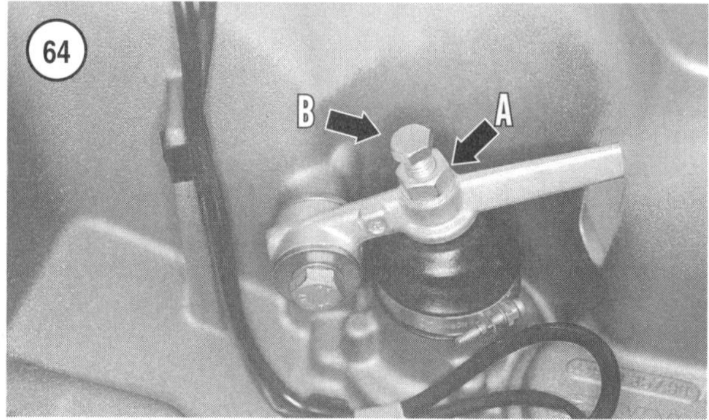

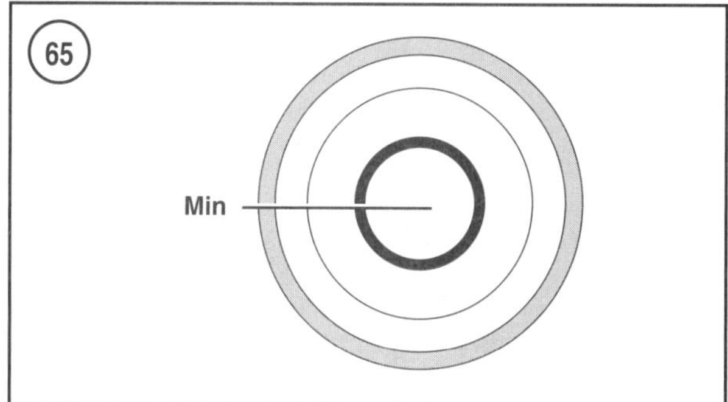

1. Loosen the locknut and turn the adjusting bolt (**Figure 60**) in either direction until the desired height is achieved.
2. Hold the adjusting bolt and tighten the locknut securely.

CLUTCH

Clutch Adjustment (Cable Operated Models)

Adjust the clutch at the interval indicated in **Table 1**.

1. Slowly pull the clutch lever until resistance is felt. The free play in the clutch cable (**Figure 61**) should be the amount listed in **Table 6**.
2. Measure the distance between the locknut and adjuster as shown in **Figure 62**. Refer to **Table 6** for the specification. When servicing, if either the free play or the distance between the locknut and adjuster are not as specified, perform Step 3-7.
3. At the clutch hand lever loosen the locknut (A, **Figure 63**) and turn the cable adjuster (B) in either direction until the distance between the locknut and adjuster (**Figure 63**) is correct.
4. Tighten the cable adjuster locknut (A, **Figure 63**) securely.

NOTE
Figure 64 *is shown with the transmission removed to better illustrate the step.*

5. Access the clutch release lever adjuster from the right side of the motorcycle and use a 13-mm wrench and loosen the locknut (A, **Figure 64**) on the release lever adjuster bolt. Use a 10-mm wrench and turn the adjuster bolt (B, **Figure 64**) until correct free play is achieved.
6. Tighten the locknut securely.
7. Road test the motorcycle and make sure the clutch fully disengages when the lever is pulled in; if the it does not, the motorcycle will creep in gear when stopped. If the clutch does not fully engage, it will slip, particularly when accelerating in high gear.
8. For a quick adjustment of free play between service intervals, perform Step 3 and disregard the distance between the locknut and adjuster. Always perform Steps 3-7 when servicing.
9. If the proper adjustment cannot be achieved, the cable is stretched and must be replaced. Refer to Chapter Six.

Clutch Master Cylinder Fluid Level (R850C, R1100S, All R1150 and R1200C Models)

The clutch hydraulic system requires DOT 4 brake fluid specified for disc brakes.

1A. On R850C, R1100S and R1200C models, perform the following:

a. Place the motorcycle on level ground on an auxiliary stand.
b. Move the handlebars to the full right side position.

1B. On all R1150 models, perform the following:

a. Place the motorcycle on level ground on the centerstand.
b. Move the handlebars to the straight ahead, or centered, position.

2. The fluid level must be half-way up the center marking ring (**Figure 65**) on the master cylinder reservoir (**Figure**

66). If the clutch fluid level is at or below the lower level mark, continue to Step 3.

NOTE
If the master cylinder is empty, air has probably entered the brake system. Bleed the clutch system as described in Chapter Six.

3. Clean any dirt from the area around the cover prior to removing the cover.

4. Remove the screws securing the cover (**Figure 67**). Remove the cover and the diaphragm.

5. Add fresh DOT 4 brake fluid to fill the reservoir until the level is at the half-way up the center marking ring on the clutch master cylinder reservoir.

6. Reinstall the diaphragm and cover. Tighten the screws securely.

7. If the clutch fluid level was low, check the clutch friction plate for excessive wear as described in Chapter Six.

NOTE
A low clutch fluid level usually indicates clutch friction plate wear. As the plate wear and become thinner, the clutch fluid level drops in the system. However, if the clutch fluid level is low and the clutch friction plate is not worn excessively, check the clutch release cylinder and all clutch hoses for leaks.

Clutch Hydraulic Hose (R850C, R1100S, All R1150 and R1200C Models)

Check the clutch hydraulic hose assembly between the master cylinder and the slave cylinder. If there is any leakage, tighten the connections and bleed the clutch system as described in Chapter Six. If this does not stop the leak or if a clutch hydraulic brake line is obviously damaged, cracked or chafed, replace the clutch hydraulic line and bleed the system as described in Chapter Six.

FUEL FILTER REPLACEMENT

A cartridge fuel filter is located in the fuel tank; refer to Chapter Nine. There is also a fuel strainer attached to the inlet end of the fuel pump. Remove and clean the fuel strainer if there is evidence of fuel blockage and whenever the cartridge fuel filter has been replaced. Replace the fuel filter at the intervals listed in **Table 1**.

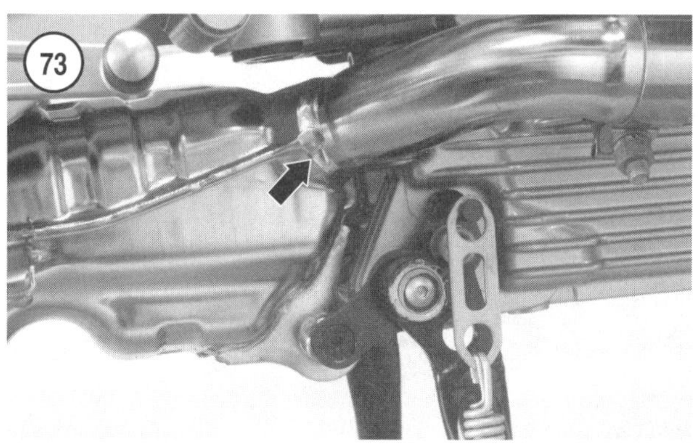

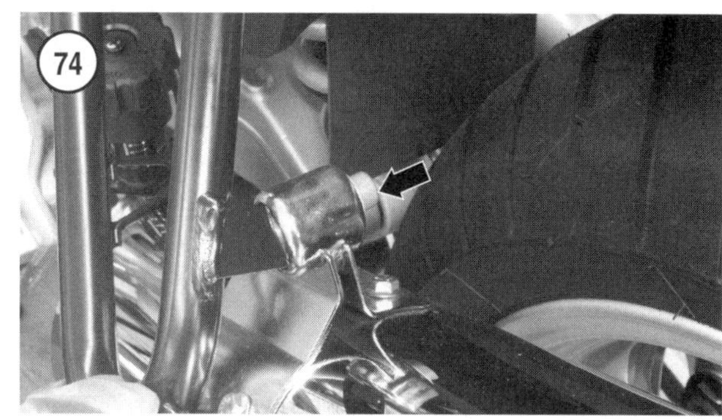

FUEL HOSE INSPECTION

Inspect the fuel feed and return hoses (**Figure 68**, typical) from the fuel tank to their respective components. If either is cracked or starting to deteriorate it must be replaced. Make sure the hose clamps are in place and holding securely.

WARNING
A damaged or deteriorated fuel line presents a very dangerous fire hazard to both the rider and the motorcycle.

CRANKCASE BREATHER INSPECTION

Inspect the breather hose (**Figure 69**) from the crankcase outlet to the air filter air box. If it is cracked or starting to deteriorate it must be replaced. Make sure the hose clamps are in place and holding securely.

EVAPORATIVE EMISSION CONTROL SYSTEM

On models with an evaporative emission control system, the fuel and fuel vapor in the fuel tank expand due to engine heat and ambient temperature. This fuel vapor is routed into a charcoal canister (**Figure 70**) and is stored until the engine is started.

When the engine is restarted, the vacuum in the air intake system pulls the fuel vapor from the canister and mixes it with the incoming fresh air, thus burning it in the engine.

There is no routine maintenance for the evaporation emission control system. Inspect the hoses whenever the fuel tank is removed as described in Chapter Nine.

EXHAUST SYSTEM

Check for leakage at the fittings (**Figure 71-75**, typical). Tighten all bolts and nuts. Replace any gaskets if necessary. Refer to *Exhaust System* in Chapter Nine.

75

76

HANDLEBARS

Inspect the individual handlebars for any evidence of damage. A bent or damaged handlebar(s) must be replaced. Check the tightness of the mounting bolts as follows:

1. On R850R, R1100R and all RT models, check the mounting bolts **Figure 76**. Tighten to 21 N•m (15 ft.-lb.).
2. On R1150R and all GS models, check the mounting bolts and clamps (**Figure 77**). Tighten to 21 N•m (15 ft.-lb.).
3. On RS models, remove the trim cap (**Figure 78**) and check the tightness of the mounting bolts and nuts. Tighten to 20 N•m (15 ft.-lb.). Check the tightness of the handlebar adjusting bolt (**Figure 79**) on each side. Tighten securely.
4. On R1100S models, make sure the locating bolt and both pinch bolts are tight (**Figure 80**). Tighten the locating bolt to 9 N•m (80 in.-lb.) and tighten the pinch bolts to 25 N•m (18 ft.-lb.).
5. On R850C and R1200C models, check the mounting bolts **Figure 81**. Tighten to 21 N•m (15 ft.-lb.).

77

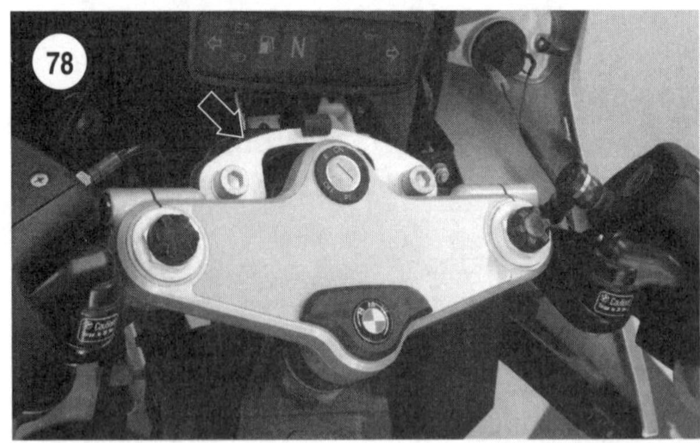
78

HANDLEBAR GRIPS

Inspect the handlebar grips (**Figure 82**) for tearing, looseness or excessive wear. Install new grips when required as described in Chapter Twelve.

FRONT SUSPENSION INSPECTION

1. Apply the front brake and pump the suspension up and down vigorously. Check for smooth operation and any oil leakage.

2A. On RS models, make sure the upper fork bridge bolt (**Figure 83**) is tight on each side.

2B. On R1100S models, make sure the handlebar clamping bolt (**Figure 84**) is tight on each side.

79

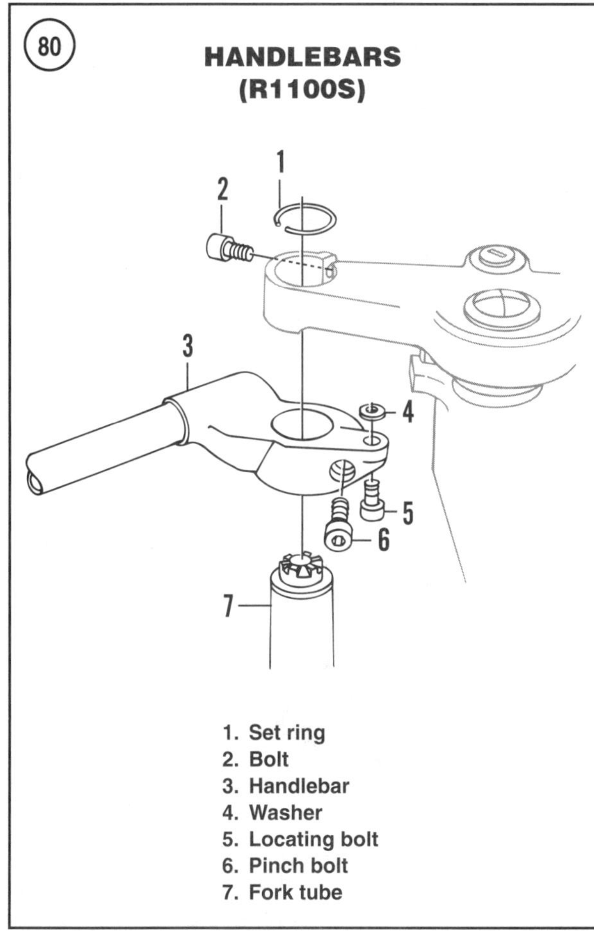

3A. On R1150R models, perform the following:

a. Remove the handlebar assembly (A, **Figure 85**).

b. Remove the trim cap (B, **Figure 85**) on the upper fork bridge.

3B. On R850C and R1200C models, remove the trim cap (**Figure 86**) on the upper fork bridge.

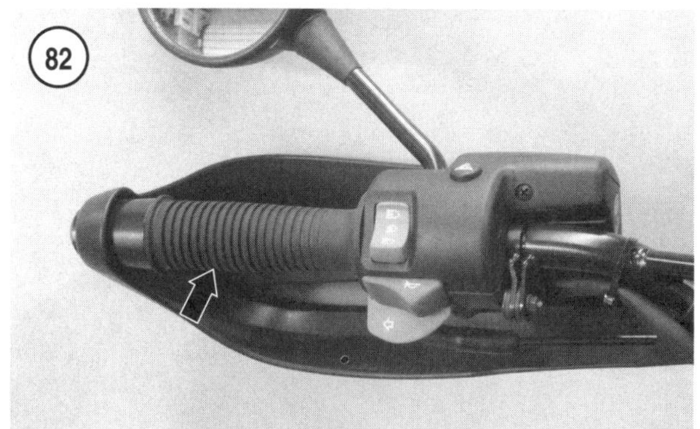

3C. On all models except R850C, R1100S and R1200C, remove the trim cap (**Figure 87**) on the upper fork bridge. Check the tightness of the threaded connector (**Figure 88**).

4A. On GS and S models, make sure the Allen bolts (**Figure 89**, typical) securing the lower fork bridge are tight.

4B. On R850C and R1200C models, make sure the Allen bolts securing the lower fork bridge (**Figure 90**) are tight.

4C. On all models except R850C, R1100S and R1200C, make sure all Allen bolts (**Figure 91**) securing the fork tubes to the lower bridge are tight.

5. Make sure the front axle clamp bolts (A, **Figure 92**) are tight.

6. On the left side, check the tightness of the front axle bolt (B, **Figure 92**).

7. Check the front strut mounting bolts and nuts for tightness. Refer to **Figure 93** for the upper nut and **Figure 94** for the lower bolt and nut.

8. Check the front suspension A-arm mounting nut and pivot shaft bolt for tightness. Refer to **Figure 95** for the front mounting nut and **Figure 96** for the pivot shaft bolt.

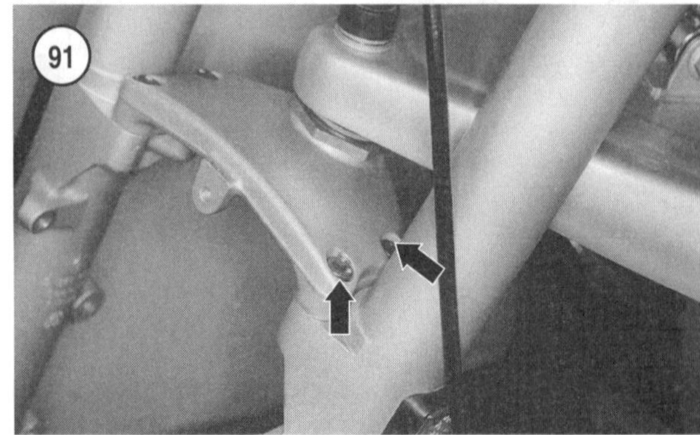

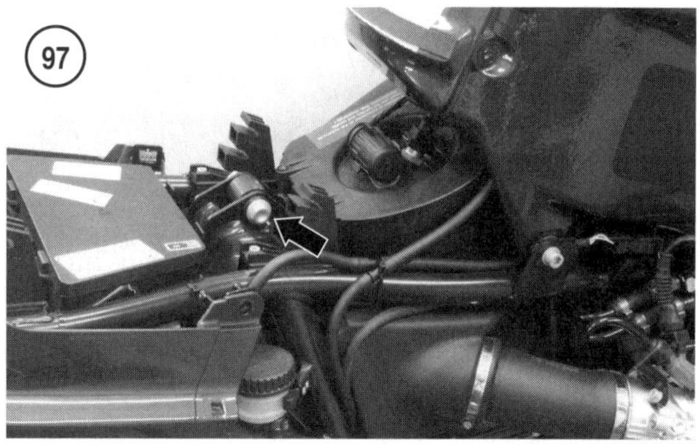

9. On R850R and R1100R models, check the steering damper mounting bracket bolts and the pivot bolts for tightness. Move the handlebar from side to side and check for smooth operation of the damper unit. Make sure there is no binding at any handlebar location.

WARNING

If any of the previously mentioned bolts and nuts are loose, refer to Chapter Ten for tightening procedures and torque specifications.

REAR SUSPENSION INSPECTION

1. Place a wooden block(s) under each side of the crankcase to support it securely with the rear wheel off the ground.
2. Push hard on the rear wheel (sideways) to check for side play in the rear swing arm bearings. Remove the wooden block(s).
3. Check the tightness of the shock absorber upper bolt (**Figure 97**).

4A. On R850C and R1200C models, check the tightness of the lower bolt (**Figure 98**) securing the shock absorber to the swing arm.

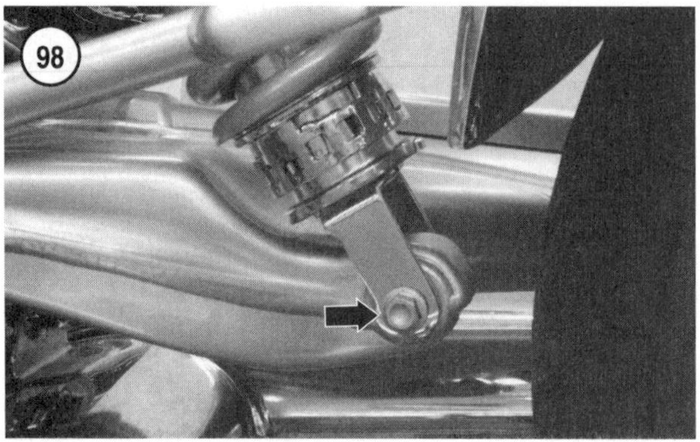

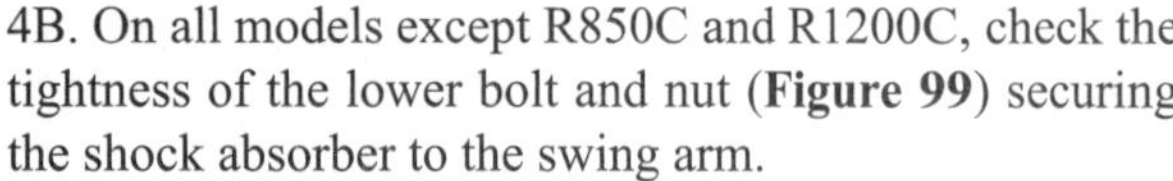

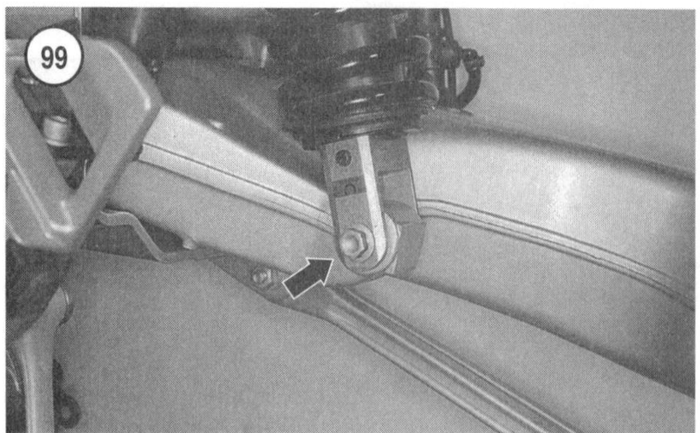

4B. On all models except R850C and R1200C, check the tightness of the lower bolt and nut (**Figure 99**) securing the shock absorber to the swing arm.

5A. On R850C, R1100S and R1200C models, make sure the swing arm pivot pins and locknut are tight as follows:

a. Refer to **Figure 100** for the right side pivot pin.

b. Refer to A, **Figure 101** for the left side locknut.

c. Refer to B, **Figure 101** for the adjustable pivot pin.

5B. On R1100S models, make sure the swing arm pivot pins and locknut are tight as follows:

a. Refer to **Figure 102** for the right side pivot pin.

b. Refer to A, **Figure 103** for the left side locknut.

c. Refer to B, **Figure 103** for the adjustable pivot pin.

5C. On all models except R850C, R1100S and R1200C, make sure the swing arm pivot pins and locknut are tight as follows:

a. Refer to **Figure 104** for the right pivot pin.

b. Refer to A, **Figure 105** for the left side locknut.

c. Refer to B, **Figure 105** for the adjustable pivot pin.

6. Make sure the rear wheel bolts are tight. Refer to **Figure 106** for wire wheel models or **Figure 107**, typical for cast wheel models.

WARNING

If any of the previously mentioned bolts and nuts are loose, refer to Chapter Thirteen for tightening procedures and torque specifications.

REAR FRAME INSPECTION

Inspect the rear frame sections for cracks or other damage. Check all welded sections attached to the main frame spar. Check the tightness of the rear frame mounting bolts and tighten securely if necessary. Refer to Chapter Fifteen for additional information.

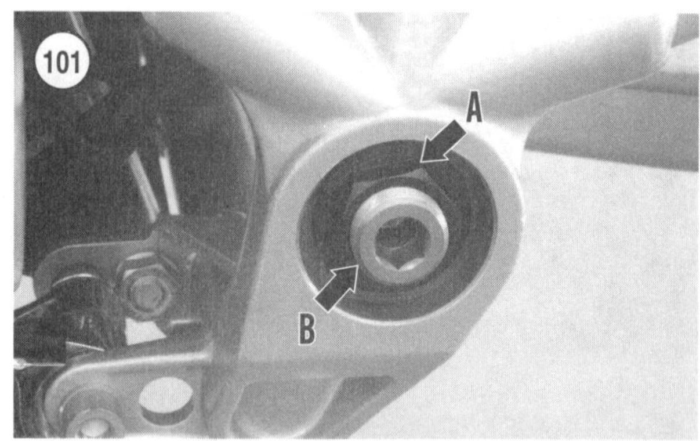

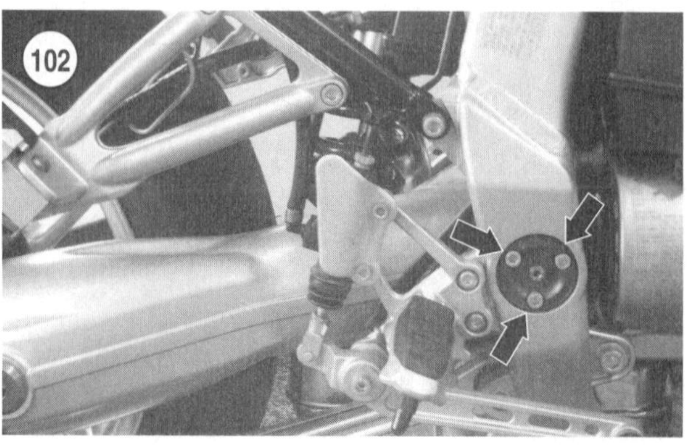

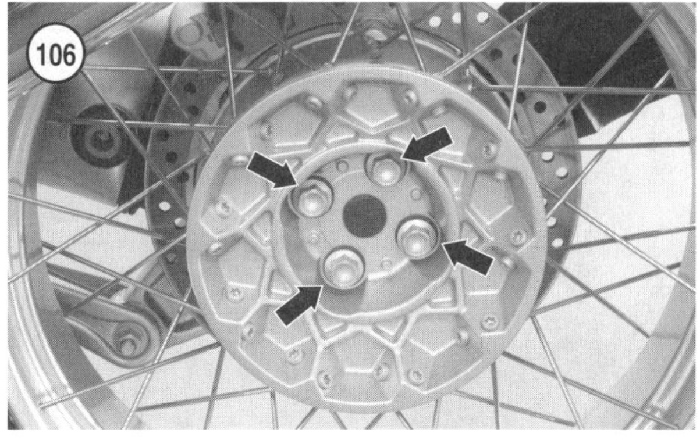

FASTENER INSPECTION

Constant vibration can loosen many of the fasteners on the motorcycle. Check the tightness of all fasteners, especially those on:

1. Engine mounting hardware.
2. Engine crankcase covers.
3. Handlebar and front suspension.
4. Gearshift lever.
5. Brake pedal and lever.
6. Swing arm and shock absorber.
7. Exhaust system.
8. Lighting equipment.
9. Body panels and luggage.

TUNE-UP PROCEDURES

Perform a complete tune-up by following the intervals listed in **Table 1** for the individual items. Refer to **Table 7** for tune-up specifications. More frequent service to some items may be required if thc motorcycle is ridden in stop and go traffic and other extreme conditions.

There is no provision for cam chain tensioner adjustment. The correct tension is maintained automatically on both camshaft chains.

Perform a tune-up in the following order:

1. Tighten cylinder head bolts.
2. Adjust valve clearance.
3. Check ignition timing.
4. Replace the air filter element.
5. Run a compression test.
6. Replace the spark plugs.
7. Set the idle speed and synchronize the fuel injector throttles.
8. Adjust the alternator drive belt.

CYLINDER HEAD FASTENERS

The cylinder head nuts and Torx bolt must be re-tightened after the first 600 miles (1000 km).

The cylinder head fastener tightening procedure must be performed with the engine cool (maximum cylinder head temperature is 35° C [95° F]).

Refer to Steps 9-12 of *Valve Clearance* in this section to tighten the cylidner head nuts and bolt.

VALVE CLEARANCE

The valve clearance procuedure must be performed with the engine cool (maximum cylinder head temperature 35° C [95° F]).

1A. On models so equipped, place the motorcycle on the centerstand with the front wheel off of the ground.

1B. On models without a centerstand, place a suitable size jack under the engine to support the motorcycle with the front wheel off the ground.

2. On RT and S models, remove the lower fairing panels as described in Chapter Fifteen.

3. On the right rear side of the crankcase, remove the rubber plug (**Figure 108**) covering the inspection hole for the timing mark (**Figure 109**).

4. On models so equipped, remove the mounting bolts and the engine guard (**Figure 110**) from each cylinder head.

NOTE
On dual-plug models, it is only necessary to remove the primary spark plug.

5. Remove the spark plug from each cylinder head as described in this chapter. This will make it easier to rotate the engine during this procedure.

6. Place a drain pan under the cylinder head as some oil may drain when the cylinder head cover is removed.

7. Using a crisscross pattern, loosen the bolts (**Figure 111**) securing the cylinder head cover. Remove the bolts, the cover and the rubber gasket.

NOTE
A cylinder at top dead center (TDC) on its compression stroke will have free play in both rocker arms, indicating that both sets of intake and exhaust valves are closed.

NOTE
There are two methods of rotating the engine to bring it to top dead center (TDC) on the compression stroke. Use the method that is the easiest to achieve. Either cylinder can be worked on first.

108

109

110

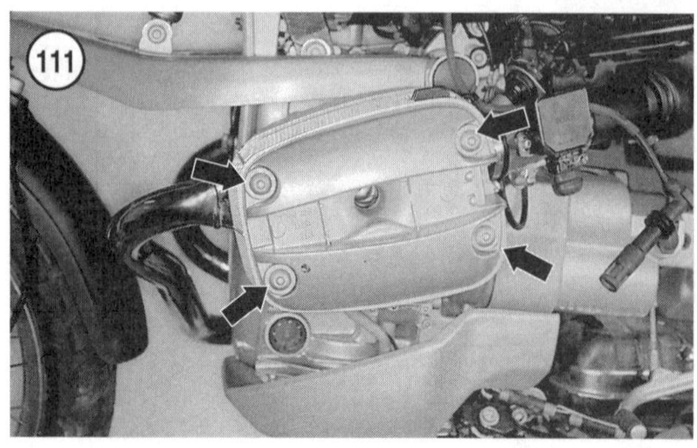
111

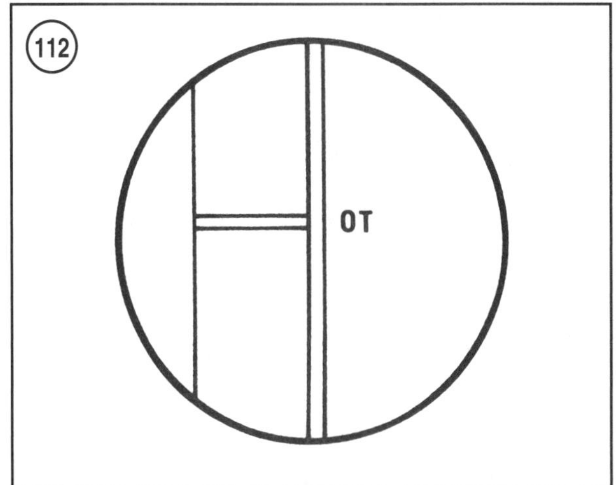

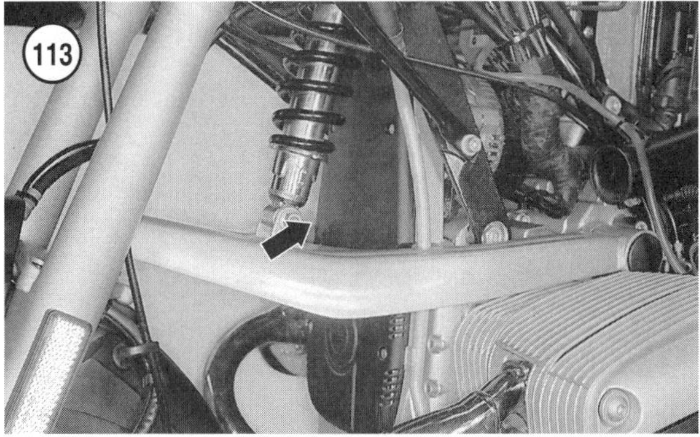

8A. Rotate the engine using the rear wheel until the left piston is at top dead center (TDC) on its compression stroke. To determine TDC for the left cylinder, perform the following:

a. Shift the transmission into fifth gear.
b. Rotate the rear wheel, in normal forward rotation, until the camshaft has completely opened the *intake* valves and then allowed them to close.

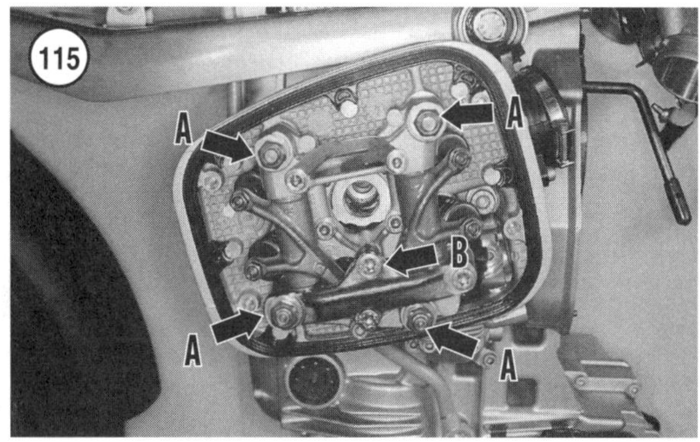

c. Using a small flashlight, direct the light into the spark plug hole to observe the piston as it moves up in the cylinder.
d. Continue to rotate the rear wheel until the left cylinder's piston reaches the top of its stroke. This is TDC on the compression stroke with the timing mark OT centered in the inspection hole in the crankcase (**Figure 112**). At this point all four valves will be closed and there will be a slight clearance between both rocker arms and all four valve stems.

8B. To rotate the engine without using the rear wheel, perform the following:

a. Remove the bolts securing the alternator cover (**Figure 113**) and remove the cover.
b. Install a wrench onto the crankshaft pulley bolt (**Figure 114**).
c. As viewed from the front of the engine, rotate the engine *clockwise* until the left piston is at top dead center (TDC) on its compression stroke.
d. Using a small flashlight, direct the light into the spark plug hole to observe the piston as it moves up in the cylinder.
e. Continue to rotate the crankshaft pulley until the left cylinder's piston reaches the top of its stroke. This is TDC on the compression stroke with the timing mark OT centered in the inspection hole in the crankcase (**Figure 112**). At this point all four valves will be closed and there will be clearance between both rocker arms and all four valve stems.

NOTE
Steps 9-12 are only required during the 600 miles (1000 km) service.

9. Loosen each cylinder head nut (A, **Figure 115**) 1/4 turn maximum—do *not* loosen the nuts any more than specified as it will place undue stress on the valve train.

10. Using a crisscross pattern, tighten the cylinder head mounting nuts (**Figure 116**) to the preliminary torque of 20 N•m (15 ft.-lb.).
11. Attach a degree wheel (**Figure 117**) to the wrench and tighten the nuts an additional 180°.
12. Loosen the 10–mm Torx bolt (B, **Figure 115**) 1/4 turn, then tighten the bolt to 40 N•m (29 ft.-lb.).

CAUTION

Each rocker arm operates two valves at the same time; therefore, the clearance measurement must be measured at the same time using two flat feeler gauges.

NOTE

*The correct valve clearance is listed in **Table 6**. The intake valves are located at the rear of the cylinder head and the exhaust valves are located at the front.*

13. With the left cylinder in this position, inspect and measure the valve clearance as follows:
    a. Check the clearance by inserting two flat metric feeler gauges between the rocker arm and the valve stems (**Figure 118**). If the clearance is correct, there will be a slight drag on the feeler gauges as they are inserted and withdrawn.
    b. Measure the valve clearance for the intake and exhaust valves on the left cylinder.
14. To adjust the clearances, perform the following:
    a. Leave the feeler gauge in place on both valves.
    b. Loosen the valve adjuster locknut (A, **Figure 119**) and turn the adjuster (B) in either direction until there is a slight drag on the feeler gauge.
    c. Hold the adjuster and tighten the locknut to 8 N•m (70 in.-lb.). Repeat if necessary for the other valve.
    d. Recheck the clearances to make sure the adjuster did not turn when the locknuts were tightened. Readjust if necessary.
15. Repeat Steps 7-14 for the right cylinder head.
16. Re-inspect all valve clearances as described in this procedure. Repeat this procedure until all clearances are correct.
17. Make sure the cylinder head cover gasket is in good condition and is in place.
18. If removed, install the spark plug opening gasket (**Figure 120**) on the cylinder head cover.
19. Make sure the rubber bumper (**Figure 121**) is in place.
20. Install the cylinder head cover and tighten the bolts (**Figure 111**) in a crisscross-cross pattern. Tighten the bolts securely.

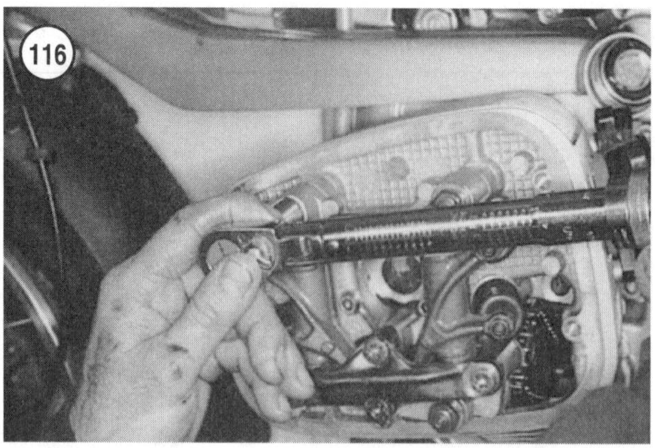

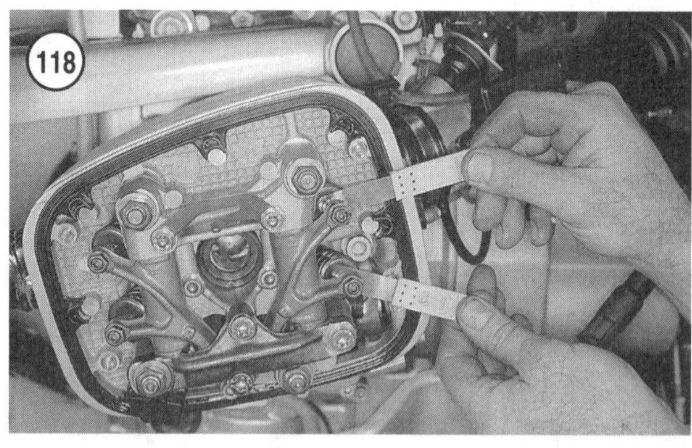

21. Install the spark plugs as described in this chapter.
22. On models so equipped, install the engine guard (**Figure 110**) onto each cylinder head and tighten the bolts securely.
23. On the right rear side of the crankcase, install the rubber plug (**Figure 108**) securely into the hole in the crankcase.
24. On RT and S models, install the lower fairing panels as described in Chapter Fifteen.

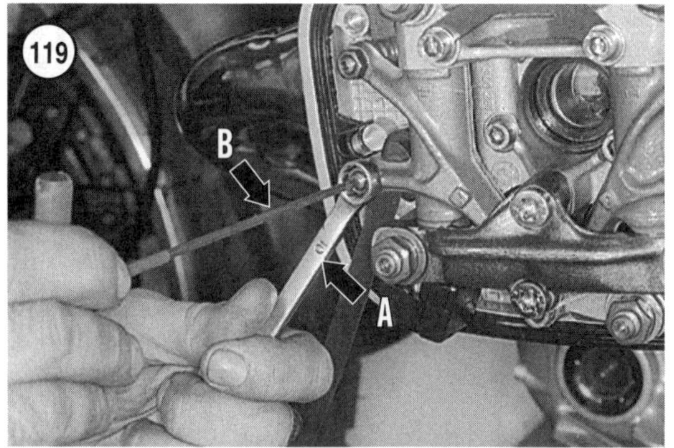

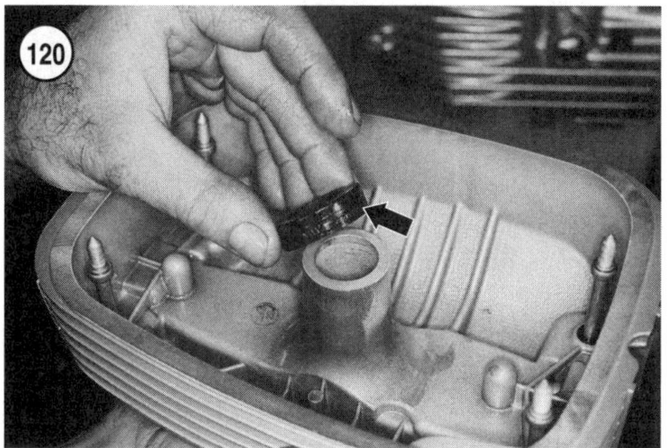

IGNITION TIMING

On early models, to check the ignition timing, it is necessary to remove the alternator drive belt and the lower sprocket. Refer to *Ignition System* in Chapter Ten.

On later models, the ignition timing must be checked by a BMW dealership using the MoDiTec diagnostic equipment.

ENGINE COMPRESSION TEST

3

A cranking compression test is a quick way to check the internal condition of the engine (piston rings, pistons, head gasket, valves and cylinders). It is a good idea to check compression at each tune-up, record it in the maintenance log at the end of this manual and compare it with subsequent readings.

Use the spark plug tool included in the motorcycle's tool kit and a screw-in compression gauge with a flexible adapter. Before using the gauge, check that the rubber gasket on the end of the adapter is not cracked or damaged; this gasket seals the cylinder to ensure accurate compression readings.

NOTE
Make sure the socket used to remove the spark plugs is equipped with a rubber insert that secures the spark plug. This type of socket is included in the standard tool kit and is necessary for both removal and installation, since the spark plugs are located in the cylinder head receptacles. It is not possible to remove or install the spark plugs by hand.

1. Make sure the battery is fully charged to ensure proper engine cranking speed.
2. Run the engine until it reaches normal operating temperature, then turn it off.

NOTE
On dual-plug models, it is only necessary to remove the primary spark plug.

3. Remove the spark plug from each cylinder head as described in this chapter. Reconnect each spark plug lead to each spark plug and ground it on the engine.

CAUTION
Each spark plug must be grounded to the cylinder head to prevent damage to the ignition system.

4. Remove the fuel tank as described in Chapter Nine.
5. Disconnect the primary connector from the ignition coil as described in Chapter Ten.
6. Disconnect the multi-pin electrical connector from the Motronic control unit as described in Chapter Ten.
7. Lubricate the threads of the compression gauge adapter with a small amount of antiseize compound and carefully thread the gauge into the left cylinder following the manufacturer's instructions.

CAUTION

Do not crank the engine more than is absolutely necessary. When the spark plug leads are disconnected, the electronic ignition will produce the highest voltage possible and the coil may overheat and be damage.

8. Open the throttle completely and using the starter, crank the engine over until there is no further rise in pressure. Maximum pressure is usually reached within 4-7 seconds of engine cranking. Record the reading with a left or right cylinder identification.

9. Repeat Steps 7 and 8 for the other cylinder.

10. When interpreting the results, note any difference between the cylinders. A compression range is specified in **Table 7**. Abnormally low compression indicates worn or broken rings, leaky or sticky valves, blown head gasket or a combination of all three.

If a low reading is obtained on a cylinder, pour about a teaspoon of engine oil into the spark plug hole. Turn the engine over once to distribute the oil, then take another compression test and record the reading. If the compression increases significantly, the valves are good but the rings are defective on that cylinder. If compression does not increase, the valves require servicing.

11. Connect the multi-pin electrical connector onto the Motronic control unit as described in Chapter Ten.

12. Connect the primary connector to the ignition coil as described in Chapter Ten.

13. Install the fuel tank as described in Chapter Nine.

14. Install the spark plugs as described in this chapter.

SPARK PLUGS (SINGLE PLUG IGNITION SYSTEM)

Spark Plug Removal

1. Two special tools are required to remove and install the spark plugs. These tools are included in the motorcycle's tool kit or from a BMW dealership as follows:

   a. Spark plug cap puller (BMW part No. 12-3-520).

   b. Spark plug wrench (BMW part No. 12-3-510).

2. Place the motorcycle on level ground on the sidestand.

3. Remove the spark plug cover as follows:

   a. Pull out on the front of the cover (A, **Figure 122**) and disengage it from the cylinder head cover.

   b. Pull the rear of the cover (B, **Figure 122**) out of the cylinder head cover receptacle and remove the cover.

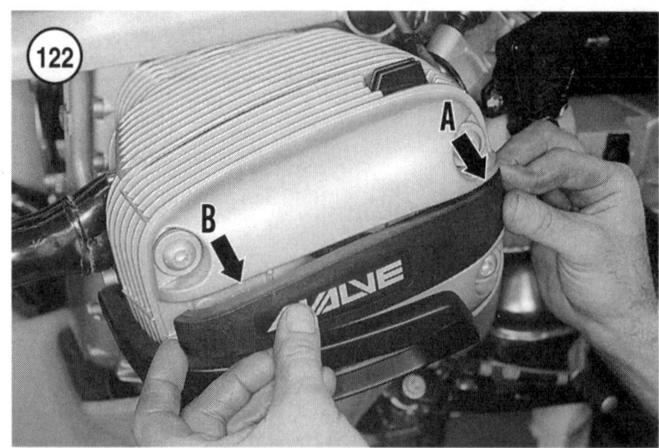

CAUTION

The spark plug cap puller must be used to disengage the spark plug wire/cap assembly from the spark plug. If the tool is not used, the spark plug wire/cap assembly will be damaged during removal.

4. Attach the spark plug puller (**Figure 123**) to the front of the spark plug/cap assembly and slide it on until it stops.

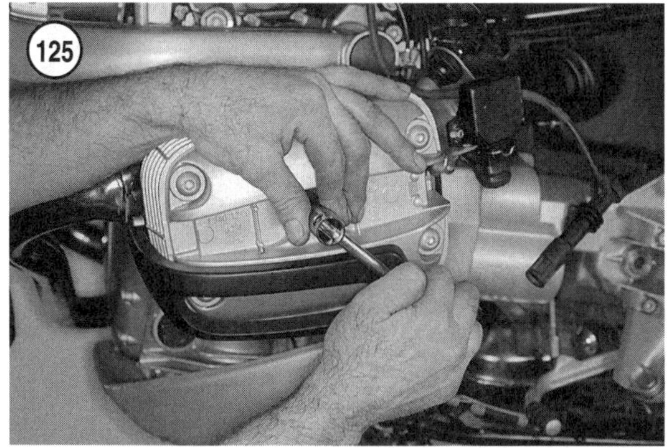

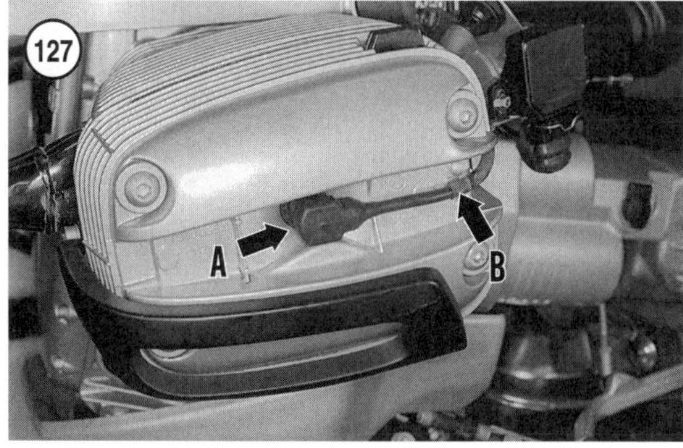

5. Insert an index finger through the ring and slowly pull straight out on the puller (**Figure 124**). Completely disengage the cap from the spark plug. Remove the puller from the spark plug cap.

CAUTION

Whenever the spark plugs are removed, dirt around them can fall into the spark plug hole. This can cause serious engine damage.

6. Use compressed air and blow away any debris from the cylinder head and the cavity around the spark plug well.

7. Remove the spark plug with the BMW spark plug wrench, or equivalent (**Figure 125**). Mark the spark plug as to which cylinder it was removed from (left cylinder and right cylinder).

NOTE

If the plug is difficult to remove, spray some penetrating oil around the base of the plug and let it soak for about 10-20 minutes.

8. Repeat Steps 3-7 for the other spark plug.

9. Inspect the spark plugs carefully. Look for broken center porcelain, excessively eroded electrodes and excessive carbon or oil fouling. If deposits are light, the plugs may be reused.

Spark Plug Installation

1. Apply a *small* amount of aluminum antiseize compound on the threads of the spark plug before installing it. Remove any compound that contacts the plug's firing tips. Do not use engine oil on the threads.

CAUTION

The cylinder head is aluminum. If the spark plug is cross-threaded into the cylinder head, the internal threads will be damaged.

2. Insert the spark plug (**Figure 126**) into the spark plug wrench and make sure it is properly seated and square in the wrench.

3. Insert the spark plug and wrench into the receptacle in the cylinder head and cover.

4. Carefully screw the spark plug in by hand until it seats. Very little effort is required. If force is necessary, the plug may be cross-threaded; unscrew it and try again.

5A. If installing new spark plugs, tighten the spark plug an additional 1/2 turn after the gasket makes contact with the cylinder head.

5B. If reinstalling used spark plugs and are reusing the old gaskets, only tighten an additional 1/4 turn after the gasket makes contact with the cylinder head.

CAUTION

Do not overtighten the spark plug. This will only crush the gasket and destroy its sealing ability. It may also damage the spark plug threads in the cylinder head.

6. Install the spark plug wire onto the spark plug and push it until it stops (A, **Figure 127**).

3

7. Route the spark plug wire in the cylinder head cavity (B, **Figure 127**) as noted during removal.
8. Install the spark plug cover as follows:
   a. Insert the locating tab (**Figure 128**) into the rear of the cylinder head cover receptacle.
   b. Push the rear portion into place (A, **Figure 122**), hold it there, and push the front portion into place (B). Make sure both ends are properly installed to avoid losing the cover when riding.

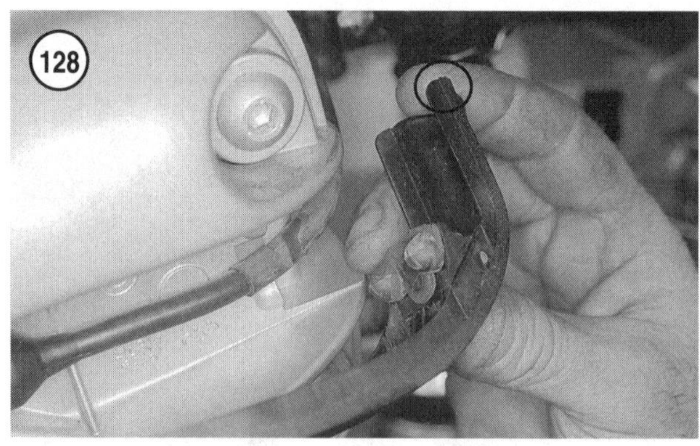

SPARK PLUGS (DUAL-PLUG IGNITION SYSTEM)

Primary Spark Plug Removal

1. Two special tools are required to remove and install the spark plugs. These special tools are included in the motorcycle's tool kit or from a BMW dealership as follows:
   a. Spark plug cap puller (BMW part No. 12-3-520).
   b. Spark plug wrench (BMW part No. 12-3-510).

2A. On models so equipped, place the motorcycle on the centerstand with the front wheel off of the ground.

2B. On models without a centerstand, place a suitable size jack under the engine to support the motorcycle with the front wheel off the ground.

3. Remove the spark plug cover as follows:
   a. Pull out on the rear of the cover (A, **Figure 129**) and disengage it from the cylinder head cover.
   b. Pull the front of the cover (B, **Figure 129**) out of the cylinder head cover receptacle and remove the cover.
4. Attach the spark plug puller to the front of the direct ignition coil assembly (**Figure 130**) and slide it on until it stops.
5. Insert an index finger through the ring and slowly pull straight out on the puller. Completely disengage the direct ignition coil from the spark plug, then remove the puller.
6. Disconnect the electrical connector from the direct ignition coil.

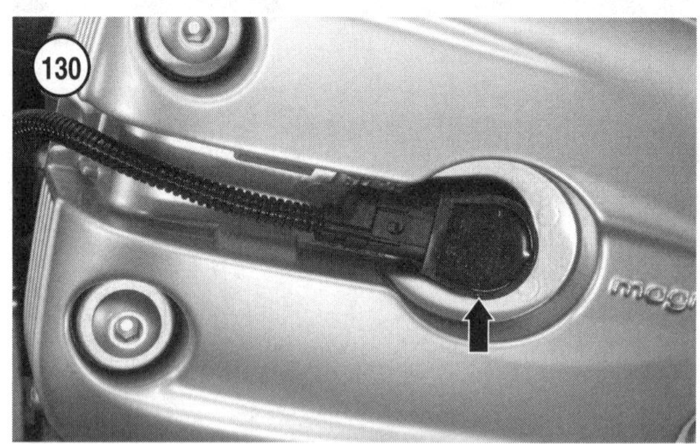

CAUTION
Whenever the spark plugs are removed, dirt around them can fall into the spark plug hole. This can cause serious engine damage.

7. Use compressed air and blow away any debris from the cylinder head and the cavity around the spark plug well.
8. Remove the spark plug with the BMW spark plug wrench, or equivalent. Mark the primary spark plug as to which cylinder it was removed from (left or right).

NOTE
If the plug is difficult to remove, spray some penetrating oil around the base of the plug and let it soak for about 10-20 minutes.

9. Repeat Steps 3-8 for the other spark plug.
10. Inspect the spark plug carefully. Look for broken center porcelain, excessively eroded electrodes and excessive carbon or oil fouling. If deposits are light, the plug may be reused.

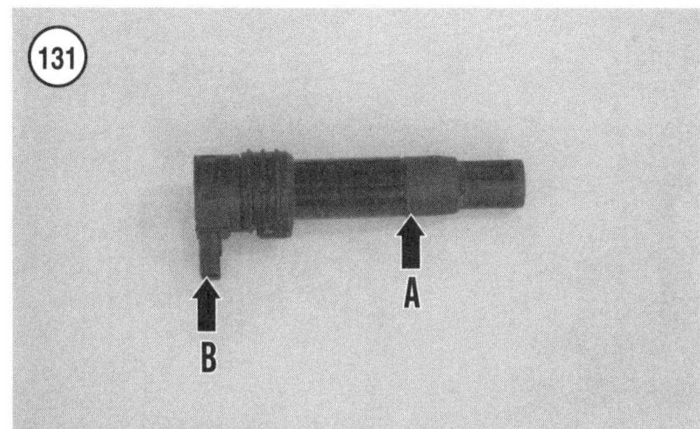

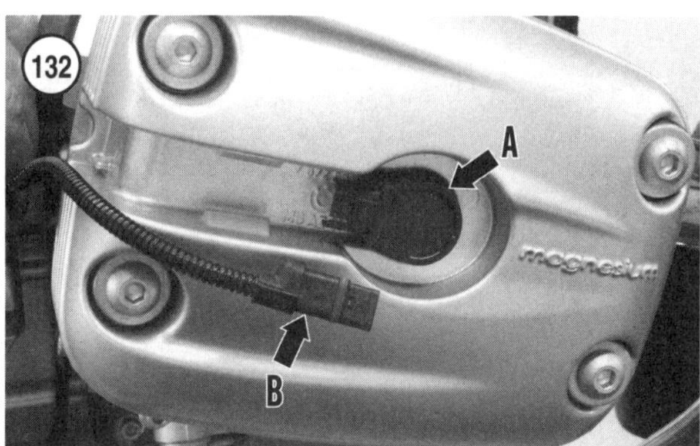

11. Also inspect the direct ignition coil (A, **Figure 131**) for external wear or damage. Inspect the 2-pin electrical connector (B, **Figure 131**) for corrosion or damage.

Primary Spark Plug Installation

1. Apply a *small* amount of aluminum antiseize compound on the threads of the spark plug before installing it. Remove any compound that contacts the plug's firing tips. Do not use engine oil on the threads.

CAUTION

The cylinder head is aluminum. If the spark plug is cross-threaded into the cylinder head, the internal threads will be damaged.

2. Insert the spark plug into the spark plug wrench and make sure it is properly seated and square in the wrench.
3. Insert the spark plug and wrench into the receptacle in the cylinder head and cover.
4. Slowly and carefully screw the spark plug in by hand until it seats. Very little effort is required. If force is necessary, the plug may be cross-threaded; unscrew it and try again.

5A. If installing new spark plugs, tighten the spark plug an additional 1/2 turn after the gasket makes contact with the cylinder head.

5B. If reinstalling used spark plugs and are reusing the old gaskets, only tighten an additional 1/4 turn after the gasket makes contact with the cylinder head.

CAUTION

Do not overtighten the spark plug. This will only crush the gasket and destroy its sealing ability. It may also damage the spark plug threads in the cylinder head.

6. Install the direct ignition coil onto the spark plug and push it straight on until it stops (A, **Figure 132**).
7. Connect the electrical connector (B, **Figure 132**) onto the direct ignition coil. Push it on until it locks into place (**Figure 130**).
8. Route the spark plug wire in the cylinder head cavity and into the groove in the cylinder head cover.
9. Install the spark plug cover as follows:
   a. Insert the front locating tab into the front of the cylinder head cover receptacle (B, **Figure 129**).
   b. Push the rear portion into place (A, **Figure 129**), hold it there, and push the front portion into place (B). Make sure both ends are properly installed to avoid losing the cover when riding.

Secondary Spark Plug Removal

1. Place the motorcycle on level ground on the sidestand.
2. On models so equipped, remove the screw securing the cylinder head guard (**Figure 133**) and remove the guard.
3. On the underside of the cylinder head, remove the two screws securing the spark plug cover and remove the cover.

4. Slowly pull straight out and completely disengage the cap from the spark plug (**Figure 134**).

CAUTION
Whenever the spark plugs are removed, dirt around them can enter into the spark plug hole. This can cause serious engine damage.

5. Use compressed air and blow away any debris from the cylinder head and the cavity around the spark plug well.
6. Remove the spark plug (**Figure 135**) with the BMW spark plug wrench, or equivalent. Mark the secondary spark plug as to which cylinder it was removed from (left or right).

NOTE
If the plug is difficult to remove, spray some penetrating oil around the base of the plug and let it soak for about 10-20 minutes.

7. Repeat Steps 2-6 for the other spark plug.
8. Inspect the spark plug carefully. Look for broken center porcelain, excessively eroded electrodes and excessive carbon or oil fouling. If deposits are light, the plug may be reused.

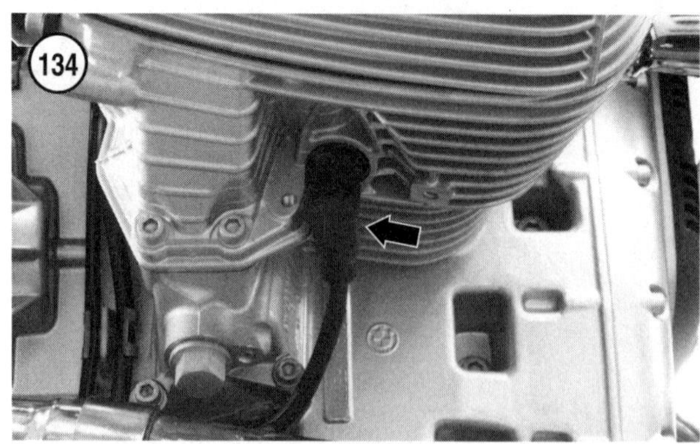

Secondary Spark Plug Installation

1. Apply a *small* amount of aluminum antiseize compound on the threads of the spark plug before installing it. Remove any compound that contacts the plug's firing tips. Do not use engine oil on the threads.

CAUTION
The cylinder head is aluminum. If the spark plug is cross-threaded into the cylinder head, the internal threads will be damaged.

2. Insert the spark plug into the spark plug wrench and make sure it is properly seated and square in the wrench.
3. Insert the spark plug and wrench into the receptacle in the cylinder head and cover.
4. Slowly and carefully screw the spark plug (**Figure 135**) in by hand until it seats. Very little effort is required. If force is necessary, the plug may be cross-threaded; unscrew it and try again.
5A. If installing new spark plugs, tighten the spark plug an additional 1/2 turn after the gasket makes contact with the cylinder head.
5B. If reinstalling used spark plugs and are reusing the old gaskets, only tighten an additional 1/4 turn after the gasket makes contact with the cylinder head.

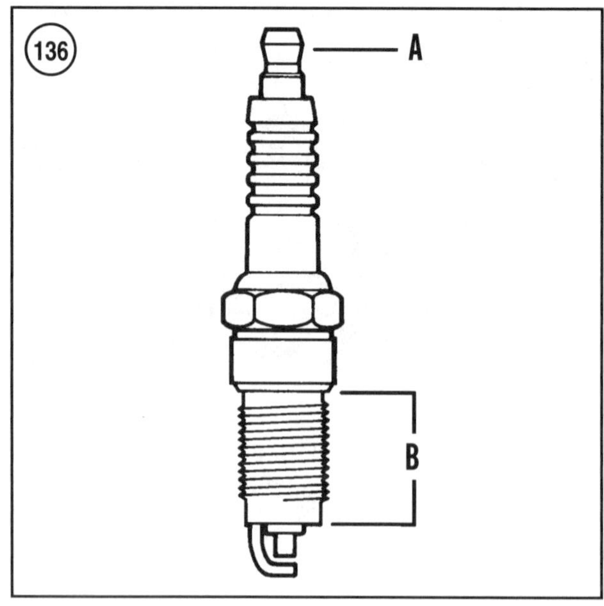

CAUTION
Do not overtighten the spark plug. This will only crush the gasket and destroy its sealing ability. It may also damage the spark plug threads in the cylinder head.

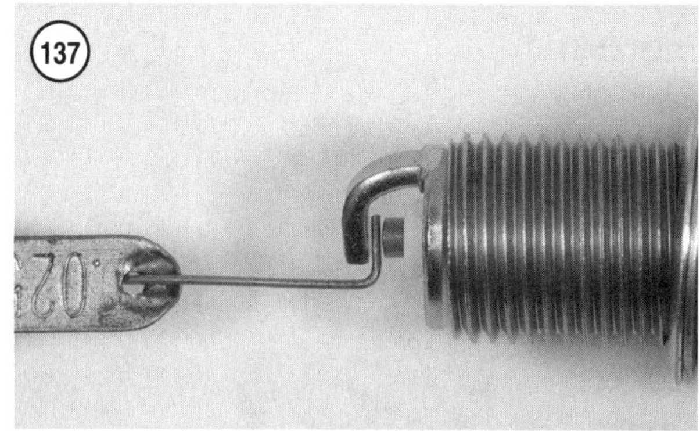

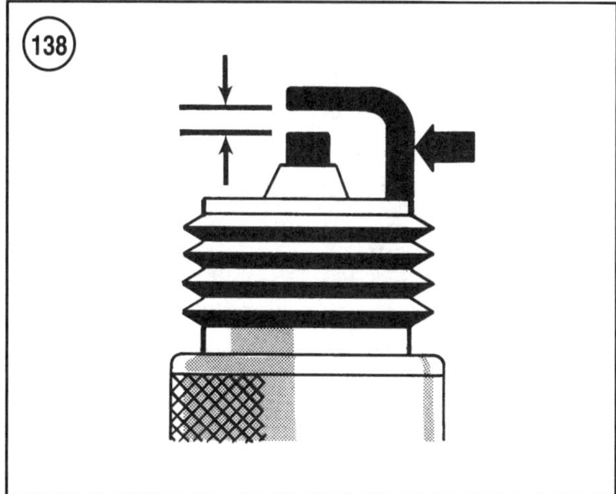

6. Install the spark plug wire onto the spark plug and push it straight on until it stops (**Figure 134**).

7. Install the spark plug cover and two screws. Tighten the screws securely.

8. On models so equipped, install the cylinder head guard (**Figure 133**) and tighten the screws securely.

SPARK PLUG INSPECTION

Spark Plug Gap

Carefully adjust the electrode gap on new spark plugs to ensure a reliable, consistent spark. To do this, use a spark plug gap gapping tool with a wire gauge.

1. Remove the new spark plugs from the box. If removed, install the terminal nut onto the spark plug (A, **Figure 136**).

CAUTION
BMW does not recommend re-gapping a used spark plug. The side electrode (ground) may be weakened and break off after the spark plug has been in use. Only set the gap on new spark plugs.

2. Insert a round feeler gauge between the center and each side electrode of the plug and the gap (**Figure 137**, typical). The correct gap (**Figure 138**) is listed in **Table 6**. If the gap is correct, a slight drag will be felt as the gauge is pulled through. If there is no drag or the gauge will not pass through, bend the side electrode with the gapping tool (**Figure 139**) to set the gap.
3. Repeat for the other spark plug(s).

NOTE
A round feeler gauge must be used since the ground electrodes are notched to fit close to the center electrode. A flat feeler gauge will give a false reading.

Spark Plug Reading

Reading the spark plugs can provide a significant amount of information regarding engine performance. Reading plugs that have been in use will give an indication of spark plug operation, air/fuel mixture composition and engine condition (oil consumption, pistons, etc.). Before checking new spark plugs, operate the motorcycle under a medium load for approximately 6 miles (10 km). Avoid prolonged idling before shutting off the engine. Remove the spark plugs as described in this chapter. Examine each plug and compare it to those in **Figure 140**.

Spark Plug Heat Range

Spark plugs are available in various heat ranges, hotter or colder than the plugs originally installed by the manufacturer.

Select a plug with a heat range designed for the loads and conditions under which the motorcycle will be oper-

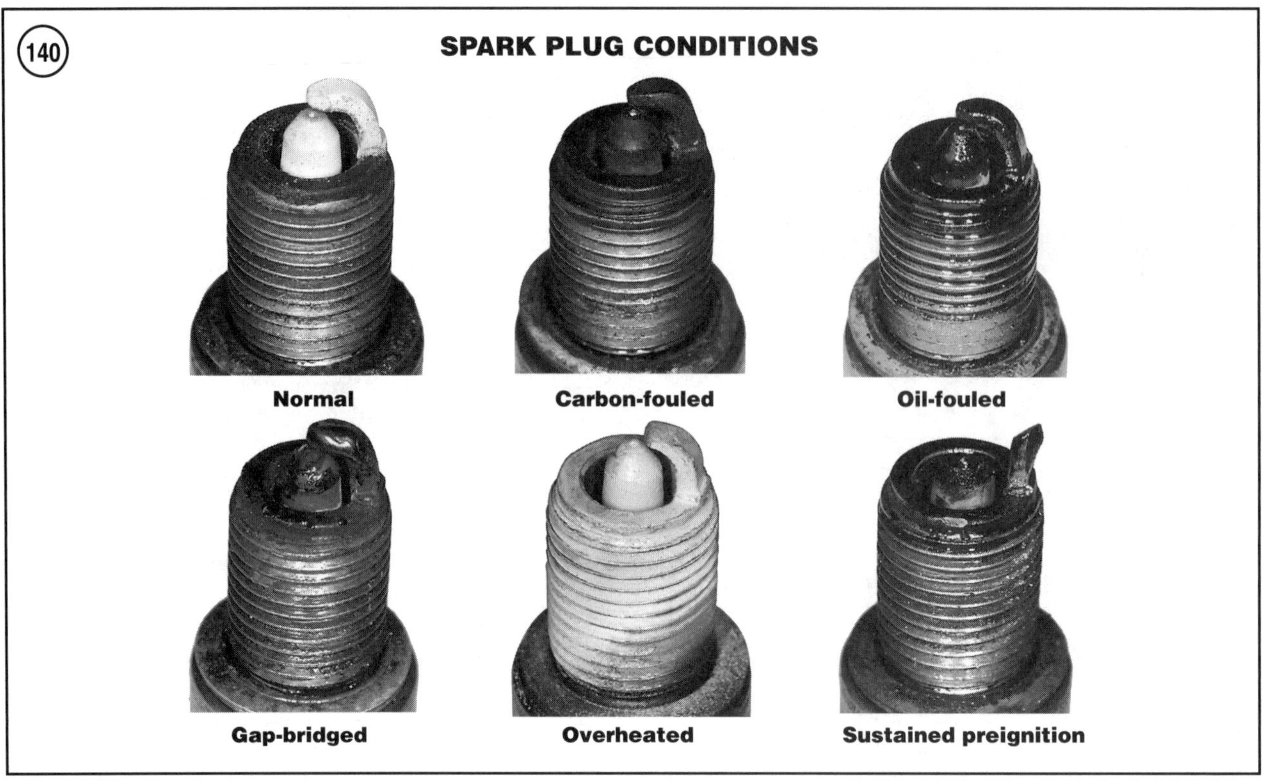

ated. A plug with an incorrect heat range can foul, overheat and cause piston damage.

In general, use a hot plug for low speeds and low temperatures. Use a cold plug for high speeds, high engine loads and high temperatures. The plug should operate hot enough to burn off unwanted deposits, but not so hot that it is damaged or causes preignition. To determine if the plug heat range is correct, remove each spark plug and examine the insulator.

Do not change the spark plug heat range to compensate for adverse engine or air/fuel mixture conditions. Compare the insulator to those in **Figure 140** when reading plugs.

When replacing plugs, make sure the reach (B, **Figure 136**) is correct. A longer than standard plug could interfere with the piston, causing engine damage.

Refer to **Table 6** for recommended spark plugs.

Normal condition

If the plug has a light tan- or gray-colored deposits and no abnormal gap wear or erosion, good engine, fuel system and ignition condition are indicated. The plug in use is of the proper heat range and may be returned to use.

Carbon fouled

Soft, dry, sooty deposits covering the entire firing end of the plug are evidence of incomplete combustion. Even though the firing end of the plug is dry, the plug's insulation decreases when in this condition. The carbon forms an electrical path that bypasses the spark plug electrodes resulting in a misfire condition. One or more of the following can cause carbon fouling:

1. Rich fuel mixture.
2. Cold spark plug heat range.
3. Clogged air filter.
4. Improperly operating ignition component.
5. Ignition component failure.
6. Low engine compression.
7. Prolonged idling.

Oil fouled

The tip of an oil fouled plug has a black insulator tip, a damp oily film over the firing end and a carbon layer over the entire nose. The electrodes are not worn. Oil fouled spark plugs may be cleaned in an emergency, but it is better to replace them. It is important to correct the cause of the fouling before the engine is returned to service. Common causes for this condition are:

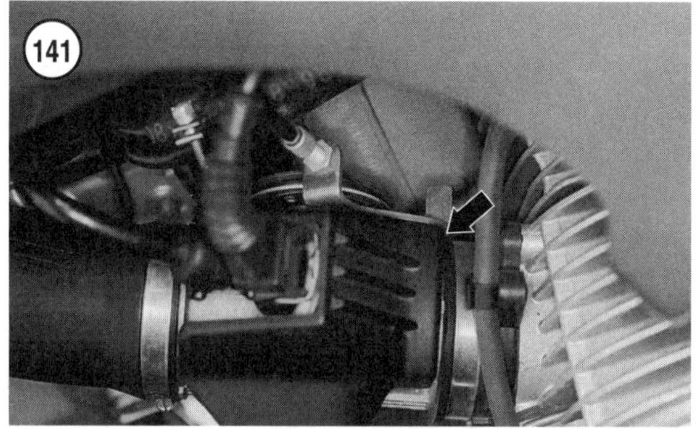
141

1. Incorrect air/fuel mixture.
2. Low idle speed or prolonged idling.
3. Ignition component failure.
4. Cold spark plug heat range.
5. Engine still being broken in.
6. Valve guides worn.
7. Piston rings worn or broken.

Gap bridging

Plugs with this condition exhibit gaps shorted out by combustion deposits between the electrodes. If this condition is encountered, check for excessive carbon or oil in the combustion chamber. Be sure to locate and correct the cause of this condition.

Overheating

Badly worn electrodes and premature gap wear are signs of overheating, along with a gray or white blistered porcelain insulator surface. The most common cause for this condition is using a spark plug of the wrong heat range (too hot). If the spark plug is in the correct heat range and is overheating, consider the following causes:
1. Lean air/fuel mixture.
2. Improperly operating ignition component.
3. Engine lubrication system malfunction.
4. Engine air leak.
5. Wrong spark plug heat range (too hot).
6. Improper spark plug installation.
7. No spark plug gasket.

Worn out

Corrosive gasses formed by combustion and high voltage sparks have eroded the electrodes. A spark plug in this condition requires more voltage to fire under hard acceleration. Replace with a new spark plug.

Preignition

If the electrodes are melted, preignition is almost certainly the cause. Check for intake air leaks at the manifolds and throttle bodies, and advanced ignition timing. It is also possible that a plug of the wrong heat range (too hot) is being used. Find the cause of the preignition before returning the engine into service.

THROTTLE AND CHOKE CABLE ADJUSTMENT (ALL MODELS EXCEPT R850C AND 1200C MODELS)

On the 1993-1995 models there is only one throttle cable. This single cable runs from the throttle grip to the left throttle wheel and then across the engine to the right throttle wheel. This single cable controls both throttle bodies. The system used on 1996-on models uses three short throttle cables and a junction box on the right side of the motorcycle. The first cable runs from the throttle grip to the distribution disc in the junction box. From the junction box, two separate throttle cables leave the distribution disc and connect to each throttle body. Be sure to follow the correct procedure for the specific year motorcycle being worked on.

1993-1995 Models

1. Start the engine and let it reach normal operating temperature. Stop and go riding of 10-15 minutes is sufficient. Shut off the engine.
2. Place the motorcycle on the sidestand.
3. Shift the transmission into neutral.
4. On RS and RT models, remove the front fairing side panels as described in Chapter Fifteen.
5. On models so equipped, remove the throttle body cover (**Figure 141**).

NOTE
Step 6 is very important since the throttle wheel on the throttle body is subjected to road debris. Any debris trapped between the throttle wheel and the cable may fall out after this adjustment procedure is complete. If this happens, the slack in the throttle cable will increase and adversely affect the synchronization.

6. Thoroughly check and remove any debris trapped between the throttle cables and the throttle wheels on both throttle bodies. Open and close the throttle several times and check for debris on the throttle wheel and/or cable. Apply compressed air to ensure a thorough cleaning.

7. To adjust the cold-start (choke) cable free play, perform the following:
   a. At the handlebar, move the choke lever from the full on (cold start) position (**Figure 142**) and then back to the full off position (A, **Figure 143**). Perform this several times and leave the choke lever in the full OFF position.
   b. At the left throttle body, use needlenose pliers and gently pull up on the choke cable sheath at the throttle wheel. There must be at least 1 mm (0.04 in.) of free play (**Figure 144**). If necessary, loosen the locknut and turn the adjusting nut to correct the free play. Tighten the locknut.
8. To adjust the throttle cable free play, perform the following:
   a. Turn the front wheel and handlebar to the full right position.
   b. Use needlenose pliers and gently pull up on the throttle grip cable sheath at the throttle wheel. There must be at least 0.5 mm (0.02 in.) of free play (A, **Figure 145**). If necessary, loosen the locknut and turn the adjuster to correct the free play.
   c. Use needlenose pliers and gently pull up on the throttle cross-over cable sheath at the throttle wheel. There must be at least 0.5 mm (0.02 in.) of free play (B, **Figure 145**). If necessary, loosen the locknut and turn the adjuster to correct the free play. Tighten the locknut.
9. Synchronize the throttle bodies and adjust the idle speed as described in the this chapter.

1996-on Models

1. Start the engine and let it reach normal operating temperature. Stop and go riding of 10-15 minutes is sufficient. Shut off the engine.
2. Place the motorcycle on the sidestand.
3. Shift the transmission into neutral.
4. On RS, RT and S models, remove the front fairing side panels as described in Chapter Fifteen.
5. On models so equipped, remove the throttle body cover (**Figure 141**).

NOTE

Step 6 is very important since the throttle wheel on the throttle body is subjected to road debris. Any debris trapped between the throttle wheel and the cable may fall out after this adjustment procedure is complete. If this happens, the slack in the throttle cable will increase and adversely affect the synchronization.

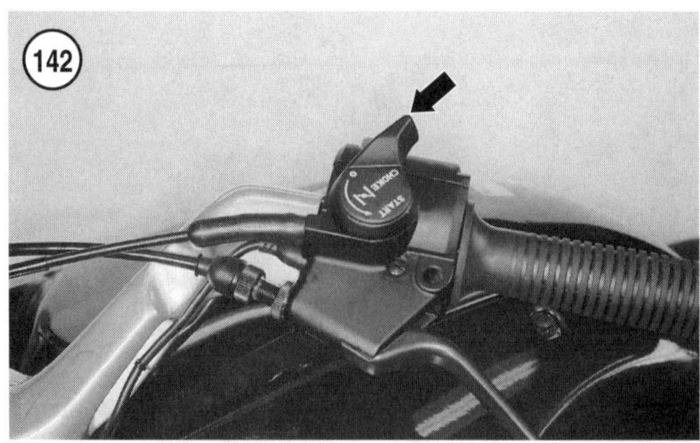

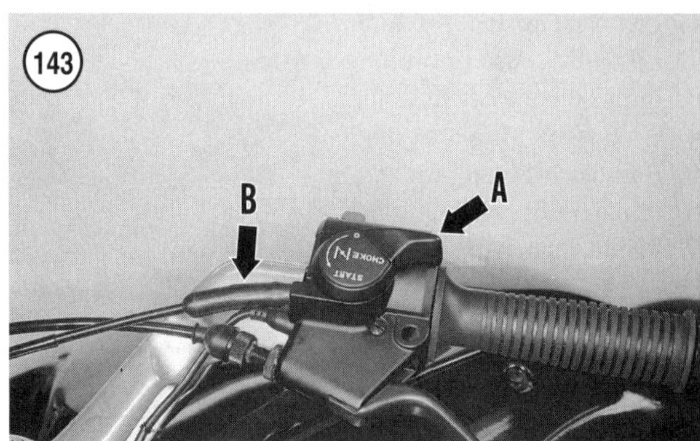

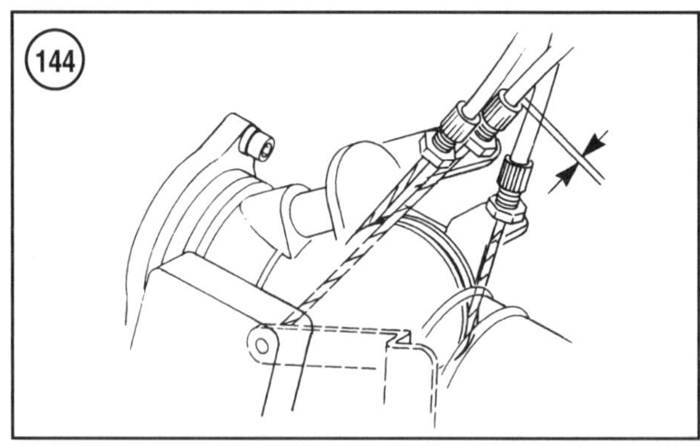

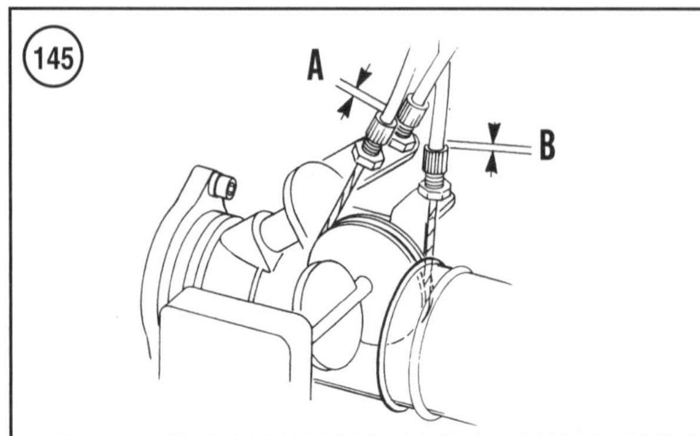

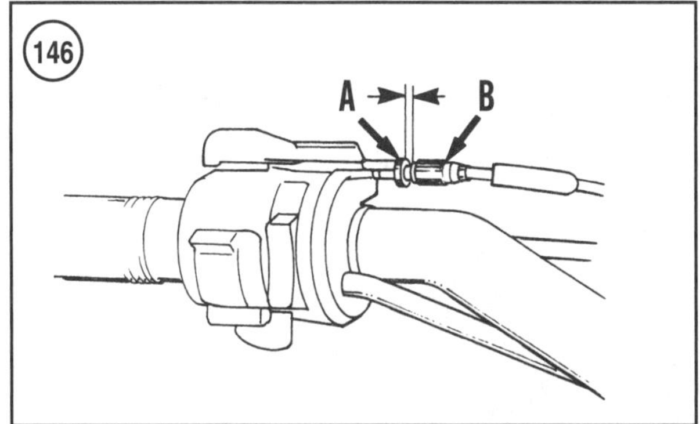

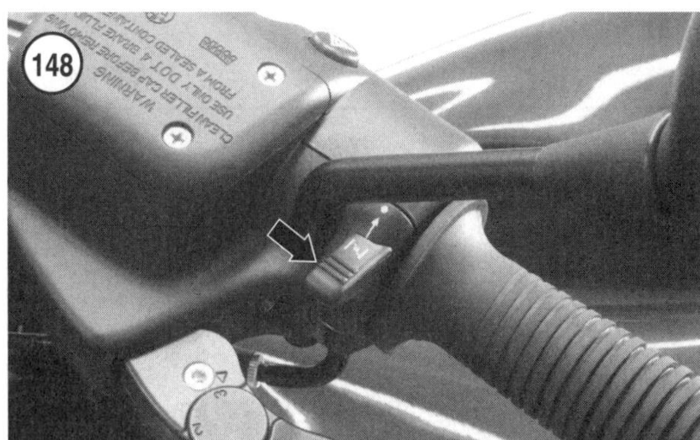

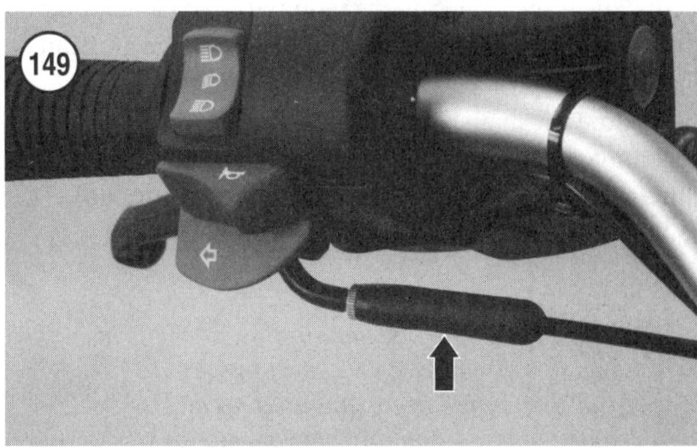

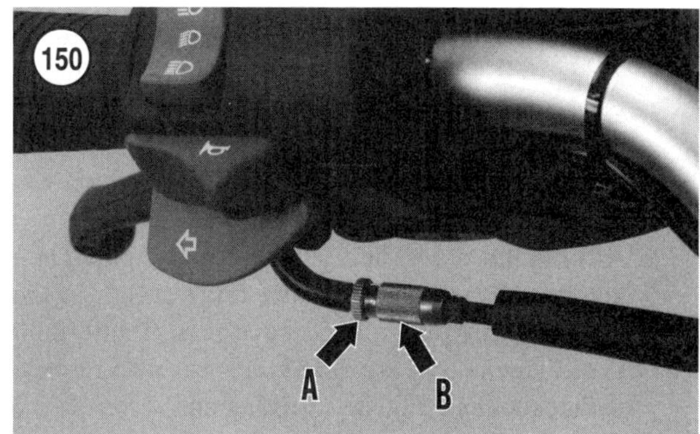

6. Thoroughly check and remove debris that may be trapped between the throttle cables and the throttle wheels on both throttle bodies. Open and close the throttle several times and check for debris on the throttle wheel and/or cable. Apply compressed air to ensure a thorough cleaning.

7A. On early models, to adjust the cold-start (choke) cable free play, perform the following:

a. At the handlebar, move the choke lever from the full on (cold start) position (**Figure 142**) and then back to the full off position (A, **Figure 143**). Perform this several times and leave the choke lever in the full OFF position.
b. At the choke lever, slide the rubber boot (B, **Figure 143**) off the adjuster and onto the cable.
c. Loosen the locknut (A, **Figure 146**) and turn the adjuster (B) in either direction until there is a 1 mm (0.04 in.) gap between the locknut and the adjuster. Tighten the locknut.

7B. On later models, to adjust the cold-start (choke) cable free play, perform the following:

a. At the handlebar, move the choke lever from the full on (cold start) position (**Figure 147**) and then back to the full off position (**Figure 148**). Perform this several times and leave the choke lever in the full OFF position.
b. At the choke lever, slide the rubber boot **Figure 149** off the adjuster and onto the cable.
c. Loosen the locknut (A, **Figure 150**) and turn the adjuster (B) in either direction until there is a 1 mm (0.04 in.) gap between the locknut and the adjuster. Tighten the locknut.

8A. On early models, to adjust the throttle cable free play, perform the following:

a. At the handlebar, open and close the throttle several times, then move it back to the full OFF position.

b. At the throttle grip, slide the rubber boot (**Figure 151**) off the adjuster and onto the throttle cable.
c. Loosen the locknut and turn the adjuster in either direction until there is a 1 mm (0.04 in.) gap between the locknut and the adjuster. Tighten the locknut.
d. At both throttle bodies, use needlenose pliers and gently pull up on the throttle cable sheath at the throttle wheel. There must be at least 2 mm (0.08 in.) of free play (**Figure 152**). If necessary, loosen the locknut and turn the adjusting nut to correct the free play. Tighten the locknut.

8B. On later models, to adjust the throttle cable free play, perform the following:

a. At the handlebar, open and close the throttle several times, then move it back to the full OFF position.
b. At the throttle grip, slide the rubber boot (**Figure 153**) off the adjuster and onto the throttle cable.
c. Loosen the locknut (A, **Figure 154**) and turn the adjuster (B) in either direction until there is a 1 mm (0.04 in.) gap between the locknut and the adjuster. Tighten the locknut.
d. At both throttle bodies, use needlenose pliers and gently pull up on the throttle cable sheath at the throttle wheel. There must be at least 2 mm (0.08 in.) of free play (**Figure 152**). If necessary, loosen the locknut and turn the adjusting nut to correct the free play. Tighten the locknut.

9. Synchronize the throttle bodies and adjust the idle speed as described in this chapter.

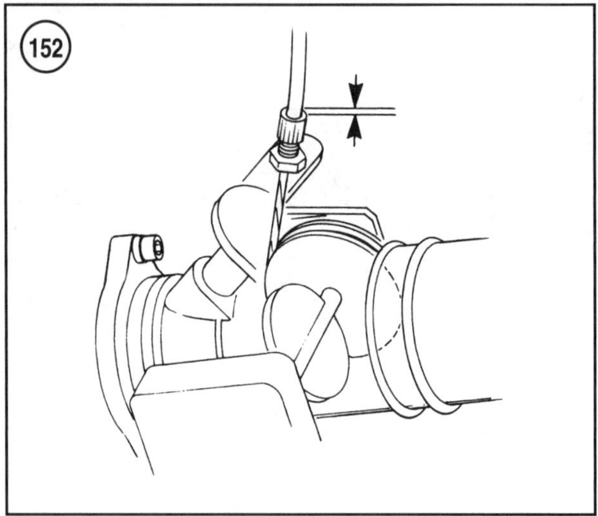

THROTTLE CABLE ADJUSTMENT (1993-1995 R850C AND R1200C MODELS)

A single throttle cable runs from the throttle grip to the throttle body. These models are not equipped with a cold-start (choke) cable or system.

1. Start the engine and let it reach normal operating temperature. Stop and go riding of 10-15 minutes is sufficient. Shut off the engine.
2. Place the motorcycle on the sidestand.
3. Shift the transmission into neutral.
4. At the handlebar, open and close the throttle several times, then move it back to the full OFF position.
5. At the throttle grip, slide the rubber boot (**Figure 153**) off the adjuster and onto the throttle cable.
6. Loosen the locknut (A, **Figure 154**) and turn the adjuster (B) in either direction until there is a 0.05 mm (0.02 in.) gap between the locknut and the adjuster. Tighten the locknut.

THROTTLE BODY SYNCHRONIZATION AND IDLE SPEED ADJUSTMENT

All Models Except R850C, All R1150 and R1200C

Throttle body synchronization ensures that both throttle valves open and close at exactly the same time. A set of vacuum gauges that measures the intake vacuum of both cylinders at the same time is required. The tachometer on these motorcycles is accurate in the low range and can be used for this procedure.

A home mechanic can perform this procedure, but it is recommended that a BMW dealership perform the procedure using the BMW Synchrotester diagnostic tool. This tool is more accurate than typical vacuum gauges.

WARNING

The engine must be running when performing this procedure. When doing so, do not run the engine in an enclosed area. The exhaust gasses contain carbon monoxide, a

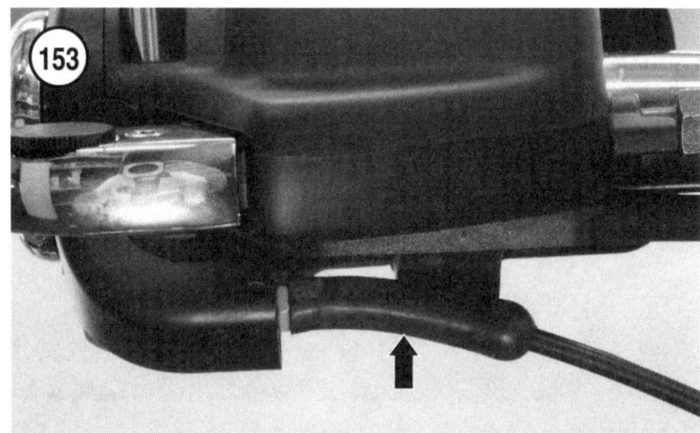

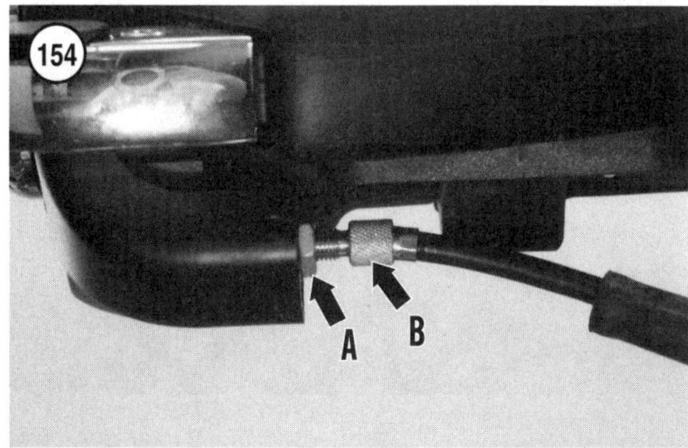

colorless, tasteless, poisonous gas. Carbon monoxide levels build quickly in enclosed areas and can cause unconsciousness and death in a short time. Start and run the engine in an area with adequate ventilation.

CAUTION

Since the engine is air-cooled, do not run the engine for more than 20 minutes in a stationary position. If possible, direct a cooling fan across the cylinders from the front of the motorcycle.

NOTE

Prior to synchronizing the throttle bodies, the air filter element must be clean and the valve clearance properly adjusted.

1. Adjust the throttle and cold-start (choke) cables as previously described.
2. Slowly and carefully turn the air screw (A, **Figure 155**) in until it *lightly* seats, then back it out 1 1/4 to 1 1/2 turns.
3. Remove the clamps, or disconnect the vacuum hose (B, **Figure 155**) from the throttle body vacuum fitting.
4. Install the vacuum gauge set to the vacuum fittings following the manufacturer's instructions.
5. Start the engine and let it idle.

6. Balance the vacuum gauge set, following its manufacturer's instructions, prior to using it in this procedure.
7. If the throttle bodies are correctly balanced, the vacuum level will be the same for both cylinders.
8. If adjustment is necessary, loosen the locknut located at the end of the throttle cable at the throttle body. Turn the adjuster as required to equalize the vacuum readings.
9. Open and close the throttle several times and note the gauge readings throughout the speed range. The readings must remain equal at all speeds.
10. Hold the adjusters and tighten the locknuts. Recheck the readings after the locknuts are tightened to make sure the adjusters do not move. Readjust if necessary.
11. To adjust the idle speed, perform the following:
    a. Slowly turn the air screw (A, **Figure 155**) on each throttle body in either direction until achieving the correct idle speed.
    b. The throttle bodies must remain synchronized during this step. If necessary, turn either or both air screws until the correct idle speed and synchronization is achieved.
    c. Open and close the throttle several times and recheck the idle speed and gauge readings. Readjust if necessary.
12. Shut off the engine and disconnect the vacuum gauge set.
13. Install the caps or vacuum hoses onto the throttle body fittings. Make sure they are properly seated to avoid a vacuum leak.
14. On models so equipped, install the throttle body cover (**Figure 141**).
15. On RS, RT and C models, install the front fairing side panels as described in Chapter Fifteen.

R850C, All R1150 and R1200C Models

There is no synchronization procedure on these models. This service must be performed by a BMW dealership using the MoDiTec diagnostic tool.

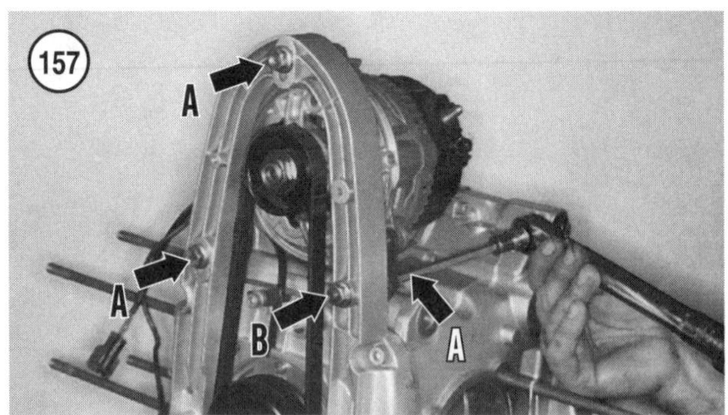

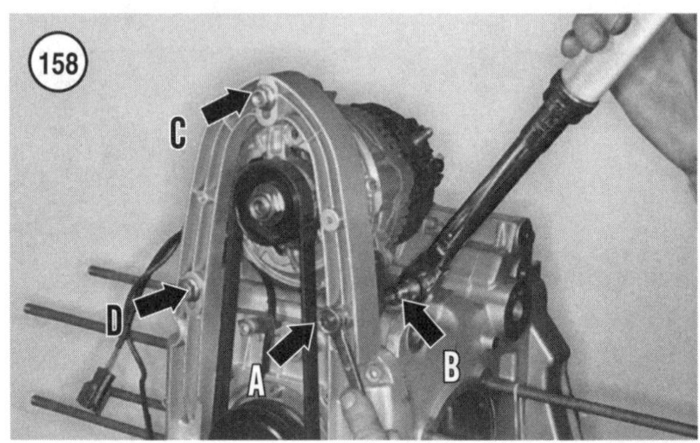

ALTERNATOR DRIVE BELT ADJUSTMENT

Adjust the alternator drive belt at the intervals listed in **Table 1**. Replace the drive belt at the intervals listed in **Table 1**. Refer to Chapter Nine for instructions.

1A. On models so equipped, place the motorcycle on the centerstand with the front wheel off of the ground.

1B. On models without a centerstand, place a suitable size jack under the engine to support the motorcycle with the front wheel off the ground.

2. Remove the fuel tank as described in Chapter Nine.
3. On RS, RT and S models, remove both side fairing panels as described in Chapter Fifteen.
4. Remove the bolts securing the alternator cover (**Figure 156**) and remove the cover.

NOTE
The following steps are shown with the engine removed and partially disassembled to better illustrate the steps. This procedure can be accomplished with the engine assembled and in the frame.

5. Slightly loosen all alternator mounting bolts and nuts (A, **Figure 157**).

NOTE
Models equipped with the Resilient Poly-V or ELAST alternator drive belt are identified by a small raised triangle on the bottom edge of the alternator cover. These models require three special tool and must be adjusted at a BMW dealership.

6A. On all R1150 models, perform the following:

a. Remove the left hex nut (B, **Figure 157**) from the threaded stud with a box wrench.
b. Install the special tensioning tool (part No. 12-3-551) onto the threaded stud and torque wrench.
c. Tighten the left hex nut and preload it to 8 N•m (71 in. lb.) and maintain this pressure
d. Tighten the upper nut (A, **Figure 157**) securely and release the pressure on the left hex nut.
e. Remove the special tool from the threaded stud.
f. Install the left hex nut (B, **Figure 157**) onto the threaded stud and tighten securely

6B. On all models except R1150 models perform the following:

a. Using only your fingers, lightly tighten the left hex nut (B, **Figure 157**).
b. Secure the left hex nut (A, **Figure 158**) with a box wrench.
c. Use a torque wrench and tighten the adjust bolt (B, **Figure 158**) to 8 N•m (71 in.-lb.)
d. Securely tighten the upper mounting bolt and nut (C, **Figure 158**).
e. Slightly slacken the adjust screw (B, **Figure 158**).

7. On R1150 models, securely tighten the upper mounting bolt and nut (C, **Figure 158**).
8. Securely tighten the right mounting bolt and nut (D, **Figure 158**).
9. Install the alternator cover (**Figure 156**) and tighten the bolts securely.
10. On RS, RT and S models, install both side fairing panels as described in Chapter Fifteen.
11. Install the fuel tank as described in Chapter Nine.

Table 1 MAINTENANCE SCHEDULE[1]

Pre-ride check	Check tire pressure cold; adjust to suit load and speed Check tire and wheel rim condition Check lights and horn operation Check engine oil level; add oil if necessary Check brake fluid level and condition; add fluid if necessary Check clutch fluid level and condition; add fluid if necessary (models so equipped) Check the operation of the front and rear brakes Check throttle operation Check clutch lever operation Check fuel level in fuel tank; top off if necessary Check fuel system for leaks
Initial 600 miles (1000 km) inspection	Perform bleed test on integral ABS (with MoDiTec unit) Change engine oil and filter Change final drive lubricant Check rear wheel lug nut tightness Check swing arm bearing adjustment Check operation of side stand interlock switch Grease side stand pivot Retorque cylinder heads Check valve clearance, adjust if necessary Check throttle operation, adjust if necessary Check EFI synchronization Check tire and wheel condition Check clutch, gearshift and brake operation Check all lighting equipment Conduct complete road test
Every 6000 miles (10,000 km)	Change engine oil and filter; change more often if conditions warrant Check battery condition; clean cable connections if necessary Check battery electrolyte level; add purified water if necessary (conventional batteries) Check brake fluid level and condition; add fluid if necessary Check front and rear brake pads and discs for wear Check ABS sensor clearance and for contamination: adjust if necessary (models so equipped) Check tire condition and inflation pressure Check wheel rim condition and spoke tightness (models so equipped) Check transmission oil level; top off if necessary Check final drive unit oil level; top off if necessary Check clutch lever operation; adjust if necessary (cable operated models) Inspect spark plugs Check clutch fluid level and condition; add fluid if necessary (hydraulic operated models) Inspect the air filter element; replace if necessary Check valve clearance; adjust if necessary Adjust alternator drive belt (models not equipped with Resilient Poly-V or ELAST belt)[2] Check throttle cable operation Check enrichener (choke) cable operation (models so equipped) Check throttle play; adjust if necessary Check engine idle speed; adjust if necessary Check fuel system for leaks Check electrical switches and equipment for proper operation Check oil cooler and brake lines for leakage Check all fasteners for tightness Check swing arm bearings for play; adjust if necessary Lubricate front brake and clutch lever pivot pin Lubricate sidestand and centerstand pivot points (continued)

Table 1 MAINTENANCE SCHEDULE[1] (continued)

Every 6000 miles (10,000 km) (continued)	Grease lower pivot point of front strut Grease windshield adjuster (models so equipped) Check steering play Check and tighten fasteners Road test the motorcycle Have a BMW dealership read out and clear any fault codes within the Motronic system memory
Every 12,000 miles (20,000 km)	Perform all items listed in 6000 miles (10,000 km) plus the following: Replace air filter Replace spark plugs Check electrical switches and equipment for proper operation Check battery condition; clean cable connections if necessary Check wheel bearings; replace if necessary Check tightness of steering damper (R models so equipped)
Every 24,000 miles (40,000 km)	Perform all items listed in 12,000 miles (20,000 km) plus the following: Replace the alternator drive belt (models not equipped with Resiliant Poly V or ELAST belt)[2] Replace fuel filter Change final drive unit oil (or every 2 years)
Every 36,000 miles (60,000 km)	Perform all items listed in 24,000 miles (40,000 km) plus the following: Replace the alternator drive belt (models equipped with Resiliant Poly V or ELAST belt)[2, 3]
Annual service[4]	Change brake fluid Change clutch fluid (hydraulic operated models) Check brake hoses for wetness or deterioration; replace as necessary Perform bleed test on integral ABS (with MoDiTec unit)
Every 2 years	Change transmission oil

1. Consider this maintenance schedule a guide to general maintenance and lubrication intervals. Harder than normal use and exposure to extreme conditions will require more frequent attention to some maintenance items.
2. Resilient Poly V belt requires a one-time adjustment at 6000 miles (10,000 km) or after installation of a new belt. ELAST drive belt requires no routine adjustemnt. Models equipped with either belt are identfied with a small raised triangle on the bottom edge of the alternator cover.
3 Refer to a BMW dealership.
4. An annual inspection must be performed by a BMW dealership to maintain any applicable warranty

Table 2 TIRE INFLATION PRESSURE (COLD)*

Item	kPa	psi
Front (1993-1998 R850, R1100 models [except R1100S])		
Solo	213	31
Rider and passenger	269	39
Rider, passenger and luggage	283	41
Front (1999-on R850, R1100C, R1150 models)		
Solo	213	31
Rider and passenger	248	36
Rider, passenger and luggage	248	36
Rear (all models)		
Solo	248	36
Rider and passenger	269	39
Rider, passenger and luggage	286	42

*Tire inflation pressure is for original equipment tires. Aftermarket tires may require different inflation pressure. The use of tires other than those specified by BMW may cause instability.

Table 3 BATTERY STATE OF CHARGE

Specific gravity reading	Percentage of charge remaining
1.120-1.140	0
1.135-1.155	10
1.150-1.170	20
1.160-1.180	30
1.175-1.195	40
1.190-1.210	50
1.205-1.225	60
1.215-1.235	70
1.230-1.250	80
1.245-1.265	90
1.260-1.280	100

Table 4 BATTERY CHARGING RATES/TIMES (APPROXIMATE)

Voltage	% of charge	3 amp charger	6 amp charger	10 amp charger	20 amp charger
12.8	100%	–	–	–	–
12.6	75%	1.75 hours	50 minutes	30 minutes	15 minutes
12.3	50%	3.5 hours	1.75 hours	1 hour	30 minutes
12.0	25%	5 hours	2.5 hours	1.5 hours	45 minutes
11.8	0%	6 hours and 40 minutes	3 hours and 20 minutes	2 hours	1 hour

Table 5 RECOMMENDED LUBRICANTS AND CAPACITIES

Battery water (conventional batteries)	Distilled or purified water	
Brake fluid	–	DOT4
Clutch fluid	–	DOT4
Engine oil type		
1993-1998 R850, R1100 models (except R1100S)	HD oil API SE, SF or SG	
1999-on R850, R1100S, R1150 models	HD oil API SF, SG or SH; the suffixes CD or CE are acceptable; or HD oil CCMC G4 or G5; the suffix PD2 is acceptable	
Engine oil change		
Oil change only	3.5 L (3.7 U.S. qts.)	
Oil and filter	3.75 L (4.0 U.S. qts.)	
Difference between MIN and MAX marks	0.50 L (0.53 U.S. qt.)	
Final drive unit		Hypoid gear oil GL5
Above 5° C (41° F)	SAE 90	
Below 5° C (41° F)	SAE 80	
Alternative	SAE 80W/90W	
R850C, R1200C models		
Oil change	0.18 L (0.19 U.S. qt.)	
Rebuild	0.20 L (0.21 U.S. qt.)	
All models except R850C, R1200C models		
Oil change	0.23 L (0.24 U.S. qt.)	
Rebuild	0.25 L (0.26 U.S. qt.)	
Front fork oil	0.47 L (0.50 U.S. qt.)	BMW fork oil 5W or 10W

(continued)

Table 5 RECOMMENDED LUBRICANTS AND CAPACITIES (continued)

Grease		
Clutch splines	–	Optimoly MP3 or Microlube GL261or BelRay Total Performance Lube
Assembly paste	–	Optimoly TA
Roller bearings, final drive and drive shaft splines, chassis components	–	Retinax EP2 or Kluberplex BEM 34-132
Fuel grade		
Models with catalytic converter		Premium unleaded fuel with a minimum Octane rating of 95 (RON) or 85 (MON), AKI 91 premium
Models without catalytic converter		Premium leaded fuel with a minimum Octane rating of 95 (RON) or 85 (MON)
Transmission oil		Hypoid gear oil GL5
Above 5° C (41° F)	SAE 90	
Below 5° C (41° F)	SAE 80	
Oil change	0.81 L (0.86 U.S. qt.)	
Rebuild	1.0 L (1.06 U.S. qts.)	

Table 6 MAINTENANCE AND TUNE-UP SPECIFICATIONS

Item	Specifications
Brake pedal height	Rider preference
Clutch (cable operated models)	
Free play	5-7 mm (0.19-0.27 in.)
Locknut-to-adjuster clearance	12 mm (0.47 in.)
Cold start (choke) free play	Minimum 1 mm (0.04 in.)
Engine compression	
Good	Above 1000 kPa (145 psi)
Normal	862-1000 1000 kPa (125-145 psi)
Poor	Less than 862 kPa (125 psi)
Idle speed	
1993-1998	1000-1150 rpm
1999-on	1050-1150 rpm
Ignition timing	Non-adjustable
Rocker arm end float	
Minimum	0.05 mm (0.002 in.)
Maximum	0.40 mm (0.016 in.)
Spark plug type and gap (single-plug ignition)	
R850, R1100 (except R1100S), R1200C models	
Type	Bosch FR 6 DDC
Specified gap	0.8 mm (0.031 in.)
Gap limit	1.0 mm (0.04 in.)
Spark plug type and gap (single-spark ignition)	
R1150	
Type	NGK BKR 7 EKC
Specified gap	0.8 mm (0.031 in.)
Gap limit	1.0 mm (0.04 in.)
Spark plug type and gap (dual-plug ignition)	
R1100, R1150, R1200 models	
Primary spark plug	
Type	NGK BKR 7 EKC
Specified gap	0.8 mm (0.031 in.)
Gap limit	1.0 mm (0.04 in.)
	(continued)

Table 6 MAINTENANCE AND TUNE-UP SPECIFICATIONS (continued)

Item	Specifications
Spark plug type and gap (dual-plug ignition)	
R1100, R1150, R1200 models (continued)	
Secondary spark plug	
Type	NGK DCPR 8 EKC or Bosch YR 6 LDE
Specified gap	0.8 mm (0.031 in.)
Gap limit	1.0 mm (0.04 in.)
Throttle cable free play	
1993-1995	Minimum 0.5 mm (0.02 in.)
1996-on	Minimum 2 mm (0.08 in.)
Throttle synchronization*	
Maximum allowable difference in BMW Synchronizer bars	5 mm (0.19 in.)
Valve clearance (cold)	
Intake	0.17-0.23 mm (0.007-0.009 in.)
Exhaust	0.25-0.31 mm (0.010-0.012 in.)

* All R850C, R1100S, R1150 and R1200C models must be adjusted using the BMW MoDiTec diagnostic unit.

Table 7 MAINTENANCE AND TUNE UP TORQUE SPECIFICATIONS

Item	N•m	in.-lb.	ft.-lb.
Alternator drive belt bolt	8	71	–
Cylinder head			
10–mm Torx bolt	40	–	29
Nuts			
Preliminary	20	–	15
Final	an additional 180°		
Engine oil drain plug	32	–	24
Final drive unit			
Drain plug	23	–	17
Oil fill cap	23	–	17
Handlebar			
R1100S models			
Locating bolt	9	80	–
Pinch bolt	25	–	18
All models except R1100S			
Mounting bolt	21	–	15
Oil filter cartridge	11	98	–
Transmission			
1999-on R850C, R1100S, R1200C models			
Drain plug	55	–	41
Oil filler cap	23	–	17
R1150 models			
Drain plug	30	–	22
Oil filler cap	30	–	22
All models except 1999-on R850C, R1100S, R1150, R1200 models			
Drain plug	23	–	17
Oil fill cap	23	–	17
Valve adjuster locknut	8	70	–

CHAPTER FOUR

ENGINE TOP END

This chapter provides service procedures for the engine top end. The engine lower end is covered in Chapter Five.

The engine is an air/oil cooled, single overhead camshaft (SOHC), four-valve opposed twin. The valves on each cylinder head are operated via a single chain-driven camshaft, pushrods and rocker arms.

The lubrication system is a wet sump type with the oil supply housed in the lower crankcase. The chain-driven oil pump delivers oil directly to the oil cooler(s). These components are covered in Chapter Five.

Engine specifications are in **Tables 1-3** at the end of the chapter.

ENGINE SERVICE NOTES

An important part of successful engine service is preparation. Before servicing the engine, note the following:

1. Review the *Basic Service Methods* and *Precision Measuring Tools* sections of Chapter One. Accurate measurements are critical to a successful engine rebuild.
2. Clean the entire engine and frame with a commercial degreaser before removing engine components. A clean motorcycle is easier to work on and this will help prevent debris from falling into the engine.
3. Have all the necessary tools and parts on hand before starting the procedure(s). Store parts in boxes, plastic bags and containers. Use masking tape and a permanent, waterproof marking pen to label parts. Record the location, position and thickness of all shims and washers as they are removed.
4. Use an assortment of vacuum hose identifiers (Lisle part No. 74600) to identify hoses and fittings during engine services.
5. Throughout the text there are references to the left and right side of the engine. This refers to the engine as it is mounted in the frame, not how it may sit on the workbench.
6. When inspecting components described in this chapter, compare the measurements to the service specifications listed in **Table 2** or **Table 3**. Replace any part that is out of specification, worn to the service limit or damaged.
7. Always replace worn or damaged fasteners with those of the same size, type and torque requirements. If a specific torque value is not listed in the text or in **Table 4**, refer to the general torque specifications in Chapter One.
8. Use a vise with protective jaws to hold parts.
9. Use a press or special tools when force is required to remove and install parts. Do not try to pry, hammer or otherwise force them on or off.

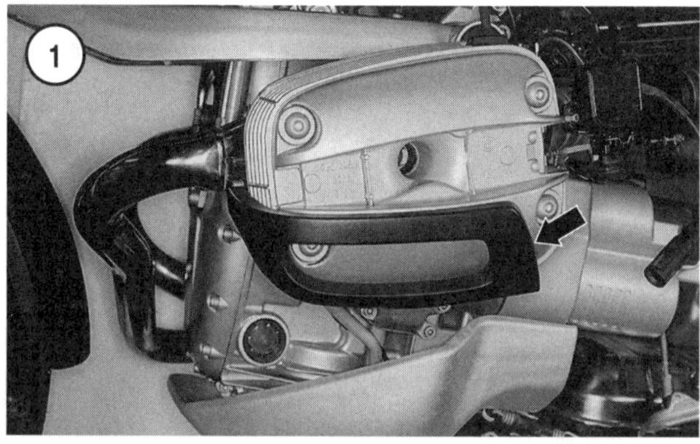

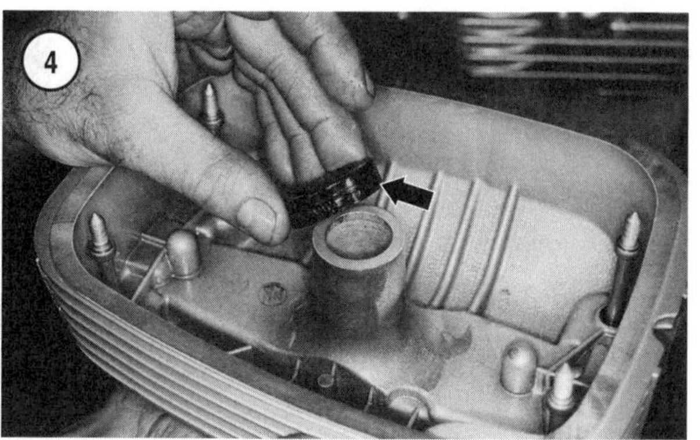

10. Replace all O-rings and seals with *new* ones during assembly. Set aside old seals and O-rings so they can be compared with the new ones if necessary. Apply a small amount of grease to the inner lips of each new oil seal to prevent damage when the engine is first started.

CYLINDER HEAD COVER

The cylinder head cover can be removed with the engine mounted in the frame. Some of this procedure is shown with the transmission case removed to better illustrate the steps.

Removal

1. Place the motorcycle on level ground on the centerstand.
2. Remove the seat as described in Chapter Fifteen.
3. On RS, RT and S models remove the front fairing side panels as described in Chapter Fifteen.
4. Disconnect the battery negative lead as described in Chapter Three.
5. Remove the spark plugs as described in Chapter Three.
6. On models so equipped, remove the mounting bolts and the engine guard (**Figure 1**) from each cylinder head.
7. Place a drain pan under the cylinder head as some oil may drain out when the cylinder head cover is removed.
8. Following a crisscross pattern, loosen the cylinder head cover bolts (**Figure 2**). Remove the bolts and special washers securing the cylinder head cover.
9. Pull the cover straight up and off the cylinder head and remove the cover.
10. The gasket will usually stay attached to the cylinder head. Remove it from the cylinder head or cover.
11. Remove the rubber gasket from the spark plug tower in the cylinder head cover.
12. Inspect all parts as described in this section.

Installation

1. Thoroughly clean all oil and grease residue from the gasket surface on the cylinder head and cylinder head cover to achieve a leak-free seal.
2. Install the cylinder head cover gasket onto the cylinder head (**Figure 3**). Press the gasket down to make sure it seats correctly.
3. Install the gasket onto the spark plug tower in the cover (**Figure 4**). Press the gasket down to make sure it seats correctly.
4. Make sure the rubber grommet (A, **Figure 5**) and the special washer (B) are in place under each bolt.

5. Install the cylinder head cover onto the cylinder head and make sure it seats correctly.

6. Hand tighten the cylinder head cover bolts (**Figure 2**) until the cover seats correctly against the cylinder head. Tighten the bolts in a crisscross pattern to 8 N•m (71 in.-lb.).

7. On models so equipped, install the engine guard (**Figure 1**) and tighten the bolts securely.

8. Install the spark plug as described in Chapter Three.

9. Connect the battery negative lead as described in Chapter Three.

10. Install the seat as described in Chapter Fifteen.

11. Start the engine and check for oil leaks.

12. On RS, RT and S models install the front fairing side panels as described in Chapter Fifteen.

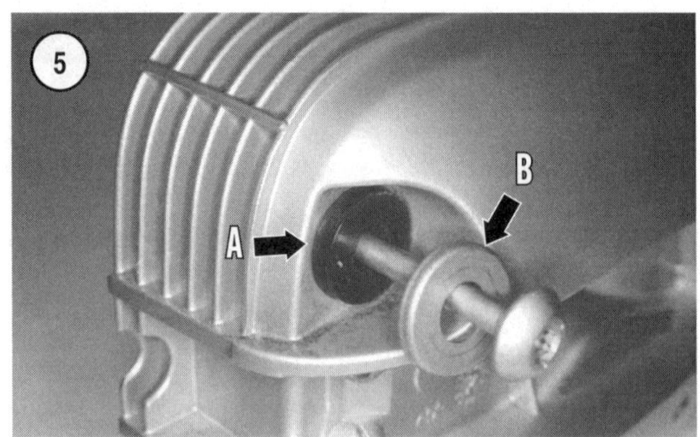

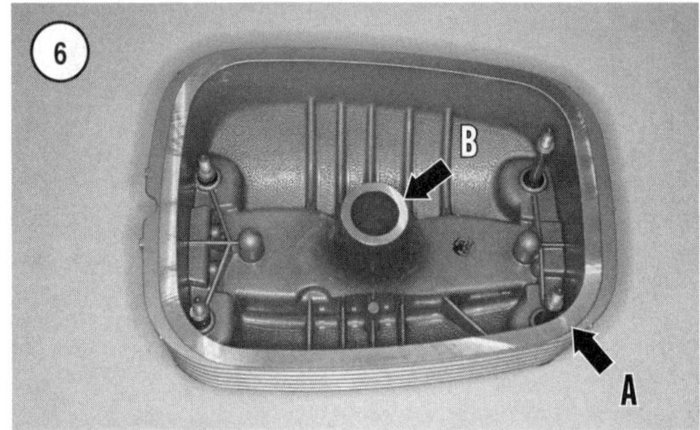

Inspection

1. Inspect the cylinder head cover gasket around its perimeter for wear or damage. Replace if it is starting to deteriorate or harden.

2. Check the cylinder head cover for warp, cracks or damage. Replace it if necessary.

3. Inspect the cylinder head cover gasket surface (A, **Figure 6**) and spark plug tower gasket surface (B) for scratches or gouges that could cause an oil leak. Repair if possible or replace the cover.

4. Inspect the cylinder head gasket surface and spark plug tower gasket surface for scratches or gouges that could lead to an oil leak. Repair if possible or replace the cylinder head.

5. Check the cooling fins (**Figure 7**) for debris, cracked or missing fins.

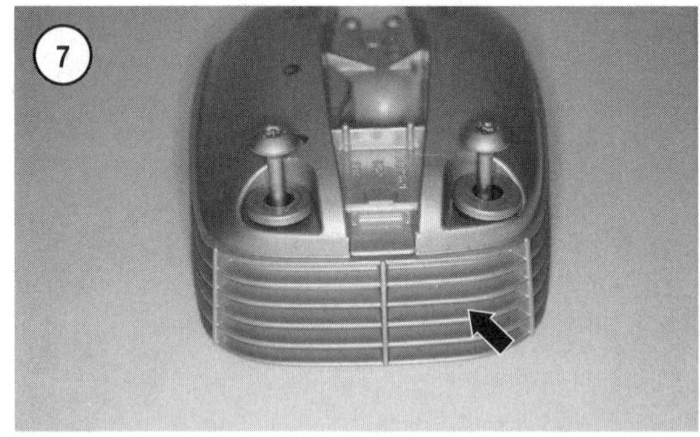

CYLINDER HEAD

Removal

1A. On models so equipped, place the motorcycle on the centerstand with the rear wheel off of the ground.

1B. On models without a centerstand, place a suitable size jack under the engine to support the motorcycle with the rear wheel off the ground.

2. Remove the throttle body assembly from the cylinder head and air box as described in Chapter Nine.

3. Remove the cylinder head cover (A, **Figure 8**) as described in this chapter.

4. Remove the camshaft drive chain sprocket cover (B, **Figure 8**) from the rear surface of the cylinder head.

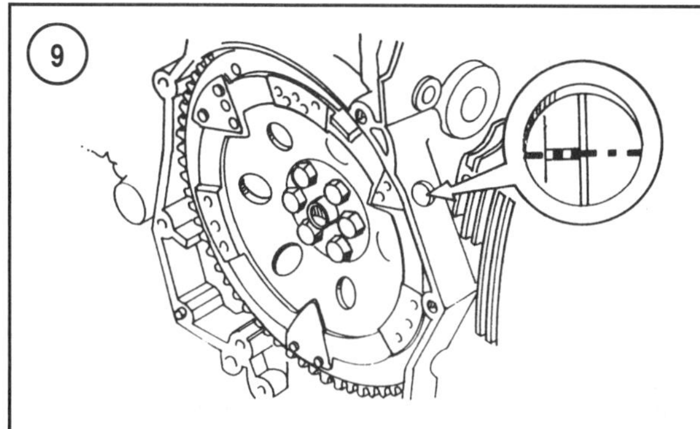

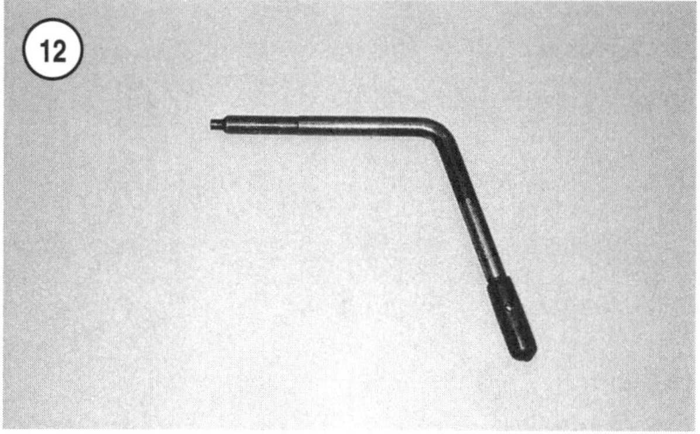

NOTE
There are two methods of rotating the engine. Use the method that is easiest. Either cylinder can be worked on first.

5A. Rotate the engine with the rear wheel until the piston is at top dead center (TDC) on its compression stroke. To determine TDC for that cylinder, perform the following:

a. Shift the transmission into top gear.
b. Rotate the rear wheel, in normal forward rotation, until the intake valves open, then close.
c. With a small flashlight, direct light into the spark plug hole to observe the piston as it moves up in the cylinder.
d. Continue to rotate the rear wheel until the left cylinder's piston reaches the top of its stroke. This is TDC on the compression stroke with the timing mark OT centered in the inspection hole in the crankcase (**Figure 9**). At this point all four valves will be closed and there will be a slight clearance between both rocker arms and all four valve stems.

5B. To rotate the engine without using the rear wheel, perform the following:

a. Remove the bolts securing the alternator cover (**Figure 10**) and remove the cover.
b. Insert a socket or wrench into the crankshaft pulley bolt (**Figure 11**).
c. As viewed from the front of the engine, rotate the engine in a *clockwise* direction until the left piston is at top dead center (TDC) on its compression stroke.
d. With a small flashlight, direct light into the spark plug hole to observe the piston as it moves up in the cylinder.
e. Continue to rotate the crankshaft pulley until that cylinder's piston reaches the top of its stroke. This is TDC on the compression stroke with the timing mark OT centered in the inspection hole in the crankcase (**Figure 9**). At this point, all four valves will be closed and there will be clearance between both rocker arms and all four valve stems.

6. Insert the TDC locking pin (**Figure 12**) as follows:

a. On the rear left side of the crankcase, above the starter, remove the TDC pin cover plug (**Figure 13**).

NOTE
***Figure 14** is shown with the transmission case removed to better show the flywheel hole and the crankcase receptacle.*

b. Insert the TDC locking pin (BMW part No. 11-2-650) through the crankcase hole (**Figure 15**),

4

through the flywheel and into the receptacle in the backside of the crankcase (**Figure 14**). Push it in until it locks into place. If necessary, slightly rotate the engine in either direction to align the flywheel hole properly to the crankcase receptacle, then push the locking pin into place. After the TDC pin locks into place, try to rotate the engine—the engine should not rotate even the slightest amount. If the engine does rotate, the locking pin is not engaged properly; reposition the locking pin until there is no engine movement.

NOTE

This procedure is shown on the left side of the engine. This procedure is applicable to the right side with the exception of the chain tensioner location and shape of the tensioner inner body. If disassembling both sides of the engine, keep all parts separate so that they will be installed on the correct side of the engine.

7A. On the left cylinder, loosen the camshaft chain tensioner (**Figure 16**) located on the top surface of the cylinder. Unscrew and remove the tensioner and washer (**Figure 17**).

7B. On the right cylinder, loosen the camshaft chain tensioner located on the bottom surface of the cylinder. Unscrew and remove the tensioner and washer.

NOTE

*In Step 8, if the camshaft driven sprocket is not going to be removed, it must be secured to the drive chain with a tie wrap (**Figure 18**). If not secured, it will disengage from the drive chain and roll down into the crankcase.*

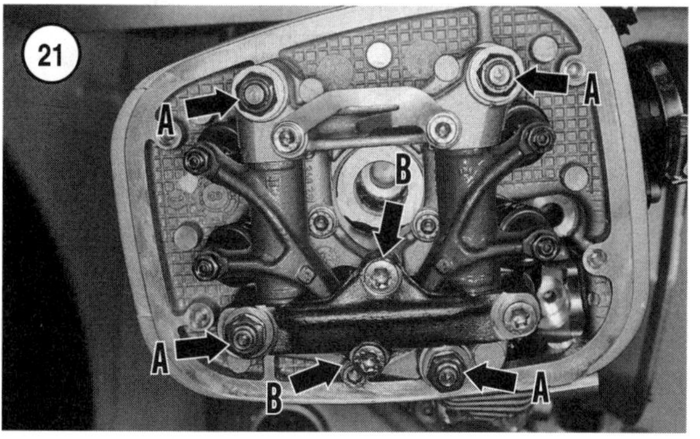

8. Loosen the Allen bolt (**Figure 19**) securing the camshaft driven sprocket to the camshaft.

9. Hold onto the sprocket and remove the Allen bolt and washer. If necessary, secure the sprocket to the drive chain with a tie wrap.

10. Remove the Allen bolts and washers (**Figure 20**) at the base of the cylinder head.

11. Following a crisscross pattern, loosen the cylinder head mounting nuts (A, **Figure 21**).

12. If the rocker arms are going to be disassembled, loosen the bearing cap Torx bolts (B, **Figure 21**) at this time.

13. Remove the nuts and washers loosened in Step 11.

14. Slowly pull the cylinder straight off of the crankcase studs (**Figure 22**) and remove it. Take it to the workbench for further service or place it in a plastic bag and box to protect it.

15. Remove the cylinder head gasket and secure the camshaft drive chain and driven sprocket to the exterior of the engine. Do not lose the locating dowels on the crankcase studs.

16. Inspect all parts as described in this section.

Installation

NOTE

If both cylinder head assemblies are removed, the right cylinder head must be installed first to ensure correct camshaft timing.

1A. On R1100S and all R1150 models, when installing the right cylinder head assembly, refer to the following:

a. Position the piston at top dead center (TDC) on its compression stroke.

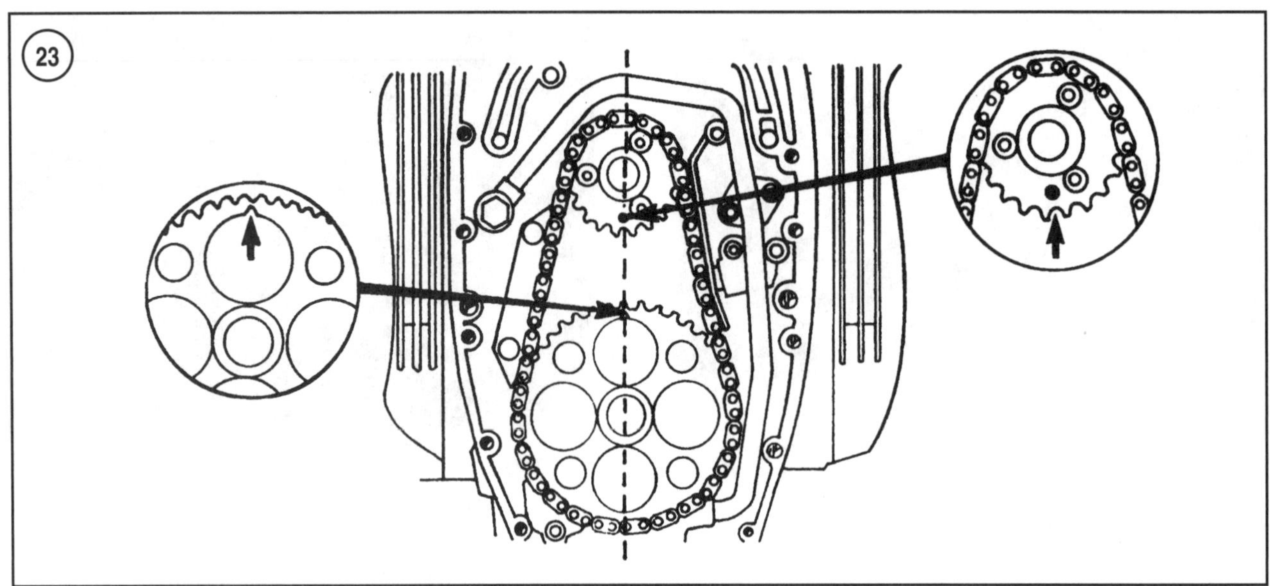

b. Refer to Step 5 of *Removal* to ensure that the piston is positioned properly. Also refer to **Figure 23** and **Figure 24** for timing marks.

1B. On all models except R1100S and all R1150, when installing the right cylinder head assembly, refer to the following:

a. Position the piston at top dead center (TDC) on its compression stroke.
b. Refer to Step 5 of *Removal* to ensure that the piston is positioned properly. Also refer to **Figure 23** and **Figure 25** for timing marks.

1C. On R1100S and all R1150 models, when installing the left cylinder head assembly, refer to the following:

a. Position the cylinder at top dead center (TDC) on its compression stroke.
b. Refer to Step 5 of *Removal* to ensure that the piston is positioned properly. Also refer to **Figure 26** and **Figure 27** for timing marks.

1D. On all models except R1100S and all R1150, when installing the left cylinder head assembly, refer to the following:

a. Position the cylinder at top dead center (TDC) on its compression stroke.
b. Refer to Step 5 of *Removal* to ensure that the piston is positioned properly. Also refer to **Figure 26** and **Figure 28** for timing marks.

2. Make sure the cylinder head and cylinder mating surfaces are clean of all gasket material.
3. If removed, install the locating dowels (**Figure 29**) on the crankcase studs. Push them down until seated correctly.

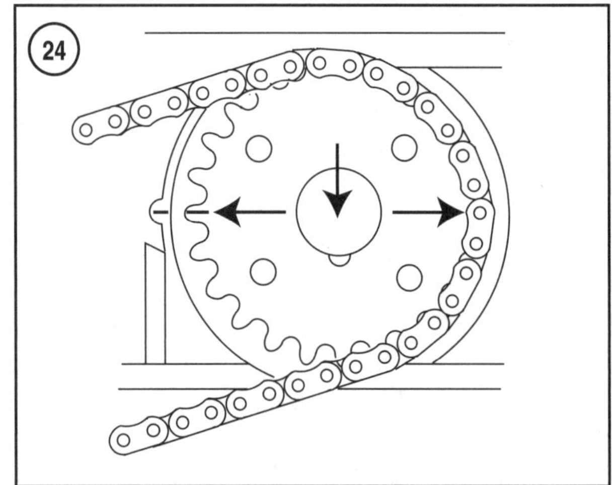

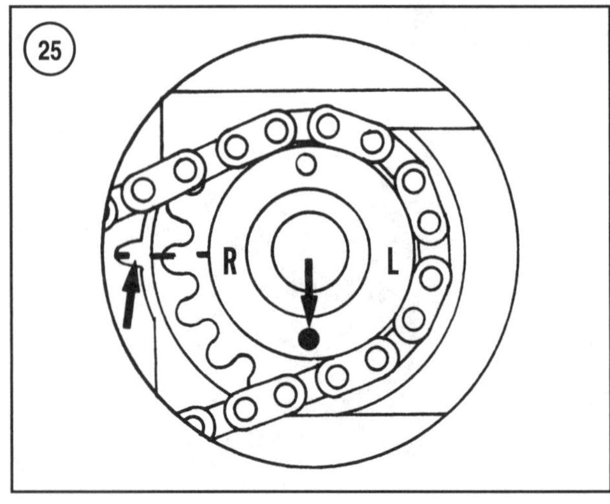

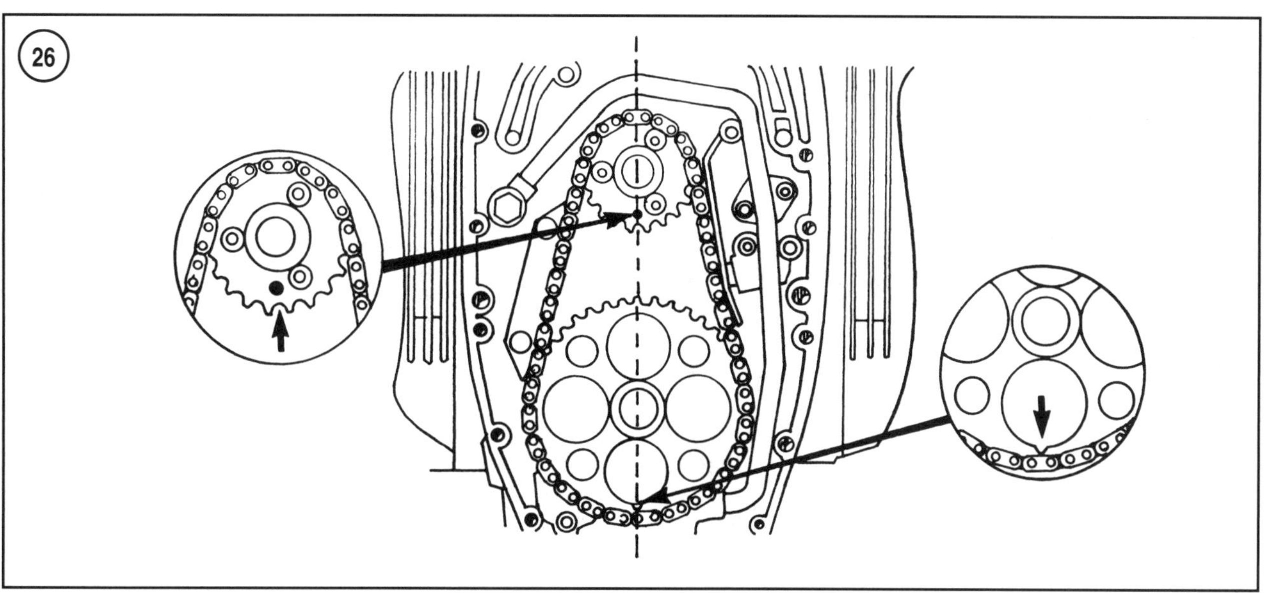

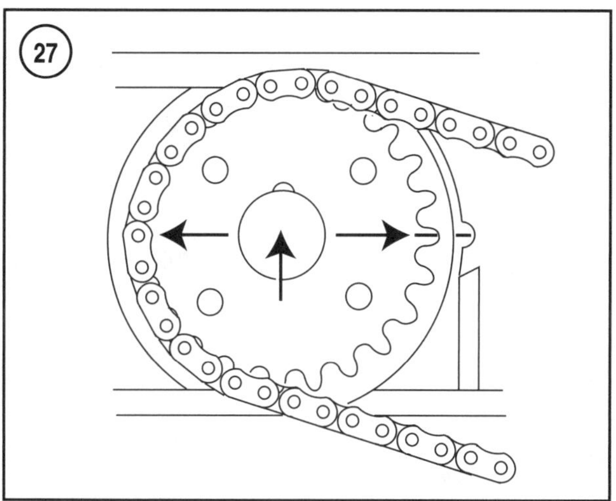

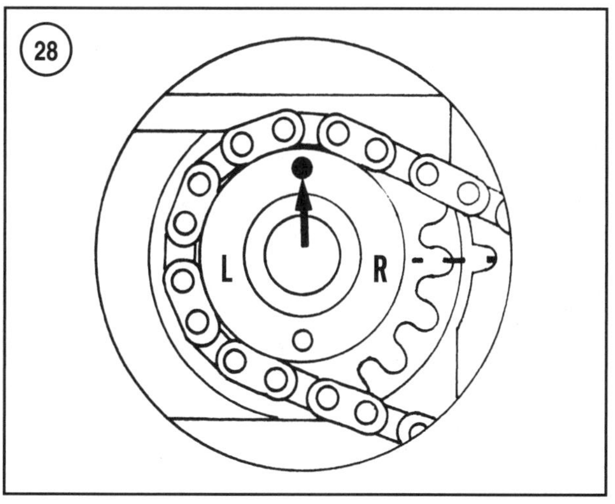

4. Untie the camshaft drive chain and driven sprocket from the exterior of the engine.

5. Install a *new* cylinder head gasket (**Figure 30**). Make sure all cylinder holes align with the new gasket holes.

NOTE

*If the camshaft driven sprocket was removed from the drive chain, ensure that the sprocket side with the timing marks (**Figure 31**) face toward the **rear** of the engine.*

6. For preliminary alignment, pull the camshaft driven sprocket and drive chain straight out from the cylinder. The arrows must be horizontal; readjust the sprocket on the drive chain if necessary.

7. Position the cylinder head onto the crankcase studs and slowly push it part-way down. Hold the cylinder head with one hand and guide the camshaft driven sprocket and

drive chain into the cylinder head chain tunnel (**Figure 32**).

8. Push the cylinder head farther down. Use an angled pick and pull the sprocket and chain into position (**Figure 33**), then push the cylinder head down until it seats. Make sure the locating dowels engage the cylinder head.

NOTE

If the sprocket bolt hole does not align with the camshaft bolt hole, the drive chain is not engaged correctly with the auxiliary shaft drive sprocket.

9. Pull out the camshaft drive chain and make sure it engages properly with the auxiliary shaft sprocket before continuing.

10A. On right side cylinder head, confirm that the driven sprocket arrow aligns with the cylinder head timing notch (**Figure 34**). Readjust if necessary. Refer to the following:

a. On R1100S and all R1150models, refer to **Figure 24**.

b. On all models except R1100S and R1150, refer to **Figure 25**.

10B. On left side cylinder head, confirm that the driven sprocket arrow aligns with the cylinder head timing notch (**Figure 34**). Readjust if necessary. Refer to the following:

a. On R1100S and all R1150 models, refer to **Figure 27.**

b. On all models except the R1100S and all R1150, refer to **Figure 28**.

11. Make sure the crankcase stud threads, washers and nuts are clean. If dirty or corroded they will resist tightening and will result in the in the incorrect torque specification.

12. Install the washers (A, **Figure 35**) onto the crankcase studs (**Figure 36**).

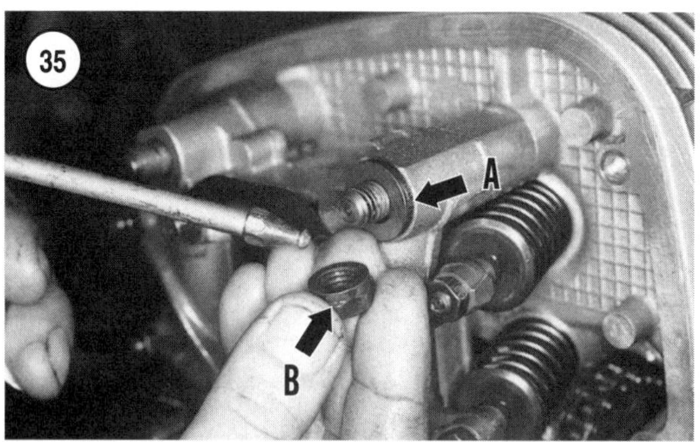

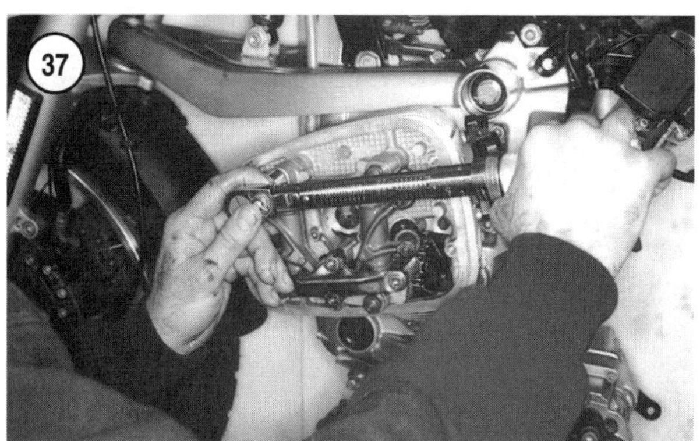

13. Apply clean engine oil to the nuts. Position the nuts with the collar side (B, **Figure 35**) facing the washers and install the nuts.

14. Following a crisscross pattern tighten (**Figure 37**) the cylinder head mounting nuts (A, **Figure 38**) to the preliminary torque of 20 N•m (15 ft.-lb.).

15. Attach a degree wheel (**Figure 39**) to the wrench and tighten the nuts an additional 180°.

16. Install the Allen bolts and washers (**Figure 40**) at the base of the cylinder head and tighten to 9 N•m (80 in.-lb.).

CAUTION

The mounting nuts must be tightened again after the motorcycle has been run approximately 600 miles (1000 km).

17. After 600 miles (1000 km), perform the following:
    a. Following a crisscross pattern, tighten (**Figure 37**) the cylinder head mounting nuts (A, **Figure 38**) to the preliminary torque of 20 N•m (15 ft.-lb.).
    b. Attach a degree wheel (**Figure 39**) to the wrench and tighten the nuts an additional 180°.

18. Check the rocker arm end play as follows:
    a. Insert a flat feeler gauge between the lower surface of the rocker arm and the rocker arm bearing cap. Refer to **Figure 41** and **Figure 42**.

b. Refer to the specified axial play in **Table 2** or **Table 3**.
c. If the axial play is within specification, tighten the bearing cap mounting Torx bolts (B, **Figure 38**) to 15 N•m (11 ft.-lb.).
d. If the end play is not correct, carefully move the bearing cap as necessary to achieve the correct end play, then tighten the bearing cap mounting Torx bolts (**Figure 40**) to 15 N•m (11 ft.-lb.).

19. Remove the tie wrap securing the drive chain to the camshaft driven sprocket.
20. Install the driven sprocket onto the end of the camshaft.
21. Install the washer (**Figure 43**) onto the Allen bolt and install the Allen bolt. Tighten the Allen bolt to 65 N·m (48 ft.-lb.).
22. Confirm that the driven sprocket arrow still aligns with the cylinder head timing notch (**Figure 44**). Readjust if necessary.

CAUTION
*Do not intermix the camshaft chain tensioner assemblies (**Figure 45**) as they are unique and must be installed in the correct location. If removed, install the spring and plunger into the tensioner housing (**Figure 46**) prior to installation.*

23A. On the left cylinder, install the camshaft chain tensioner and washer on the top surface of the cylinder block. Tighten the tensioner to 32 N•m (24 ft.-lb.).
23B. On the right cylinder, install the camshaft chain tensioner and washer on the bottom surface of the cylinder. Tighten the tensioner to 32 N•m (24 ft.-lb.).
24. On the rear left side of the crankcase, above the starter, remove the locking pin (**Figure 47**) and install the TDC pin cover plug.
25. Apply a light coat of clean engine oil to the O-ring on the camshaft drive chain sprocket cover (A, **Figure 48**). Install the cover and tighten the bolts securely.
26. Adjust the valves as described in Chapter Three.
27. Install the cylinder head cover (B, **Figure 48**) as described in this chapter.
28. Install the throttle body assembly onto the cylinder head and air box as described in Chapter Nine.

Inspection

Before removing the valves from the cylinder head, perform a solvent test to check the valve face-to-valve seat seal.

1. Remove the cylinder head as described in this section.

41

42

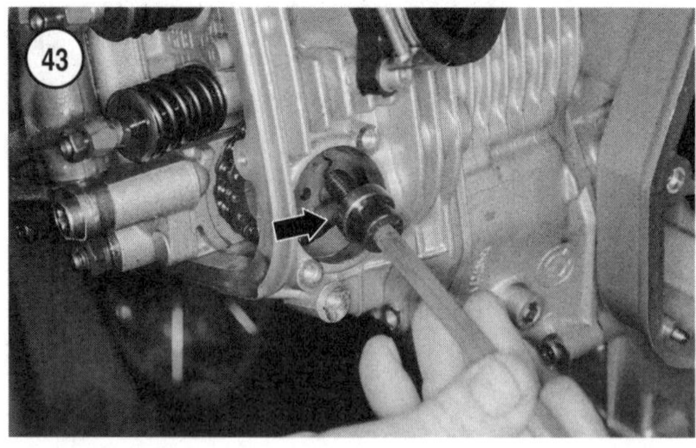
43

44

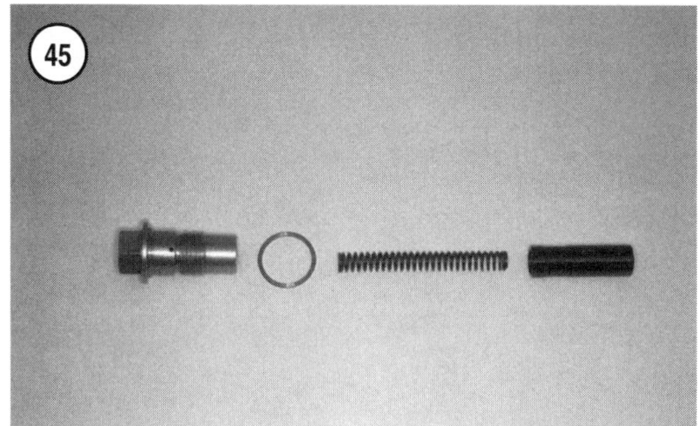

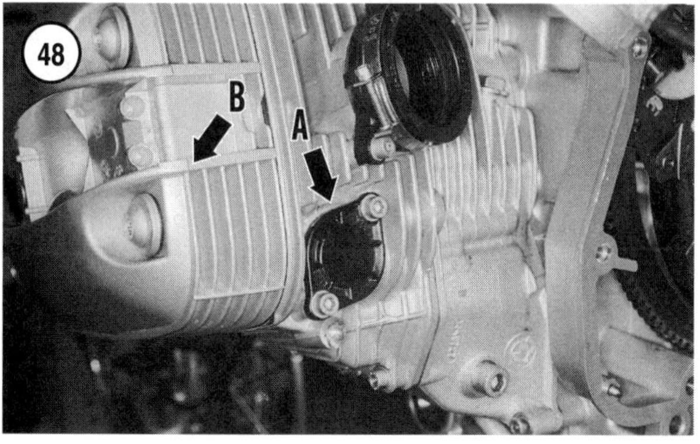

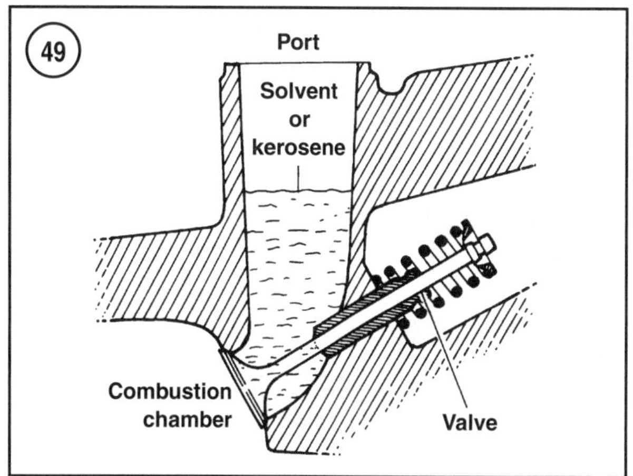

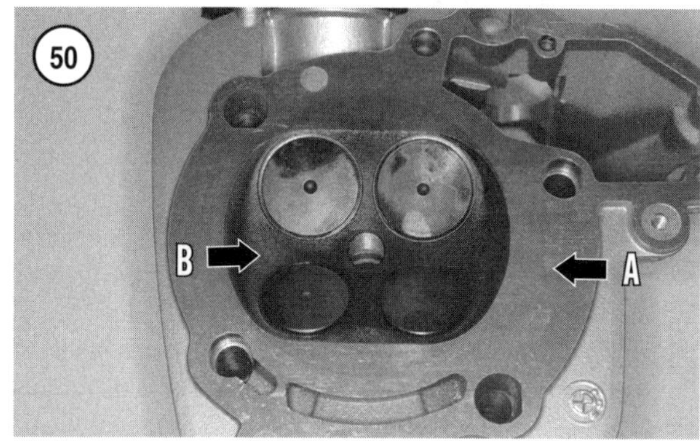

2. Support the cylinder head with the exhaust port facing up (**Figure 49**). Then pour solvent or kerosene into the port. Immediately check the combustion chamber for fluid leaking past the exhaust valve.

3. Repeat Step 2 for the intake valves.

4. If there is fluid leakage around one or both sets of valves, the valve(s) is not seating correctly. The following conditions will cause poor valve seating:

   a. A bent valve stem.

   b. A worn or damaged valve seat.

   c. A worn or damaged valve face.

   d. A crack in the combustion chamber.

5. Remove the valve gear holder assembly as described in this chapter.

6. Remove all traces of gasket residue from the cylinder head (A, **Figure 50**) and cylinder (A, **Figure 51**) mating surfaces. Do not scratch the gasket surfaces.

7. Without removing the valves, remove all carbon deposits from the combustion chamber (B, **Figure 50**). Use a fine wire brush dipped in solvent or make a scraper from hardwood. Take care not to damage the head, valves or spark plug threads.

CAUTION

Cleaning the combustion chamber with the valves removed can damage the valve seat surfaces. A damaged or even slightly scratched valve seat will cause poor valve seating.

8. Examine the spark plug threads (**Figure 52**) in the cylinder head for damage. If damage is minor or if the threads are dirty or clogged with carbon, use a spark plug thread tap to clean the threads. Install a steel thread insert if thread damage is severe. Thread insert kits can be purchased at automotive supply stores or can be installed at a BMW dealership or machine shop.

NOTE

When using a tap to clean spark plug threads, coat the tap with an aluminum tap cutting fluid or kerosene.

NOTE

Aluminum spark plug threads are commonly damaged due to galling, cross-threading and overtightening. Apply an antiseize compound on the plug threads before installation to prevent galling, and do not overtighten the plugs.

9. After removing all carbon from the combustion chambers and valve ports and after repairing the spark plug thread hole, clean the entire head in solvent and dry with compressed air.

10. Examine the piston crown (B, **Figure 51**). The crown(s) should show no signs of wear or damage. If the crown appears pecked or spongy-looking, also check the spark plug, valves and combustion chamber for aluminum deposits. If aluminum transfer is noted, the cylinder has overheated due to a lean fuel mixture or preignition.

11. Inspect the inlet pipe (**Figure 53**) for cracks or other damage that would allow unfiltered air to enter the engine. If necessary, remove the inlet pipes and discard them. Install a *new* O-ring seal between the inlet pipe and the cylinder head. Install each inlet pipe and tighten the screws securely.

12. Check for cracks in the combustion chamber, intake port and exhaust port. A cracked head must be replaced.

13. Inspect the threads on the exhaust pipe mounting studs for damage. If necessary, repair the threads with an appropriate size metric die.

14. Check for cracked or missing cooling fins. If you find damage, have it repaired at a shop specializing in the repair of precision aluminum castings or replace the cylinder head.

15. Make sure the cooling fins are clean. Clean them out with a stiff brush and wash with solvent. Blow them off with compressed air.

16. After the head is thoroughly clean, check the cylinder head gasket surface for nicks or damage that could cause an air leak and result in overheating. If deep nicks are found, the cylinder head must be resurfaced or replaced.

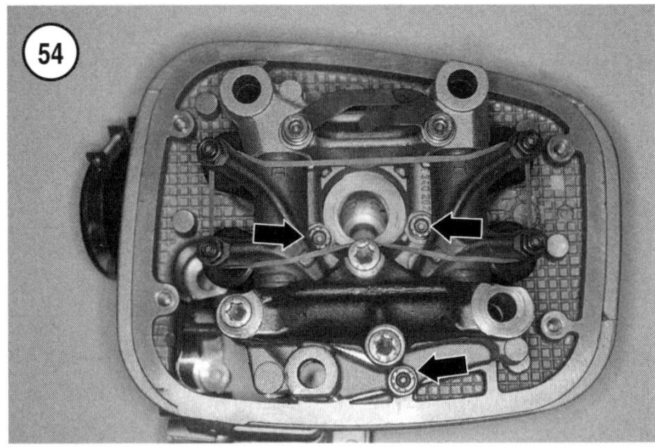

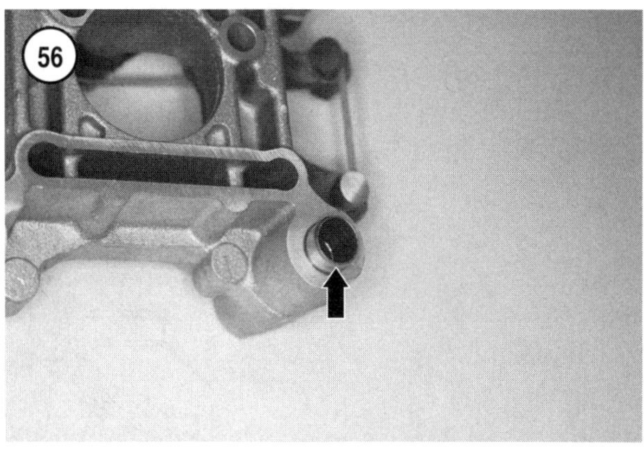

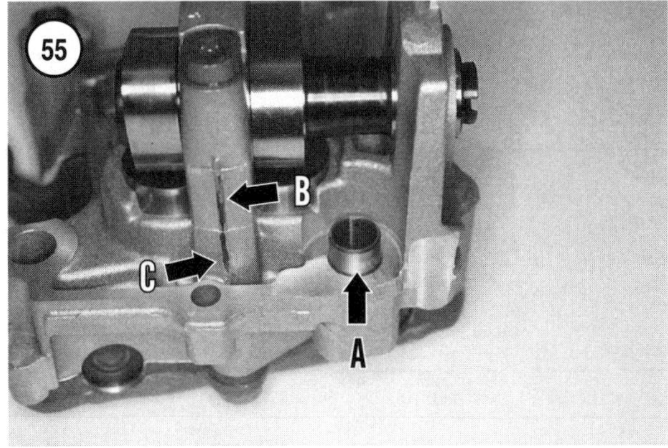

Refer to a BMW dealership or a machine shop experienced in this type of work.

VALVE GEAR HOLDER

Removal/Installation

The valve gear holder contains the camshaft, tappets, pushrods and rocker arm assemblies.

1. Remove the cylinder head as described in this chapter.
2. Place a rubber band around the rocker arm valve adjusters to hold the rocker arms in the raised position.
3. Remove the bolts (**Figure 54**) securing the valve gear holder to the cylinder head and remove the holder assembly. Do not lose the locating dowels on the base of the holder assembly.
4. Inspect all parts as described in this section.
5. If removed, install the locating dowels. Refer to A, **Figure 55** and **Figure 56**.
6. Apply clean engine oil to the camshaft and rocker arms.
7. Install the valve gear holder onto the cylinder head.
8. Install the bolts and tighten them in a crisscross pattern to 15 N·m (11 ft.-lb.).
9. Remove the rubber band.
10. Install the cylinder head as described in this chapter.

Disassembly

Refer to **Figure 57** and **Figure 58**.

1. Remove the valve gear holder as described in this section.
2. Place a rubber band around the rocker arm valve adjusters to hold the rocker arms in the raised position.
3. Loosen the bolts (**Figure 59**) securing the camshaft bearing caps. Do not remove at this time.
4. Remove the Torx bolts (A, **Figure 60**) securing the rocker arm shaft bearing cap. Remove the bearing cap (B, **Figure 60**).
5. Remove the Torx bolts (A, **Figure 61**) securing the contact plate and remove the contact plate (B).
6. Withdraw the rocker arm shafts (**Figure 62**) from the rocker arms and from the end of the valve gear holder. If necessary, insert an appropriate size drill bit into the hole in the end of the shaft and pull the rocker arm shaft free.
7. Remove the rubber band and both rocker arms (**Figure 63**).
8. Remove the short pushrods (**Figure 64**) from the tappets.

NOTE
There is a lightly marked alignment line on the bearing caps and holder and it is sometimes hard to see. Be sure to make the alignment marks in Step 8. Use either a scribe or permanent marker pen.

9. Prior to removing the camshaft bearing caps, make alignment marks on both caps (B, **Figure 55**) and the

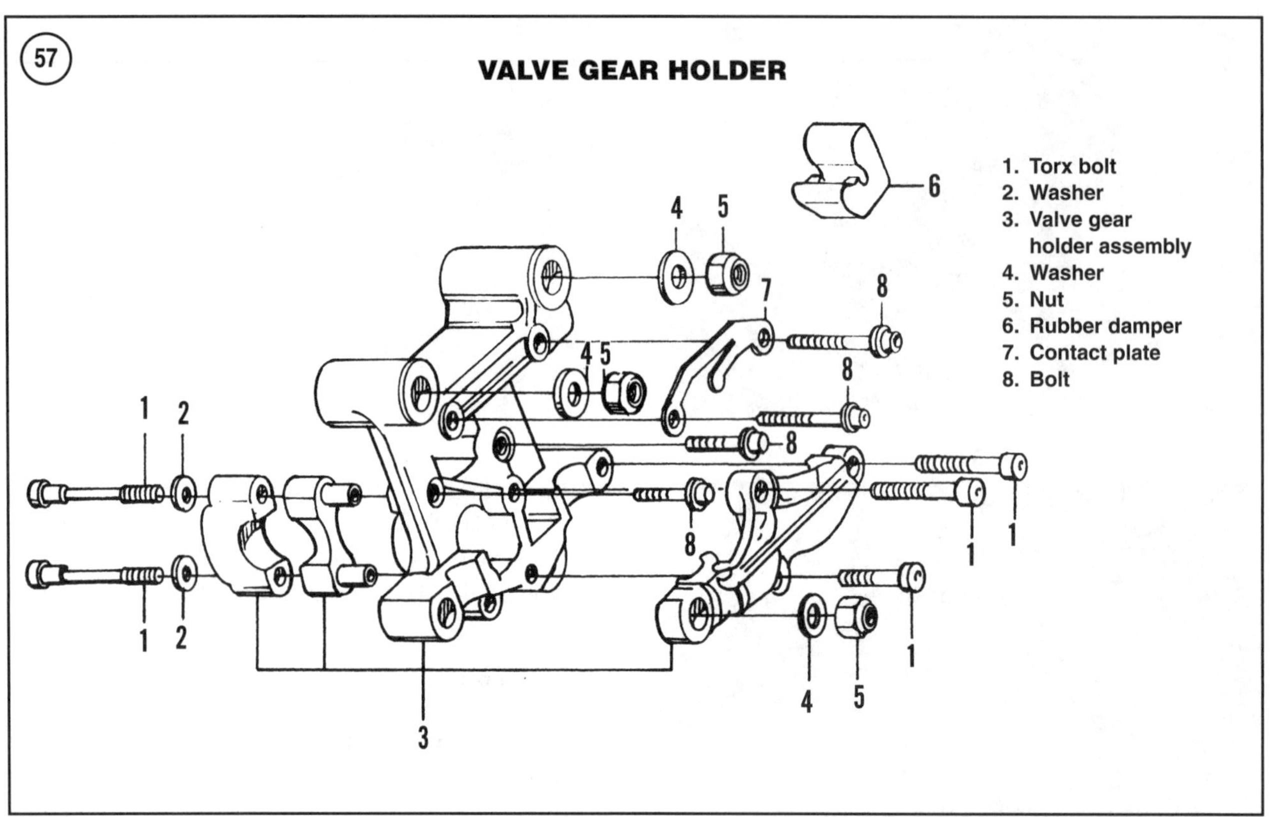

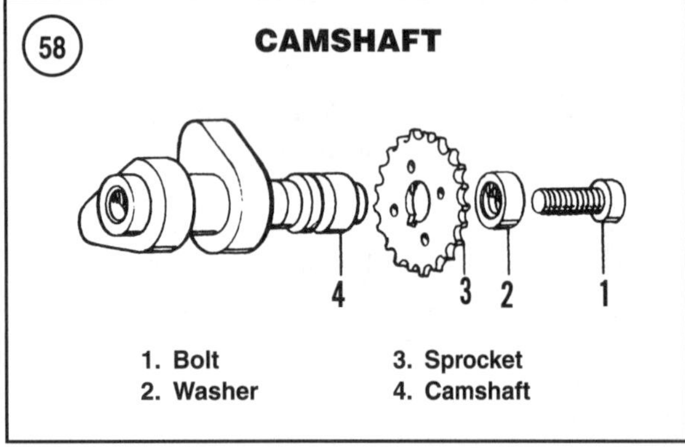

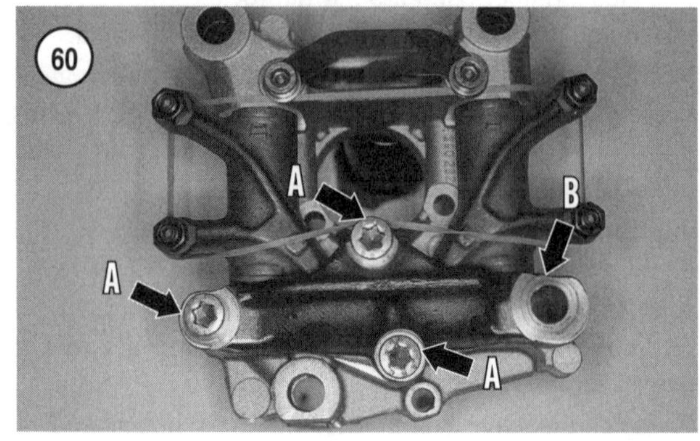

holder (C). This will ensure correct alignment of all three parts during assembly.

10. Remove the bolts and washers (**Figure 59**) loosened in Step 3, securing the camshaft bearing caps.

11. Remove both bearing caps, then the camshaft.

12. Carefully withdraw both tappets (**Figure 65**) from the holder.

13. Inspect all parts as described in this section.

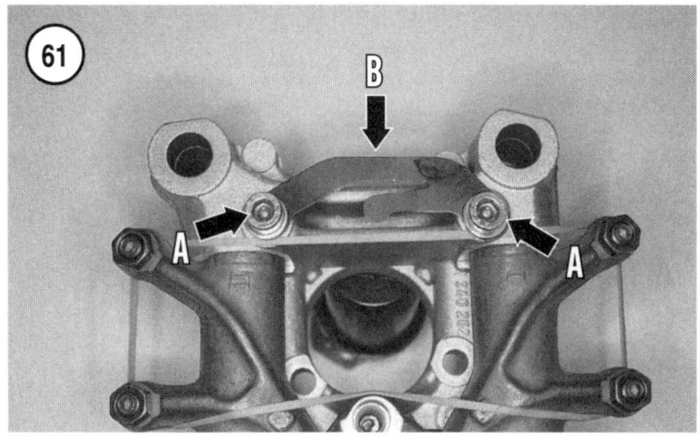

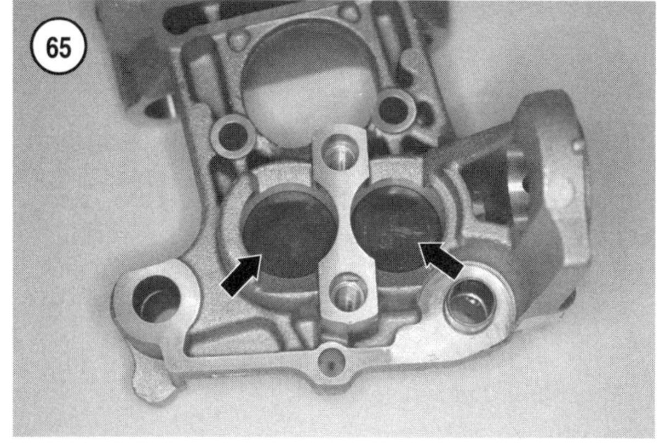

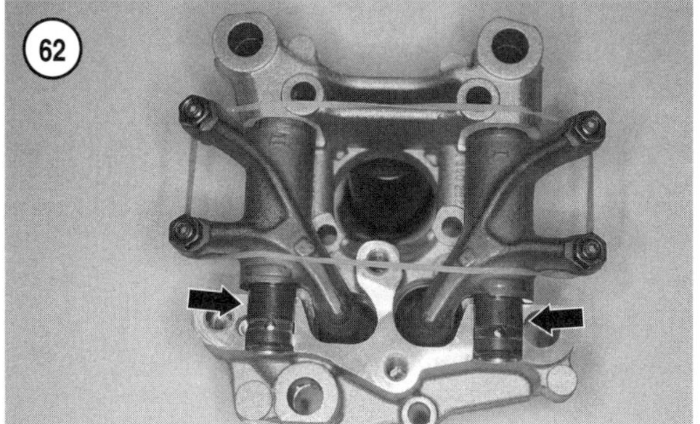

Assembly

1. Apply clean engine oil to the outside of the tappets and to the inner walls of the tappet bores in the valve gear holder.

2. Turn the valve gear holder upside down on the workbench.

3. Position the tappets with the closed side facing out (**Figure 66**) and install both tappets. Push the tappets down until they bottom (**Figure 65**).

4. Apply clean engine oil to the camshaft bearing surfaces and lobes. Also apply clean engine oil to the bearing surfaces in the valve gear holder and the bearing caps.

5. Correctly position the lower bearing cap onto the valve gear holder aligning the marks on each part (**Figure 67**).

6. Install the camshaft into the bearing bore in the valve gear holder and onto the lower bearing cap (**Figure 68**). Push the camshaft into place and slightly rotate it to make sure it seats properly on both parts.

7. Install the locating dowels into the upper bearing cap.

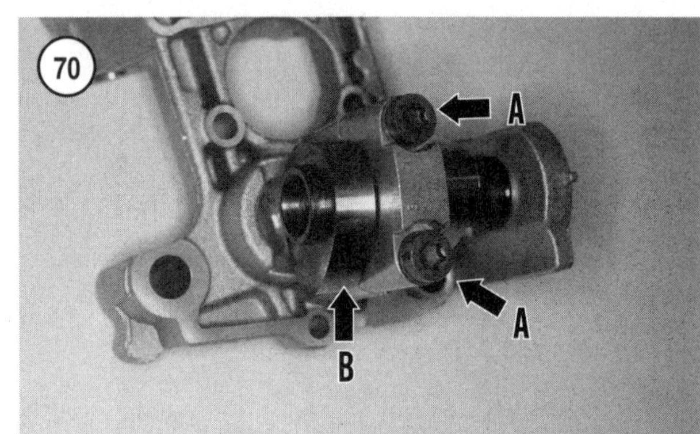

8. Position the upper bearing cap (A, **Figure 69**) onto the lower bearing cap (B), aligning the marks on each part.

9. Install the Torx bolts and washers (A, **Figure 70**) and tighten to 15 N• m (11 ft.-lb.).

10. Position the camshaft with the lobes facing down (B, **Figure 70**) toward the bottom surface of the valve gear holder where it seats against the cylinder head.

11. Turn the valve gear holder upside down.

12. Install the short pushrods (A, **Figure 71**) into the tappet pockets (B).

NOTE
***Figure 72** is shown without the rocker arm in place to better illustrate the rocker arm shaft notch.*

13. Install the rocker arms, then the shafts. Align the rocker arm shaft notch (A, **Figure 72**) with the mounting bolt hole (B) in the valve gear holder. This alignment is necessary so the mounting bolts can pass through and also lock the rocker arm shafts in place.

14. After the installation of the rocker arm shafts, look through the mounting bolt holes (**Figure 73**) and check for correct alignment of the rocker arm shaft notch. If not properly aligned, insert an appropriate size punch into the

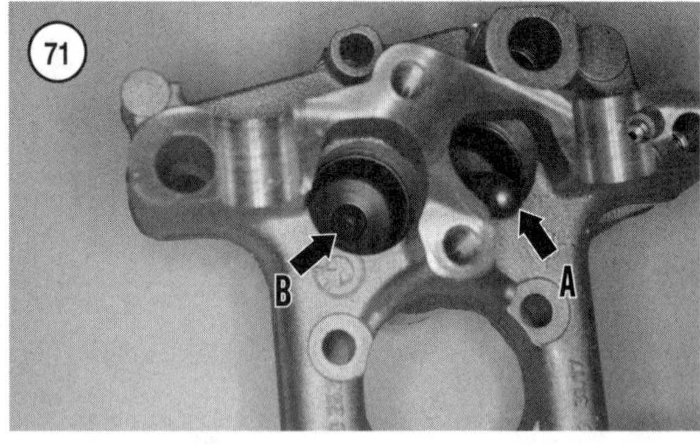

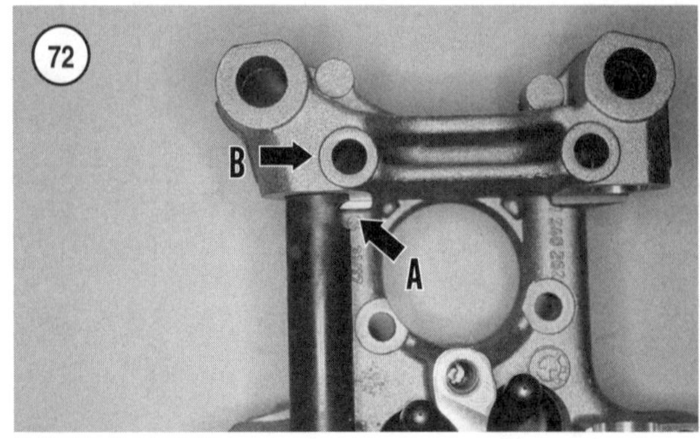

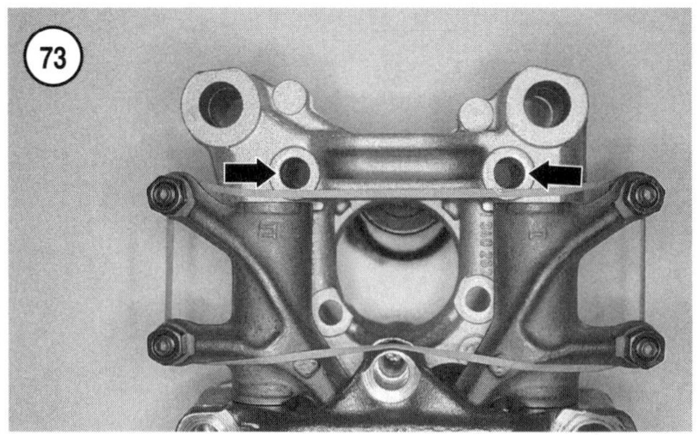
73

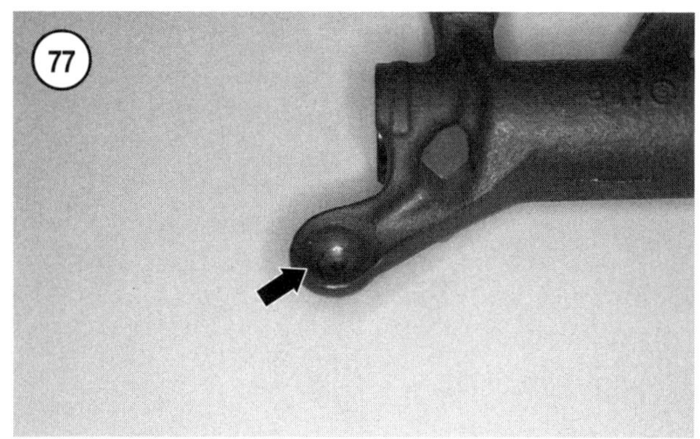
77

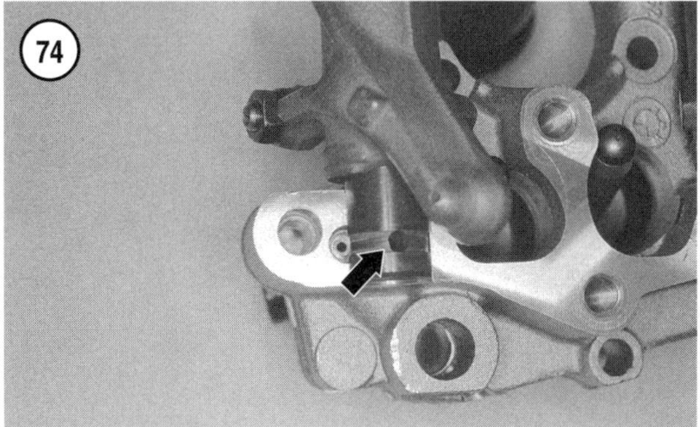
74

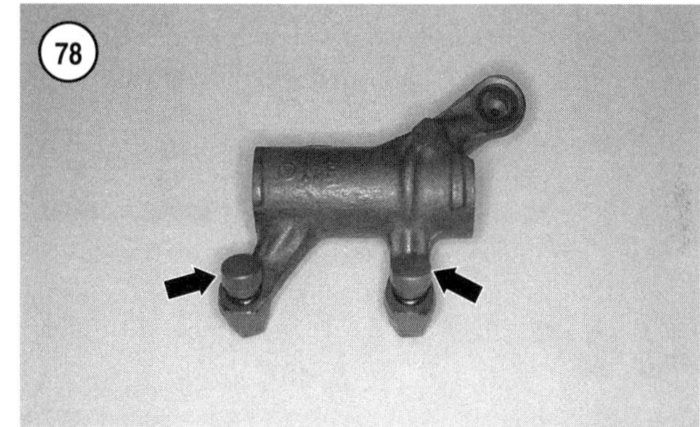
78

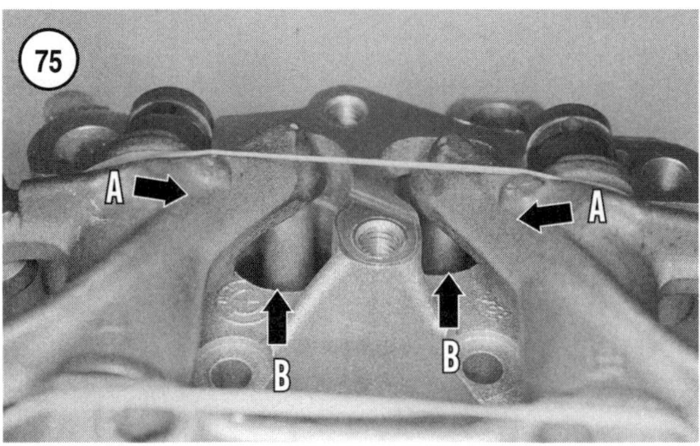

75

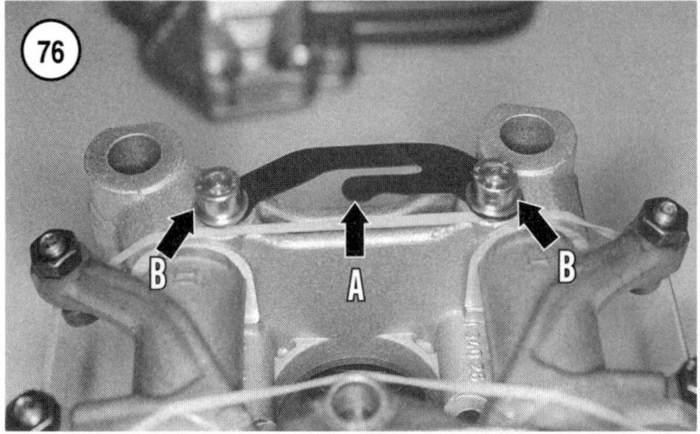

76

rocker arm shaft hole (**Figure 74**) and slightly rotate the shaft until alignment is correct.

15. Pull the rocker arms (A, **Figure 75**) up and position the pocket against the end of the short pushrods (B). Make sure they are properly aligned, then install a rubber band to hold them in this position.
16. Install the contact plate as shown (A, **Figure 76**) and install the Torx bolts (B). Tighten the Torx bolts securely.
17. Install the rocker arm shaft bearing cap (B, **Figure 60**) and bolts (A). Tighten the bolts to15 N•m (11 ft.-lb.).
18. Install the valve gear holder as described in this chapter.

Inspection

Rocker arms and shafts

1. Clean all parts in solvent and with compressed air.
2. Inspect the rocker arms for wear or damage.
3. Inspect the rocker arm pocket (**Figure 77**) where the pushrod rides. Check for scoring or cracks.
4. Check the rocker arm pads (**Figure 78**) where they ride on the valve stems. If the pad(s) is scratched or worn unevenly, replace the rocker arm. Also check the valve stem for wear or damage. Replace if necessary.

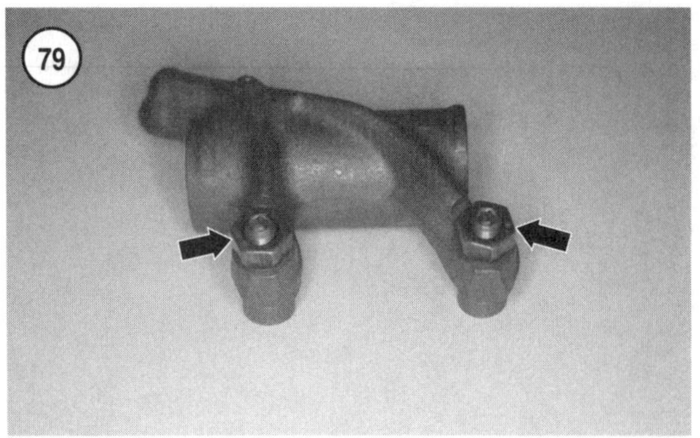

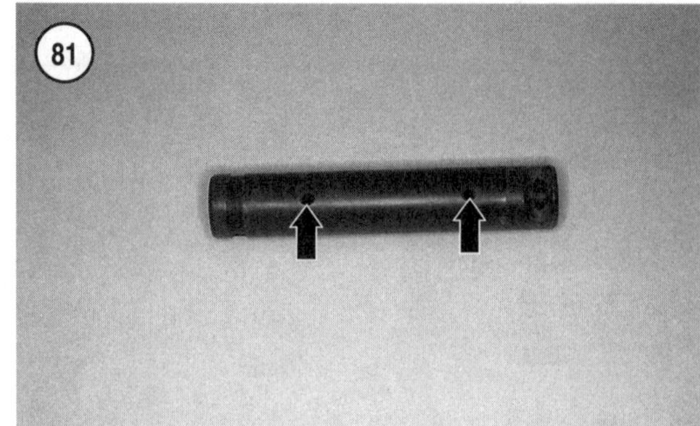

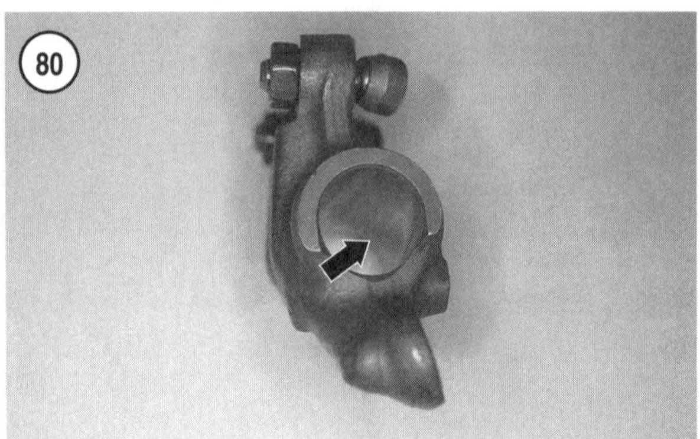

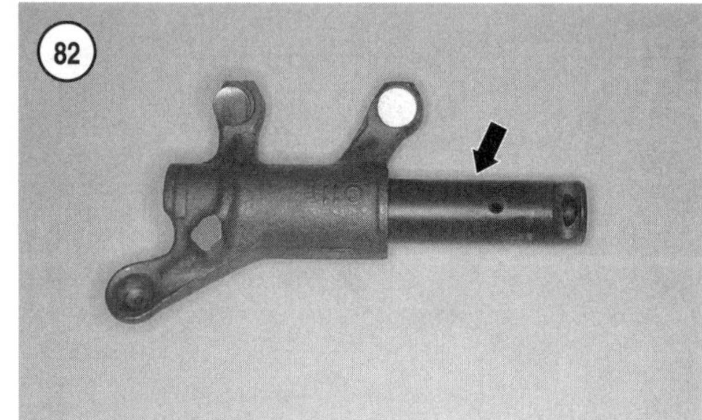

5. Inspect the rocker arm adjusters (**Figure 79**). Loosen the locknut and rotate the adjuster back-and-forth and check for binding. Clean up the threads of all parts if necessary.
6. Inspect the rocker arm bore (**Figure 80**) for wear or scoring.
7. Inspect the rocker arm shaft for wear or scoring. Make sure the oil control holes (**Figure 81**) are clear. Blow out with compressed air if necessary.
8. Insert each rocker arm shaft (**Figure 82**) into the rocker arm. Move it in and out and rotate it slowly and check for binding or looseness.
9. Calculate the rocker arm shaft clearance as follows:
   a. Measure the rocker arm bore inside diameter (**Figure 83**) in several locations with a small bore gauge, then measure the gauge with a micrometer (**Figure 84**) and record the measurement.
   b. Measure the rocker arm shaft diameter (**Figure 85**) in several locations and record the measurement.
   c. Subtract the measurement in substep b from the measurement in substep a to determine rocker arm-to-shaft oil clearance. Replace the rocker arm and shaft if the clearance is worn to the service limit listed in **Table 2** or **Table 3**.
10. Repeat for the other rocker arm assembly.

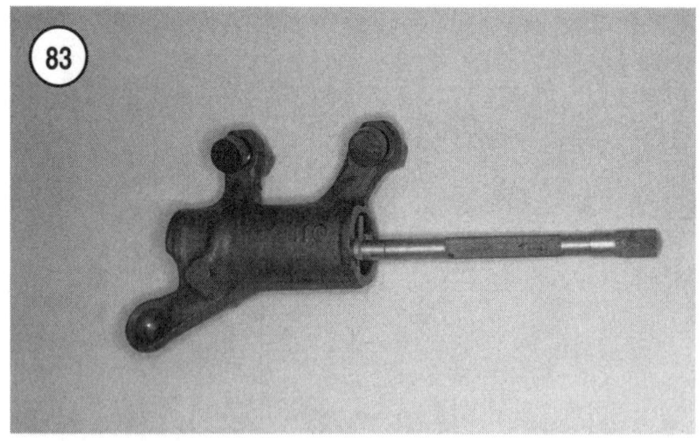

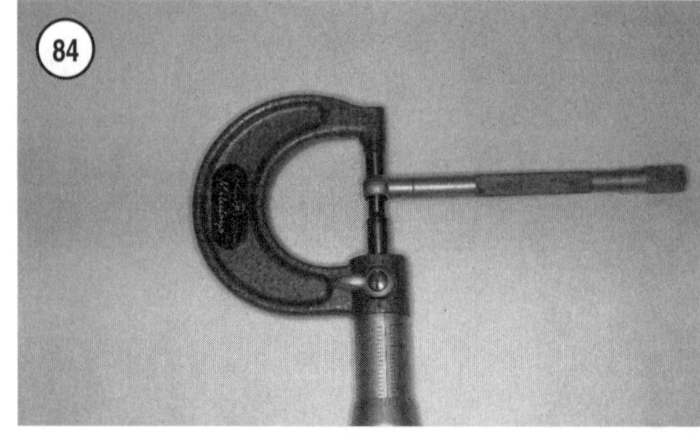

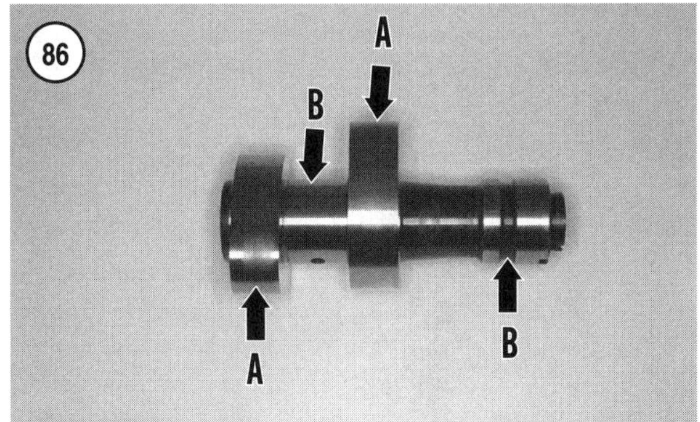

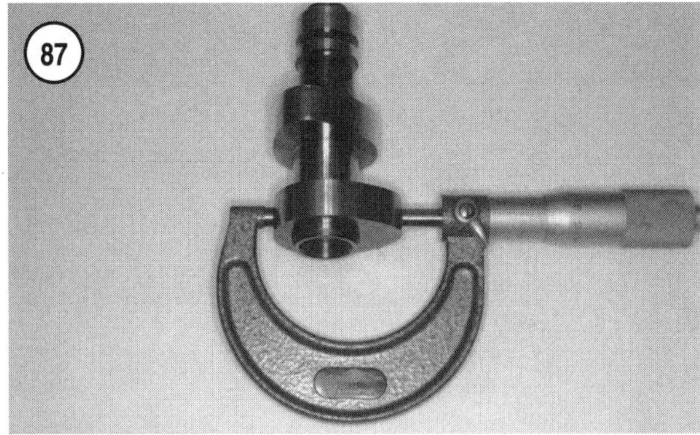

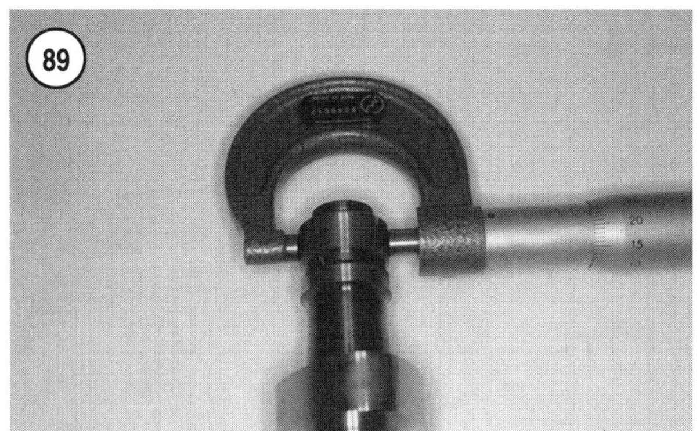

Camshaft, tappets and pushrods

When measuring the camshafts in this section, compare the measurements to the specifications in **Table 2** or **Table 3**. Replace worn or damaged parts as described in this section.

1. Check the camshaft lobes (A, **Figure 86**) for wear. The lobes should not be scored and the edges should be square.

2. Measure the height of each lobe (**Figure 87**) with a micrometer.

3. Check each camshaft bearing journal (B, **Figure 86**) for wear and scoring.

4. Measure each camshaft bearing journal with a micrometer. Refer to **Figure 88** and **Figure 89**.

5. If the bearing journals are severely worn or damaged, check the bearing surfaces in the valve gear holder (**Figure 90**) and bearing caps (**Figure 91**). They should not be scored or excessively worn. If any of the bearing surfaces are worn or scored, the valve gear holder assembly must be replaced as a set. Individual parts are not available.

6. Inspect the camshaft sprocket for broken or chipped teeth. Also check the teeth for cracking or rounding. If the camshaft sprocket(s) is damaged or worn, replace the

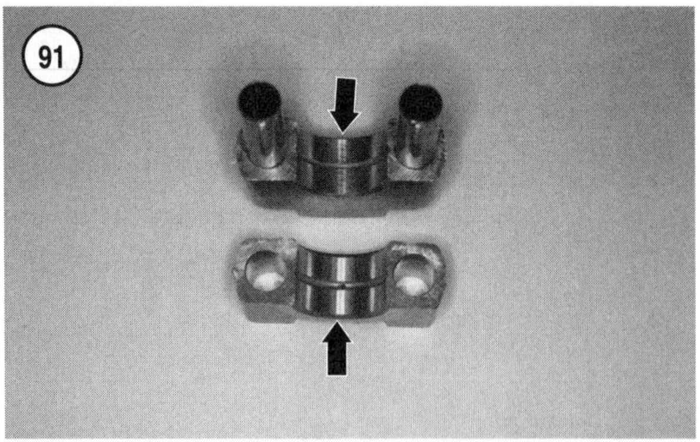

camshaft. Also, inspect the drive (lower) sprocket located on the crankshaft as described in Chapter Five.

NOTE

If the camshaft sprockets are worn, check the camshaft drive chain, chain guides and chain tensioner for wear or damage.

7. Inspect the sides of the tappets (**Figure 92**) for wear and scoring. If damaged, inspect the inner surfaces of the tappet bores in the valve gear holder for possible wear or damage. Replace the tappets if necessary.
8. Calculate the tappet clearance as follows:
   a. Measure the tappet bore diameter (**Figure 93**), in several locations, with a small hole gauge, then measure the small hole gauge with a micrometer and record the measurement.
   b. Measure the tappet diameter (**Figure 94**), in several locations, and record the measurement.
   c. Subtract the measurement in substep b from the measurement in substep a to determine the tappet oil clearance. Replace the tappet if the oil clearance exceeds the service limit in **Table 2** or **Table 3**.
9. Repeat for the other tappet.
10. Inspect the pushrod ends (**Figure 95**) where they ride in the tappet and rocker arm pocket. Check for wear, scoring or rough areas. Place the pushrod into the rocker arm pocket, rotate it (**Figure 96**) and check for smooth operation. Replace if necessary.

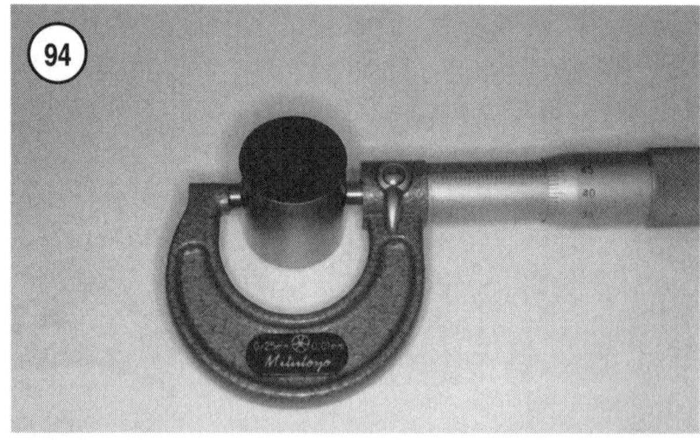

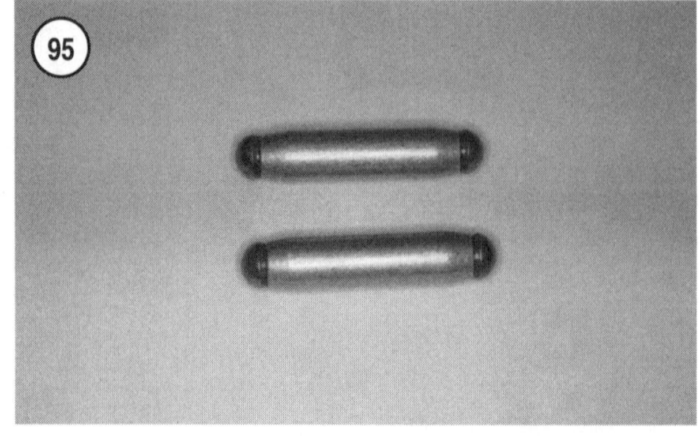

Camshaft bearing clearance measurement

Wipe all oil residue from each camshaft bearing journal and from the bearing surfaces of the valve gear holder and the bearing caps.

1. Measure each camshaft bearing journal with a micrometer. Refer to **Figure 88** and **Figure 89**.

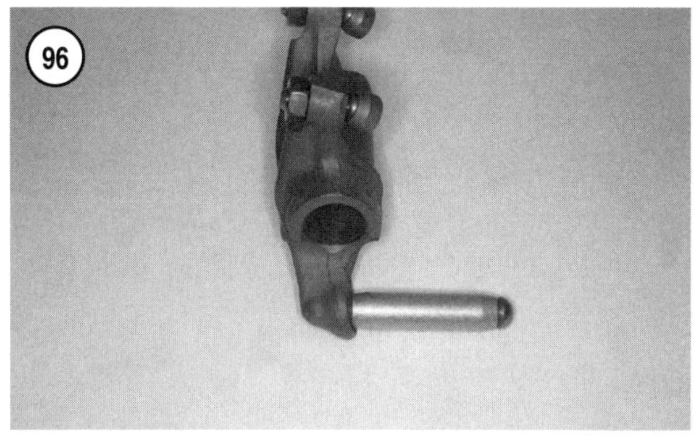
96

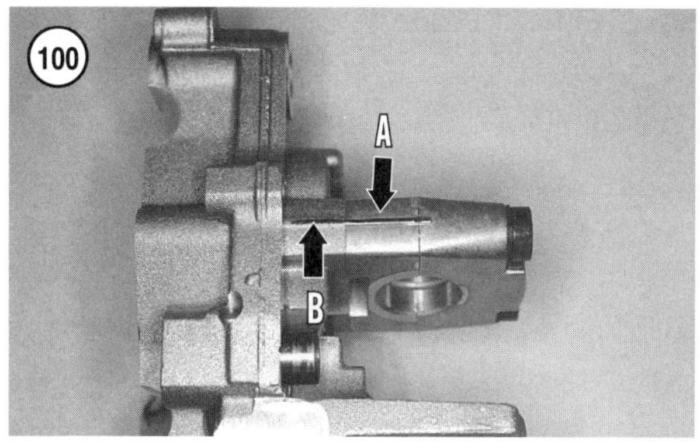

100

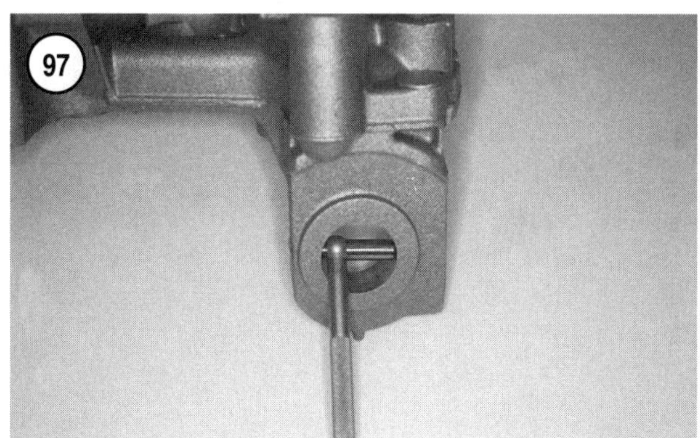
97

101

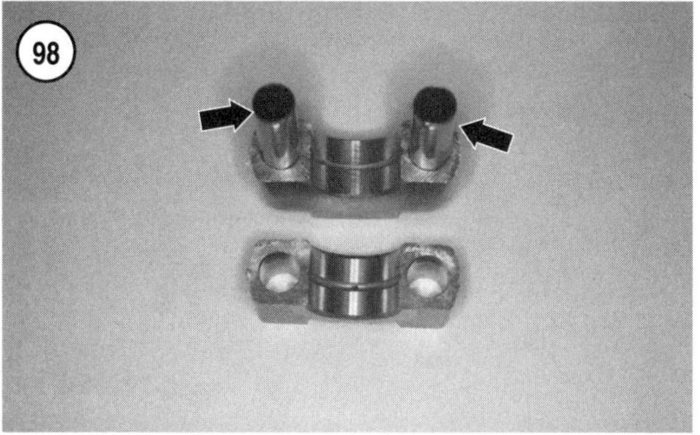
98

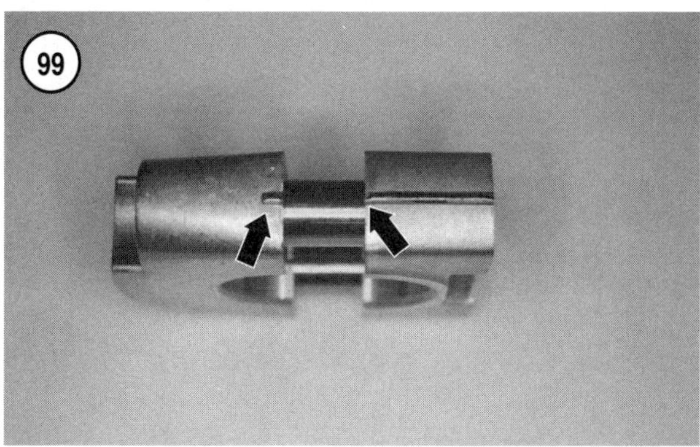
99

2. Measure the inside diameter of the fixed bearing journal with a telescoping gauge (**Figure 97**), then measure the gauge with a micrometer and record the measurement.
3. Assemble the bearing caps as follows:
   a. If removed, install the locating dowels (**Figure 98**).
   b. Align the alignment marks (**Figure 99**) and assemble the bearing caps. Press them together until they are bottomed.
   c. Align the bearing cap assembly alignment marks (A, **Figure 100**) with the mark on the valve gear holder (B) and install the bearing cap assembly onto the valve gear holder.
   d. Install the bolts and washers (**Figure 101**). Tighten the bolts to 15 N•m (11 ft.-lb.).
4. Measure the inside diameter of the bearing journal assembly with a telescoping gauge (**Figure 102**), then measure the gauge with a micrometer and record the measurement.
5. Subtract the camshaft journal's outer diameter from the bearing journal's inner diameter to determine camshaft oil clearance. Replace the camshaft and/or valve gear holder assembly if the oil clearance exceeds the service limit listed in **Table 2** or **Table 3**.
6. Disassemble the bearing caps from the valve gear holder.

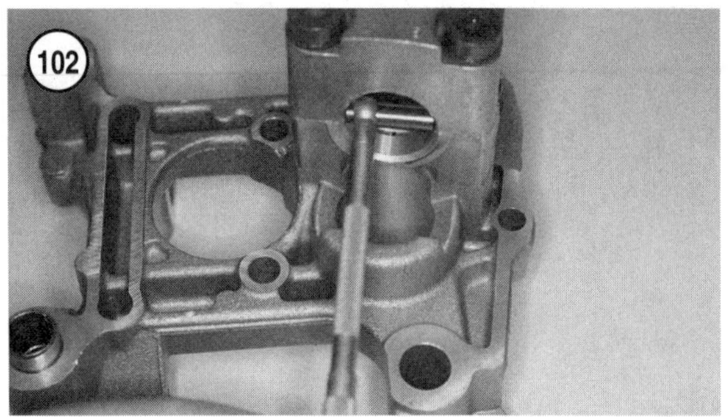

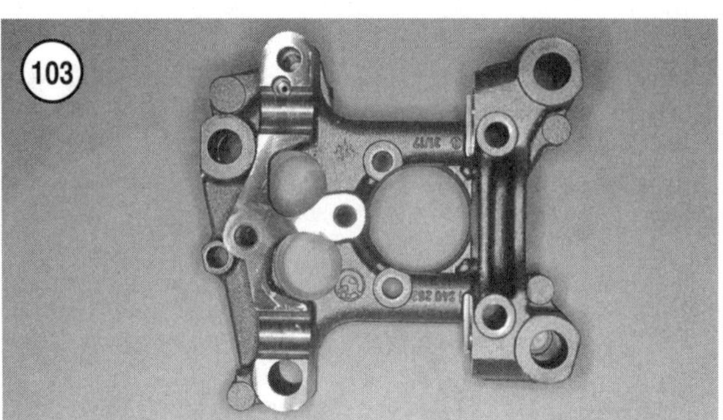

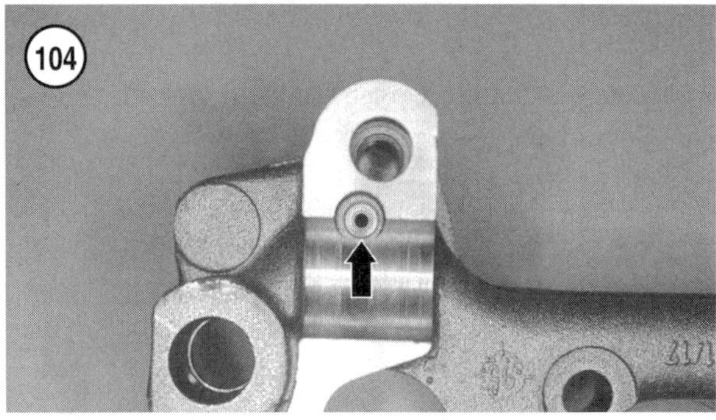

Valve gear holder and bearing cap

1. Check the valve gear holder (**Figure 103**) for wear or damage.
2. Make sure the oil control hole (**Figure 104**) is clear. If necessary, clean it out with solvent and clear with compressed air.
3. Check the rocker arm shaft bearing surfaces in the valve gear holder (**Figure 105**) and the bearing cap (**Figure 106**). They should not be scored or excessively worn. If any of the bearing surfaces are worn or scored, the valve gear holder assembly must be replaced as a set. Individual parts are not available.
4. Check the rocker arm bearing cap (**Figure 107**) for wear or damage.

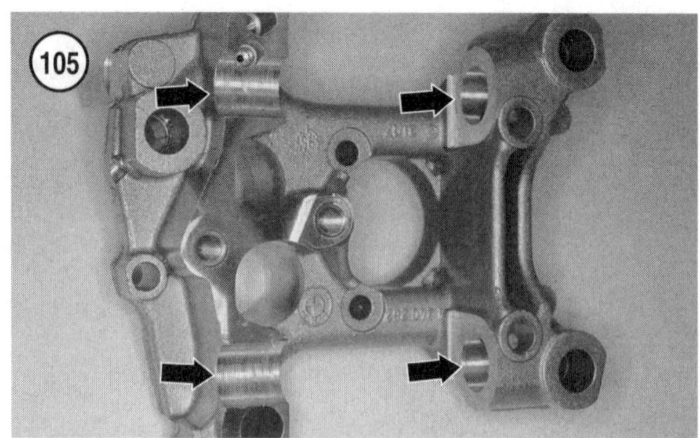

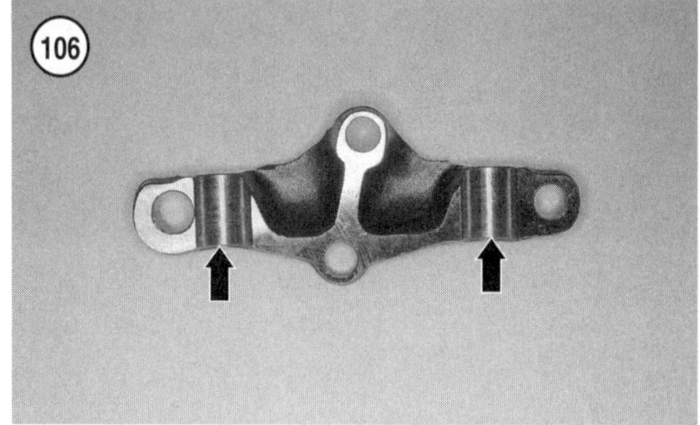

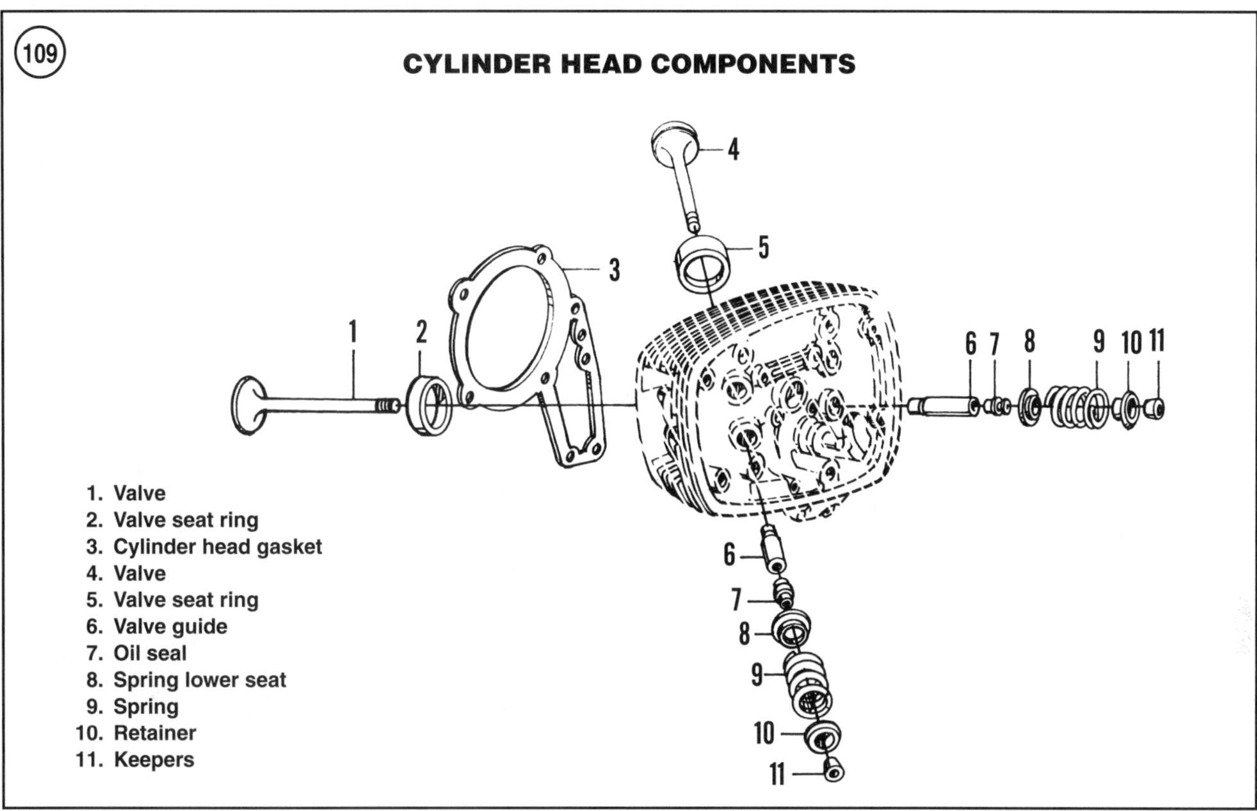

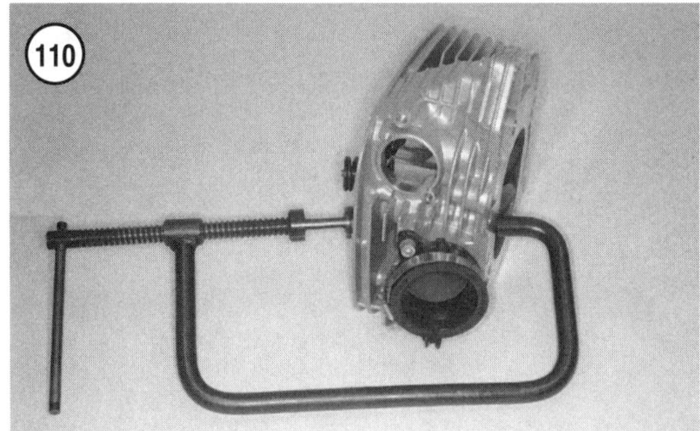

VALVES AND VALVE COMPONENTS

Due to the number of special tools and the skills required to use them, it is general practice for those who perform their own service to remove the cylinder heads and entrust valve service to a BMW dealership or machine shop. The following procedures describe how to check for valve component wear and to determine what type of service is required.

A valve spring compressor (BMW part No. 11-5-690 [**Figure 108**] or equivalent) is required to remove and install the valves.

Valve Removal

Refer to **Figure 109** for this procedure.

1. Remove the cylinder head(s) as described in this chapter.
2. Install a valve spring compressor squarely over the valve spring retainer (**Figure 110**) and place the other end of the tool against the valve head (**Figure 111**).
3. Tighten the valve spring compressor until the valve keepers separate from the valve stem. Lift the valve keepers out through the valve spring compressor with a magnet or needlenose pliers.

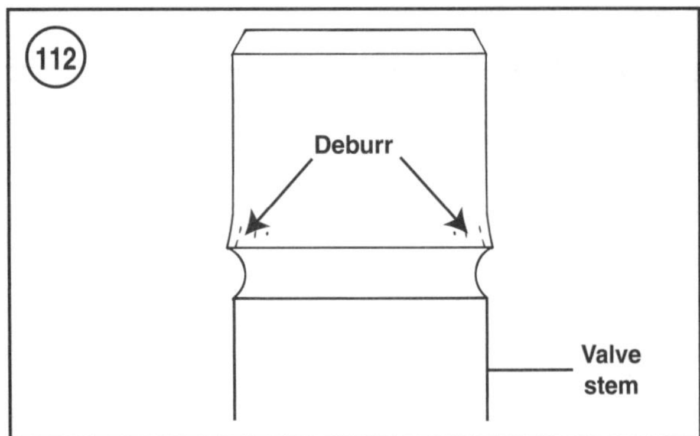

4. Gradually loosen the valve spring compressor and remove it from the cylinder head.
5. Remove the spring retainer and the valve spring.

CAUTION

*Remove any burrs from the valve stem groove (**Figure 112**) before removing the valve; otherwise the valve guides will be damaged.*

6. Remove the valve from the cylinder head.

NOTE

If the valve is difficult to remove, it may be bent, causing it to stick in the valve guide. This condition will require valve and valve guide replacement.

7. Remove the spring seat.
8. Pull the valve stem seal off of the valve guide. Discard the seal.

CAUTION

*All parts of each valve assembly must be kept together (**Figure 113**). Place each set in a plastic bag, divided carton or into separate small boxes. Label the sets as to which cylinder and either intake or exhaust valves. This will keep them from getting mixed up and will make installation simpler. Do not intermix components from the valves or excessive wear may result.*

9. Mark all parts as they are removed to ensure that they will be installed in their same locations.
10. Repeat Steps 2-9 and remove the remaining valves—keep all valve sets separate.

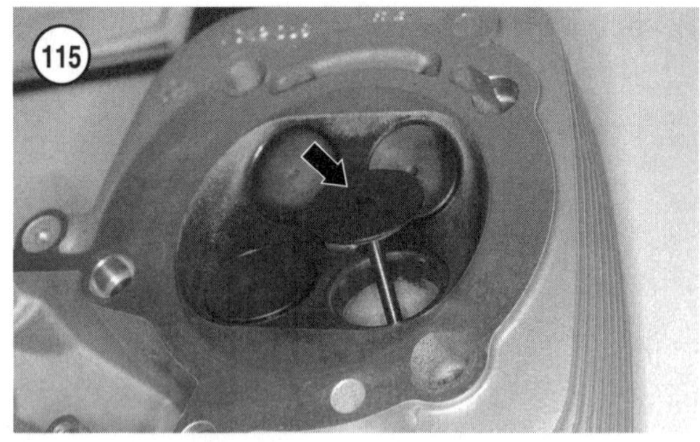

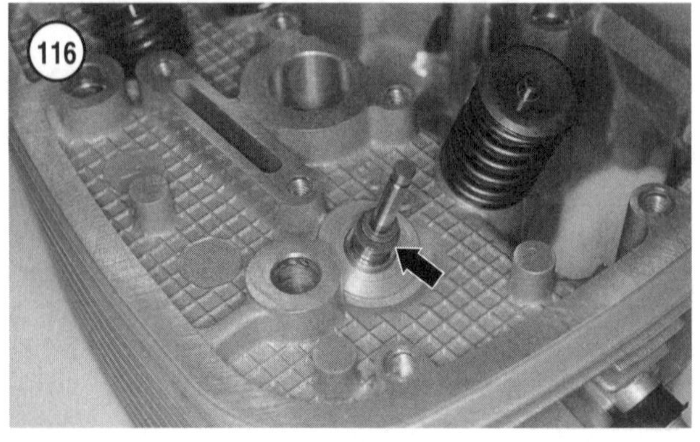

Valve Installation

1. Clean the end of the valve guide.

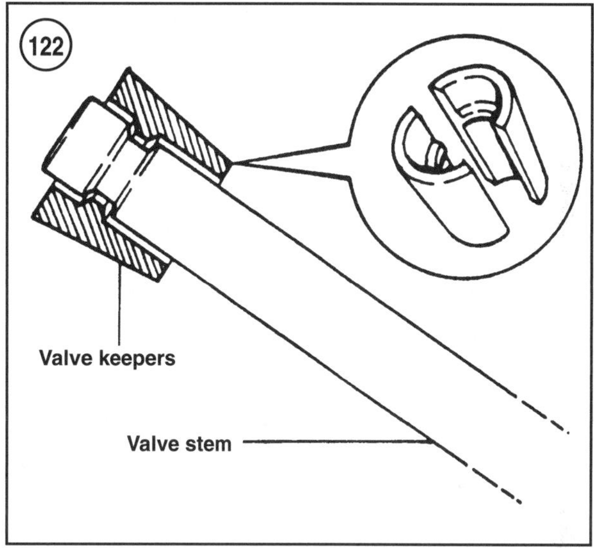

2. Apply clean engine oil to the new valve stem seal and install it over the end of the valve guide. Push it down until it completely seats on the cylinder head surface (**Figure 114**).
3. Coat a valve stem with molybdenum disulfide paste. Install the valve (**Figure 115**) part way into the guide. Then, slowly turn the valve as it enters the valve seal (**Figure 116**) and continue turning it until the valve installs all the way.
4. Install the lower spring seat over the valve seal (**Figure 117**) and push it down until it is completely seated on the cylinder head surface.
5. Install the valve spring (**Figure 118**) and make sure it is properly seated on the lower spring seat.
6. Install the retainer on top of the valve spring (**Figure 119**).
7. Compress the valve springs with a valve spring compressor (**Figure 120**) and install the valve keepers (**Figure 121**). Make sure the keepers fit correctly into the rounded groove in the valve stem (**Figure 122**).

8. Remove the valve spring compressor tool.

CAUTION

If Step 9 is not performed, the valve keepers may pop out of the valve stem groove after the cylinder head has been installed and the engine started. This may result in engine damage.

9. Place a drift onto the top of the valve stem (**Figure 123**) and tap on the end with a hammer several times to ensure the keepers are seated correctly. If the keepers are not installed correctly, they will pop out at this time.
10. Repeat Steps 1-9 for the remaining valves.
11. Install the cylinder head as described in this chapter.
12. After installing the cylinder head, adjust the valve clearance as described in Chapter Three.

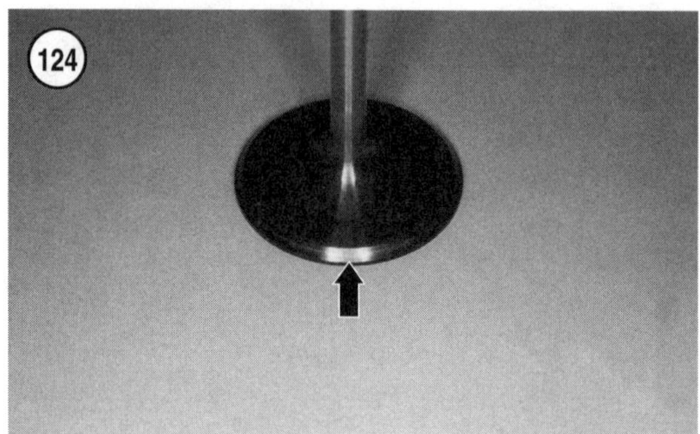

Valve and Valve Seat Inspection

When measuring the valve components in this section, compare the measurements to the specifications listed in **Table 2** or **Table 3**. Replace parts that are damaged or out of specification as described in this section.

1. Clean the valves in solvent. Do not damage the valve seating surface.
2. Inspect the valve face (**Figure 124**) for burning, pitting or other signs of wear. Unevenness of the valve face is an indication that the valve is not serviceable. If the wear on a valve is too extensive to be corrected by hand-lapping the valve into its seat, replace the valve. The face on the valve cannot be ground. Replace the valve if defective.
3. Inspect the valve stem for wear and roughness.
4. Measure each valve head edge thickness (**Figure 125**).
5. Measure the outside diameter of each valve head.
6. Check the valve head runout with a V-block and dial indicator as shown in **Figure 126**.
7. Remove all carbon and varnish from the valve guides (**Figure 127**) with a stiff spiral wire brush before measuring wear. Then clean the valve guides with solvent to wash out all debris. Dry with compressed air.
8. Measure each valve stem outside diameter with a micrometer (**Figure 128**). Note the following:
    a. If a valve stem is out of specification, replace the valve.
    b. If a valve stem is within specification, record the measurement so it can be used to determine the valve stem-to-guide clearance in Step 11.
9. Insert each valve into its respective valve guide and move it up and down by hand. The valve should move smoothly.

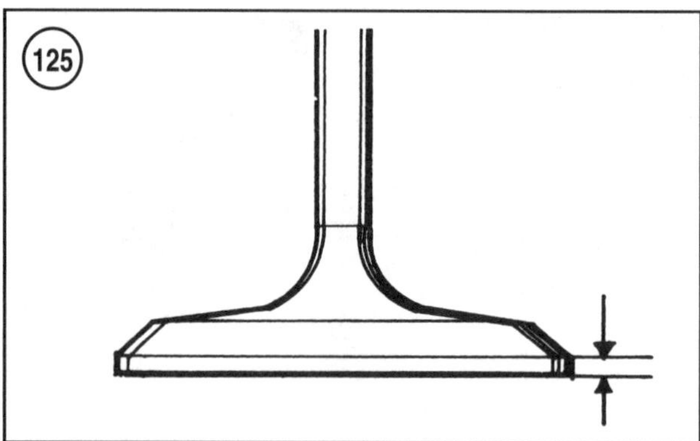

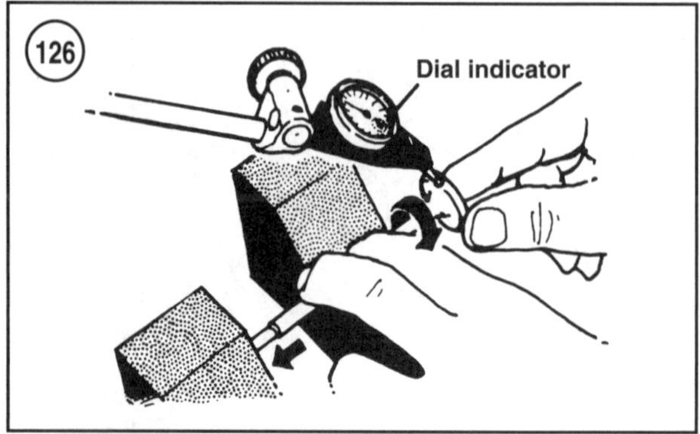

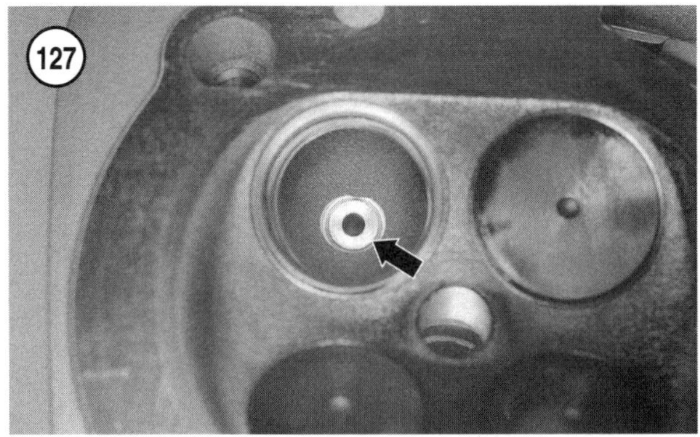

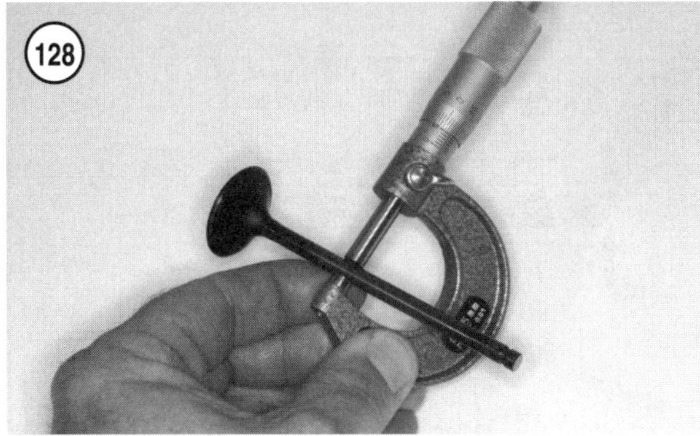

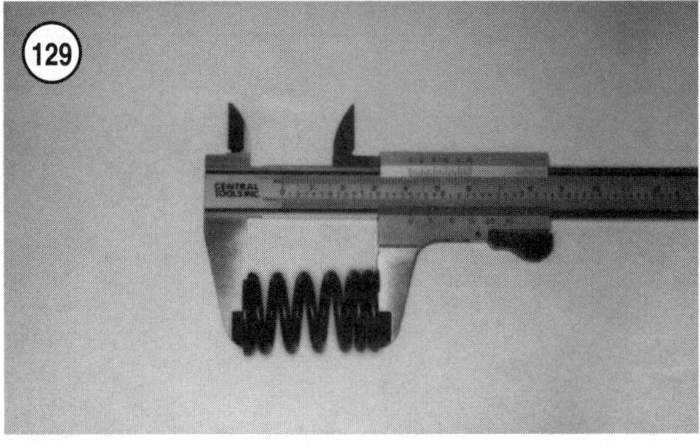

10. Measure each valve guide inside diameter with a small bore gauge and record the measurements. Note the following:

NOTE
Because valve guides wear unevenly (oval shape), measure each guide at different positions. Use the largest bore diameter measurement when determining its size.

a. If a valve guide is out of specification, replace it as described in this section.
b. If a valve guide is within specification, record the measurement so it can be used to determine the valve stem-to-guide clearance in Step 11.

11. Subtract the measurement made in Step 8 from the measurement made in Step 10 to determine the valve stem-to-guide clearance. Note the following:

a. If the clearance is out of specification, determine if a new guide would bring the clearance within specification.
b. If the clearance would be out of specification with a new guide, replace the valve and valve guide as a set.

12. Inspect the valve springs as follows:

a. Inspect each spring for any cracks, distortion or other damage.
b. Measure the free length of each valve spring with a vernier caliper (**Figure 129**).
c. Replace the defective spring(s).

13. Check the upper retainer and valve keepers. If they are in good condition, they may be reused; replace in pairs as necessary.

14. Inspect the valve seats as described under *Valve Seat Inspection* in this section.

4

Valve Guide Replacement

If valve guides are excessively worn, the guides must be replaced. Due to the number of special tools and the skills required to use them, it is general practice for those who perform their own service to remove the cylinder heads and entrust valve guide service to a BMW dealership or machine shop. If the valve guide is replaced, also replace the respective valve.

Valve Seat Inspection

The most accurate method for checking the valve seal is to use a marking compound (machinist's dye), available from auto parts and tool stores. Marking compound is used to locate high or irregular spots when checking or making close fits. Follow the manufacturer's directions.

NOTE
Because of the close operating tolerances within the valve assembly, the valve stem and guide must be within tolerance; otherwise the inspection results will be inaccurate.

1. Remove the valves as described in this chapter.
2. Clean the valve seat in the cylinder head and valve mating areas with contact cleaner.

3. Thoroughly clean all carbon deposits from the valve face with solvent and dry thoroughly.
4. Spread a thin layer of marking compound evenly on the valve face.
5. Slowly insert the valve into its guide.
6. Support the valve with two fingers and tap the valve up and down in the cylinder head (**Figure 130**). Do *not* rotate the valve or a false reading will result.
7. Remove the valve and examine the impression left by the marking compound. If the impression on the valve or in the cylinder head is not even and continuous and the valve seat width (**Figure 131**) is not within the specified tolerance (**Table 2** or **Table 3**) the valve seat in the cylinder head must be reconditioned.
8. Closely examine the valve seat in the cylinder head (**Figure 132**). It should be smooth and even with a polished seating surface.
9. If the valve seat is not in good condition have a BMW dealership or machine shop recondition the valve seat.
10. Repeat for the other valves.

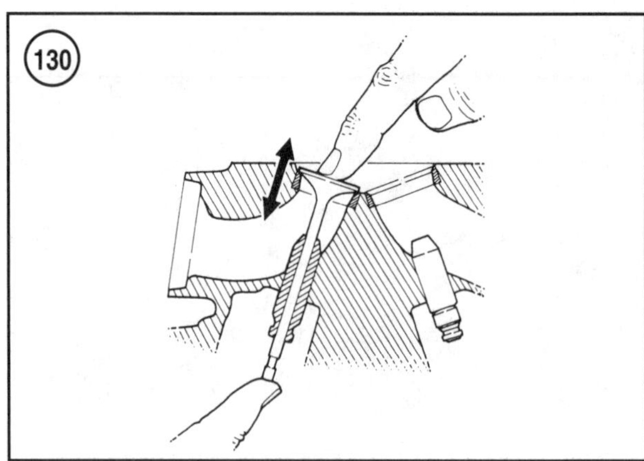

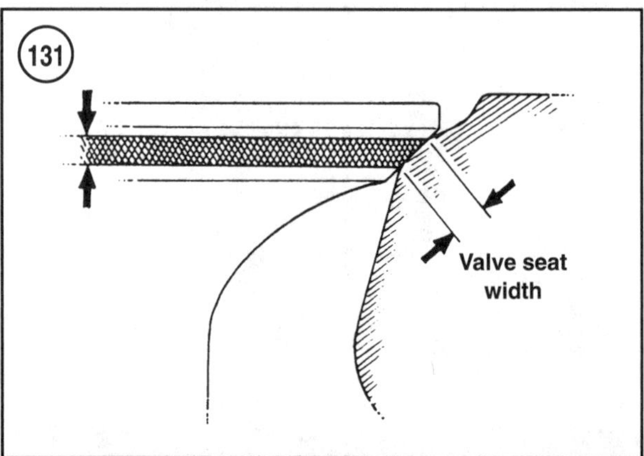

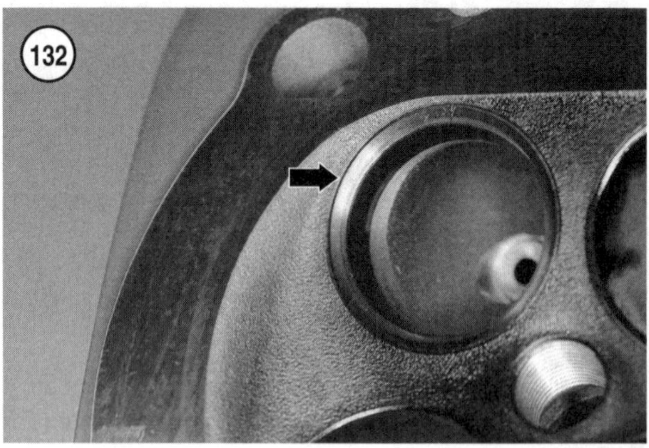

Valve Seat Reconditioning

Due to the number of special tools and the skills required to use them, it is general practice for those who perform their own service to remove the cylinder heads and entrust valve service to a BMW dealership or machine shop.

Valve Lapping

Valve lapping can restore the valve seat without machining if the amount of wear or distortion is not too great.

This procedure should only be performed after determining that the valve seat width and outside diameter are within specifications.

1. Apply a light coating of fine grade valve lapping compound on the valve face seating surface.
2. Insert the valve into the head.
3. Wet the suction cup of the lapping stick and stick it onto the head of the valve. Spin the tool in both directions, while pressing it against the valve seat and lap the valve to the seat. Every 5 to 10 seconds, lift and rotate the valve 180° in the valve seat. Continue until the mating surfaces on the valve and seat are smooth and equal in size.
4. Closely examine the valve seat in the cylinder head (**Figure 132**). It should be smooth and even with a polished seating ring.
5. Repeat Steps 1-4 for the other valves.
6. Thoroughly clean the valves and cylinder head in solvent and then with hot soapy water to remove all valve grinding compound. Dry thoroughly.

CAUTION
Any compound left on the valves or in the cylinder head causes excessive wear to the engine components.

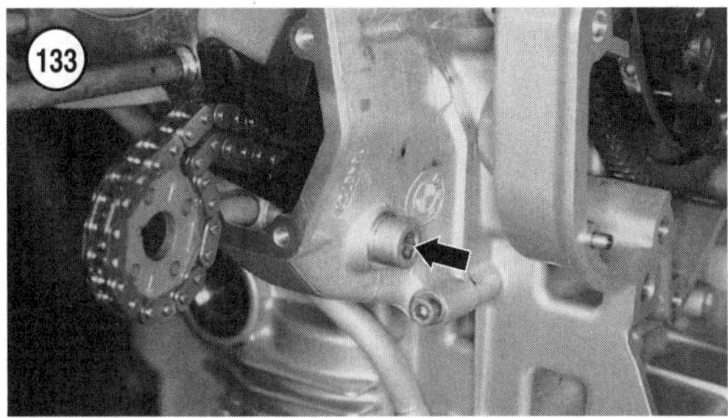
133

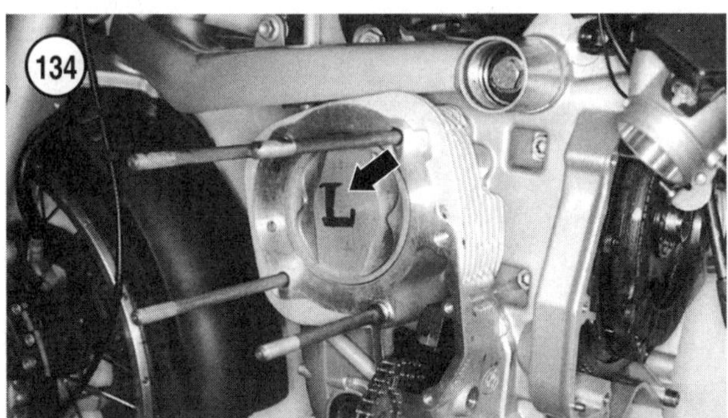
134

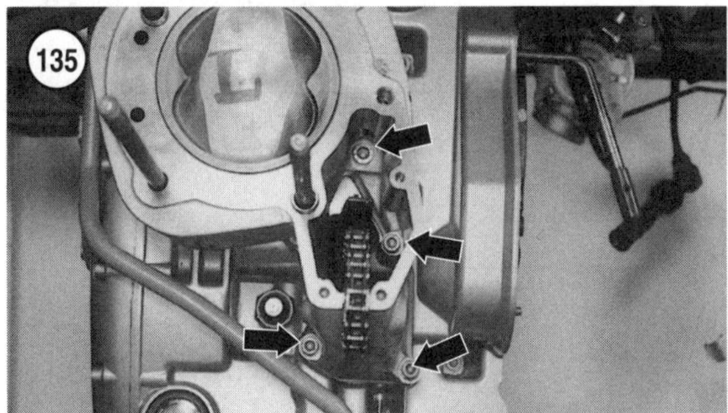
135

7. Install the valve assemblies as described in this chapter.

8. After the lapping is completed and the valves are reinstalled in the head, perform the solvent test under *Cylinder Head, Inspection* in this chapter. There should be no leakage past the seat. If leakage occurs, the combustion chamber appears wet. If fluid leaks past any of the seats, disassemble that valve assembly and repeat the lapping procedure until there is no leakage.

NOTE
This solvent test does not ensure long-term durability or maximum power. It merely ensures maximum compression will be available on initial start-up after assembly.

136

9. If the cylinder head and valve components are cleaned in detergent and hot water, apply a light coat of engine oil to all bare metal surfaces to prevent rust formation.

CYLINDER AND PISTON

The alloy cylinders use a pressed-in, cast iron liner that can be bored 0.50 mm (0.020 in.) oversize. Oversize pistons and rings are available from BMW dealerships.

The pistons are made of aluminum alloy. The piston pin is made of steel and is a precision fit in the pistons. The piston pins are held in place by an external snap ring at each end.

NOTE
Due to the size of the cylinder bore it is recommended that the cylinder and piston be removed from the crankcase as an assembly. By doing this it will make piston removal and installation easier and lessen the chance of piston ring and cylinder wall damage.

Removal

1. Remove the cylinder head as described in this chapter.
2. Remove the camshaft drive chain guide rail bearing bolt and washer (**Figure 133**).
3. Mark the top of the piston with the identification letter L (left cylinder) (**Figure 134**) or R (right cylinder). The left side refers to a rider sitting on the seat facing forward. These marks make it easier to ensure that the pistons are installed onto the correct connecting rods and into the correct cylinder bores.
4. Remove the Allen bolts and washers (**Figure 135**) mounting the cylinder to the crankcase.
5. Loosen the cylinder by tapping around the perimeter with a rubber or plastic mallet.
6. When the cylinder is free, pull the cylinder (**Figure 136**) straight out part-way to gain access to the piston pin

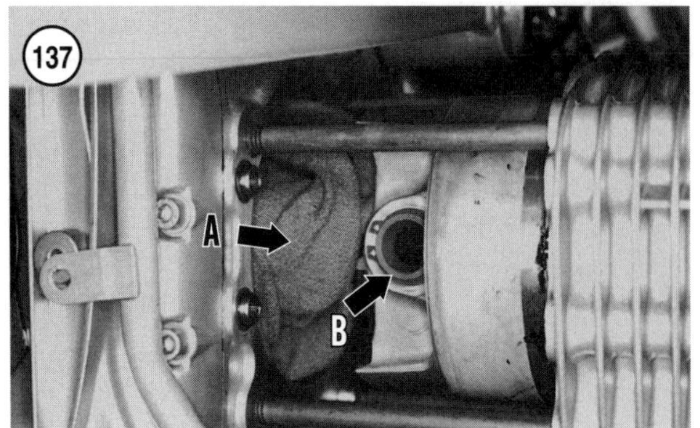

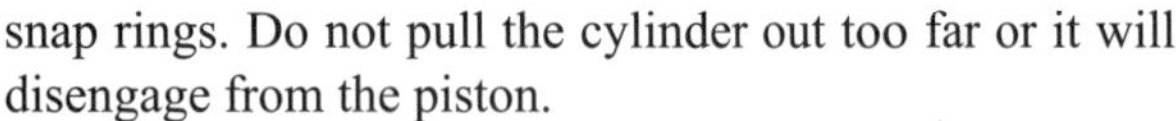

snap rings. Do not pull the cylinder out too far or it will disengage from the piston.

7. Place a clean shop cloth (A, **Figure 137**) into the crankcase opening to prevent a snap ring from falling into the opening.

8. Remove the front snap ring (B, **Figure 137**).

9. Remove the rear snap ring (**Figure 138**).

10. Slowly press the piston pin (**Figure 139**) out of the piston and connecting rod by hand. If the pin is tight, use a tool (**Figure 140**) and remove it. Do not drive the piston pin out as this action may damage the piston pin, connecting rod or piston. Remove the piston pin.

11. Slowly slide the cylinder and piston assembly farther away from the crankcase and carefully lower the connecting rod (**Figure 141**).

12. Slowly slide the cylinder and piston assembly completely off of the crankcase studs.

13. Suspend the connecting rod's outer ends with rubber bands secured to the crankcase studs as shown in **Figure 142**. This will lessen the chance of damage to both the connecting rods and to the crankcase openings if the crankshaft must be rotated.

14. If loose, remove the cylinder locating dowels and O-rings. Discard the O-rings.

15. Turn the cylinder upside down on several shop cloths. Carefully withdraw the piston from the cylinder.

16. Cover the crankcase opening to prevent debris from entering the crankcase.

17. Repeat for the other cylinder and piston if necessary.

18. Inspect all parts as described in this section.

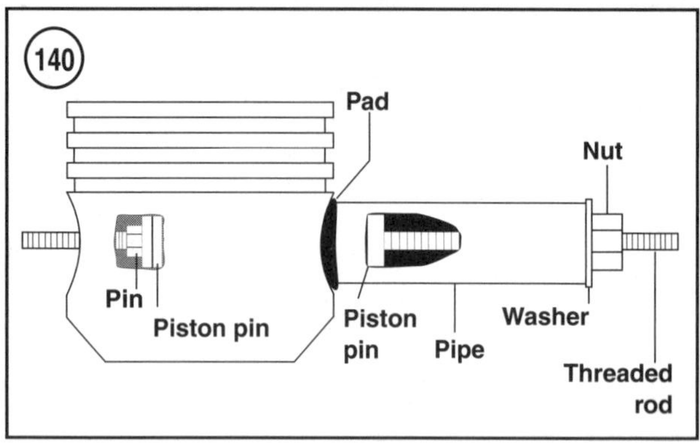

Installation

1. Apply clean engine oil to the cylinder bore, piston skirt, piston ring grooves and rings.

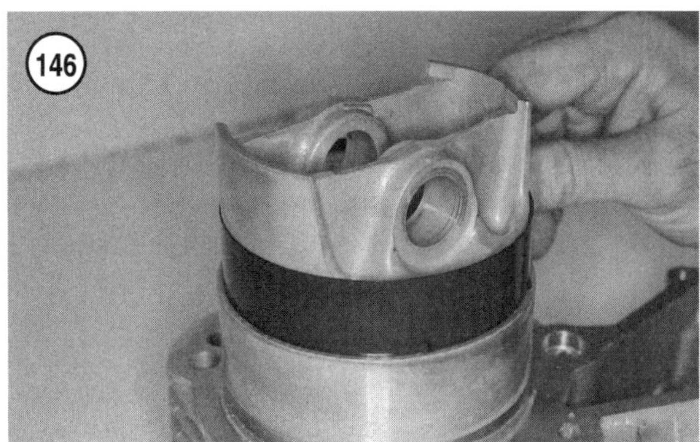

NOTE
Install the correct piston into the correct cylinder. Refer to the marks made during removal Step 3.

2. Rotate the oil ring to position the gap toward the top of the cylinder. Stagger each remaining ring 120° apart.
3. Install a piston ring compressor onto the piston (**Figure 143**).

CAUTION
The leading surface of the cylinder and cylinder head are tilted down from true horizontal. But the valves are positioned in a true horizontal plane with the crankcase. The piston therefore must be installed correctly in the cylinder to align the piston crown reliefs with the valves. If the piston is installed backward, the valves will contact the piston crown at TDC.

4. Position the piston with the location mark (**Figure 144**) facing toward the exhaust side of the cylinder. The arrow (**Figure 145**) must face toward the front, or exhaust side, of the engine.
5. Insert the piston into the base of the cylinder (**Figure 146**).
6. Hold the ring compressor tightly against the piston rings and slowly press the piston and rings into the cylinder bore. Push the piston in until all rings are inside the cylinder bore (**Figure 147**), then stop and remove the ring compressor. Do not press the piston in any farther as the piston pin bore must be exposed for piston pin installation.
7. Clean the crankcase mating surface of all gasket material.
8. Verify that the top and bottom of the cylinder surfaces are clean of all gasket material.
9. Remove the rubber band suspending the connecting rod.

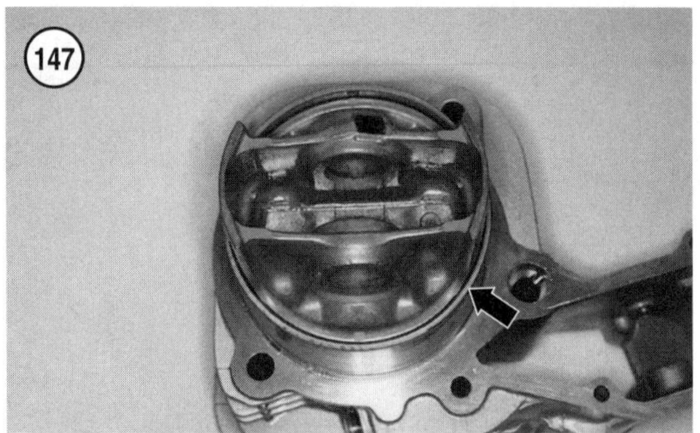

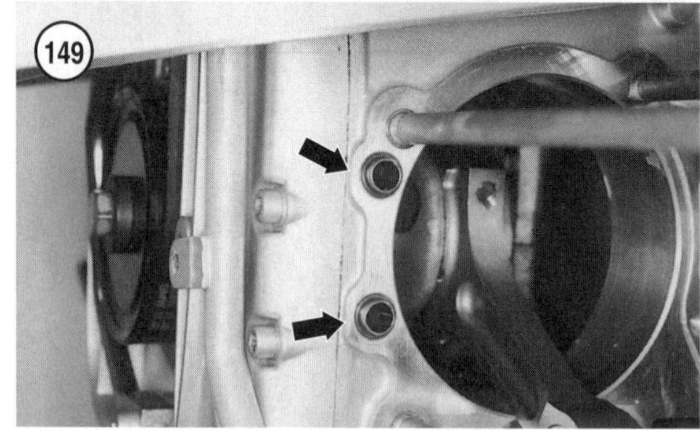

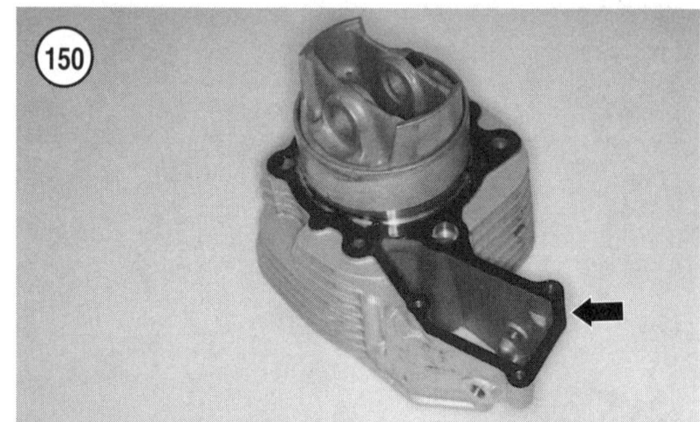

10. Install the cylinder rear locating dowel (**Figure 148**) and the two front locating dowels with new O-ring seals (**Figure 149**) into the crankcase. Press the new O-rings into the locating rings in the crankcase.

11. Apply a light, even coat of ThreeBond 1209 gasket sealer to the lower gasket surface of the cylinder (**Figure 150**).

12. Install the cylinder and piston assembly onto the crankcase studs (**Figure 151**). Slowly slide the assembly toward the crankcase and the connecting rod.

13. Align the piston pin bore with the connecting rod small end bore to facilitate piston pin installation. Slightly rotate the piston as necessary.

14. Apply clean engine oil to the piston pin and install it part-way into the piston (**Figure 152**). Push it in until it is flush with the inner surface of the piston boss.

15. With one hand, raise the connecting rod (**Figure 153**) and align it with the piston and piston pin. With the other hand, slowly push the cylinder and piston assembly toward the connecting rod until the small end is aligned with the piston pin.

16. Press the piston pin in through the connecting rod and part way into the piston boss on the other side (**Figure 154**).

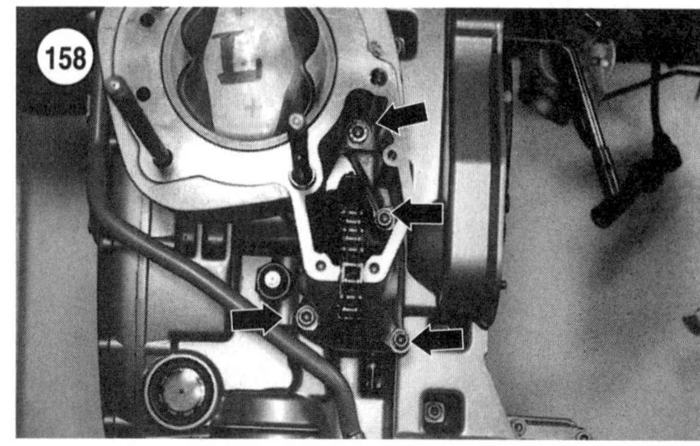

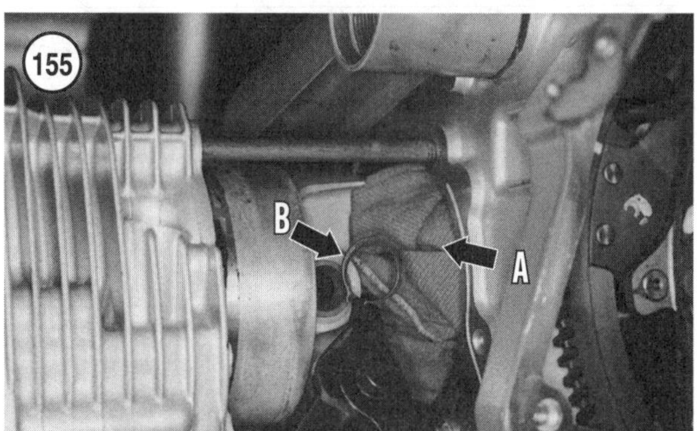

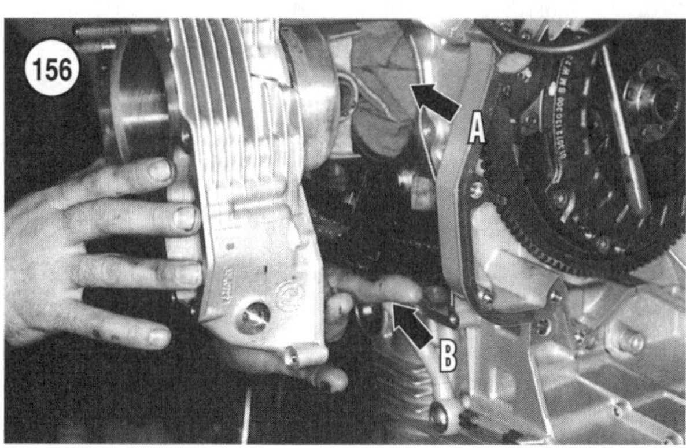

17. Place a clean shop cloth (A, **Figure 155**) into the crankcase opening to prevent a snap ring from falling into the opening.
18. Install a new snap ring (B, **Figure 155**) onto the piston pin. Make sure the snap ring seats correctly in the piston pin groove.
19. Push the piston pin through the piston until it stops.
20. Install a new snap ring onto the other end of the piston pin. Make sure the snap ring seats correctly in the piston pin groove.
21. Remove the shop cloth (A, **Figure 156**) from the crankcase.
22. With one hand, push the camshaft drive chain and slipper (B, **Figure 156**) up and guide the camshaft driven sprocket and drive chain into the cylinder block chain tunnel.
23. Continue to hold the camshaft drive chain and chain guide rail (**Figure 157**) by hand, then push the cylinder down until it stops on the crankcase mating surface. Ensure the cylinder seats correctly against the crankcase around its entire perimeter.
24. Install the Allen bolts and washers (**Figure 158**) to secure the cylinder to the crankcase. Follow a crisscross pattern and tighten to the following:
   a. 6–mm Allen bolts 9 N•m (80 in.-lb.)

b. 8–mm Allen bolts 20 N•m (15 ft.-lb.)

25. Install the camshaft chain guide rail bolt (A, **Figure 159**) and washer (B) and tighten to 18 N•m (13 ft.-lb.).

26. Install the cylinder head as described in this chapter.

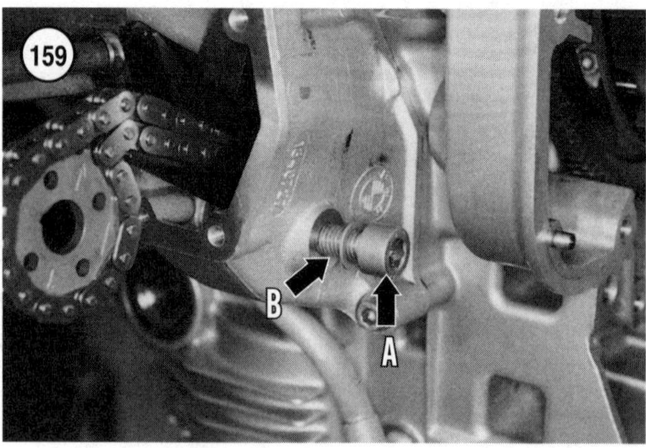

Inspection

NOTE

Piston and piston ring inspection are covered under ***Piston and Piston Rings*** *in this chapter. A bore gauge and micrometer are required to measure the cylinder bore accurately. If these tools are not available, entrust the measurements to a BMW dealership or machine shop.*

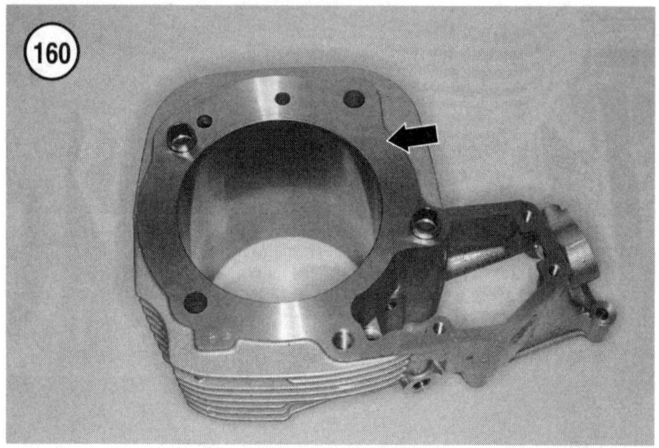

1. Remove all gasket material from the cylinder top (**Figure 160**) and bottom gasket surfaces. Both surfaces must be free of all completely clean.
2. Wash the cylinder in solvent and dry with compressed air.
3. Check the crankcase locating dowel holes (**Figure 161**) at the bottom surface for cracks or other damage.
4. Check the threads of the camshaft chain tensioner (**Figure 162**) for wear or damage (right side cylinder shown). If necessary, repair the threads with an appropriate size metric tap.
5. Check each cylinder bore (**Figure 163**) for scoring, rusting or other visible damage.
6. Measure the cylinder bore inner diameter, taper and out-of-round with a bore gauge or inside micrometer. Measure the cylinder bore at the two positions, measured down from the top or lower surface (**Figure 164**) listed in **Table 2** or **Table 3**. Measure aligned with the piston pin and 90° to the pin. Check all measurements against the specifications. If any measurement is greater that the service limit, the cylinders must be rebored to the next oversize. Rebore both cylinders even if only one is worn.

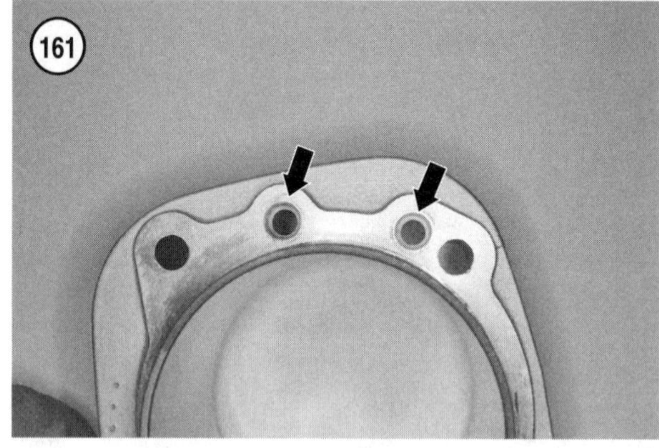

NOTE

Obtain new pistons before the cylinders are bored so that the pistons can be measured. Each cylinder must be bored to match the corresponding piston.

7. If the cylinder bore is within specifications, determine piston-to-cylinder clearance as described under *Piston Clearance* in this chapter.
8. After the cylinders are serviced, wash the bores in hot soapy water and rinse completely to remove the fine grit material left from the bore, or honing, job. After washing a cylinder, run a clean white cloth through it. The cylinder walls should show no traces of grit or other debris. If the rag is dirty, the cylinder walls are not clean and must be re-washed. When the cylinder bores are thoroughly cleaned, lubricate the bores with clean engine oil to prevent the cylinders from rusting.

CAUTION

A combination of soap and water is the only solution that will completely clean the cylin-

162

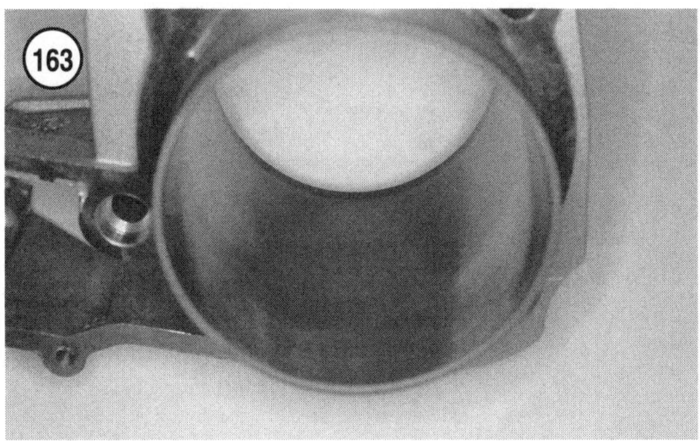
163

164

165

der bores. Solvent and kerosene cannot wash fine grit out of cylinder crevices. Grit remaining in the cylinder will cause premature wear to the new rings.

9. After the cylinder is thoroughly clean, check for nicks in the cylinder sealing surfaces that could cause air or oil leakage. If damaged, the cylinder(s) must be resurfaced or replaced. Entrust resurfacing to a BMW dealership or machine shop experienced with this type of work.

PISTON AND PISTON RINGS

Piston

The pistons are made of aluminum alloy. The piston pin is made of steel and is a precision fit within the pistons. The piston pins are held in place by an external snap ring at each end.

Removal/installation

Piston removal and installation are covered under *Cylinder and Piston* in this chapter.

Inspection

1. If necessary, remove the piston rings as described in this chapter.
2. Carefully clean the carbon from the piston crown (**Figure 165**) with a soft scraper or wire wheel mounted in a drill. Large carbon accumulation reduces piston cooling and results in detonation and piston damage.

CAUTION
Do not gouge or damage the piston when removing carbon. Never use a wire brush to clean the piston skirt or ring grooves. Do not attempt to remove carbon from the sides of the piston above the top ring or from the cylinder bore near the top. Removal of carbon from these two areas may cause increased oil consumption.

3. After cleaning the piston, examine the crown. The crown should not be worn or damaged. If the crown appears pecked or spongy-looking, also check the spark plug, valves and combustion chamber for aluminum deposits. If aluminum transfer is noted, the engine is overheating.
4. Examine each ring groove (**Figure 166**) for burrs, dented edges or other damage. Pay particular attention to the top compression ring groove as it usually wears more

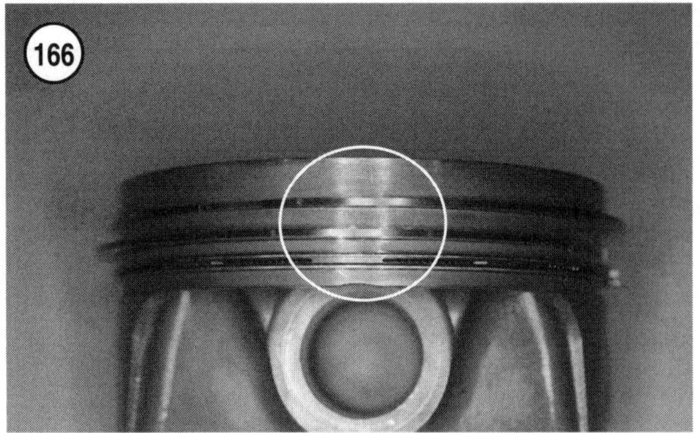

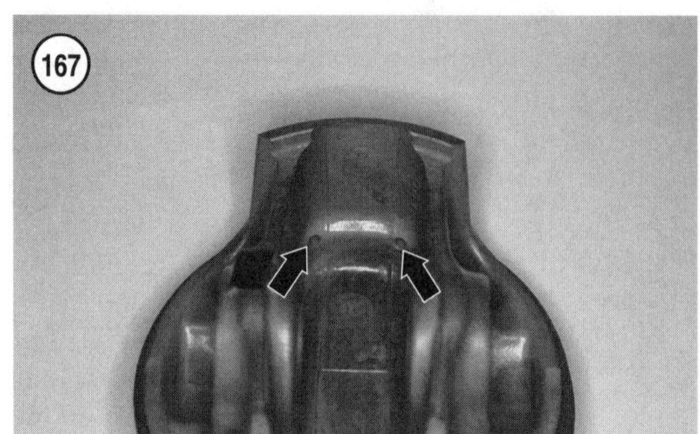

than the others. Because the oil rings are constantly bathed in oil, these rings and grooves wear little compared to compression rings and their grooves. If there is evidence of oil ring groove wear or if the oil ring assembly is tight and difficult to remove, the piston skirt may be collapsed due to excessive heat and is permanently deformed. Replace the piston.

5. Check the oil control holes in the piston for carbon or oil sludge buildup. Refer to **Figure 167** and **Figure 168**. Carefully clean the holes with wire and blow them out with compressed air.

6. Check the piston skirt (**Figure 169**) for cracks or other damage. If a piston has evidence of partial seizure (bits of aluminum transfer on the piston skirt), replace the piston and bore the cylinder (oversize, if necessary) to reduce the possibility of engine noise and further piston seizure.

NOTE
If the piston skirt is worn or scuffed unevenly from side to side, the connecting rod may be bent or twisted.

7. Measure piston-to-cylinder clearance as described under *Piston Clearance* in this section.

8. If necessary, select a new piston as described under *Piston Clearance* in this section. If the piston, rings and cylinder are not damaged and are dimensionally correct, they can be reused.

9. Calculate piston-to-piston pin clearance as follows:

   a. Measure the piston pin bore inside diameter (**Figure 170**) at both ends with a small bore gauge, then measure the small bore gauge with a micrometer and record the measurement.

   b. Measure the piston pin outside diameter (**Figure 171**) in several locations, and record the measurement.

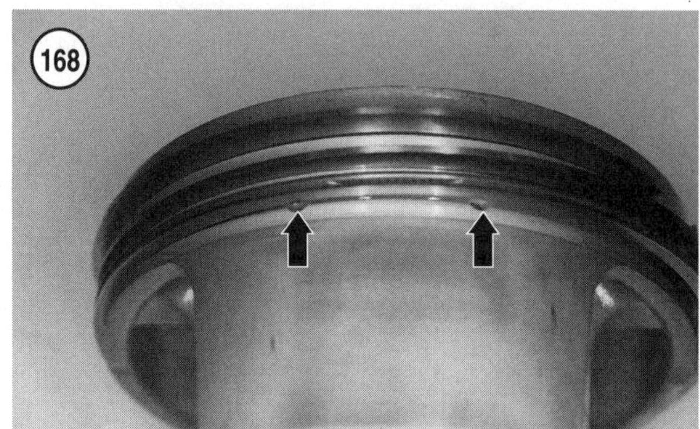

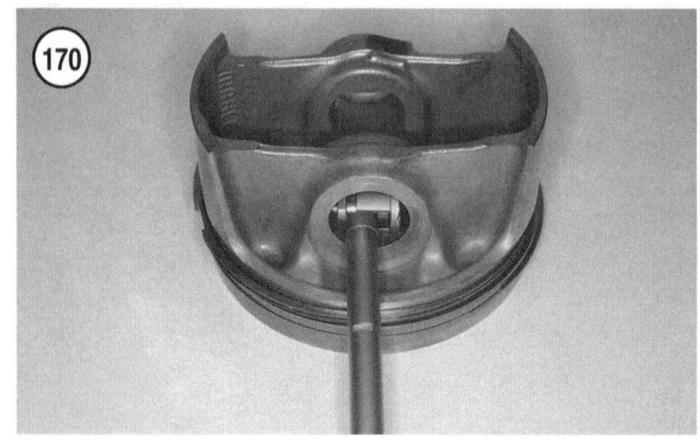

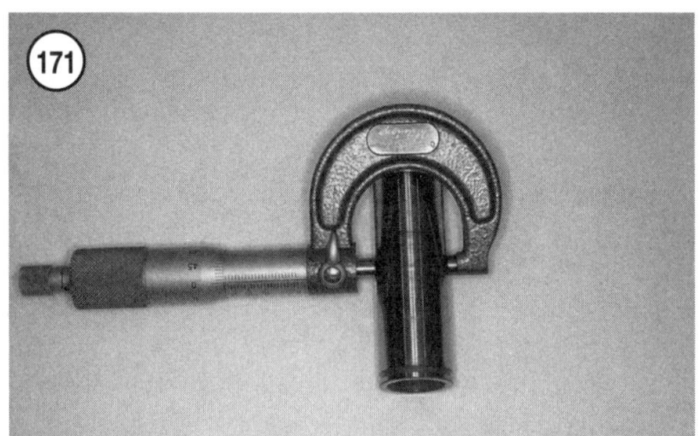

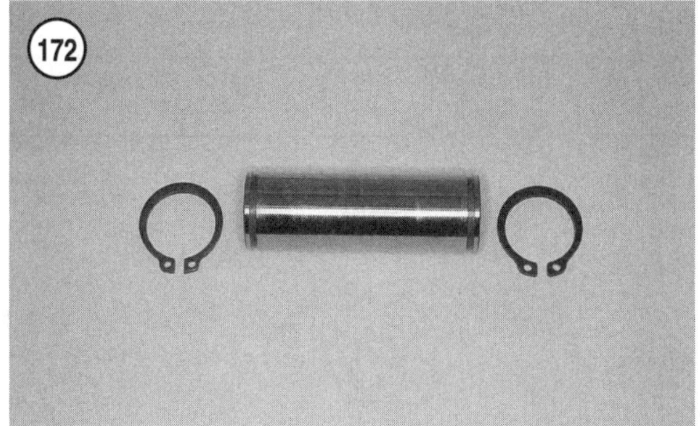

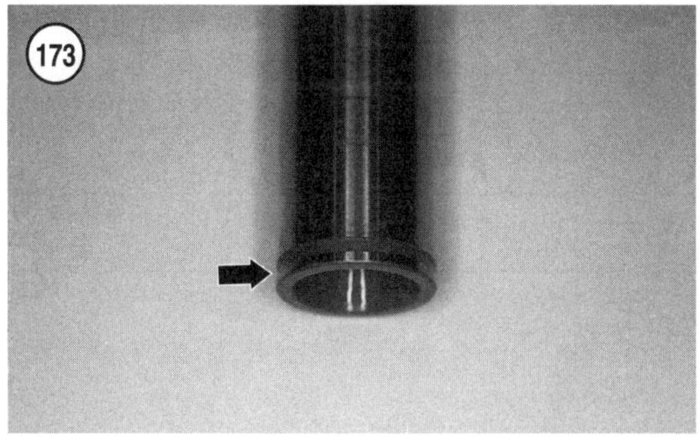

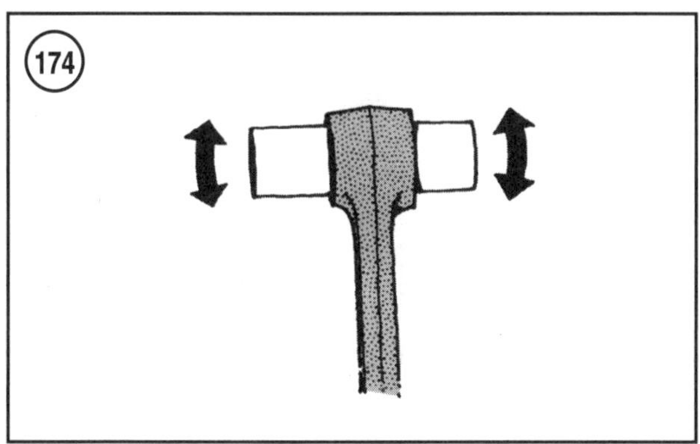

NOTE
The piston pin can be replaced separately. If the piston requires replacement, the piston and pin must be replaced as a matching set.

c. Subtract the measurement in substep b from the measurement in substep a and determine piston-to-piston pin oil clearance. Replace the piston and/or piston pin if the clearance exceeds the service limit in **Table 2** or **Table 3**.

Piston Pin Inspection

1. Clean the piston pin in solvent and dry thoroughly.
2. Inspect the piston pin (**Figure 172**) for chrome flaking or cracks. Replace it if necessary.
3. Check the snap ring groove (**Figure 173**) on each end for wear, cracks or other damage. If the grooves are in questionable condition, check the snap ring fit by installing a new snap ring into each groove and then attempt to move the snap ring from side to side. If the snap ring has any side play, the groove is worn and the piston pin must be replaced.
4. Oil the piston pin and install it in the connecting rod. Slowly rotate the piston pin and check for any radial play (**Figure 174**).
5. Oil the piston pin and install it in the piston (**Figure 175**) and check for excessive play.
6. Replace the piston pin and/or piston or connecting rod if necessary.

Piston Clearance

1. Make sure the piston skirt and cylinder walls are clean and dry.
2. Measure the cylinder bore as described in this chapter. Record the bore diameter.
3. Measure the piston diameter with a micrometer at a right angle to the piston pin bore. Measure up 6 mm

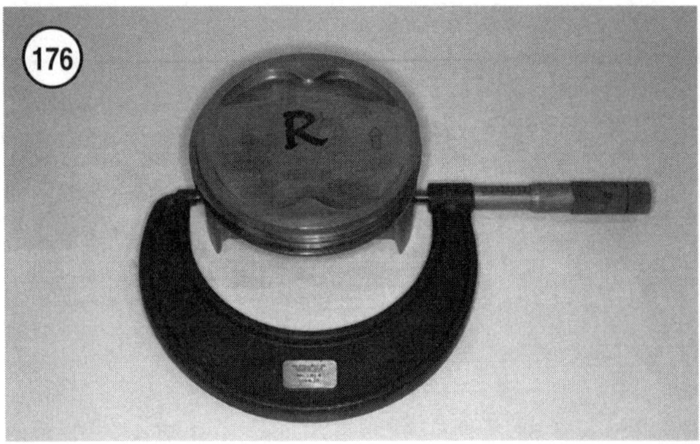

(0.236 in.) from the bottom edge of the piston skirt as shown in **Figure 176**.

4. Subtract the piston diameter from the largest bore diameter; the difference is piston-to-cylinder bore clearance. If the clearance exceeds the specification in **Table 2** or **Table 3**, the pistons should be replaced and the cylinders bored oversize and then honed. Purchase the new pistons first. Measure the piston diameters and add the specified clearance to determine the proper cylinder bore oversize diameter.

Piston Ring

Inspection and removal

A three-ring piston and ring assembly is used. The top and second rings are compression rings. The lower ring is an oil control ring assembly (consisting of two ring rails and an expander spacer).

When measuring the piston rings and piston in this section, compare the measurements to the specifications in **Table 2** or **Table 3**. Replace worn or damaged parts as described in this section.

1. Measure the side clearance of each compression ring in its groove with a flat feeler gauge (**Figure 177**). If the clearance is greater than specified, the rings must be replaced. If the clearance is still excessive with the new rings, the piston(s) must be replaced.

WARNING

The edges of all piston rings are very sharp. Be careful when handling them to avoid cutting fingers.

NOTE

Store the old rings in the order in which they are removed.

2. Remove the compression rings with a ring expander tool (**Figure 178**) or by carefully spreading the ring ends

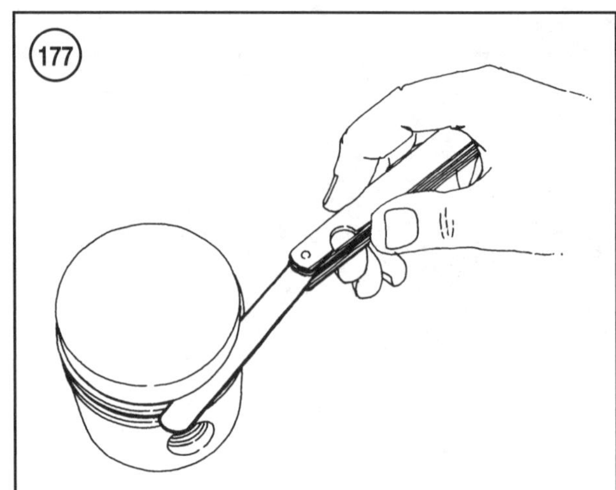

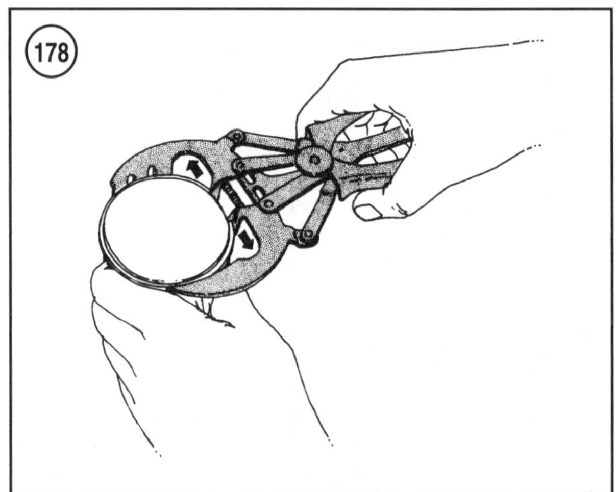

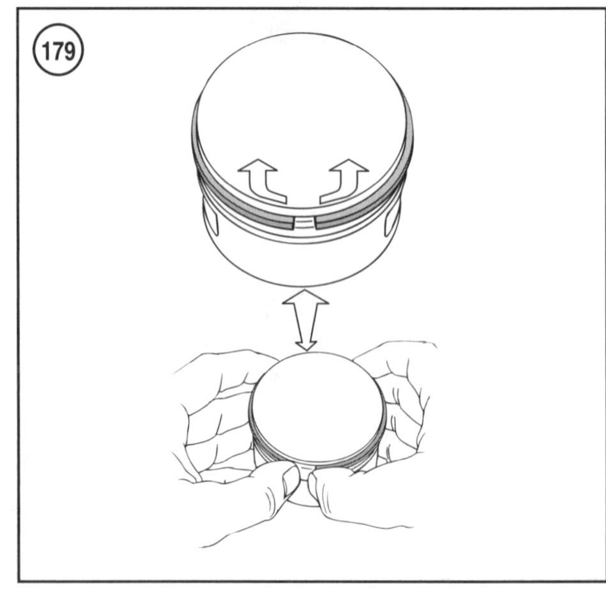

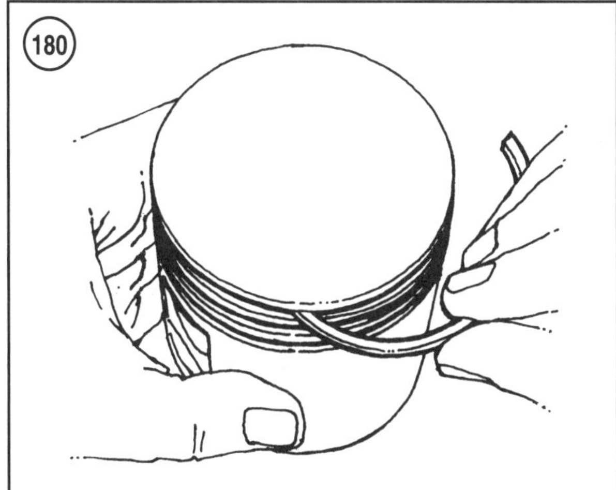
180

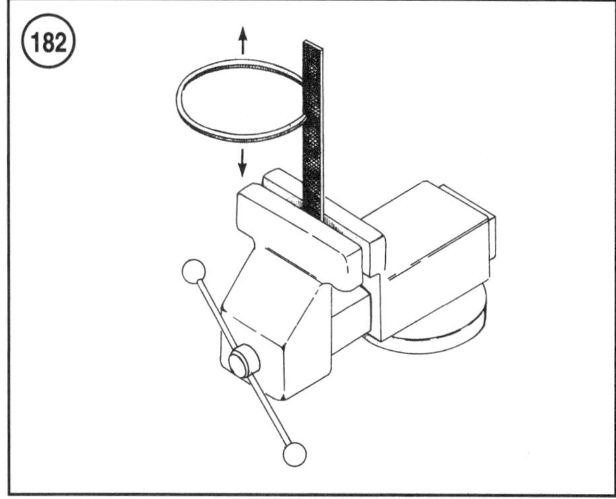
182

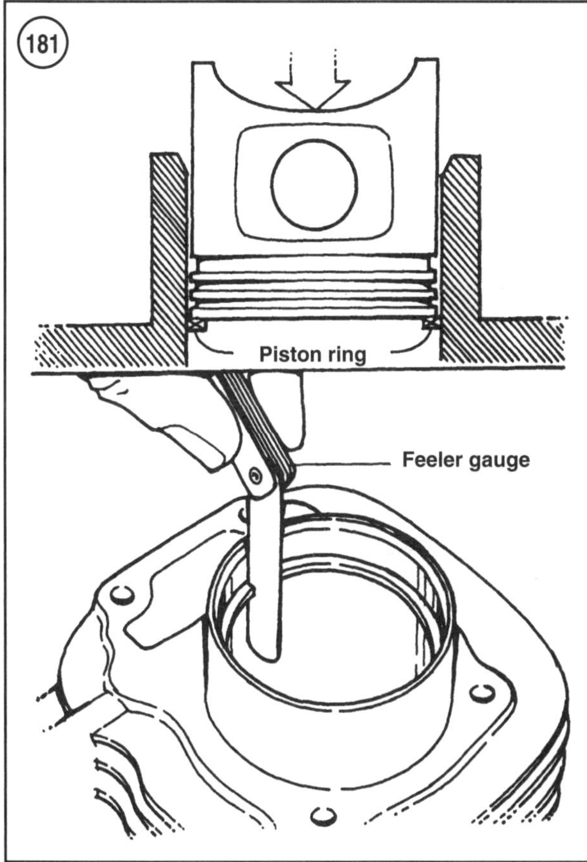

181

by hand and evenly lifting the rings up (**Figure 179**) off the top of the piston.

3. Remove the upper and then the lower oil ring rails followed by the expander spacer.

4. Use a broken piston ring and carefully remove carbon and oil residue from the piston ring grooves (**Figure 180**). Do not remove aluminum material from the ring grooves as this will increase ring side clearance.

5. Measure each compression ring groove and the oil ring groove width with a vernier caliper. Measure each groove at several points around the piston. Replace the piston if any groove width exceeds the service limit.

6. Inspect the grooves carefully for burrs, nicks, or broken or cracked lands. Replace the piston if necessary.

7. Insert the piston ring into the bottom of the cylinder bore. Tap the ring with the piston to position the ring squarely in the bore. Measure the ring end gap with a feeler gauge (**Figure 181**). Replace the piston ring if the end gap exceeds the specification in **Table 2** or **Table 3**. If the end gap of a new compression ring is smaller than specified, clamp a small file in a vise (**Figure 182**) and carefully enlarge the ring gap as necessary.

Installation

1. If new rings are installed, the cylinder bores must be deglazed or honed to seat the new rings. If necessary, refer honing service to a BMW dealership. After honing, measure the end gap of each ring and compare to the specifications in **Table 2** or **Table 3**.
2. Clean the piston and rings. Dry with compressed air.
3. Install the piston rings as follows:

NOTE
Install the piston rings in this order: first the bottom, then the middle and then the top ring.

a. Carefully spread the ends by hand and then slip the rings over the top of the piston. The piston rings must be installed with the marks on them facing toward the top of the piston. Incorrectly installed piston rings can wear rapidly and/or allow oil to escape past them.

b. Install the oil ring assembly into the bottom ring groove.
c. Install the compression rings with the manufacturer's TOP mark facing up.

NOTE
When installing aftermarket piston rings, follow their manufacturer's directions.

d. Install the second or middle compression ring.
e. Install the top compression ring.

4. Make sure the rings seat completely in their grooves all the way around the piston and that the end gaps are distributed around the piston as shown in **Figure 183**. The ring gaps must not align with each other during installation to prevent compression pressures from escaping past them.
5. If installing oversize compression rings, check the number to make sure the correct rings are being installed. The ring numbers should be the same as the piston oversize number.
6. If new parts are installed, break-in the engine just as though it were new. Refer to Engine *Break-In* in Chapter Five.

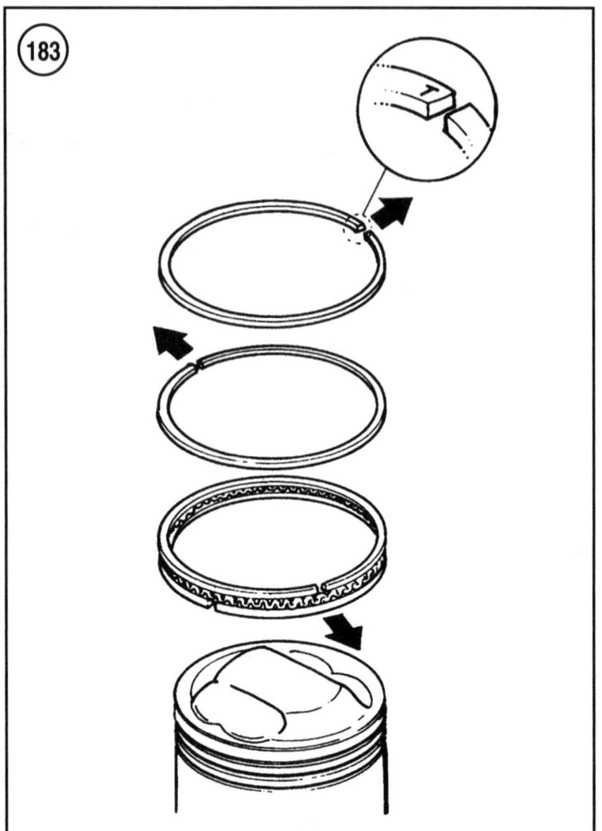

Table 1 ENGINE GENERAL SPECIFICATIONS

Item	Specification
Cylinder arrangement	Opposed twin
Engine type	4-stroke, SOHC, 4-valve head
Bore × stroke	
850 cc	87.5 × 70.5 mm (3.444 × 2.775 in.)
1100 cc	99 × 70.5 mm (3.897 × 2.775 in.)
1150 cc	101 × 70.5 mm (3.976 × 2.775 in.)
1200 cc	101 × 73 mm (3.976 × 2.87 in.)
Displacement	
850 cc	848 cc
1100 cc	1085 cc
1150 cc	1130 cc
1200 cc	1170 cc
Compression ratio	
850 cc	10.3 to 1
1100 cc	
R, GS models	10.3 to 1
RS, RT models	10.7 to 1
S models	11.3 to 1
	(continued)

Table 1 ENGINE GENERAL SPECIFICATIONS (continued)

Item	Specification
Compression ratio (continued)	
1150 models	
R, GS models	10.3 to 1
RS, RT models	11.3 to 1
R1200 models	10.0 to 1
Ignition system	
Type	Motronic
Ignition trigger	Hall-effect sensors
Ignition timing (non-adjustable)	
At idle	0°
Full advance	43°
Direction of rotation	Clockwise (as viewed from front of engine)
Lubrication system	Wet sump with oil cooler(s)
Cooling system	Air/oil cooled

Table 2 ENGINE TOP END SPECIFICATIONS—850 CC AND 1200 CC MODELS

Item	Specification mm (in.)
Rocker arms and shafts	
Rocker arm bore inside diameter	16.016-16.027 (0.6305-0.6309)
Rocker arm shaft outside diameter	15.973-15.984 (0.6289-0.6293)
Rocker arm-to-shaft oil clearance	
Standard	0.032-0.054 (0.0013-0.0021)
Service limit	0.1 (0.004)
Rocker arm axial play	
Maximum	0.40 (0.016)
Minimum	0.05 (0.002)
Camshafts	
Camshaft lift (1993-1998)	
Intake	9.68 (0.3811)
Exhaust	9.26 (0.3645)
Camshaft lift (1999-on)	
Intake	8.23 (0.3240)
Exhaust	8.23 (0.3240)
Camshaft bearing outside diameter	20.97-21.00 (0.8256-0.8267)
Camshaft bearing bore inside diameter	21.02-21.04 (0.8275-0.8283)
Oil clearance	
Standard	0.02-0.07 (0.0008-0.0027)
Service limit	0.15 (0.0059)
Camshaft bearing width	16.0-16.05 (0.6299-0.6318)
Valve gear holder width	15.92-15.95 (0.6267-0.6279)
Axial play	
Standard	0.08-0.13 (0.0031-0.0051)
Service limit	0.25 (0.0098)
Tappets	
Tappet outside diameter	23.947-23.960 (0.9427-0.9433)
Tappet bore inside diameter	24.000-24.021 (0.9448-0.9457)
Oil clearance	
Standard	0.040-0.074 (0.0016-0.0029)
Service limit	0.18 (0.0070)
Valves	
Valve head outside diameter (850 cc)	
Intake	32 (1.2598)
Exhaust	27 (1.0629)

(continued)

Table 2 ENGINE TOP END SPECIFICATIONS—850 CC AND 1200 CC MODELS (continued)

Item	Specification mm (in.)
Valves (continued)	
Valve head outside diameter (1200 cc)	
Intake	34 (1.34)
Exhaust	29 (1.14)
Valve stem outside diameter	
Intake	
Standard	4.966-4.980 (0.1955-0.1961)
Service limit	4.946 (0.1947)
Exhaust	
Standard	4.956-4.970 (0.1951-0.1956)
Service limit	4.936 (0.1943)
Valve head edge thickness (1993-1998)	
Intake	
Standard	0.8-1.2 (0.0315-0.0472)
Service limit	0.5 (0.0196)
Exhaust	
Standard	1.45-1.65 (0.0571-0.0728)
Service limit	1.0 (0.0394)
Valve head edge thickness (1999-on)	
Intake	
Standard	0.8-1.2 (0.0315-0.0472)
Service limit	0.5 (0.0196)
Exhaust	
Standard	0.8-1.2 (0.0315-0.0472)
Service limit	0.5 (0.0196)
Valve head runout (maximum)	
Intake and exhaust	0.035 (0.0014)
Valve seat width	
Intake	0.85-1.25 (0.033-0.049)
Exhaust	0.8-1.2 (0.031-0.047)
Valve guides	
Guide inside diameter	5.00-5.012 (0.1968-0.1973)
Guide outside diameter	12.533-12.544 (0.4934-0.4938)
Guide bore in cylinder head	
Outside diameter	12.500-12.518 (0.4921-0.4928)
Replacement guide outside diameter	12.550-12.561 (0.4941-0.4945)
Oversize guide outside diameter	12.733-12.744 (0.5013-0.5017)
Valve stem-to-guide clearance	
Intake	
Standard	0.020-0.046 (0.0008-0.0018)
Service limit	0.15 (0.0059)
Exhaust	
Standard	0.030-0.056 (0.0012-0.0022)
Service limit	0.17 (0.0067)
Valve springs overall free length	
Standard	41.1 (1.618)
Service limit	39.0 (1.535)
Cylinder (850 cc)	
Bore inside diameter	
Type A	
Standard	87.492-87.500 (3.4446-3.4449)
Service limit	87.558 (3.447)
Type B	
Standard	87.500-87.508 (3.4449-3.4452)
Service limit	87.558 (3.447)
Out of round service limit	
20 mm (0.78 in.) from top edge	0.03 (0.0012)
100 mm (3.94 in.) from lower edge	0.04 (0.0016)

(continued)

Table 2 ENGINE TOP END SPECIFICATIONS—850 CC AND 1200 CC MODELS (continued)

Item	Specification mm (in.)
Cylinder (1200 cc)	
Bore inside diameter	
Type A	
Standard	100.992-101.000 (3.9761-3.9764)
Bore inside diameter	
Type A	
Service limit	101.050 (3.9784)
Type B	
Standard	101.000-101.008 (3.9764-3.9768)
Service limit	101.058 (3.9787)
Out of round service limit	
20 mm (0.78 in.) from top edge	0.03 (0.0012)
100 mm (3.94 in.) from lower edge	0.04 (0.0016)
Pistons	
Outside diameter (850 cc)	
Type A	
Standard	87.465-87.477 (3.4435-3.4439)
Service limit	87.39 (3.4405)
Type B	
Standard	87.477-87.485 (3.4439-3.4443)
Service limit	87.400 (3.4409)
Type AB	
Standard	87.473-87.481 (3.4438-3.4441)
Service limit	87.395 (3.4407)
Outside diameter (1200 cc)	
Type A	
Standard	100.992-101.00 (3.9761-3.9764)
Service limit	101.050 (3.9784)
Type B	
Standard	101.000-101.008 (3.9764-3.9768)
Service limit	101.058 (3.9787)
Type AB	
Standard	100.979-100.987 (3.9756-3.9759)
Service limit	100.900 (3.9725)
Piston-to-cylinder clearance	
Standard	0.011-0.035 (0.0004-0.0013)
Service limit	0.12 (0.005)
Piston pin bore inside diameter	22.005-22.011 (0.8663-0.8666)
Piston pin outside diameter	
Standard	21.995-22.000 (0.8659-0.8661)
Service limit	21.980 (0.8653)
Piston-to-piston pin oil clearance	
Standard	0.005-0.016 (0.0002-0.0006)
Service limit	0.070 (0.0027)
Piston rings	
Top ring	
Ring height	
Standard	1.170-1.190 (0.0461-0.0469)
Service limit	1.1 (0.0433)
Gap clearance	
Standard	0.1-0.3 (0.004-0.012)
Service limit	0.8 (0.0315)
Side clearance	
Standard	0.030-0.070 (0.0012-0.0027)
Service limit	0.15 (0.006)
Second ring	
Ring height	
Standard	1.170-1.190 (0.0461-0.0469)
Service limit	1.10 (0.0433)
	(continued)

Table 2 ENGINE TOP END SPECIFICATIONS—850 CC AND 1200 CC MODELS (continued)

Item	Specification mm (in.)
Piston rings (continued)	
Second ring	
Gap clearance (R850R, R850GS)	
Standard	0.30-0.50 (0.0118-0.0196)
Service limit	1.00 (0.03937)
Gap clearance (R850C, R1200C)	
Standard	0.20-0.40 (0.008-0.016)
Service limit	1.00 (0.040)
Side clearance	
Standard	0.030-0.070 (0.0012-0.0027)
Service limit	0.15 (0.0059)
Oil ring	
Ring height (R850R, R850GS)	
Standard	2.470-2.490 (0.0972-0.0980)
Service limit	2.400 (0.0945)
Ring height (R850C, R1200C)	
Standard	1.970-1.990 (0.0776-0.0783)
Service limit	1.90 (0.075)
Gap clearance (R850R, R850GS)	
Standard	0.30-0.60 (0.0118-0.0236)
Service limit	1.20 (0.0472)
Gap clearance (R850C, R1200C)	
Standard	0.30-0.55 (0.0118-0.022)
Service limit	1.20 (0.0472)
Side clearance	
Standard	0.020-0.060 (0.0008-0.0023)
Service limit	0.15 (0.0059)

Table 3 ENGINE TOP END SPECIFICATIONS—1100 CC AND 1150 CC MODELS

Item	Specification mm (in.)
Rocker arms and shafts	
Rocker arm bore inside diameter	16.016-16.027 (0.6305-0.6309)
Rocker arm shaft outside diameter	15.973-15.984 (0.6289-0.6293)
Rocker arm-to-shaft oil clearance	
Standard	0.032-0.054 (0.0013-0.0021)
Service limit	0.1 (0.004)
Rocker arm axial play	
Maximum	0.05 (0.002)
Minimum	0.40 (0.016)
Camshaft	
Camshaft lift (1100 cc)	
Intake	9.68 (0.3811)
Exhaust	9.26 (0.3645)
Camshaft lift (1150 cc)	
Intake	9.68 (0.3811)
Exhaust	8.60 (0.3386)
Camshaft bearing outside diameter	20.97-21.00 (0.8256-0.8267)
Camshaft bearing bore inside diameter	21.02-21.04 (0.8275-0.8283)
Oil clearance	
Standard	0.02-0.07 (0.0008-0.0027)
Service limit	0.015 (0.0006)
Camshaft bearing width	16.0-16.05 (0.6299-0.6318)
Valve gear holder width	15.92-15.95 (0.6267-0.6279)
Axial play	
Standard	0.08-0.13 (0.0031-0.0051)
Service limit	0.25 (0.0098)
	(continued

Table 3 ENGINE TOP END SPECIFICATIONS—1100 CC AND 1150 CC MODELS (continued)

Item	Specification mm (in.)
Camshaft (continued)	
End float (1150 cc)	
Standard	0.05-0.13 (0.0020-0.0051)
Service limit	0.25 (0.0098)
Tappets	
Tappet outside diameter	23.947-23.960 (0.9427-0.9433)
Tappet bore inside diameter	24.000-24.021 (0.9448-0.9457)
Oil clearance	
Standard	0.040-0.074 (0.0016-0.0029)
Service limit	0.18 (0.0070)
Valves (1100 cc 1993-1995)	
Valve head outside diameter	
Intake	36 (1.4173)
Exhaust	29 (1.1417)
Valve stem outside diameter	
Intake	
Standard	5.960-5.975 (0.2346-0.2352)
Service limit	5.940 (0.2338)
Exhaust	
Standard	5.945-5.960 (0.2340-0.2346)
Service limit	5.925 (0.2333)
Valve head edge thickness	
Intake	
Standard	0.8-1.2 (0.0315-0.0472)
Service limit	0.5 (0.0196)
Exhaust	
Standard	1.45-1.65 (0.0571-0.0649)
Service limit	1.0 (0.0394)
Valve head runout (maximum)	
Intake and exhaust	0.035 (0.0014)
Valves (1100 cc 1996-on, 1150 cc)	
Valve head outside diameter	
Intake	34 (1.1338)
Exhaust	29 (1.1417)
Valve stem outside diameter	
Intake	
Standard	4.966-4.980 (0.1955-0.1961)
Service limit	4.946 (0.1947)
Exhaust	
Standard	4.956-4.970 (0.1951-0.1956)
Service limit	4.936 (0.1943)
Valve head edge thickness	
Intake	
Standard	0.8-1.2 (0.0315-0.0472)
Service limit	0.5 (0.0196)
Exhaust (R1100RT)	
Standard	0.8-1.2 (0.0315-0.0472)
Service limit	0.5 (0.0196)
Exhaust (models other than R1100RT and R1150)	
Standard	1.45-1.85 (0.0571-0.0728)
Service limit	1.0 (0.0394)
Exhaust (1150 cc)	
Standard	0.7-1.1 (0.0275-0.0433)
Service limit	0.5 (0.0197)
Valve head runout (maximum)	
Intake and exhaust	0.035 (0.0014)

(continued)

4

Table 3 ENGINE TOP END SPECIFICATIONS—1100 CC AND 1150 CC MODELS (continued)

Item	Specification mm (in.)
Valve guides	
Guide inside diameter	
1993-1995	6.00-6.012 (0.2362-0.2367)
1996-on	5.00-5.012 (0.1968-0.1973)
Guide outside diameter	12.533-12.544 (0.4934-0.4938)
Guide bore in cylinder head	
Outside diameter	12.500-12.518 (0.4921-0.4928)
Replacement guide outside diameter	12.550-12.561 (0.4941-0.4945)
Oversize guide outside diameter	12.733-12.744 (0.5013-0.5017)
Valve stem-to-guide clearance (1993-1995)	
Intake	
Standard	0.025-0.055 (0.0009-0.0022)
Service limit	0.15 (0.0059)
Exhaust	
Standard	0.040-0.079 (0.0016-0.0031)
Service limit	0.17 (0.0067)
Valve stem-to-guide clearance (1996-on)	
Intake	
Standard	0.020-0.046 (0.0008-0.0018)
Service limit	0.15 (0.0059)
Exhaust	
Standard	0.030-0.056 (0.0012-0.0022)
Service limit	0.17 (0.0067)
Valve springs overall free length	
Standard	41.1 (1.618)
Service limit	39.0 (1.535)
Cylinder (1100 cc)	
Bore inside diameter	
Type A	
Standard	98.992-99.000 (3.8973-3.9876)
Service limit	99.50 (3.9173)
Type B	
Standard	99.000-99.008 (3.8976-3.8979)
Service limit	99.058 (3.899)
Out of round service limit	
20 mm (0.78 in.) from top edge	0.03 (0.0012)
100 mm (3.94 in.) from lower edge	0.04-0.0016)
Cylinder (1150 cc)	
Bore inside diameter	
Type A	
Standard	100.992-101.000 (3.9761-3.9764)
Service limit	101.050 (3.9784)
Type B	
Standard	101.000-101.008 (3.9764-3.9768)
Service limit	101.058 (3.9787)
Out of round service limit	
20 mm (0.78 in.) from top edge	0.03 (0.0012)
100 mm (3.94 in.) from lower edge	0.04 (0.0016)
Pistons	
Outside diameter (1100 cc)	
Type A	
Standard	98.965-98.988 (3.8962-3.8972)
Service limit	98.89 (3.8933)
Type B	
Standard	98.977-98.989 (3.8967-3.8972)
Service limit	98.900 (3.8937)
Type AB	
Standard	98.973-98.981 (3.8966-3.8969)
Service limit	98.895 (3.8935)
	(continued)

Table 3 ENGINE TOP END SPECIFICATIONS—1100 CC AND 1150 CC MODELS (continued)

Item	Specification mm (in.)
Pistons (continued)	
Outside diameter (1150 cc)	
Type A	
Standard	100.971-100.983 (3.9753-3.9758)
Service limit	100.895 (3.9723)
Outside diameter (1150 cc)	
Type B	
Standard	100.983-100.995 (3.9757-3.9763)
Service limit	100.905 (3.9727)
Type AB	
Standard	100.979-100.987 (3.9756-3.9759)
Service limit	100.900 (3.9725)
Piston-to-cylinder clearance	
1100 cc	
Standard	0.011-0.035 (0.0004-0.0013)
Service limit	0.12 (0.005)
1150 cc	
Standard	0.005-0.029 (0.0002-0.0011)
Service limit	0.12 (0.005)
Piston pin bore inside diameter	22.005-22.011 (0.8663-0.8666)
Piston pin outside diameter	
Standard	21.995-22.000 (0.8659-0.8661)
Service limit	21.980 (0.8653)
Piston pin-to-bore oil clearance	
Standard	0.005-0.016 (0.0002-0.0006)
Servce limit	0.070 (0.0027)
Piston rings	
Top ring	
Ring height	
Standard	1.175-1.190 (0.0462-0.0469)
Service limit	1.1 (0.0433)
Gap clearance	
Standard	0.1-0.3 (0.004-0.012)
Service limit	0.8 (0.0315)
Side clearance (1100cc)	
Standard	0.040-0.075 (0.0016-0.0029)
Service limit	0.15 (0.006)
Side clearance (1150cc)	
Standard	0.030-0.070 (0.0012-0.0027)
Service limit	0.15 (0.006)
Second ring	
Ring height	
Standard	1.175-1.190 (0.0462-0.0469)
Service limit	1.10 (0.0433)
Gap clearance (1100 cc)	
Standard	0.10-0.30 (0.0039-0.0118)
Service limit	0.80 (0.03149)
Gap clearance (1150 cc)	
Standard	0.20-0.40 (0.0078-0.0157)
Service limit	1.00 (0.03937)
Side clearance	
Standard	0.030-0.065 (0.0012-0.0027)
Service limit	0.15 (0.0059)
Oil ring	
Ring height (1100 cc)	
Standard	2.475-2.490 (0.0974-0.0980)
Service limit	2.400 (0.0945)

(continued)

4

Table 3 ENGINE TOP END SPECIFICATIONS—1100 CC AND 1150 CC MODELS (continued)

Item	Specification mm (in.)
Piston ring (continued)	
Oil ring	
Ring height (1150 cc)	
Standard	1.97-1.99 (0.0776-0.0783)
Service limit	1.900 (0.0748)
Gap clearance	
Standard	0.30-0.55 (0.0118-0.022)
Service limit	1.20 (0.0472)
Side clearance (1100 cc)	
Standard	0.020-0.055 (0.0008-0.0022)
Service limit	0.150 (0.0059)
Side clearance (1150 cc)	
Standard	0.020-0.060 (0.0008-0.0024)
Service limit	0.150 (0.0059)

Table 4 ENGINE TOP END TORQUE SPECIFICATIONS

Item	N•m	in.-lb.	ft.-lb.
Camshaft chain guide rail bolt	18	–	13
Camshaft chain tensioner	32	–	24
Camshaft driven sprocket Allen bolt	65	–	48
Cylinder head base Allen bolts	9	80	–
Cylinder head cover bolt	8	71	–
Cylinder head mounting nuts*			
Preliminary	20	–	15
Final	Additional 180°		
Cylinder block mounting Allen bolts	9	80	–
Rocker arm bearing cap Torx bolts	15	–	11
Valve gear holder bolts	15	–	11

*Lubricate fasteners threads and head seating surface with engine oil.

5

CHAPTER FIVE

ENGINE LOWER END

This chapter describes service procedures for the lower end engine components. Engine removal and installation procedures are also included. **Table 1** and **Table 2** are located at the end of the chapter. The following service procedures are included in this chapter:

1. Flywheel.
2. Ignition trigger mechanism (Hall sensor unit).
3. Auxiliary drive shaft mechanism.
4. Oil pump.
5. Crankcase assembly.
6. Crankshaft.
7. Connecting rods.

ENGINE SERVICE NOTES

Before removing and installing the engine in the frame, note the following:

1. Park the motorcycle on level ground.
2. A hydraulic floor jack is required to support the engine.
3. Due to the weight and bulk of the engine, it is essential that a minimum of two, preferably three, people perform engine removal and installation.
4. Label all electrical connectors and hoses with tape and a permanent pen prior to disconnecting them.
5. Due to the external configuration of the engine, an engine stand and adapter are required to avoid damage to the crankcase and crankcase studs. The engine adapter (BMW part No. 11-0-630) can be easily mounted to a typical engine stand.

SERVICING THE ENGINE IN FRAME

Many components can be serviced with the engine mounted in the frame.

1. Transmission case.
2. Clutch.
3. Alternator.
4. Cylinder heads, cylinders and pistons.
5. Starter.

ENGINE
(R, GS, RS AND RT MODELS)

Removal/Installation

The front and rear suspension assemblies as well as the rear frame are attached to the engine. During engine removal it is necessary to use several special tools to secure the suspension components together during and after engine removal.

1. The special tools required for engine removal are as follows:
   a. Auxiliary frame (BMW part No. 46-5-630 [A, **Figure 1**]).
   b. Frame support adapter (BMW part No. 46-5-623 [B, **Figure 1**]).
   c. Frame support (BMW part No. 46-5-6203 [C, **Figure 1**]).

NOTE

The engine can be removed for service by lifting the suspension components and interconnecting parts off of the engine and transmission case, but this is a more labor intensive way of performing this procedure.

2A. On models so equipped, place the motorcycle on the centerstand with the rear wheel off of the ground.

2B. On models without a centerstand, place a suitable size jack under the engine to support the motorcycle with the rear wheel off the ground.

3. Remove all fairing assemblies and both seats as described in Chapter Fifteen.

4. Drain the engine oil and remove the oil filter as described in Chapter Three.

5. Disconnect the negative battery cable as described in Chapter Three.

6. Remove the fuel tank as described in Chapter Nine.

7. Remove the air filter housing as described in Chapter Nine.

8. Remove the exhaust system as described in Chapter Nine.

9. Disconnect the spark plug leads and tie them out of the way. Refer to Chapter Three.

10. Remove the Motronic unit as described in Chapter Ten.

11. On models so equipped, disconnect the ABS brake lines (**Figure 2**, typical) from the right side of the crankcase.

12. Remove both front footrests as described in Chapter Fifteen.

13. Remove the battery holder (**Figure 3**) as described in Chapter Nine.

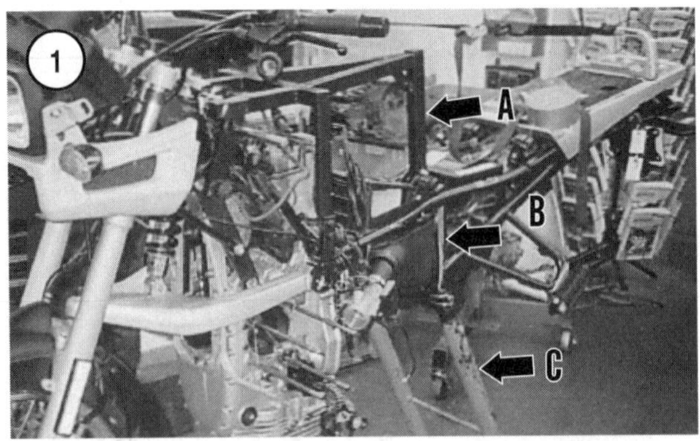

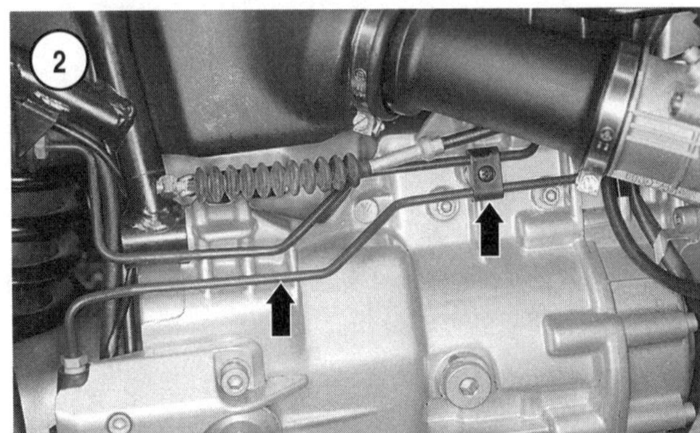

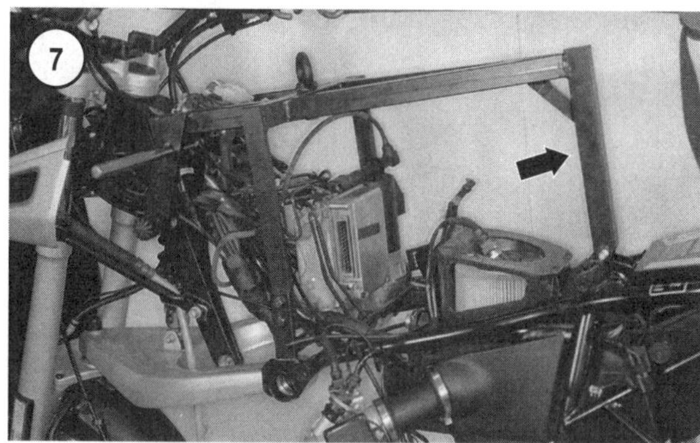

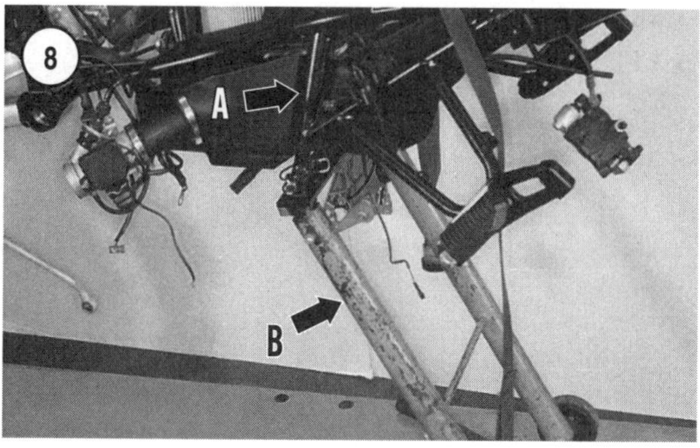

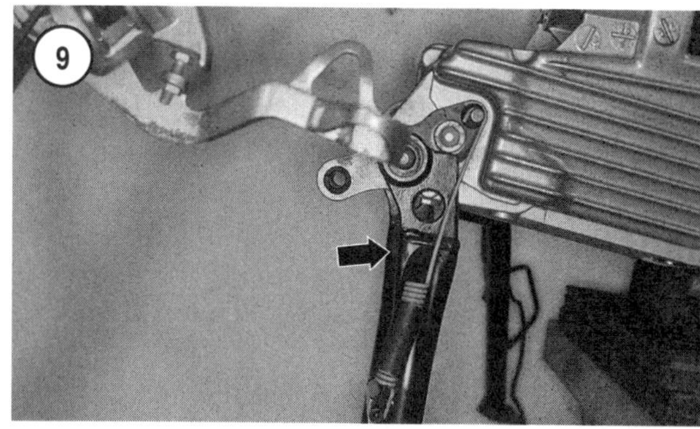

14. Remove all tie wraps (**Figure 4**, typical) and release the electrical cables from the cable guide on top of the crankcase.
15. Remove the starter as described in Chapter Ten.
16. Disconnect the oil cooler lines from the crankcase as described in this chapter.
17. If disassembling the engine for service, remove the following subassemblies:
   a. Cylinder head and pistons from each side.
   b. Cylinder from each side.
   c. Transmission.
18. Disconnect the following electrical connectors:
   a. Engine ground cable (**Figure 5**).
   b. Hall sensor unit.
   c. Alternator.
   d. Neutral indicator.
   e. Oil temperature switch.
   f. Oxygen sensor (models with catalytic converter).
   g. Oil pressure switch.
   h. Sidestand interlock switch.
19. Move all electrical wires, harnesses and hoses out of the way.
20. Place a jack underneath the engine (**Figure 6**). Raise the jack so that the pad rests just against the bottom of the engine. Place a thick wood block on the jack pad to protect the crankcase.

NOTE
The following illustrations are shown with the engine assembly removed to better illustrate the step.

21. Install the following tools onto the suspension components following the manufacturer's instructions:
   a. Auxiliary frame (**Figure 7**).
   b. Frame support adapter (A, **Figure 8**).
   c. Frame support (B, **Figure 8**).
22. On models so equipped, remove the centerstand and sidestand assembly (**Figure 9**) from the crankcase as described in Chapter Fifteen.

23. Remove the bolt, nut and washers (**Figure 10**, typical) securing the front strut to the front suspension arm.

24. Lower the front suspension arm (**Figure 11**) to gain access to the front mounting fasteners on each side.

25. Apply several layers of duct tape (A, **Figure 12**) to the top surface of the front suspension arm to protect the finish. Apply it to both sides.

26. Loosen and remove the nut (B, **Figure 12**) from the front mounting bolt.

27. Withdraw the front mounting bolt from one side (**Figure 13**).

28. Raise the front suspension arm and reinstall the front strut and the mounting bolt and nut. Tighten the nut securely.

NOTE
The rear mounting bolt differs among the various models and years. It may be a long bolt with a washer and nut on the other end, or a long rod with threads on each end and secured with a nut and washer at each end.

29. Have an assistant hold the engine in place. Remove the nut(s) and washer(s) from the rear mounting bolt (**Figure 14**) and withdraw the bolt from one side.

CAUTION
When lowering the engine, continually check on both sides to make sure all wiring and components are disconnected from the engine. Also, make sure the engine does not snag any component as it is being lowered.

30. Have an assistant hold the engine and slowly lower the engine out of the front suspension and special tool assembly.

31. Completely lower the engine. Carefully remove the engine from the jack and place the engine on a sheet of plywood or a heavy blanket.

CAUTION
*If the engine stand is not going to be used, place the engine in a strong wood box (**Figure 15**) fabricated to accept the lower end of the crankcase. This is not recommended, but if used, make sure the wooden box is strong enough to securely support this very top-heavy engine. Also the crankcase has very long crankcase studs protruding from each side. If the engine should tilt to one side when removing a component, there is a good chance that the crankcase studs will be bent and/or damaged.*

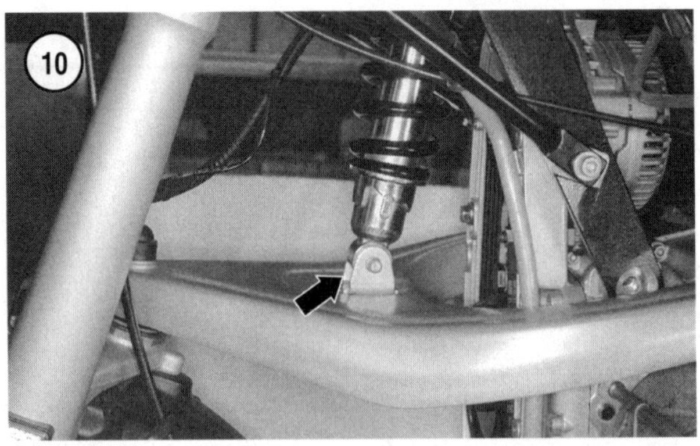

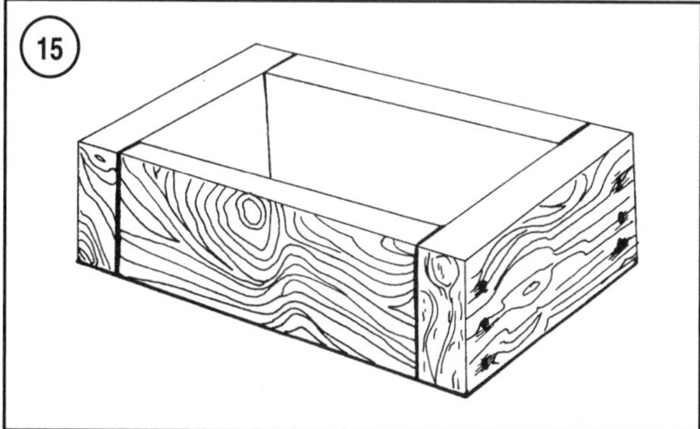

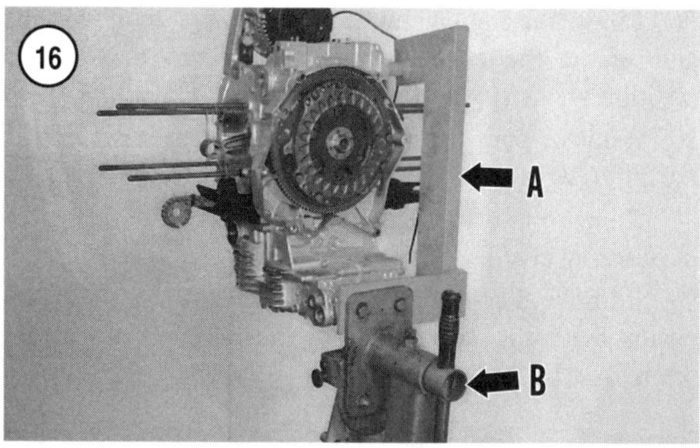

32. Install the engine onto the engine adapter (BMW part No. 11-0-630 [A, **Figure 16**]), then install the engine adapter onto an engine stand (B) for further disassembly.

33. While the engine is removed, check the engine frame mounts for cracks or other damage. Check the mounting bolts for thread damage and repair them, if necessary.

34. Remove corrosion from bolts using a wire wheel. Check the threads on all parts for wear or damage. Repair the threads with the appropriate size metric tap or die and clean with solvent.

35. Installation is the reverse of removal while noting the following:

CAUTION
Do not tighten any of the engine mounting bolts or nuts until all of them are installed. This will ensure proper alignment of all bolt holes in the engine and frame. After all mounting bolts and nuts are installed, then tighten the bolts and nuts.

a. Install both engine mounting bolts and tighten the nuts finger-tight initially. After both mounting bolts and nuts are installed and hand-tightened, torque the fasteners to the specifications listed in **Table 2**.
b. Make sure all electrical connections are free of corrosion and oil. Securely tighten all connections.

5

ENGINE (R1100S MODELS)

Removal/Installation

The front and rear suspension assemblies as well as the main and rear frames are attached to the engine. Unlike GS, R, RS and RT models, there are no BMW special tools for this model to secure the suspension components together during and after engine removal.

This procedure must be carried out by a minimum of two to three people. The engine must be stabilized after each of the suspension and frame components are removed.

1. Place a jack underneath the engine. Raise the jack so that the pad rests just against the bottom of the engine. Place a thick wood block on the jack pad to protect the crankcase. Support the motorcycle with the rear wheel off the ground.
2. Remove all fairing assemblies and the seat as described in Chapter Fifteen.
3. Drain the engine oil and remove the oil filter as described in Chapter Three.
4. Disconnect the negative battery cable as described in Chapter Three.
5. Remove the fuel tank as described in Chapter Nine.
6. Remove the exhaust system as described in Chapter Nine.
7. Disconnect the spark plug leads and tie them out of the way. Refer to Chapter Three.
8. Remove the Motronic unit as described in Chapter Ten.
9. On models so equipped, remove the ABS pressure modulator as described in Chapter Fourteen.

10. Remove the battery and battery holder as described in Chapter Nine.
11. Remove the starter as described in Chapter Ten.

NOTE
Mark the locations of all tie wraps securing the electrical cables and hoses where they attach to the engine and frame assemblies.

12. Remove the tie wraps and release the electrical cables from the engine, front frame, rear frame and main frame.
13. Disconnect the oil cooler lines from the crankcase as described in this chapter.
14. If disassembling the engine for service, remove the following subassemblies:
   a. Cylinder head and pistons from each side.
   b. Cylinder from each side.
15. Disconnect the following electrical connectors:
   a. Engine ground cable.
   b. Hall sensor unit.
   c. Alternator.
   d. Neutral indicator.
   e. Oil temperature switch.
   f. Oxygen sensor.
   g. Oil pressure switch.
   h. Sidestand interlock switch.
16. Disconnect all electrical connectors securing the rear portion of the wiring harness to the main harness.
17. Move all electrical wires, harnesses and hoses out of the way.
18. Disconnect the gearshift lever from the crankcase as described in Chapter Eight.
19. Remove the rear wheel as described in Chapter Eleven.
20. Remove the swing arm, final drive assembly and drive shaft as described in Chapter Thirteen.
21. Make sure all electrical cables have been disconnected from the rear frame. Remove the rear frame as described in Chapter Fifteen.
22. Remove the rear main frame as described in Chapter Fifteen.
23. Remove the transmission case as described in Chapter Eight.
24. Make sure all electrical cables have been disconnected from the front frame member.
25. Remove the front wheel as described in Chapter Eleven.

CAUTION
Do not allow the engine and front suspension assembly to tip to one side as the crankcase studs will be damaged.

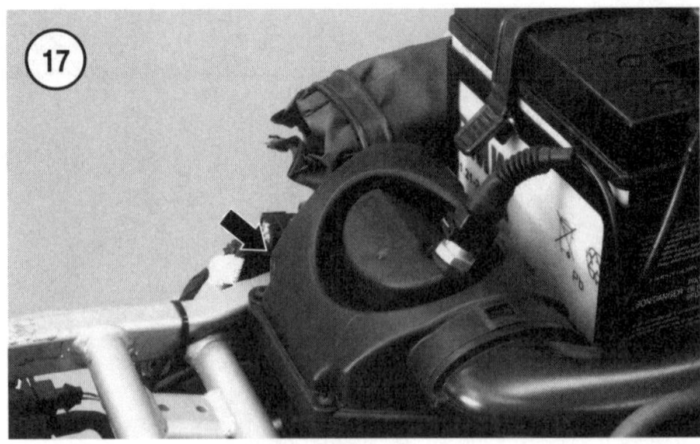

26. Lower the engine and front suspension to the ground and remove the jack. Support the assembly in a vertical position on a sheet of plywood or a heavy blanket.
27. Remove both front fork assemblies as described in Chapter Twelve.
28. Remove the front suspension A-arm as described in Chapter Twelve.
29. Remove the nut on one side of the through bolts securing the front frame member and rear supports to the crankcase.

NOTE
The electrical harness and central electrical module will remain with the front fairing bracket attached to the front frame member.

30. Have one assistant secure the engine in an upright position and have another steady the front frame member. Withdraw both through bolts, then lift up and remove the front frame member assembly from the engine.

CAUTION
*If the engine stand is not going to be used, place the engine in a strong wood box **(Figure 15)** fabricated to accept the lower end of the crankcase. This is not recommended, but*

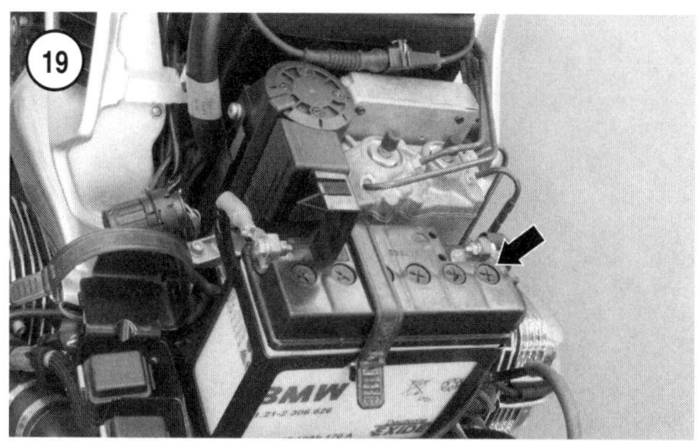

if used, make sure the wooden box is strong enough to securely support this very top-heavy engine. The crankcase has very long crankcase studs protruding from each side. If the engine should tilt to one side when removing a component, there is a good chance that the crankcase studs will be bent and/or damaged.

31. Install the engine onto the engine adapter (BMW part No. 11-0-630 [A, **Figure 16**]), then install the engine adapter onto an engine stand (B) for further disassembly.
32. While the engine is removed, check the engine frame mounts for cracks or other damage. Check the mounting bolts for thread damage and repair them, if necessary.
33. Remove corrosion from bolts using a wire wheel. Check the threads on all parts for wear or damage. Repair the threads with the appropriate size metric tap or die and clean with solvent.
34. Installation is the reverse of removal while noting the following:

CAUTION
Do not tighten any of the engine mounting bolts or nuts until all of them are installed. This will ensure proper alignment of all bolt holes in the engine and frame. After all mounting bolts and nuts are installed, then tighten the bolts and nuts.

a. Install both engine mounting through bolts and tighten the nuts finger-tight initially. After both mounting bolts and nuts are installed, tighten both nuts to 82 N•m (60 ft.-lb.).
b. Refer to the appropriate chapters for the torque specifications for the various frame members.
c. Make sure all electrical connections are free of corrosion and oil. Securely tighten all connections.

5

ENGINE (R850C AND R1200C MODELS)

Removal/Installation

The front and rear suspension assemblies as well as the main and rear frames are attached to the engine. Unlike R, GS, RS and RT models, there are no BMW special tools for this model to secure the suspension components together during and after engine removal.

This procedure must be carried out by a minimum of two to three people. The engine must be stabilized after each of the suspension and frame components are removed.

1A. Place a jack underneath the engine. Raise the jack so that the pad rests just against the bottom of the engine. Place a thick wooden block on the jack pad to protect the crankcase. Support the motorcycle with the rear wheel off the ground.
1B. If available, support the motorcycle on the auxiliary stand (BMW part No. 00-1-550) with the rear wheel off the ground.
2. Drain the engine oil and remove the oil filter as described in Chapter Three.
3. Remove the seat as described in Chapter Fifteen.
4. Remove the side trims and the fuel tank described in Chapter Nine.
5. Remove the exhaust system as described in Chapter Nine.
6. Disconnect the spark plug leads and tie them out of the way. Refer to Chapter Three.
7. Remove the air filter element and top cover assembly (**Figure 17**) as described in Chapter Three.
8. Remove the Motronic unit (**Figure 18**) as described in Chapter Ten.
9. Remove the battery (**Figure 19**) and battery holder (A, **Figure 20**) as described in Chapter Nine.
10. Remove the ABS pressure modulator (B, **Figure 20**) as described in Chapter Fourteen.

11. Remove the starter as described in Chapter Ten.

NOTE
Mark the locations of all tie wraps securing the electrical cables and hoses where they attach to the engine and frame assemblies.

13. Remove the tie wraps and release the electrical cables from the engine and rear frame.
14. Disconnect the oil cooler lines from the crankcase as described in this chapter.
15. Disconnect the gearshift lever from the crankcase as described in Chapter Eight.
16. If disassembling the engine for service, remove the following subassemblies:
   a. Cylinder head and pistons from each side.
   b. Cylinder from each side.
17. Disconnect the following electrical connectors:
   a. Engine ground cable.
   b. Hall sensor unit.
   c. Alternator.
   d. Neutral indicator.
   e. Oil temperature switch.
   f. Oxygen sensor.
   g. Oil pressure switch.
   h. Sidestand interlock switch.
18. Disconnect all additional electrical connections at the central electrical equipment box (A, **Figure 21**).
19. Remove the ignition coil (B, **Figure 21**) as described in Chapter Ten.
20. On the right side, separate the plug for the throttle position sensor and throttle potentiometer.
21. Disconnect both fuse boxes at the plug retaining plate.
22. If the cylinder heads were not removed, remove the fuel injectors and stub pipes as described in Chapter Nine.
23. On the right side, disconnect the rear brake light switch.
24. Disconnect the throttle cable at the hand grip; see chapter Twelve.
25. Make sure all electrical cables have been disconnected from the rear frame. Remove the rear frame as described in Chapter Fifteen.
26. If used, remove auxiliary stand installed in Step 1B.
27. Remove the footrest assembly as described in Chapter Fifteen.
28. Remove the rear wheel as described in Chapter Eleven.
29. Remove the swing arm, final drive assembly and drive shaft as described in Chapter Thirteen.
30. Remove the transmission as described in Chapter Seven.

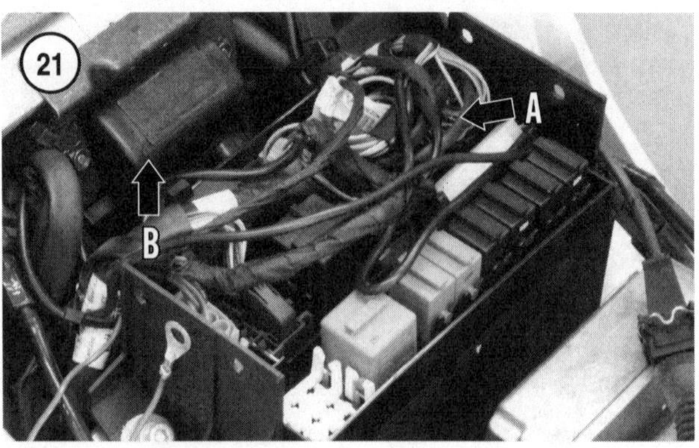

31. Remove the headlight, turn signals and instrument cluster as described in Chapter Ten.
32. Disconnect the engine ground strap from the top of the crankcase.
33. Make sure all electrical cables have been disconnected from the front frame member.
34. Remove the handlebar assembly as described in Chapter Twelve.
35. Remove the front wheel as described in Chapter Eleven.

CAUTION
Do not allow the engine and front suspension assembly to tip to one side as the crankcase studs will be damaged.

36. Lower the engine and front suspension to the ground and remove the jack. Support the assembly in a vertical position on a sheet of plywood or a heavy blanket.
37. Remove both front fork assemblies as described in Chapter Twelve.
38. Remove the front suspension A-arm as described in Chapter Twelve.
39. On the right side, remove the nut from the front through bolt.
40. On the right side, remove the nut and washer from the rear through bolt.
41. Have one assistant secure the engine in an upright position and have another steady the front frame member. Withdraw both through bolts, then pull the front frame member forward and off the engine.

CAUTION
*If the engine stand is not going to be used, place the engine in a strong wood box (**Figure 15**) fabricated to accept the lower end of the crankcase. This is not recommended, but if used, make sure the wooden box is strong enough to securely support this very top-heavy engine. The crankcase has very*

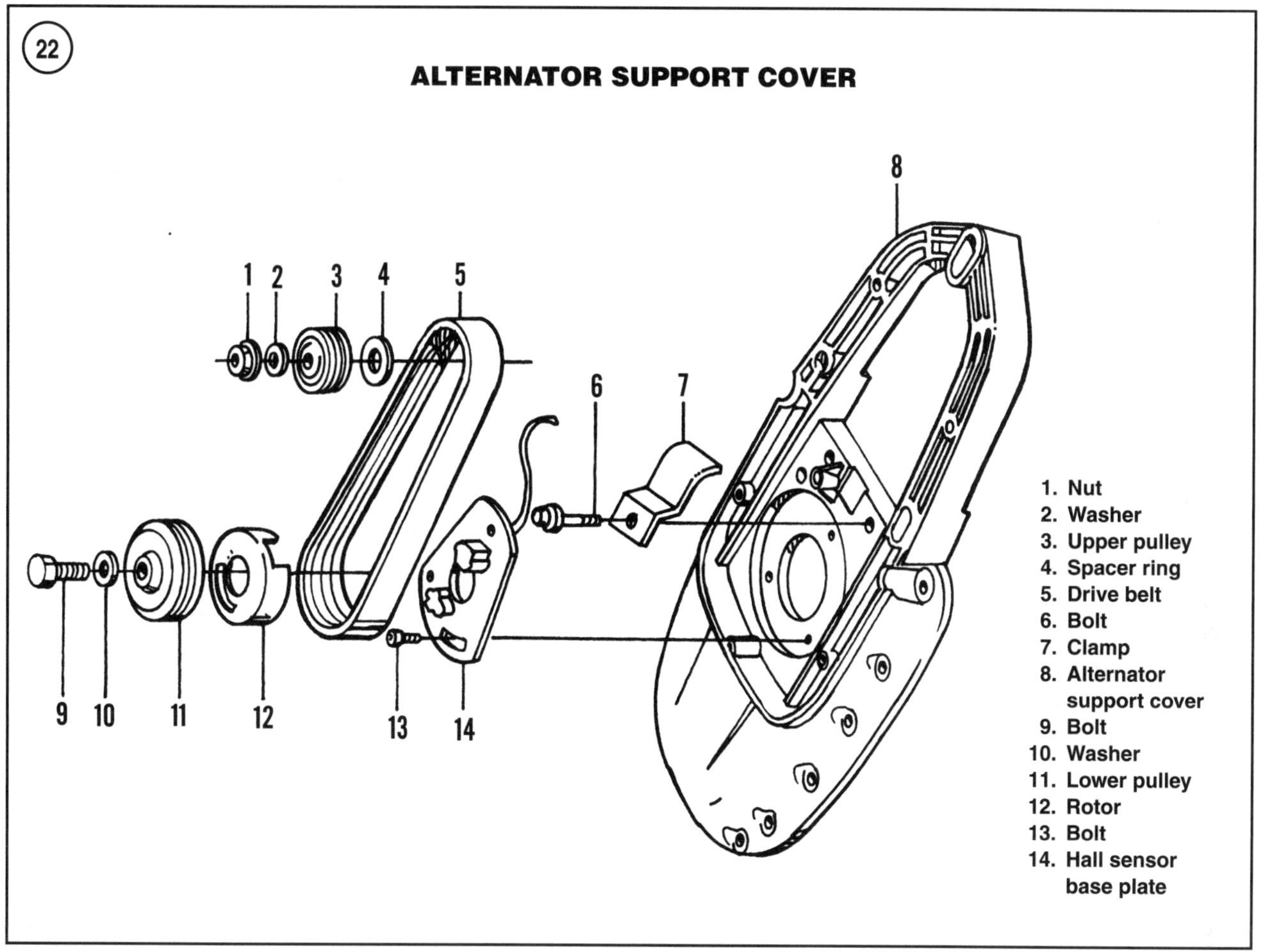

long crankcase studs protruding from each side. If the engine should tilt to one side when removing a component, there is a good chance that the crankcase studs will be bent and/or damaged.

42. Install the engine onto the engine adapter (BMW part No. 11-0-630 [A, **Figure 16**]), then install the engine adapter onto an engine stand (B) for further disassembly.
43. While the engine is removed, check the engine frame mounts for cracks or other damage. Check the mounting bolts for thread damage and repair them, if necessary.
44. Remove corrosion from bolts using a wire wheel. Check the threads on all parts for wear or damage. Repair the threads with the appropriate size metric tap or die and clean with solvent.
45. Installation is the reverse of removal while noting the following:

CAUTION
Do not tighten any of the engine mounting bolts or nuts until all of them are installed. This will ensure proper alignment of all bolt holes in the engine and frame. After all mounting bolts and nuts are installed, then tighten the bolts and nuts.

a. Install both engine mounting through bolts and tighten the nuts finger-tight initially. After both mounting bolts and nuts are installed, tighten the front nut to 82 N•m (60 ft.-lb.) and the rear nut to 58 N•m (43 ft.-lb.)
b. Refer to the appropriate chapters for the torque specifications for the various frame members.
c. Make sure all electrical connections are free of corrosion and oil. Securely tighten all connections.

ALTERNATOR SUPPORT COVER

Removal

Refer to **Figure 22**.

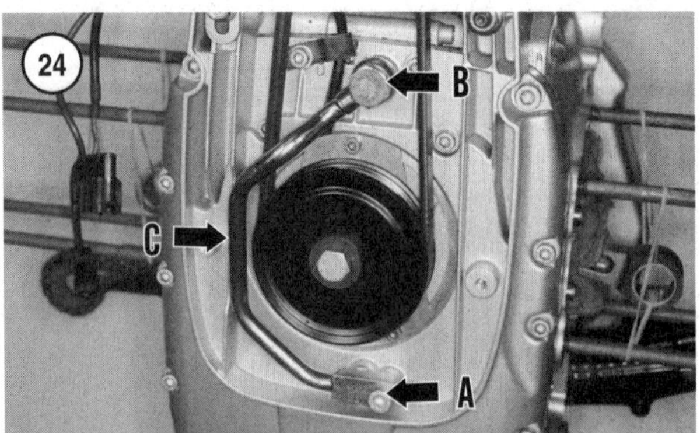

1. Remove the screws securing the front cover (**Figure 23**) and remove the cover.
2. Remove the engine as described in this chapter.
3. On models equipped with the rotary breather pipe, perform the following:
   a. Remove the lower bolt (A, **Figure 24**) and the upper banjo bolt (B) and sealing washers securing the rotary breather pipe (C).
   b. Remove the rotary breather pipe and the O-ring located on the lower bolt hole locating pin between the pipe and the alternator support cover.
4. Remove the alternator as described in Chapter Ten.
5. Remove the belt from both pulleys.
6. Loosen the clamp bolt (**Figure 25**) on the wiring harness clamp. Move the wire out from under the clamp.
7. Remove the bolt and washer (A, **Figure 26**) and remove the lower pulley (B) from the crankshaft.

NOTE
The Hall sensor unit does not have to be removed unless it is going to be replaced.

8. If necessary, remove the Hall sensor unit, as follows:
   a. Make an alignment mark on the edge of the base plate and on the engine (**Figure 27**). This will make certain that the base plate will be reinstalled in its original position.
   b. Remove the screws and washers (A, **Figure 28**) securing the base plate to the alternator support cover.
   c. Carefully pull the base plate assembly (B, **Figure 28**) from the alternator support cover and remove it.
9. Remove the Allen bolts and washers securing the alternator support cover (**Figure 29**) and remove the cover. Do not lose the locating dowels.

Installation

1. Make sure the cover sealing surface is free of old sealant residue.

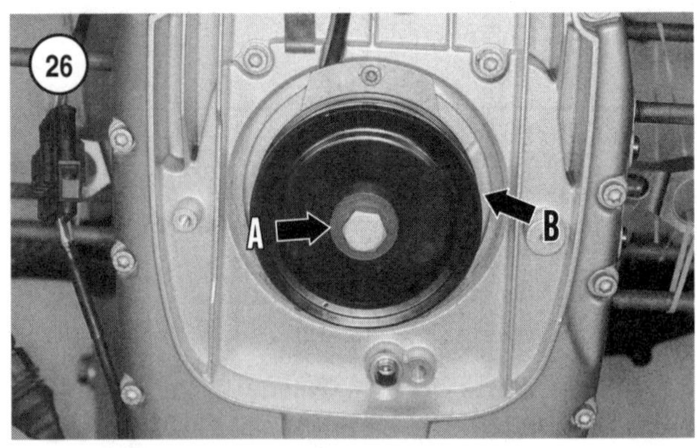

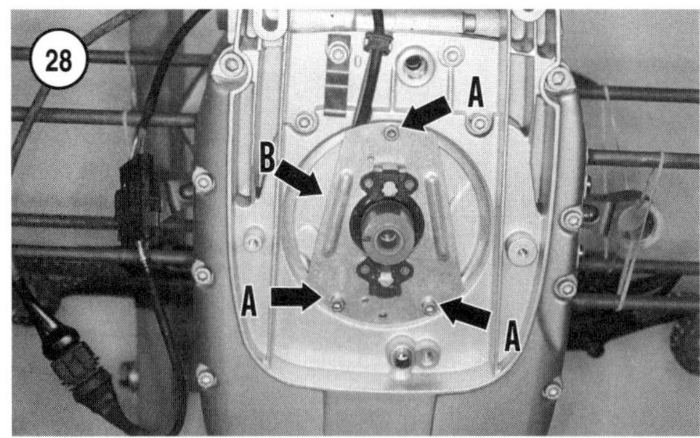

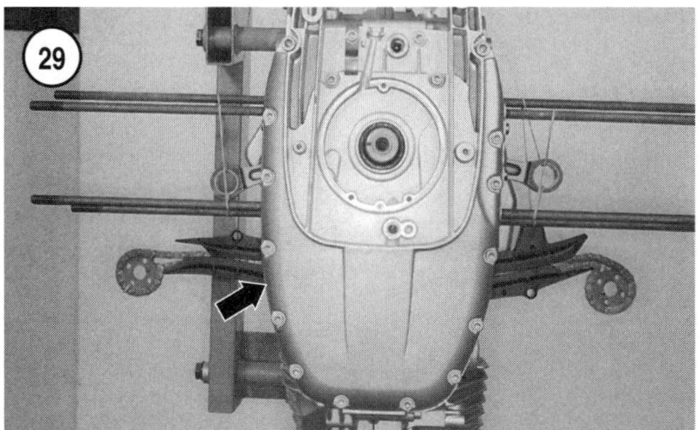

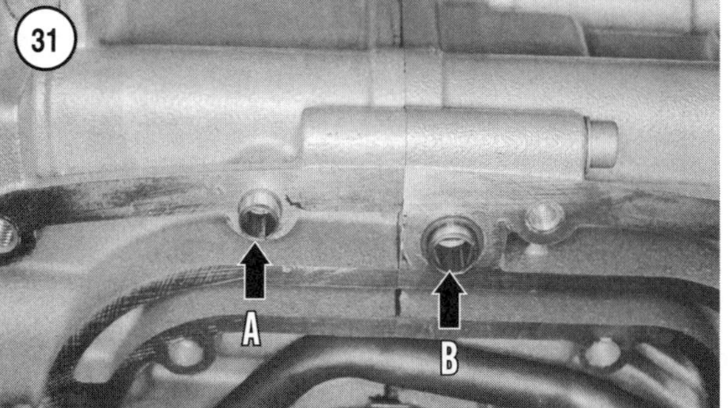

2. Apply a light coat of non-hardening liquid gasket sealer, such as ThreeBond 1209, or an equivalent, onto the cover sealing surface of the crankcase (**Figure 30**).

3. If removed, install the upper right locating dowel (A, **Figure 31**) and the upper left locating dowel and new O-ring (B). Install the lower locating dowel (**Figure 32**).

4. Apply a light coat of Tri-flow lubrication to the crankshaft (**Figure 33**). This will lessen the chance of damage to the radial oil seal on the cover.

5. Install the alternator support cover straight onto the front of the crankcase. Tap the cover on until it is seated around the perimeter.

CAUTION

When properly aligned, the alternator support cover should fit against the crankcase mating surface. If the cover does not fit completely, do not attempt to pull them together with the bolts.

6. Install the Allen bolts and washers securing the alternator support cover (**Figure 29**). Using a crisscross pattern, tighten the bolts in several stages to 20 N•m (15 ft.-lb.).

7. If the Hall sensor unit was removed, perform the following:

a. Refer to the alignment marks made during removal and install the base plate (B, **Figure 28**) onto the alternator support cover. Install the screws and washers (A, **Figure 28**). Tighten the screws securely. After the screws are tightened, recheck the alignment marks and readjust if necessary.

b. If installing a new Hall sensor unit, install the base plate (B, **Figure 28**) onto the alternator support cover. Install the screws and washers (A, **Figure 28**). Tighten the screws securely.

c. Move the wire harness and rubber grommet back under the clamp and tighten the clamp bolt (**Figure 25**).

NOTE

It is important that the ignition timing be checked at this time.

d. To ensure proper installation and alignment of the base plate, check the ignition timing at this time as described in Chapter Ten.

8. Align the raised tab on the pulley (A, **Figure 34**) with the crankshaft groove (B) and install the pulley onto the crankshaft (**Figure 35**). Make sure the raised tab is properly located in the crankshaft groove.

9. Install the bolt and washer and tighten to 50 N•m (37 ft.-lb.).

10. Install the alternator as described in Chapter Ten. Install the belt onto both pulleys.

11. On models equipped with the rotary breather pipe perform the following:

a. Install a new O-ring seal onto the locating dowel (**Figure 36**) and push it in until it seats properly. Apply a light coat of clean engine oil to the O-ring and locating dowel.

b. Install the rotary breather pipe (C, **Figure 24**) onto the alternator support cover. Push the lower porting into place over the locating dowel and O-ring. Install the lower bolt (A, **Figure 24**) and tighten finger-tight.

c. Install a new inner sealing washer between the pipe and the support, then install the upper banjo bolt and new sealing washer through the pipe and the inner sealing washer. Make sure both sealing washers are in place (**Figure 37**) on the upper banjo bolt. Tighten the upper banjo bolt and the lower bolt securely.

12. Install the engine as described in this chapter.

13. Install the front cover (**Figure 23**) and tighten the bolts securely.

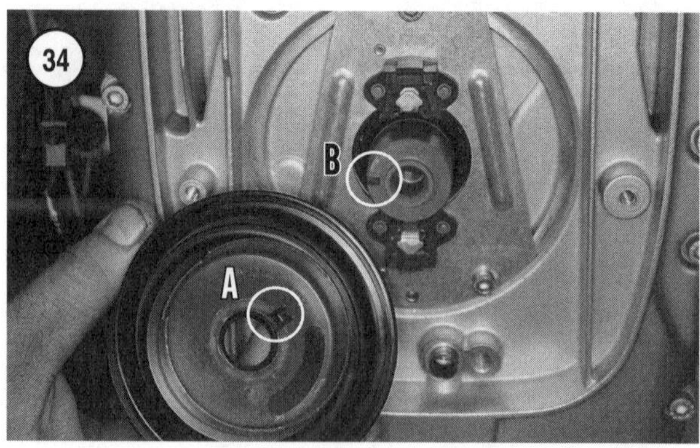

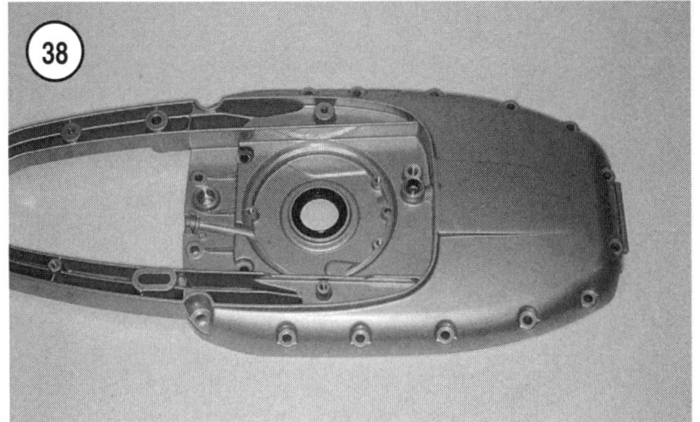

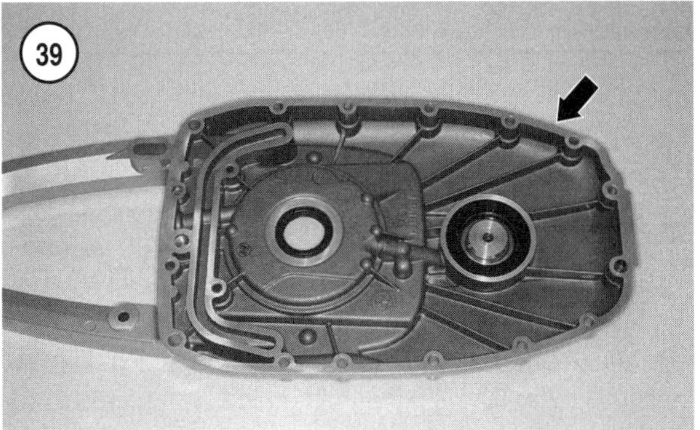

Inspection

1. Clean the inside and outside surfaces of the alternator support cover with solvent and dry with compressed air.
2. Remove all traces of gasket sealant from the inner sealing surface.
3. Inspect the alternator support cover (**Figure 38**) for cracks or damage.
4. Carefully check the sealing surface (**Figure 39**) for gouges or nicks that may cause an oil leak.
5. On models with the rotary breather, make sure the locating dowel (**Figure 40**) is in place and is secure.

Crankshaft Radial Seal Replacement

CAUTION
After the new seal is installed, do not start the engine for approximately one hour. This allows the seal lips to form correctly against the crankshaft and avoid a possible oil leak.

1. Carefully pry the oil seal (**Figure 41**) from the cover.
2. Thoroughly clean the seal bore with solvent and dry with compressed air.
3. Apply a light coat of Tri-flow lubricant to the crankshaft (**Figure 33**).
4. Install the cover as described in this chapter.
5. Pre-form the seal with your fingers. Press the sealing lips out with several fingers until it is even all around. The inner lip must be moved out so it will clear the crankshaft taper during installation.
6. Position the seal with the open end facing toward the crankcase. Carefully slide the new seal onto the crankshaft and push it part way into the cover.
7. Use a driver that matches the outside diameter of the seal and carefully tap the new seal straight into place until it stops.

Rotary Breather Radial Seal Replacement (Models So Equipped)

CAUTION
After the new seal is installed, do not start the engine for approximately one hour. This allows the seal lips to form correctly against the auxiliary shaft.

1. Carefully pry the seal from the cover.
2. Thoroughly clean out the seal bore in the cover with cleaning solvent and dry with compressed air.
3. Position the new seal onto the crankshaft with the open side facing down (A, **Figure 42**).

4. Pre-form the seal with your fingers. Press the sealing lips in with several fingers until it is even all around. The inner lip must be moved in so it will clear the shaft during installation.

5. Use a large socket or driver (B, **Figure 42**) that matches the outer diameter of the oil seal and press the new seal squarely into the cover until it seats completely. Make sure it seats correctly around its entire perimeter.

6. Apply a light coat of Tri-flow lubricant to the new oil seal inner lips. This will lessen the chance of damage to the radial oil seal during installation.

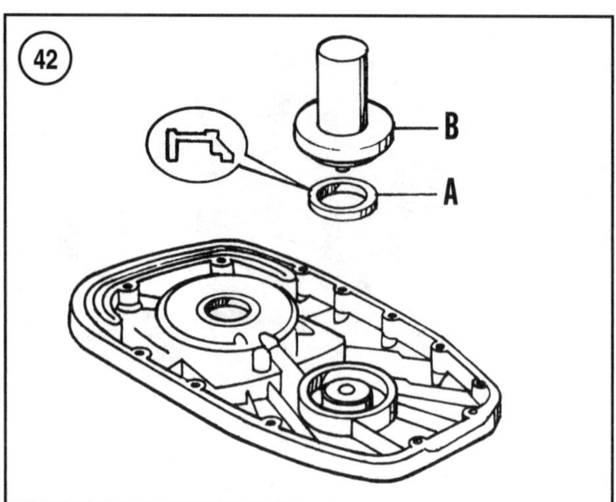

AUXILIARY DRIVE SHAFT MECHANISM

Removal

Refer to **Figure 43**.

1. Remove the engine as described in this chapter.
2. Remove the alternator support cover as described in this chapter.

CAUTION
*If the pistons are removed, suspend the connecting rod outer ends with rubber bands secured to the crankcase studs as shown in **Figure 44**. This will lessen the chance of damage to both the connecting rods and to the crankcase openings if the crankshaft is rotated.*

3. Rotate the crankshaft until the timing marks on both sprockets align as shown in **Figure 45**.
4. Remove the oil pipe as follows:
   a. Remove the ventilation valve or union bolt and sealing washers (A, **Figure 46**) securing the oil pipe to the crankcase.
   b. Remove the mounting bolts (B, **Figure 46**) securing the oil pipe to the crankcase.
   c. Pivot the oil pipe (C, **Figure 46**) down and release it from the left side of the oil pump.
5. Remove the bolts (A, **Figure 47**) securing the chain tensioner to the crankcase and remove the tensioner assembly (B). Hold the end of the tensioner piston to keep it from falling out along with the spring.
6. Remove the snap ring and washer (A, **Figure 48**) securing the tensioner rail and remove the tensioner rail (B) from the post.
7. Remove the snap rings and washers (A, **Figure 49**) securing the guide rail and remove the guide rail (B).
8. To keep the crankshaft from rotating in the next step insert the locking device (BMW part No. 11-5-640) into the flywheel gear teeth and crankcase (**Figure 50**).

9A. On models equipped with the rotary breather, perform the following:
   a. Remove the bolt and washer (A, **Figure 51**) securing the rotary breather and auxiliary shaft sprocket.
   b. Remove the rotary breather (B, **Figure 51**) and the auxiliary shaft sprocket (**Figure 52**).

9B. On all other models, remove the bolt and washer securing the auxiliary shaft sprocket and remove the auxiliary shaft sprocket (**Figure 52**).

10. Remove the chain (**Figure 53**) from the crankshaft sprocket.

Installation

Refer to **Figure 43**.

1. Install the chain (**Figure 53**) onto the crankshaft sprocket.

2A. On models equipped with the rotary breather, perform the following:
   a. Align the sprocket raised locating boss (A, **Figure 54**) with the depression (B) on the auxiliary shaft end and install the sprocket (**Figure 52**) onto the auxiliary shaft. Make sure both parts align correctly.
   b. Confirm that the timing marks on both sprockets are aligned as shown in **Figure 45**.
   c. Install the rotary breather and bolt (**Figure 55**). Tighten the bolt to 70 N•m (52 ft.-lb.).

2B. On all other models, perform the following:
   a. Align the sprocket raised locating boss (A, **Figure 54**) with the depression (B) on the auxiliary shaft end and install the sprocket (**Figure 52**) onto the auxiliary shaft.
   b. Confirm that the timing marks on both sprockets are aligned as shown in **Figure 45**.
   c. Install the bolt and tighten to70 N•m (52 ft.-lb.).

43

AUXILIARY DRIVE SHAFT MECHANISM

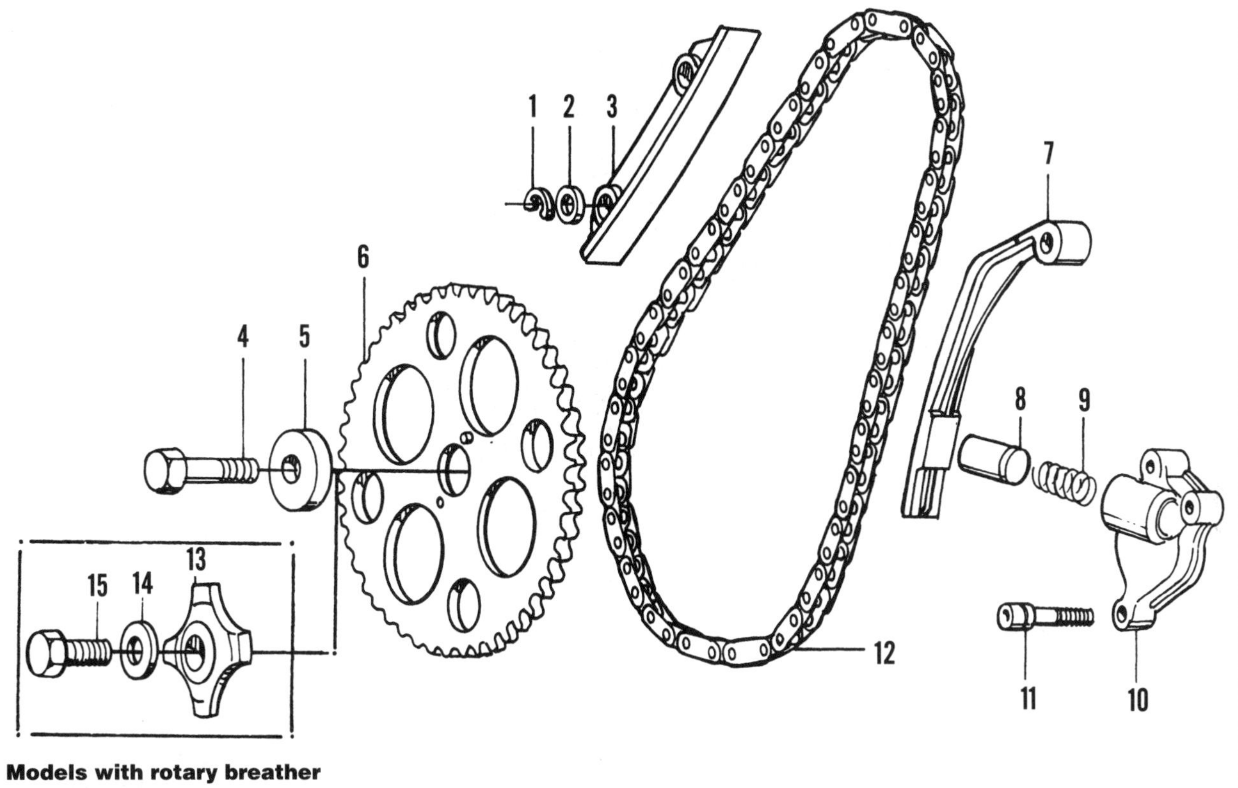

1 2 3 4 5 6 7 8 9 10 11 12 13 14 15

Models with rotary breather

1. E-clip
2. Washer
3. Guide rail
4. Bolt
5. Washer
6. Auxillary shaft sprocket
7. Tensioner rail
8. Piston
9. Spring
10. Chain tensioner
11. Allen bolt
12. Chain
13. Rotary breather
14. Washer
15. Bolt

3. Remove the locking device from the flywheel gear teeth and crankcase (**Figure 50**).

4. Position the guide rail with the long end (C, **Figure 49**) facing down. This will place the manufacturer's marks facing toward the crankcase. Install the guide rail (B, **Figure 49**) onto the posts and install the washers and E-clips (A). Make sure the E-clips seat properly in the groove in each post.

5. Install the tensioner rail (B, **Figure 48**) and the washer and E-clip (A). Make sure the E-clip seats properly in the groove in the post.

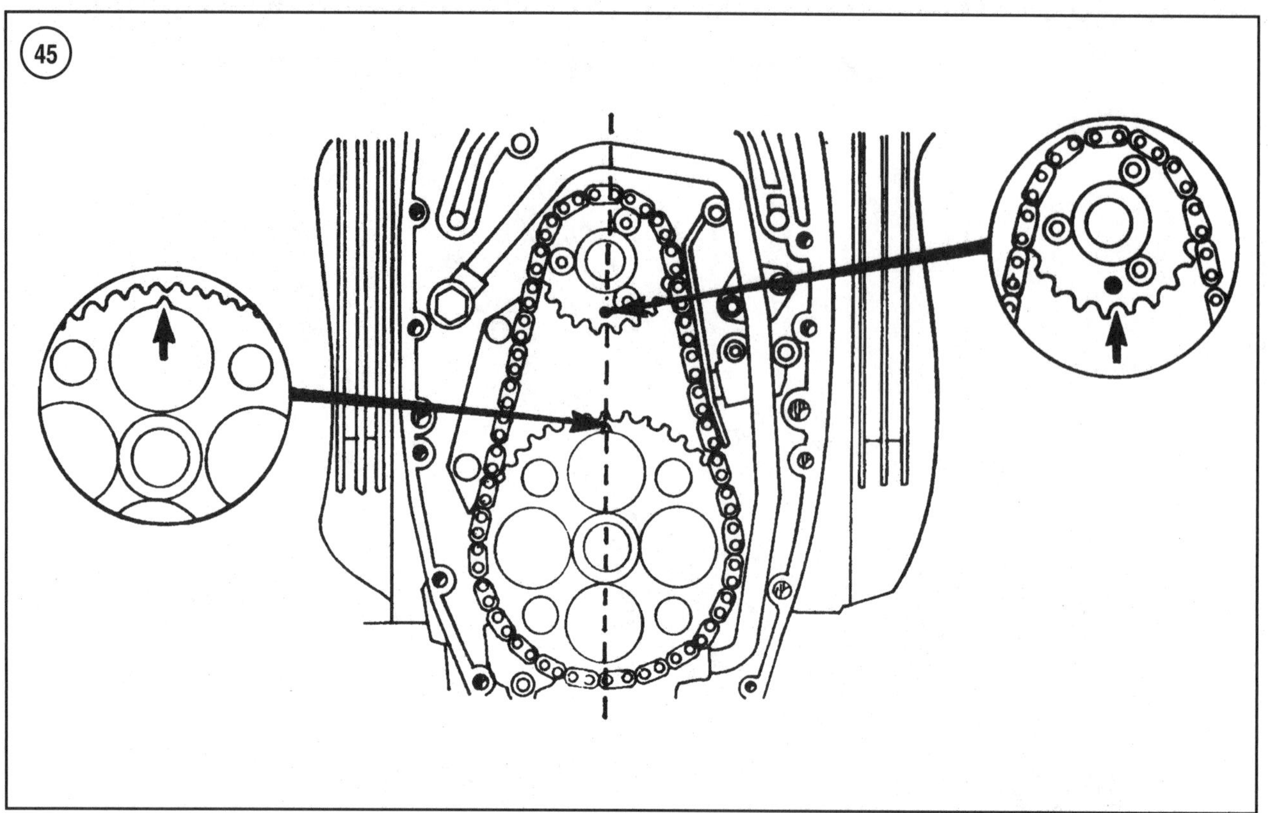

6. Install the spring and piston into the chain tensioner housing. Compress the piston and spring and install the tensioner housing (B, **Figure 47**) onto the crankcase. Install the mounting bolts (A, **Figure 47**) securing the chain tensioner to the crankcase and tighten to 32 N•m (24 ft.-lb.).

7. Install the oil pipe as follows:

   a. Install a new O-ring seal onto the oil pump end of the oil pipe and insert it into the oil pump.

   b. Move the oil pipe (C, **Figure 46**) up into position and install the ventilation valve, or union bolt and sealing washers securing the oil pipe to the crankcase. Be sure to install a sealing washer on each side of the fitting (**Figure 56**). Tighten the valve or bolt to 25 N•m (18 ft.-lb.).

   c. Install the mounting bolts and tighten to 20 N•m (15 ft.-lb.).

8. After installation is complete, make sure the timing marks on both sprockets are still aligned as shown in **Figure 45**.

9. Install the alternator support cover as described in this chapter.

10. Install the engine as described in this chapter.

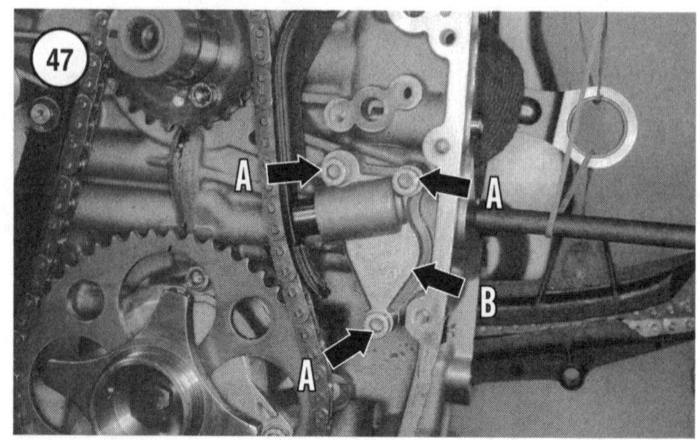

48
A
B

52

49
A
B
A
C

53

50

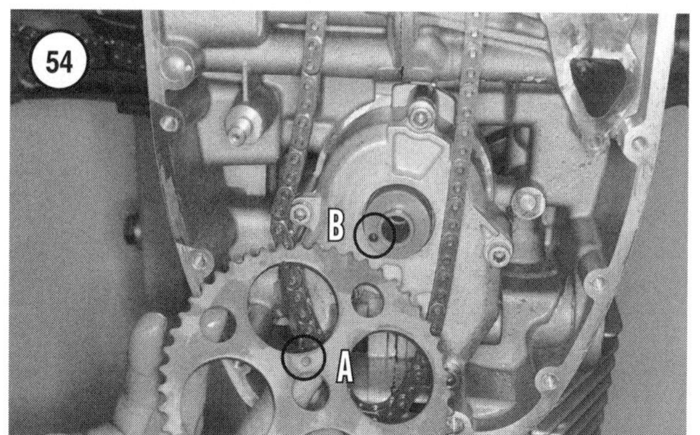
54
B
A

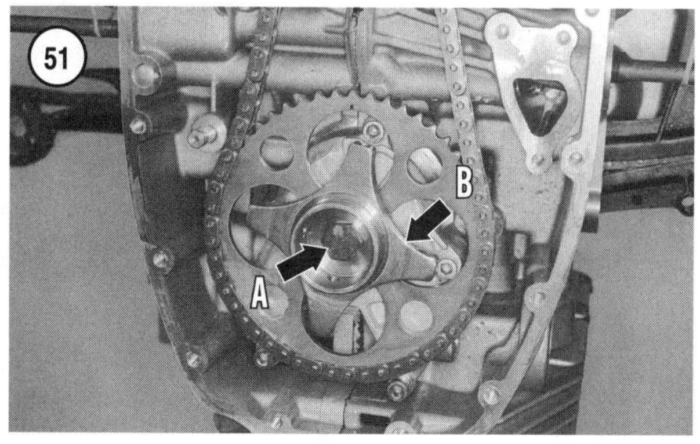
51
B
A

55

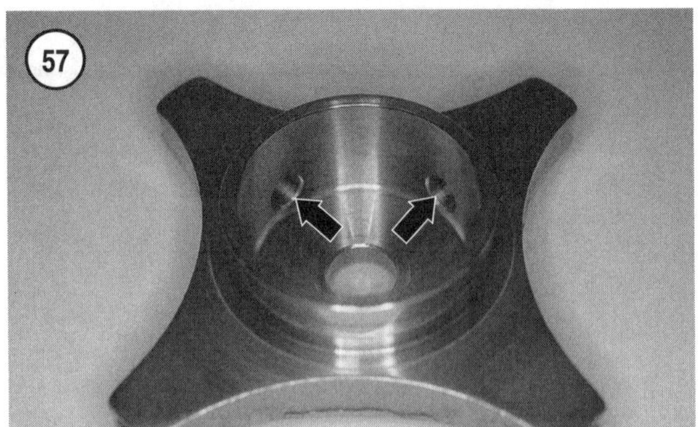

Inspection

1. Thoroughly clean all parts in solvent and dry with compressed air.
2. On models so equipped, inspect the rotary breather as follows:
   a. Make sure all openings are clean. Refer to **Figure 57** and **Figure 58**.
   b. Check the rotary breather for external damage (**Figure 59**).
3. Withdraw the piston and spring from the tensioner and visually inspect all parts for wear (**Figure 60**). If any portion is damaged, replace the entire assembly.
4. Check the chain bearing surface of the guide rail and tensioner rail (**Figure 61**) for wear or damage. Replace as necessary.
5. Inspect the sprocket for damaged or missing teeth (**Figure 62**). If damaged, replace the sprocket. If damage is severe, also check the chain and the crankshaft sprocket for damage.
6. Check the entire length of the chain (**Figure 63**) for abnormal wear or damage.
7. On models so equipped, check the ventilation valve for clogged openings. Refer to **Figure 64** and **Figure 65**. Clean it out if necessary.
8. Inspect the oil pipe for damage (**Figure 66**). Apply light air pressure to one end and make sure it is clear.

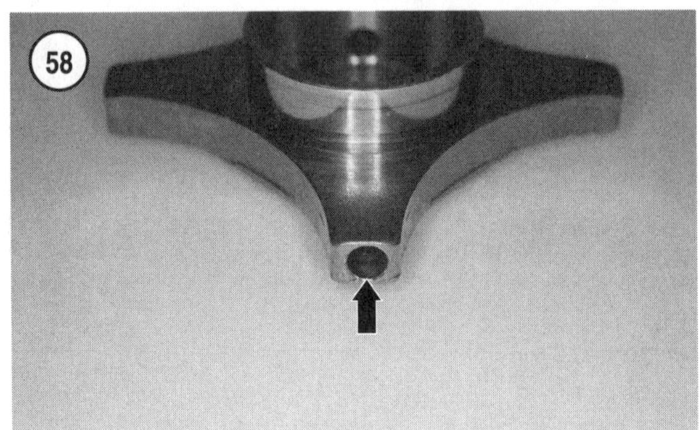

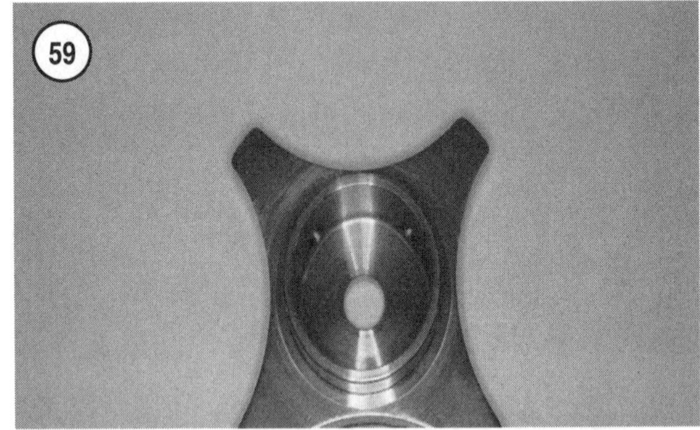

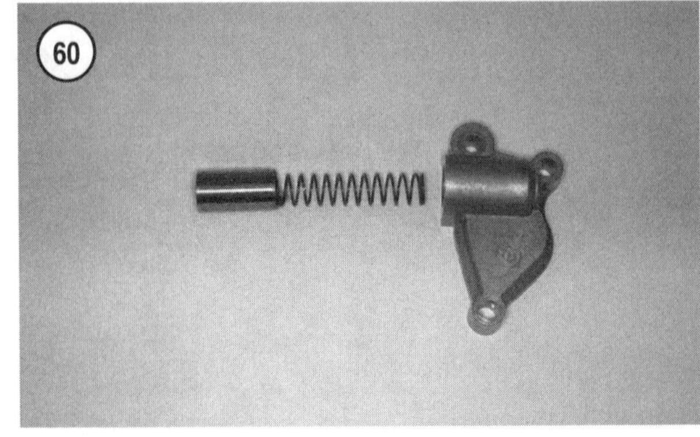

OIL PUMP

The oil pump is mounted on the front surface of the crankcase behind the auxiliary drive sprocket. The oil pump is equipped with two different sets of rotors.

The outer rotor set circulates the oil through the oil cooler and part of the engine. The inner set circulates oil throughout the engine. The outer rotors are dimensionally different and cannot be intermixed.

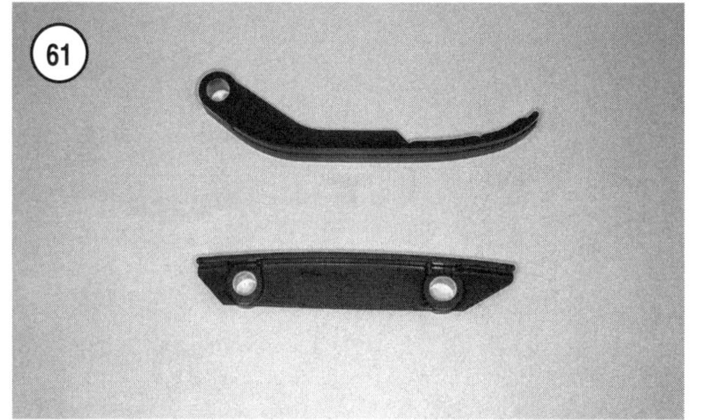

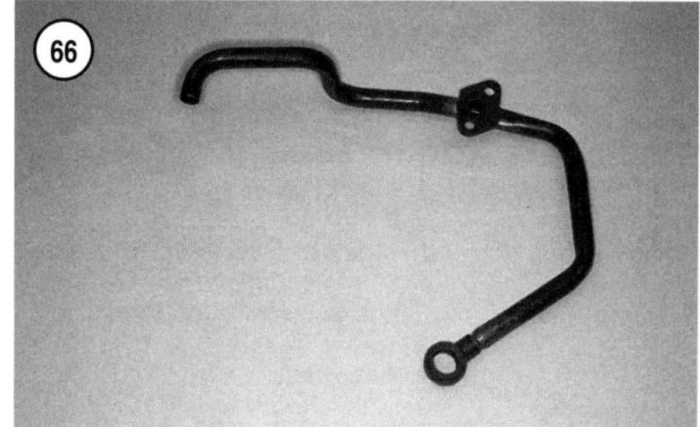

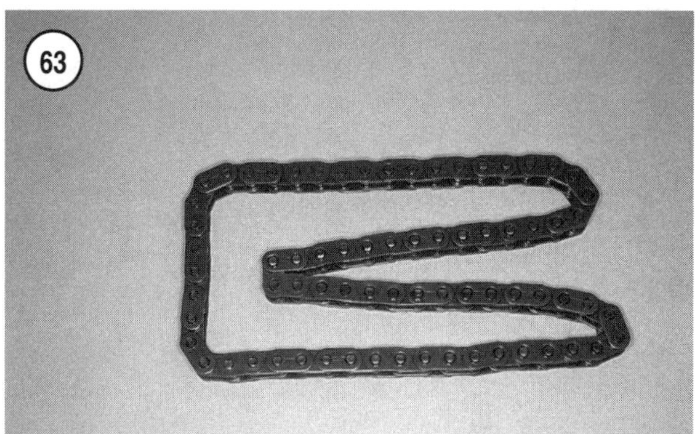

Removal/Disassembly

Refer to **Figure 67**.

1. Remove the auxiliary shaft drive mechanism as described in this chapter.

NOTE
Some models have a bolt and washer and others have a flange bolt with no washer.

2. Remove the bolts and washers securing the cover to the oil pump body (**Figure 68**).
3. Remove the oil cooler inner (A, **Figure 69**) and outer (B) rotors from the auxiliary shaft.
4. Remove the Woodruff key from the auxiliary shaft.

CAUTION
The engine oil pump outer rotor will usually come off with the pump body. Place a finger on to the backside of the body when removing it from the crankcase to avoid dropping it.

NOTE
The engine oil pump inner rotor is an integral part of the intermediate shaft and will

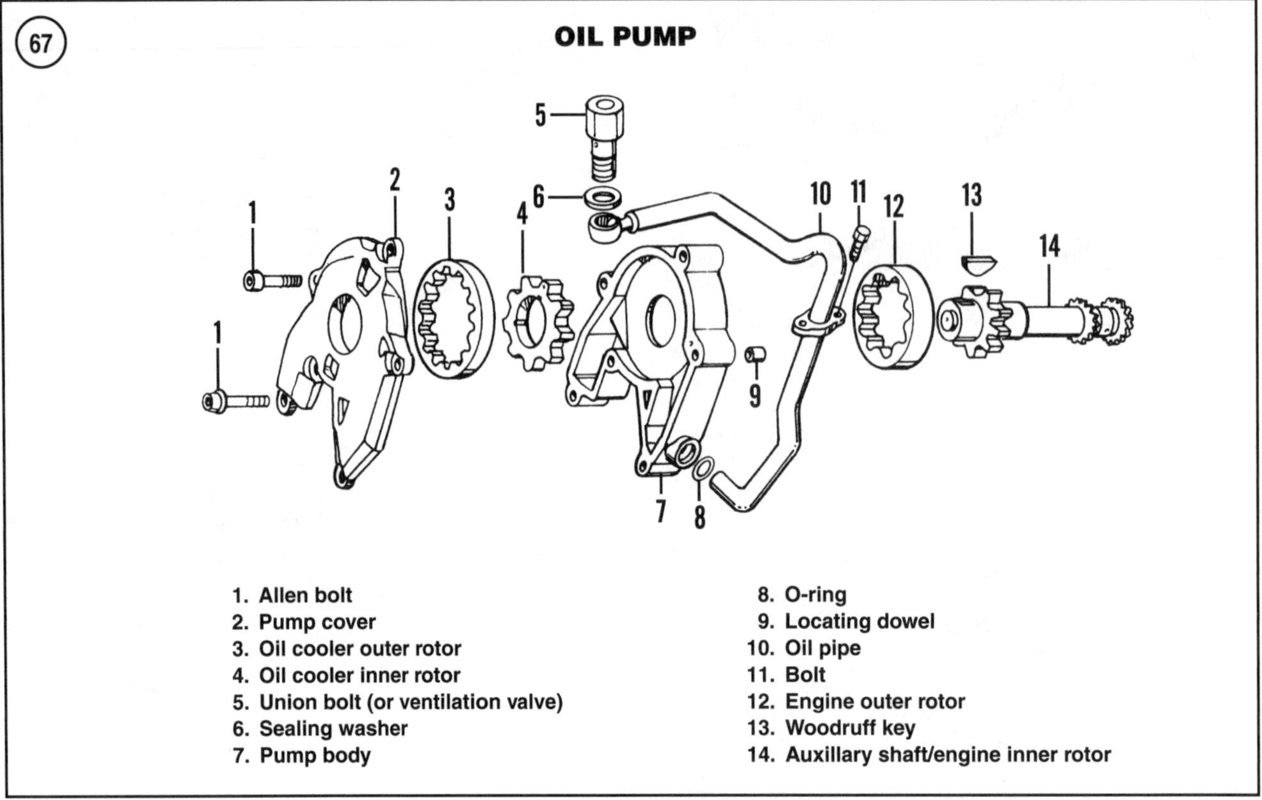

not come off when the oil pump body is removed.

5. Pull the oil pump body (**Figure 70**) straight off the crankcase. Do not lose the locating dowels.
6. Remove the engine oil pump outer rotor (A, **Figure 71**).
6. Remove the O-ring seal (**Figure 72**) from the oil pump body and discard it.
7. Inspect the oil pump as described in this chapter.

Assembly/Installation

Refer to **Figure 67**.

1. Apply clean engine oil to all parts prior to assembly. Be sure to lubricate the engine inner rotor (**Figure 73**) on the end of the auxiliary shaft.
2. Install a *new* O-ring (**Figure 74**) into the pump body. Make sure it is seated correctly (**Figure 72**).
3. If removed, install the locating dowels (B, **Figure 71**) into the backside of the pump body.
4. Position the engine pump outer rotor with the mark facing out (toward the front of the engine) and install the outer rotor (A, **Figure 71**) into the backside of the pump body.

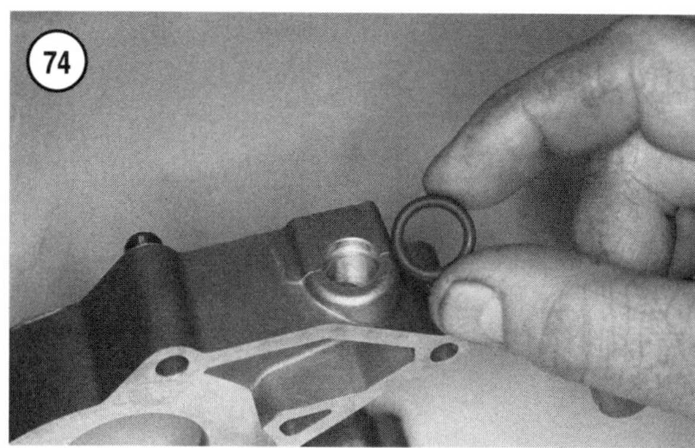

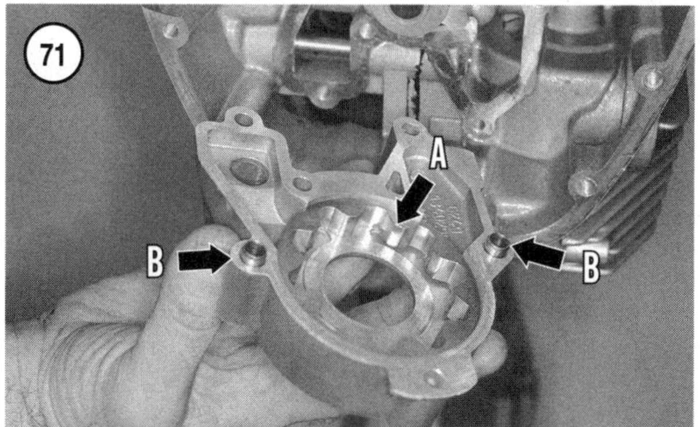

CAUTION
In Step 5, do not force the pump body onto the crankcase as the engine pump of rotors may not be aligned properly.

5. Carefully and slowly install the oil pump body onto the crankcase while aligning the inner and outer rotors. If necessary, slightly rotate the body back and forth to achieve alignment of the rotors. Once aligned properly, push the oil pump body (**Figure 70**) onto the crankcase until it bottoms. Make sure the locating dowels are installed correctly.

CAUTION
When properly aligned, the oil pump body fits against the crankcase mating surface. If the oil pump body does not fit completely, do not attempt to pull it down with the cover bolts. Remove the oil pump body and correct the problem at this time.

6. Install the Woodruff key into the auxiliary shaft groove.

7. Position the oil cooler outer rotor with the mark (**Figure 75**) facing out, and install the outer rotor. Push it in until it stops.

76

78

77

79

8. Position the oil cooler inner rotor with the mark (**Figure 76**) facing out. Align the rotor locating groove with the Woodruff key, and install the inner rotor. Push it in until it stops.

9. Make sure the mark on both rotors is facing out.

10. Install the cover (**Figure 68**), bolts and washers. Follow a crisscross pattern and tighten the bolts to 9 N•m (80 in.-lb.).

11. Install the auxiliary shaft drive mechanism as described in this chapter.

80

Inspection

When measuring the oil pump components in this section, compare the measurements to the specifications listed in **Table 1**. Replace worn or damaged parts as described in this section.

1. Clean all parts in solvent and thoroughly dry them.

2. Inspect the inner (**Figure 77**) and outer surfaces (**Figure 78**) of the pump body for wear, cracks or damage. Check the inner walls for abrasions.

3. Inspect the inner surfaces of the cover (**Figure 79**) for wear, cracks, abrasions or damage.

81

82

83

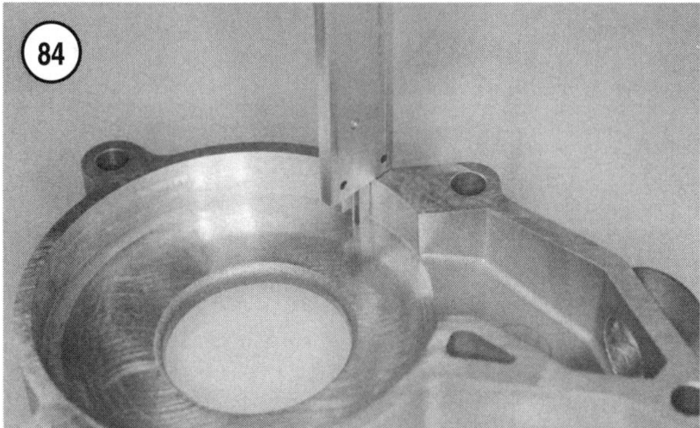
84

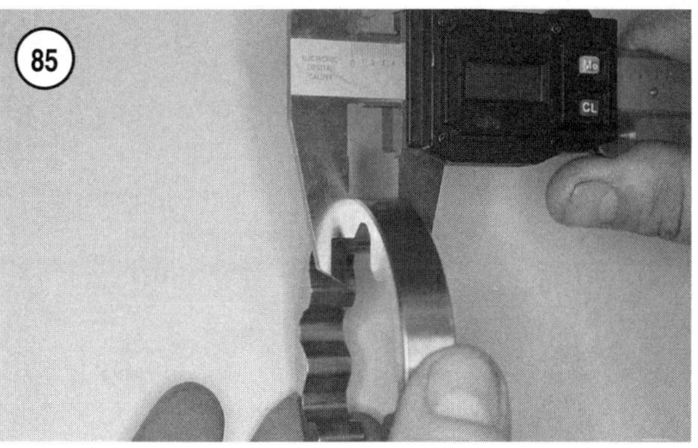
85

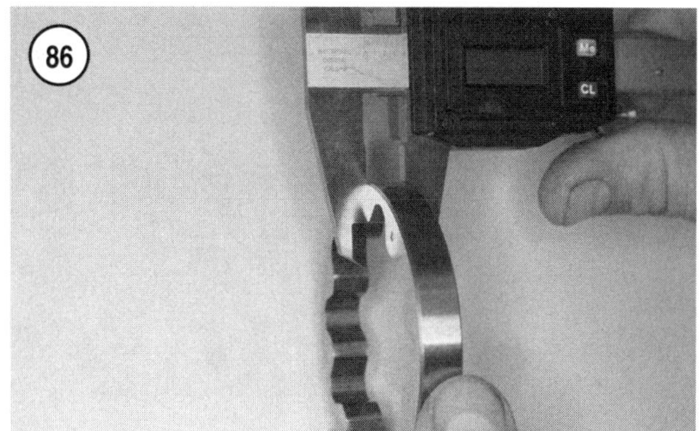
86

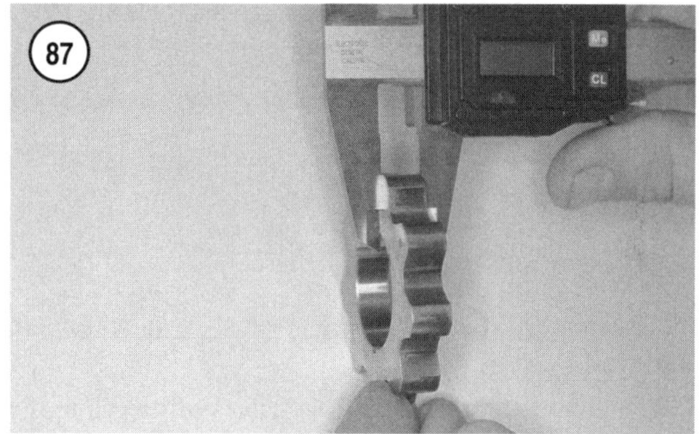
87

4. Inspect the oil cooler rotors (**Figure 80**) and the engine outer rotor (**Figure 81**) for abrasion, wear, cracks or damage.

5. Inspect the engine inner rotor (**Figure 82**) for abrasion, wear, cracks or damage.

6. Use a depth gauge or vernier caliper and measure the depth of the pump body. Measure the engine pump depth (**Figure 83**) and the oil cooler pump depth (**Figure 84**).

7. Use a vernier caliper and measure the thickness of the outer rotors. Measure the thickness of engine pump rotor (**Figure 85**) and the oil cooler pump rotor (**Figure 86**).

NOTE

To measure the engine pump inner rotor attached to the intermediate shaft, place a piece of metal, like a thick flat feeler gauge, behind the inner rotor to establish the back surface of the rotor.

8. Use a vernier caliper and measure the thickness of the inner rotors. Measure the engine inner rotor thickness and the oil cooler inner rotor thickness (**Figure 87**).

88

9. Install the oil cooler inner and outer rotors in the pump body. Insert a flat feeler gauge between the rotor tips (**Figure 88**) and measure the axial play.

10. Replace the oil pump assembly if any part of the oil pump is worn or damaged.

CRANKCASE

Disassembly of the crankcase assembly requires engine removal.

The crankcase is made in two halves of precision die cast aluminum alloy. To avoid damage, do not hammer or pry on any of the interior or exterior projected walls—excessive force will damage these areas. The crankcase halves are assembled with a sealant. No gasket is used. The crankcase halves are sold as a matched set only. If one crankcase half is damaged, both case halves must be replaced as a set.

Remember that the right and left sides of the engine relate to the engine as it sits in the frame, not as it is mounted in the engine. Keep this in mind when working on the engine in the stand.

Disassembly

This procedure describes disassembly of the crankcase halves. When the crankcase assembly is disassembled, all internal components remain in the right crankcase half.

1. Remove the cylinder heads, cylinders and pistons as described in Chapter Four.

2. Remove the engine as described in this chapter.

3. Install the engine into the engine adapter (BMW part No. 11-0-630 [**Figure 89**]). Fasten the engine adapter to the right crankcase half.

4. Remove the alternator (A, **Figure 90**) as described in Chapter Ten.

89

90

91

92

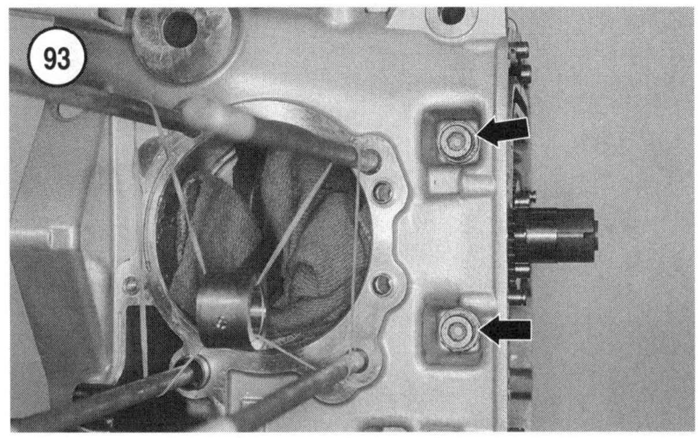

93

94

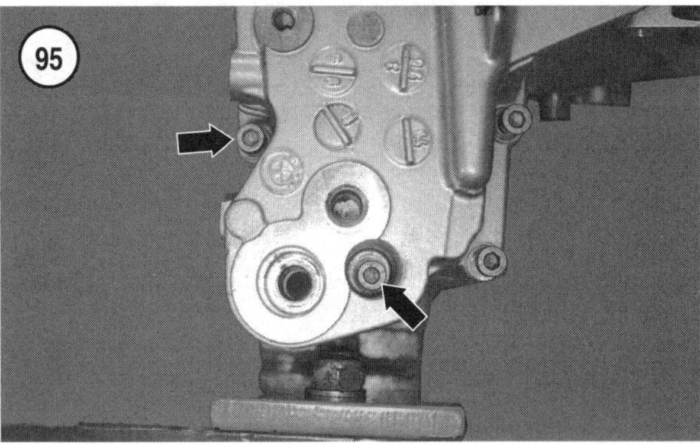

95

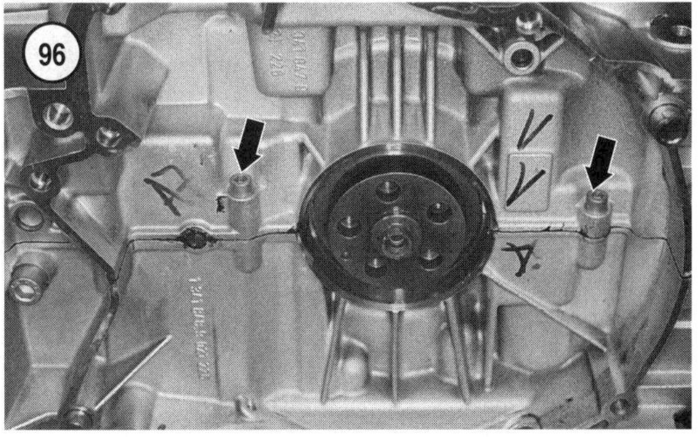

96

97

5

NOTE
The rubber mounts are very difficult to loosen and will usually be damaged during removal. To loosen, use locking pliers and clamp down hard on the rubber portion as close to the crankcase surface as possible.

5. Remove the rubber mounts (B, **Figure 90**) securing the electrical cable bracket and the ABS unit/battery holder bracket (C).
6. Remove the intermediate shaft drive mechanism as described in this chapter.
7. Remove the oil pump assembly as described in this chapter.

CAUTION
*Suspend the connecting rod outer ends with rubber bands secured to the crankcase studs as shown in **Figure 91**. This will lessen the chance of damage to both the connecting rods and to the crankcase openings if the crankshaft must be rotated.*

NOTE
To help keep track of the crankcase bolts, draw the crankcase outline on a piece of cardboard, then number and punch holes to correspond with each bolt location. On the left side there are three different length 6–mm bolts. After removal, insert the bolts in their appropriate locations. Leave any cable clamps on its respective bolt.

8. On the right side of the crankcase perform the following:
   a. Loosen all 8–mm bolts (**Figure 92**) in three stages, then remove them.
   b. Loosen the 10–mm bolts (**Figure 93**) in three stages, then remove them.
9. On the left side of the crankcase perform the following:
   a. Loosen the 6 mm bolts in three stages. Refer to **Figures 94-99**. Remove all bolts.

b. Loosen the 10–mm bolts (**Figure 100**) in three stages, then remove them.

10. Make sure that all of the bolts are removed.

11. Tap around the perimeter of the crankcase with a plastic or soft-faced mallet and separate the crankcase halves.

12. Carefully lift the left crankcase off the right upper crankcase. Turn the left crankcase over immediately and be careful that the crankcase main bearing inserts do not fall out. If necessary, reinstall them immediately into their original positions.

13. If loose, remove the crankcase dowel pins. Do not remove if they are secure.

14. Remove the camshaft drive chains and intermediate shaft as an assembly as described in this chapter.

15. Remove the crankshaft/connecting rod assembly as described in this chapter.

16. If necessary, remove the oil pressure switch (**Figure 101**) from the left crankcase half.

CAUTION
There are two different sizes and shapes of main bearing inserts. The front inserts are smaller in diameter while the rear are larger and shouldered. If the inserts are going to be reused, they must be reinstalled in their original positions to prevent lower end damage.

17. If the main bearing inserts are going to be removed, they must be identified. After removing the insert, mark the backside of the insert with an R (right) or L (left).

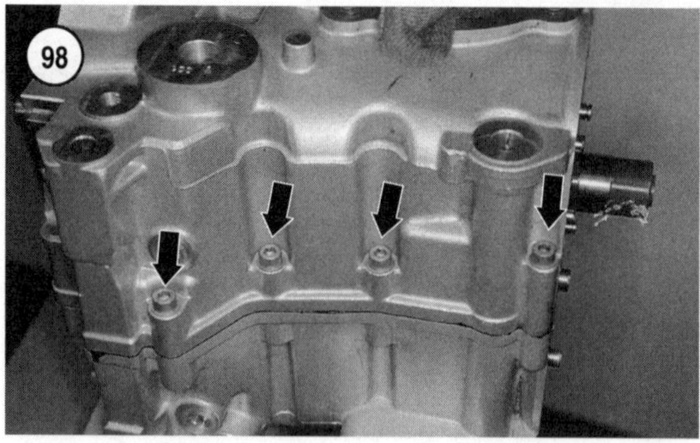

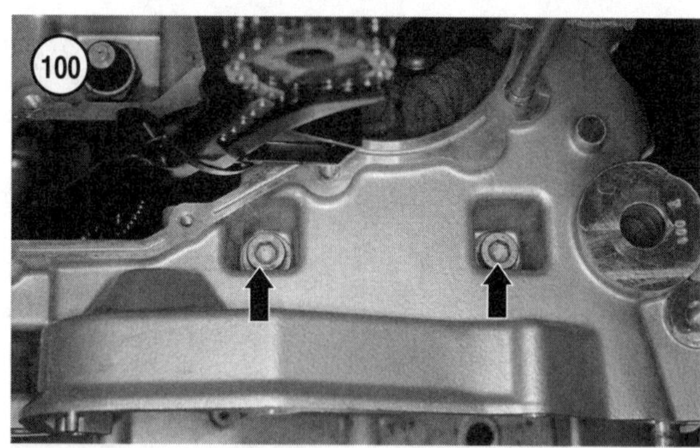

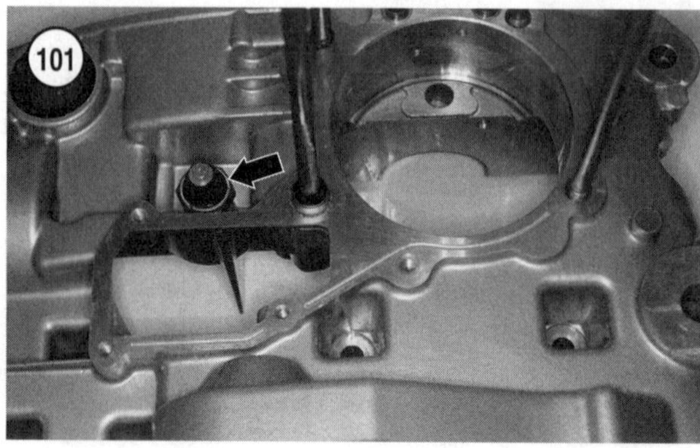

Assembly

NOTE
If reusing the old bearing inserts, install the in the correct locations as noted during removal. Apply assembly oil or clean engine oil to all bearing surfaces.

1. If removed, install the crankshaft main bearing inserts as follows:
   a. Make sure the bearing insert surfaces in both crankcase halves are clean. Check that the oil control hole at each journal is clear.
   b. Wipe clean both sides of the bearing insert with a lint-free cloth.
   c. Install the inserts into the correct locations (**Figure 102**) and carefully press the insert into position with your finger or thumb. Make sure the inserts are locked in place (**Figure 103**).
2. Apply clean engine oil to all main bearing inserts.

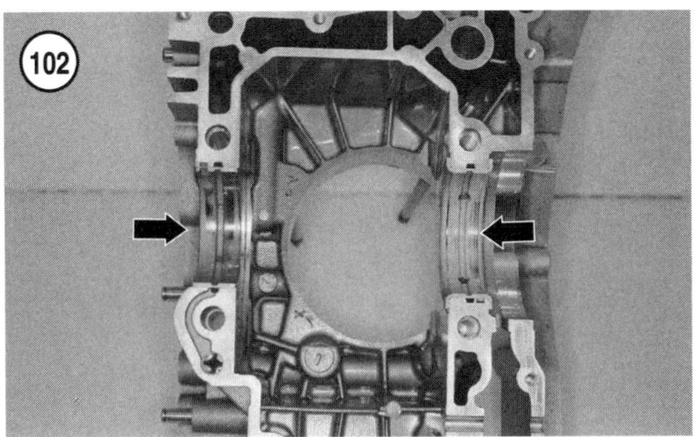

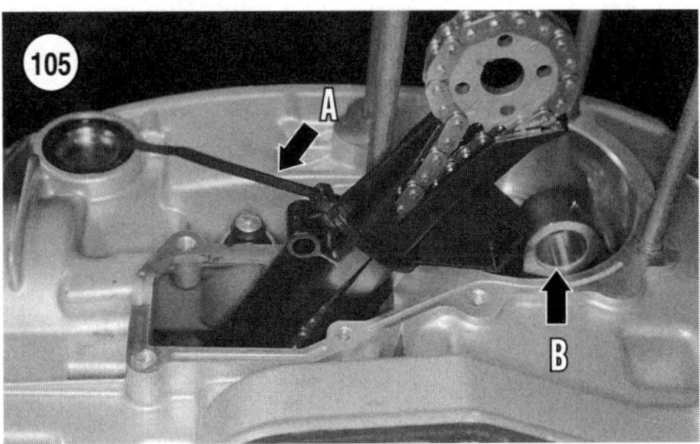

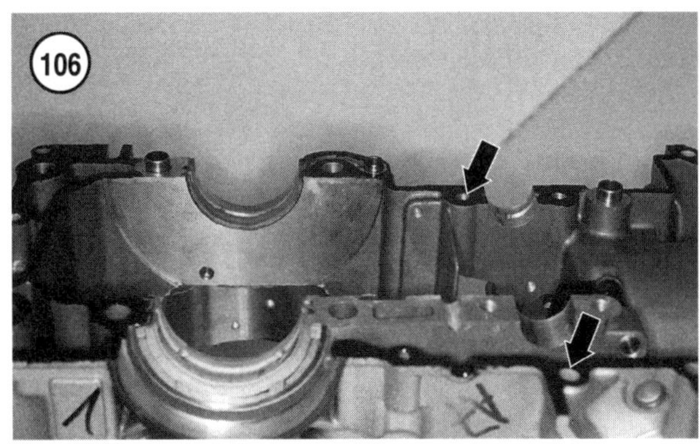

3. If removed, install the oil pressure switch (**Figure 101**) into the left crankcase half and tighten to 30 N•m (22 ft.-lb.).

4. Install the crankshaft/connecting rod assembly as described in this chapter.

5. Check each end of the crankshaft to make sure it seats properly in the crankcase. Rotate the crankshaft so the left piston is at bottom dead center. This will position the small end of the connecting rod down as far as possible for ease of left crankcase half installation.

6. Install the camshaft drive chains and intermediate shaft as described in this chapter.

7. If removed, install the four locating dowels (**Figure 104**) in the left crankcase half. If not removed, make sure all four are in place.

8. On the left side, install the camshaft driven sprocket onto the chain and secure the chain, tensioner and guide together with a tie wrap (A, **Figure 105**).

9. Make sure both crankcase mating surfaces are free of old sealant material or other residue.

10. Apply a light coat of non-hardening liquid gasket sealer, such as ThreeBond 1209, or equivalent, onto the left crankcase half mating surface (**Figure 106**). When selecting an equivalent, avoid thick and hard setting materials. Cover only flat surfaces, *not curved* bearing surfaces. Make the coating as thin as possible, but still completely covered.

CAUTION

When properly aligned, the left crankcase half slides over the shafts and seats against the opposite case half. If the crankcase halves do not fit together completely, do not attempt to pull them together with the crankcase bolts. Make sure the connecting rod is inside the opening in the left crankcase half (B, ***Figure 105****). Separate the crankcase halves and correct the cause of the interference. Crankcase halves are* *matched; do not risk damage by trying to force them together.*

11. Position the left crankcase half onto the right crankcase half. Guide the left camshaft chain and tensioner assembly (A, **Figure 107**) and connecting rod small end (B) up through the openings in the crankcase. Push the left crankcase half down until it seats on the right crankcase half around the entire perimeter.

12. Join both halves and tap them together lightly with a plastic or soft-faced mallet—do not use a metal hammer as this will damage the cases.

NOTE

Apply a light coat of clean engine oil to the 8 mm and 10 mm bolt threads prior to installation.

NOTE

*The crankcase bolts are several different lengths. Make certain that the bolts are installed in their correct locations (**Figure 108**, typical).*

13. Install and tighten the left crankcase half mounting bolts as follows:
    a. Use a crisscross pattern and tighten the 10 mm bolts (**Figure 100**) in three stages to 45 N•m (33 ft.-lb.).
    b. Use a crisscross pattern and tighten the 6 mm bolts in three stages to 9 N•m (80 in.-lb.). Refer to **Figures 94-99**.

CAUTION

*Suspend both connecting rod outer ends with rubber bands secured to the crankcase studs as shown in **Figure 91**. This will lessen the chance of damage to both the connecting rods and to the crankcase openings.*

14. Turn the engine over in the engine stand so the right crankcase half is facing up.

15. Install and tighten the right crankcase half mounting bolts in the correct locations as follows:
    a. Follow a crisscross pattern and tighten the 10 mm bolts (**Figure 93**) in three stages to 45 N•m (33 ft.-lb.).
    b. Follow a crisscross pattern and tighten the 8 mm bolts (**Figure 92**) in three stages to 20 N•m (15 ft.-lb.).

16. Rotate the crankshaft to make sure that the crankshaft rotates freely. If not, disassemble the crankcase and correct the problem.

17. Install the oil pump assembly as described in this chapter.

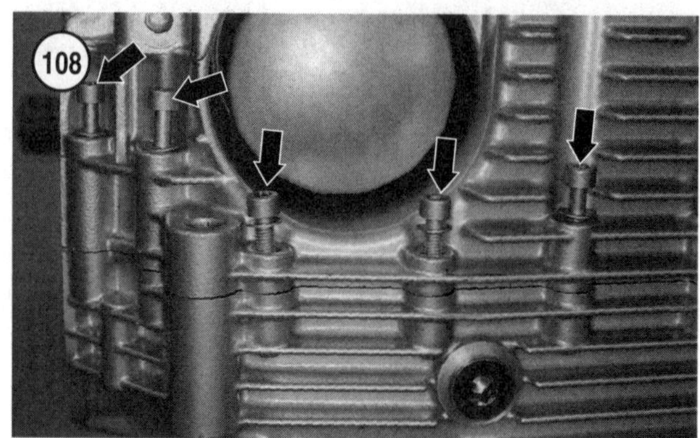

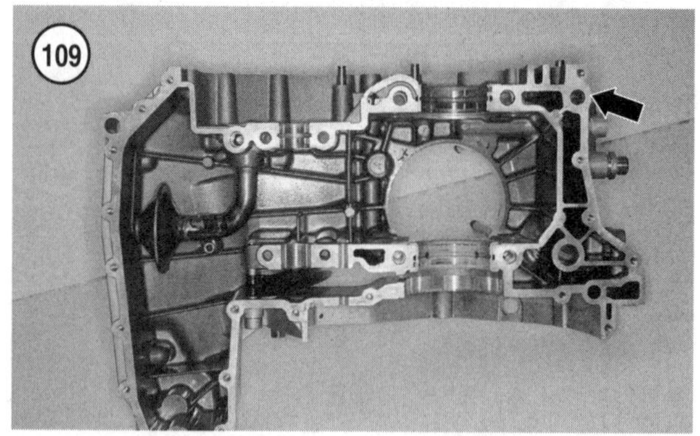

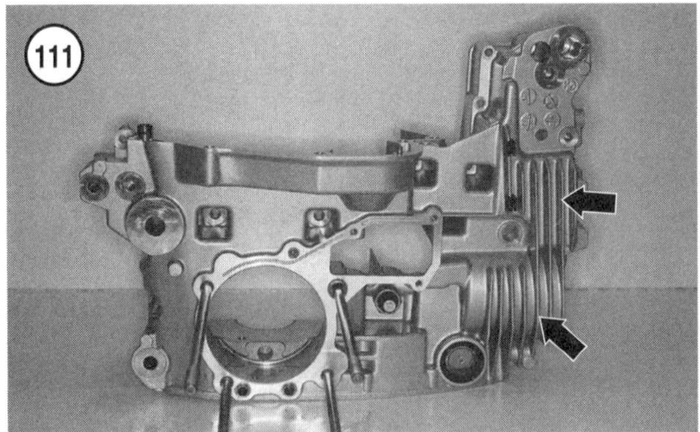
111

112

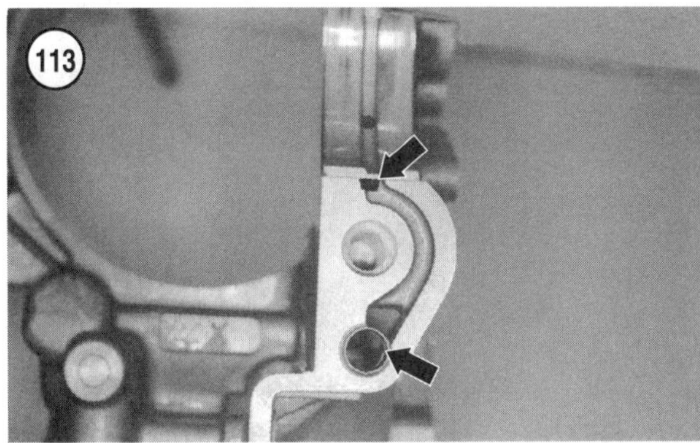
113

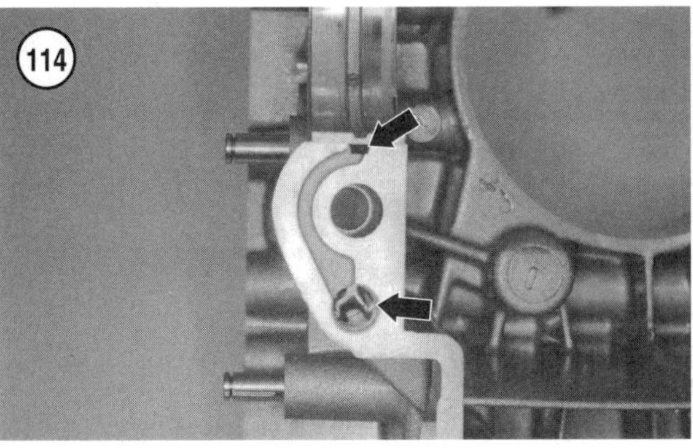
114

18. Install the intermediate shaft drive mechanism as described in this chapter.
19. Install the electrical cable bracket and ABS unit/battery holder bracket (C, **Figure 90**) onto the crankcase. Install the new rubber mounts (B, **Figure 90**) and tighten securely.
20. Install the alternator (A, **Figure 90**) as described in Chapter Ten.
21. With the aid of an assistant, remove the crankcase assembly from the engine adapter (**Figure 89**).
22. Install the engine as described in this chapter.
23. Install the cylinders, pistons and the cylinder heads as described in Chapter Four.

Inspection

1. Clean both crankcase halves and all crankcase bearings with cleaning solvent. Thoroughly dry them with compressed air. Make sure there is no solvent residue left in the case halves as it will contaminate the new engine oil.
2. Use a scraper and carefully remove any remaining sealant from all crankcase gasket surfaces as follows:
   a. Crankcase halves.
   b. Cylinder mating surface.
   c. Alternator support cover.
3. Inspect the sealing surface of both crankcase halves. Refer to **Figure 109** and **Figure 110**. Check for gouges or nicks that may cause an oil leak.
4. Clean all crankcase oil passages with compressed air.
5. Inspect the cases for cracks and fractures, especially in the lower cooling fin areas (**Figure 111**) where they are vulnerable to rock damage. Check the areas around the stiffening ribs and around bearing bosses and threaded holes for damage. If damage is found, have it repaired at a shop specializing in the repair of precision aluminum castings or replace the damaged crankcase.
6. Check the threaded holes in both crankcase halves for thread damage, dirt or oil buildup. If necessary, clean or repair the threads with a suitable size metric tap. Coat the tap threads with kerosene or an aluminum tap fluid before use.
7. Check the crankcase studs (**Figure 112**) for straightness, cracks and thread damage. Repair thread damage with a suitable size metric die. The studs cannot be replaced.
8. Check the oil filter threaded fitting for thread damage, dirt or oil buildup. If necessary, clean or repair the threads with a suitable size metric tap. Coat the tap threads with kerosene or an aluminum tap fluid before use.
9. Inspect all oil control openings. Refer to **Figure 113-115**. Clean out with solvent and apply compressed air.

10. Check the stud (**Figure 116**) that supports the camshaft chain tensioners and guides for wear or damage. The stud cannot be replaced.
11. Check the studs (**Figure 117**) that support the auxiliary shaft chain guide rail for wear or damage. The studs cannot be replaced.
12. Inspect the oil level view port (**Figure 118**) for leakage. Replace it if necessary.
13A. On models with two oil pickup baskets, remove the bolt and washer securing both oil pickup baskets (**Figure 119**). Pivot the pickup baskets out and remove them from the crankcase. Remove the O-ring from the end of each basket and discard them.
13B. On models with a single oil pickup basket, remove the bolt and washer (A, **Figure 120**) securing the oil pickup basket (B). Pivot the pickup basket up and remove it from the crankcase. Remove the O-ring from the end of the basket and discard it.
14. Check the oil cooler outlet fitting (**Figure 121**) on the left crankcase half for damage that could result in an oil leak. Replace if necessary.

115

116

REAR MAIN SEAL REPLACEMENT

R1100S and all R1150 Models

The rear main seal must be installed with the BMW special tools. If the tools are not used the seal will not fit correctly and leak.

The special tools hold the seal in the correct position to install it squarely in the crankcase bore.

NOTE
The rear main can be replaced without removing the engine. This procedure is shown with the engine removed to better illustrate the procedure.

1. Remove the clutch as described in Chapter Six.
2. Carefully remove the rear main seal from the crankcase.
3. Thoroughly clean the crankshaft surface and crankcase bore with solvent and dry with compressed air. Be sure to remove all sludge or hardened oil from the seal bore and from the crankshaft surface. Both of these parts must be completely clean for the new seal to work properly.
4. Apply a light coat of Tri-flow lubricant to the outer circumference of the crankshaft (**Figure 122**).
5. Pre-form the seal with your fingers. Press the sealing lips out with two fingers until it is even all around. The inner lip must be moved out so it will clear the crankshaft taper during installation.

117

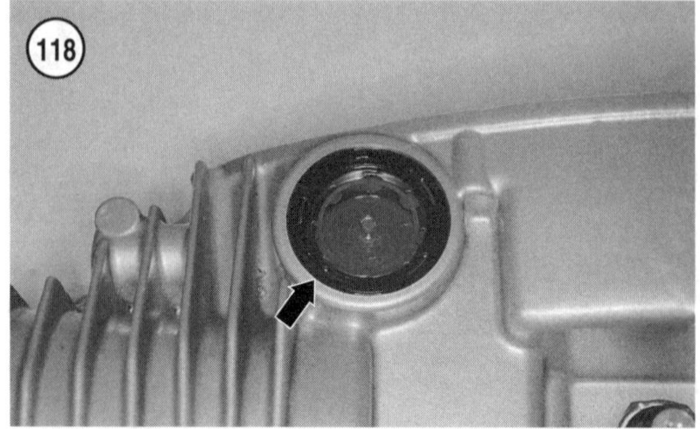
118

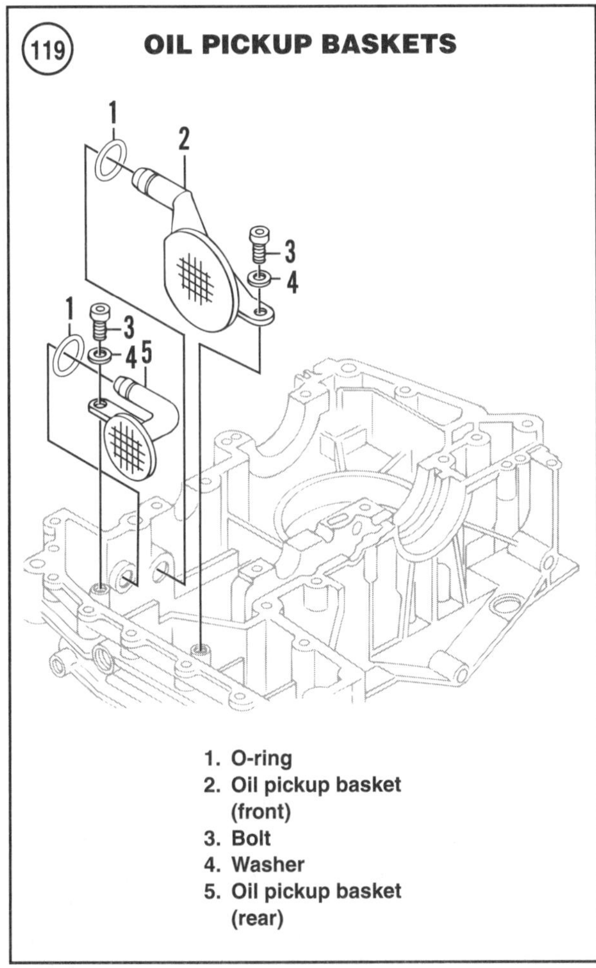

6. Position the seal with the open end facing out (A, **Figure 123**) and install it onto the sliding sleeve (BMW part No. 11-5-702) and then farther back onto the sleeve (part No. 11-5-703 [B]).

7. Remove the sliding sleeve from the sleeve.

8. To center the tool onto the crankshaft (C, **Figure 123**), position the recessed portion of the tool onto the raised boss on the end of the crankshaft (**Figure 124**).

9. Install drift (BMW part No. 11-5-701[D, **Figure 123**]) and securely hold the tool against the crankshaft and crankcase. Tap the new seal into the crankcase recess (**Figure 125**). Tap the seal in until it stops.

10. Remove the special tool and inspect the seal. Make sure it seats squarely and completely in the recess.

11. Install the clutch as described in Chapter Six.

All Models Except R1100S and R1150

The rear main seal must be installed with the BMW special tool. If the tool is not used the seal will not fit correctly and leak.

The special tool holds the seal in the correct position to install it squarely in the crankcase bore.

NOTE
The rear main seal can be replaced without removing the engine. This procedure is

shown with the engine removed to better illustrate the procedure.

1. Remove the clutch as described in Chapter Six.
2. Carefully remove the rear main seal from the crankcase.
3. Thoroughly clean the crankshaft surface and crankcase bore with solvent and dry with compressed air. Be sure to remove all sludge or hardened oil from the seal bore and from the crankshaft surface. Both of these parts must be completely clean for the new seal to work properly.
4. Apply a light coat of Tri-flow lubricant to the outer circumference of the crankshaft (**Figure 122**).
5. Pre-form the seal with your fingers. Press the sealing lips out with two fingers until it is even all around. The inner lip must be moved out so it will clear the crankshaft taper during installation.
6. Position the seal with the open end facing out (A, **Figure 126**) and install it onto the sliding sleeve (BMW part No. 11-5-660 [B]) as shown in **Figure 127**.
7. Remove the inner portion (C, **Figure 126**) of the tool as shown in **Figure 128**.
8. To center the tool onto the crankshaft (D, **Figure 126**), position the recessed portion of the tool (**Figure 129**) onto the raised boss on the end of the crankshaft (**Figure 124**).
9. Securely hold the special tool against the crankshaft and crankcase. Tapthe new seal into the crankcase recess (**Figure 125**). Tap the seal in until it stops.
10. Remove the tool and inspect the seal. Make sure it seats squarely and completely in the recess.
11. Install the clutch as described in Chapter Six.

AUXILIARY DRIVE SHAFT, CAMSHAFT CHAINS AND TENSIONER ASSEMBLIES

Refer to **Figure 130** (crankshaft, auxiliary drive shaft, camshaft chains and tensioner assemblies) and **Figure 131** (camshaft chain and tensioner assemblies).

Removal

1. Separate the crankcase as described in this chapter.
2. Carefully lift up and remove the camshaft drive chain tensioner and guide pin as an assembly (**Figure 132**).
3. Carefully lift up and remove the camshaft drive chains and auxiliary shaft as an assembly (**Figure 133**).
4. On the right crankcase half, remove the bolt (A, **Figure 134**) securing the camshaft chain tensioner (B) and remove the tensioner.
5. On the left crankcase, remove the E-clip securing the camshaft chain guide rail and remove the guide rail.

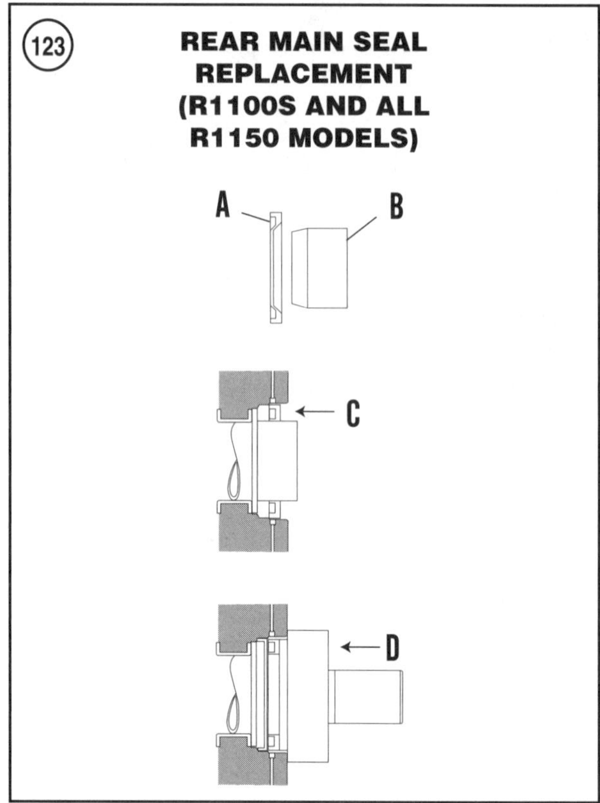

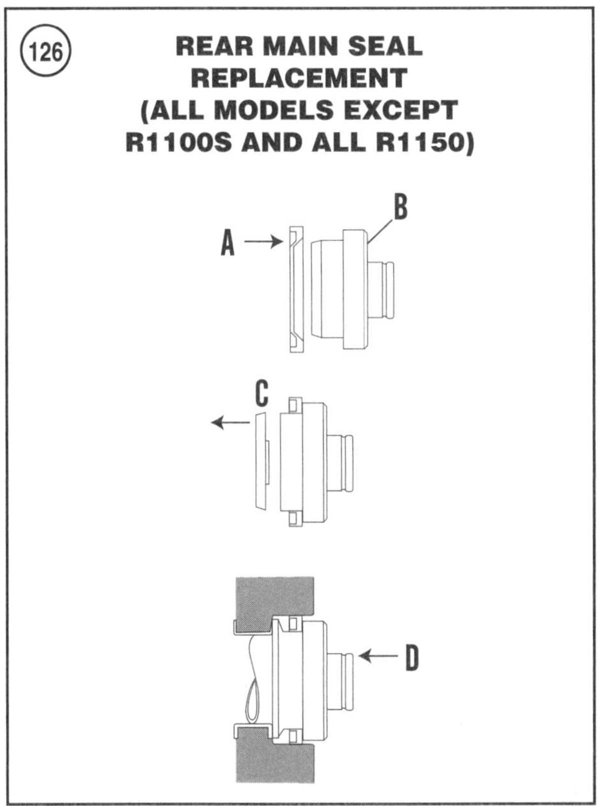

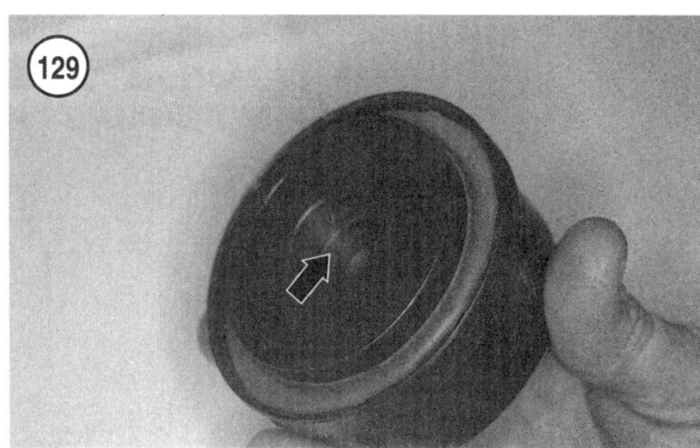

5

Installation

1. On the clutch side of the crankcase, apply a light coat of non-hardening liquid gasket sealer, such as ThreeBond 1209, or an equivalent, onto the guide pin receptacles (**Figure 135**) on the right crankcase half. This is necessary to prevent a possible oil leak in the clutch area.
2. On the left crankcase half, install the camshaft guide rail onto the post (**Figure 136**) and install the snap ring. Make sure the snap ring seats properly.
3. On the right crankcase half, insert the camshaft chain tensioner through the crankcase opening (**Figure 137**) and install the bolt (A, **Figure 134**). Tighten the bolt securely.
4. Install the camshaft chains onto the auxiliary shaft (**Figure 133**) and lower the assembly into the right crankcase half. Make sure the auxiliary shaft seats correctly in the crankcase bearing area (**Figure 138**).
5. Install the camshaft drive chain tensioner and guide pin assembly (**Figure 132**). Make sure the guide pin seats correctly in the crankcase (**Figure 139**).
6. Pull the camshaft chain tight onto the auxiliary sprockets to make sure they properly engage. Refer to **Figure 140** and **Figure 141**.
7. Pull the camshaft chain and sprocket tight and lay the chain onto the chain tensioner (**Figure 142**). Secure the camshaft chain and sprocket onto the tensioner with a tie wrap.
8. Assemble the crankcase as described in this chapter.

Inspection

1. Install one of the driven sprockets onto the camshaft chain and pull the chain tightly against the sprocket (A, **Figure 143**). Check for proper engagement between the two parts.
2. Inspect the individual camshaft driven sprockets (B, **Figure 143**) for broken or chipped teeth. Check the teeth

(130)

CRANKSHAFT, AUXILIARY DRIVE SHAFT, CAMSHAFT CHAINS AND TENSIONER ASSEMBLIES

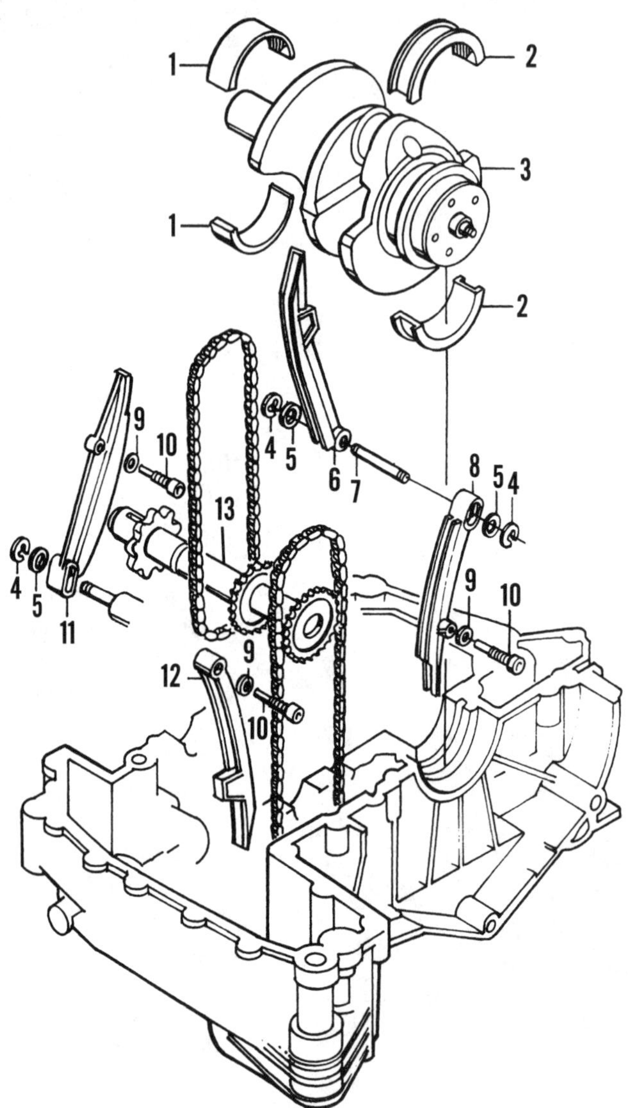

1. Front bearing insert
2. Rear bearing insert
3. Crankshaft
4. E-clip
5. Washer
6. Chain tensioner
7. Guide pin
8. Chain guide rail
9. Washer
10. Bolt
11. Chain guide rail
12. Chain tensioner
13. Auxiliary drive shaft

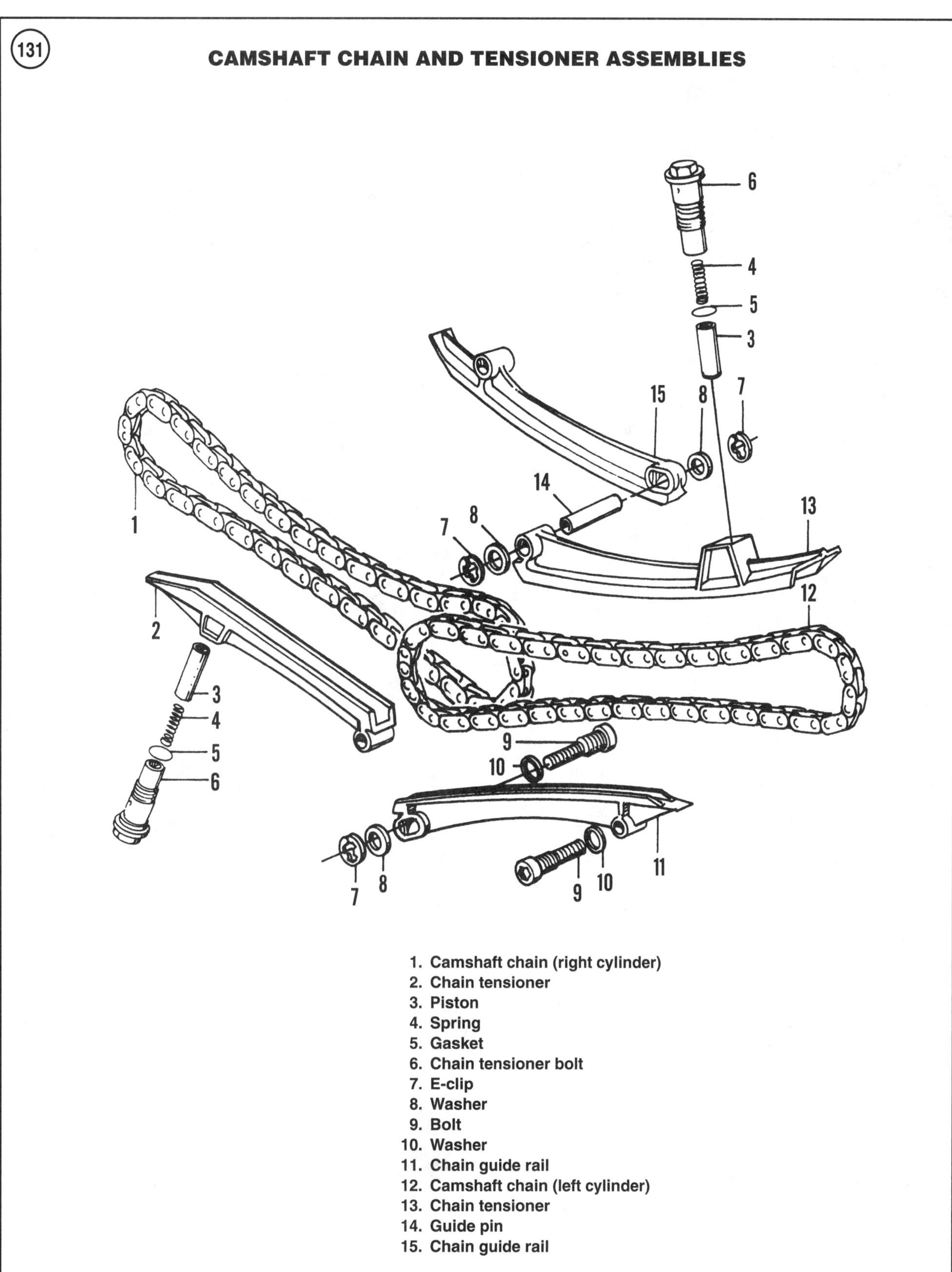

CAMSHAFT CHAIN AND TENSIONER ASSEMBLIES

1. Camshaft chain (right cylinder)
2. Chain tensioner
3. Piston
4. Spring
5. Gasket
6. Chain tensioner bolt
7. E-clip
8. Washer
9. Bolt
10. Washer
11. Chain guide rail
12. Camshaft chain (left cylinder)
13. Chain tensioner
14. Guide pin
15. Chain guide rail

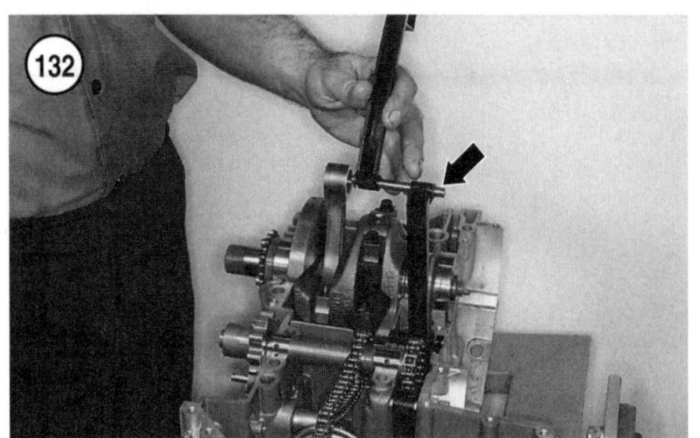

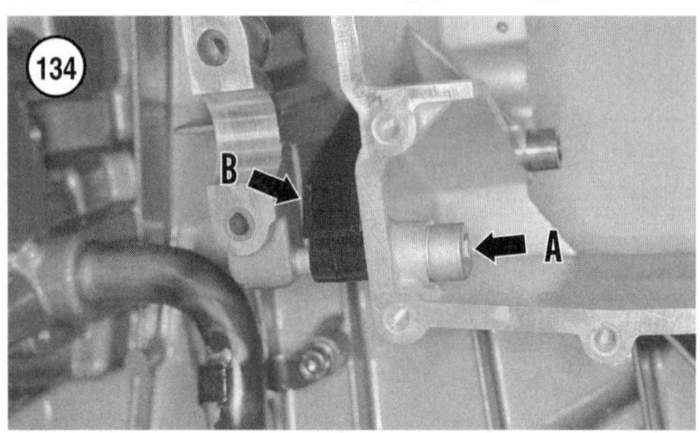

for cracking or rounding (**Figure 144**). If either of the camshaft sprockets are damaged or excessively worn, replace both driven sprockets.

3. On the auxiliary shaft, inspect the camshaft drive sprockets (**Figure 145**) for broken or chipped teeth. Check the teeth for cracking or rounding (**Figure 144**). If either one of the camshaft drive sprockets are damaged or excessively worn, replace the intermediate shaft.

CAUTION
If the camshaft driven sprockets or the auxiliary shaft are replaced, also replace both

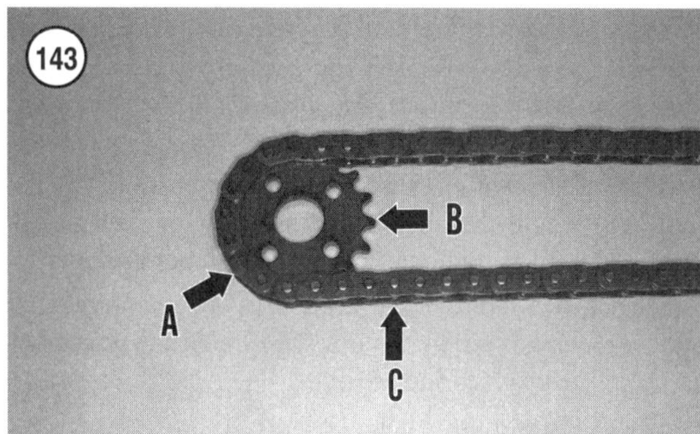

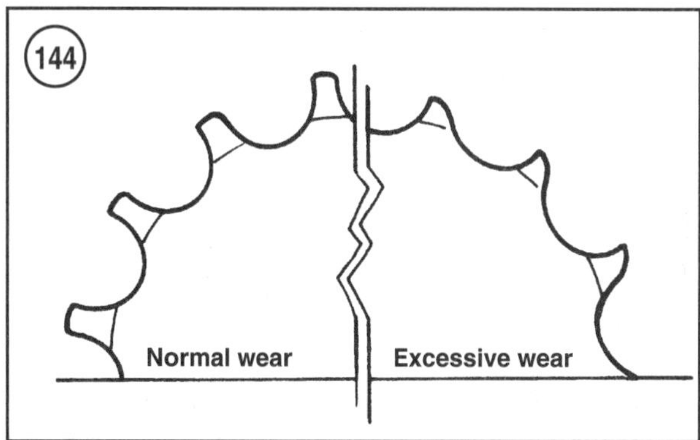

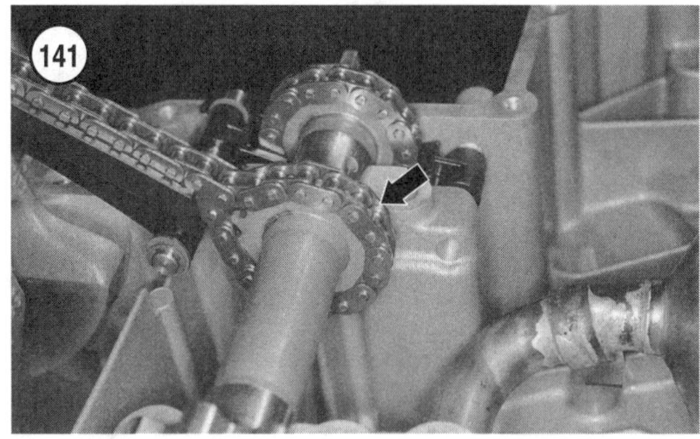

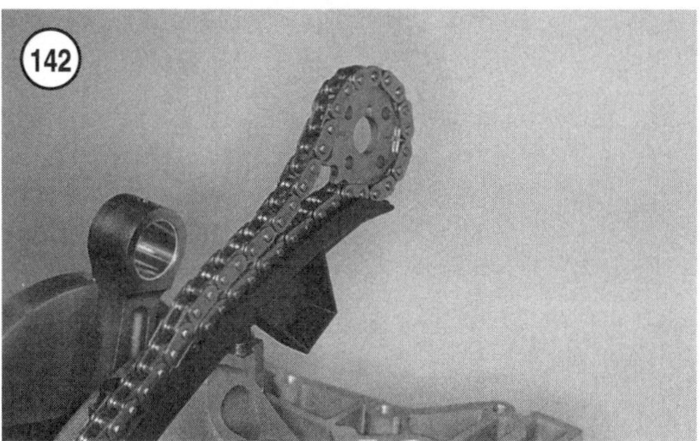

camshaft chains. Never install a new chain over a worn sprocket or a worn chain over new sprockets as this will lead to premature wear to the new parts.

NOTE

If the camshaft sprockets are worn, inspect the camshaft drive chain, chain guides and chain tensioner for damage.

4. Check for wear or abrasion on the inner and outer plates and link pins of both chains (C, **Figure 143**). If they are worn, replace both chains as a set.

5. Inspect the auxiliary shaft for wear on the bearing surfaces (**Figure 146**). Replace the shaft if worn or scored. Check the bearing surface (**Figure 147**) in the crankcase for wear.

6. Inspect the chain guide rails and both tensioners (**Figure 148**) where the chain rides for wear or damage. If damaged, replace the guide rail and tensioner as a pair.

7. Check the guide pin (A, **Figure 149**) for straightness and wear. Make sure the E-clips (B, **Figure 149**) seat correctly in the grooves and are tight.

8. Check the mounting holes (**Figure 150**) for elongation and wear.

9. Inspect the camshaft chain tensioner assemblies (**Figure 151**) for wear or damage. Make sure the oil control hole (**Figure 152**) is clear.

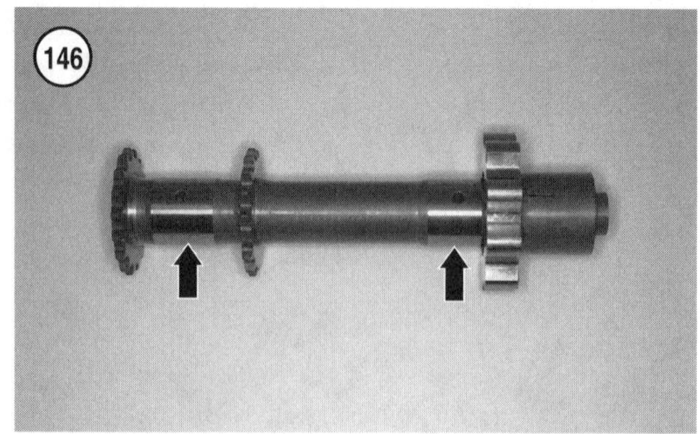

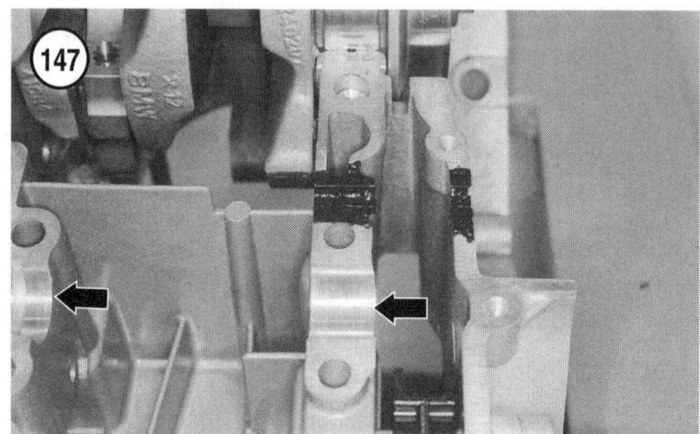

Auxiliary Shaft Oil Clearance Inspection

Wipe all oil residue from each auxiliary shaft bearing journal and from the bearing surface of both crankcase bearing surfaces.

1. Measure each auxiliary shaft bearing journal with a micrometer. Refer to **Figure 153** and **Figure 154**.

2. Assemble the crankcase halves without any internal components.

3. Install and tighten all crankcase bolts. Refer to *Crankcase Assembly* in this chapter for bolt locations and torque specifications.

4. Measure the inside diameter of the fixed bearing journal with a small bore gauge, then measure the gauge with a micrometer and record the measurement.

5. Subtract the measurement of the auxiliary shaft bearing journal's diameters from the crankcase bearing journal's bore to determine the auxiliary shaft oil clearance. Replace the auxiliary shaft and/or the crankcase assembly if the clearance exceeds the service limit in **Table 1**.

6. Remove the bolts and separate the crankcase halves.

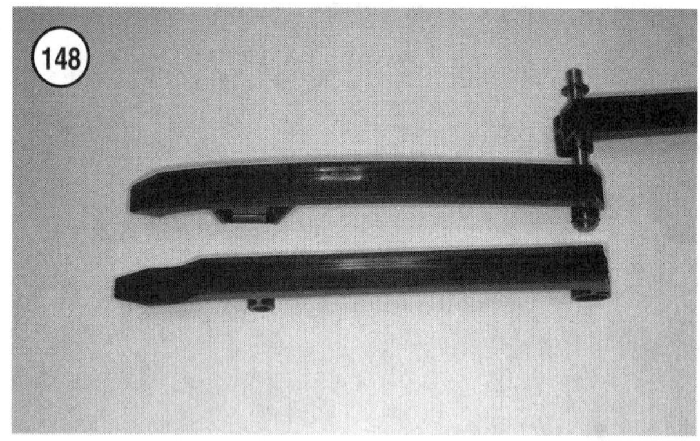

CRANKSHAFT

Removal/Installation

Refer to **Figure 155**.

1. Remove the engine and separate the crankcase as described in this chapter.

2. Remove the auxiliary drive shaft, camshaft chains and tensioner assemblies as described in this chapter.

3. Hold the exposed connecting rods and carefully lift and remove the crankshaft assembly (**Figure 156**).

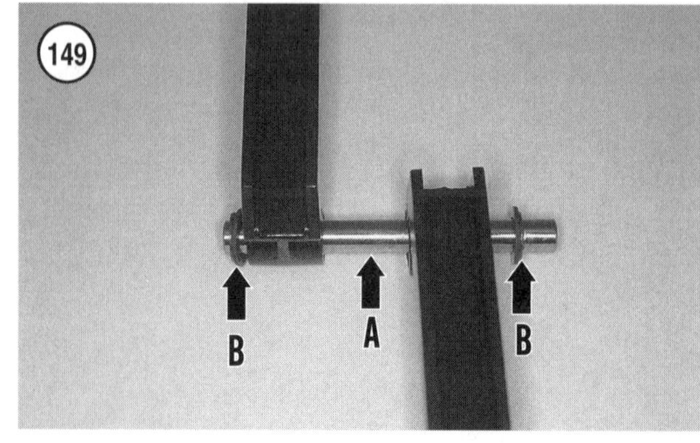

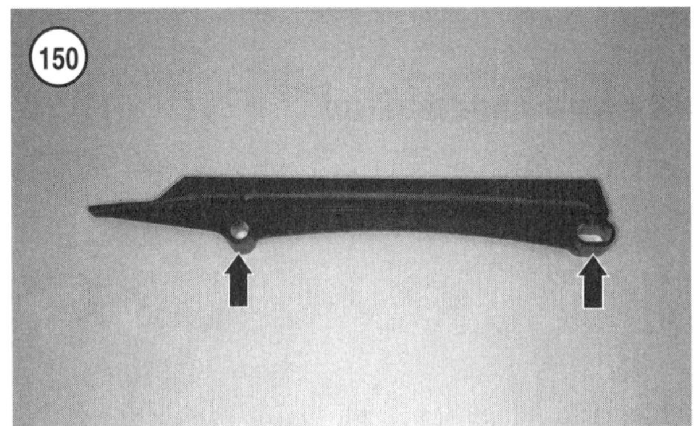
150

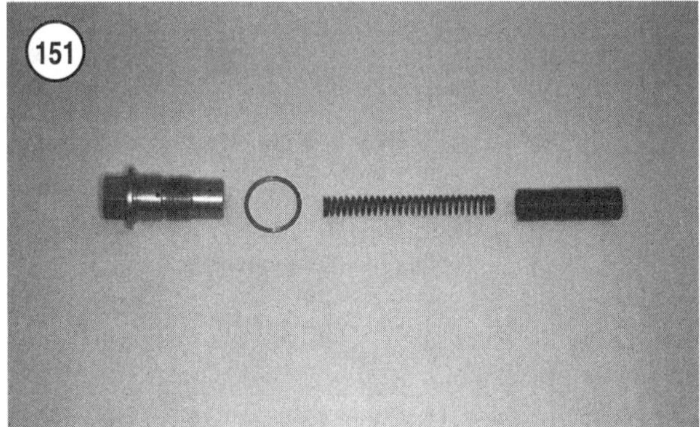
151

152

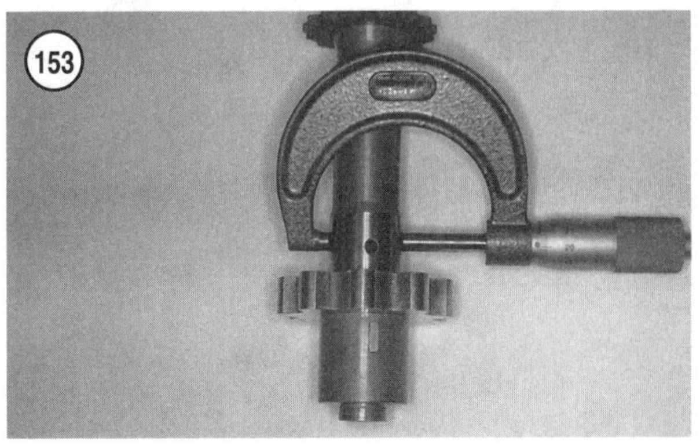
153

154

CAUTION
There are two different sizes and shapes of main bearing inserts. The front inserts are smaller in diameter while the rear guide bearings are larger and have a shoulder on each side. If you reuse the inserts, they must be reinstalled in the correct location in the crankcase to prevent lower end damage.

4. If the main bearing inserts are going to be removed, they must be identified. After removing the insert, mark the backside of the insert with R (right) or L (left).
5. Inspect the crankshaft and main bearings as described in this chapter.
6. Slowly lower the crankshaft and connecting rod assembly into the right crankcase half. Verify that the crankshaft seats properly in the bearings (**Figure 157**). Hold the exposed connecting rod and slowly rotate the crankshaft and check for smooth operation.
7. Install the auxiliary drive shaft, camshaft chains and tensioner assemblies as described in this chapter.
8. Assemble the crankcase and install the engine as described in this chapter.

Inspection

1. Clean the crankshaft thoroughly with solvent. Clean the crankshaft oil passageways (**Figure 158**) with compressed air. If necessary, clean them out with rifle cleaning brushes, then flush out with solvent. Dry the crankshaft with compressed air. Lubricate all of the bearing surfaces with a light coat of engine oil.
2. Inspect each crankshaft main journal (A, **Figure 159**) and each connecting rod journal (B) for scratches, ridges, scoring, nicks or heat discoloration. Very small nicks and scratches may be removed with crocus cloth. More serious damage must be removed at a machine shop.
3. If the surface finish on all crankshaft main bearing journals is satisfactory, measure the main journals in two

155

CRANKSHAFT, AUXILIARY DRIVE SHAFT, CAMSHAFT CHAINS AND TENSIONER ASSEMBLIES

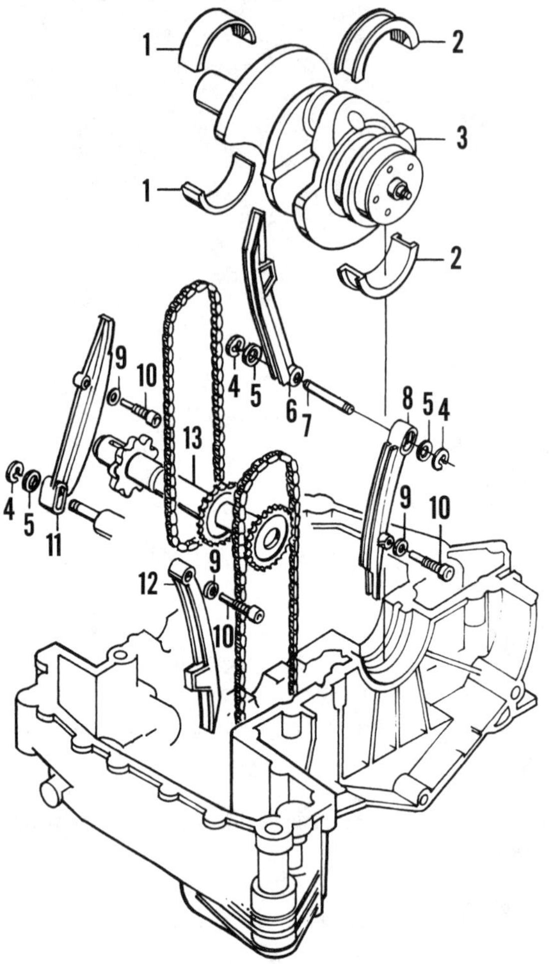

1. Front bearing insert
2. Rear bearing insert
3. Cranshaft
4. E-clip
5. Washer
6. Chain tensioner
7. Guide pin
8. Chain giude rail
9. Washer
10. Bolt
11. Chain guide rail
12. Chain tensioner
13. Auxiliary drive shaft

directions, 90° apart with a micrometer (**Figure 160**). Check out-of-roundness, taper and wear on all journals against measurements listed in **Table 1**.

4. If the surface finish on all connecting rod bearing journals is satisfactory, measure the rod journals in two directions, 90° apart with a micrometer (**Figure 161**). Check out-of-roundness, taper and wear on all journals against measurements listed in **Table 1**.

5. On the front of the crankshaft, inspect the auxiliary shaft drive sprocket teeth (**Figure 162**) for broken or chipped teeth. Check the teeth for cracking or rounding (**Figure 163**). If the sprocket is damaged or worn, replace the sprocket as follows:

   a. Have an assistant hold the crankshaft on the work bench.

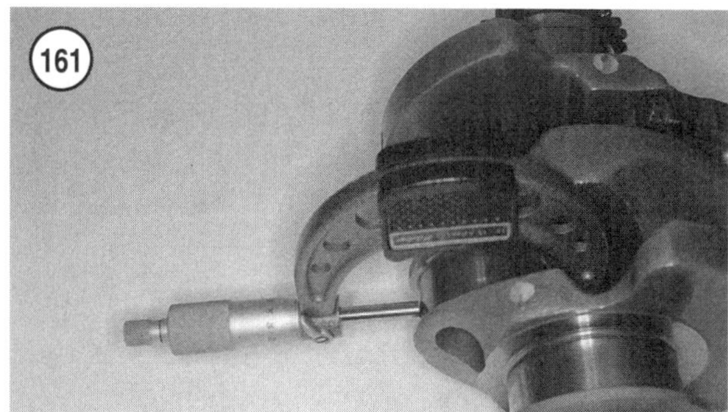

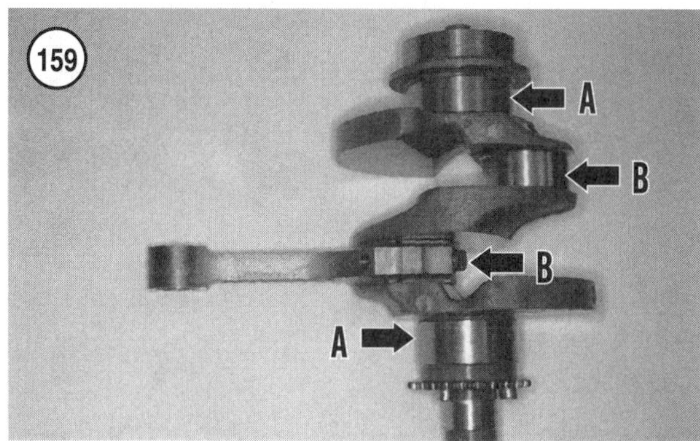

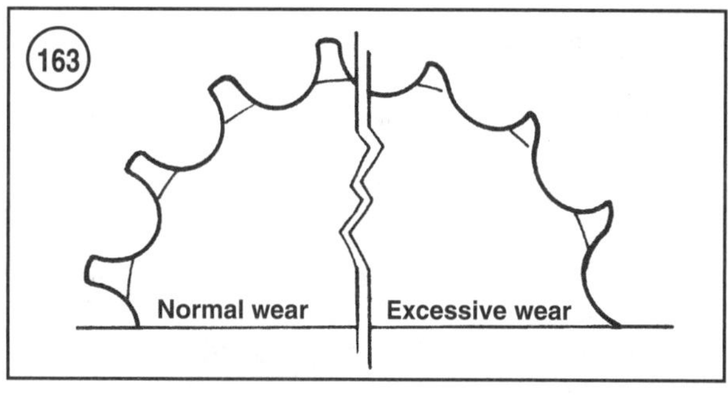

b. Remove the Allen bolts (**Figure 164**) securing the sprocket to the front of the crankshaft.

c. Remove the sprocket.

d. Install the new sprocket onto the crankshaft and install new bolts.

e. Tighten the Allen bolts in three stages to 70 N•m (52 ft.-lb.).

CAUTION

If the sprocket is damaged, also inspect the auxiliary shaft sprocket and chain as they probably are damaged also.

CAUTION

If the crankshaft auxiliary shaft chain sprocket is replaced, also replace the sprocket on the auxiliary shaft and the

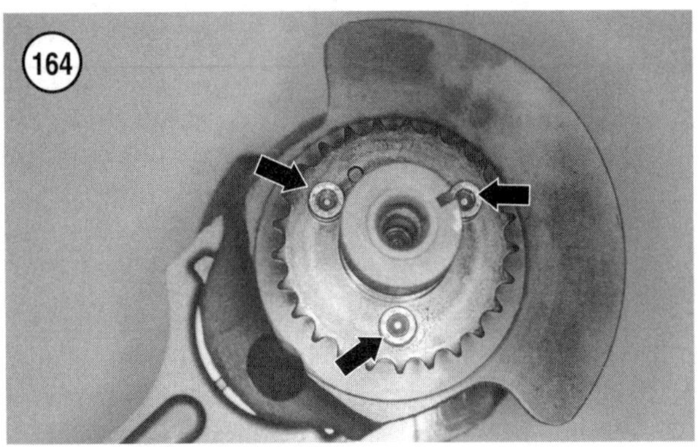

chain. Never install a new chain over a worn sprocket or a worn chain over new sprockets as this will lead to premature wear to the new parts.

6. On the rear or clutch end of the crankshaft, inspect the clutch housing mounting bolt hole threads (**Figure 165**). Clean or repair the threads with a suitable size metric tap. Coat the tap threads with kerosene or an aluminum tap fluid before use.

Main Bearing Oil Clearance Measurement

1. Check the crankshaft main bearing inserts (**Figure 166**) for wear, abrasion and scoring. If the bearing inserts are good they may be reused. If any insert is questionable, replace the entire set.
2. Clean the bearing surfaces of the crankshaft and the bearing inserts for the crankshaft.
3. If removed, install all existing crankshaft bearing inserts in both the right and left crankcase halves in their original locations. Make sure they are locked in place (**Figure 167**).
4. Assemble the crankcase halves without any internal components or sealant.
5. Install and tighten all crankcase bolts. Refer to *Crankcase Assembly* in this chapter for bolt locations and torque specifications.
6. Measure the inside diameter of the bearing journals with a bore gauge. Measure the front bearing (**Figure 168**) and the rear bearing (**Figure 169**) and record the measurements.
7. Measure the crankshaft main bearing journals in two directions, 90° apart with a micrometer (**Figure 170**). Measure the front and rear bearing journals. Record the measurements.
8. Subtract the main journal diameter from the crankcase bearing bore diameter to determine main bearing clear-

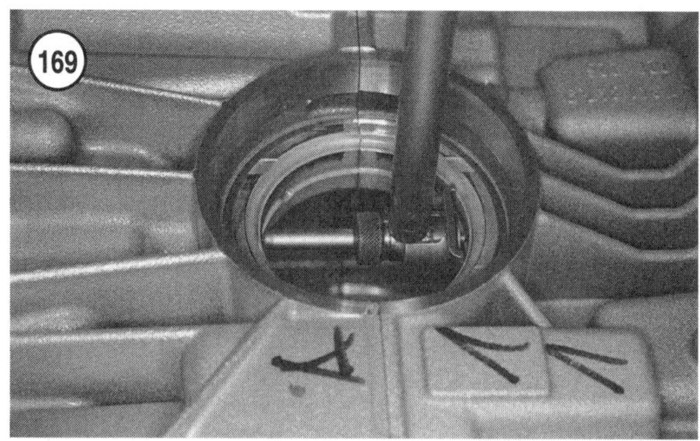

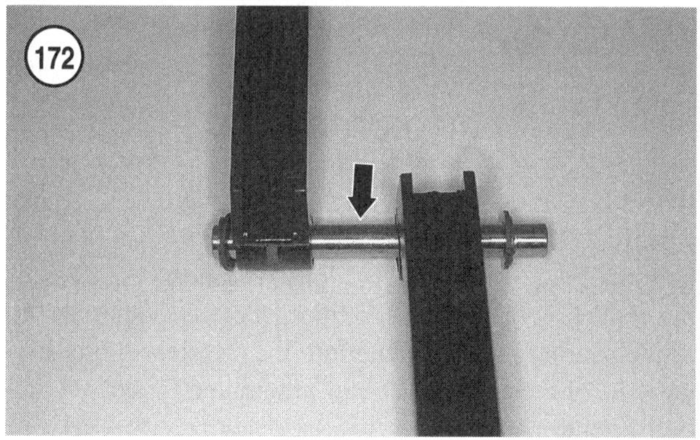

5

ance. Replace the bearing inserts if the oil clearance exceeds the service limit in **Table 1**.

9. Remove the bolts and separate the crankcase halves.

End Play Inspection

The rear main bearing (guide bearing) controls crankshaft axial or end play. Normally, replacing the rear main bearing ensures that crankshaft end play is within the specification in **Table 1**. However, if end play is still excessive after rear main bearing replacement, the crankshaft may be excessively worn and require replacement.

1. Apply clean engine oil to the crankshaft main bearing inserts.
2. Slowly lower the crankshaft and connecting rod assembly into the right crankcase half. Confirm that the crankshaft seats properly in the bearings (**Figure 171**).
3. Install the left crankcase half and tighten the bolts finger-tight.
4. Disassemble the camshaft chain tensioner and guide assembly and remove the guide pin (**Figure 172**).
5. To correctly center the two crankcase halves without the internal parts in place, insert the guide pin into its receptacle (**Figure 173**) in the backside of the crankcase assembly.
6. Install and tighten all crankcase bolts. Refer to *Crankcase Assembly* in this chapter for bolt locations and torque specifications.
7. Securely attach a dial indicator to the backside of the crankcase.
8. Push the crankshaft toward the front of the crankcase until it stops.
9. Zero the dial indicator.
10. From the front of the engine, slowly push the crankshaft toward the rear of the crankcase and note the reading. This indicates the amount of crankshaft end play.

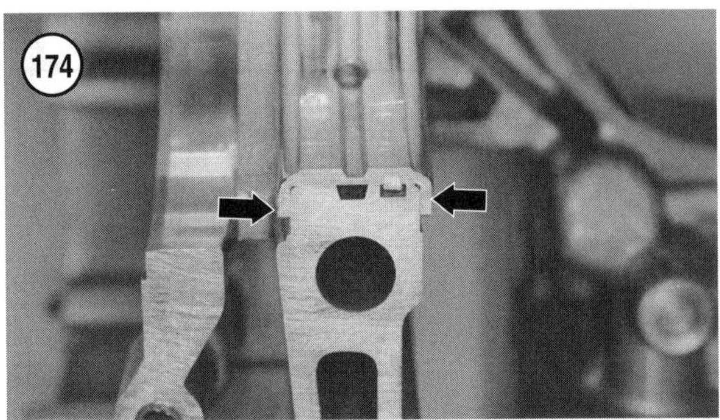

11. If the end play exceeds the specification listed in **Table 1**, either the rear bearing inserts or the crankshaft must be replaced.
12. Separate the crankcase halves and remove the crankshaft.
13. To determine which part is out of specification, perform the following:
    a. Use a micrometer and measure the overall width of both bearing inserts (**Figure 174**). Refer to the specification listed in **Table 1**.
    b. If the bearing inserts are within specification, measure the crankshaft rear bearing journal width (**Figure 175**) with a vernier caliper. Refer to the specification listed in **Table 1**.
    c. Replace the necessary parts to achieve the correct amount of end play.

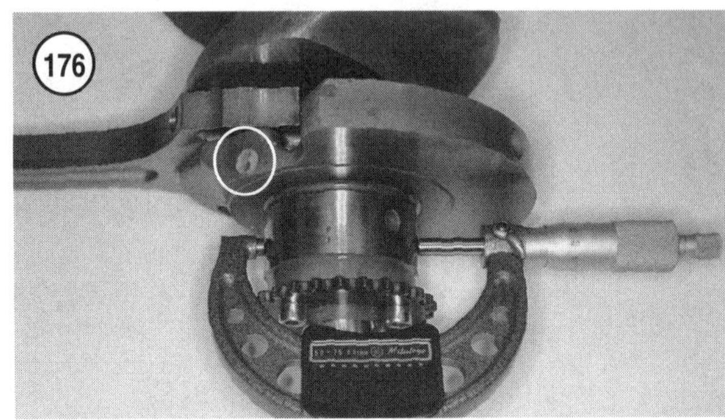

Main Bearing Selection

The crankshaft main bearings are available in two sizes, standard size and 0.25 mm oversize. If oversize bearings are required to obtain the specified bearing clearance, the crankshaft must be machined to accommodate the 0.25 mm oversize bearings. However, the crankshaft can only be machined once; if further wear occurs, replace the crankshaft.

1. The crankshaft front main bearing journal is marked on the counterbalance web with a green or yellow paint mark (**Figure 176**). Refer to **Table 1** for the bearing journal outer diameter and color mark. Measure the journal if necessary.
2. The bearing inserts are also marked with either a green or yellow paint mark. Refer to **Table 1** for the bearing journal insert inner diameter and color mark.
3. The color mark of the insert and crankshaft color mark must always match.
4. Always replace all four inserts at the same time.
5. After installing new bearing inserts, recheck the clearance by repeating *Main Bearing Oil Clearance Measurement* procedure in this section. If the clearance is still out of specification, either the crankshaft or the crankcase is excessively worn and requires replacement.

CONNECTING RODS

The connecting rods can be removed with the crankshaft installed in the crankcase. However, this is a difficult task since the work must be done within the confines of the crankcase opening. In addition, there is the possibility of the bearing inserts falling into the crankcase. It is suggested that the crankcase be disassembled for connecting rod service.

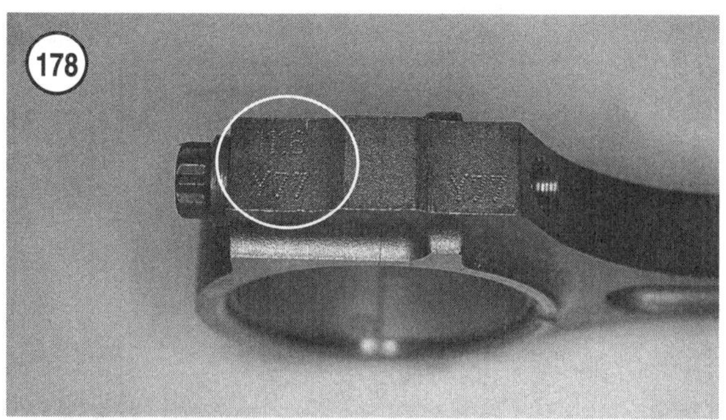

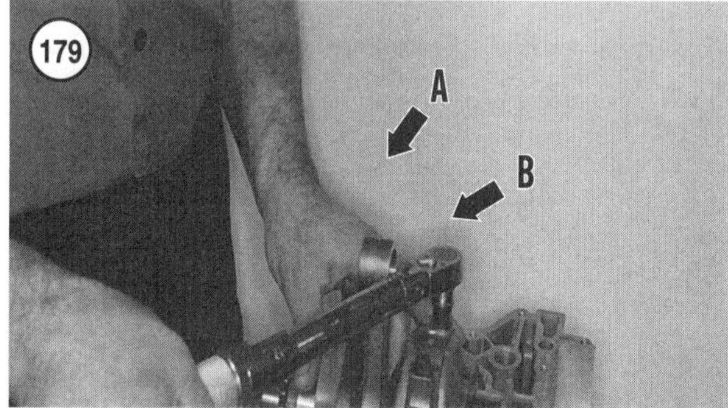

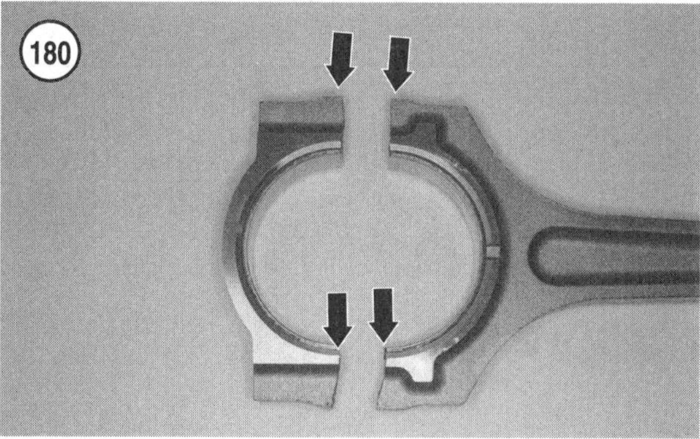

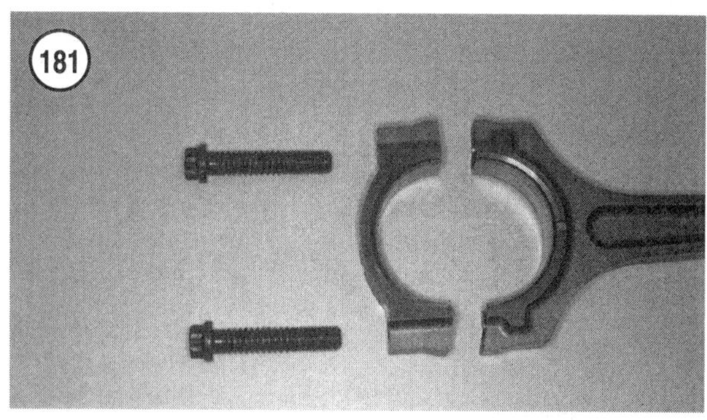

Removal/Installation

CAUTION
Leave the crankshaft and connecting rod assembly in place in the right crankcase half. The crankcase offers a great holding fixture—but the crankshaft must be held securely in place to avoid damage to the right main bearing inserts.

1. Separate the crankcase as described in this chapter.

2. Remove the auxiliary drive shaft, camshaft chains and tensioner assemblies as described in this chapter.

3. With the connecting rods properly installed on the crankshaft, measure the big end side clearance. Insert a flat feeler gauge between the connecting rod and the crankshaft machined web (**Figure 177**). Refer to the specifications listed in **Table 1**. Check both connecting rods. Refer to *Connecting Rod Inspection* in this section for the connecting rod's big end width. Replace the connecting rod(s) or crankshaft as necessary.

NOTE
Prior to disassembly, mark the connecting rods and caps with a L (left) or R (right).

NOTE
*The connecting rod weight mark (**Figure 178**) must face UP when installed.*

4. With one hand, securely hold the crankshaft in place in the crankcase (A, **Figure 179**) and loosen the connecting rod bolts (B) on both connecting rods.

5. Remove the crankshaft and connecting rod assembly from the crankcase.

NOTE
*The connecting rod is manufactured and then the cap is removed from the rod portion using the cracked-cap method. This results in an uneven fracture line between the two parts (**Figure 180**) and only these two parts can be reassembled with a very tight and even set. Do not intermix the rods and caps as they will not fit together.*

6. Remove the bolts and remove the cap and separate the rod from the crankshaft. Keep each cap with its original rod (**Figure 181**) with the weight mark on the end of the cap matching mark on the rod (**Figure 178**).

CAUTION
*The connecting rod bolts are thin and light and designed to stretch when tightened; **never reuse** the bolts.*

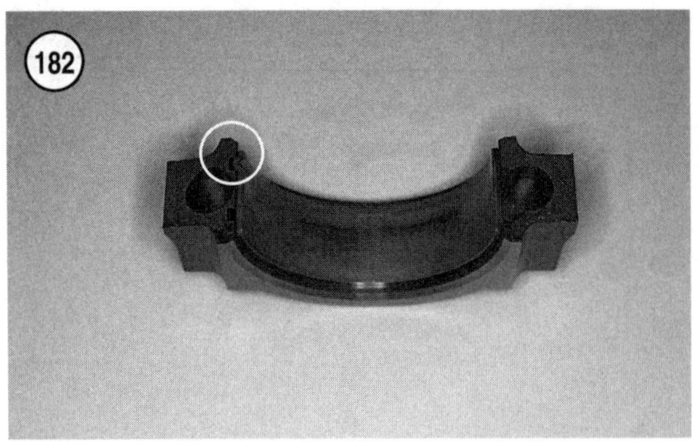

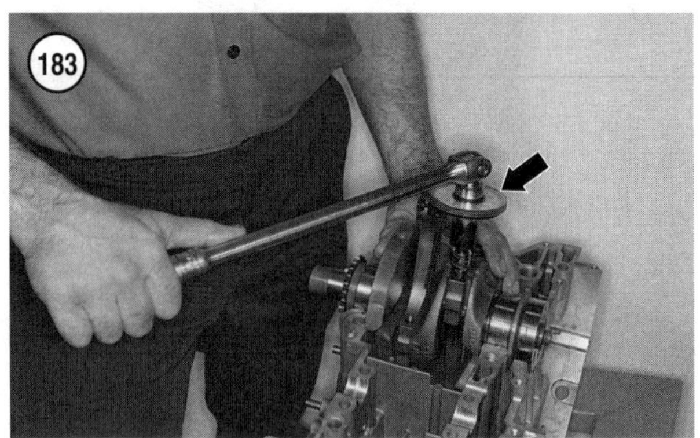

7. Remove the connecting rod cap bolts and set them aside. Use the old bolts for the *Oil Clearance Measurement* procedure later in this section. After completing that procedure, discard the bolts as they cannot be reused. New bolts must be used when the connecting rods are installed.

CAUTION
Keep each bearing insert in its original place in the connecting rod and cap. If you are going to assemble the engine with the original inserts, they must be reinstalled exactly as they were removed to prevent rapid wear.

8. Inspect the connecting rods and bearings as described in this chapter.
9. If new bearing inserts are going to be installed, check the bearing clearance as described in this chapter.
10. Apply a light even coat of clean engine oil to the connecting rod bearing journals and to the inner surface of the connecting rod inserts.
11. Insert *new* connecting rod bolts into all connecting rods.
12. Make sure the inserts are locked in place (**Figure 182**). Apply clean engine oil to the bearing surface of both upper and lower bearing inserts.
13. Thoroughly clean the new bolts and nuts with solvent and thoroughly dry them with compressed air. Apply a light coat of clean engine oil to the bolt threads and to the underside of the bolt head. This is necessary to achieve the correct torque specification.
14. Install the connecting rods onto the crankshaft in the correct location and with the weight mark (**Figure 178**) facing toward the top of the engine. Be careful not to damage the bearing surface of the crankshaft with the sharp edge of the rod during installation.
15. Install the correct rod cap, then install the *new* rod bolts and tighten finger-tight.
16. If removed, install the other connecting rod, cap and bolts.

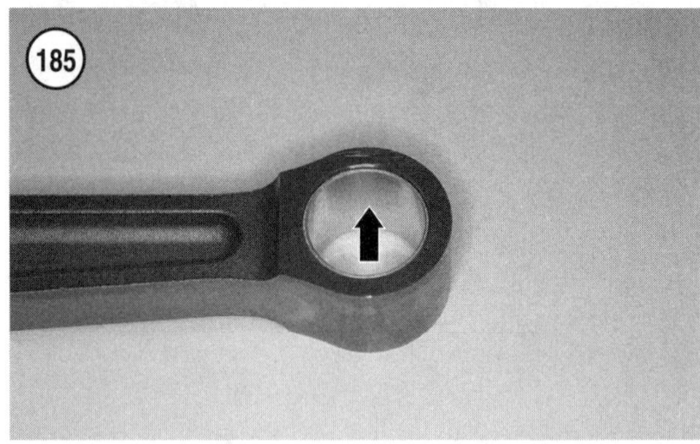

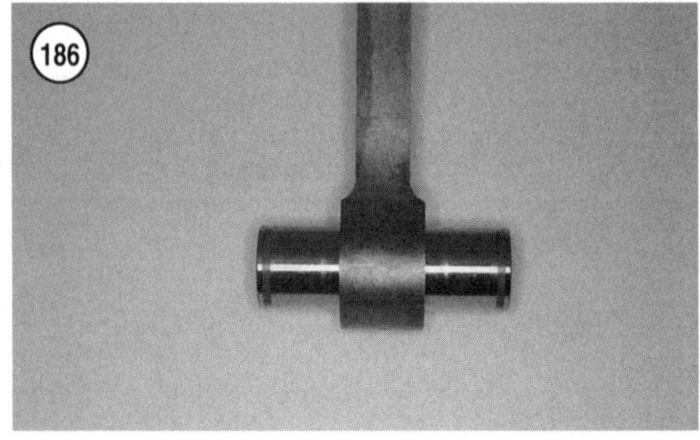

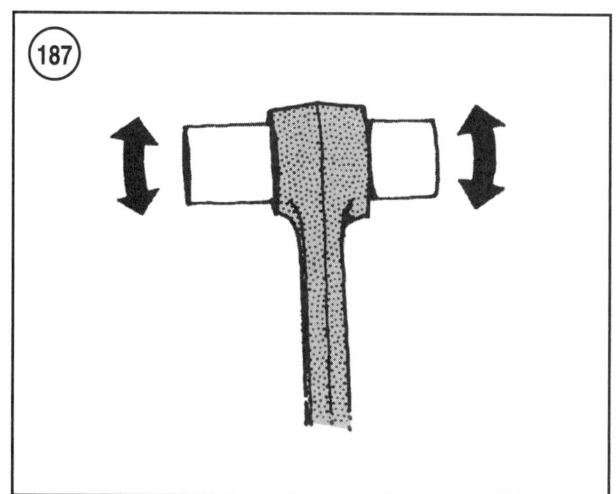

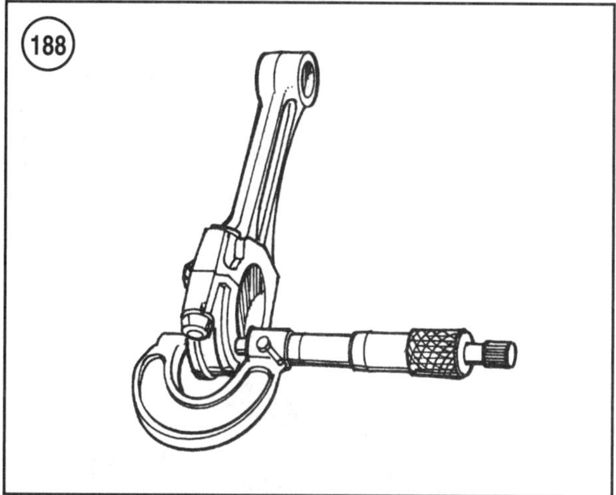

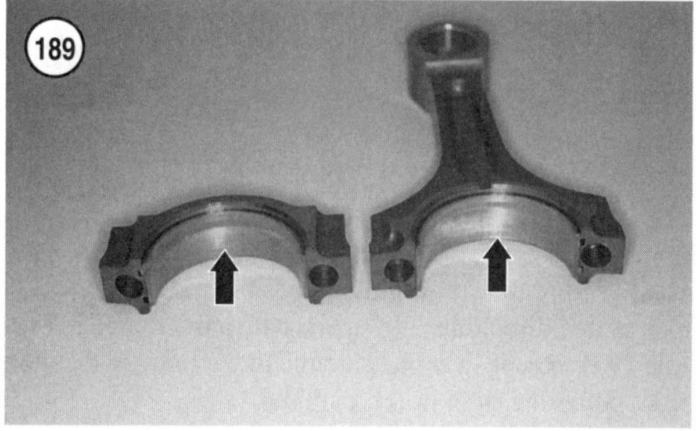

17. Install the crankshaft and connecting rod assembly into the crankcase.

18. Following a crisscross pattern, tighten the bolts to the preliminary torque specification of 20 N•m (15 ft.-lb.).

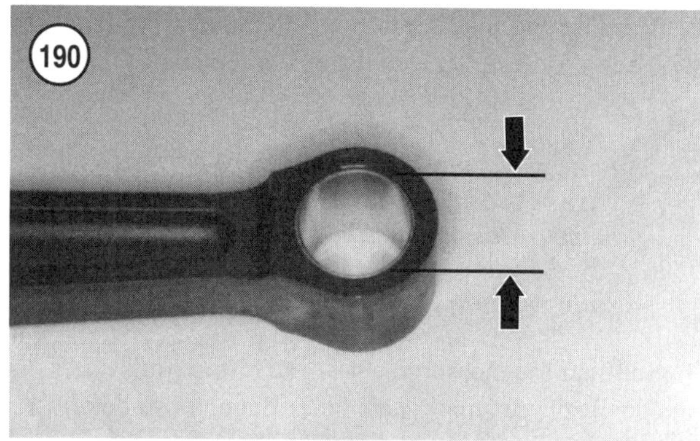

19. Attach a degree wheel (**Figure 183**) to the wrench and place the stopper against the other connecting rod (**Figure 184**). Zero the degree wheel, then tighten the bolt an additional 80°. Repeat for the other bolt.
20. Repeat Step 18 and Step 19 for the remaining connecting rod assembly.
21. After installing the connecting rods and correctly tightening the cap bolts, rotate the connecting rod on the crankshaft and check that there is no binding.

Inspection

1. Check each connecting rod assembly for obvious damage such as cracks or burns.
2. Make sure the small end oil hole is clean.
3. Check the piston pin for chrome flaking or cracks. Replace it if necessary.
4. Check the piston pin contact surface in the connecting rod small end (**Figure 185**) for wear or abrasion.
5. Lubricate the piston pin with clean engine oil and install it in the connecting rod (**Figure 186**). Slowly rotate the piston pin and check for radial play (**Figure 187**).
6. Measure the width of the big end bearing with a micrometer (**Figure 188**). Compare to the dimension listed in **Table 1**.
7. Have the connecting rods checked for excessive bending or twisting at a BMW dealership or machine shop.
8. Examine the bearing inserts (**Figure 189**) for wear, scoring or burned surfaces. They are reusable if in good condition. Make a note of the bearing color identification on the side of the insert if discarding the bearing. A previous owner may have used oversized bearings.

Piston Pin Oil Clearance Measurement

1. Measure the connecting rod small end inner diameter with a snap gauge (**Figure 190**) and measure the snap gauge with a micrometer. Record the measurement.

2. Measure the piston pin outer diameter (**Figure 191**) with a micrometer. Record the measurement.

NOTE
If the piston pin is replaced, check the clearance between the new piston pin and the existing piston as described in this procedure. The clearance between these parts must remain within specification.

3. Subtract the measurement of the piston pin's outer diameter from the small end's inner diameter to determine piston pin radial clearance. Replace the piston pin and/or connecting rod if the radial clearance is worn to the service limit listed in **Table 1**.

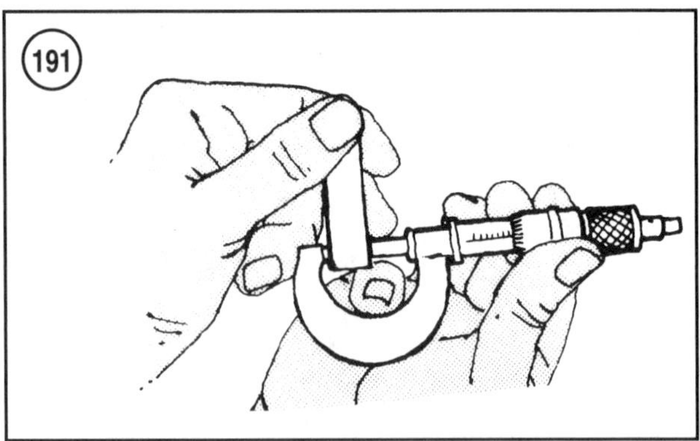
191

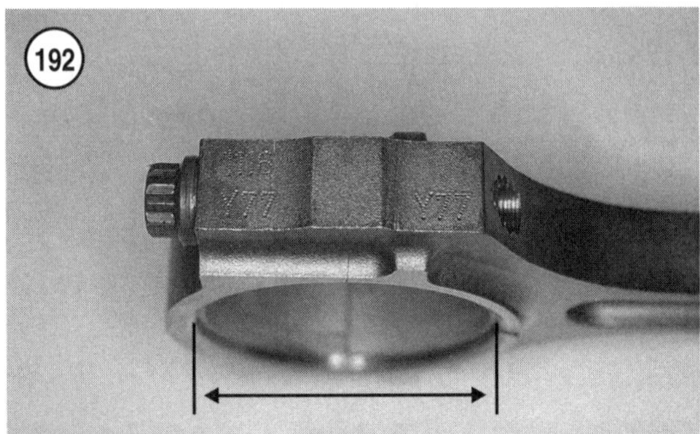
192

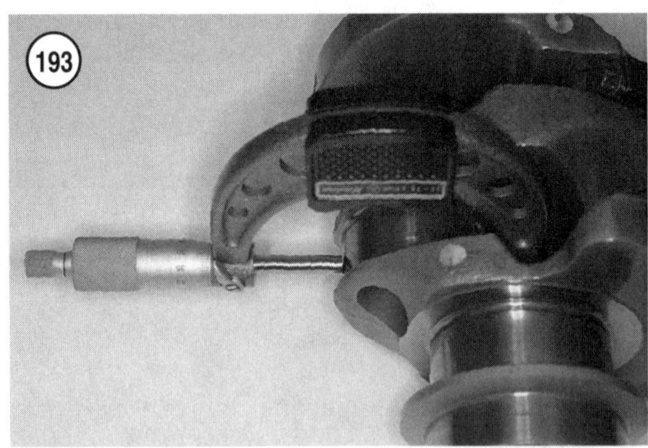
193

Connecting Rod Bearing Oil Clearance Measurement

NOTE
Do not use new bolts for this procedure as they will stretch and cannot be reused during final installation

1. Check the connecting rod inserts (**Figure 189**) for evidence of wear, abrasion and scoring. If the bearing inserts are in good condition they may be reused. If any insert is questionable, replace as a set.
2. Clean the connecting rod bearing surfaces of the crankshaft and the connecting rod bearing inserts.
3. If removed, install the existing bearing inserts into the connecting rod and cap. Make sure they are locked into place (**Figure 182**).
4. Install the connecting rod in a vise with soft jaws.
5. Apply a light coat of clean engine oil to the old bolt threads and to the under side of the bolt head.
6. Install the correct rod cap, then install the old rod bolts and tighten finger-tight.
7. Following a crisscross pattern, tighten the bolts to the preliminary torque specification of 20 N•m (15 ft.-lb.).
8. Attach a degree wheel to the wrench and place the stopper against the vise. Zero the degree wheel, then tighten the bolt an additional 80°. Repeat for the other bolt.
9. Measure the inside diameter of the connecting rod bearing inserts (**Figure 192**) with a bore gauge. Record the measurements, noting its location for either the right or left cylinder.

NOTE
The connecting rod bearing journal at the front of the crankshaft is for the left cylinder's connecting rod.

10. Measure the crankshaft connecting rod bearing journals in two directions, 90° apart, with a micrometer (**Figure 193**). Record the measurements, noting its location from either the right or left cylinder.

11. Subtract the measurement of the crankshaft connecting rod bearing journals outer diameters from the connecting rod bearing journals inner diameter to determine connecting rod bearing oil clearance. Replace the bearing inserts if the oil clearance is worn to the service limit listed in **Table 1**.

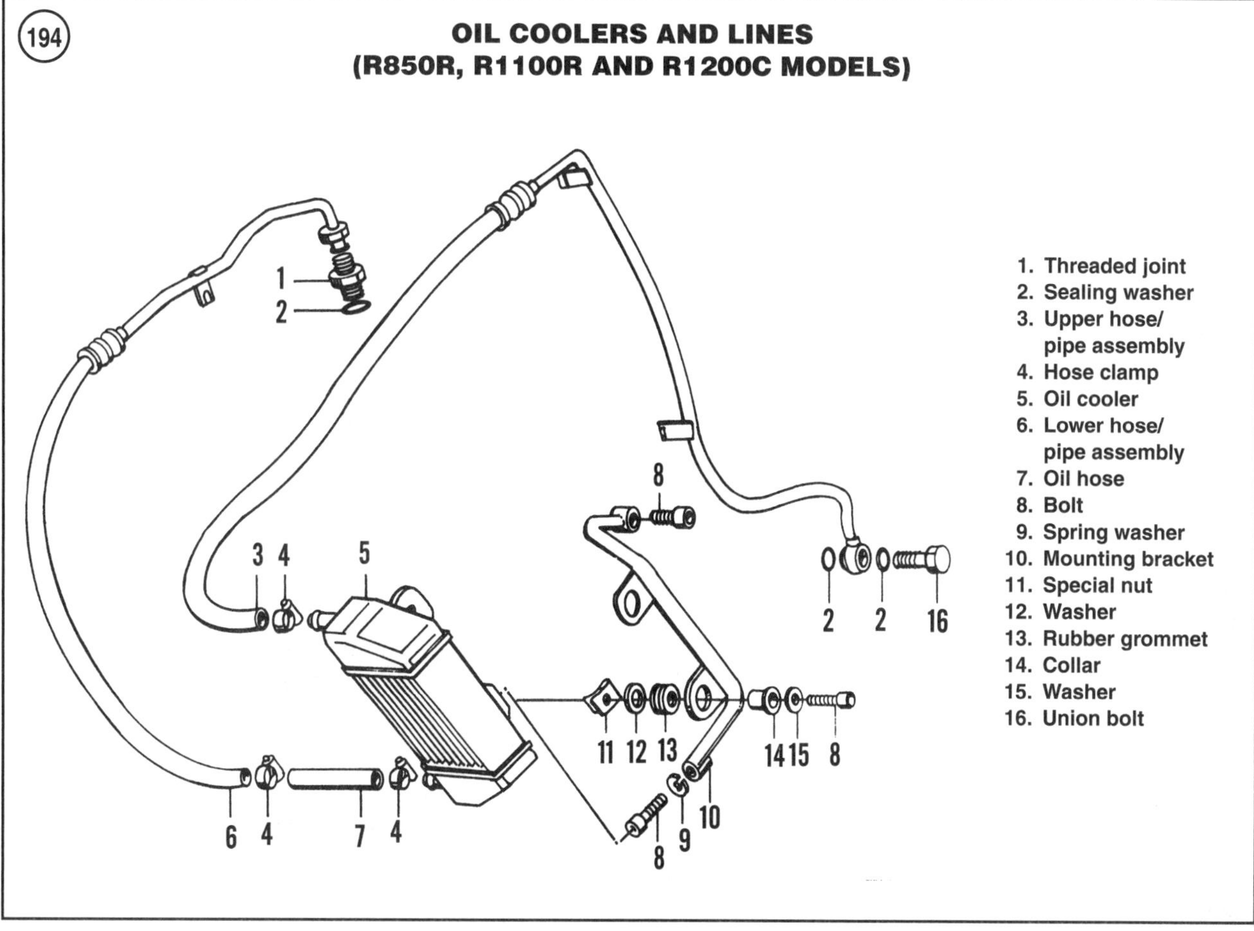

12. Remove the old bolts and separate the connecting rods. Discard the old bolts at this time.
13. If the bearing clearance is greater than specified, select new bearings as described in this chapter.

Connecting Rod-to-Crankshaft Bearing Selection

The crankshaft main bearings are available in two sizes, standard size and 0.25 mm oversize. If oversize bearings are required to obtain the specified bearing clearance, the crankshaft must be machined to accommodate the 0.25 mm oversize bearings. However, the crankshaft can only be machined once; if further wear occurs, replace the crankshaft.

1. Install new bearing inserts into the connecting rod and repeat the *Connecting Rod Bearing Oil Clearance Measurement*.
2. If the clearance is still greater than specified in **Table 1**, the crankshaft can be machined and oversized bearing inserts installed.
3. Always replace both inserts in each connecting rod at the same time.
4. After new oversized bearing inserts have been installed, recheck the clearance by repeating the *Crankshaft Main Bearing Oil Clearance Measurement*. If the clearance is still excessive, either the crankshaft or the connecting rod is excessively worn and requires replacement.

OIL COOLERS AND HOSES

Oil Cooler Removal/Installation

Refer to **Figure 194-199**.

NOTE

***Figure 194** shows only the left oil cooler. The R850C, R850R, R1100R and R1200C models are equipped with an oil cooler on each side and the right oil cooler is identical to the left side.*

195

OIL COOLERS AND LINES (R1150R MODELS)

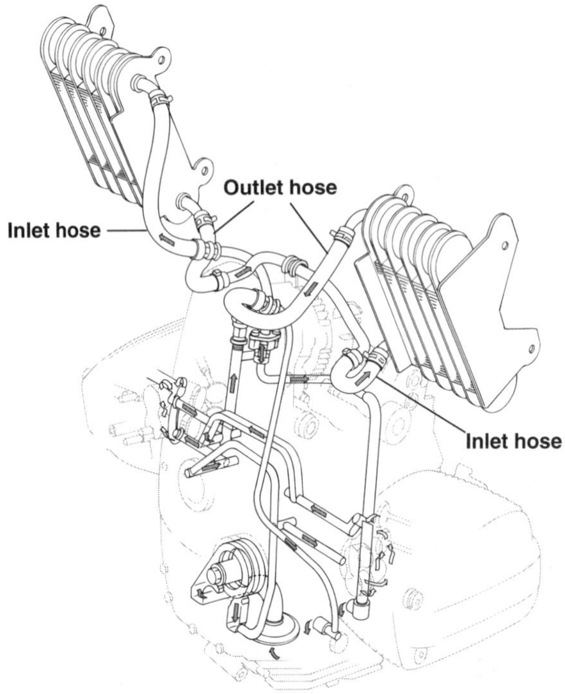

Outlet hose

Inlet hose

Inlet hose

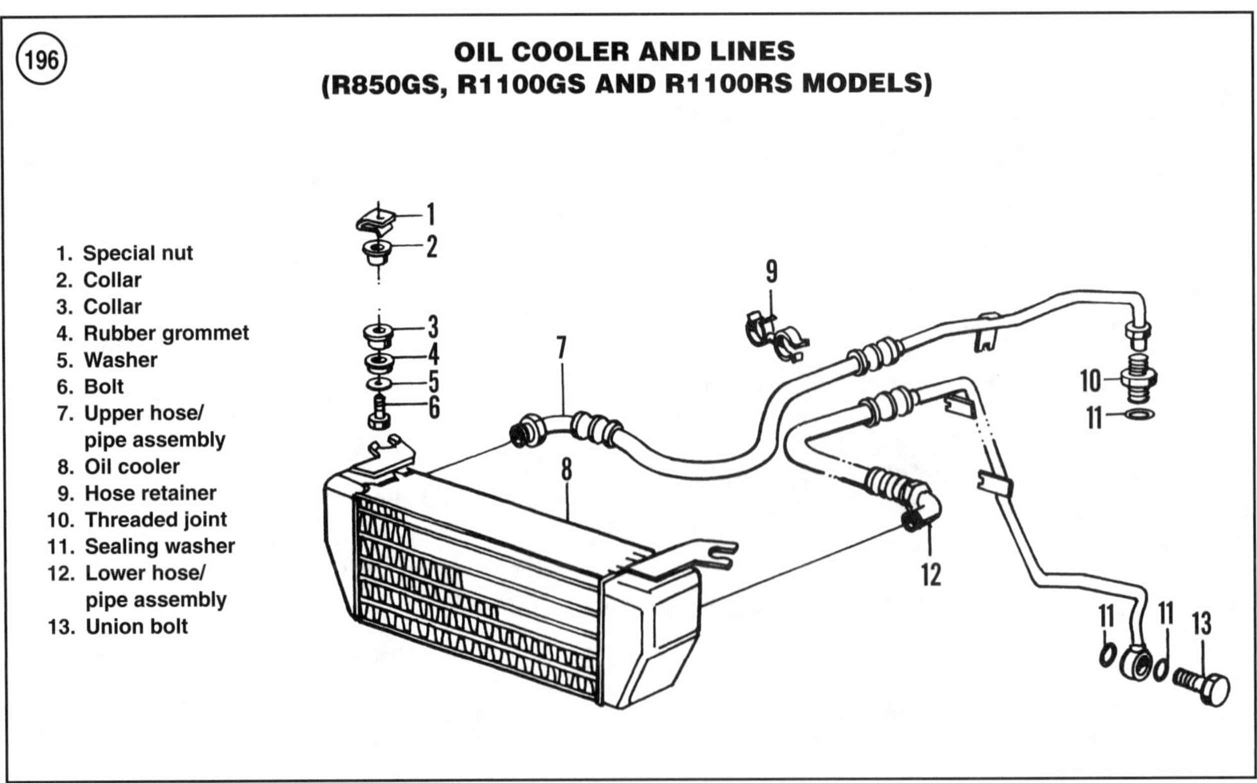

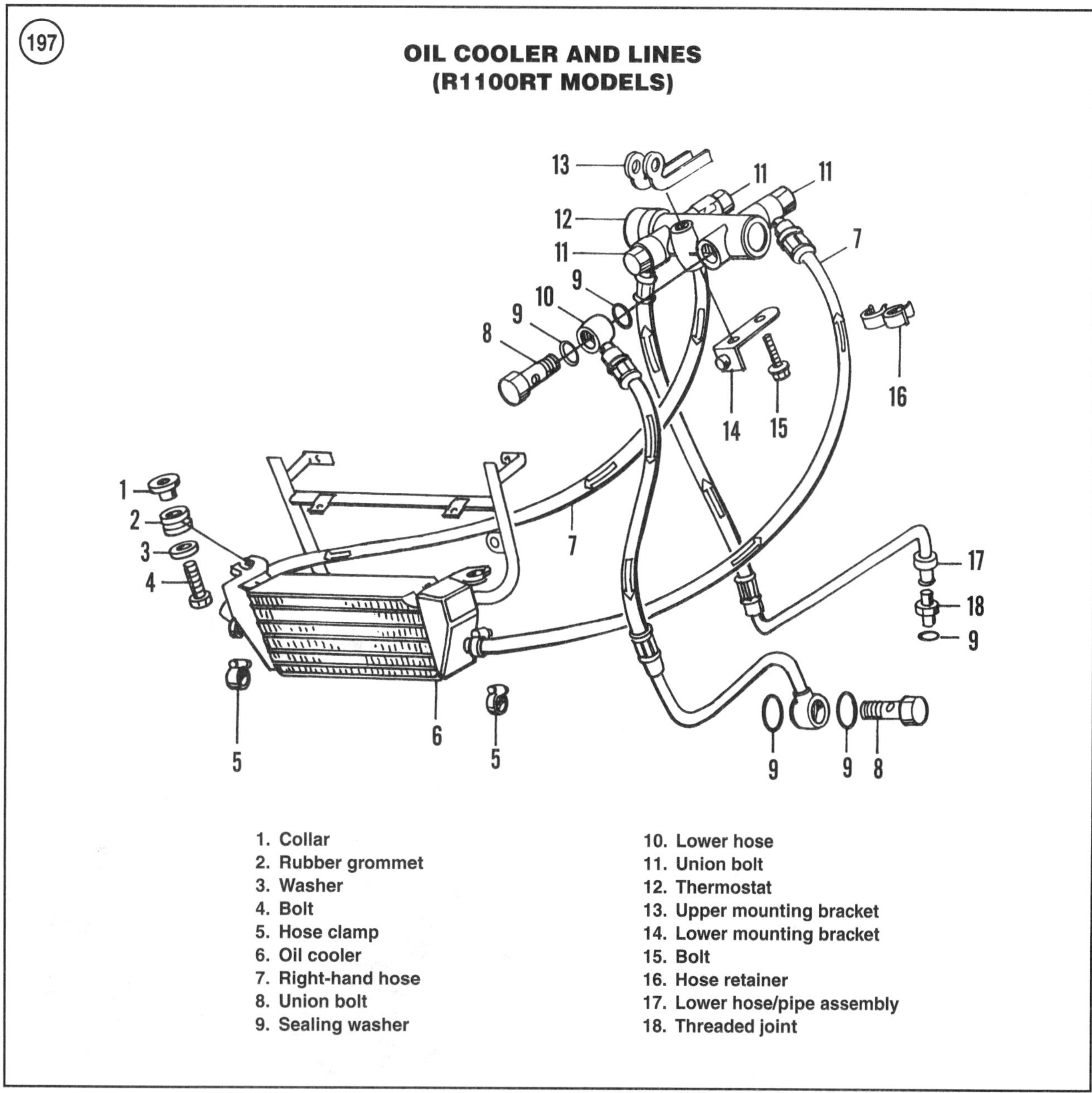

1. Collar
2. Rubber grommet
3. Washer
4. Bolt
5. Hose clamp
6. Oil cooler
7. Right-hand hose
8. Union bolt
9. Sealing washer
10. Lower hose
11. Union bolt
12. Thermostat
13. Upper mounting bracket
14. Lower mounting bracket
15. Bolt
16. Hose retainer
17. Lower hose/pipe assembly
18. Threaded joint

1. Remove the fuel tank as described in Chapter Nine.

2A. On GS models, remove the mud guard and the side trim from each side as described in Chapter Fifteen.

2B. On RS, RT and S models, remove the front fairing lower side panels as described in Chapter Fifteen.

3. Drain the engine oil as described in Chapter Three.

4. On R850R, R1100R, GS and RS models, remove the two left bolts securing the front cover. These two bolts also secure the left oil pipe to the engine.

5. Place a drain pan under the oil cooler fittings as some residual oil may drain when the hoses are disconnected from the oil cooler.

6A. On R850R and R1100R models, remove the bolts and washers securing the oil cooler and air duct/trim piece to the mounting bracket. Repeat for the oil cooler on the other side.

6B. On R1150R models, loosen the hose clamps securing both hoses (**Figure 200**) to the oil cooler and remove the oil cooler. Repeat for the oil cooler on the other side.

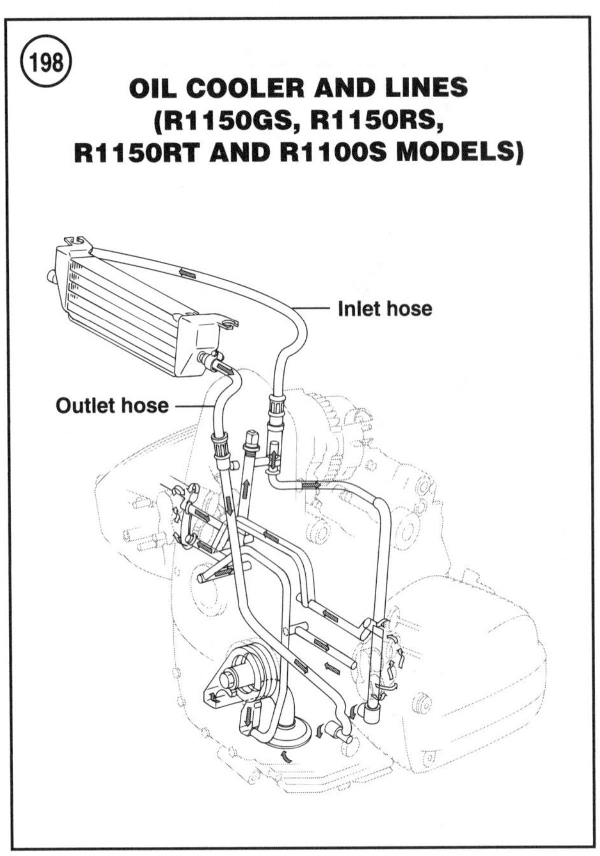

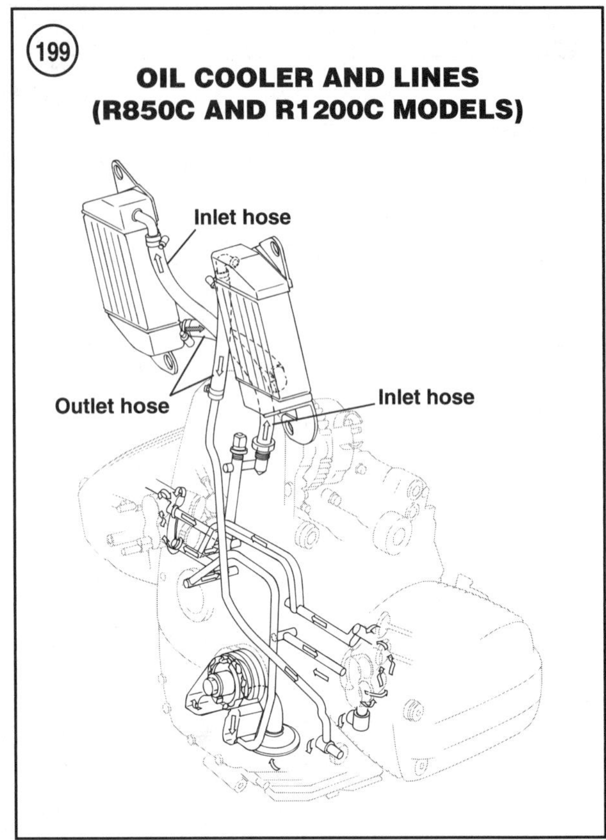

6C. On GS, RS, RT and S models, remove the bolts and washers (A, **Figure 201**, typical) on each side securing the oil cooler to the mounting bracket.

6D. On R850C and R1200C models, perform the following:

a. Remove the front frame as described in Chapter Fifteen.
b. Remove the bolts and washers securing the oil cooler to the backside of the front frame and remove the oil cooler.
c. Repeat for the oil cooler on the other side.

NOTE
If the oil cooler(s) is going to be reinstalled, drain any residual oil, close off the fittings with duct tape and place it in a reclosable plastic bag to avoid contamination.

7A. On R and RT models, loosen the screws on the hose clamps securing the oil hoses to the oil cooler fittings. Remove the hoses from the fittings and plug the ends of the hoses to prevent contamination. Remove the oil cooler(s) from the motorcycle.

7B. On GS and RS models, loosen the fittings (B, **Figure 201**) securing the oil hose assembly to the oil cooler. Re-

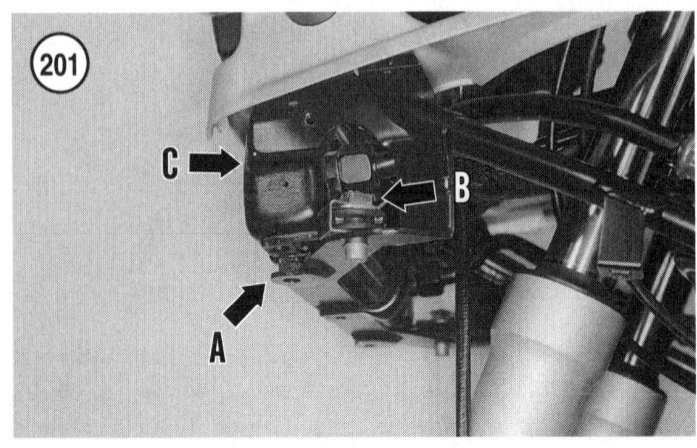

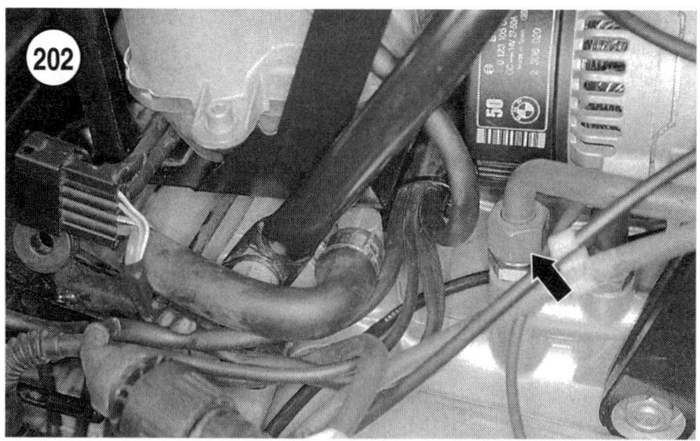

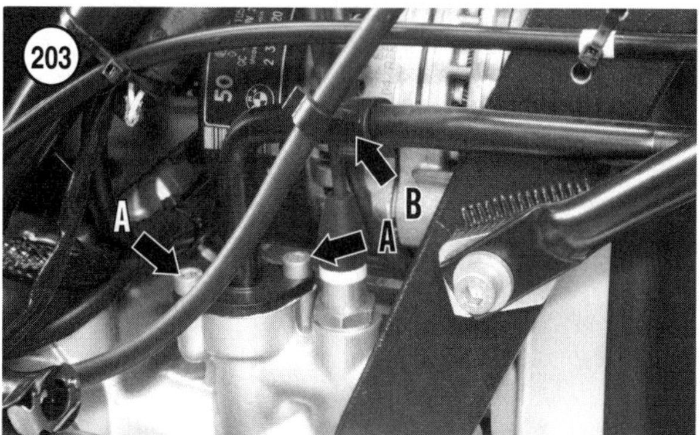

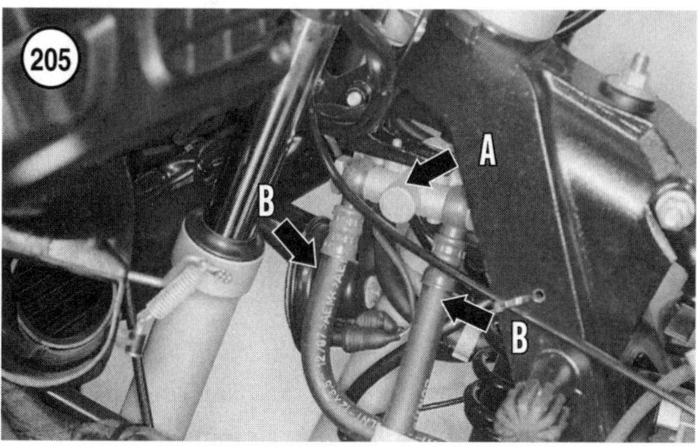

move the hoses from the fittings and plug the ends of the hoses to prevent contamination. Remove the oil cooler (C, **Figure 201**) from the motorcycle.

8. To remove the hoses, refer to the next procedure.
9. Installation is the reversal of these removal steps. Refill the engine oil as described in Chapter Three.

Oil Cooler Hoses Removal/Installation

5

Refer to **Figure 194-199**.

NOTE
The following procedure includes the removal of all oil cooler hoses. If only replacing one hose, follow the steps relating to removal of that hose.

1. Remove the fuel tank as described in Chapter Eight.

2A. On early models, on the right side of the crankcase perform the following:
   a. Unscrew the fitting (**Figure 202**) securing the right hose to the top fitting on the crankcase.
   b. Loosen, but do not remove, the bolt securing the right hose to the front frame. Slide the hose mounting bracket out from under the bolt.

2B. On later models, on the right side of the crankcase perform the following:
   a. Remove the Allen bolts (**Figure 203**) securing the right hose/fitting to the top fitting on the crankcase.
   b. Unhook the clip securing the hose to the cable.

3. Place a drain pan under this fitting as some residual oil may drain out. On the left side of the crankcase, unscrew the union bolt and sealing washers (**Figure 204**) securing the left hose to the crankcase. Do not lose the sealing washer on each side of the hose fitting.

4A. On R850GS, R1100GS and R1100RS models, loosen the fittings (B, **Figure 201**) securing the oil hose assembly to the oil cooler. Remove the hoses from the fittings and plug the end of the hoses to prevent contamination.

4B. On models other than R850GS, R1100GS and R1100RS, loosen the screws on the hose clamps securing the oil hoses to the oil cooler fittings. Remove the hoses from the fittings and plug the end of the hoses to prevent contamination.

5. On R1100RT models, perform the following:
   a. Remove the bolts securing the thermostat (A, **Figure 205**) to the front frame.
   b. Lower the thermostat and disconnect the union bolt and sealing washers securing the oil hose(s) (B, **Figure 205**) to the thermostat. Do not lose the sealing washer on each side of the hose fitting.

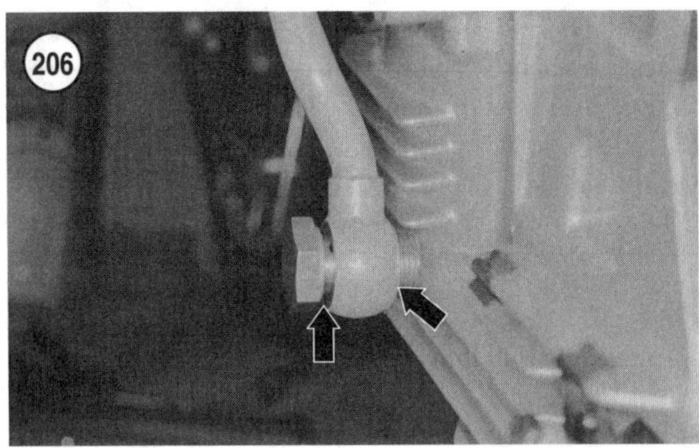

6. Follow the oil hose through the frame and remove any tie wraps securing the hose to the engine or frame or to any electrical cable.
7. Carefully remove the hose(s) from the frame and engine noting its path.
8. Install by reversing these removal steps while noting the following:
   a. Refill the engine with oil as described in Chapter Three.
   b. Be sure to install new sealing washers on each side of the applicable fittings (**Figure 206**). Tighten all fittings securely.
   c. On oil leak will occur if the union bolt on the left hose fitting (**Figure 206**) is not tightened sufficiently. Due to the air flow around the engine, any leaking oil will flow around the crankcase toward the rear and up into the clutch area. This will give a false indication of a leaking rear main seal.

Oil Cooler Thermostat (R1150R Models)

Refer to **Figure 207**.

1. Remove the fuel tank as described in Chapter Nine.
2. Drain the engine oil as described in Chapter Three.
3. Remove the Allen bolts (**Figure 208**) securing the oil cooler line to the top of the crankcase.
4. Place a shop cloth around the oil cooler line and move the line out of the way. Plug the end of the line to prevent contamination.
5. Remove the support plate, plunger and spring from the crankcase receptacle.
6. Clean all parts in solvent and dry.
7. Inspect the plunger and spring for damage or fatigue; replace as necessary.
8. Installation is the reversal of these removal steps while noting the following:
   a. Tighten the bolts to 9 N•m (80 in.-lb.).

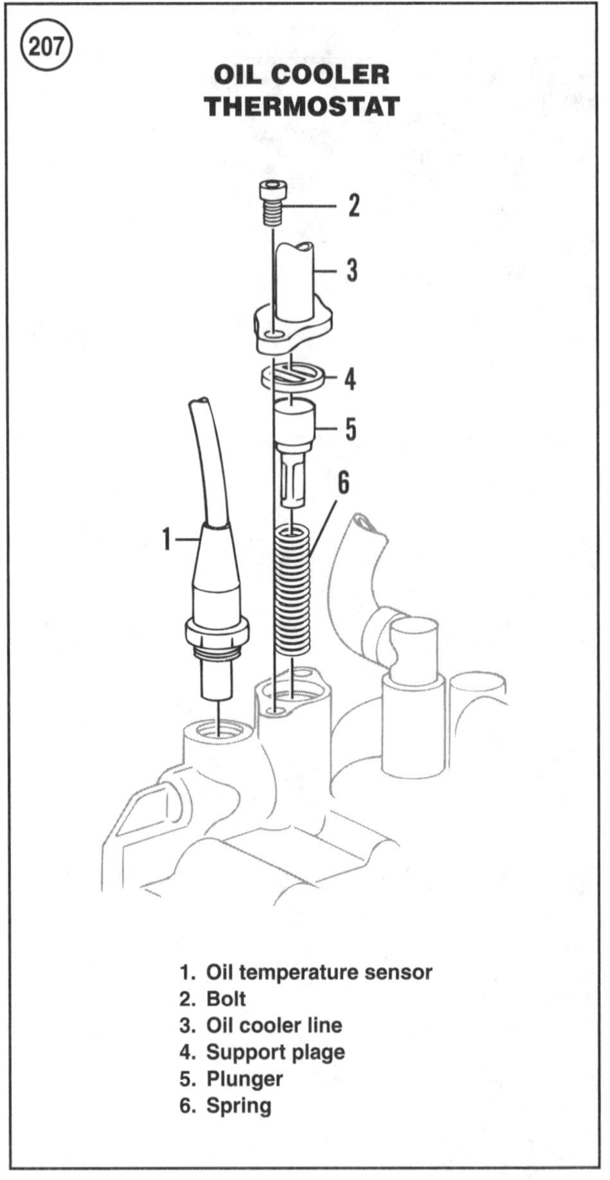

   b. Refill the engine oil as described in Chapter Three.
   c. Install the fuel tank as described in Chapter Nine.

ENGINE BREAK-IN

When replacing top end components or performing major lower end work, the engine should be broken in just as though it were new. The performance and service life of the engine depend greatly on a careful and sensible break-in.

During break-in, oil consumption will be higher than normal. It is important to check and correct the oil level frequently (Chapter Three). Never allow the oil level to

drop below the minimum level. If the oil level is low, the oil will become overheated resulting in insufficient lubrication and increased wear.

BMW designates the first 10 hours of operation as the break-in period. During this period, do not exceed 1/2 throttle.

After the break-in period, change the engine oil and filter as described in Chapter Three. It is essential to perform this service to remove all the particles produced during break-in from the lubrication system. The small added expense is a smart investment that will pay off in increased engine life.

Table 1 ENGINE LOWER END SPECIFICATIONS

Item	Specification mm (in.)
Auxiliary drive shaft	
Shaft bearing surface outer diameter	
front and rear	24.959-24.980 (0.9826-0.9835)
Bore inside diameter in crankcase	
front and rear	25.020-25.041 (0.9850-0.9858)
Oil clearance	
Standard	0.040-0.082 (0.0016-0.0032)
Service limit	0.18 (0.0071)
Oil pump (850 cc, 1100 cc, 1200 cc)	
Engine set of rotors (inner set)	
Rotor thickness	9.95-9.98 (0.3917-0.3929)
Pump body depth	10.02-10.05 (0.3945-0.3957)
Oil cooler set of rotors (outer set)	
Rotor thickness	11.95-11.98 (0.4705-0.4716)
Pump body depth	12.02-12.05 (0.4732-0.4744)
Axial play	
Standard	0.04-0.1 (0.0016-0.0039)
Service limit	0.25 (0.0098)
Oil pump (1150 cc)	
Engine set of rotors (inner set)	
Rotor thickness	9.965-9.98 (0.3923-0.3929)
Pump body depth	10.02-10.05 (0.3945-0.3957)
Oil cooler set of rotors (outer set)	
Rotor thickness	10.965-10.98 (0.4317-0.4323)
Pump body depth	11.02-11.05 (0.4339-0.4350)
Axial play	
Standard	0.04-0.1 (0.0016-0.0039)
Service limit	0.25 (0.0098)
Crankshaft (850cc, 1100 cc, 1200 cc)	
Front main bearing	
Inside diameter in crankcase	60.000-60.019 (2.3622-2.3629)
Bearing shell inside diameter	
Green mark	54.998-55.039 (2.1652-2.1668)
Yellow mark	55.008-55.049 (2.1656-2.1673)
Bearing journal outside diameter	
Green mark	54.971-54.980 (2.1643-2.2039)
Yellow mark	54.981-55.990 (2.1646-2.2043)
Oil clearance	
Standard	00.018-0.068 (0.0007-0.0027)
Service limit	0.13 (0.0051)
	(continued)

Table 1 ENGINE LOWER END SPECIFICATIONS (continued)

Item	Specification mm (in.)
Crankshaft (1150cc)	
Front main bearing	
Inside diameter in crankcase	64.949-64.969 (2.5571-2.5579)
Bearing shell inside diameter	
Green mark	59.965-59.999 (2.3608-2.3621)
Yellow mark	59.979-60.013 (2.3614-2.3628)
Bearing journal outside diameter	
Green mark	59.939-59.948 (2.3598-2.3602)
Yellow mark	59.949-59.958 (2.3602-2.3606)
Oil clearance	
Standard	0.018-0.060 (0.0007-0.0023)
Service limit	0.1 (0.0039)
Rear main (guide) bearing (850cc, 1100 cc, 1200cc)	
Inside diameter in crankcase	64.949-64.969 (2.5571-2.5579)
Bearing shell inside diameter	
Green mark	59.964-60.003 (2.3609-2.3624)
Yellow mark	59.974-60.013 (2.3612-2.3628)
Bearing journal outside diameter	
Green mark	59.939-59.948 (2.3598-2.3602)
Yellow mark	59.949-59.958 (2.3602-2.3606)
Oil clearance	
Standard	0.015-0.064 (0.0006-0.0025)
Service limit	0.1 (0.0039)
Bearing width	24.890-24.940 (0.9799-0.9819)
Rear main (guide) bearing (1150 cc)	
Inside diameter in crankcase	64.949-64.969 (2.5571-2.5579)
Bearing shell inside diameter	
Green mark	59.965-59.999 (2.3608-2.3621)
Yellow mark	59.979-60.013 (2.3614-2.3628)
Bearing journal outside diameter	
Green mark	59.939-59.948 (2.3598-2.3602)
Yellow mark	59.949-59.958 (2.3602-2.3606)
Oil clearance	
Standard	0.017-0.060 (0.0007-0.0023)
Service limit	0.1 (0.0039)
Bearing width	24.890-24.940 (0.9799-0.9819)
Axial play (850 cc, 1100 cc, 1200 cc)	
Standard	0.080-0.163 (0.0031-0.0064)
Service limit	0.2 (0.008)
Axial play (1150 cc)	
Standard	0.125-0.208 (0.0049-0.0082)
Service limit	0.2 (0.008)
Crankpin outside diameter (rod bearing)	47.975-47.991 (1.8887-1.8889
Crankshaft identification	
Unground stage zero	No paint mark on counterbalance weight
Ground +0.25 mm (0.0098 in.)	Stage 1 paint mark (subtract 0.25 mm [0.0098 in.] from all previous specifications)
Connecting rods	
Big end	
Bore inside diameter	51.000-51.013 (2.0079-2.0083)
Bearing insert inside diameter	48.016-48.050 (1.8904-1.8917)
Bearing width	21.883-21.935 (0.8615-0.8635)
Oil clearance	
Standard	0.025-0.075 (0.0009-0.0029)
Wear limit	0.13 (0.0051)
Oil clearance	
Standard	0.130-0.312 (0.0051-0.0122)
Service limit	0.5 (0.0196)

(continued)

Table 1 ENGINE LOWER END SPECIFICATIONS (continued)

Item	Specification mm (in.)
Connecting rods (continued)	
Maximum twist at 150 mm (5.905 in.) spacing	
850 cc, 1100 cc, 1200 cc	0.07 (0.0027)
1150 cc	0.02 (0.0008)
Small end bearing bore	22.015-22.025 (0.8667-0.8671)
Radial clearance	
Standard	0.015-0.030 (0.0006-0.0012)
Service limit	0.06 (0.002)
Side clearance	
Standard	0.130-0.312 (0.0051-0.0123)
Service limit	0.5 (0.0197)

Table 2 ENGINE LOWER END TORQUE SPECIFICATIONS

Item	N•m	in.-lb.	ft.-lb.
Alternator			
Support cover bolts	20	–	15
Lower pulley bolt	50	–	37
Auxiliary shaft			
Sprocket bolts	70	–	52
Chain tensioner mounting bolt	9	80	–
Camshaft chain tensioner	32	–	24
Connecting rod cap bolts			
Preliminary	20	–	15
Final	additional 80°		
Crankcase bolts			
6–mm	9	80	–
8–mm	20	–	15
10–mm	45	–	33
Crankshaft auxiliary shaft sprocket bolt	10	88	–
Engine front mounting bolts and nuts	82	–	60
Engine rear mounting bolts and nuts			
C, GS, R models	58	–	43
RS, RT models	47	–	35
S models	82	–	60
Oil line (without rotary breather)			
Oil line mounting bolt	20	–	15
Ventilation valve or union bolt	25	–	18
Oil line at oil cooler thermostat	9	80	–
Oil pressure switch	30	–	22
Oil pump cover	9	80	–
Rotary breather			
Mounting bolt	70	–	52
Ventilation valve or union bolt	25	–	18

CHAPTER SIX

CLUTCH

This chapter provides service procedures for the clutch and both hydraulically and cable-operated clutch release mechanisms.

The dry single-plate clutch mounts at the rear portion of the engine. The clutch design is similar to an automotive clutch instead of the usual wet multiplate unit found on most motorcycles. The clutch friction plate is splined to the transmission input shaft and is sandwiched between the clutch pressure plate and the clutch housing cover. The clutch housing is bolted to the flywheel. The clutch housing cover, pressure plate and diaphragm spring rotate with the engine and when the clutch is engaged. The friction plate also turns with this assembly, thus turning the transmission input shaft.

On cable operated models, the clutch release pushrod rides within the hollow channel in the transmission's input shaft. The clutch lever on the handlebar controls the pushrod. The release lever is mounted on the rear of the transmission housing. When the clutch lever on the handlebar is pulled in, the clutch cable actuates the clutch release lever on the transmission housing and pushes the release pushrod forward. This type of clutch requires routine adjustment since the cable will stretch with use. Refer to Chapter Three for adjustment procedures.

On hydraulic operated models, the clutch release pushrod rides within the hollow channel in the transmission's input shaft. It is controlled by the clutch master cylinder on the handlebar and slave cylinder mounted on the rear of the transmission housing. When the clutch lever on the handlebar is pulled in, the hydraulic pressure generated by the master cylinder activates the clutch slave cylinder, which in turn pushes the release pushrod forward.

The forward end of the release push rod has a conical steel tip that rides against the center of the diaphragm spring. As the release pushrod moves forward, the spring pressure is released, thus allowing the clutch housing assembly to rotate freely without rotating the friction plate and transmission input shaft.

Table 1 and **Table 2** are located at the end of this chapter.

CLUTCH

Removal

Refer to **Figure 1** and **Figure 2**.

The clutch assembly can be removed with the engine in the frame, but the transmission must be removed.

1. Remove the transmission as described in Chapter Seven or Chapter Eight.

CAUTION

*The housing cover and pressure plate are installed as a balanced assembly. The relationship of these two parts must remain the same or **severe vibration** may result. Prior to performing Step 2, check to see if there is*

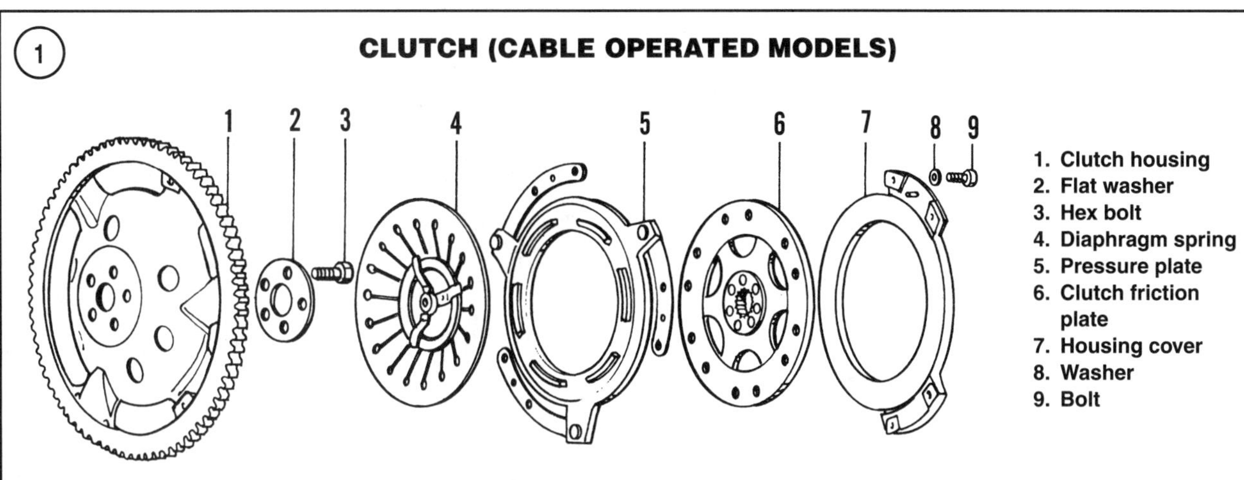

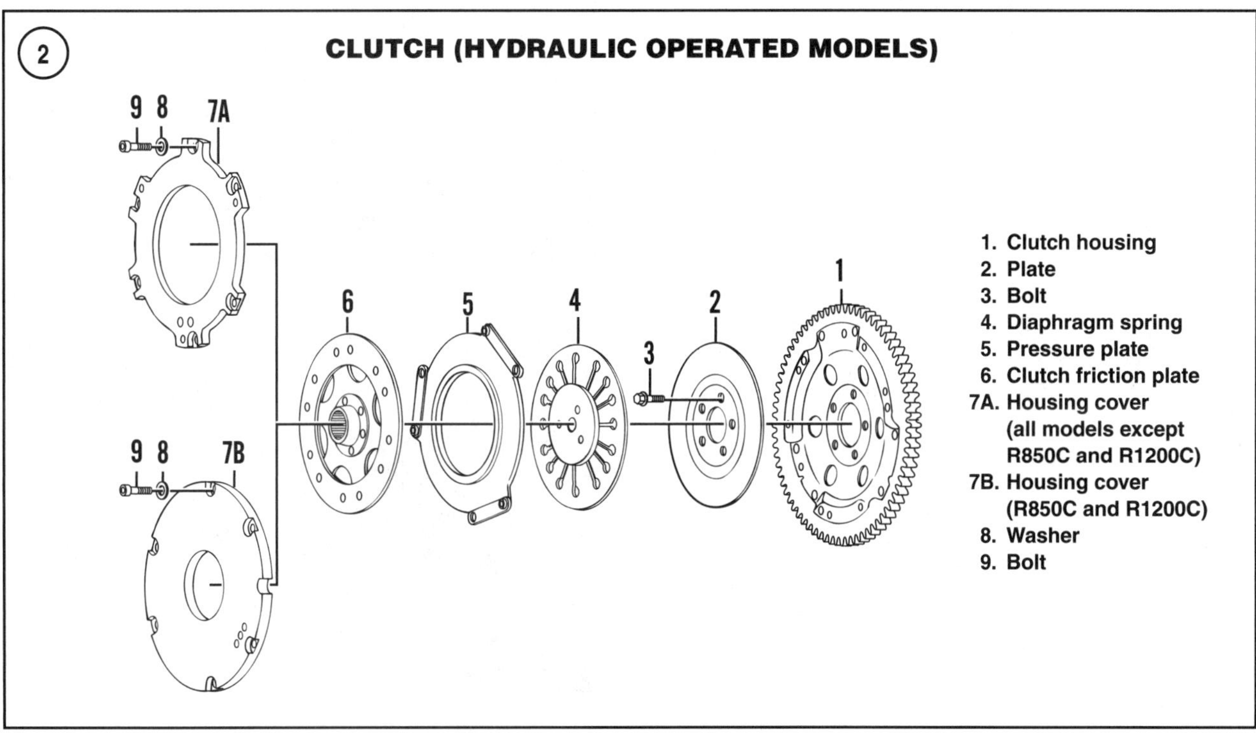

a yellow or white paint balance mark on each of these two parts. These parts are not symmetrical in shape or weight and the marks are placed at the ***heaviest portion*** *of each part. The parts are installed with the balance marks spaced 180° apart from each other. This spreads out the weight imbalance in order to equalize the assembly into a balanced assembly.*

2. Following a crisscross pattern, loosen and then remove the clutch housing cover and washers (**Figure 3**). Discard the bolts, as new ones must be used during installation.

NOTE

In Step 3, be prepared to catch the diaphragm spring when the assembly is removed.

3. Remove the housing cover, friction plate and pressure plate as an assembly. Do not separate these parts until they are marked for alignment. Use a permanent marking pen

and make an alignment mark between the housing cover pin (A, **Figure 4**) and the pressure plate arm (B).

4. Remove the diaphragm spring.
5. To keep the clutch housing from rotating in the following step, install the special tool (BMW part No. 11-5-640). Mesh it with the gear teeth and the crankcase receptacle (**Figure 5**). Push the tool in until it bottoms.

CAUTION
The clutch hex bolts have a very shallow head and are easily damaged during removal.

6. To loosen the clutch hex bolts, perform the following:
   a. Use a 6-point socket. Do not use a 12-point as the bolt head is easily rounded off.
   b. Apply a light coat of valve grinding compound to the inner surface of the socket where it contacts the bolt head. This ensures maximum grip on the bolt head.
   c. Use an impact driver and impact socket to loosen the bolts or, if using a regular socket, push very hard on the socket and wrench to ensure the socket presses securely against the bolt head.
7. Following a crisscross pattern, loosen the clutch hex bolts (A, **Figure 6**).

8A. On cable operated models, perform the following:
   a. Hold the clutch housing and remove the clutch hex bolts and flat washer (A, **Figure 6**). Discard the bolts since new ones must be used during installation.
   a. Remove the clutch housing and flat washer (B, **Figure 6**).

8B. On hydraulic operated models, perform the following:
   a. Hold the clutch housing and remove the clutch bolts and plate. Discard the bolts since new ones must be used during installation.
   b. Remove the clutch housing and the plate.

9. Inspect all clutch components as described in this section.

Installation

Refer to **Figure 1** and **Figure 2**.

CAUTION
Use only the BMW recommended lubricant, Optimoly MP3 or Microlube GL261, during the following assembly procedure. For the clutch to operate effectively and smoothly, the recommended lubricant must be used. This lubricant is available from a BMW

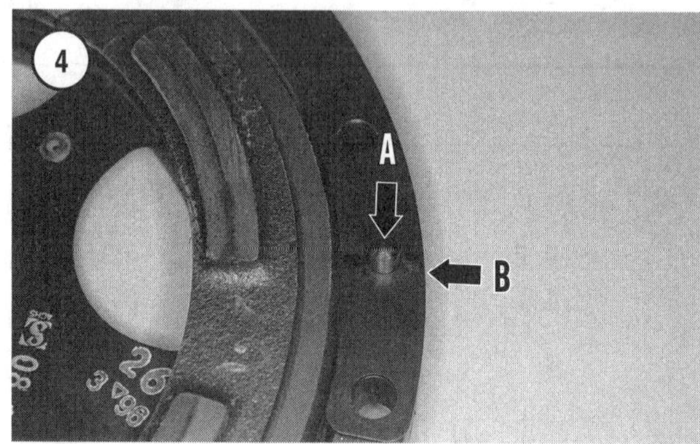

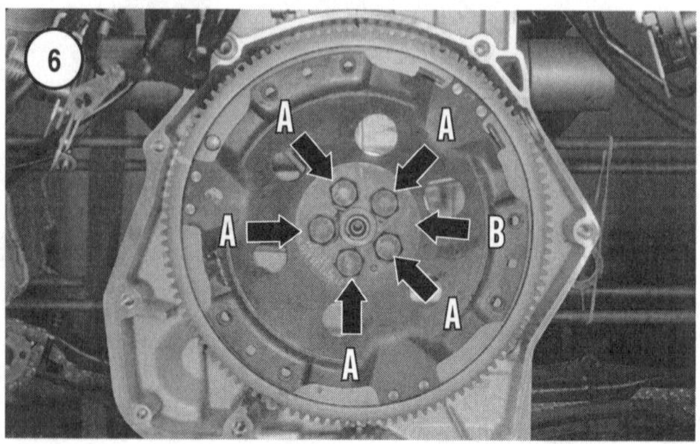

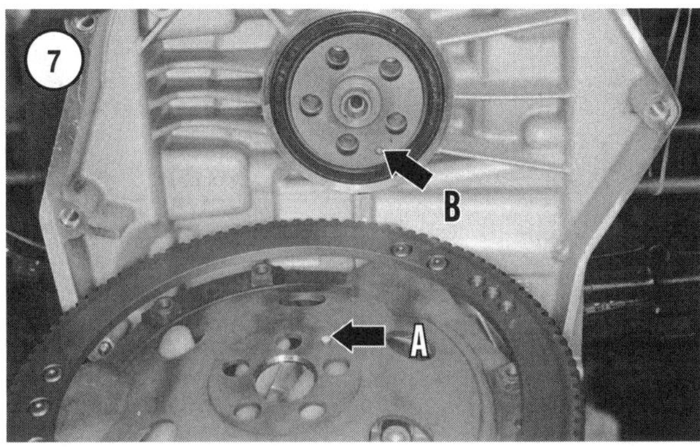

dealership. Bel Rey Total Performance Lube is a suitable substitute.

CAUTION

When applying lubricant, ***apply only a thin coat*** *and only to the designated areas. If too much lubricant is used or is applied in the wrong place, it will be thrown off and may contaminate the clutch friction plate.*

1. Align the clutch housing index mark (A, **Figure 7**) with the crankshaft index mark (B) and install the clutch housing onto the end of the crankshaft.

NOTE

Apply a light coat of clean engine oil to the hex bolt threads prior to installation.

2A. On cable operated models, hold the clutch housing in place and install the flat washer (B, **Figure 6**) and *new* clutch hex bolts (A). Tighten the hex bolts finger tight.

2B. On hydraulic operated models, hold the clutch housing in place and install the plate and *new* clutch hex bolts. Tighten the hex bolts finger tight.

3. Use the same tool (**Figure 5**) used during removal to keep the clutch housing from rotating when tightening the clutch bolts. Push the tool in until it bottoms.

4. Following a crisscross pattern, tighten the hex bolts to 40 N•m (29 ft.-lb.). After all bolts are tightened to this specification, tighten an additional 32° as follows:
   a. Install a degree wheel (A, **Figure 8**) onto the bolt head and attach a long socket wrench (B) onto the tool.
   b. Position the locating leg (C, **Figure 8**) into one of the holes to keep the tool from rotating.
   c. Zero the dial on the tool and tighten the hex bolt an additional 32°.
   d. Repeat for each remaining hex bolt.

5. Apply a light coat of BMW Microlube GL261 or Bel Rey Total Performance Lube, to the perimeter (**Figure 9**) of the diaphragm spring where it contacts the pressure plate.

CAUTION

As noted during removal, the clutch cover and pressure plate must be installed in a specific arrangement in order to form a balanced assembly. The relationship of these two parts must be correct or ***severe vibration*** *will result, leading to costly clutch and/or engine damage.*

NOTE

*The balance mark on the pressure plate (**Figure 10**) must be positioned 180° from*

6

*the balance mark on the clutch cover (**Figure 11**). If there were no marks, refer to the marks made in Step 3 of **Removal** as shown in **Figure 3**.*

6. Place the clutch cover on the work bench with the locating pins facing upward (A, **Figure 12**).
7. Position the clutch friction disc with the long side of the spline section facing down so that the flush side is up (A, **Figure 13**) and install the clutch friction plate (B) onto the clutch cover.
8. Install the clutch pressure plate as follows:
   a. Apply a light coat of multipurpose grease to the locating pins (C, **Figure 13**) on the housing cover to prevent corrosion.
   b. Align the paint marks 180° apart.
   c. Align the mounting holes in the pressure plate with the locating pins on the housing cover.
   d. Install the clutch pressure plate (**Figure 14**) onto the housing cover and friction disc.
   e. Push the clutch pressure plate onto the locating dowels and make sure it is completely seated.
9. Apply a light coat of BMW Microlube GL 261 or Bel Rey Total Performance Lube, (**Figure 15**) to the raised bosses on the pressure plate (**Figure 16**).
10. Pick up the clutch assembly and, from the backside, install the friction plate centering tool (BMW part No. 21-3-680) into the center of the friction plate (A, **Figure 17**).
11. Position the diaphragm spring (B, **Figure 17**) with the concave side facing toward the engine and install the diaphragm spring onto the clutch assembly and the special tool.

NOTE

*Do **not** try to reassemble and install the clutch assembly without the clutch plate centering tool. The alignment of the friction plate to the crankshaft pilot bushing is critical. During transmission installation, the transmission's input shaft slides through the friction plate's center splines and into the pilot bushing in the end of the crankshaft. If this alignment is not correct, the transmission can not be installed.*

12. Install the clutch assembly (A, **Figure 18**) onto the engine. Carefully insert the end of the friction plate centering tool (B) into the end of the crankshaft.
13. Align the mounting bolt holes of the clutch assembly with the holes in the clutch housing.
14. Install *new* clutch assembly mounting bolts (**Figure 3**) no more than finger-tight at this time.

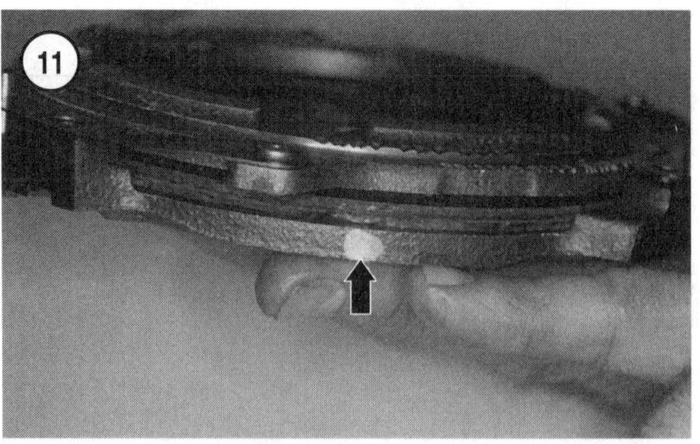

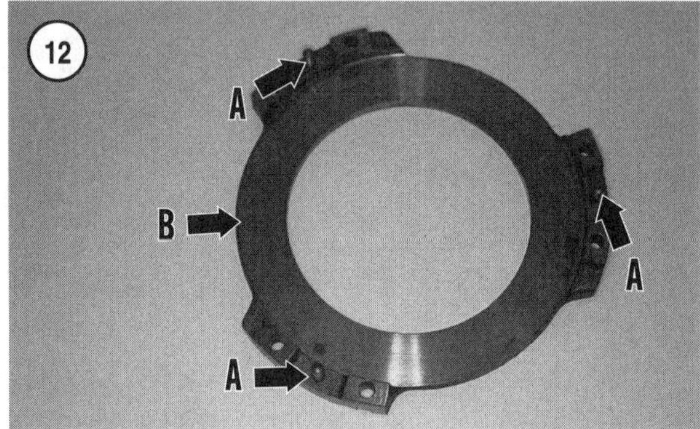

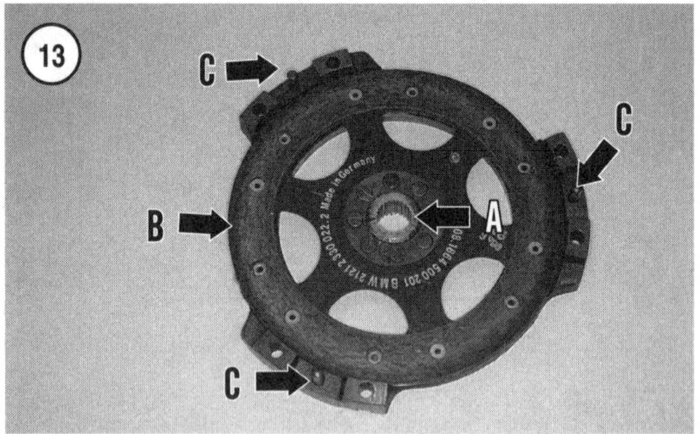

15. Following a crisscross pattern, tighten the clutch housing bolts in 2-3 stages to the following:

   a. On cable operated models:18 N•m (13 ft.-lb.).
   b. On hydraulically operated models:12 N•m (106 in.-lb.).

16. Remove the centering tool (B, **Figure 18**) from the friction plate.

CAUTION
Remove the clutch housing holding tool from the clutch housing prior to installing the transmission housing. If left in place, the engine will be unable to start since the clutch housing and crankshaft cannot rotate. If the tool has not been removed, it can be removed through the opening on the left-hand side of the transmission housing.

17. Remove the clutch housing holding tool (**Figure 5**) installed in Step 3 from the clutch housing teeth and crankcase receptacle.

18. Prior to installing the transmission, apply a light coat of Microlube GL 261or Bel Rey Total Performance Lube, to the following areas:

   a. The release push rod end.
   b. Inner splines of the friction plate (**Figure 19**).
   c. Outer splines of the transmission input shaft where it rides in the friction plate.

19. Install the transmission as described in Chapter Seven or Chapter Eight.

Inspection

When measuring the clutch components, compare the actual measurements to the specifications in **Table 1**.

To maintain maximum performance from the clutch assembly, replace any part(s) that is in questionable condition.

1. Check all parts for oil or grease contamination. If the friction plate is fouled with oil or grease, it must be replaced.
2. If the housing cover, pressure plate, diaphragm spring or clutch housing is contaminated with oil and/or grease, perform the following:
   a. Thoroughly clean all parts in solvent and dry them with compressed air.
   b. After cleaning in solvent, clean the surfaces of the housing cover and pressure plate with lacquer thinner and/or contact cleaner and remove any solvent residue.
   c. Dry with a lint free cloth.
3. If there is oil and/or grease contamination on the clutch parts, inspect the rear main crankshaft seal (**Figure 20**) on the engine. Replace the seal, if necessary, as described in Chapter Five.
4. Inspect the housing cover locating pins (A, **Figure 21**) and the locating pin holes in the pressure plate and clutch housing (A, **Figure 22**) for wear or damage. Replace any defective parts.
5. Check the clutch housing bolt hole threads (B, **Figure 22**). If damaged, clean with an appropriate size metric tap, then clean with solvent and blow dry with compressed air.
6. Inspect the starter ring gear teeth (A, **Figure 23**) on the clutch housing for wear or damaged teeth. Minor roughness can be repaired with a file, but there is little point in attempting to remove deep scars.
7. Check the clutch housing mounting bolt holes (B, **Figure 23**) for elongation or any radial cracks emanating from the hole(s). Replace the clutch housing if necessary.
8A. On cable operated models, inspect the flat washer for elongation or any radial cracks emanating from the hole(s) (**Figure 24**). Replace the flat washer if necessary.
8B. On hydraulic operated models, inspect the plate for elongation or any radial cracks emanating from the hole(s). Replace the plate if necessary.
9. Inspect the clutch friction plate surface (A, **Figure 25**) for damage or wear. Replace the friction plate if the friction material is worn close to the rivets.
10. Measure the clutch friction plate surface-to-rivet head depth at several places around the plate with a depth gauge or vernier caliper (B, **Figure 25**). Replace the clutch friction plate if it is worn to the service limit.
11. Inspect the inner splines (A, **Figure 26**) in the clutch friction plate for cracks, nicks or galling where they contact the transmission input shaft. If any damage is evident, the friction plate must be replaced. If the splines are damaged, the clutch action may be erratic. Inspect the transmission input shaft splines for wear or damage. If the transmission input shaft is damaged, refer to Chapter

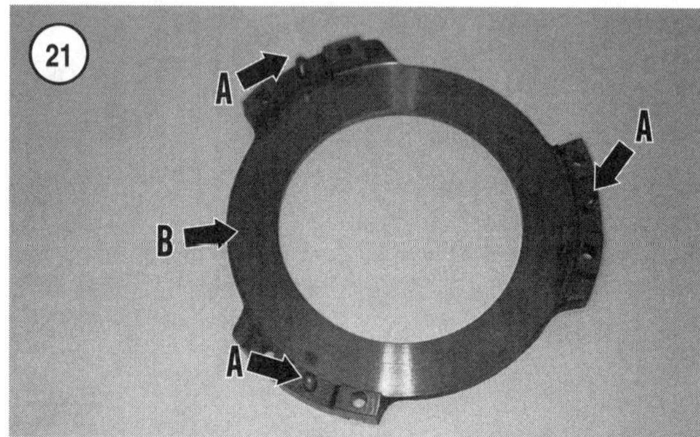

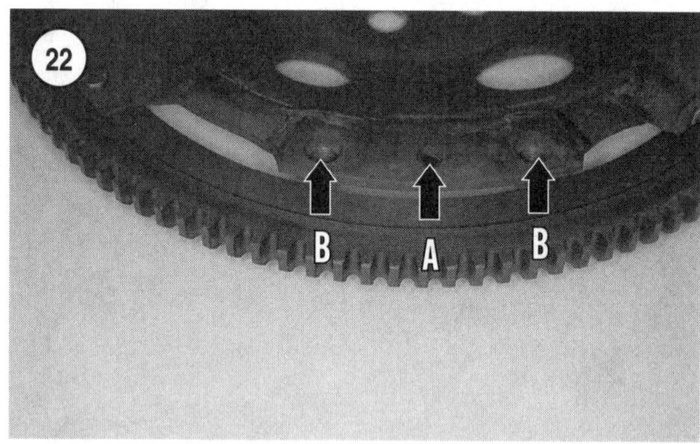

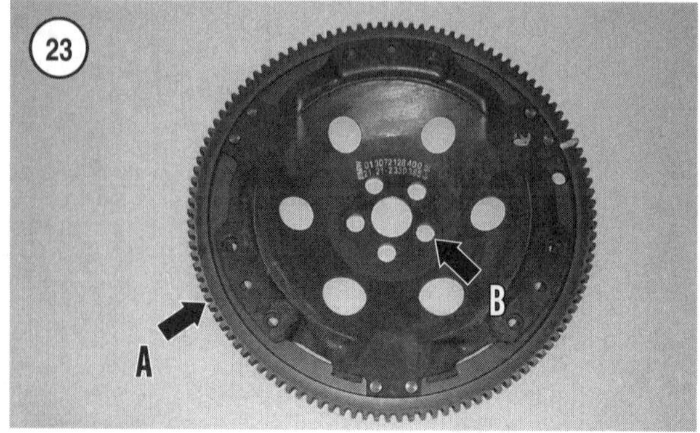

24

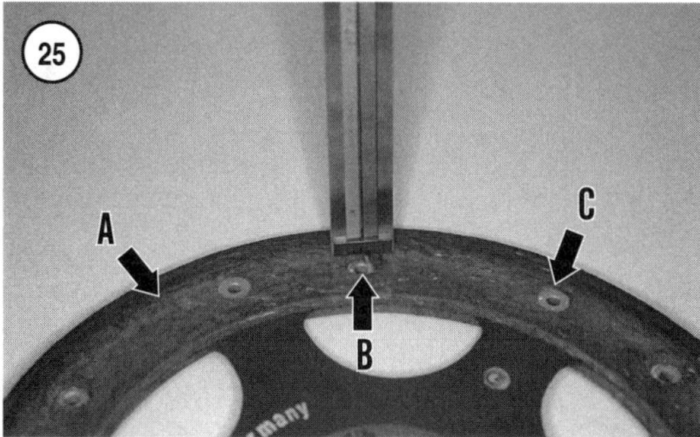

25

26

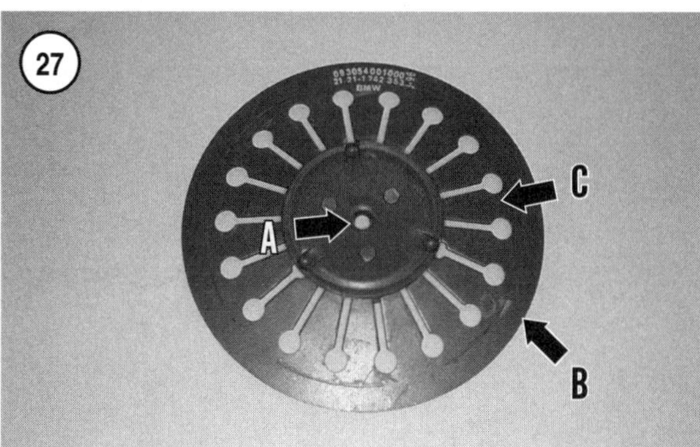

27

Seven or Chapter Eight for the transmission shaft replacement procedure.

12. Inspect the rivets (B, **Figure 26**) securing the inner spline portion to the clutch friction plate and the rivets securing the friction material to each side of the disc (C, **Figure 25**). If any of the rivets are loose or damaged; replace the clutch friction plate.

13. Inspect the clutch friction plate contact surface of both the pressure plate and the housing cover (B, **Figure 21**). Check for wear, cracks or scoring caused by friction disc rivet contact. If any of these conditions are found, replace either or both parts.

14. Inspect the diaphragm spring as follows:
   a. Check the center portion (A, **Figure 27**) where the release push rod makes contact for wear or damage.
   b. Check the outer portion (B, **Figure 27**) where the spring contacts the pressure plate for wear or damage.
   c. Check the spring for cracked or broken spring fingers (C, **Figure 27**).
   d. Check the spring for weakness. If the clutch has been slipping and the clutch release mechanism is properly adjusted, the spring may be weak.
   e. Replace the diaphragm spring if any of these faults are found.

CLUTCH RELEASE MECHANISM (CABLE OPERATED MODELS)

Refer to **Figure 28**.

Removal

The clutch release bearing can be removed with the engine and transmission in the frame. The following photographs are shown with the transmission removed to better illustrate the steps.

1A. On models equipped with a centerstand, place the motorcycle on the centerstand with the rear wheel off the ground.

1B. On models without a centerstand, place a suitable size jack under the engine to support the motorcycle with the rear wheel off the ground.

2. At the clutch hand lever on the handlebar, loosen the locknut (A, **Figure 29**) and turn the adjuster (B) all the way in to provide the maximum clutch cable slack.

3. Remove the swing arm and drive shaft as described in Chapter Thirteen.

4. Disconnect the clutch cable from the clutch release lever (**Figure 30**) at the rear of the transmission housing.

5. Remove the bolt and washers (A, **Figure 31**) securing the clutch release lever.

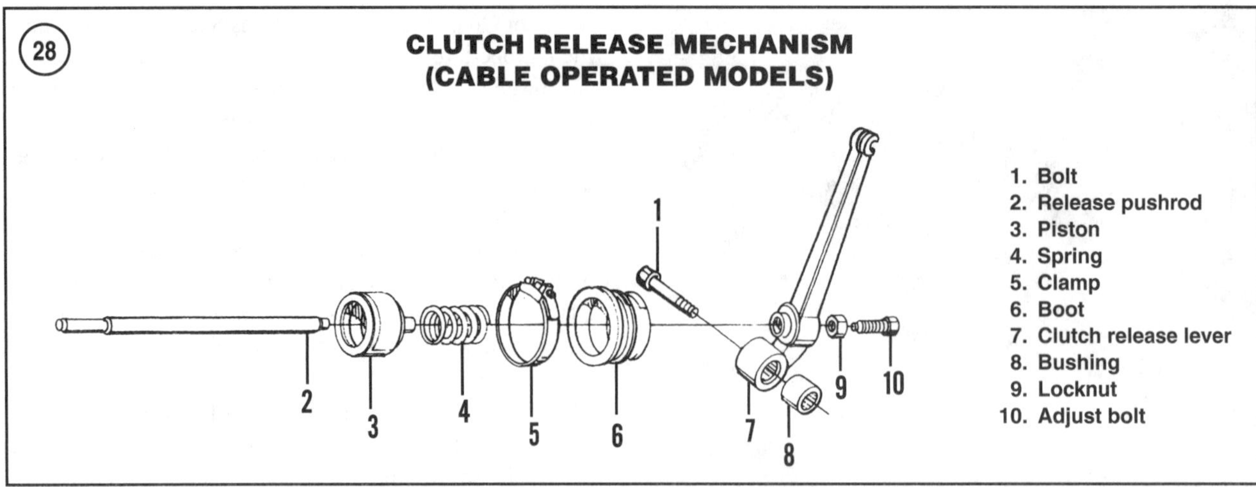

6. Remove the clutch release lever (B, **Figure 31**) from the transmission housing.
7. Loosen the clamp (A, **Figure 32**), and remove the boot and spring (B).
8. Use needlenose pliers and remove the piston (**Figure 33**).

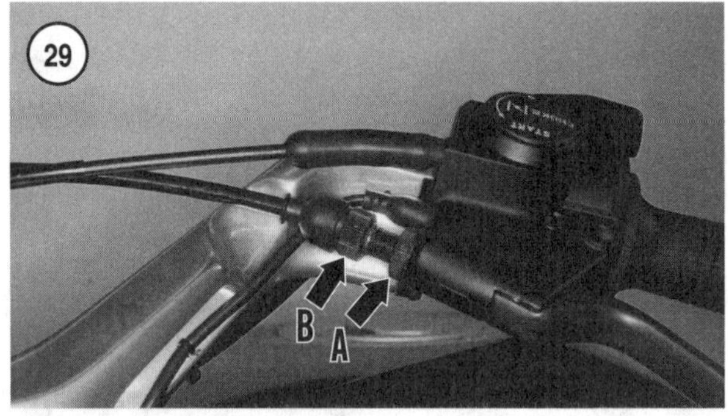

Installation

1. Position the piston with the raised pad facing up and install the piston (**Figure 34**). Push the piston down until it bottoms.
2. Install the spring (**Figure 35**) into the piston (B).
3. Hold the spring in place within the boot and install the assembly onto the transmission case. Push the rubber boot down until it seats on the transmission case, then securely tighten the clamp (A, **Figure 32**).
4. Apply a light coat of Microlube GL261 or Optimoly MP3 paste grease to the end of the release lever adjust bolt where it contacts the piston.
5. Insert the clutch release lever (B, **Figure 31**) through the opening in the transmission housing.
6. Install a large washer on each side of the release lever and position the lever against the mounting boss. Install the bolt and washer (A, **Figure 31**) and tighten securely.
7. Move the release lever up and down to ensure that there is no binding after tightening the mounting bolt.
8. Connect the clutch cable onto the clutch release lever (**Figure 30**) at the rear of the transmission housing.
9. If removed, install the drive shaft and swing arm as described in Chapter Thirteen.
10. Adjust the clutch hand lever free play as described in Chapter Three.

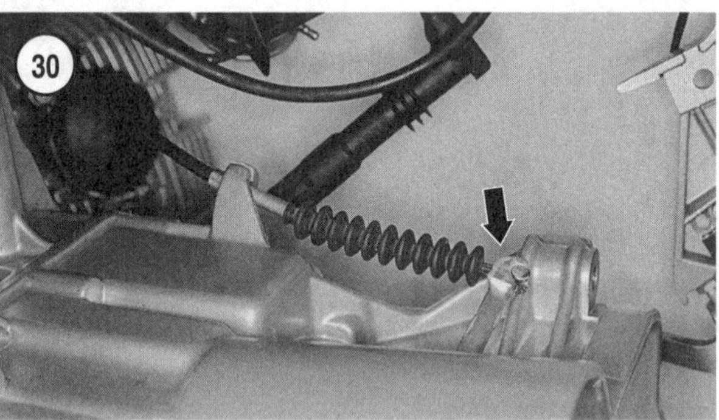

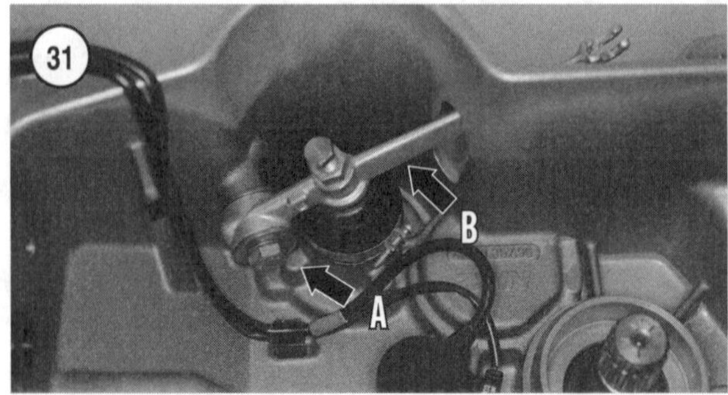

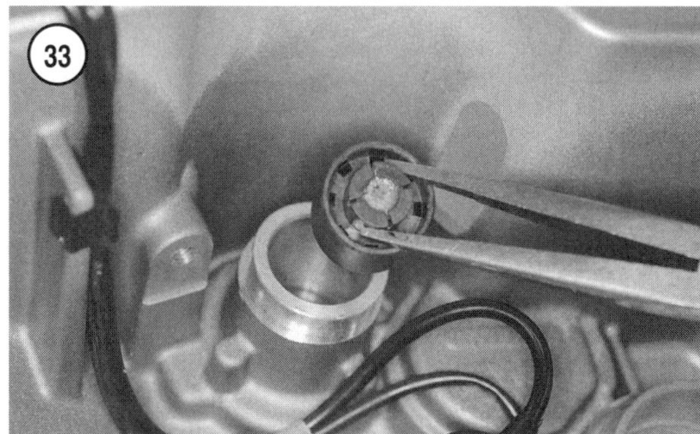

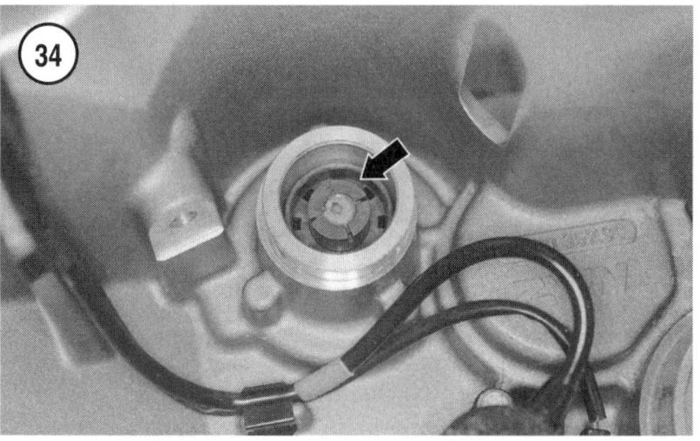

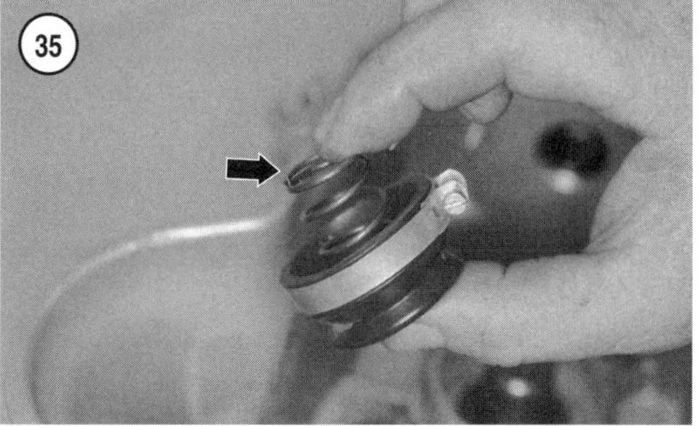

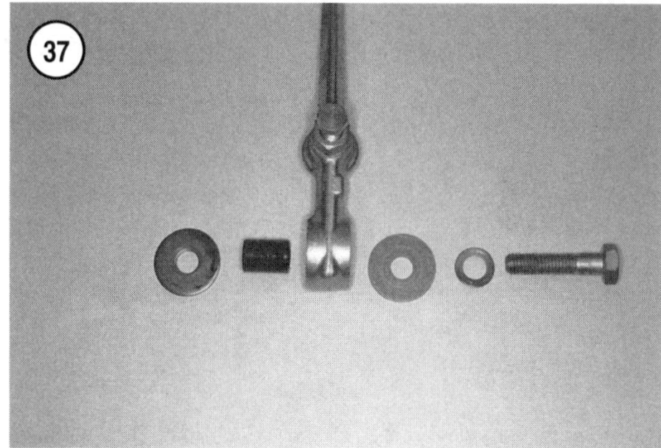

Inspection

1. Inspect the rubber boot for damage, tears or deterioration; replace it if necessary.
2. Inspect the spring for sagging or damage. Replace if it is in questionable condition.
3. Roll the release push rod on a surface plate or plate glass to check its straightness. The rod must be perfectly straight to prevent it from binding inside the transmission input shaft.
4. Inspect the release push rod end where it contacts the diaphragm spring. Make sure it is not damaged or rough. Replace it if necessary.
5. Inspect the piston for wear or damage.
6. Inspect the release lever needle bearing (**Figure 36**) for wear or damage. If damaged, replace the release lever. If the bearing is good, apply a light coat of BMW Microlube GL261, or Bel Rey Total Performance Lube, to the inner surface of the needle bearing. Insert the bushing into the needle bearing.
7. Check the release lever, bushing and washers (**Figure 37**) for wear or damage. Replace any worn or damaged part.

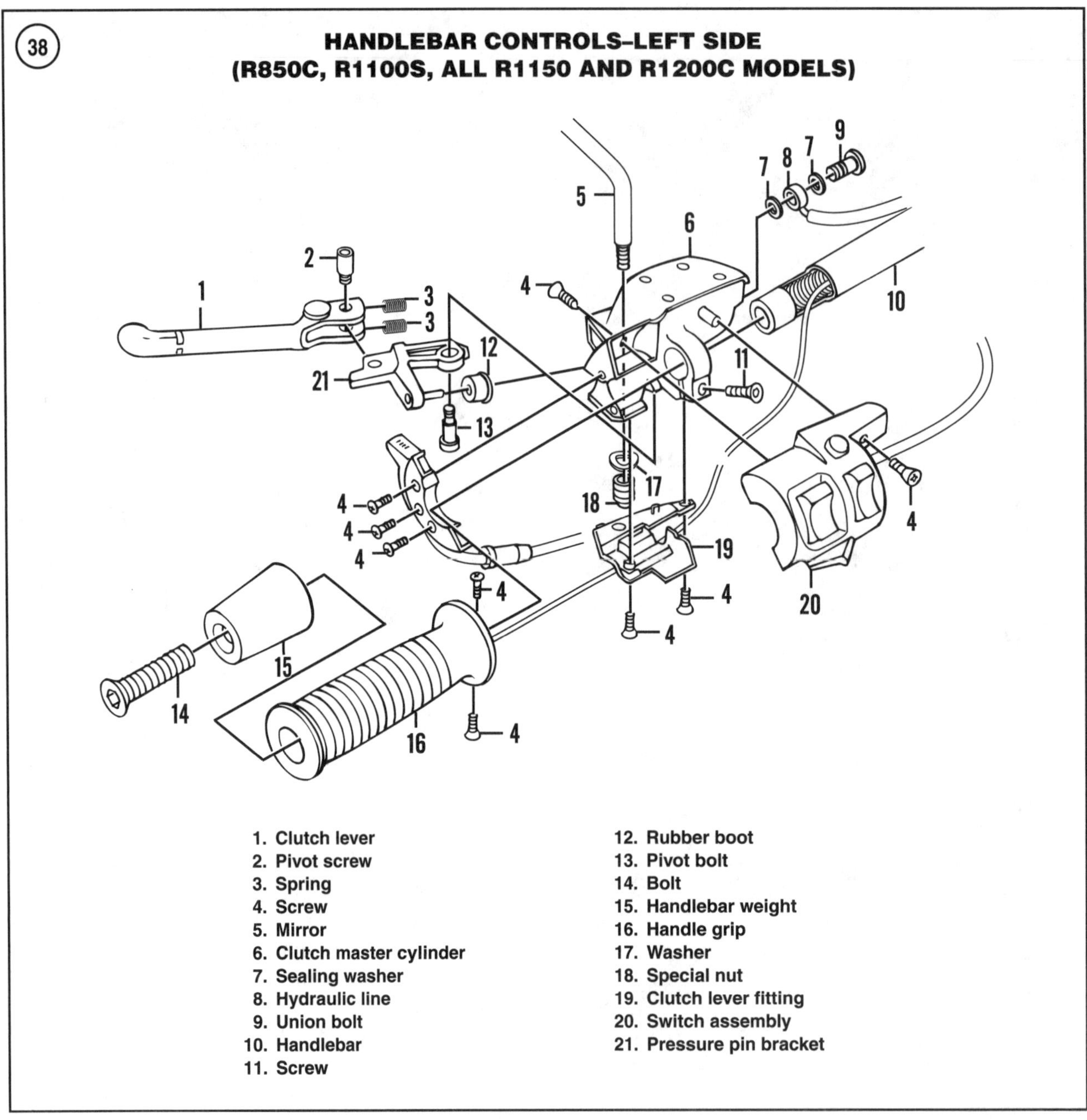

(38) **HANDLEBAR CONTROLS–LEFT SIDE (R850C, R1100S, ALL R1150 AND R1200C MODELS)**

1. Clutch lever
2. Pivot screw
3. Spring
4. Screw
5. Mirror
6. Clutch master cylinder
7. Sealing washer
8. Hydraulic line
9. Union bolt
10. Handlebar
11. Screw
12. Rubber boot
13. Pivot bolt
14. Bolt
15. Handlebar weight
16. Handle grip
17. Washer
18. Special nut
19. Clutch lever fitting
20. Switch assembly
21. Pressure pin bracket

8. Inspect the clutch release lever adjustment bolt and locknut for wear or damage. Replace if necessary.

CLUTCH CABLE

Replacement

1A. On models equipped with a centerstand, place the motorcycle on the centerstand with the rear wheel off of the ground.

1B. On models without a centerstand, place a suitable size jack under the engine to support the motorcycle with the rear wheel off the ground.

2. Remove the fuel tank as described in Chapter Nine.

3. On RS and RT models, remove the fairing right side panels as described in Chapter Fifteen.

4. At the clutch hand lever on the handlebar, loosen the locknut (A, **Figure 29**) and turn the adjuster (B) all the way in to provide maximum clutch cable slack.

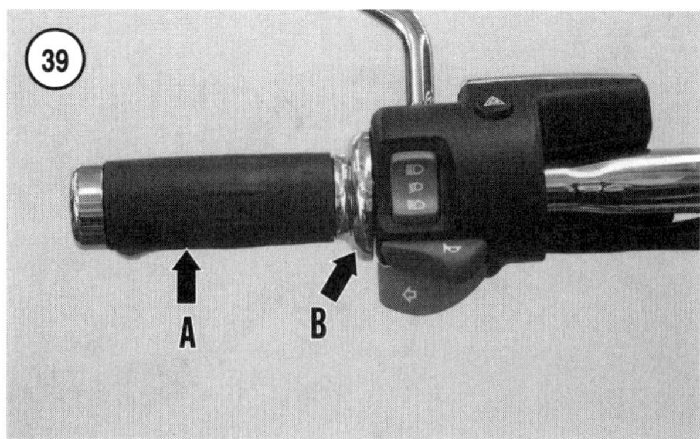

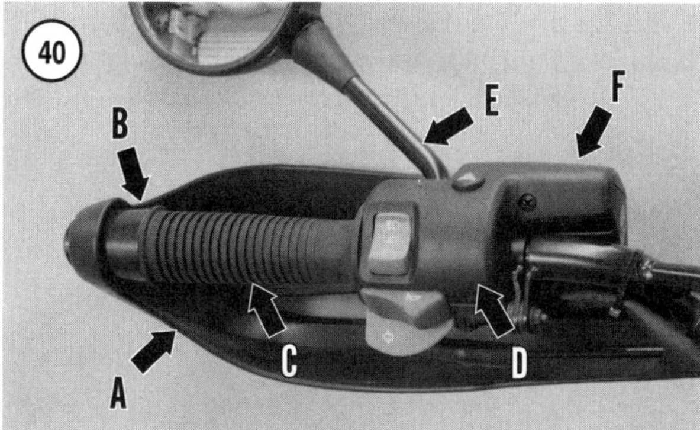

5. Disconnect the clutch cable from the clutch release lever (**Figure 30**) at the rear of the transmission housing.
6. Remove any straps securing the clutch cable to the frame.

NOTE
Prior to removing the cable, make a drawing of the cable routing through the frame. Replace the cable exactly as it was, avoiding any sharp turns.

7. Pull the clutch cable out from behind the steering head area and out of the frame.
8. Remove the cable and replace it with a new cable.
9. Install by reversing the removal steps. Adjust the clutch as described in Chapter Three.

CLUTCH MASTER CYLINDER

Refer to **Figure 38**.

Removal/Installation

CAUTION
Cover the fuel tank and front fairing with a heavy cloth or plastic tarp to protect them from accidental brake fluid spills. Brake fluid will damage the finish on any plastic, painted or plated surface. Immediately wash any spilled brake fluid from the motorcycle. Use soapy water, and rinse the area completely.

1. Clean all dirt and foreign matter from top of the master cylinder.
2A. On R850C and R1200C models, perform the following:
   a. Remove the screw securing the handgrip (A, **Figure 39**) and pull off the handgrip.
   b. Remove the two screws securing the trim plate (B, **Figure 39**) and remove the trim plate.

6

2B. On all models except R850C and R1200C, perform the following:
   a. On GS models so equipped, remove the bolt securing the hand guard (A, **Figure 40**) and handlebar weight (B).
   b. On all other models, remove the bolt securing the handlebar weight (B, **Figure 40**) and remove the weight.
   c. Remove the two screws securing the handgrip (C, **Figure 40**).
   d. On models so equipped, disconnect the electrical connector and release the cable shoe for the heated hand grip.
   e. Slide the hand grip (C, **Figure 40**) off the handlebar.
3. Remove the screws securing the lower section of the clutch lever fitting and remove the fitting.
4. On all models except R850C and R1200C, remove the screws securing the increase idle (choke) lever and move the lever out of the way.
5. Remove the screws securing the handlebar switch (D, **Figure 40**) and move the switch away from the handlebar.
6. On models so equipped, remove the rear view mirror (E, **Figure 40**)
7. Remove the screws securing the top cover (F, **Figure 40**). Remove the top cover, plate and diaphragm from the master cylinder reservoir.
8. If a shop syringe is available, draw all of the brake fluid out of the master cylinder reservoir. Temporarily reinstall the diaphragm, plate and cover. Tighten the cover finger tight.
9. Remove the clutch lever position switch from the underside of the master cylinder.
10A. On models equipped with a banjo bolt, perform the following:
   a. Place a rag beneath the banjo bolt and remove the bolt.

b. Separate the clutch hose from the master cylinder. Do not lose the two sealing washers, one from each side of the clutch hose fitting.

10B. On models equipped with a clutch line fitting (**Figure 41**), perform the following:

a. Place a wrench on one side of the fitting and loosen the other portion of the fitting.

b. Separate the clutch hose from the master cylinder.

11. Place the loose end of the clutch hose in a reclosable plastic bag to prevent brake fluid from dribbling onto the motorcycle. Tie the loose end of the hose up to the handlebar.

12. Loosen the master cylinder clamp bolt and slide the master cylinder off the end of the handlebar.

13. Drain any residual brake fluid from the master cylinder and reservoir. Dispose of fluid properly.

14. If the master cylinder is not going to be serviced; place it in a reclosable plastic bag to protect it from contamination.

15. Install by reversing the removal steps while noting the following:

a. Position the clutch master cylinder onto the left handlebar, and align the mark on the master cylinder with the handlebar punch mark.

b. On models equipped with a banjo bolt, install a *new* sealing washer onto each side of the hose fitting and tighten the banjo bolt to 14 N•m (124 in.-lb.).

c. Refill the master cylinder and reservoir with fresh DOT 4 brake fluid and bleed the clutch system as described in this chapter.

Disassembly

Refer to **Figure 42**.

1. Remove the clutch master cylinder assembly as described in this chapter.
2. Remove the pivot bolt securing the hand lever to the master cylinder body. Remove the hand lever.
3. Remove the rubber boot from the cylinder bore on the master cylinder.
4. Press the piston into the cylinder bore and use snap ring pliers to remove the internal snap ring from the bore.
5. Remove the piston assembly and the spring from the cylinder bore.
6. Inspect the components as described in this chapter.

Assembly

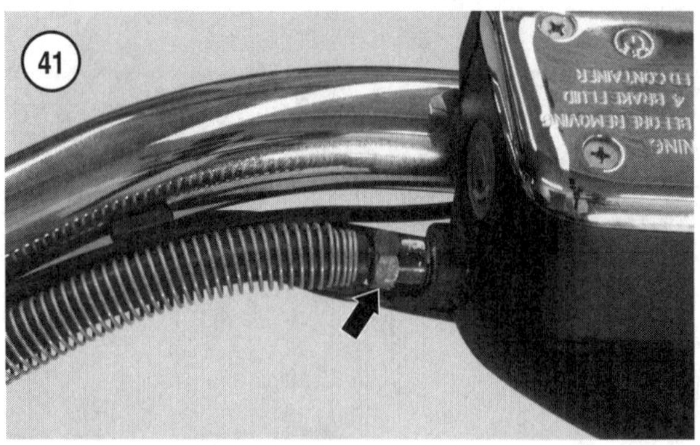
41

1. Soak the new cups and the new piston assembly in fresh DOT 4 brake fluid for at least 15 minutes to make them pliable. Coat the inside of the cylinder bore with fresh brake fluid prior to the assembly of parts.
2. If removed, install the primary cup onto the spring and install the secondary cup onto the piston.

CAUTION
When installing the piston assembly, do not allow the cups to turn inside out. They will be damaged and allow brake fluid leakage within the cylinder bore.

3. Install the spring and piston assembly. Push them into the cylinder until they bottom in the bore.
4. Press the piston assembly into the cylinder and install the snap ring. Make sure it is correctly seated in the snap ring groove.
5. Install the hand lever onto the master cylinder. Guide the pushrod into the opening in the rubber boot. Make sure the metal tab on the clutch position switch is correctly positioned against the clutch lever.
6. Align the bolt holes and install the pivot bolt and nut. Tighten the pivot bolt securely. Make sure the hand lever operates freely within the master cylinder with no binding.
7. Operate the clutch lever and make sure the switch plunger moves in and out with no binding.
8. Install the clutch master cylinder as described in this chapter.

Inspection

There are no specifications available for the clutch master cylinder. If any part is faulty replace the master cylinder as an assembly.

1. Clean all parts in isopropyl alcohol or fresh DOT 4 brake fluid. Inspect the cylinder bore surface for signs of wear or damage. If less than perfect, replace the master cylinder assembly. The body cannot be replaced separately.

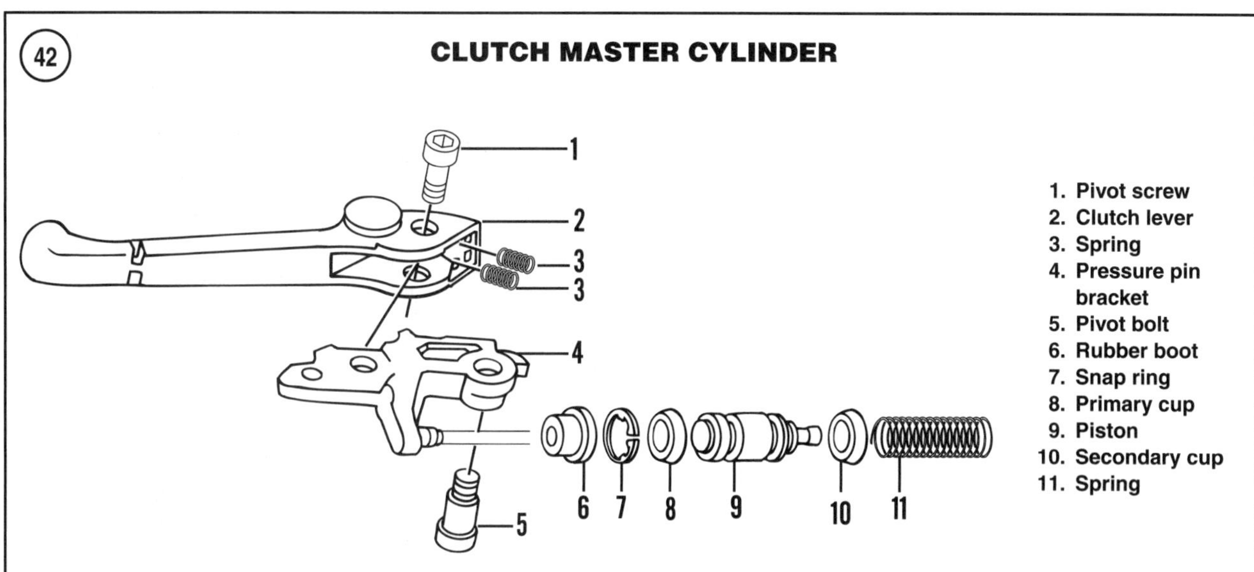

2. Inspect the piston cups for signs of wear and damage. If less than perfect, replace the piston assembly. Individual cups cannot be replaced.

3. Inspect the piston contact surfaces for signs of wear and damage. If less than perfect, replace the piston assembly.

4. Check the end of the piston for wear caused by the hand lever pushrod.

5. Inspect the pivot hole in the hand lever. If worn or elongated the lever must be replaced.

6. Inspect the hand lever pivot lugs on the master cylinder for cracks or other signs of damage.

7. Make sure the fluid passage in the bottom of the reservoir is clear. Clean it if necessary.

8. Inspect the banjo bolt threads in the cylinder bore. If worn or damaged, clean the threads with a metric thread tap or replace the master cylinder assembly.

9. Check the top cover, diaphragm and diaphragm plate for damage and deterioration; replace as necessary.

10. Inspect the adjuster on the hand lever. If worn or damaged replace the hand lever as an assembly.

CLUTCH RELEASE CYLINDER

CAUTION

Cover the frame with a heavy cloth or plastic tarp to protect it from accidental brake fluid spills. Brake fluid will damage the finish on any plastic, painted or plated surface. Immediately wash any spilled brake fluid from the motorcycle. Use soapy water, and rinse the area completely.

Removal/Installation

R850C and R1200C models

1. Place a suitable size jack under the engine to support the motorcycle with the rear wheel off the ground.
2. Remove the fuel tank as described in Chapter Nine.
3. Release the clutch bleeder valve from the frame clip (**Figure 43**). Open the bleed screw and continue to apply the clutch lever until the clutch fluid is drained from the hydraulic line. Close the bleed screw.
4. Remove the three bolts securing the release cylinder (**Figure 44**). Pull the release cylinder straight back and away from the transmission case.
5. Remove the union bolts securing the brake lines to the slave cylinder and remove the release cylinder.

6

6. Install by reversing these removal steps while noting the following:
   a. Make sure the snap ring (**Figure 45**) is secure within the release cylinder housing.
   b. Tighten all mounting bolts securely.
   c. Install a *new* sealing washer each side of the clutch hose fitting. Install the banjo bolt and tighten to the specification listed in **Table 2**.
   d. Bleed the clutch system as described in this chapter.

All models except R850C and R1200C

1A. On models equipped with a centerstand, place the motorcycle on the centerstand with the rear wheel off of the ground.

1B. On models without a centerstand, place a suitable size jack under the engine to support the motorcycle with the rear wheel off the ground.

2. Remove the seat as described in Chapter Fifteen.
3. Remove the rear wheel as described in Chapter Eleven.
4. Remove the rear shock absorber as described in Chapter Thirteen.
5. Remove the central electrical box from the frame as described in Chapter Ten.
6. Remove the bracket securing the brake line to the rear frame.
7. Remove the rear brake master cylinder reservoir from the frame holder.
8. Release the clutch bleeder valve from the frame clip (**Figure 43**). Open the bleed screw and continue to apply the clutch lever until the clutch fluid is drained from the hydraulic line. Close the bleed screw.
9. Partially remove the right and left side footrest assembly from the frame as described in Chapter Fifteen. It is not necessary to completely remove the assemblies, just move them away from the frame.
10. Remove the bolts securing the rear frame. Partially move the rear frame to the rear by 15 mm (0.60 in.).
11. Remove the three bolts (A, **Figure 46**) securing the release cylinder. Pull the release cylinder straight back and away from the transmission case.
12. Remove the union bolts (B, **Figure 46**) securing the brake lines to the release cylinder and remove the release cylinder.
13. Install by reversing these removal steps while noting the following:
    a. Make sure the snap ring (**Figure 45**) is secure within the slave cylinder housing.
    b. Tighten all mounting bolts securely.

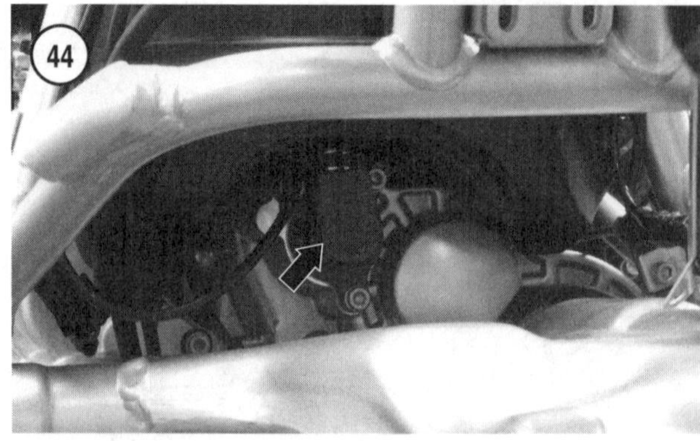

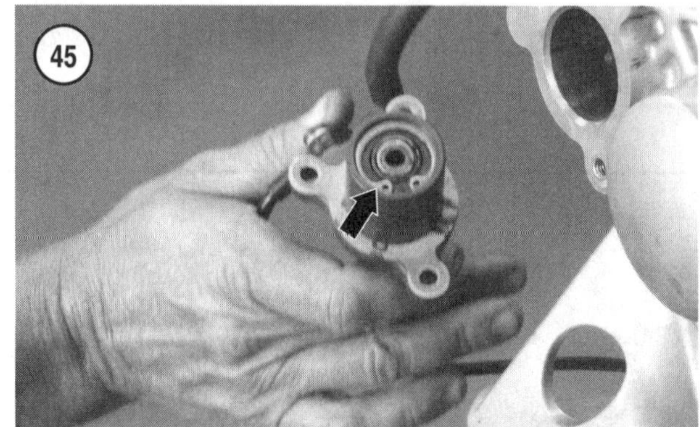

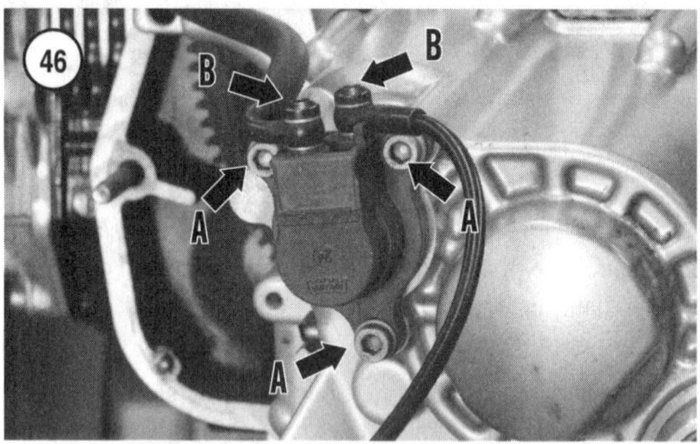

    c. Install a *new* sealing washer each side of the clutch hose fitting. Install the union bolt and tighten to the specification listed in **Table 2**.
    d. Bleed the clutch system as described in this chapter.

Inspection

Replacement parts are not available for the release cylinder. If the release cylinder is leaking hydraulic brake fluid, replace it.

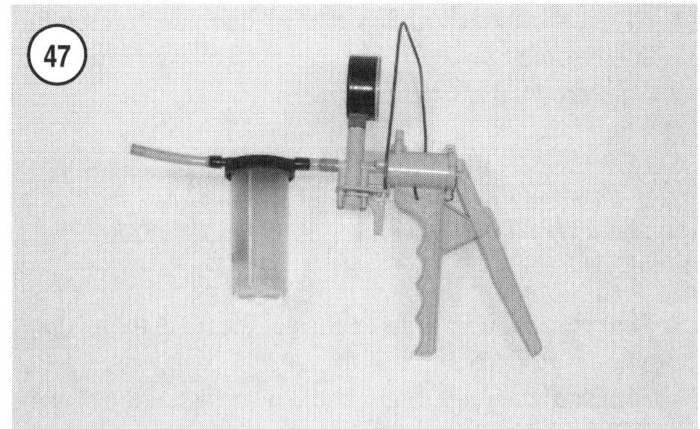

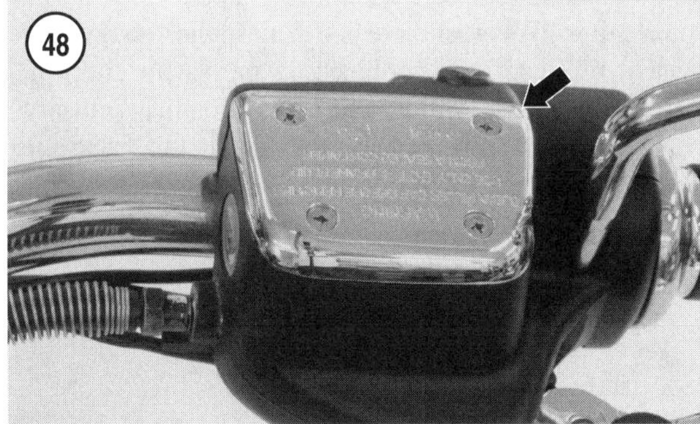

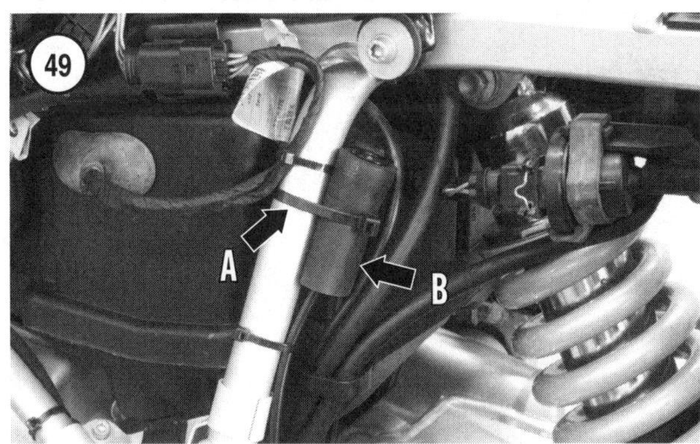

CLUTCH HYDRAULIC SYSTEM

The clutch is actuated by hydraulic fluid pressure and is controlled by the hand lever on the clutch master cylinder. As clutch components wear, the fluid level drops in the master cylinder and automatically adjusts for wear. There is no routine clutch adjustment necessary or possible.

When working on the clutch hydraulic system, the work area and all tools must be absolutely clean. Clutch master cylinder and release cylinder components can be damaged by even tiny particles of grit that enter the clutch system. Do not use sharp tools inside the master cylinder or release cylinder or on the pistons.

If there is any doubt about the ability to correctly and safely service the clutch components, refer the job to a BMW dealership or other qualified specialist.

Bleeding the clutch hydraulic system removes air from the clutch system. Air in the clutch system increases clutch lever travel while causing it to feel spongy and less responsive. Under extreme circumstances, it can cause complete loss of clutch action.

The clutch system can be bled manually or with the use of a Mityvac vacuum pump (**Figure 47**). When adding brake fluid during the bleeding process, use fresh DOT 4 brake fluid. Do not reuse old brake fluid or use DOT 5 (silicone based) brake fluid.

6

Brake fluid damages most surfaces, so wipe up any spill immediately with soapy water and rinse completely.

NOTE

When bleeding the clutch, check the master cylinder frequently to prevent it from running dry, especially when using a vacuum pump. If air enters the system it must be fled again.

1. Clean the top of the master cylinder of all dirt and foreign matter.
2. Remove the screws securing the clutch master cylinder top cover (**Figure 48**) and remove the cover, plate and diaphragm.
3. Fill the reservoir almost to the top with DOT 4 brake fluid and reinstall the diaphragm and cover. Leave the cover in place during this procedure to prevent the entry of dirt.

NOTE

As brake fluid exits the system, the level in the reservoir drops. Add brake fluid as necessary to keep the fluid level 10 mm (3/8 in.) below the reservoir top so air will not be drawn into the system.

4. Remove the tie wrap (A, **Figure 49**) and slide back the protective hose (B) from the bleeder valve.
5. Wrap a shop towel around the filler adapter assembly.
6. Remove the Allen head grub screw from the filler adapter.
7. Assemble the Mityvac tool according to its manufacturer's instructions. Secure it to the caliper bleed valve.
8. Connect the brake caliper bleed screw into the filler adapter and screw it in all the way with the valve in the closed position.

9. Open the bleed screw approximately 1/2 turn.
10. Operate the pump several times to create a vacuum in the line, then open the bleed valve. Brake fluid will quickly draw from the release cylinder into the pump's reservoir. Tighten the bleed valve before the fluid stops flowing through the hose. To prevent air from being drawn through the release cylinder, add fluid to maintain its level at the top of the reservoir.

NOTE
Do not allow the master cylinder reservoir to empty during the bleeding operation or more air will enter the system. If this occurs, the procedure must be repeated.

11. Continue the bleeding process until the fluid drawn from the release cylinder is bubble free. If bubbles are withdrawn with the brake fluid, more air is trapped in the line. Repeat Step 10, making sure to refill the master cylinder to prevent air from being drawn into the system.
12. When the brake fluid is free of bubbles, tighten the bleed valve and remove the brake bleeder assembly. Reinstall the bleed valve dust cap.

NOTE
Dispose of the brake fluid expelled during the bleeding process. Do not reuse the brake fluid.

13. If necessary, add fluid to correct the level in the master cylinder reservoir.
14. Reinstall the diaphragm and cover. Install the screws and tighten securely.
15. Test the feel of the clutch lever. It must be firm and offer the same resistance each time it is operated. If it feels spongy, it is likely that there is still air in the system and it must be bleed again. After bleeding the system, check for leaks and tighten all fittings and connections as necessary.
16. Test ride the motorcycle slowly at first to make sure the clutch is operating properly.

Table 1 CLUTCH SPECIFICATIONS

Item	Specification mm (in.)
Clutch friction plate (1993-1998 R850, all R1100 [except R1100S] models)	
Outer diameter	165 (6.4960)
Thickness service limit	4.8 (0.1890)
Clutch friction plate (1999-on R850, R1100S, R1150, R1200 models)	
Outer diameter	180 (7.0866)
Thickness service limit	4.5 (0.1771)

Table 2 CLUTCH TORQUE SPECIFICATIONS

Item	N•m	in.-lb.	ft.-lb.
Clutch housing bolts			
Cable operating	18	–	13
Hydraulic operated	12	106	–
Clutch housing hex bolts			
Preliminary	40	–	29
Final	additional 32°		
Clutch master cylinder union bolt	14	124	–

CHAPTER SEVEN

FIVE SPEED TRANSMISSION AND GEARSHIFT MECHANISMS

7

The transmission shafts and the gearshift mechanism are all located inside a transmission housing and cover that is bolted to the back of the engine.

The engine driven input shaft is splined to the clutch friction plate and is equipped with a shock damper to dampen engine-to-transmission shock loads. The rear of the input shaft has a helical-cut gear which mates to a similar gear on the intermediate shaft. The intermediate shaft transmits engine power from the input shaft to the output shaft. With the exception of the one helical-cut gear on the input and intermediate shaft, all the other gears are straight-cut.

Some of the components of the transmission housing require heat to loosen and remove them. A heat gun capable of generating 120° C (248° F) is required. A heat gun is also required for disassembly of some of the front and rear suspension components.

Table 1 and **Table 2** are located at the end of the chapter.

TRANSMISSION CASE

Removal

CAUTION

*To prevent damaging the clutch release pushrod and transmission input shaft, install guide pins (BMW part No. 23-1-820) or modified long bolts (**Figure 1**) after two of the transmission case mounting holes have been removed. The guide pins, or bolts, ensure that the weight of the transmission will not bend the pushrod.*

NOTE

BMW recommends removal of the transmission case from the engine prior to removing the engine if both components are going to be serviced.

1. Remove all fairing assemblies and both seats as described in Chapter Fifteen.
2. Disconnect the negative battery cable as described in Chapter Three.
3. Remove the fuel tank as described in Chapter Nine.
4. Remove the throttle body assemblies from each side as described in Chapter Nine.
5. Remove the air filter housing as described in Chapter Nine.
6. Remove the exhaust system as described in Chapter Nine.
7. Remove the Motronic unit as described in Chapter Ten.
8. Remove both front footrests as described in Chapter Fifteen.
9. Remove the battery holder (**Figure 2**) as described in Chapter Ten.
10. Remove the starter as described in Chapter Ten.
11. Disconnect the gearshift linkage from the transmission as described in this chapter.
12. If the transmission is going to be disassembled, drain the transmission oil as described in Chapter Three.
13. Remove the rear wheel as described in Chapter Eleven.
14. Remove the final drive unit and the swing arm as described in Chapter Thirteen.
15. Disconnect the clutch cable from the clutch release lever (A, **Figure 3**) and remove the cable from the retaining boss (B) on the transmission housing.
16. Disconnect the electrical connector from the transmission gear position switch and the neutral switch.
17. Check to make sure all electrical wiring and connectors are disconnected and moved away from the area where the transmission case will be exiting.
18. Place wood blocks or a small floor jack under the transmission housing.
19. Remove the transmission case mounting bolts in the following order:
   a. Loosen the two lower bolts.
   b. Remove the right bolt (A, **Figure 4**) and install a guide pin into the threaded hole.
   c. Remove the left bolt (B, **Figure 4**) and the connecting strap (C).
   d. Loosen the left bolts. Remove the upper bolt (A, **Figure 5**) and install a guide pin into the threaded hole.
   e. Remove the lower bolt (B, **Figure 5**).

CAUTION
Make sure the transmission case is secure on the wooden blocks or jack prior to removing the final two bolts.

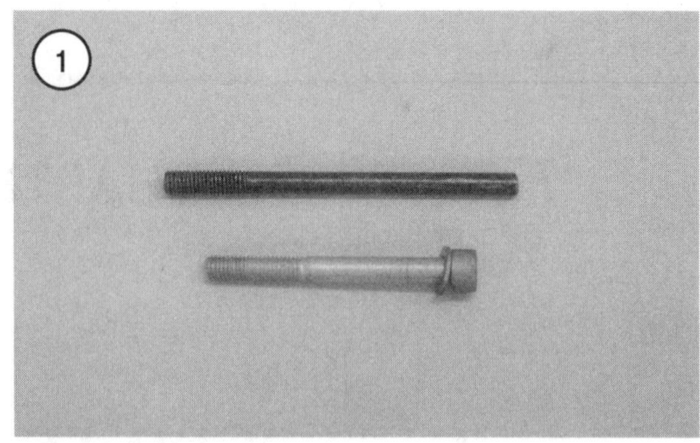

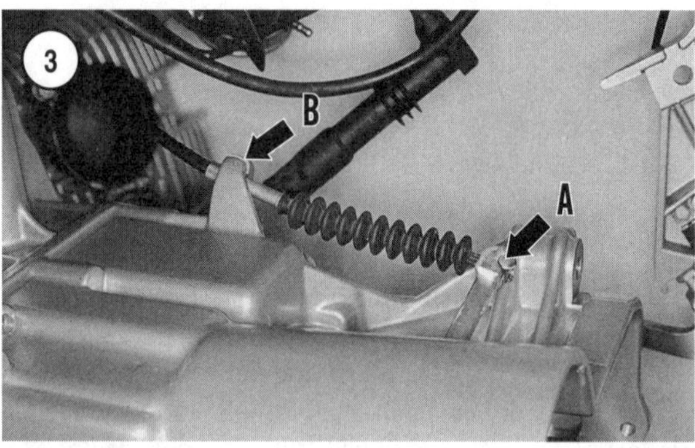

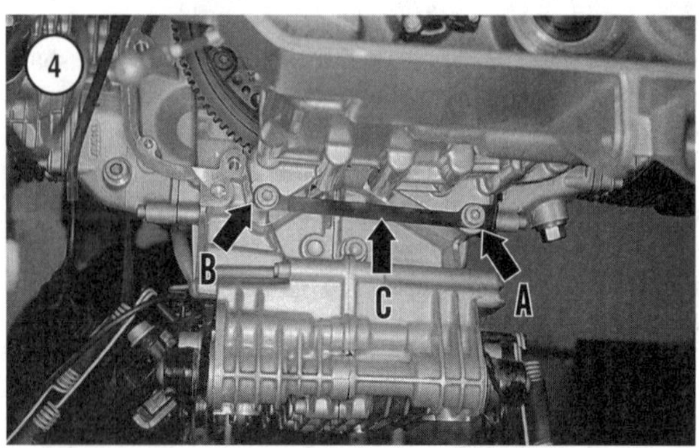

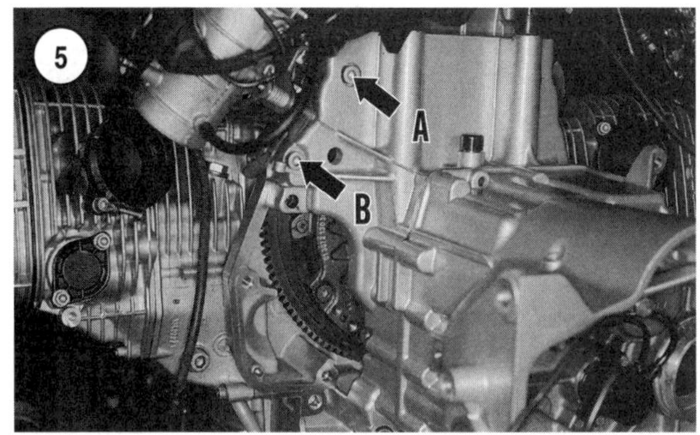

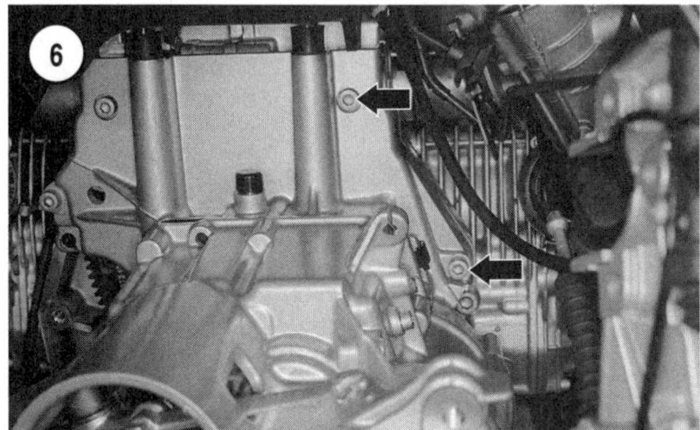

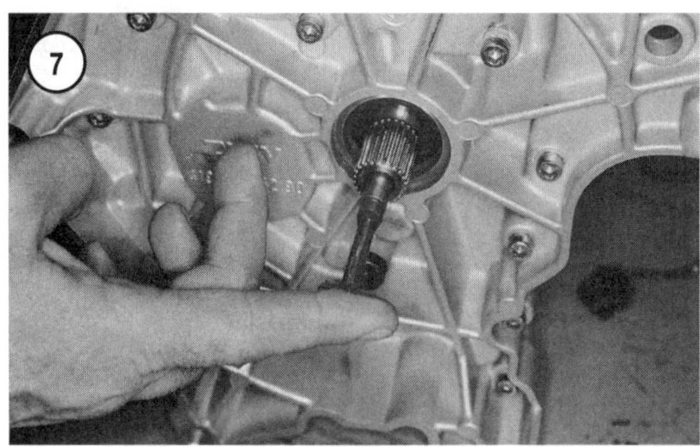

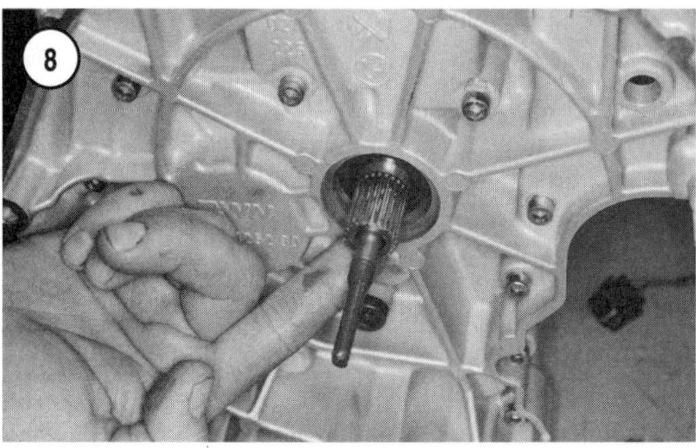

f. Remove both bolts (**Figure 6**) from the right side.

CAUTION
In the following step, to prevent damage to the transmission input shaft and clutch release push rod, pull the transmission case straight back until it is disengaged from the clutch assembly and guide pins.

20. Use a rubber mallet and tap around the perimeter of the transmission case to break it loose from the rear of the engine.

NOTE
The transmission case should separate easily from the engine. If it will not, confirm that all external components are removed. If the motorcycle has high-mileage or if it has been subjected to saltwater or road salt, the two locating pins may be corroded at the guide pin locations. Apply Liquid Wrench (or an equivalent) penetrating oil to the locating pins and let it sit for 15 minutes.

21. Pull the transmission case *straight back* until it is free of the engine, the clutch assembly and the clutch pushrod.
22. Lower the transmission case and take it to the workbench.
23. If necessary, remove the clutch assembly as described in Chapter Six.

Installation

1. If the transmission shaft assemblies were disassembled, rotate the input shaft and shift the transmission through all five gears. Make sure all shafts rotate smoothly and all gears engage.
2. Shift the transmission into fifth gear and leave it engaged to prevent the input shaft from rotating in the following steps.
3. Clean the mating surfaces of both the engine and the transmission housing of any corrosion.
4. If removed, position the clutch release pushrod with the short ball-end going in first and insert it into the transmission input shaft. Push it in until it stops. Apply a light coat of Optimoly MP3 or BMW Microlube GL261 to the release push rod end (**Figure 7**).
5. Apply a light coat of BMW Microlube GL261, or Bel Rey Total Performance Lube, to the transmission input shaft outer splines (**Figure 8**) where it rides in the clutch friction plate.

6. If removed, install the clutch assembly (A, **Figure 9**) as described in Chapter Six.
7. Apply a light coat of multipurpose grease to the guide pins (**Figure 10**) and the transmission housing receptacles to ease installation and prevent corrosion.
8. If removed, install the guide pins (B, **Figure 9**) into the mounting bolt holes. Press the guide pins into the engine receptacles until they bottom.
9. Shift the transmission into fifth gear.
10. Raise the transmission case and align it with the back surface of the engine.

CAUTION
To prevent damage to the transmission input shaft and clutch release push rod, push the transmission housing straight forward until it is properly engaged with the clutch assembly.

11. Slowly push the transmission case forward and align the input shaft outer splines with the inner splines of the clutch friction plate. Slightly rotate the output shaft at the rear of the transmission until alignment is achieved. Align the transmission housing with the guide pins on the engine.

CAUTION
When properly aligned, the transmission case should fit directly against the engine mounting surface with no gap. If not properly aligned, do not attempt to pull the transmission housing up against the engine with the mounting bolts. Separate the transmission housing and investigate the cause of the interference.

12. Push the transmission case forward until it is tight against the engine mating surface around the entire perimeter.
13. Install the transmission case mounting bolts in the following order:
   a. Install the upper three mounting bolts and tighten securely.
   b. Remove the upper left side guide pin and install the remaining bolt. Tighten it securely.

NOTE
*Make sure to install the strap (C, **Figure 4**) on the bottom two bolts.*

   c. Remove the lower right guide pin, then install the lower right bolt and lower left bolt. Tighten the bolts securely.
   d. Tighten all six bolts to 22 N•m (16 ft.-lb.).

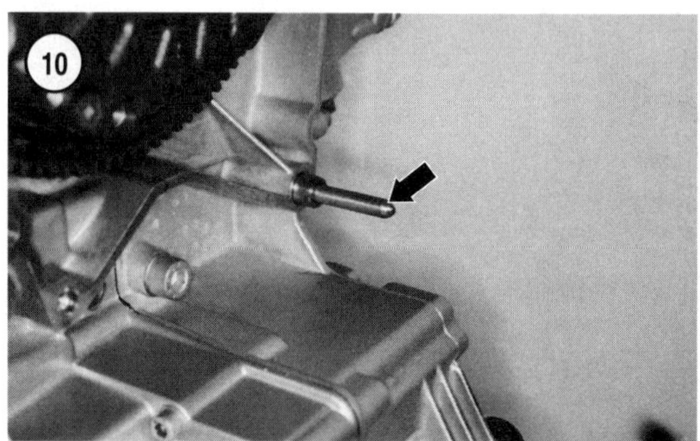

14. Connect the electrical connector onto the transmission gear position switch and the neutral switch.
15. Insert the clutch cable into the retaining boss (B, **Figure 3**) on the transmission housing. Connect the clutch cable onto the clutch release lever (A, **Figure 3**). Adjust the clutch as described in Chapter Three.
16. Connect the electrical connector onto the transmission gear position switch and the neutral switch.
17. Install the final drive unit and the swing arm as described in Chapter Thirteen.
18. Install the rear wheel as described in Chapter Eleven.

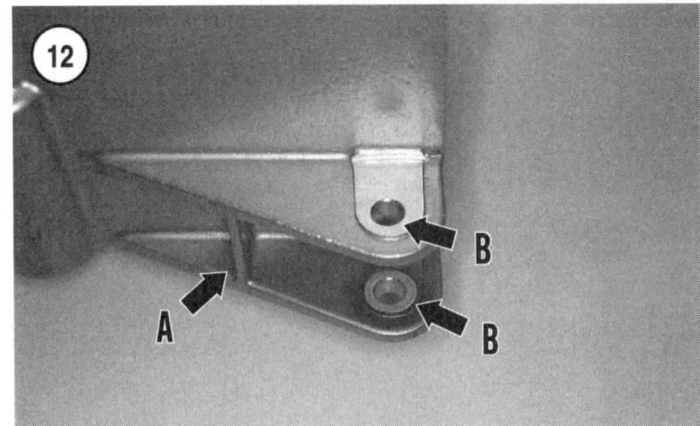

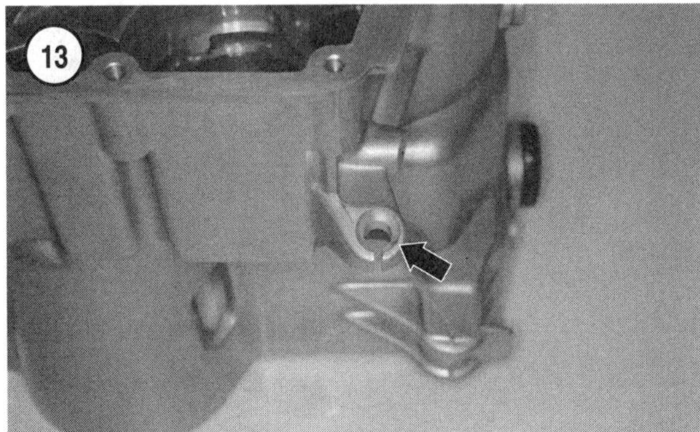

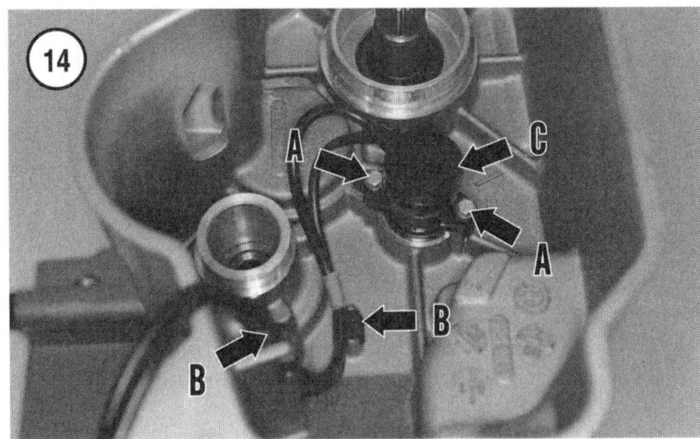

19. Connect the gearshift linkage onto the transmission as described in this chapter.

20. Install the starter as described in Chapter Ten.

21. Install the battery holder (**Figure 2**) as described in Chapter Ten.

22. Install both front footrests as described in Chapter Fifteen.

23. Install the Motronic unit as described in Chapter Ten.

24. Install the exhaust system as described in Chapter Nine.

25. Install the air filter housing as described in Chapter Nine.

26. Install the throttle body assemblies from each side as described in Chapter Nine.

27. Install the fuel tank as described in Chapter Nine.

28. Connect the negative battery cable as described in Chapter Three.

29. Install all fairing assemblies and both seats as described in Chapter Fifteen.

30. If the transmission was serviced, refill the transmission with oil as described in Chapter Three.

31. Ride the motorcycle slowly at first to make sure the clutch and the transmission are operating properly.

Inspection

7

1. Thoroughly clean the housing in solvent and dry it with compressed air.
2. Inspect the housing for any cracks or damage. Check around the ribs and the transmission sealing surface (**Figure 11**). If it is damaged, replace the cover and/or housing.
3. Inspect the final drive torque link mounting brackets (A, **Figure 12**) for any cracks or damage. Check the bolt holes (B, **Figure 12**) for elongation or damage.
4. Inspect the clutch cable mounting bracket (**Figure 13**) for any cracks or damage.

NEUTRAL SWITCH AND GEAR POSITION SWITCH

Removal/Installation

NOTE
If the motorcycle is equipped with the gear position switch, it is mounted on top of the neutral switch. Both switches are secured with the same two bolts and are removed at the same time. The switches can be replaced separately.

1. Remove the bolts (A, **Figure 14**) securing the neutral switch and the gear position switch, if so equipped.
2. Unhook the electrical cable clamps (B, **Figure 14**) from the transmission housing bosses.
3. Remove the switch(es) (C, **Figure 14**) and electrical cable(s) from the transmission housing.

NOTE
If replacing the neutral switch, also order an oil seal. It is not included with the switch.

15

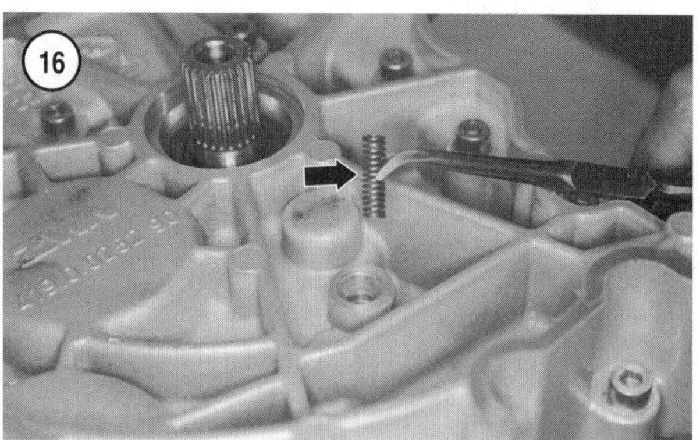

16

4. Install the switch(es) onto the transmission case and install the bolts (A, **Figure 14**). Tighten the bolts securely.

CAUTION
The electrical cable(s) must be secured properly to the transmission case bosses to keep them away from moving parts to avoid a possible short.

5. Install the electrical cable(s) and clamps (B, **Figure 14**) onto the transmission housing bosses.

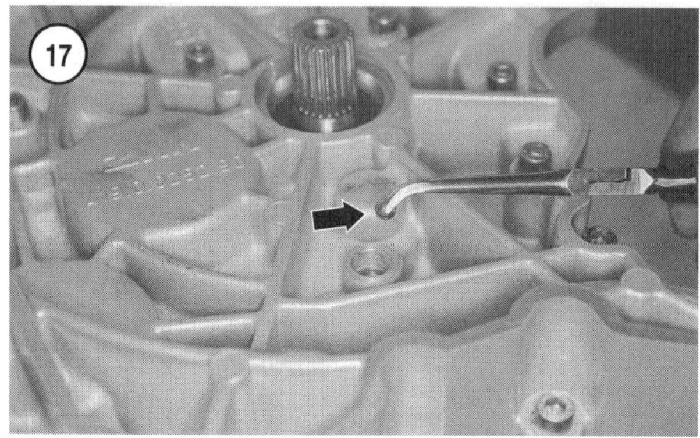

17

TRANSMISSION HOUSING COVER

Removal

1. Remove the neutral detent Allen bolt plug (**Figure 15**). Use a small magnetic tool, remove the spring (**Figure 16**) and ball (**Figure 17**) from the receptacle in the cover.
2. Following a crisscross pattern, loosen, then remove the silver colored inner bolts and lockwashers securing the housing cover (**Figure 18**).
3. Following a staggered pattern, loosen, then remove the four bronze colored outer bolts and lockwashers securing the housing cover (**Figure 19**).
4. Make sure all bolts and washers are removed prior to proceeding to the next steps.

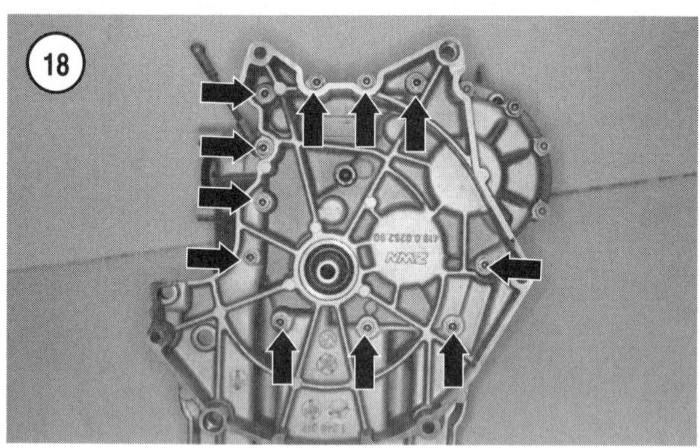

18

NOTE
BMW recommends heating the cover to 120° C (248° F) to release the cover from the transmission bearings. The motorcycle being working on may not require this heating procedure. First try to remove the cover without the use of heat. If not successful, perform Step 5.

CAUTION
Do not heat the cover with any type of propane or acetylene torch flame as they generate a heat range much greater than required

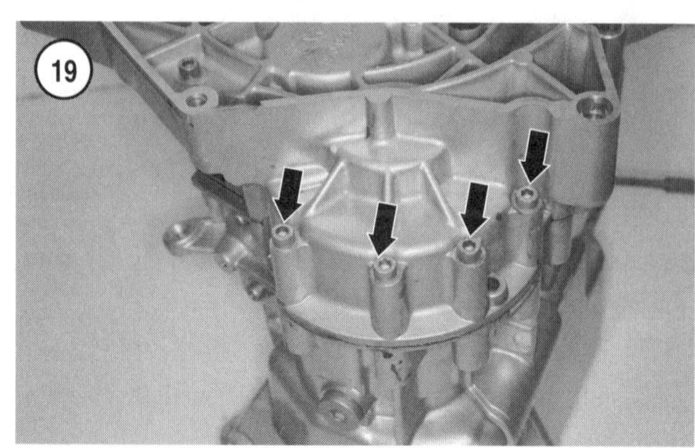

19

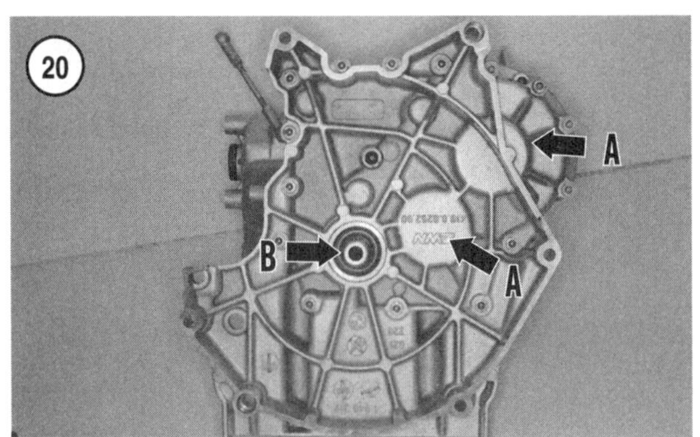

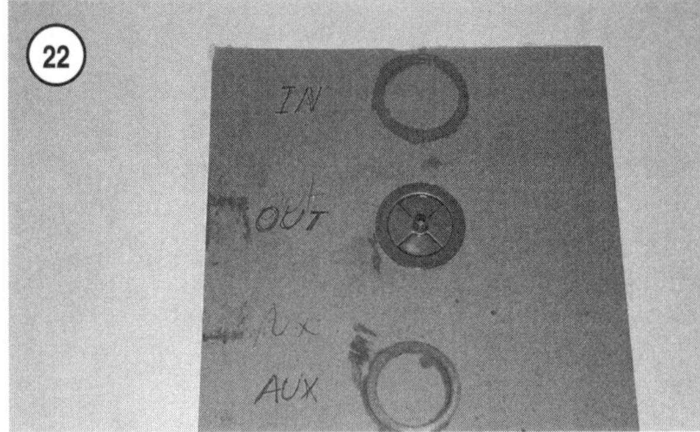

and may also discolor the transmission cover's finish.

7

5. Heat the cover with a heat gun in the area of the transmission shaft bearings (A, **Figure 20**) to 120° C (248° F).

6. Use a rubber or plastic mallet and carefully tap around the perimeter of the housing cover to loosen it from the housing.

7. Tap on the end of the input shaft (B, **Figure 20**) with a rubber or plastic mallet. If necessary, *carefully* pry the cover loose and remove the cover from the housing.

8. Do not lose the two end play shims (A, **Figure 21**) and the shim/oil guide (B) that will either stay on the end of the transmission shafts or in the cover bearing bores. They must be reinstalled on the same transmission shafts during assembly.

9. Remove the shims and the shim/oil guide. Place them on a piece of cardboard and label them as to which shaft they belong (**Figure 22**). Tape the shims and oil guide in place to avoid inter-mixing them.

10. Thoroughly clean and inspect the cover as described in this chapter.

11. Clean all old gasket sealer from the mating surface of the cover and the transmission housing with solvent and dry with compressed air.

12. After the surfaces are clean, clean them again with contact cleaner and a lint free cloth to remove any traces of solvent.

Installation

1. Assemble the shims and oil guides as follows:
   a. Position the output shaft oil guide with the long shoulder facing upward (**Figure 23**). This long shoulder fits into the end of the output shaft.
   b. Install the shim (A, **Figure 24**) and the oil guide (B) for the output shaft.

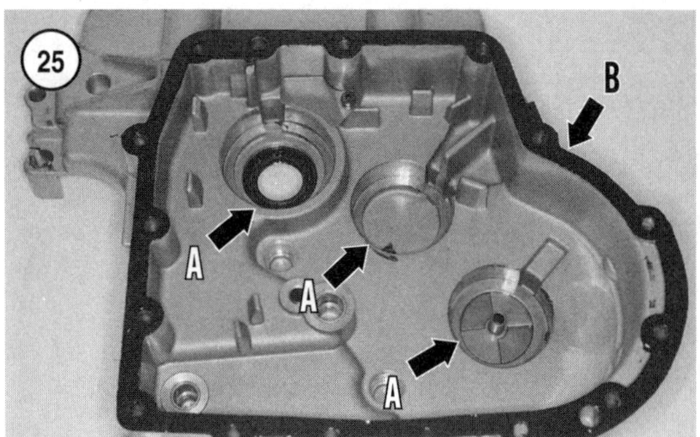

2. Apply a light coat of grease to the end play shims and place them in their proper locations in the cover (A, **Figure 25**). They must be reinstalled onto the same transmission shafts.

3. Apply a light, even coat of Loctite 573, or an equivalent, gasket sealer to the mating surface of the transmission housing cover (B, **Figurc 25**).

4. Wrap the output shaft splines (C, **Figure 21**) with two layers of clear smooth adhesive tape. Do not use masking tape or duct tape as it may scratch the cover seal during installation.

5. If removed, install the locating dowels. Refer to **Figure 26** and **Figure 27**.

6. Move the detent lever arm into position on the shift drum (**Figure 28**) and position the spring end (**Figure 29**) toward the outer surface of the housing and hold it in this position.

7. Apply a light coat of transmission gear oil or engine oil to the outer surfaces of the transmission shaft ball bearings and to the gearshift drum where it rides in the transmission housing cover. This will make cover installation easier.

8. Position the cover onto the transmission housing and start it down into place. If necessary, move the ends of the transmission shafts to where the bearings are aligned with their respective bores in the cover.

9. Heat the cover with a heat gun in the area of the transmission shaft outer bearings (A, **Figure 20**) to 120° C (248° F).

10. Push the cover down until the bearings start to enter the cover.

11. Move the detent lever arm spring arm into position on the inner surface of the cover and hold it in this position.

12. After the bearings are properly started, and the spring is positioned correctly, *carefully* tap the cover into place with a rubber or plastic mallet. Tap on the cover directly over the bearing locations and around the perimeter until

30

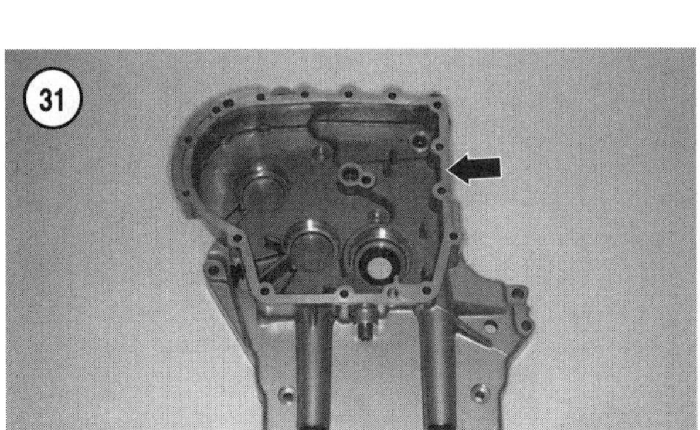
31

32

33

34

the cover seats completely against the transmission housing mating surface.

13. Install the cover bolts and lockwashers. Following a crisscross pattern, tighten the bolts to 10 N•m (88 in.-lb.).

14. Install the neutral detent ball (**Figure 17**) and spring (**Figure 16**).

15. Apply a medium strength threadlocking compound to the neutral detent Allen bolt plug threads prior to installation.

16. Install the neutral detent Allen bolt plug (**Figure 15**) and tighten to 13 N•m (115 in.-lb.).

17. Remove the tape from the transmission output shaft splines.

Inspection

1. Thoroughly clean the cover in solvent and dry it with compressed air.

2. Inspect the cover (**Figure 30**) for any cracks or damage. Check around the ribs and the transmission sealing surface (**Figure 31**). If damaged, replace the cover.

TRANSMISSION SHAFTS AND GEARSHIFT MECHANISM

Removal

1. Remove the transmission case as described in this chapter.

2. Remove the transmission case cover from the transmission housing as described in this chapter.

3. Pulling straight up, remove the large oil baffle (**Figure 32**) and the small oil baffle (**Figure 33**).

4. Withdraw both shift fork shafts (**Figure 34**).

5. Make an alignment mark on the gearshift selector shaft in relation to the split on the gearshift lever (A, **Figure 35**). This will ensure correct alignment during installation.

6. Remove the bolt and washer (B, **Figure 35**) securing the gearshift lever and remove the lever.

7. To protect the gearshift selector shaft seal, wrap two layers of clear smooth adhesive tape around the shaft splines (**Figure 36**).

8. Rotate the gearshift selector shaft arm clockwise (A, **Figure 37**), away from the shift drum.

9. Disengage the shift fork pins and rotate the gearshift forks away from the shift drum.

10. Withdraw the shift drum (B, **Figure 37**).

11. Withdraw the gearshift selector shaft (A, **Figure 37**).

NOTE
Do not lose the individual roller on each shift fork pin during removal.

12. Remove the three shift forks (**Figure 38**).

NOTE
BMW recommends heating the transmission housing to 120° C (248° F) to release the transmission shaft lower bearings from the housing. The motorcycle being working on may not require this heating procedure. Try to remove the transmission shafts without the use of heat and, if not successful, heat the cover as described in Step 13.

CAUTION
Do not apply heat to the transmission case with a propane or acetylene torch flame as they generate a heat range much greater than required and may also discolor the transmission case finish.

13. Use a heat gun and heat the base of the transmission housing in the area of the transmission shaft bearings to 120° C (248° F).

14. Withdraw the input shaft (A, **Figure 39**).

CAUTION
In the following step, both shafts must be removed as an assembly at the same time, otherwise the bevel gears (fifth gear) will be damaged.

15. Withdraw the intermediate shaft (B, **Figure 39**) and the output shaft (C) as an assembly.

16. Inspect the transmission shaft assemblies as described in this chapter.

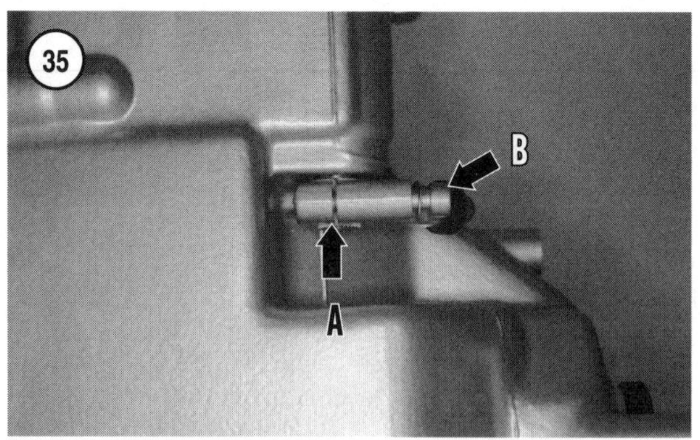

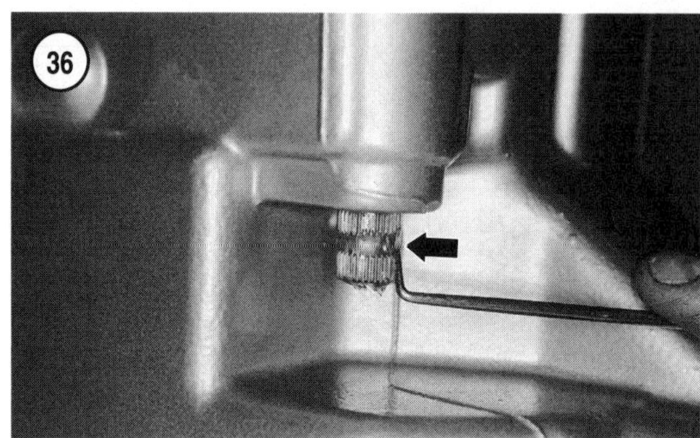

Installation

7

1. Place all three transmission shaft assemblies in a freezer for 30 minutes. This will reduce the overall size of the roller bearings and will make transmission shaft installation easier.
2. Apply SAE 90 hypoid gear oil to the bearings at each end of all three transmission shafts and to the transmission housing bearing bores (**Figure 40**).

NOTE
If heat was required to remove the transmission shafts, it may also be necessary for transmission shaft installation.

3. Heat the transmission housing in the area of the transmission shaft bearings to 120° C (248° F).

CAUTION
In the following step, do not try to install one shaft without the other shaft. The two shafts must be installed as an assembly to avoid damage to the fifth gear bevel gears.

4. Properly mesh the intermediate shaft and the output shaft together as an assembly. Install them into the transmission housing (**Figure 41**) as an assembly.
5. Make sure the bearings align properly with their respective bearing bores in the transmission housing. Carefully tap on the ends of the transmission shafts with a plastic or rubber mallet. Tap on the shafts until they seat completely in the housing receptacles.
6. Spin each transmission shaft and make sure it rotates freely. If it binds or does not spin at all, correct the problem at this time.
7. Install the input shaft (**Figure 42**) with the helical cut gear end going in first. Tilt the input shaft slightly away from the intermediate shaft already installed. It may be necessary to slightly wiggle and rotate the shaft (**Figure 43**) until it meshes properly with the intermediate shaft gear.

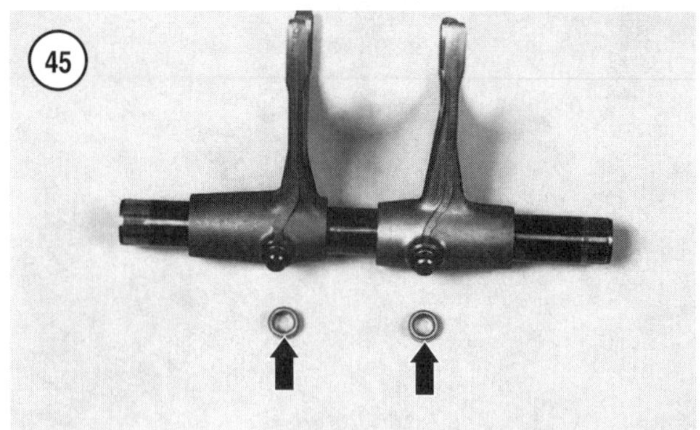

Carefully tap on the end of the shaft assembly with a plastic or rubber mallet. Tap on the shaft until it seats completely in the housing receptacle.

8. After all three transmission shafts are installed, look straight across the two gears and the bearing. All three components should align across the top surface as shown in **Figure 44**. If not aligned, one or more of the shafts did not seat properly in the transmission housing bearing receptacle. Tap on the end of the shaft(s) until proper alignment is achieved.

9. If either transmission shaft was disassembled (even for bearing replacement), have the *Transmission Shaft Preload and End Play Measurement and Adjustment* performed at a BMW dealership at this time, as described in this chapter. This procedure is necessary to maintain end play if any component has been removed.

10. Apply a light coat of multipurpose grease to each roller (**Figure 45**) and install them onto each gearshift fork. The grease will help to hold the rollers in place during installation.

11. Position the third/fourth gearshift fork with the short guide end facing down. Install the third/fourth gearshift fork into the third/fourth gear groove (**Figure 46**).

12. Position the fifth gear shift fork with the long guide end facing down and install the shift fork into the fifth gear (A, **Figure 47**).

13. Position the first/second gearshift fork with the short guide end facing down and install the shift fork into the first/second gear (B, **Figure 47**).

14. Move the shift forks toward each side to make room for the shift drum.

15. Make sure the rollers (**Figure 48**) are still in place on all shift fork cam pin followers.

16. To protect the gearshift selector shaft seal, wrap two layers of clear smooth adhesive tape around the shaft splines (**Figure 49**). Apply a light coat of grease to the outer surface of the tape.

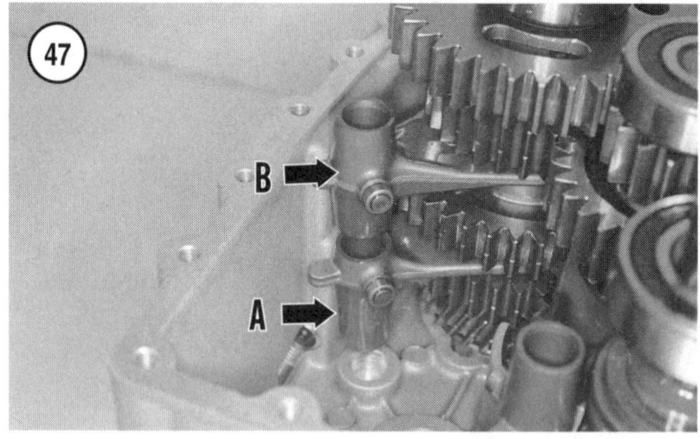

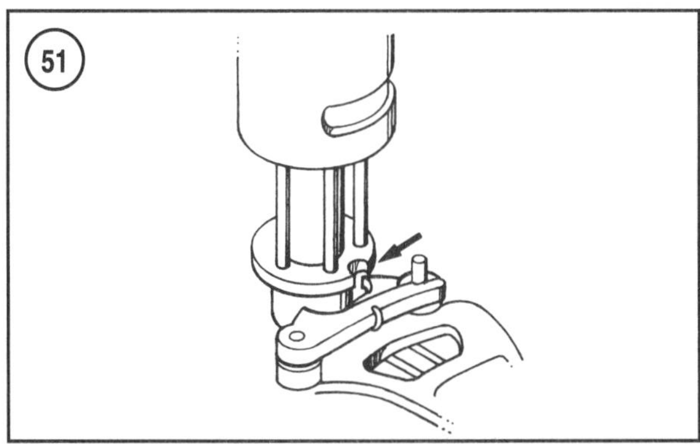

NOTE
Make sure the gearshift selector shaft seats completely in the housing, especially if the seal has been replaced. If the shaft is not seated correctly it will bind once the transmission housing cover is installed and the transmission can not be shifted.

17. Carefully install the gearshift selector shaft. Slowly push the shaft through the seal and align the return spring with the raised post (**Figure 50**). Push the gearshift selector shaft down until it stops. Confirm that the return spring still is positioned correctly on the raised post. This alignment is necessary for proper gearshift operation.

18. Remove the tape from the gearshift selector shaft splines (**Figure 36**).

19. Refer to the alignment marks made during removal and install the gearshift lever onto the gearshift selector shaft (A, **Figure 35**).

20. Install the bolt and washer (B, **Figure 35**) and tighten securely.

21. Apply transmission gear oil onto the shift drum.

22. Position the shift drum so the cutout notch aligns with the shift selector pawl (**Figure 51**) and install the shift drum (**Figure 52**). Push the shift drum down until it bottoms in the transmission case receptacle.

23. Move the shift forks into position and insert the cam pin followers into the grooves in the shift drum. It may be necessary to slightly pull up on a gear and shift fork to achieve proper alignment.

24. Apply transmission gear oil onto the shift fork shaft bores in each shift fork and to each shift fork shaft.

25. Move the gearshift selector arm over past the shift drum (A, **Figure 53**).

26. Insert the first/second gear and the fifth gear shift fork shaft (B, **Figure 53**) through the shift forks and into the bore in the base of the transmission housing.

27. Insert the third/fourth shift fork shaft through the shift fork and into the receptacle in the base of the transmission housing.
28. Ensure that both shift fork shafts seat correctly in the transmission case receptacles.
29. Move the gearshift selector arm over onto the shift drum selector cam (A, **Figure 54**). Push on the spring (B, **Figure 54**) to make sure they engage properly.

CAUTION
Correctly position the baffles in the locating bosses in the base of the transmission housing. If not located correctly, the baffles will shift and contact the moving parts in the housing.

30. Install the small oil baffle (**Figure 33**) and the large oil baffle (**Figure 32**) into the housing. Push the baffles down until seated correctly (**Figure 55**).
31. If removed, install both locating dowels (**Figure 56**) into the housing. Push them down until they bottom.
32. Temporarily install the housing cover as described in this chapter. Install several bolts to secure the cover in place.
33. Lay the transmission case on the workbench in its normal operating position.

NOTE
The following step requires the aid of an assistant.

34. Have an assistant spin the transmission input shaft while shifting through all five gears using the shift lever. Make sure the transmission can be shifted into all five gears at this time.
35. If the transmission shifts through all gears correctly, remove the housing cover, then install it as described in this chapter.

CAUTION
Step 36 must be performed to avoid bare metal parts and bearings from rusting.

36. If the transmission gear assemblies were placed into a freezer prior to installation there will be moisture on the gears and bearings after they have returned to room temperature. Fill the transmission housing with the recommended transmission oil. Repeatedly turn the transmission over from side-to-side and end-to-end to coat the gear assemblies with fresh oil to rinse away the trapped moisture. Drain this oil and dispose of it correctly.
37. Install the transmission case as described in this chapter.

38. Refill the transmission with the recommended type of oil. Ride the motorcycle several miles until the transmission is at normal operating temperature. Once again, drain the transmission oil and refill as described in Chapter Three.

Transmission Shaft Preload and End Play Measurement and Adjustment

If the transmission shafts were serviced or removed from the transmission housing, the bearing preload and shaft endplay must inspected as follows:

1. Input shaft tapered roller bearing preload (1994-1996).
2. Input shaft ball bearing endplay (1997-on).
3. Output and intermediate shaft ball bearing endplay (1994-on).

The preload is the amount of pressure applied to the tapered roller bearings after assembling the transmission housing and cover. This type of bearing requires some preload or pressure to maintain a correct roller-to-race relationship. The bearings will fail prematurely, if the preload is not correct.

The endplay is the play or free space between the end of the transmission shaft and the transmission housing cover. The ball bearings do not require a preload as do roller bearings, which must have a certain amount of endplay.

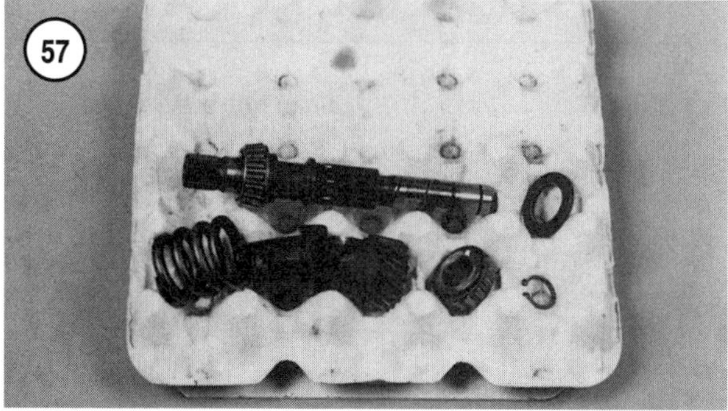

The bearings will fail prematurely if the endplay is not correct.

BMW has made several internal changes to this transmission over the years.

The input shaft tapered roller bearing was replaced with a sealed ball bearing.

The unsealed ball bearings on the input and output shafts were replaced with sealed bearings, and are referred to as a clean bearing. These bearings are sealed and operate within their own lubrication verses lubrication by the transmission lubricant.

Due to the changes, some of which were used on an interim basis, have a BMW dealership perform transmission shaft preload and endplay measurement and adjustment.

CAUTION

If the preload and endplay measurement, and adjustment is not performed correctly, the transmission shaft assemblies may be damaged.

TRANSMISSION SHAFTS

Throughout the following procedure, reference is made to the front and rear of the shaft and to front and rear bearings. The *rear* of the shaft is the end that is installed in the transmission housing. The *front* of the shaft is the end facing toward the housing cover.

Preliminary Inspection

After the transmission shafts are removed from the transmission housing, clean and inspect the shafts prior to disassembling them. Place the assembled shaft into a large can or plastic bucket and thoroughly clean with a petroleum-based solvent such as kerosene and a stiff brush. Dry with compressed air or let it sit on rags to drip dry. Repeat for all shaft assemblies.

1. Visually inspect the components of the assemblies for excessive wear. Check the gear teeth for chips, burrs or pitting, Clean up damage with an oilstone. Replace any components with damage that cannot be cleaned up. 7

NOTE

Replace defective gears and their mating gear on the other shaft as well, even though it may not show as much wear or damage.

2. Carefully check the engagement dogs. If any are chipped, worn, rounded or missing, the affected gear must be replaced.
3. Rotate the transmission bearings by hand. Check for roughness, noise and radial play. Replace any bearing that is suspect.
4. If the transmission shafts are satisfactory and are not going to be disassembled, apply clean gear oil to all components and reinstall them in the transmission housing as described in this chapter.

NOTE

If disassembling a used, high mileage transmission for the first time, pay particular attention to any additional shims not shown in the illustrations or photographs. To compensate for wear, additional shims may have been installed during the previous repair. If the transmission is being reassembled with the old parts, install these shims in their original locations since the shims have developed a wear pattern. If new parts are being used, discard the additional shims.

Service Notes

1. Parts with two different sides, such as gears, snap rings and shift forks, can be incorrectly installed. To maintain the correct alignment and position of the parts during disassembly, store each part in order and in a divided container (**Figure 57**).

2. The snap rings are a tight fit on the transmission shafts and will bend and twist during removal. Install *new* snap rings during transmission assembly.
3. To avoid bending and twisting the new snap rings during installation, use the following installation technique:
   a. Open the new snap ring with a pair of snap ring pliers while holding the back of the snap ring with a pair of pliers (**Figure 58**).
   b. Then slide the snap ring down the shaft and seat it into its correct transmission groove. Check the snap ring to make sure it seats in its groove completely.
4. When installing snap rings, align the snap ring opening with the spline groove and a spline as shown in **Figure 59**.
5. Snap rings and flat washers have one sharp edge and one rounded edge (**Figure 60**). Install the snap rings with the sharp edge facing away from the gear producing the thrust.

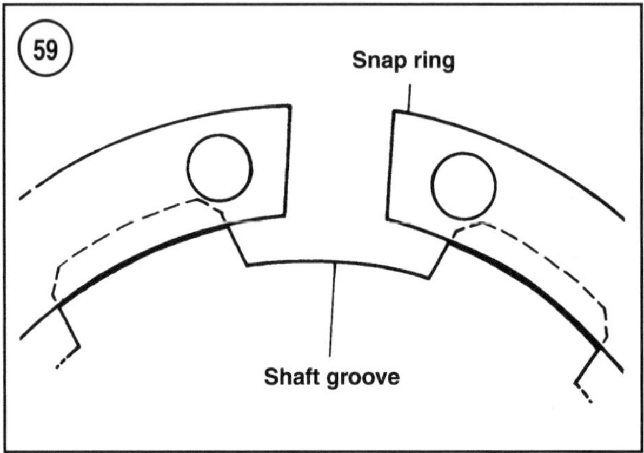

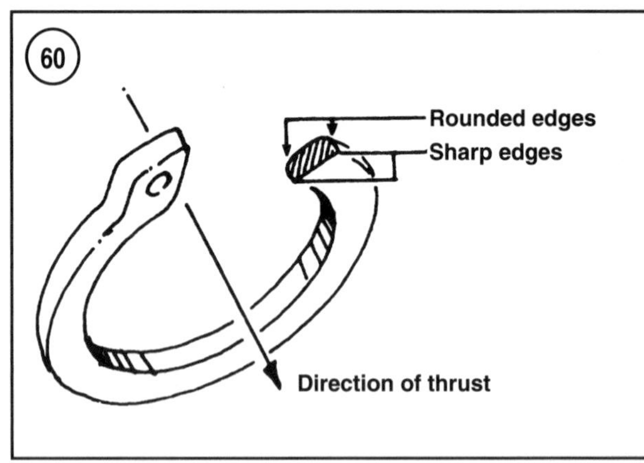

Input Shaft

Disassembly

Refer to **Figure 61**.

NOTE
*A helpful tool for transmission disassembly is the large egg flat (the type that restaurants get their eggs in) as shown in **Figure 57**. When removing a part from the shaft, set it in one of the depressions in the same position from which it was removed. This is an easy way to remember the correct relationship of all the parts.*

NOTE
This procedure is shown on a 1993-1996 model with tapered roller bearings. Where differences occur with 1997-on models they are identified.

1. Remove the input shaft as described in this chapter.
2. Attach a bearing puller to the input shaft as shown in **Figure 62**. Place the puller fingers on the edge of the shock damper front cam (**Figure 63**).
3. Tighten the bearing puller and compress the spring sufficiently to relieve the spring pressure from the shock damper rear cam.
4. Remove the snap ring (**Figure 64**) and washer from the rear of the shaft.

5A. On 1993-1996 models, perform the following:
   a. Install the insert under the rear bearing (**Figure 65**).
   b. Install the input shaft and bearing puller assembly in the hydraulic press (**Figure 66**).
   c. Place a suitable size driver (**Figure 67**) on the rear of the shaft. The driver must be small enough to pass through the inner race of the roller bearing being pressed off.
   d. Hold onto the input shaft and bearing puller assembly, slowly press the roller bearing off of the shaft.

5B. On 1997-on models, perform the following:
   a. Install the insert under the shock damper rear cam gear surface (A, **Figure 68**) below the ball bearing.

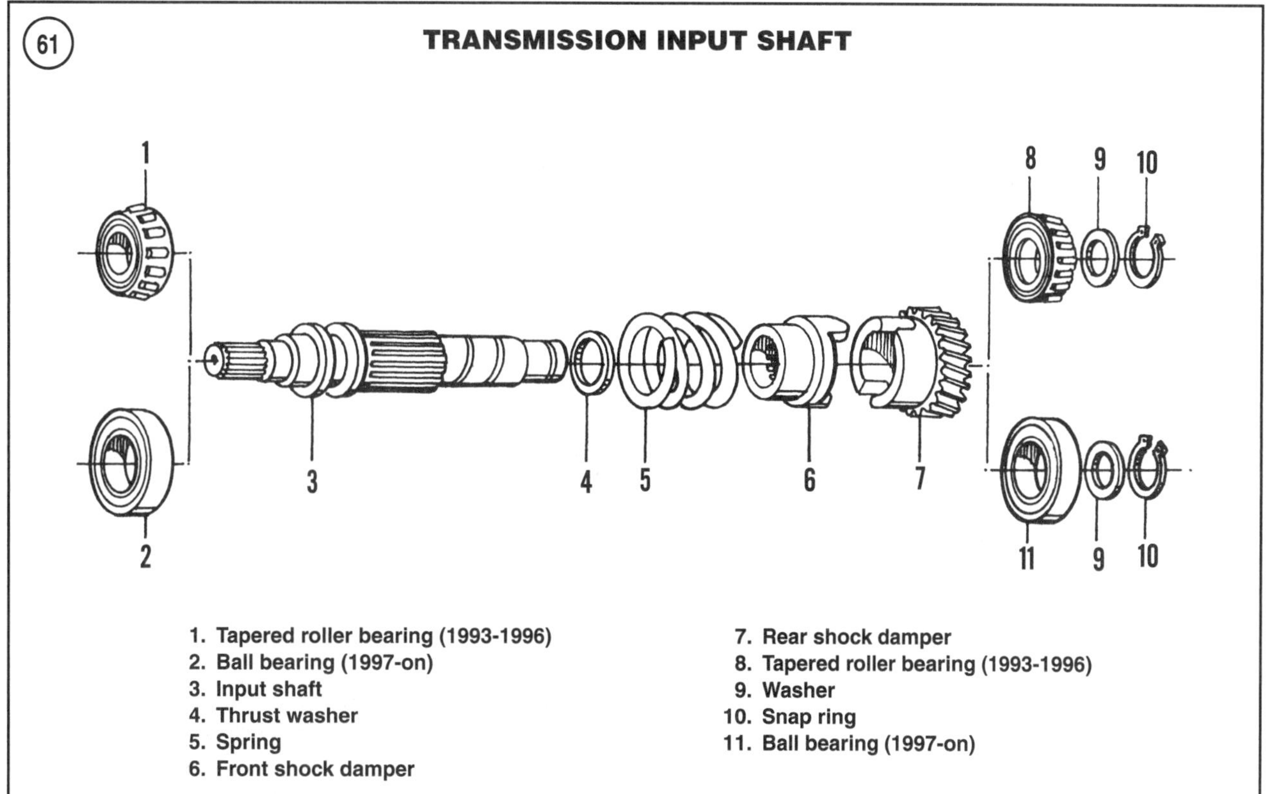
61
TRANSMISSION INPUT SHAFT
1
2
3
4
5
6
7
8
9
10
11
9
10
1. Tapered roller bearing (1993-1996)
2. Ball bearing (1997-on)
3. Input shaft
4. Thrust washer
5. Spring
6. Front shock damper
7. Rear shock damper
8. Tapered roller bearing (1993-1996)
9. Washer
10. Snap ring
11. Ball bearing (1997-on)

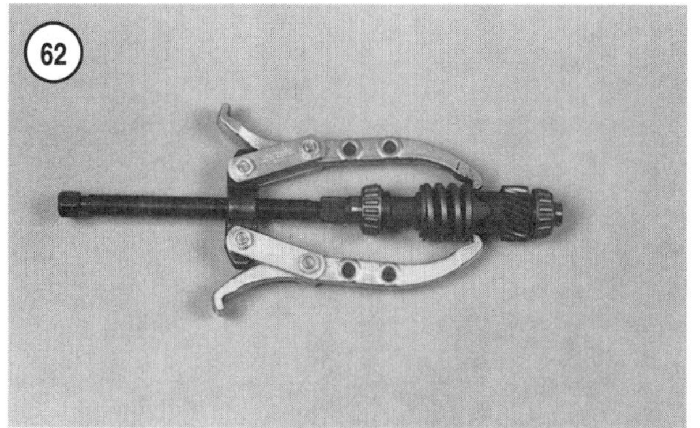
62

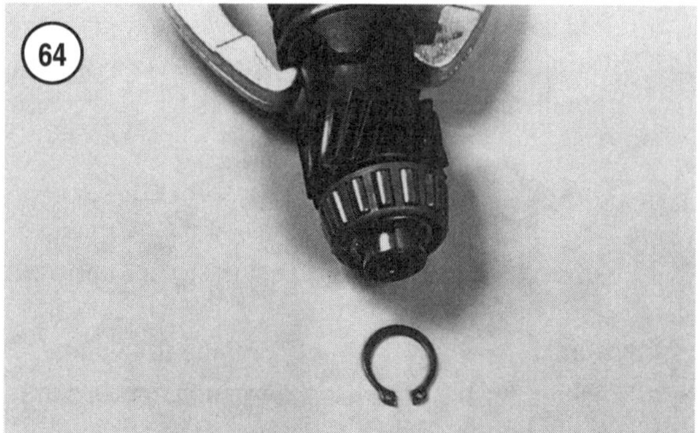
64

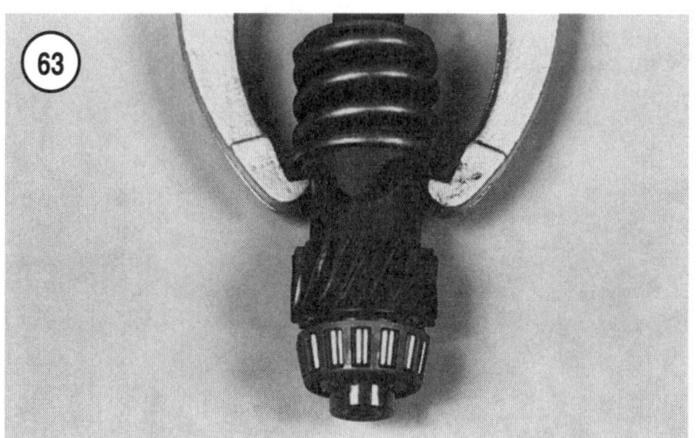
63

65

7

b. Install the input shaft and bearing puller assembly in the hydraulic press.
c. Place a suitable size driver on the rear of the shaft. The driver must be small enough to pass through the inner race of the ball bearing being pressed off.
d. Hold onto the input shaft and bearing puller assembly. Slowly press the ball bearing and rear shock damper off of the shaft.

6. Relax the hydraulic pressure and remove the shaft and bearing puller assembly from the hydraulic press.

7. Gradually loosen the bearing puller and remove it from the shaft assembly.

8A. On 1993-1996 models, slide off the rear shock damper, the front shock damper, the spring and the thrust washer.

8B. On 1997-on models, slide off the front shock damper, the spring and the thrust washer.

9. If the front bearing requires removal, perform the following:

a. Install the insert under the front bearing (**Figure 69**).
b. Install the input shaft assembly in the hydraulic press.
c. Place a suitable size driver on the front of the shaft. The driver must be small enough to pass through the inner race of the roller bearing being pressed off.
d. Hold onto the input shaft assembly, slowly press the bearing off of the shaft. Remove the shaft assembly from the hydraulic press.

Assembly

1. Apply clean engine oil to all sliding surfaces prior to installing any parts.

2. To install the front bearing, perform the following:

a. Position the bearing with the manufacturer's marks facing out and install it onto the front of the input shaft.
b. Install the input shaft assembly into the hydraulic press and set the rear of the shaft on the press plates. Have an assistant hold the shaft in place.

CAUTION

*Do **not** press the bearing into place by exerting pressure on the bearing outer race as the bearing will be damaged.*

c. Place a suitable size driver on the inner race of the front bearing. The driver must fit the inner race only and must also have a large enough inner diameter to clear the splines on the input shaft. The shaft splines

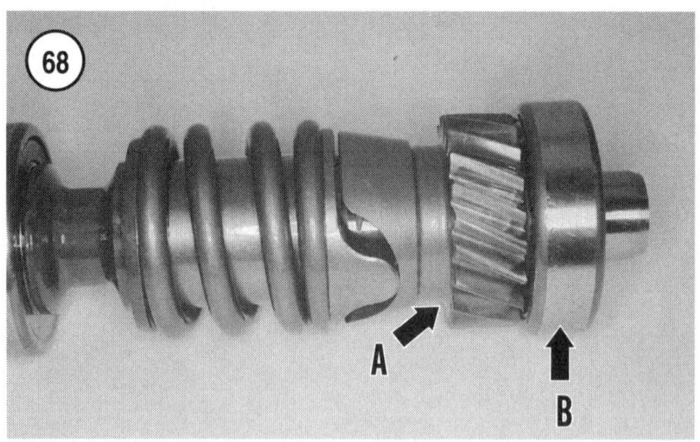

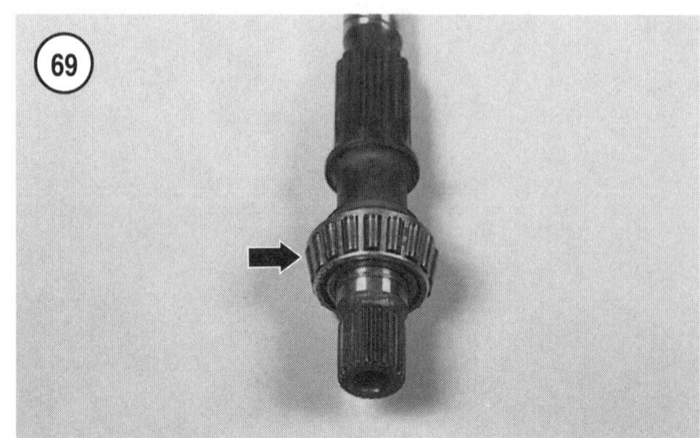

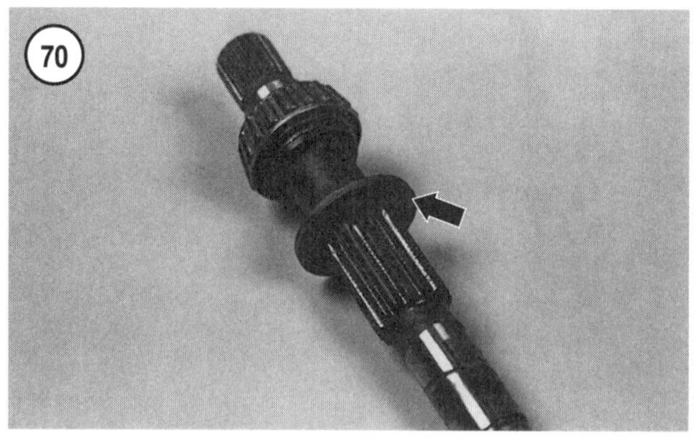

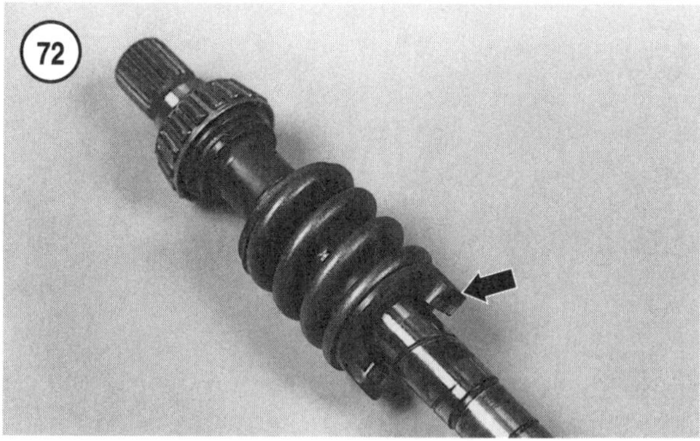

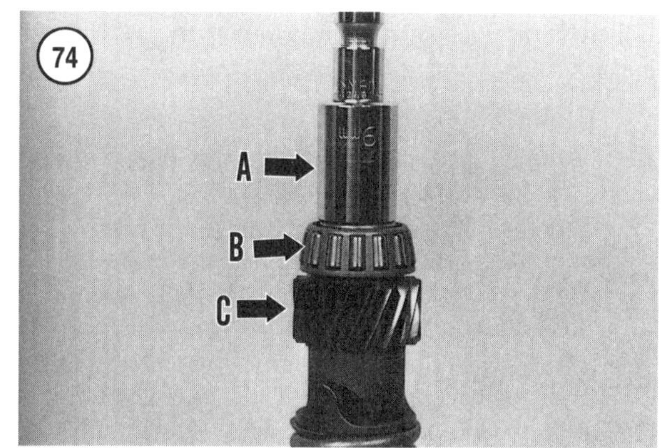

will be damaged if the inner surface of the driver touches the shaft splines.

d. Slowly press the front bearing onto the shaft. Press it on until it bottoms.

e. Remove the driver and the input shaft from the hydraulic press.

f. Rotate the bearing by hand to make sure it rotates freely and was not damaged during installation.

3. Slide the thrust washer (**Figure 70**) and spring (**Figure 71**) onto the input shaft.

4. Align the splines in both parts and slide the front shock damper (**Figure 72**) onto the input shaft.

5. Install the rear shock damper and rear bearing onto the rear of the shaft.

6. Position the rear bearing with the manufacturer's marks facing out and install it onto the input shaft assembly.

7. Install the input shaft assembly into the hydraulic press with the front of the shaft resting on the press plates (**Figure 73**). Have an assistant hold the shaft in place.

CAUTION
*Do **not** press the bearing into place by putting pressure on the bearing outer race as the bearing will be damaged.*

8. Place a suitable size driver (A, **Figure 74**) on the inner race of the rear bearing. The driver must fit onto the inner race only.

9. Slowly press the rear bearing (B, **Figure 74**) and the rear shock damper (C) onto the shaft. Press it on until it bottoms.

10. Remove the driver from the input shaft.

11. Confirm that the snap ring groove in the shaft is visible above the rear bearing. There must be additional space above the rear bearing for the washer that is located below the snap ring. If necessary, press the bearing on farther un-

til there is sufficient space to accept both the washer and the snap ring.

CAUTION
Replace the snap ring every time the transmission is disassembled to ensure proper bearing alignment. Install the snap ring onto the shaft with the rounded side going on first. Do not expand a snap ring more than necessary to slide it over the shaft.

12. Rotate the bearing by hand. Refer to **Figure 69** for 1993-1996 models or B, **Figure 68** for 1997-on models. Check for roughness, noise and radial play. Replace any bearing that is suspect.

13. Install the washer and the *new* snap ring. Make sure the snap ring seats properly in the groove in the input shaft. Refer to **Figure 75** for 1993-1996 models or **Figure 76** for 1997-on models.

14. After input shaft assembly, refer to the following photographs for correct component placement. Refer to **Figure 77** for 1993-1996 models or **Figure 78** for 1997-on models.

15. Install the input shaft as described in this chapter.

Inspection

1. Inspect the ramps of both the front and rear shock dampers. Check for excessive wear, burrs, pitting or chipped areas. Replace if necessary.

2. Inspect the inner splines of the front shock damper for wear or damage. Replace if necessary.

3. Inspect the splines for the front shock damper (A, **Figure 79**) and the clutch friction disc (B) for wear or damage. If worn or damaged, replace the shaft.

4. Make sure that the shock dampers slide smoothly on the input shaft splines and sliding surfaces.

5. Inspect the spring. If broken or weak, replace the spring.

6A. On 1993-1996 models, rotate the input shaft roller bearings (**Figure 80**) by hand. Check for roughness, noise and radial play.

6B. On 1997-on models, rotate the input shaft bearings (A, **Figure 81**) outer race by hand. Check for roughness, noise and radial play.

7. Inspect the splines (B, **Figure 81**) for wear or damage. Slight damage may be repaired with a file, but if the damage is severe, replace the shaft. If the splines are severely damaged, inspect the inner splines of the clutch friction plate for damage.

75

76

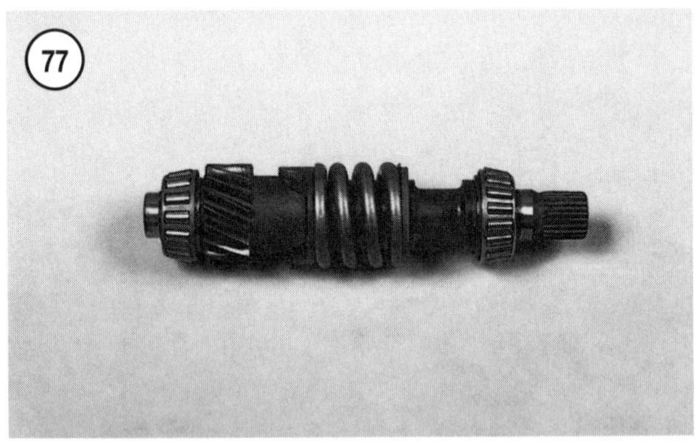
77

78

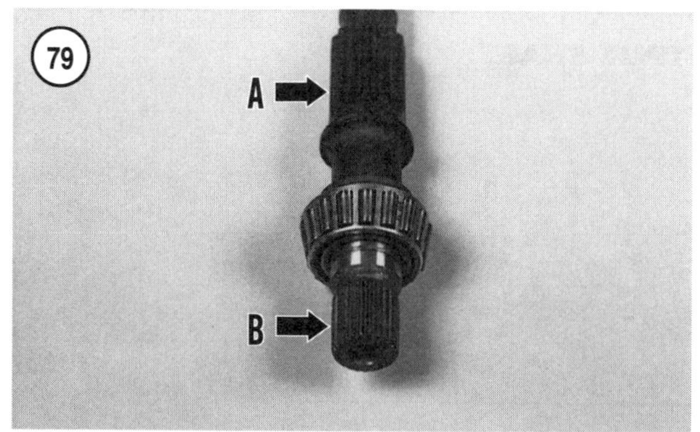

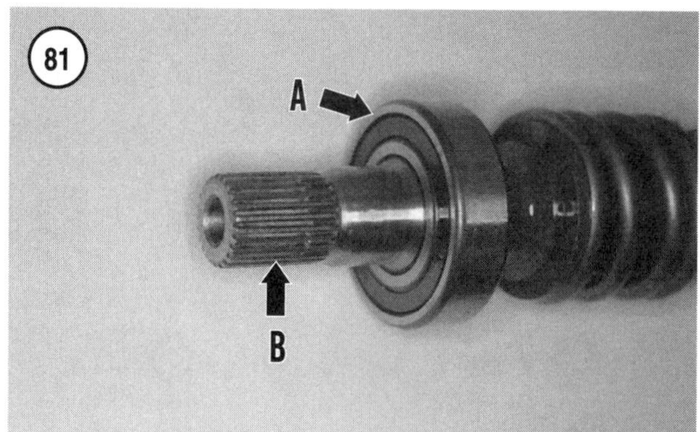

Intermediate Shaft
Inspection and Bearing Replacement

The intermediate shaft has no removable parts except for the ball bearings. If any portion of the shaft is defective, with the exception of the ball bearings, replace the entire shaft assembly.

NOTE
In the following procedure, the ball bearing at each end of the shaft can be removed either with a gear puller or with a hydraulic press and a bearing plate.

1. Remove the intermediate shaft as described in this chapter.
2. Inspect the ball bearing on each end of the shaft (**Figure 82**). Rotate the bearings by hand. Check for roughness, noise and radial play.
3. If damaged, remove the ball bearing(s) (**Figure 83**) from the end(s) of the intermediate shaft. Refer to Chapter One for typical bearing replacement.

Output Shaft

Disassembly

Refer to **Figure 84**.

NOTE
*As each part is removed from the shaft, lay it in order on a workbench (**Figure 85**). Keep the parts in this order even when cleaning. Wash one part at a time and return it to the correct location.*

1. Remove the output shaft as described in this chapter.
2. Prior to disassembly of the output shaft, measure the overall length of the shaft assembly as shown in **Figure 86**. The same exact length must be maintained during as-

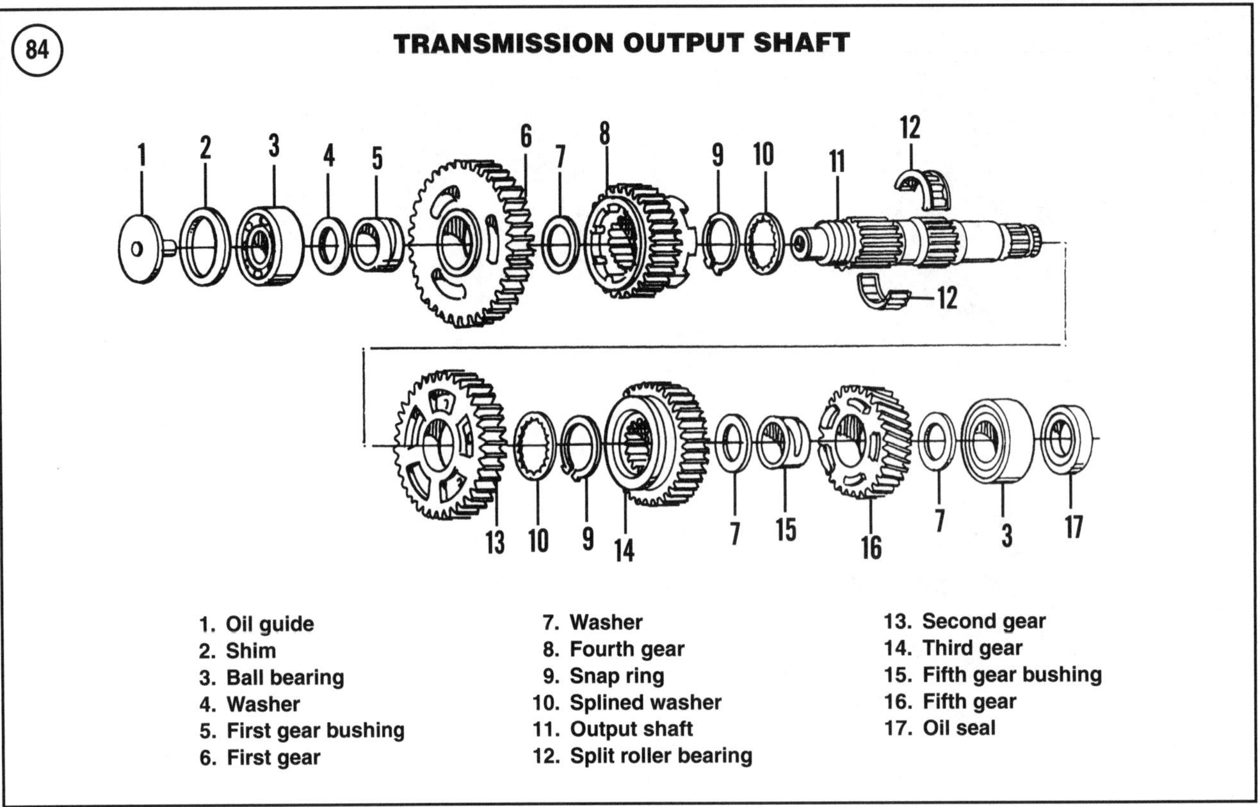

sembly for the shaft to properly fit into the transmission housing and cover.

3. To remove the rear bearing (next to the fifth gear), perform the following:
   a. Install the insert (**Figure 87**) under the bearing, next to the fifth gear.
   b. Place the shaft assembly in the hydraulic press.
   c. Hold onto the output shaft assembly and slowly press the bearing off of the shaft.
   d. Remove the shaft assembly from the hydraulic press.
4. To remove the front bearing (next to the first gear), turn the shaft assembly and perform the following:
   a. Place the shaft assembly in the hydraulic press.
   b. Position the press plates under the first gear (**Figure 88**).
   c. Place a suitable size driver, or round stock (**Figure 89**), on the front end of the shaft. The driver, or round stock, must be small enough to pass through the roller bearing inner race being pressed off.
   d. Hold onto the output shaft assembly and slowly press the bearing off of the shaft.
   e. Remove the shaft assembly from the hydraulic press.
   f. Remove the front bearing and slide off the washer and the first gear.

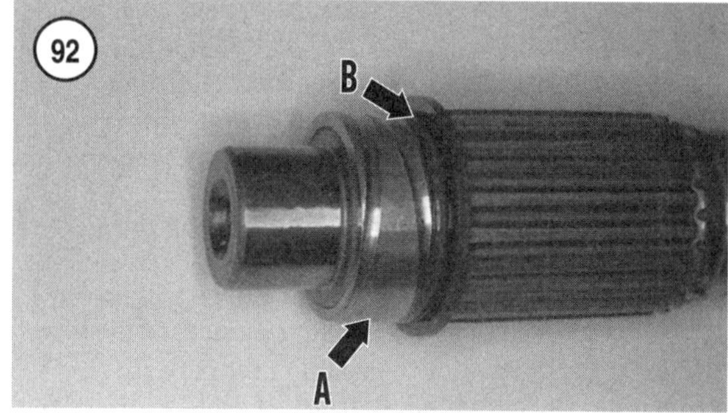

5A. From the lower end of the shaft, remove the fifth gear bushing, washer and the third gear (**Figure 90**).

NOTE
On some shafts, it may be necessary to press the fifth gear bushing off of the shaft.

5B. To remove the fifth gear bushing, perform the following:

a. Install the insert under the third gear.
b. Place the shaft assembly in the hydraulic press (**Figure 91**).
c. Hold onto the output shaft assembly, slowly press the third gear off of the shaft sufficiently for the fifth gear bushing to be released from the shaft.
d. Remove the shaft assembly from the hydraulic press.

6. Remove the snap ring and slide off the splined washer.
7. Slide off the second gear and remove the split needle bearing.
8. Slide off the splined washer and remove the snap ring.
9. Slide off the fourth gear and the washer.
10. To remove the first gear bushing (A, **Figure 92**), perform the following:

CAUTION
Do not apply heat to the transmission shaft with any type of propane or acetylene torch

as they generate a heat range much greater than required and may result in the loss of the shaft hardness.

a. Secure the transmission shaft in a vise with soft jaws.
b. Use a heat gun and heat the bushing to 80° C (176° F).
c. Wear heavy gloves since the bushing will be *hot*. Carefully pry the bushing off the end of the shaft and remove it and the washer (B, **Figure 92**).

Assembly

NOTE
Replace the snap ring every time the transmission is disassembled to ensure proper gear alignment. Install the snap ring onto the shaft with the rounded side going on first. Do not expand a snap ring more than necessary to slide it over the shaft.

1. Apply clean gear oil to all sliding surfaces of the gears, bushings and shaft prior to installing the parts.
2. If removed, install the first gear bushing (A, **Figure 92**), as follows:
   a. If possible, place the transmission shaft in the freezer for 30 minutes. This will reduce the shaft outer diameter.
   b. Place the first gear bushing on a noncombustible surface.
   c. Use a heat gun and heat the bushing 80° C (176° F).
   d. Secure the transmission shaft vertically in a vise with soft jaws.
   e. Install the washer (B, **Figure 92**).
   f. Wear heavy gloves as the bushing will be *hot*. Pick up the bushing with pliers and place it on top of the shaft. When heated to the correct temperature the bushing will slide down the shaft and rest on the washer. If necessary, carefully tap the bushing down on the shaft until it bottoms on the washer.
   g. Allow the bushing to cool.
3. Install the first gear (A, **Figure 93**) and washer (B).

CAUTION
When installing the ball bearing, apply pressure only on the ***inner race****. If pressure is applied to the outer race the bearing will be damaged.*

4. To install the front ball bearing (next to the first gear), perform the following:

97

101

98

99

100

a. Position the bearing with the manufacturer's marks facing out.

b. Install the bearing onto the end of the shaft (A, **Figure 94**).

c. Place the transmission shaft assembly on the plate of the hydraulic press (**Figure 95**).

d. Place a suitable size driver (B, **Figure 94**) onto the bearing. The driver must fit the inner race only and must have a large enough inner diameter to clear the splines on the output shaft. The shaft splines will be damaged if the inner surface of the driver touches the shaft splines.

e. Hold onto the shaft and slowly press the bearing onto the shaft. Press it on until it stops.

f. Remove the output shaft and driver from the hydraulic press.

g. After pressing the bearing (**Figure 96**) into place, rotate the bearing by hand. Check for roughness, noise and radial play.

5. Position the fourth gear (**Figure 97**)with the shift fork groove side) going on last. Slide the fourth gear into the backside of the first gear.

6. Install the snap ring and make sure it seats properly in the groove (**Figure 98**).

7. Install the splined washer (A, **Figure 99**) and, on models so equipped, the large O-ring (B). Push the splined washer onto the spline ends and move the O-ring against it to hold it in place (**Figure 100**).

8. Install the split roller bearing (**Figure 101**). Position it in the shaft groove and bring both ends together to close it. Make sure it seats properly in the shaft groove.

9. Position the third gear with the shift dog receptacle side going on first and slide on the third gear (A, **Figure 102**).

10. Install the splined washer (B, **Figure 102**) and snap ring (C). Make sure the snap ring seats properly in the shaft groove (**Figure 103**).

11. Position the third gear with the shift fork groove (**Figure 104**) side going on first. Slide on the third gear (**Figure 105**).

12. Slide on the washer (A, **Figure 106**) and fifth gear bushing (B). If the fifth gear bushing will not slide on, repeat Step 2 to install this bushing.

13. Move the washer and bushing (**Figure 107**) down until they stop against the spline ends.

14. Position the fifth gear with the shift dog side going on first. Slide on the fifth gear (A, **Figure 108**)

15. Position the washer (B, **Figure 108**) with the chamfer side going on last and slide the washer on (**Figure 109**).

16. To install the rear bearing (next to the fifth gear), perform the following:
   a. Position the bearing with the manufacturer's marks facing out.
   b. Install the bearing onto the end of the shaft (**Figure 110**).
   c. Place the transmission shaft assembly (A, **Figure 111**) on the plate of the hydraulic press.
   d. Place a suitable size driver (B, **Figure 111**) onto the inner race of the bearing. The driver must fit the inner race only and must also have a large enough inner diameter to clear the splines on the output shaft.

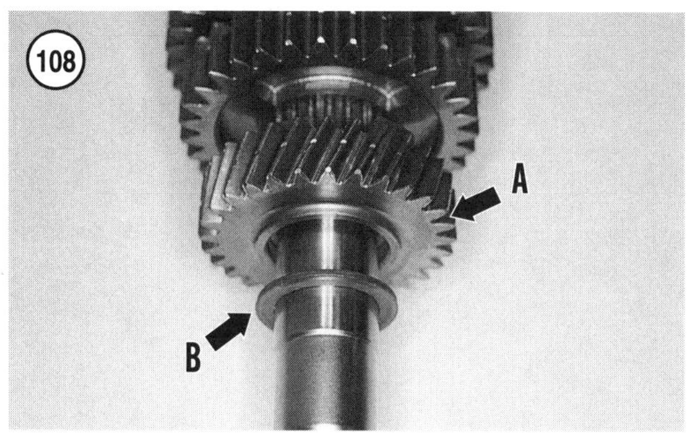

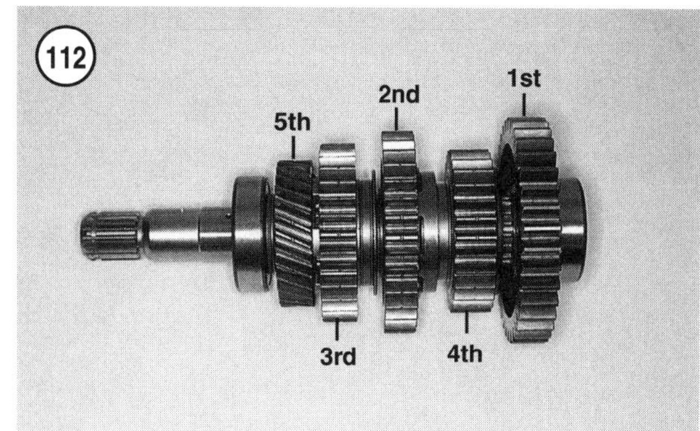

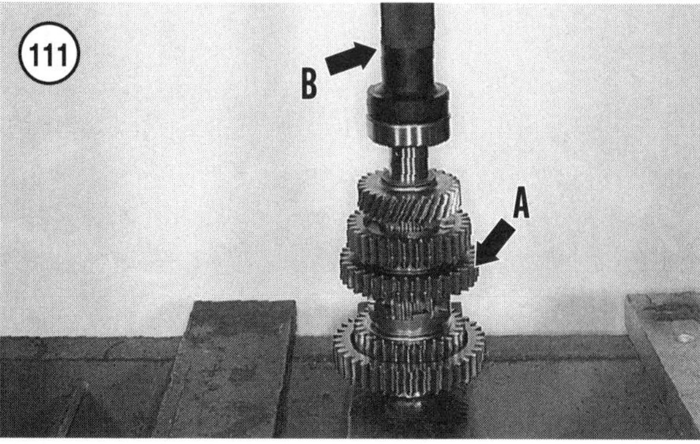

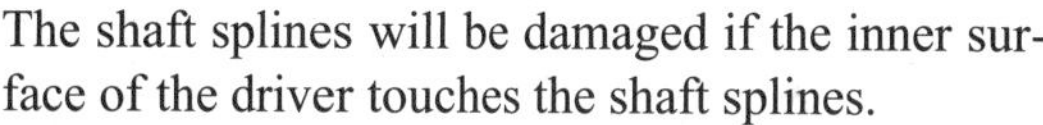

The shaft splines will be damaged if the inner surface of the driver touches the shaft splines.

e. Hold onto the shaft and slowly press the bearing onto the shaft. Press it on until it bottoms.

f. Remove the output shaft and driver from the hydraulic press.

g. After pressing the bearing into place, rotate it by hand. Check for roughness, noise and radial play.

17. Refer to **Figure 112** for correct placement of all gears. Make sure all snap rings seat correctly in the output shaft grooves.

18. Make sure each gear engages properly to the adjoining gear, where applicable.

19. After completing the transmission shaft assembly, measure the overall length of the shaft as shown in **Figure 113** and note the measurement. Refer to the measurement taken prior to disassembly as the shaft must be the exact same overall length to fit properly into the transmission housing and cover.

20. After assembling the output shaft, mesh the output shaft and the intermediate shaft together in their correct position. Confirm that all gears meet correctly.

21. Install the output shaft as described in this chapter.

Inspection

1. Check each gear for excessive wear, burrs, pitting or chipped or missing teeth (**Figure 114**).
2. Make sure the engagement dogs (**Figure 115**) on the gears are in good condition.
3. Inspect the engagement dog receptacles in each gear. Refer to **Figure 116** and **Figure 117**.
4. Check the inner splines (**Figure 118**) of the third and fourth gears for excessive wear or burrs.
5. Inspect the machined shift fork grooves in the respective gears. Check for wear, gouges or other damage, replacing the gear if necessary.
6. Check the first and fifth gear bushings (A, **Figure 119**) for excessive wear, pitting or damage. Make sure the oil hole is clear (**Figure 120**).
7. Check the bushing surface (B, **Figure 119**) in the respective gears. Apply a light coat of lubricant to the outer surface of the bushing and install into the gear (**Figure 121**). Rotate the bushing and check for ease of rotation.
8. Make sure that all gears and bushings slide smoothly on the output shaft.
9. Inspect the splines (**Figure 122**) and snap ring grooves (A, **Figure 123**) on the output shaft. If any are damaged, the shaft must be replaced.

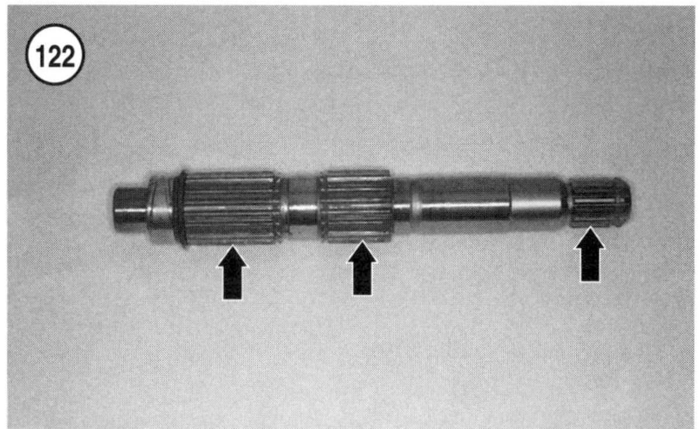

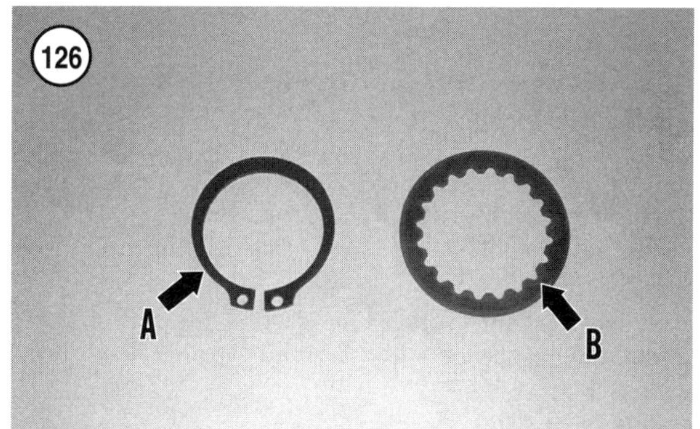

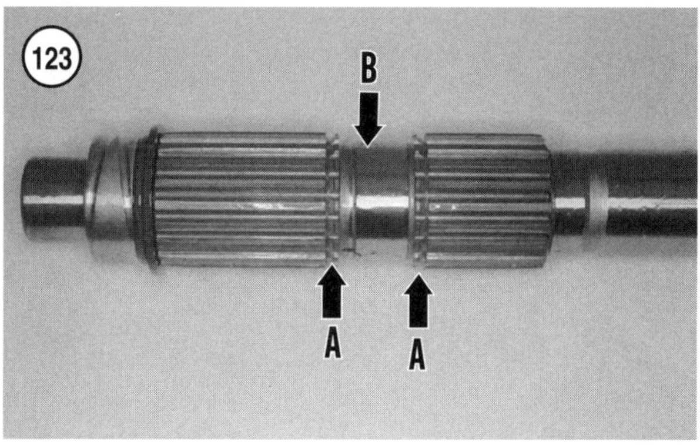

10. Inspect the shaft surface (B, **Figure 123**) where the split roller bearing rides. It must be free of burrs and damage.

11. Inspect both ball bearings (**Figure 124**) and rotate by hand. Check for roughness, noise and radial play. Replace any bearing that is suspect.

12. Inspect the split roller bearing (**Figure 125**). Check the bearing cage for cracks at the corners of the needle slots and inspect the needles themselves for cracking. If any cracks are found, the split bearing must be replaced.

13. Discard the snap rings (A, **Figure 126**) even if they appear to be in good condition.

14. Check the plain and splined washers (B, **Figure 126**) for wear or damage, and replace as necessary.

GEARSHIFT MECHANISM

Internal Gearshift Selector Shaft Inspection

Refer to **Figure 127**.

Replacement parts are not available for the gearshift selector shaft. Some smaller components can be removed for cleaning purposes only.

1. Clean the shaft assembly in solvent and dry with compressed air.
2. Inspect the gearshift shaft (**Figure 128**) for bending, wear or other damage.
3. Inspect the return spring on the following parts:
   a. Stop lever (A, **Figure 129**).
   b. Shift pawls (**Figure 130**).
   c. Torsion spring (**Figure 131**).
4. Inspect the roller (B, **Figure 129**) on the stop lever. It must rotate freely.
5. Check the movement of each pawl arm (A, **Figure 132**). It must move freely and the spring must return it to the post (**Figure 133**).
6. Make sure snap ring is tight (B, **Figure 132**) securing the pawl post to the shaft.
7. Make sure the snap ring (**Figure 134**) securing the stop lever is secure.
8. Inspect the outer splines (A, **Figure 135**) on the shaft and the inner splines (B) on the lever.

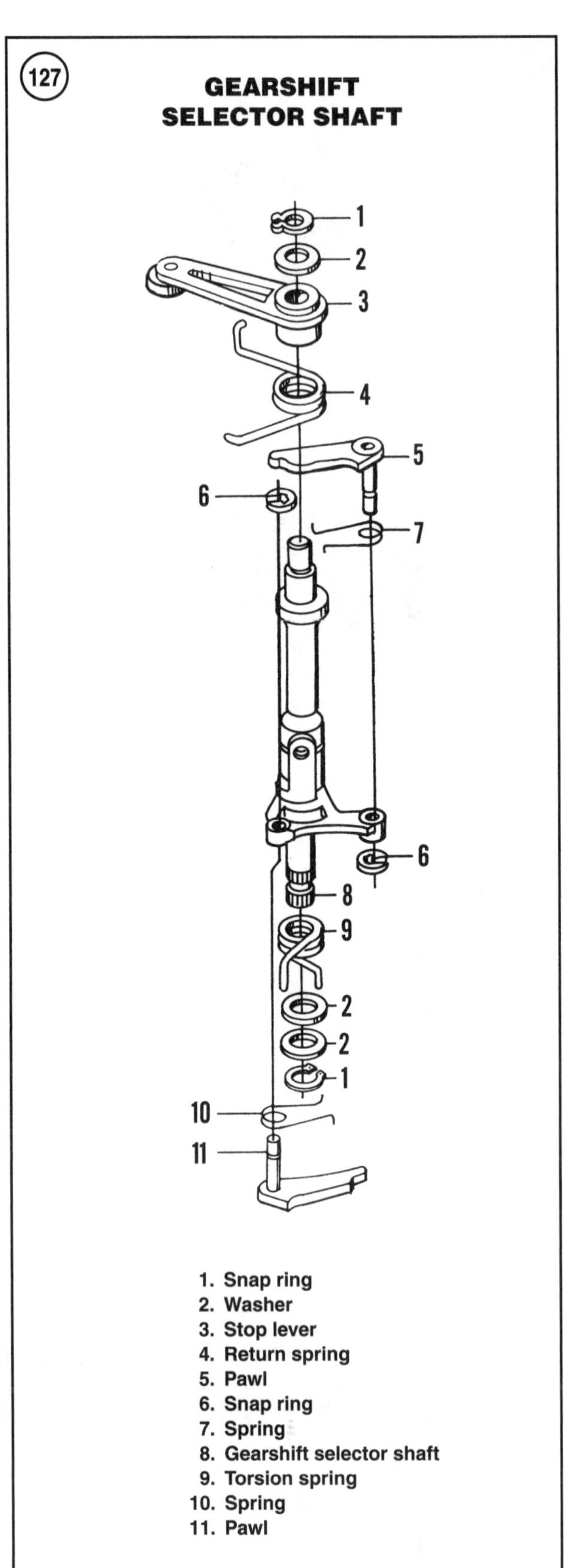

1. Snap ring
2. Washer
3. Stop lever
4. Return spring
5. Pawl
6. Snap ring
7. Spring
8. Gearshift selector shaft
9. Torsion spring
10. Spring
11. Pawl

Shift Drum and Shift Forks Inspection

Refer to **Figure 136**.

Replace the shift fork(s), the shaft(s) and shift drum if worn or damaged.

CAUTION

It is recommended that marginally worn shift forks be replaced. Worn forks can cause the transmission to slip out of gear, leading to transmission damage.

1. Inspect the ramps (A, **Figure 137**) on the selector cam for wear or damage.
2. Place the neutral switch steel ball (B, **Figure 137**) into the receptacle in the selector cam. The ball must be a tight fit.
3. Inspect the roller pins (A, **Figure 138**) in the end of the shift drum. Make sure they are a tight fit in the shift drum. If the pins (B, **Figure 138**) are loose, replace all of them as a set.

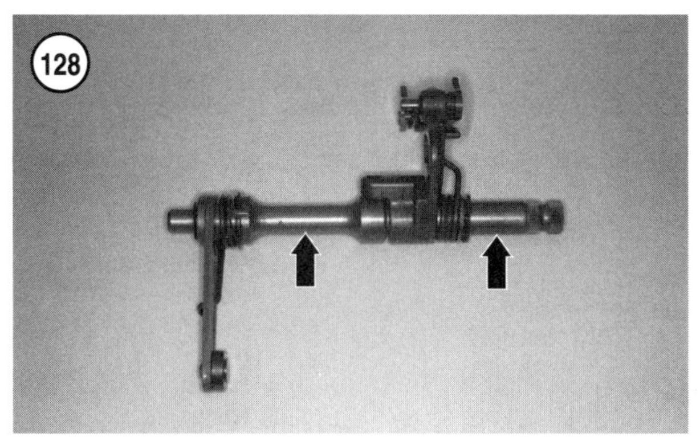
128

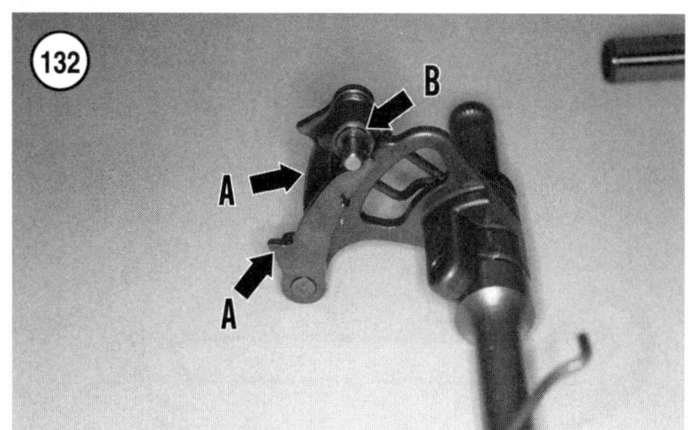
132
B
A
A

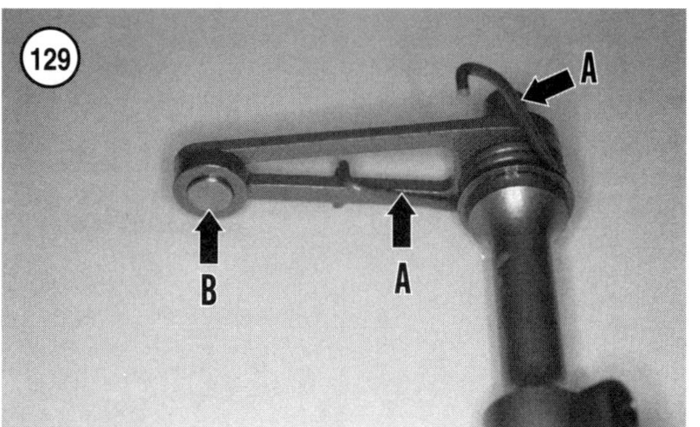
129
A
B
A

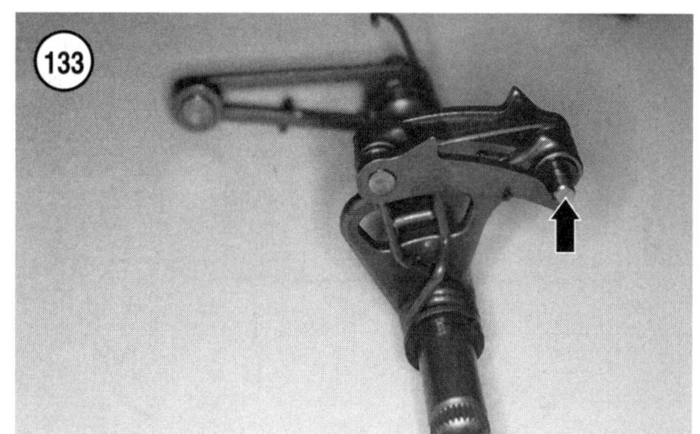
133

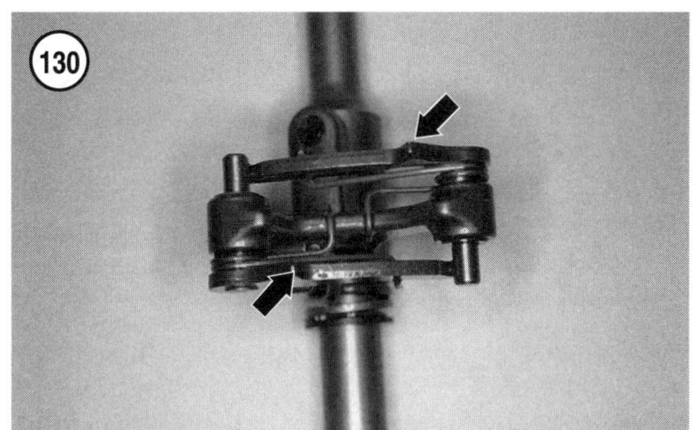
130

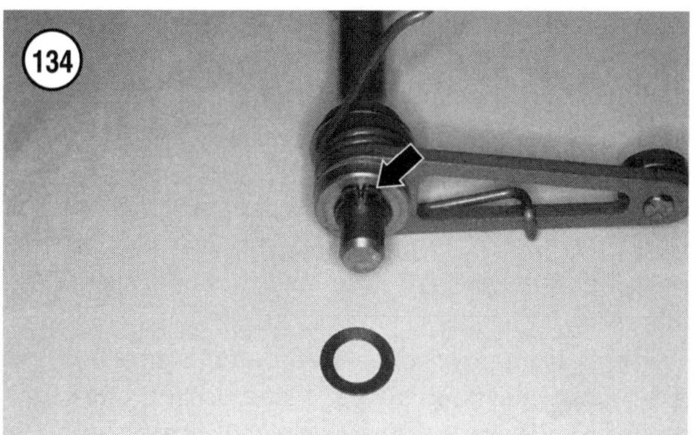
134

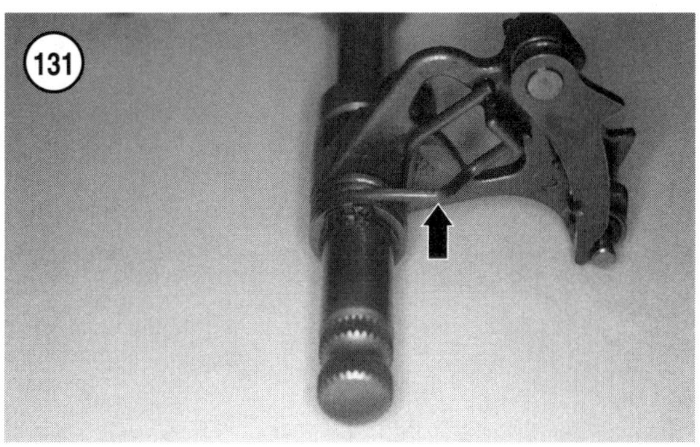
131

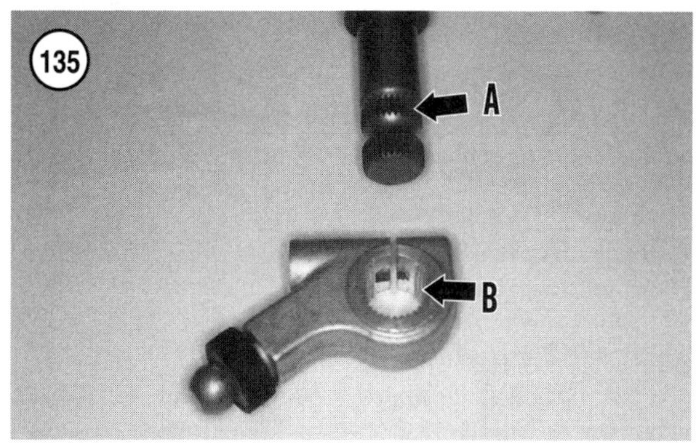
135
A
B

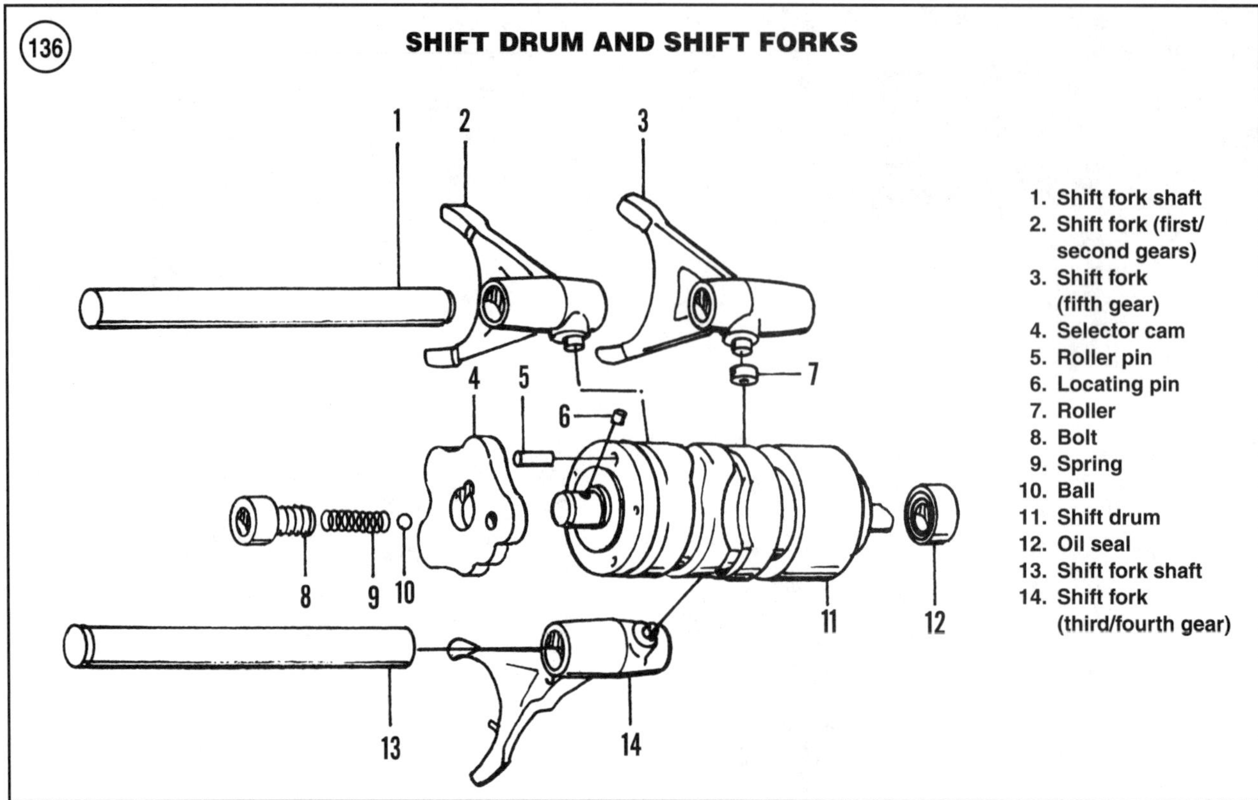

4. Inspect the end of the shift drum (**Figure 139**) where it rides in the transmission housing for wear or damage.
5. Inspect each shift fork for wear or cracking (**Figure 140**). Check for bending and make sure each fork slides smoothly on the shaft (**Figure 141**).
6. Check for any arc-shaped wear or burned marks on the shift fork fingers (**Figure 142**). This indicates that the shift fork is excessively worn and the fork must be replaced.
7. Check the grooves in the shift drum (**Figure 143**) for wear or roughness. Replace the shift drum if any of the groove profiles have excessive wear or damage.
8. Check the cam pin follower and roller (**Figure 144**) on each shift fork that rides in the shift drum for wear or damage.
9. Roll each shift fork shaft on a flat surface such as a piece of plate glass and check for bends. If the shaft is bent, it must be replaced.

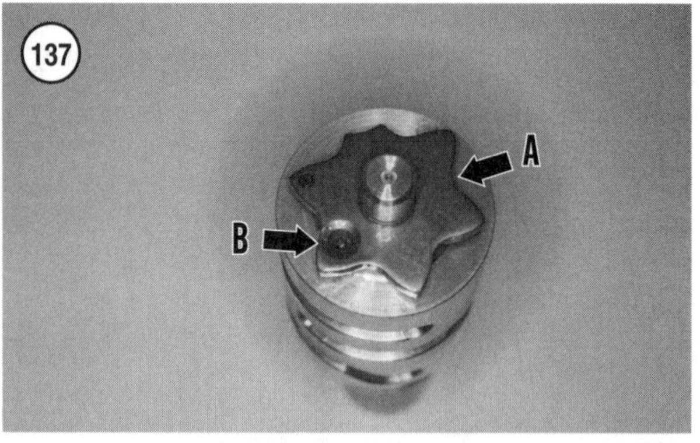

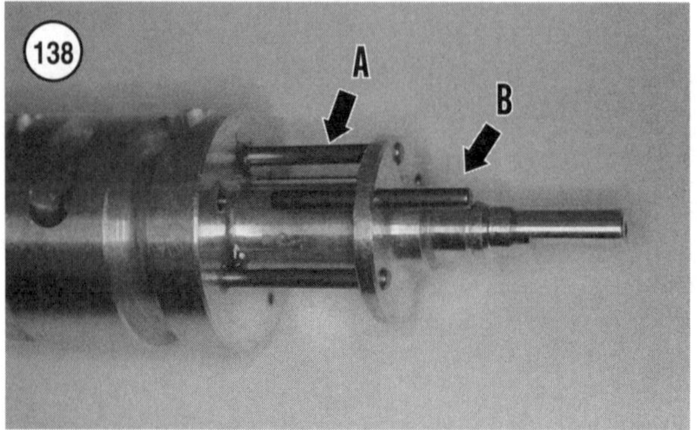

External Gearshift Mechanism Removal/Installation

Refer to **Figure 145**.

1A. On models so equipped, place the motorcycle on the centerstand with the rear wheel off the ground.

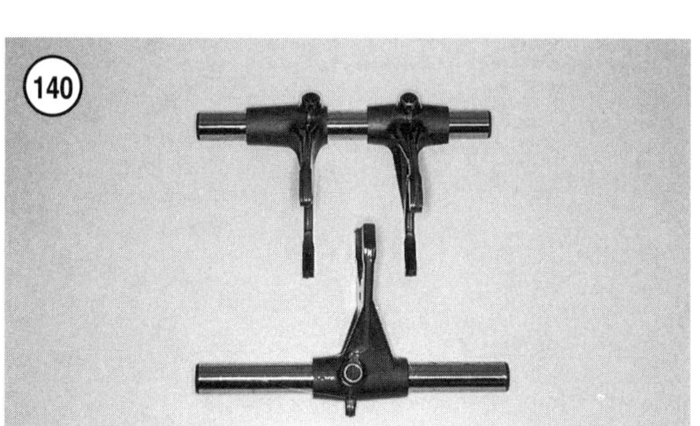

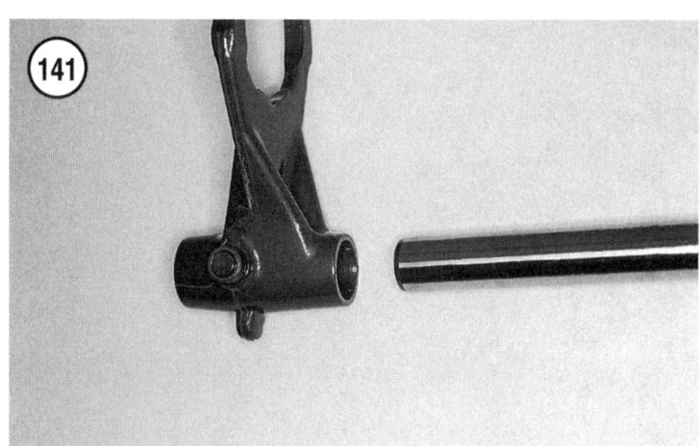

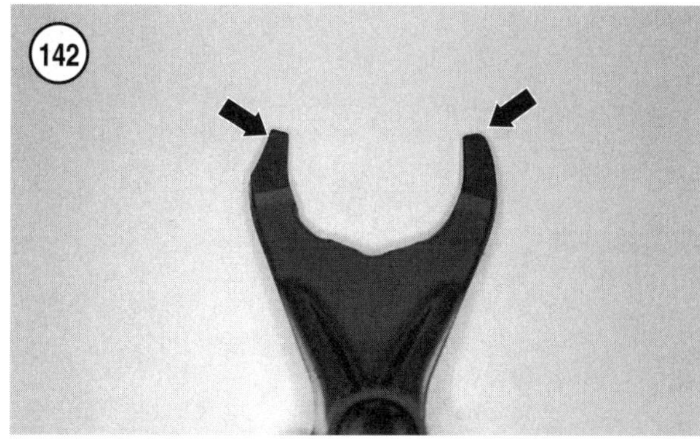

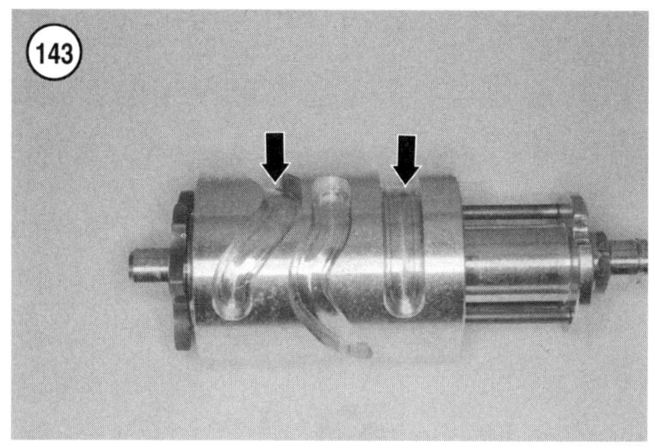

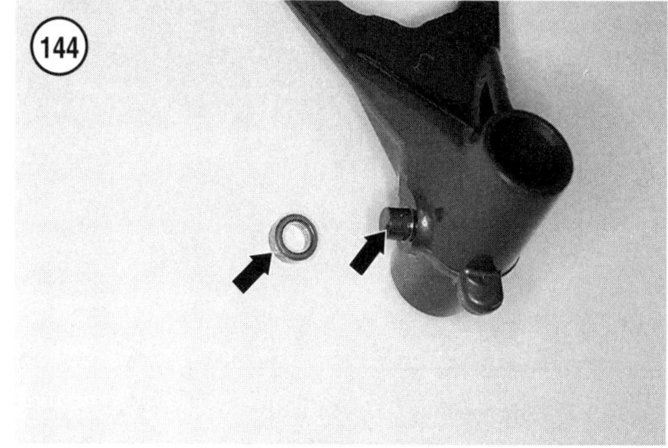

1B. On models without a centerstand, place a suitable size jack under the engine to support the motorcycle with the rear wheel off the ground.

2. Remove the clip and disconnect the connector rod from the shift lever (A, **Figure 146**, typical).

3. Remove the clip and disconnect the connector rod from the transmission housing shift lever (**Figure 147**).

4. To remove the shift lever from the left footrest, perform the following:

a. Remove the bolts (B, **Figure 146**) securing the left footrest to the crankcase. Remove the footrest.

b. Remove the bolt securing the shift lever to the backside of the footrest and remove the shift lever.

c. If necessary, remove the collar from the shift lever.

d. Apply a light coat of grease to the collar and the bushings in the shift lever pivot.

e. Install the collar into the shift lever and position the shift lever onto the footrest.

f. On R, GS and RS models, install the bolt and tighten to 35 N•m (26 ft.-lb.)

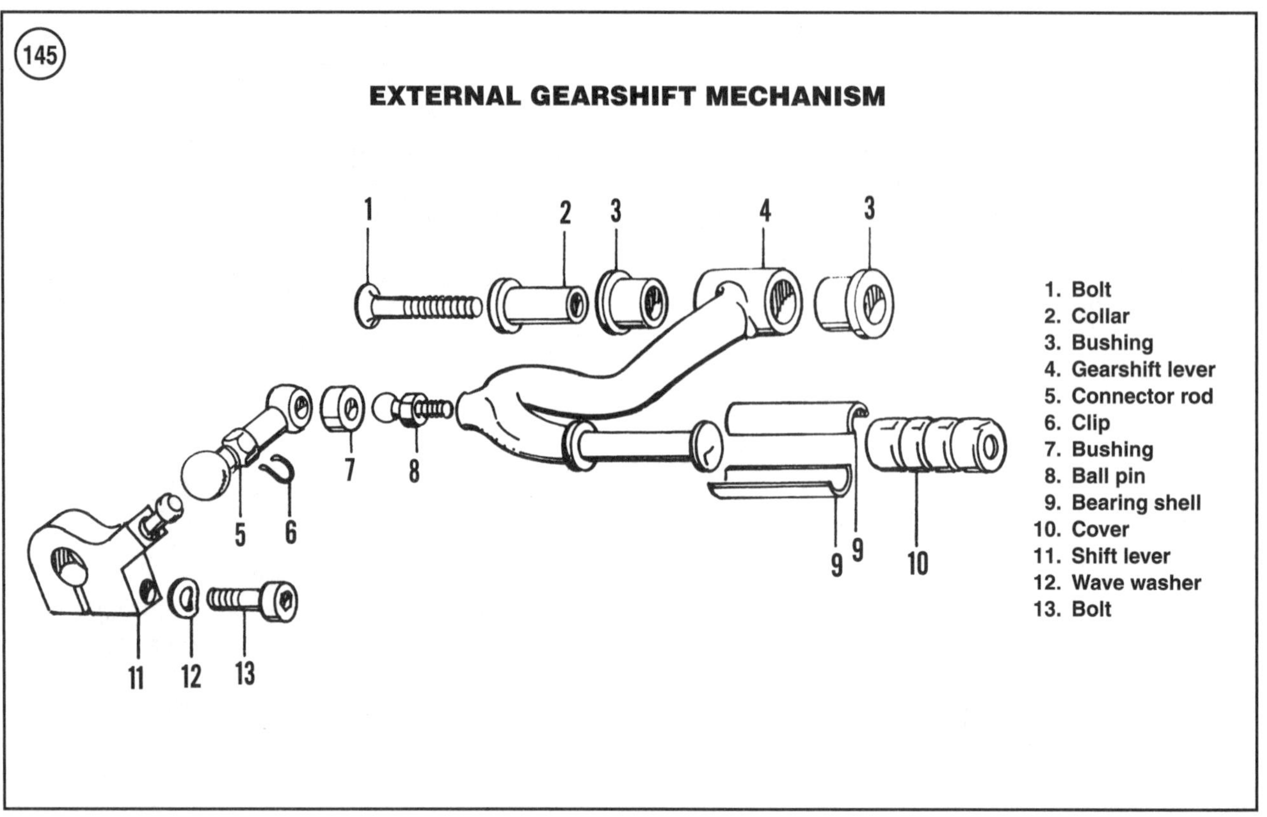

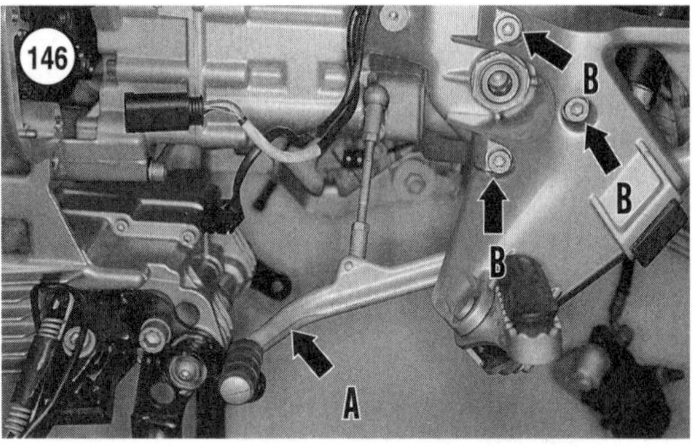

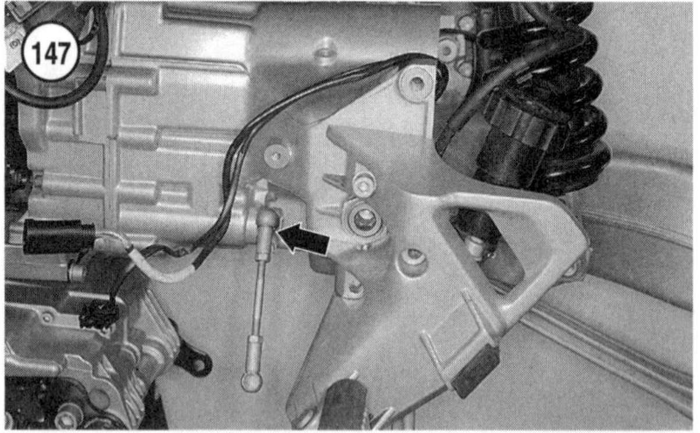

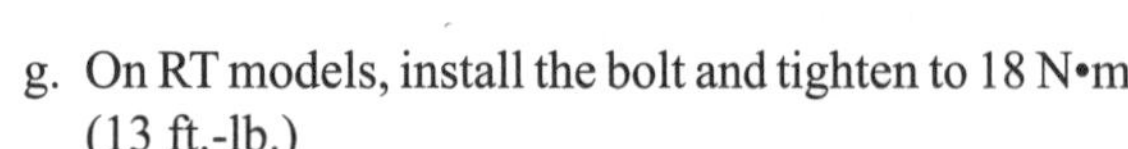

g. On RT models, install the bolt and tighten to 18 N•m (13 ft.-lb.)

5. Tighten the footrest mounting bolts to 22 N•m (16 ft.-lb.).

TRANSMISSION COVER AND HOUSING BEARINGS AND SEALS

After the transmission housing cover has been removed and the transmission shafts have been removed from the housing, inspect the bearings and seals.

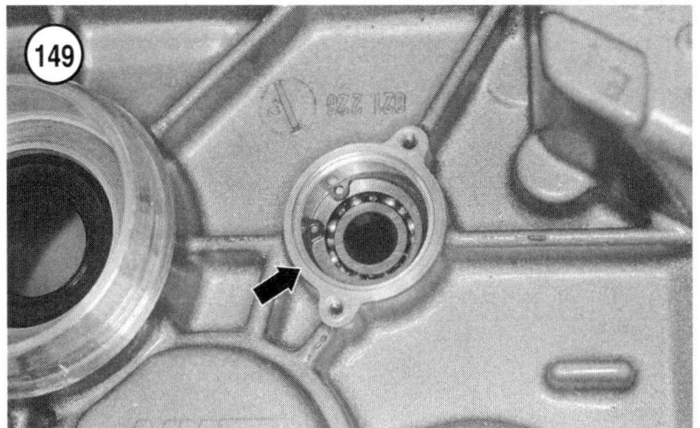

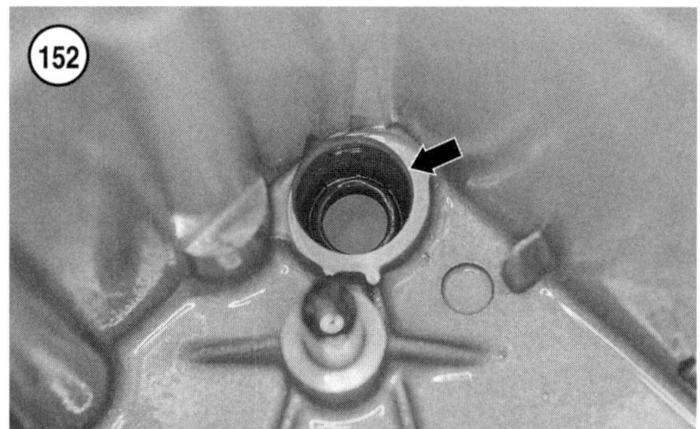

Rotate the bearings by hand. Refer to **Figure 148-152**. Check for roughness, noise and radial play.

Due to the number of BMW special tools required, it is recommended that the replacement of bearings and oil seals be performed by a BMW dealership. The bearings and seals must be installed to a specific depth in the housing bores using the special tools. If the bearings and seals are installed incorrectly in the housing, the seal, the bearing and possibly the transmission shafts may be damaged.

Table 1 FIVE-SPEED TRANSMISSION SPECIFICATIONS

Type	Five speed constant mesh transmission with integral spring damper Claw-type shift fork shifting mechanism
Gear ratios (1993 models)	
First gear	4.030
Second gear	2.576
Third gear	1.886
Fourth gear	1.538
Fifth gear	1.318
Gear ratios (1994-on models)	
First gear	4.163
Second gear	2.914
Third gear	2.133
Fourth gear	1.740
Fifth gear	1.450

Table 2 FIVE-SPEED TRANSMISSION TORQUE SPECIFICATIONS

Item	N•m	in.-lb.	ft.-lb.
Footrest mounting bolts	22	–	16
Neutral detent Allen bolt plug	13	115	–
Shift lever-to-footrest bolt			
GS, R, RS models	35	–	26
RT	18	–	13
Transmission case bolts	22	–	16
Transmission housing cover bolts	10	88	–

CHAPTER EIGHT

SIX SPEED TRANSMISSION AND GEARSHIFT MECHANISMS

The transmission shafts and the gearshift mechanism are all located inside a transmission housing that is bolted to the back of the engine.

The engine driven input shaft is splined to the clutch friction plate and is equipped with a shock damper to dampen engine-to-transmission shock loads. The rear of the input shaft has a helical-cut gear which mates to a similar gear on the intermediate shaft. The intermediate shaft transmits engine power from the input shaft to the output shaft. With the exception of the one helical-cut gear on the input and intermediate shaft, all the other gears are straight-cut.

Some of the components of the transmission housing require heat to loosen and remove them. A heat gun capable of generating 120° C (248° F) is required. A heat gun is also required for disassembly of some of the front and rear suspension components.

The R1100S and all R1150 models are equipped with a 6-speed transmission. The R850C and R1200C models uses the same transmission, but it is referred to as a 5-speed transmission. The R850C/R1200C 5-speed transmission has all of the same gears as the 6-speed, but they are referred to differently as noted in the exploded views and the text.

The figures in this chapter are based on the short length transmission case equipped on the R850C, R1100S and R1200C models. The rear swing arm, on these models, pivots on the rear frame instead of on the long extensions of the transmission case typical of all other models.

Table 1 and **Table 2** are located at the end of the chapter.

TRANSMISSION CASE

Removal

NOTE
BMW recommends removal of the transmission case from the engine prior to removing the engine if both components are going to be serviced.

CAUTION
To prevent damaging the clutch release pushrod and transmission input shaft, in-

*stall guide pins (BMW part No. 23-1-820) or modified long bolts (**Figure 1**) after two of the transmission case mounting holes have been removed. These guide pins, or bolts, ensure that the weight of the transmission will not bend the clutch pushrod.*

1. Remove all fairing assemblies and the seat(s) as described in Chapter Fifteen.
2. Disconnect the negative battery cable as described in Chapter Three.
3. Remove the fuel tank as described in Chapter Nine.
4. Remove the throttle body assembly (**Figure 2**) from each side as described in Chapter Nine.
5. Remove the air filter housing (A, **Figure 3**) as described in Chapter Nine.
6. Remove the exhaust system as described in Chapter Nine.
7. On R1100S models, remove the Motronic unit as described in Chapter Ten.
8. Remove both front footrests as described in Chapter Fifteen.
9. Remove the battery and the holder (B, **Figure 3**) as described in Chapter Nine.
10. Remove the starter as described in Chapter Ten.
11. If the transmission is going to be disassembled, drain the transmission oil as described in Chapter Three.
12. Remove the rear wheel as described in Chapter Eleven.
13. Remove the final drive unit and the swing arm as described in Chapter Thirteen.

14A. On R850C, R1100S and R1200C models, perform the following:

a. Remove the sidestand/footrest assembly as described in Chapter Fifteen.
b. Remove the rear main frame as described in Chapter Fifteen.

14B. On all models except R850C, R1100S and R1200C, remove or raise the rear frame section as described in Chapter Fifteen.

15. Remove the clutch release cylinder (**Figure 4**) as described in Chapter Six.
16. Disconnect the electrical connector from the transmission gear position switch.
17. Check to make sure all electrical wiring and connectors are disconnected and moved away from the area where the transmission case will be exiting.
18. Place wood blocks or a small floor jack under the transmission housing.
19. Remove the transmission case mounting bolts in the following order:

a. Loosen the two lower bolts.

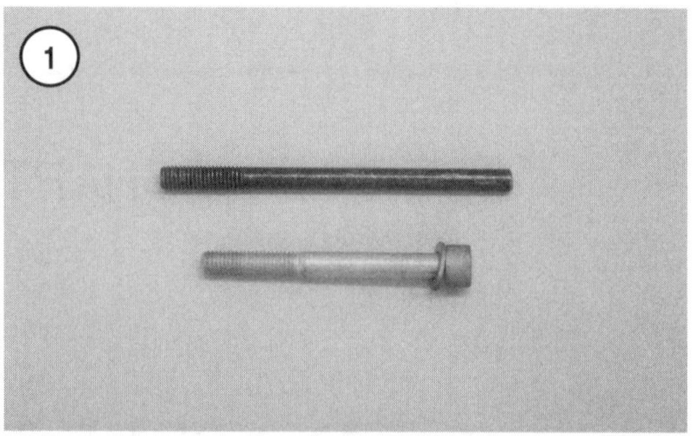

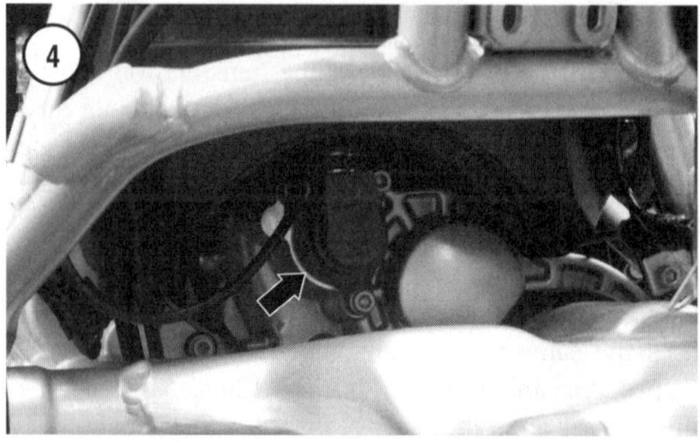

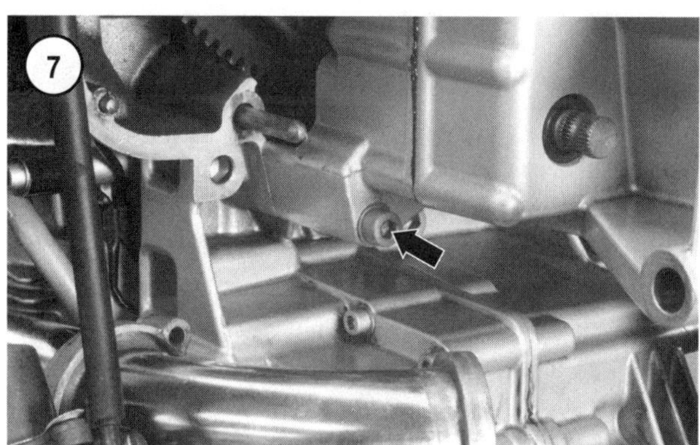

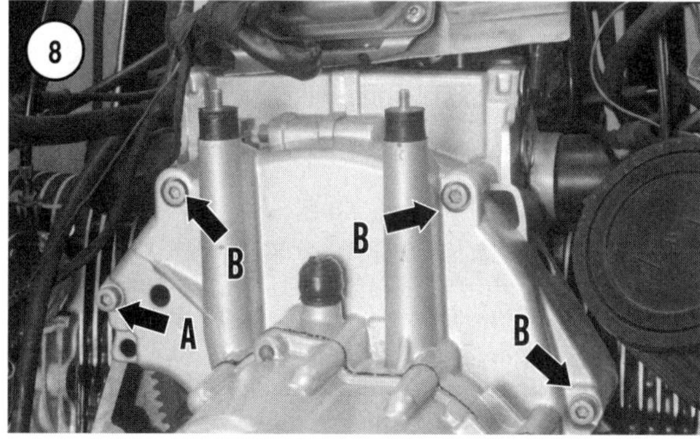

b. Remove the right lower bolt (**Figure 5**) and install a guide pin into the threaded hole (**Figure 6**).
c. Remove the left lower bolt (**Figure 7**).
d. Remove the upper left bolt (A, **Figure 8**) and install a guide pin into the threaded hole (**Figure 9**).

CAUTION
Make sure the transmission housing is secure on the wooden blocks or jack prior to removing the final three bolts.

e. Remove the three remaining upper bolts (B, **Figure 8**).

CAUTION
In the following step, to prevent damage to the transmission input shaft and clutch release push rod, pull the transmission housing straight back until it is disengaged from the clutch assembly and guide pins.

20. Using a soft faced mallet, tap around the perimeter of the transmission housing to break it loose from the rear of the engine.

NOTE
The transmission case should separate easily from the engine. If not, confirm that all external components are removed. If the motorcycle has high-mileage or if it has been subjected to saltwater or road salt, the two locating pins may be corroded at the two locations where the guide pins were installed. Apply Liquid Wrench (or an equivalent) penetrating oil to the locating pins and let it sit for 15 minutes.

21. Pull the transmission housing *straight back* until it is free of the engine, the clutch assembly and the clutch pushrod.
22. Lower the transmission housing and take it to the workbench.

8

23. If necessary, remove the clutch assembly as described in Chapter Six.

Installation

1. If the transmission shaft assemblies were disassembled, rotate the input shaft and shift the transmission through all gears. Make sure all shafts rotate smoothly and all gears engage.
2. Shift the transmission into sixth gear and leave it engaged to prevent the input shaft from rotating for ease of transmission installation.
3. Clean the mating surfaces of both the engine and the transmission housing of any corrosion.
4. If the clutch release pushrod was removed, perform the following:
   a. Install a new felt sleeve (**Figure 10**) into the groove in the pushrod.
   b. Apply Microlube GL261, or Bel Rey Total Performance Lube, to the felt sleeve.
   c. Position the pushrod with the short ball-end (**Figure 11**) going in first and insert it part way into the transmission input shaft. Carefully insert the felt sleeve (**Figure 12**) into the transmission input shaft. Ensure it stays within the pushrod groove.
   d. Push it in until it is flush with the end of the input shaft stops. Apply a light coat of Microlube GL261 or Bel Rey Total Performance Lube to the release push rod end (A, **Figure 13**).
5. Apply a light coat of Microlube GL261 or Bel Rey Total Performance Lube to the outer splines of the transmission input shaft (B, **Figure 13**) where it rides in the clutch friction plate.
6. If removed, install the upper left locating dowel (A, **Figure 14**) and guide pin (B).
7. If removed, install the lower right locating dowel (A, **Figure 15**) and guide pin (B).
8. If removed, install the clutch assembly as described in Chapter Six.
9. Shift the transmission into sixth gear.
10. Raise the transmission housing and align it with the back surface of the engine.

CAUTION
To prevent damage to the transmission input shaft, push the transmission housing straight forward until it is properly engaged with the clutch assembly.

11. Slowly push the transmission housing forward and align the input shaft outer splines with the inner splines of the clutch friction plate. Slightly rotate the output shaft at the rear of the transmission until alignment is achieved. Also, align the transmission housing with the guide pins on the engine.

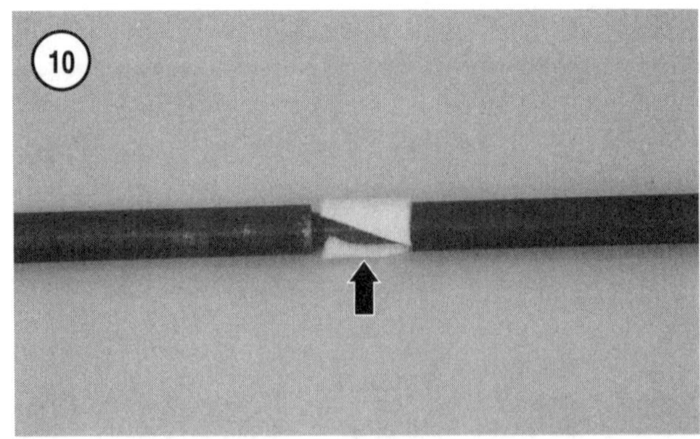

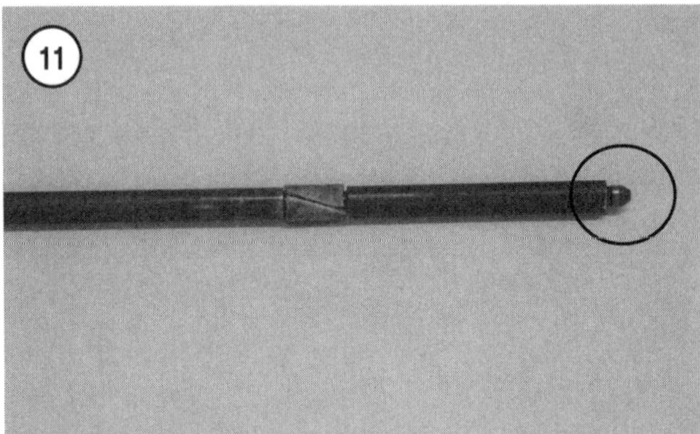

CAUTION
When properly aligned, the transmission case should fit directly against the engine mounting surface with no gap. If not properly aligned, do not attempt to pull the transmission housing up against the engine with the mounting bolts. Separate the trans-

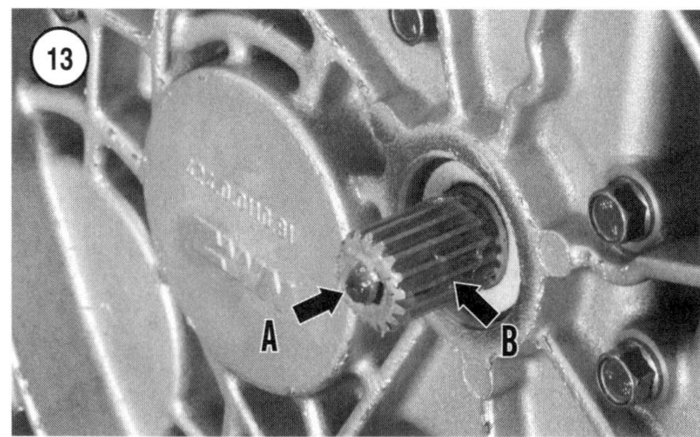

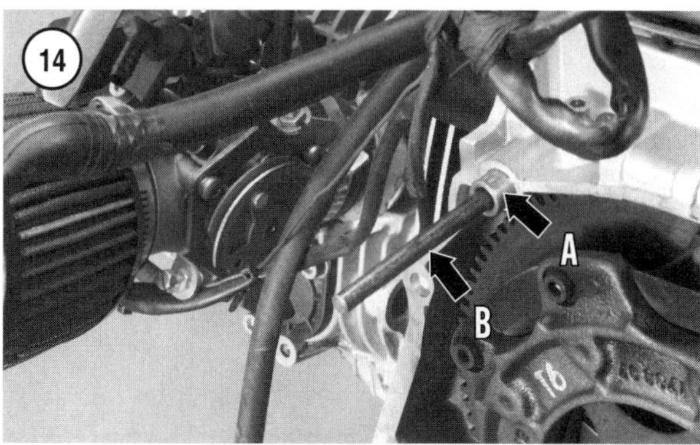

mission housing and investigate the cause of the interference.

12. Push the transmission case forward until it is tight against the engine mating surface around the entire perimeter.

13. Install the transmission case mounting bolts in the following order:

   a. Install the upper three mounting bolts (B, **Figure 8**) and tighten securely.
   b. Remove the upper left side guide pin and install the remaining bolt. Tighten it securely.
   c. Remove the lower right guide pin (**Figure 6**), then install the lower right bolt (**Figure 5**) and lower left bolt (**Figure 7**). Tighten the bolts securely.
   d. Tighten all six bolts to 22 N•m (16 ft.-lb.).

14. Connect the electrical connector onto the transmission gear position switch and the neutral switch.
15. Install the clutch release cylinder (**Figure 4**) as described in Chapter Six.
16A. On R850C, R1100S and R1200C models, perform the following:
   a. Install the sidestand/footrest assembly as described in Chapter Fifteen.
   b. Install the rear main frame as described in Chapter Fifteen.

16B. On all models except R850C, R1100S and R1200C, install or lower the rear frame section as described in Chapter Fifteen.
17. Install the final drive unit and the swing arm as described in Chapter Thirteen.
18. Install the rear wheel as described in Chapter Eleven.
19. If the transmission was disassembled, refill the transmission oil as described in Chapter Three.
20. Install the starter as described in Chapter Ten.
21. Install the battery and the holder (B, **Figure 3**) as described in Chapter Nine.
22. Install both front footrests as described in Chapter Fifteen.
23. On R1100S models, install the Motronic unit as described in Chapter Ten.
24. Install the exhaust system as described in Chapter Nine.
25. Install the air filter housing (A, **Figure 3**) as described in Chapter Nine.
26. Install the throttle body assemblies (**Figure 2**) onto each side as described in Chapter Nine.
27. Install the fuel tank as described in Chapter Nine.
28. Connect the negative battery cable as described in Chapter Three.
29. Install all fairing assemblies and both seats as described in Chapter Thirteen.
30. Ride the motorcycle slowly at first to make sure the clutch and the transmission are operating properly.

Inspection

1. Thoroughly clean the housing and cover in solvent and dry it with compressed air.
2. Inspect the housing and cover for any cracks or damage. Check around the ribs and the transmission sealing

surface (**Figure 16**). If it is damaged, replace the cover and/or housing.

3. On all models except the R850C, R1100S and R1200C, inspect the final drive torque link mounting brackets for any cracks or damage. Check the bolt holes for elongation or damage.

16

NEUTRAL/GEAR POSITION SWITCH

Removal/Installation

1. Compress the spring securing the neutral/gear position switch to the backside of the transmission housing.
2. Unhook the electrical cable clamps from the transmission housing bosses.
3. Remove the switch and electrical cable from the transmission housing.

NOTE
If replacing the switch, also order the oil seal. It is not included with the switch.

4. Install the switch onto the transmission housing. Push it in until it bottoms, then make sure the spring secures the switch to the transmission housing.

CAUTION
The electrical cable must be secured properly to the transmission housing bosses to keep it away from moving parts to avoid a possible short.

5. Install the electrical cable and clamps onto the transmission housing bosses.

17

18

TRANSMISSION HOUSING

Removal

1. If still in place, remove the gearshift selector lever.
2. Place the transmission case on the workbench with the cover facing down.

NOTE
It may be necessary to heat the area surrounding the alignment studs to loosen them.

3. Use a drift and carefully tap the alignment studs from the transmission housing and into the transmission cover. Refer to **Figure 17** and **Figure 18**. Just tap on the studs until they exit the transmission housing flange.

19

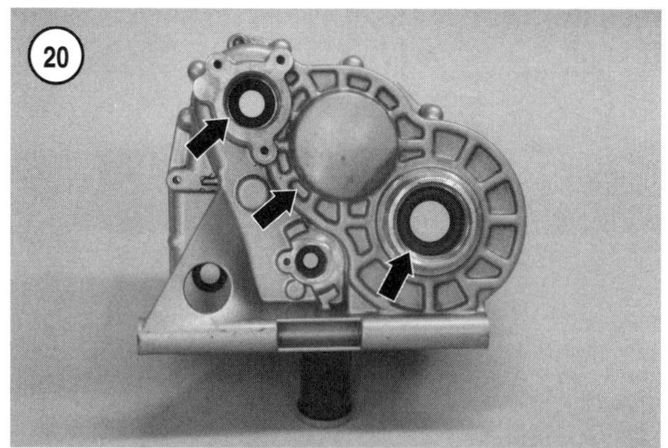
20

21

22

4. Using a crisscross pattern, loosen, then remove all inner and outer bolts and lockwashers securing the housing cover (**Figure 19**).

5. Make sure all bolts and washers are removed prior to proceeding to the next steps.

NOTE

BMW recommends heating the housing to 120° C (248° F) to release the housing from the transmission bearings. The motorcycle being working on may not require this heating procedure. First try to remove the housing without the use of heat, if not successful, perform Step 6.

CAUTION

Do not heat the housing with any type of propane or acetylene torch flame as they generate a heat range much greater than required and may also discolor the transmission housing's finish.

6. Heat the housing with a heat gun in the area of the transmission's three shaft's outer bearing races (**Figure 20**) to 120° C (248° F).

WARNING

The housing is very hot. Make sure to wear protective gloves when removing the housing in the next step.

7. Turn the transmission case over with the cover facing down on the workbench.
8. Use a rubber or plastic mallet and carefully tap around the perimeter of the transmission housing to loosen it from the cover.
9. Tap on the end of the output shaft with a plastic mallet to assist in removal. If necessary, *carefully* pry the housing loose and remove the housing from the cover and transmission gears.
10. Do not lose the thrust washer (**Figure 21**) on the top end of the shift drum. It must be reinstalled on the shift drum during assembly.
11. Thoroughly clean and inspect the housing cover as described in this chapter.

8

Installation

NOTE

*If the transmission was serviced and the selector shaft removed, refer to Step 16 of **Transmission Shaft and Gearshift Mechanism Installation** in this chapter. Make sure the torsion spring on the selector shaft is aligned correctly in order to accept the post (**Figure 22**) in the housing.*

1. If removed, install the thrust washer (**Figure 21**) on the top end of the shift drum.
2. Apply a light, even coat of Loctite 574, or an equivalent, gasket sealer to the mating surface of the transmission housing cover (**Figure 23**). Follow the manufacturer's instructions regarding the set time.
3. Wrap the splines on the output shaft (A, **Figure 24**) and the selector shaft (B) with two layers of clear smooth

adhesive tape. Do not use masking tape or duct tape as it may scratch the housing seals during installation.

4. Apply a light coat of transmission gear oil or engine oil to the outer surfaces of the transmission shaft ball bearings and to the gearshift drum where it rides in the transmission housing.

NOTE
There are two different ways to install the transmission housing onto the gears onto the cover.

5A. If a refrigerator freezer is available, place the transmission gear and cover assembly in a freezer for 30 minutes. This will reduce the outer diameter of the bearings and make installation easier without the use of heat.

5B. If the freezer is not available, heat the housing with a heat gun in the area of the transmission's three shaft's outer bearing races (**Figure 20**) to 120° C (248° F).

6. Position the transmission housing over the transmission gears and the cover. Slowly push it down into place. If necessary, move the ends of the transmission shafts to where the bearings are aligned with their respective bores in the housing.

7. Push the housing down until the bearings start to enter the housing (**Figure 25**).

NOTE
If the transmission housing will not fit flush with the cover there may be a problem with the overall length of the transmission shaft(s). If either the input or output shaft were disassembled one or more of the bearings may not be completely seated onto the shaft. Correct the problem at this time.

8. After the bearings are properly started, *carefully* tap the housing into place with a plastic mallet. Tap on the housing directly over the bearing locations and around the perimeter until the housing seats completely against the transmission cover mating surface.

9. Carefully turn the transmission case assembly over and rest it on the bottom surface.

10. Install the cover bolts and lockwashers (**Figure 19**). Using a crisscross pattern, tighten the bolts to 9 N•m (80 in.-lb.).

11. Remove the tape from the transmission output shaft splines.

NOTE
*Insert the drift into the hole (**Figure 26**) in the front surface of the cover to tap on the upper alignment stud.*

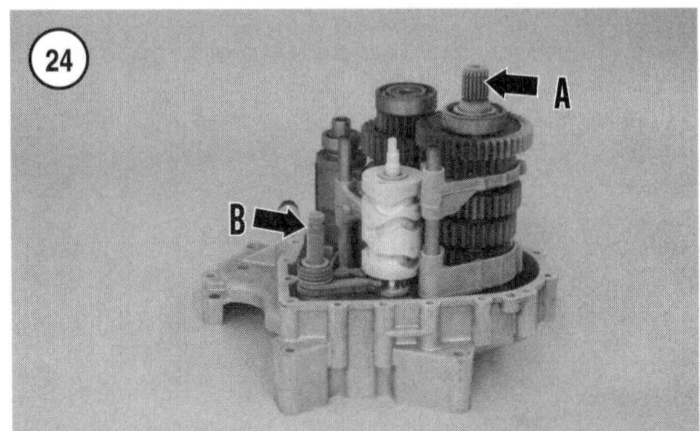

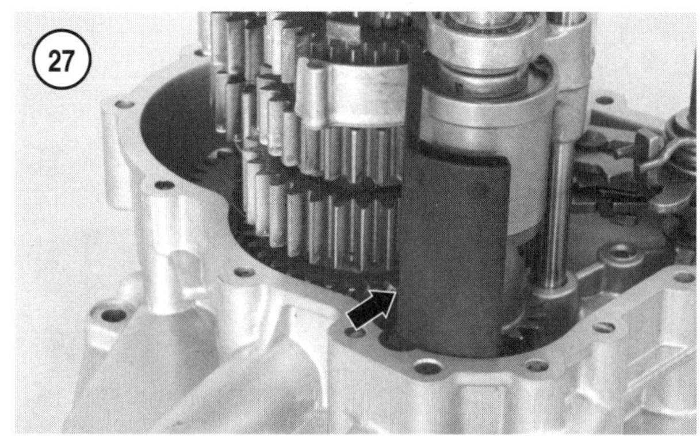

12. Use a drift and carefully tap the alignment studs back from the cover and into the transmission housing. Refer to **Figure 17** and **Figure 18**. Just tap on the studs until they enter into the transmission housing flange.

8

TRANSMISSION SHAFTS AND GEARSHIFT MECHANISM

Removal

1. Remove the transmission case as described in this chapter.
2. Remove the transmission housing from the transmission cover as described in this chapter.
3. Place the transmission cover and gear assembly on the workbench with the cover facing down.
4. Pulling straight up, remove the breather tube (**Figure 27**).
5. Pull the selector shaft guide plate (**Figure 28**) back and release it from the shift drum.
6. Pull straight up and withdraw the selector shaft assembly from the transmission cover. Remove the washer below the selector shaft and keep it with the selector shaft assembly.
7. Withdraw both shift fork shafts (**Figure 29**).
8. Move the shift forks away from the shift drum, then remove the shift drum (**Figure 30**). Also, remove the shim and the thrust washer under the shift drum. Keep all parts together.
9. Remove the two shift forks (**Figure 31**) from the output shaft.
10. Turn the transmission cover and transmission shaft assembly on its side.

NOTE

BMW recommends heating the cover to 120° C (248° F) to release the cover from the transmission bearings. The motorcycle being working on may not require this heat-

ing procedure. First try to remove the cover without the use of heat, if not successful, perform Step 11.

CAUTION
Do not heat the cover with any type of propane or acetylene torch flame as they generate a heat range much greater than required and may also discolor the transmission cover's finish.

11. Heat the base of the transmission cover with a heat gun in the area of the transmission's three shaft's outer bearing races (**Figure 32**) to 120° C (248° F).

WARNING
The cover is very hot. Make sure to wear protective gloves when securing the cover to the workbench next steps.

12. Turn the transmission assembly over with the cover facing down on the workbench.

CAUTION
In the following step, all three shafts and the shift fork must be removed as an assembly at the same time, otherwise the bevel gears (sixth gear) will be damaged.

13. Have an assistant secure the transmission cover to the workbench.

14. Withdraw the input shaft (A, **Figure 33**), the intermediate shaft (B), the output shaft (C) and the shift fork (D) as an assembly. If necessary, use a plastic mallet and carefully tap on the transmission shafts to loosen them from the cover.

15. Inspect the transmission shaft assemblies as described in this chapter.

16. Inspect the transmission cover as described in this chapter.

Installation

NOTE
There are two different ways to install the transmission shafts into the cover.

1. Apply SAE 90 hypoid gear oil to the bearings at each end of all three transmission shafts and to the bearing bores (**Figure 34**) in the base of the transmission housing.

2. Install the *C* shift fork (A, **Figure 35**) into the mesh with the intermediate shaft.

3A. If a refrigerator freezer is available, place the transmission gear assembly in a freezer for 30 minutes. This

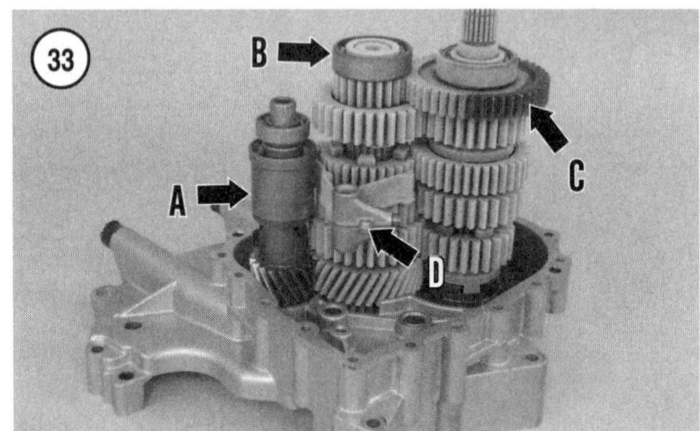

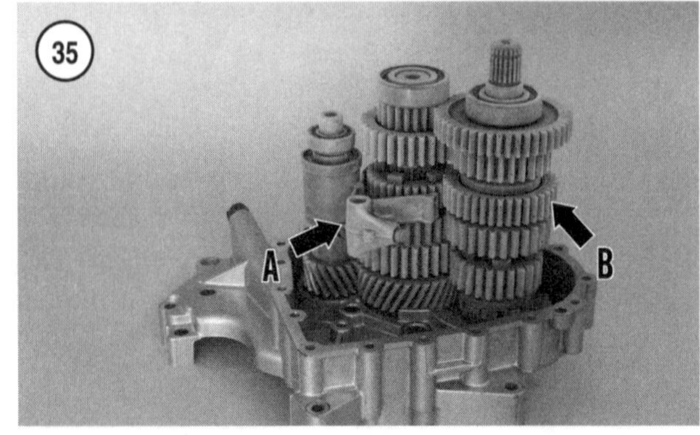

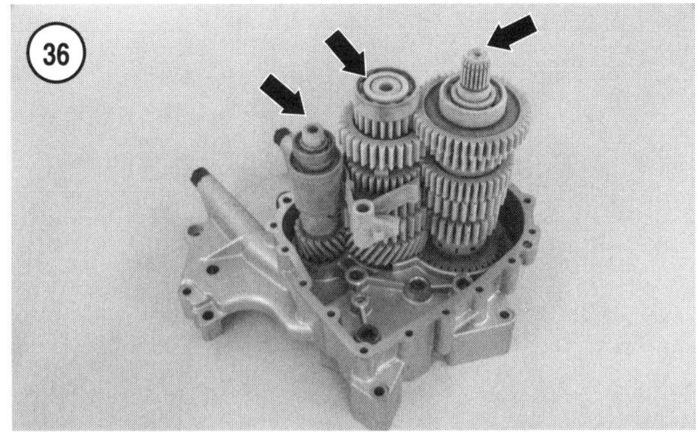

will reduce the outer diameter of the bearings and make installation easier without the use of heat.

3B. If the freezer is not available, heat the cover with a heat gun in the area of the transmission's three shaft's outer bearing races (**Figure 32**) to 120° C (248° F).

WARNING
If heat was applied in Step 3b, the cover is very hot. Make sure to wear protective gloves when handling the cover in the next step.

4. Place the cover on the workbench with the bearing receptacles facing up.

CAUTION
In the following step, do not try to install one shaft without the other shaft as the bevel gears (sixth gear) will be damaged. The three shafts must be installed as an assembly.

5. Properly mesh all three transmission shafts together as an assembly. Install them into the transmission cover (B, **Figure 35**) as an assembly.
6. Make sure the bearings align properly with their respective bearing bores in the transmission cover. Carefully tap on the ends of the transmission shafts with a plastic or rubber mallet. Tap on the shafts (**Figure 36**) until they seat completely in the cover receptacles.
7. Spin each transmission shaft and make sure it rotates freely. If it binds or does not spin at all, correct the problem at this time.
8. Apply a light coat of multipurpose grease to each shift fork roller.
9. Install the *B* shift fork into the fifth gear groove (**Figure 37**).
10. Install the *A* shift fork into the sixth gear groove (**Figure 38**).
11. Move the shift forks away from the shift drum area.
12. Install the shim and the thrust washer (**Figure 39**) onto the lower end of the shift drum and install the shift drum. Ensure that the shim and thrust washer (A, **Figure 40**) are still in place after the shift drum is in place.
13. Move all three shift forks into mesh with the shift drum (B, **Figure 40**).
14. Install the intermediate shaft shift fork shaft (**Figure 41**). Push it down until it bottoms in the cover receptacle.
15. Install the output shaft shift fork shaft (**Figure 42**). Push it down until it bottoms in the cover receptacle.
16. Install the selector shaft assembly as follows:

a. If removed, install the washer (**Figure 43**) on the bottom of the selector shaft assembly.
b. Compress the lower torsion spring (A, **Figure 44**) with channel lock pliers.
c. Hold the washer in place by hand (B, **Figure 44**) and move the shaft partway into the cover.
d. Pull the guide plate back to clear the shift drum (**Figure 45**).
e. Move the outer finger of the torsion spring in and down against the inner surface of the cover (A, **Figure 46**) and release the pliers.
f. Ensure the washer (B, **Figure 46**) is still in place, then move the shaft assembly into place in the cover receptacle (C). Push it down until it bottoms.
g. Ensure that the upper torsion spring is still properly engaged with the selector shaft post (**Figure 47**). This alignment is necessary for proper gearshift operation.
h. Move the guide plate back and forth (**Figure 48**) to make sure it moves freely.
i. To correctly align the selector shaft with the post in the transmission housing, insert a punch between the fingers of the upper torsion spring (A, **Figure 49**) into the cover receptacle (B). Remove the punch.

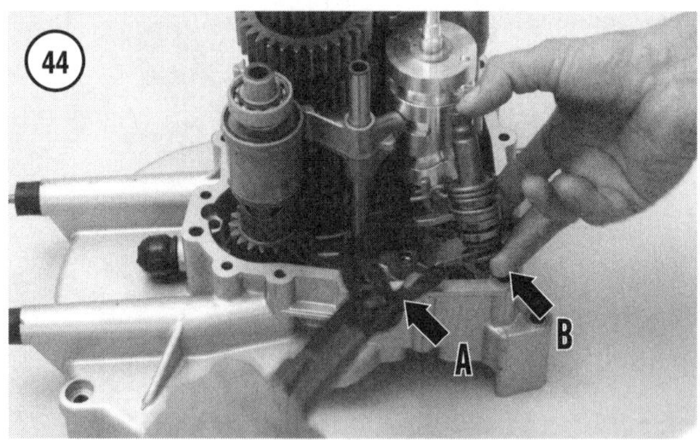

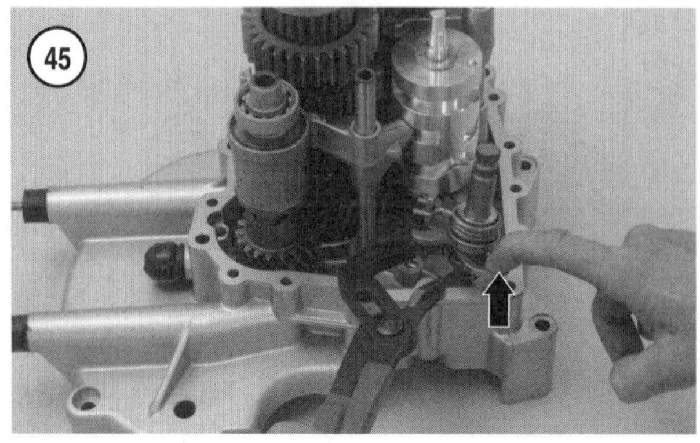

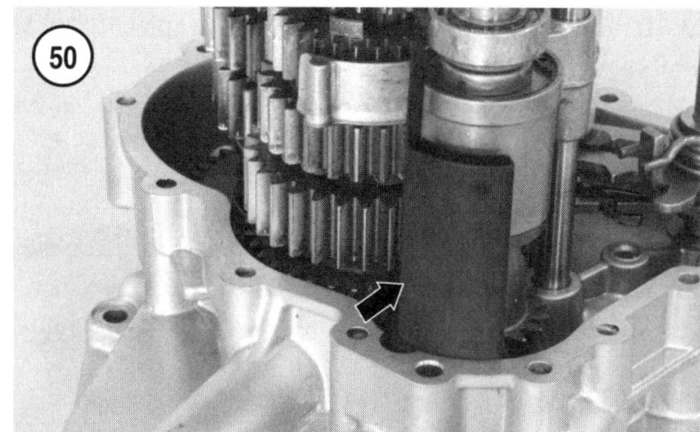

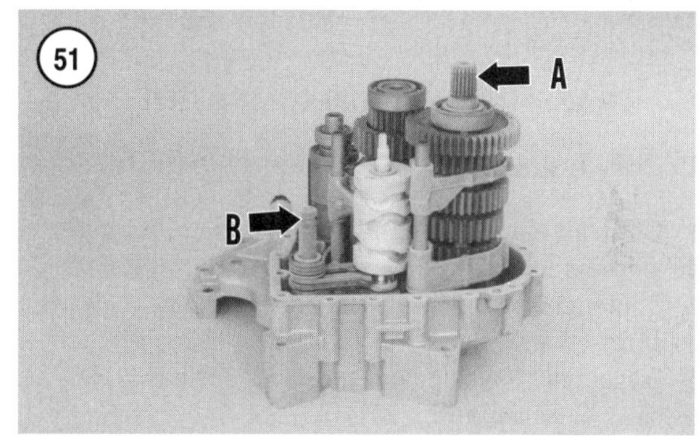

17. Install the breather tube (**Figure 50**) and push it down until it bottoms.

18. Lay the transmission assembly partway down to the normal horizontal position on the workbench.

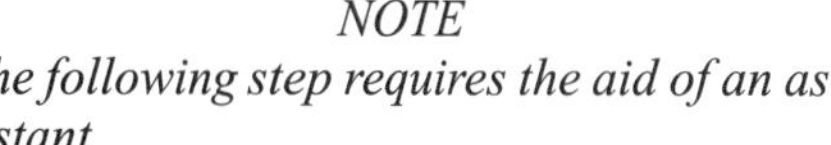

NOTE

The following step requires the aid of an assistant.

19. Have an assistant spin the transmission input shaft while shifting through all gears using the shift lever. Make sure the transmission can be shifted into each gear at this time.

20. Remove the shift lever from the selector shaft.

21. Wrap the splines on the output shaft (A, **Figure 51**) and the selector shaft (B) with two layers of clear smooth adhesive tape. Do not use masking tape or duct tape as it may scratch the housing seals during installation.

22. Install the transmission housing onto the transmission cover as described in this chapter.

CAUTION

Step 23 must be performed to avoid bare metal parts and bearings from rusting.

23. If the transmission gear assemblies were placed into a freezer prior to installation there will be moisture on the gears and bearings after they have returned to room temperature. Fill the transmission housing with the recommended type of transmission oil. Repeatedly turn the transmission case over from side-to-side and end-to-end to coat the gear assemblies with fresh oil to rinse away the trapped moisture. Drain this oil and dispose of it correctly.
24. Install the transmission case as described in this chapter.
25. Refill the transmission with the recommended oil. Drive the motorcycle several miles until the transmission is at normal operating temperature. Once again, drain the transmission oil and refill as described in Chapter Three.

TRANSMISION HOUSING AND COVER

Housing Inspection

1. Clean all old gasket sealer from the mating surface of the housing with solvent and dry with compressed air.
2. Thoroughly clean the hosing in solvent and dry it with compressed air.
3. Inspect the housing (A, **Figure 52**) for any cracks or damage. Check around the ribs for any fractures.
4. Inspect the sealing surface (**Figure 53**) for gouges or damage.
5. Make sure the post (**Figure 54**) for the gearshift selector shaft is secure.
6. Inspect the small O-ring seal (**Figure 55**) for the gearshift selector shaft. Replace if necessary.
7. Inspect the seals (B, **Figure 52**) for hardness or leakage; replace if necessary as described later in this chapter.
8. After the surfaces are clean, clean them again with contact cleaner and a lint free cloth to remove any traces of solvent.

Cover Inspection

1. Clean all old gasket sealer from the mating surface of the cover with solvent and dry with compressed air.
2. Thoroughly clean the cover in solvent and dry it with compressed air.
3. Inspect the cover (**Figure 56**) for any cracks or damage. Check around the ribs for any fractures.
4. Inspect the sealing surface (**Figure 57**) for gouges or damage.
5. Remove the one-way pressure relief valve (**Figure 58**) from the cover. Gently move back the outer cover (A, **Figure 59**) and inspect the valve (B). Clean out with solvent if necessary. Push the valve back into the cover and make sure it seats correctly.

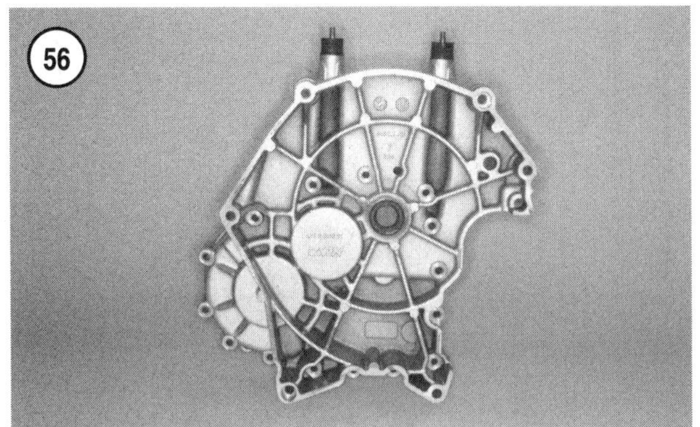

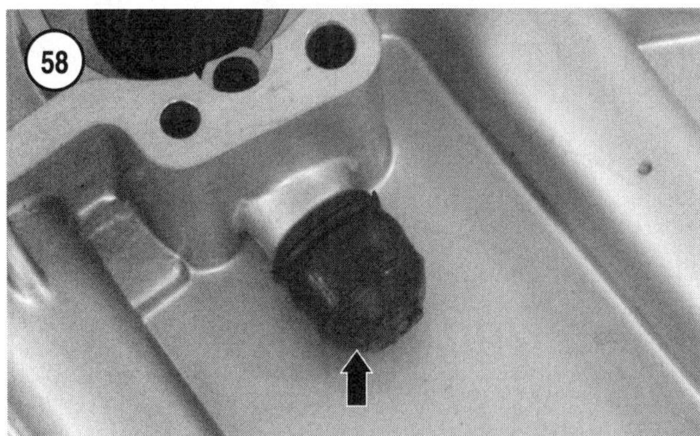

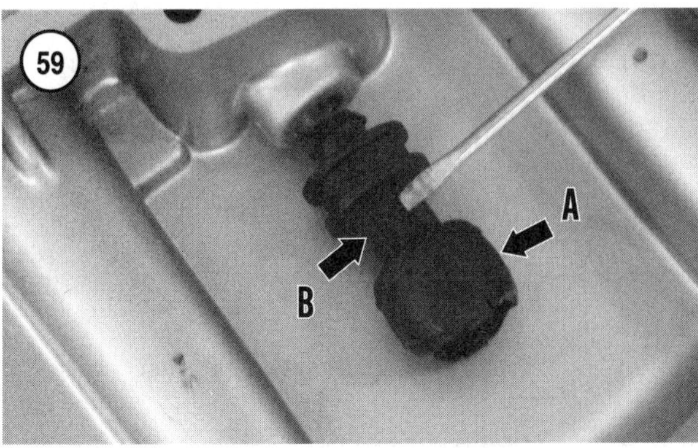

6. After the surfaces are clean, clean them again with contact cleaner and a lint free cloth to remove any traces of solvent.

TRANSMISSION SHAFTS

Throughout the following procedure, reference is made to the front and rear of the shaft and front and rear bearings. The *rear* of the shaft is the end that is installed in the transmission housing. The *front* of the shaft is the end facing toward the housing cover.

Preliminary Inspection

After the transmission shafts are removed from the transmission housing, clean and inspect the shafts prior to disassembling them. Place the assembled shaft into a large can or plastic bucket and thoroughly clean with a petroleum-based solvent such as kerosene and a stiff brush. Dry with compressed air or let it sit on rags to drip dry. Repeat for all shaft assemblies.

1. Visually inspect the components of the assemblies for excessive wear. Check the gear teeth for chips, burrs or pitting, Clean up damage with an oilstone. Replace any components with damage that cannot be cleaned up.

NOTE
Replace defective gears and their mating gear on the other shaft as well, even though it may not show as much wear or damage.

2. Carefully check the engagement dogs. If any are chipped, worn, rounded or missing, the affected gear must be replaced.
3. Rotate the transmission bearings by hand. Check for roughness, noise and radial play. Replace any bearing that is suspect.
4. If the transmission shafts are satisfactory and are not going to be disassembled, apply clean gear oil to all components and reinstall them in the transmission housing as described in this chapter.

NOTE
If disassembling a used, high mileage transmission for the first time, pay particular attention to any additional shims not shown in the illustrations or photographs. To compensate for wear, additional shims may have been installed during the previous repair. If the transmission is being reassembled with the old parts, install these shims in their original locations since the shims have de-

veloped a wear pattern. If new parts are being used, discard the additional shims.

Transmission Service Notes

1. Prior to disassembling the input and/or the output shaft, measure the overall length of each shaft assembly from bearing-to-bearing and record this dimension. The shafts and bearings must be reassembled to the exact same overall length, or a little less, in order to fit into the transmission case. If the shaft assemblies are too long they will not allow the cover to completely close down on the housing as required resulting in a gap.
2. Parts that have two different sides, such as gears, snap rings and shift forks, can be installed backward. To maintain the correct alignment and position of the parts during disassembly, store each part in order and in a divided container (**Figure 60**).
3. The snap rings are a tight fit on the transmission shafts and will bend and twist during removal. Install *new* snap rings during transmission assembly.
4. To avoid bending and twisting the new snap rings during installation, use the following installation technique:
   a. Open the new snap ring with a pair of snap ring pliers while holding the back of the snap ring with a pair of pliers (**Figure 61**).
   b. Then slide the snap ring down the shaft and seat it into its correct transmission groove. Check the snap ring to make sure it seats in its groove completely.
5. When installing snap rings, align the snap ring opening with the spline groove and a spline as shown in **Figure 62**.
6. Snap rings and flat washers have one sharp edge and one rounded edge (**Figure 63**). Install the snap rings with the sharp edge facing away from the gear producing the thrust.
7. A universal bearing puller is required for the disassembly of both the input and intermediate shaft assemblies. The puller used in the following procedures is the Kawasaki Steering Stem Bearing Puller tool (part No. 57001-135). A similar special tool is also available from BMW (part No. 00-7-500).

Input Shaft

Disassembly

Refer to **Figure 64**.

1. Remove the input shaft as described in this chapter.
2. Measure the overall length of the input shaft from bearing-to-bearing (**Figure 65**). Record this measurement since the shaft and bearings must be reassembled to the *exact same overall length*, or a little less, in order to fit

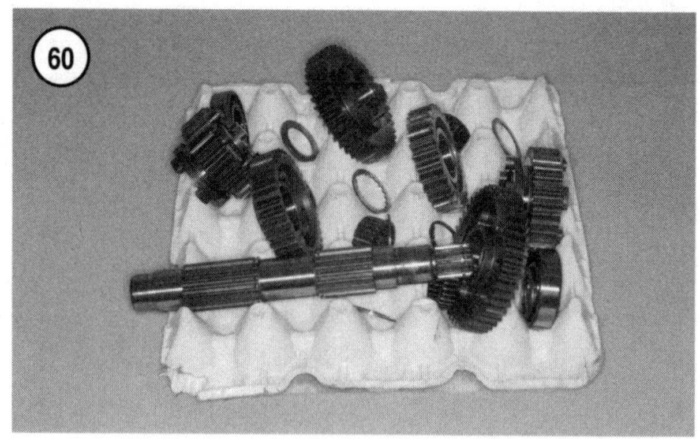

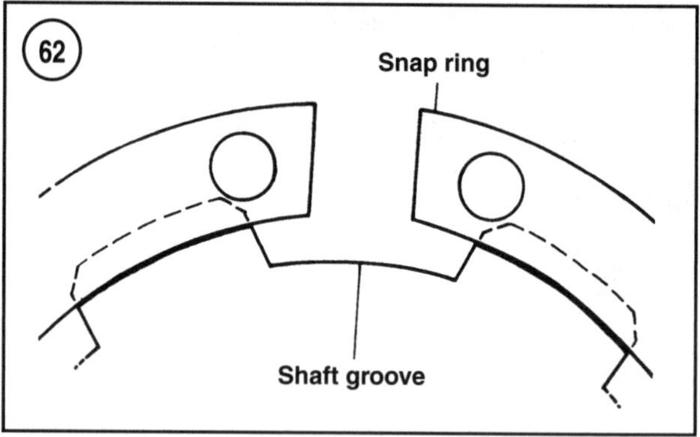

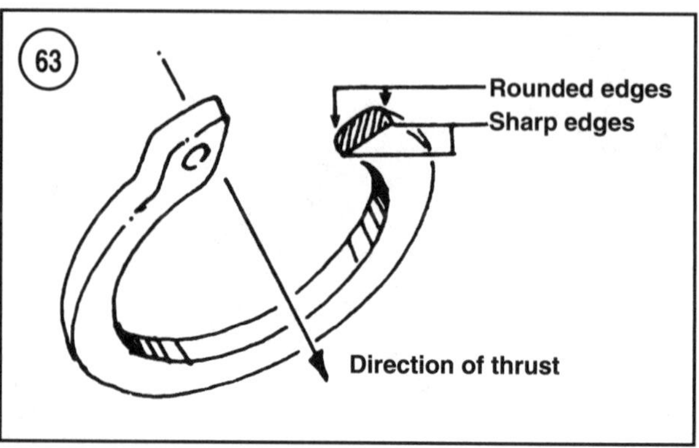

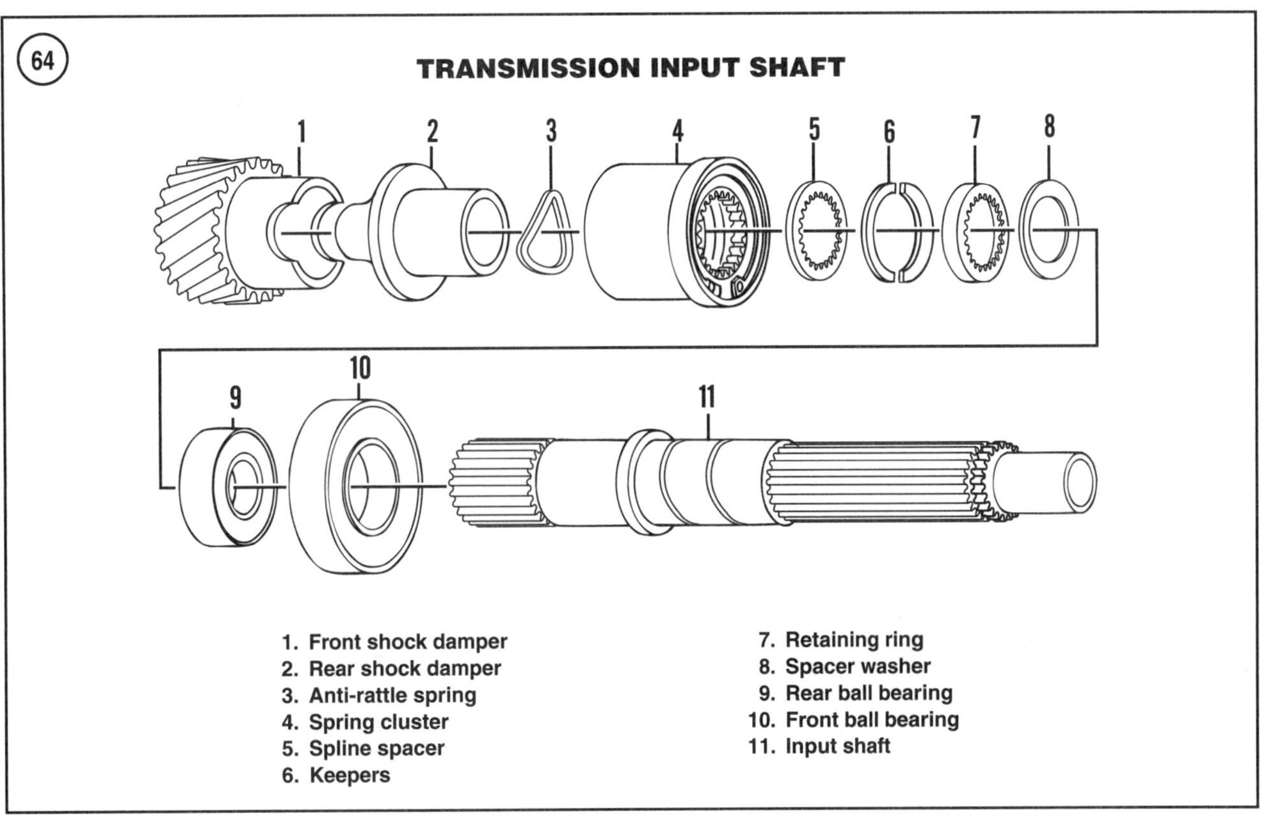

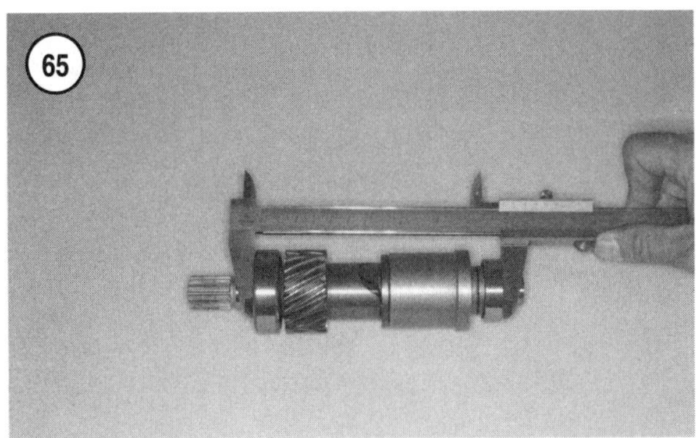

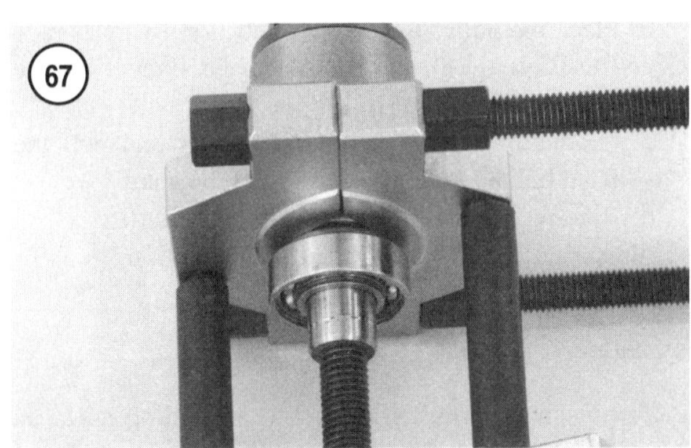

into the transmission case. If the shaft assemblies are too long the transmission case cannot be assembled correctly.

3. To remove the rear ball bearing, perform the following:

   a. Attach a bearing puller to the input shaft as shown in **Figure 66**.
   b. Place the puller fingers against the spacer washer (**Figure 67**).
   c. Gradually tighten the bearing puller and pull the rear ball bearing and spacer washer off the rear of the shaft.

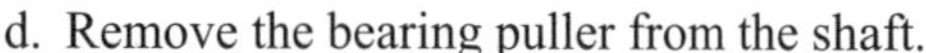

d. Remove the bearing puller from the shaft.

4. Slide the spacer washer (**Figure 68**) and the retaining ring off the shaft.

5. Remove the two keepers (**Figure 69**) from the shaft.

6. Slide the spline spacer (**Figure 70**) off the shaft.

7. Slide the spring cluster (A, **Figure 71**) off the shaft.

8. Slide the anti-rattle spring (**Figure 72**) off the shaft.

9. Slide the rear shock damper (A, **Figure 73**) and the front shock damper (B) off the shaft.

10. If necessary to remove the front ball bearing, perform the following:

   a. Attach a bearing puller to the input shaft as shown in **Figure 74**.

   b. Place the puller fingers on the bearing's inner race (A, **Figure 75**). Do not place the fingers on the shaft's raised boss (B, **Figure 75**).

   c. Gradually tighten the bearing puller and pull the front ball bearing off the front of the shaft.

   d. Remove the bearing puller from the shaft.

11. Inspect all parts as described in this section.

Assembly

1. Apply clean transmission oil to all sliding surfaces prior to installing any parts.

2. To install the front bearing, perform the following:

   a. Position the bearing on the front end of the input shaft with the manufacturer's marks facing out.

   b. Install the input shaft assembly into the hydraulic press and set the rear of the shaft on the press plates. Have an assistant hold the shaft in place.

CAUTION

*Do **not** press the bearing into place by exerting pressure on the bearing outer race as the bearing will be damaged.*

   c. Place a suitable size driver on the inner race of the front bearing. The driver must fit the inner race only

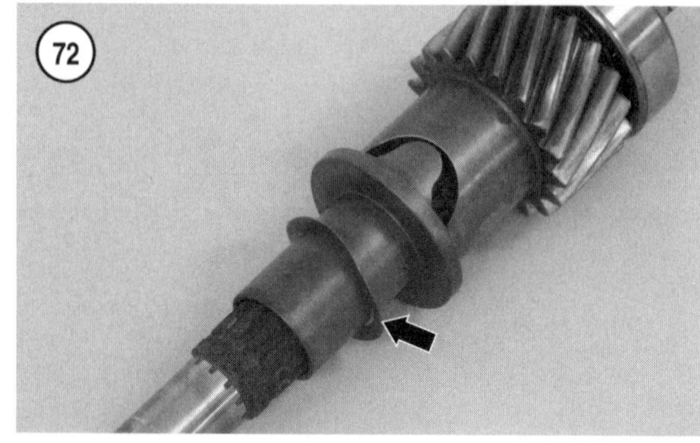

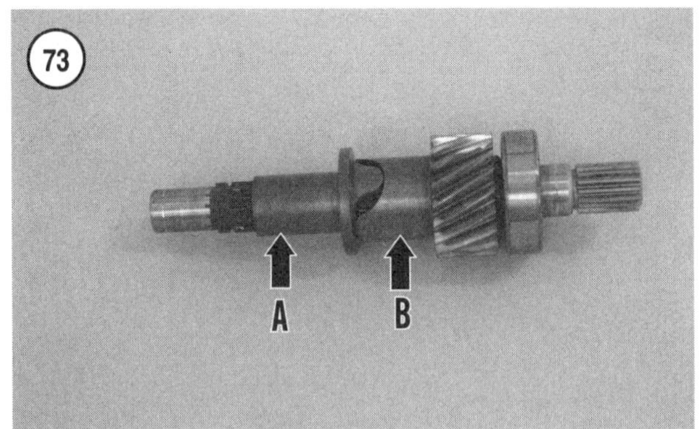

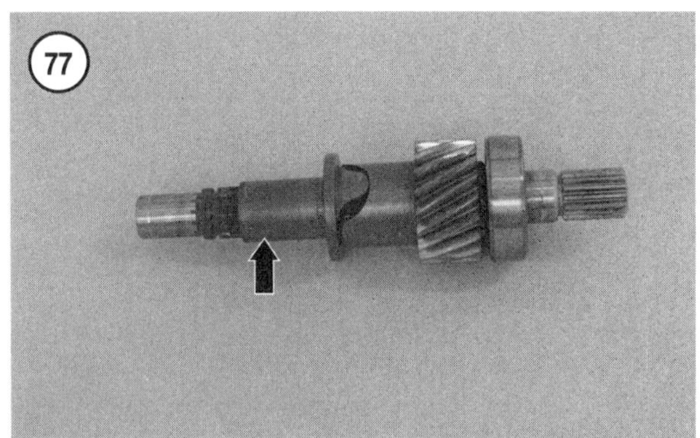

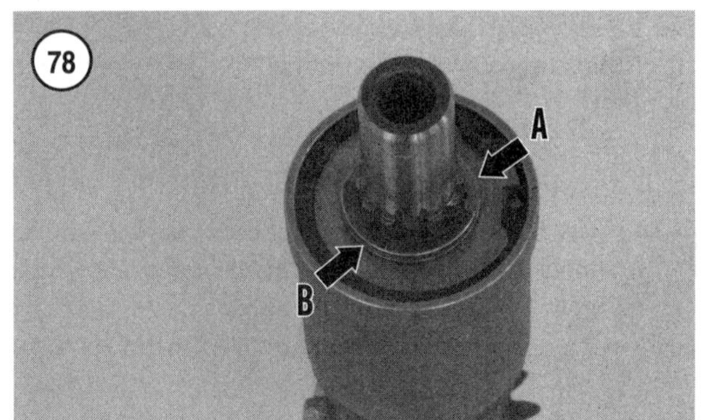

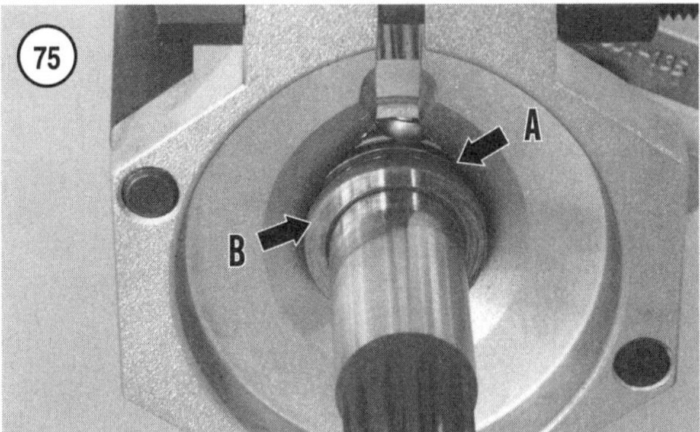

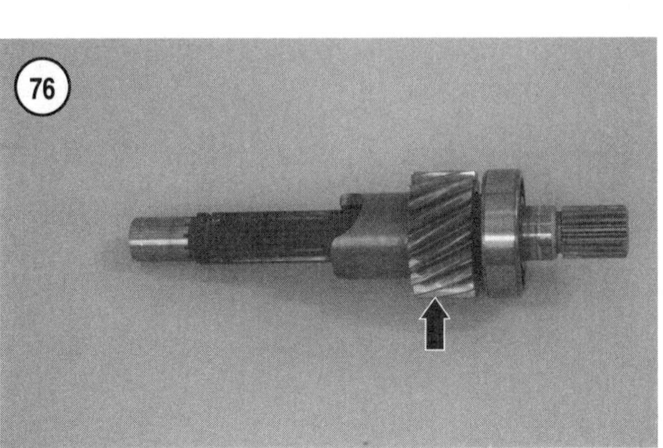

and must also have a large enough inner diameter to clear the splines on the input shaft. The shaft splines will be damaged if the inner surface of the driver touches the shaft splines.

d. Slowly press the front bearing onto the shaft. Press it on until it bottoms.

e. Remove the driver and the input shaft from the hydraulic press.

f. Rotate the bearing by hand to make sure it rotates freely and was not damaged during installation.

3. Slide the front shock damper (**Figure 76**) and the rear shock damper (**Figure 77**) onto the shaft. Push them on until they bottom.

4. Slide the anti-rattle spring (**Figure 72**) onto the shaft.

5. Position the spring cluster with the open end (B, **Figure 71**) going on last and slide the spring cluster (A) onto the shaft.

6. Slide the spline spacer (**Figure 70**) onto the shaft.

7. Turn the input shaft up on the front end.

8. Push the spline spacer down (A, **Figure 78**) and install one of the keepers (B). Install the remaining keeper and make sure they are indexed into the shaft's groove (**Figure 69**).

9. Install the retaining ring (**Figure 79**) onto the shaft and lock both keepers in place (**Figure 80**).

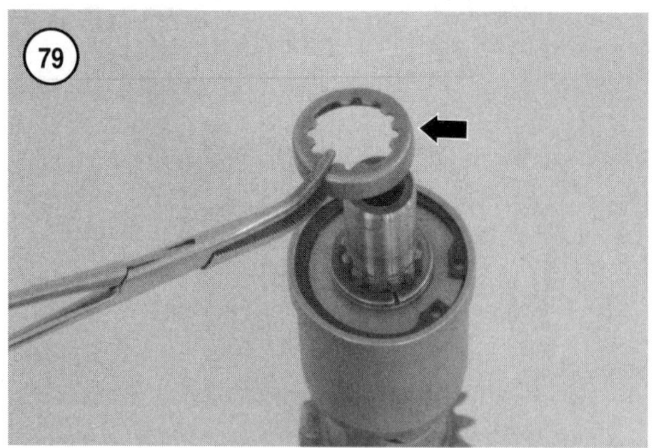
79

80

10. At this time check the end float of the spring cluster as follows:

a. Push down on the retaining ring to ensure the keepers are indexed into the shaft's groove.
b. Insert a flat feeler gauge between the rear shock damper surface and the spring cluster as shown in **Figure 81**.
c. The specified end float is 0.4-0.6 mm (0.0157-0.0236 in.).
d. If the end float is out of specification, install a spline spacer of a different thickness.

11. Slide the spacer washer (**Figure 82**) onto the shaft against the retaining ring.

12. To install the rear ball bearing, perform the following:

a. Apply a light coat of oil to the inner surface of the bearing's inner race and onto the input shaft.
b. Position the rear bearing (**Figure 83**) with the manufacturer's marks facing out and install the bearing onto the end of the shaft.
c. Place the transmission shaft assembly on the plate of the hydraulic press (A, **Figure 84**).
d. Place a suitable size driver (B, **Figure 84**) onto the ball bearing (C). The driver must fit the inner race only and must have a large enough inner diameter to clear the splines on the output shaft. The shaft splines will be damaged if the inner surface of the driver touches the shaft splines.
e. Hold onto the shaft and *slowly* press the ball bearing onto the shaft. Frequently stop and measure the overall length of the input shaft. If pressed on too far, the ball bearing must be pressed part way back off and then pressed back on again to obtain the correct overall length.
f. Remove the output shaft and driver from the hydraulic press.

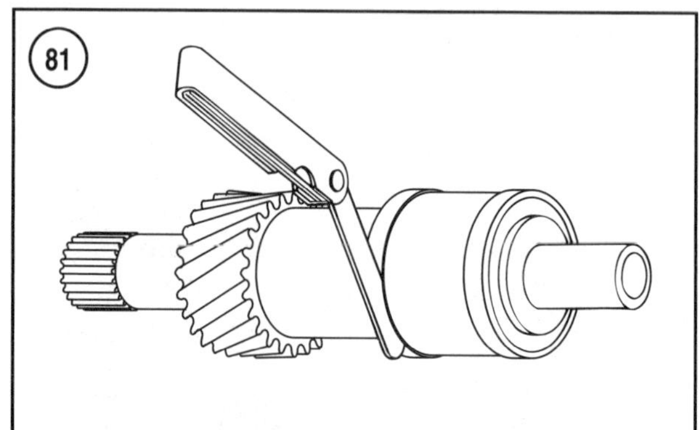
81

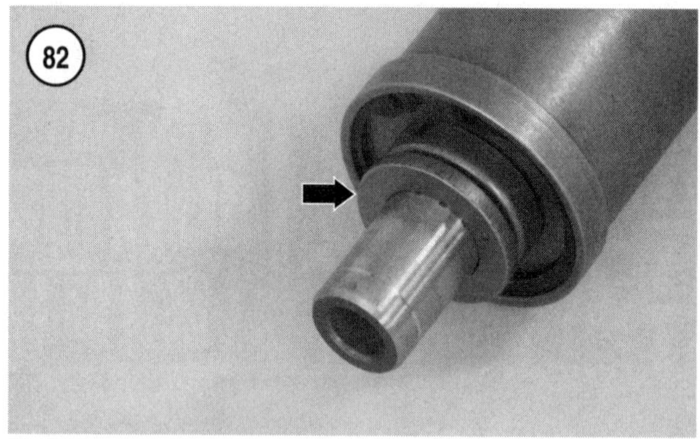
82

83

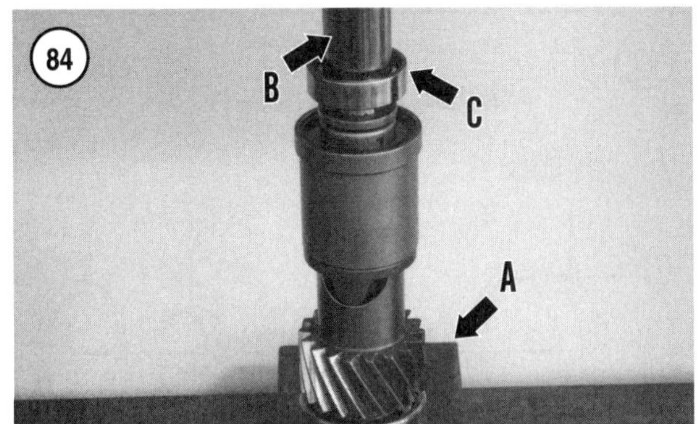

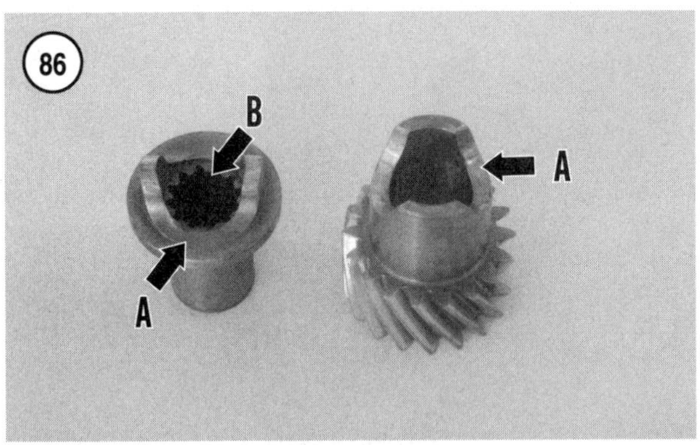

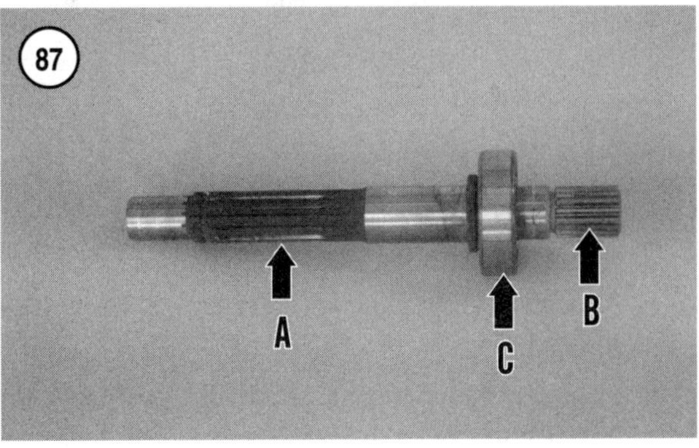

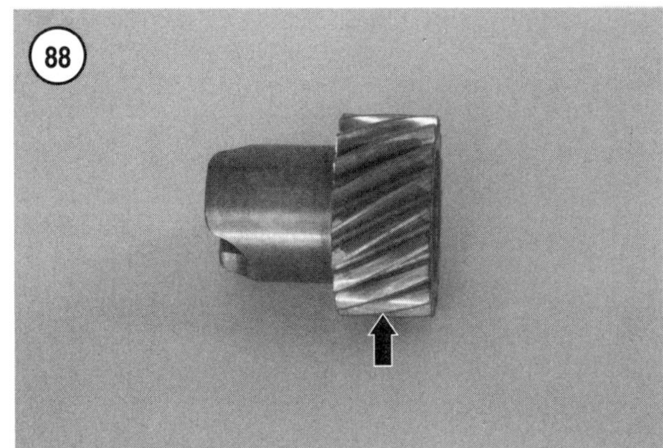

g. After pressing the bearing into place, rotate the bearing by hand. Check for roughness, noise and radial play.

13. Re-measure the overall length of the input shaft from bearing-to-bearing (**Figure 65**). Check against the dimension recorded in Step 2 of *Disassembly*. The overall length must exactly the same, or a little less, in order to fit into the transmission case. If the shaft assemblies are too long the transmission case cannot be assembled correctly.

14. Refer to **Figure 85** for the correct location of all parts.

15. Install the input shaft as described in this chapter.

8

Inspection

1. Inspect the ramps of both the front and rear shock dampers (A, **Figure 86**). Check for excessive wear, burrs, pitting or chipped areas. Replace if necessary.
2. Inspect the inner splines (B, **Figure 86**) of the rear shock damper for wear or damage. Replace if necessary.
3. Inspect the shaft splines for the rear shock damper (A, **Figure 87**) and the clutch friction disc (B) for wear or damage. If worn or damaged, replace the shaft.
4. Make sure both shock dampers slide smoothly on the input shaft splines and sliding surfaces.
5. Check the front shock damper gear (**Figure 88**) for shipped or missing teeth. If damaged, inspect the mating teeth on the intermediate shaft for damage.
6. Check the spacer washer, retaining ring, keepers and spline spacer (**Figure 89**) for wear or damage.
7. Inspect the spring cluster (**Figure 90**) as follows:
   a. Press down on the spline washer (A, **Figure 91**) and check for a broken or worn spring (**Figure 92**).
   b. Make sure the snap ring (B, **Figure 91**) is secure within the housing.

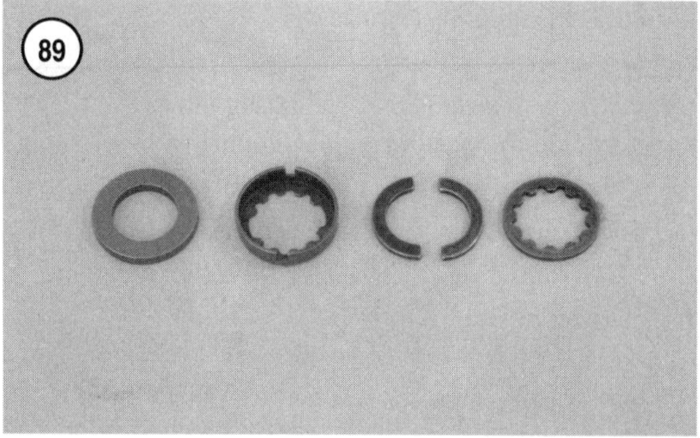

89

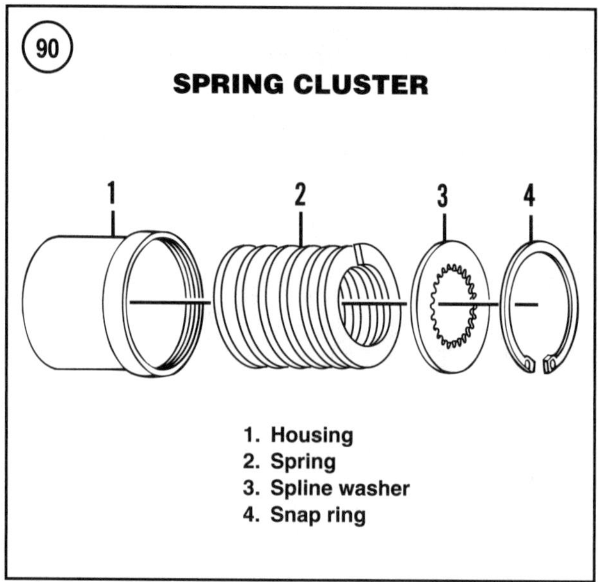

90

c. Inspect the spline washer (C, **Figure 91**) for damage.
d. If necessary, compress the spring, remove the snap ring and remove the spline washer and spring. Install the snap ring and make sure it seats correctly.

8. Rotate the input shaft bearings outer race by hand, Refer to C, **Figure 87** and **Figure 93**. Check for roughness, noise and radial play. Replace as necessary.

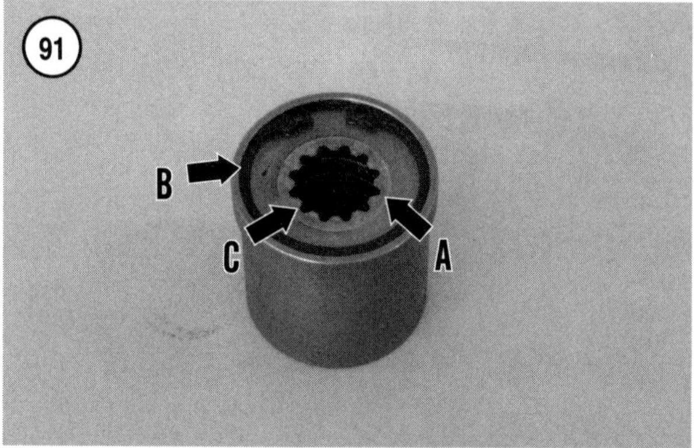

91

92

Intermediate Shaft Inspection and Bearing Replacement

The intermediate shaft has no removable parts except for the ball bearings. If any portion of the shaft is defective, with the exception of the ball bearings, replace the entire shaft assembly.

NOTE
In the following procedure, the ball bearing at each end of the shaft can be removed either with a gear puller or with a hydraulic press and a bearing plate.

1. Remove the intermediate shaft as described in this chapter.
2. Inspect the ball bearing on each end of the shaft (**Figure 94**). Rotate the bearings by hand. Check for roughness, noise and radial play.
3. Inspect the teeth on all six gears for chipped or missing teeth. If any are damaged, inspect the mating gears on the output shaft.
4. Measure the overall length of the intermediate shaft from bearing-to-bearing (**Figure 95**). Record this measurement since the bearings must be reinstalled to the exact same overall length, or a little less, in order to fit into the transmission case. If the shaft assemblies are too long the transmission housing will not fit flush onto the transmission case.
5. To remove the ball bearings, perform the following:

a. Attach a bearing puller to the intermediate shaft as shown in **Figure 96**.
b. Place the puller fingers against the bearing outer race (**Figure 97**).

93

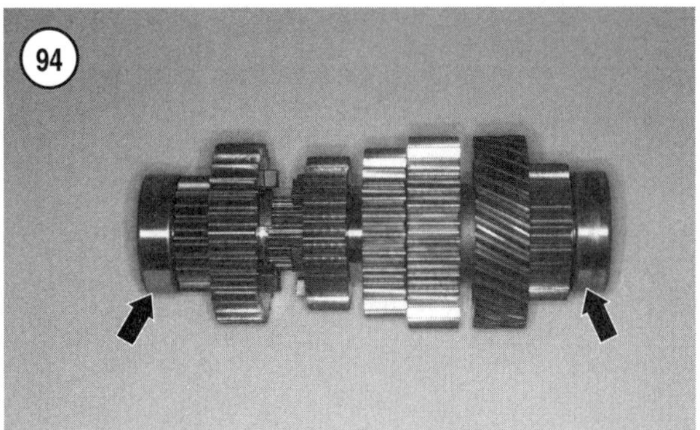
94

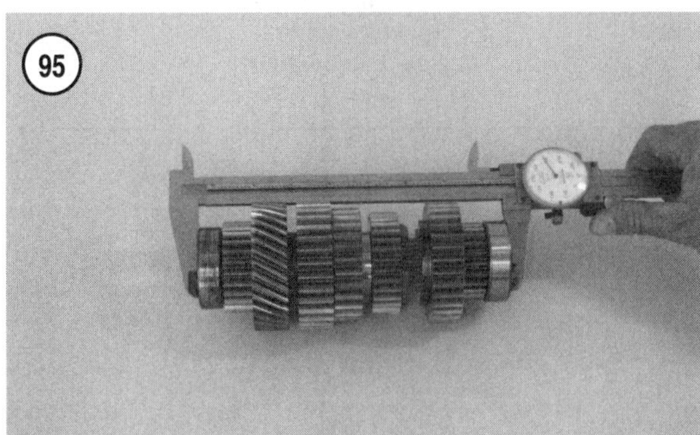
95

96

97

c. Gradually tighten the bearing puller and pull the ball bearing off the shaft.

d. Remove the bearing puller from the shaft.

e. If necessary, repeat for the bearing on the other end of the shaft.

6. To install the rear ball bearing, perform the following:

a. Apply a light coat of oil to the inner surface of the bearing's inner race and onto the intermediate shaft.

b. Position the bearing with the manufacturer's marks facing out and install the rear ball bearing onto the end of the shaft.

c. Place the transmission shaft assembly on the plate of the hydraulic press.

d. Place a suitable size driver onto the ball bearing. The driver must fit the inner race only.

e. Hold onto the shaft and *slowly* press the ball bearing onto the shaft. Frequently stop and measure the overall length of the intermediate shaft. If pressed on too far, the ball bearing must be pressed part way back off and then pressed back on again to obtain the correct overall length.

f. Remove the output shaft and driver from the hydraulic press.

g. After pressing the bearing, rotate the bearing by hand. Check for roughness, noise and radial play.

h. If necessary, repeat for the bearing on the other end of the shaft.

7. Repeat Step 4.

Output Shaft

Disassembly

Refer to **Figure 98**.

NOTE

*To maintain the correct alignment and position of the parts during disassembly, store each part in order and in a divided container (**Figure 99**).*

98

TRANSMISSION OUTPUT SHAFT

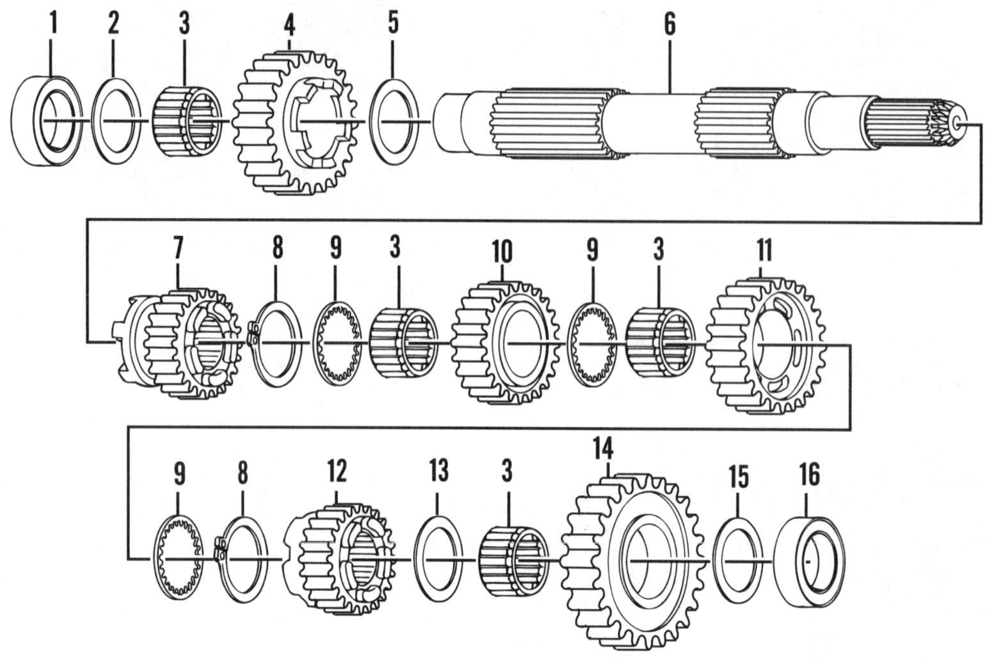

1. Front ball bearing
2. Shim
3. Split needle bearing
4. Second gear
5. Thrust washer
6. Output shaft
7. Sixth gear (or sliding gear)
8. Snap ring
9. Spline washer
10. Fourth gear
11. Third gear
12. Fifth gear
13. Spacer washer
14. First gear
15. Spacer washer
16. Rear ball bearing

1. Remove the output shaft as described in this chapter.
2. Measure the overall length of the output shaft from bearing-to-bearing (**Figure 100**). Record this measurement since the shaft and bearings must be reassembled to the exact same overall length, or a little less, in order to fit into the transmission case. If the shaft assemblies are too long the transmission case cannot be assembled correctly.
3. To remove the front bearing, perform the following:
   a. Attach a bearing puller to the output shaft as shown in **Figure 101**.
   b. Place the puller fingers on the ledge behind the second gear (**Figure 102**).
   c. Gradually tighten the bearing puller and pull the front ball bearing, the shim and the second gear off the front of the shaft.
   d. Remove the bearing puller from the shaft.
4. Remove the split needle bearing and thrust washer.
5. Slide off the sixth gear (or sliding gear).
6. Remove the snap ring and slide off the spline washer.

7. Slide off the fourth gear, then remove the split needle bearing.
8. Slide off the spline washer and the third gear.
9. Remove the split needle bearing and slide off the spline washer.
10. Remove the snap ring, then slide off the fifth gear.

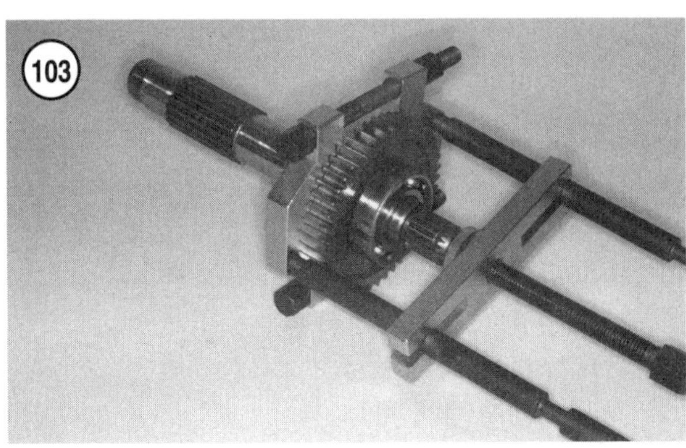

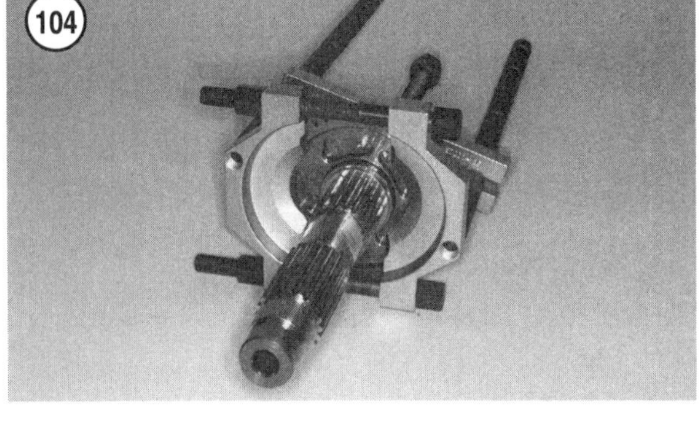

11. To remove the rear bearing, perform the following:
   a. Attach a bearing puller to the output shaft as shown in **Figure 103**.
   b. Place the puller fingers on the ledge behind the first gear (**Figure 104**).
   c. Gradually tighten the bearing puller and pull the rear ball bearing, the spacer washer and the first gear off the front of the shaft.
   d. Remove the bearing puller from the shaft.

12. Remove the split needle bearing and the spacer washer.

Assembly

CAUTION

Replace the snap ring every time the transmission is disassembled to ensure proper gear alignment. Install the snap ring onto the shaft with the rounded side going on first. Do not expand a snap ring more than necessary to slide it over the shaft.

CAUTION

Install the split roller bearings into the shaft grooves and bring both ends together to close it. Make sure they seat properly in the shaft grooves. If necessary, install new bearings.

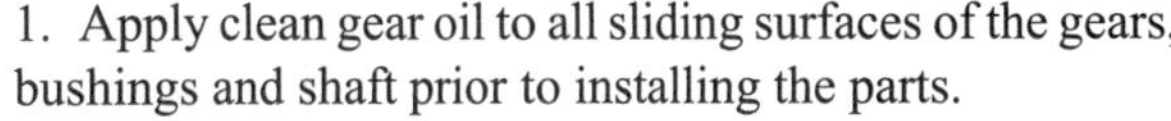

1. Apply clean gear oil to all sliding surfaces of the gears, bushings and shaft prior to installing the parts.
2. Slide on the spacer washer (A, **Figure 105**), then install the split needle bearing (B).
3. Position the first gear with the flush side going on last and slide on the first gear (A, **Figure 106**). Slide on the spacer washer (B, **Figure 106**).

CAUTION

*When installing the ball bearing, apply pressure only on the **inner race**. If pressure*

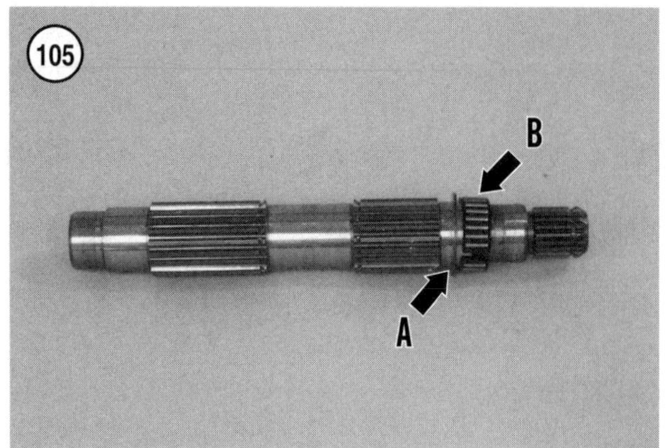

is applied to the outer race the bearing will be damaged.

4. To install the rear ball bearing (next to the first gear), perform the following:
   a. Apply transmission oil to the inner surface of the bearing's inner race and to the outer surface of the transmission shaft.
   b. Position the bearing with the manufacturer's marks facing out.
   c. Install the ball bearing onto the end of the shaft (**Figure 107**).
   d. Place the transmission shaft assembly on the plate of the hydraulic press (A, **Figure 108**).
   e. Place a suitable size driver (B, **Figure 108**) onto the ball bearing. The driver must fit the inner race only and must have a large enough inner diameter to clear the splines on the output shaft. The shaft splines will be damaged if the inner surface of the driver touches the shaft splines.
   f. Hold onto the shaft and slowly press the ball bearing (C, **Figure 108**) onto the shaft. Press it on until it bottoms on the shaft's flange.

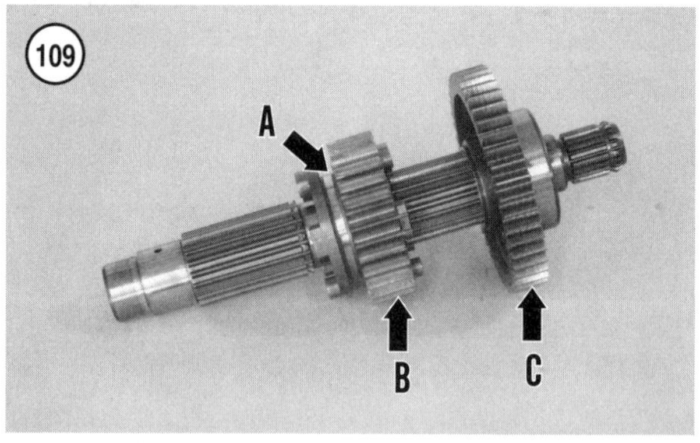

g. Remove the output shaft and driver from the hydraulic press.

h. After pressing the bearing into place, rotate the bearing by hand. Check for roughness, noise and radial play.

5. Position the fifth gear with the shift fork groove side (A, **Figure 109**) going on last. Slide the fifth gear (B, **Figure 109**), then push it into the backside of the first gear (C).

6. Install the snap ring (**Figure 110**) and make sure it seats properly in the groove (**Figure 111**).

7. Slide on the spline washer (**Figure 112**). Push it up against the snap ring (**Figure 113**) and into mesh with the shaft splines.

8. Hold the spline washer against the snap ring and install the split roller bearing (**Figure 114**) into the shaft groove. Bring both ends together to close it.

9. Position the third gear with the shift dog receptacle side going on first. Slide the third gear (**Figure 115**) onto the split needle bearing.

10. Install the splined washer (**Figure 116**) and push it against the third gear.

11. Install the split roller bearing (**Figure 117**) onto the shaft groove. Bring both ends together to close it.

12. Position the fourth gear with the shift dog receptacle side going on last. Slide on the fourth gear (**Figure 118**) onto the split needle bearing.

13. Install the spline washer (**Figure 119**) and snap ring (**Figure 120**). Make sure the snap ring seats properly in the shaft groove (**Figure 121**).

14. Position the sixth gear, or sliding gear, with the shift fork groove (A, **Figure 122**) side going on last. Slide on the sixth gear (B, **Figure 122**).

15. Slide on the thrust washer (**Figure 123**), then install the split roller bearing (**Figure 124**) onto the end of the shaft. Bring both ends together to close it.

16. Position the second gear with the flush side going on last and install the second gear (**Figure 125**).

17. Install the shim (**Figure 126**) onto the end of the shaft and up against the second gear.

18. To install the front ball bearing (next to the second gear), perform the following:
    a. Apply transmission oil to the inner surface of the bearing's inner race and to the outer surface of the transmission shaft.
    b. Position the ball bearing with the manufacturer's marks facing out.
    c. Install the ball bearing onto the front end of the shaft.
    d. Place the transmission shaft assembly on the plate of the hydraulic press.
    e. Place a suitable size driver onto the ball bearing. The driver must fit the inner race only.
    f. Hold onto the shaft and slowly press the ball bearing onto the shaft. Press it on until it bottoms on the shaft's flange.
    g. Remove the output shaft and driver from the hydraulic press.

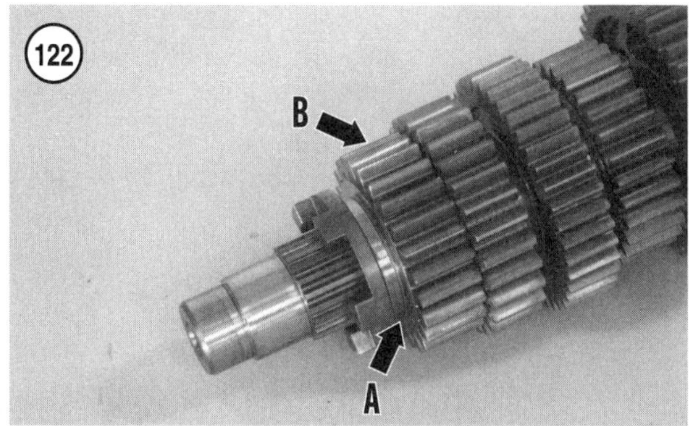

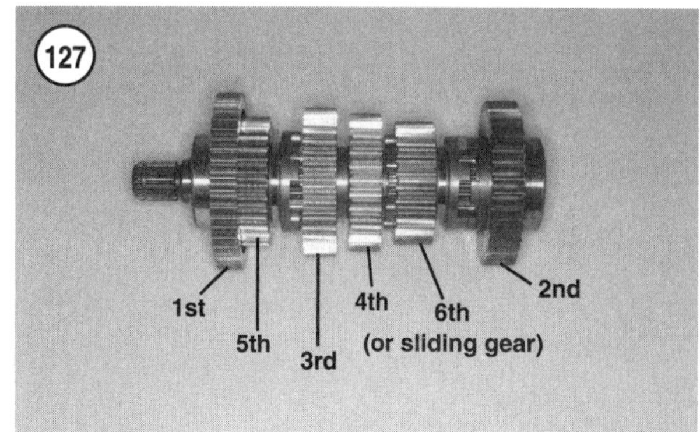

h. After pressing the bearing into place, rotate the bearing by hand. Check for roughness, noise and radial play.

19. Refer to **Figure 127** for placement of all gears. Make sure all snap rings seat correctly in the output shaft grooves.

20. Make sure each gear engages properly to the adjoining gear, where applicable.

21. After completing the transmission shaft assembly, measure the overall length of the shaft as shown in **Figure 100** and note the measurement. Refer to the measurement taken prior to disassembly as the shaft must be the exact same overall length. If the shaft assemblies are too long the transmission case cannot be assembled correctly.

22. After assembling the output shaft, mesh the output shaft and the intermediate shaft together in their correct position. Confirm that all gears meet correctly.

23. Install the output shaft as described in this chapter.

Inspection

1. Check each gear for excessive wear, burrs, pitting or chipped or missing teeth. Refer to **Figure 128** and **Figure 129**.

128

131

129

132

130

133

2. Make sure the engagement dogs (**Figure 130**) on the gears are in good condition.

3. Inspect the engagement dog receptacles (**Figure 131**) in each gear.

4. Check the inner splines (**Figure 132**) of the third and fourth gears for excessive wear or burrs.

5. Inspect the machined shift fork grooves (**Figure 133**) in the respective gears. Check for wear, gouges or other damage, replacing the gear if necessary.

6. Check the bearing surface (**Figure 134**) in the respective gears.

134

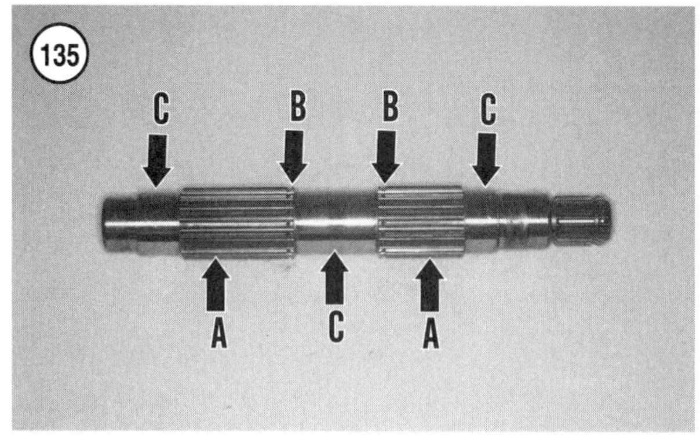

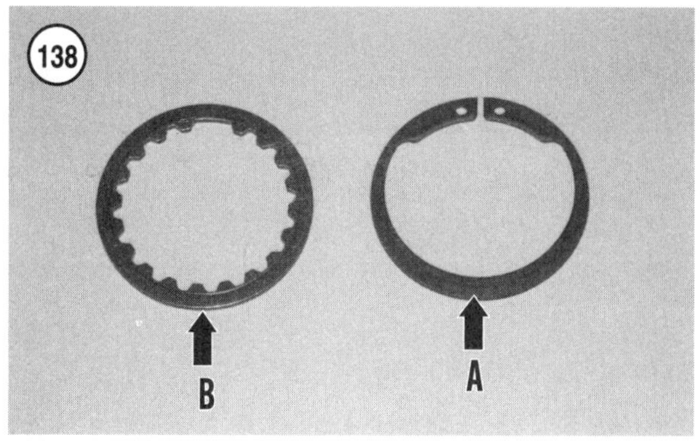

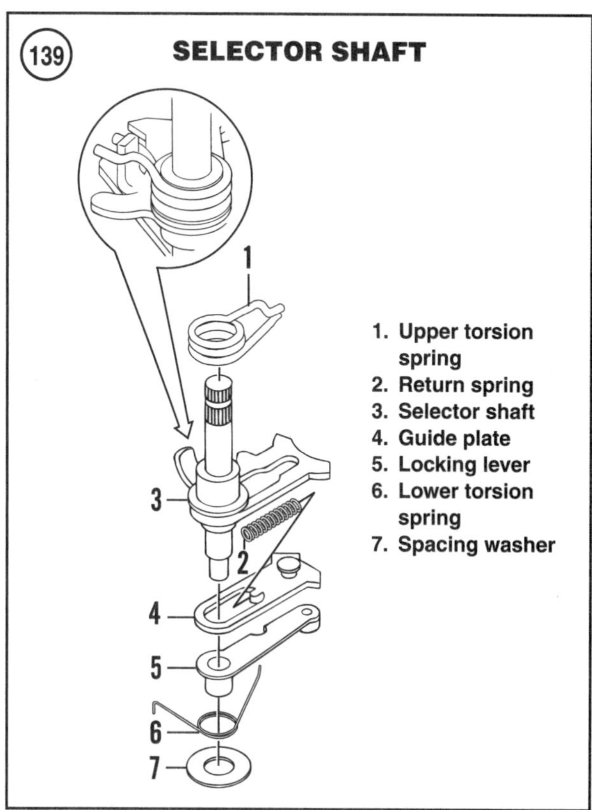

7. Make sure that all gears slide smoothly on the output shaft.

8. Inspect the splines (A, **Figure 135**) and snap ring grooves (B) on the output shaft. If any are damaged, the shaft must be replaced.

9. Inspect the shaft surface (C, **Figure 135**) where the split roller bearing rides. It must be free of burrs and damage.

10. Inspect the split needle bearing (**Figure 136**). Check the bearing cage for cracks at the corners of the needle slots and inspect the needles themselves for cracking. If any cracks are found, the split bearing must be replaced.

11. Inspect both ball bearings (**Figure 137**) and rotate by hand. Check for roughness, noise and radial play. Replace any bearing that is suspect.

12. Discard the snap rings (A, **Figure 138**) even it they appear to be in good condition.

13. Check the spline washers (B, **Figure 138**) for wear or damage, and replace as necessary.

GEARSHIFT MECHANISM

Internal Gearshift Selector Shaft Inspection

Refer to **Figure 139**.

8

Replacement parts are not available for the gearshift selector shaft. Some smaller components can be removed for cleaning purposes only.

1. Remove the internal gearshift selector shaft as described in this chapter.
2. If necessary, disassemble the selector shaft as follows:
   a. Remove the washer (A, **Figure 140**) and the lower torsion spring (B).
   b. Slide the locking lever (**Figure 141**) off the selector shaft.
   c. If necessary, remove the spring and slide the guide plate (**Figure 142**) off the selector shaft.
   d. Remove the upper torsion spring (**Figure 143**) from the selector shaft.
3. Clean the shaft assembly in solvent and dry with compressed air.
4. Inspect the gearshift shaft (A, **Figure 144**) for bending, wear or other damage.
5. Inspect the outer splines (B, **Figure 144**) on the shaft and the inner splines on the lever.
6. Inspect the guide plate return spring (**Figure 145**) for weakness.
7. Inspect the upper torsion spring (A, **Figure 146**) for weakness.
8. Inspect the lower torsion spring (A, **Figure 147**) for weakness.
9. Check the movement of the locking lever (**Figure 148**). It must move freely and the spring must return to it locked position.
10. Check the movement of the guide plate (**Figure 149**). It must move freely back and forth and return to the extended position.
11. Inspect the roller (B, **Figure 147**) on the locking lever. It must rotate freely.
12. If the selector shaft was disassembled, perform the following:

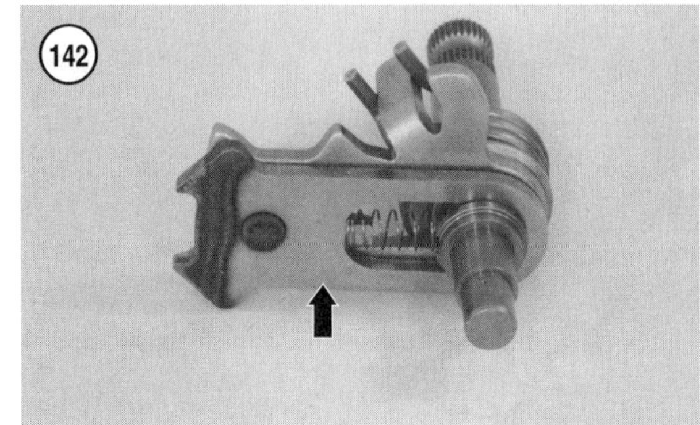

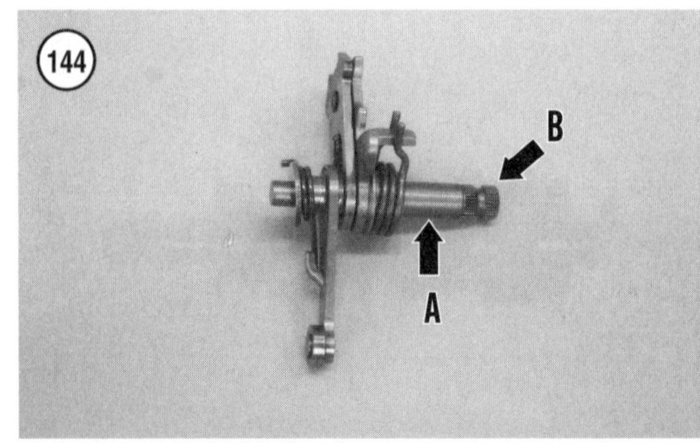

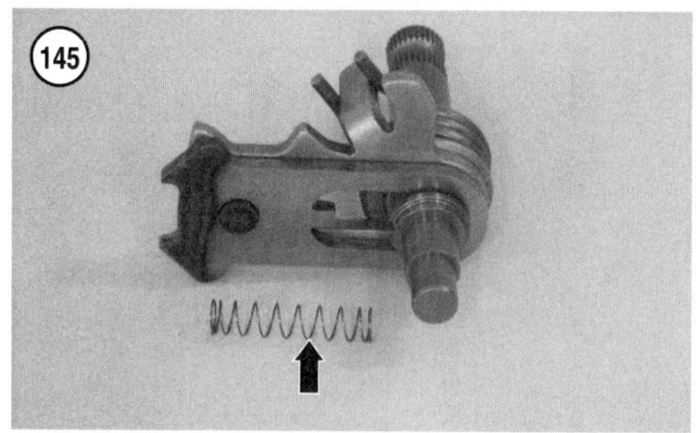

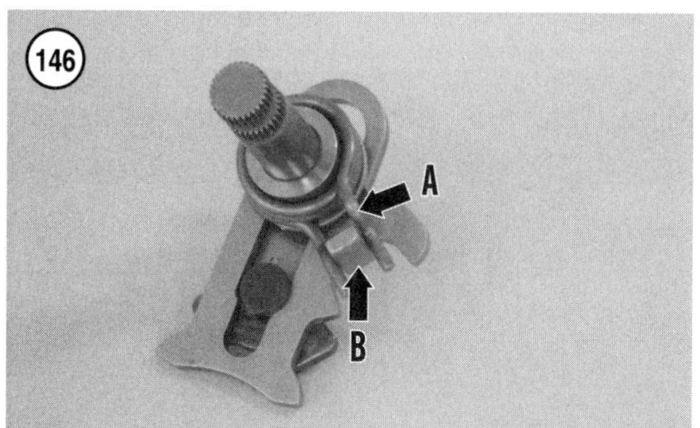

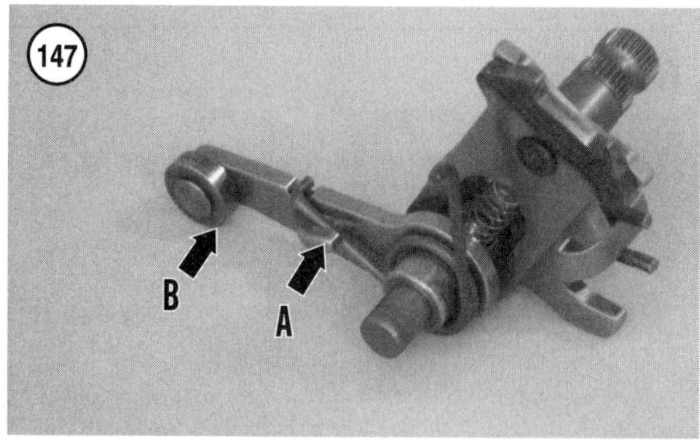

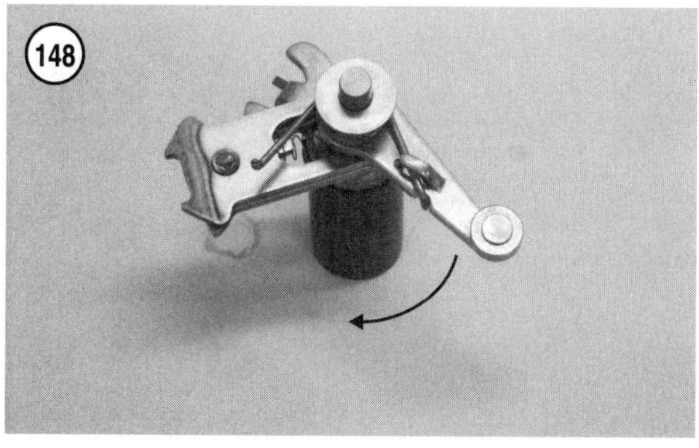

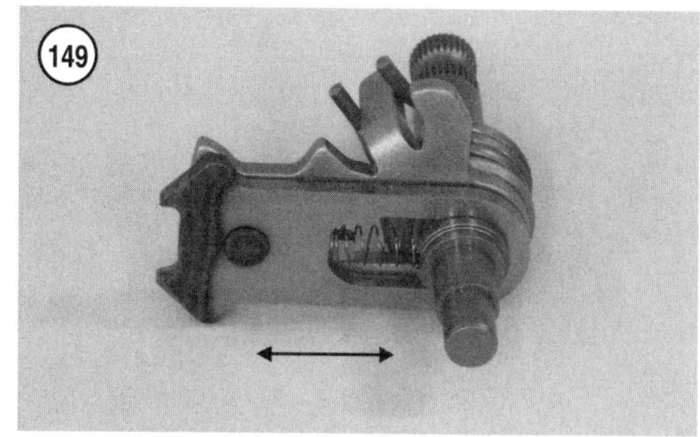

a. Install the upper torsion spring (**Figure 143**) onto the selector shaft and lock it into place on the selector shaft tab (B, **Figure 146**).

b. Install the guide plate and spring (**Figure 142**). Push the guide plate back and forth and make sure it moves freely.

c. Install the locking lever (**Figure 141**) onto the selector shaft.

d. Install the lower torsion spring (B, **Figure 140**) and index it into the groove and locating tab on the locking lever.

e. Install the washer (A, **Figure 140**) onto the end of the shaft.

8

Selector Shaft End Float Inspection

If the selector shaft and/or the transmission case are replaced, the correct amount of selector shaft end float must be maintained. If the clearance is less than specified the shaft will bind with the case. The specified clearance is 0.1-0.3 mm (0.0039-0.0118 in.).

The spacer washer located at the base of the selector shaft determines end float and is available in various thickness.

1. Disassemble the transmission case as described in this chapter.

2. Thoroughly clean the transmission housing and cover in solvent and dry with compressed air.

3. Measure the distance from the top surface of the transmission cover to the top surface of the bushing (**Figure 150**) as shown in **Figure 151**. This is dimension A.

4. Measure the distance from the top surface of the transmission housing to the top surface of the bushing (**Figure 152**) as shown in **Figure 153**. This is dimension B.

5. Measure the selector shaft from the shoulder to the back of the sleeve (**Figure 154**) as shown in **Figure 155**. This is dimension C.

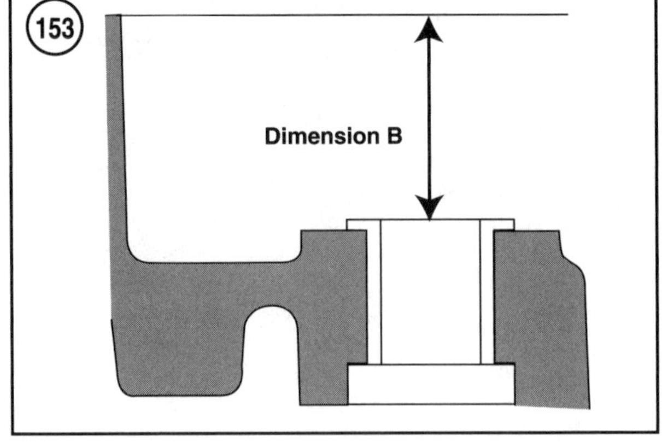

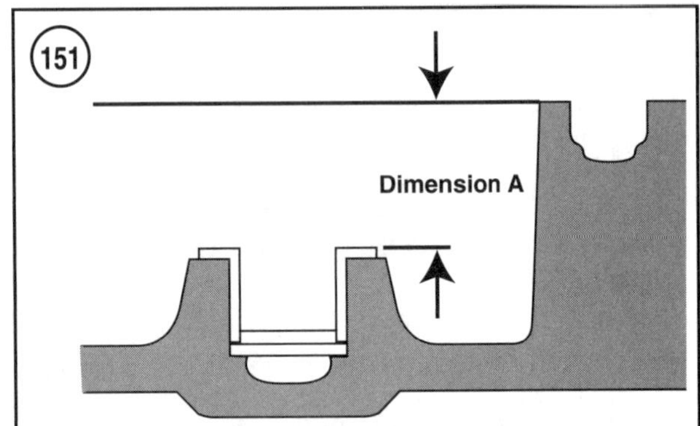

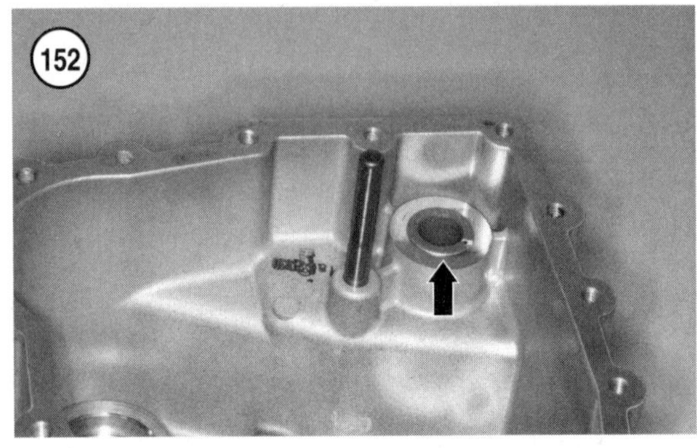

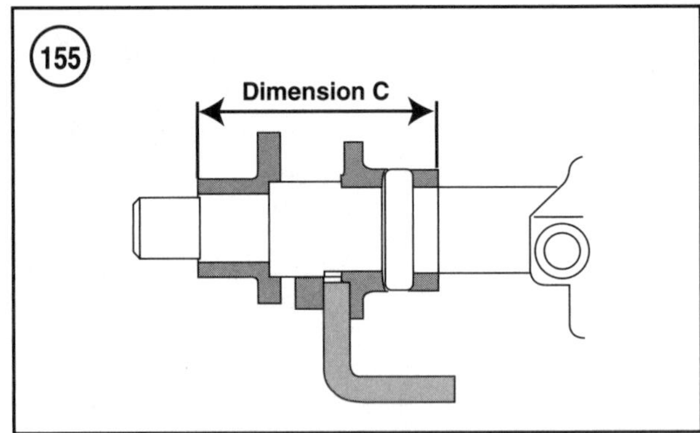

6. Determine the thickness of the new spacer washer (*W*) with the following equation:
   a. W = (A + B) - C
   b. *W* is the thickness of the new spacing washer.
   c. *A* is the distance from the top surface of the transmission cover to the top surface of the bushing.
   d. *B* is the distance from the top surface of the transmission housing to the top surface of the bushing.
   e. *C* is the measured length from the shoulder to the back of the sleeve.

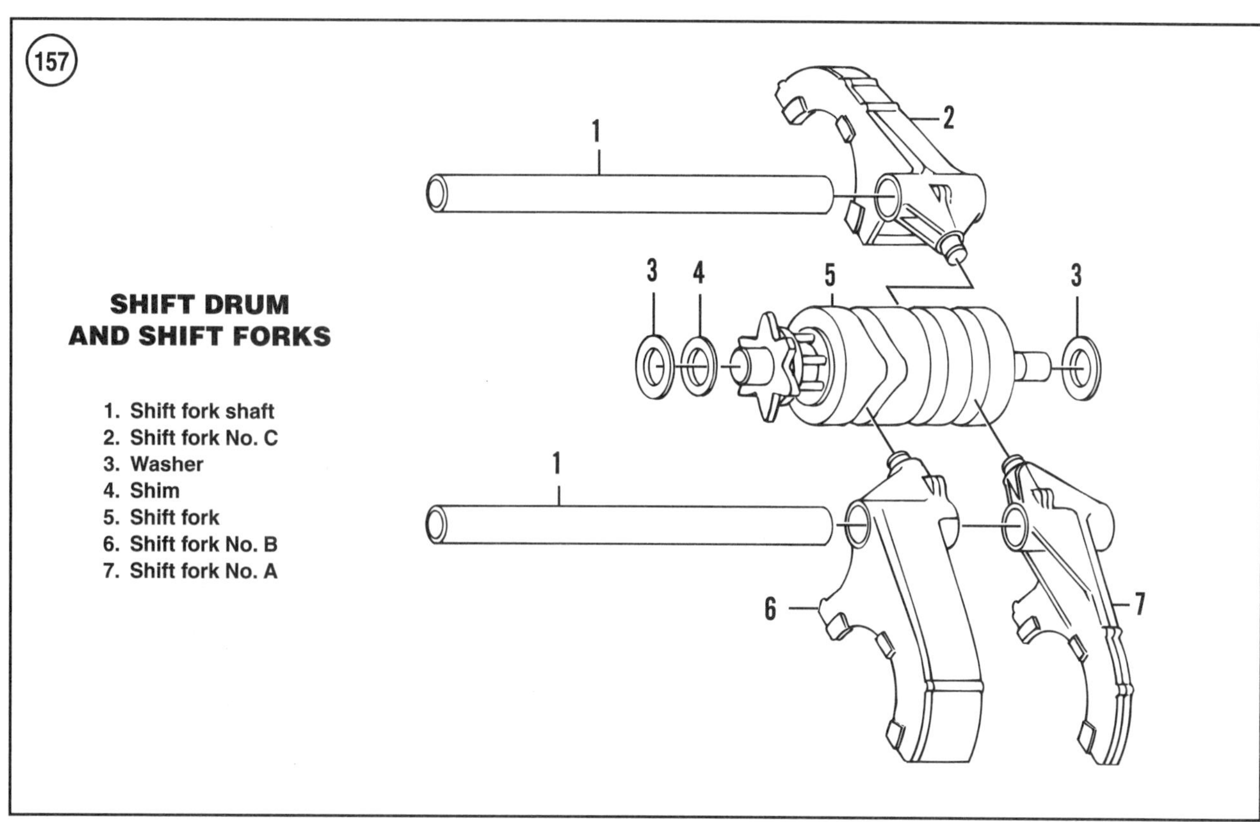

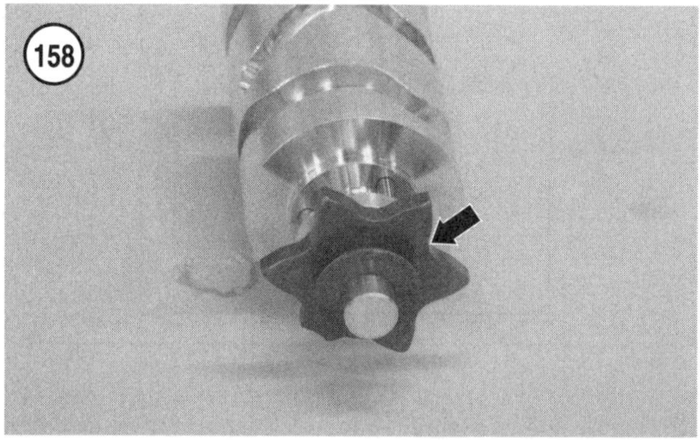

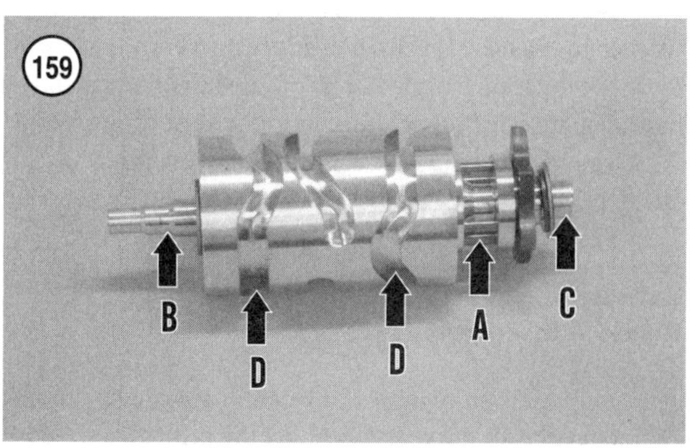

7. If the end float is out of specification, install a new spacing washer (**Figure 156**) onto the selector shaft assembly.
8. Assemble the transmission case as described in this chapter.

Shift Drum and Shift Forks Inspection

Refer to **Figure 157**.

Replace the shift fork(s), the shaft(s) and shift drum if worn or damaged.

CAUTION
It is recommended that marginally worn shift forks be replaced. Worn forks can cause the transmission to slip out of gear, leading to serious transmission damage.

1. Remove the shift drum and shift forks as described in this chapter.
2. Inspect the ramps (**Figure 158**) on the selector cam for wear or damage.
3. Inspect the roller pins (A, **Figure 159**) in the end of the shift drum. Make sure they are a tight fit in the shift drum. Replace all as a set if any are loose.

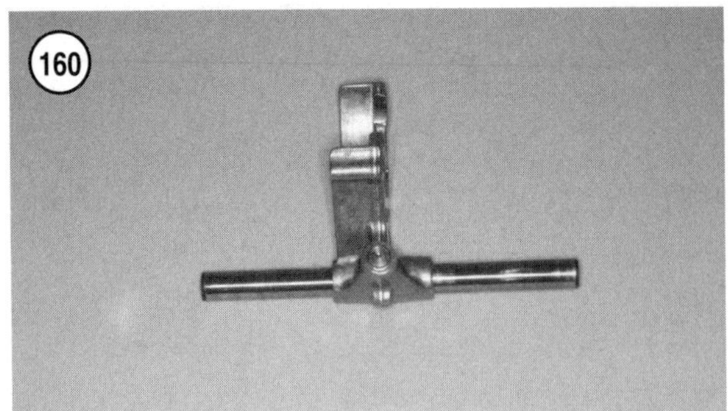
160

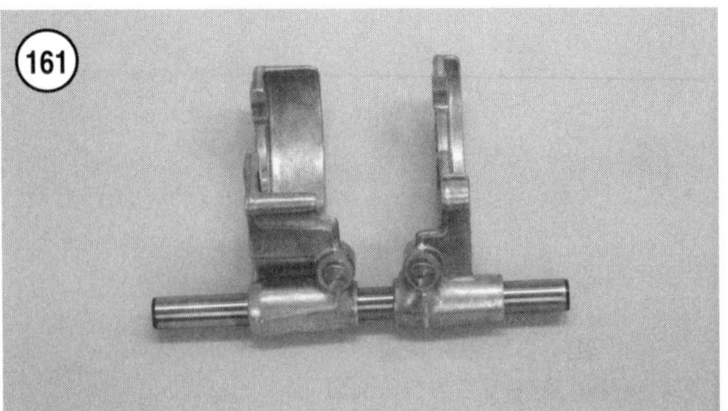
161

4. Inspect the end of the shift drum where it rides in the transmission housing (B, **Figure 159**) and transmission cover (C) for wear or damage.
5. Check the grooves in the shift drum (D, **Figure 159**) for wear or roughness. Replace the shift drum if any of the groove profiles have excessive wear or damage.
6. Inspect the washers and the spacing washer, shim, on the shift drum for wear or distortion.
7. Inspect each shift fork for wear or cracking. Check for bending and make sure each fork slides smoothly on the shaft. Refer to **Figure 160** and **Figure 161**.
8. Inspect each shift fork for wear or cracking. Check for any arc-shaped wear or burned marks on the shift fork fingers (A, **Figure 162**). This may indicate that the shift fork is excessively worn and the fork must be replaced.
9. Check the cam pin follower and roller (B, **Figure 162**) on each shift fork that rides in the shift drum for wear or damage.
10. Roll each shift fork shaft on a flat surface such as a piece of plate glass and check for bends. If the shaft is bent, it must be replaced.

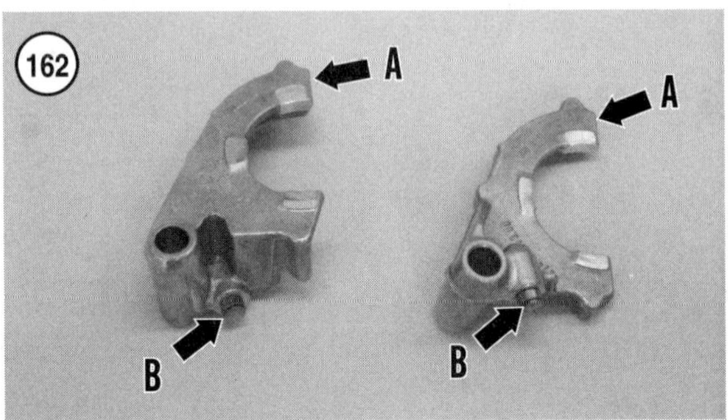

162

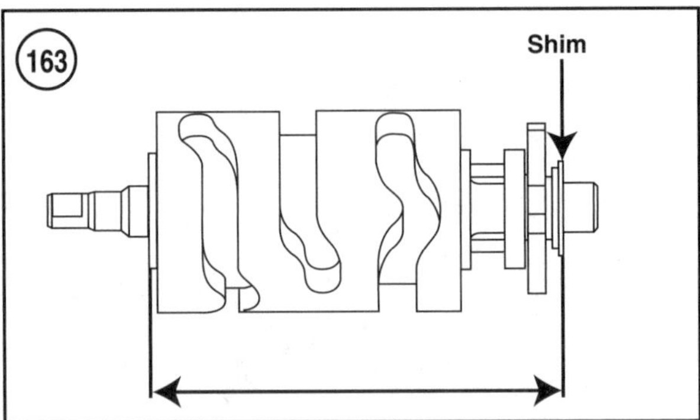

163

Shift Drum Overall Length Inspection

If the shift drum and/or the transmission case are replaced, the overall length of the shift drum must be maintained. If the overall length is greater than specified the shift drum will bind with the case. The specified overall length is 111.80-111.90 mm (4.4015-4.4055 in.).

The spacing washer, or shim, located under the washer at the base of the shift drum determines the overall length of the shift drum and is available in various thickness at a BMW dealership.

1. Disassemble the transmission case as described in this chapter.
2. Thoroughly clean the shift drum, washers and shim in solvent and dry with compressed air.
3. Install the washer on the top surface of the shift drum.
4. Install the existing spacing washer, or shim, and washer on the base of the shift drum.
5. Measure the overall length of the shift drum from washer-to-washer as shown in **Figure 163**.
6. If the overall length is out of specification, install a new spacing washer, or shim, onto the shift drum.
7. Assemble the transmission case as described in this chapter.

External Gearshift Mechanism Removal/Installation

1A. On models so equipped, place the motorcycle on the centerstand with the rear wheel off the ground.

(164)

EXTERNAL SHIFT LEVER ASSEMBLY (TYPICAL)

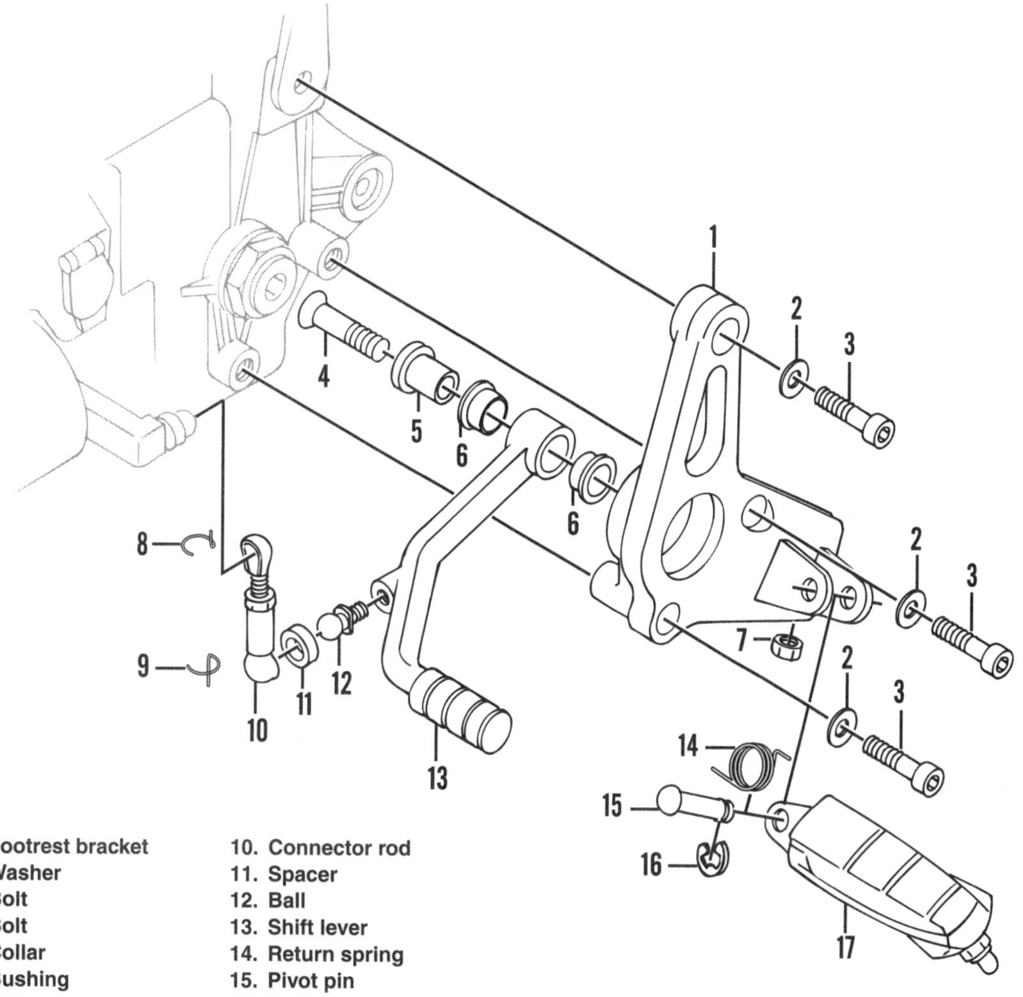

1. Footrest bracket
2. Washer
3. Bolt
4. Bolt
5. Collar
6. Bushing
7. Nut
8. Clip
9. Clip
10. Connector rod
11. Spacer
12. Ball
13. Shift lever
14. Return spring
15. Pivot pin
16. E-clip
17. Foot rest

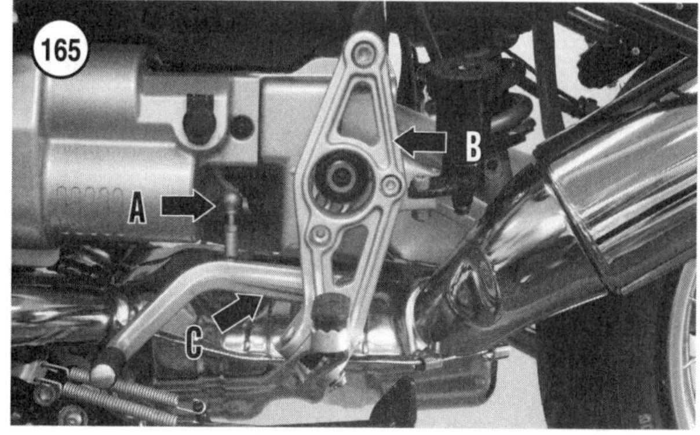

1B. On models without a centerstand, place a suitable size jack under the engine to support the motorcycle with the rear wheel off the ground.

2A. On R1150GS, R1150R, R1150RS and R1150RT models, refer to **Figure 164**, typical, and perform the following:

a. Remove the clip and disconnect the connector rod from the transmission housing shift lever ball (A, **Figure 165**).

b. Remove the left side footpeg assembly (B, **Figure 165**) as described in Chapter Fifteen.

c. Remove the bolt securing the gearshift lever (C, **Figure 165**) to the footpeg assembly to the backside of the footpeg assembly and remove it.
d. Do not lose the bushings or collar from the backside of the gearshift lever.

2B. On R1150RT models, perform the following:

a. Remove the left fairing panel as described in Chapter Fifteen.
b. Remove the clip and disconnect the connector rod from the transmission housing shift lever.
c. Remove the left footrest assembly as described in Chapter Fifteen.
d. Remove the bolt securing the gearshift lever to the backside of the footrest assembly and remove it.

2C. On R1100S models, perform the following:

a. Remove the clip (A, **Figure 166**) and disconnect the connector rod from the transmission housing shift lever.
b. Remove the bolt and washer (B, **Figure 166**) securing the gearshift lever to the main frame and remove the gearshift lever assembly (C).

2D. On R850C and R1200C models, perform the following:

a. Working under the gearshift pedal area, remove the clip and disconnect the connector rod from the transmission housing shift lever.
b. Remove the bolt and washer (A, **Figure 167**) securing the gearshift lever to the main frame and remove the gearshift lever assembly (B).

3. Apply a light coat of grease to the collar and the bushings in the shift lever pivot.
4. Install the gearshift levers and tighten the mounting bolts to the following:

a. R1150R, R1150GS, R1150RS and R1150RT models: 35 N•m (26 ft.-lb.).
b. R1100S models: 21 N•m (15 ft.-lb.).
c. R850C and R1200C models: 41 N•m (30 ft.-lb.).

5. Install all fairing and footpeg assemblies as described in Chapter Fifteen.

TRANSMISSION COVER AND HOUSING OIL SEALS

Whenever the transmission case has been disassembled the oil seals must be replaced to avoid an oil leak.

Transmission Cover Oil Seal Replacement

Use BMW replacement oil seal part No. 2312-7667-733.

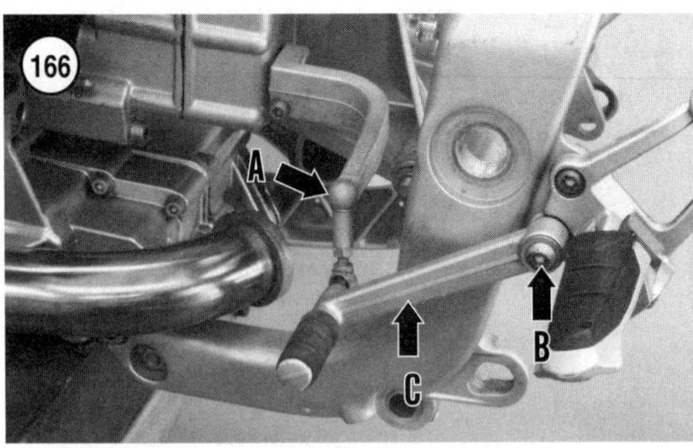

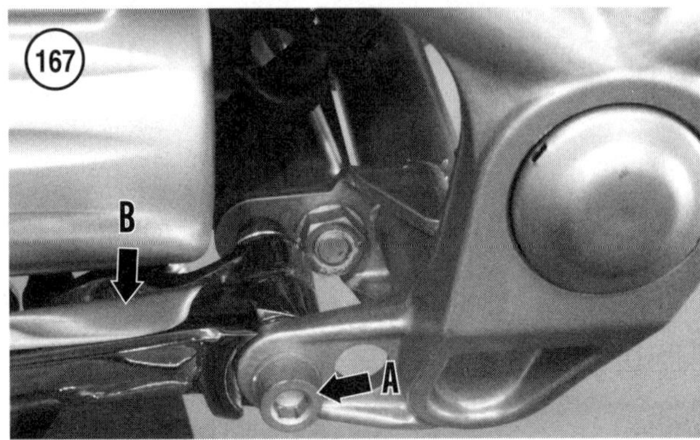

1. Disassemble the transmission cover as described in this chapter.
2. Thoroughly clean the transmission cover in solvent and dry with compressed air.
3. Use a suitable size socket and drive the old oil seal (**Figure 168**) out from the outside surface of the cover.
4. Clean the oil seal receptacle (**Figure 169**) and check for any burrs or damage.
5. The oil seal floats within the receptacle and must be backed up from the inside surface to ensure correct installation.
6. Place an appropriate size socket on a spacer (**Figure 170**) and set then on the workbench.
7. Position the cover with the outside surface facing up and rest it on the socket and spacer. Make sure the socket is flush with the bottom surface of the cover receptacle (**Figure 171**). This will control the installation depth of the oil seal.
8. Apply clean transmission oil to the outer edge of the oil seal and the cover receptacle.
9. Place the *new* oil seal with the closed side facing out and rest it on the cover receptacle (**Figure 172**).
10. Use a suitable size socket and carefully drive the new oil seal (**Figure 173**) into cover. Tap it in until it bottoms on the socket face below it (**Figure 174**).
11. Assemble the transmission case as described in this chapter.

8

Transmission Housing Oil Seal Replacement

Input shaft oil seal

Use BMW replacement oil seal part No. 2312-7656-019.

1. Disassemble the transmission case as described in this chapter.

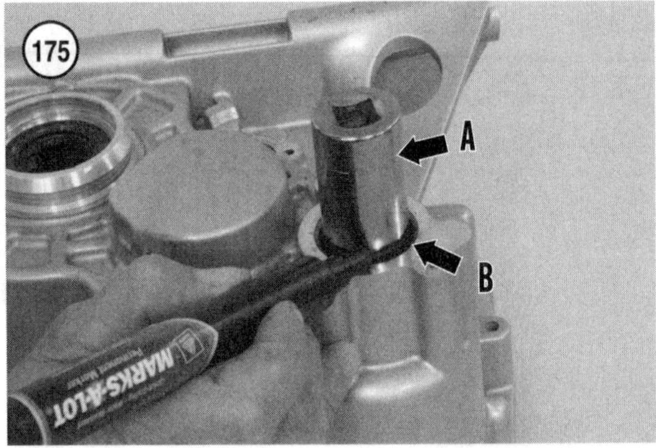

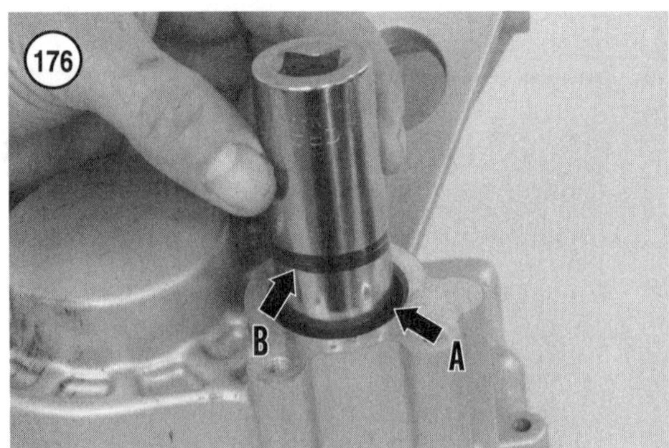

2. Thoroughly clean the transmission housing in solvent and dry with compressed air.

3. The oil seal floats within the receptacle and the specified depth must be established prior to removing the old oil seal. Insert an appropriate size socket into the oil seal receptacle from the outside surface of the housing (A, **Figure 175**) and make a perimeter mark on the socket (B) with a permanent marking pen.

4. Use a suitable size socket and drive the old oil seal out from the outside surface of the cover.

5. Clean the oil seal receptacle and check for any burrs or damage.

6. Position the housing with the outside surface facing up.

7. Apply clean transmission oil to the outer edge of the oil seal and the cover receptacle.

8. Place the *new* oil seal (A, **Figure 176**) with the closed side facing out and rest it on the housing receptacle.

9. Use the socket with the perimeter mark (B, **Figure 176**) and carefully drive the new oil seal into the housing to the specified dimension.

10. Turn the housing over and make sure that the new oil seal's outer lip is clear of the oil flow channel in the housing as shown in **Figure 177**. Oil flow will be restricted if the seal lip interferes with the oil path.

11. Assemble the transmission case as described in this chapter.

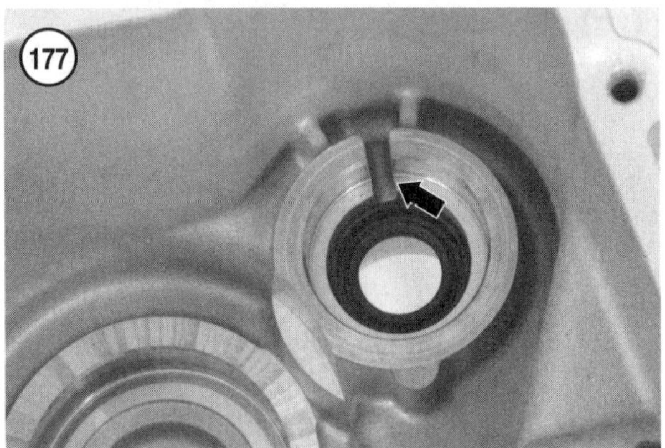

Output shaft oil seal

Use BMW replacement oil seal part No. 2312-1340-324.

1. Disassemble the transmission case as described in this chapter.

2. Thoroughly clean the transmission housing in solvent and dry with compressed air.

3. Carefully pry the old oil seal out from the outside surface of the cover.

4. Clean the oil seal receptacle and check for any burrs or damage.

5. Position the housing with the outside surface facing up.

6. Apply clean transmission oil to the outer edge of the oil seal and the cover receptacle.

7. Place the *new* oil seal with the closed side facing out and rest it on the housing receptacle.

8. Use a suitable size socket and drive the *new* oil seal (**Figure 178**) into the outside surface of the cover.

9. Drive the oil seal in until it bottoms in the flange (**Figure 179**).

10. Assemble the transmission case as described in this chapter.

Shift drum oil seal

Use BMW replacement oil seal part No. 2312-2332-884.

1. Disassemble the transmission case as described in this chapter.
2. Thoroughly clean the transmission housing in solvent and dry with compressed air.
3. Carefully pry the old oil seal (**Figure 180**) out from the outside surface of the cover.
4. Clean the oil seal receptacle and check for any burrs or damage.
5. Position the housing with the outside surface facing up.
6. Apply clean transmission oil to the outer edge of the oil seal and the cover receptacle.
7. Place the *new* oil seal with the closed side facing out and rest it on the housing receptacle.
8. Use a suitable size socket and drive the *new* oil seal (**Figure 181**) into the outside surface of the cover.
9. Drive the oil seal in until it bottoms in the flange.
10. Assemble the transmission case as described in this chapter.

Shift shaft oil seal

Use BMW replacement oil seal part No. 2312-2330-139.

1. Disassemble the transmission case as described in this chapter.
2. Thoroughly clean the transmission housing in solvent and dry with compressed air.
3. Carefully pry the old oil seal (**Figure 182**) out from the outside surface of the cover.
4. Clean the oil seal receptacle and check for any burrs or damage.

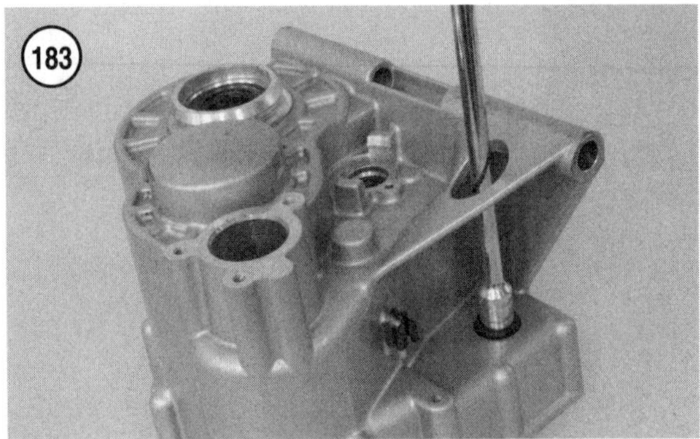

5. Position the housing with the outside surface facing up.
6. Apply clean transmission oil to the outer edge of the oil seal and the cover receptacle.
7. Place the *new* oil seal with the closed side facing out and rest it on the housing receptacle.
8. Use a suitable size socket and drive the *new* oil seal (**Figure 183**) into the outside surface of the cover.
9. Drive the oil seal in until it bottoms in the flange (**Figure 184**).
10. Assemble the transmission case as described in this chapter.

Table 1 SIX-SPEED TRANSMISSION SPECIFICATIONS

Transmission type	Six speed constant mesh transmission with integral spring damper Claw-type shift fork shifting mechanism
Gear ratios	
First gear	3.864
Second gear	3.022
Third gear	2.393
Fourth gear	1.962
Fifth gear	1.700
Sixth gear	1.511
Selector shaft end float	0.1-0.3 mm (0.0039-0.0118 in.)
Spring cluster end float	0.4-0.6 mm (0.0157-0.0236 in.)
Shift drum overall length	111.80-111.90 mm (4.4015-4.4055 in.)

Table 2 SIX-SPEED TRANSMISSION TORQUE SPECIFICATIONS

Item	N•m	in.-lb.	ft.-lb.
Footrest mounting bolt	22	–	16
Shift lever-to-footrest bolt			
GS, R, RS, RT	35	–	26
R1100S	21	–	15
R850C, R1200C	41	–	30
Transmission housing-to-engine bolts	22	–	16
Transmission housing cover bolts	9	80	–

CHAPTER NINE

FUEL, EMISSION CONTROL AND EXHAUST SYSTEMS

This chapter covers the fuel injection system. Complete service of the system requires the BMW MoDiTec diagnostic tool and a number of additional specialty tools. System fault codes can only be retrieved using the MoDiTec tool in conjunction with the motorcycle's diagnostic connector (**Figure 1**). However, basic troubleshooting diagnosis is no different on a fuel-injected machine than on a carbureted one. If there is a drivability problem, make sure all electrical connections are clean and secure. A high or erratic idle speed may indicate a vacuum leak. Make sure there is an adequate supply of fresh gasoline. If basic tests fail to reveal the cause of a problem, refer service to a BMW dealership. Incorrectly performed diagnostic procedures can result in damage to the fuel injection system.

CAUTION

*Servicing the electronic fuel injection requires special precautions to prevent damage to the Motronic control unit. Common electrical system service procedures acceptable on other motorcycles may damage parts of this system. Refer to **Fuel Injection System Precautions** in this chapter.*

The fuel system consists of the fuel tank, two fuel injector and throttle body assemblies, a fuel pump, a fuel filter and an air filter assembly. Air filter service is covered in Chapter Three, but service to the air filter case is covered in this chapter.

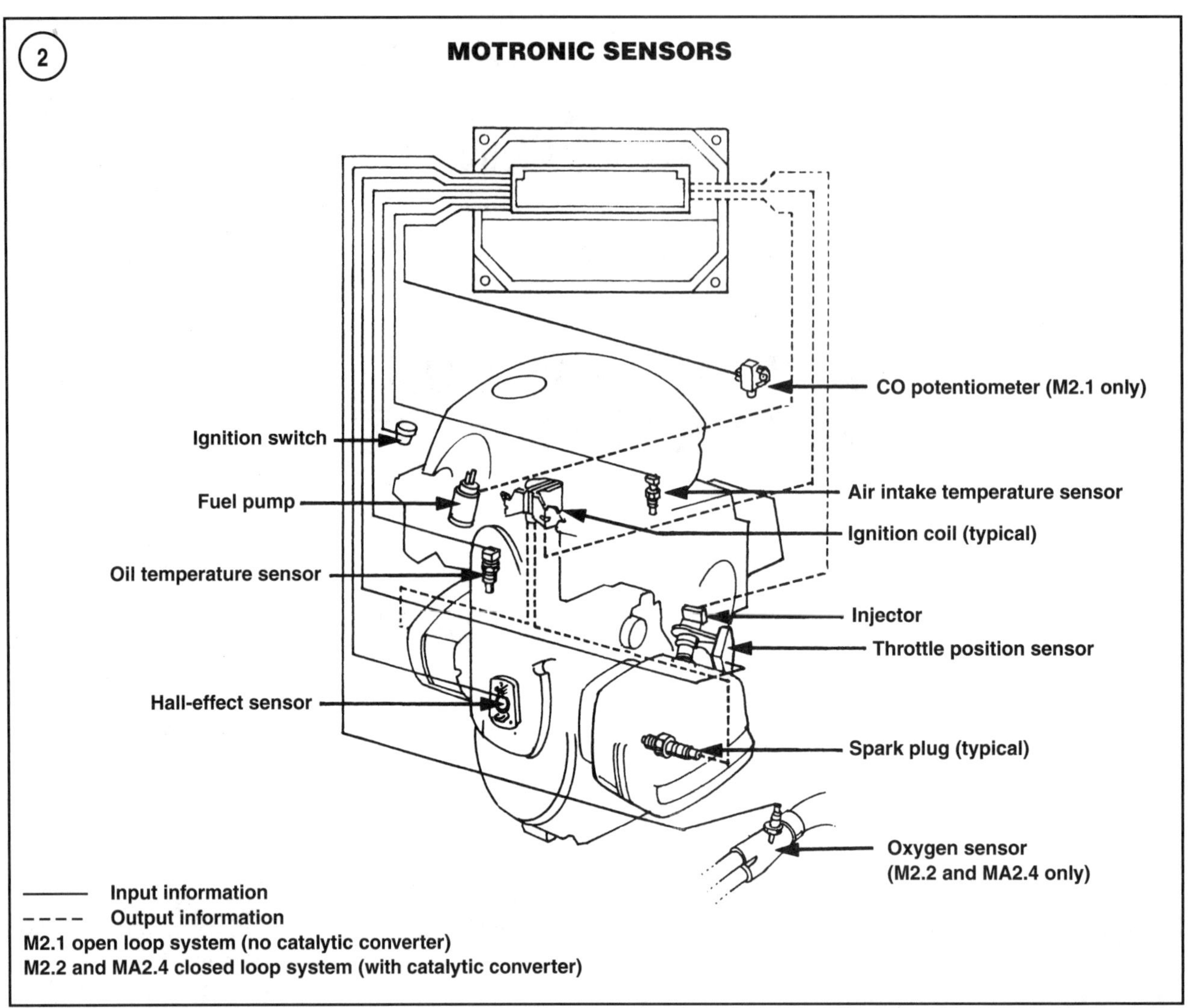

Table 1 and **Table 2** are located at the end of the chapter.

MOTRONIC SYSTEM

The Motronic system controls the fuel injection system and the ignition system. Since these systems interact with each other, the single control unit monitors all aspects of both systems to accomplish maximum torque characteristics, greater fuel economy and low exhaust emissions due to the matching of the air/fuel ratio and ignition point depending upon load conditions. Refer to **Figure 2** and **Figure 3**.

Two Motronic systems are used. The more recent version is the M2.2/MA2.4 which is a *closed loop* system and incorporates a catalytic converter and a Lambda or oxygen sensor. This system is standard on U.S., Canada and U.K. models and is optional on motorcycles sold in other countries. The M2.1 system is an *open loop* system with no catalytic converter and has an oxygen potentiometer instead of the oxygen sensor.

During operation, the Motronic system monitors engine temperature, intake air temperature, engine speed, engine load and exhaust gas oxygen content. It processes this information and determines the correct amount of fuel and spark advance to provide optimum performance at all engine speeds and load conditions.

Fuel System

Based on information input from various sensors, the Motronic control unit determines the opening time of the injectors, and the timing spark advance to provide maximum performance and optimum fuel economy.

MOTRONIC SYSTEM

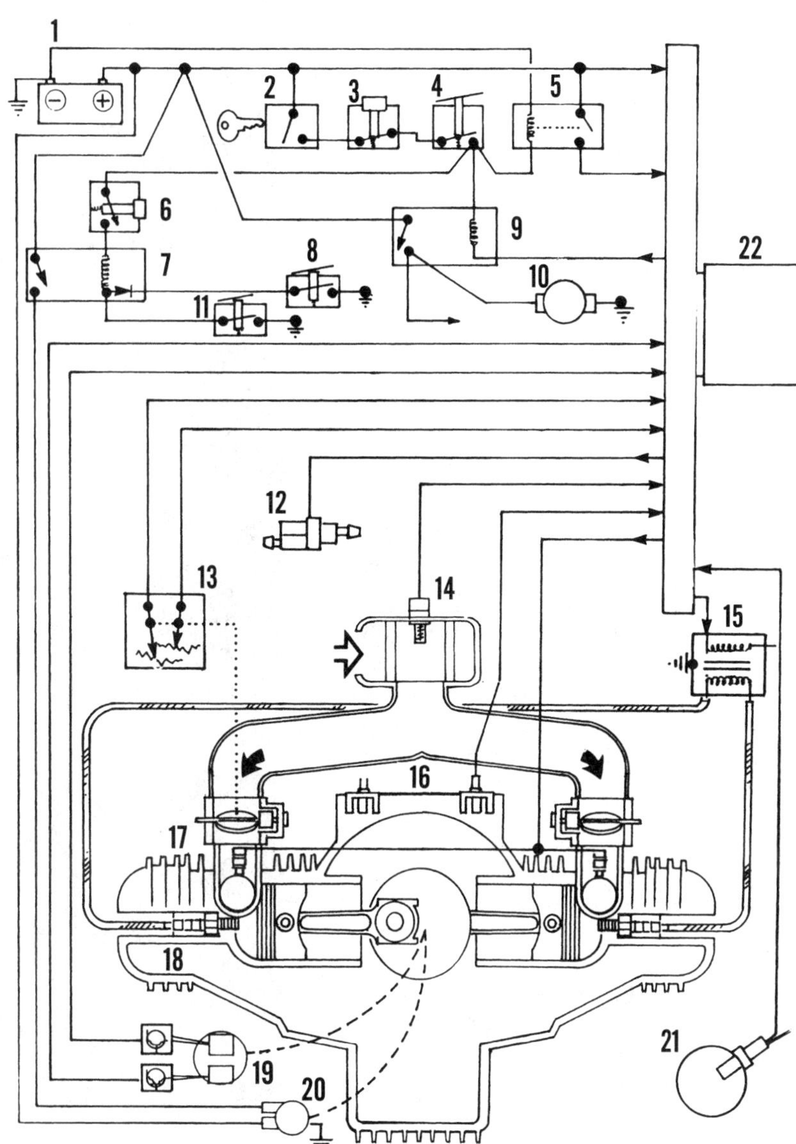

1. Battery
2. Ignition switch
3. Engine stop switch
4. Sidestand interlock switch
5. Motronic relay
6. Start button
7. Starter relay
8. Neutral switch
9. Fuel pump relay
10. Fuel pump
11. Clutch interlock switch
12. Purge valve (CA models only)
13. Throttle position sensor
14. Air temperature sensor
15. Ignition coil
16. Oil temperature sensor
17. Throttle body
18. Spark plug
19. Hall-effect sensor I and II
20. Starter
21. Oxygen sensor
22. Control unit

The Motronic system also processes engine temperature, air intake temperature and air mass information to provide the correct air/fuel ratio for cold starting and engine warm-up. This is in addition to the increased idle speed (choke) feature found on most models.

Ignition System

Refer to *Ignition System* in Chapter Ten.

FUEL INJECTION SYSTEM COMPONENTS

An understanding of the function of the fuel injection components and their relationship to one another is a valuable aid for locating a source of fuel injection problems.

Motronic Control Unit

The Motronic unit (**Figure 4**) performs the following functions.

1. Receives input from the sensors to calculate the correct air/fuel ratio. Based on data from the sensors, the control unit activates the injectors in one of two basic modes; one for small throttle openings and one for large throttle openings. The length of time that the injectors are open determines the air/fuel ratio.
2. Controls the fuel pump.
3. Determines the optimum ignition timing.

Hall Sensor

The Hall sensor assembly (**Figure 5**) is located at the front of the engine and is driven by the front of the crankshaft. The unit provides crankshaft position and ignition information to the Motronic control unit.

Throttle Valves

The throttle valves located in the throttle bodies control the amount of air that enters the engine. The throttle valves are attached to the throttle linkage and are connected together by the interconnecting throttle cables.

Fuel Pump and Filters

The fuel pump and filters are located within the fuel tank. The fuel pump delivery rate specification is approximately 100 liters/hour (26.4 U.S. gal/hour) at a constant pressure. The fuel is filtered prior to entering the fuel pump and then again after leaving the pump to protect the fuel injectors.

4

5

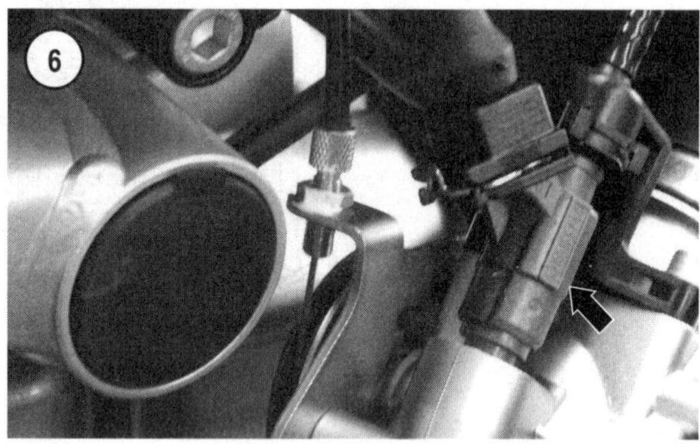
6

Pressure Regulator

The pressure regulator, located between the fuel tank and the fuel injectors, maintains a constant fuel pressure of 300 kPa (43.5 psi). If the specified fuel pressure is exceeded, the pressure regulator valve opens, allowing the fuel to return to the fuel tank via a separate return hose.

The pressure regulator maintains a constant fuel pressure to the fuel injectors at all times and under all conditions.

Fuel Injectors

The fuel injectors (**Figure 6**), mounted on the throttle bodies, are a solenoid-actuated constant-stroke pintle type consisting of a solenoid, plunger, needle valve and housing. When the control unit applies a pulsed ground to the solenoid coil, the valve is lifted and fuel is injected into the throttle body and into the intake passage way adjacent to the dual intake valves.

The size of the fuel injector's opening is fixed and fuel pressure is constant at all times. The amount of fuel injected is controlled by the injector open time period of 1.5 to 9 milliseconds and is controlled by the Motronic unit. The injector open time depends on engine speed and air intake volume.

Throttle Position Sensor

The throttle position sensor (TPS) is located on the left side throttle body (**Figure 7**) and is attached directly to the throttle shaft. This sensor indicates the throttle angle and sends this information to the Motronic unit.

Air Intake Temperature Sensor

The air intake temperature sensor (**Figure 8**) is located on top of the air filter cover. This sensor determines the air density and adjusts the fuel injector opening time based on input from this sensor.

DEPRESSURIZING THE FUEL SYSTEM

The fuel system is under pressure at all times, even when the engine is not operating. The fuel system is not equipped with a port for relieving the fuel pressure, so if a fuel line or fitting is loosened or removed, gasoline will spray from the fitting unless the system pressure is relieved.

WARNING
Always wear eye protection when working on the fuel system.

1. Prior to disconnecting any fuel line or fitting, use a clamp and pinch off both the pressurized and return fuel hoses (**Figure 9**) on the right side of the fuel tank.
2. Disconnect the fuel hoses from the fittings and place the ends in a container. Loosen the clamp and allow the pressurized fuel to drain into the container. Dispose of the fuel correctly.
3. When disconnecting any fuel line or fitting, wrap the surrounding area with a clean shop cloth to catch any spilled fuel.
4. Properly dispose of any fuel soaked rags.

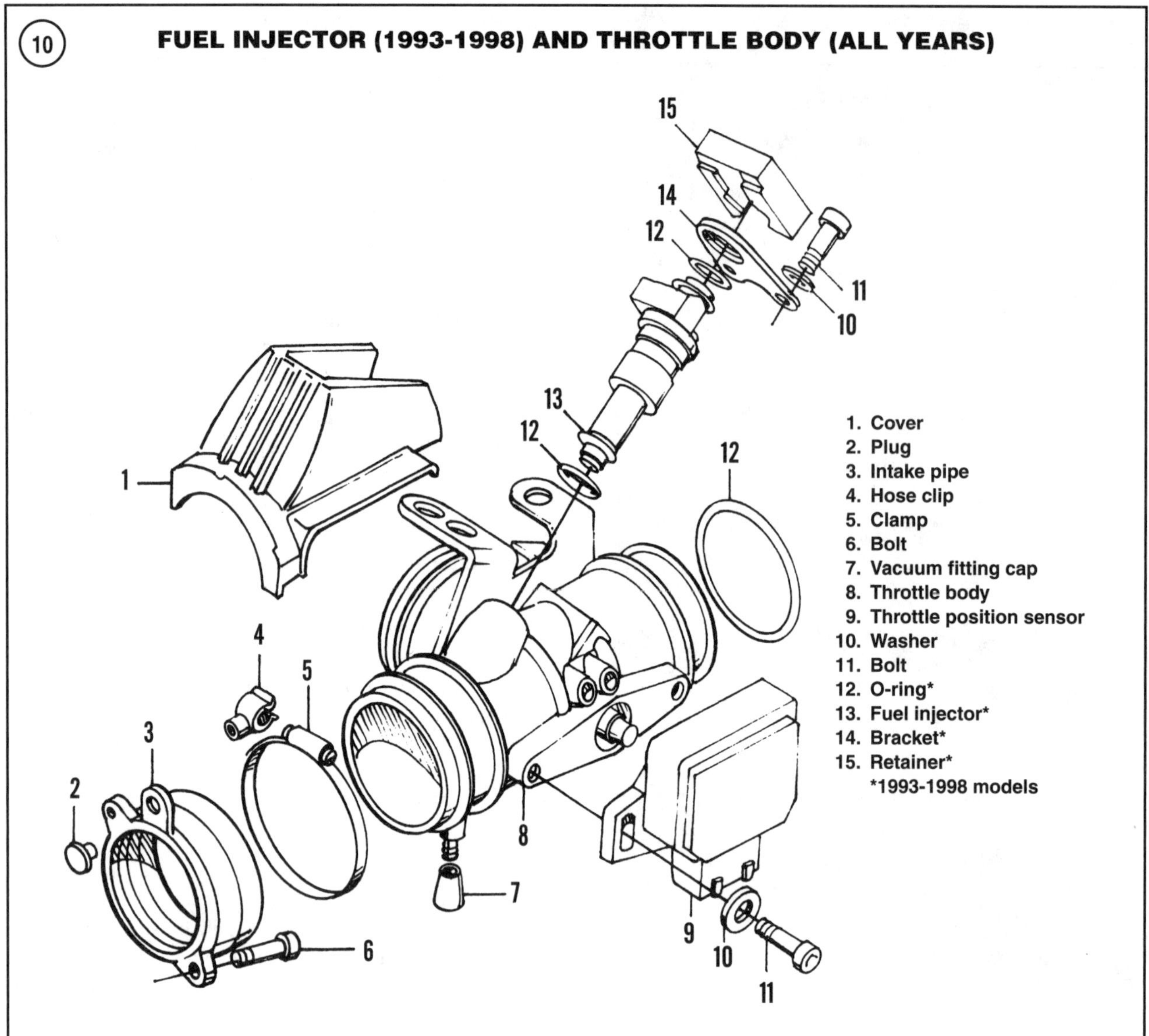

FUEL INJECTION SYSTEM PRECAUTIONS

CAUTION
Servicing the fuel injection system requires special precautions to prevent damage to the Motronic control unit. Common electrical system service procedures acceptable for other motorcycles may damage several parts of this system.

Motronic Control Unit

1. Unless otherwise specified in a procedure, do not start the engine while any electrical connectors are disconnected. Do not disconnect the battery cables or any electrical connector while the ignition switch is on. If these instructions are not followed, the Motronic control unit will be damaged.

2. Before disconnecting any electrical connector, turn the ignition switch *off*.

3. When repairs are completed, do not try to start the engine without first confirming that all fuel injection system electrical connectors are free from corrosion and are securely attached. Faulty connectors may damage the control unit and its related components.

4. Do not disconnect the battery while the engine is running.

5. Do not connect the battery cables backward (cross polarity).

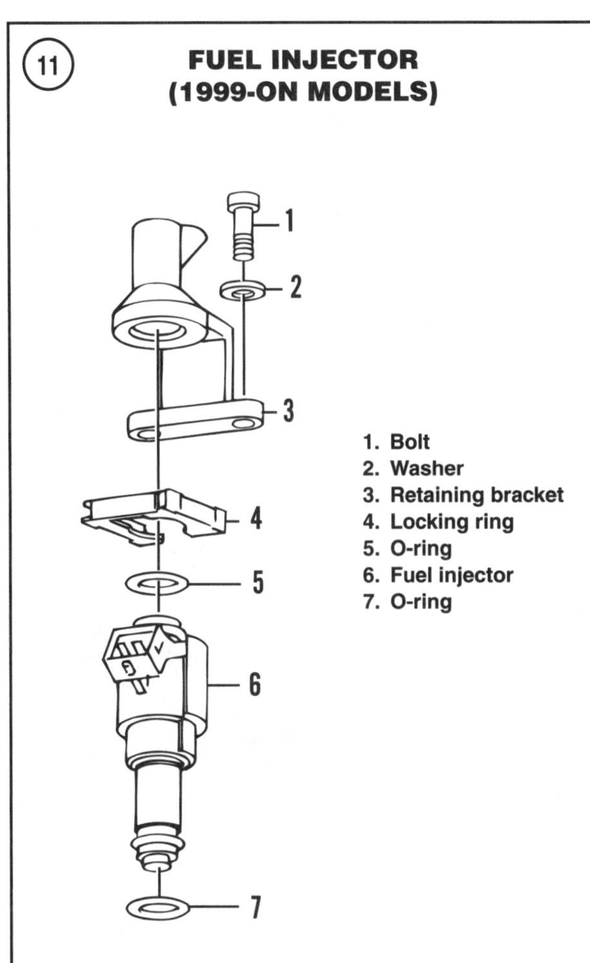

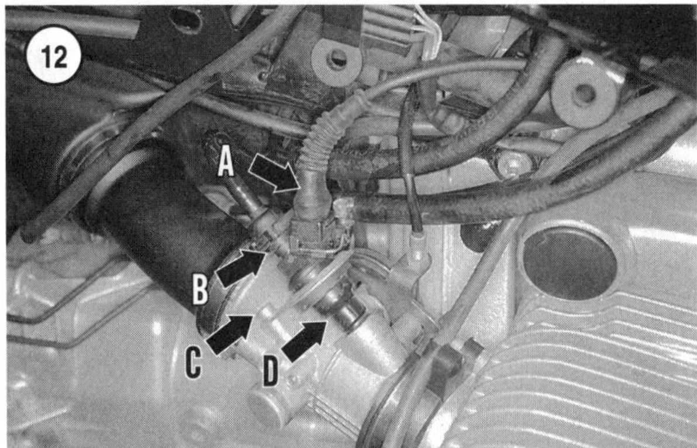

6. Do not apply anything other than a 12-volt battery to the motorcycle's electrical system. The motorcycle's battery must be removed from the motorcycle before attaching a battery charger.

7. Do not use any piece of electrical test equipment that has its own power supply (ohmmeter, multimeter, megger or self-powered test lamp) as the applied voltage may damage the sensitive circuits in the system. Use only the specified BMW test equipment listed in the test procedures.

Fuel System

1. The fuel system is pressurized, so wear eye protection whenever working on the fuel system, especially when disconnecting any fuel lines.
2. The fuel pump is cooled, and the bearings are lubricated, by the fuel passing through the unit. Refill the fuel tank when there is a 1/4 tank of fuel remaining. If the fuel pump is operated without fuel, its bearings will be damaged. If damaged, the fuel pump must be replaced as a unit.
3. Do not add any lubricants, fuel preservatives or additives to the gasoline as the fuel system may become corroded or clogged.

Troubleshooting

Complete troubleshooting of the system requires the BMW MoDiTec diagnostic tool and a number of additional specialty tools. Therefore, entrust all service work on the Motronic control unit to a BMW dealership. If any service work relating to the control unit is performed by unauthorized BMW personnel, it will void any applicable warranty.

FUEL INJECTORS

Removal

Refer to **Figure 10** and **Figure 11**.

1. Disconnect the battery's negative lead as described in Chapter Three.
2. On RS, RT and S models, remove the front faring side panels as described in Chapter Fifteen.
3. Depressurize the fuel system as described in this chapter.

4A. On 1993-1998 models, perform the following:

a. Press in on the spring catch and carefully disconnect the multi-pin electrical connector (A, **Figure 12**) from the top of the fuel injector.

NOTE
Place a clean shop cloth under the fuel hose to catch any remaining fuel in the hose.

b. Unfasten the fuel hose retainer and disconnect the fuel hose (B, **Figure 12**) from the fuel injector. Plug

9

the end of the fuel hose to prevent the entry of debris and to prevent fuel leakage.

c. Remove the bolt and washer securing the fuel injector retaining bracket (C, **Figure 12**). Remove the retaining bracket.

NOTE

The air intake hose is removed to better illustrate the steps on some of the 1999-on model photos.

4B. On 1999-on models, perform the following:

a. Press in on the spring catch, then carefully disconnect the multi-pin electrical connector (A, **Figure 13**) from the top of the fuel injector.

b. Loosen the hose clamp (B, **Figure 13**) and disconnect the fuel hose from the fuel injector. Plug the end of the fuel hose to prevent the entry of debris and to prevent fuel leakage.

c. Remove the bolts and washers (**Figure 14**) securing the fuel injector retaining bracket to the throttle body.

4C. On R850C and R1200C models, perform the following:

a. Press in on the spring catch, then carefully disconnect the multi-pin electrical connector from the top of the fuel injector. Refer to A, **Figure 15** and A, **Figure 16**.

NOTE

*The fuel pressure regulator is equipped with a flexible hose (B, **Figure 15**) going to the left side fuel injector and a rigid fuel pipe (**Figure 17**) to the right side fuel injector.*

b. Unfasten the retainer and pull the pipe, or hose, from the fuel injector. Refer to C, **Figure 15** and B, **Figure 16**. Plug the end of the fuel pipe (right side), or fuel hose (left side) to prevent the entry of debris and to prevent fuel leakage.

5. Use compressed air to remove all debris from around the fuel injector prior to removing it. If any debris falls into the opening in the throttle body, it will fall into the cylinder head assembly and cause internal engine wear/damage.

NOTE

If the existing fuel injectors are going to be reinstalled, mark them with R (right side) and L (left side) so they will be reinstalled in the same location.

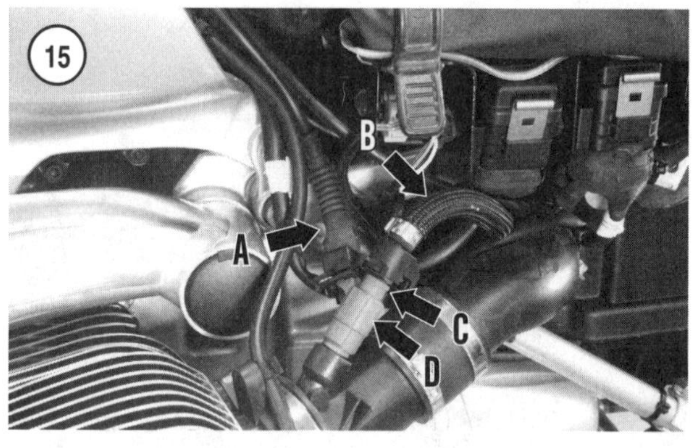

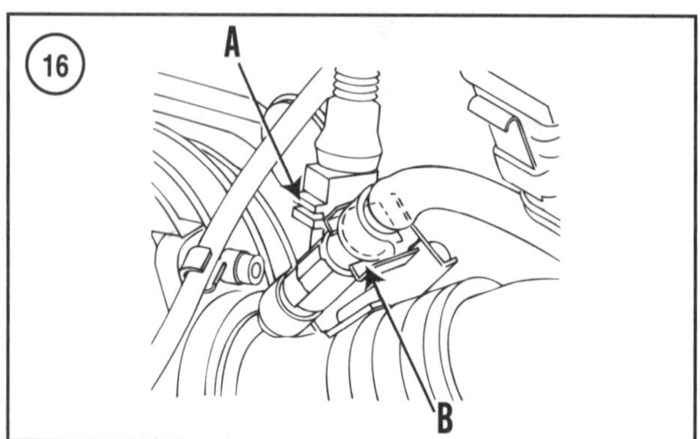

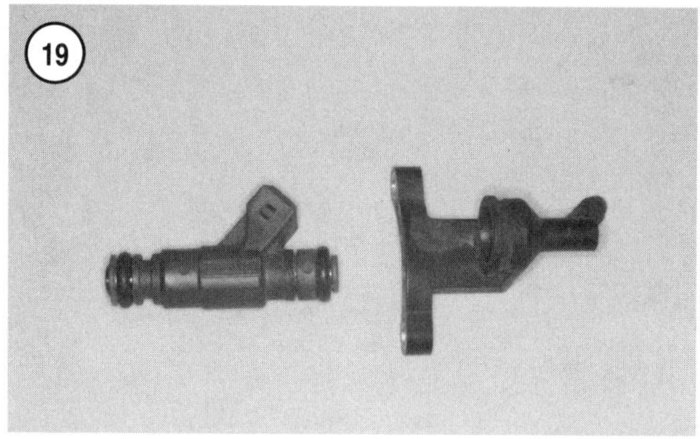

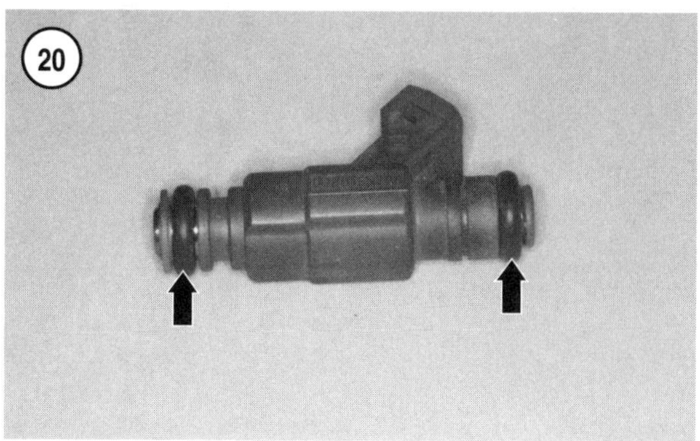

6A. On 1993-1998 models, carefully pull straight out and remove the fuel injector (D, **Figure 12**) from the throttle body.

6B. On 1999-on models, perform the following:

a. Carefully pull straight out and remove the fuel injector (**Figure 18**) from the throttle body.

b. Separate the fuel injector from the retainer (**Figure 19**).

6C. On R850C and R1200C models, carefully pull straight out and remove the fuel injector (D, **Figure 15**) from the intake pipe.

7. Remove the O-ring seal (**Figure 20**) from each end of the fuel injectors. The O-rings must be replaced every time the fuel injector is removed to maintain a leak free seal.

Installation

1. Clean out any old fuel residue or corrosion, from the fuel injector receptacle (**Figure 21**) in the throttle body.
2. Coat the *new* O-rings (**Figure 20**) with clean engine oil and install them onto the fuel injector. Make sure they seat properly in the fuel injector grooves.

CAUTION

Carefully push the fuel injector into the receptacle to avoid damage to the O-ring seal. If the O-ring is damaged during installation, it will result in a fuel leak.

NOTE

If the existing fuel injectors are being reinstalled, refer to the marks made during removal and reinstall them in the same location.

3A. On 1993-1998 models, carefully push the fuel injector (D, **Figure 12**) squarely into the throttle body. Push it in until it bottoms.

3B. On 1999-on models, perform the following:

9

a. Install the fuel injector onto the retainer (**Figure 22**).
b. Carefully push the fuel injector squarely into the throttle body (**Figure 18**). Push it in until it bottoms.

3C. On R850C and R1200C models, push the fuel injector squarely into the intake pipe (D, **Figure 15**). Push it in until it bottoms.

4A. On 1993-1998 models, perform the following:

a. Install the retaining bracket (C, **Figure 12**) onto the fuel injector. Make sure it sits correctly on the fuel injector and throttle body. Install the washer and bolt and tighten them securely.
b. Remove the plug from the end of the fuel hose.
c. Connect the fuel hose (B, **Figure 12**) onto the end of the fuel injector and push it on until it bottoms. Attach the fuel hose retainer and make sure it secures properly.
d. Make sure the wiring harness electrical connector is free of corrosion. Connect the multi-pin electrical connector (A, **Figure 12**) onto the top of the fuel injector. Push the connector onto the fuel injector and make sure it is on tight. Install the spring catch and make sure it holds the connector on securely.

4B. On 1999-on models, perform the following:

a. Install the fuel injector retaining bracket (**Figure 14**) mounting bolts and washers. Tighten the bolts securely.
b. Connect the fuel hose onto the fuel injector and tighten the hose clamp (B, **Figure 13**).
c. Make sure the wiring harness electrical connector is free of corrosion. Connect the multi-pin electrical connector (A, **Figure 13**) onto the top of the fuel injector. Push the connector onto the fuel injector and make sure it is on tight. Install the spring catch and make sure it holds the connector on securely.

4C. On R850C and R1200C models, perform the following:

a. Push the pipe or hose into the fuel injector. Push it in until it bottoms.
b. Install the retainer from the inside of the fuel injector so the open end of the retainer is facing out as shown in B, **Figure 16**. This is necessary to prevent the fuel injector from rotating within the throttle body receptacle. Make sure the retainer is engaged correctly so it will not pop out.
c. Make sure the wiring harness electrical connector is free of corrosion. Connect the multi-pin electrical connector onto the top of the fuel injector. Refer to A, **Figure 15** and A, **Figure 16**. Push the connector onto the fuel injector and make sure it is on tight.
d. Install the spring catch and make sure it holds the connector on securely.

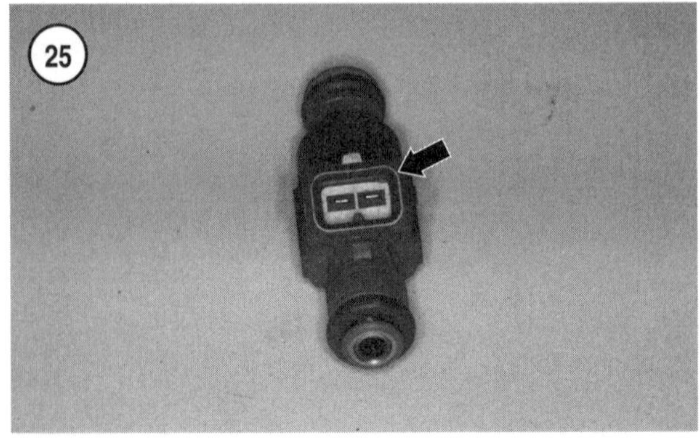

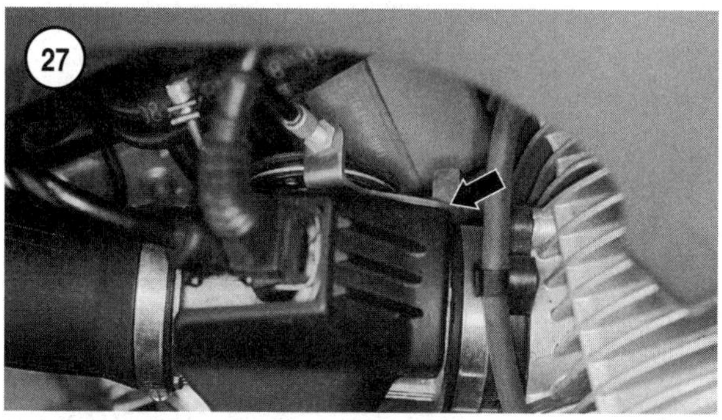

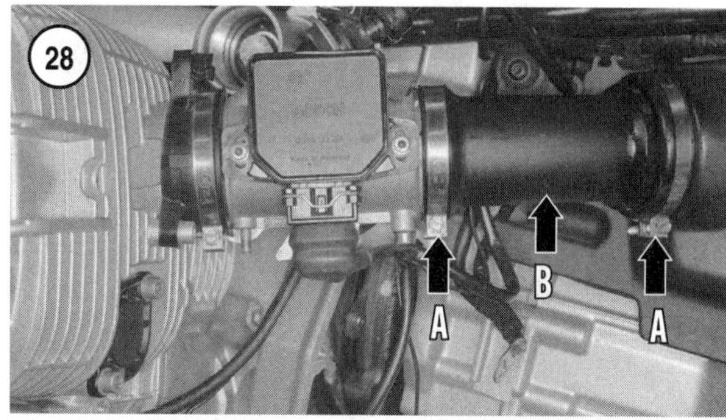

WARNING
In Step 5, do not allow the engine to start in case there is a fuel leak at the fuel injector connection.

5. After the fuel hoses are attached correctly, turn the ignition switch on, but do not operate the starter. After the fuel pump runs for approximately 2 seconds the fuel pressure in the fuel hose will rise. Turn the ignition switch off and check for fuel leaks.

WARNING
Do not start the engine if there is the slightest fuel leak. Any type of fuel leak can lead to a dangerous fire.

6. Repeat Step 5 two or three times to check for leaks. Fix any leaks before starting the engine.
7. Start the engine and once again check for any fuel leaks.
8. On RS, RT and S models, install the front faring side panels as described in Chapter Fifteen.

Inspection

CAUTION
Do not attempt to clean the fuel injectors. They will be damaged.

1. Confirm that the opening at each end of the fuel injector is open and clean. Refer to **Figure 23** and **Figure 24**.
2. Inspect the fuel injector receptacle (**Figure 21**) in the throttle body. If necessary, remove the throttle body as described in this chapter and clean off any old fuel residue or corrosion. After cleaning, apply a light coat of clean engine oil to the receptacle.
3. Make sure the electrical connections (**Figure 25**) are free of corrosion.
4. Inspect the fuel injector for any evidence of damage and replace if necessary.
5. On 1999-on models, inspect the retaining bracket (**Figure 26**) for damage.

THROTTLE BODY

During certain procedures, such as cylinder head removal, it is more efficient to remove the throttle body along with the fuel injector and control cable as an assembly. However, if only partial disassembly is necessary, refer to *Partial Removal/Installation* in this section.

Partial Removal/Installation

Refer to **Figure 10** and **Figure 11**.

1. Disconnect the negative battery cable as described in Chapter Three.
2. On RS, RT and S models, remove the front fairing side panels as described in Chapter Fifteen.
3. On models so equipped, remove the cover (**Figure 27**) from the throttle body.
4. On the left side, perform the following:
   a. Loosen both hose clamps (A, **Figure 28**) and remove the flexible inlet hose (B) from the throttle body and air filter case.
   b. Disconnect the vacuum hose from the fitting on the base of the throttle body.

c. Loosen the hose clamp (A, **Figure 29**) and carefully withdraw the throttle body (B) from the inlet pipe on the cylinder head.
5. On the right side, perform the following:
a. Loosen both hose clamps (A, **Figure 30**) and remove the flexible inlet hose (B) from the throttle body and air filter air case.
b. Disconnect the vacuum hose (C, **Figure 30**) from the fitting on the base of the throttle body.
c. Loosen the hose clamp (D, **Figure 30**) and carefully withdraw the throttle body (E) from the inlet pipe on the cylinder head.
6. Move the throttle body out of the way. Place the assembly in a reclosable plastic bag to avoid contamination.
7. Insert a clean, lint-free cloth into the opening in the air filter air box to keep out debris.
8. Install by reversing these removal steps while noting the following:
a. Install a *new* O-ring seal (**Figure 31**) onto the throttle body groove. Make sure it seats correctly, then apply a light coat of clean engine oil to the O-ring.
b. Correctly index the raised tab on the throttle body with the groove on the inlet pipe on the cylinder head (**Figure 32**).

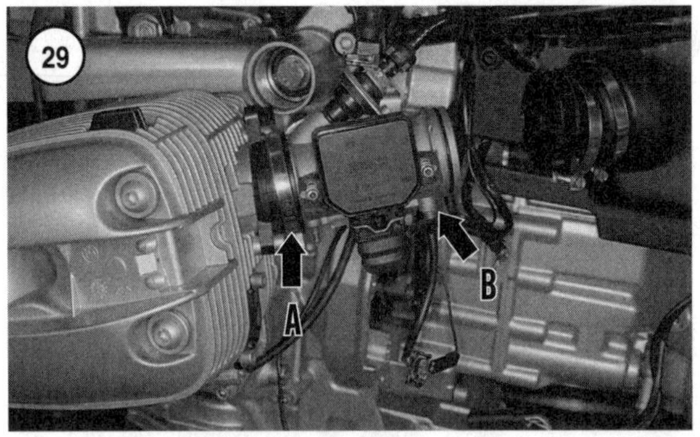

Complete Removal/Installation

Refer to **Figure 10** and **Figure 11**.
1. Remove the fuel injectors from the throttle bodies as described in this section.
2. Perform *Partial Removal/Installation* in this section.
3. On the left side, disconnect the throttle and choke cables from the throttle housing as described under *Throttle Cable Replacement* and *Choke Cable Replacement* in this chapter.
4. On the right side, disconnect the interconnecting throttle cable from the throttle housing as described under *Throttle Cable Replacement* in this chapter.
5. Install by reversing these removal steps. Adjust the idle speed and throttle valve synchronization as described in Chapter Three.

PRESSURE REGULATOR

Removal/Installation

Refer to **Figure 33-36**.
1. Remove the fuel tank as described in this chapter.
2. Depressurize the fuel system as described in this chapter.
3. Remove the air filter air box as described in this chapter.

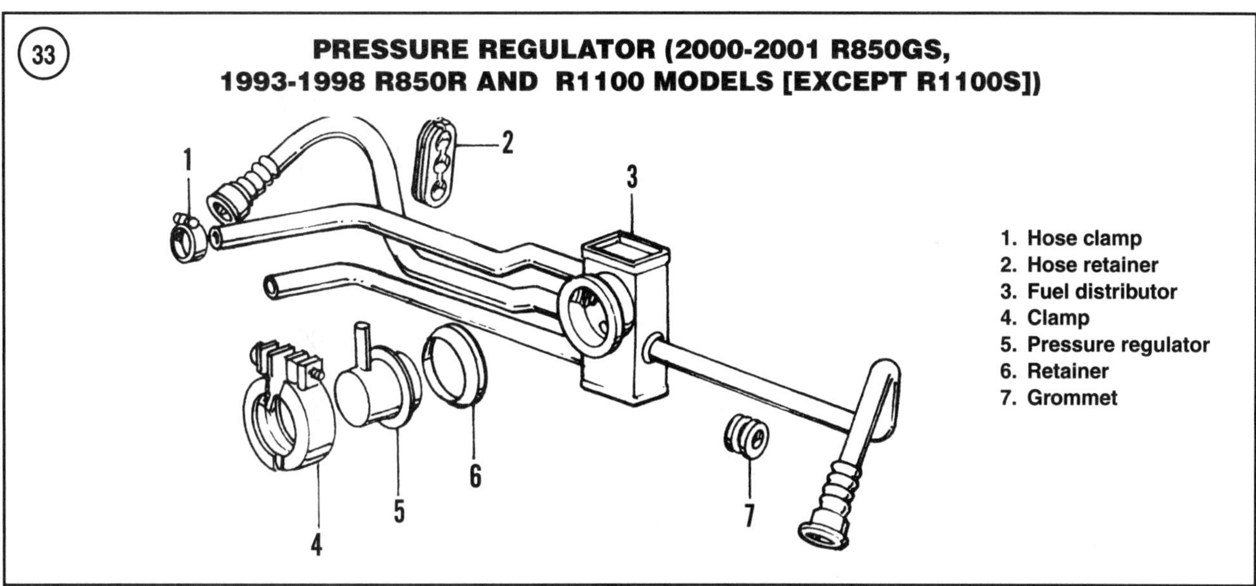

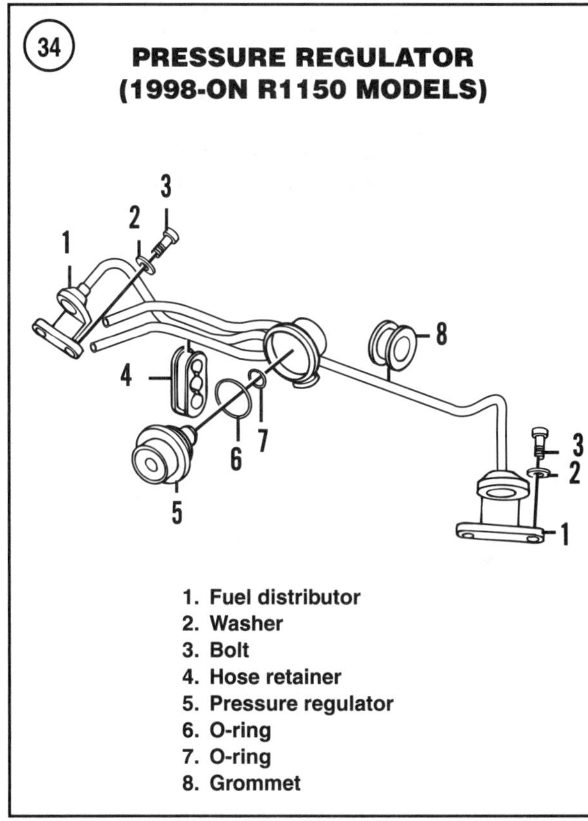

4. Remove the transmission case assembly as described in Chapter Seven or Chapter Eight.

5A. On 1993-1998 models, remove the screw and nut securing the pressure regulator clamp to the fuel distributor. Remove the clamp.

5B. On 1999-on models, slide off the retainer clip securing the pressure regulator to the fuel distributor.

NOTE
Place a clean shop cloth under the pressure regulator to catch any fuel remaining within the fuel distributor.

6A. On 1993-1998 models only, perform the following:
  a. Disconnect the return hose from the fitting on top of the pressure regulator.
  b. Withdraw the pressure regulator from the fuel distributor.
  c. Discard the retainer.
  d. Install a new retainer onto the pressure regulator.

6B. On 1999-on models, withdraw the pressure regulator from the fuel distributor.

7A. On 1993-1998 models, perform the following:
  a. Position the pressure regulator with the fitting facing up and install the pressure regulator into the fuel distributor. Push it in until it bottoms.
  b. Install the clamp and tighten the screw and nut securely.
  c. Connect the hose onto the fitting on top of the pressure regulator.

7B. On 1999-on models, perform the following:
  a. Install the pressure regulator into the fuel distributor. Push it in until it bottoms.
  b. Slide on the retainer clip securing the pressure regulator to the fuel distributor. Make sure it has seated correctly.

8. Install the transmission case assembly as described in Chapter Seven or Chapter Eight.

9

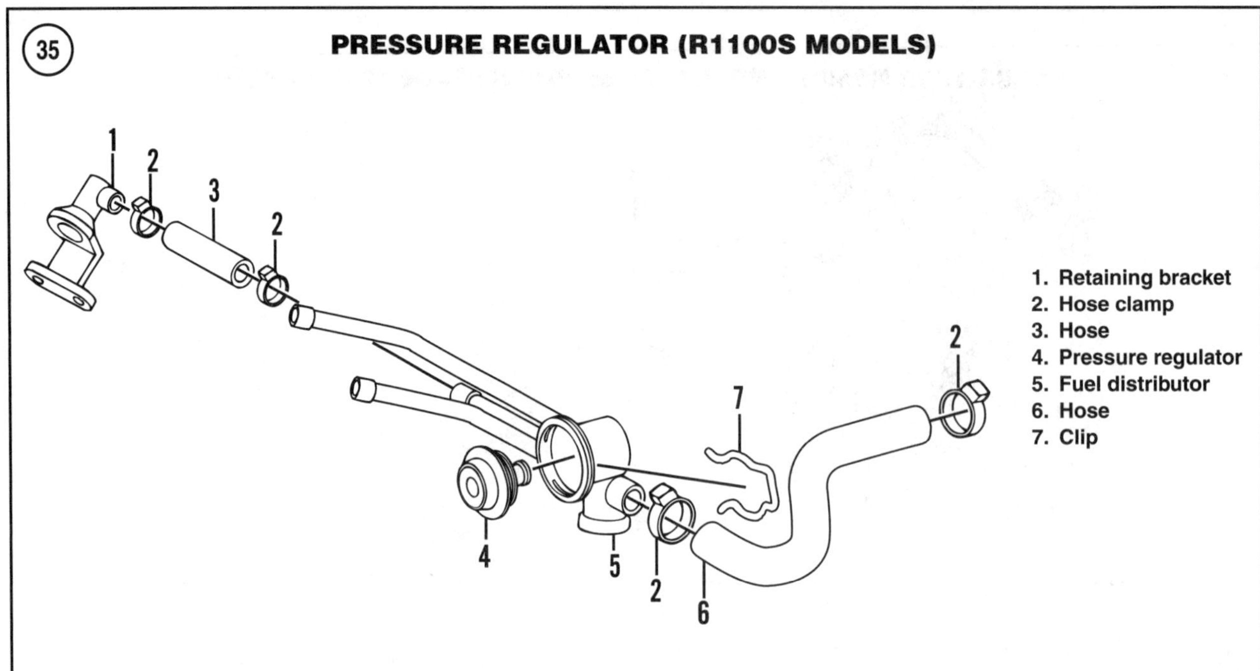

9. Install the air filter air box as described in this chapter.

MOTRONIC CONTROL UNIT

Removal/Installation

All models except R850C and R1200C

1. Disconnect the battery negative lead as described in Chapter Three.
2. Remove the fuel tank as described in this chapter.
3A. On 1993-1998 models, perform the following:
   a. Unhook the clips and carefully disconnect the multi-pin electrical connector (A, **Figure 37**) from the Motronic control unit.
   b. On the right side, remove the screws and washers (B, **Figure 37**) securing the Motronic control unit to the frame mounting brackets.
   c. On the left side, remove the screws and washers (A, **Figure 38**) securing the Motronic control unit to the frame mounting brackets. Note the location of the ground wire (B, **Figure 38**) on the lower screw.
   d. Carefully pull the Motronic control unit (C, **Figure 37**) straight up and out of the frame
3B. On 1999-on models, perform the following:
   a. On some models, it is necessary to move or disconnect some of the electrical connector assemblies (A, **Figure 39**) out of the way to gain access to the multi-pin electrical connector (B).

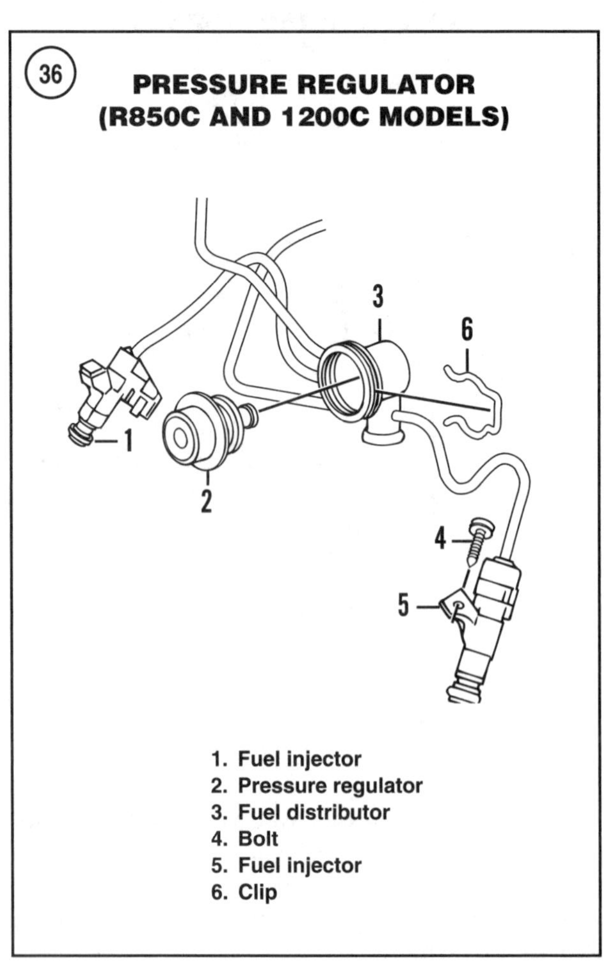

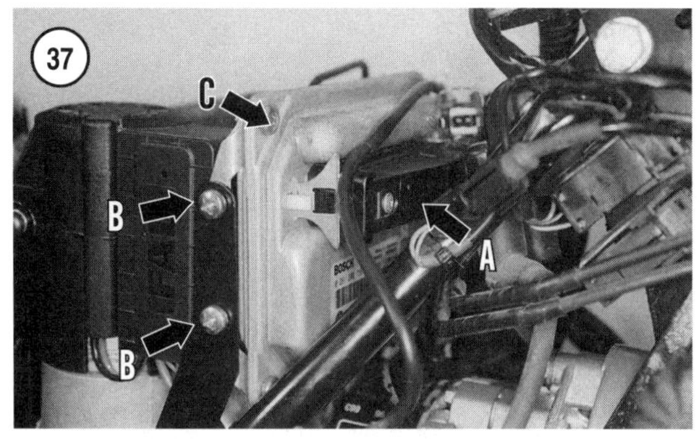

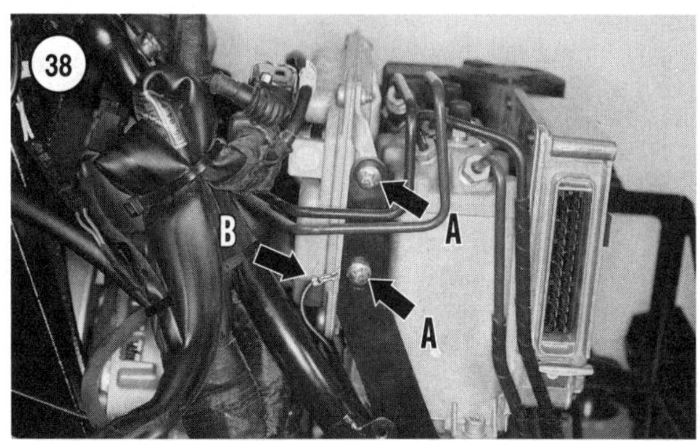

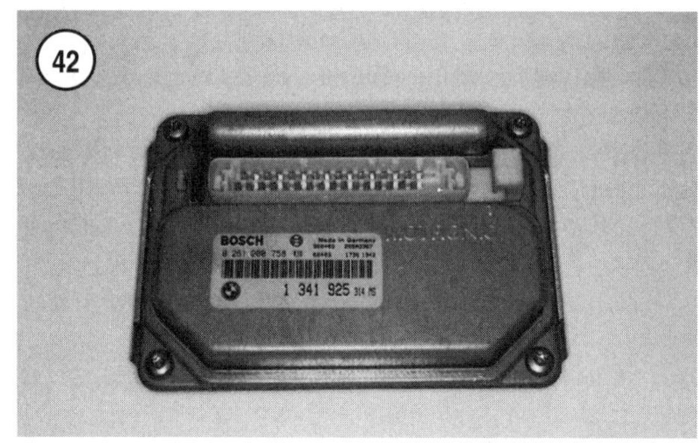

b. Unhook the clips and carefully disconnect the multi-pin electrical connector (B, **Figure 39**) from the Motronic control unit.

c. On the right side, remove the screws and washers (**Figure 40**) securing the Motronic control unit to the frame mounting brackets.

d. On the left side, remove the screws and washers (A, **Figure 41**) securing the Motronic control unit to the frame mounting brackets. Note the location of the ground wire (B, **Figure 41**) on the upper screw.

e. Carefully pull the Motronic control unit (C, **Figure 39**) straight up and out of the frame.

4. Inspect the Motronic control unit (**Figure 42**) for damage. Check for bent or corroded terminals on the multi-pin electrical connector. Straighten or clean them as necessary.

5. Install by reversing these removal steps while noting the following:

a. Make sure the multi-pin electrical connector is pushed on tight and locked in place.

b. Make sure the ground wire is located under the mounting screw and is tight.

R850C and R1200C models

1. Disconnect the battery negative lead as described in Chapter Three.
2. Remove the fuel tank as described in this chapter.
3. Unhook the clips and carefully disconnect the multi-pin electrical connector (A, **Figure 43**) from the Motronic control unit.
4. On the right side, remove the screws and washers (**Figure 44**) securing the Motronic control unit to the central electrical equipment box mounting brackets.
5. On the left side, remove the screws and washers (A, **Figure 45**) securing the Motronic control unit to the frame mounting brackets. Note the location of the ground wire (B, **Figure 45**) on the front screw.
6. Carefully remove the Motronic control unit (B, **Figure 43**) straight up and out of the frame.
7. Inspect the Motronic control unit (**Figure 42**) for damage. Check for bent or corroded terminals on the multi-pin electrical connector. Straighten or clean them as necessary.
8. Install by reversing these removal steps while noting the following:
   a. Make sure the multi-pin electrical connector is pushed on tight and locked in place.
   b. Make sure the ground wire is located under the front mounting screw and is tight.

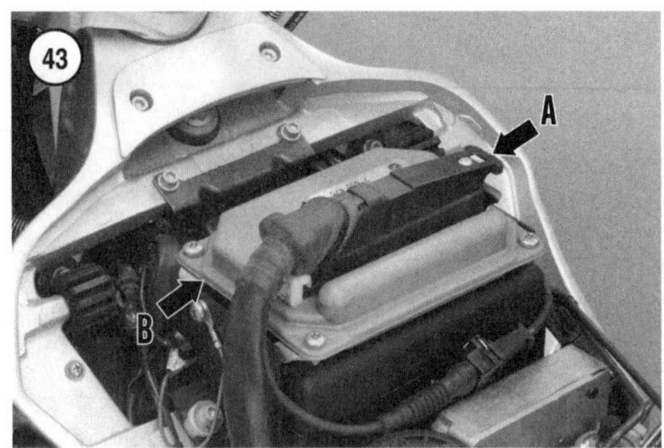

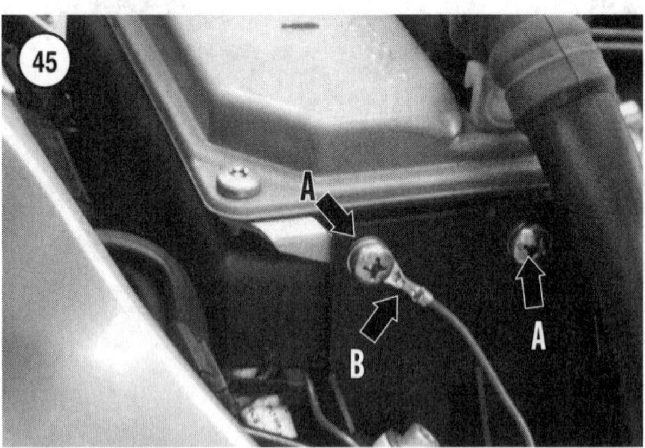

THROTTLE POSITION SENSOR

Removal/Installation

All models except R850C and R1200C

Refer to **Figure 46**.

The throttle position sensor is located only on the left side throttle body and is attached directly to the throttle shaft.

CAUTION
Do not remove the throttle position sensor unless it is going to be replaced.

1. Disconnect the negative battery cable as described in Chapter Three.
2. On RS, RT and S models, remove the front faring side panels as described in Chapter Fifteen.
3. Push on the spring catch (A, **Figure 47**) and disconnect the multi-pin connector (B) from the throttle position sensor.
4. Make alignment marks on the throttle position sensor and the throttle body to establish a basic alignment point for the installation of new sensor.
5. Remove the screws and washers (C, **Figure 47**) securing the throttle position sensor to the right throttle body.
6. Carefully pull the sensor off of the throttle body and remove it.
7. Install by reversing these removal steps while noting the following:
   a. Install the new sensor in the same location as the prior sensor.

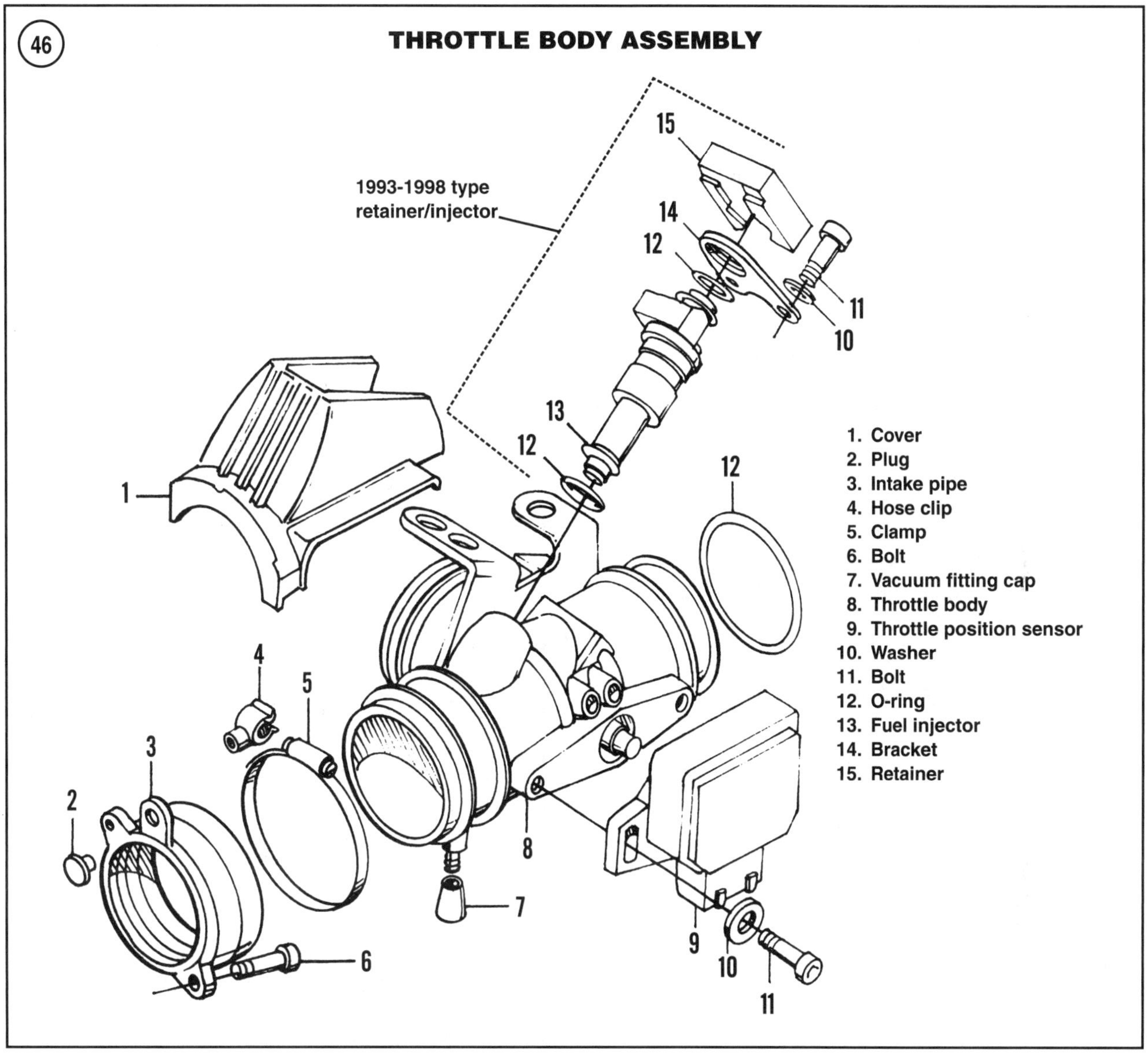

(46)

THROTTLE BODY ASSEMBLY

1993-1998 type retainer/injector

1. Cover
2. Plug
3. Intake pipe
4. Hose clip
5. Clamp
6. Bolt
7. Vacuum fitting cap
8. Throttle body
9. Throttle position sensor
10. Washer
11. Bolt
12. O-ring
13. Fuel injector
14. Bracket
15. Retainer

b. Tighten the screws securely.

c. Have the throttle position sensor adjusted at a BMW dealership. On 1999-on models, it must be adjusted with the MoDiTec diagnostic tool.

R850C and R1200C models

Refer to **Figure 46**.

The throttle position sensor is located on the left side throttle stub pipe within the air filter air case and is attached directly to the throttle shaft.

CAUTION
Do not remove the throttle position sensor unless it is going to be replaced.

1. Disconnect the negative battery cable as described in Chapter Three.
2. Remove the air filter case as described in this chapter.
3. Make alignment marks on the throttle position sensor and the throttle stub pipe to establish a basic alignment point for installation of the new sensor.
4. Remove the screws and washers securing the throttle position sensor to the throttle stub pipe.
5. Carefully pull the sensor off of the throttle stub pipe and remove it.
6. Install by reversing these removal steps while noting the following:
   a. Install the new sensor in the same location as the prior sensor.
   b. Tighten the screws securely.
   c. Have the throttle position sensor adjusted at a BMW dealership with the MoDiTec diagnostic tool.

AIR FILTER ASSEMBLY

Removal/Installation

GS, R, RS and RT models

Refer to **Figure 48**.

1. Remove the seat(s) as described in Chapter Fifteen.
2. On RS and RT models, remove the side sections of the front fairing as described in Chapter Fifteen.
3. Remove the fuel tank as described in this chapter.
4. Remove the front mounting bolt (A, **Figure 49**) and remove the intake air pipe (B).
5. Disconnect the air intake temperature sensor multi-pin electrical connector (A, **Figure 50**) from the air filter case cover.
6. Unhook the clips and remove the air filter case cover (B, **Figure 50**). Remove the element.
7. Remove the rear brake master cylinder reservoir and hose (**Figure 51**) from the frame mounting bracket. It is not necessary to disconnect the brake hose.
8. Disconnect the rear brake light switch from the rear brake master cylinder as described in Chapter Fourteen.
9. Remove all electrical cables clipped to the side of the air box. Move the cables out of the way.
10. Disconnect the electrical connectors from the neutral switch and the sidestand switch.
11. Loosen the clamps (A, **Figure 52**) and remove the inlet pipes (B) from both throttle bodies.

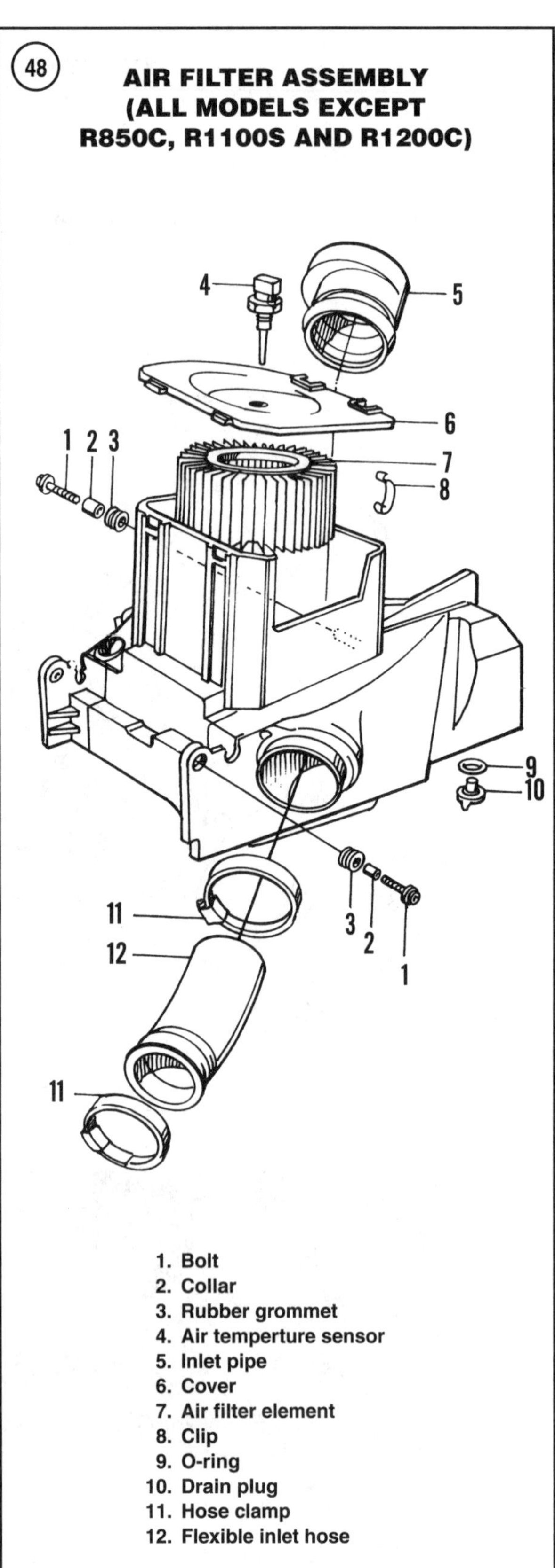

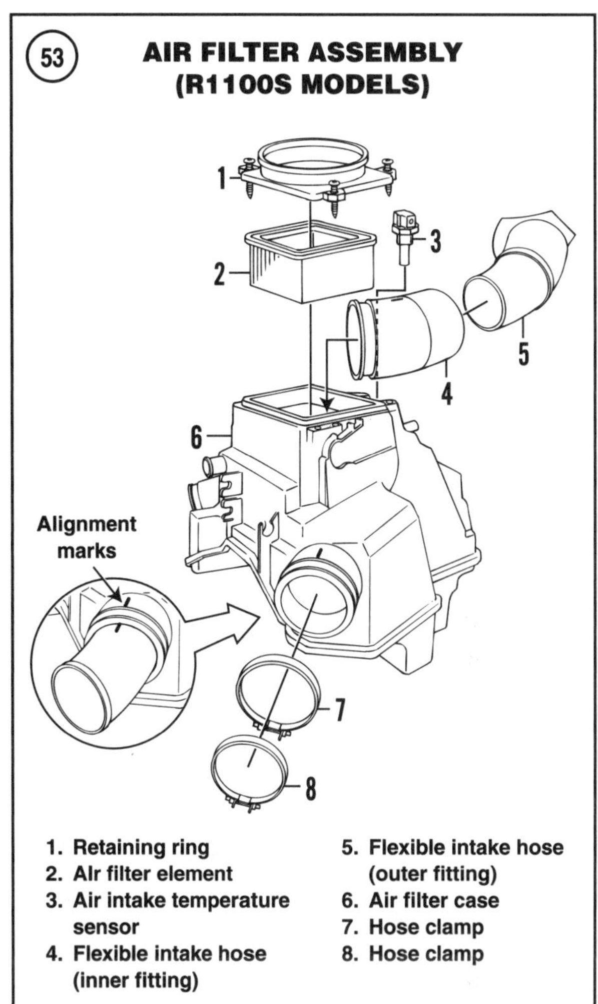

1. Retaining ring
2. Air filter element
3. Air intake temperature sensor
4. Flexible intake hose (inner fitting)
5. Flexible intake hose (outer fitting)
6. Air filter case
7. Hose clamp
8. Hose clamp

12. On models so equipped, disengage the throttle cables at the Bowden cable divider as described in this chapter.
13. Remove the muffler as described in this chapter.
14. Remove the rear wheel as described in Chapter Eleven.
15. Remove the rear shock absorber as described in Chapter Thirteen.
16. Raise the rear frame member assembly as described in Chapter Fifteen.
17. Disconnect the crankcase breather hose from the air case.
18. Remove the air filter case from the frame.
19. Install by reversing these removal steps.

S models

Refer to **Figure 53**.

1. Remove the seat(s) as described in Chapter Fifteen.
2. Remove the side sections of the front fairing as described in Chapter Fifteen.
3. Remove the fuel tank as described in this chapter.
4. Disconnect the air intake temperature sensor multi-pin electrical connector (A, **Figure 54**) from the air filter case cover.
5. Unhook the diagnostic connector (B, **Figure 54**) from the air filter cover and move it out of the way.
6. Remove the screws securing the air filter cover (C, **Figure 54**).
7. Hinge up the cover and carefully release the locating tabs from the slots in the air box. Do not pull on the cover until the tabs are released, otherwise the tabs will break off.
8. Remove the cover and set it aside.
9. Remove the element (A, **Figure 55**) from the air box.
10. Remove the front mounting bolt and remove the intake air pipe (B, **Figure 55**).
11. Remove all electrical cables clipped to the side of the air box. Move the cables out of the way.
12. Disconnect the crankcase breather hose from the air case.
13. Remove the throttle body assembly (**Figure 56**) from each side as described in this chapter.
14. Disengage the throttle cables at the Bowden cable divider as described in this chapter.
15. Remove the exhaust system as described in this chapter.
16. Remove the transmission as described in Chapter Seven.
17. Remove the air filter case from the frame.
18. Install by reversing these removal steps.

R850C and R1200C models

Refer to **Figure 57**.

1. Place a suitable size jack under the engine to support the motorcycle with the rear wheel off the ground.
2. Disconnect the negative battery cable as described in Chapter Three.
3. Remove the seat as described in Chapter Fifteen.
4. Remove the fuel tank as described in this chapter.
5. Disconnect the air intake temperature sensor multi-pin electrical connector (**Figure 58**) from the air filter case cover.
6. Remove the screws securing the air filter cover (**Figure 59**).
7. Remove the cover and intake tube and set it aside.
8. Remove the element (**Figure 60**) from the air box.

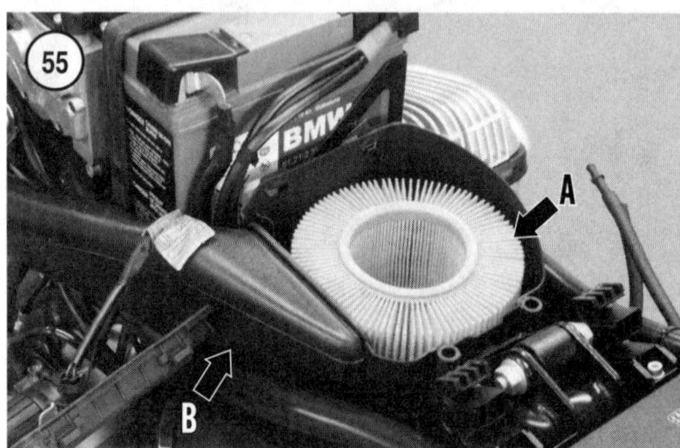

9. Loosen the clamps (A, **Figure 61**) on the flexible intake tube (B) and remove the tube from the air filter case and the intake pipe.
10. Unhook the straps (A, **Figure 62**) and remove the tool kit (B) from the brackets.
11. Pull up on the fuse boxes (**Figure 63**) and partially move them out of the way.
12. Remove the bolts and washers securing the fuse box/tool kit holder to the air filter air box. Leave the fuse boxes and holder in place.

57

AIR FILTER AND THROTTLE BODY ASSEMBLY (R850C AND R1200C MODELS)

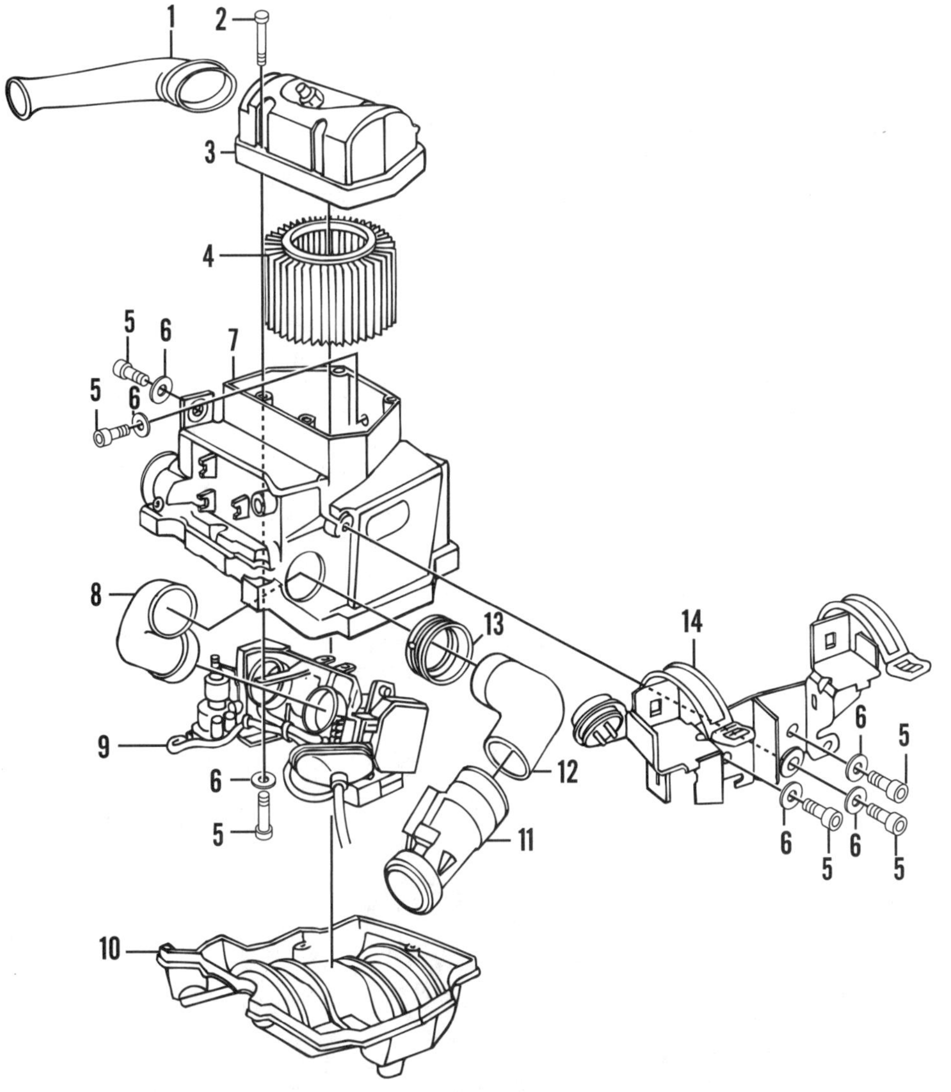

1. Intake tube
2. Screw
3. Cover
4. Air filter element
5. Bolt
6. Washer
7. Air filter case
8. Flexible intake hose (right side)
9. Throttle body
10. Air filter case bottom cover
11. Intake pipe
12. Flexible intake hose (left side)
13. Hose clamp
14. Fuse box/tool kit holder

58

59

13. Remove the rear frame as described in Chapter Fifteen.
14. Remove the air filter case from the main frame.
15. Install by reversing these removal steps.

THROTTLE CABLES

The 1993-1995 models are equipped with a single throttle cable that controls both throttle bodies. The single cable runs from the throttle grip to the left throttle body throttle wheel and then across the engine to the right side throttle wheel.

The system used on 1996-on models, except R850C and R1200C models, uses three short throttle cables and a Bowden cable junction box on the right side of the motorcycle. The first cable runs from the throttle grip to the distribution disc within the junction box. From the junction box, two separate throttle cables leave the distribution disc and connect to each throttle body.

The R850C and R1200C models are equipped with a single throttle cable that controls the throttle body assembly located within the air filter case. The single cable runs from the throttle grip to the right side where it enters the air filter box and is attached to the throttle wheel.

Removal/Installation

1993-1995 models

1. Disconnect the negative battery cable as described in Chapter Three.
2. Remove both seats as described in Chapter Fifteen.
3. On RS and RT models, remove the side sections of the front fairing as described in Chapter Fifteen.
4. Remove the fuel tank as described in this chapter.
5. Remove the screw (A, **Figure 64**) securing the switch assembly (B) to the handlebar. Move the switch assembly out of the way.
6. Remove the throttle cable cover (**Figure 65**) and disconnect the throttle cable (**Figure 66**) from the throttle grip.
7. Partially remove both throttle body assemblies to gain access to the backside of the assembly as described in this chapter.
8. On the right side, perform the following:
   a. Carefully rotate the throttle body around to gain access to the throttle wheel on the backside of the assembly.
   b. Unhook the throttle cable from the bracket (A, **Figure 67**).
   c. Remove the retaining spring and disconnect the throttle cable end from the throttle wheel (B, **Figure 67**).

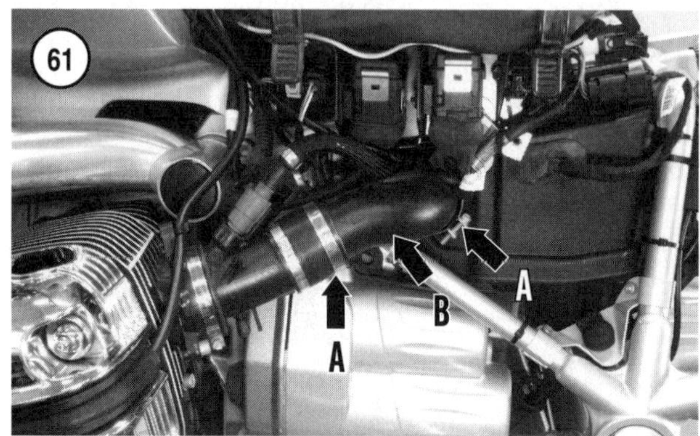

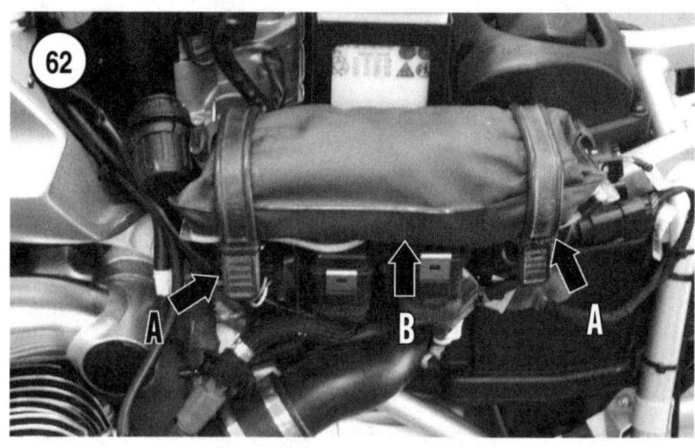

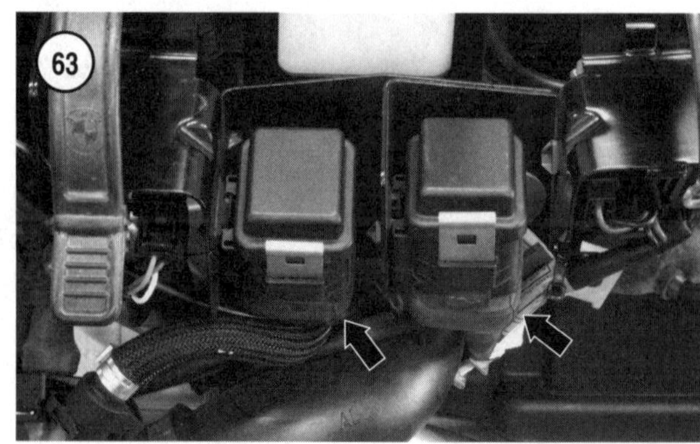

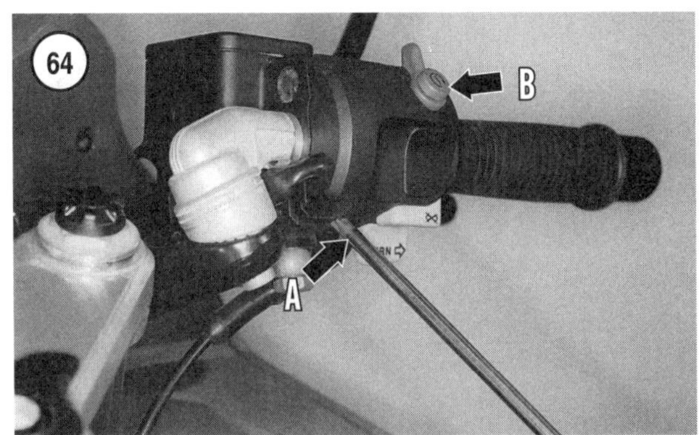

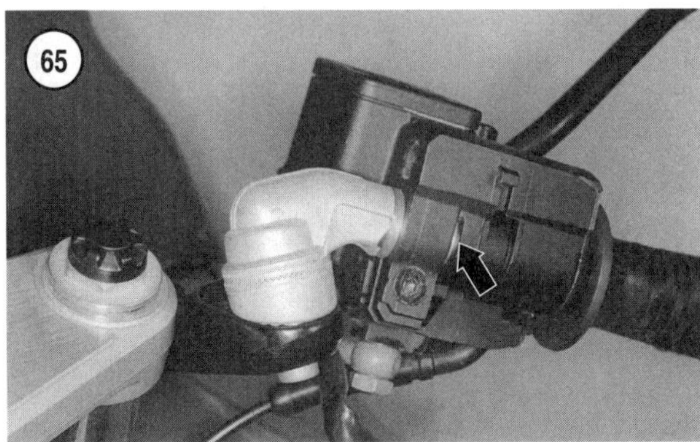

9. On the left side, perform the following:
   a. Carefully rotate the throttle body around to gain access to the throttle wheel on the backside of the assembly.

NOTE
Prior to disconnecting the throttle cables, mark their position on the throttle wheel to ensure correct location during installation.

   b. Loosen both locknuts and turn both adjusters (A, **Figure 68**) to allow slack in the throttle cable.

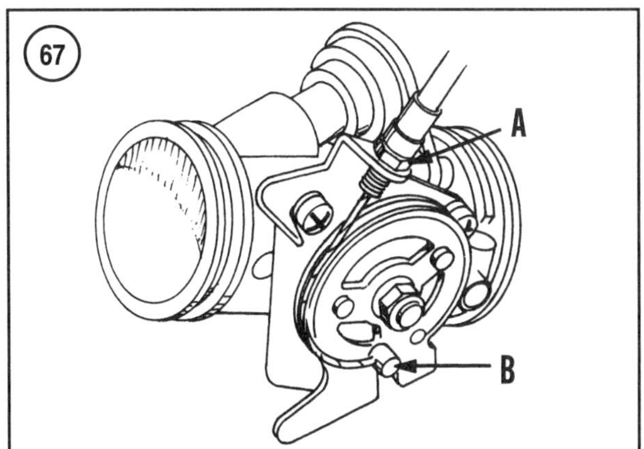

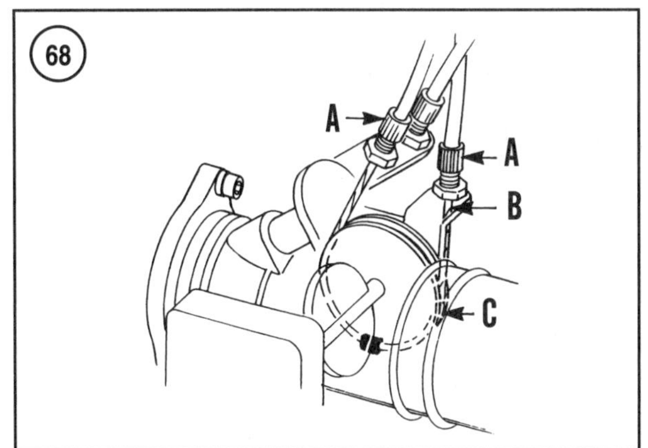

   c. Unhook the throttle cable from the bracket (B, **Figure 68**).
   d. Remove the retaining spring and disconnect the throttle cable nipple from the throttle wheel.
   e. Remove and disconnect the throttle cable ends from the throttle wheel (C, **Figure 68**).

10. Disconnect the throttle cable from any clips and/or tie wraps securing it to the handlebar and frame.

11. Make a note of the cable routing path through the frame, then remove it.

12. If not nylon lined, lubricate the new cable as described in Chapter Three.

13. Install by reversing these removal steps while noting the following:
   a. On the left side, be sure to install the throttle cable into the correct location on the throttle wheel as noted during removal.
   b. Operate the throttle lever and make sure the throttle body linkage operates correctly without binding. If not, correct the problem at this time.
   c. Adjust the throttle cable as described in Chapter Three.

d. Start the engine and allow it to idle. Turn the handlebar from side to side, making sure the idle speed does not increase. If the idle speed increases, the throttle cable is incorrectly adjusted or the throttle cable is improperly routed.

WARNING
An improperly adjusted or incorrectly routed throttle cable(s) can cause the throttle to stick open, resulting in an accident. Do not ride the motorcycle until the throttle cable operation is correct.

1996-on models (except R850C and R1200C)

1. Disconnect the negative battery cable as described in Chapter Three.
2. Remove both seats as described in Chapter Fifteen.
3. On RS, RT and S models, remove the side sections of the front fairing as described in Chapter Fifteen.
4. Remove the fuel tank as described in this chapter.

5A. On early models, perform the following:
  a. Remove the screw (A, **Figure 64**) securing the switch assembly (B) to the handlebar. Move the switch assembly out of the way.
  b. Remove the throttle cable cover (**Figure 65**) and disconnect the throttle cable (**Figure 66**) from the throttle grip.

5B. On later models, perform the following:
  a. Remove the screw securing the throttle grip cover (**Figure 69**) and remove the cover.
  b. Unscrew the throttle cable adjust screw and disengage the throttle cable from the throttle grip.

6. Partially remove both throttle body assemblies to gain access to the backside of each assembly as described in this chapter.
7. On the right side, perform the following:
  a. Carefully rotate the throttle body around to gain access to the throttle wheel on the backside of the assembly.
  b. Unhook the throttle cable from the bracket (A, **Figure 70**).
  c. Remove the retaining spring and disconnect the throttle cable end from the throttle wheel (B, **Figure 70**).
8. On the left side, perform the following:
  a. Carefully rotate the throttle body around to gain access to the throttle wheel on the backside of the assembly.

69

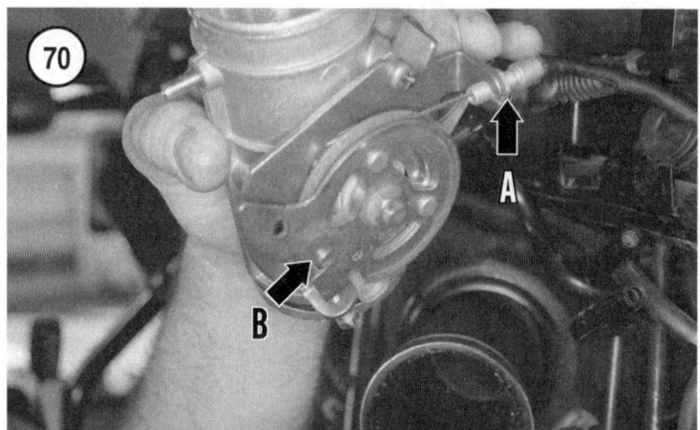

70

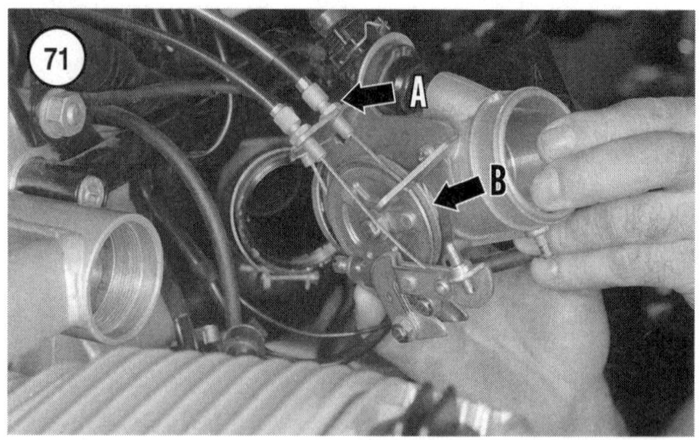

71

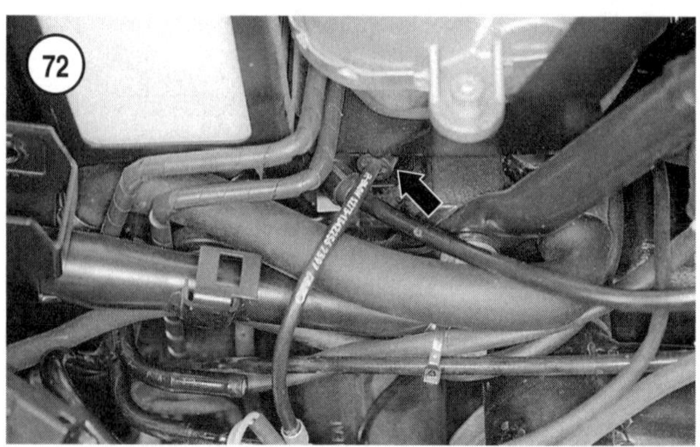
72

73

BOWDEN CABLE DIVIDER (EARLY MODELS)

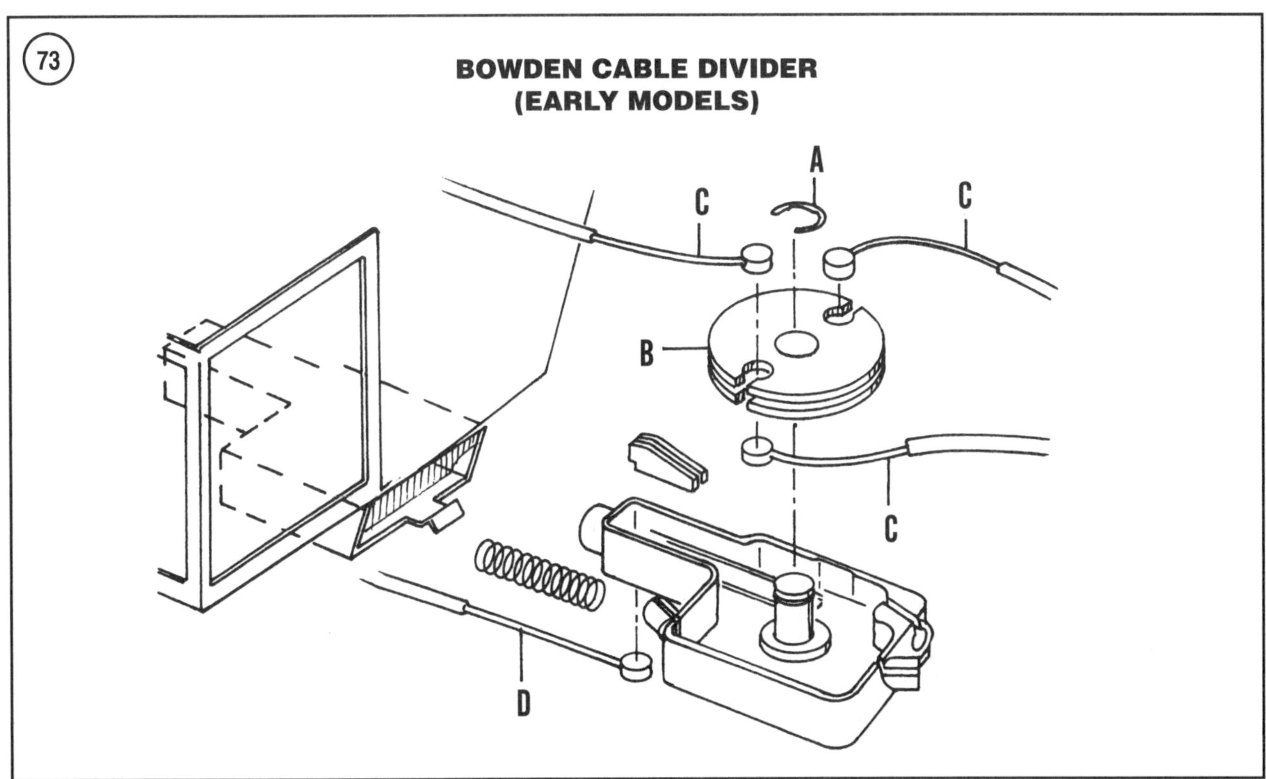

74

NOTE
Prior to disconnecting the throttle cables, mark their position on the throttle wheel to ensure correct location during installation.

b. Unhook the throttle cable from the bracket (A, **Figure 71**).

c. Remove the retaining springs and disconnect the throttle cable end from the throttle wheel (B, **Figure 71**).

9A. On early models, perform the following:

a. On the right side of the motorcycle, release the clip and carefully withdraw the cable distribution block (**Figure 72**) from under the ABS unit.

b. Remove the E-clip (A, **Figure 73**) and pull the distribution disc (B) up off of the pivot post.

c. Mark the location of the three throttle cables on the disc prior to removal, then remove the cables (C, **Figure 73**) from the disc.

9B. On later models, perform the following:

a. On the right side of the motorcycle, release the clip and carefully withdraw the cable distribution block (**Figure 74**) from under the ABS unit.

b. Remove the E-clip (A, **Figure 75**) and pull the distribution disc (B) up off of the pivot post.

c. Mark the location of the three throttle cables on the disc prior to removal, then remove the cables (C, **Figure 73**) from the disc.

10. Disconnect the throttle cables from any clips and/or tie wraps securing them to the handlebar and frame.

11. Make a note of the cable routing path through the frame, then remove them.

12. On non-nylon lined cables, lubricate the new cables as described in Chapter Three.

13. Install by reversing these removal steps while noting the following:

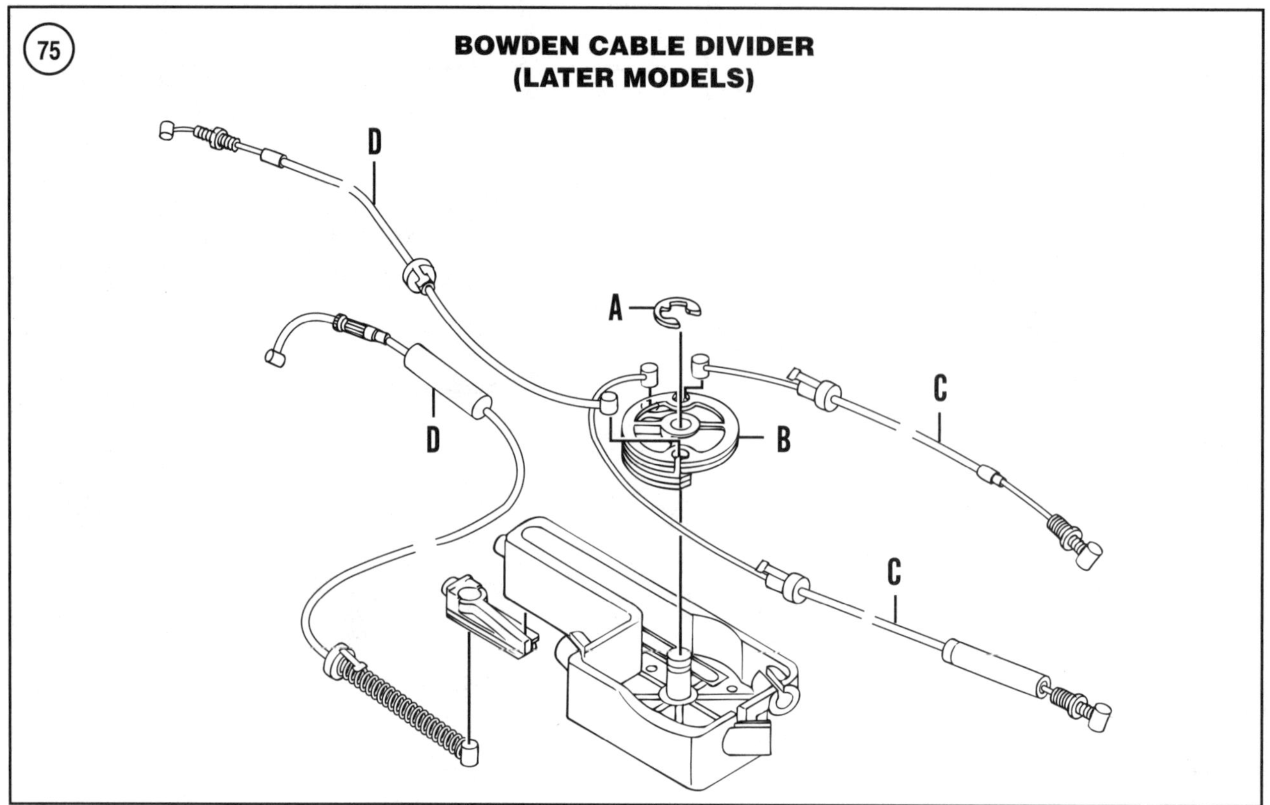

a. On the left side, be sure to install the throttle cable into the correct location on the throttle wheel as noted during removal.
b. Operate the throttle lever and make sure the throttle body linkage operates correctly without binding. If not, correct the problem at this time.
c. Adjust the throttle cable as described in Chapter Three.
d. Start the engine and allow it to idle. Turn the handlebar from side to side, making sure the idle speed does not increase. If idle speed increases, the throttle cable is incorrectly adjusted or the throttle cable is improperly routed.

WARNING
An improperly adjusted or incorrectly routed throttle cable(s) can cause the throttle to stick open, resulting in an accident. Do not ride the motorcycle until the throttle cable operation is correct.

R850C and R1200C models

1. Disconnect the negative battery cable as described in Chapter Three.
2. Remove both seats as described in Chapter Fifteen.

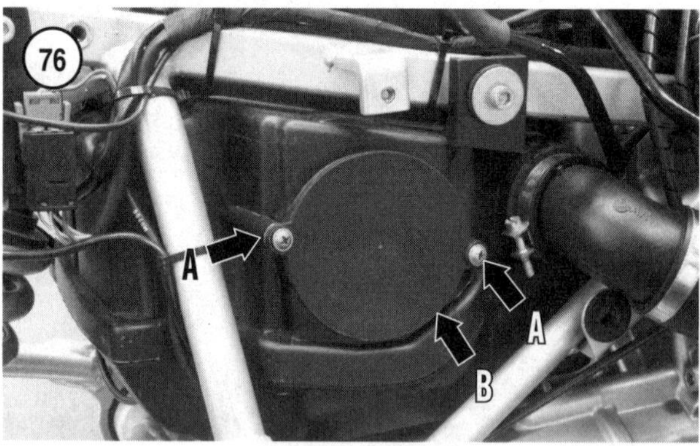

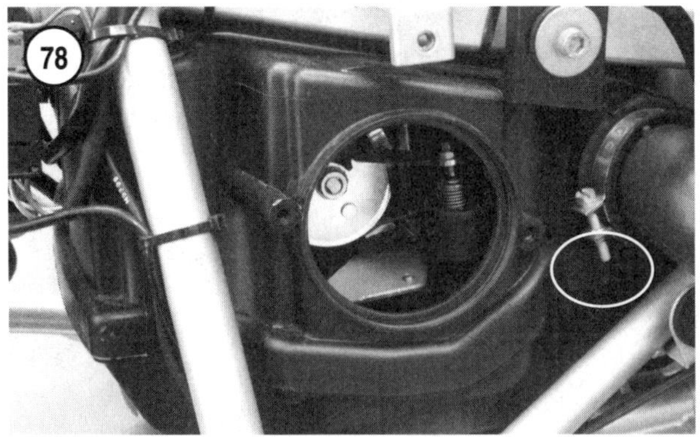

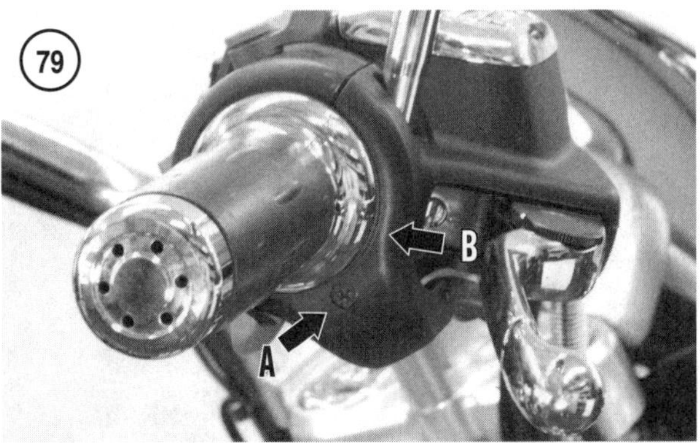

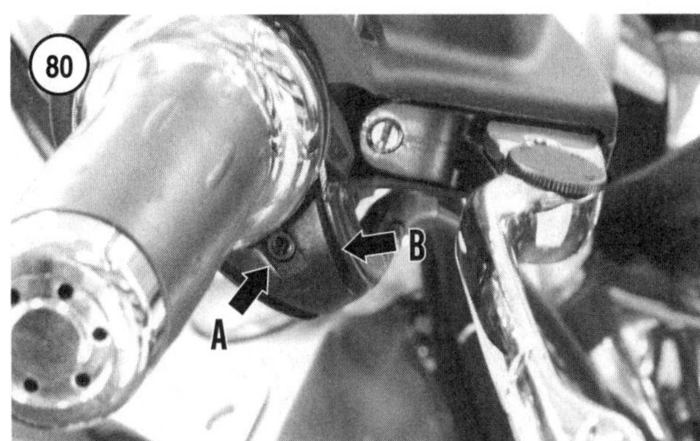

3. Remove the fuel tank as described in this chapter.

4. Remove the screws (A, **Figure 76**) securing the throttle cable cover (B) on the air filter case and remove the cover.

5. Within the air filter case, disconnect the throttle cable end from the throttle wheel (**Figure 77**).

6. Working at the front, lower right side of the air filter case (**Figure 78**), press the throttle cable rubber nipple out of the case.

7. Carefully withdraw the throttle cable out of the air filter case.

8. At the throttle grip on the handlebar, perform the following:

   a. Remove the screw (A, **Figure 79**) securing the throttle cable cover and remove the cover (B).
   b. On models so equipped, remove the screw (A, **Figure 80**) securing the throttle cable guide and remove the guide (B).
   c. Disconnect the throttle cable end (**Figure 81**) from the grip assembly.
   d. Disconnect the throttle cable from the throttle grip assembly.

9. Disconnect the throttle cable from any clips and/or tie wraps securing them to the handlebar and frame.

10. Make a note of the cable routing path through the frame, then remove it.

11. On a non-nylon lined cable, lubricate the new cable as described in Chapter Three.

12. Install by reversing these removal steps while noting the following:

   a. Make sure the throttle cable rubber nipple is secure in the air filter case to guard against moisture.
   b. Inspect the O-ring gasket (**Figure 82**) on the throttle cable cover. Replace if necessary and tighten the cover screws securely.
   c. Operate the throttle lever and make sure the throttle body assembly operates correctly without binding. If not, correct the problem at this time.

d. Adjust the throttle cable as described in Chapter Three.
e. Start the engine and allow it to idle. Turn the handlebar from side to side, making sure the idle speed does not increase. If idle speed increases, the throttle cable is incorrectly adjusted or the throttle cable is improperly routed.

WARNING
An improperly adjusted or incorrectly routed throttle cable can cause the throttle to stick open, resulting in an accident. Do not ride the motorcycle until the throttle cable operation is correct.

INCREASE IDLE (CHOKE) CABLE REPLACEMENT (ALL MODELS EXCEPT R850C AND R1200C)

NOTE
The R850C and R1200C models are not equipped with an increase idle (choke) system.

1. Disconnect the battery negative lead as described in Chapter Three.
2. Remove the seat (s) as described in Chapter Fifteen.
3. On RS, RT and S models, remove the side sections of the front fairing as described in Chapter Fifteen.
4. Remove the fuel tank as described in this chapter.

5A. On R850R and all R1100 models (except R1100S), disconnect the increase idle (choke) cable as follows:
a. Carefully pry off the cover from the operating lever.
b. Unscrew the large flat screw (**Figure 83**) and special washer (**Figure 84**).
c. Remove the lever (A, **Figure 85**) from the housing and disconnect the cable (B) from the lever.
d. Push the cable sleeve out and remove the cable (C, **Figure 85**) from the slot in the cable housing.

5B. On all other models, perform the following:
a. On GS models so equipped, remove the bolt securing the hand guard (A, **Figure 86**) and handlebar weight (B).
b. On all other models, remove the bolt securing the handlebar weight (B, **Figure 86**) and remove the weight.
c. Remove the two screws securing the handgrip (C, **Figure 86**).
d. On models so equipped, disconnect the electrical connector and release the cable shoe for the heated handlebar grip.
e. Slide the grip (A, **Figure 87**) off the handlebar.

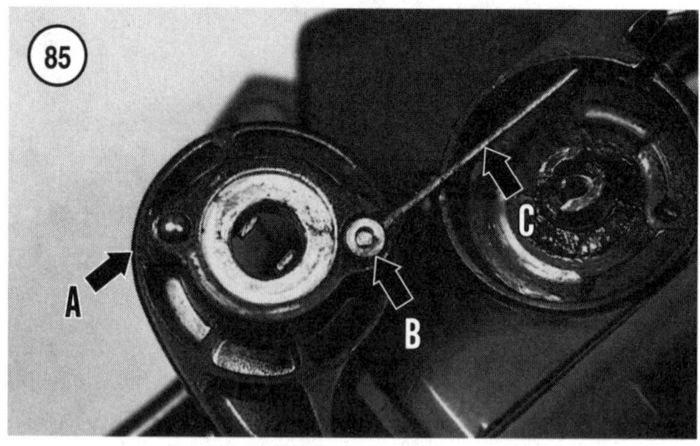

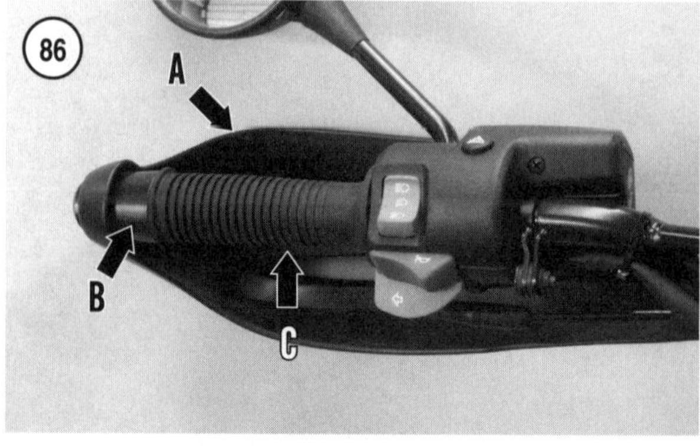

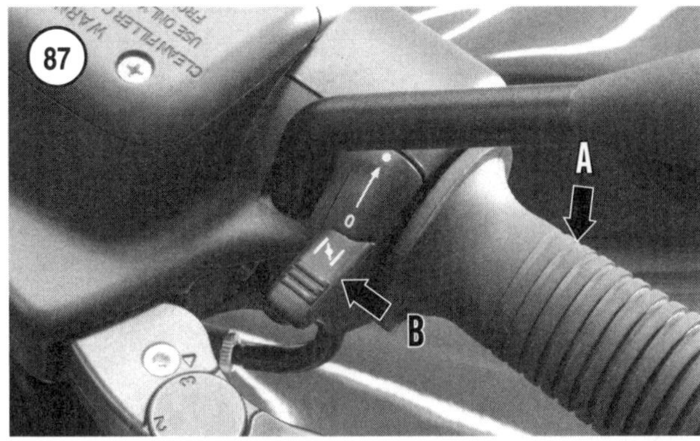

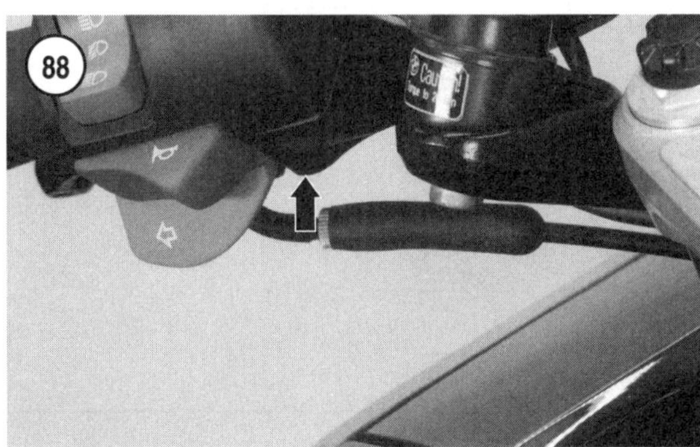

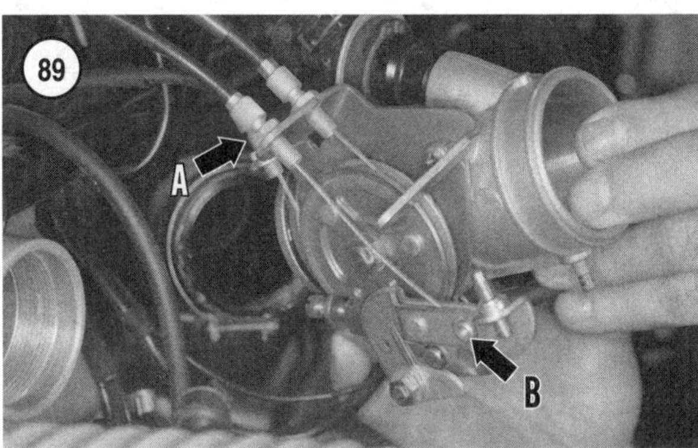

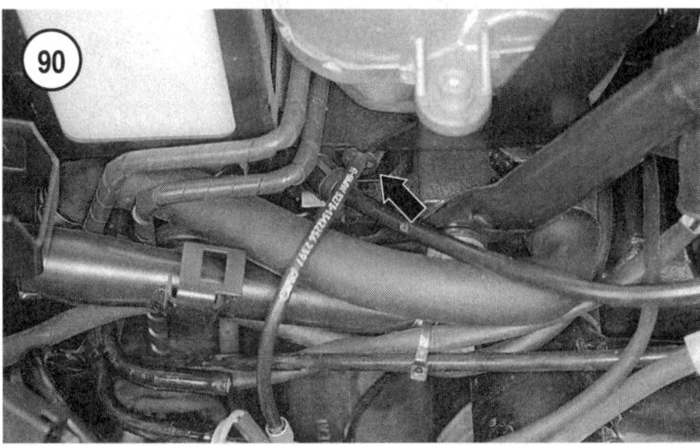

   f. Remove the screws securing the lower section of the clutch lever fitting (**Figure 88**) and remove the fitting.
   g. Remove the screws securing the increase idle (choke) lever (B, **Figure 87**) and move the lever out of the way.

6. Partially remove the left side throttle body assembly to gain access to the backside of the throttle body assembly.
7. Carefully rotate the throttle body around to gain access to the throttle wheel on the backside of the assembly.
8. Unhook the choke cable from the bracket (A, **Figure 89**).
9. Remove the retaining spring and disconnect the choke cable end from the linkage (B, **Figure 89**).

10A. On early models, perform the following:
   a. On the right side of the motorcycle, release the clip and carefully withdraw the cable distribution block (**Figure 90**) from under the ABS unit.
   b. Remove the E-clip (A, **Figure 91**) and pull the distribution disc (B) up off of the pivot post.
   c. Mark the location of the choke cable on the disc prior to removal, then remove the cable (D, **Figure 91**) from the disc.

10B. On later models, perform the following:
   a. On the right side of the motorcycle, release the clip and carefully withdraw the cable distribution block (**Figure 92**) from under the ABS unit.
   b. Remove the E-clip (A, **Figure 93**) and pull the distribution disc (B) up off of the pivot post.
   c. Mark the location of the choke cable on the disc prior to removal, then remove the cable (D, **Figure 93**) from the disc.

11. Disconnect the choke cable from any clips and/or tie wraps securing them to the handlebar and frame.
12. Make a note of the cable routing path through the frame, then remove it.
13. On a non-nylon lined cable, lubricate the new cable as described in Chapter Three.
14. Install by reversing these removal steps while noting the following:
   a. Operate the choke lever and make sure the throttle body linkage operates correctly without binding. If operation is incorrect or there is binding, make sure that the cables attach correctly and there are no tight bends in either cable.
   b. Adjust the choke cable as described in Chapter Three.
   c. Start the engine and allow to idle. Then turn the handlebar from side to side, making sure the idle speed does not increase. If it does, the choke cable is adjusted incorrectly or the choke cable is routed improperly.

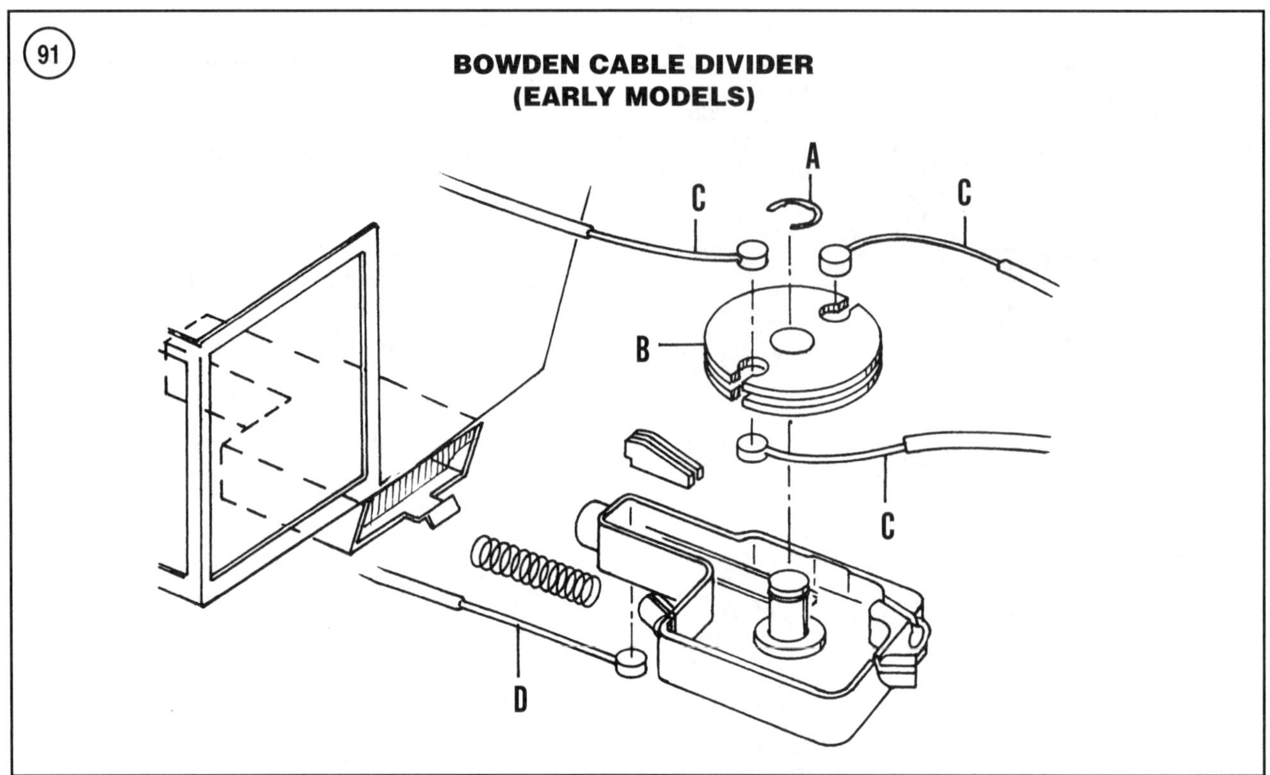

WARNING
An improperly adjusted or incorrectly routed throttle cable can cause the throttle to stick open, resulting in an accident. Do not ride the motorcycle until the throttle cable operation is correct.

FUEL TANK

WARNING
Some fuel may spill from the fuel tank hoses when during the following procedures.

Because gasoline is extremely flammable and explosive, perform this procedure away from all open flames, including appliance pilot lights, and sparks. Do not smoke or allow anyone to smoke in the work area, as an explosion and fire may occur. Always work in a well-ventilated area. Wipe up any spills immediately.

WARNING
Route the fuel vapor hoses so they cannot contact hot engine or exhaust components. These hoses contain flammable vapors.

WARNING
A small amount of fuel will drain out of the fuel tank when the fuel lines are disconnected from the base of the tank. Place several shop cloths under the fuel line fittings to catch spilled fuel prior to disconnecting them. Discard the shop cloths in a safe manner.

Removal/Installation

R850R, R1100GS, R1100R and R1100RS models

Refer to **Figure 94** and **Figure 95**.

1A. On models so equipped, place the motorcycle on the centerstand with the front wheel off the ground.

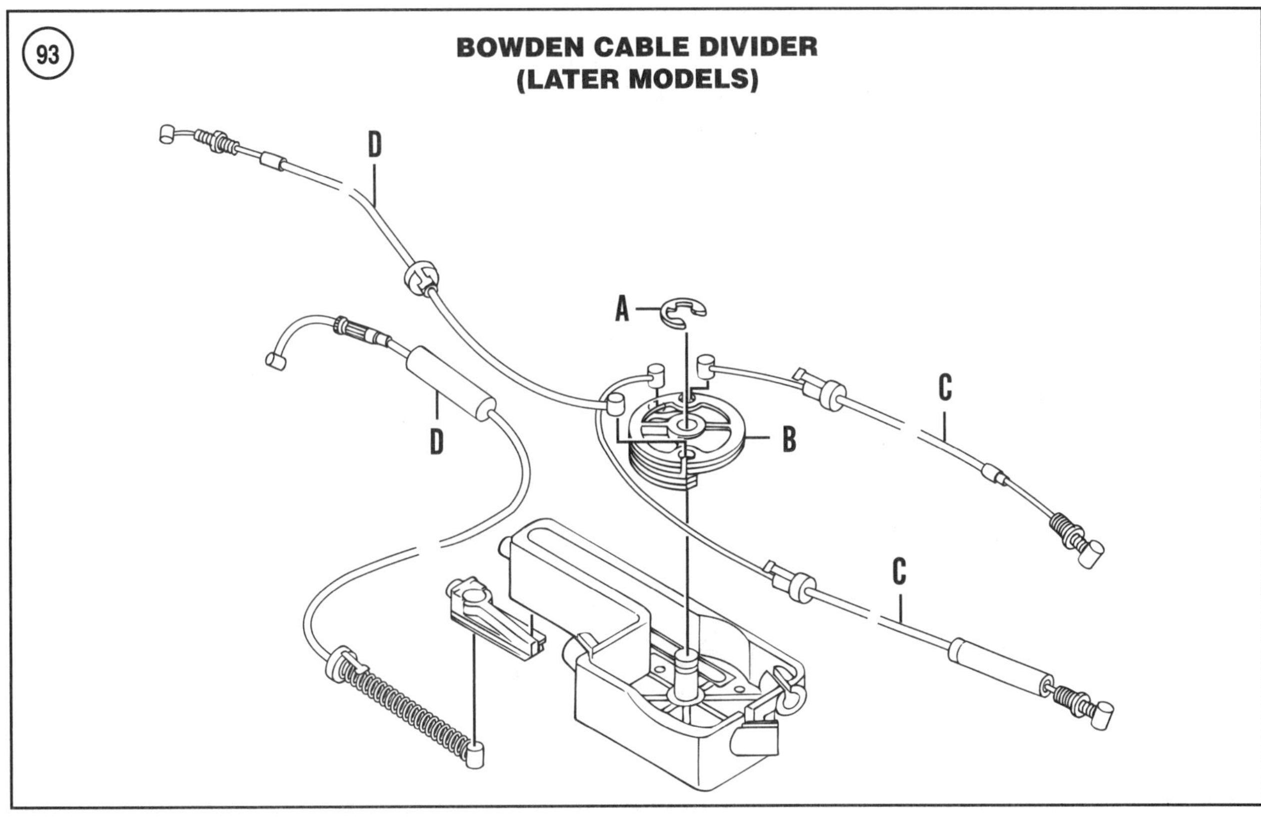
93
BOWDEN CABLE DIVIDER
(LATER MODELS)
D
A
D
B
C
C

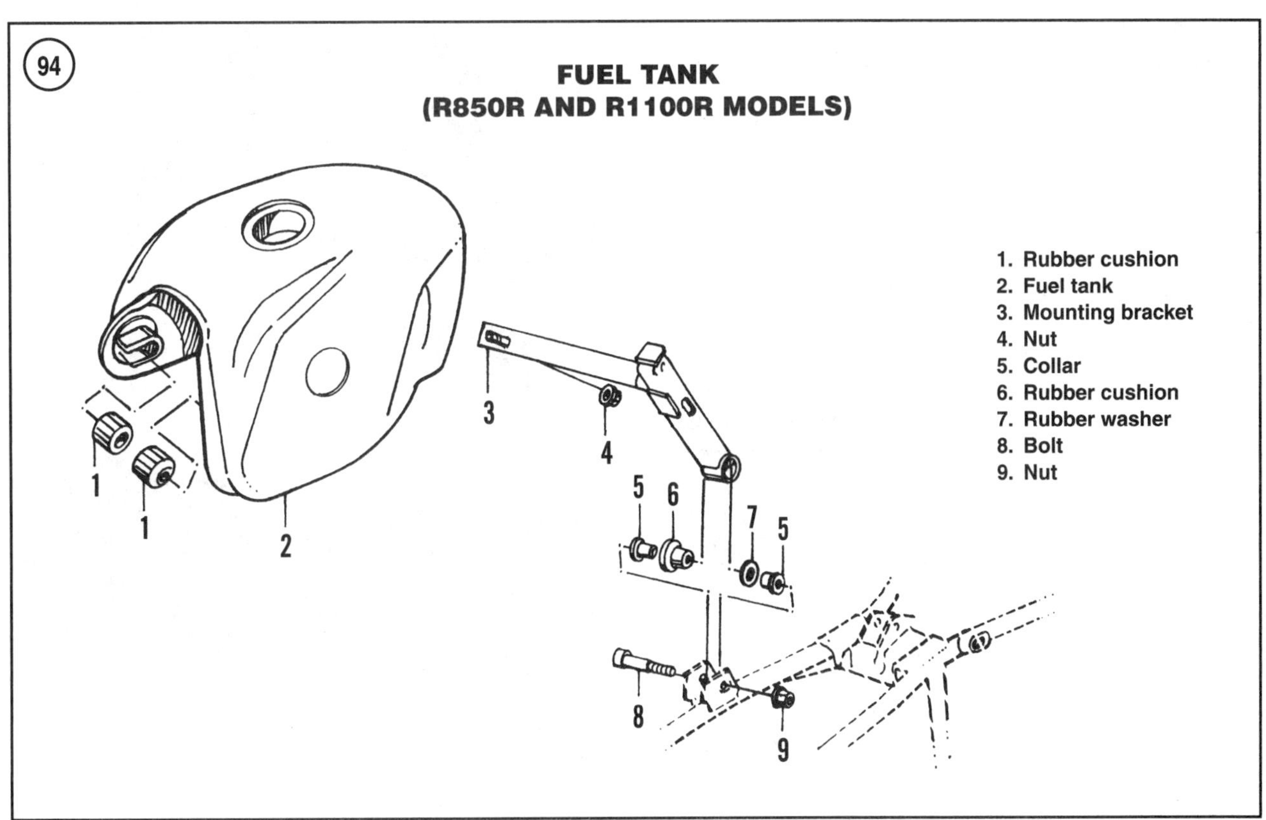
94
FUEL TANK
(R850R AND R1100R MODELS)
1. Rubber cushion
2. Fuel tank
3. Mounting bracket
4. Nut
5. Collar
6. Rubber cushion
7. Rubber washer
8. Bolt
9. Nut
1
1
2
3
4
5
6
7
5
8
9

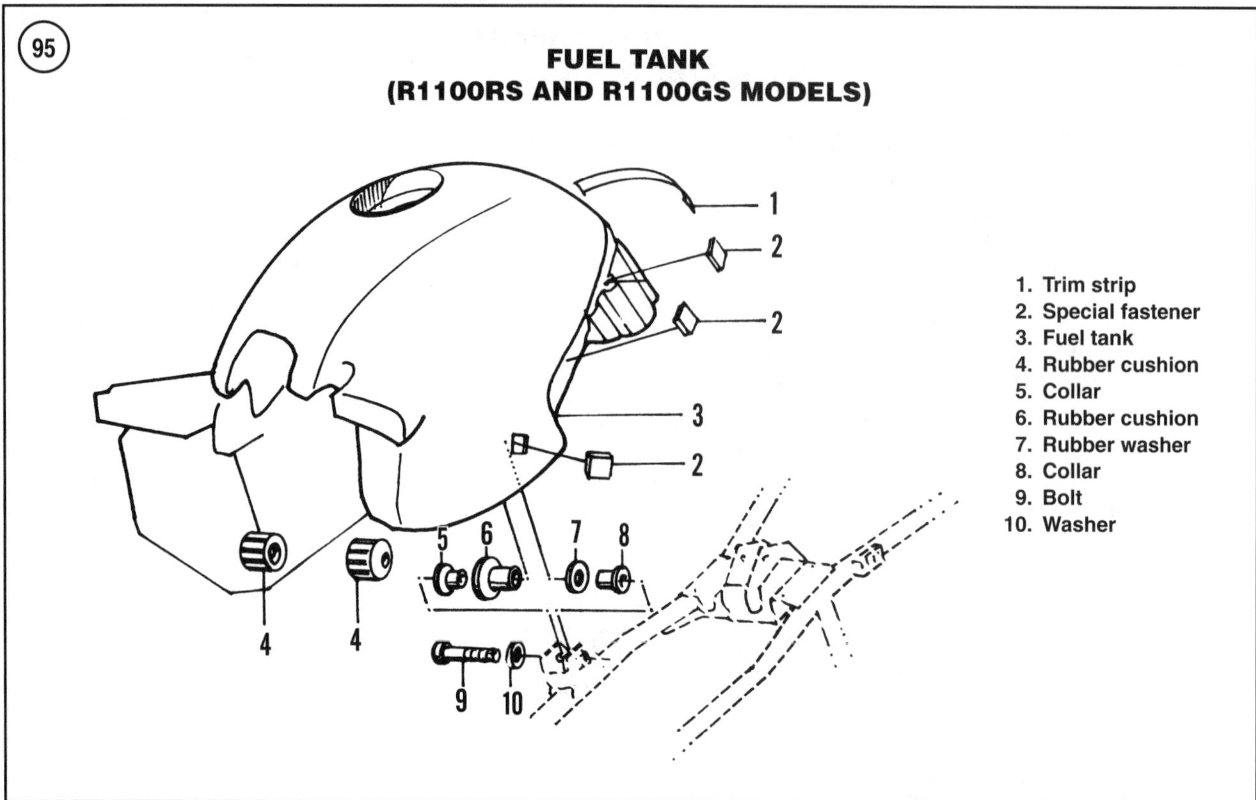

1B. On models without a centerstand, place a suitable size jack under the engine to support the motorcycle with the front wheel off the ground.

2. Remove the seat(s) as described in Chapter Fifteen.

3. Disconnect the negative battery cable as described in Chapter Three.

4. On RS models, remove the front fairing side panels and the inner panels as described in Chapter Fifteen.

5. Disconnect the fuel pump multi-pin electrical connector (**Figure 96**).

6. Remove the tie wrap (**Figure 97**) securing the fuel feed and return lines to the frame crossmember.

7. Remove the bolt and washer (**Figure 98**) securing the rear of the fuel tank to the frame. On models so equipped, do not lose the spacer (**Figure 99**) between the frame mounting bracket and the fuel tank mounting bracket.

8. Raise the rear of the fuel tank to gain access to the fuel lines.

9. Prior to disconnecting the fuel lines, mark them so they will be reconnected to the correct fitting during installation.

10. Depressurize the fuel system as described in this chapter.

11. Disconnect the fuel return line (**Figure 100**) and the fuel pressure line (**Figure 101**).

12. Plug the fuel lines and vacuum lines.

98

99

100

101

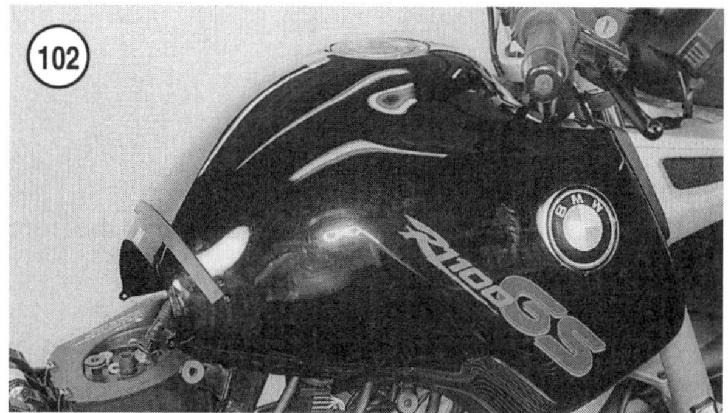
102

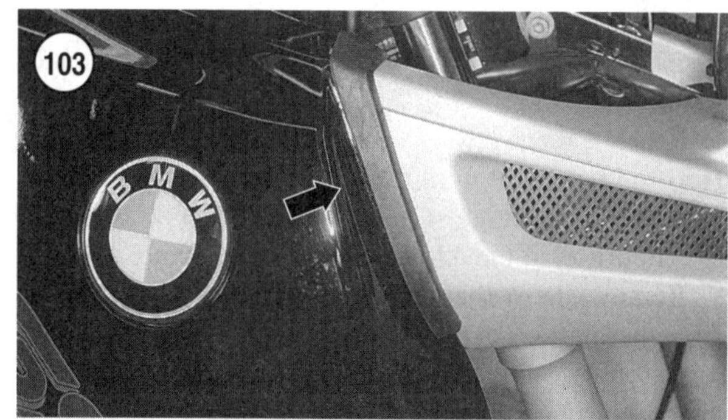
103

104

13. Carefully remove the fuel tank (**Figure 102**, typical) and mounting bracket (R models) from the frame.
14. Inspect the fuel tank as described in this chapter.
15. Install by reversing the removal steps while noting the following:
   a. Connect the fuel hoses onto the correct fittings.
   b. Check for fuel leakage at all hose connections after completing installation.
   c. On GS models, align the leading edge of the fuel tank with the rubber grommet (**Figure 103**) on the mudguard side trim.
   d. Make sure the rubber grommet (**Figure 104**) and sleeve (**Figure 105**) are in place on the rear mounting bracket, then install the mounting bolts.

e. Tighten the mounting bolts securely.

R1150R models

Refer to **Figure 106**.

1. Place the motorcycle on the centerstand with the front wheel off the ground.
2. Remove the seat as described in Chapter Fifteen.
3. Disconnect the negative battery cable as described in Chapter Three.
4. Remove the screws (A, **Figure 107**) securing the lower portion of the side panel (B) to the fuel tank.
5. Lift straight up on the side panel to release the top posts from the oil cooler assembly and remove the side panel.
6. Remove the screws securing the lower panel (**Figure 108**) and remove it from the fuel tank.
7. Remove the three screws (**Figure 109**) securing the lower portion of the oil cooler to the fuel tank.
8. Remove the two upper screws (**Figure 110**) securing the upper portion of the oil cooler to the fuel tank.
9. Carefully move the oil cooler, air guide and inter-connecting hose away from the fuel tank.
10. Do not lose the small washers (**Figure 111**) located within the rubber grommets on the fuel tank.
11. Disconnect the fuel pump electrical connector (**Figure 112**).
12. Place a shop cloth or towel (**Figure 113**) between the top surface of the fuel tank and the upper fork bridge to protect the fuel tank finish.
13. Press on the tabs on the quick disconnect fitting on both fuel lines (**Figure 114**). Disconnect both fuel lines from the fuel tank.
14. Disconnect the vent line(s) (A, **Figure 115**). On models equipped with two vent lines, leave the connector on the fuel tank side on one of the lines and the connector on the outlet side of the line. This will ensure the vent lines will be re-connected correctly.
15. Remove the bolt and washer (B, **Figure 115**) securing the rear of the fuel tank. Do not lose the bushings on the mounting bracket .
16. Carefully pull straight up and toward the rear and remove the fuel tank and mounting bracket from the frame.
17. Plug the fuel lines and vacuum lines.
18. Inspect the fuel tank as described in this chapter.
19. Install by reversing the removal steps while noting the following:
    a. Make sure the O-ring seals are correctly seated within the quick disconnect fittings and are in good condition; replace if necessary.
    b. Connect the fuel hoses onto the correct fittings. Push the hoses together until they lock into place.

    c. Check for fuel leakage at all hose connections after completing installation.
    d. Make sure the small washers are in place in the rubber grommet (**Figure 111**).
    e. Tighten the mounting bolt to 22 N•m (16 ft.-lb.).
    f. Insert the side panel top posts (**Figure 116**) into the rubber grommets (**Figure 117**) on top of the oil cooler assembly. Push the side panel down until it bottoms then install the lower bolts (A, **Figure 107**).

R850GS and R1150GS models

Refer to **Figure 118**.

1. Place the motorcycle on the centerstand with the front wheel off the ground.
2. Remove the seat as described in Chapter Fifteen.
3. Disconnect the negative battery cable as described in Chapter Three.
4. Remove the screws securing the side cover (**Figure 119**).
5. Remove the bolt, washer and nut (**Figure 120**) securing the rear of the fuel tank. Do not lose the collars on the mounting bracket.
6. Disconnect the fuel pump electrical connector (A, **Figure 121**).
7. Place a shop cloth or towel between the top surface of the fuel tank and the upper fork bridge to protect the fuel tank finish.

8A. On 2000-2001 models, perform the following:
    a. Prior to disconnecting the fuel lines, mark them so they will be reconnected to the correct fitting during installation.
    b. Depressurize the fuel system as described in this chapter.
    c. Disconnect the fuel return line and the fuel pressure line.
    d. Plug the fuel lines.

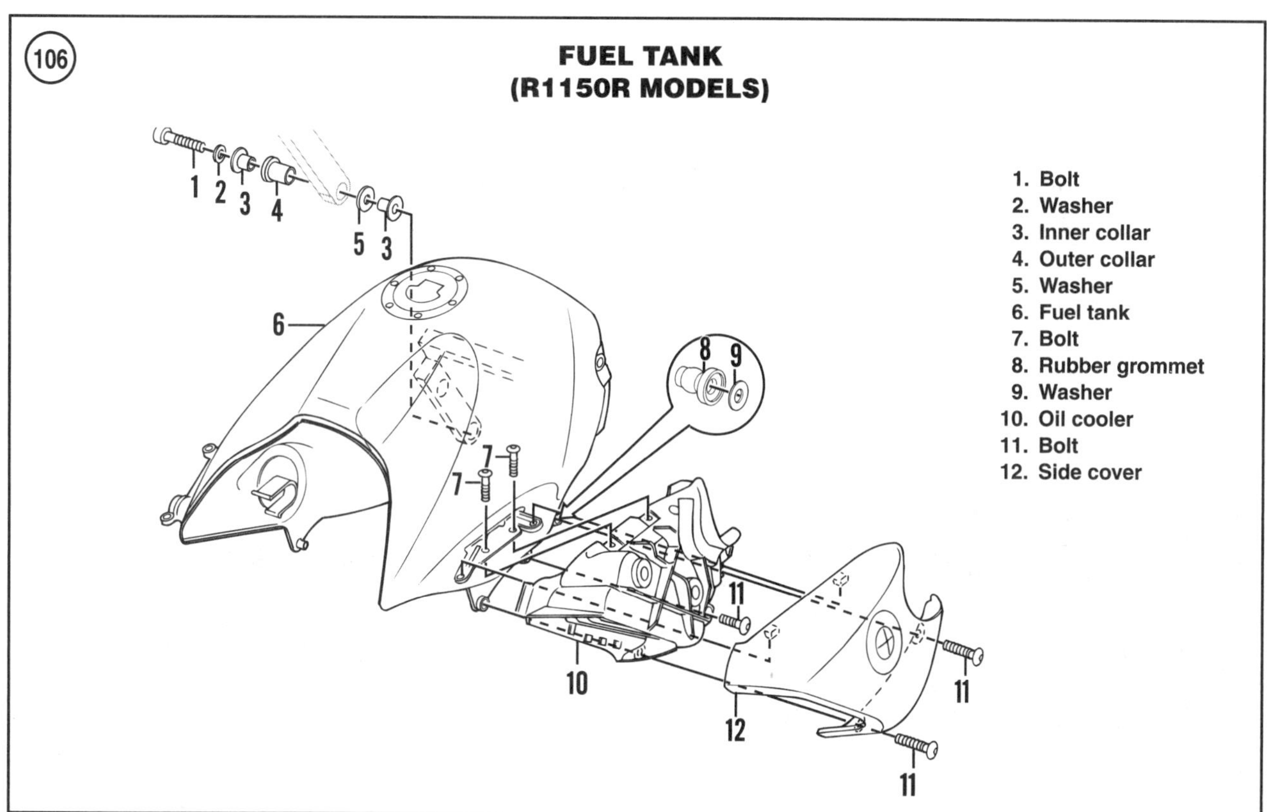
106
FUEL TANK
(R1150R MODELS)
1. Bolt
2. Washer
3. Inner collar
4. Outer collar
5. Washer
6. Fuel tank
7. Bolt
8. Rubber grommet
9. Washer
10. Oil cooler
11. Bolt
12. Side cover
1
2
3
4
5
3
6
7
7
8
9
10
11
11
11
12

107
A
A
B

109

108

110

9

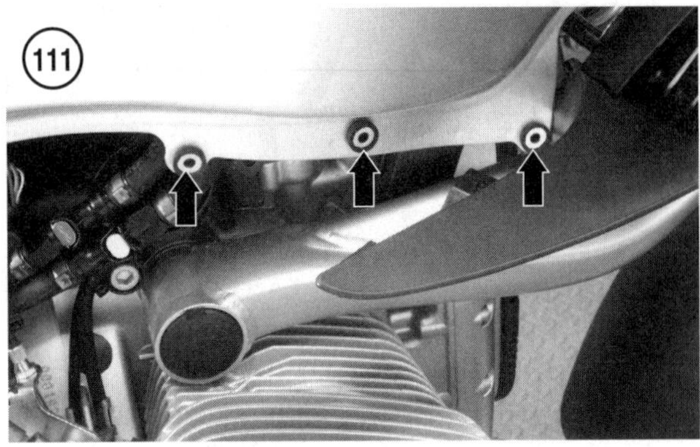
111

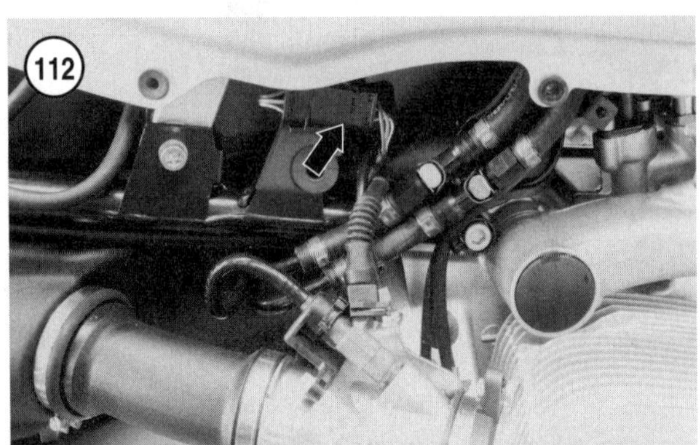
112

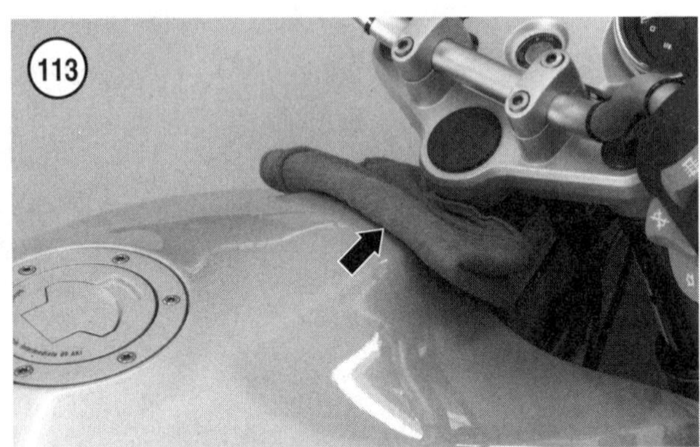
113

114

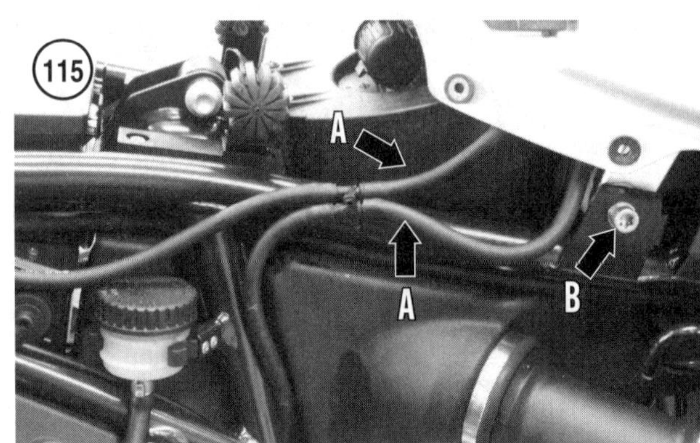

115

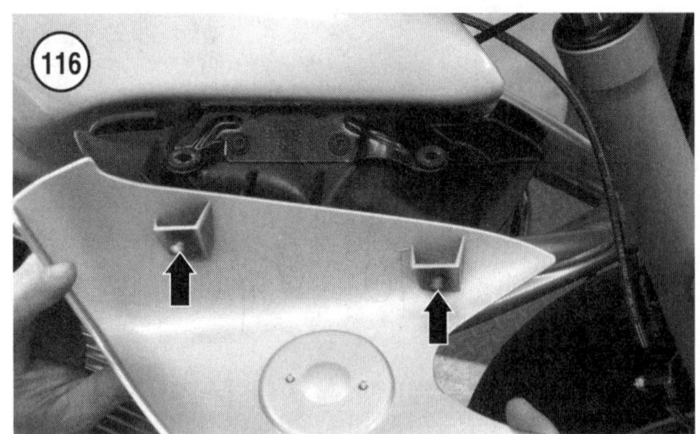
116

117

8B. On 2002-on models, press on the tabs on the quick disconnect fitting on both fuel lines (B, **Figure 121**). Disconnect both fuel lines from the fuel tank.

NOTE

On models equipped with two vent lines, leave the connector attached on fuel tank side on one of the lines and the connector attached on the outlet side of the other line. This will ensure the vent lines will be re-connected correctly.

9. Disconnect the vent line(s) (**Figure 122**).

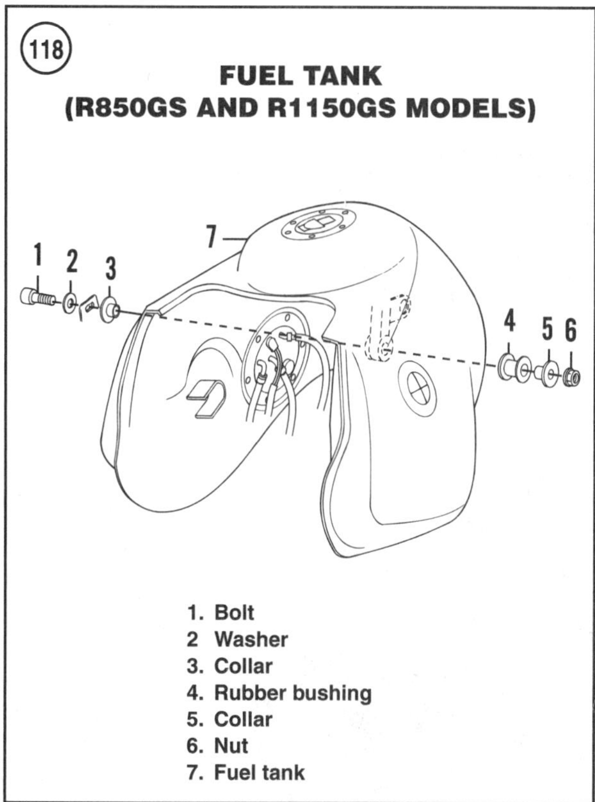

10. Carefully pull straight up and toward the rear and remove the fuel tank and mounting bracket from the frame.

11. Plug the fuel lines and vacuum lines.

12. Inspect the fuel tank as described in this chapter.

13. Install by reversing the removal steps while noting the following:

   a. On 2002-on models, make sure the O-ring seals are correctly seated within the quick disconnect fittings and are in good condition; replace if necessary.
   b. Connect the fuel hoses onto the correct fittings. Push the hoses together until they lock into place.
   c. Check for fuel leakage at all hose connections after completing installation.
   d. Tighten the mounting bolt to 22 N•m (16 ft.-lb.).

R1150RS models

Refer to **Figure 123**.

1. Place the motorcycle on the centerstand with the front wheel off of the ground.

2. Remove the seat as described in Chapter Fifteen.

3. Disconnect the negative battery cable as described in Chapter Three.

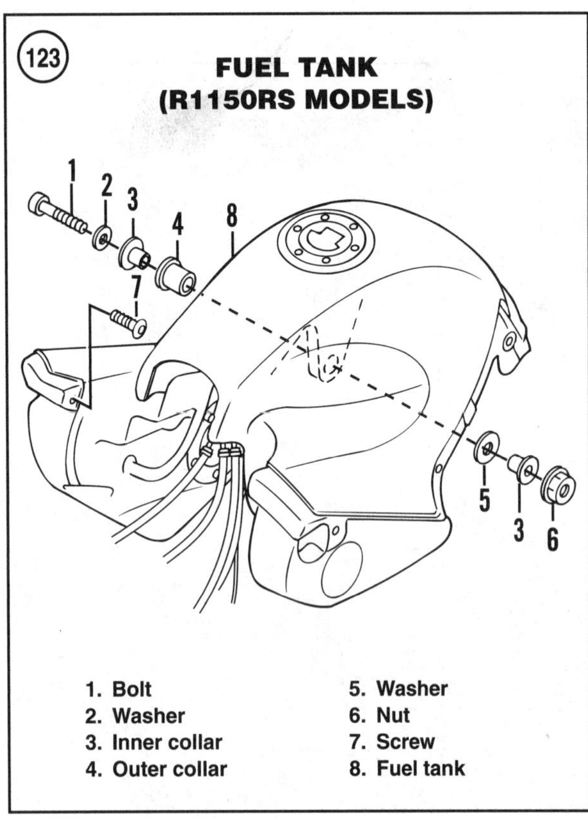

4. Remove the front fairing side panels as described in Chapter Fifteen.

5. Remove the screw (**Figure 124**) on each side securing the front fairing to the fuel tank.

NOTE

On models equipped with two vent lines, leave the connector attached on fuel tank side on one of the lines and the connector attached on the outlet side of the other line. This will ensure the vent lines will be re-connected correctly.

6. Disconnect the vent line(s) (**Figure 125**).

7. Remove the bolt, washer and nut (**Figure 126**) securing the rear of the fuel tank. Do not lose the collars on the mounting bracket.

8. Place a shop cloth or towel between the top surface of the fuel tank and the upper fork bridge to protect the fuel tank finish.

9. Press on the quick disconnect fitting tabs on both fuel lines (**Figure 127**). Disconnect both fuel lines from the fuel tank.

10. Disconnect the fuel pump electrical connector (**Figure 128**).

11. Carefully pull straight up and toward the rear and remove the fuel tank and mounting bracket from the frame.

12. Plug the fuel lines and vacuum lines.

13. Inspect the fuel tank as described in this chapter.

14. Install by reversing the removal steps while noting the following:

   a. Make sure the O-ring seals are correctly seated within the quick disconnect fittings and are in good condition; replace if necessary.

   b. Connect the fuel hoses onto the correct fittings. Push the hoses together until they lock into place.

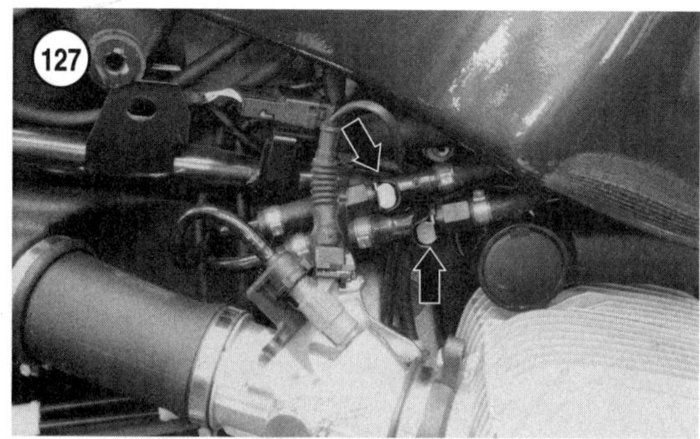

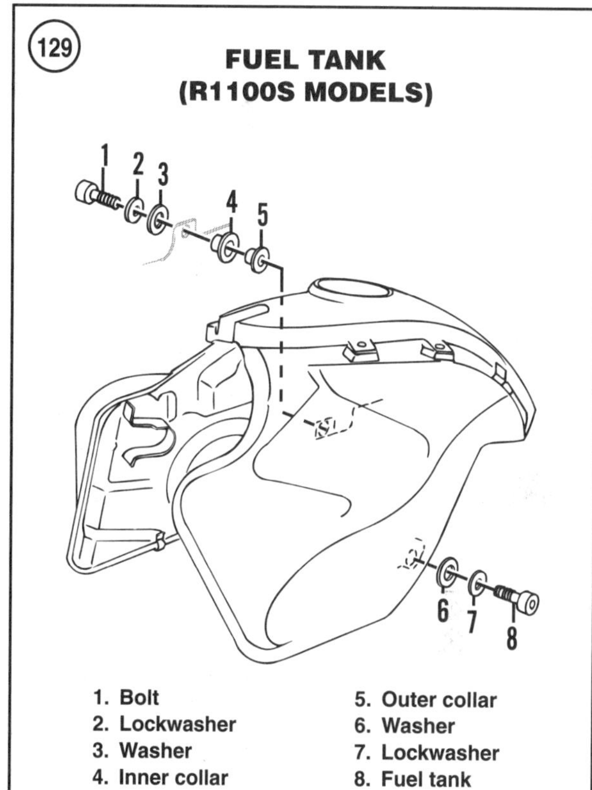

c. Check for fuel leakage at all hose connections after completing installation.
d. Tighten the mounting bolt to 22 N•m (16 ft.-lb.).

R1100S models

Refer to **Figure 129**.

1. Place a suitable size jack under the engine to support the motorcycle with the front wheel off the ground.
2. Remove the seat as described in Chapter Fifteen.
3. Disconnect the negative battery cable as described in Chapter Three.
4. Remove the front fairing side panels as described in Chapter Fifteen.
5. On the left side, remove the screws and washers securing the air filter air intake to the frame and air filter case. Remove the air intake air.
6. Disconnect the fuel pump electrical connector.
7. On the right side, remove the bolt, lockwasher and washer securing the rear of the fuel tank.
8. On the left side, remove the bolt, lockwasher and washer securing the rear of the fuel tank. Do not lose the collars on the mounting bracket.
9. Place a shop cloth or towel between the top surface of the fuel tank and the upper fork bridge to protect the fuel tank finish.
10. Raise the rear of the fuel tank to gain access to the fuel lines.
11. Prior to disconnecting the fuel lines, mark them so they will be reconnected to the correct fitting during installation.
12. Despressurize the fuel system as described in this chapter.
13. Disconnect the fuel return line and the fuel pressure line.
14. Disconnect the vent line(s). On models equipped with two vent lines, leave the connector on fuel tank side on one of the lines and the connector on the outlet side of the line. This will ensure the vent lines will be re-connected correctly.
15. Plug the fuel lines and vacuum lines.
16. Carefully pull straight up and toward the rear and remove the fuel tank and mounting bracket from the frame.
17. Inspect the fuel tank as described in this chapter.
18. Install by reversing the removal steps while noting the following:
    a. Connect the fuel hoses onto the correct fittings.
    b. Check for fuel leakage at all hose connections after completing installation.

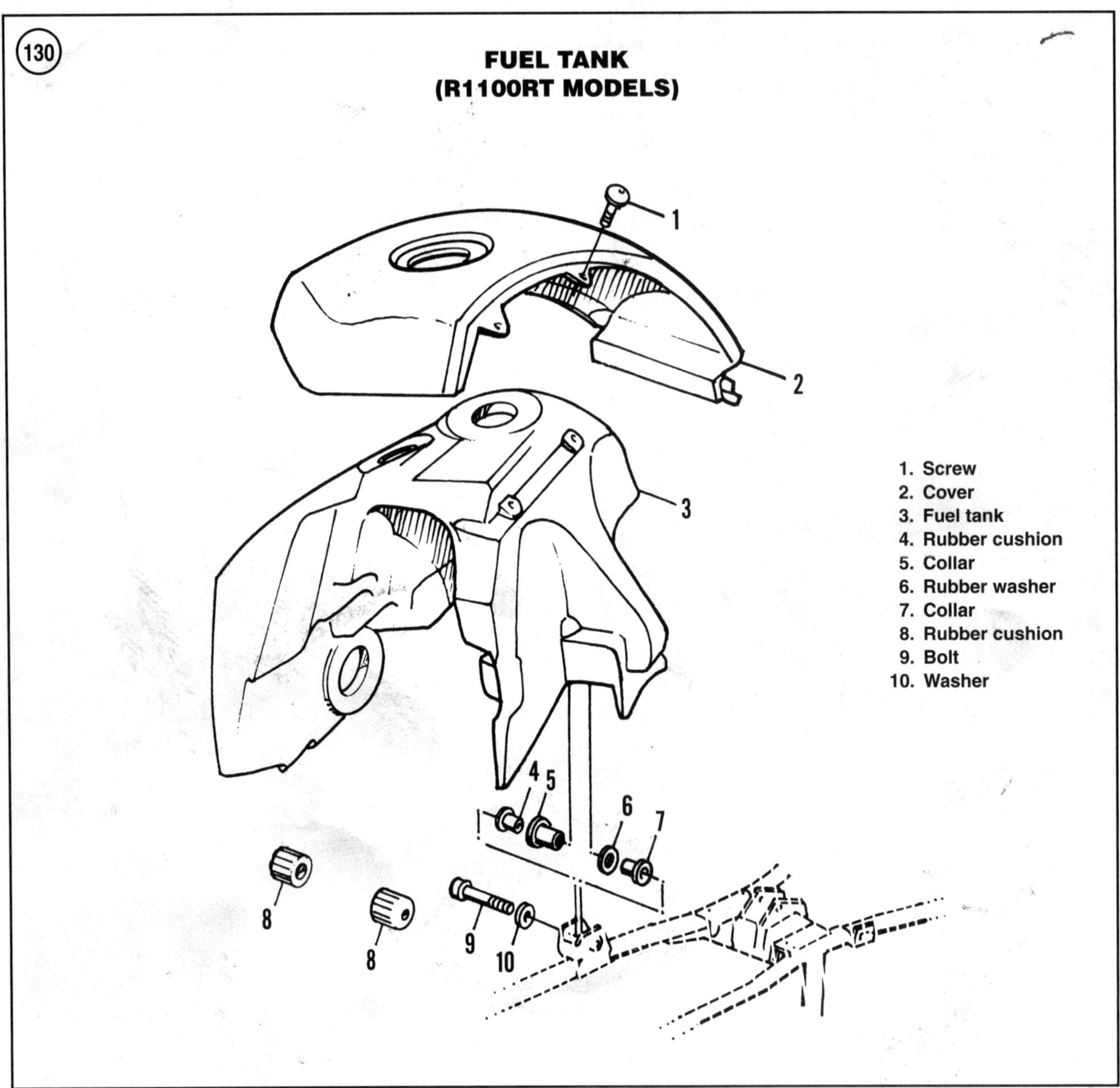

c. Tighten the mounting bolts to 9 N•m (80 in.-lb.).

R1100RT and R1150RT models

Refer to **Figure 130** and **Figure 131**.

1. Place the motorcycle on the centerstand with the front wheel off of the ground.
2. Remove the seat as described in Chapter Fifteen.
3. Remove the side sections of the front fairing as described in Chapter Fifteen.
4. Disconnect the negative battery cable as described in Chapter Three.
5. On R1150RT models, perform the following on the right side:
   a. Remove the screws and washer securing the radio compartment support. Remove the support.
   b. Remove the special nut securing the radio compartment to the threaded stud on the fuel tank.
   c. Remove the screws securing the radio compartment and the right side of the fuel tank to the frame.
   d. Move the radio compartment out of the way and suspend it to the frame with a bungee cord.
6. Disconnect the fuel pump multi-pin electrical connector.

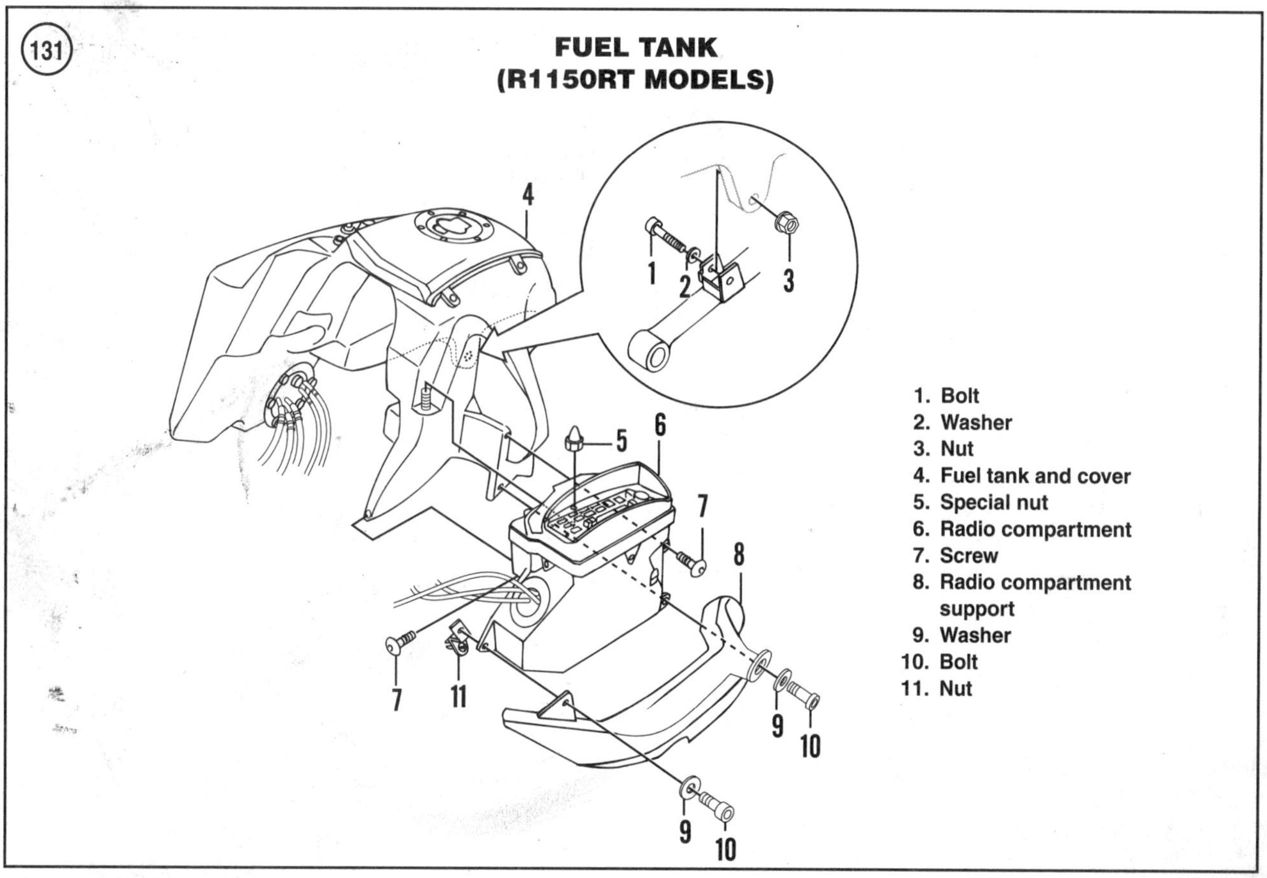

131
FUEL TANK
(R1150RT MODELS)
1
2
3
4
5
6
7
8
7
11
9
10
9
10
1. Bolt
2. Washer
3. Nut
4. Fuel tank and cover
5. Special nut
6. Radio compartment
7. Screw
8. Radio compartment support
9. Washer
10. Bolt
11. Nut

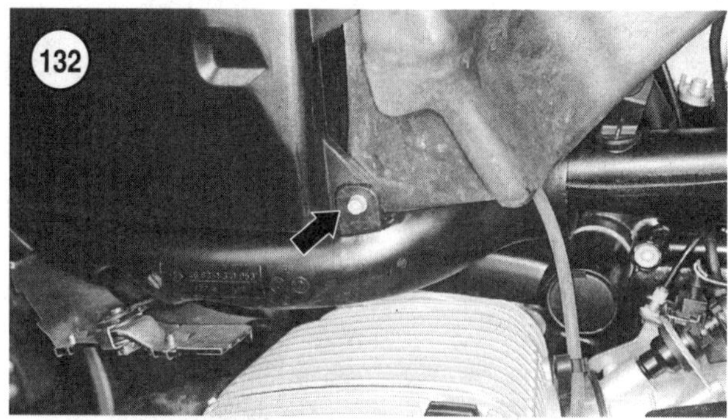

132

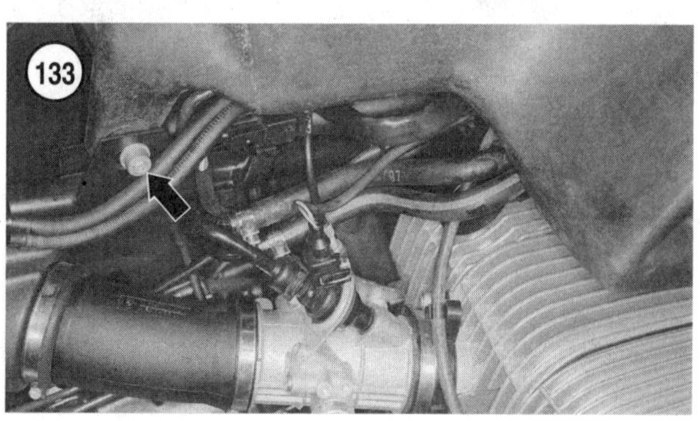

134

133

7. Remove the tie wrap securing the fuel feed and return lines to the frame crossmember.

8. Remove the bolt and washer from each side securing the rear of the fuel tank to the frame. Refer to **Figure 132** and **Figure 133**.

9. Raise the rear of the fuel tank (**Figure 134**) to gain access to the fuel lines.

10. Prior to disconnecting the fuel lines, mark them so they will be reconnected to the correct fitting during installation.

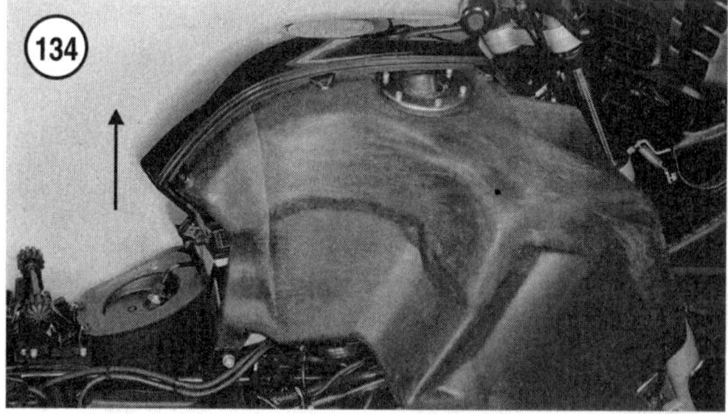

11A. On 1995-2001 models, perform the following:

a. Prior to disconnecting the fuel lines, mark them so they will be reconnected to the correct fitting during installation.
b. Depressurize the fuel system as described in this chapter.
c. Disconnect the fuel return line (**Figure 135**) and the fuel pressure line (**Figure 136**).
d. Plug the fuel lines.

11B. On 2002-on models, press on the tabs on the quick disconnect fitting on both fuel lines. Disconnect both fuel lines from the fuel tank.

12. Plug the fuel lines and vacuum lines to prevent contamination and leakage.
13. Carefully remove the fuel tank from the frame.
14. If necessary, remove the fuel tank cover as follows:
    a. Using a Torx screwdriver (**Figure 137**), remove the screws and the fuel filler cap assembly (A, **Figure 138**).
    b. Remove the mounting screws (B, **Figure 138**) and remove the cover (C).
15. Inspect the fuel tank as described in this chapter.
16. Install by reversing the removal steps while noting the following:
    a. On 1995-2001 models, be sure to reconnect the fuel hoses onto the correct fittings.
    b. On 2002-on models, make sure the O-ring seals are correctly seated within the quick disconnect fittings and are in good condition; replace if necessary.
    c. Connect the fuel hoses onto the correct fittings.
    d. On 2002-on models, push the hoses together until they lock into place.
    e. Check for fuel leakage at all hose connections after completing installation.
    f. Tighten the mounting bolt to 22 N•m (16 ft.-lb.).

R850C and R1200C models

Refer to **Figure 139**.

1. Place a suitable size jack under the engine to support the motorcycle with the front wheel off the ground.
2. Remove the seat as described in Chapter Fifteen.
3. Disconnect the negative battery cable as described in Chapter Three.
4. Pull straight out and release the posts on the chrome trim panel (**Figure 140**) from the rubber grommets on the fuel tank. Remove the chrome trim panel. Repeat for the other side.
5. Remove screws (A, **Figure 141**) securing the lower trim panel (B). Repeat for the other side.
6. Disconnect the fuel pump electrical connector (A, **Figure 142**).

135

136

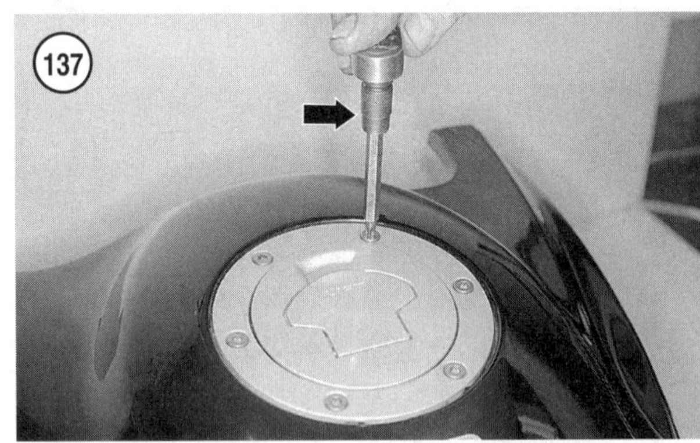
137

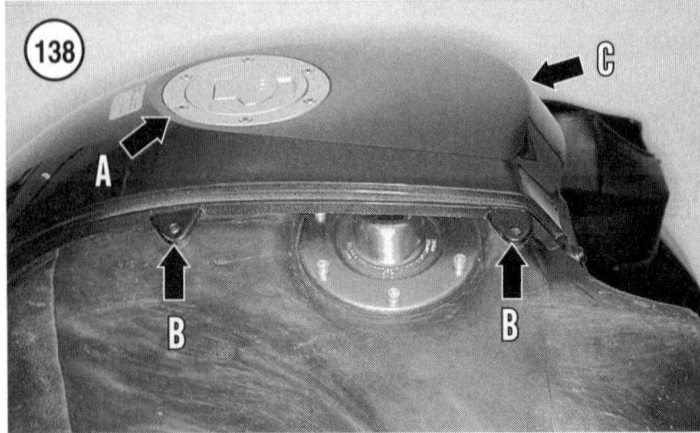

138

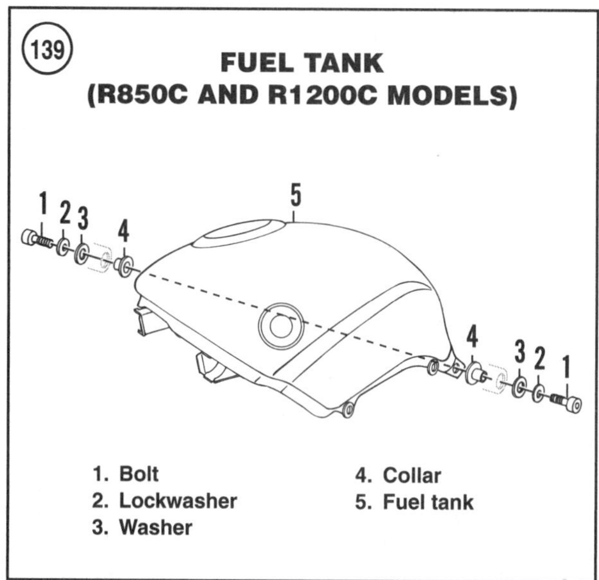

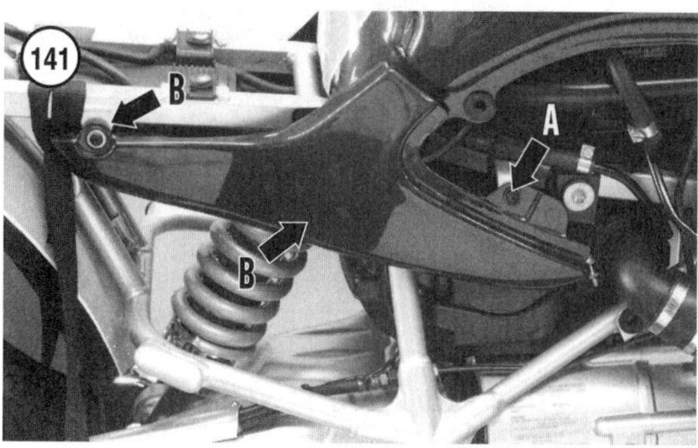

7. On each side, remove the bolt, lockwasher and washer (B, **Figure 142**) securing the rear of the fuel tank. Do not lose the collars on the fuel tank mounting brackets.

8. Prior to disconnecting the fuel lines, mark them so they will be reconnected to the correct fitting during installation.

9. Depressurize the fuel system as described in this chapter.
10. Disconnect the fuel return line and the fuel pressure line (**Figure 143**).
11. Disconnect the vent line(s). On models equipped with two vent lines, leave the connector on fuel tank side on one of the lines and the connector on the outlet side of the line. This will ensure the vent lines will be re-connected correctly.
12. Plug the fuel lines and vacuum lines.
13. Carefully pull straight up and toward the rear and remove the fuel tank from the frame.
14. Inspect the fuel tank as described in this chapter.
15. Install by reversing the removal steps while noting the following:

   a. Connect the fuel hoses onto the correct fittings.
   b. Check for fuel leakage at all hose connections after completing installation.
   c. Tighten the mounting bolt to 22 N•m (16 ft.-lb.),

Inspection (All Models)

1. Inspect the rear mounting bracket (**Figure 144**, typical) for wear, cracks or damage. If damaged, replace the fuel tank.
2. Inspect the front mounting bracket (**Figure 145**, typical) for deterioration. If damaged, replace the fuel tank.

3. On later models, inspect the mounting bracket nuts (**Figure 146**) for tightness. Tighten securely if necessary.

4. On R1150R models, inspect the oil cooler assembly mounting bracket (A, **Figure 147**) for damage. Make sure the mounting bolts (B, **Figure 147**) are tight.

5. Inspect the rubber cushions, grommets and spacer for damage or deterioration, and replace them if necessary.

6. Inspect the entire fuel tank for leakage or damage. Repair or replace the fuel tank if any fuel leakage is found.

7. To remove the outer portion of the fuel fill cap, perform the following:

   a. Use the ignition key and open the fuel filter cap. Inspect the fuel fill cap gasket (**Figure 148**). If the cap gasket is damaged or starting to deteriorate, replace the cap. The gasket cannot be replaced separately.

   b. Remove the screws and remove the cap (**Figure 149**).

   c. Install a new O-ring seal and a new cap, then securely tighten the screws.

ROLLOVER VALVE (ALL R1150 MODELS)

Removal/Installation

1. Place the motorcycle on the centerstand with the rear wheel off the ground.

2. On R1150RT models, perform the following:

   a. Remove the front fairing side panels as described in Chapter Fifteen.

   b. Remove the fuel fill cap and the fuel tank cover as described under *Fuel Tank Removal/Installation, R1100RT and R1150RT models* in this chapter.

3. On all models except R1150RT, remove the screws securing the fuel fill cap and remove the fill cap.

4. Carefully pull the reducer unit with the rollover valve assembly partially up and out of the fuel tank.

5. Mark the fuel hoses and fittings to ensure correct installation, then disconnect the hoses from the assembly. Remove the reducer unit with the rollover valve assembly from the fuel tank.

6. Remove the large O-ring seal.

7. Install by reversing these removal steps while noting the following:

   a. Install the hoses to the correct fittings on the reducer unit with the rollover valve assembly.

   b. Install *new* hose clamps and tighten securely.

   c. Install a *new* large O-ring seal if necessary.

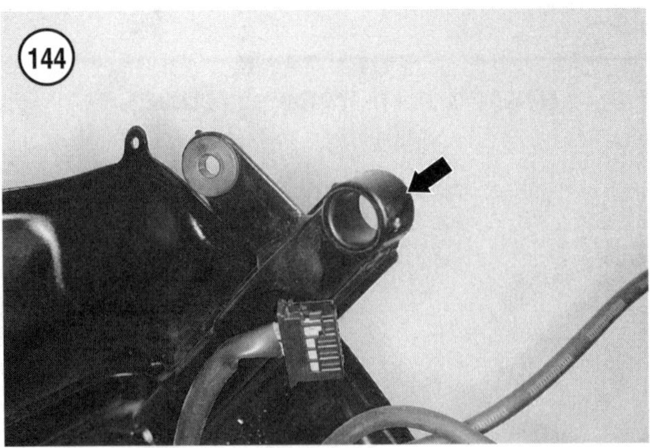

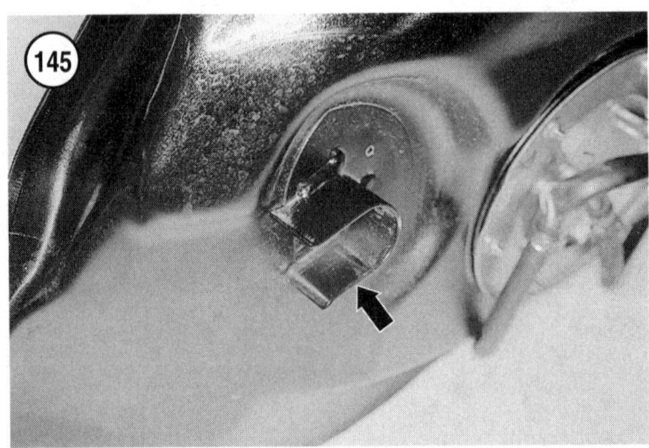

FUEL FILTER REPLACEMENT

Removal/Installation

Refer to **Figure 150-154**.

The cartridge fuel filter is located in the fuel tank. There is also a fuel strainer attached to the inlet end of the fuel pump. Remove and clean the fuel strainer if there is evidence of fuel blockage and whenever the cartridge fuel

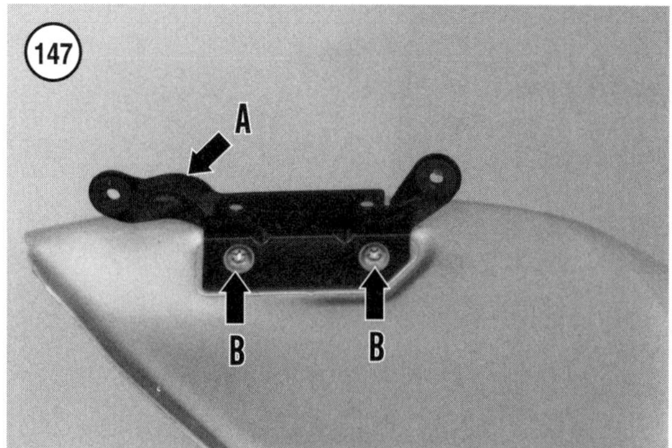

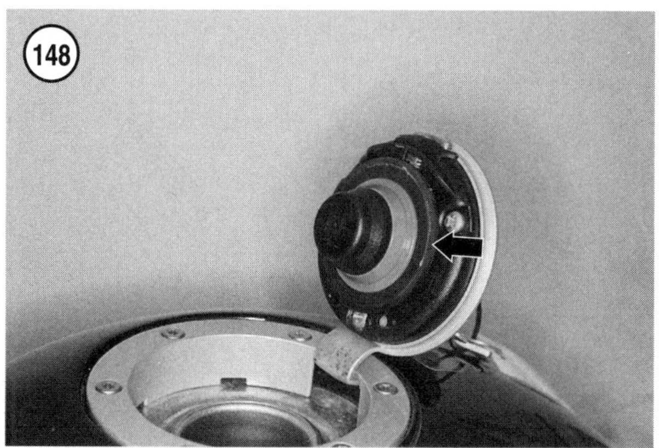

filter has been replaced. Replace the fuel filter at the intervals listed in **Table 1** in Chapter Three.

NOTE
*The BMW hose clamps used to secure the internal hoses to the fuel filter fittings are not reusable. The clamps are unique and require special pliers (BMW part No. 13-1-500) to install and secure. A good quality screw-type hose clamp (**Figure 155**) can be used in place of the original BMW clamp.*

1. Remove the fuel tank as described in this section.
2. Siphon all fuel from the tank and store it in a suitable, sealed container. This fuel can be returned to the fuel tank.
3. If compressed air is available, blow out the interior of the fuel tank to evacuate the majority of the fumes.
4. Place a blanket or several towels on the workbench to protect the fuel tank finish.
5. Turn the fuel tank upside down on the workbench. Thoroughly clean the underside of the fuel tank of all debris surrounding the fuel gauge mounting flange (**Figure 156**).
6. Make an alignment mark (A, **Figure 157**) on the fuel tank and the fuel gauge mounting flange (A) to ensure proper installation.
7. Remove the nuts (B, **Figure 157**) securing the flange to the fuel tank.
8. Carefully pull the assembly away from the side of the fuel tank. Remove the large ring gasket and discard it.
9. Apply hemostats, or a similar type of small clamps, to the fuel lines (**Figure 158**) in the fuel tank.
10. Mark the internal fuel lines in relation to the external fuel lines on the assembly. On some early models, the external overflow fuel line is marked with a series of X marks (C, **Figure 157**). This ensures correct attachment during installation.
11. Open the hose clamps (**Figure 159**) and disconnect the hoses from the fittings. Discard the BMW hose clamps.
12. *Carefully* withdraw the assembly (**Figure 160**) from the fuel tank being careful not to damage the fuel gauge arm and float (models so equipped).
13. Remove the hose clamps (**Figure 161**) from the fuel filter. Discard the BMW hose clamps.
14. Install the new fuel filter with the arrow (**Figure 162**) pointing in the correct direction of fuel flow.
15. Install *new* hose clamps and tighten securely.
16. Note the location of the fuel strainer in relation to the fuel pump. The strainer must be reinstalled correctly to not interfere with the fuel gauge float and arm. Carefully remove the strainer (**Figure 163**) from the fuel pump.
17. Clean the strainer with solvent and a soft toothbrush to remove any debris. Check the strainer for any broken areas that would allow any dirt or debris to pass through. Replace the strainer if damaged in any way. Install the strainer onto the fuel pump.
18. Apply a small amount of gasket sealant to the *new* large ring seal and install it (**Figure 164**) into the recess in the mounting flange.

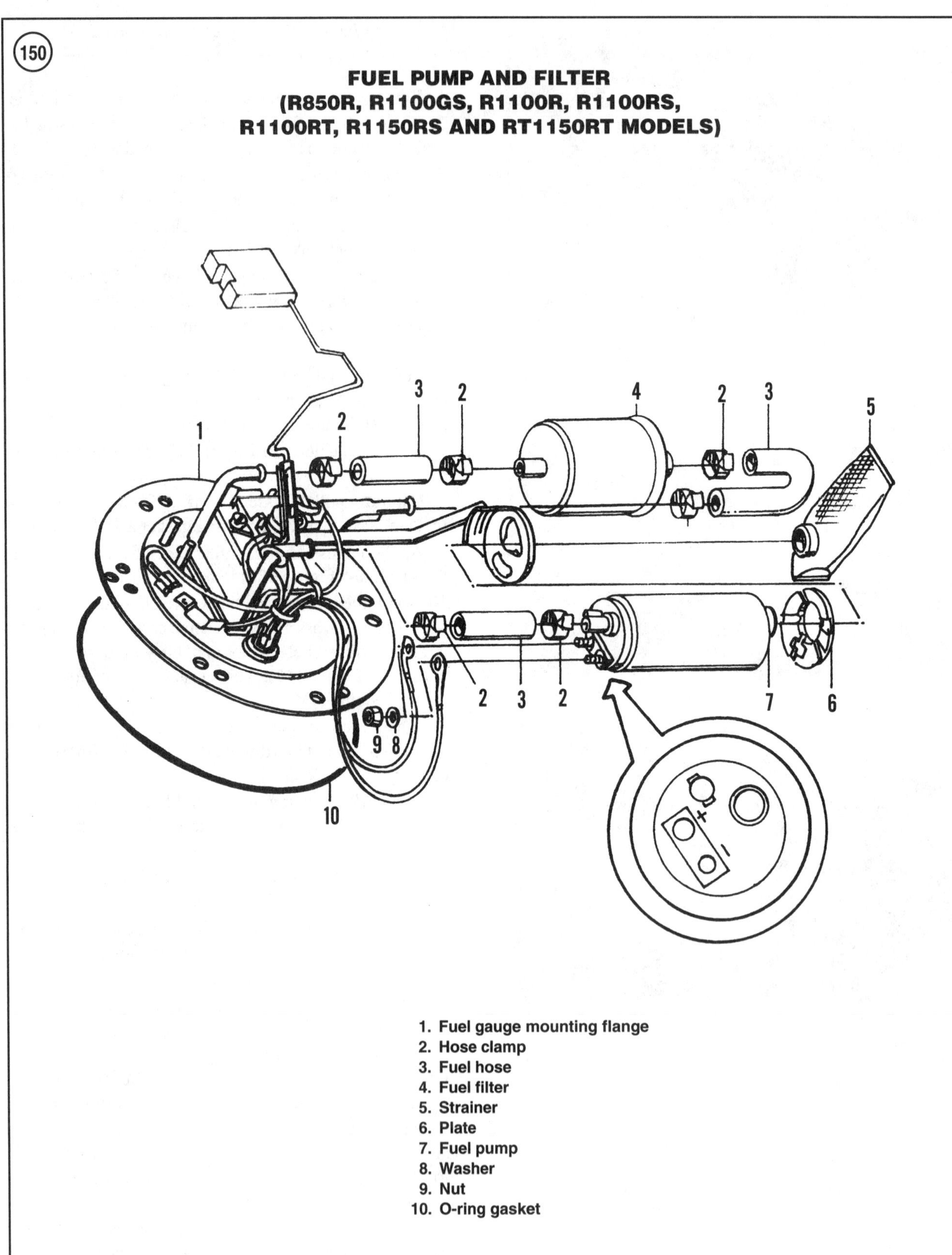
150
FUEL PUMP AND FILTER
(R850R, R1100GS, R1100R, R1100RS,
R1100RT, R1150RS AND RT1150RT MODELS)
1
2
3
2
4
2
3
5
2
3
2
7
6
9
8
10
+
–
1. Fuel gauge mounting flange
2. Hose clamp
3. Fuel hose
4. Fuel filter
5. Strainer
6. Plate
7. Fuel pump
8. Washer
9. Nut
10. O-ring gasket

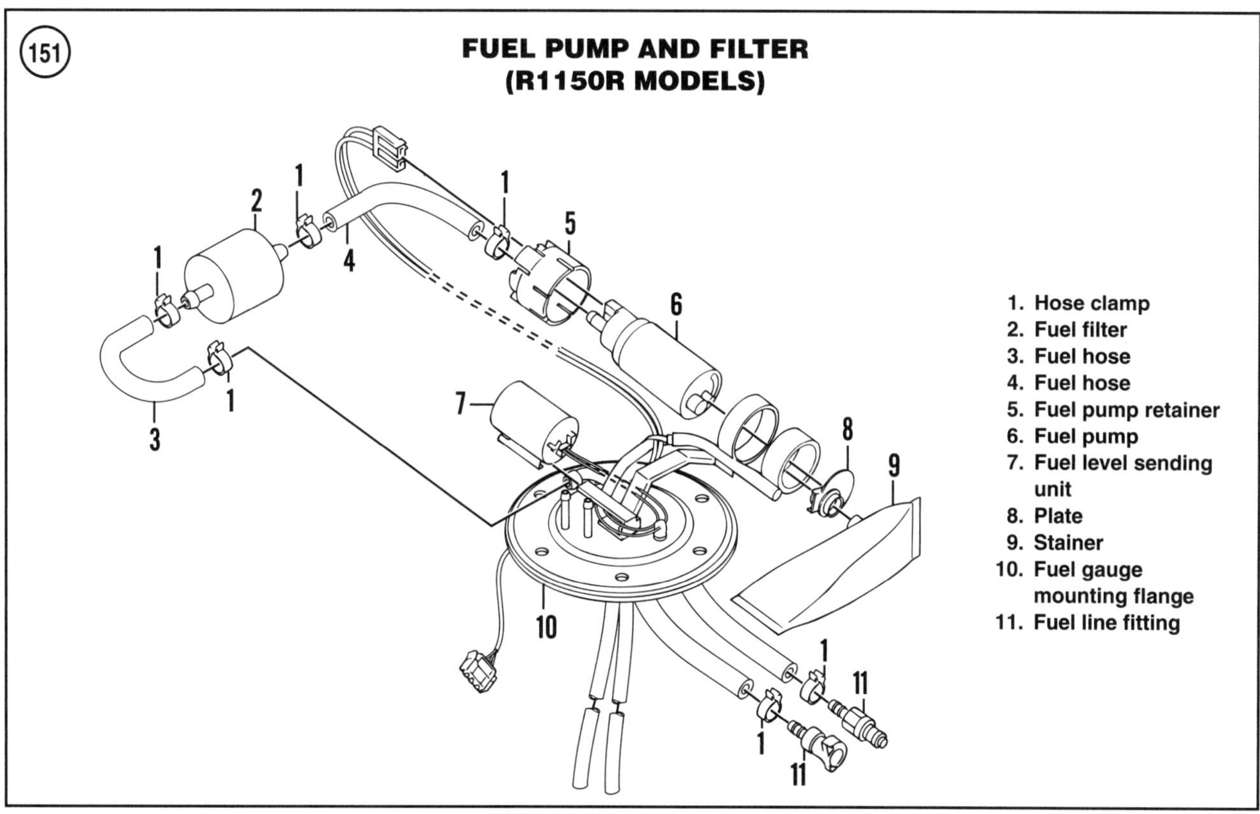
151
FUEL PUMP AND FILTER
(R1150R MODELS)
1. Hose clamp
2. Fuel filter
3. Fuel hose
4. Fuel hose
5. Fuel pump retainer
6. Fuel pump
7. Fuel level sending unit
8. Plate
9. Stainer
10. Fuel gauge mounting flange
11. Fuel line fitting

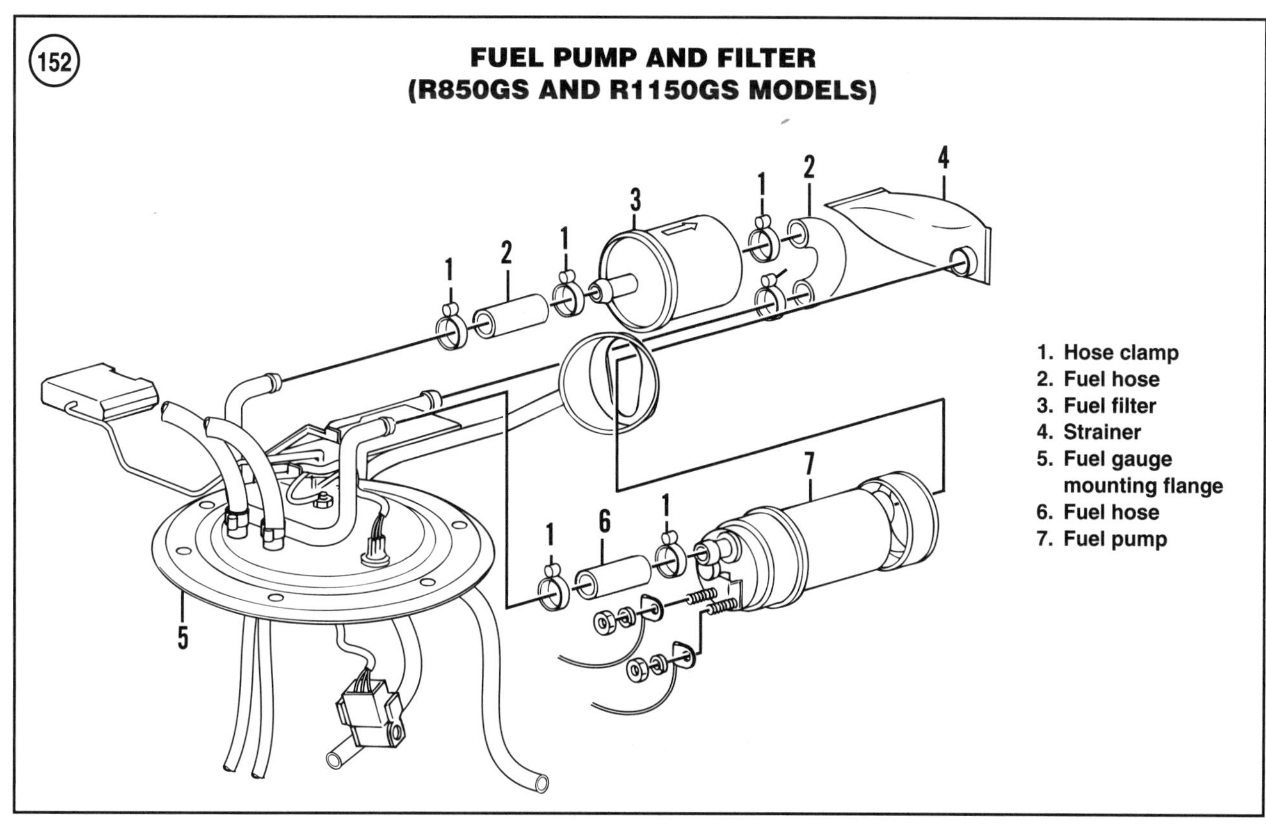
152
FUEL PUMP AND FILTER
(R850GS AND R1150GS MODELS)
1. Hose clamp
2. Fuel hose
3. Fuel filter
4. Strainer
5. Fuel gauge mounting flange
6. Fuel hose
7. Fuel pump

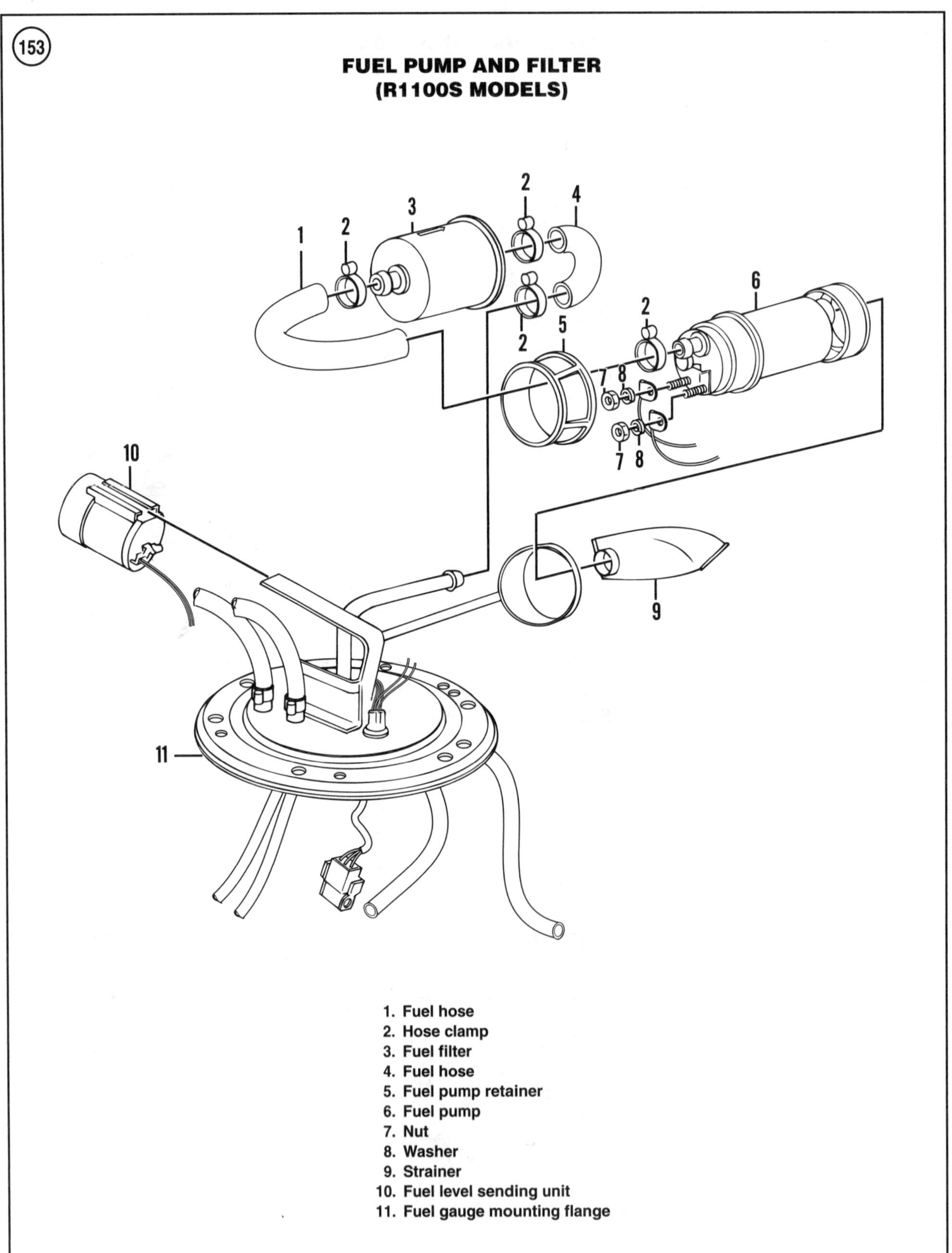
153
FUEL PUMP AND FILTER
(R1100S MODELS)
1
2
3
2
4
6
2
2
5
7
8
7
8
10
9
11
1. Fuel hose
2. Hose clamp
3. Fuel filter
4. Fuel hose
5. Fuel pump retainer
6. Fuel pump
7. Nut
8. Washer
9. Strainer
10. Fuel level sending unit
11. Fuel gauge mounting flange

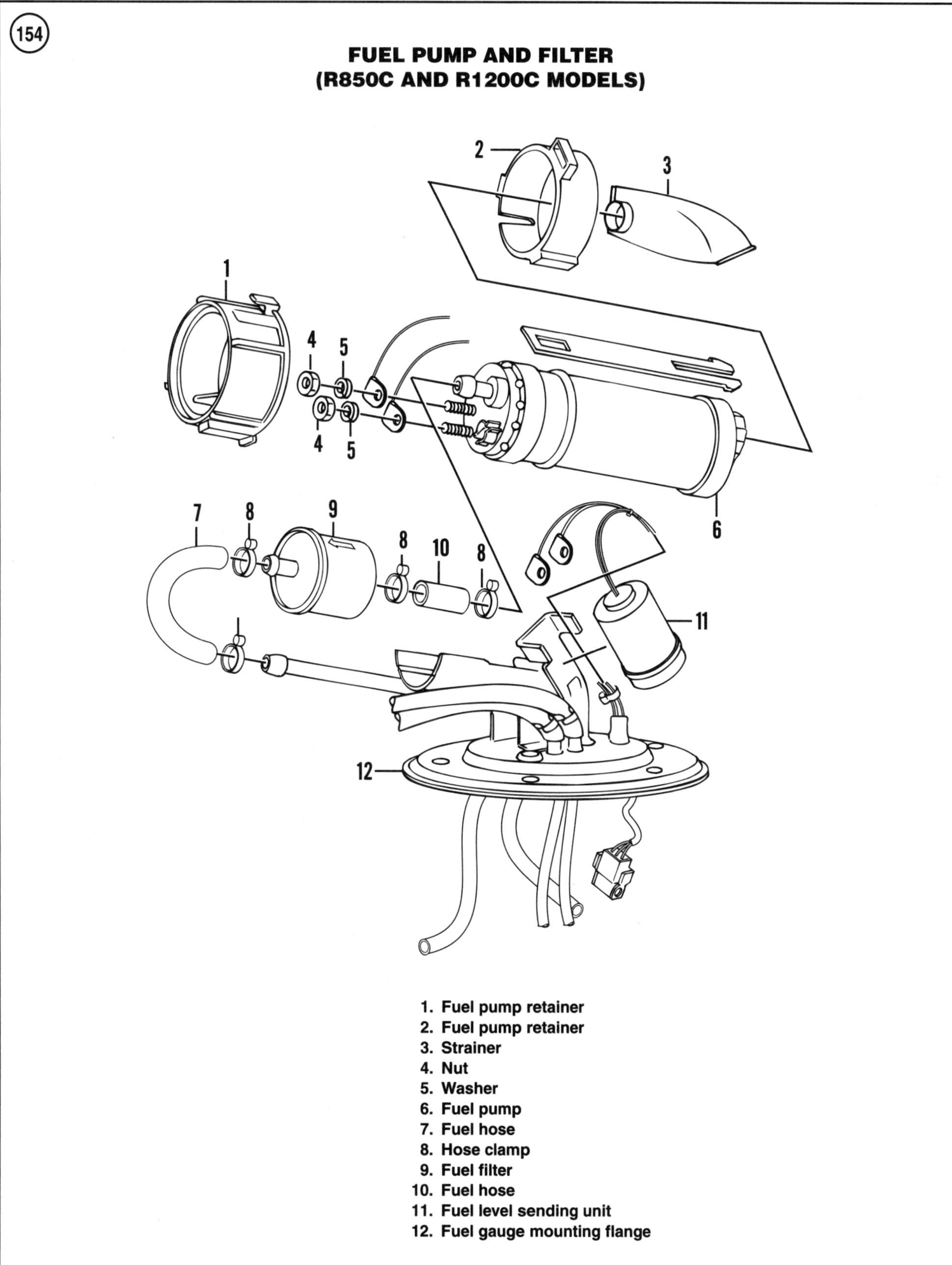

1. Fuel pump retainer
2. Fuel pump retainer
3. Strainer
4. Nut
5. Washer
6. Fuel pump
7. Fuel hose
8. Hose clamp
9. Fuel filter
10. Fuel hose
11. Fuel level sending unit
12. Fuel gauge mounting flange

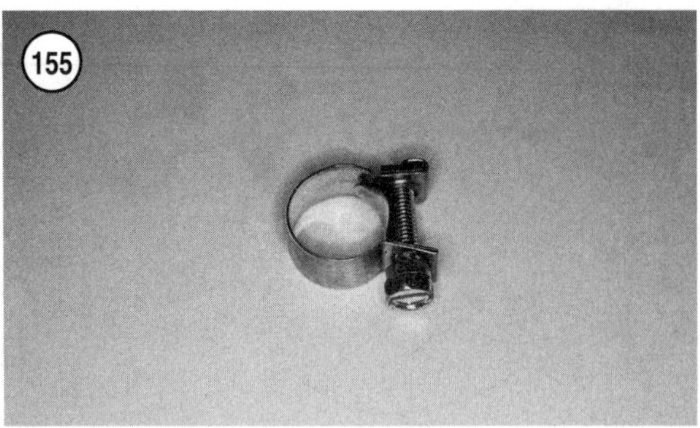

19. Reattach the fuel lines to the correct fittings on the flange and remove the hemostats or clamps from the hoses. Refer to the marks made during Step 6 for correct location.
20. *Carefully* install the assembly (**Figure 165**) into the fuel tank being careful to not damage the fuel gauge arm and float (models so equipped).

WARNING
Make sure the new large ring seal is still in position on the mounting flange. If it is not, the flange will not seat correctly to the side of the fuel tank, resulting in a fuel leak that could cause a dangerous fire.

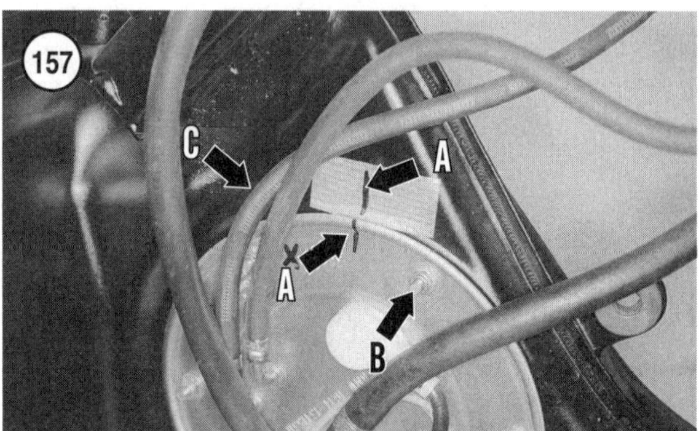

21. Align the alignment marks (A, **Figure 157**) made during removal and install the flange onto the mounting studs on the fuel tank.
22. Install the mounting nuts (B, **Figure 157**) and tighten securely.
23. Partially refill the fuel tank with gasoline. Move the fuel tank so the gasoline is covering the backside of the fuel gauge assembly and leave it in this position for several minutes. Check for any fuel leakage at this time. If there is a leak, either the nuts are not tightened sufficiently or the large ring seal is not seated correctly. Immediately correct this problem.
24. Install the fuel tank as described in this chapter.

FUEL PUMP

Removal/Installation

Refer to **Figure 150-154**.

NOTE
The BMW hose clamps used to secure the internal hoses to the fuel filter fittings are not reusable. The clamps are unique require special pliers (BMW part No. 13-1-500) to install and secure. A good quality screw

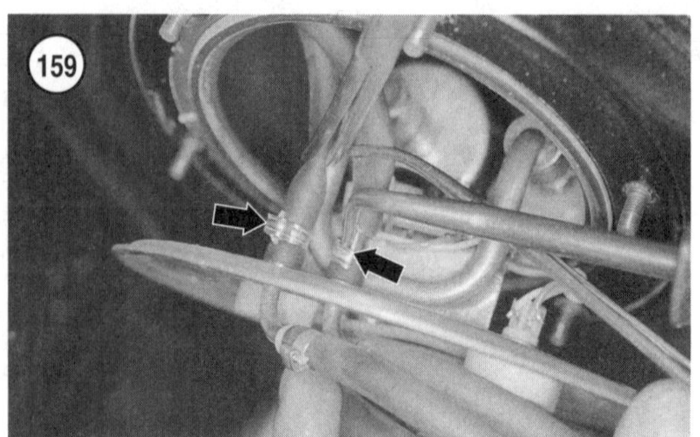

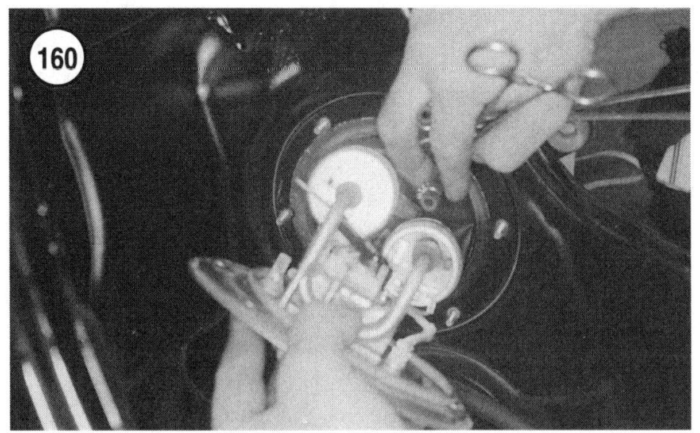
160

161

162

163

164

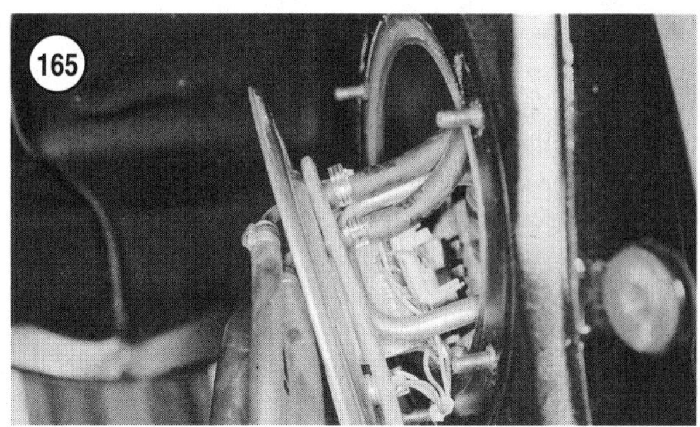
165

9

*hose clamp (**Figure 155**) can be used in place of the original BMW clamp.*

1. Remove the fuel tank as described in this chapter.
2. Siphon all fuel from the tank and store it in a suitable, sealed container. This fuel can be returned to the fuel tank.
3. If compressed air is available, blow out the interior of the fuel tank to evacuate the majority of the fumes.
4. On all models with a painted fuel tank, place a blanket or several towels on the workbench to protect the fuel tank finish.
5. Turn the fuel tank upside down on the workbench. Thoroughly clean the underside of the fuel tank of all debris surrounding the fuel gauge mounting flange (**Figure 156**).
6. Make an alignment mark (A, **Figure 157**) on the fuel tank and the fuel gauge mounting flange (A) to ensure proper installation.
7. Remove the nuts (B, **Figure 157**) securing the flange to the fuel tank.
8. Carefully pull the assembly away from the side of the fuel tank. Remove the large ring gasket and discard it.
9. Apply hemostats, or a similar type of small clamps, to the fuel lines (**Figure 158**) in the fuel tank.
10. Mark the internal fuel lines in relation to the external fuel lines on the assembly. On some early models, the ex-

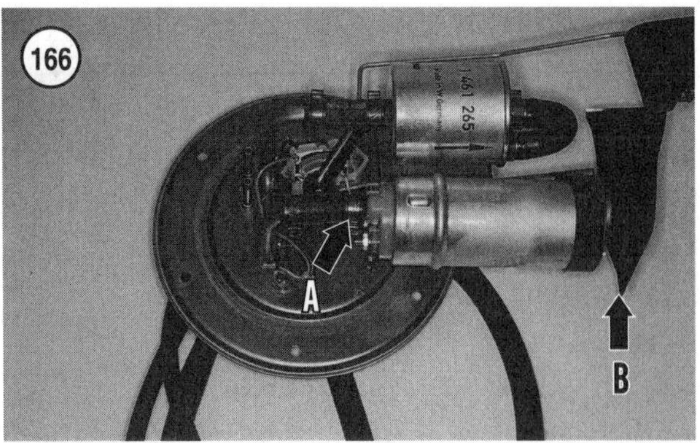

ternal overflow fuel line is marked with a series of X marks (C, **Figure 157**). This ensures correct attachment during installation.

11. Open the hose clamps (**Figure 159**) and disconnect the hoses from the fittings. Discard the BMW hose clamps.
12. *Carefully* withdraw the assembly (**Figure 160**) from the fuel tank being careful not to damage the fuel gauge arm and float (models so equipped).
13. Remove the nuts and washers securing the electrical connectors (A, **Figure 166**) to the fuel pump.
14. Remove the fuel strainer (B, **Figure 166**) from the inlet end of the fuel pump.
15. Remove the hose clamp (**Figure 167**) from the fuel pump. Discard the BMW hose clamp.
16. Install the *new* fuel pump and connect the electrical connectors. Tighten the nuts securely.
17. Install a *new* hose clamp and tighten securely.
18. Note the location of the fuel strainer in relation to the fuel pump. The strainer must be reinstalled correctly to not interfere with the fuel gauge float and arm. Carefully remove the strainer (**Figure 163**) from the fuel pump.
19. Clean the strainer with solvent and a soft toothbrush to remove any debris. Check the strainer for any broken areas that would allow any dirt or debris to pass through. Replace the strainer if damaged in any way. Install the strainer onto the fuel pump
20. Apply a small amount of gasket sealant to the *new* large ring seal and install it (**Figure 164**) into the recess in the mounting flange.
21. Reattach the fuel lines to the correct fittings on the flange and remove the hemostats, or clamps, from the hoses. Refer to the marks made in Step 6 for correct location.
22. *Carefully* install the assembly (**Figure 165**) into the fuel tank being careful to not damage the fuel gauge arm and float (models so equipped).

WARNING

Make sure the new large ring seal is still in position on the mounting flange. If it is not, the flange will not seat correctly to the side of the fuel tank, resulting in a fuel leak that could cause a dangerous fire.

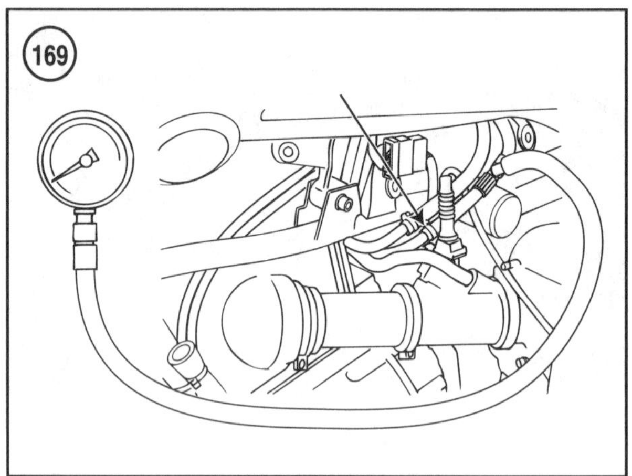

23. Align the alignment marks (A, **Figure 157**) made during removal and install the flange onto the mounting studs on the fuel tank.
24. Install the mounting nuts (B, **Figure 157**) and tighten securely.

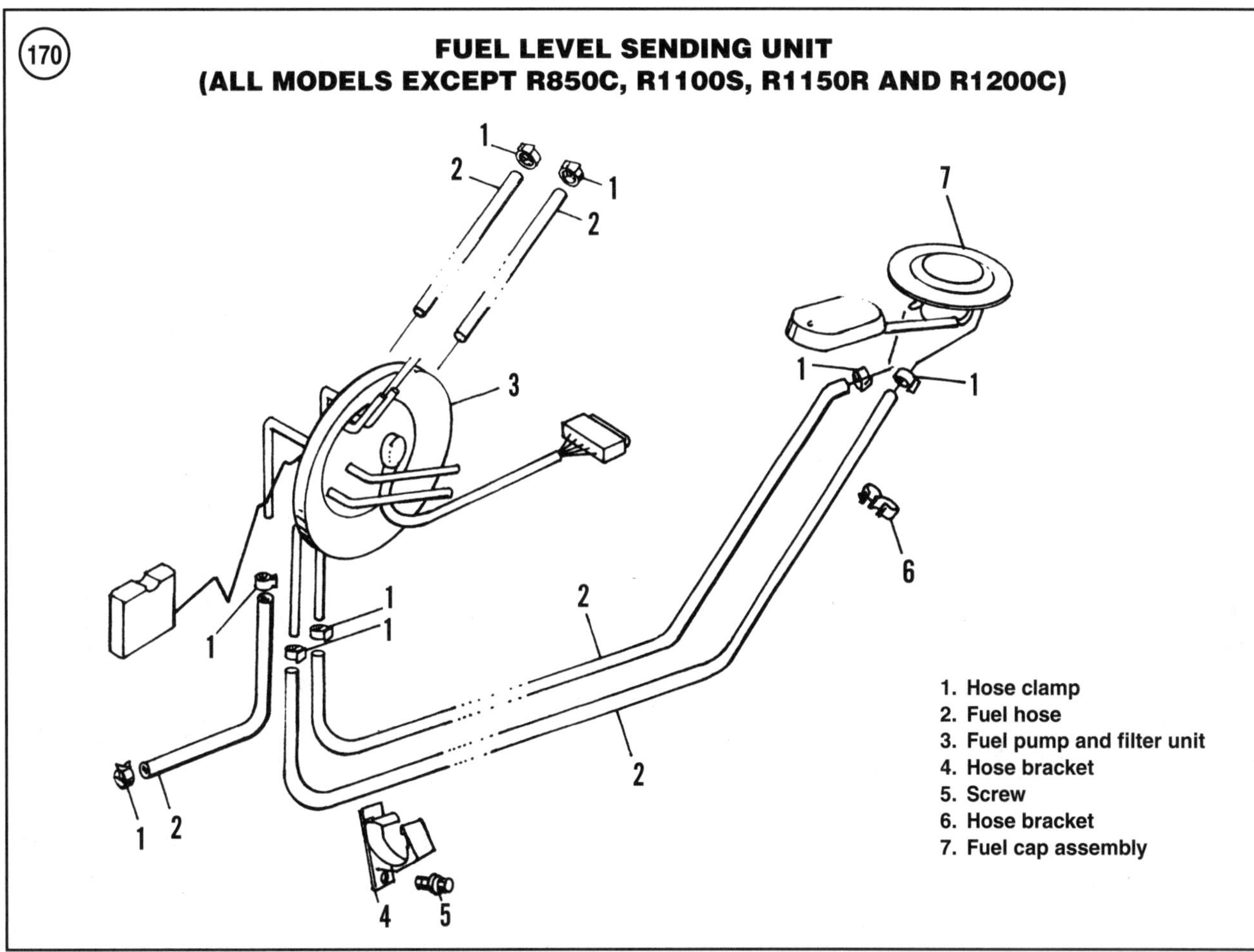

25. Partially refill the fuel tank with gasoline. Move the fuel tank so the gasoline is covering the backside of the fuel gauge assembly and leave it in this position for several minutes. Check for any fuel leakage at this time. If there is a leak, either the nuts are not tightened sufficiently or the large ring seal is not seated correctly. Immediately correct this problem.

26. Install the fuel tank as described in this chapter.

FUEL PUMP PRESSURE TEST

1. Remove the seat as described in Chapter Fifteen.

2. On RS, RT and S models, remove the side sections of the front fairing as described in Chapter Fifteen.

3. Disconnect the pressure side fuel hose (**Figure 168**, purple arrow).

4A. On models without quick disconnect fitting, connect the pressure gauge (BMW part No. 16-1-500) onto the fuel hose (**Figure 169**, typical).

4B. On models with a quick disconnect fitting, perform the following:

a. Attach the quick release coupling (BMW part No. 16-1-503) to the fuel hose.
b. Connect the pressure gauge (BMW part No. 16-1-500) onto the quick release coupling (**Figure 169**, typical).

FUEL LEVEL SENDING UNIT

Removal/Installation

All models except R850C, R1100S, R1150R and R1200C

Refer to **Figure 170**.

NOTE

There is no test available to check the fuel level sending unit. There are also no replacement parts available. If the unit is faulty, the fuel pump and filter mounting bracket assembly must be replaced as an assembly.

1. Remove the fuel level sending unit, fuel filter and fuel pump as described in the section.
2. Remove the fuel pump and screen (A, **Figure 171**) from the assembly as described in this chapter.
3. Remove the fuel filter (B, **Figure 171**) from the assembly as described in Chapter Three.
4. Install the fuel pump, screen and the filter to the *new* fuel level sending unit as described in this section.

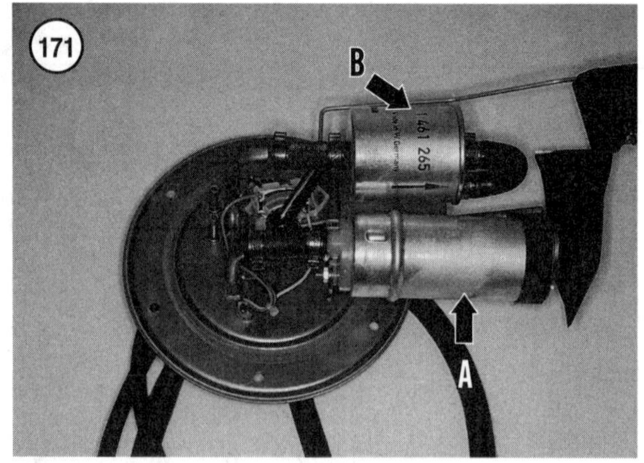

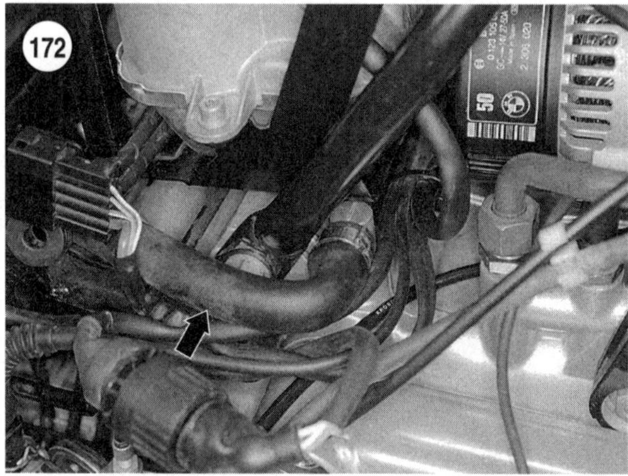

R850C, R1100S, R1150R and R1200C models

Refer to **Figure 151**, **153** and **154**.

NOTE
There is no test available to check the fuel level sending unit.

1. Remove the fuel level sending unit, fuel filter and fuel pump as described in the section.

2A. On R1150R and R1100S models, perform the following:

  a. Slide the fuel level sending unit and wiring harness off the bracket on the assembly.
  b. Slide the new unit back onto the bracket until it bottoms.

2B. On R850C and R1200C models, perform the following:

  a. Remove the tie wraps securing the fuel level sending unit to the mounting bracket and remove it and the wiring harness from the assembly.
  b. Install the new unit onto the mounting bracket and secure with new tie wraps.

3. Install the fuel level sending unit, fuel filter and fuel pump as described in the section.

CRANKCASE BREATHER SYSTEM (U.S. MODELS ONLY)

All U.S. models are equipped with a closed crankcase breather system. This system routes the combustion gasses from the crankcase to the air box where they enter the engine to be burned.

Inspection and Cleaning

Inspect the breather hose (**Figure 172**) from the crankcase outlet to the air filter air box. If it is cracked or starting to deteriorate, it must be replaced. Make sure the hose clamps are in place and holding securely.

Remove the drain plug from the left rear corner of the air box and drain all residue. Perform this procedure more frequently if a considerable amount of riding is done at full throttle or in the rain.

EVAPORATIVE EMISSION CONTROL SYSTEM (CALIFORNIA MODELS ONLY)

To prevent fuel vapors from evaporating into the atmosphere, the vapor from the tank is routed into a charcoal canister while the engine is not running (**Figure 173**). When the engine is started, the vapor is drawn from the charcoal canister into the engine and burned during the combustion process. **Figure 174** shows a typical evaporative emission component layout. Due to the various manufacturing changes, always refer to the Emission Control label located on the underside of the seat.

(173)

EVAPORATIVE EMISSION CONTROL SYSTEM (CALIFORNIA MODELS ONLY, TYPICAL)

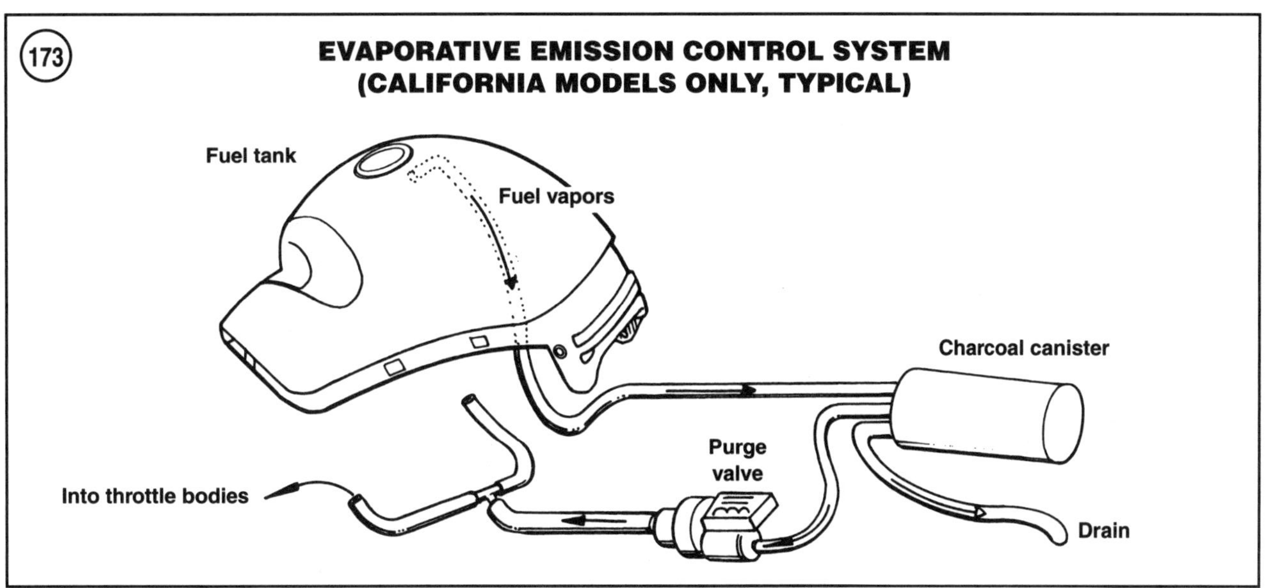

(174)

EVAPORATIVE EMISSION CONTROL SYSTEM (CALIFORNIA MODELS ONLY, TYPICAL)

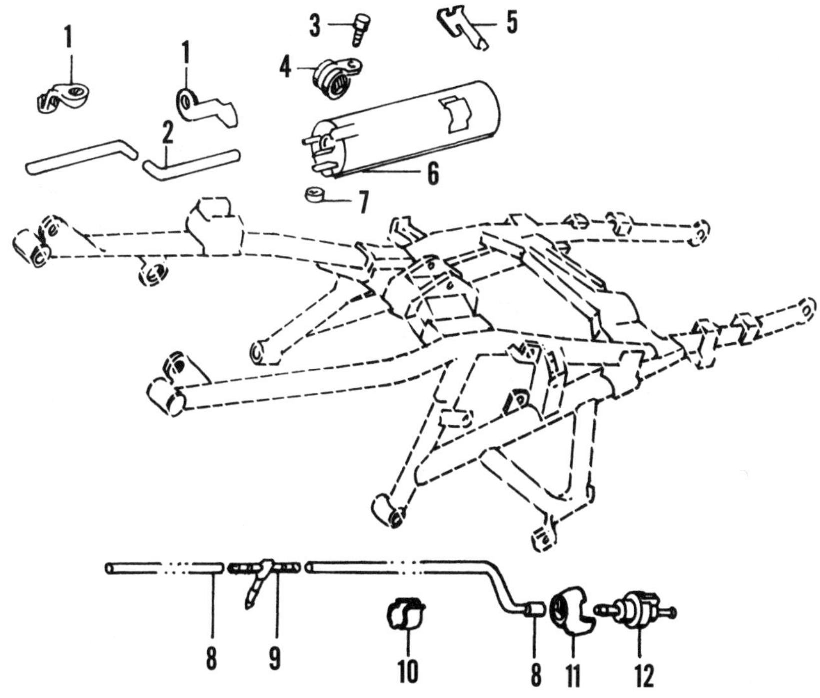

1. Bracket
2. Fuel vapor hose
3. Screw
4. Clamp
5. Mounting bracket
6. Charcoal canister
7. Nut
8. Vacuum hose
9. T-fitting
10. Clamp
11. Bracket
12. Fuel tank breather valve

Charcoal Canister

Inspection

Before removing the hoses from any of the parts, mark the hose and fitting with a piece of masking tape to identify them.

1. Check all emission control lines and hoses to make sure they are correctly routed and connected.

WARNING
Make sure the fuel tank vapor hoses are routed so they cannot contact hot engine or exhaust components. These hoses contain flammable vapor. If a hose melts from contact with a hot part, leaking vapor may ignite, causing severe motorcycle damage and rider injury.

2. Make sure there are no kinks in the lines or hoses. Also inspect the hoses and lines routed near engine hot spots for excessive wear or burning.
3. Check the physical condition of all lines and hoses in the system. Check for cuts, tears or loose connections. These lines and hoses are subjected to various temperatures and operating conditions, and eventually become brittle and crack. Replace damaged lines and hoses.
4. Check all components in the emission control system for damage, such as broken fittings.

Replacement

1A. On models so equipped, place the motorcycle on the centerstand with the front wheel off the ground.

1B. On models without a centerstand, place a suitable size jack under the engine to support the motorcycle with the front wheel off the ground.

2. On all models, mark the two hoses (A, **Figure 175**) and the canister fittings prior to disconnecting the hoses from the fittings.
3. Remove the seat(s) as described in Chapter Fifteen.
4. On models so equipped, remove the rear side panels as described in Chapter Fifteen.

5A. On R1100S models, loosen the clamps (B, **Figure 175**) securing the charcoal canister to the rear frame rail.

5B. On R850C and R1200C models, remove the bolt (A, **Figure 176**) securing the charcoal canister (B) and remove it from the rear frame rail.

5C. On all models except R850C, R1100S and R1200C, remove the bolts and clamps (A, **Figure 177**) securing the charcoal canister (B) and remove it from the rear frame rail.

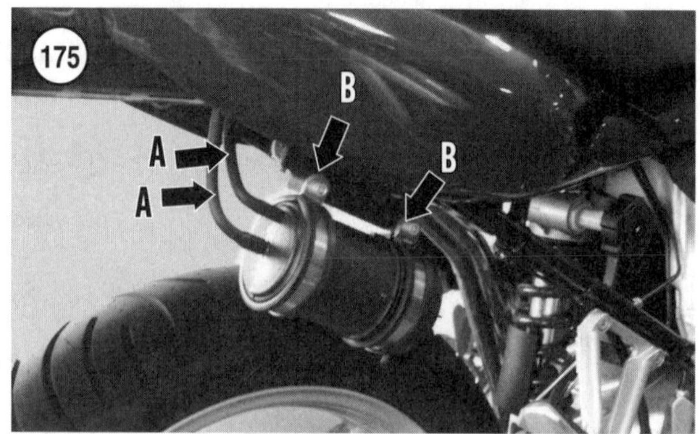

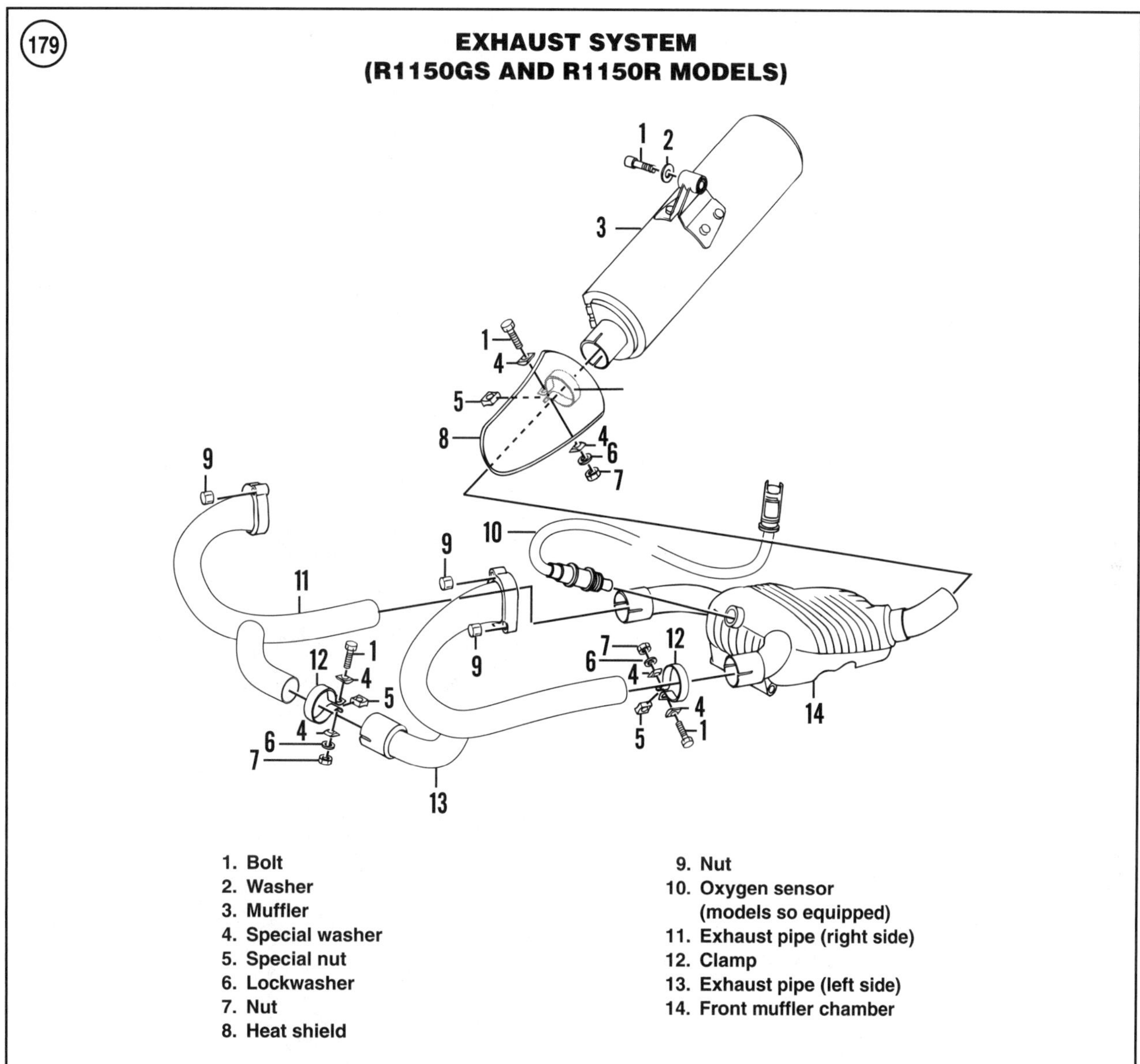

1. Bolt
2. Washer
3. Muffler
4. Special washer
5. Special nut
6. Lockwasher
7. Nut
8. Heat shield
9. Nut
10. Oxygen sensor (models so equipped)
11. Exhaust pipe (right side)
12. Clamp
13. Exhaust pipe (left side)
14. Front muffler chamber

6. Disconnect the charcoal canister from the mounting bracket and lower it from the rear frame rail.

7. Disconnect the hoses from the canister fittings and remove the canister and the rollover valve (**Figure 178**).

8. Installation is the reverse of removal. Ensure that all hoses are connected to the correct fittings and are secure.

EXHAUST SYSTEM

R1150GS and R1150R Models Removal/Installation

Refer to **Figure 179**.

1. Place the motorcycle on the centerstand with the rear wheel off the ground.

CAUTION
The oxygen sensor wire harness is fragile, do not pull on it as it will be damaged.

2. On models so equipped, perform the following:
   a. Follow the oxygen sensor wire harness from the muffler to the main harness and disconnect it.
   b. Remove any tie wraps securing the sensor wiring harness to the frame or engine components.

3. Remove the bolt and washer (**Figure 180**) securing the muffler to the rear frame.

4. Loosen the clamp securing the front of the muffler to the front muffler.
5. Remove the muffler.
6. Loosen the bolt and nut on the clamp (**Figure 181**) at the front crossover section. Slide the clamp off the pipe.
7. Remove the nuts (**Figure 182**) securing the exhaust pipe to the cylinder head.
8. Pull the exhaust pipe forward and out of the cylinder head and remove the exhaust pipe from the motorcycle. Remove the gaskets from the exhaust port in each cylinder.
9. Repeat Step 7 and Step 8 for the exhaust pipe on the other cylinder head.
10. To remove the front muffler chamber, perform the following:
   a. Place a support under the front muffler chamber.
   b. Remove the special Allen bolt (A, **Figure 183**) securing the front muffler chamber to the side stand mounting bracket.
   c. Lower the front muffler chamber (B, **Figure 183**) and remove it from the engine and frame. Note the path of the oxygen sensor wire harness through the frame.
11. Inspect the exhaust system as described in this section.
12. Install by reversing these removal steps while noting the following:
   a. Ensure the oxygen sensor wire harness is routed correctly and secured to the frame with tie wraps.
   b. Apply a light coat of antiseize compound to the exhaust pipe-to-muffler clamp bolts prior to installation.
   c. Tighten all clamp bolts and nuts to 45 N•m (33 ft, lb.).
   d. Tighten cylinder head nuts to 21 N•m (15 ft.-lb.).
   e. Tighten front muffler chamber Allen bolt 15 N•m (132 in.-lb.).
   f. After installation is complete, start the engine and make sure there are no exhaust leaks.

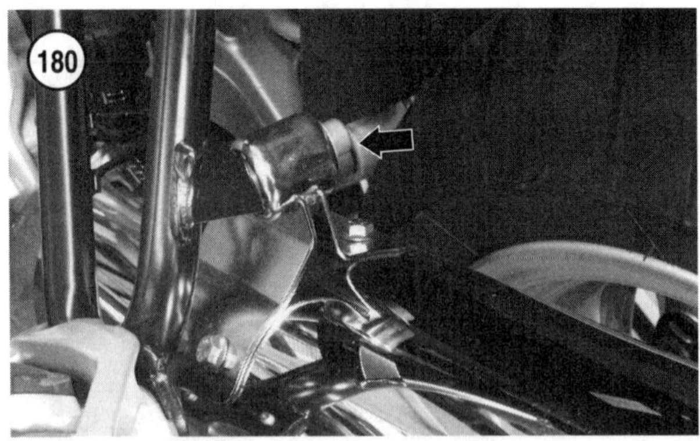

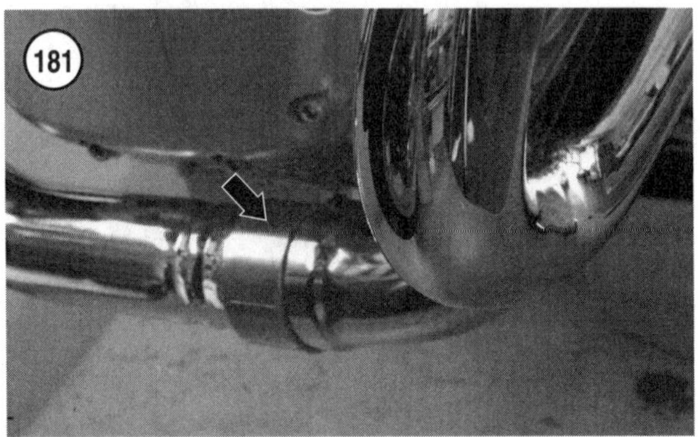

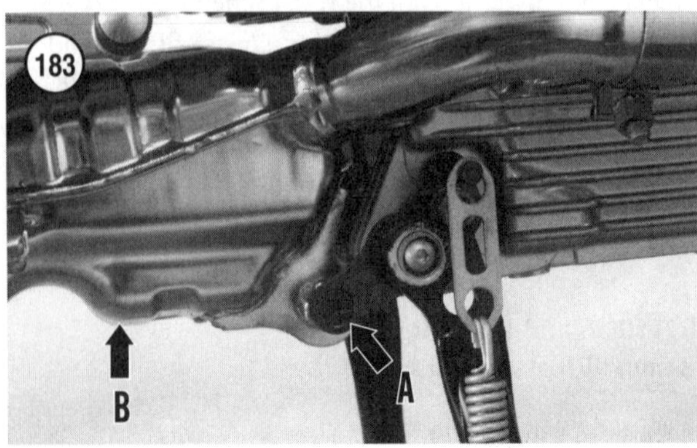

R1100S Models Removal/Installation

Refer to **Figure 184**.

1. Place the motorcycle on the centerstand with the front wheel off the ground.

CAUTION
The oxygen sensor wire harness is fragile, do not pull on it as it will be damaged.

2. On models so equipped, perform the following:

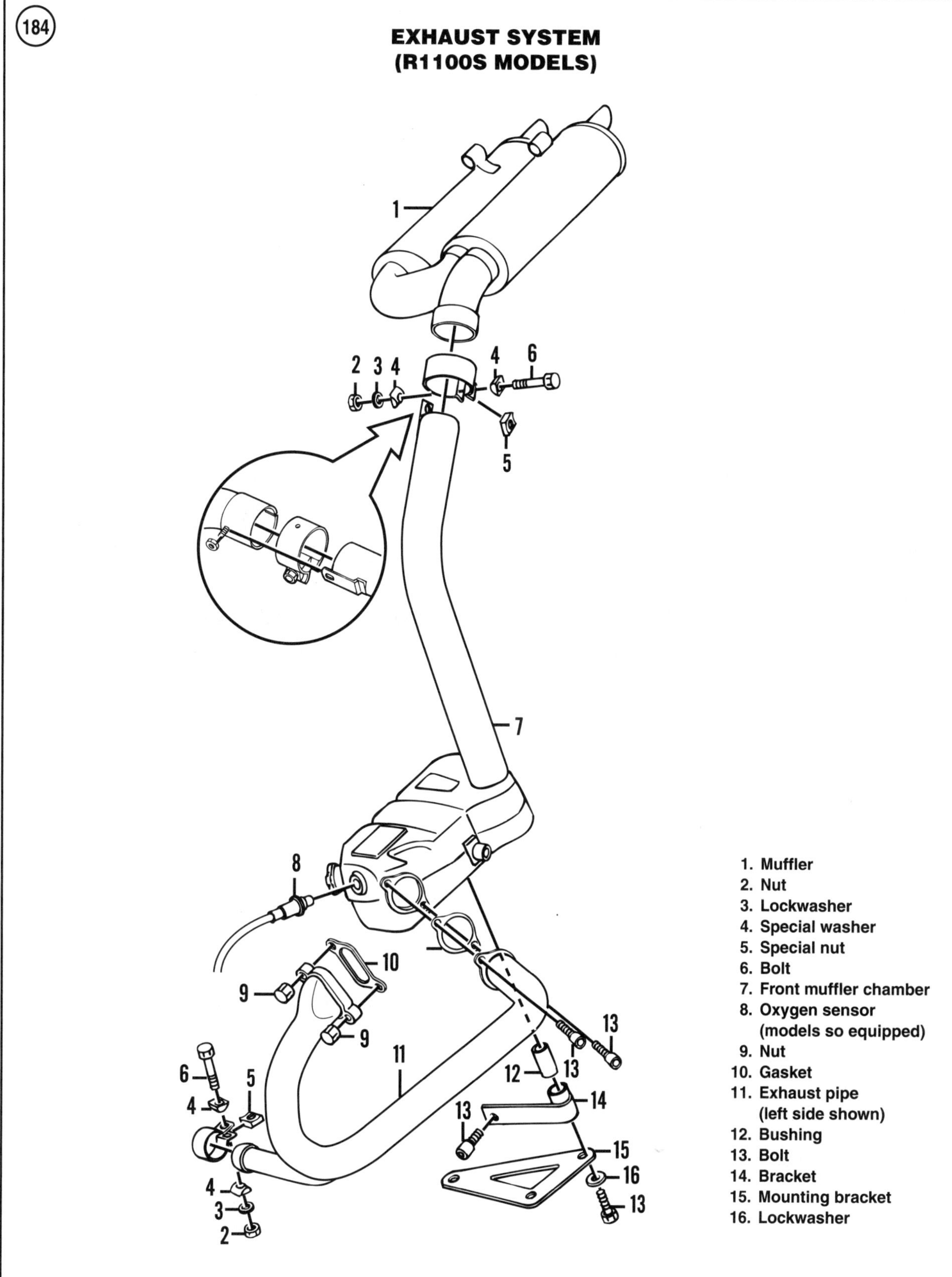
184
EXHAUST SYSTEM
(R1100S MODELS)
1
2 3 4
4 6
5
7
8
10
9
9
11
13
13
12
14
13
15
16
13
6
5
4
4
3
2
1. Muffler
2. Nut
3. Lockwasher
4. Special washer
5. Special nut
6. Bolt
7. Front muffler chamber
8. Oxygen sensor
(models so equipped)
9. Nut
10. Gasket
11. Exhaust pipe
(left side shown)
12. Bushing
13. Bolt
14. Bracket
15. Mounting bracket
16. Lockwasher

a. Follow the oxygen sensor wire harness from the muffler to the main harness and disconnect it.
b. Remove any tie wraps securing the sensor wiring harness to the frame or engine components.

3. Remove the seat (A, **Figure 185**) as described in Chapter Fifteen.
4. Remove both rear side panels (B, **Figure 185**) as described in Chapter Fifteen.
5. Remove the fuel tank as described in this chapter.
6. Remove the license plate light assembly (C, **Figure 185**) as described in Chapter Ten.
7. Remove the nut on the securing the tab washer on the front muffler. If necessary, straighten the tab washer.
8. Loosen the clamp securing the rear muffler to the front muffler chamber.
9. Pull the rear muffler straight back and off the locating post on the frame. Remove the rear muffler.
10. Loosen the bolt and nut on the clamp (**Figure 181**) at the front cross over section. Slide the clamp off the pipe.
11. Remove the bolts (**Figure 186**) securing the exhaust pipe to the front muffler.
12. Remove the nuts (**Figure 182**) securing the exhaust pipe to the cylinder head.
13. Pull the exhaust pipe forward and out of the cylinder head and remove the exhaust pipe and gaskets.
14. Repeat Step 12 and Step 13 for the exhaust pipe on the other side.
15. To remove the front muffler chamber, perform the following:
   a. Place a support under the front muffler chamber.
   b. Remove the bolts and washers securing the mounting brackets securing the front muffler chamber to the under side of the crankcase. Do not lose the bushing between the upper bracket and the crankcase.
   c. Lower the front muffler chamber and pipe down through the frame and remove it from the engine and frame. Note the path of the oxygen sensor wire harness through the frame.
16. Inspect the exhaust system as described in this section.
17. Install by reversing these removal steps while noting the following:
   a. Ensure the oxygen sensor wire harness is routed correctly and secured to the frame with tie wraps.
   b. Apply a light coat of antiseize compound to the exhaust pipe-to-muffler clamp bolts prior to installation.
   c. Tighten all clamp bolts and nuts to 45 N•m (33 ft, lb.).
   d. Tighten cylinder head nuts to 21 N•m (15 ft.-lb.).

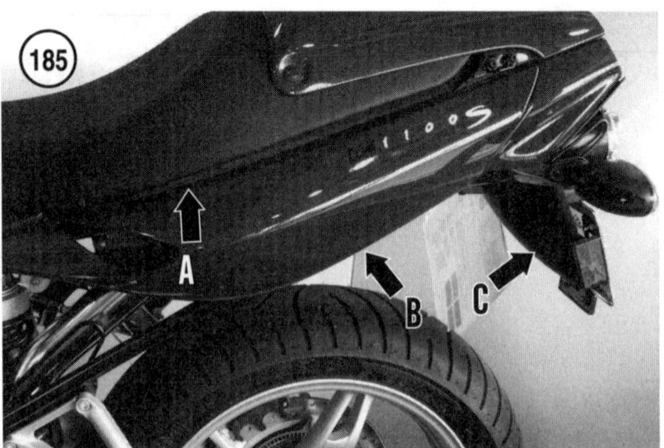

   e. Tighten front muffler chamber Allen bolt 12 N•m (106 in.-lb.).
   f. After installation is complete, start the engine and make sure there are no exhaust leaks.

R850C and R1200C Models Removal/Installation

Refer to **Figure 187**.

1. Place a suitable size jack under the engine to support the motorcycle with the rear wheel off the ground.

CAUTION
The oxygen sensor wire harness is fragile, do not pull on it as it will be damaged.

2. On models so equipped, perform the following:
   a. Follow the oxygen sensor wire harness from the muffler to the main harness and disconnect it.
   b. Remove any tie wraps securing the sensor wiring harness to the frame or engine components.
3. Remove the fuel tank as described in this chapter.

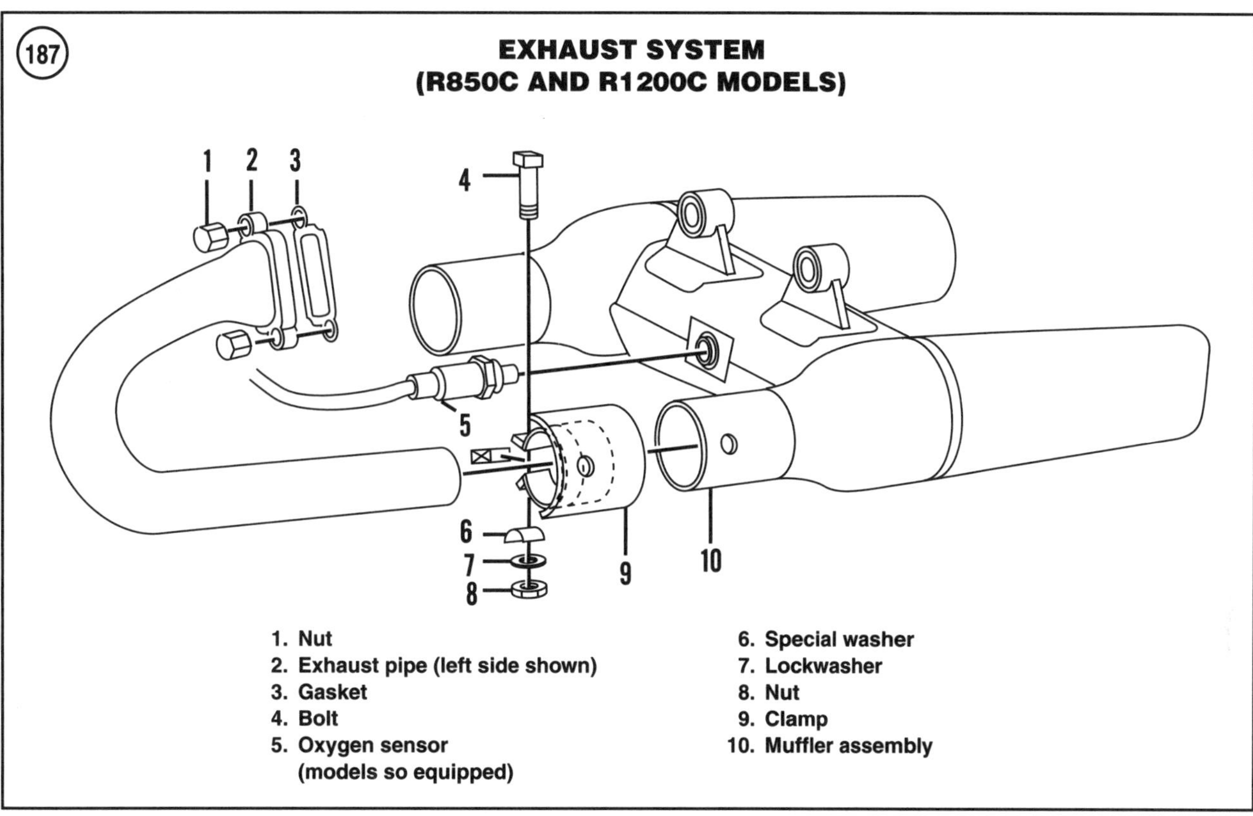

4. Loosen the bolt and nut on the backside of the clamp (**Figure 188**) securing the exhaust pipe to the muffler assembly.

5. Repeat Step 4 for the exhaust pipe on the other side.

6. Remove the nuts (**Figure 189**) securing the exhaust pipe to the cylinder head.

7. Pull the exhaust pipe forward and out of the cylinder head and remove the exhaust pipe and gaskets.

8. Repeat Steps 4-7 for the exhaust pipe on the other side.

9. Place a box under the muffler assembly since it is heavy and will drop down after being released form the locating posts in Step 6.

10. Pull the muffler assembly straight back and off the locating posts on the frame (**Figure 190**). Remove the muffler assembly.

11. Inspect the exhaust system as described in this section.

12. Install by reversing these removal steps while noting the following:

   a. Ensure the oxygen sensor wire harness is routed correctly and secured to the frame with tie wraps.

   b. Apply a light coat of antiseize compound to the exhaust pipe-to-muffler clamp bolts prior to installation.

c. Align the hole in the clamp with the embossed dot on the muffler (arrows on **Figure 187**) then tighten the clamp bolt and nut to 55 N•m (40 ft.-lb.).

d. Tighten cylinder head nuts to 24 N•m (17 ft.-lb.).

e. After installation is complete, start the engine and make sure there are no exhaust leaks.

All Models Except R850C, R1100S, R1150GS, R1150R and R1200S Removal/Installation

Muffler

Refer **Figure 191** and **Figure 192**.

1A. On models so equipped, place the motorcycle on the centerstand with the front wheel off the ground.

1B. On models without a centerstand, place a suitable size jack under the engine to support the motorcycle with the front wheel off the ground.

CAUTION
The oxygen sensor wire harness is fragile, do not pull on it as it will be damaged.

2. On models so equipped, perform the following:
   a. Follow the oxygen sensor wire harness from the muffler to the main harness and disconnect it.
   b. Remove any tie wraps securing the sensor wire harness to the frame or engine components.

3. Loosen the front clamp bolt (**Figure 193**) securing the muffler to the exhaust pipe assembly.

4. Remove the bolt from each side (**Figure 194**) securing the muffler to the centerstand support plate. There is a washer between the support plate and the rubber cushion on the muffler mount. These washers may fall out when the bolts are removed. Do not lose the washers as they must be reinstalled.

5A. On R and GS models, remove the bolt (**Figure 195**) securing the muffler to the frame.

5B. On RS and RT models, remove the bolt and washer securing the muffler retainer to the frame.

6. Pull the muffler back and out of the exhaust pipe opening and carefully lower it to the ground. Note the path of the oxygen sensor wire harness through the frame.

7. Remove the muffler assembly.

8. On models so equipped, do not remove the oxygen sensor (**Figure 196**) unless it is going to be replaced.

9. Install by reversing these removal steps while noting the following:
   a. Ensure the oxygen sensor wire harness is routed correctly and secured to the frame with tie wraps.

   b. Apply a light coat of antiseize compound to the exhaust pipe-to-muffler clamp bolt prior to installation.
   c. Tighten the muffler-to-rear frame (R and GS models) bolts to 24 N•m (18 ft.-lb.).
   d. Tighten the muffler-to-footrest (RS and RT) bolt and nut to 35 N•m (26 ft.-lb.).
   e. Tighten muffler-to-centerstand support plate bolt 20 N•m (15 ft.-lb.).
   f. After installation is complete, start the engine and make sure there are no exhaust leaks.

Exhaust pipe assembly

Refer **Figure 191** and **Figure 192**.

1. On RT models, remove the front fairing side panels as described in Chapter Fifteen.

2. Loosen the front clamp bolt (**Figure 193**) securing the exhaust pipe assembly to the muffler.

3. Remove the three nuts (**Figure 197**) securing the exhaust pipe assembly to each cylinder head outlet.

4. Pull the exhaust pipe assembly (**Figure 198**) forward and out of the cylinder head and remove the exhaust pipe assembly from the motorcycle. Remove the gaskets from the exhaust ports in each cylinder.

5. Install a new exhaust pipe gasket onto each exhaust pipe fitting. Apply a small amount of cold grease to the gaskets to hold them in place.

6. Install the exhaust pipe assembly onto the cylinder head and muffler.

7. Install by reversing the removal steps while noting the following:
   a. Apply a light coat of antiseize compound to the exhaust pipe-to-muffler clamp bolt prior to installation.

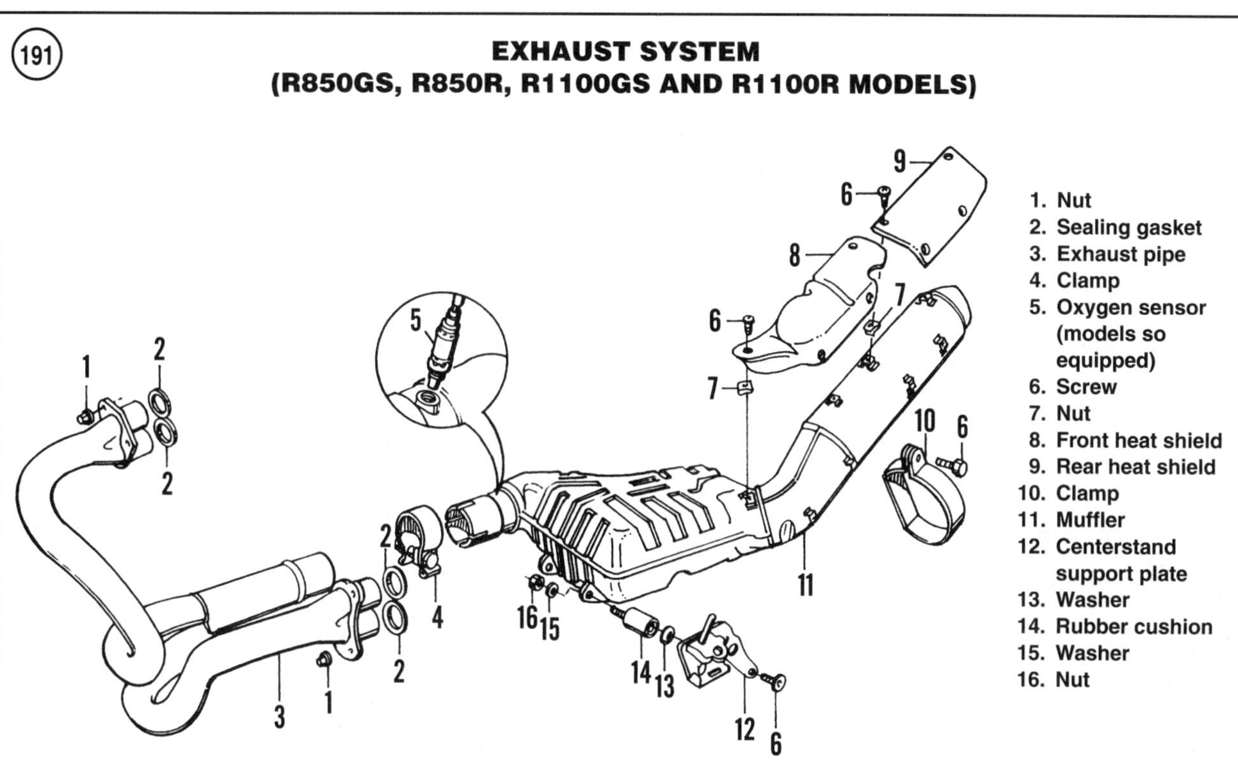
191
EXHAUST SYSTEM
(R850GS, R850R, R1100GS AND R1100R MODELS)
1. Nut
2. Sealing gasket
3. Exhaust pipe
4. Clamp
5. Oxygen sensor (models so equipped)
6. Screw
7. Nut
8. Front heat shield
9. Rear heat shield
10. Clamp
11. Muffler
12. Centerstand support plate
13. Washer
14. Rubber cushion
15. Washer
16. Nut

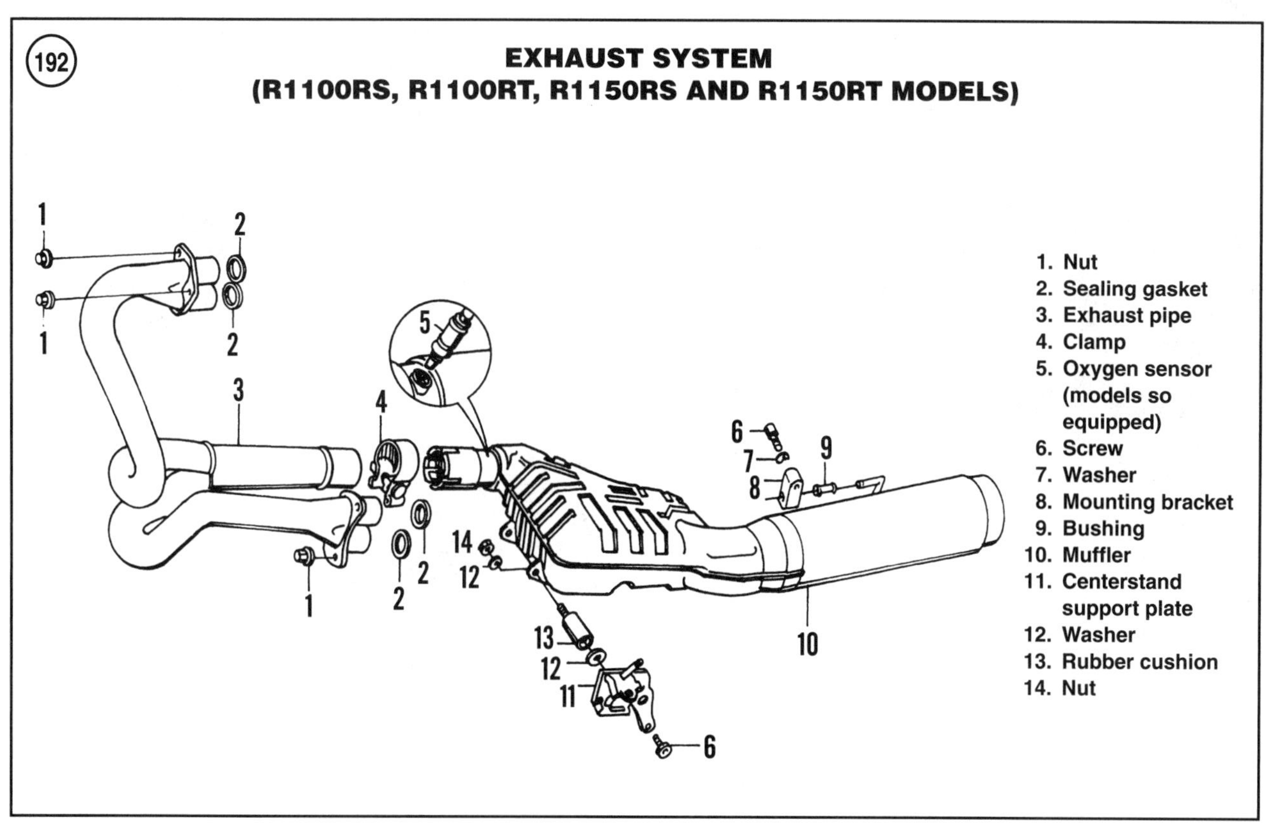
192
EXHAUST SYSTEM
(R1100RS, R1100RT, R1150RS AND R1150RT MODELS)
1. Nut
2. Sealing gasket
3. Exhaust pipe
4. Clamp
5. Oxygen sensor (models so equipped)
6. Screw
7. Washer
8. Mounting bracket
9. Bushing
10. Muffler
11. Centerstand support plate
12. Washer
13. Rubber cushion
14. Nut

9

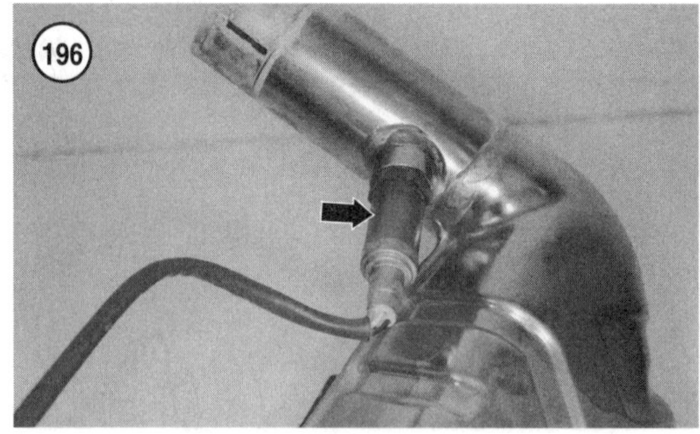

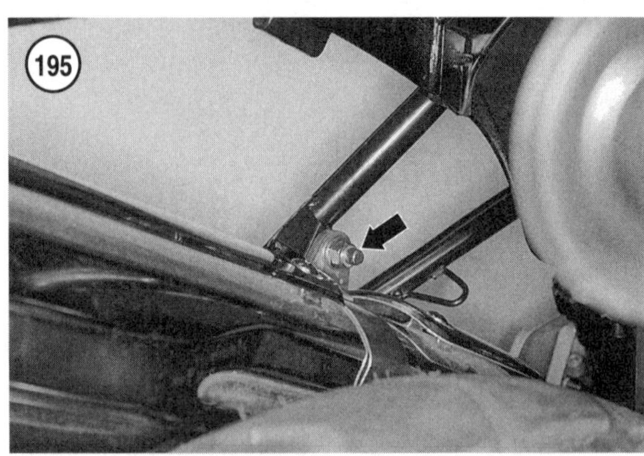

b. Tighten the exhaust pipe-to-muffler clamp bolt to 50 N•m (37 ft.-lb.).

c. Tighten the exhaust pipe-to-cylinder head nuts (with plate) to 22 N•m (16 ft.-lb.).

d. Tighten the exhaust pipe-to-cylinder head nuts (without plate) to 18 N•m (13 ft.-lb.).

e. After installation is complete, start the engine and make sure there are no exhaust leaks.

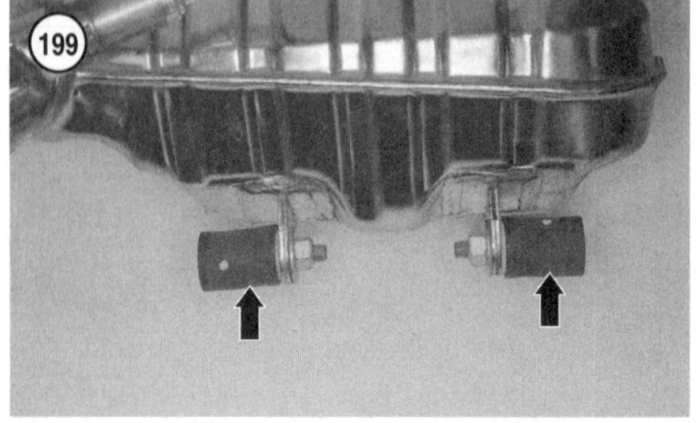

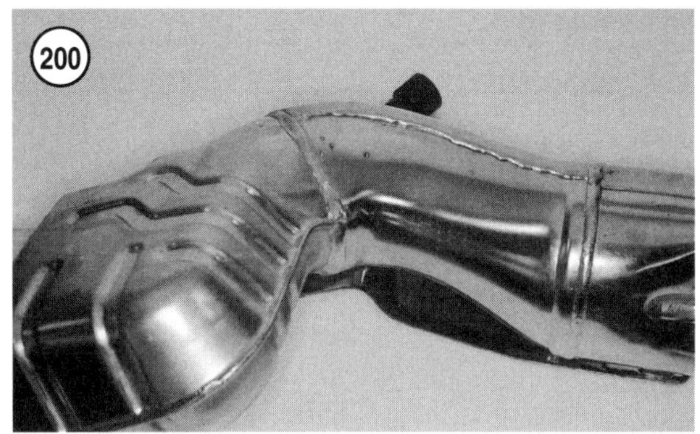

200

201

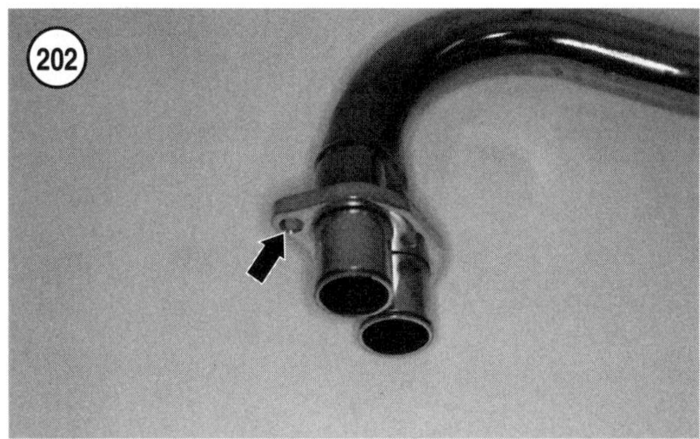

202

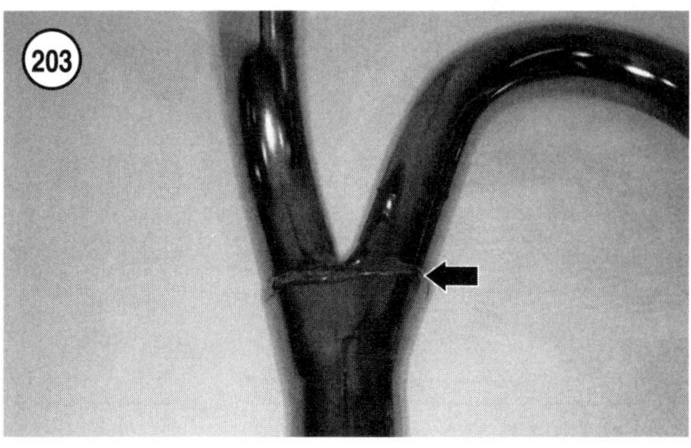

203

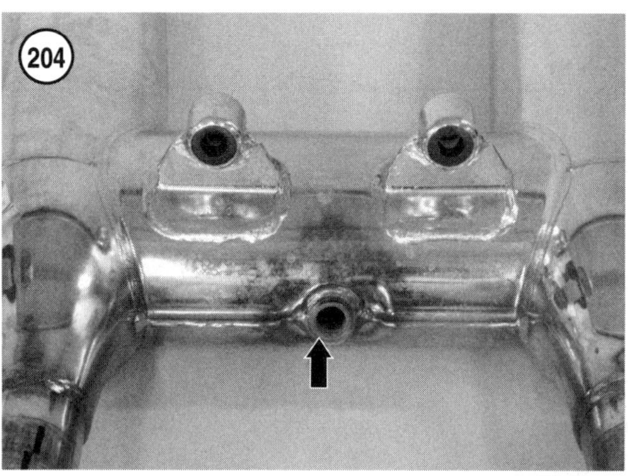

204

205

Inspection (All Models)

1. Check the rubber grommets (**Figure 199**) at the front mounting brackets. Replace the rubber grommets if they are starting to harden or deteriorate.

2. Inspect all of the welds (**Figure 200**) for leakage or corrosion.

3. On models so equipped, check the heat shields (**Figure 201**) and the mounting bolts. Tighten if necessary.

4. Check the exhaust pipe-to-cylinder head flange (**Figure 202**) for corrosion, burned areas or damage.

5. Inspect all welds (**Figure 203**) for leakage or corrosion.

6. On models so equipped, inspect the threads for the oxygen sensor (**Figure 204**) for thread damage. Repair if necessary.

7. Inspect all clamps (**Figure 205**, typical) for rust and damage.

Table 1 FUEL SYSTEM SPECIFICATIONS

Item	Specification
Fuel grade	
Models with catalytic converter	Premium unleaded fuel with a minimum Octane rating of 95 (RON) or 85 (MON), AKI 91 premium
Models without catalytic converter	Premium leaded fuel with a minimum Octane rating of 95 (RON) or 85 (MON)
Fuel tank capacity[1]	
R models	21 L (5.54 U.S. gal)
R1100GS	25 L (6.60 U.S. gal)
R1150GS	22 L (5.80 U.S. gal)
R1100RS	23 L (6.07 U.S. gal)
R1150RS	22.5 L (5.95 U.S. gal)
R1100RT	26 L (6.86 U.S. gal)
R1150RT	25.2 L (6.66 U.S. gal)
R1100S	18 L (4.80 U.S. gal)
R850C, R1200C	17 L (4.50 U.S. gal)
Throttle body bore inner diameter	45 mm (1.772 in.)
Throttle butterfly angle at idle[2]	
R1100R and R1100GS models	5°
R1100RS and R1100RT models	10°
Air filter element	Replaceable paper element

1. Includes reserve.
2. Information for all other models not available.

Table 2 FUEL AND EXHAUST SYSTEM TORQUE SPECIFICATIONS

Item	N•m	in.-lb.	ft.-lb.
Exhaust system			
All Models Except R850C, R1100S, R1150GS, R1150R, and R1200C			
Muffler-to-rear frame			
R, GS models	24	–	18
Muffler-to-footrest bolt and nut			
RS, RT models	35	–	26
Muffler-to-centerstand support plate bolt	20	–	15
Exhaust pipe-to-muffler clamp bolt	50	–	37
Exhaust pipe-to-cylinder head nuts			
With plate	22	–	16
Without plate	18	–	13
All clamp bolts	45	–	33
R1150GS, R1150R models			
Exhaust pipe-to-cylinder head nuts	21	–	15
Front muffler chamber Allen bolts	15	132	–
All clamp bolts	45	–	33
R1100S models			
Exhaust pipe-to-cylinder head nuts	21	–	15
Front muffler chamber Allen bolts	12	106	–
All clamp bolts	45	–	33
R850C and R1200C models			
Exhaust pipe-to-cylinder head nuts	24	–	17
All clamp bolts and nuts	55	–	40
Fuel system			
Fuel tank mounting bolts			
R1100S	9	80	–
All other models	22	–	16

CHAPTER TEN

ELECTRICAL SYSTEM

Electrical system specifications are located in **Tables 1-3** at the end of this chapter. Wiring diagrams are at the end of the book. For spark plug and battery procedures, refer to Chapter Three.

ELECTRICAL COMPONENT REPLACEMENT

Most motorcycle dealerships and parts suppliers will not accept returns of electrical parts. If you cannot determine the *exact* cause of any electrical system malfunction, have a BMW dealership retest that specific system to verify your test results. If you purchase a new electrical component(s), install it, and then find that the system still does not work properly, you will probably not be able to return the unit for a refund.

CHARGING SYSTEM

The charging system consists of the battery and a three-phase 12-volt alternator with an integral electronic voltage regulator.

The alternating current generated by the alternator is rectified to direct current. The voltage regulator maintains the voltage to the battery and additional electrical loads at a constant voltage, regardless of variations in engine speed and load.

A Poly-V drive belt, driven off the crankshaft, runs the alternator.

Current Leakage (Draw) Test

Perform this test before performing the *Regulated Voltage Test.*

1. Turn the ignition switch off.
2. Disconnect the negative battery cable as described in Chapter Three.

CAUTION
Before connecting the ammeter into the circuit in Step 3, set the meter to its highest amperage scale. This prevents a large current flow from damaging the meter or blowing the meter's fuse.

3. Connect an ammeter between the negative battery cable and the negative battery terminal (**Figure 1**).
4. Switch the ammeter to its lowest scale and note the reading. The maximum current must be 2.0 mA or less. A current draw that exceeds 2.0 mA will discharge the battery.
5. Dirt and/or electrolyte on top of the battery or a crack in the battery case can create a path for battery current to flow. If an excessive current draw is noted, remove and

clean the battery as described in Chapter Three, then repeat the drain test.

6. If the current draw is still excessive, consider the following probable causes:
   a. Faulty voltage regulator/rectifier.
   b. Damaged battery.
   c. Short circuit in the system.
   d. Loose, dirty or faulty electrical connectors in the charging circuit.

7. To find the short circuit causing a current draw, refer to the wiring diagrams at the end of this manual. Then continue to measure the current draw while disconnecting different connectors in the electrical system one by one. When the current draw rate returns to an acceptable level, the circuit is indicated. Test the circuit further to find the problem.

8. Disconnect the ammeter.

9. Reconnect the negative battery cable.

Regulated Voltage Test

If a charging system malfunction is suspected, make sure the battery is fully charged and in good condition before going any further. Clean and test the battery as described in Chapter Three.

1. Turn the ignition switch on. The battery charge light on the instrument cluster should come on. If the light does not come on, refer to *Instrument Panel* in this chapter and see if the charge light bulb is burned out.

2. Start the motorcycle and increase idle speed. The battery charge light should now go off. If the light does not go off, shut off the engine and check the alternator brushes and slip rings as they are usually the primary problem. Refer to *Voltage Regulator/Brush Unit Replacement* in this chapter.

3. Start the motorcycle and let it reach normal operating temperature. Usually 10-15 minutes of stop-and-go riding is sufficient. Shut off the engine.

4. Remove the rider's seat as described in Chapter Fifteen.

5. Make sure that the battery cables are attached securely to the battery terminals and that the terminals are clean. If necessary, clean the terminals and cables.

6. Leave the battery terminal protective covers hinged up as the terminals must be accessible.

7. Connect a portable tachometer, following its manufacturer's instructions.

8. Start the engine and let it run at approximately 1400 rpm.

9. Connect a voltmeter to the battery terminals (**Figure 2**). The reading should be 13-14 volts.

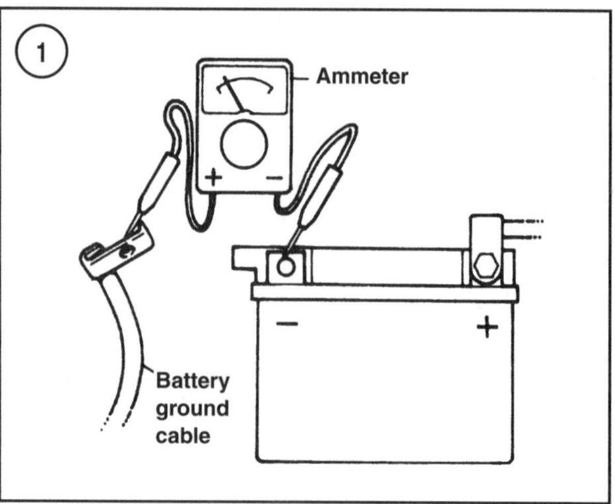

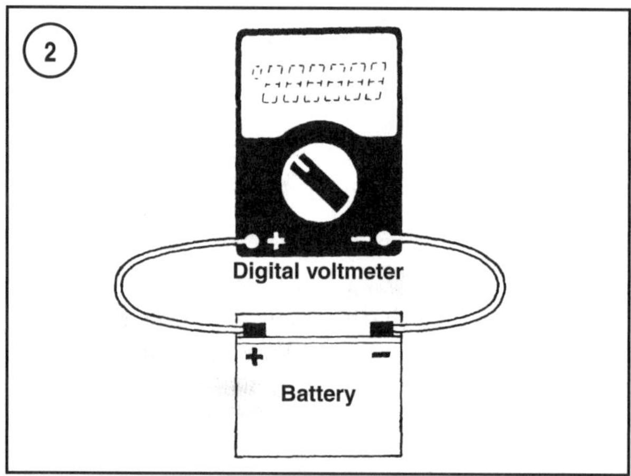

10. Turn on all lights and accessories. The voltage reading should remain 13-14 volts.

11. If the voltage is less than specified, inspect the alternator brushes and slip rings as described in this chapter.

12. If the voltage is more than specified, the voltage regulator is probably faulty and must be replaced as described in this chapter.

13. Shut off the engine and disconnect the voltmeter and portable tachometer.

14. Hinge the battery terminal protective covers down to the closed position.

15. Install the rider's seat as described in Chapter Fifteen.

ALTERNATOR

Removal (All Models Except R850C and R1200C)

Refer to **Figure 3**.

1. Remove both seats as described in Chapter Fifteen.

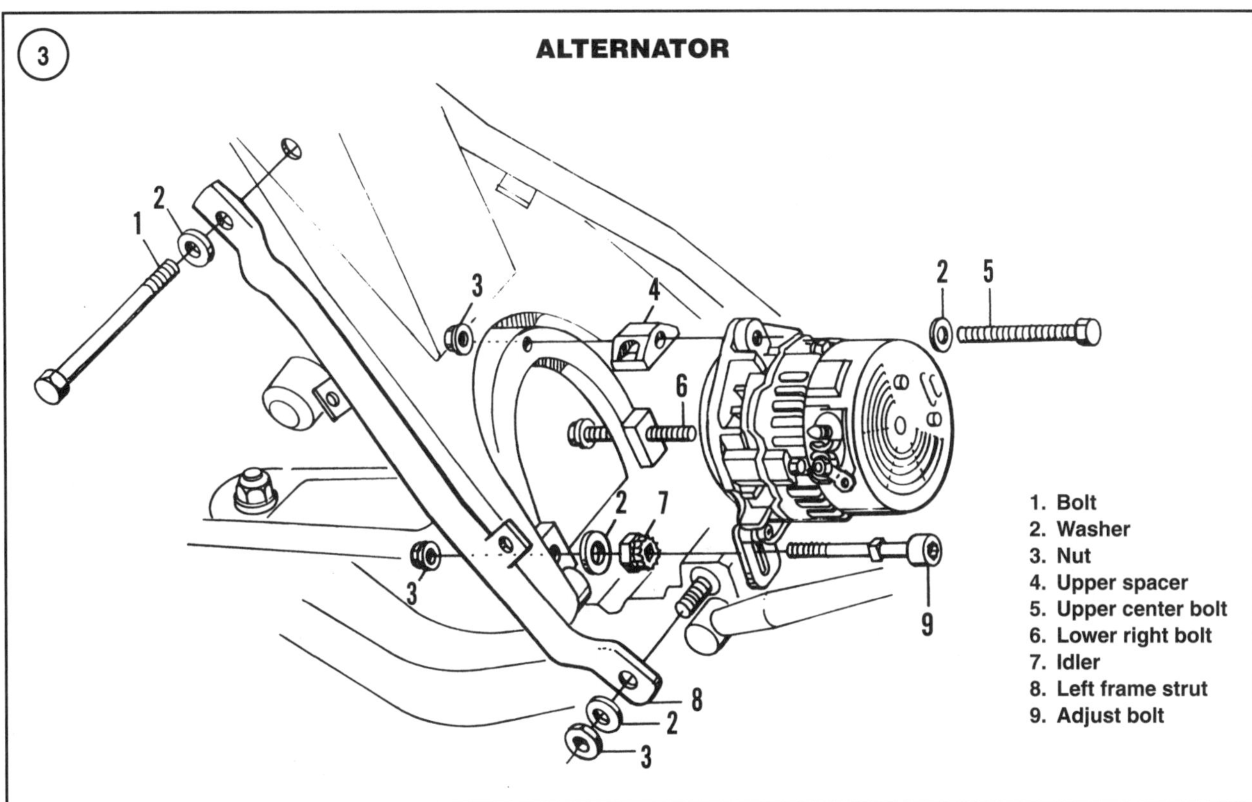

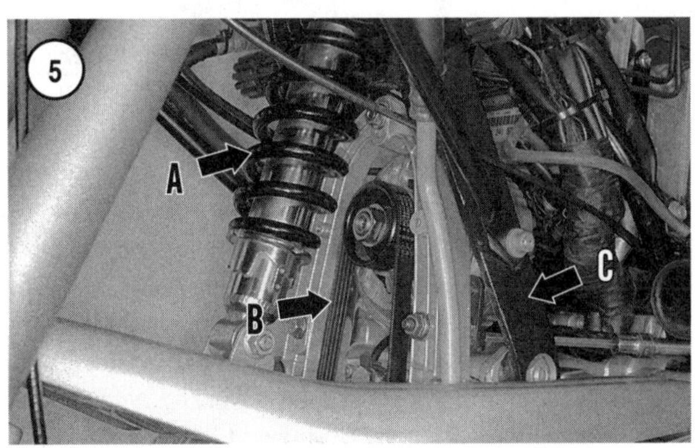

2. On RS, RT and S models, remove the front fairing side sections as described in Chapter Fifteen.
3. Disconnect the negative battery cable as described in Chapter Three.
4. Remove the fuel tank as described in Chapter Nine.
5. On the left side of S models, remove the bolts and washers securing the air filter air intake duct to the frame and the air filter housing. Remove the duct.
6. Remove the screws securing the front cover (**Figure 4**) and remove the cover.
7. Remove the front strut (A, **Figure 5**) as described in Chapter Twelve.
8. Remove the Motronic control unit as described in Chapter Nine.

WARNING
The ABS brake system ***must*** *be bled with a power bleeder after the ABS unit is reinstalled. After installation, trailer the motorcycle to a BMW dealership to have the system bled.*

9. Remove the ABS unit, or ABS pressure modulator, as described in Chapter Twelve.
10. On the left rear side of the alternator, remove the insulated cap (**Figure 6**) from the large nut. Remove the nut

(A, **Figure 7**) securing the large electrical wire to the alternator terminal. Disconnect the smaller electrical connector from the spade terminal (B, **Figure 7**).

11. Loosen the alternator mounting bolts and nuts sufficiently to allow slack in the drive belt.

12. On models so equipped remove the rotary breather pipe as follows:

   a. Remove the lower bolt and the upper banjo bolt and sealing washers securing the rotary breather pipe.
   b. Remove the rotatry breather pipe and the O-ring located on the lower bolt hole locating pin between the pipe and the alternator support cover.

13. Remove the drive belt (B, **Figure 5**) from the alternator pulley.

14. Remove the bolts and nuts securing the alternator to the alternator support cover. Do not lose the adjusting bolt idler and washer on the adjusting bolt, located between the alternator and the support cover.

14. On all R1100 and R1150GS models, remove the bolts and nuts securing the left frame strut (C, **Figure 5**) and remove the strut.

16. Remove the alternator from the crankcase.

Installation (All Models Except R850C and R1200C)

Refer to **Figure 3**.

1. Install the alternator onto the alternator support cover.

2. On all 1100 cc and R1150GS models, install the left frame strut (C, **Figure 5**) and the bolts and nuts. Tighten the bolts and nuts securely.

NOTE

This procedure is shown with the engine removed to better illustrate the steps.

NOTE

*The adjusting bolt has a unique square shoulder (A, **Figure 8**) that fits into the square receptacle in the idler (B). This bolt must be installed on the lower left mount to be used with the adjusting bar on the alternator (**Figure 9**) for drive belt tension adjustment.*

NOTE

In Steps 3-6, tighten the bolts and nuts only tight enough to securely hold the alternator in place in the crankcase. After installation is complete, adjust the drive belt, then tighten the bolts securely.

3. Install the upper center bolt (**Figure 10**), upper spacer (A, **Figure 11**) and nut (B). Tighten only finger-tight at this time.

6

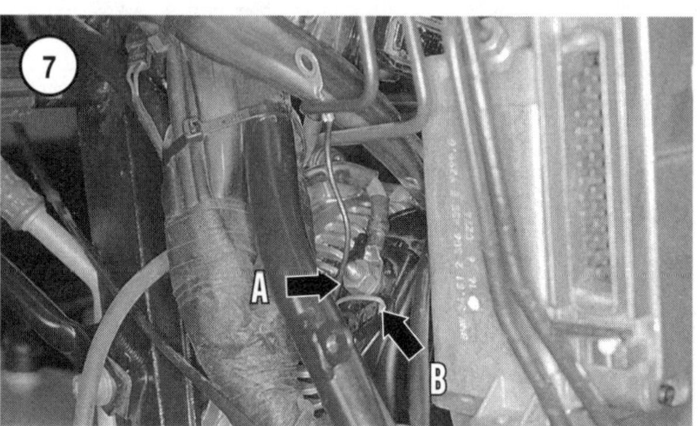
7

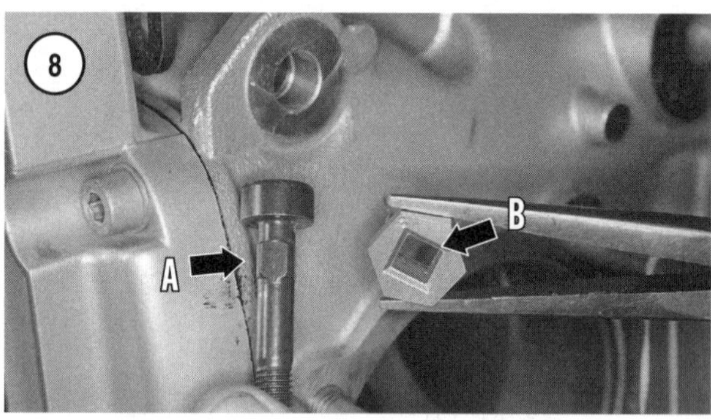
8

4. Install the lower right bolt into the alternator mounting bracket.

5. Position the idler with the barbed side (B, **Figure 8**) facing toward the alternator adjusting bolt (A).

6. Install a washer between the idler and the crankcase. Install the adjusting bolt through the idler aligning the square shoulder with the square receptacle and install the nut onto the adjusting bolt.

7. On models so equipped remove the rotary breather pipe as follows:

   a. Install a new O-ring seal onto the locating dowel and push it in until it seats properly. Apply a light coat of clean engine oil to the O-ring and locating dowel.

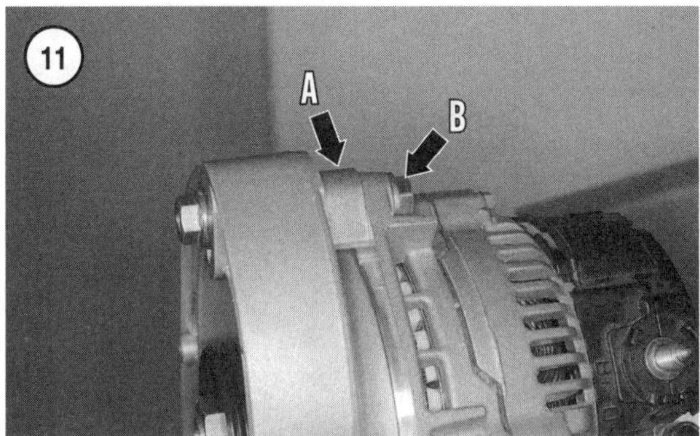

b. Install the rotatory breather pipe onto the alternator support cover. Push the lower porting into place over the locating dowel and O-ring. Install the lower bolt and tight finger-tight.

c. Install a new inner sealing washer between the pipe and the support, then install the upper banjo bolt and new sealing washer through the pipe and the inner sealing washer. Make sure both sealing washers are in place on the upper banjo bolt. Tighten the upper banjo bolt and the lower bolt securely.

8. Ensure the drive belt is installed correctly on the crankcase pulley, then install the belt onto the alternator pulley (B, **Figure 5**).

9. On the left rear side of the alternator, install the large electrical wire onto the alternator terminal and tighten the nut (A, **Figure 7**). Connect the smaller electrical connector (B) onto the spade terminal. Push it on until it bottoms.

10. Install the ABS unit, or ABS pressure regulator, as described in Chapter Twelve.

11. Install the Motronic control unit as described in Chapter Nine.

12. Adjust the alternator drive belt as described in Chapter Three.

13. Install the front strut (A, **Figure 5**) as described in Chapter Twelve.

14. Install the front cover (**Figure 4**) and tighten the screws securely.

15. On the left side of S models, install the air filter air intake duct onto the air filter housing. Install the bolts and washers and tighten securely.

16. Install the fuel tank as described in Chapter Nine.

17. Connect the negative battery cable as described in Chapter Three.

18. On RS, RT and S models, install the front fairing side sections as described in Chapter Fifteen.

19. Install both seats as described in Chapter Fifteen.

10

Removal (R850C and R1200C Models)

Refer to **Figure 3**.

1. Remove the seat as described in Chapter Fifteen.

2. Disconnect the negative battery cable as described in Chapter Three.

3. Drain the engine oil as described in Chapter Three.

4. Remove the fuel tank as described in Chapter Nine.

5. Remove the horn and the holder (**Figure 12**) as described in this chapter.

6. Remove the screws securing the front cover (**Figure 13**) and remove the cover.

7. Remove the starter as described in this chapter.

8. Disconnect the oil cooler return line as described in Chapter Five.

9. Place a suitable size jack under the front portion of the engine. Block the rear wheel so the motorcycle will not move and apply jack pressure to release all weight from the front wheel. Secure the motorcycle it in this position.

10. Remove the bolt (**Figure 14**) securing the front strut (A, **Figure 15**) to the front suspension A-arm.

11. Disconnect the left throttle body (B, **Figure 15**) from the cylinder head as described in Chapter Nine.

12. Remove the left exhaust pipe (C, **Figure 15**) as described in Chapter Nine.

13. Remove the front suspension A-arm pivot shaft as described in Chapter Twelve. Carefully move the front wheel and front suspension (D, **Figure 15**) forward to gain access to the alternator support cover.

NOTE
The following steps are shown with the engine removed and partially disassembled to better illustrate the steps.

14. Remove the rotary breather pipe as follows:
   a. Remove the lower bolt (A, **Figure 16**) and the upper banjo bolt (B) and sealing washers securing the rotary breather pipe (C).
   b. Remove the rotary breather pipe and the O-ring located on the lower bolt hole locating pin between the pipe and the alternator support cover.

15. Loosen the alternator mounting bolts and nuts sufficiently to allow slack in the drive belt.

16. Remove the bolts and nuts securing the alternator to the alternator support cover. Do not lose the adjusting bolt idler and washer on the adjusting bolt, located between the alternator and the support cover.

17. Remove the belt (D, **Figure 16**) from both pulleys.

18. Loosen the clamp bolt (**Figure 17**) on the wiring harness clamp. Move the wire out from under the clamp.

19. Remove the bolt and washer (A, **Figure 18**) and remove the lower pulley (B) from the crankshaft.

NOTE
The Hall sensor unit does not have to be removed unless it is going to be replaced. Disregard Step 20 if the Hall sensor unit is to be left in place.

20. To remove the Hall sensor unit, perform the following:
   a. Make an alignment mark on the edge of the base plate and on the engine (**Figure 19**). This will make certain that the base plate will be reinstalled in its original position.

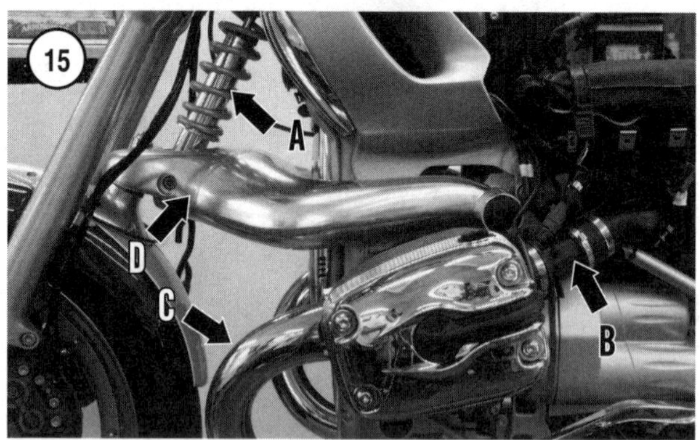

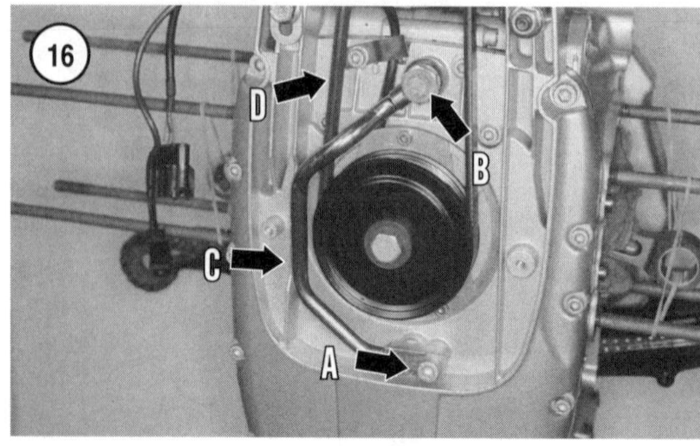

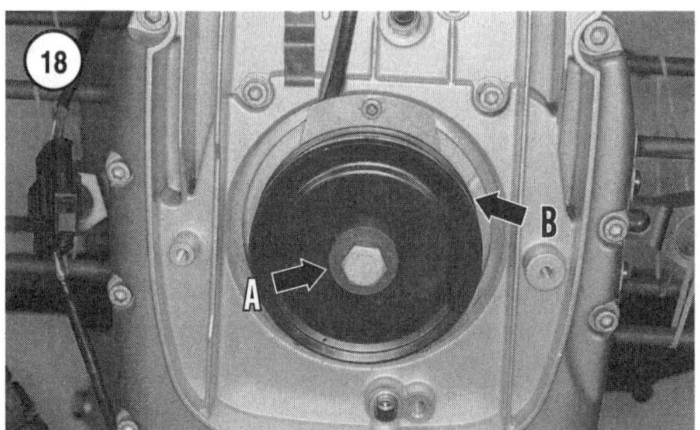

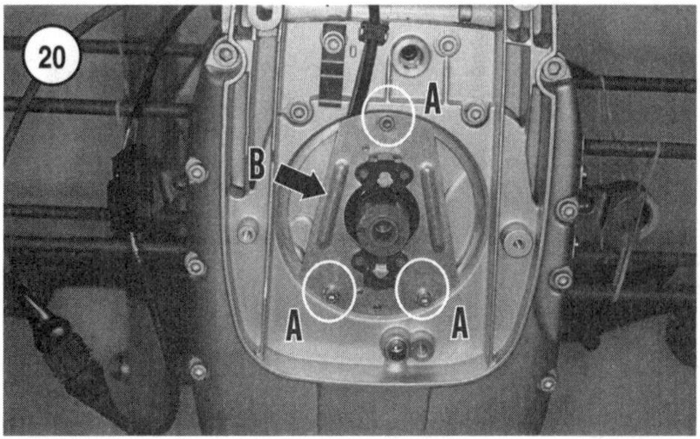

b. Remove the screws and washers (A, **Figure 20**) securing the base plate to the alternator support cover.

c. Carefully pull the base plate assembly (B, **Figure 20**) from the alternator support cover and remove it.

21. Remove the Allen bolts and washers securing the alternator support cover (**Figure 21**) and remove the cover. Do not lose the locating dowels.

22. Remove the mounting hardware and raise the central electrical equipment box.

23. On the left rear side of the alternator, remove the insulated cap from the large nut. Remove the nut securing the large electrical wire to the alternator terminal. Disconnect the smaller electrical connector from the spade terminal.

24. Remove the alternator from the crankcase.

10

Installation (R850C and R1200C Models)

1. Move the alternator into position on top of the crankcase.

NOTE
Make sure the electrical connectors are free of corrosion.

2. On the left rear side of the alternator, install the large electrical wire onto the alternator terminal and tighten the nut. Connect the smaller electrical connector onto the spade terminal. Push it on until it bottoms.

3. Lower the central electrical equipment box, install the mounting hardware and tighten securely.

4. Make sure the alternator support cover mating surface is free of old sealant residue.

5. Apply a light coat of non-hardening liquid gasket sealer, such as ThreeBond 1209, or an equivalent, onto the crankcase cover sealing surface (**Figure 22**).

6. If removed, install the upper right locating dowel (A, **Figure 23**) and the upper left locating dowel and new O-ring (B). Install the lower locating dowel (**Figure 24**).

7. Apply a light coat of Tri-flow lubrication to the crankshaft (**Figure 25**). This will lessen the chance of damage to the radial oil seal on the cover.

8. Install the alternator support cover straight onto the front of the crankcase. Tap the cover on until it is seated around the perimeter.

CAUTION

When properly aligned, the alternator support cover should fit against the crankcase mating surface. If the cover does not fit completely, do not attempt to pull them together with the bolts. Remove the cover and solve the problem.

9. Install the Allen bolts and washers securing the alternator support cover (**Figure 21**). Using a crisscross pattern, tighten the bolts in several stages to 20 N•m (15 ft.-lb.).

10. If the Hall sensor unit was removed, perform the following:

   a. Refer to the alignment marks made during removal and install the base plate (B, **Figure 20**) onto the alternator support cover. Install the screws and washers (A, **Figure 20**). Tighten the screws securely. After the screws are tightened, recheck the alignment marks and readjust if necessary.

   b. If installing a new Hall sensor unit, install the base plate (B, **Figure 20**) onto the alternator support cover. Install the screws and washers (A, **Figure 20**). Tighten the screws securely.

   c. Move the wire harness and rubber grommet back under the clamp and tighten the clamp bolt (**Figure 17**).

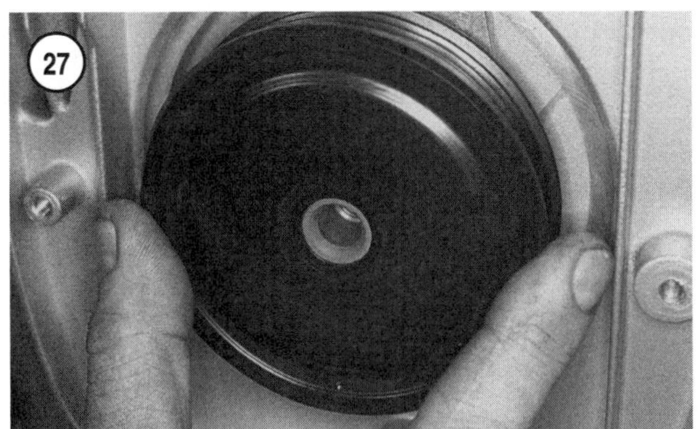
27

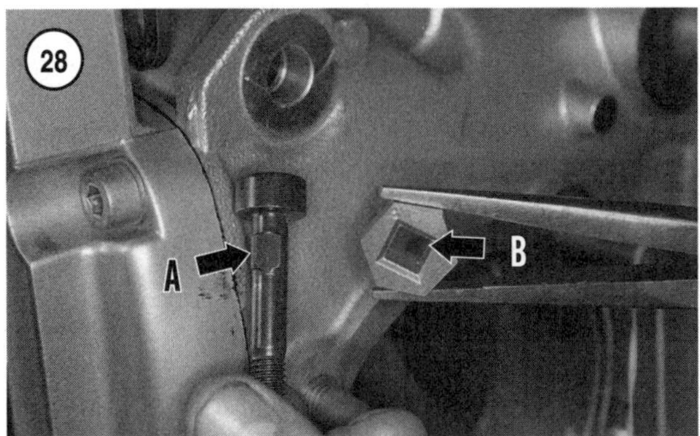

28

29

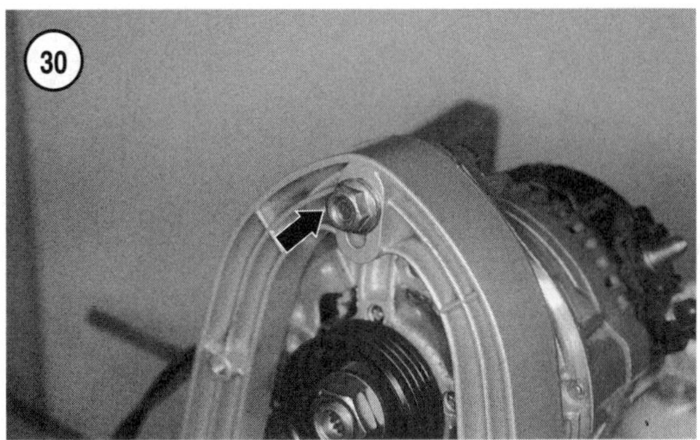
30

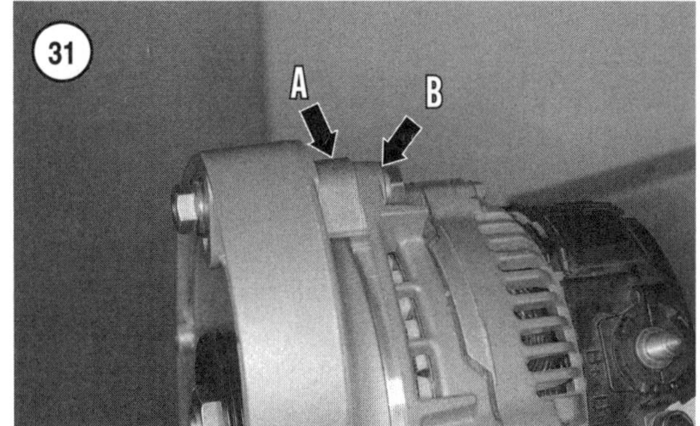

31

NOTE
It is important that the ignition timing be checked at this time.

d. To ensure proper installation and alignment of the base plate, check the ignition timing at this time as described in this chapter.

11. Align the raised tab on the lower pulley (A, **Figure 26**) with the crankshaft groove (B) and install the pulley onto the crankshaft (**Figure 27**). Make sure the raised tab is properly located in the crankshaft groove.

12. Install the bolt and washer and tighten to 50 N•m (37 ft.-lb.).

13. Move the wire back into position and install the clamp bolt (**Figure 17**) on the wiring harness. Tighten the bolt securely.

14. Install the belt onto both pulleys.

15. Install the bolts and nuts securing the alternator to the alternator support cover as follows:

NOTE
*The adjusting bolt has a unique square shoulder (A, **Figure 28**) that fits into the square receptacle in the idler (B). This bolt must be installed on the lower left mount to be used with the adjusting bar on the alternator (**Figure 29**) for drive belt tension adjustment.*

NOTE
In Steps 2-5, tighten the bolts and nuts only tight enough to securely hold the alternator in place in the crankcase. After installation is complete, adjust the drive belt, then tighten the bolts securely.

a. Install the upper center bolt (**Figure 30**), upper spacer (A, **Figure 31**) and nut (B). Tighten only finger-tight at this time.
b. Install the lower right bolt into the alternator mounting bracket.

c. Position the idler with the barbed side (A, **Figure 28**) facing toward the alternator adjusting bolt (B).
d. Install a washer between the idler and the crankcase. Install the adjusting bolt through the idler aligning the square shoulder with the square receptacle and install the nut onto the adjust bolt.
e. Ensure the drive belt is installed correctly on the crankcase pulley, then install the belt onto the alternator pulley.

16. Install the rotary breather pipe as follows:
 a. Install a new O-ring seal onto the locating dowel (**Figure 32**) and push it in until it seats properly. Apply a light coat of clean engine oil to the O-ring and locating dowel.
 b. Install the rotary breather pipe (C, **Figure 16**) onto the alternator support cover. Push the lower portion into place over the locating dowel and O-ring. Install the lower bolt (A, **Figure 16**) and tighten finger-tight.
 c. Install a new inner sealing washer between the pipe and the support, then install the upper banjo bolt and new sealing washer through the pipe and the inner sealing washer. Make sure both sealing washers are in place (**Figure 33**) on the upper banjo bolt. Tighten the upper banjo bolt and the lower bolt securely.

17. Carefully move the front wheel and front suspension back into position. Install the front suspension A-arm pivot shaft as described in Chapter Twelve.

18. Install the left exhaust pipe (C, **Figure 15**) as described in Chapter Nine.

19. Connect the left throttle body (B, **Figure 15**) onto the cylinder head as described in Chapter Nine.

20. Install the bolt (**Figure 14**) securing the front strut to the front suspension A-arm and tighten to 40 N•m (29 ft.-lb.).

21. Remove the jack from under the front portion of the engine.

22. Connect the oil cooler return line as described in Chapter Five.

23. Install the starter as described in this chapter.

24. Install the front cover (**Figure 13**) and tighten the screws securely.

25. Install the horn and the holder (**Figure 12**) as described in this chapter.

26. Install the fuel tank as described in Chapter Nine.

27. Refill the engine oil as described in Chapter Three.

28. Connect the negative battery cable as described in Chapter Three.

29. Install the seat as described in Chapter Fifteen.

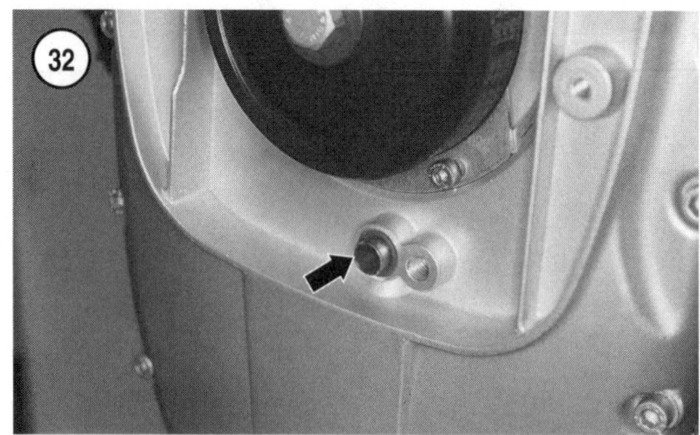
32

33

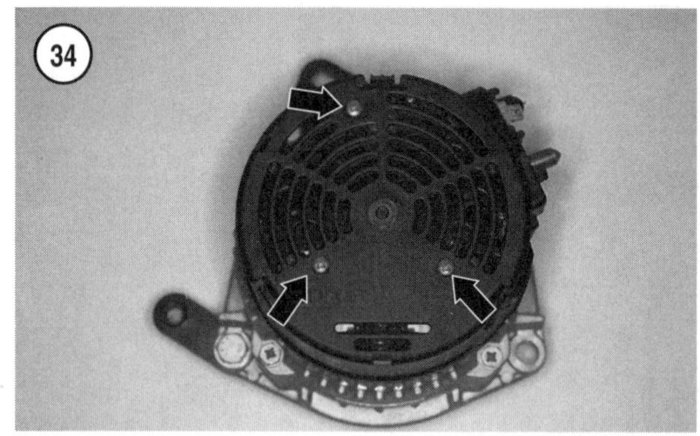
34

35

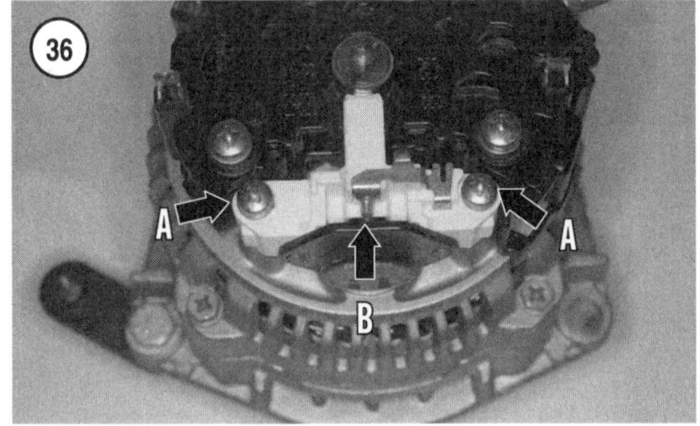

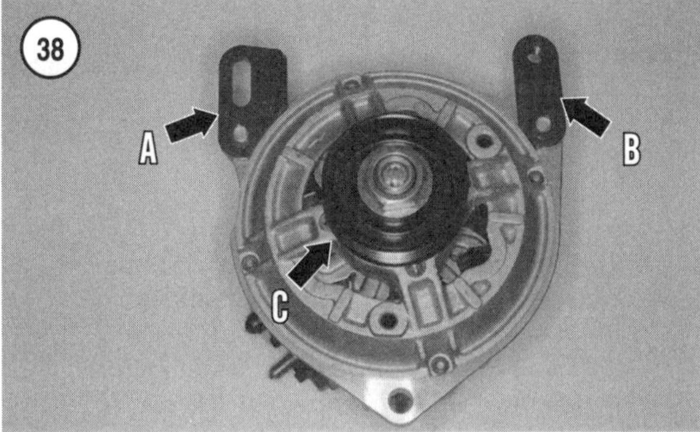

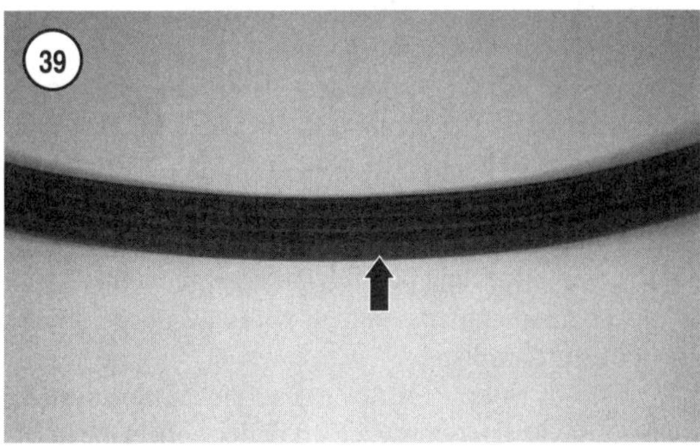

Disassembly/Assembly and Voltage Regulator/Brush Unit Replacement

The only replaceable part of the alternator is the voltage regulator/brush unit and the pulley. If defective, the alternator must be replaced; it cannot be serviced.

1. Remove the alternator as described in this chapter.
2. Remove the screws (**Figure 34**) securing the cover.
3. Press in and release the three retaining clips (**Figure 35**) and remove the cover.
4. Remove the screws (A, **Figure 36**) securing the voltage regulator/ brush unit (B) and withdraw the unit from the rear of the alternator.
5. To remove the pulley, perform the following:
   a. Secure the pulley (A, **Figure 37**) to keep it from rotating.
   b. Loosen, then remove the nut (B, **Figure 37**), washer and pulley.
6. Assemble by reversing these disassembly steps. Tighten the pulley nut to 50 N•m (37 ft.-lb.).

Inspection (All Models)

NOTE
*The alternator pulley on models equipped with the Resilient Poly-V or ELAST belt will freewheel in the **counterclockwise direction**. Models equipped with these drive belts are identified by a small raised triangle on the bottom edge of the alternator cover.*

1. Check the adjusting bar (A, **Figure 38**) and mounting bracket (B) for wear or damage. Replace if necessary.
2. Rotate the pulley (C, **Figure 38**) by hand and make sure the rotor bearings rotate freely. If the bearings are noisy or there is any indication of binding, replace the alternator assembly.
3. Check the grooves in the pulley for wear or damage and replace the pulley if necessary. Check the grooves in the crankshaft pulley for wear or damage.
4. Measure the outer diameter of the pulley at the tips of the teeth. Replace the pulley if wear exceeds the service limit listed in **Table 2**.
5. Inspect the drive belt (**Figure 39**) for stretching or damage. Replace if necessary.

NOTE
The brushes are an integral part of the voltage regulator and cannot be replaced separately.

6. The new brush assembly length is approximately 14 mm (0.55 in.). If the brushes are worn to about one-half of that length, replace the unit assembly.

7. Inspect the brushes for chips or cracks. If damaged, replace the unit assembly.
8. Clean the slip rings with an aerosol electrical contact cleaner and wipe dry with a lint-free cloth.

Testing (1993-1998 Models)

NOTE
On 1999-on models, the alternator must be tested with the BMW MoDiTec test equipment.

NOTE
This test should be performed using the BMW Diagnostic Meter (part No. 61-1-510). If a different ohmmeter is used, the resistance reading may differ.

1. Remove the back cover to gain access to the slip rings as described in this chapter.
2. Calibrate the BMW meter as follows prior to using it:
   a. Touch the yellow (+) and green (–) test probes together.
   b. Press the OHM key and hold it down until the digital display reads 0.00 ohm.
3. Measure the resistance between both slip rings (**Figure 40**) and compare to the specification listed in **Table 2**.
4. Measure the resistance between the outer slip ring and the case (**Figure 41**) and compare to the specification listed in **Table 2**.
5. If the alternator fails either of these tests, replace the alternator.
6. Install the back cover as described in this chapter.

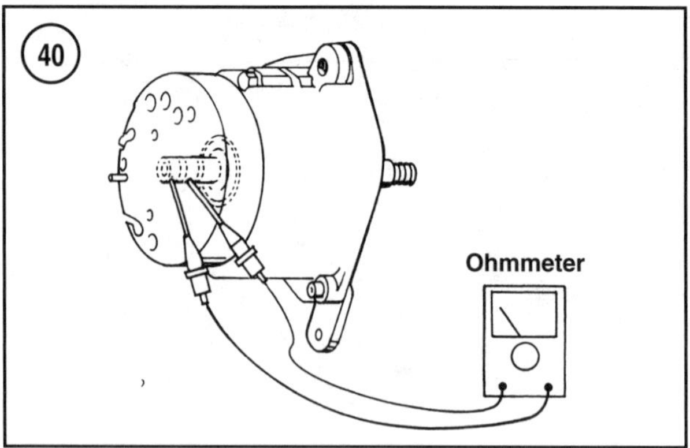

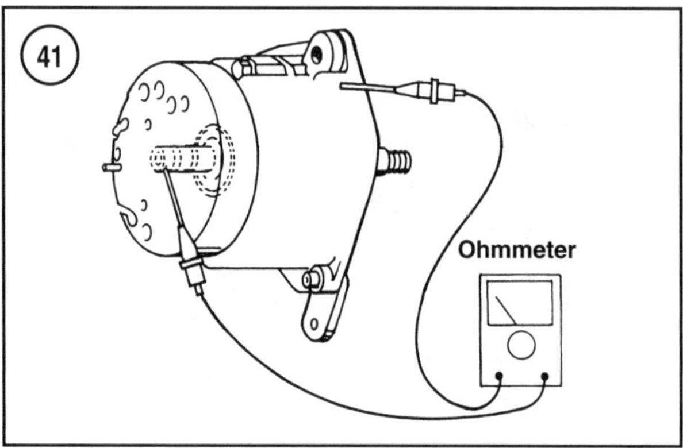

IGNITION SYSTEM

The ignition system consists of the Motronic control unit and a Hall sensor unit. On 1993-2003 models, the main ignition coil fires an individual spark plug for each cylinder. 2004 models use a dual-plug ignition system. The main ignition coil also fires the secondary spark plugs located at the lower portion of the cylinder heads. The primary spark plugs located on top of the cylinder heads are fired by the direct ignition coils located atop the spark plugs.

Both systems provide an efficient spark throughout the entire speed range of the engine. Ignition timing is fixed and no adjustment is possible.

The Hall sensor is attached to the front of the crankshaft and is driven at direct crankshaft speed. This transmitter triggers the ignition signal and sends the signal to the Motronic control unit. The Motronic control unit then evaluates this information and directs voltage to the primary side of the ignition coils.

Precautions

Refer to the following to prevent ignition system damage.

WARNING
This ignition system produces a very high electrical output that could be fatal if any of the components or any un-insulated electrical connections are touched while the engine is running or if the ignition switch is on.

1. Always keep the battery fully charged. Make sure the electrolyte level is correct (non-maintenance free battery). Refer to *Battery* in Chapter Three.
2. Never connect the battery backward. If the battery polarity is reversed, the components in the ignition system will be damaged.
3. Do not disconnect the battery while the engine is running. A voltage surge will occur which will damage the ignition components and possibly burn out the lights.
4. Never jump start the engine with an outside source greater than 16 volts.
5. Whenever working on any part of the ignition system, always turn the ignition switch off or disconnect the nega-

tive battery negative cable. Move the negative cable out of the way and insulate it to avoid the accidental contact with the battery negative terminal.

6. With the ignition switch on or with the engine running, *never* disconnect the ignition coil electrical connectors (primary or secondary). A severe (maybe fatal) electrical shock is possible and the ignition coil/Motronic control unit may be damaged.

7. Never try to test either the Hall sensor assembly or the Motronic control unit with a piece of electrical test equipment (ohmmeter, multimeter, meggar or self-powered test lamp) that has its own power source. The applied voltage may damage the circuits in the system. Use only the specified BMW test equipment in the test procedures or have the unit tested by a BMW dealership.

8. Keep all connections between the various units clean and tight. Make sure that the wiring connections are pushed firmly together to help keep out moisture.

9. Use only genuine BMW components whenever replacing any faulty component. These components are matched to the Motronic control unit. If another type or brand is used, the system may not function properly and may also be damaged.

10. If the ignition component is mounted in a rubber vibration isolator, always be sure that the isolator is in place when installing these units.

11. Make sure all ground wires are attached properly and are free of oil and corrosion.

12. Do not try to modify or change any of the components of the ignition system. The original ignition system is a closed loop system where all components are designed to work with each other and with the fuel injection system.

Troubleshooting

Complete troubleshooting of the system requires the BMW MoDiTec diagnostic tool and a number of additional specialty tools. Therefore, entrust all service work on the Motronic control unit to a BMW dealership. If any service work relating to the control unit is performed by unauthorized BMW personnel, it will void any applicable warranty.

HALL SENSOR UNIT

Testing

Testing of the Hall sensor trigger unit requires special precautions to prevent damage to the unit. Common electrical system service procedures acceptable on other motorcycles may cause damage to this unit. This component must be serviced at a BMW dealership.

All Models Except R850C and R1200C

Removal

NOTE

This procedure is shown with the engine removed from the frame for clarity. The Hall sensor unit can be removed with the engine in place.

1. Remove both seats as described in Chapter Fifteen.
2. On RS, RT and S models, remove the front fairing side sections as described in Chapter Fifteen.
3. Disconnect the negative battery cable as described in Chapter Three.
4. Remove the front portion of the exhaust system as described in Chapter Nine.
5. Remove the front wheel as described in Chapter Ten.
6. Remove the fuel tank as described in Chapter Nine.
7. On the right rear side of the crankcase, remove the rubber plug (**Figure 42**) covering the inspection hole for the timing mark (**Figure 43**).
8. Remove both spark plugs as described in Chapter Three. This will make it easier to rotate the engine.

9. Remove the screws securing the front cover and remove the cover.

10. On the right side, adjacent to the alternator, disconnect the Hall sensor unit multi-pin electrical connector (**Figure 44**, typical) from the main electrical harness.

11. Install a socket and wrench onto the crankshaft pulley bolt (**Figure 45**).

12. As viewed from the front of the engine, rotate the engine in a *clockwise* direction and have an assistant observe the timing hole until the timing mark *OT* centers in the inspection hole in the crankcase (**Figure 46**).

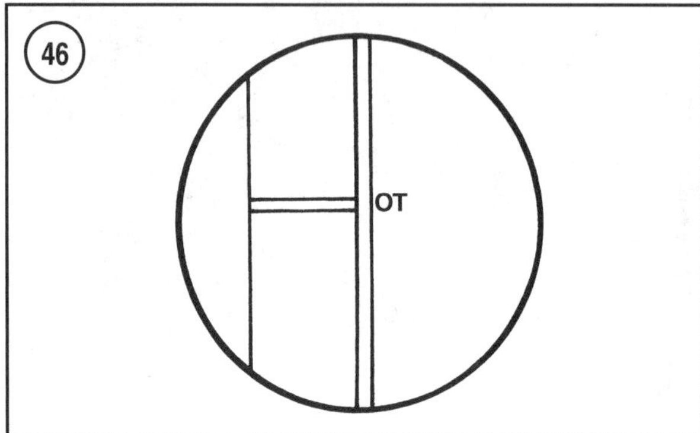

13. Insert the TDC locking pin (**Figure 47**) as follows:

a. On the rear left side of the crankcase, above the starter, remove the TDC pin cover plug.

NOTE

***Figure 48** is shown with the transmission case removed to better show the flywheel hole and the crankcase receptacle.*

b. Insert the TDC locking pin (BMW part No. 11-2-650) through the crankcase hole, through the flywheel and into the receptacle in the backside of the crankcase (**Figure 48**). Push it in until it locks into place. If necessary, slightly rotate the engine in either direction to properly align the flywheel hole to the crankcase receptacle, then push the locking pin into place. After the TDC pin is locked in place, try to rotate the engine—the engine should not rotate even the slightest amount. If the engine does rotate, the locking pin is not engaged properly; reposition the locking pin until there is no engine movement.

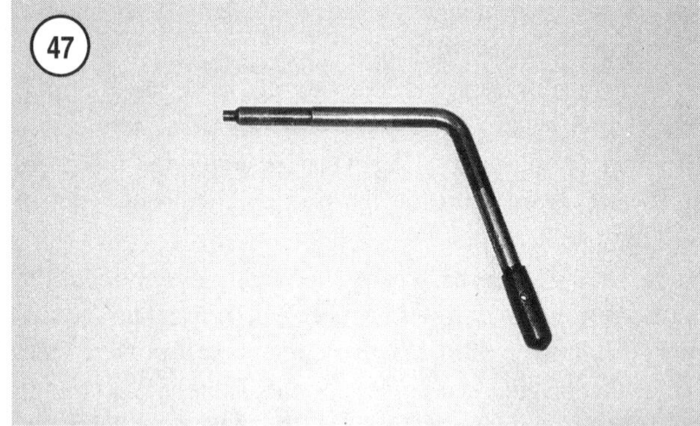

14. On models equipped with the rotary breather pipe, perform the following:

a. Remove the lower bolt (A, **Figure 49**) and the upper banjo bolt (B) and sealing washers securing the rotary breather pipe (C).

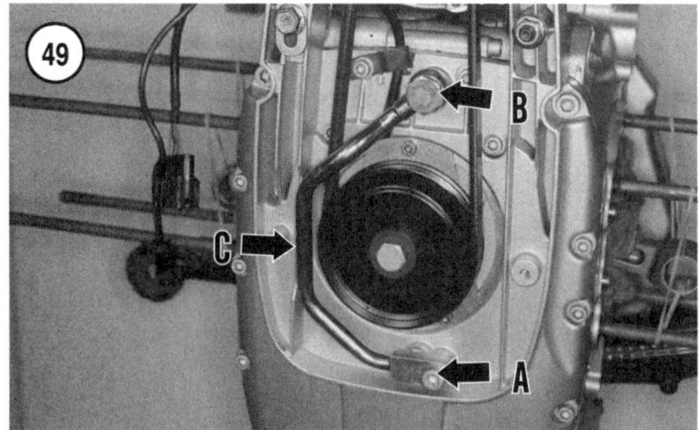

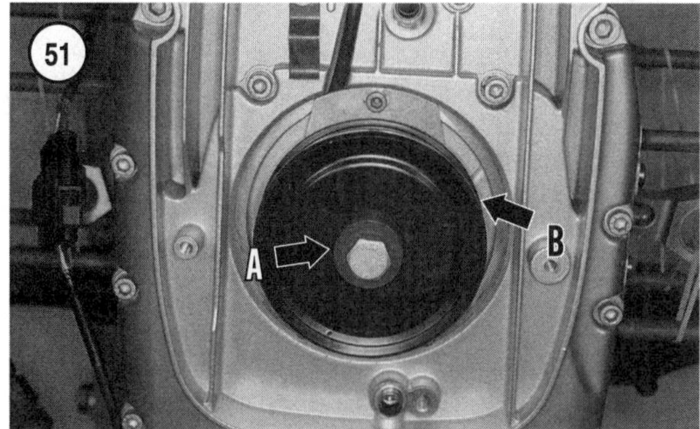

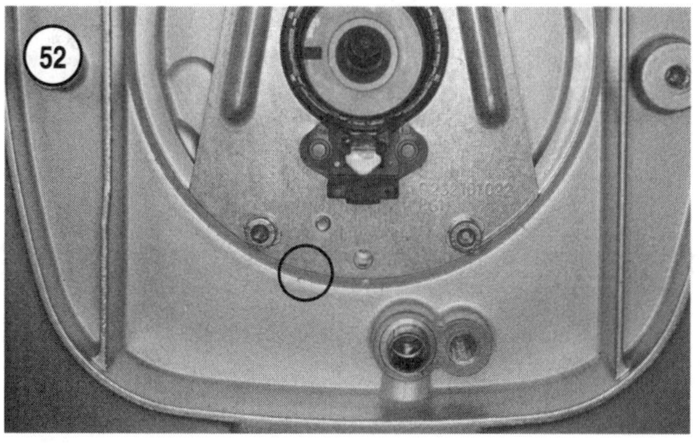

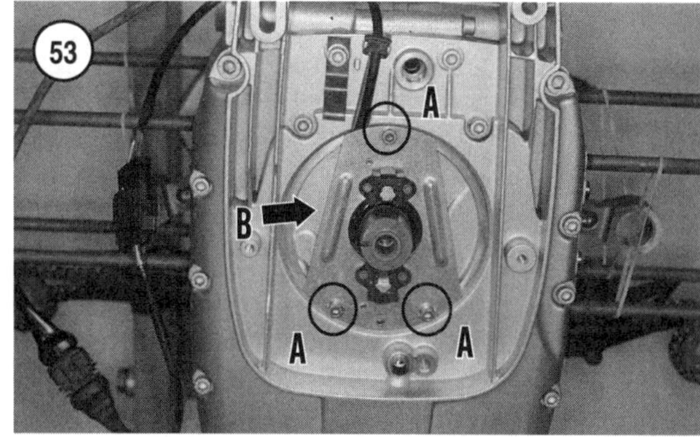

b. Remove the rotary breather pipe and the O-ring located on the lower bolt hole locating pin between the pipe and the alternator support cover.

15. Loosen the alternator mounting bolts to allow slack in the drive belt. Remove the belt from both pulleys.

16. Loosen the clamp bolt (**Figure 50**) on the wiring harness clamp. Move the wire out from underneath the clamp.

17. Remove the bolt and washer (A, **Figure 51**) and remove the lower pulley (B) from the crankshaft.

18. Make an alignment mark on the edge of the base plate and on the engine (**Figure 52**). This will make certain that the base plate will be reinstalled in its original position.

19. Remove the screws and washers (A, **Figure 53**) securing the base plate to the alternator support cover.

20. Carefully pull the base plate assembly (B, **Figure 53**) from the alternator support cover and remove it.

Installation

1A. If installing the original Hall sensor unit, refer to the alignment marks made in Step 18 of *Removal* and install the base plate (B, **Figure 53**) onto the alternator support cover. Install the screws and washers (A, **Figure 53**) and tighten securely. After the screws are tightened, recheck the alignment marks and readjust if necessary.

1B. If installing a new Hall sensor unit, install the base plate (B, **Figure 53**) onto the alternator support cover. Install the screws and washers (A, **Figure 53**) and tighten securely.

2. Move the wire harness and rubber grommet back under the clamp and tighten the clamp bolt (**Figure 51**).

NOTE
It is important that the ignition timing be checked at this time.

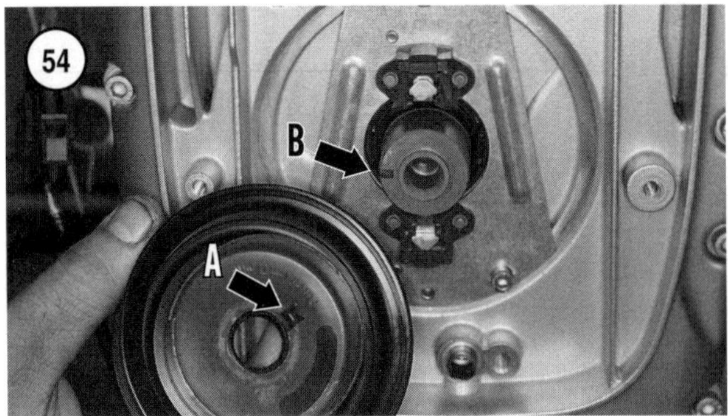

3. To ensure the base plate was installed and aligned correctly, check the ignition timing as described in the following procedure.
4. Align the raised tab on the pulley (A, **Figure 54**) with the crankshaft groove (B) and install the pulley onto the crankshaft. Make sure the raised tab is located properly within the crankshaft groove.
5. Install the bolt and washer and tighten to 50 N•m (37 ft.-lb.).
6. Install the drive belt onto both pulleys.
7. On models equipped with the rotary breather pipe perform the following:
   a. Install a new O-ring seal onto the locating dowel (**Figure 55**) and push it in until it seats properly. Apply a light coat of clean engine oil to the O-ring and locating dowel.
   b. Install the rotary breather pipe (C, **Figure 49**) onto the alternator support cover. Push the lower portion into place over the locating dowel and O-ring. Install the lower bolt (A, **Figure 49**) and tighten finger-tight.
   c. Install a new inner sealing washer between the pipe and the support, then install the upper banjo bolt and new sealing washer through the pipe and the inner sealing washer. Make sure both sealing washers are in place (**Figure 56**) on the upper banjo bolt. Tighten the upper banjo bolt and the lower bolt securely.
8. Remove the TDC locking pin (**Figure 57**), installed in Step 13, from the engine and install the TDC pin cover plug (**Figure 58**).
9. On the right side, adjacent to the alternator, connect the Hall sensor unit multi-pin electrical connector (**Figure 44**) to the main harness. Make sure the electrical connector is free of corrosion and engages properly. Pull the rubber boot back over the connector.
10. Install the front cover and tighten the screws securely.
11. Install both spark plugs as described in Chapter Three.

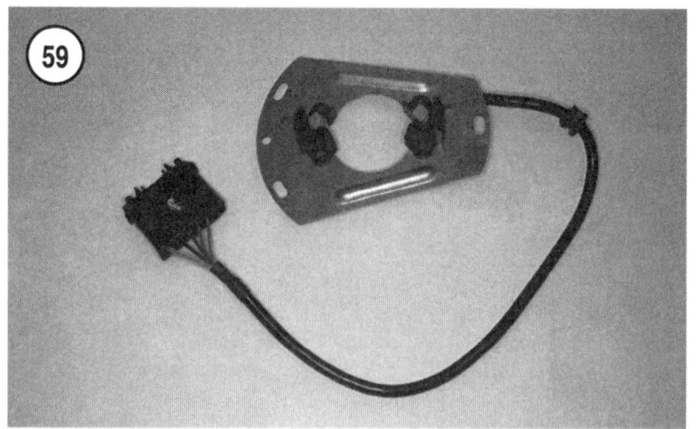

59

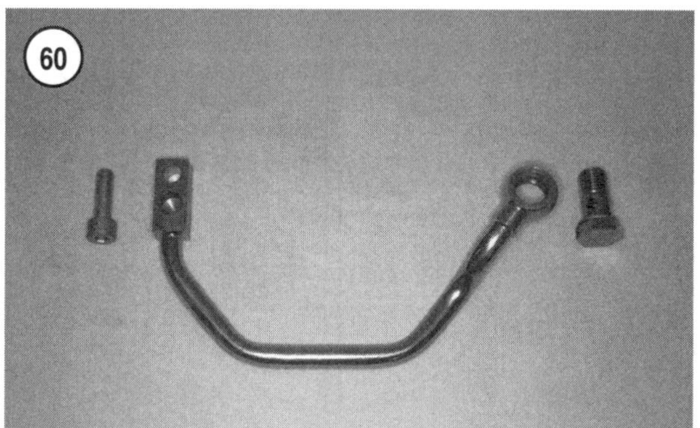

60

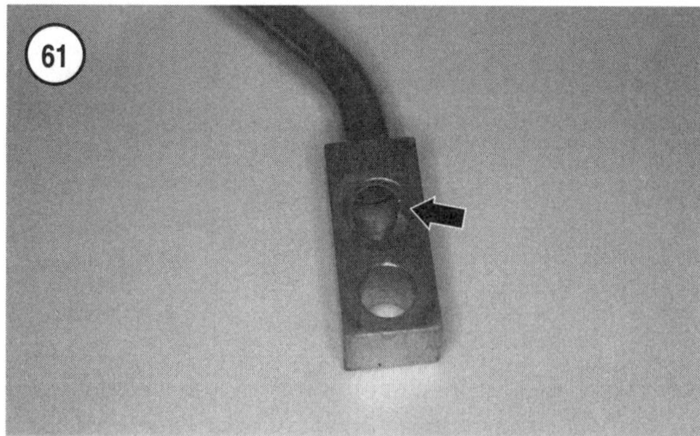

61

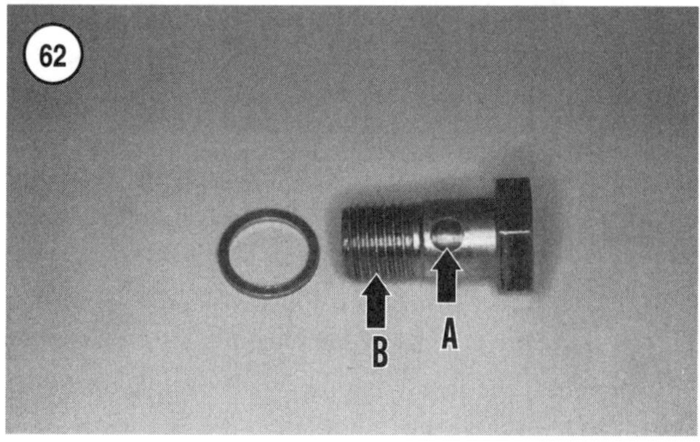

62

63

12. Install the front wheel as described in Chapter Ten.
13. Install the front portion of the exhaust system as described in Chapter Nine.
14. Install the fuel tank as described in Chapter Nine.
15. Reconnect the battery negative cable as described in Chapter Three.
16. On RS, RT and S models, install the front fairing side sections as described in Chapter Fifteen.
17. Install both seats as described in Chapter Fifteen.

R850C and R1200C Models

Removal

Perform Steps 1-20 *Alternator, Removal (R850C and R1200C Models)* in this chapter.

Installation

Perform Steps 10-28 *Alternator, Installation (R850C and R1200C Models)* in this chapter.

Inspection (All Models)

1. Inspect the Hall sensor unit (**Figure 59**) for damage. Check the electrical harness and connector for damage and corrosion. Replace if necessary.
2. On models equipped with the rotary breather pipe, perform the following:
   a. Insect the rotary breather pipe (**Figure 60**) for damage. Make sure the opening in the lower end (**Figure 61**) is clear.
   b. Confirm that the opening (A, **Figure 62**) in the upper banjo bolt is clear.
   c. Check the banjo bolt threads (B, **Figure 62**) for damage. If necessary, repair the threads with an appropriate size metric thread die.
3. Inspect the lower pulley for wear or damage. Check the raised ribs (**Figure 63**) for damage.

10

4. On 1995-on models, the rotor is secured to the backside of the lower pulley with Loctite instant adhesive, or an equivalent. If the rotor is loose, perform the following:
   a. Remove the rotor from the pulley.
   b. Thoroughly clean the mating surfaces of both parts.
   c. Use an aerosol electrical contact cleaner and clean both mating surfaces.
   d. Apply the new Loctite instant adhesive following its manufacturer's instructions.
   e. Install the rotor onto the backside of the pulley and press into place.
   f. Install the pulley onto the crankshaft and tighten the bolt securely and allow the adhesive to cure following the manufacturer's instructions.
   g. Remove the bolt and lower pulley.

Ignition Timing Inspection (1993-1998 Models)

NOTE
On 1999-on models, the alternator must be tested with the BMW MoDiTec test equipment.

1. The following BMW tools are required to inspect ignition timing as follows:
   a. Ignition tester—BMW part No. 12-3-650.
   b. Test lead—BMW part No. 12-3-652.
2. Connect the test lead (A, **Figure 64**) to the Hall sensor unit electrical connector.
3. Connect the ignition tester (B, **Figure 64**) to the test lead.
4. Refer to *Hall Sensor Unit Removal* and make sure the engine is still on TDC as follows:
   a. Install a wrench into the crankshaft pulley bolt.
   b. Make sure the timing mark OT still is centered in the inspection hole in the crankcase (**Figure 65**).
   c. As viewed from the front of the engine, rotate the engine in a *clockwise* direction, if necessary, have an assistant observe the timing hole until the timing mark OT centers in the inspection hole in the crankcase (**Figure 65**).
5. With the engine in the TDC position, the LED on the BMW timing box will be ON.

NOTE
The base plate will only move a minimum amount in either direction. It is not necessary to try to advance or retard the timing with base plate. Once the LED light goes OUT, the Motronic unit will have a base point of reference to set the ignition timing.

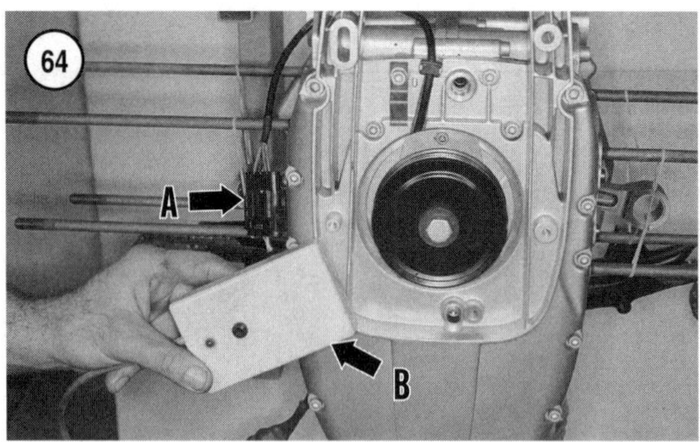

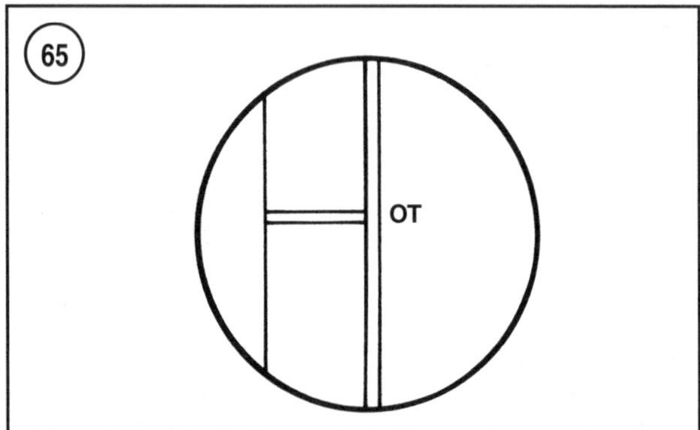

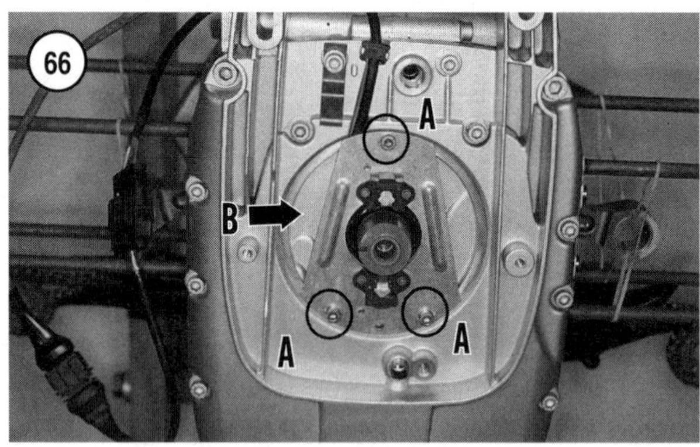

6. Loosen the base plate Allen screws (A, **Figure 66**) and gradually rotate the base plate assembly (B) in either direction until the LED goes OUT. When the LED goes OUT, the base ignition timing is correct.
7. Once again, gradually rotate the base plate assembly until the LED goes OUT—stop and tighten the base plate mounting screws securely.
8. Refer to *Hall Sensor Unit Removal* and remove the TDC locking pin and install the plug into the crankcase.
9. Disconnect the BMW ignition tester and the test lead from the Hall sensor unit connector.

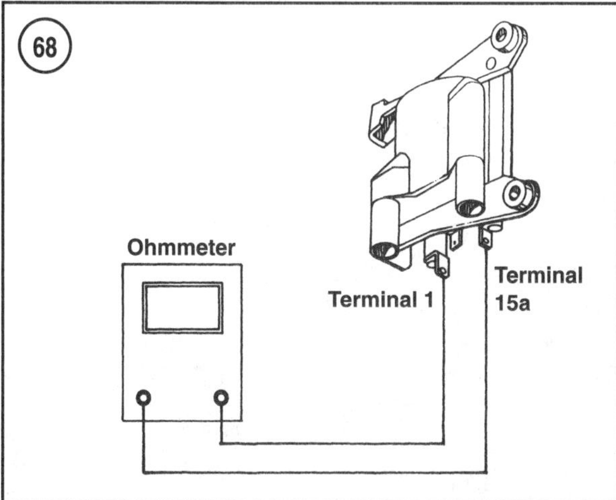

10. Make sure the Hall sensor unit connector is free of corrosion, then reconnect it. Pull the rubber boot back over the connector.
11. If the ignition timing is still inaccurate, have the ignition system tested at a BMW dealership. There may be a fault code in the Motronic unit.

MAIN IGNITION COIL

On 1993-2003 models, the main ignition coil (**Figure 67**) fires the one spark plugs for each cylinder. On 2004 models with the dual-plug ignition system, the main ignition coil also fires the secondary spark plugs located at the lower portion of each cylinder head. The primary spark plugs located on top of the cylinder heads are fired by the direct ignition coils located on top of the spark plugs.

Performance Test

1A. On 1993-2003 models, disconnect the high voltage lead from one of the spark plugs. Remove the spark plug from the top of the cylinder head as described in Chapter Three.
1B. On 2004-on models, disconnect the high voltage lead from one of the secondary spark plugs. Remove the spark plug from the lower portion of the cylinder head as described in Chapter Three.

CAUTION
The spark plug must be securely grounded to the cylinder head or cylinder. If not securely grounded, the Motronic control unit may be damaged.

2. Connect a new or known-good spark plug to the high voltage lead and securely ground the spark plug base on the engine cylinder head or cylinder. Position the spark plug so the electrodes can be seen.

WARNING
If the engine is flooded, do not perform this test. Fuel that may ejected through the spark plug hole can be ignited by the firing of the spark plug.

WARNING
If it is necessary to hold the high voltage lead, do so with an insulated pair of pliers. The high voltage generated could produce serious or fatal shocks.

3. Push the starter button and turn the engine over a couple of times. If a fat blue spark occurs, the coil is in good condition; if not, it must be replaced. Make sure that you are using a known-good spark plug for this test. If the spark plug used is defective, the test results will be incorrect. Repeat for the other cylinder.
4. Reinstall the spark plug in the cylinder head, as described in Chapter Three, and reconnect the spark plug lead.

Resistance Test

1. Remove the main ignition coil as described in the following procedure.
2. Measure the coil primary resistance using an ohmmeter.. Measure resistance between the primary terminals 1 and 15a shown in **Figure 68**. See **Table 1** for test specifications.
3. Measure the secondary resistance using an ohmmeter. Measure the resistance between the secondary leads 4a and 4b (spark plug leads) as shown in **Figure 69**. See **Table 1** for test specifications.

4. If the coil resistance does not meet either of these specifications, the coil must be replaced. If the coil exhibits visible damage, it should be replaced.
5. Take the faulty ignition coil to a BMW dealership and have the ignition coil tested on their diagnostic tester to confirm your test results.

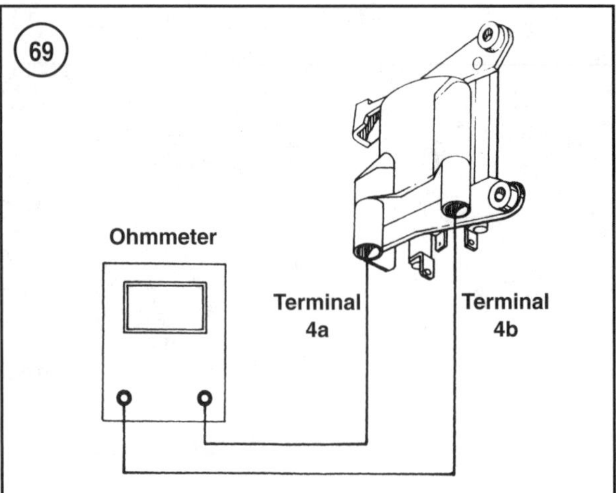

Removal/Installation

CAUTION
Do not turn the engine over with the starter or try to run the engine with any of the spark plug leads disconnected since this will damage the ignition system.

1A. On models so equipped, place the motorcycle on the centerstand with the front wheel off the ground.
1B. On models without a centerstand, place a suitable size jack under the engine to support the motorcycle with the front wheel off the ground.
2. Disconnect the negative battery lead as described in Chapter Three.
3. Turn the ignition switch off.
4. Remove the seats as described in Chapter Fifteen.
5. On RS, RT and S models, remove the front fairing side sections as described in Chapter Fifteen.
6. Depending on model and year, it may be necessary to remove the Motronic control unit as described in Chapter Nine. On other models, it may be necessary to remove various electrical panels and connectors (A, **Figure 70**) to gain access to the ignition coil (B).

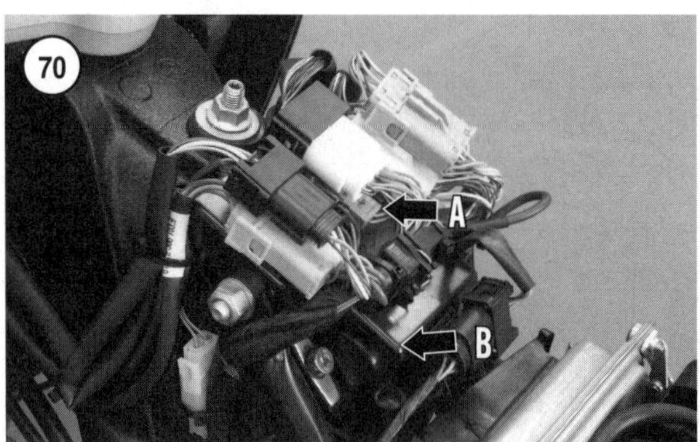

NOTE
The ignition coil is mounted on the top of the frame section and its location varies slightly among the different models and years. To locate the coils, follow one of the secondary ignition wires from the spark plug to the ignition coil.

7. Remove the bolts (A, **Figure 71**) securing the ignition coil to the front frame.

NOTE
To avoid the crossing of the secondary wires, remove only one wire at a time.

8. Carefully pull the ignition coil (B, **Figure 71**) away from the front frame and disconnect both secondary wires (C).
9. Carefully pull the ignition coil farther away from the front frame and disconnect the primary wire electrical connector.
10. Remove the ignition coil. Do not lose the rubber mounts or metal plates at each mounting hole on the front frame.
11. Install by reversing the removal steps while noting the following:
   a. Be sure to install the rubber mounts and metal plates along with the mounting bolts. Tighten the bolts securely.

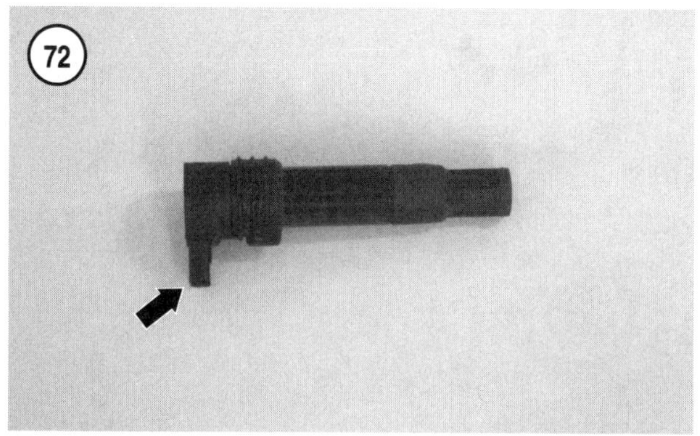

b. Make sure all electrical connections are tight and free of corrosion.
c. Route the spark plug wires to the correct cylinder.

DIRECT IGNITION COILS

Performance Test

1. Disconnect the high voltage lead from one of the primary spark plugs atop the cylinder head. Remove the primary spark plug as described in Chapter Three.

CAUTION
The spark plug must be securely grounded to the cylinder head or cylinder. If not grounded securely, the Motronic unit may be damaged.

2. Connect a new or known-good spark plug to the high voltage lead and securely ground the spark plug base on the engine cylinder head or cylinder. Position the spark plug so you can see the electrodes.

WARNING
If the engine is flooded, do not perform this test. Fuel that may ejected through the spark plug hole can be ignited by the firing of the spark plug.

WARNING
If it is necessary to hold the high voltage lead, do so with an insulated pair of pliers. The high voltage generated could produce serious or fatal shocks.

3. Push the starter button and turn the engine over a couple of times. If a fat blue spark occurs, the coil is in good condition; if not, it must be replaced. Make sure that you are using a known-good spark plug for this test. If the spark plug used is defective, the test results will be incorrect. Repeat for the other cylinder.
4. Reinstall the spark plug in the cylinder head, as described in Chapter Three, and reconnect the spark plug lead.

Resistance Test

There is no secondary resistance specification.

1. Remove the direct ignition coil as described in the following procedure.
2. Measure the coil primary resistance between the primary terminals (**Figure 72**) at the top of the coil. Refer to **Table 2** for the test specifications. 10
3. If the coil primary resistance does not meet specifications, the coil must be replaced. If the coil exhibits visible damage, it should be replaced.
4. Take the faulty ignition coil to a BMW dealership and have the ignition coil tested on their diagnostic tester to confirm your test results.

Removal/Installation

1A. On models so equipped, place the motorcycle on the centerstand with the front wheel off the ground.
1B. On models without a centerstand, place a suitable size jack under the engine to support the motorcycle with the front wheel off the ground.
2. Remove the spark plug cover as follows:
   a. Pull out on the rear of the cover (A, **Figure 73**) and disengage it from the cylinder head cover.
   b. Pull the front of the cover (B, **Figure 73**) out of the cylinder head cover receptacle and remove the cover.
3. Attach the spark plug puller to the front of the direct ignition coil assembly (**Figure 74**) and slide it on until it stops.

4. Insert an index finger through the ring and slowly pull straight out on the puller. Completely disengage the direct ignition coil from the spark plug, then remove the puller.
5. Disconnect the electrical connector from the direct ignition coil.
6. Install the direct ignition coil onto the spark plug and push it straight on until it stops (A, **Figure 75**).
7. Connect the electrical connector (B, **Figure 75**) onto the direct ignition coil. Push it on until it locks into place (**Figure 74**).
8. Route the spark plug wire in the cylinder head cavity and into the groove in the cylinder head cover.
9. Install the spark plug cover as follows:
   a. Insert the front locating tab into the front of the cylinder head cover receptacle (B, **Figure 73**).
   b. Push the rear portion into place (A, **Figure 73**), hold it there, and push the front portion into place (B). Make sure both ends are properly installed to avoid losing the cover when riding.

SPARK PLUG SECONDARY WIRES

Removal

CAUTION
Do not turn the engine over with the starter or try to run the engine with any of the spark plug leads disconnected since the ignition system will be damaged.

1A. On models so equipped, place the motorcycle on the centerstand with the front wheel off the ground.
1B. On models without a centerstand, place a suitable size jack under the engine to support the motorcycle with the front wheel off the ground.
2. Disconnect the battery negative lead as described in Chapter Three.
3. Turn the ignition switch off.
4. Remove the seats as described in Chapter Fifteen.
5. Remove the fuel tank as described in Chapter Nine.
6. On RS, RT and S models, remove the front fairing side sections as described in Chapter Fifteen.
7. Depending on model and year, it may be necessary to remove the Motronic control unit as described in Chapter Nine. On other models, it may be necessary to remove various electrical panels and connectors (A, **Figure 70**) to gain access to the ignition coil (B).

NOTE
The ignition coil is mounted on the top of the frame section and its location varies slightly among the different models and years. To locate the coils, follow one of the secondary

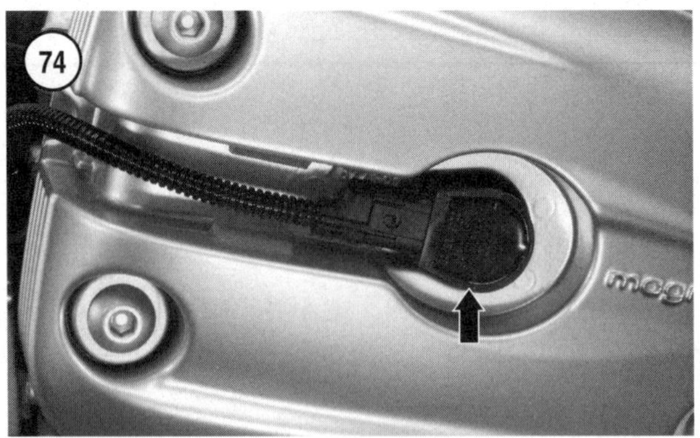

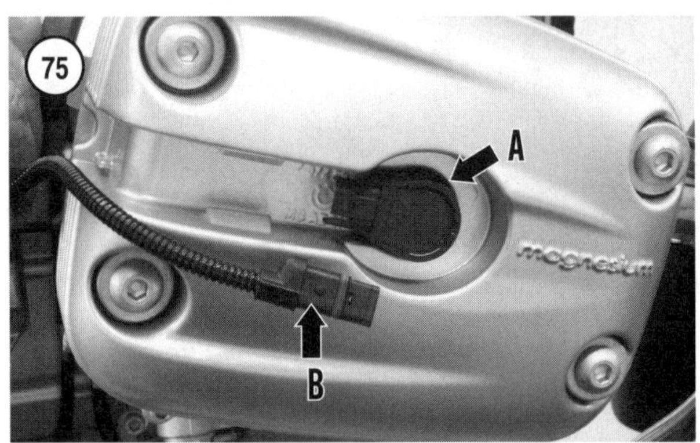

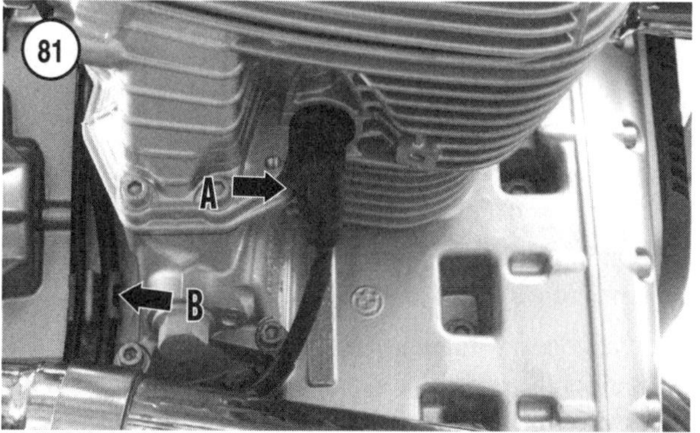

ignition wires from the spark plug to the ignition coil.

8. Remove the bolts (A, **Figure 71**) securing the ignition coil to the front frame.

NOTE
To avoid the crossing of the secondary wires, remove only one wire at a time.

9. Carefully pull the ignition coil (B, **Figure 71**) up away from the front frame and disconnect one of the secondary wires (C).

10. Prior to removing the spark plug wires, note the routing of the wires through the frame and engine areas. The wires must be rerouted in this manner to keep from being damaged.

CAUTION
If the wires are being reused, pull on the wires carefully to prevent damaging them during removal.

11A. On single plug ignition system, perform the following:

a. Pull out on the front of the cover (A, **Figure 76**) and disengage it from the cylinder head cover.
b. Pull the rear of the cover (B, **Figure 76**) out of the cylinder head cover receptacle and remove the cover.

CAUTION
The special spark plug cap puller tool must be used to disengage the spark plug wire/cap from the spark plug. If the special tool is not used, the spark plug wire/cap will be damaged.

c. Attach the spark plug puller (**Figure 77**) to the front of the spark plug cap and slide it on until it stops.
d. Slowly pull straight out on the puller (**Figure 78**). Completely disengage the assembly from the spark plug. Remove the puller from the spark plug cap.
e. Disconnect the secondary wire from the clips on the engine (**Figure 79**) and frame, then remove the wire.

11B. On dual-plug ignition system, perform the following:

a. On models so equipped, remove the screw securing the cylinder head guard (**Figure 80**) and remove the guard.
b. On the underside of the cylinder head, remove the two screws securing the spark plug cover and remove the cover.
c. Slowly pull straight out and completely disengage the cap (A, **Figure 81**) from the spark plug.

d. Disconnect the secondary wire from the clip(s) on the engine (B, **Figure 81**) and frame, then remove the wire.

12. Repeat Steps 9-11 for the remaining spark plug wire.

Installation

NOTE
Install original equipment BMW spark plug wires as they have the correct wire resistance and are of the correct length.

1. Install the *new* spark plug wires, one at a time, and route them correctly through the frame and engine. Connect the secondary wire onto the clips on the engine and frame.

2A. On single plug ignition models, perform the following:
   a. Connect the secondary wire onto the clips on the engine (**Figure 79**) and frame.
   b. Install the spark plug wire onto the spark plug and push it straight on until it stops (A, **Figure 82**).
   c. Route the spark plug wire in the cylinder head cavity (B, **Figure 82**).
   d. Insert the locating tab (**Figure 83**) into the rear cylinder head cover receptacle.
   e. Push the rear portion into place (A, **Figure 84**), hold it there and then push the front portion into place (B). Make sure both ends install properly to avoid loosing the cover when riding.

2B. On dual-plug ignition models, perform the following:
   a. Connect the secondary wire onto the clip(s) on the engine (B, **Figure 81**).
   b. Install the spark plug wire onto the spark plug and push it straight on until it stops (A, **Figure 81**).
   c. On the underside of the cylinder head, install the spark plug cover and tighten the screws securely.
   d. On models so equipped, install the cylinder head guard (**Figure 80**) and tighten the screws securely.

3. Connect the secondary wires (C, **Figure 71**) onto the ignition coil (B).

4. Be sure to install the rubber mounts and metal plates along with the mounting bolts (A, **Figure 71**). Tighten the bolts securely.

5. On models so removed, install the Motronic control unit as described in Chapter Nine.

6. On RS, RT and S models, install the front fairing side sections as described in Chapter Fifteen.

7. Install the fuel tank as described in Chapter Nine.

8. Install the seats as described in Chapter Fifteen.

9. Connect the battery negative lead as described in Chapter Three.

10. Start the motorcycle and make sure it idles smoothly. If there is an ignition related misfire, the probable cause is that one of the wires is not properly connected to the ignition coil and/or spark plug.

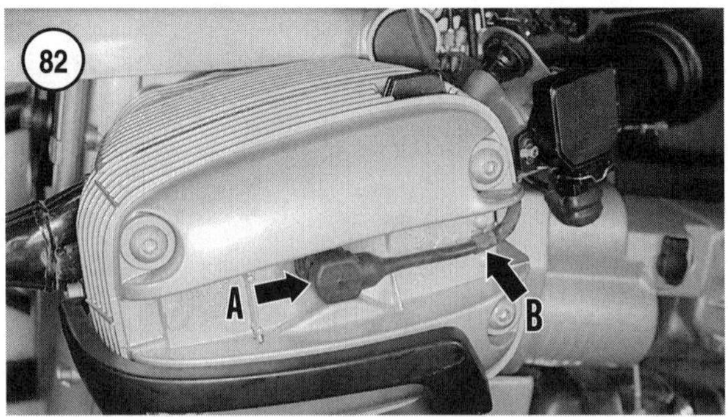

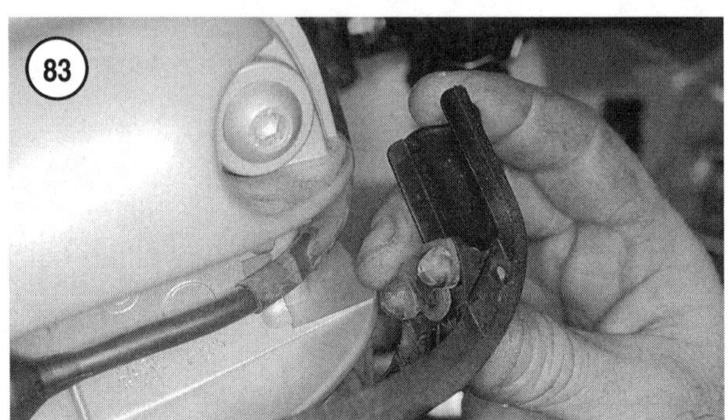

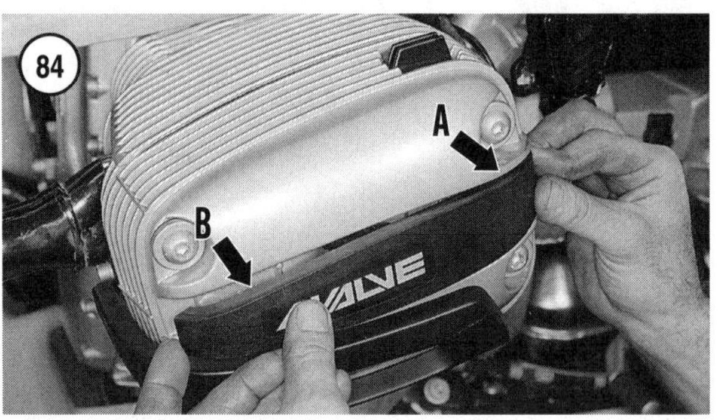

SPARK PLUG PRIMARY WIRES (DUAL-PLUG MODELS)

Removal

1A. On models so equipped, place the motorcycle on the centerstand with the front wheel off of the ground.

1B. On models without a centerstand, place a suitable size jack under the engine to support the motorcycle with the front wheel off the ground.

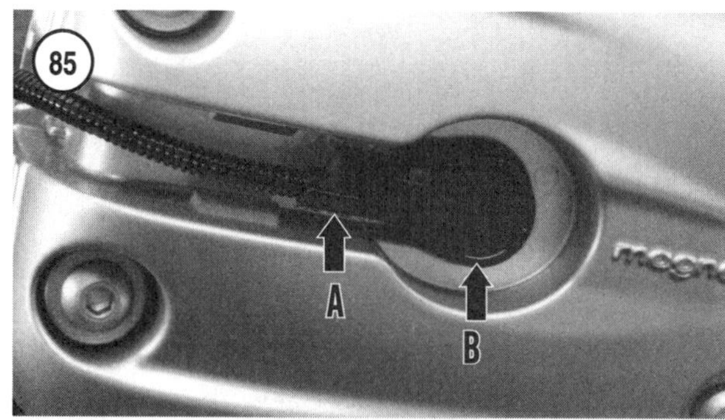

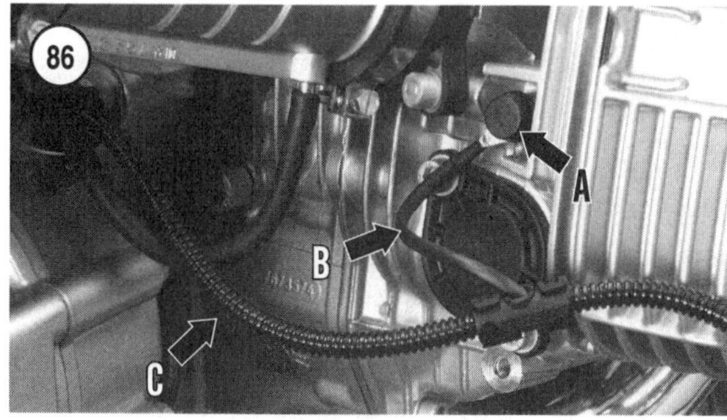

2. Disconnect the negative battery cable as described in Chapter Three.
3. Turn the ignition switch off.
4. Remove the seats as described in Chapter Fifteen.
5. Remove the fuel tank as described in Chapter Nine.
6. On RS, RT and S models, remove the front fairing side sections as described in Chapter Fifteen.
7. Remove the spark plug cover as follows:
   a. Pull out on the rear of the cover (A, **Figure 73**) and disengage it from the cylinder head cover.
   b. Pull the front of the cover (B, **Figure 73**) out of the cylinder head cover receptacle and remove the cover.
8. Disconnect the electrical connector (A, **Figure 85**) from the direct ignition coil (B).
9. Remove the cap (A, **Figure 86**), then remove the screw and disconnect the ground lead (B) from the cylinder head.
10. Follow the primary spark plug lead (C, **Figure 86**) through the chassis to the Motronic control unit and disconnect it.
11. Disconnect the secondary wire from the clips on the engine (B, **Figure 81**) and frame, then remove the wire.
12. Repeat Steps 7-11 for the remaining spark plug wire.

Installation

1. Connect the primary wire to the Motronic control unit.
2. Install one spark plug lead at a time, and route it correctly through the frame and engine. Connect the primary lead onto the clips on the engine and frame.
3. Connect the ground wire (B, **Figure 86**) to the cylinder head and tighten the screw securely, then install the cap (A).
4. Install the connector (A, **Figure 85**) onto the direct ignition coil (B) and push it on until it locks into place.
5. Route the spark plug wire in the cylinder head cavity and into the groove in the cylinder head cover.
6. Install the spark plug cover as follows:
   a. Insert the front locating tab into the front of the cylinder head cover receptacle (B, **Figure 73**).
   b. Push the rear portion into place (A, **Figure 73**), hold it there, and push the front portion into place (B). Make sure both ends are properly installed to avoid losing the cover when riding.
7. On RS, RT and S models, install the front fairing side sections as described in Chapter Fifteen.
8. Install the fuel tank as described in Chapter Nine.
9. Install the seats as described in Chapter Fifteen.
10. Connect the battery negative lead as described in Chapter Three.
11. Start the motorcycle and make sure it idles smoothly. If there is an ignition related misfire, the probable cause is that one of the wires is not properly connected to the ignition coil and/or spark plug.

STARTING SYSTEM

The starting system consists of the starter, starter relay and the starter button.

When the starter button is pressed, it allows current to flow from the battery, through the starter relay, to the starter.

CAUTION
Do not operate the starter for more than 5 seconds at a time. Let it cool approximately 10 seconds before operating it.

STARTER

Removal/Installation

1. Remove both seats as described in Chapter Fifteen.
2. On RS, RT and S models, remove the front fairing left side cover as described in Chapter Fifteen.
3. On models so equipped, perform the following:
   a. Remove the screw (A, **Figure 87**) securing the starter cover (B).

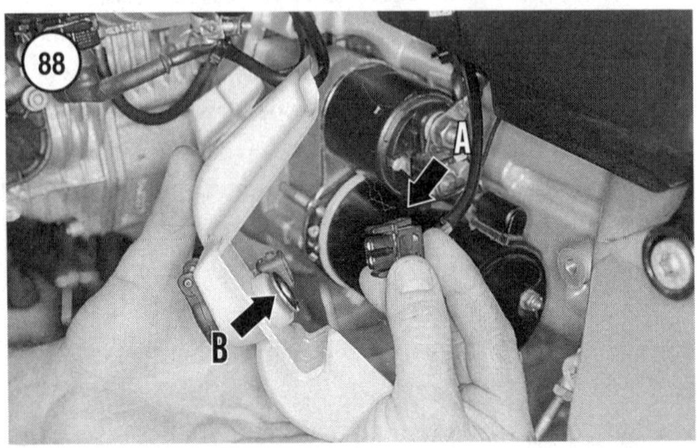

b. Pull the cover part way out and disconnect the electrical connector (A, **Figure 88**) from the backside of the auxiliary power socket (B). Remove the cover.

4. Carefully slide the electrical connector (**Figure 89**) off of the spade terminal.

5. Remove the nut securing the remaining electrical connector and remove the connector (**Figure 90**).

6. Cut and remove the tie wrap (**Figure 91**) securing the wires to the starter assembly.

NOTE
*In **Figure 92**, only one of the mounting bolts is visible; remove both bolts.*

7. Remove both bolts and washers (A, **Figure 92**) securing the starter to the transmission housing.

8. Carefully withdraw the starter (B, **Figure 92**) straight back and out of the transmission housing.

9. Install by reversing the removal steps while noting the following:

a. Position the two wires (**Figure 93**) behind the starter prior to installing the starter.

b. Install the starter and secure the two wires to the starter with a tie wrap (**Figure 94**).

c. Make sure the electrical terminals (**Figure 95**) are clean and free of corrosion.

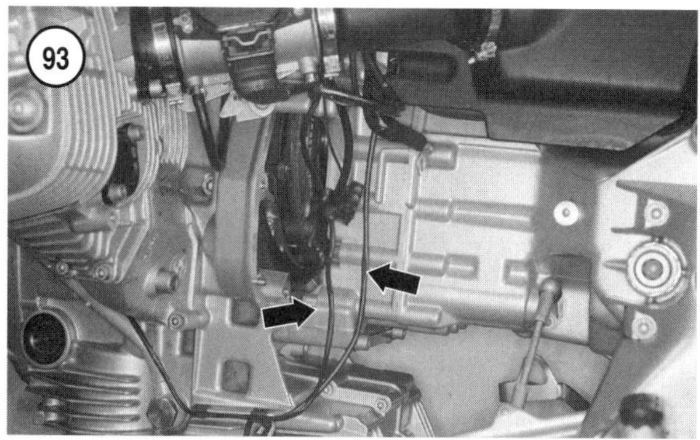

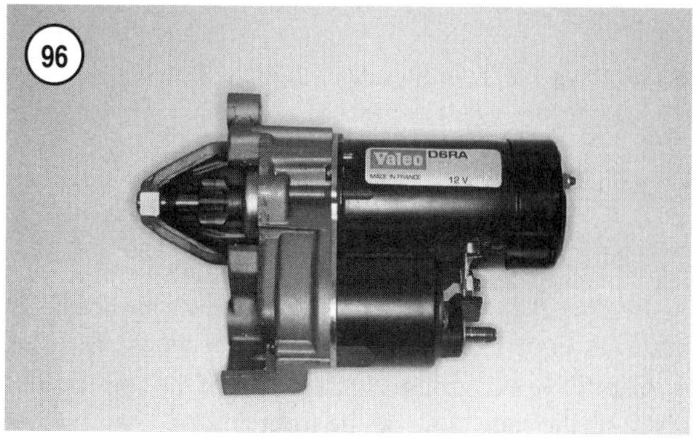

d. Make sure the wire connections are tight.
e. Make sure to connect the electrical connector (A, **Figure 88**) onto the backside of the auxiliary power socket (B).

Inspection

The starter cannot be serviced; if faulty, the entire unit must be replaced.

1. Inspect the starter assembly (**Figure 96**) for external damage.
2. Inspect the gear (**Figure 97**) for chipped or missing teeth. If damaged, check the gear teeth on the flywheel for possible damage.

STARTER RELAY

Removal/Installation

The starter relay is located in the central electrical equipment box under the rider's seat or fuel tank.

1A. On C models, remove the fuel tank as described in Chapter Nine.
1B. On all models except C, remove the rider's seat as described in Chapter Fifteen.
2. Disconnect the negative battery cable as described in Chapter Three.
3. Remove the cover from the central electrical equipment box as described in this chapter.
4. Pull straight up and remove the starter relay (**Figure 98**, typical).
5. Install by reversing the removal steps.

LIGHTING SYSTEM

The lighting system consists of a headlight, taillight/brake light combination, license plate light, turn signals, indicator lights and illumination lights for the speedometer and tachometer. **Table 2** lists replacement bulbs for these components.

Always use the correct wattage bulb. The use of a larger bulb rating will give a dim light and a smaller will burn out prematurely.

Troubleshooting

If the bulb has been replaced and is still inoperative, check the following:

1. If none of the lights are operating correctly, check the battery for a full charge and make sure the battery cable terminals are tight, clean and free of corrosion. Refer to Chapter Three.
2. Make sure the replacement bulb is good and has the correct rating. Check the bulb terminals for oxidation and check the element to make sure it is not broken.
3. Inspect the socket terminals for dirt, oily film or corrosion. Clean off and spray with a contact cleaner.
4. Use jumper wires and connect the bulb directly to the battery. If the bulb illuminates, check the wiring leading to the socket. Check for breaks and/or frayed or missing insulation.
5. Make sure all ground connections are in good order with no corrosion.
6. If the wiring is good, the switch may be faulty or if the circuit is protected by a relay, the relay may be defective.

HEADLIGHT

CAUTION

All models are equipped with a quartz-halogen bulb. Do not touch the bulb glass. Traces of oil on the bulb will drastically reduce the life of the bulb. Clean any traces of oil from the bulb with a cloth moistened in alcohol or lacquer thinner.

WARNING

If the headlight has just burned out or just turned off, it will be hot. To avoid burned fingers, allow the bulb to cool prior to removal.

Headlight and Parking Light Bulb Replacement

R models

Refer to **Figure 99** and **Figure 100**.

1. Turn the ignition switch off.
2. Remove the screw from the base of the trim ring or headlight assembly (**Figure 101**).

98

3. On R1100R models, carefully pull out on the bottom of the trim ring and disengage it from the headlight housing.
4. Carefully pull the headlight lens assembly, or headlight assembly, part way out of the housing and disconnect the electrical connector (**Figure 102**) from the backside of the bulb.
5. Unhook the set spring and remove and discard the blown bulb (**Figure 103**).
6. Align the tangs on the new bulb with the notches in the headlight lens and install the bulb.
7. Securely hook the headlight clip onto the new bulb.
8. Correctly align the electrical plug. Push it *straight on* until it bottoms on the bulb and the connector cover.
9. Disconnect the electrical connector (**Figure 104**) from the parking light bulb.
10. Carefully withdraw the parking light bulb from the reflector (**Figure 105**) and install a new one. Push the bulb in until it seats completely.
11. Check headlight operation.
12. Complete the installation by reversing the removal steps while noting the following:
    a. Make sure the electrical connectors are corrosion free and secure.
    b. Check headlight adjustment as described in this section.

R850GS and R1100GS models

Refer to **Figure 106**.

1. Turn the ignition switch off.
2. Place a shop cloth (A, **Figure 107**) on top of the front fender.
3. Remove the screws and washers securing the headlight bezel (B, **Figure 107**) and remove the bezel.
4. Carefully pull the headlight lens out of the housing and rest it on the shop cloth on the front fender.

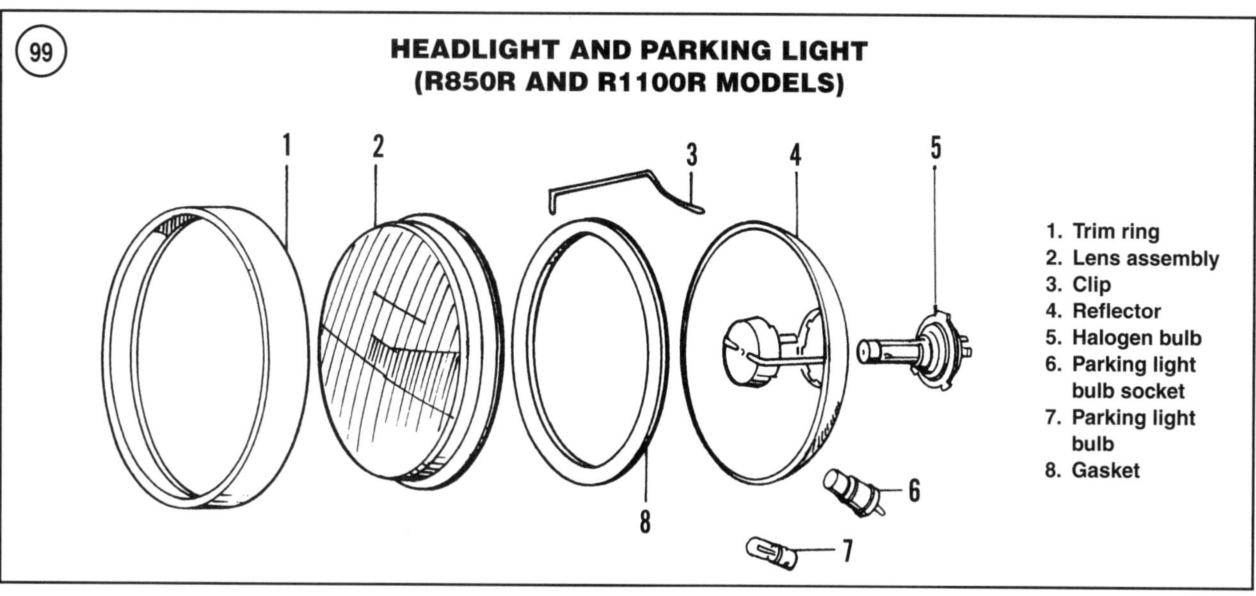

HEADLIGHT AND PARKING LIGHT (R850R AND R1100R MODELS)

1. Trim ring
2. Lens assembly
3. Clip
4. Reflector
5. Halogen bulb
6. Parking light bulb socket
7. Parking light bulb
8. Gasket

(100)

HEADLIGHT AND TURN SIGNAL ASSEMBLY (R1150R MODELS)

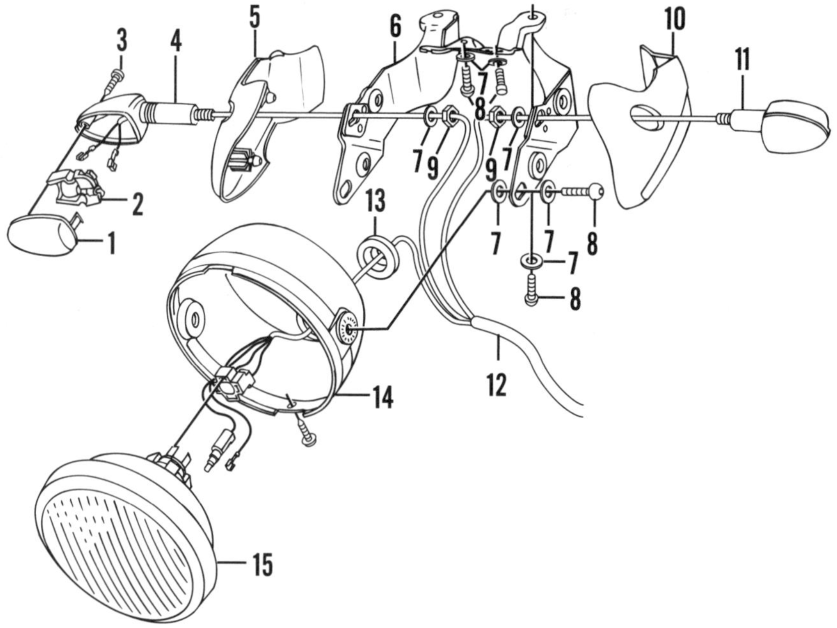

1. Lens
2. Reflector
3. Screw
4. Housing
5. Trim panel (right side)
6. Headlight mounting bracket
7. Washer
8. Bolt
9. Nut
10. Trim panel (left side)
11. Turn signal assembly
12. Wiring harness
13. Rubber grommet
14. Headlight housing
15. Headlight assembly

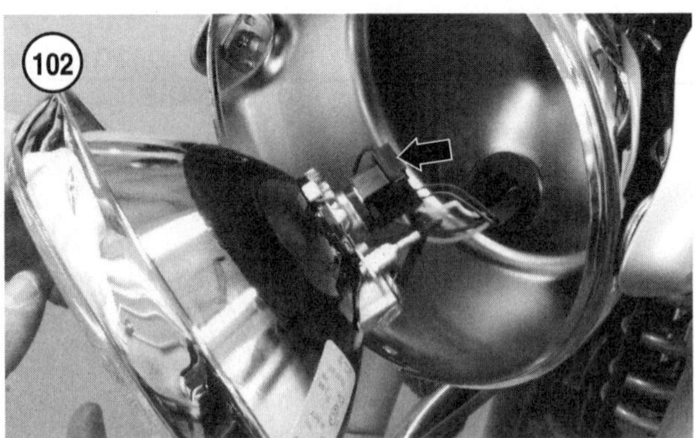

5. Disconnect the electrical connector (**Figure 108**) from the base of the lens assembly.
6. Carefully withdraw the parking light bulb and socket assembly (**Figure 109**) from the lens assembly. If necessary, remove the bulb and install a new one.
7. Remove the rubber boot (**Figure 110**) from the base of the lens assembly.
8. Rotate the retaining ring and spring (**Figure 111**) and remove it.
9. Remove and discard the blown bulb.
10. Align the tangs on the new bulb with the notches in the headlight lens and install the bulb (**Figure 112**).
11. Securely hook the headlight clip onto the new bulb.
12. Position the rubber boot with the UP mark facing up (**Figure 113**).
13. Correctly align the electrical plug. Push it *straight on* until it bottoms on the bulb and the connector cover.
14. Check headlight operation.
15. Complete the installation by reversing the removal steps while noting the following:
    a. Make sure the electrical connectors are corrosion free and secure.
    b. Check headlight adjustment as described in this section.

R1150GS and Rockster models

Refer to **Figure 114**.

NOTE
This procedure is shown with the headlight assembly removed to better illustrate the steps.

1. Turn the ignition switch off.

2A. To replace the low beam, perform the following:
    a. Turn the handlebar to the full right position.
    b. Turn the left side cover (A, **Figure 115**) *counter-clockwise*, unlock it and swing it down.

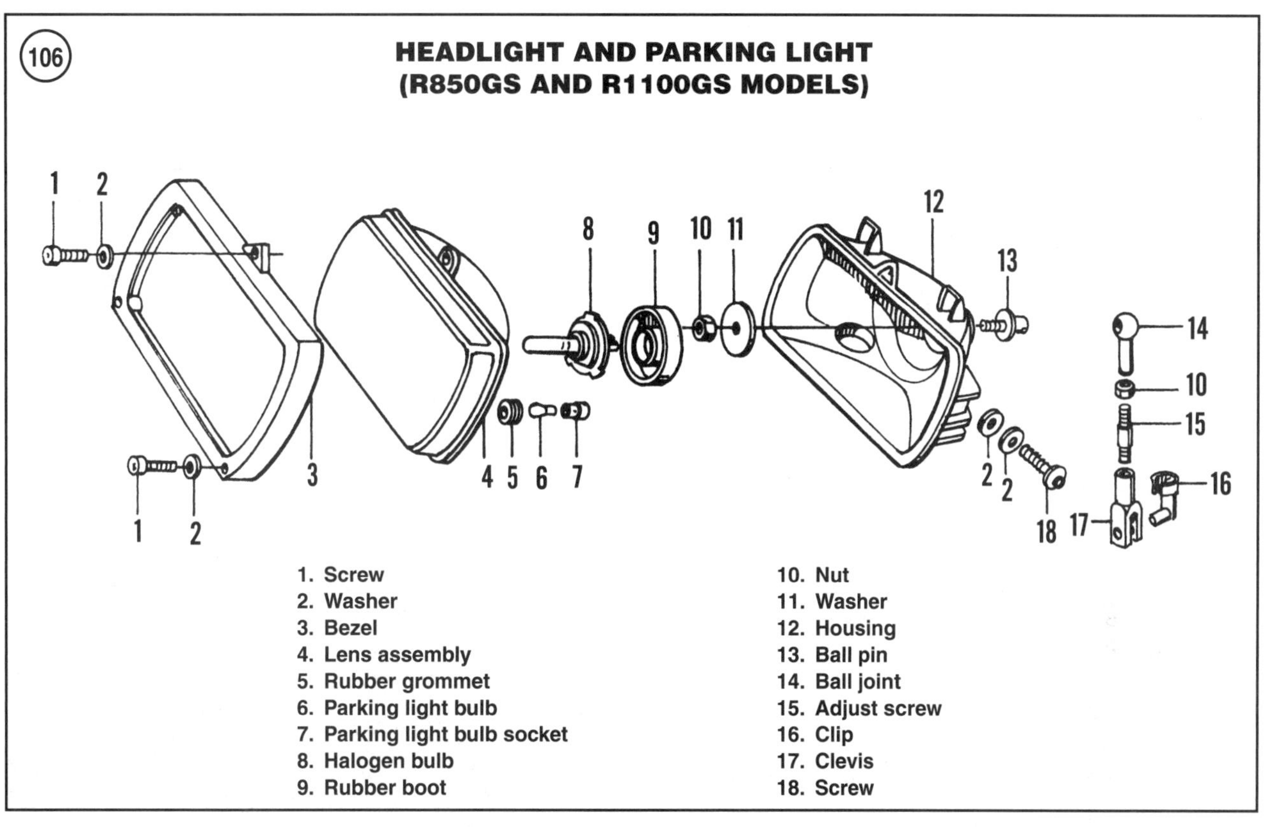

HEADLIGHT AND PARKING LIGHT
(R850GS AND R1100GS MODELS)

1. Screw
2. Washer
3. Bezel
4. Lens assembly
5. Rubber grommet
6. Parking light bulb
7. Parking light bulb socket
8. Halogen bulb
9. Rubber boot
10. Nut
11. Washer
12. Housing
13. Ball pin
14. Ball joint
15. Adjust screw
16. Clip
17. Clevis
18. Screw

10

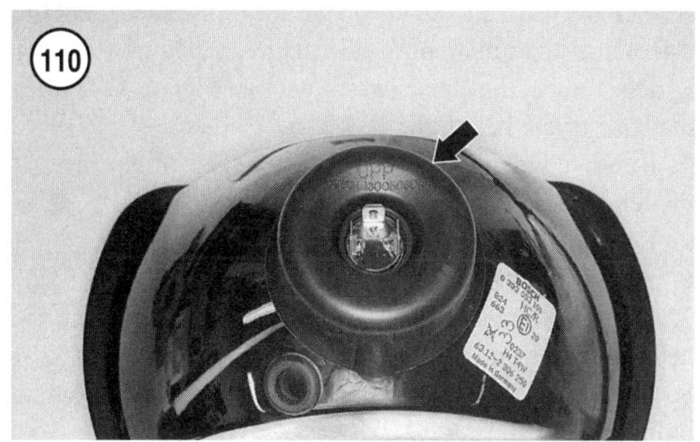

2B. To replace the high beam, perform the following:

a. Turn the handlebar to the full left position.

b. Turn the right side cover (B, **Figure 115**) *counter-clockwise*, unlock it and swing it down.

NOTE
The remainder of this procedure is shown on the low beam bulb. The high beam bulb replacement is identical.

3. Release the spring clip (**Figure 116**) and release the bulb.
4. Disconnect the electrical connector (A, **Figure 117**), remove and discard the blown bulb (B).
5. Align the tangs on the new bulb with the notches in the headlight lens and install the bulb.
6. Securely hook the headlight spring clip onto the new bulb.
7. Correctly align the electrical plug. Push it *straight on* until it bottoms on the bulb.
8. Move the left side cover into position and turn it *clockwise* and lock it in place.
9. Check high beam headlight operation. Check headlight adjustment as described in this section.
10. Repeat for the high beam bulb (**Figure 118**) if necessary.
11. To replace the parking light bulb, perform the following:

a. Turn the handlebar to the full right position.

b. Turn the left side cover (A, **Figure 115**) *counter-clockwise*, unlock it and swing it down.

c. Located below the left side housing, pull straight out and remove the parking light housing.

d. Push the bulb in, turn it *counterclockwise*, and remove the bulb (A, **Figure 119**) from the housing (B).

RS models

1. Turn the ignition switch off.
2. Remove the front fairing right side inner panel as described in Chapter Fifteen. Do not forget to disconnect the riders information display electrical connector.
3. Disconnect the electrical connector (**Figure 120**) from the base of the headlight.
4. Remove the rubber boot (**Figure 121**) from the base of the lens assembly.
5. Release the spring clip and release the bulb.
6. Remove and discard the bulb assembly (**Figure 122**).
7. Align the tangs on the new bulb with the notches in the headlight lens and install the bulb.
8. Securely hook the headlight spring clip onto the new bulb.

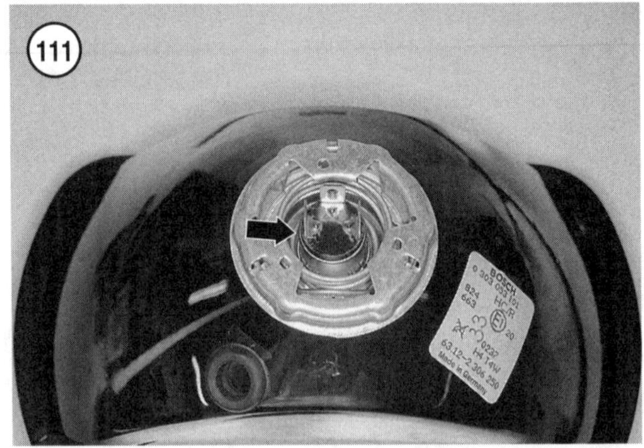

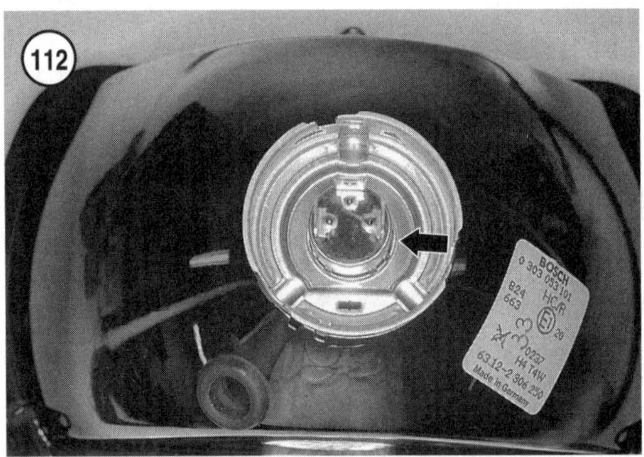

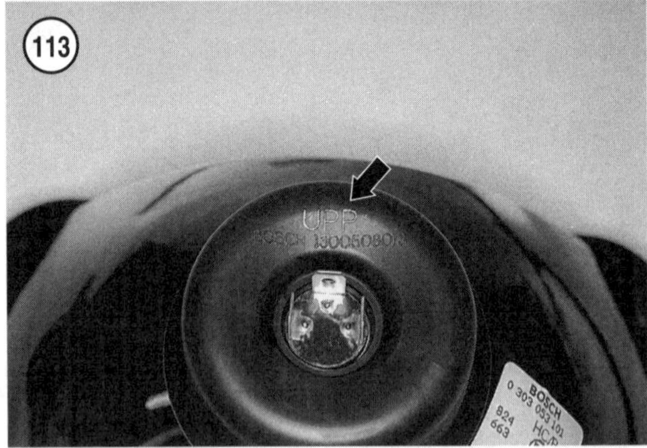

9. Position the rubber boot with the UP mark facing up and install the boot.
10. Correctly align the electrical plug. Push it *straight on* until it bottoms on the bulb.
11. Carefully withdraw the parking light bulb and socket from the lens assembly. If necessary, remove the bulb and install a new one.

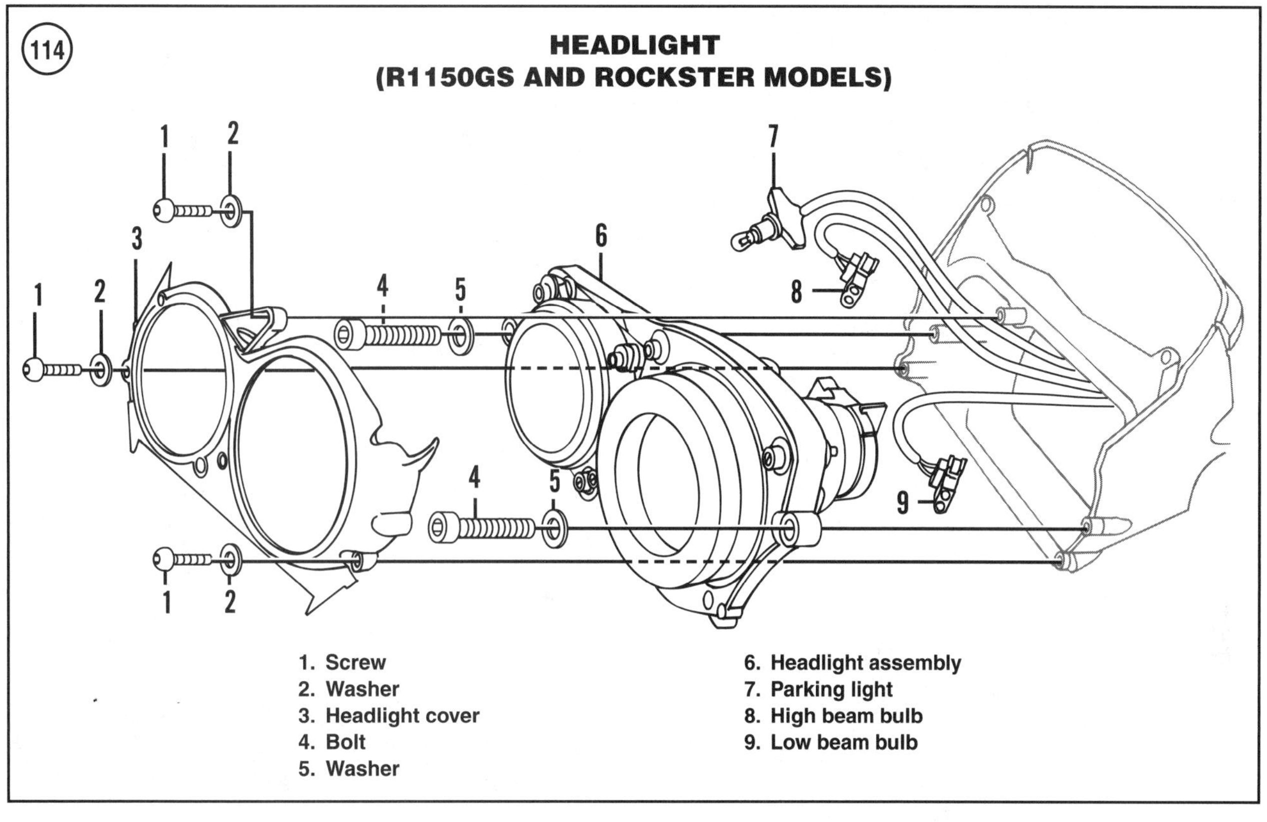
114
HEADLIGHT
(R1150GS AND ROCKSTER MODELS)
1. Screw
2. Washer
3. Headlight cover
4. Bolt
5. Washer
6. Headlight assembly
7. Parking light
8. High beam bulb
9. Low beam bulb

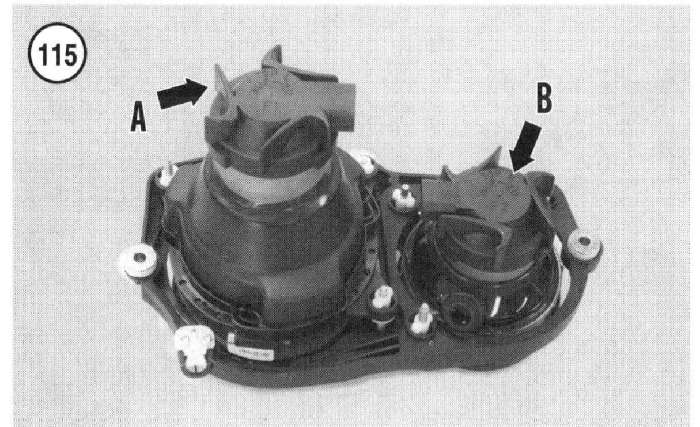
115
A
B

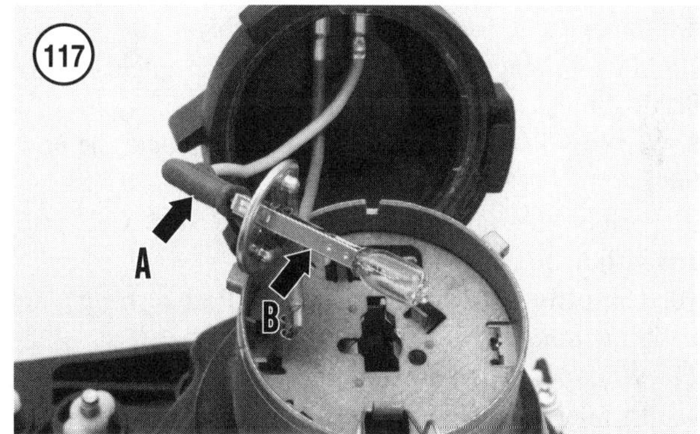
117
A
B

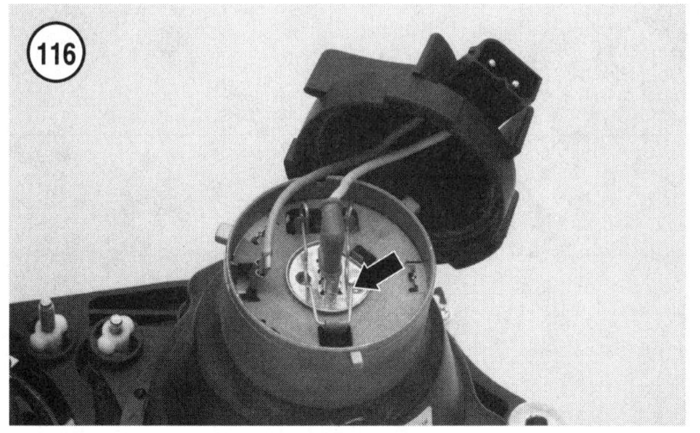
116

118

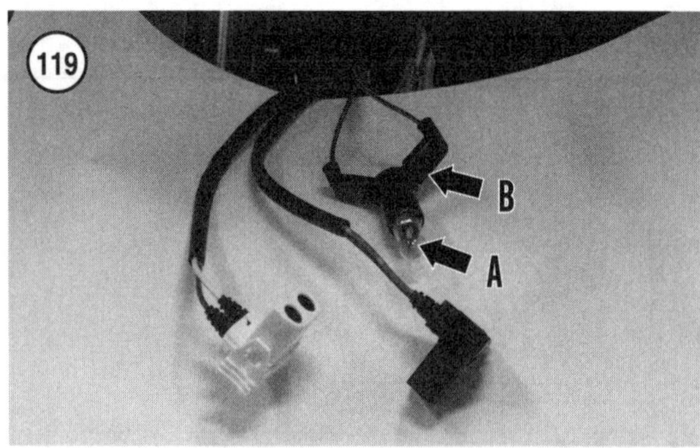

12. Check high beam headlight operation. Check headlight adjustment as described in this section.

RT models

1. Turn the ignition switch off.
2. Turn the handlebar to the full right position.
3. Disconnect the electrical connector (**Figure 123**) from the base of the headlight.
4. Remove the rubber boot (**Figure 124**) from the base of the lens assembly.
5. Release the spring clip and release the bulb (**Figure 125**).
6. Remove and discard the bulb assembly.
7. Align the tangs on the new bulb with the notches in the headlight lens and install the bulb.
8. Securely hook the headlight spring clip onto the new bulb.
9. Position the rubber boot with the UP mark facing up and install the boot.
10. Correctly align the electrical plug. Push it *straight on* until it bottoms on the bulb.
11. Working under the headlight assembly in the oil cooler inlet area, carefully withdraw the parking light bulb and socket (**Figure 126**) from the base of the lens assembly. If necessary, remove the bulb (**Figure 127**) and install a new one.
12. Check high beam headlight operation. Check headlight adjustment as described in this section.

S models
High beam bulb

1. Turn the ignition switch off.
2. Turn the handlebar to the full left position.
3. Reach under the handlebar and instrument panel and remove the rubber boot from the right side of the base of the headlight assembly.

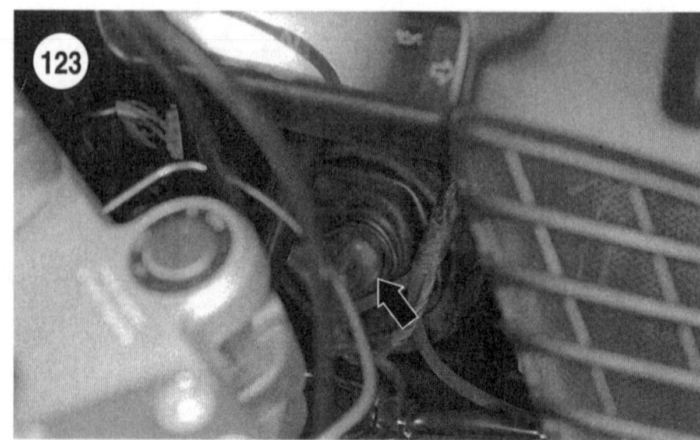

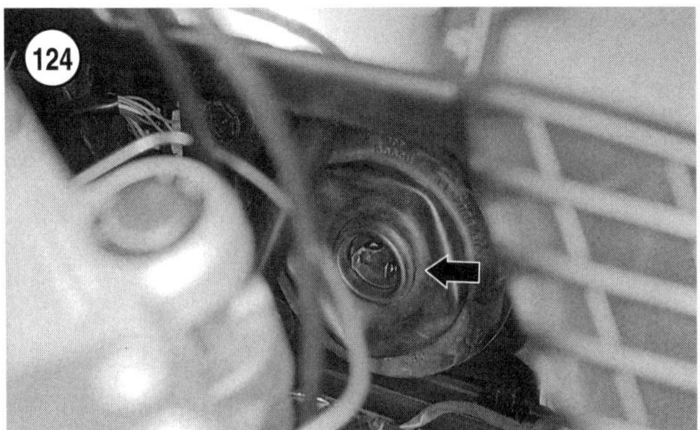
124

125

126

127

128

4. Disconnect the electrical connector from the base of the headlight.

5. Release the spring clip and release the bulb.

6. Remove and discard the bulb assembly.

7. Align the tab on the new bulb with the notch in the headlight lens and install the bulb.

8. Securely hook the headlight spring clip onto the new bulb.

9. Correctly align the electrical plug. Push it *straight on* until it bottoms on the bulb.

10. Install the rubber boot.

11. Check high beam headlight operation. Check headlight adjustment as described in this section.

S models
Low beam bulb

1. Turn the ignition switch off.

2. Turn the handlebar to the full right position.

3. Reach under the handlebar and instrument panel (**Figure 128**) and remove the rubber boot from the left side of the base of the headlight assembly.

4. Disconnect the electrical connector from the base of the headlight.

5. Release the spring clip and release the bulb.

6. Remove and discard the bulb assembly.

7. Position the beveled surface of the bulb to the bottom left and install the bulb.

8. Securely hook the headlight spring clip onto the new bulb.

9. Correctly align the electrical plug. Push it *straight on* until it bottoms on the bulb.

10. Install the rubber boot.

11. Check low beam headlight operation. Check headlight adjustment as described in this section.

S models

Parking light bulb

1. Turn the ignition switch off.
2. Turn the handlebar to the full right position.
3. Reach under the handlebar and instrument panel and remove the rubber boot from the left side of the base of the headlight assembly.
4. Rotate the small parking light bulb holder *clockwise* and withdraw it from the headlight case.
5. Remove and discard the bulb assembly.
6. Insert the holder, rotate it *counterclockwise* and lock it into place.
7. Install the rubber boot onto the left side of the headlight assembly.
8. Check parking light operation.

C models

1. Turn the ignition switch off.
2. Loosen, but do not remove, the screw at the base of the headlight assembly (**Figure 129**).
3. Carefully pull out on the bottom of the trim ring and disengage it from the headlight housing.
4. Carefully pull the headlight assembly part way out of the housing and disconnect the electrical connector (**Figure 130**) from the backside of the bulb.
5. Unhook the set spring and remove and discard the blown bulb (**Figure 131**).
6. Align the tangs on the new bulb with the notches in the headlight lens and install the bulb.
7. Securely hook the headlight clip onto the new bulb.
8. Correctly align the electrical plug. Push it *straight on* until it bottoms on the bulb and the connector cover.
9. Check headlight operation. Check headlight adjustment as described in this section.
10. Carefully withdraw the parking light bulb socket assembly (**Figure 132**) from the reflector.
11. Hold onto the socket assembly (A, **Figure 133**), push in on the bulb, turn *counterclockwise* and remove the bulb (B).
12. Install a new bulb and turn it *clockwise*, then install the socket assembly into the headlight assembly. Push it in until it bottoms.
13. Check parking light operation.

129

130

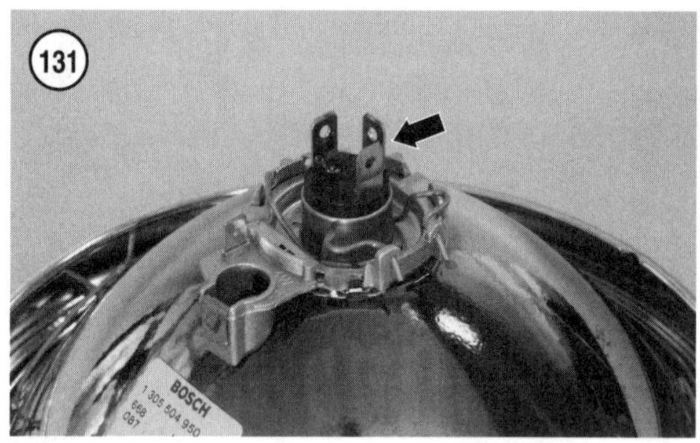

131

132

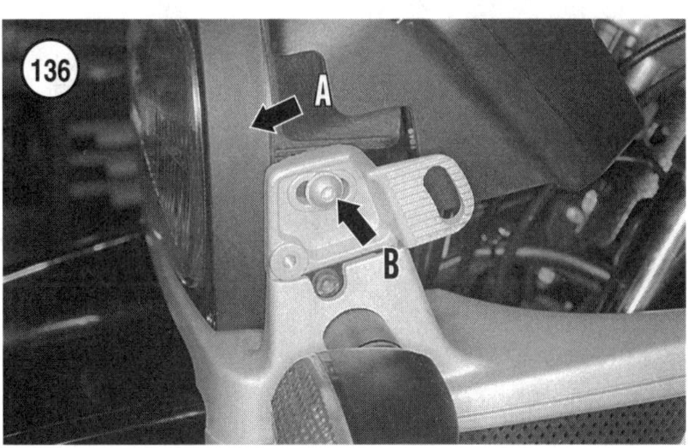

Headlight Case Assembly Removal/Installation

R850R and R1100R models

1. Remove the headlight lens and bulb as described in this section.
2. Reach under the headlight case and disconnect the horizontal adjustment linkage.
3. Within the headlight case, remove the nut and washer on each side securing the headlight case to the mounting bracket.
4. Carefully pull the wire harness out through the backside of the headlight case.
5. Remove the headlight case.
6. Install by reversing the removal steps. Check headlight adjustment as described in this section.

R1150R models

Refer to **Figure 100**.

1. Remove the headlight lens and bulb (A, **Figure 134**) as described in this section.
2. Reach behind the mounting bracket and unscrew the nut (**Figure 135**) securing the front turn signal unit on each side.
3. Carefully pull the turn signal unit (B, **Figure 134**) away from the mounting bracket and allow it to hang from the wiring harness.
4. Carefully pull the trim panel's posts (C, **Figure 134**) free from the mounting bracket.
5. Remove the Allen bolt on each securing the headlight housing to the mounting bracket and remove the housing. Do not lose the washer on each side of the mounting bracket.
6. Carefully pull the wire harness out through the backside of the headlight case.
7. Remove the headlight case.
8. Install by reversing the removal steps. Check headlight adjustment as described in this section.

R850GS and R1100GS models

Refer to **Figure 106**.

1. Remove the headlight lens and bulb (A, **Figure 136**) as previously described.
2. Remove the front fender side trim panel as described in Chapter Fifteen.

NOTE
The rubber washer is located between the headlight case and the mounting bracket.

10

Be sure to reinstall it in the same location.

3. Remove from each side the bolt, washer and rubber washer (B, **Figure 136**) securing the headlight housing to the mounting bracket.

4. Within the headlight case, remove the center screw and washer (A, **Figure 137**) securing the headlight case to the mounting bracket.

5. Partially pull the headlight housing forward and disconnect the vertical adjustment linkage, securing the headlight case to the mounting bracket.

6. Carefully pull the wire harness out through the backside of the headlight case (B, **Figure 137**).

7. Remove the headlight case.

8. Install by reversing the removal steps. Check headlight adjustment as described in this section.

R1150GS and Rockster models

Refer to **Figure 114**.

1. Turn the ignition switch off.

2A. On the R1150 GS models, perform the following:

   a. Remove the screw (A, **Figure 138**) securing the windscreen on each side.
   b. Carefully pull out on the windscreen at the pivot post (B, **Figure 138**) and remove the windshield.
   c. Remove the Phillips screw (**Figure 139**) on each side securing the top cover and remove the top cover.
   d. Remove the screws securing the headlight cover (**Figure 140**) and remove the cover.

2B. On Rockster models, remove the screws securing the headlight cover (**Figure 141**) and remove the cover.

3. Remove the Phillips screws and washers (**Figure 142**) securing the headlight assembly to the instrument panel mount.

4. Use flat blade screwdriver and release the low beam adjuster (**Figure 143**).

5. Partially pull the headlight assembly forward and disconnect the low beam connector (A, **Figure 144**), high beam connector (B) and parking lamp connector (not shown).

6. Remove the headlight assembly.

7. Install by reversing the removal steps. Check headlight adjustment as described in this section.

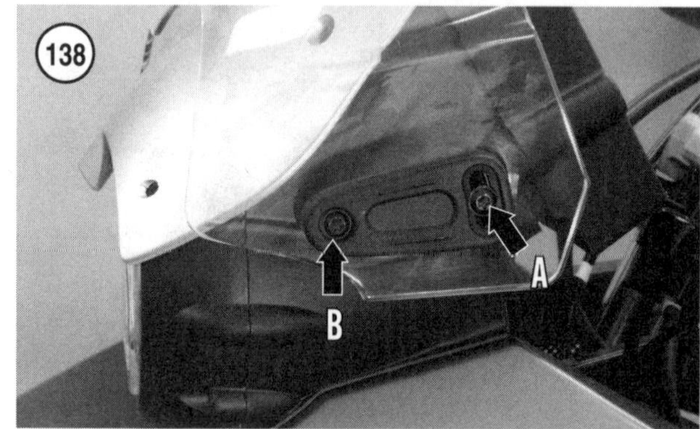

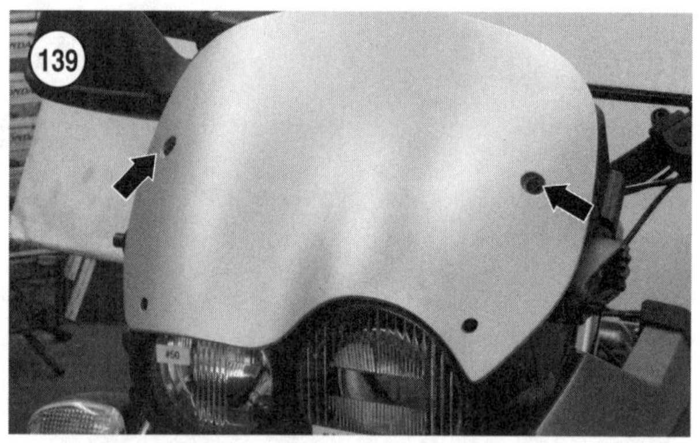

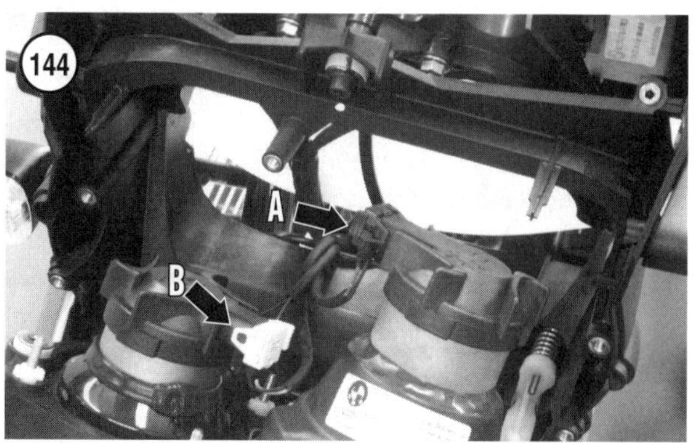

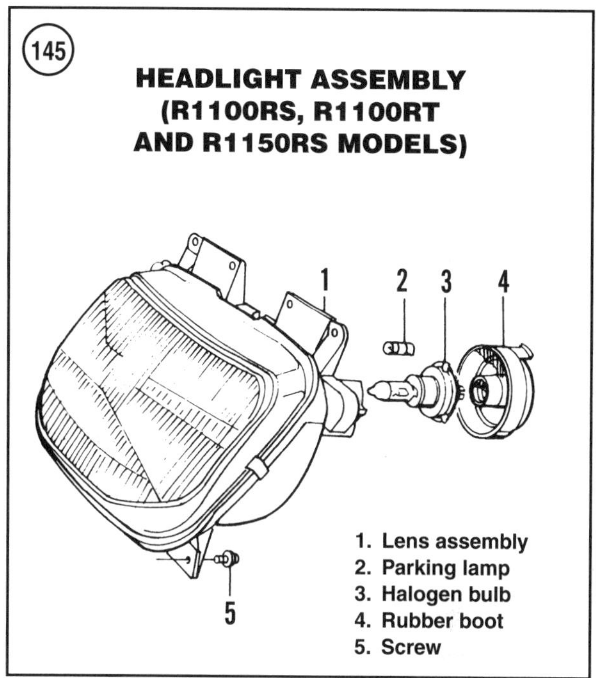

Headlight Lens Assembly Removal/Installation

RS models

Refer to **Figure 145**.

1. Remove the headlight bulb as described in this section.
2. Remove the front fairing as described in Chapter Fifteen.
3. Remove the windshield holder from the headlight.
4. On the backside of the headlight lens assembly, remove the nuts and washers securing the headlight lens to the front fairing mounting bracket.
5. Remove the headlight lens assembly.
6. Install by reversing the removal steps. Check headlight adjustment as described in this section.

RT models

Refer to **Figure 145** and **Figure 146**.

1. Remove the headlight bulb as described in this section.
2. Remove the front fairing as described in Chapter Fifteen.
3. Turn the front fairing upside down on several blankets to protect the finish.
4. Remove the screws securing the headlight lens assembly to the backside of the upper fairing front fairing.
5. Remove the headlight lens assembly.

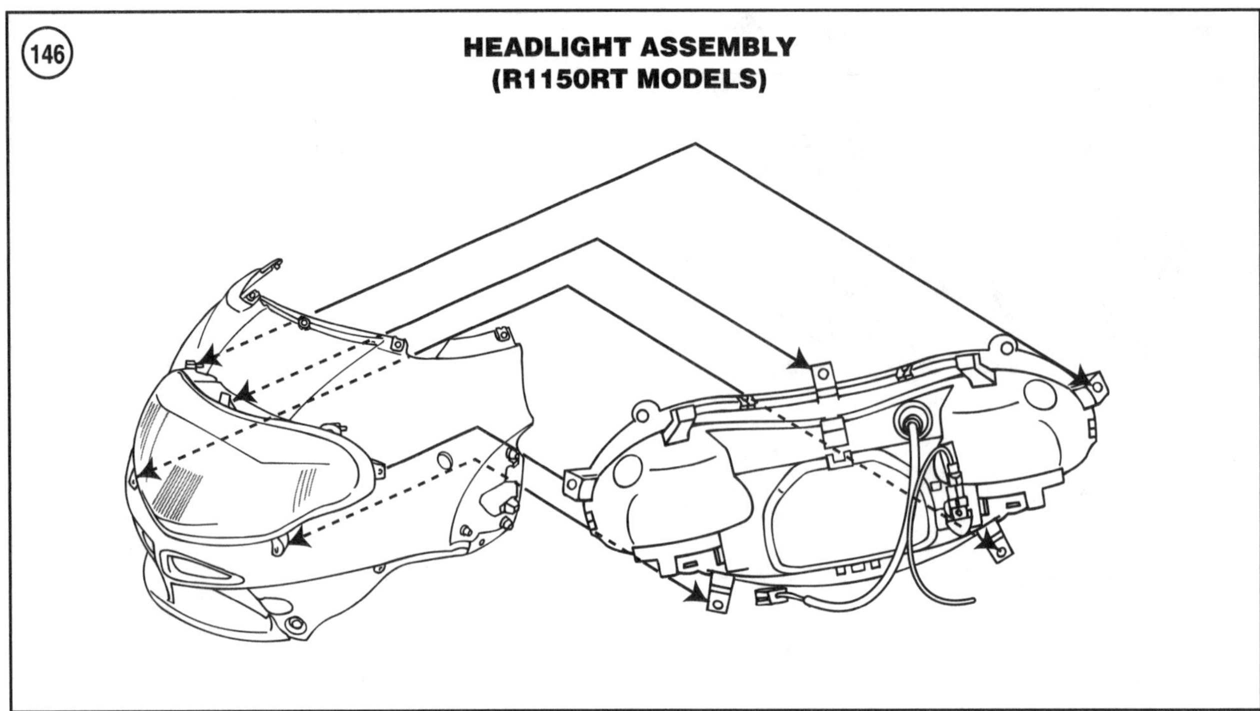

6. Install by reversing the removal steps while noting the following:
   a. Do not over-tighten the mounting screws as the plastic mounting bosses on the trim may be fractured.
   b. Check headlight adjustment as described in this section.

S models

Refer to **Figure 147**.

1. Remove the headlight bulb as described in this section.
2. Remove the windshield (A, **Figure 148**) and front fairing (B) as described in Chapter Fifteen.
3. Turn the front fairing upside down on several blankets to protect the finish.
4. Remove the screws and washers securing the headlight lens assembly to the backside of the upper fairing front fairing.
5. Remove the headlight lens assembly.
6. Install by reversing the removal steps while noting the following:
   a. Move the lower trim panel into position prior to installing any screws.
   b. Do not over-tighten the mounting screws as the plastic mounting bosses on the trim may be fractured.
   c. Check headlight adjustment as described in this section.

Headlight Adjustment

Adjust the headlight according to the local Department of Motor Vehicle regulations.

R models

1. For horizontal adjustment, on the left lower side of the headlight rotate the adjuster (**Figure 149**) until the aim is correct.

2A. On R1100R models, for vertical adjustment, perform the following:
   a. Loosen the headlight case mounting screws on each side.
   b. Turn the headlight case up or down until aim is correct.
   c. Tighten the mounting screws on each side.

2B. On R1150R models, for vertical adjustment, perform the following:
   a. Reach behind the mounting bracket and unscrew the nut (**Figure 135**) securing the front turn signal unit on each side.
   b. Carefully pull the turn signal unit away from the mounting bracket and allow it to hang from the wiring harness.
   c. Carefully pull the trim panel's posts free from the mounting brackct.

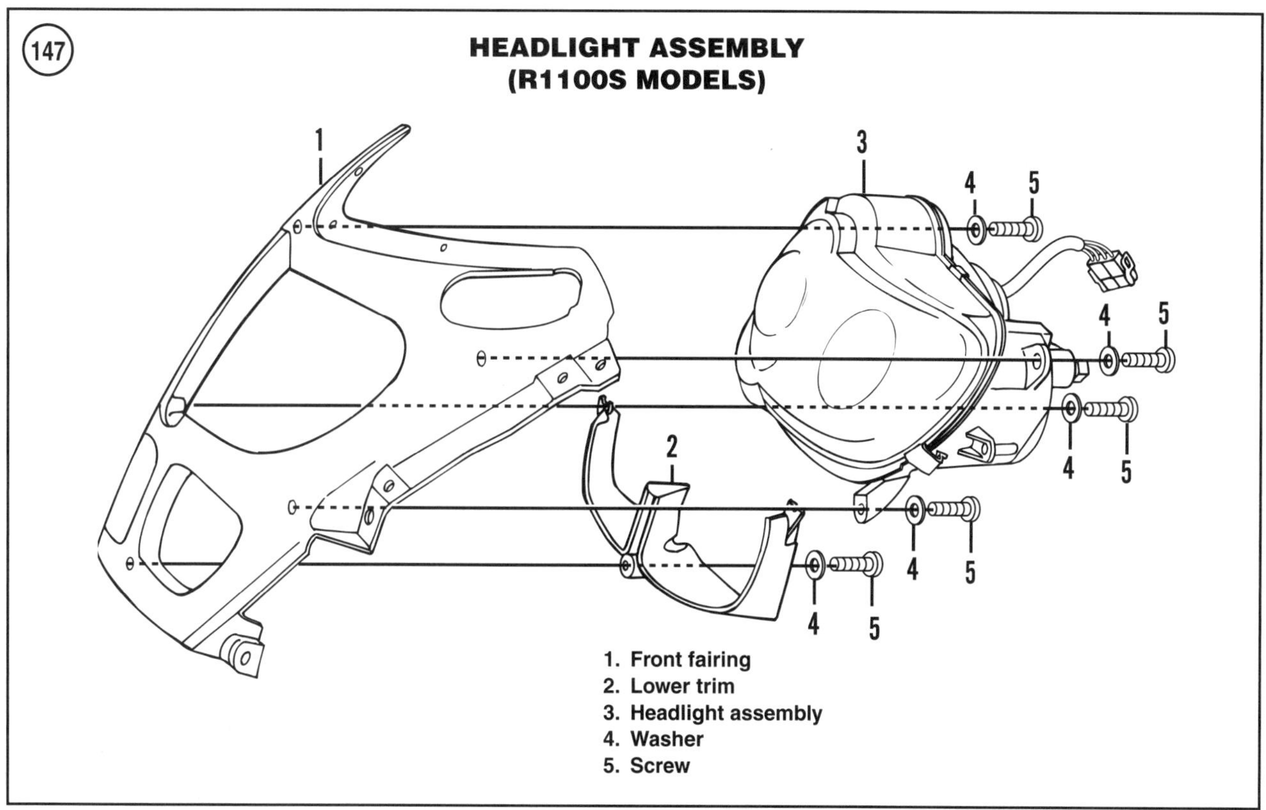

d. Loosen the Allen bolt on each securing the headlight housing.
e. Move the headlight case up or down until aim is correct.
f. Tighten the mounting screws on each side.
g. Push the trim panel back into position on the mounting bracket.
h. Install the turn signal unit onto the mounting bracket and tighten the nut securely.

R850GS and R1100GS models

1. For horizontal adjustment, perform the following:
   a. Remove the front fender side trim panel as described in Chapter Fifteen.
   b. Loosen the bolt (B, **Figure 136**) on each side securing the headlight housing to the mounting bracket.
   c. Slowly move the headlight housing to either side until aim is correct.
   d. Tighten the bolts securely.
2. For vertical adjustment, perform the following:
   a. On the right lower side of the headlight, loosen the adjuster locknut.

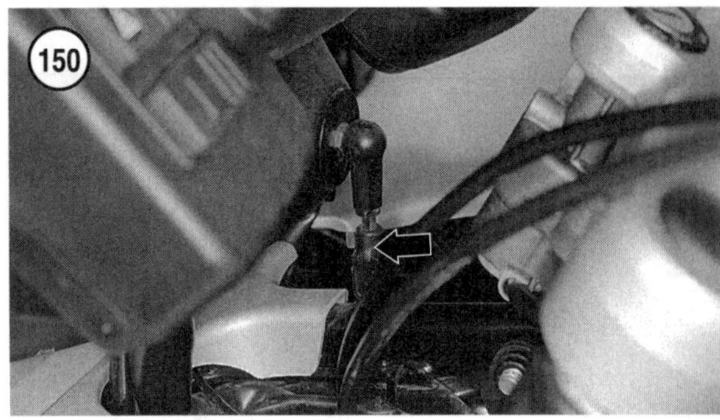

b. Rotate the adjuster (**Figure 150**) until the aim is correct. Tighten the locknut.

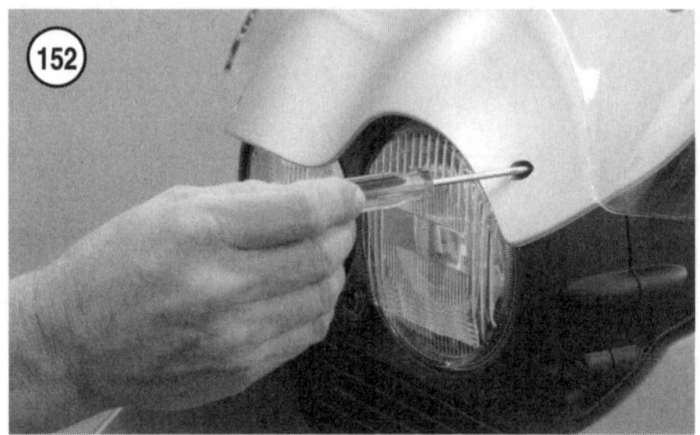

R1150GS and Rockster models

1. For horizontal adjustment, turn the lower beam lower screw (**Figure 151**) in either direction.
2. For basic vertical adjustment, turn the low beam upper screw (**Figure 152**) in either direction.
3. For vertical load adjustment, perform the following:
   a. Solo riding and minimum load: position the pivot lever in the neutral position (**Figure 153**).
   b. Dual riding or heavy load: position the pivot lever *counterclockwise* 90° to the high load position.

RS and RT models

1. For horizontal adjustment, on the left side rotate the adjust screw (**Figure 154**) in either direction until aim is correct.
2. For vertical adjustment, perform the following:
   a. On the right side, move the lever to the up position.
   b. Rotate the adjusting screw until the aim is correct. Move the lever to the down position (**Figure 155**).

S models

For vertical load adjustment, perform the following:

1. Solo riding and minimum load: position the pivot lever, located below the tachometer portion of the instrument panel (**Figure 156**), in the up position.
2. Dual riding or heavy load: position the lever in the down position.

C models

There is no horizontal adjustment

1. For vertical adjustment, perform the following:

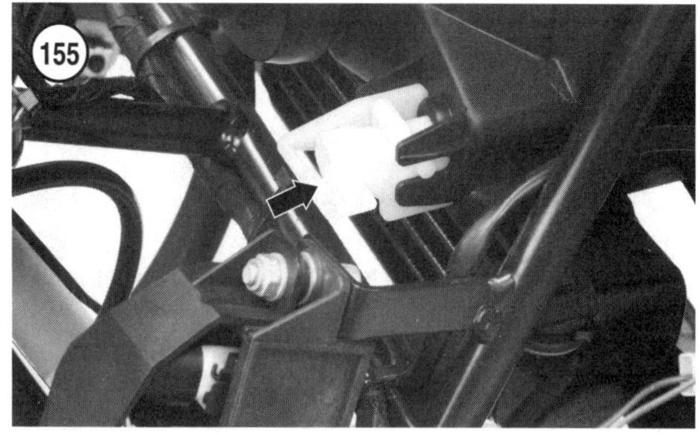

a. Loosen the Allen bolt (**Figure 157**) on each side securing the headlight housing to the mounting bracket.

b. Slowly move the headlight housing either up or down until aim is correct.

c. Tighten the bolts securely.

TAILLIGHT/BRAKE LIGHT AND LICENSE PLATE LIGHT

Bulb Replacement and Lens Assembly Removal/Installation

R850R, R1100R, R850GS and R1100GS models

1. Turn the ignition switch off.
2. Remove the screws (**Figure 158**) securing the lens and remove the lens and gasket from the light assembly.
3. Push in on the bulb (A, **Figure 159**), turn it *counterclockwise* and remove the bulb from the reflector.
4. Wash the inside and outside of the lens with a mild detergent and wipe dry.
5. Carefully wipe the reflector (B, **Figure 159**) clean with a soft lint-free cloth.
6. Inspect the socket. If damaged, replace the light assembly.
7. Install the new bulb. Turn it *clockwise* until it stops.
8. Apply either brake to make sure the new bulb operates correctly.
9. Install the lens and tighten the screws securely. Do not overtighten the screws as the lens or screw bosses may be damaged.
10. To remove the reflector assembly, perform the following:
    a. Work under the rear fender and remove the mounting bolts.
    b. Disconnect the electrical connector from the main wiring harness and remove the reflector assembly.

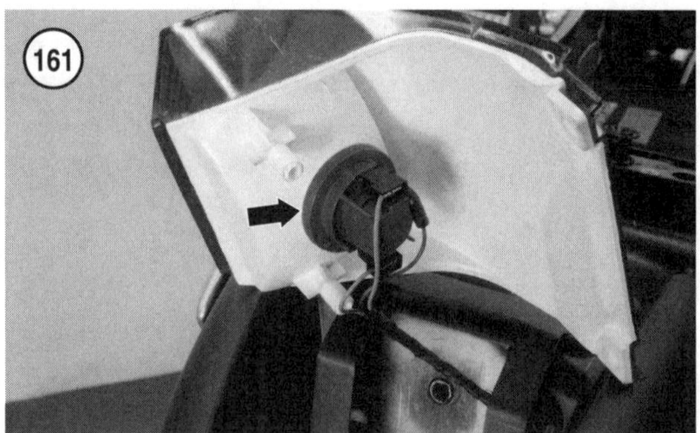

c. Install the lens assembly and tighten bolts securely. Do not overtighten the bolts as the lens assembly may be damaged.

R1150R models

1. Turn the ignition switch off.
2. Remove the pillion seat as described in Chapter Fifteen.
3. Remove the screws (A, **Figure 160**) securing the taillight assembly (B).
4. Partially pull the taillight assembly up, turn bulb socket assembly (**Figure 161**) *counterclockwise* and remove it from the taillight assembly.
5. Push in on the bulb (**Figure 162**) *counterclockwise* and remove it from the socket assembly.
6. Install the new bulb. Turn it *clockwise* until it stops.
7. Apply either brake to make sure the new bulb operates correctly.
8. Install the bulb socket assembly into the taillight assembly (**Figure 161**) and turn it *clockwise* until it stops.
9. Install the taillight assembly and tighten the screws securely. Do not overtighten the screws as the taillight assembly may be damaged.
10. Install the pillion seat as described in Chapter Fifteen.

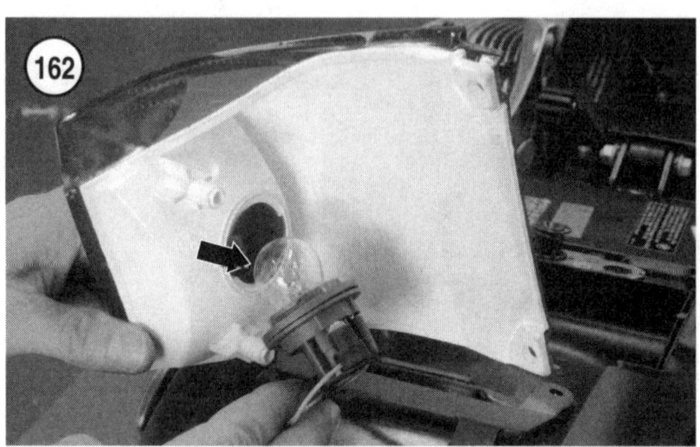

RS models

Refer to **Figure 163**.

1. Turn the ignition switch off.
2. Remove the seat as described in Chapter Fifteen.
3. Within the under seat storage area, unscrew the knurled knobs (**Figure 164**) securing the light assembly to the rear cowl.
4. Partially pull the lens assembly (**Figure 165**) out from the rear cowl and disconnect the electrical connector from the main harness.
5. To remove the taillight/brake light bulb, perform the following:

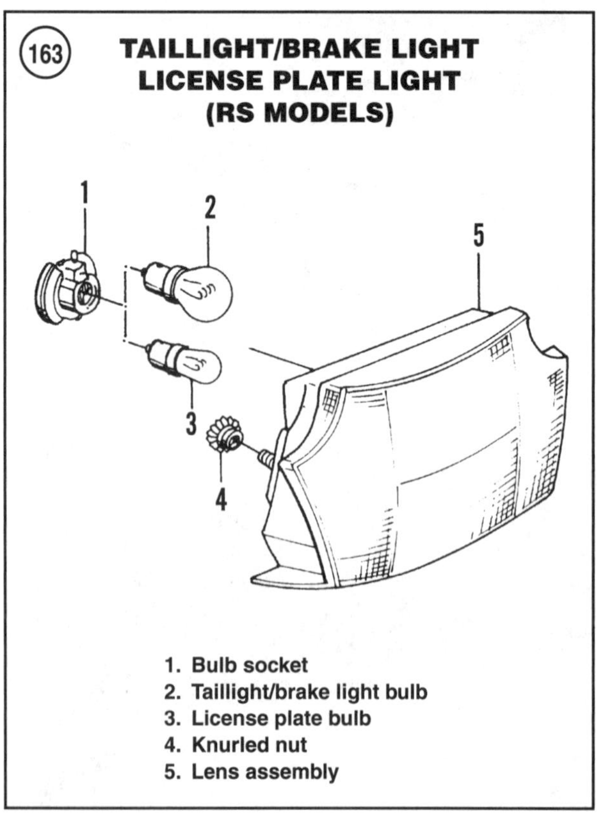

164

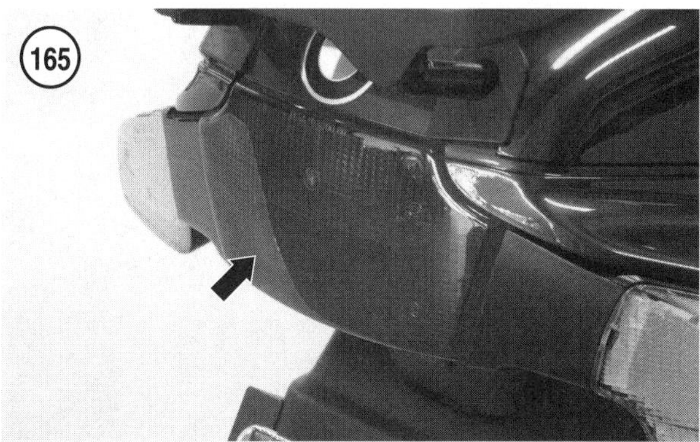
165

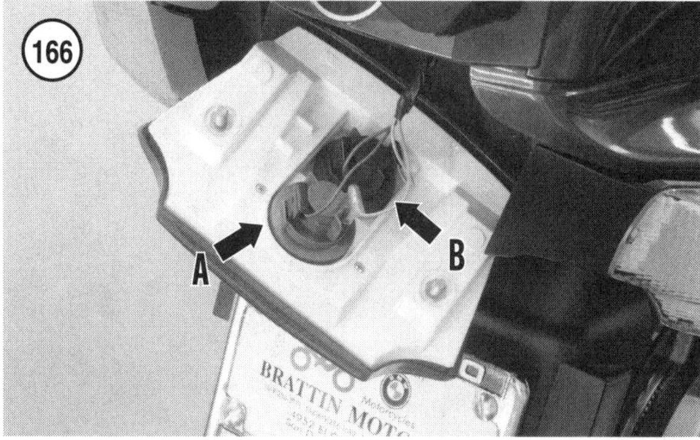

166

167

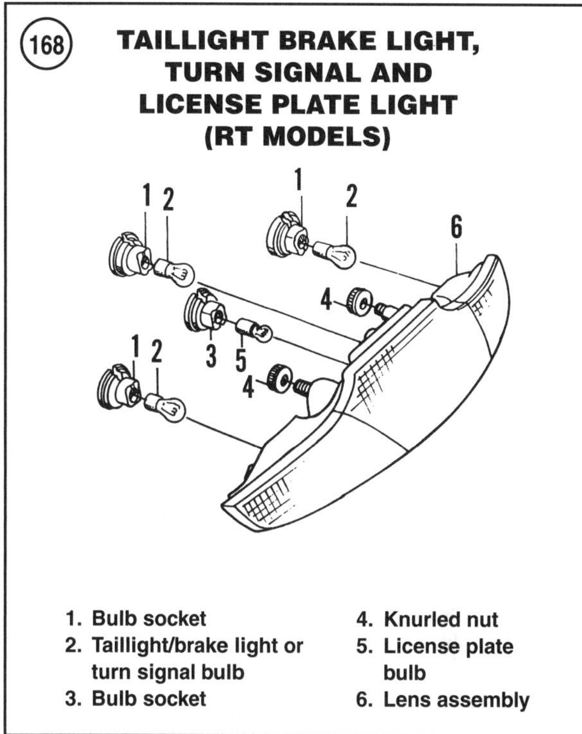

168 **TAILLIGHT BRAKE LIGHT, TURN SIGNAL AND LICENSE PLATE LIGHT (RT MODELS)**

1. Bulb socket
2. Taillight/brake light or turn signal bulb
3. Bulb socket
4. Knurled nut
5. License plate bulb
6. Lens assembly

a. Push in on the taillight/brake light socket (A, **Figure 166**), turn it *counterclockwise* and remove the socket from the light assembly.

b. Push in on the bulb (**Figure 167**), turn it *counterclockwise* and remove the bulb from the socket.

6. To remove the license plate bulb, perform the following:

a. Push in on the light socket (B, **Figure 166**), turn it *counterclockwise* and remove the socket from the light assembly.

b. Push in on the bulb, turn it *counterclockwise* and remove the bulb from the socket.

7. Inspect the light and the socket assemblies. Replace the light assembly if damaged or deteriorated.

8. Install the new bulb(s).

9. Connect the electrical connector to the main harness.

10. Apply either brake to make sure the new bulbs operate correctly.

11. Install the light assembly into the rear cowl and position it correctly.

12. Install the knurled knobs (**Figure 164**) and tighten securely.

13. Install the seat as described in Chapter Fifteen.

RT models

Refer to **Figure 168**.

1. Turn the ignition switch off.
2. Remove the seat as described in Chapter Fifteen.
3. Within the under seat storage area, unscrew the knurled knobs (**Figure 164**) securing the light assembly to the rear cowl.
4. Pull the lens assembly (**Figure 169**) out from the rear cowl and disconnect the electrical connector from the main harness.
5. To remove the taillight/brake light bulb, perform the following:
   a. Push in on the taillight/brake light socket (A, **Figure 170**), turn it *counterclockwise* and remove the socket from the light assembly.
   b. Push in on the bulb, turn it *counterclockwise* and remove the bulb from the socket.
6. To remove the license plate bulb, perform the following:
   a. Push in on the license plate light socket (B, **Figure 170**), turn it *counterclockwise* and remove the socket from the light assembly.
   b. Push in on the bulb, turn it *counterclockwise* and remove the bulb from the socket.
7. Inspect the light and the socket assemblies. Replace the light assembly if damaged or deteriorated.
8. Install the new bulb(s).
9. Connect the electrical connector to the main harness.
10. Apply either brake to make sure the new bulbs operate correctly.
11. Install the light assembly into the rear cowl and position it correctly.
12. Install the knurled knobs (**Figure 164**) and tighten securely.
13. Install the seat as described in Chapter Fifteen.

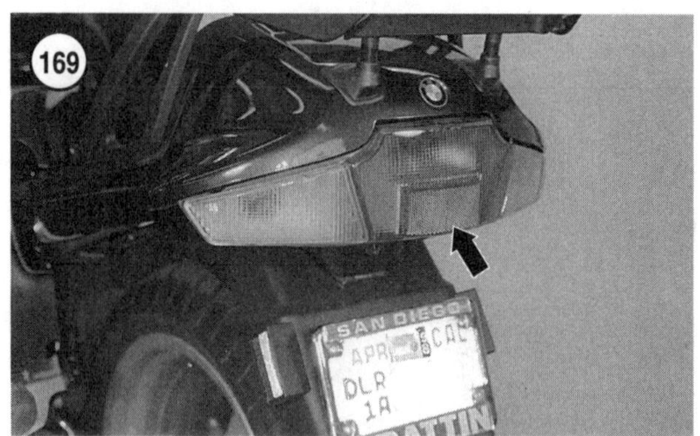

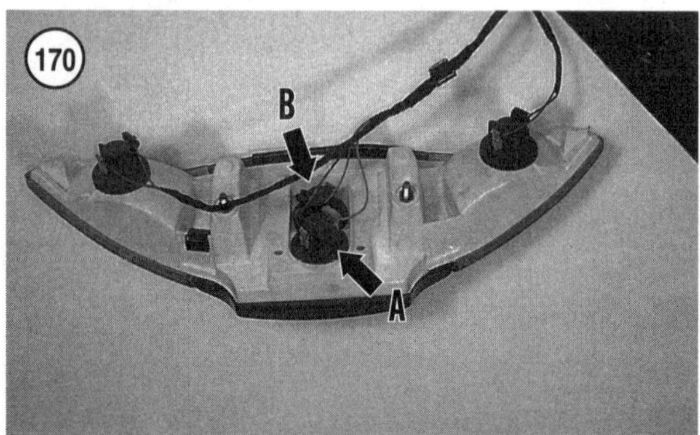

S models

1. Turn the ignition switch off.
2. Remove the screws (**Figure 171**) securing the lens and remove the lens and gasket from the light assembly.
3. Push in on the bulb, turn it *counterclockwise* and remove the bulb from the reflector.
4. Wash the inside and outside of the lens with a mild detergent and wipe dry.
5. Carefully wipe the reflector clean with a soft lint-free cloth.
6. Inspect the socket. If damaged, replace the light assembly.
7. Install the new bulb. Turn it *clockwise* until it stops.
8. Apply either brake to make sure the new bulb operates correctly.

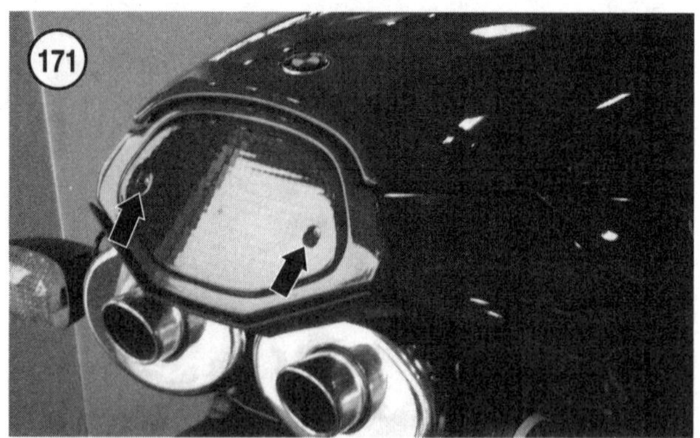

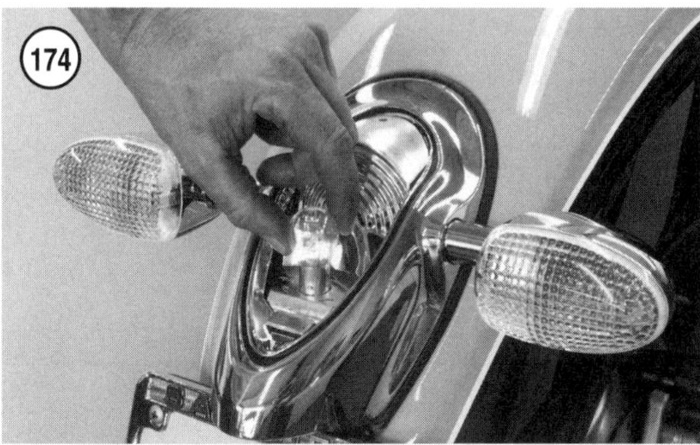

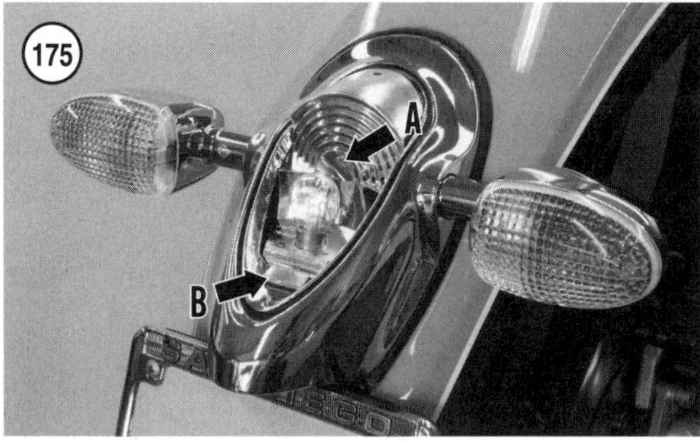

9. Install the lens and tighten the screws securely. Do not overtighten the screws as the lens or screw bosses may be damaged.
10. To remove the license plate light, perform the following:
   a. Remove the screws securing the license plate light assembly to the bracket below the muffler outlets.
   b. Lower the assembly and remove the bulb from the two spring clips on the assembly.
   c. Install a new bulb and install the assembly into the bracket. Tighten the screws securely.

C models

1. Turn the ignition switch off.
2. Remove the screw (**Figure 172**) securing the lens.

CAUTION
Do not lift up on the lens since the locating tab will break.

3. Slide and move the lens (**Figure 173**) straight back off the reflector.
4. Push in on the bulb (**Figure 174**), turn it *counterclockwise* and remove the bulb from the reflector.
5. Wash the inside and outside of the lens with a mild detergent and wipe dry.
6. Carefully wipe the reflector (A, **Figure 175**) clean with a soft lint-free cloth.
7. Inspect the socket. If damaged, replace the light assembly.
8. Install the new bulb. Turn it *clockwise* until it stops.
9. Apply either brake to make sure the new bulb operates correctly.
10. Slide the lens on from the rear and push it on until it stops. Install the screw and tighten securely. Do not overtighten the screw as the lens or screw bosses may be damaged.
11. To remove the license plate light, perform the following:
   a. Carefully lift the lower portion of the reflector (B, **Figure 175**) up out of the taillight housing.
   b. Push in on the bulb, turn it *counterclockwise* and remove the bulb from the underside of the reflector.
   c. Install the new bulb. Turn it *clockwise* until it stops.
   d. Lower the reflector into the housing and push it down until it bottoms.

TURN SIGNALS

Front and Rear Turn Signal Bulb Replacement (R850GS, R850R, R1100GS and R1100R Models)

Refer to **Figure 176**.

1. Turn the ignition switch off.
2. Remove the screw from the backside of the turn signal housing.
3. Carefully pull the lens (**Figure 177**) away from the housing.
4. Turn the bulb *counterclockwise* and remove the bulb from the socket.
5. Inspect the lens and the socket. Replace the lens if damaged or deteriorated.
6. Wash the inside and outside of the lens with a mild detergent and wipe dry.

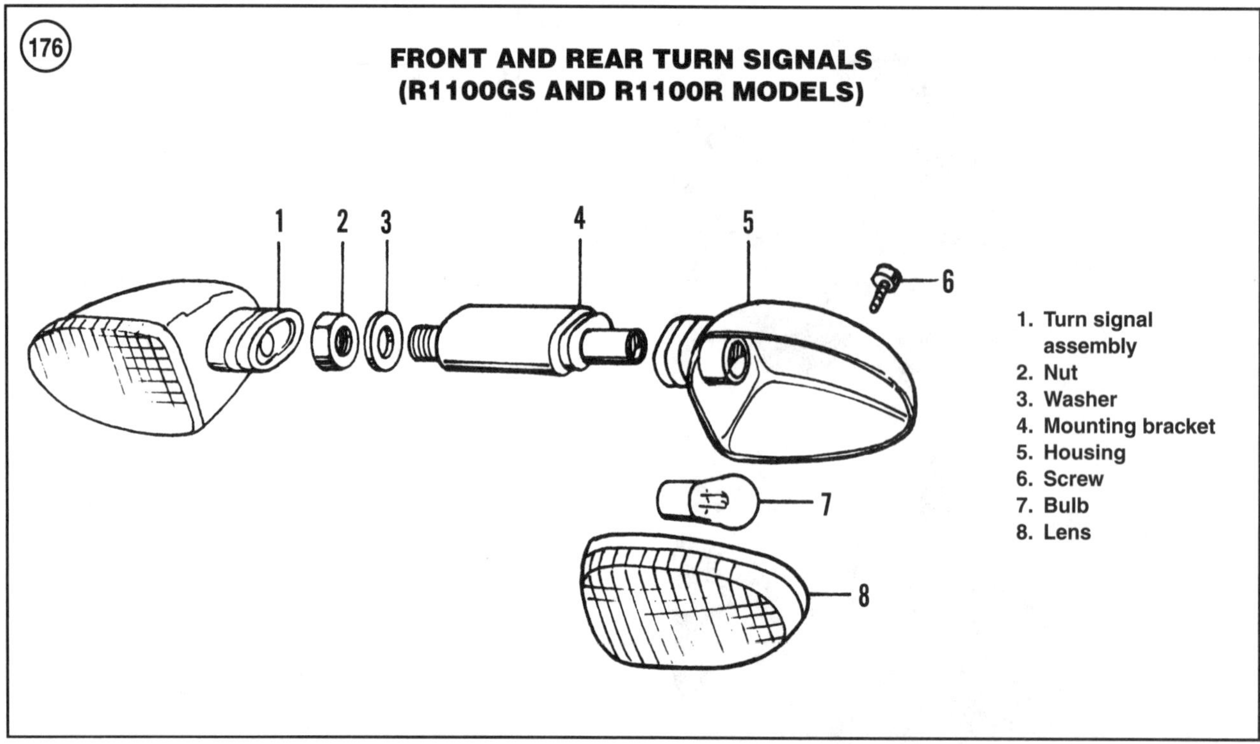

7. Install the new bulb. Turn it *clockwise* until it stops.
8. Operate the turn signal lever to make sure the new bulb operates correctly.
9. Install the lens and install the screw. Tighten the screw securely. Do not overtighten the screws as the plastic lens may be damaged.

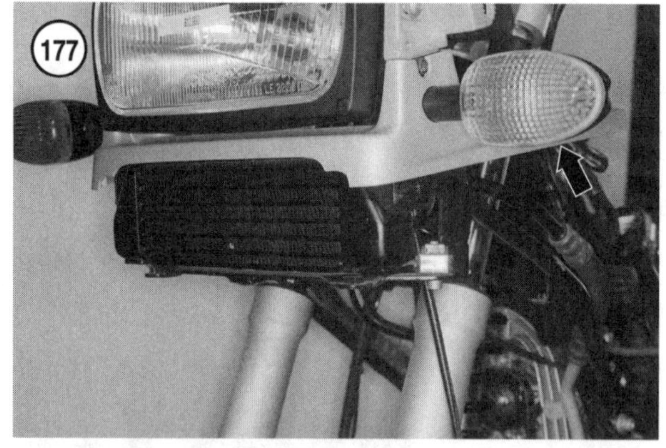

Front and Rear Turn Signal Bulb Replacement (R1150R and Rockster Models)

1. Turn the ignition switch off.
2. Remove the screw from the backside of the turn signal housing. Refer to **Figure 178** or **Figure 179**.
3. Carefully pull the lens away from the housing.
4. Turn the bulb *counterclockwise* and remove the bulb from the socket.
5. Inspect the lens and the socket. Replace the lens if damaged or deteriorated.
6. Wash the inside and outside of the lens with a mild detergent and wipe dry.
7. Install the new bulb. Turn it *clockwise* until it stops.
8. Operate the turn signal lever to make sure the new bulb operates correctly.
9. Install the lens and install the screw. Tighten the screw securely. Do not overtighten the screws as the plastic lens may be damaged.

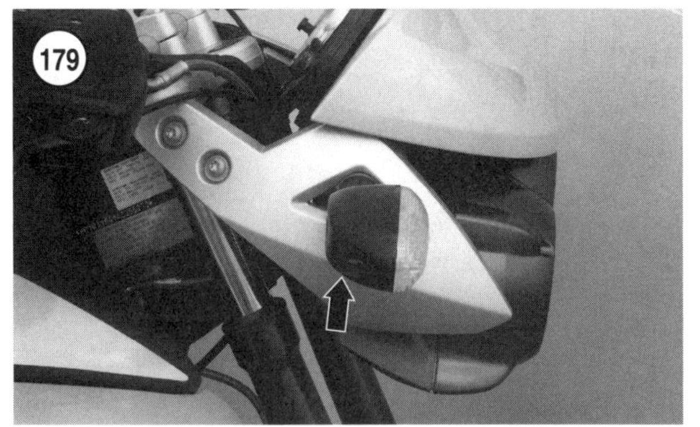

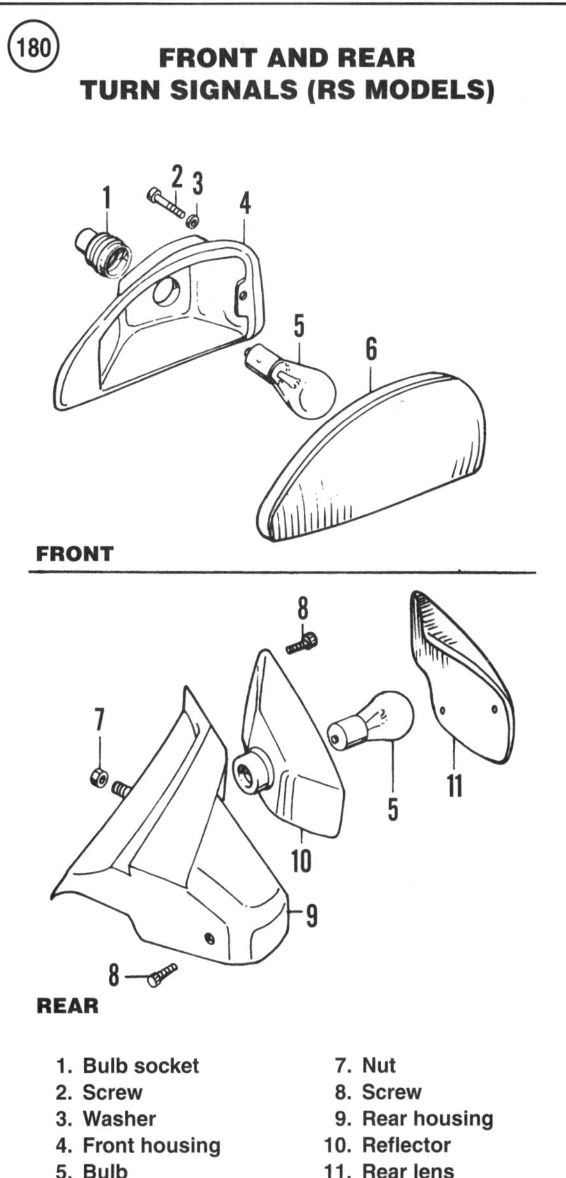

Front Turn Signal Bulb Replacement (RS Models)

Refer to **Figure 180**.

1. Turn the ignition switch off.
2. Remove the front fairing front inner panel as described in Chapter Fifteen.
3. Turn the socket/bulb assembly (**Figure 181**) *counterclockwise* and remove it from the front fairing main panel.
4. Turn the bulb (**Figure 182**) *counterclockwise* and remove the bulb from the socket.
5. Inspect the lens and the socket. Replace the lens if damaged or deteriorated.
6. Install the new bulb. Turn it *clockwise* until it stops.
7. Operate the turn signal lever to make sure the new bulb operates correctly.
8. Install the socket/bulb into the front fairing main panel and turn it *clockwise*.
9. Install the front fairing front inner panel as described in Chapter Fifteen.

Rear Turn Signal Bulb Replacement (RS Models)

Refer to **Figure 180**.

1. Turn the ignition switch off.
2. Remove the screw from the backside of the turn signal housing.
3. Carefully pull the lens (**Figure 183**) away from the housing.
4. Turn the bulb (**Figure 184**) *counterclockwise* and remove the bulb from the socket.
5. Inspect the lens and the socket. Replace the lens if damaged or deteriorated.
6. Wash the inside and outside of the lens with a mild detergent and wipe dry.
7. Install the new bulb. Turn it *clockwise* until it stops.
8. Operate the turn signal lever to make sure the new bulb operates correctly.
9. Install the lens and the screw. Tighten the screw securely. Do not overtighten the screw as the plastic lens may be damaged.

Front Turn Signal Bulb Replacement (RT Models)

Refer to **Figure 185**.

1. Turn the ignition switch off.
2. Remove the rear view mirror as described in Chapter Fifteen.
3. Carefully turn the socket *counterclockwise* and remove it from the backside of the rear view mirror.
4. Turn the bulb (**Figure 186**) *counterclockwise* and remove the bulb from the socket.
5. Inspect the lens and the socket. Replace the lens if damaged or deteriorated.
6. Install the new bulb. Turn it *clockwise* until it stops.
7. Operate the turn signal lever to make sure the new bulb operates correctly.
8. Carefully install the socket into the rear view mirror and turn it *clockwise* to lock it into place.
9. Install the rear view mirror as described in Chapter Fifteen.

Rear Turn Signal Bulb Replacement (RT Models)

Refer to **Figure 168**.

1. Turn the ignition switch off.
2. Remove the seat as described in Chapter Fifteen.
3. Within the under seat storage area, unscrew the knurled knobs (**Figure 187**) securing the light to the rear cowl.

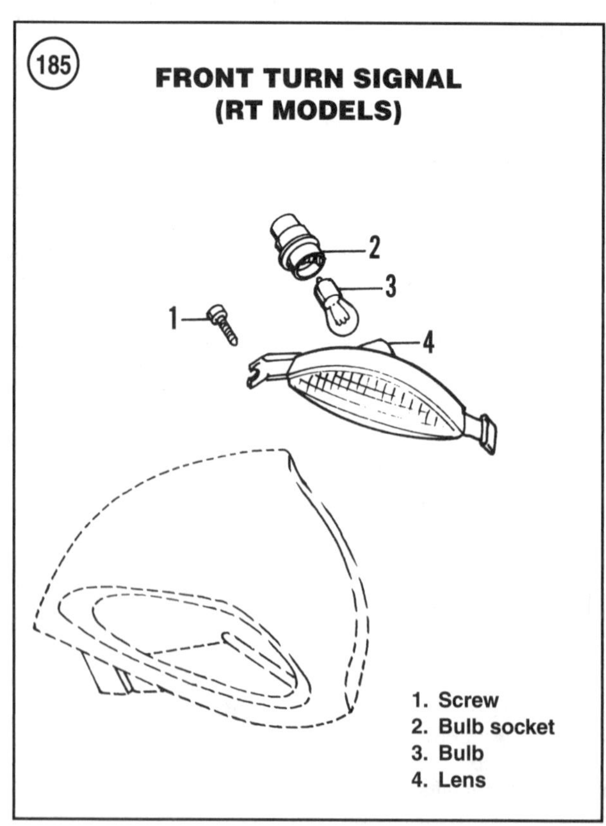

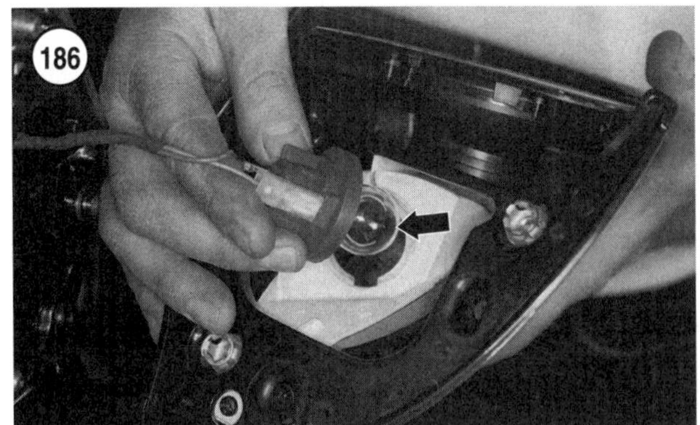

186

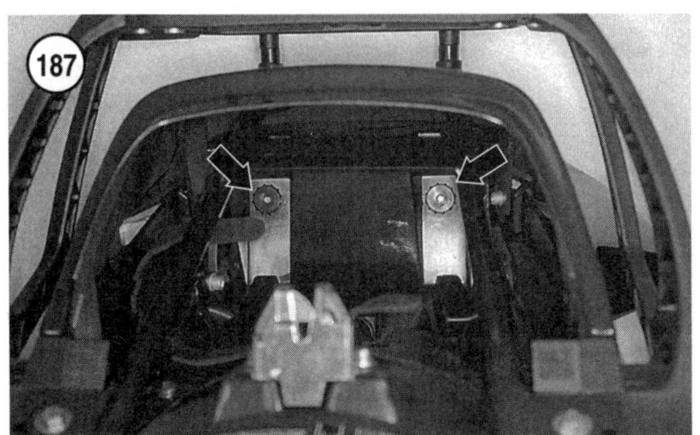

187

188

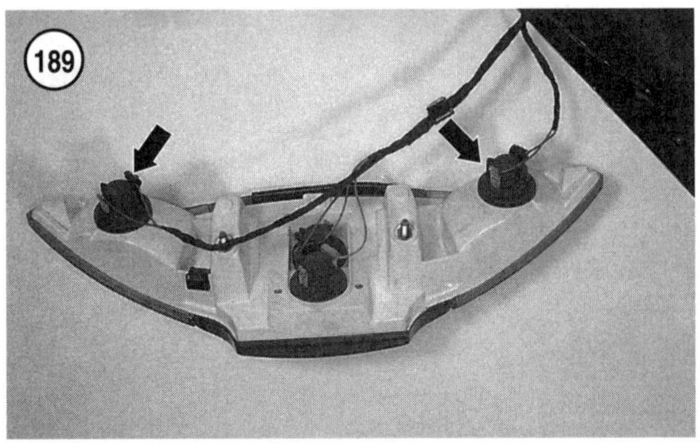

189

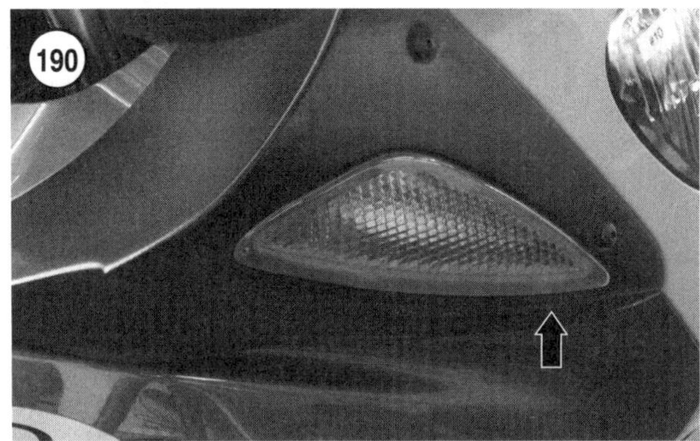

190

4. Pull the light (**Figure 188**) out from the rear cowl and disconnect the electrical connector from the main harness.
5. To remove the rear turn signal light bulb, perform the following:
   a. Push in on the turn signal light socket (**Figure 189**), turn it counterclockwise and remove the socket from the light.
   b. Push in on the bulb, turn it counterclockwise and remove the bulb from the socket.
6. Inspect the lens and socket assembly(ies). Replace the lens if damaged or deteriorated.
7. Install the new bulb(s). Turn it *clockwise* until it stops.
8. Connect the electrical connector to the main harness.
9. Operate the turn signal lever to make sure the new bulb operates correctly.
10. Install the light into the rear cowl and position it correctly.
11. Install the knurled knobs (**Figure 187**) and tighten securely.
12. Install the seat as described in Chapter Fifteen.

Front Turn Signal Bulb Replacement (S Models)

1. Turn the ignition switch off.
2. Insert a small flat blade screwdriver into the notch (**Figure 190**) at the front of the lens and carefully release the lower edge of the assembly from the housing.
3. Carefully pull the assembly from the front fairing panel.
4. Hold the lens assembly, turn the socket *counterclockwise* and remove the socket and bulb from the lens assembly.
5. Turn the bulb *counterclockwise* and remove the bulb from the socket.
6. Inspect the lens assembly and the socket. Replace the lens assembly if damaged or deteriorated.

7. Wash the outside of the lens with a mild detergent and wipe dry.
8. Install the new bulb. Turn it *clockwise* until it stops.
9. Hold the lens assembly, turn the socket *clockwise* and install the socket and bulb into the lens assembly.
10. Operate the turn signal lever to make sure the new bulb operates correctly.
11. Insert the lens assembly into the front fairing panel at the top, then snap the lower edge into place. Make sure it is secured in place.

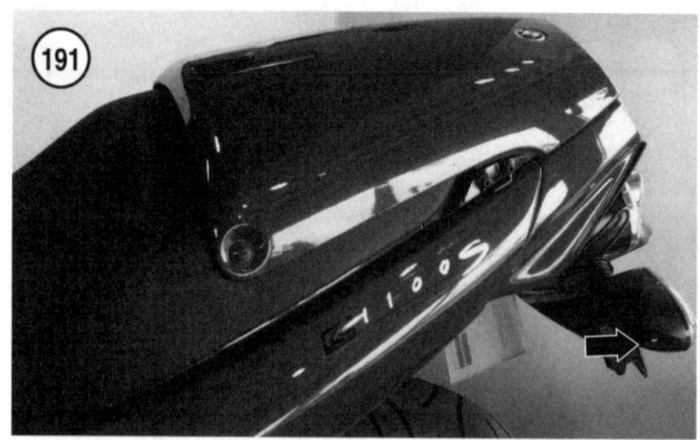

Rear Turn Signal Bulb Replacement (S Models)

1. Turn the ignition switch off.
2. Remove the screw from the backside of the turn signal housing (**Figure 191**).
3. Carefully pull the lens away from the housing.
4. Turn the bulb *counterclockwise* and remove the bulb from the socket.
5. Inspect the lens and the socket. Replace the lens if damaged or deteriorated.
6. Wash the inside and outside of the lens with a mild detergent and wipe dry.
7. Install the new bulb. Turn it *clockwise* until it stops.
8. Operate the turn signal lever to make sure the new bulb operates correctly.
9. Install the lens and install the screw. Tighten the screw securely. Do not overtighten the screws as the plastic lens may be damaged.

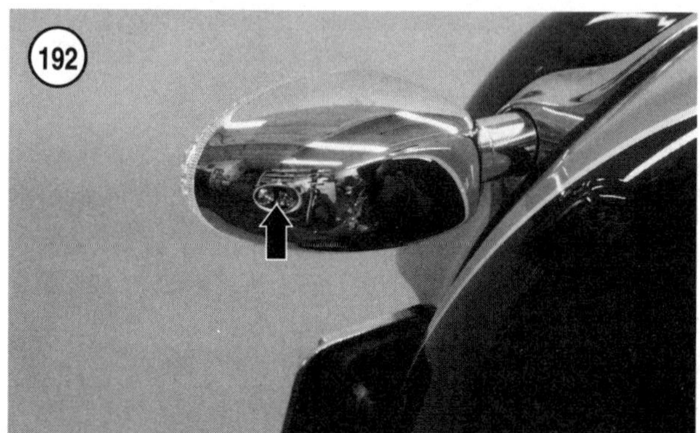

Front and Rear Turn Signal Bulb Replacement (C Models)

1. Turn the ignition switch off.
2. Remove the screw (**Figure 192**) from the backside of the turn signal housing.
3. Carefully pull the lens (**Figure 193**) away from the housing.
4. Turn the bulb (**Figure 194**) *counterclockwise* and remove the bulb from the socket.
5. Inspect the lens and the socket. Replace the lens if damaged or deteriorated.
6. Wash the inside and outside of the lens with a mild detergent and wipe dry.
7. Install the new bulb. Turn it *clockwise* until it stops.
8. Operate the turn signal lever to make sure the new bulb operates correctly.
9. Install the lens and install the screw. Tighten the screw securely. Do not overtighten the screws as the plastic lens may be damaged.

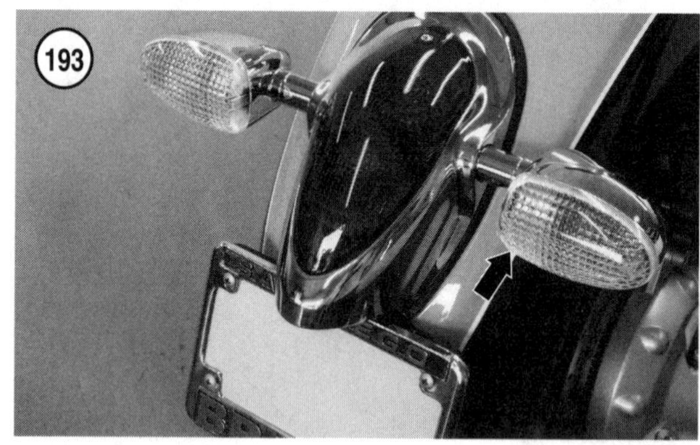

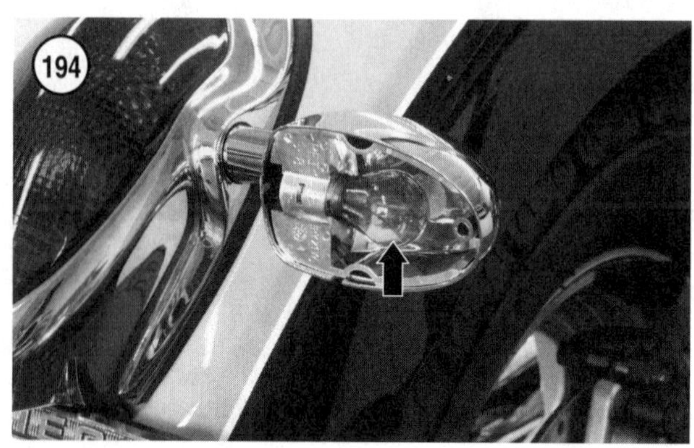

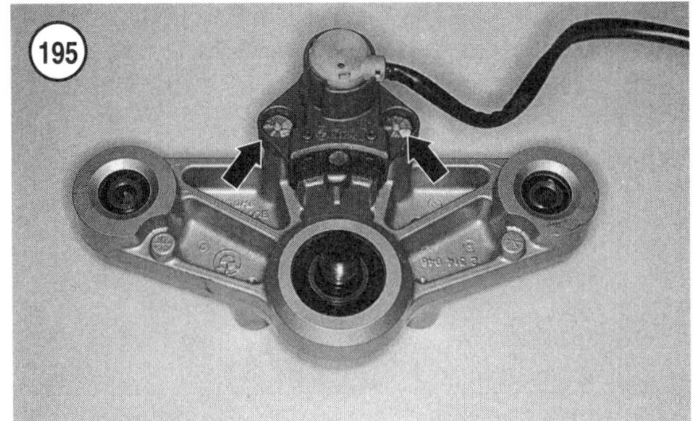

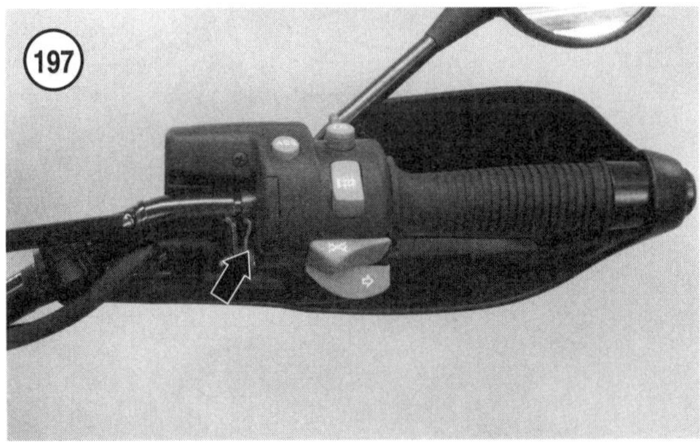

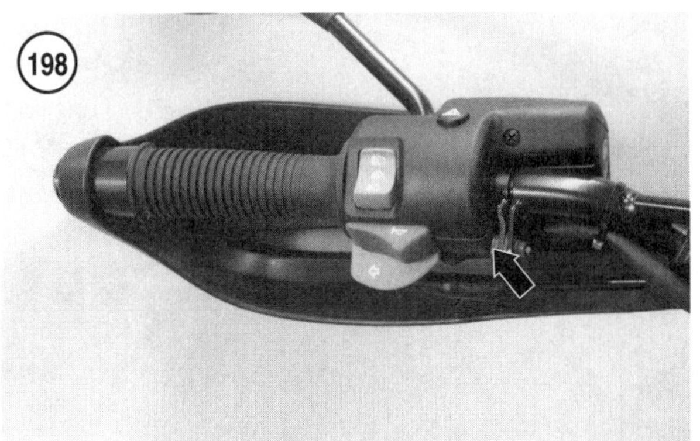

SWITCHES

Ignition Switch Removal/Installation

NOTE
Two new switch mounting bolts are required to install the ignition switch. Purchase these bolts prior to removing the switch.

1. Disconnect the negative battery cable as described in Chapter Three.
2. Remove the upper fork bridge as described in Chapter Twelve.
3. To remove the mounting bolts, perform the following:
   a. Center punch the exact center of the special bolt heads (**Figure 195**).
   b. Drill a small hole in the center of the bolt and use a screw extractor to loosen and remove the bolt. Remove both bolts.
   c. Remove the ignition switch (**Figure 196**) from the upper fork bridge.
4. Install the new ignition switch into the upper fork bridge and install *new* bolts. Tighten the bolts securely.
5. Install the upper fork bridge as described in Chapter Twelve.
6. Connect the negative battery cable as described in Chapter Three.
7. Check the ignition switch for proper operation.

Right and Left Combination Switches Removal/Installation

The right combination switch (**Figure 197**) contains the engine stop switch, starter button, right side turn signal switch, heated handlebar grip switch (optional) and light switch (on models so equipped).

The left side combination switch (**Figure 198**) contains the headlight high/low switch, the horn button, left turn signal switch, hazard warning flasher switch, and on RT models the windshield adjustment switch.

All of the switches are an integral part of their respective combination switch and if any portion of the switch is inoperative the entire switch must be replaced.

To remove either the switches refer to *Handlebar Controls* in Chapter Twelve.

Auxiliary Switches (R1100RS) Removal/Installation

1. Disconnect the negative battery cable as described in Chapter Three.

2. Partially remove the front fairing left inner panel (**Figure 199**) containing the auxiliary switches as described in Chapter Fifteen.

3. Remove the screws securing the auxiliary switch (**Figure 200**) to the inner panel. Remove the auxiliary switch from the inner panel.

4. Follow the auxiliary switch wire harness to the main wiring harness.

5. Disconnect the electrical connectors (**Figure 201**).

6. Remove any tie wraps securing the switch wire to the chassis and/or fairing brackets.

7. Carefully pull on the switch and wire harness and follow the electrical wires through the frame and remove the switch and wire harness.

8. Install a new switch assembly by reversing the removal steps while noting the following:

   a. Make sure all electrical connections are corrosion free and secure.

   b. Move the electrical wires back into position and secure with tie wraps.

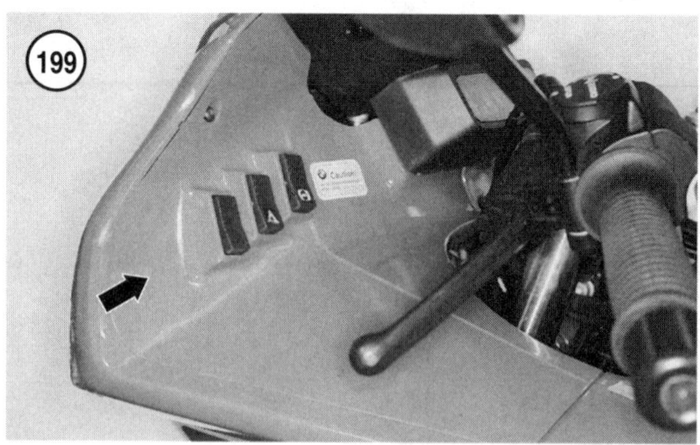

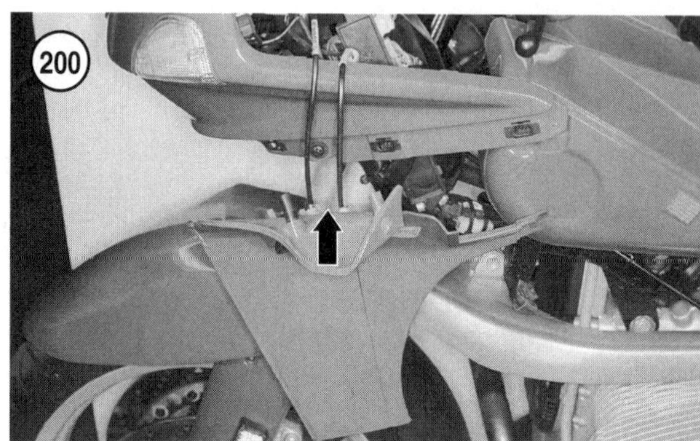

Front Brake Light Switch Removal/Installation

1. Disconnect the negative battery cable as described in Chapter Three.

2A. On early models, remove the screw (A, **Figure 202**) securing the master cylinder front cover and remove the cover (B).

2B. On later models, remove the screw (A, **Figure 203**) and separate the right side switch assembly (B).

3. Follow the front brake light switch wire harness to the main wiring harness.

4. Disconnect the electrical connector.

5. Remove any tie wraps securing the switch wire to the handlebar and/or fairing brackets.

6. Remove the screw securing the switch to the base of the master cylinder or to the brake lever.

7. Carefully pull on the switch and wire harness and follow the electrical wire along the handlebar and remove the switch and wire harness.

8. Install by reversing the removal steps while noting the following:

   a. Make sure all electrical connections are corrosion free and secure.

   b. Move the electrical wires back into position and secure with tie wraps.

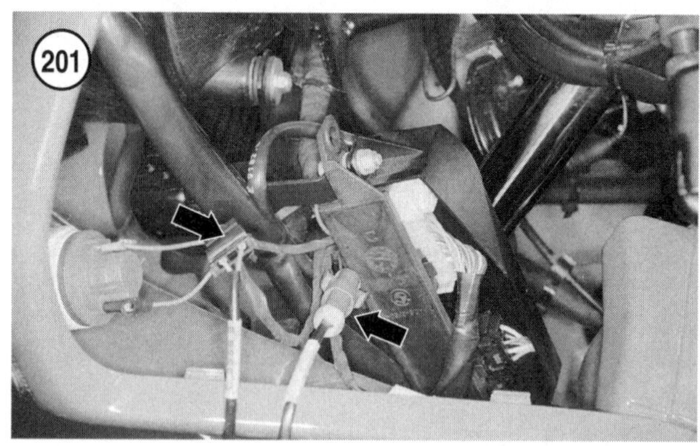

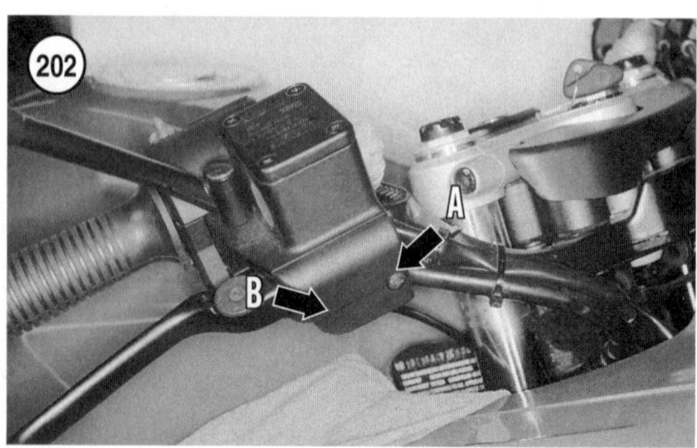

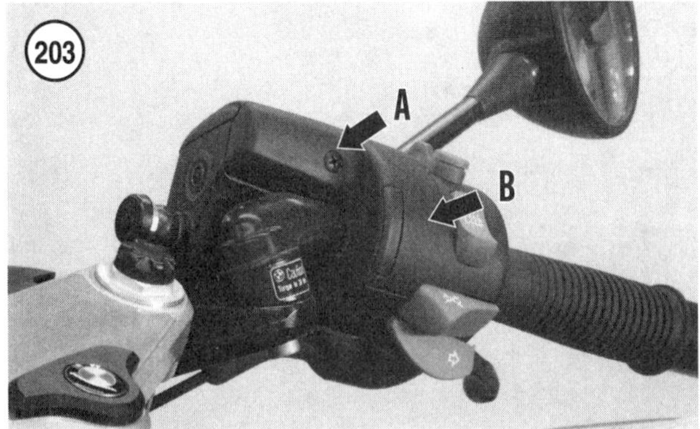

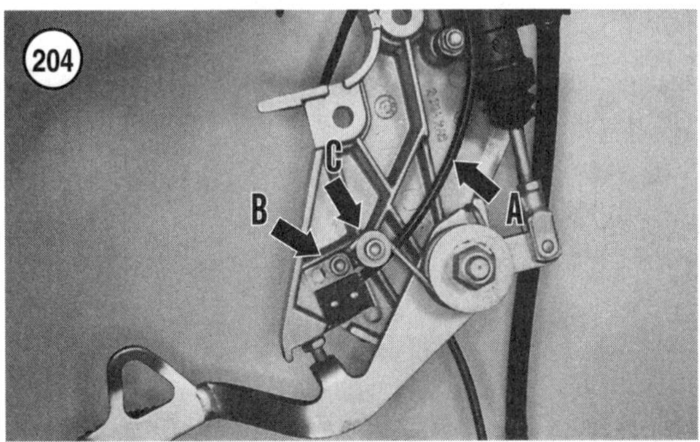

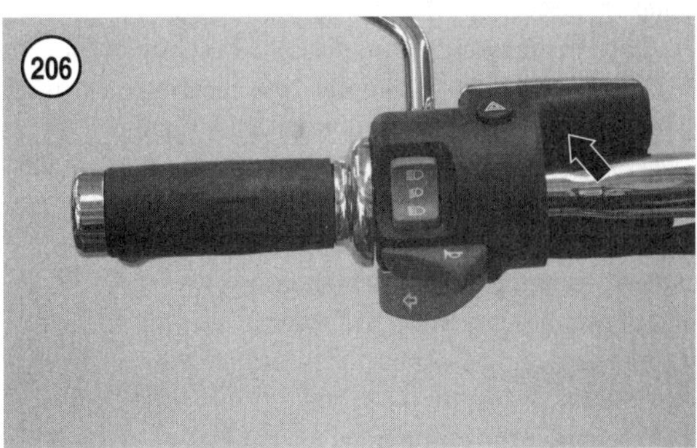

Rear Brake Light Switch Removal/Installation

1. Partially remove the front footpeg and bracket as described in Chapter Fifteen.
2. Follow the rear brake light switch wire harness (A, **Figure 204**, typical) to the main wiring harness.
3. Disconnect the electrical connector.
4. Remove any tie wraps securing the switch wire assembly to the front footpeg.
5. Remove the screw (B, **Figure 204**) securing the switch to the front footpeg assembly.
6. Carefully pull on the switch and wire harness and follow the wire along the footpeg and frame and remove the switch and wire harness.
7. Install by reversing the removal steps while noting the following:
   a. Install the wire harness under the rear brake pedal return spring as shown in C, **Figure 204**.
   b. Make sure all electrical connections are tight and free of corrosion.
   c. Move the electrical wires back into position and secure with tie wraps.

Clutch Interlock Switch Removal/Installation

1. Disconnect the negative battery cable as described in Chapter Three.

2A. On early models, perform the following:
   a. Remove the nut securing the clutch interlock switch (**Figure 205**) to the clutch lever bracket.
   b. Follow the clutch interlock switch wire harness to the main wiring harness.

2B. On later models, perform the following:
   a. Remove the screw and separate the left side switch assembly (**Figure 206**).
   b. Disconnect the switch from the clutch lever.
   c. Follow the clutch interlock switch wire harness to the main wiring harness.

3. Disconnect the electrical connector.
4. Remove any tie wraps securing the switch wire assembly to the handlebar and/or fairing brackets.
5. Carefully pull on the switch and wire and follow the wire harness along the handlebar and remove the switch and wire harness.
6. Install by reversing the removal steps while noting the following:
   a. Make sure all electrical connections are corrosion free and secure.
   b. Move the electrical wires back into position and secure with tie wraps.

Sidestand Interlock Switch Removal/Installation

The switch is attached to the backside of the sidestand.

1. Disconnect the negative battery cable as described in Chapter Three.

2A. On models so equipped, place the motorcycle on the centerstand with the rear wheel off of the ground.

2B. On models without a centerstand, place a suitable size jack under the engine to support the motorcycle with the rear wheel off the ground.

NOTE

__Figure 207__ is shown with some of the components removed from the engine for clarity.

3A. On early models, perform the following:

   a. Remove the screw securing the sidestand switch (A, **Figure 207**) to the sidestand.
   b. Remove any tie wraps securing the switch wire assembly to thc framc.
   c. Carefully pull on the switch and wire harness (B, **Figure 207**) along the frame and remove the switch and wire harness.

3B. On later models, perform the following:

   a. Move the sidestand to the raised position.
   b. Remove the snap ring (A, **Figure 208**) securing the switch to the post on the sidestand mounting bracket.
   c. Remove the switch (B, **Figure 208**) from the post.
   d. Remove any tie wraps securing the switch wire assembly to the frame.
   e. Follow the wire (C, **Figure 208**) from the switch back to where the electrical connector is located at the main wiring harness.

4. Disconnect the electrical connector.

5. Install by reversing the removal steps while noting the following:

   a. Make sure the electrical connection is corrosion free and secure.
   b. Move the electrical wire back into position and secure with tie wraps.

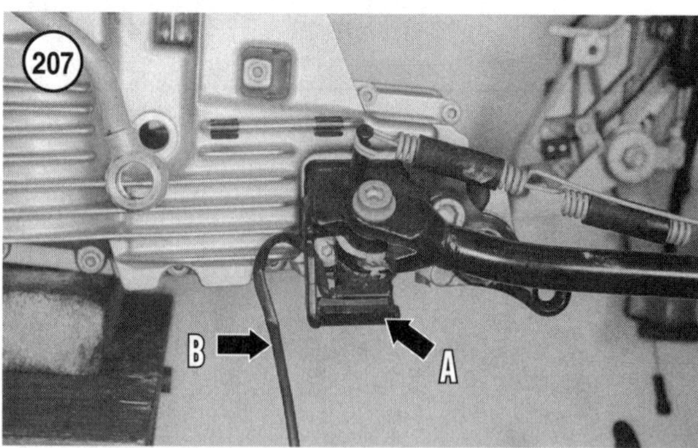

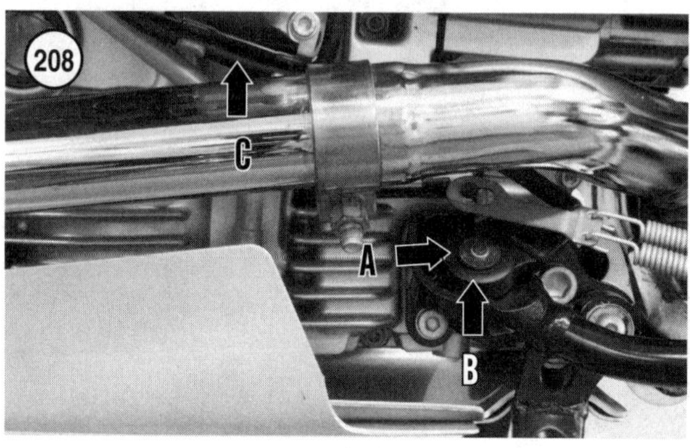

Neutral Switch and Gear Position Switch (Five-Speed Transmission) Removal/Installation

NOTE

If the motorcycle is equipped with the gear position switch, it is mounted on top of the neutral switch. Both switches are secured with the same two bolts and are removed at the same time. The switches can be replaced separately.

The gear position switch is located on the backside of the transmission housing. If the gear position on the instrument panel is incorrect or is not working at all, check all electrical connections. If the electrical connections are in acceptable condition, replace the switch.

The switch can be removed with the engine and transmission assembly in the frame. In the following procedure the engine and transmission are removed to better illustrate the steps.

1. Disconnect the negative battery cable as described in Chapter Three.
2. Remove the swing arm as described in Chapter Eleven.
3. Remove the bolts (A, **Figure 209**) securing the neutral switch and the gear position switch, if so equipped.
4. Unhook the electrical cable clamps (B, **Figure 209**) from the transmission housing bosses.
5. Remove the switch(es) (C, **Figure 209**) and electrical cable(s) from the transmission housing.
6. Follow the wire from the switch assemblies back to where the electrical connector is located at the main wiring harness.
7. Disconnect the electrical connector(s).

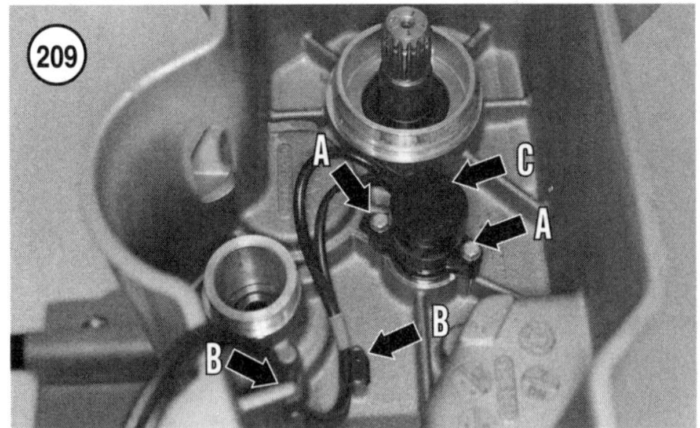

8. Remove any tie wraps securing the switch wire assembly to the frame.

NOTE

If replacing the neutral switch, also order the oil seal. It is not included with the new switch.

9. Install the switch(es) onto the transmission case and install the bolts (A, **Figure 209**). Tighten the bolts securely.

CAUTION

The electrical cable(s) must be secured properly to the transmission case bosses to keep them away from moving parts to avoid a possible short.

10. Install the electrical cable(s) and clamps (B, **Figure 209**) onto the transmission housing bosses.

11. Make sure all electrical connections are tight and free of corrosion.

12. Move the wires back into position and secure them with tie wraps.

13. Install the swing arm as described in Chapter Eleven.

Neutral/Gear Position Switch (Six-Speed Transmission) Removal/Installation

The neutral/gear position switch is located on the backside of the transmission housing. If the gear position on the instrument panel is incorrect or is not working at all, check all electrical connections. If the electrical connections are in acceptable condition, replace the switch.

The switch can be removed with the engine and transmission assembly in the frame.

1. Disconnect the negative battery cable as described in Chapter Three.

2. Remove the swing arm as described in Chapter Eleven.

NOTE

***Figure 210** shows switch location only. The switch has been removed to better illustrate the steps.*

3. Compress the spring securing the neutral/gear position switch to the backside of the transmission housing (**Figure 210**).

4. Unhook the electrical cable clamps from the transmission housing bosses.

5. Remove the switch and electrical cable from the transmission housing.

6. Follow the wire from the switch assembly back to where the electrical connector is located at the main wiring harness.

7. Disconnect the electrical connector.

8. Remove any tie wraps securing the switch wire assembly to the frame.

9. Install the switch onto the transmission housing. Push it in until it bottoms, then make sure the spring secures the switch to the transmission housing.

CAUTION

The electrical cable must be secured properly to the transmission housing bosses to keep it away from moving parts to avoid a possible short.

10. Make sure all electrical connections are tight and free of corrosion.

11. Move the wires back into position and secure them with tie wraps.

12. Install the swing arm as described in Chapter Eleven.

Oil Pressure Warning Switch Replacement

The oil pressure warning light on the instrument panel must come on when the ignition is turned on. As soon as the engine is started and the oil pressure rises to the correct level, the warning light should go out.

If the light fails to come on, check the bulb as described under *Instrument Panel* in this chapter. Replace the bulb if necessary.

If the oil warning light stays on after the engine is running, stop the engine and check the oil level as described under *Engine Oil Level* in Chapter Three. If the oil level is correct, the oil pressure switch may be faulty or the oil pressure may be low.

The oil pressure warning switch is located on the lower left side of the engine below the left cylinder.

1A. On models so equipped, remove the engine lower guard as described in Chapter Fifteen.

1B. On RS, RT and S models, remove the front fairing left lower side panel as described in Chapter Fifteen.

2. Remove the screw securing the electrical connector to the switch.

3. Turn the ignition switch on.

4. Have an assistant observe the oil pressure warning light on the instrument cluster.

5. Briefly touch the electrical connector to a good engine ground. The warning light should turn on. If the light still does not light, the switch is faulty and must be replaced.

6. Disconnect the negative battery cable as described in Chapter Three.

7. Unscrew the oil pressure switch (**Figure 211**) from the crankcase.

8. Apply a light coat of sealant to the upper portion of the switch threads.

9. Install the new oil pressure switch and tighten securely.

10. Attach the wire and screw to the switch. Make sure the connection is free from oil and corrosion. Tighten the screw securely.

11A. On models so equipped, install the engine lower guard as described in Chapter Fifteen.

11B. On RS, RT and S models, install the front fairing left lower side panel as described in Chapter Fifteen.

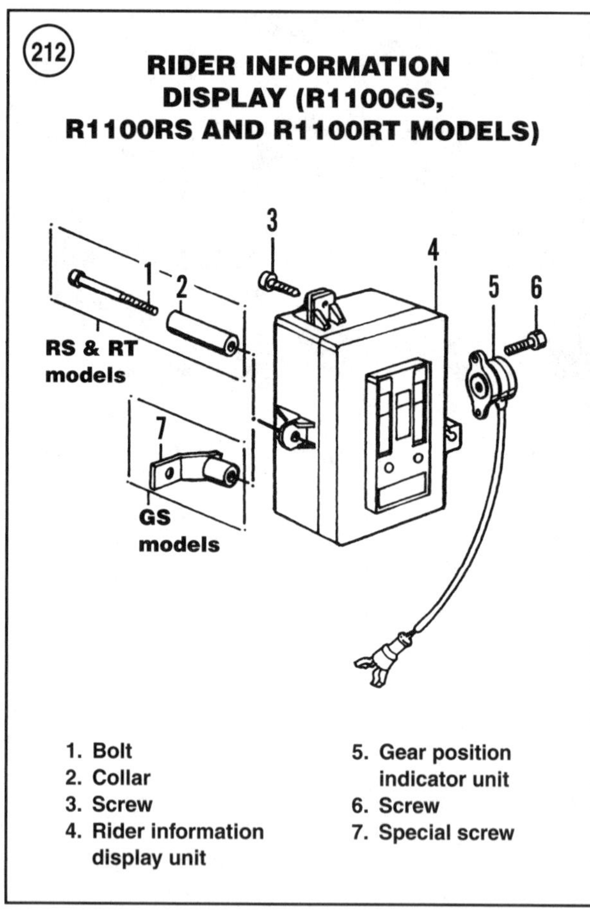

RIDER INFORMATION DISPLAY (1993-1998 GS, RS AND RT MODELS)

Removal/Installation

Refer to **Figure 212** for this procedure.

1. Disconnect the battery negative lead as described in Chapter Three.

2A. On GS models, perform the following:

a. Remove the instrument panel as described in this chapter.

b. Remove the screws securing the rider information display to the backside of the top cover.

2B. On RS and RT models, perform the following:

a. Partially remove the front fairing right inner panel containing the rider information display.

b. Remove the two short screws (A, **Figure 213**) and the long screw and collar (B). Remove the display unit (C, **Figure 213**).

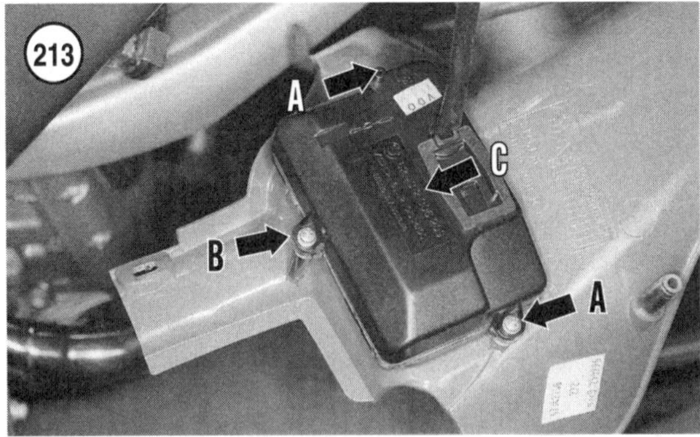

3. Follow the wire harness from the display back to where the electrical connector is located at the main wiring harness.

4. Disconnect the electrical connector (**Figure 214**, typical) and remove the display assembly.

5. Install by reversing the removal steps while noting the following:
   a. Make sure the electrical connection is tight and free of corrosion.
   b. Move the electrical wires back into position and tighten the screws securely.

INSTRUMENT PANEL

Removal/Installation

R850R and R1100R models

Refer to **Figure 215-217**.

1. Disconnect the negative battery cable as described in Chapter Three.

2. Remove the headlight case as described in this chapter.

3. On models equipped with the cowl panels, perform the following:
   a. Disconnect the front turn signal electrical connectors.
   b. Remove the nuts securing the front turn signals to the headlight bracket.
   c. Remove the screws securing the cowl panel on each side and remove both panels.

4. Remove the mounting screws and remove the trip reset knob assembly.

5. Remove the nuts and washers securing the speedometer to the housing.

6. Unscrew the speedometer cable from the base of the speedometer.

7. Disconnect the electrical connector from the speedometer.

8. Remove the trim panel.

9. Disconnect the indicator panel electrical connector from the wiring harness.

10. Remove the indicator panel.

11. On models equipped with the auxiliary instrument(s), perform the following:
   a. On the backside of the mounting bracket remove the bolts securing the instrument to the bracket.
   b. Carefully pull the instrument part way out of the bracket and disconnect the electrical connector.
   c. Remove the instrument and housing from the mounting bracket.

12. Install by reversing the removal steps while noting the following:
   a. Align the pegs on the base of the speedometer with the receptacles in the speedometer housing and install the speedometer.
   b. Tighten the screws and bolts securely. Do not overtighten the screws or bolts as the mounting bosses may be damaged.
   c. Make sure the electrical connectors are free of corrosion and are tight.

R1150R models

Refer to **Figure 218**.

1. Disconnect the battery negative lead as described in Chapter Three.

2. Remove the headlight lens and case (A, **Figure 219**) as described in this chapter.

3. Unscrew and disconnect the speedometer cable (**Figure 220**) from the backside of the speedometer.

4. Remove the screws securing the rear cover (B, **Figure 219**) and remove the rear cover.

5. Disconnect the lighting electrical connector for the speedometer and remove the speedometer (A, **Figure 221**).

(215)

INSTRUMENT PANEL AND SPEEDOMETER ASSEMBLY (R850R AND R1100R MODELS)

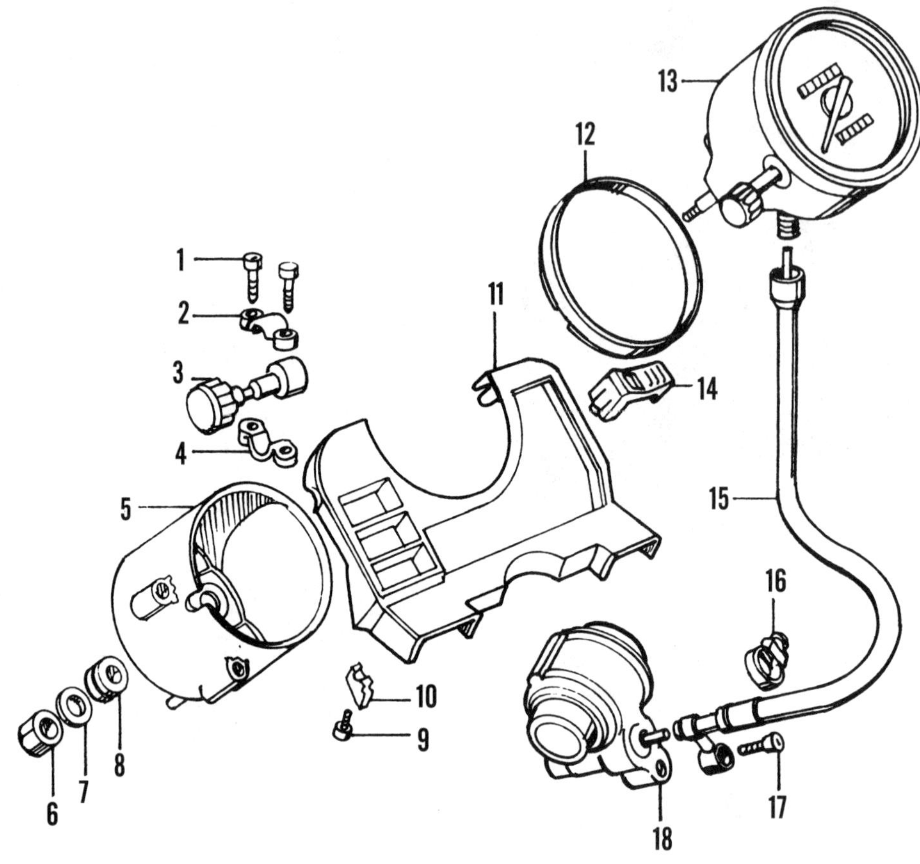

1. Bolt
2. Upper bracket
3. Reset knob
4. Lower bracket
5. Speedometer housing
6. Nut
7. Washer
8. Rubber grommet
9. Screw
10. Spacer
11. Trim panel
12. Damper ring
13. Speedometer
14. Switch cover
15. Speedometer cable
16. Support clip
17. Bolt
18. Speedometer drive unit

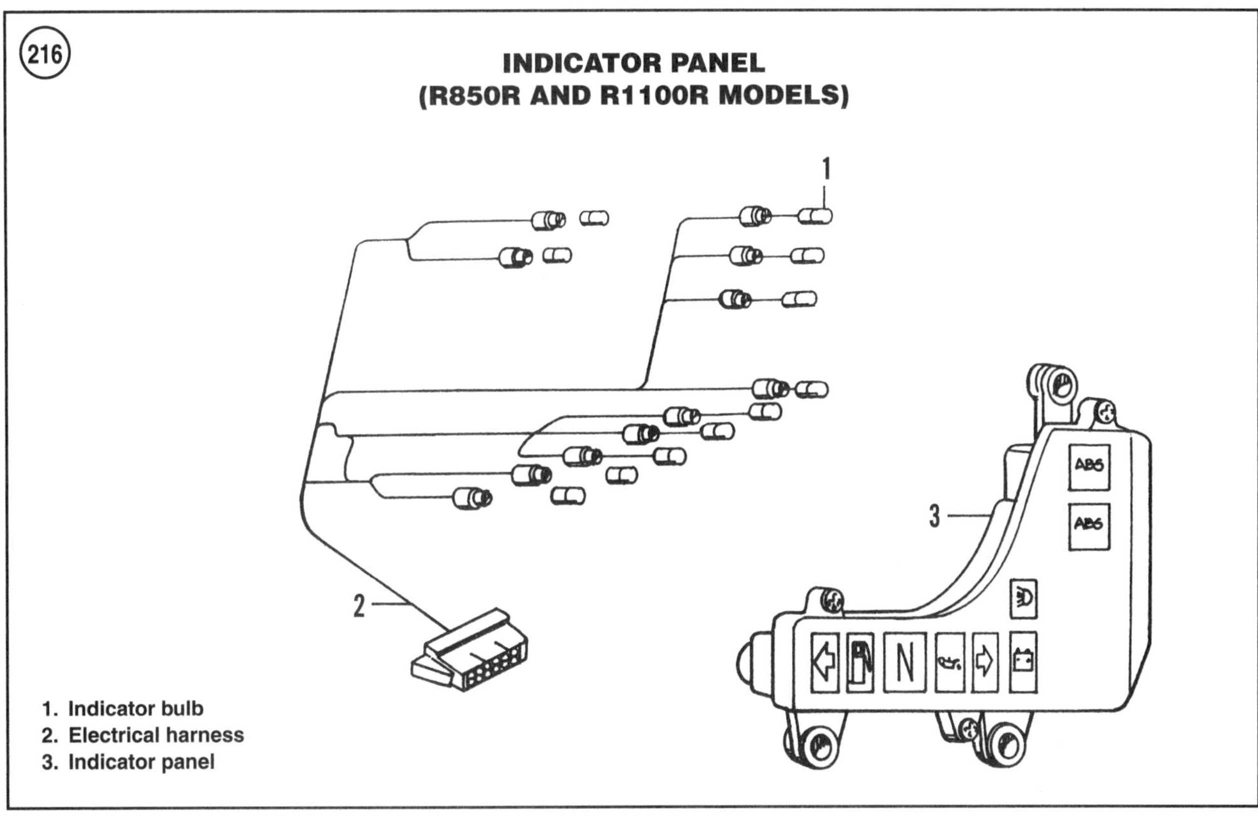

1. Indicator bulb
2. Electrical harness
3. Indicator panel

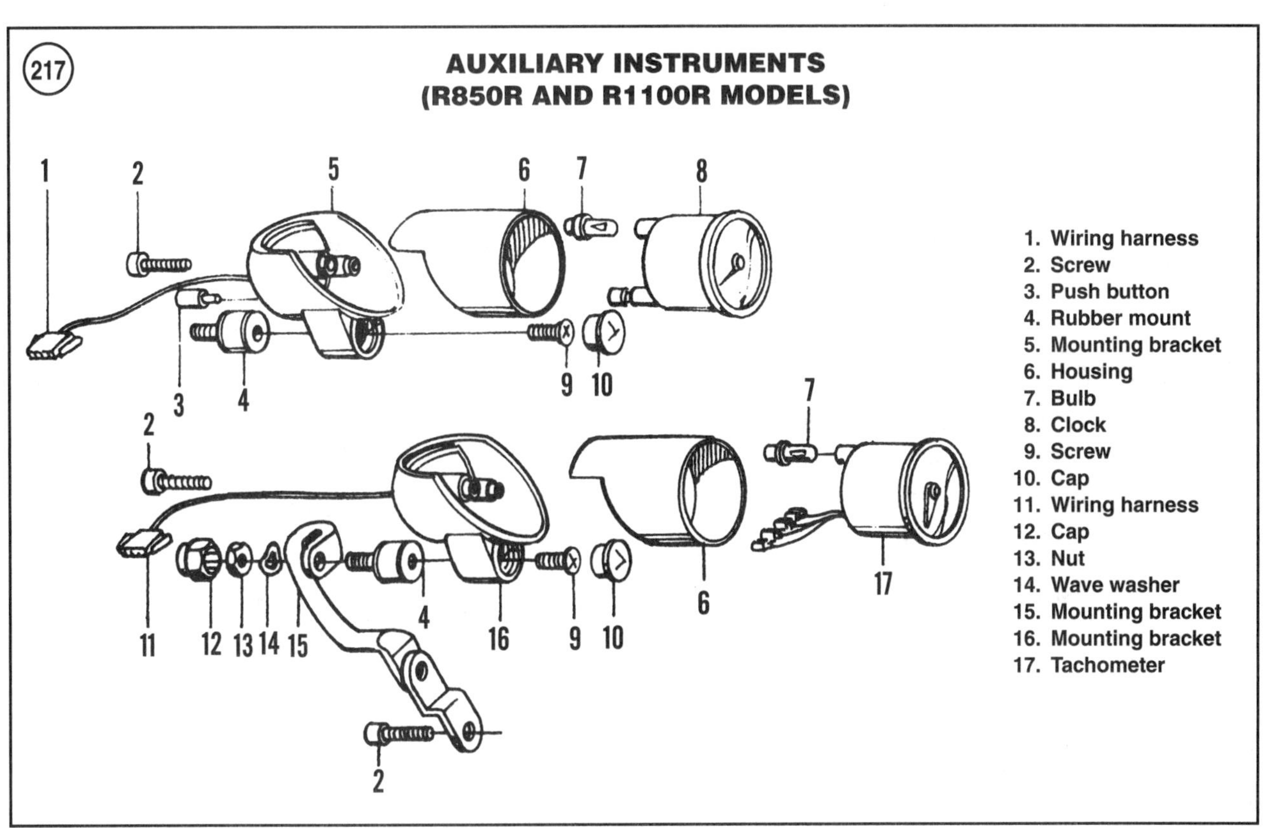

1. Wiring harness
2. Screw
3. Push button
4. Rubber mount
5. Mounting bracket
6. Housing
7. Bulb
8. Clock
9. Screw
10. Cap
11. Wiring harness
12. Cap
13. Nut
14. Wave washer
15. Mounting bracket
16. Mounting bracket
17. Tachometer

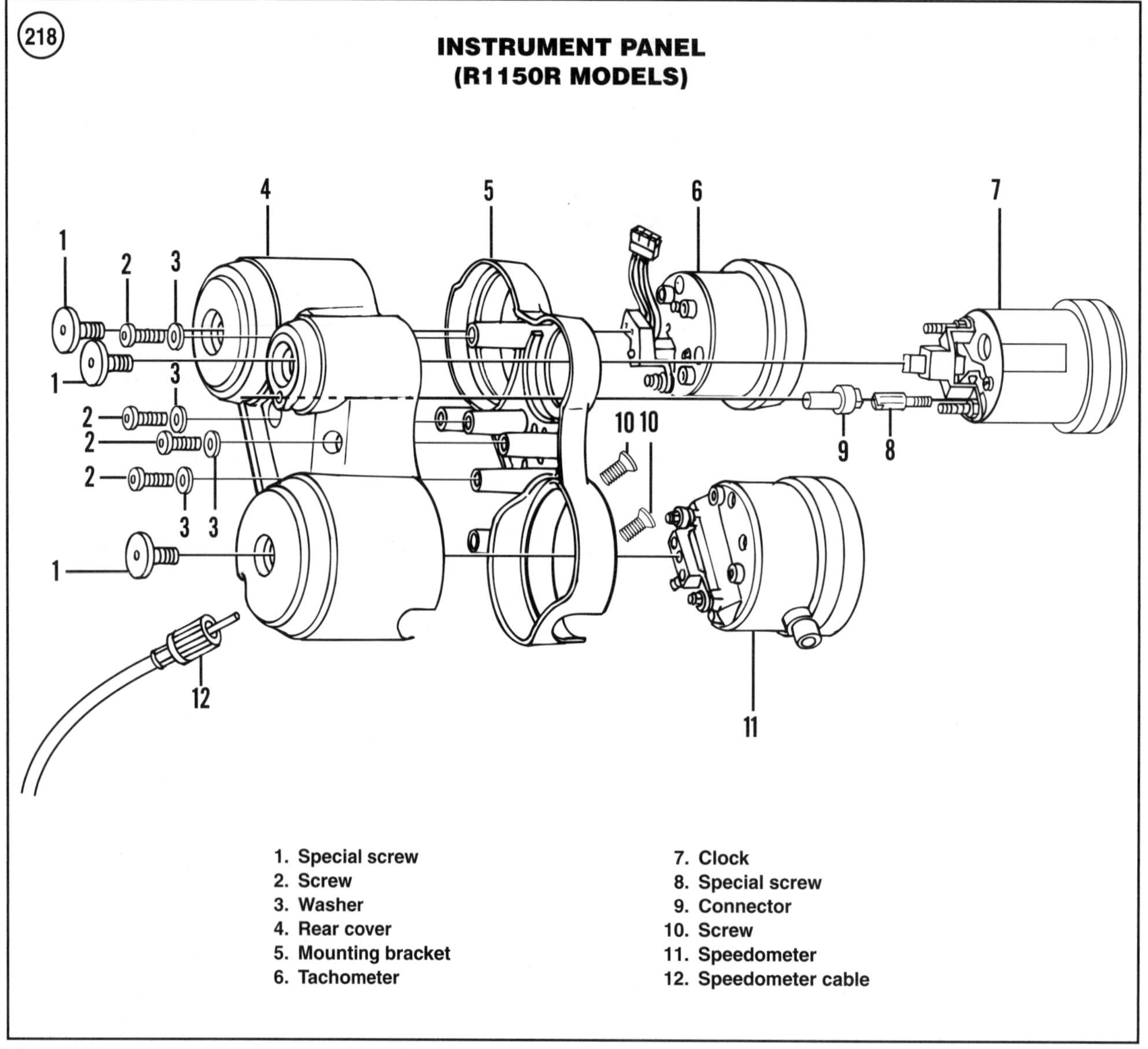

6. Disconnect the lighting electrical connector for the tachometer and remove the tachometer (B, **Figure 221**).

7. Disconnect the lighting electrical connector for the clock and remove the clock (C, **Figure 221**).

8. Working under the instrument panel, remove the two screws and washers securing the mounting bracket to the under side of the upper fork bridge.

9. On the front side of the mounting bracket, perform the following:

   a. Very carefully, pry out both turn signal indicator caps (D, **Figure 221**).

   b. Carefully push both turn signal indicator LED units inward and out of the mounting bracket.

10. Directly under the both turn signal indicator cap locations, remove the two screws securing the mounting bracket to the top surface of the upper fork bridge.

11. Remove the mounting bracket assembly from the upper fork bridge.

12. Install by reversing the removal steps while noting the following:

   a. Tighten the screws securely. Do not overtighten the screws as the mounting bosses may be damaged.

   b. Make sure the electrical connectors are corrosion free and secure.

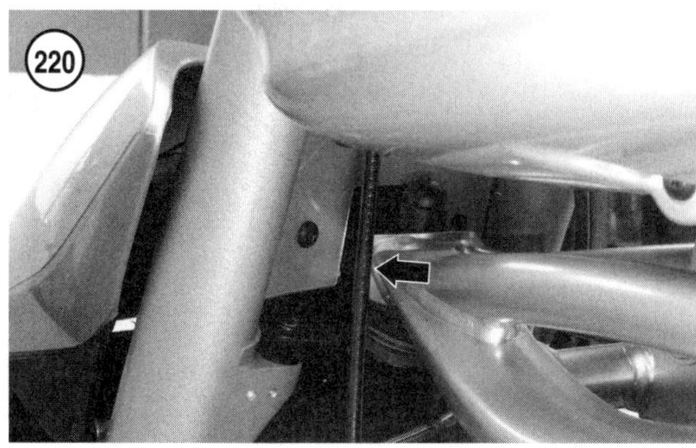

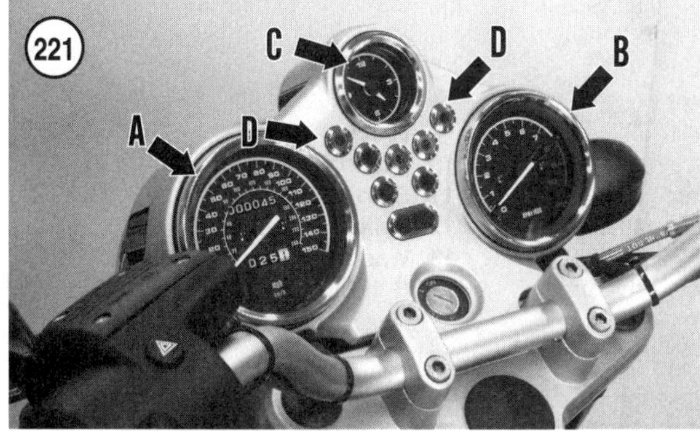

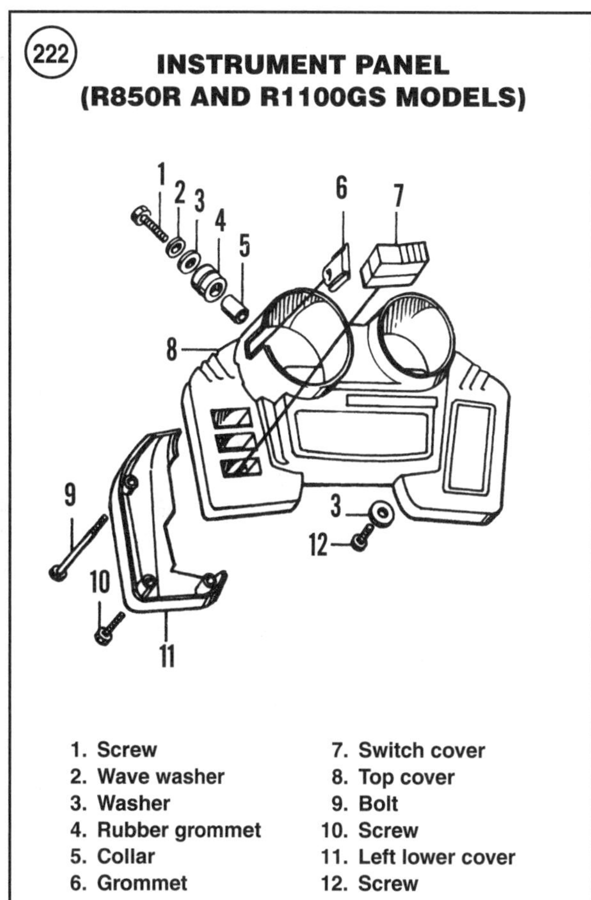

1. Screw
2. Wave washer
3. Washer
4. Rubber grommet
5. Collar
6. Grommet
7. Switch cover
8. Top cover
9. Bolt
10. Screw
11. Left lower cover
12. Screw

R850GS and R1100GS models

Refer to **Figure 222** and **Figure 223**.

1. Disconnect the battery negative lead as described in Chapter Three.

2. Remove the headlight lens assembly as described in this chapter.

3. Unscrew and disconnect the speedometer cable from the backside of the speedometer.

4. Remove the screws and remove the lower left cover from the instrument panel top cover.

5. Carefully disconnect the electrical connectors from both instruments and the indicator panel.

6. If so equipped, disconnect the electrical connector for the rider's information display unit.

7. Working within the headlight housing, remove the two nuts securing the instrument panel to the headlight housing and remove the instrument panel (**Figure 224**).

8. To remove the meters from the case, perform the following:

   a. Remove the nuts and lockwashers securing the meters to the top cover and remove the meters.

   b. Remove the screws and washers securing the indicator panel to the top cover and remove the panel.

9. Install by reversing these removal steps while noting the following:

   a. Tighten the screws securely. Do not overtighten since the mounting bosses may be damaged.

   b. Make sure the electrical connectors are corrosion free and secure.

223

INSTRUMENTS (R1100GS AND R1100RS MODELS)

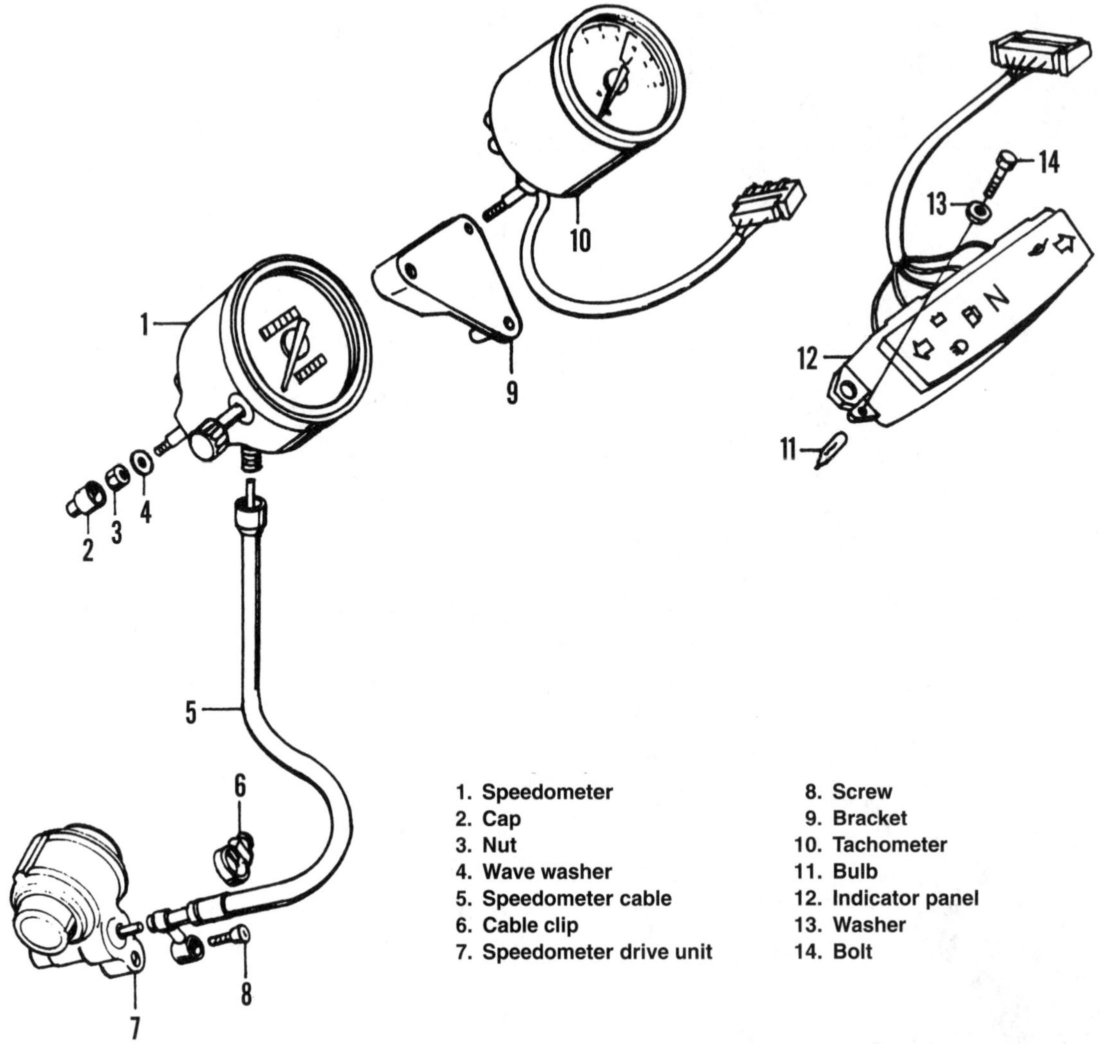

1. Speedometer
2. Cap
3. Nut
4. Wave washer
5. Speedometer cable
6. Cable clip
7. Speedometer drive unit
8. Screw
9. Bracket
10. Tachometer
11. Bulb
12. Indicator panel
13. Washer
14. Bolt

R1150GS models

Refer to **Figure 225**.

1. Disconnect the negative battery cable as described in Chapter Three.
2. Remove the headlight assembly as described in this chapter.
3. Carefully pull the bulb/socket assemblies (**Figure 226**) from the backside of the speedometer and tachometer.
4. Remove the Allen bolt and washer (**Figure 227**) securing the instrument panel and mounting bracket to the headlight mounting bracket.

224

225

**INSTRUMENT PANEL
(R1150GS MODELS)**

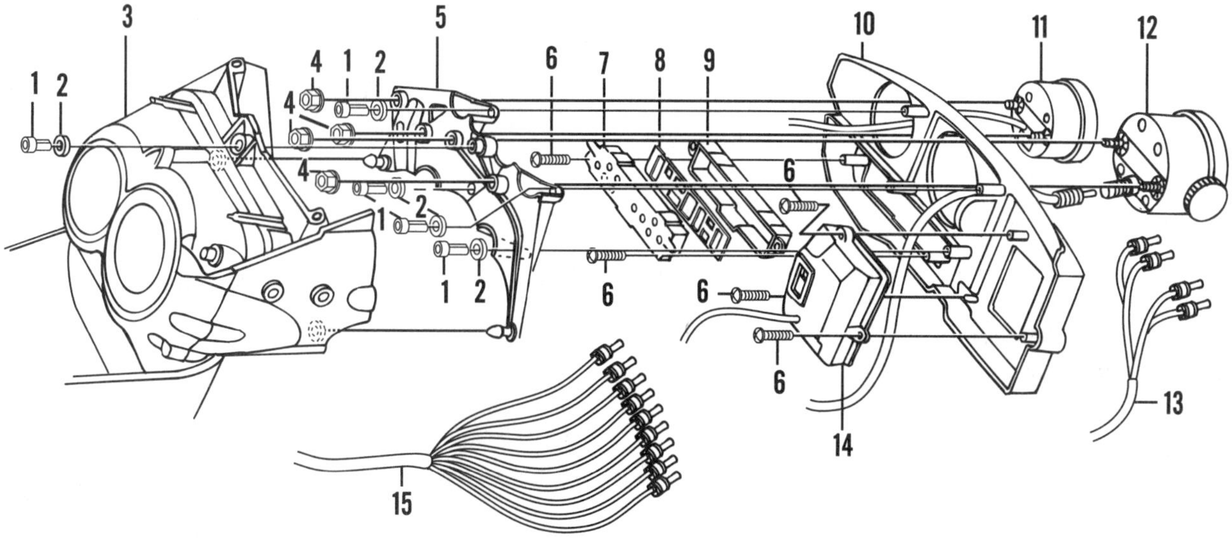

1. Screw
2. Washer
3. Headlight mounting bracket
4. Nut
5. Mounting bracket
6. Screw
7. Indicator light assembly
8. Screen
9. Lens
10. Top cover
11. Tachometer
12. Speedometer
13. Wiring harness
14. Rider information display
15. Wiring harness (indicator lights)

226

227

5. Pull out on the lower corner posts (**Figure 228**) of the instrument panel mounting bracket and release the mounting posts from the headlight mounting bracket.
6. Unscrew and disconnect the speedometer cable (A, **Figure 229**) from the backside of the speedometer.
7. Remove the screws securing the indicator light assembly (B, **Figure 229**) to the top cover.
8. On model so equipped, remove the screws securing the rider information display to the top cover.
9. Remove the instrument panel (**Figure 230**) from the headlight mounting bracket.
10. If necessary, remove the speedometer and tachometer from the top cover and the mounting bracket.
11. Install by reversing these removal steps while noting the following:
   a. Tighten the Allen bolt securely. Do not overtighten since the mounting boss may be damaged.
   b. Make sure the electrical connectors are corrosion free and secure.

RS models

Refer to **Figure 223** and **Figure 231**.

1. Disconnect the negative battery cable as described in Chapter Three.
2. Remove both fairing front inner panels (**Figure 232**) as described in Chapter Fifteen.
3. Rotate the windshield adjuster knob (**Figure 233**) all the way *counterclockwise*, disconnect and remove it.
4. Unscrew and disconnect the speedometer cable (**Figure 234**) from the backside of the speedometer.
5. Remove the bolt and washer (**Figure 235**) on each side securing the meter case to the mounting bracket.
6. Place a shop cloth or towel (**Figure 236**) over the upper fork bridge to protect the instrument panel.
7. Pull the meter case part way out (**Figure 237**) and carefully disconnect the electrical connectors from the speedometer, tachometer and the indicator panel.
8. To remove the meters from the case, perform the following:
   a. Remove the nuts and lockwashers securing the meters to the meter case and remove the meters.
   b. Remove the screws and washers securing the indicator panel to the top cover and remove the panel.
9. Install by reversing these removal steps while noting the following:
   a. Tighten the bolts and nuts securely. Do not overtighten since the mounting bosses may be damaged.
   b. Make sure the electrical connectors are corrosion free and secure.

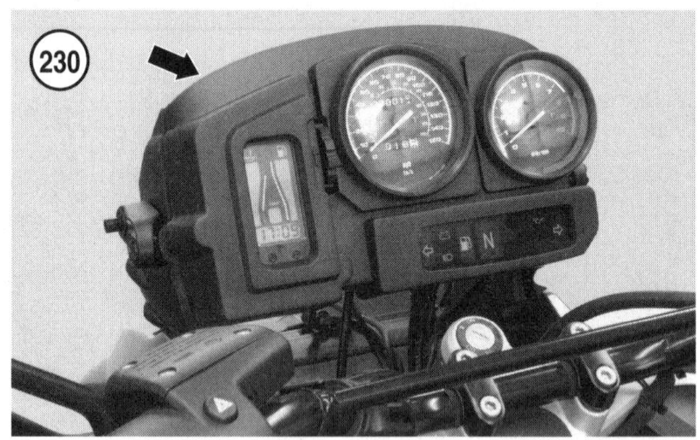

RT models

Refer to **Figure 238**.

1. Disconnect the negative battery cable as described in Chapter Three.
2. Remove the windshield (A, **Figure 239**) and the front fairing inner panel (B) as described in Chapter Fifteen.
3. Remove the four bolts from each side securing the meter case (C, **Figure 239**) to the mounting bracket.
4. Pull the meter case part way out and perform the following:

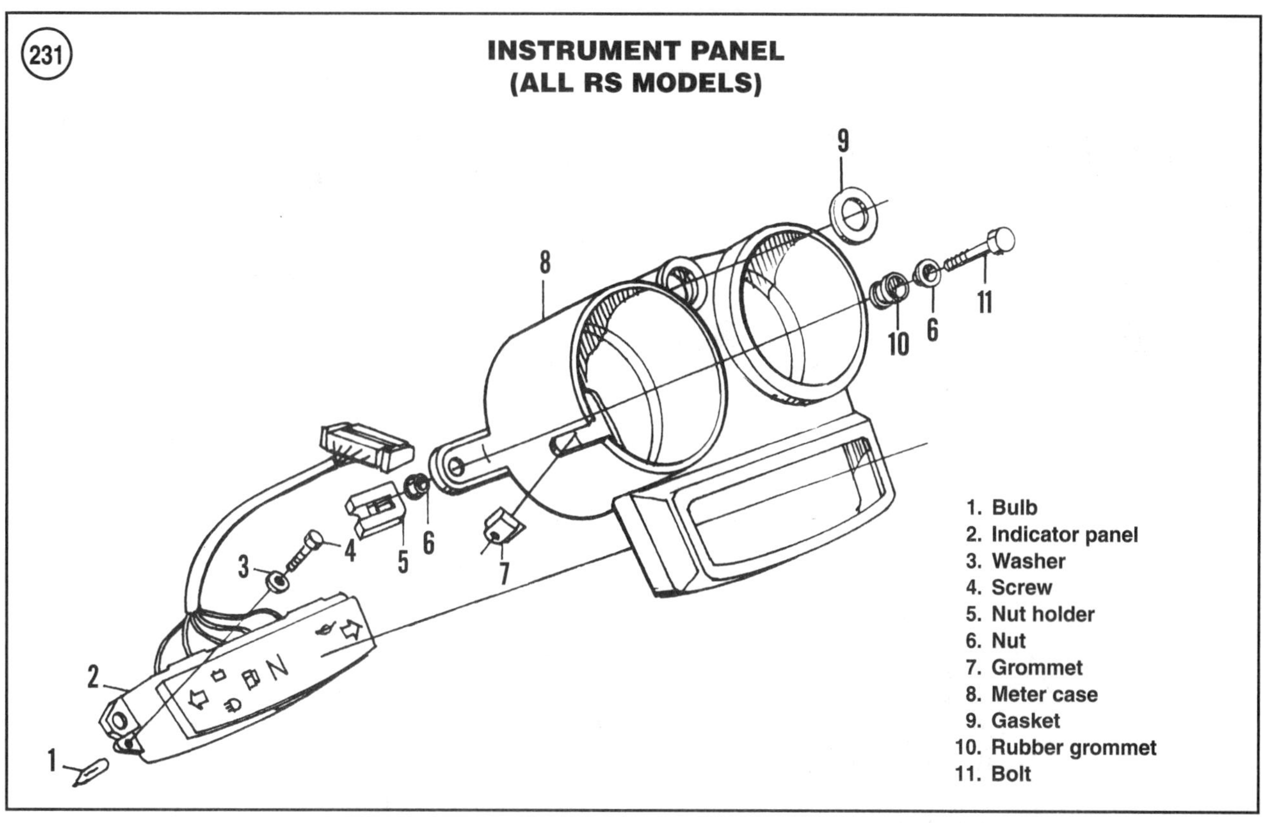
231
INSTRUMENT PANEL
(ALL RS MODELS)
1. Bulb
2. Indicator panel
3. Washer
4. Screw
5. Nut holder
6. Nut
7. Grommet
8. Meter case
9. Gasket
10. Rubber grommet
11. Bolt

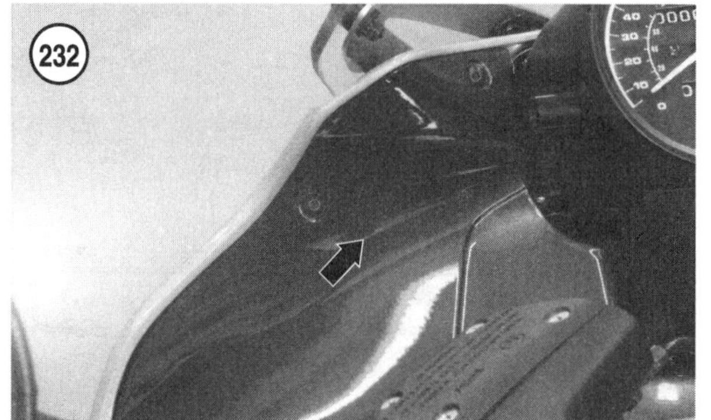
232

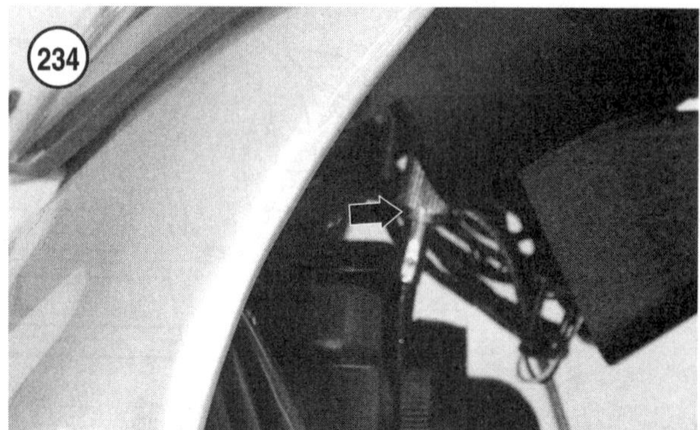
234

233

235

236

237

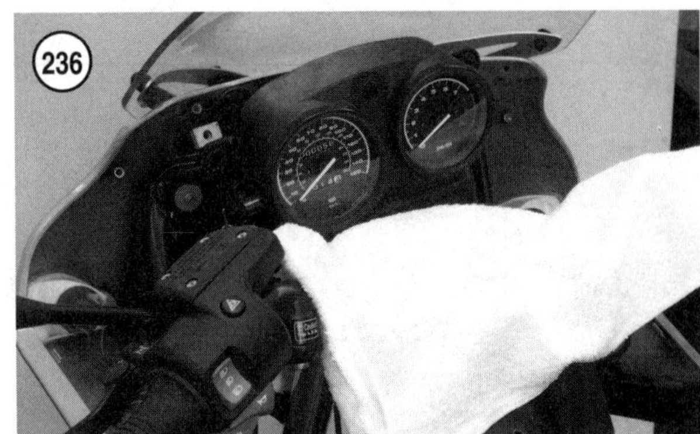

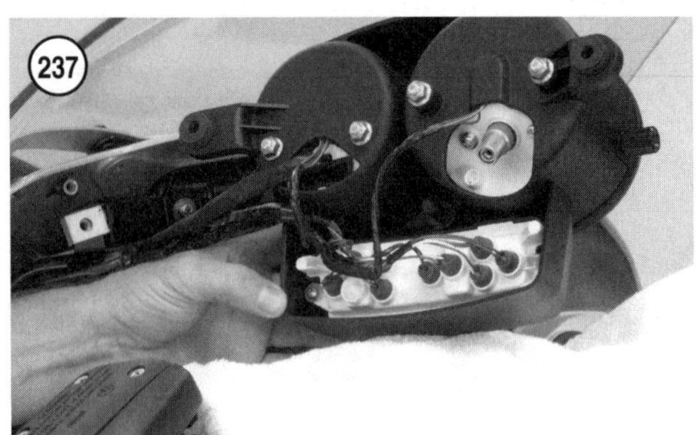

238

**INSTRUMENT PANEL
(ALL RT MODELS)**

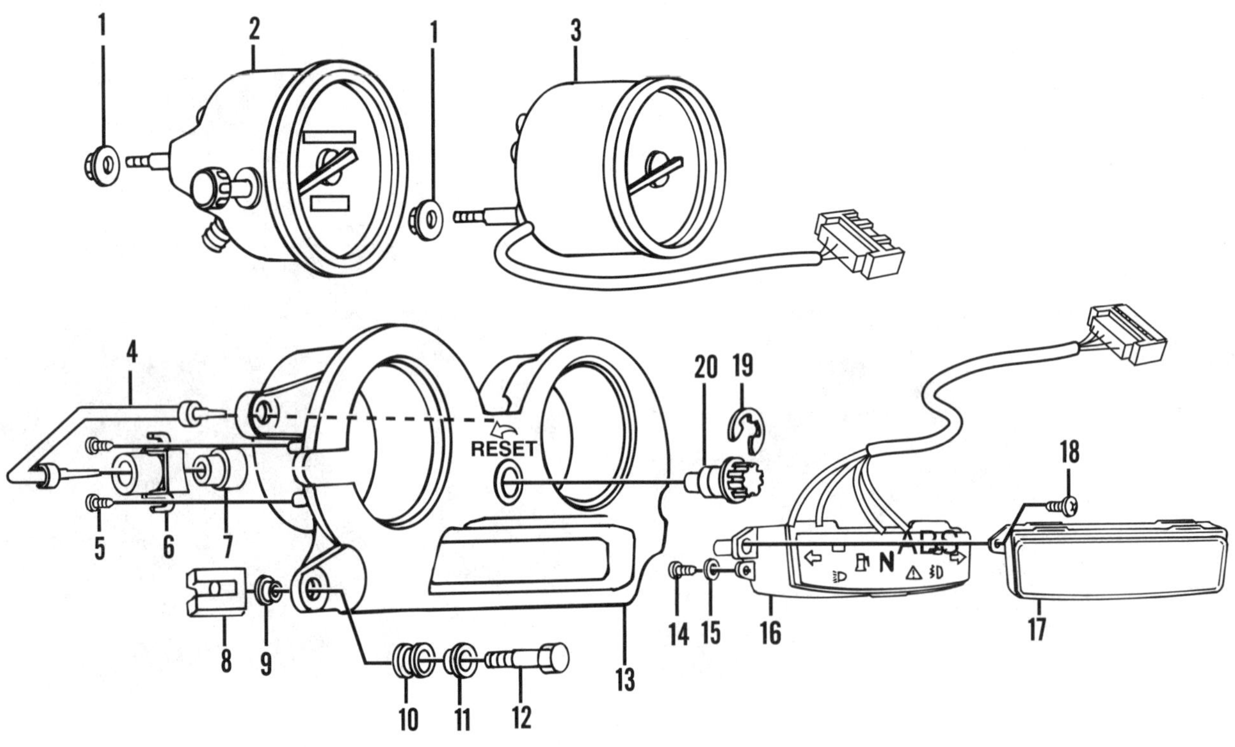

1. Nut
2. Speedometer
3. Tachometer
4. Odometer reset cable
5. Screw
6. Housing
7. Grommet
8. Special nut
9. Collar
10. Rubber grommet
11. Collar
12. Bolt
13. Case
14. Screw
15. Washer
16. Indicator panel
17. Lens cover
18. Screw
19. E-clip
20. Odometer reset knob

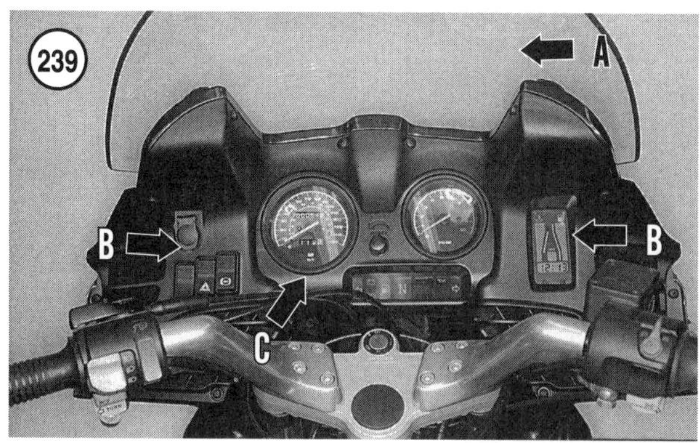

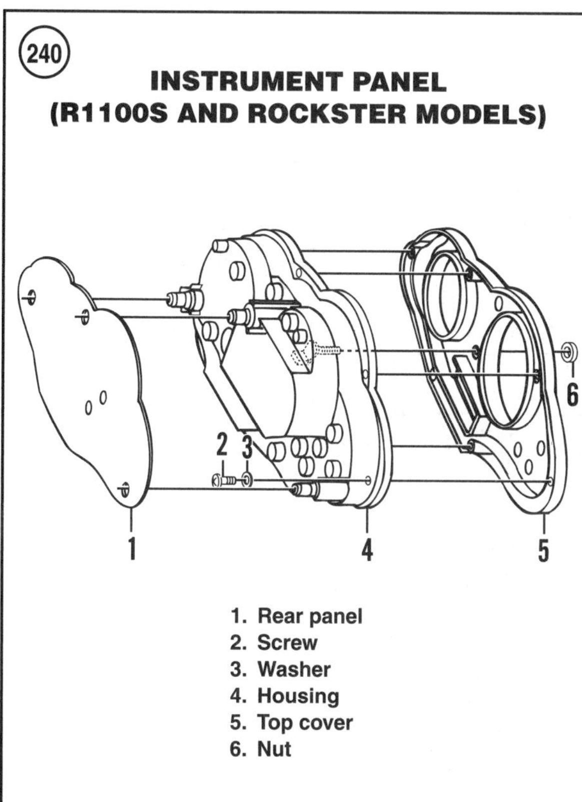

INSTRUMENT PANEL (R1100S AND ROCKSTER MODELS)

1. Rear panel
2. Screw
3. Washer
4. Housing
5. Top cover
6. Nut

a. Unscrew and disconnect the speedometer cable from the backside of the speedometer.

b. Carefully disconnect the electrical connectors from the meters and the indicator panel.

5. To remove the meters from the case, perform the following:

a. Remove the nuts and lockwashers securing the meters to the meter case and remove the meters.

b. Remove the screws and washers securing the indicator panel to the top cover and remove the panel.

6. Install by reversing these removal steps while noting the following:

a. Tighten the bolts securely. Do not overtighten since the mounting bosses may be damaged.

b. Make sure the electrical connectors are corrosion free and secure.

S models

Refer to **Figure 240**.

1. Disconnect the negative battery cable as described in Chapter Three.
2. Remove both side fairing panels as described in Chapter Fifteen.
3. Remove the windshield, the front fairing and both side mirrors (A, **Figure 241**) as described in Chapter Fifteen.
4. On the right side, open the central electrical module.
5. Locate and disconnect the electrical connector and the fuse for the instrument panel.
6. Working under the front fairing mounting bracket, disconnect the three special fasteners from the plastic mounting posts on the instrument panel housing.
7. Pull straight up and remove the instrument panel (B, **Figure 241**) and wiring harness from the mounting bracket.
8. Install by reversing these removal steps while noting the following:

a. Push the three special fasteners all the way onto the mounting posts to secure the panel in place.

b. Make sure the electrical connector is corrosion free and secure.

C models

Refer to **Figure 242**.

1. Disconnect the negative battery cable as described in Chapter Three.
2. Remove the fuel tank as described in Chapter Nine.
3. Follow the wiring harness from the instrument panel to the electrical connector panel (**Figure 243**) and disconnect the instrument panel wiring harness connector.

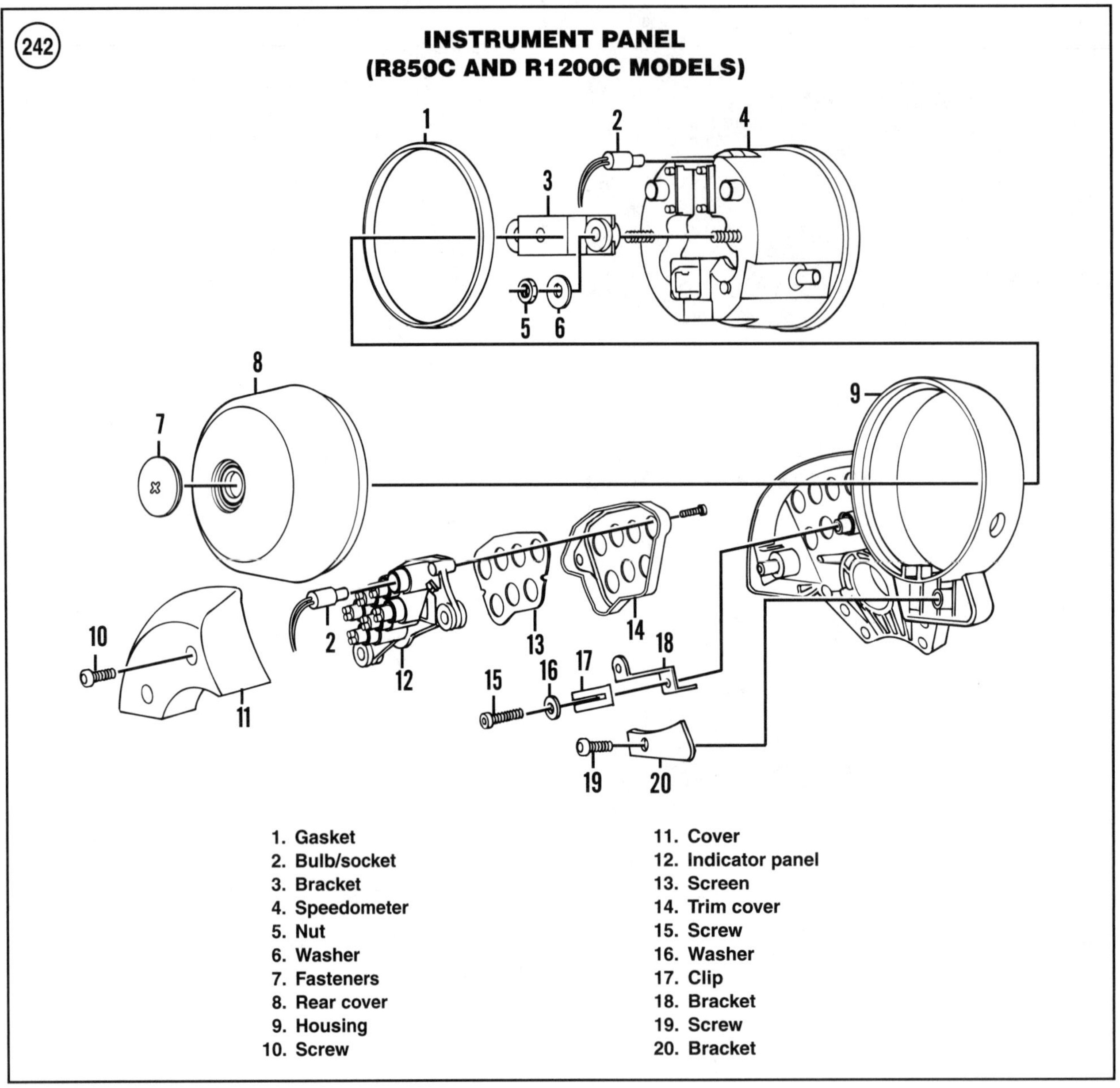

4. At the central electrical control box, remove the fuse for the instrument panel.

5. Remove the four bolts (**Figure 244**) securing the instrument panel to the upper fork bridge.

6. Pull straight up and remove the instrument panel and wiring harness from the mounting bracket.

7. To remove the speedometer from the housing, perform the following:

   a. Remove the screw and the trip reset knob from the side of the speedometer.

   b. Unscrew the fastener from the backside of the rear cover and remove the rear cover.

   c. Disconnect the electrical connector and the LED/socket from the speedometer.

   d. Make sure everything is disconnected from the speedometer, then remove the speedometer from the housing.

8. Install by reversing these removal steps while noting the following:

   a. Tighten the screws securely.

   b. Make sure the electrical connectors are corrosion free and secure.

243

244

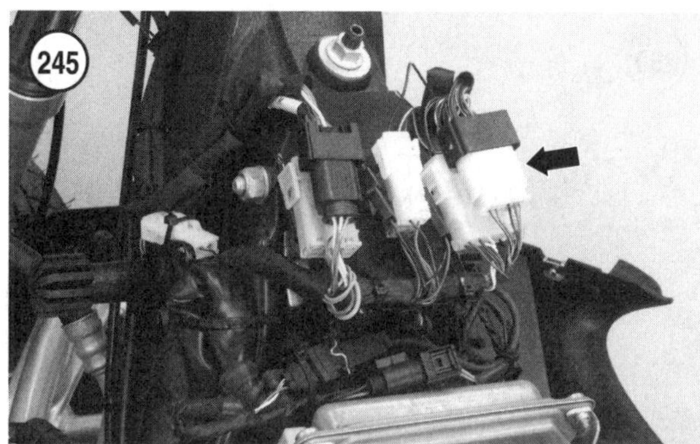

245

246

247

Rockster models

1. Disconnect the negative battery cable as described in Chapter Three.
2. Remove the fuel tank as described in Chapter Nine.
3. Remove the headlight case as described under *Headlight Case Assembly Removal/Installation* in this chapter.
4. Follow the wiring harness from the instrument panel to the electrical connector panel (**Figure 245**) on top of the frame and disconnect the wiring harness connector.
5. At the central electrical control box, remove the fuse for the instrument panel.
6. Working under the headlight mounting bracket, disconnect the three special fasteners from the plastic mounting posts on the instrument panel housing.
7. Pull straight up and remove the instrument panel (**Figure 246**) and wiring harness from the mounting bracket.
8. Install by reversing these removal steps while noting the following:
   a. Push the three special fasteners all the way onto the mounting posts to secure the panel in place.
   b. Make sure the electrical connector is corrosion free and secure.

CENTRAL ELECTRICAL EQUIPMENT BOX OR MODULES

The central electrical equipment box or modules houses the relays and fuses used to operate and protect the various electrical systems within the motorcycle. These relays and fuses are located on the top surface of the central electrical equipment box, or modules.

On R1100S models, the central electrical equipment modules are located on each side of the frame rail under the fuel tank. On all models other than R1100S, the central electrical equipment box is located either under the seat (**Figure 247**) or under the fuel tank.

RELAYS

BMW does not provide service information for the relays. If a relay is suspect, thoroughly inspect the circuit prior to replacing the relay.

Replacement

S models

1. Remove the fuel tank as described in Chapter Nine.
2. Remove the both faring side panels as described in Chapter Fifteen.
3. Remove the relay(s) from the equipment module(s).
4. Install by reversing these removal steps. Make sure the electrical connector(s) is corrosion free and secure.

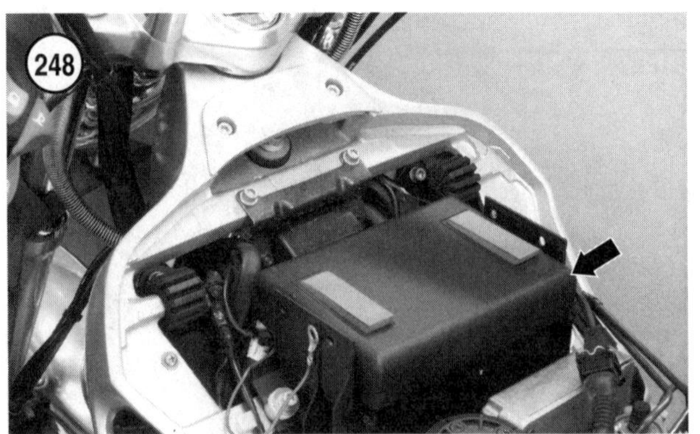
248

249

C models

1. Remove the Motronic control unit from the top cover as described in Chapter Nine.
2. Remove the top cover (**Figure 248**).
3. Remove the relay(s) (**Figure 249**) from the equipment box.
4. Install by reversing these removal steps. Make sure the electrical connector(s) is corrosion free and secure.

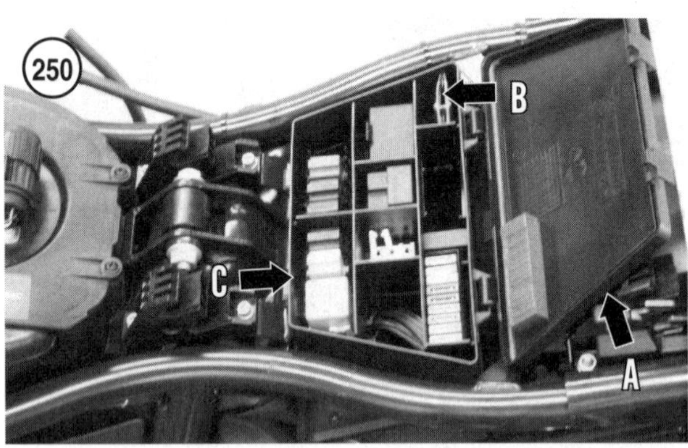

250

All models except S and C

1. Remove the seat(s) as described in Chapter Fifteen.
2. Open the cover (A, **Figure 250**) from the equipment box.
3. Use the relay removal tool (B, **Figure 250**) provided in the equipment box and remove the relay(s) (C).
4. Install by reversing these removal steps. Make sure the electrical connectors are corrosion free and secure.

251

FUSES

All models are equipped with a series of fuses to protect the electrical system. The number of fuses varies depending on the model and year and are in different locations. Refer to the wiring diagrams at the end of the manual.

Whenever a fuse blows, find the reason for the failure before replacing the fuse. Usually the trouble is a short circuit in the wiring. This may be caused by worn-through insulation or a disconnected wire shorted to ground. Check the circuit that the fuse protects.

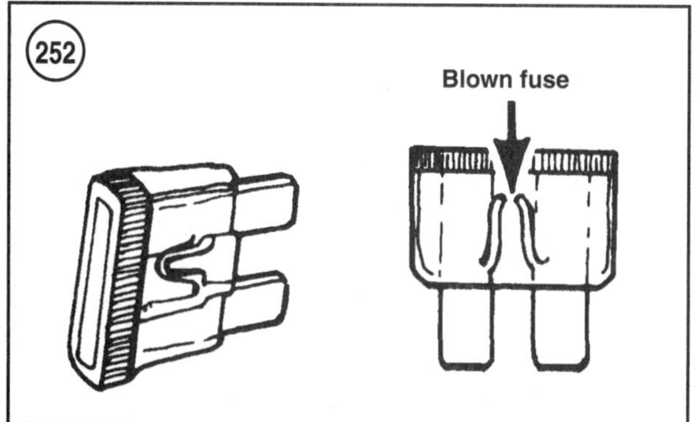

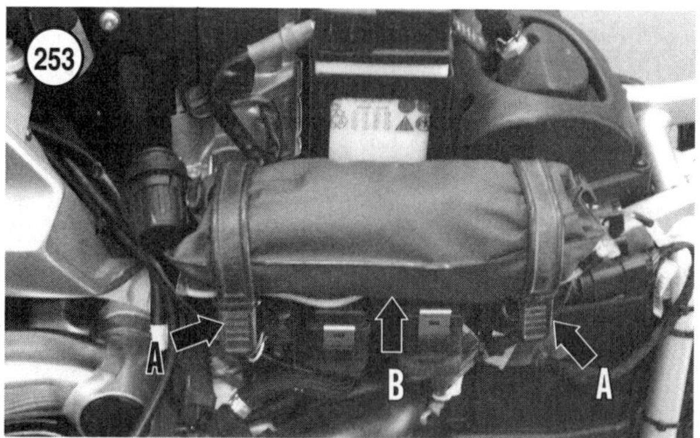

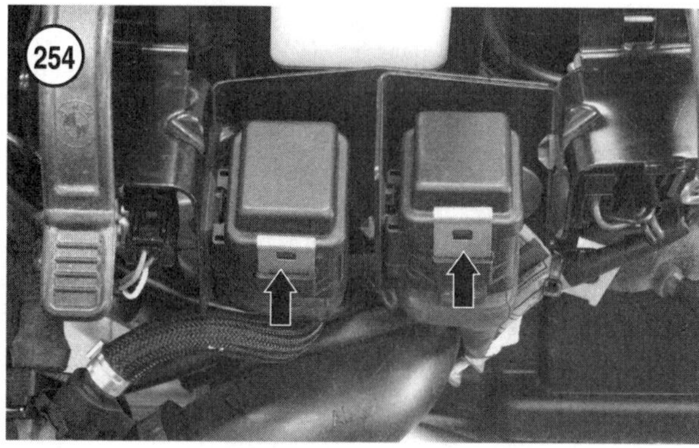

Replacement

All models except S and C

1. Remove the seat(s) as described in Chapter Fifteen.
2. Open the cover (A, **Figure 251**) from the equipment box.
3. Remove the fuse(s) (B, **Figure 251**) from the fuse box and inspect it. If the fuse is blown, there will be a break in the element as shown in **Figure 252**.
4. Install a new fuse and push it all the way down until it seats completely.
5. Install by reversing these removal steps. Make sure the electrical connectors are free of corrosion and are tight.
6. Install the cover onto the equipment box and make sure it is secure to keep out moisture.
7. Install the seat(s) as described in Chapter Fifteen.

S models

NOTE

There is a fuse box on each side of the frame above the central electrical modules. The only fuse in the right side fuse box is for the heated handlebar grips.

1. Remove the seat as described in Chapter Fifteen.
2. Remove the fuel tank as described in Chapter Nine.
3. Remove the both fairing side panels as described in Chapter Fifteen.
4. Release the hook and remove the fuse box cover.
5. Remove the fuse(s) from the fuse box and inspect it. If the fuse is blown, there will be a break in the element as shown in **Figure 252**.
6. Install a new fuse and push it all the way down until it seats completely.
7. Install the cover onto the fuse box and secure with the strap to keep out moisture.
8. Install the both faring side panels as described in Chapter Fifteen.
9. Install the fuel tank as described in Chapter Nine.
10. Install the seat as described in Chapter Fifteen.

C models

1. Remove the seat as described in Chapter Fifteen.
2. Remove the fuel tank as described in Chapter Nine.
3. Unhook the straps (A, **Figure 253**) and remove the tool kit (B) from the brackets.
4. Release the hook(s) (**Figure 254**) and remove the fuse box cover(s) (**Figure 255**).

5. Remove the fuse(s) (**Figure 256**) from the fuse box and inspect it. If the fuse is blown, there will be a break in the element as shown in **Figure 252**.
6. Install a new fuse and push it all the way down until it seats completely.
7. Install the cover(s) onto the fuse box(s) and secure with the straps to keep out moisture.
8. Install the tool kit onto the brackets and secure with both straps.
9. Install the fuel tank as described in Chapter Nine.
10. Install the seat as described in Chapter Fifteen.

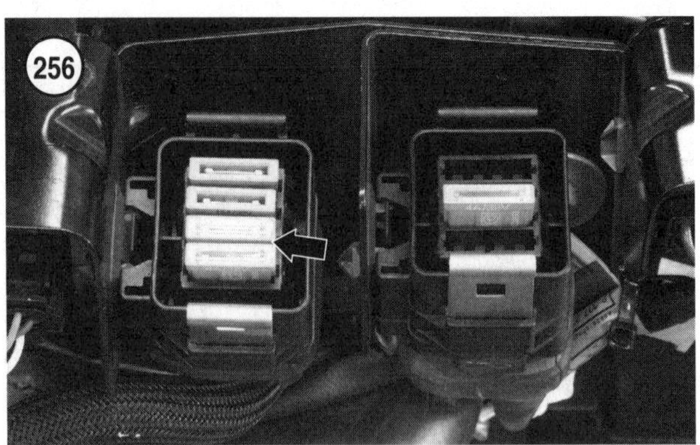

BATTERY CASE

Removal/Installation

On all models except S and C

1A. On models so equipped, place the motorcycle on the centerstand with the front whccl off thc ground.
1B. On models without a centerstand, place a suitable size jack under the engine to support the motorcycle with the front wheel off the ground.
2. Remove the seat as described in Chapter Fifteen.
3. Remove the fuel tank as described in Chapter Nine.
4. On RS and RT models, remove the front fairing side panels as described in Chapter Fifteen.
5. On 2002-on models, remove the screws securing the air intake stub pipe and remove it from the frame and air filter air box.
6. Remove the battery (A, **Figure 257**) as described in Chapter Three.
7. Remove the Motronic control unit (B, **Figure 257**) as described in Chapter Nine.
8A. On 1993-2001 models, perform the following:
   a. Disconnect the multi-pin electrical connector (**Figure 258**) from the ABS Unit.
   b. Loosen the bolts securing the ABS unit. Refer to **Figure 259** and **Figure 260**. It is not necessary to remove the ABS unit, just be able to move it up to gain access to the battery case mounting bolts below it.
   c. Remove the three visible nuts and washers (**Figure 261**). Remove the last nut and washer (**Figure 262**) under the ABS unit.
   d. Move the battery case toward the left and remove it from the frame.
8B. On 2002-on models, perform the following:
   a. Remove the ABS unit (C, **Figure 257**, or ABS pressure modulator, as described in Chapter Fourteen.
   b. Remove the nuts and washers securing the battery case.

260

261

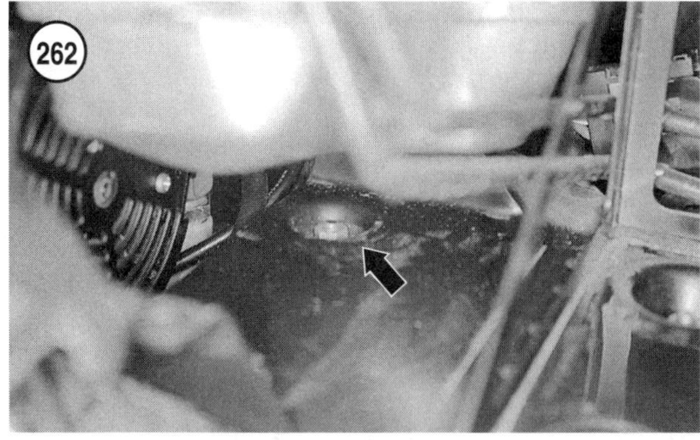

262

263

c. Move the battery case toward the left and remove it from the frame.

9. Inspect the rubber mounts (**Figure 263**) for wear or deterioration. Replace if necessary.

10. Install by reversing these removal steps while noting the following:

a. Make sure the electrical connectors corrosion free and secure.

b. Tighten the mounting bolts and nuts securely.

S models

1. Place the motorcycle on the centerstand with the front wheel off of the ground.
2. Remove the seat as described in Chapter Fifteen.
3. Remove the fuel tank as described in Chapter Nine.
4. Remove the front fairing side panels as described in Chapter Fifteen.
5. Remove the battery as described in Chapter Three.
6. Remove the Motronic control unit as described in Chapter Nine.
7. Remove the ABS unit, or ABS pressure module, as described in Chapter Fourteen.
8. Remove the nuts and washers securing the battery case.
9. Move the battery case toward the left and remove it from the frame.
10. Inspect the rubber mounts for wear or deterioration. Replace if necessary.
11. Install by reversing these removal steps while noting the following:

a. Make sure the electrical connectors are corrosion free and secure.

b. Tighten the mounting bolts and nuts securely.

C models

1. Place a suitable size jack under the engine to support the motorcycle with the front wheel off the ground.
2. Remove the seat as described in Chapter Fifteen.
3. Remove the fuel tank as described in Chapter Nine.
4. Remove the battery (**Figure 264**) as described in Chapter Three.
5. Remove the ABS unit (A, **Figure 265**) as described in Chapter Fourteen.

NOTE

*B, **Figure 265** only shows two of the mounting nuts and washers. Be sure to remove all nuts and washers.*

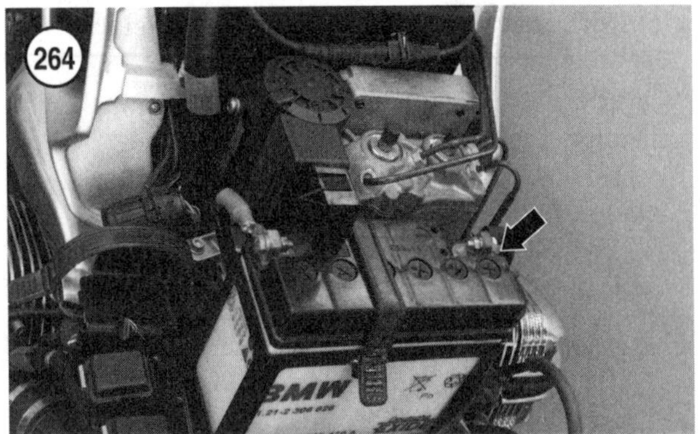

6. Remove the nuts and washers (B, **Figure 265**) securing the battery case.
7. Move the battery case toward the left and remove it from the frame.
8. Inspect the rubber mounts (**Figure 263**) for wear or deterioration. Replace if necessary.
9. Install by reversing these removal steps while noting the following:
   a. Make sure the electrical connectors corrosion free and secure.
   b. Tighten the mounting bolts and nuts securely.

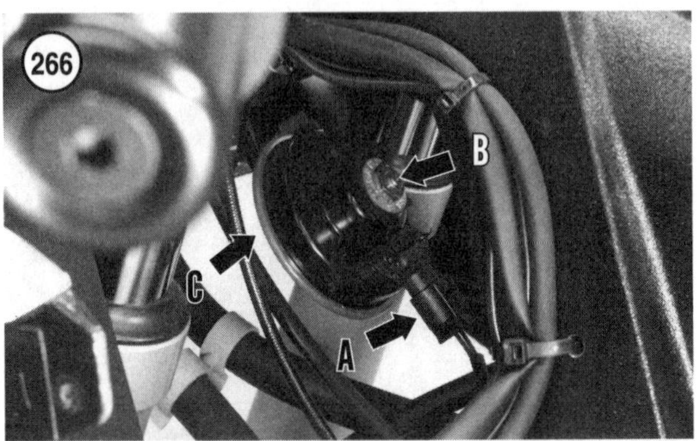

HORN

Removal/Installation

1. Disconnect the negative battery cable as described in Chapter Three.
2. Remove the fuel tank as described in Chapter Nine.
3. On RS, RT and S models, remove the front fairing lower left section as described in Chapter Fifteen.
4. Disconnect the electrical connectors (A, **Figure 266**) from the horn.
5. Remove the nut (B, **Figure 266**) securing the horn and remove the horn (C).
6. Install by reversing the removal steps while noting the following:
   a. Tighten the nut securely.
   b. Make sure the electrical connectors are corrosion free and secure.

Horn Testing

Remove the horn as described in this chapter. Connect a 12-volt battery to the horn. If the horn is good, it will sound. If not, replace it.

WIRING DIAGRAMS

Wiring diagrams are located at the end of this manual.

Table 1 ELECTRICAL SYSTEM SPECIFICATIONS

Alternator	
Type	Three-phase AC with integral electronic voltage regulator
Maximum output rating	700 watts/14 volts
Maximum current	
At 1000 rpm	18 amps
At 4000 rpm	50 amps
Alternator pulley outer diameter tip of teeth	55.5 mm (2.18 in.)
Resistance between slip rings	3 ohms
Resistance between outer slip ring and case	0 ohms
Starter	
Type	Permanent magnet motor with a planetary gear drive
Gear ratio	Planetary gears 5.5 to 1
Power rating	1100 watts
Ignition system	
Type	Motronic mapped characteristic control
Ignition trigger	Hall-effect sensors (2)
Ignition timing	
At idle	0° BTDC
Full advance	43° BTDC
Ignition coil resistance (single-spark ignition)	
Primary	0.5 ohm
Secondary	1300 ohms
Ignition coil resistance (dual-plug ignition)	
Primary spark plugs with direct ignition coil	
Primary	0.87 ohm
Secondary	not measurable
Secondary spark plugs with traditional ignition coil	
Primary	0.50 ohm
Secondary	7500 ohms

10

Table 2 REPLACEMENT BULBS

Item	Wattage
Headlight—high/low beam	
1993-1998	H4 60/55W
1991-on	
R850C, R1150R, R1150RS, R1200C	H4 60/55W
Headlight–low beam	
R1100S, R1150GS, Rockster	H1 55W
R1150RT	H7 55W
Headlight–high beam	
R1150GS, Rockster	H1 65W
R1150RT	H3 55W
R1100S	H7 55W
Fog lamps R1150RT	H3 55W
Position light*	
1993-1998	5W
1999-on	4W
Front and rear turn signals	21W
Tail/brake light	
R1100S, R1150GS, R1150R, R850C, R1200C	21/5W
Taillight	
R850R, R850GS, R1100GS, R1100R	
R1100RT, R1100RS, R1150RS, R1150RT	10W

(continued)

Table 2 REPLACEMENT BULBS (continued)

Item	Wattage
Brake light	
R850GS, R850R, R1100GS, R1100RS,	
R1100RT, R1150RT	21W
License plate light	
R850C, R1150R, Rockster, R1200C	6W
All models except R850C, R1150R,	
Rockster, R1200C	5W
Instrument panel (1993-1998)	
Turn signal, high beam indicator	3W
All other indictors and illumination	1.7W
Instrument panel (1999-on)	
Turn signal, high beam indicator	4W
All other indictors and illumination	
R850C, R1200C	1.7W
All models except R850C, R1200C	3W

*Position light on models so equipped.

Table 3 ELECTRICAL SYSTEM TORQUE SPECIFICATIONS

Item	N•m	in.-lb.	ft.-lb.
Alternator pulley nut			
Upper and lower	50	–	37
Alternator support cover	20	–	15
Positive lead to alternator	12	106	–
Starter			
Mounting bolts	20	–	15
Cover bolts	7	62	–
Positive lead-to-starter	10	88	–

CHAPTER ELEVEN

WHEELS, HUBS AND TIRES

This chapter describes service procedures for the wheels, wheel bearings and tires.

Table 1 and **Table 2** are at the end of this chapter.

FRONT WHEEL

Removal

Refer to **Figure 1** and **Figure 2**.

1A. On models so equipped, place the motorcycle on the centerstand with the front wheel off the ground.

1B. On models without a centerstand, place a suitable size jack under the engine to support the motorcycle with the front wheel off the ground.

2. Remove the front fender as described in Chapter Fifteen.

3. On ABS equipped models, remove the screws securing the ABS trigger sensor (A, **Figure 3**) and remove the sensor and shim (models so equipped) from the left side fork slider. Move the sensor and wire out of the way.

4. On model so equipped, remove the screw securing the speedometer cable (B, **Figure 3**). Withdraw the cable and move the cable out of the way.

5. Loosen the axle clamping screws (A, **Figure 4**) on both fork sliders.

6. Loosen the axle bolt (B, **Figure 4**) on the left fork slider.

7. Remove both the right and left side brake calipers as follows:

   a. Push the brake caliper in (toward wheel) by hand. Doing so pushes the caliper pistons into the caliper to provide additional brake pad clearance when reinstalling the caliper.

   b. Remove both brake calipers (C, **Figure 3**) as described in Chapter Fourteen.

   c. Tie the calipers up to take the strain off of the hydraulic brake hoses.

NOTE

Insert a spacer in the calipers to hold the brake pads in place. Then, if the brake lever is inadvertently squeezed, the pistons will not be forced out of the calipers. If this does happen, the calipers must be disassembled to reseat the pistons and the system will have to be bled.

NOTE

Before removing the front wheel, note the direction of the rim and tire rotation arrows. The wheel must be reinstalled so the arrows point in the direction of forward rotation. The wheel can be installed in either direc-

(1)

FRONT WIRE WHEEL AND HUB (TYPICAL)

1. Cap
2. Front axle
3. Bushing
4. Bearing
5. Wire wheel
6. Distance collar
7. Bushing
8. Snap ring
9. Speedometer drive dog
10. Seal
11. Speedometer drive unit
12. Bolt

(2)

FRONT ALLOY WHEEL AND HUB (TYPICAL)

1. Cap
2. Front axle
3. Bushing
4. Bearing
5. Distance collar
6. Bushing
7. Snap ring
8. Speedometer drive dog
9. Seal
10. Speedometer drive nut
11. Bolt
12. Cast wheel
13. Valve

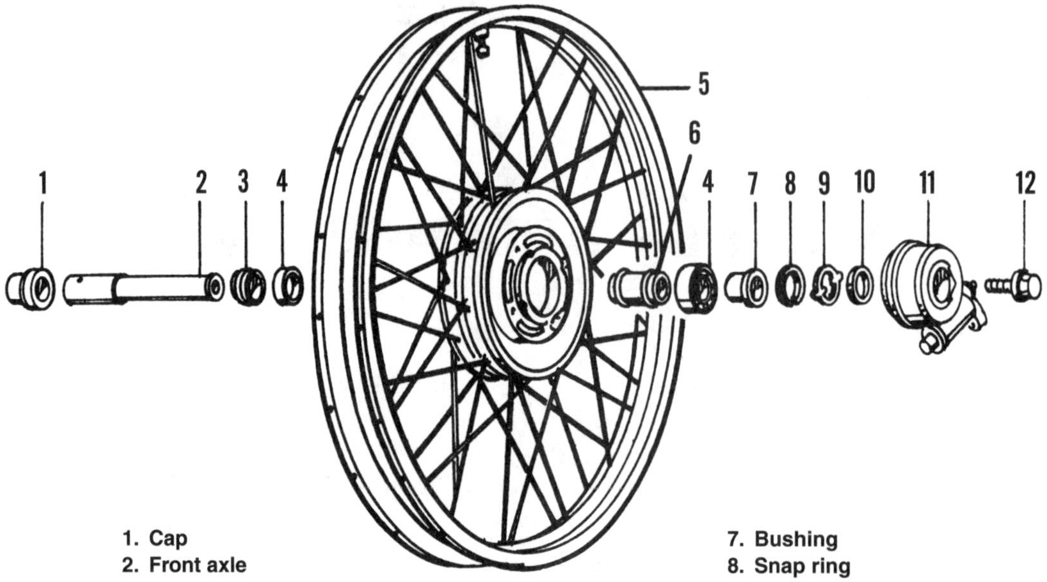

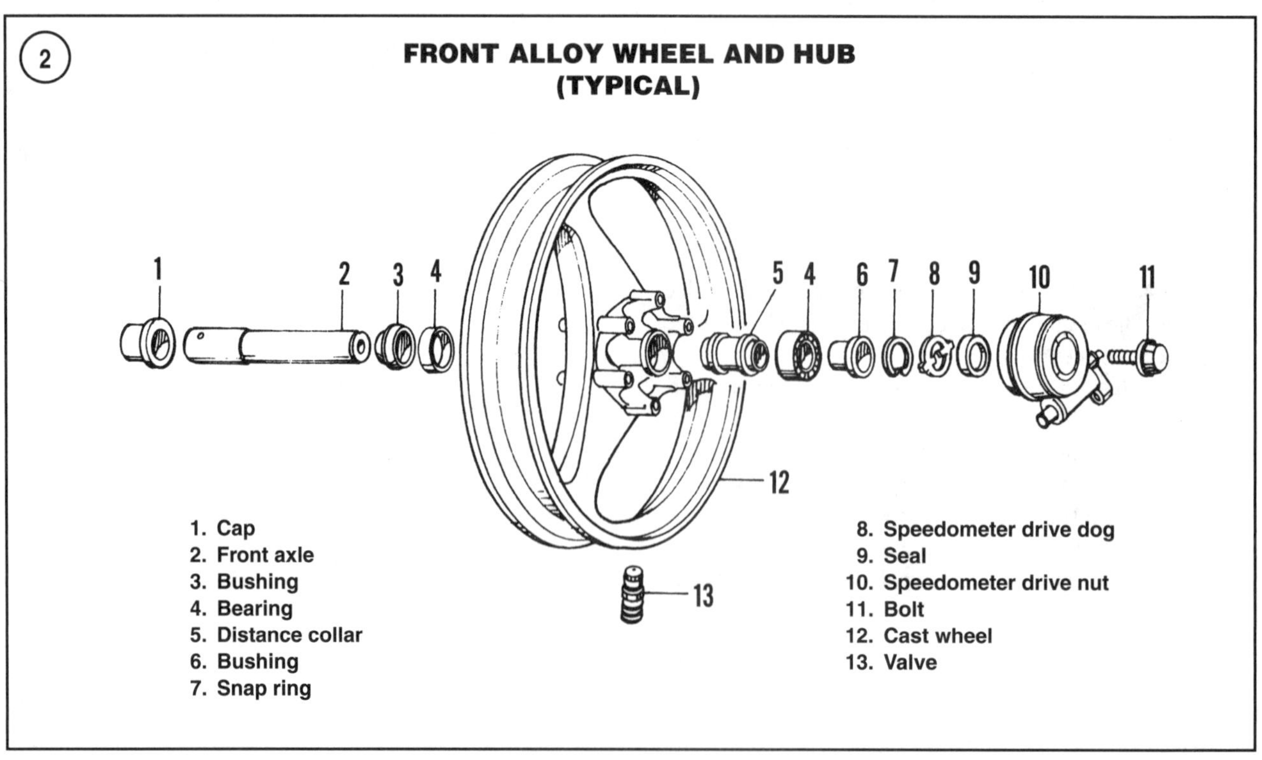

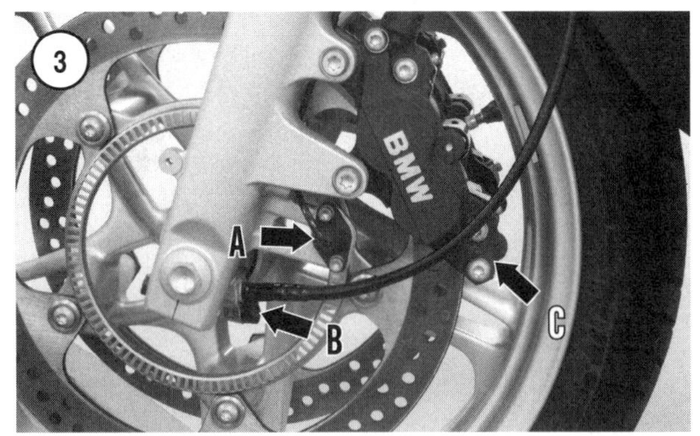

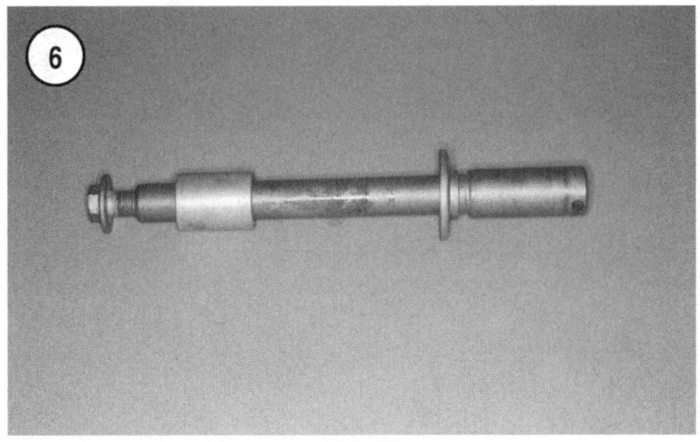

tion. On ABS equipped models, the ABS rotor must be installed on the left side.

8. Insert a drift or screwdriver into the hole (**Figure 5**) in the right side of the front axle. Rotate the axle back and forth and withdraw the front axle from both fork tubes.

NOTE

On S and C models, the wheel collars on the left and right sides are different. Identify the collars before removing them and mark them after wheel removal.

9A. On R850C, R1100S and R1200C models, let the wheel come down and forward so it can be removed. Do not lose the spacers on both sides of the front hub.

9B. On all models except R850C, R1100S and R1200C, let the wheel come down and forward and remove it. Do not lose the spacer from the right side or the speedometer drive unit from the left side of the front hub.

CAUTION

Do not set the wheel down on the disc surface, as it may be damaged.

10. Install the spacers (and speedometer drive unit on models so equipped) and axle bolt onto the front axle (**Figure 6**) to avoid misplacing them.

11. Inspect the front wheel as described in this chapter.

Installation

1. Make sure the axle bearing surfaces of both fork tubes and the axle are free from burrs and nicks.
2. Apply a small amount of cold grease to the inner surface of the spacer(s) to help hold it in place.
3. Apply a light coat of BMW Kluberplex BEM 34-132 grease, or an equivalent waterproof bearing grease, to the front axle prior to installation.
4. Lubricate both seal lips (**Figure 7**) with a waterproof bearing grease grease.

5A. On R850C, R1100S and R1200C models, install the front axle spacers onto the correct side of the front hub as noted during removal.

5B. On all models except R850C, R1100S and R1200C, install the spacer on the right side and the speedometer drive unit on the left side of the front hub.

6A. On non-ABS models, install the wheel between the fork tubes with the wheel's rim and tire arrow marks facing in the direction of forward rotation.

6B. On ABS equipped models, install the wheel between the fork tubes with the ABS rotor located on the left side.

7. Position the front wheel between the fork sliders. Raise the wheel assembly up and align it with the front axle holes in the fork sliders.

8. Install the axle from the left side and push it through until it bottoms.

9. Install the axle bolt (B, **Figure 4**) and tighten it finger-tight.

10. Insert a drift or screwdriver into the hole (**Figure 5**) in the right side of the front axle.

11. Hold the axle and tighten the front axle bolt (B, **Figure 4**) to 30 N•m (22 ft.-lb.).

12A. On R850C, R1100S and R1200C models, check that both the right side (**Figure 8**) and the left side (**Figure 9**) axle spacer are correctly in place.

12B. On all models except R850C, R1100S and R1200C, perform the following:

a. Check that the right side spacer (**Figure 10**) and the speedometer drive unit (A, **Figure 11**) are correctly in place.
b. Make sure the raised boss on the speedometer drive unit is located correctly in front of the raised locating tab on the fork tube (B, **Figure 11**). This is necessary for proper speedometer operation.

13. Install both the right and left side brake calipers (C, **Figure 3**) as described in Chapter Fourteen. Spin the front wheel and apply the front brake to reposition the brake pads in both calipers.

14. On ABS equipped models, install the ABS trigger sensor (A, **Figure 3**) and shim (models so equipped) onto the left side fork slider.

15. Take the motorcycle off the centerstand or jack.

16. Apply the front brakes and pump the front suspension up and down several times to seat and center the front axle in the fork tube.

17. Tighten the right axle clamp bolt (A, **Figure 4**) on both sides to 22 N•m (16 ft.-lb.).

18. Rotate the wheel several times and apply the brakes to make sure the wheel rotates freely and that the brake pads are against both discs correctly.

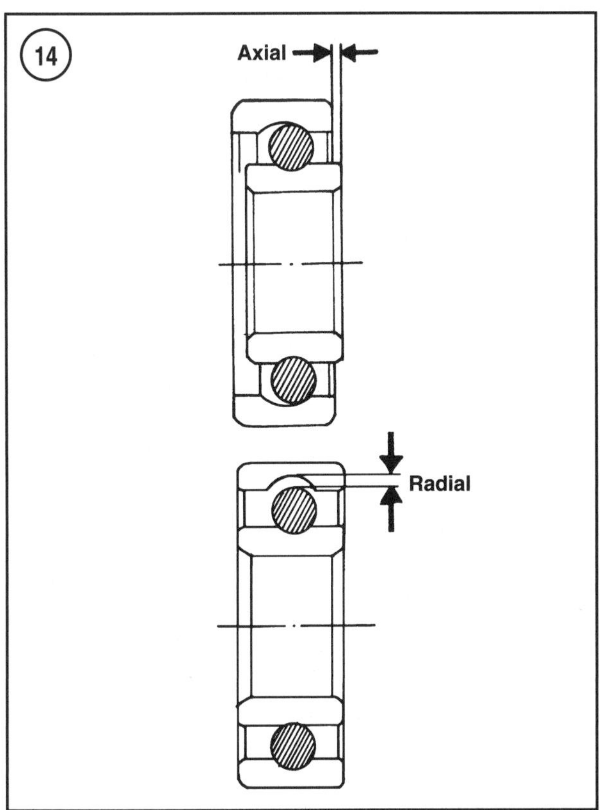

WARNING
If the distance between the trigger sensor and pulse generating wheel is not maintained correctly, the ABS system ***will not function properly****.*

19. On ABS equipped models, inspect the distance between the ABS sensor and the pulse generating wheel (**Figure 12**) as described in Chapter Fourteen.
20. Install the front fender as described in Chapter Fifteen.

Inspection

Replace worn or damaged parts as described in this section.

1. Clean the axle and collars in solvent to remove all grease and dirt.
2. Remove any corrosion on the front axle and collars with a piece of fine emery cloth.
3. Check the axle surface for any cracks or other damage. Check the axle operating areas for any nicks or grooves that can cut and damage the seals.
4. Check the axle bolt (**Figure 13**) and axle threads for damage. Replace the axle and axle bolt if their corners are damaged.
5. Clean the seals with a rag. Then inspect the seals (**Figure 7**) for wear, hardness, cracks or other damage. If necessary, replace the seals as described under *Front Hub* in this chapter.
6. Turn each bearing inner race by hand. The bearing must turn smoothly. Some axial play is normal, but radial play, or side play, must be negligible. Refer to **Figure 14**. If one bearing is damaged, replace both bearings as a set. Refer to *Front Hub* in this chapter.
7. Check the brake disc bolts (**Figure 15**) for tightness. To service the brake disc, refer to Chapter Fifteen.

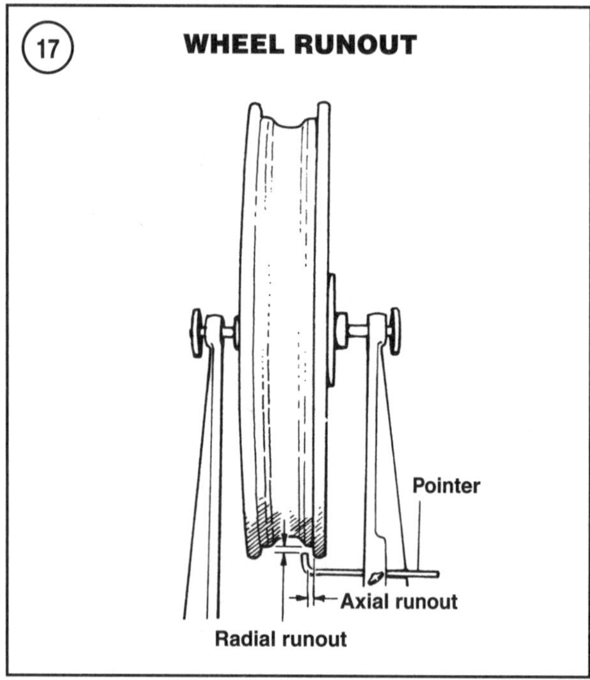

8. On ABS equipped models, check the pulse generating wheel mounting Torx bolts (**Figure 16**) for tightness. To service the pulse generating wheel bolts, refer to Chapter Fifteen.

9. Measure the axial (side to side) and radial (up and down) runout of the front wheel with a dial indicator as shown in **Figure 17**. Refer to **Table 1** for the maximum allowable runout with the tire installed on the rim.

10. On models so equipped, inspect the speedometer drive unit for wear or damage and replace it if necessary.

11. Check the axle for wear and straightness. Use V-blocks and a dial indicator as shown in **Figure 18**. If the runout is 0.2 mm (0.01 in.) or greater, replace the axle.

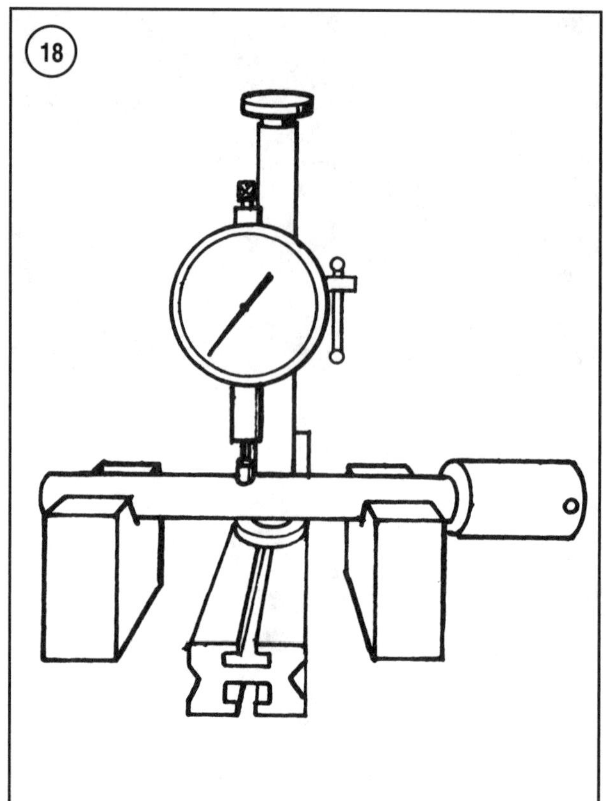

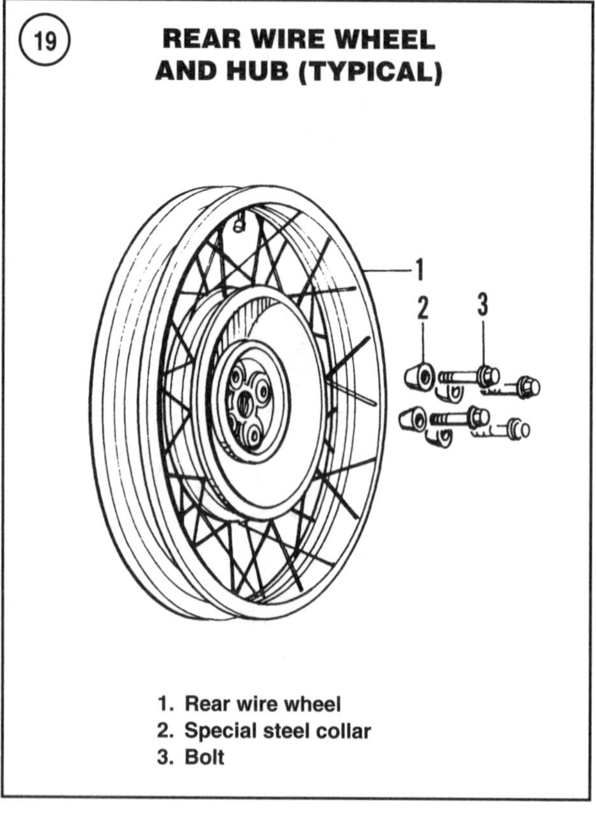

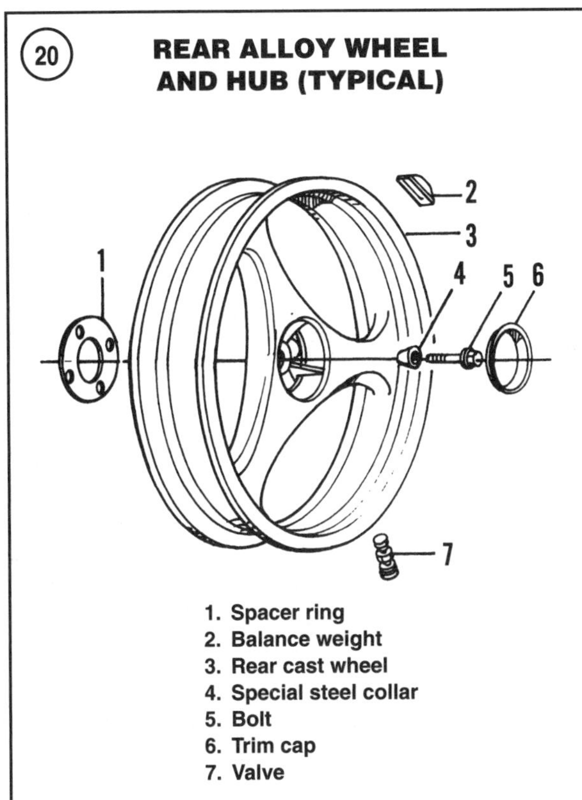

REAR WHEEL

Removal/Installation

Refer to **Figure 19** and **Figure 20**.

1A. On models so equipped, place the motorcycle on the centerstand with the rear wheel off the ground.

1B. On models without a centerstand, place a suitable size jack under the engine to support the motorcycle with the rear wheel off the ground.

2. On models so equipped, remove the left saddlebag to gain additional working room as described in Chapter Fifteen.

11

3. On GS models, remove the bolts and washers (A, **Figure 21**) securing the rear mud guard and remove the mud guard (B).

4. On R850C and R1200C models, remove the rear fender as described in Chapter Fifteen.

NOTE

Depending on tire size, it may be necessary to remove the license plate bracket assembly to allow the rear wheel to clear the back of the fender area. If necessary, refer to Chapter Fifteen.

5. On alloy wheels so equipped, carefully pry the center trim cap (**Figure 22**) loose and remove it.

6. Either shift the transmission into top gear or have an assistant apply the rear brake to prevent the rear wheel from rotating.

7A. On wire wheels, following a crisscross pattern, loosen the bolts (**Figure 23**) securing the rear wheel to the final drive unit.

7B. On alloy wheels, following a crisscross pattern, loosen the bolts securing the rear wheel to the final drive unit. Refer to **Figure 24** or **Figure 25**.

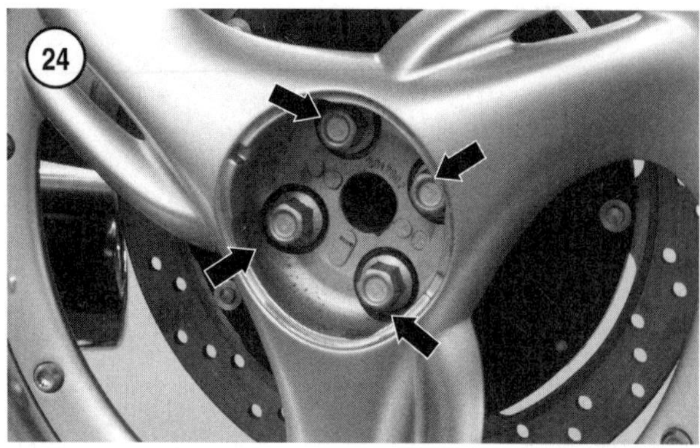

8. Remove the rear brake caliper as described in Chapter Fourteen.

9. Remove the bolts and special steel collars. Place the bolts and collars in a container to avoid misplacing them.

10. Pull the rear wheel toward the left side to disengage it from the final drive unit. If still in place, carefully push the license plate bracket assembly toward the right side and slowly roll the wheel toward the rear and remove it.

11. On alloy wheels, remove the spacer ring (**Figure 26**) from the backside of the wheel or from the final drive unit.

12. Inspect the rear wheel as described in this chapter.

13. Make sure the following mating surfaces are free of *all* road dirt and grease:

a. The rear wheel surface (**Figure 27** or **Figure 28**).

b. The rear brake disc carrier (**Figure 29**).

c. The final drive unit.

d. On alloy wheels, the spacer ring.

14. On alloy wheels, install the spacer ring (**Figure 30**) onto the backside of the wheel or from the final drive unit.

15. Make sure the tapered recesses in the wheel are free of dirt and any gouges or burrs. Refer to **Figure 31** for wire wheels or **Figure 32** for alloy wheels. Clean off all surfaces so the steel collars will seat properly.

15. Correctly position the rear wheel next to the final drive unit and align the bolt holes.

WARNING

*Never install the bolts without the special steel collars (**Figure 33**). The taper on the collar matches the bolt hole taper in the wheel and correctly locates the rear wheel onto the final drive unit. Without the collars the wheel will not be centered onto the final drive unit and will result in severe vibration and possible loss of the wheel while riding. Use only the correct length wheel bolts. The bolt length is marked on the bolt head. Do **not** apply lubricant to the bolt threads.*

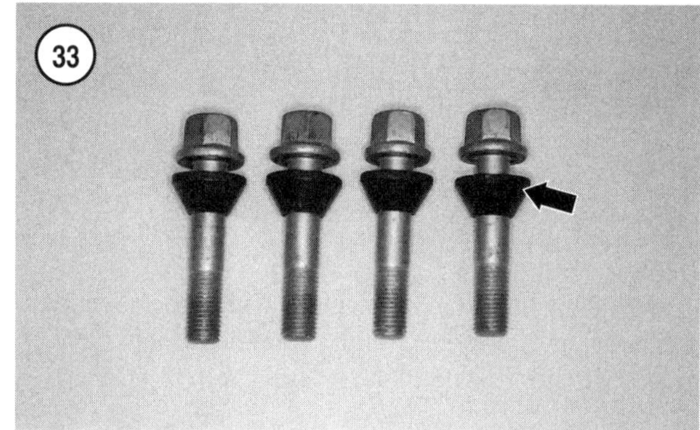

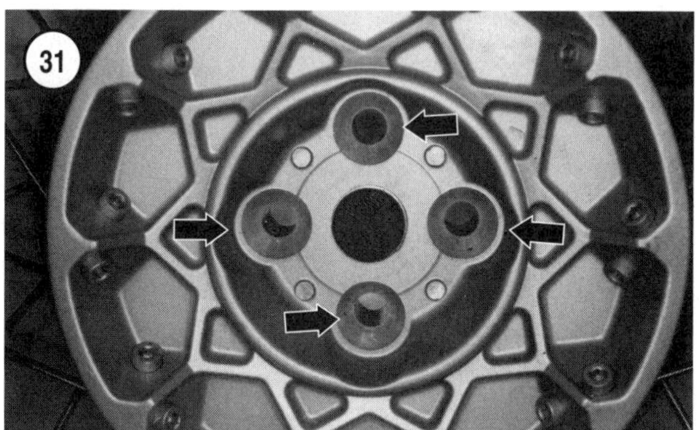

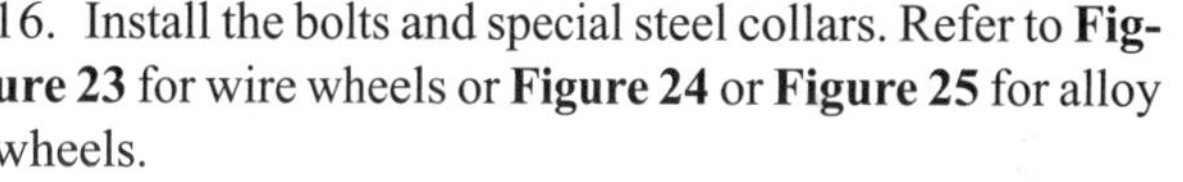

16. Install the bolts and special steel collars. Refer to **Figure 23** for wire wheels or **Figure 24** or **Figure 25** for alloy wheels.

11

17. Shift the transmission into fifth gear to prevent the rear wheel from rotating.

18. Following a crisscross pattern, first tighten the bolts to the initial torque, then to the final torque as follows:

   a. R1150GS: 72 N•m (53 ft.-lb.), final 105 N•m (77 ft.-lb.).

   b. All models except R1150GS: 50 N•m (37 ft.-lb.), final 105 N•m (77 ft.-lb.).

19. On alloy wheels so equipped, install the center trim cap retainer (A, **Figure 34**) into the rear wheel recess (B). Press it in until it bottoms (**Figure 22**) and snaps into place.

19. Install the rear brake caliper as described in Chapter Fourteen.

20. If removed, install the license plate bracket as described in Chapter Fifteen.

21. On GS models install the mud guard (B, **Figure 21**) and the bolts and washers (A). Tighten the bolts securely—do not overtighten as the mud guard mounting bosses may be damaged.

22. On R850C and R1200C models, install the rear fender as described in Chapter Fifteen.

23. If removed, install the left saddlebag.

Inspection

The rear wheel is not equipped with wheel bearings. The bearings are located in the final drive unit. Service procedures for the final drive are covered in Chapter Thirteen.

1. Inspect the wheel for cracks, fractures, dents or bends. Replace if damaged.

2. Inspect the tapered recesses in the wheel for dirt, gouges or burrs. Clean off all surfaces so the steel collars seat properly. Refer to **Figure 31** for wire wheels or **Figure 32** for alloy wheels. Clean off all surfaces so the steel washers will seat properly.

3. Check the mounting flange in the hub center (**Figure 28**, typical) for cracks or damage. If damaged, replace the wheel.

4. Make sure the raised shoulder (**Figure 35**) that fits into the final drive unit, or rear brake disc carrier, is in good condition. Replace the rear wheel if this shoulder is damaged.

5. Check the spacer ring (**Figure 36**) for wear or damage. It must be flat and free of burrs. Replace if necessary.

6. On R850C and R1200C models, check the Torx bolts (**Figure 37**) securing the modular wheel components for tightness. If loose, tighten securely.

Runout Check

Perform rear wheel runout inspection with the wheel installed on the motorcycle final drive unit.

1A. On models so equipped, place the motorcycle on the centerstand with the rear wheel off the ground.

1B. On models without a centerstand, place a suitable size jack under the engine to support the motorcycle with the rear wheel off the ground.

2. Shift the transmission into neutral.

3. Attach a dial indicator to the right side of the swing arm and measure the runout at the rim surface.

4. Slowly rotate the wheel and measure the axial and radial runout of the wheel with a dial indicator. Refer to **Table 1** for the maximum allowable runout.

35

36

37

FRONT HUB

Pre-Inspection

Inspect each wheel bearing as follows:

1A. On models so equipped, place the motorcycle on the centerstand with the rear wheel off of the ground.

1B. On models without a centerstand, place a suitable size jack under the engine to support the motorcycle with the rear wheel off the ground.

2. Hold the wheel along its sides (180° apart) and try to rock it back and forth. If there is any noticeable play at the

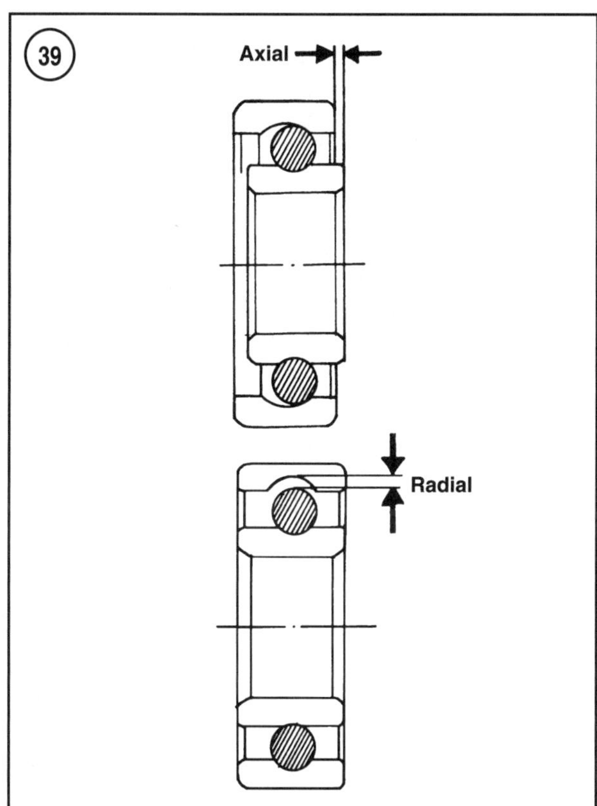

axle, the wheel bearings are worn or damaged and require replacement. Then have an assistant apply the front brake while rocking the wheel again. On severely worn bearings, play is detected at the bearings even though the wheel is locked in position.

3. Push the front calipers in by hand to move the brake pads away from the brake disc. This makes it easier to spin the wheel.

4. Spin the wheel and listen for excessive wheel bearing noise. A grinding or catching noise indicates worn bearings.

5. Apply the front brake several times to reposition the brake pads in the calipers.

CAUTION
Do not remove the wheel bearings for inspection purposes, as they may be damaged during removal. Remove the wheel bearings only if they require replacement.

6. To check any questionable bearing, remove the front wheel as described in this chapter.

CAUTION
When handling the wheel assembly in the following steps, do not lay the wheel down where it is supported by the brake disc as this could damage the disc. Support the wheel on wooden blocks.

7. Pry the seals out of the hub (**Figure 38**) and discard them. Support the tool with a rag or thin piece of wood to avoid damaging the hub or brake disc.

CAUTION
If a seal is hard to remove, do not damage the mounting bore by trying to force it out. Remove the seal with a seal removal tool as described in Chapter One.

9. Remove any burrs created during seal removal. Use emery cloth to smooth the mounting bore. Do not enlarge the mounting bore.

11

NOTE
Before removing the wheel bearings, check the tightness of the bearings in the hub by pulling the bearing up and then from side to side. The outer bearing race should be a tight fit in the hub with no movement. If the outer bearing race is loose and wobbles, the bearing bore in the hub may be cracked or damaged. Remove the bearings as described in this section and check the hub bore carefully. If any cracks or damage are found, replace the wheel. It cannot be repaired.

9. Turn each bearing inner race by hand. The bearing must turn smoothly with no roughness, catching, binding or excessive noise. Some axial play is normal, but radial play must be negligible (**Figure 39**).

10. Check the bearing's outer seal (A, **Figure 40**) for buckling or other damage that would allow dirt to enter the bearing.

11. If one bearing is damaged, replace both bearings as a set.

12. If the seals were removed, perform the following:
   a. Pack the lip of each *new* seal with waterproof grease.
   b. Place the seal squarely against the bore opening with the closed side facing out. Use an appropriate size socket (**Figure 41**) and drive the seal into the bore until it is flush with the outside of the hub's mounting bore.

Disassembly

Refer to **Figure 42** and **Figure 43**.

The distance collar fits tightly between both bearings. There is a shoulder at each end of the distance collar and it covers the inner bearing race. This shoulder makes it impossible to move the distance collar over to one side in order to tap the first bearing out of the hub with a drift and hammer.

The wheel bearings are a tight fit in the wheel hub. BMW recommends heating the front hub area to 80° C (176° F) to expand the hub bearing bore. Use an industrial type heat gun capable of creating the specified temperature to heat the surrounding area.

CAUTION
Do not heat the hub area with a propane or acetylene torch; never bring an open flame into contact with the bearing bore of the front hub. The direct heat will destroy the painted finish and could lead to wheel warp.

1. The following special tools are required to remove and install the bearings. Refer to a BMW dealership for part numbers for the wheel being serviced.
   a. Clamp arbor.
   b. Spacing ring.
   c. Counter support.
   d. Internal puller.
   e. Industrial type heat gun, capable of 80° C (176° F).
2. Remove the front wheel as described in this chapter.
3. Inspect the wheel bearings as described in this chapter. If they must be replaced, proceed as follows.
4. On models so equipped, carefully remove the bushing from the right side of the hub.
5. On the left side, perform the following:
   a. Carefully remove the axle seal (A, **Figure 44**) and the speedometer drive dog (B) on models so equipped.
   b. Remove the snap ring securing the left bearing.

NOTE
The front hub bearings are two different sizes. The larger bearing is located on the left side of the hub.

6. To remove the left bearing, perform the following:
   a. Clamp the arbor in a vise.
   b. Position the wheel with the right side facing up and place it directly onto the arbor. Make sure the left bearing seats correctly onto the arbor.
   c. Place the seating ring (A, **Figure 45**) into the center of the right side of the hub.
   d. Install the internal puller (B, **Figure 45**) and counter support (C) on top of the seating ring and into the left bearing.
   e. Heat the hub surrounding the outer bearing race to a minimum of 80° C (176° F).

WARNING
The special tools and wheel hub are now very hot. Make sure to wear protective gloves when handling the tools.

   f. Tighten the internal puller and withdraw the left bearing from the hub center. Discard the bearing.
   g. Remove the special tools.

42

FRONT WIRE WHEEL AND HUB (TYPICAL)

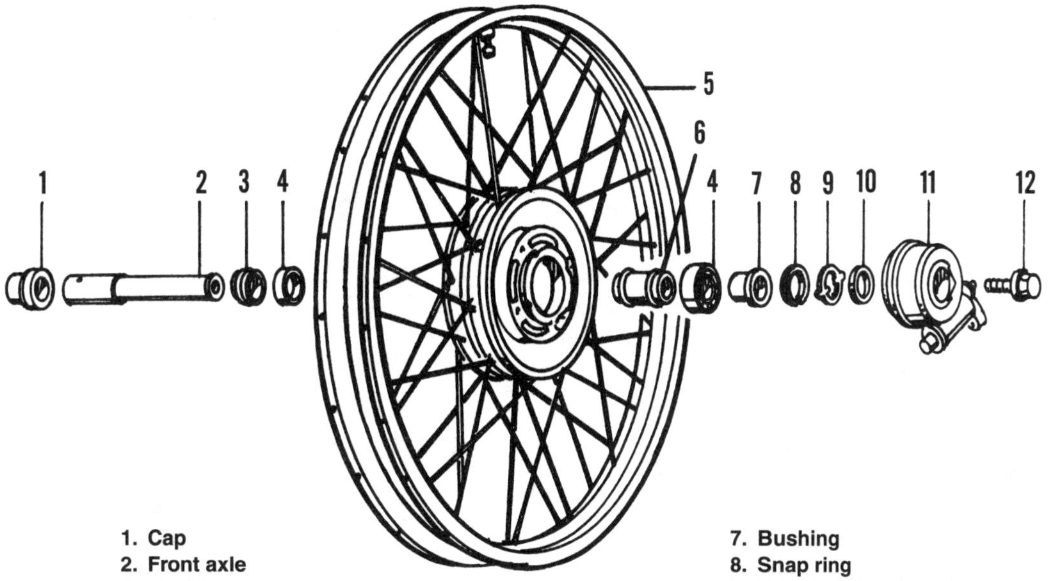

1. Cap
2. Front axle
3. Bushing
4. Bearing
5. Wire wheel
6. Distance collar
7. Bushing
8. Snap ring
9. Speedometer drive dog
10. Seal
11. Speedometer drive unit
12. Bolt

43

FRONT ALLOY WHEEL AND HUB (TYPICAL)

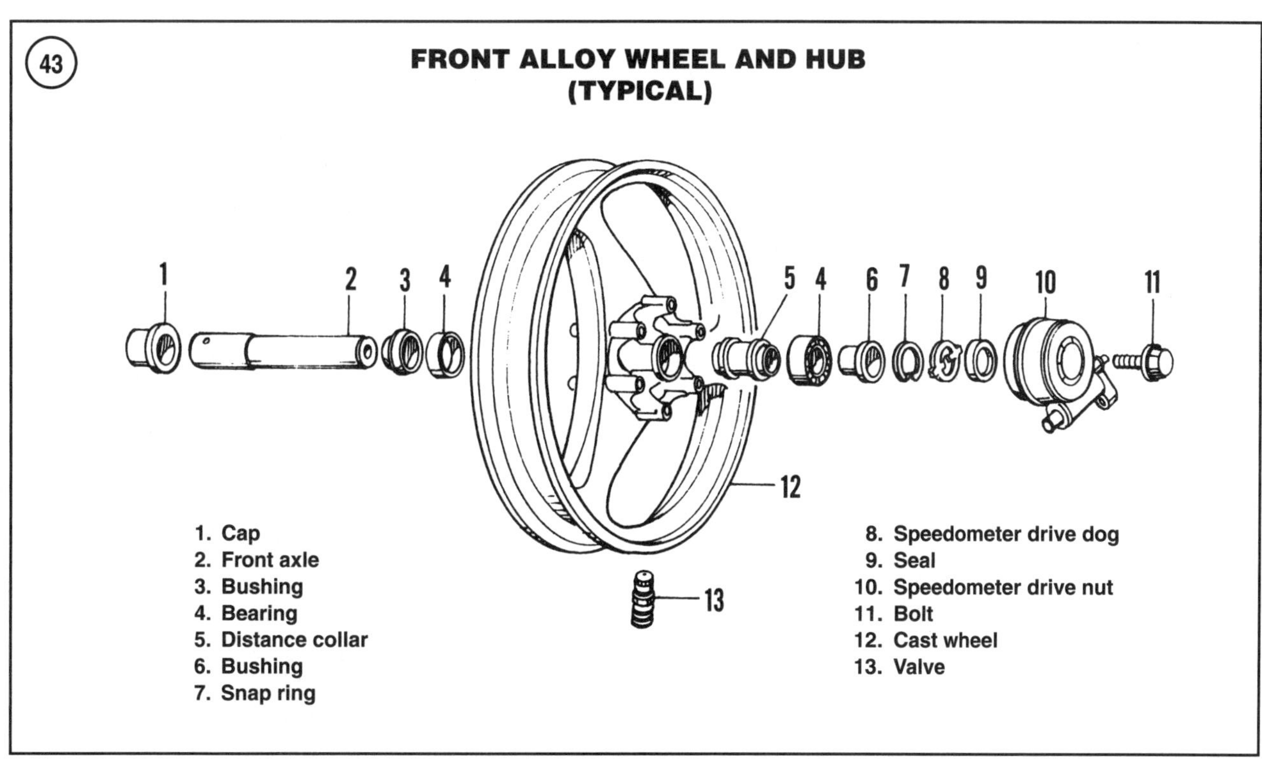

1. Cap
2. Front axle
3. Bushing
4. Bearing
5. Distance collar
6. Bushing
7. Snap ring
8. Speedometer drive dog
9. Seal
10. Speedometer drive nut
11. Bolt
12. Cast wheel
13. Valve

h. Remove the wheel from the arbor and vise.

7. To remove the right bearing and distance collar, perform the following on a workbench:

a. Heat the hub surrounding the right bearing outer race to a minimum of 80° C (176° F).

WARNING
The wheel hub is very hot. Make sure to wear protective gloves when handling the parts and the wheel.

b. Position the wheel with the right side facing up.

c. Place the wheel on two wood blocks so the wheel contacts the blocks at the wheel rim and tire area. Do not let the left brake disc contact the workbench.

d. Insert the BMW drift (A, **Figure 46**) into the hub and center it onto the distance collar (B).

e. Carefully drive the right bearing (C, **Figure 46**) out of the hub.

f. Remove the distance collar (B, **Figure 46**) from the hub.

8. After the wheel has cooled down, clean the inside and the outside of the hub with solvent and dry with compressed air.

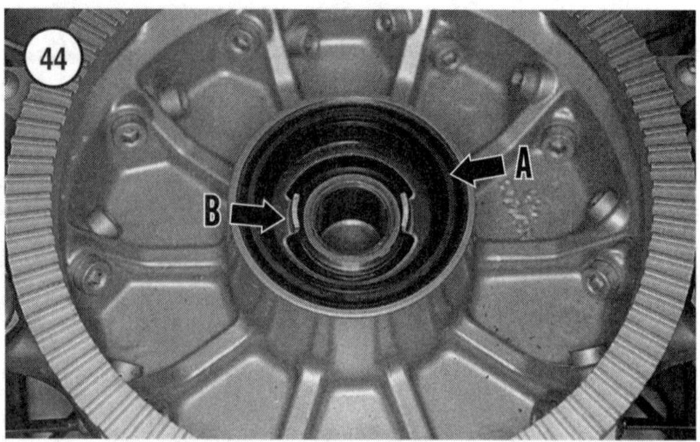

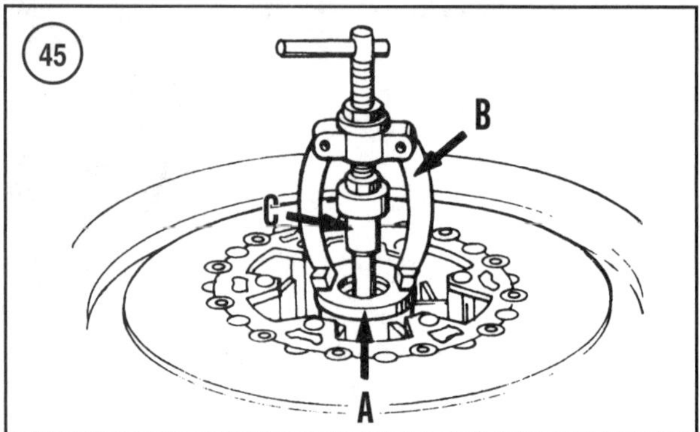

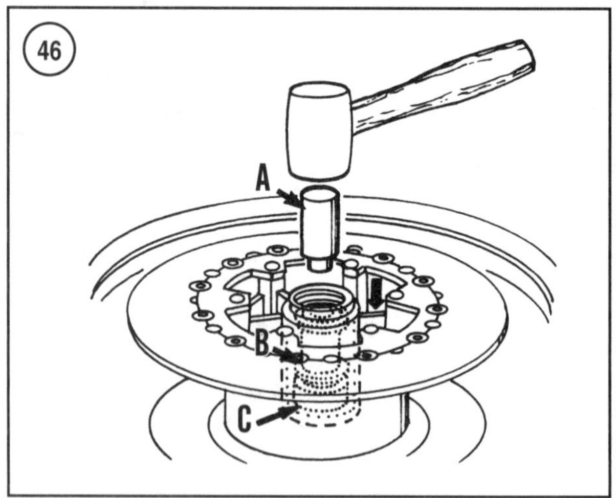

Inspection

1. Check the hub mounting bore for cracks or other damage. If one bearing is a loose fit, the mounting bore is damaged. Replace the wheel.

2. Inspect the distance collar for cracks, corrosion or other damage. Then check the distance collar ends. If the ends appear compressed or damaged, replace the distance collar. Do not try to repair the distance collar by cutting or grinding its end surfaces, as this shortens the distance collar.

CAUTION
The distance collar operates against the wheel bearing inner races to prevent them from moving inward when the axle is tightened. If the ends of the distance collar are damaged, shortened, or if it is not installed in the hub, the inner bearing races will move inward and bind as the axle is tightened, causing bearing damage and seizure.

Assembly

CAUTION
Do not heat the hub area with a propane or acetylene torch; never bring a direct flame into contact with the front hub. The direct heat will destroy the painted finish and could lead to wheel warp.

1. On unsealed bearings, pack the bearings with a good quality anti-friction waterproof bearing grease. Thoroughly work the grease in between the balls; turn the bearing by hand a couple of times to ensure the grease is distributed evenly inside the bearing.

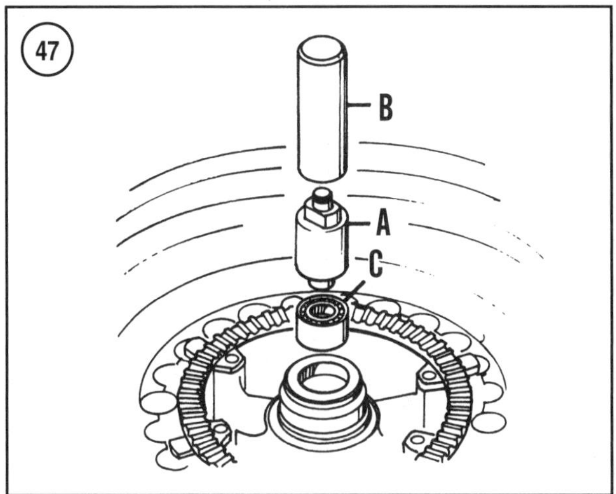

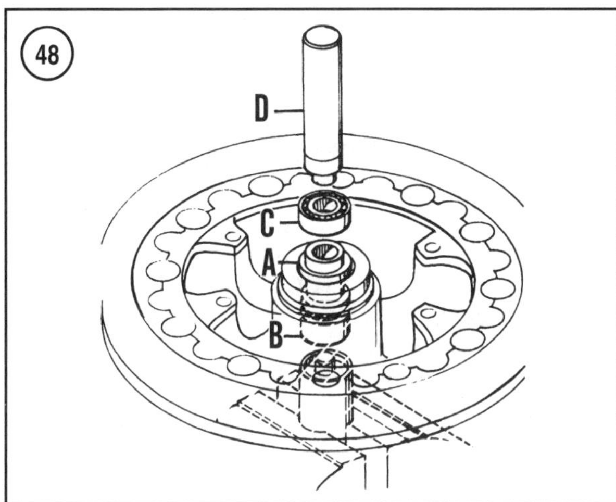

2. Blow any debris out of the hub prior to installing the bearings.

3. Place the new wheel bearings in a freezer if possible. Chilling them will slightly reduce their overall diameter while the hot wheel hub is slightly larger due to heat expansion.

4. Install the left bearing first.

CAUTION
Install the bearings with the sealed side facing outward.

5. To install the left bearing, perform the following:

a. Heat the hub surrounding the left bearing outer race to a minimum of 80° C (176° F).

WARNING
The wheel hub is now very hot. Make sure to wear protective gloves when handling the parts and the wheel.

b. Position the wheel with the left side facing up.
c. Place the wheel on two wood blocks so the wheel contacts the blocks at the wheel rim and tire area. Do not let the right brake disc contact the workbench.
d. Remove the bearing from the freezer.
e. Correctly position the bearing into the hub and tap it squarely into place on the outer race only. Use the BMW drift (A, **Figure 47**) and BMW handle (B). Do not tap on the inner race or the bearing might be damaged.
f. Carefully drive the left bearing (C, **Figure 47**) into the hub until the snapring groove is visible.
g. Install the snapring to maintain the left bearing in the correct location in the hub.
h. Remove the special tools.

6. To install the right bearing, perform the following:
a. Clamp the arbor in the vise.
b. Position the wheel with the right side facing up and place it directly onto the arbor. Make sure the left bearing seats correctly onto the arbor.
c. Heat the hub surrounding the right bearing outer race to a minimum of 80° C (176° F).

WARNING
The wheel hub is now very hot. Make sure to wear protective gloves when handling the parts and the wheel.

d. Install the distance collar (A, **Figure 48**) into the left bearing inner race (B). Make sure the collar seats correctly in the bearing. If installed incorrectly, the right bearing cannot be installed.
e. Remove the bearing from the freezer.
f. Correctly position the bearing (C, **Figure 48**) into the hub and tap it squarely into place. Use the BMW drift and BMW handle (D, **Figure 48**). Do not tap on the inner race or the bearing might be damaged.
g. Carefully drive the right bearing (C, **Figure 48**) into the hub until it seats against the distance collar.
h. Remove the special tools.
i. On models so equipped, install the speedometer drive dog.

7. Install *new* seals as follows:
a. Pack the lip of each seal with waterproof grease.
b. Place the seal squarely against the bore opening with the closed side facing out. Use an appropriate size socket (**Figure 41**) and drive the seal into the

11

bore until it is flush with the outside of the hub's mounting bore.

8. Install the front wheel as described in this chapter.

Removing Damaged Bearings

If worn or rusted wheel bearings are used too long, the inner race can break apart and fall out of the bearing leaving the outer race pressed in the hub. Because the outer race seats against a shoulder inside the hub, its removal is difficult because only a small part of the race is accessible above the hub's shoulder.

This presents a small and difficult target to drive against. To remove the bearing's outer race under these conditions, first heat the bulb evenly with a heat gun. Then drive out the outer race with a drift and hammer. Grind a clearance tip on the end of the drift, if necessary, to avoid damaging the hub's mounting bore. Check this before heating the hub. When removing the race, apply force in opposite points around the race to prevent it from rocking and binding in the mounting bore as soon as it starts to move. After removing the race, inspect the hub mounting bore carefully for cracks or other damage.

If rust is present in the mounting bore, thoroughly clean it out with crocus cloth and solvent. Clean out with solvent and dry with compressed air.

WHEEL RUNOUT AND BALANCE

Proper wheel inspection includes visual inspection, checking rim runout and wheel balance. Checking runout and wheel balance requires a truing or wheel balancing stand. If these tools are not available, refer the service to a BMW dealership.

Replace the wheel if it is dented or damaged in any way. If there is any doubt as to wheel condition, take it to a BMW dealership or wheel specialist and have the wheel inspected.

Runout Inspection

1. Clean the wheel rim to remove all road grit, chain lube and other debris. Any material left on the rim affects its runout. This includes any surface roughness caused by peeled or uneven paint and corrosion.

2. Inspect the wheel rim for dents, bending or cracks. Check the rim and rim sealing surface for scratches that could cause the tire to leak air.

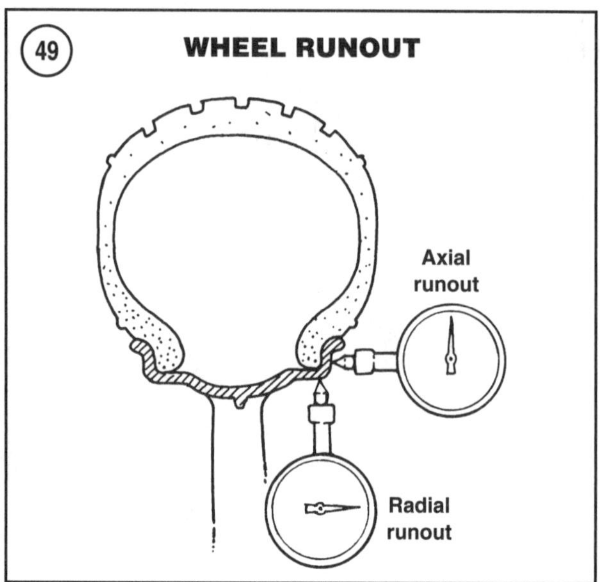

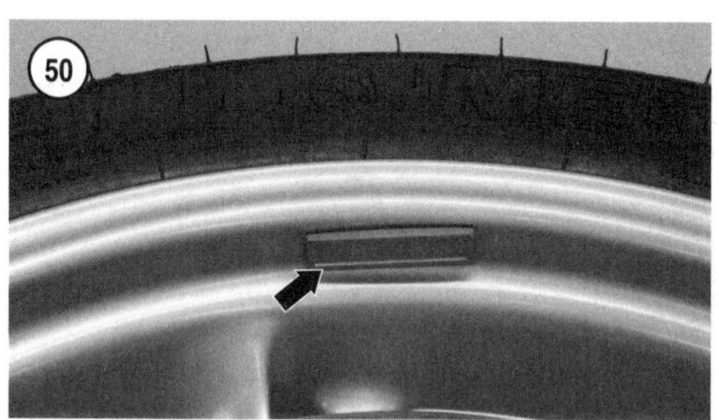

NOTE
The runout check can be performed with the tire mounted on the rim.

3. Mount the wheel on a truing stand. Refer to **Figure 49** for the dial indicator inspection points.

4. Spin the wheel slowly by hand and measure the radial (up and down) runout with a dial indicator as shown in **Figure 49**. If the runout (**Table 1**) is excessive, go to Step 6.

5. Spin the wheel slowly by hand and measure the axial (side to side) runout with a dial indicator as shown in **Figure 49**. If the runout (**Table 1**) is excessive, go to Step 6.

6. If the runout is excessive, remove the wheel from the truing stand and turn each bearing inner race (B, **Figure 40**) by hand. If necessary, remove the seal and closely check the bearings. Each bearing must turn smoothly and be a tight fit in its mounting bore. Some axial play is normal, but radial play must be negligible. Then check the bearing for visual damage. If a bearing turns roughly, replace both bearings as a set. If a bearing is loose in its

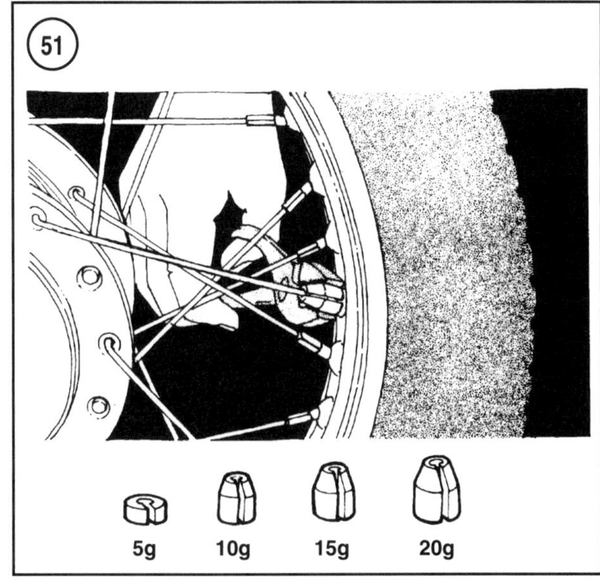

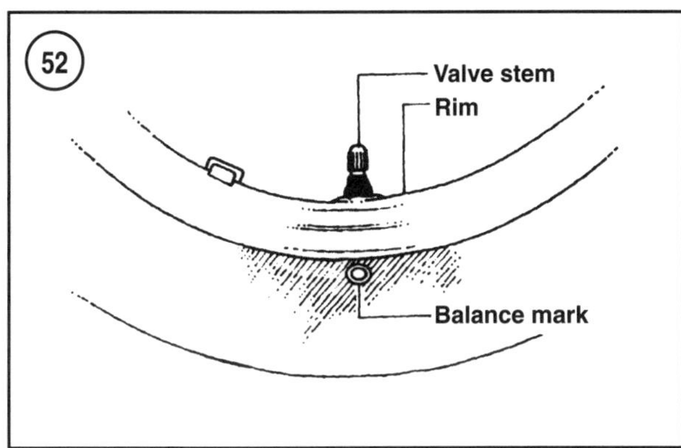

mounting bore, the hub is probably damaged. Remove the bearings and check the mounting bore for any cracks, gouges or other damage.

7. If the wheel bearings and hub are in good condition but the runout is out of specification, replace the damaged wheel.

Front Wheel Balance

A BMW balancing stand and five BMW special tools are required to balance the rear wheel. Refer this service to a BMW dealership.

A wheel that is not balanced is unsafe because it seriously affects the steering and handling of the motorcycle. Depending on the degree of unbalance and the speed of the motorcycle, anything from a mild vibration to a violent shimmy, may occur, which may result in loss of control. An imbalanced wheel also causes abnormal tire wear.

Motorcycle wheels can be checked for balance either statically or dynamically. This section describes how to static balance the wheels using a wheel balancing stand. To obtain a higher degree of accuracy, take the wheel to a BMW dealership and have them balanced with a dynamic wheel balancer. This machine spins the wheel to accurately detect any imbalance.

To balance alloy wheels, weights are attached to the rim (**Figure 50**). A kit of adhesive backed weights may be purchased from most dealerships or motorcycle supply stores. This kit contains test weights and strips of adhesive-backed weights that can be cut to the desired weight and attached directly to the rim.

To balance wire wheels, the weight is attached directly to the spoke (**Figure 51**).

The wheel must be able to rotate freely when checking wheel balance. Because excessively worn or damaged wheel bearings affect the accuracy of this procedure, check the front wheel bearings as described in this chapter. Check the wheel hub for cracks and other damage. Also confirm that the tire balance mark, a paint mark on the tire, is aligned with the valve stem (**Figure 52**). If not, break the tire loose from the rim and align the balance mark with the valve stem. Refer to *Tire Changing* in this chapter.

11

NOTE
When balancing the wheel, leave the brake discs attached to the wheel.

1. Remove the wheel as described in this chapter.
2. Clean the seals and inspect the wheel bearings as described under in this chapter.
3. Clean the tire and rim. Remove any stones or pebbles stuck in the tire tread.
4. Mount the wheel on a balance stand (**Figure 53**).

NOTE
To check the original balance of the wheel, leave the existing weights in place on the rim.

5. Spin the wheel by hand and let it coast to a stop. Mark the tire at its bottom point with chalk.
6. Spin the wheel several more times. If the same spot on the tire stops at the bottom each time, the wheel is out of balance. This is the heaviest part of the tire. When an unbalanced wheel is spun, it always comes to rest with the heaviest spot at the bottom.
7. Attach a test weight to the wheel at the point opposite the heaviest spot and spin the wheel again.
8. Experiment with different weights until the wheel, when spun, comes to rest at a different position each time. When a wheel is correctly balanced, the weight of the tire and wheel assembly is distributed equally around the wheel.
9. Remove the test weight and install the correct size weight to the rim. On alloy wheels, adhere the weight directly to the rim (**Figure 50**). On wire wheels, attach the weight directly to the spoke (**Figure 51**).
10. Record the number and position of weights on the wheel. Then, if the motorcycle experiences a handling or vibration problem at a later time, first check for any missing weights.
11. Install the wheel as described in this chapter.

SPOKE WHEEL SERVICE

Due to the unique design of the wheel and the spokes, wheel service must be performed at a BMW dealership as a special fixture is required. Each spoke has a 4 mm setscrew located inside the end of each spoke nipple. This setscrew applies pressure to the spoke and nipple threads and keeps the spoke from working loose.

TIRE CHANGING

All models are equipped with tubeless tires on both wire and alloy wheels.

Tools

NOTE
Before purchasing a bead breaker, make sure it will work on BMW tire and wheel sizes.

To change the tires, the following tools are required:
1. A set of tire levers or flat-handled tire irons with rounded ends (**Figure 54**).
2. Bead breaker.
3. Spray bottle filled with soapy water.
4. Plastic rim protectors for each tire iron.

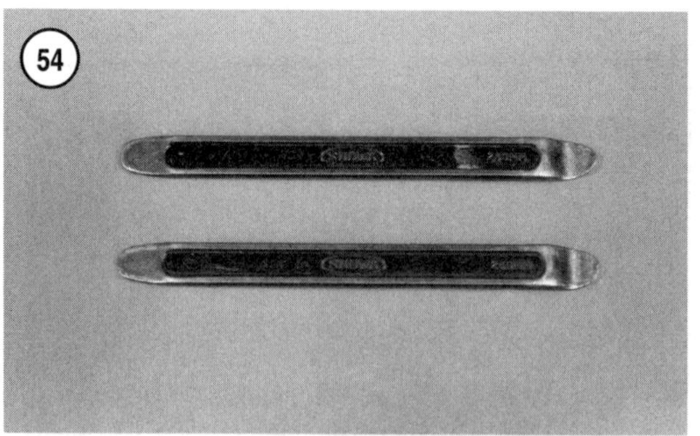

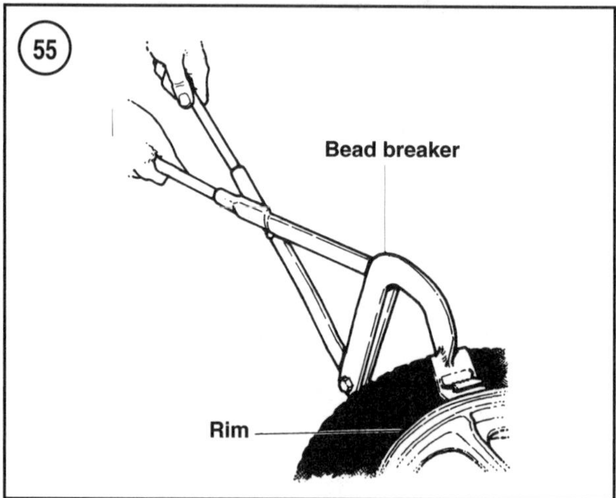

Removal

CAUTION
The wheels can be damaged easily during tire removal. Work carefully to avoid damaging the tire beads, inner liner of the tire or the wheel rim flange that form the sealing surfaces. As described in the text, insert rim protectors between the tire irons and rim to protect the rim from damage.

NOTE
Tires are harder to replace when the rubber is hard and cold. If the weather is hot, place the wheels and new tires in the sun or in a closed automobile. The heat helps soften the rubber, easing removal and installation. If the weather is cold, place the tires and wheels inside a warm building.

NOTE
It is easier to replace tires when the wheel is mounted on some type of raised platform. A popular item used by many home mechanics

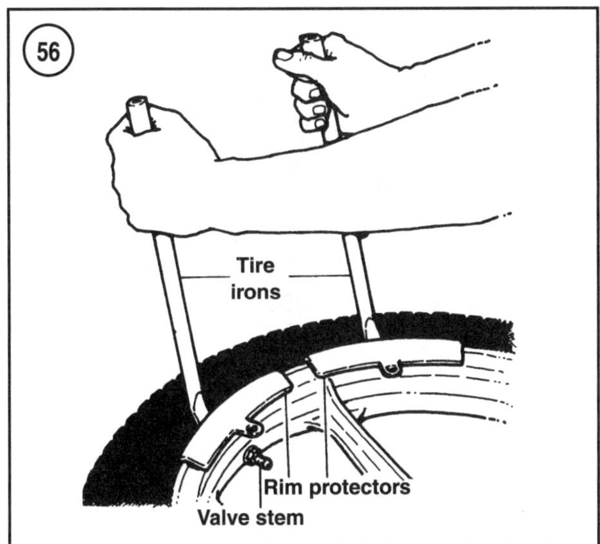

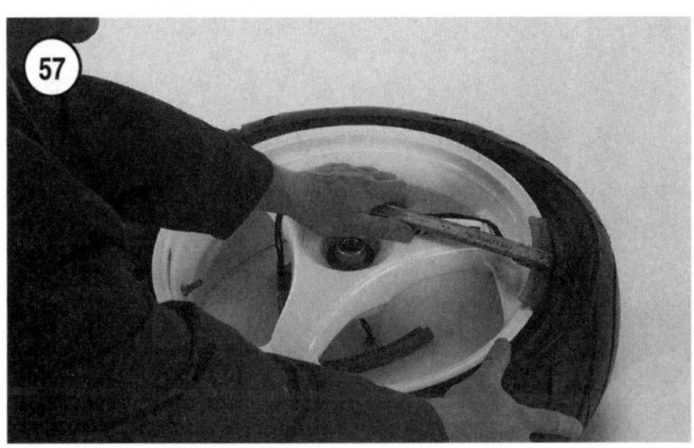

is a metal drum. Before placing the wheel on a drum, cover the drum edge with a length of garden or heater hose, split lengthwise and secured in place with plastic ties. When changing a tire at ground level, support the wheel on two wood blocks to prevent the brake disc from contacting the floor.

1. If the tire is going to be reused, mark the valve stem location on the tire so the tire can be installed in the same position for easier balancing.
2. Remove the valve core to deflate the tire.

CAUTION

The inner rim and tire bead areas are sealing surfaces on a tubeless tire. Do not scratch the inside of the rim or damage the tire bead. Do not attempt to force the bead off the rim with any type of leverage, such as a long tire iron. It is very easy to damage the tire bead surface on the tire and rim. It is also possible to crack or break the alloy wheel. Removing tubeless tires from their rims can be difficult because of the exceptionally tight bead and rim seal. If unable to break the tire bead with a bead breaker, take the wheel to a motorcycle dealership and have them change the tire.

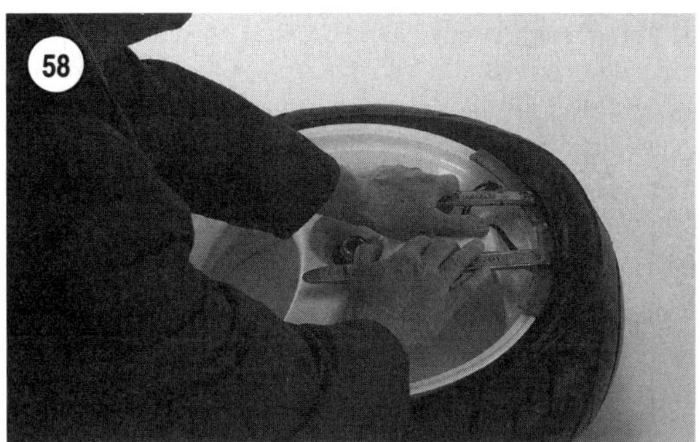

3. Use a bead breaker and break the bead all the way around the tire (**Figure 55**). Do not try to force the bead with tire irons. Make sure that both beads are clear of the rim beads.
4. Lubricate the tire beads with soapy water on the side to be removed first.

CAUTION

*Always use rim protectors (**Figure 56**) between the tire irons and the rim to protect the rim from damage.*

5. Insert the tire iron under the bead next to the valve (**Figure 57**). Force the bead on the opposite side of the tire into the center of the rim and pry the bead over the rim with the tire iron.
6. Insert a second tire iron next to the first (no more than 20.3 cm [8 in.] apart) to hold the bead over the rim. Then work around the tire with the first tool prying the bead over the rim (**Figure 58**). Work slowly by taking small bites with the tire irons. Taking large bites or using excessive force can damage the tire bead or rim.

NOTE

If the tire is tight and hard to pry over the rim, use a third tire iron and a rim protector. Use one hand and arm to hold the first two tire irons, then use the other hand to operate the third tire iron when prying the tire over the rim.

7. Turn the wheel over. Insert a tire iron between the second bead and the same side of the rim that the first bead

was pried over (**Figure 59**). Force the bead on the opposite side from the tool into the center of the rim. Pry the second bead off the rim, working around the wheel with the two rim protectors and tire irons.

8. Remove the valve stem and discard it. Remove all rubber residue from the valve stem hole and inspect the hole for cracks and other damage.

9. Remove old balance weights from the rim surface.

10. Carefully clean the rim bead with a brush—do not use excessive force or damage the sealing surface of the rim. Then inspect the sealing surface for any cracks, corrosion or other damage.

NOTE
If there is any doubt as to wheel condition, take it to a BMW dealership for a thorough inspection.

Installation

1A. If installing the original tire, carefully inspect the tire for any damage.

1B. If installing a new tire, remove all stickers from the tire tread.

2. Lubricate both beads of the tire with soapy water.

3. Make sure the correct tire, either front or rear is installed on the correct wheel and that the direction arrow on the tire faces in the direction of wheel rotation.

4. Place the backside of the tire into the center of the rim. The lower bead should go into the center of the rim and the upper bead outside. Use both hands to push the backside of the tire into the rim (**Figure 60**) as far as possible. Use tire irons when it becomes difficult to install the tire by hand (**Figure 61**).

5. Press the upper bead into the rim opposite the valve. Pry the bead into the rim on both sides of the initial point with a tire tool, working around the rim to the valve (**Figure 62**).

6. Check the bead on both sides of the tire for an even fit around the rim. Align the paint spot near the bead indicating the lightest point of the tire with the valve stem.

7. Lubricate both sides of the tire with soapy water.

WARNING
Always wear eye protection when seating the tire beads onto the rim. Never exceed 56 psi (4.0 k/cm^2) inflation pressure as the tire could burst causing severe injury. Never stand directly over the tire while inflating it.

8. Inflate the tire until the beads seat into place. A loud pop should be heard as each bead seats against its side of the rim.

9. After inflating the tire, check to see that the beads are fully seated and that the tire rim lines (**Figure 63**) are the same distance from the rim all the way around the tire. If one or both beads do not seat, deflate the tire, re-lubricate the rim and beads with soapy water and re-inflate the tire.

10. Inflate the tire to the required pressure listed in Chapter Three, **Table 2**. Screw on the valve stem cap.

11. Balance the wheel as described in this chapter.

NOTE
After installing new tires, follow the tire manufacturer's instructions for breaking-in (scuffing) the tire.

TIRE REPAIRS

Only use tire plugs as an emergency repair. Refer to the manufacturer's instructions to install and note the vehicle weight and speed restrictions. After performing an emergency tire repair with a plug, consider the repair temporary and replace the tire at the earliest opportunity.

Refer all tire repairs to a BMW dealership or other qualified motorcycle technician.

11

Table 1 WHEEL SERVICE SPECIFICATIONS

Item	Specification
Front wheel runout limit	
Axial	0.5 mm (0.0197 in.)
Radial	0.5 mm (0.0197 in.)
Rear wheel runout limit	
Axial	0.3 mm (0.0118 in.)
Radial	0.3 mm (0.0118 in.)

Table 2 WHEEL TORQUE SPECIFICATIONS

Item	N•m	in.-lb.	ft.-lb.
ABS sensor bolt	4	35	–
Front brake caliper bolts	30	–	22
Front axle bolt	30	–	22
Front axle clamp bolt	22	–	16
Rear axle nut	93	–	69
Rear sprocket nut	88	–	65
Rear wheel bolts			
All models except R1150GS			
Initial	50	–	37
Final	105	–	77
R1150GS			
Initial	72	–	53
Final	105	–	77

CHAPTER TWELVE

FRONT SUSPENSION AND STEERING

This chapter describes repair and maintenance of the front suspension, front fork and the steering components.

The Telelever front suspension incorporates two fork tubes that are joined by a steel front suspension A-arm. The rear portion of the A-arm attaches to pivot points on the engine crankcase while the front attaches to the lower fork bridge via a ball joint.

The top end of the fork tubes are attached to the upper fork bridge with pot-type joints (most models) that are pressed into the upper fork bridge. The upper fork bridge has an integral ball bearing and attaches to the front frame. There are no springs or damper rods within the fork tubes as they only contain oil for lubrication but provide no damping. This design eliminates any stiction associated with a conventional fork suspension.

The single adjustable Showa front strut (shock absorber) attaches to the front suspension A-arm and to the front frame and fulfills the suspension damping duties.

Some of the components of the front suspension must be heated for removal. A heat gun capable of generating 120° C (248° F) is required.

Table 1 and **Table 2** are at the end of this chapter.

HANDLEBAR

Removal/Installation (Controls in Place)

R850R, R1100R, R1100RT and R1150RT models

Refer to **Figure 1**.

1. If necessary, remove the left and right controls as described in this chapter.

2. Remove the Allen bolts securing the individual handlebars (**Figure 2**) to the upper fork bridge.

3. Remove the individual handlebar.

4. If the right controls were not removed, carefully move the handlebar assembly out of the way and lay it over the frame. Keep the brake master cylinder reservoir in the upright position to minimize a loss of brake fluid and to keep air from entering into the brake system.

5. On R1150RT models, if the left controls were not removed, carefully move the handlebar assembly out of the way and lay it over the frame. Keep the clutch master cylinder reservoir in the upright position to minimize a loss of brake fluid and to keep air from entering into the clutch hydraulic system.

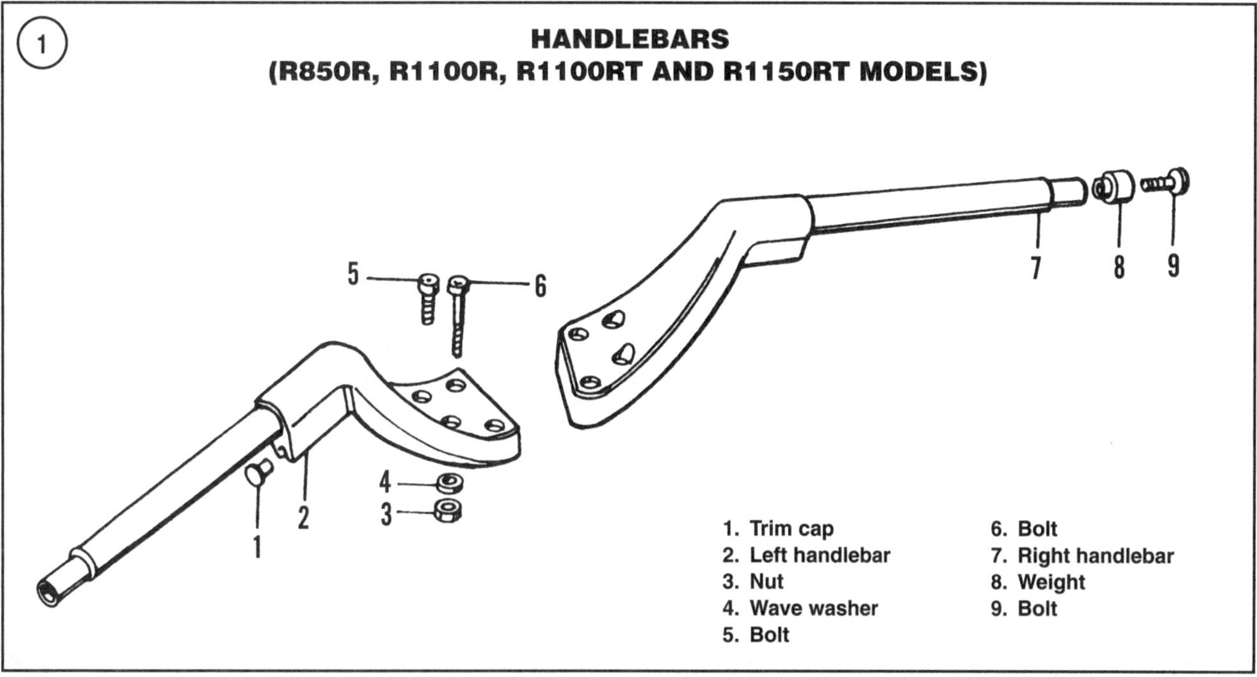

6. Install the handlebars and tighten the Allen bolts to 21 N•m (15 ft.-lb.).

R1150R models

Refer to **Figure 3**.

1. If necessary, remove the left and right controls as described in this chapter.
2. Remove the Allen bolts (**Figure 4**) securing the handlebar upper holders to the upper fork bridge.
3. Remove the handlebar.
4. If the right controls were not removed, carefully move the handlebar assembly out of the way and lay it over the frame. Keep the front master cylinder reservoir in the upright position to minimize a loss of brake fluid and to keep air from entering into the brake system.
5. If the left controls were not removed, keep the clutch master cylinder reservoir in the upright position to minimize loss of brake fluid and to keep air from entering into the clutch hydraulic system.
6. Install the handlebars and align the index mark with the split line of the upper holders (**Figure 5**). Tighten the front bolts first and then the rear bolts to 21 N•m (15 ft.-lb.).

R850GS, R1100GS and R1150GS models

Refer to **Figure 3**.

1. If necessary, remove the left and right controls as described in this chapter.
2. Remove the Allen bolts securing the handlebar upper holders (**Figure 6**) to the upper fork bridge.
3. Remove the handlebar.
4. If the right controls were not removed, carefully move the handlebar assembly out of the way and lay it over the frame. Keep the front master cylinder reservoir in the upright position to minimize a loss of brake fluid and to keep air from entering the brake system.
5. On R1150GS models, if the left controls were not removed, keep the clutch master cylinder reservoir in the upright position to minimize loss of brake fluid and to keep air from entering into the clutch hydraulic system.

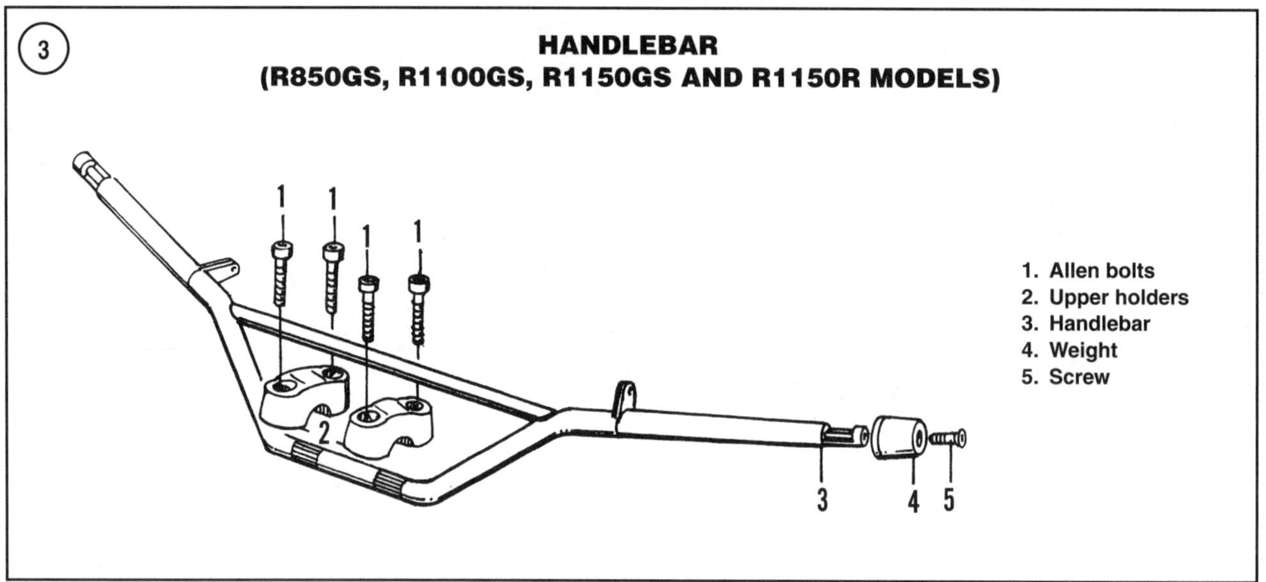

HANDLEBAR (R850GS, R1100GS, R1150GS AND R1150R MODELS)

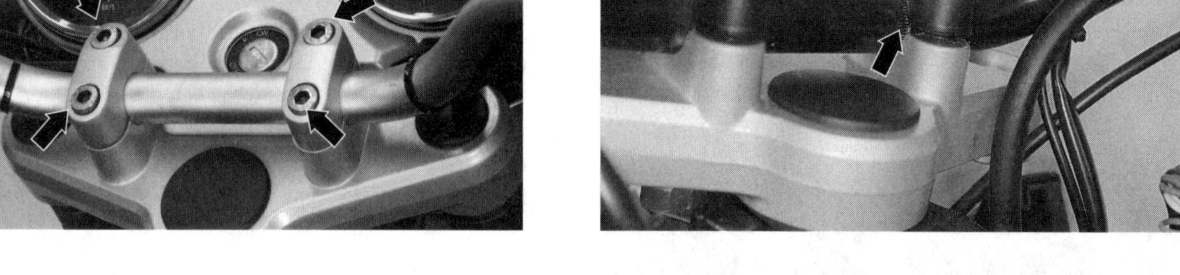

6. Install the handlebars and align the index mark with the split line of the upper holders (**Figure 5**). Tighten the front bolts first and then the rear bolts to 21 N•m (15 ft.-lb.).

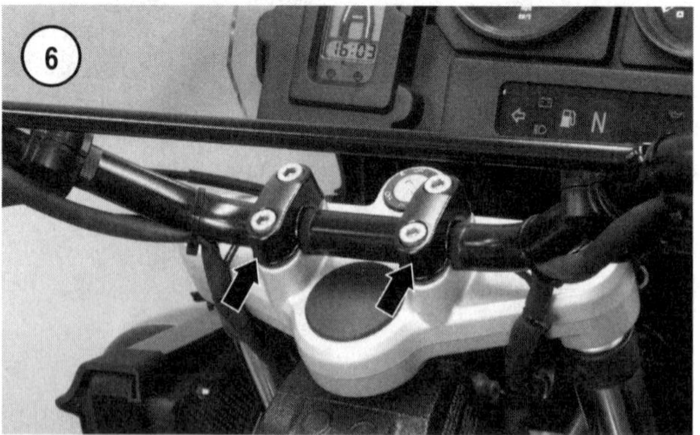

R1100RS and R1150RS models

Refer to **Figure 7**.

1. If necessary, remove the left and right controls as described in this chapter.
2. Remove the trim panel (**Figure 8**).
3. Remove the front fairing assembly as described in Chapter Fifteen.
4. Remove the bolt securing the handlebar rubber mounts (**Figure 9**) to the underside of the upper fork bridge.
5. Pull the handlebar forward and remove it.
6. If the right controls were not removed, carefully move the handlebar assembly out of the way and lay it over the frame. Keep the front master cylinder reservoir in the upright position to minimize a loss of brake fluid and to keep air from entering the brake system.
7. On R1150RS models, if the left controls were not removed, keep the clutch master cylinder reservoir in the

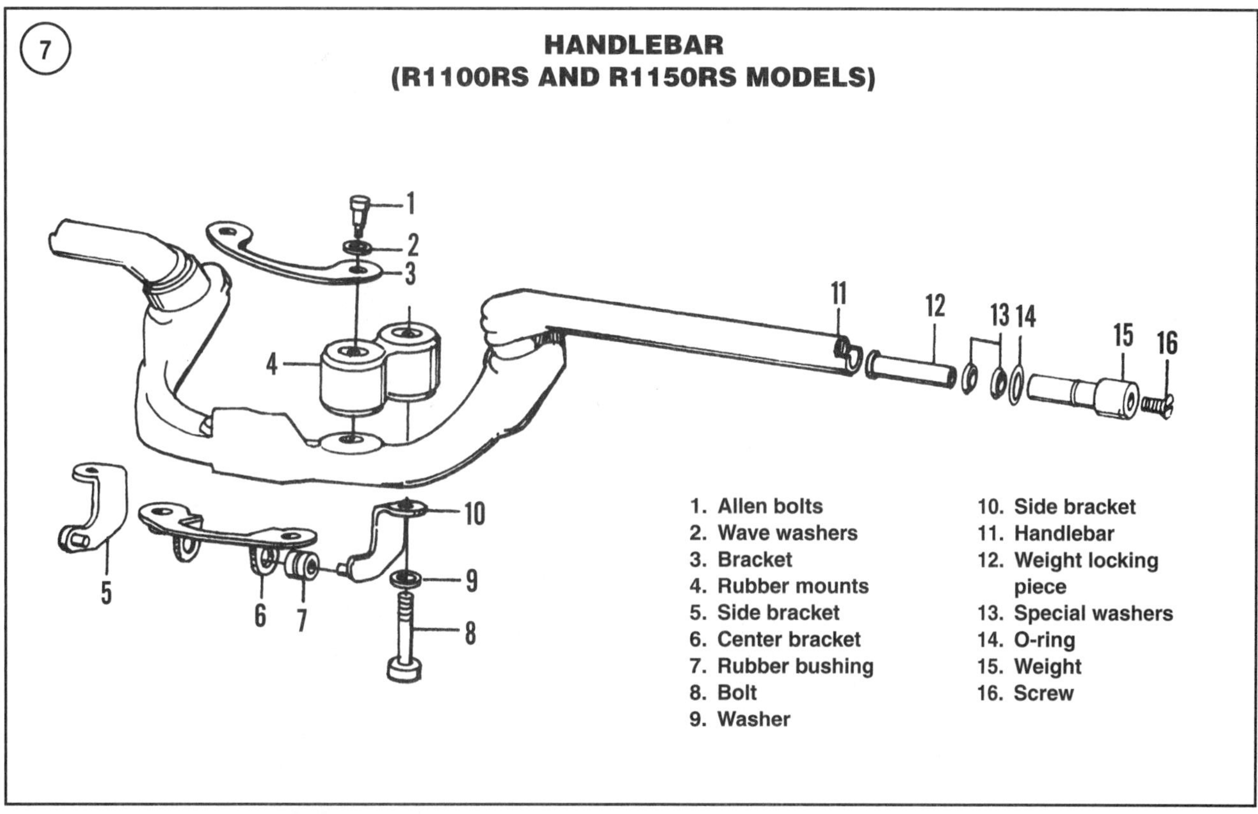

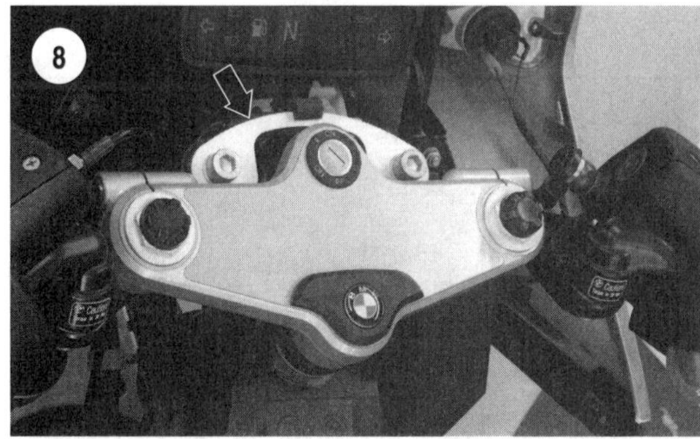

upright position to minimize loss of brake fluid and to keep air from entering the clutch hydraulic system.

8. Install the handlebars and tighten the bolts to 40 N•m (29 ft.-lb.).
9. Install the front fairing assembly as described in Chapter Fifteen.

12

R1100S models

Refer to **Figure 10**.

1. If necessary, remove the left and right controls as described in this chapter.
2. Remove the front fairing assembly as described in Chapter Fifteen.
3. Loosen the clamp bolt (A, **Figure 11**) securing the handlebar to the fork tube.
4. Partially remove the front fork tubes (B, **Figure 11**). Only lower the fork tube sufficiently to allow handlebar removal.
5. Remove the locating bolt on the under side of the handlebar and remove the handlebar (C, **Figure 11**).
6. If the left controls were not removed, keep the clutch master cylinder reservoir in the upright position to minimize loss of brake fluid and to keep air from entering the clutch hydraulic system.

7. Repeat Steps 3-5 for the other handlebar, if necessary.
8. If the right controls were not removed, carefully move the handlebar assembly out of the way and lay it over the frame. Keep the front master cylinder reservoir in the upright position to minimize a loss of brake fluid and to keep air from entering the brake system.
9. Install the handlebars and tighten the following bolts:
   a. The clamp bolt to the fork tube to 25 N•m (18 ft.-lb.).
   b. The locating bolt to 9 N•m (80 in.-lb.).

R850C and R1200C models

1. If necessary, remove the left and right controls as described in this chapter.

NOTE
The Allen bolts secure both the upper and lower handlebar holders.

2. Remove the Allen bolts securing the handlebar upper (A, **Figure 12**) and lower (B) holders to the upper fork bridge.
3. Remove the handlebar (C, **Figure 12**) and the upper and lower holders (B).
4. If the right controls were not removed, carefully move the handlebar assembly out of the way and lay it over the frame. Keep the front master cylinder reservoir in the upright position to minimize a loss of brake fluid and to keep air from entering the brake system.
5. If the left controls were not removed, keep the clutch master cylinder reservoir in the upright position to minimize loss of brake fluid and to keep air from entering the clutch hydraulic system.
6. Position the lower holders with the arrow pointing toward the front and install them.
7. Install the handlebar, the upper holders and the Allen bolts. Tighten the front bolts first and then the rear bolts to 21 N•m (15 ft.-lb.).

HANDLEBAR CONTROLS

If the handlebars are going to be removed for replacement, it is necessary to remove the controls so they can be reinstalled on the new handlebar.

R850R and All R1100 Models (Except R1100S)

Left side controls

1. Disconnect the negative battery cable as described in Chapter Three.

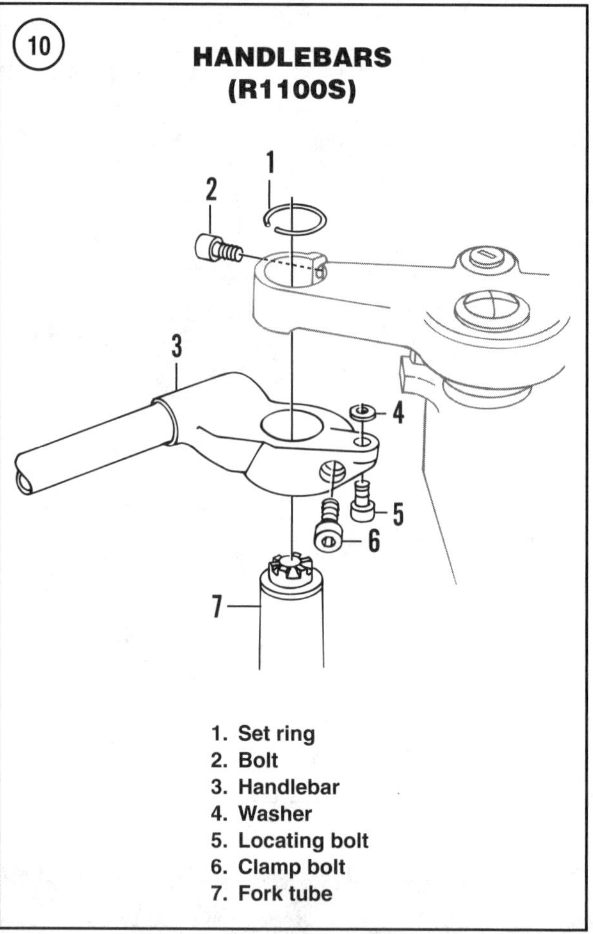

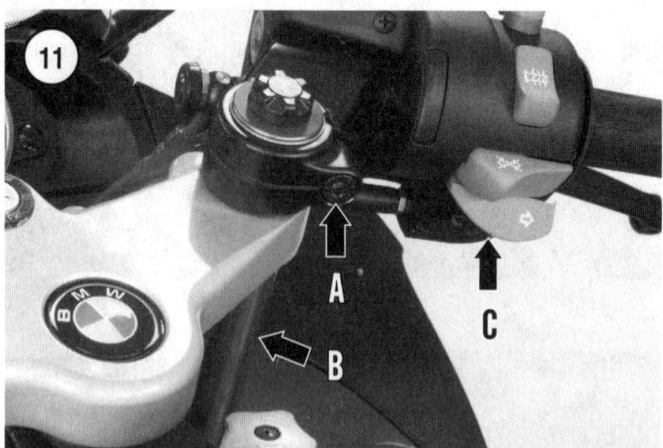

2A. On RS models, remove the left fairing panel as described in Chapter Fifteen.

2B. On GS and R models, remove the fuel tank as described in Chapter Nine.

2C. On RT models, remove the upper section of the fairing as described in Chapter Fifteen.

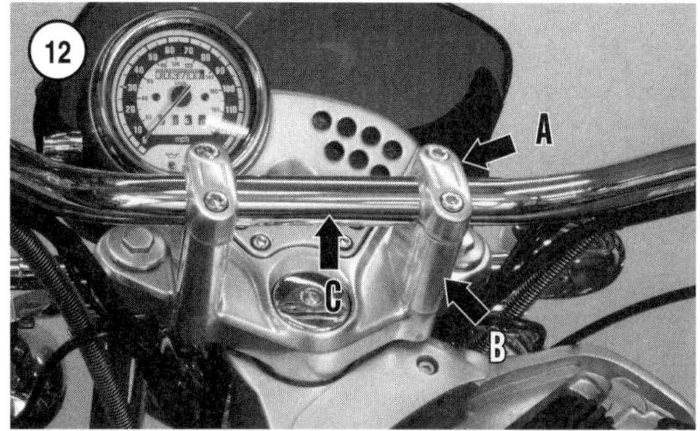

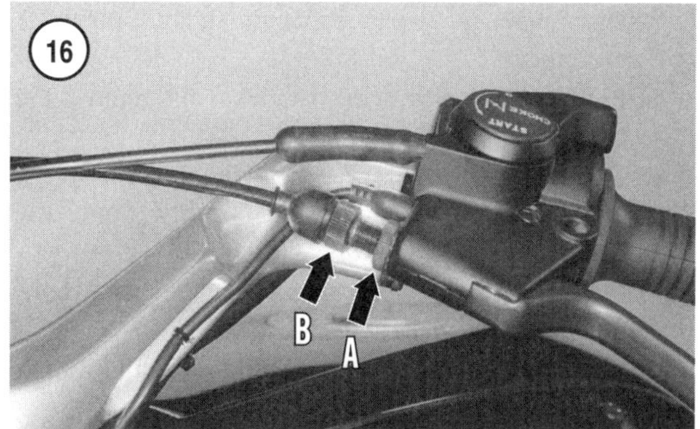

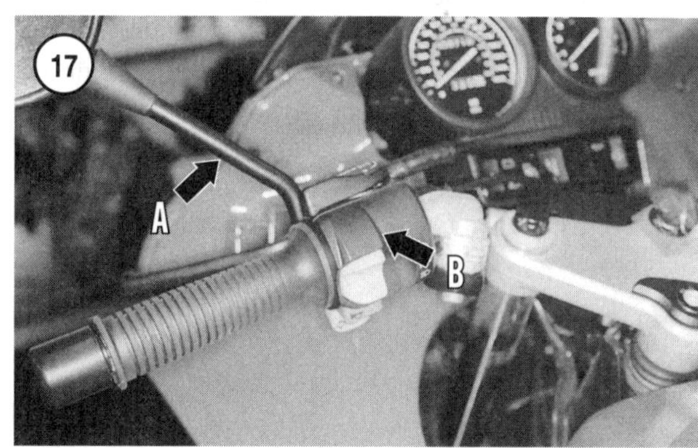

3. Follow the wires from the clutch interlock switch and disconnect the connector from the main wiring harness.
4. Disconnect the increase idle (choke) cable as follows:
   a. Carefully pry off the cover from the operating lever.
   b. Unscrew the large flat screw (**Figure 13**) and special washer (**Figure 14**).
   c. Remove the lever (A, **Figure 15**) from the housing and disconnect the cable (B) from the lever.
   d. Push the cable sleeve out and remove the cable (C, **Figure 15**) from the slot in the cable housing.
5. Disconnect the clutch cable as follows:
   a. Loosen the locknut (A, **Figure 16**) and turn the adjuster (B) in all the way. This will allow slack in the clutch cable.
   b. Disconnect the clutch cable and nipple from the underside of the clutch lever and remove the clutch cable.
6. On all models except RT models, unscrew and remove the rear view mirror (A, **Figure 17**).
7. Remove the screw and withdraw the handlebar weight.

8A. On models with non-heated grips, cut along the length of the handgrip and remove it from the handlebar.

8B. On models with heated grips, perform the following:
   a. Fold back the rubber grip at the end fitting.
   b. Remove the handgrip mounting screws.

c. Disconnect the wire connector and unfasten the wire shoes.
d. Pull the wire through the handlebar and remove the heated grip assembly.

9. Remove the screw securing the switch assembly (B, **Figure 17**) to the handlebar grip assembly. Move the switch assembly out of the way.

10. Loosen the clamping screw and slide the grip assembly off the end of the handlebar.

11. Install by reversing the removal steps while noting the following:

a. Install the grip assembly onto the handlebar and align the grip slot with the punch mark on the handlebar. Tighten the clamping screw securely.
b. On non-heated grips, apply Loctite 638, or an equivalent, to secure the grip to the handlebar. Follow the manufacturer's instructions regarding the drying time before operating the motorcycle.
c. Adjust the clutch as described in Chapter Three.

Right side controls

1. Disconnect the negative battery cable as described in Chapter Three.

2A. On RS models, remove the right fairing panel as described in Chapter Fifteen.

2B. On R and GS models, remove the fuel tank as described in Chapter Nine.

2C. On RT models, remove the upper section of the fairing as described in Chapter Fifteen.

3. Follow the wires from the front brake light switch and disconnect the connector from the main wiring harness.

4. Remove the screw (A, **Figure 18**) securing the switch assembly to the handlebar grip. Move the switch (B, **Figure 18**) out of the way.

5. Remove the throttle cable cover (**Figure 19**) and disconnect the throttle cable (**Figure 20**) from the throttle grip.

6. On all models except RT models, unscrew and remove the rear view mirror.

7. Remove the screw and withdraw the handlebar weight.

8A. For models with non-heated grips, cut along the length of the handgrip and remove it from the handlebar.

8B. For models with heated grips, perform the following:

a. Fold back the rubber grip at the end fitting.
b. Remove the handgrip mounting screws.
c. Disconnect the wire connector and unfasten the wire shoes.
d. Pull the wires through the handlebar and remove the heated grip assembly.

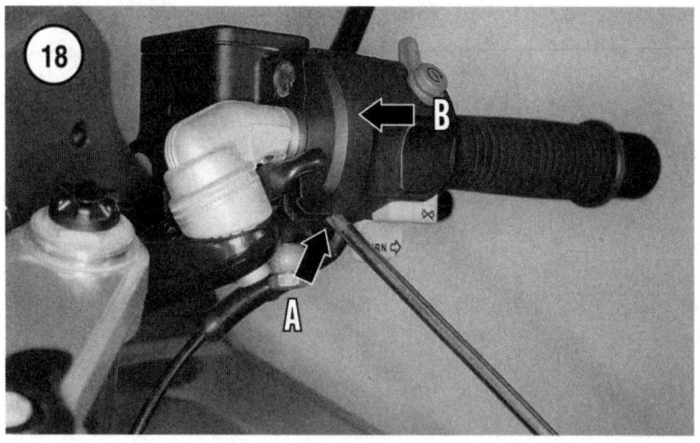

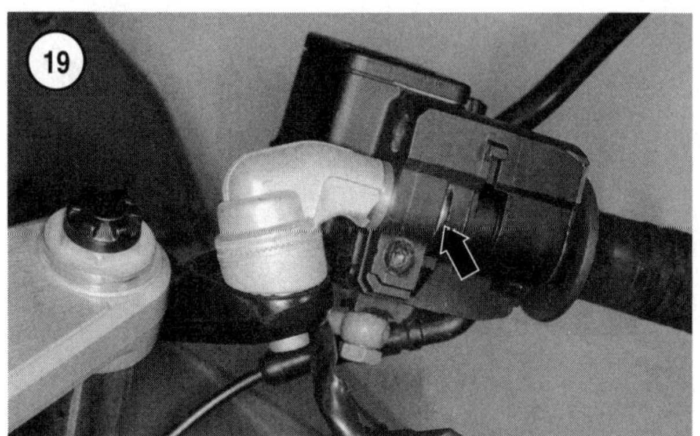

CAUTION

Cover the instrument cluster, front fairing (on models so equipped) and frame with a heavy cloth or plastic tarp to protect it from an accidental spilling of brake fluid. Wash any spilled brake fluid off any painted or plated surface immediately, as it will destroy the finish. Wash the area with soapy water and rinse thoroughly.

9. Loosen the clamping screw and slide the grip and master cylinder assembly off the end of the handlebar. Care-

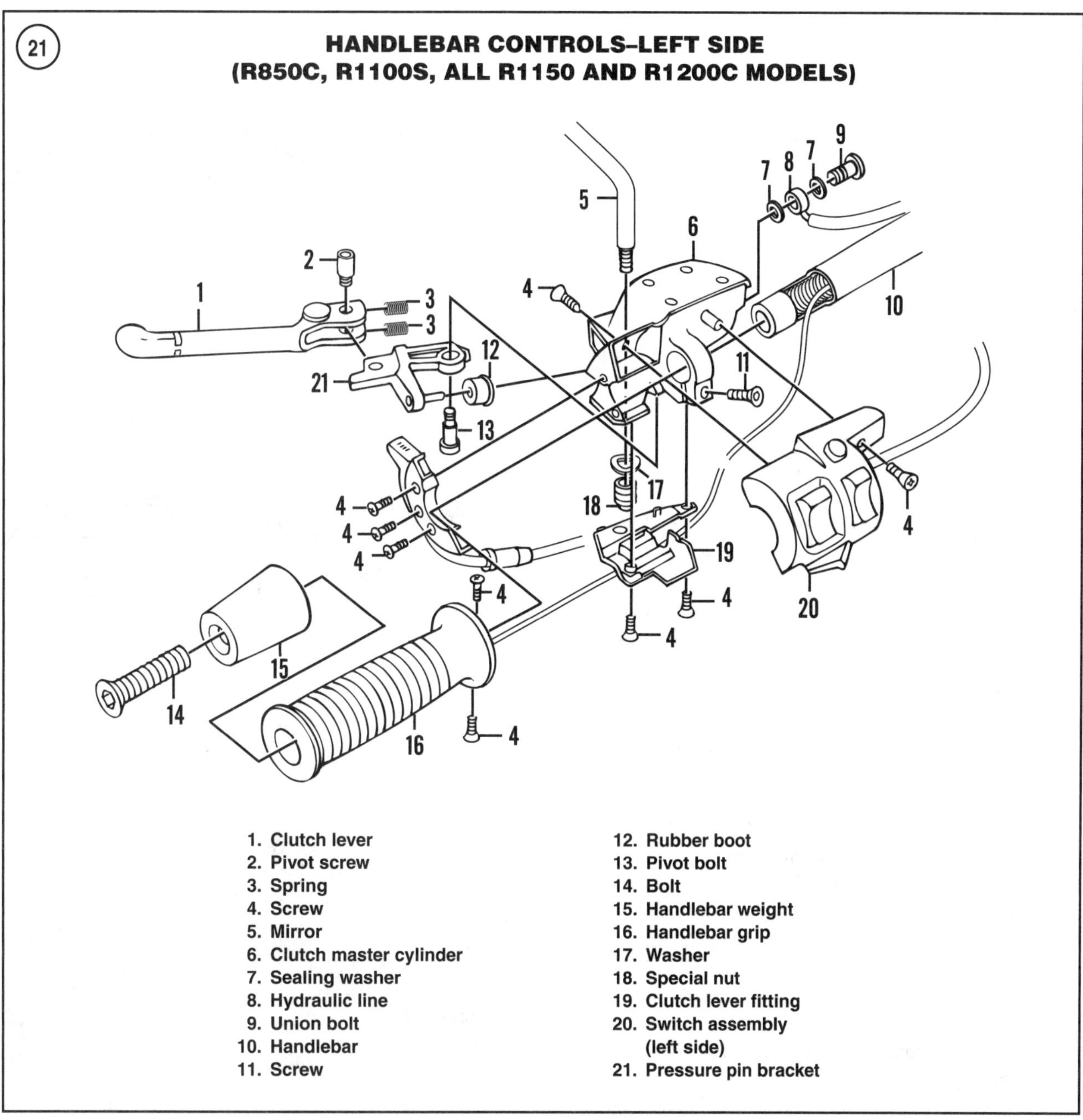

fully move the master cylinder out of the way and lay it over the frame. Keep the reservoir in the upright position to minimize loss of brake fluid and to keep air from entering into the brake system. It is not necessary to remove the hydraulic brake line.

10. Install by reversing the removal steps while noting the following:

a. Install the grip assembly onto the handlebar and align the grip slot with the punch mark on the handlebar. Tighten the clamping screw securely.

b. Check the fluid level in the front master cylinder and top it off if necessary.

R850C, R1100S, All R1150 and R1200C Models

Left side controls

Refer to **Figure 21**.

1. Disconnect the negative battery cable as described in Chapter Three.

12

2A. On RS models, remove the left fairing panel as described in Chapter Fifteen.
2B. On GS, R and C models, remove the fuel tank as described in Chapter Nine.
2C. On RT models, remove the upper section of the fairing as described in Chapter Fifteen.
3. Follow the wires from the clutch interlock switch and disconnect the connector from the main wiring harness.
4. Clean all dirt and foreign matter from top of the clutch master cylinder.
5A. On R850C and R1200C models, perform the following:

a. Remove the screw securing the handgrip (A, **Figure 22**) and pull off the handgrip.
b. Remove the two screws securing the trim plate (B, **Figure 22**) and remove the trim plate.

5B. On all models except R850C and R1200C, perform the following:

a. On GS models so equipped, remove the bolt securing the hand guard (A, **Figure 23**) and handlcbar weight (B).
b. On all other models, remove the bolt securing the handlebar weight (B, **Figure 23**) and remove the weight.
c. Remove the two screws securing the handgrip (C, **Figure 23**).
d. On models so equipped, disconnect the electrical connector and release the cable shoe for the heated hand grip.
e. Slide the hand grip (C, **Figure 23**) off the handlebar.

6. Remove the screws securing the lower section of the clutch lever fitting and remove the fitting.
7. On all models except R850C and R1200C, remove the screws securing the increase idle (choke) lever and move the lever out of the way.
8. Remove the screws securing the handlebar switch (D, **Figure 23**) and move the switch away from the handlebar.
9. On models so equipped, remove the rear view mirror (E, **Figure 23**).
10. Remove the screws securing the top cover (F, **Figure 23**). Remove the top cover, plate and diaphragm from the master cylinder reservoir.
11. If a shop syringe is available, draw all of the brake fluid out of the master cylinder reservoir. Temporarily reinstall the diaphragm, plate and cover. Tighten the cover finger tight.
12. Remove the clutch lever position switch from the underside of the master cylinder.
13A. On models equipped with a union bolt, perform the following:

a. Place a rag beneath the union bolt and remove the bolt.

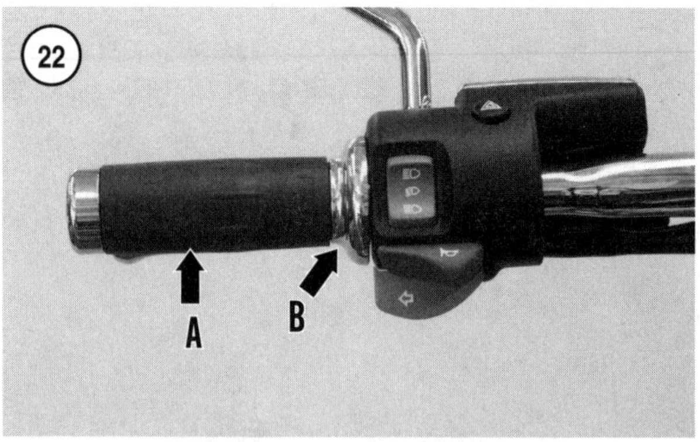

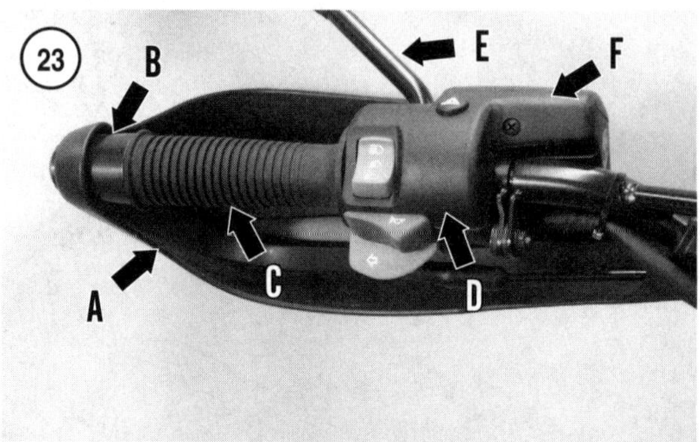

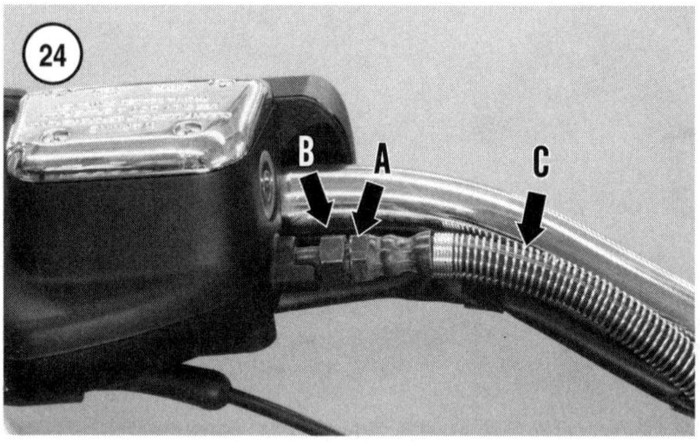

b. Separate the clutch hose from the master cylinder. Do not lose the two sealing washers, one from each side of the clutch hose fitting.

13B. On models equipped with a brake line fitting, perform the following:

a. Place a wrench on one side of the fitting (A, **Figure 24**) and loosen the other portion of the fitting (B).
b. Separate the clutch hose (C, **Figure 24**) from the master cylinder.

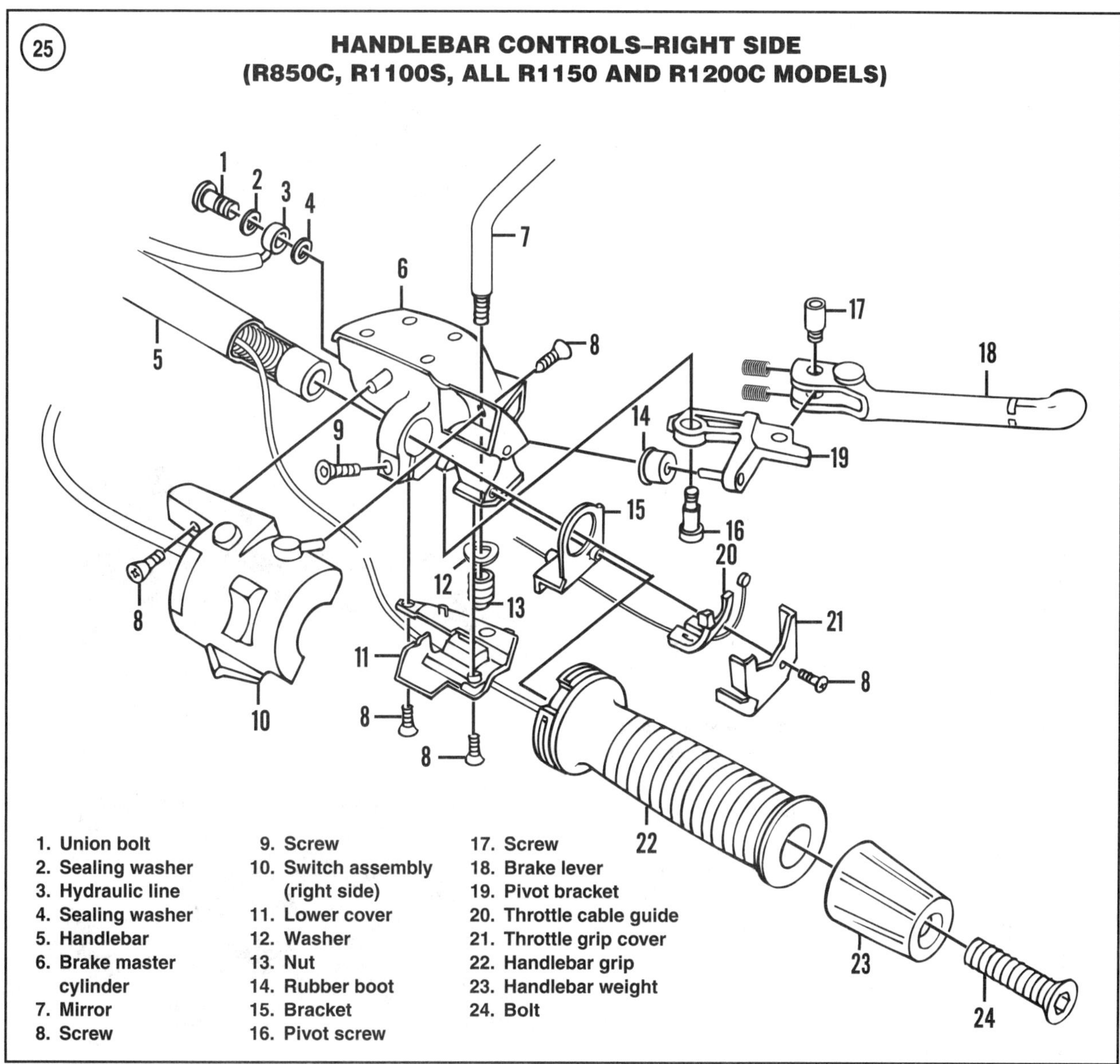

14. Place the loose end of the clutch hose in a reclosable plastic bag. Tie the loose end of the hose up to the handlebar.

15. Loosen the master cylinder clamp bolt and slide the master cylinder off the end of the handlebar.

16. Drain any residual brake fluid from the master cylinder and reservoir. Dispose of fluid properly.

17. If the master cylinder is not going to be serviced; place it in a reclosable plastic bag to protect it from contamination.

18. Install by reversing the removal steps while noting the following:

a. Position the clutch master cylinder onto the left handlebar, and align the mark on the master cylinder with the handlebar punch mark.
b. On models equipped with a union bolt, install a *new* sealing washer onto each side of the hose fitting tighten the union bolt to 14 N•m (124 in.-lb.).
c. Refill the master cylinder and reservoir with fresh DOT 4 brake fluid and bleed the clutch system as described in this chapter.

Right side controls

Refer to **Figure 25**.

12

1. Disconnect the negative battery cable as described in Chapter Three.

2A. On RS models, remove the right fairing panel as described in Chapter Fifteen.

2B. On R, GS and C models, remove the fuel tank as described in Chapter Nine.

2C. On RT models, remove the upper section of the fairing as described in Chapter Fifteen.

3. Follow the wires from the front brake light switch and disconnect the connector from the main wiring harness.

4A. On R850C and R1200C models, perform the following:

a. Remove the screw securing the throttle twist grip cover (A, **Figure 26**).

b. Remove the throttle cable adjust screw and disconnect the throttle cable from the twist grip.

c. Pull off the throttle twist grip (B, **Figure 26**).

d. Remove the screws securing the lower section of the brake lever fitting and remove the fitting (C, **Figure 26**).

4B. On all models except R850C and R1200C, perform the following:

a. On GS models so equipped, remove the bolt securing the hand guard (A, **Figure 27**) and handlebar weight (B).

b. On all other models, remove the bolt securing the handlebar weight (B, **Figure 27**) and remove the weight.

c. Remove the screw securing the throttle twist grip cover.

d. Remove the throttle cable adjust screw and disconnect the throttle cable from the twist grip.

e. Pull off the throttle twist grip (C, **Figure 27**).

f. On models so equipped, disconnect the electrical connector and release the cable shoe for the heated hand grip.

5. Remove the screws securing the lower section of the brake lever fitting and remove the fitting.

6. Remove the screws securing the handlebar switch (D, **Figure 27**) and move the switch away from the handlebar.

7. On models so equipped, remove the rear view mirror (E, **Figure 27**).

8. Clean all debris from top of the brake master cylinder.

9. Remove the screws securing the top cover (F, **Figure 27**). Remove the top cover, plate and diaphragm from the master cylinder reservoir.

10. If a shop syringe is available, draw all of the brake fluid out of the master cylinder reservoir. Temporarily reinstall the diaphragm, plate and cover. Tighten the cover finger tight.

11. Remove the clutch lever position switch from the underside of the master cylinder.

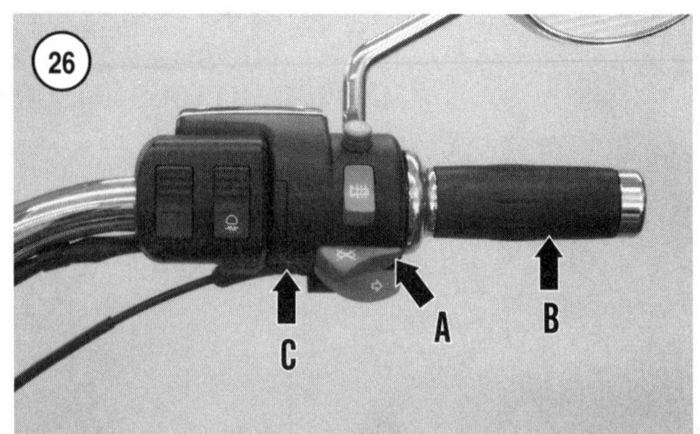

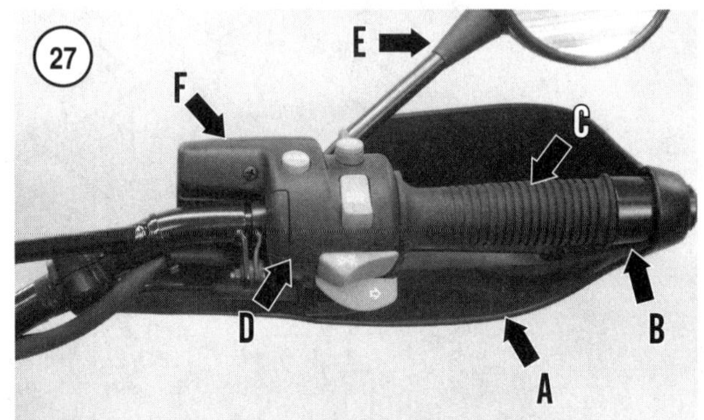

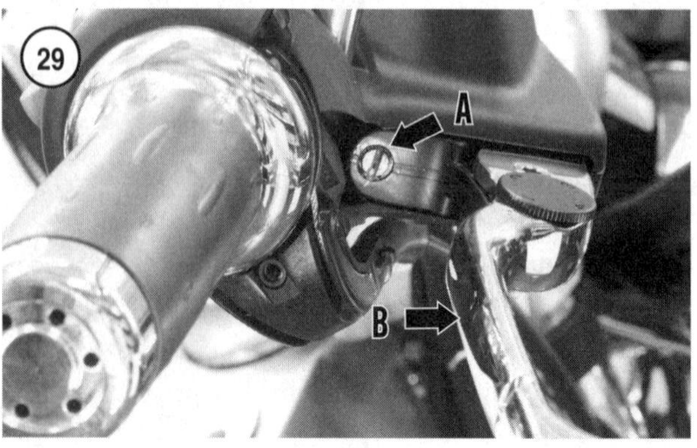

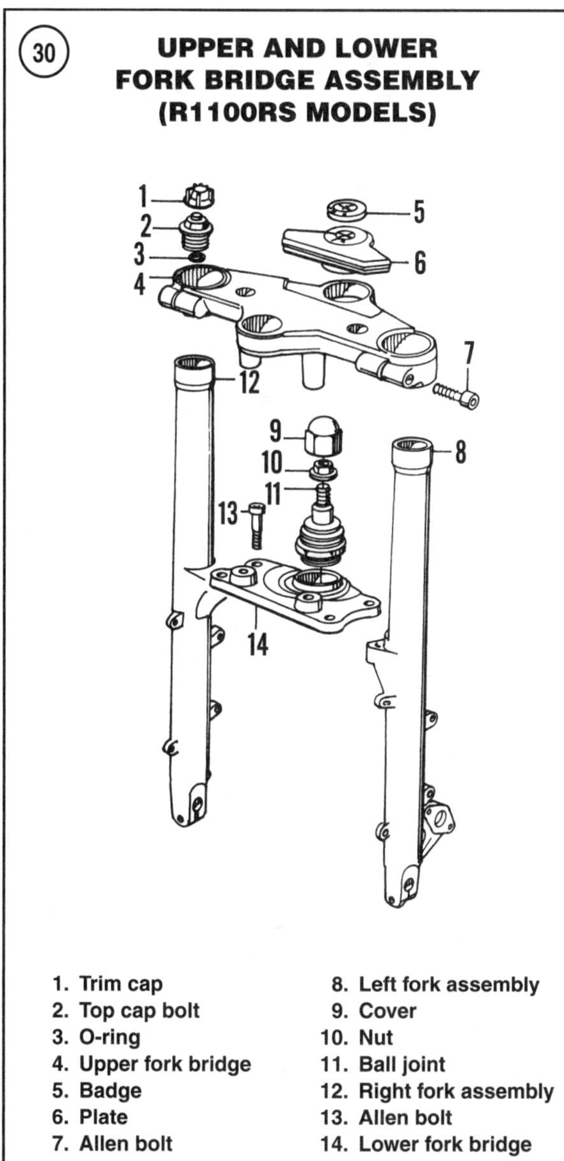

12. Place a rag beneath the union bolt and remove the bolt.

13. Separate the brake hose from the master cylinder. Do not lose the two sealing washers, one from each side of the brake hose fitting.

14. Place the loose end of the brake hose in a reclosable plastic bag to prevent brake fluid from dribbling onto the motorcycle. Tie the loose end of the hose up to the handlebar.

15. Loosen the master cylinder clamp bolt and slide the master cylinder off the end of the handlebar.

16. Drain any residual brake fluid from the master cylinder and reservoir. Dispose of fluid properly.

17. If the master cylinder is not going to be serviced; place it in a reclosable plastic bag to protect it from contamination.

18. Install by reversing the removal steps while noting the following:

a. Position the brake master cylinder onto the right handlebar, and align the mark on the master cylinder with the handlebar punch mark.
b. On models equipped with a union bolt, install a *new* sealing washer onto each side of the hose fitting tighten the union bolt to 14 N•m (124 in.-lb.).
c. Refill the master cylinder and reservoir with fresh DOT 4 brake fluid and bleed the brake system as described in this chapter.

HANDLEBAR LEVER CLEARANCE ADJUSTMENT (R1100S AND ALL R1150 MODELS)

If the brake and/or clutch lever have been removed from the handlebar the clearance must be adjusted. This procedure is shown on the brake lever. It also applies to the clutch lever.

1. Remove the screw securing the throttle grip cover (**Figure 28**) and remove the cover.
2. Unscrew and remove the adjustment screw (A, **Figure 29**).
3. Remove the lever pivot screw and remove the brake, or clutch, hand lever (B, **Figure 29**).
4. Clean all threadlocking compound from the adjustment screw threads.
5. Apply a medium strength threadlocking compound to the adjustment screw threads.
6. Apply a light coat of BMW Microlube GL 261, or Bel Rey Total Performance Lube, to the pressure pin of the adjusting screw.
7. Install the adjustment screw and screw it in a few turns.
8. Correctly position the metal tab on the brake, or clutch, switch and install the hand lever.
9. Install the hand lever pivot screw and tighten securely.
10. Tighten the adjustment screw (A, **Figure 29**) until the hand lever has zero free play, then tighten the screw an additional 90°.
11. Apply sealing lacquer to the head of the adjustment screw to prevent it from backing out.
12. Tighten the lever pivot screw to 11 N•m (97 in.-lb.).

UPPER FORK BRIDGE

Disassembly

Refer to the **Figure 30-37**.

12

31

UPPER AND LOWER FORK BRIDGE ASSEMBLY (R850R, R850GS, R1100R, R1100GS AND RT1100RT MODELS)

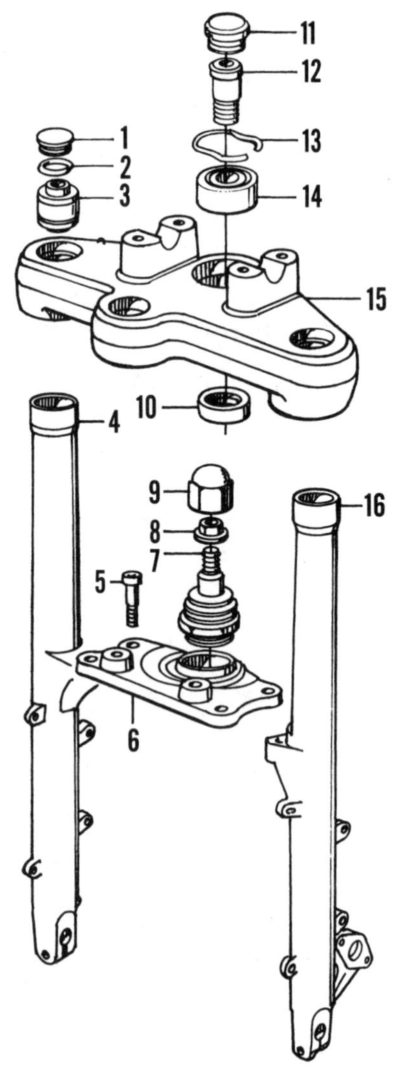

1. Trim cap
2. Circlip
3. Threaded connection
4. Right fork assembly
5. Allen bolt
6. Lower fork bridge
7. Ball joint
8. Nut
9. Cover
10. Bushing
11. Trim cap
12. Guide pin
13. Lock ring
14. Ball bearing
15. Upper fork bridge
16. Left fork assembly

32

UPPER AND LOWER FORK BRIDGE ASSEMBLY (R1150R MODELS)

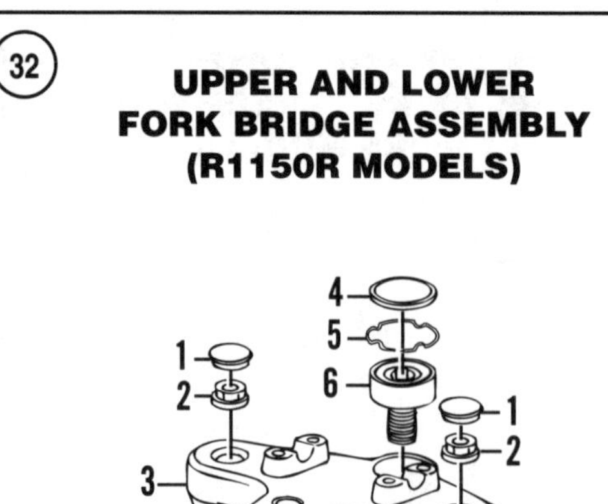

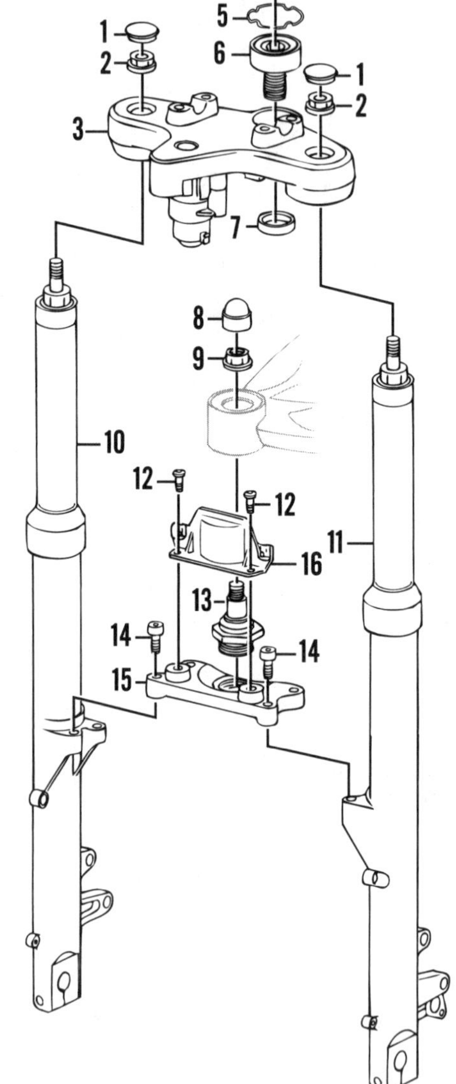

1. Trim cap
2. Nut
3. Upper fork bridge
4. Trim cap
5. Lock ring
6. Ball bearing
7. Special nut
8. Trim cap
9. Nut
10. Right fork assembly
11. Left fork assembly
12. Screw
13. Ball joint
14. Bolt
15. Lower fork bridge
16. Fender mounting bracket

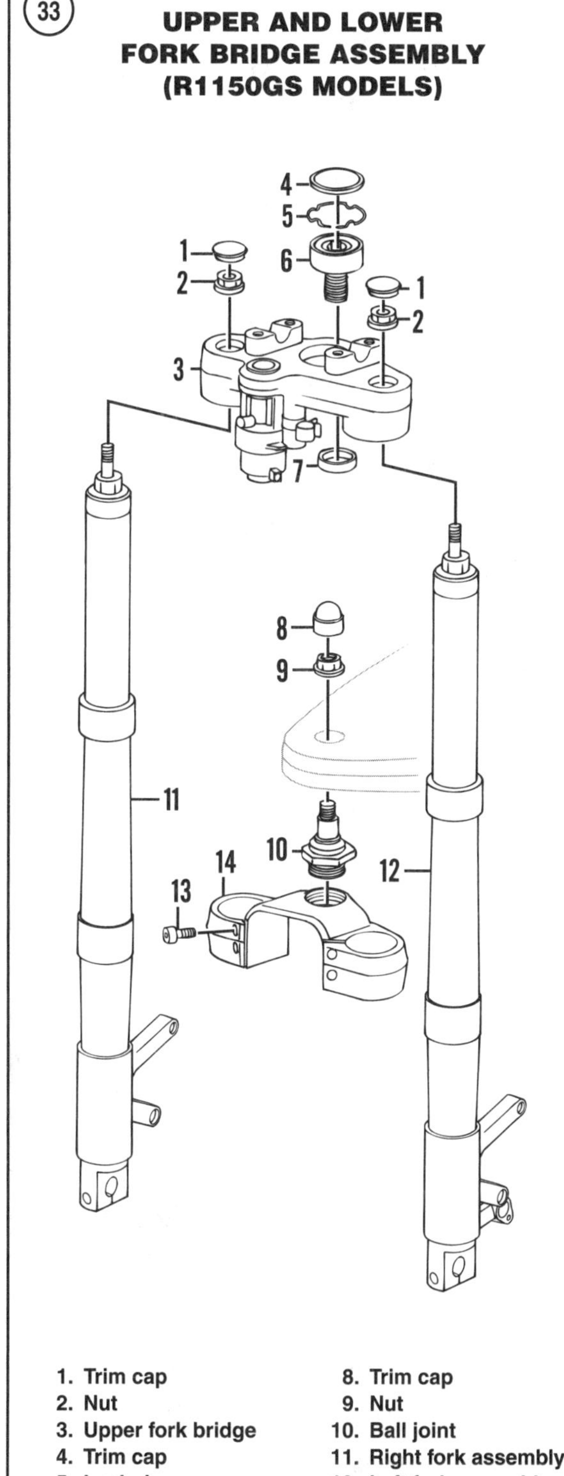

1. Trim cap
2. Nut
3. Upper fork bridge
4. Trim cap
5. Lock ring
6. Ball bearing
7. Special nut
8. Trim cap
9. Nut
10. Ball joint
11. Right fork assembly
12. Left fork assembly
13. Bolt
14. Lower fork bridge

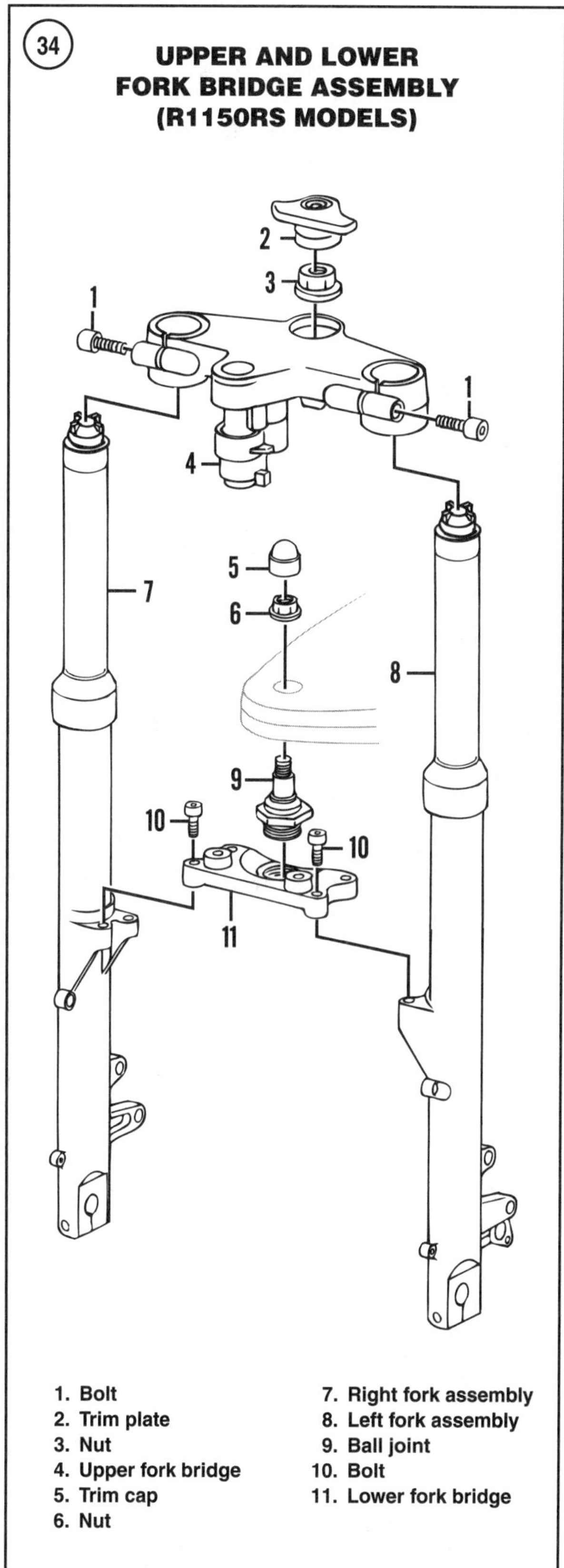

1. Bolt
2. Trim plate
3. Nut
4. Upper fork bridge
5. Trim cap
6. Nut
7. Right fork assembly
8. Left fork assembly
9. Ball joint
10. Bolt
11. Lower fork bridge

12

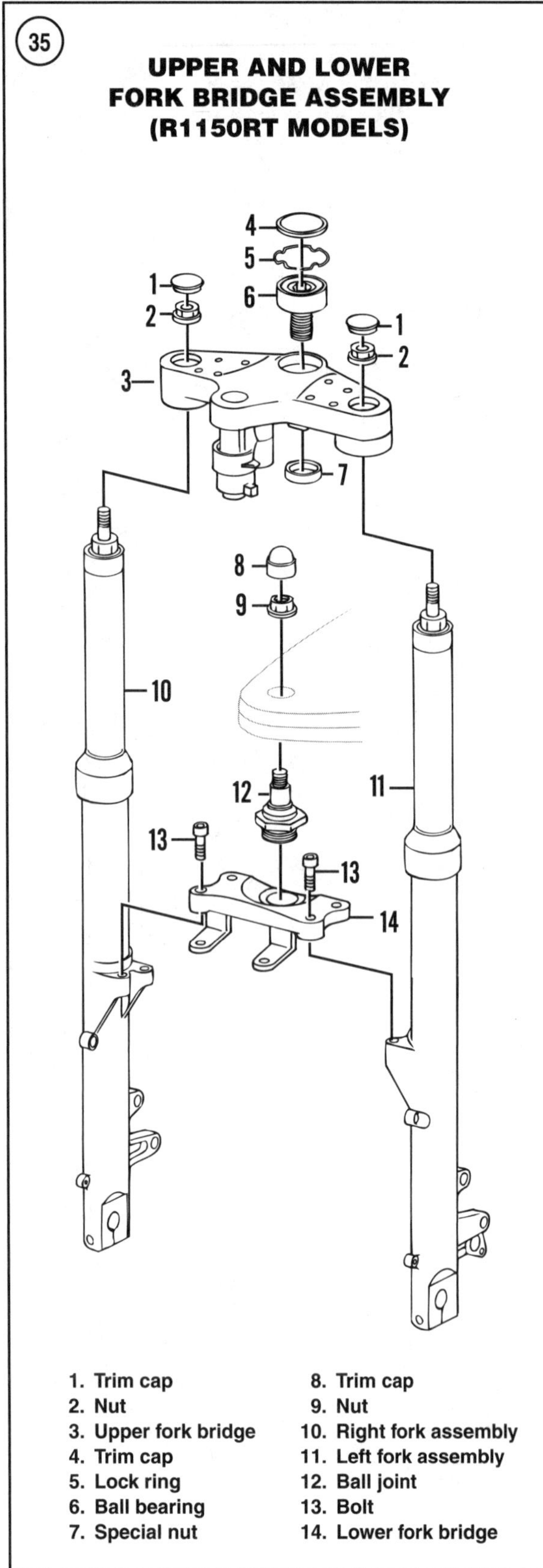

1. Trim cap
2. Nut
3. Upper fork bridge
4. Trim cap
5. Lock ring
6. Ball bearing
7. Special nut
8. Trim cap
9. Nut
10. Right fork assembly
11. Left fork assembly
12. Ball joint
13. Bolt
14. Lower fork bridge

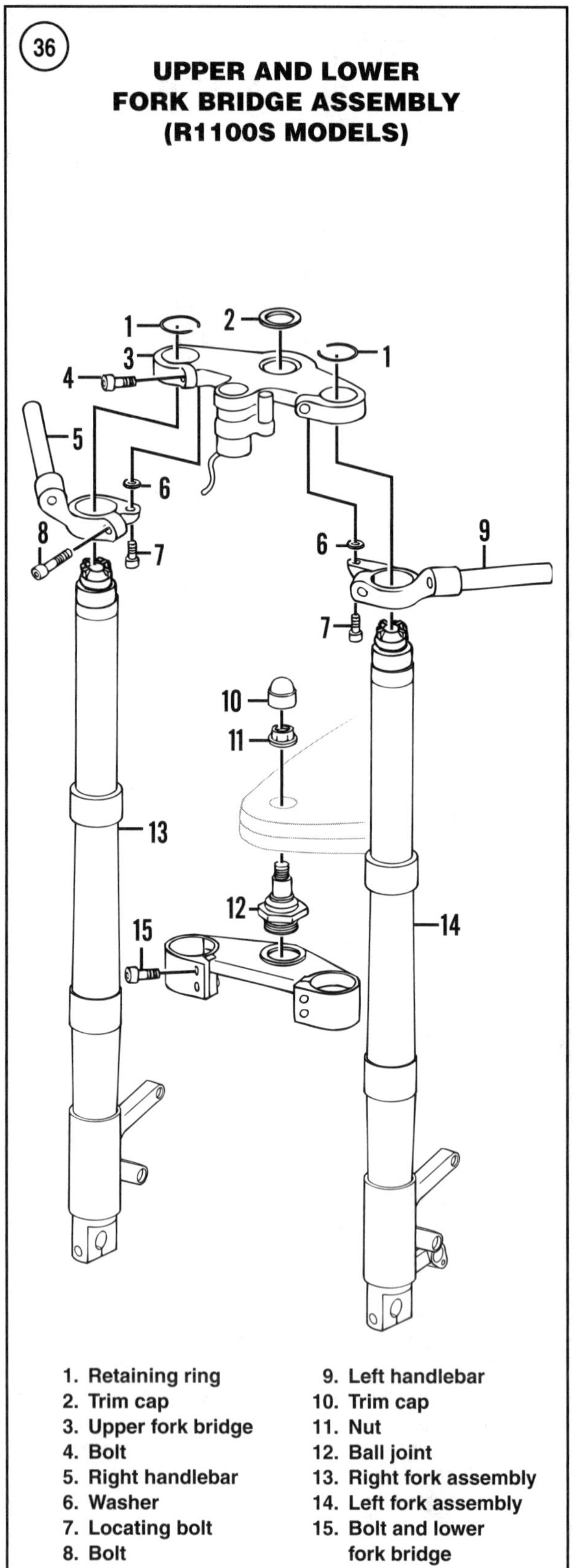

1. Retaining ring
2. Trim cap
3. Upper fork bridge
4. Bolt
5. Right handlebar
6. Washer
7. Locating bolt
8. Bolt
9. Left handlebar
10. Trim cap
11. Nut
12. Ball joint
13. Right fork assembly
14. Left fork assembly
15. Bolt and lower fork bridge

(37)

UPPER AND LOWER FORK BRIDGE ASSEMBLY (R850C AND R1200C MODELS)

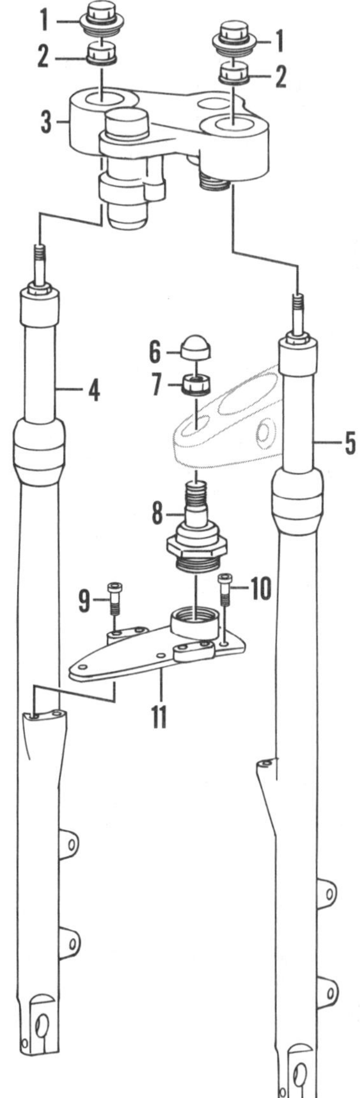

1. Cap
2. Nut
3. Upper fork bridge
4. Right fork assembly
5. Left fork assembly
6. Trim cap
7. Nut
8. Ball joint
9. Bolt
10. Bolt
11. Lower fork bridge

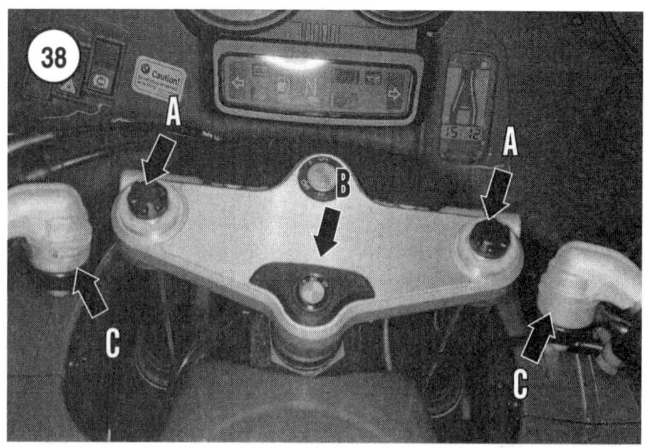

NOTE

A heat gun capable of producing 120° C (248°F) is required to loosen the Allen bolt securing the upper fork bridge to the ball joint on the front frame.

1. Remove the front wheel as described in Chapter Eleven.
2. Remove the fuel tank as described in Chapter Nine.
3. On RS, RT and S models, remove the front fairing as described in Chapter Fifteen.
4. Remove the front fork assemblies (A, **Figure 38**) as described in this chapter.
5. Disconnect the ignition switch electrical connector.

6A. On RS models, perform the following:

a. Carefully pry the trim cap (B, **Figure 38**) free and remove it.
b. Remove the handlebar (C, **Figure 38**) as described in this chapter.

CAUTION

Do not apply heat to the Allen bolt with a propane or welding torch.

c. On R1100RS models only, heat the Allen bolt securing the upper fork bridge to the ball joint on the front frame. Heat the Allen bolt to 120° C (248° F).

WARNING

The upper fork bridge is very hot. Make sure to wear protective gloves when loosening the Allen bolt in the next step.

d. Use an Allen wrench and socket handle and remove the Allen bolt. Allow the upper fork bridge to cool prior to removal.
e. Remove the upper fork bridge from the front frame.

6B. On R, GS and RT models, perform the following:

a. Remove the handlebar (A, **Figure 39**) as described in this chapter.
b. Remove the center trim cap (B, **Figure 39**).

NOTE
In substep c, the Allen bolt is pressed into the upper ball joint and the ball joint is also pressed into the upper fork bridge. Do not remove the Allen bolt, just ***loosen it****.*

c. Loosen the Allen bolt (A, **Figure 40**) securing the upper fork bridge and ball joint to the front frame.
d. Remove the upper fork bridge (B, **Figure 40**) from the front frame.
e. Remove the bushing (**Figure 41**) from the receptacle in the front frame.

6C. On S models, perform the following:
a. Carefully pry the trim cap (A, **Figure 42**) free and remove it.
b. Remove both handlebars (B, **Figure 42**) as described in this chapter.

CAUTION
Do not apply heat to the nut with a propane or welding torch.

c. Heat the nut securing the upper fork bridge to the ball joint on the lower surface of the front frame. Heat the nut to 120° C (248° F).

WARNING
The upper fork bridge is very hot. Make sure to wear protective gloves when loosening the Allen bolt in the next step.

d. Loosen and remove the nut securing the upper fork bridge. Allow the upper fork bridge to cool prior to removal.
e. Remove the fork bridge (C, **Figure 42**) from the front frame.

6D. On R850C and R1200C models, perform the following:
a. Remove the mounting screws and move the instrument panel (A, **Figure 43**) away from the upper fork bridge.
b. Remove the headlight assembly as described in Chapter Ten.
c. Remove the handlebar (B, **Figure 43**) as described in this chapter.
d. Carefully pry the trim cap (C, **Figure 43**) from above the mounting Allen bolt.
e. Remove the Allen bolt (**Figure 44**) securing the upper fork bridge to the frame.
f. Remove the upper fork bridge from the front frame.

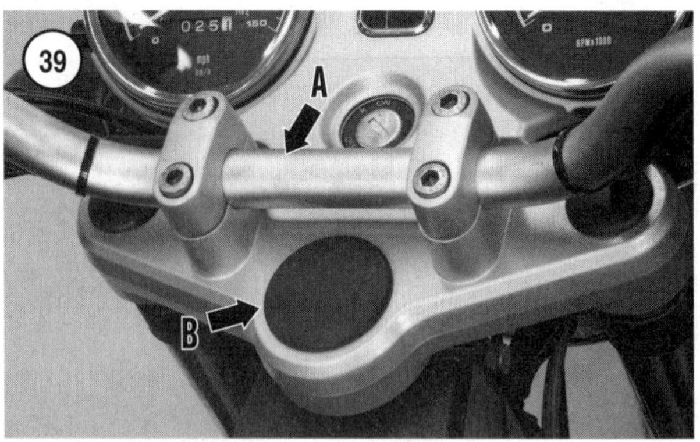

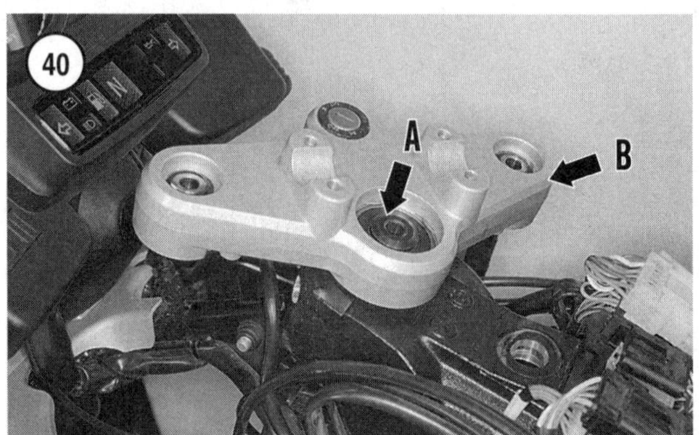

Assembly

1A. On RS models, perform the following:
a. Thoroughly clean the top surface of the front frame to ensure a clean contact surface.
b. Install the upper fork bridge onto the front frame.
c. Apply Loctite No. 2701, or an equivalent, to the Allen bolt threads and install the bolt.
d. Tighten the Allen bolt to 130 N•m (96 ft.-lb.). After tightening the Allen bolt, move the upper fork bridge from side to side to ensure ease of movement. There must be no binding.

e. Install the handlebar (C, **Figure 38**) as described in this chapter.
f. Install the trim cap (B, **Figure 38**) and make sure it seats completely.
g. Install the front fork assemblies (A, **Figure 38**) as described in this chapter.

1B. On R, GS and RT models, perform the following:

a. Thoroughly clean the top surface of the front frame to ensure a clean contact surface.
b. Install the bushing (**Figure 41**) into the receptacle in the front frame.
c. Apply Loctite No. 2701, or an equivalent, to the Allen bolt threads.
d. Install the upper fork bridge onto the front frame and start the Allen bolt into the threads by hand. Be careful not to cross-thread it.
e. Tighten the Allen bolt (A, **Figure 40**) to 130 N•m (96 ft.-lb.). After tightening the Allen bolt, move the upper fork bridge from side to side to ensure ease of movement. There must be no binding.
f. Install the center trim cap (B, **Figure 39**) and make sure it seats completely.
g. Install the handlebar assembly (A, **Figure 39**) as described in this chapter.
h. Install the front fork assembly as described in this chapter.

1C. On S models, perform the following:

a. Thoroughly clean the top surface of the front frame to ensure a clean contact surface.
b. Apply Loctite No. 2701, or an equivalent, to the nut threads.
c. Install the upper fork bridge onto the front frame and start the nut into the threads by hand. Be careful not to cross-thread it.
d. Tighten the nut to 130 N•m (96 ft.-lb.). After tightening the nut, move the upper fork bridge from side to side to ensure ease of movement. There must be no binding.
f. Install the center trim cap and make sure it seats completely.
g. Install both handlebars as described in this chapter.
h. Install the front fork assembly as described in this chapter.

1D. On R850C and R1200C models, perform the following:

a. Thoroughly clean the top surface of the front frame to ensure a clean contact surface.
b. Apply Loctite No. 243, or an equivalent, to the Allen bolt threads.
c. Install the upper fork bridge onto the front frame and start the Allen bolt (**Figure 44**) into the threads by hand. Be careful not to cross-thread it at first.
d. Tighten the Allen bolt to 130 N•m (96 ft.-lb.). After tightening the Allen bolt, move the upper fork bridge from side to side to ensure ease of movement. There must be no binding.
e. Install the trim cap (C, **Figure 43**) above the mounting bolt.
f. Install the handlebar (B, **Figure 43**) as described in this chapter.
g. Install the headlight assembly as described in Chapter Ten.

h. Move the instrument panel (A, **Figure 43**) into position and tighten the mounting screws securely.
2. Connect the ignition switch electrical connector. Make sure the connector is free of corrosion and is tight.
3. Install the fork assemblies as described in this chapter.
4. On RS, RT and S models, install the front fairing as described in Chapter Fifteen.
5. Install the fuel tank as described in Chapter Nine.
6. Install the front wheel as described in Chapter Eleven.

Inspection

The steering stem bearings are located in the ball joint located on the front frame on RS and S models or in the thrust bearing (**Figure 45**) in the upper fork bridge on R, GS and RT models. On R, GS, RT and S models, pot-type joints (**Figure 46**) are located at each side where the front forks attach.

The removal of the thrust bearing and joints should be entrusted to a BMW dealership due to a number of special tools required to remove and install these components.

1. Inspect the upper fork bridge (**Figure 47**) for wear, cracks or any additional damage, replace if necessary.
2. On R, GS, RT and S models, inspect the threads (**Figure 48**) for the Allen bolt. If damaged, clean out with the appropriate size metric tap.
3. On S models, inspect the ball joint in the upper fork bridge for wear or damage. If damaged, have it replaced at a BMW dealership.
4. If the Allen bolt or nut is going to be reused, thoroughly clean all old threadlocking compound from the bolt threads with a cleaning solvent and wire brush.

LOWER FORK BRIDGE

Removal

Refer to the **Figure 30-37**.

NOTE
A heat gun, capable of 120° C (248° F) is required to loosen the hex nut on the ball joint securing the lower fork bridge to the front suspension A-arm.

1. Remove the front wheel as described in Chapter Eleven.
2. Remove the front fender as described in Chapter Fifteen.
3. On R, RS, RT and S models, remove the fairing side panels as described in Chapter Fifteen.

45

46

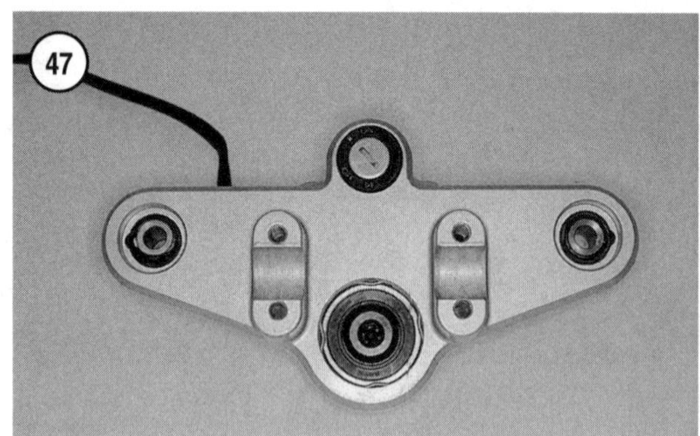
47

48

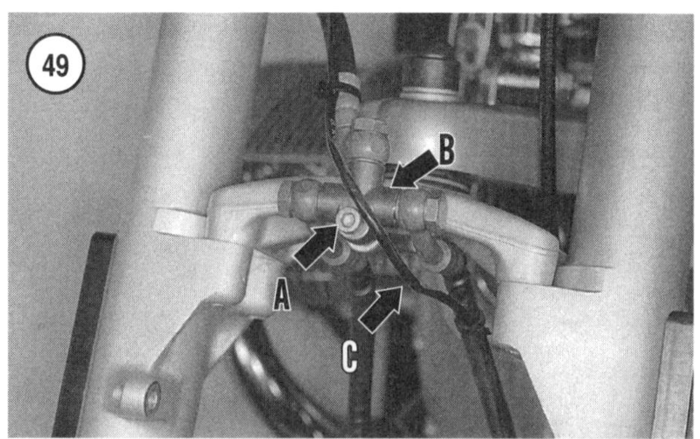

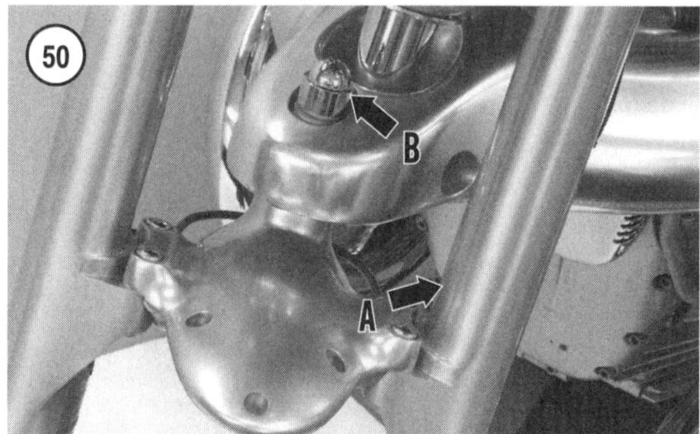

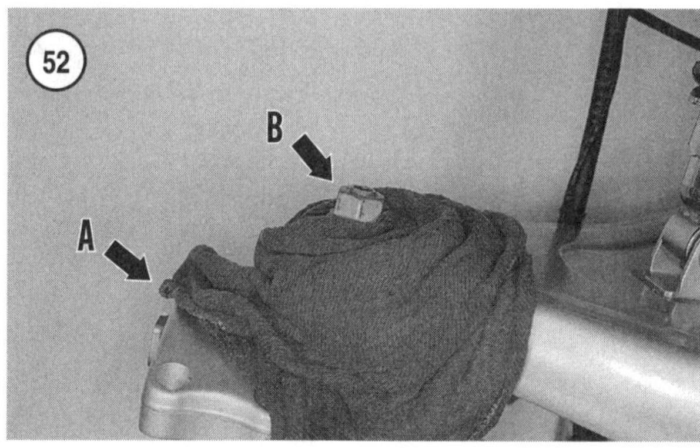

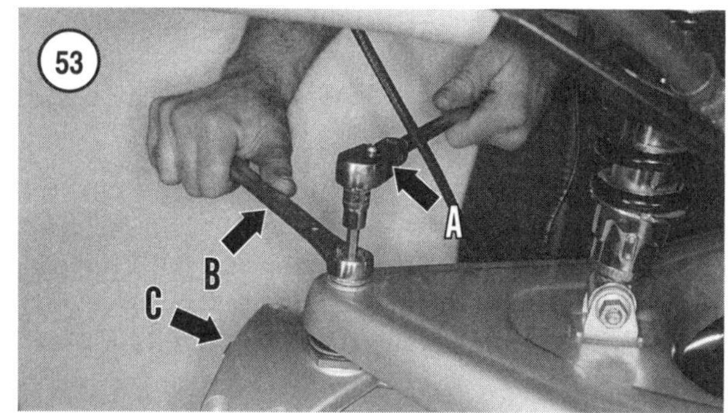

4. On R850GS and R1100GS and R1100RS models, remove the bolt (A, **Figure 49**) securing the front brake line distribution block (B) and move the block out of the way.
5. On ABS equipped models, detach the ABS sensor line (C, **Figure 49**) from the lower fork bridge. Move the sensor line out of the way.
6. On models so equipped, disconnect the steering damper from the lower fork bridge as described in this chapter.
7A. On R850C and R1200C models perform the following:
   a. Remove the front fork assemblies (A, **Figure 50**, typical) as described in this chapter.
   b. Remove the trim cap (B, **Figure 50**) from the ball joint nut.

7B. On all models except R850C and R1200C models perform the following:
   a. Remove the front fork assemblies (A, **Figure 51**, typical) as described in this chapter.
   b. Remove the trim cap (B, **Figure 51**) from the ball joint nut.

NOTE
The following photographs illustrate a typical lower steering stem removal.

CAUTION
Do not apply heat to the hex bolt with any type of open flame (propane or welding torch).

8. To protect the painted surface of the front suspension A-arm while heating the hex nut, soak several shop rags in water and place them around the hex nut on the A-arm (A, **Figure 52**).
9. Heat the hex hut (B, **Figure 52**) securing the lower fork bridge to the front suspension A-arm to 120° C (248° F).

WARNING
The front suspension A-arm is very hot. Make sure to wear protective gloves when loosening the hex nut in the next step.

10. Use an Allen wrench and socket handle (A, **Figure 53**) to secure the ball joint from rotating in the next step.

11. Loosen the hex nut (B, **Figure 53**) with a box wrench.

WARNING
The lower fork bridge may also be warm or even hot. Make sure to wear protective gloves when handling the lower fork bridge.

12. After the hex nut is loose, remove the Allen wrench and hold the lower fork bridge. Remove the hex nut and remove the lower fork bridge (C, **Figure 53**).

Installation

1. Position the lower fork bridge with the fork tube mounting holes facing toward the front of the motorcycle. Install the fork bridge into the front suspension A-arm and center it facing forward.
2. Apply Loctite No. 2701, or an equivalent, to the hex nut threads on the ball joint, then install the hex nut.
3. Use an Allen wrench and socket handle (A, **Figure 53**) to secure the ball joint from rotating in the next step.

CAUTION
Do not try to tighten the hex nut without securing the ball joint with an Allen wrench or the ball joint will be damaged.

4. Tighten the hex nut (B, **Figure 53**) with a box-end wrench to 130 N•m (96 ft.-lb.). Check to ensure the lower fork bridge is still centered and facing forward.
5. Install the trim cap (B, **Figure 51**) onto the ball joint nut.
6. Install the front fork assembly (A, **Figure 51**) as described in this chapter.
7. On models so equipped, connect the steering damper onto the lower fork bridge as described in this chapter.
8. On ABS equipped models, move the ABS sensor line (C, **Figure 49**) back into position and clip it to the lower fork bridge.
9. On R850GS and R1100GS and R1100RS models, move the front brake line distribution block (B, **Figure 49**) back into position and install the bolt (A). Tighten the bolt securely.
10. On R, RS, RT and S models, install the fairing side panels as described in Chapter Fifteen.
11. Install the front fender as described in Chapter Fifteen.
12. Install the front wheel as described in Chapter Eleven.

Inspection

The lower steering bearing is integral with the ball joint located on the lower fork bridge.

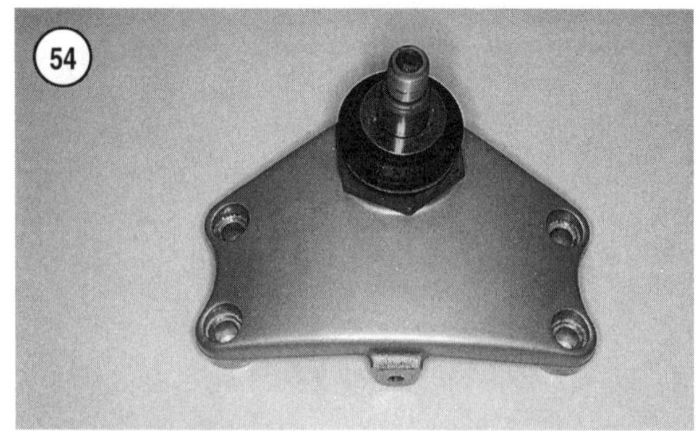

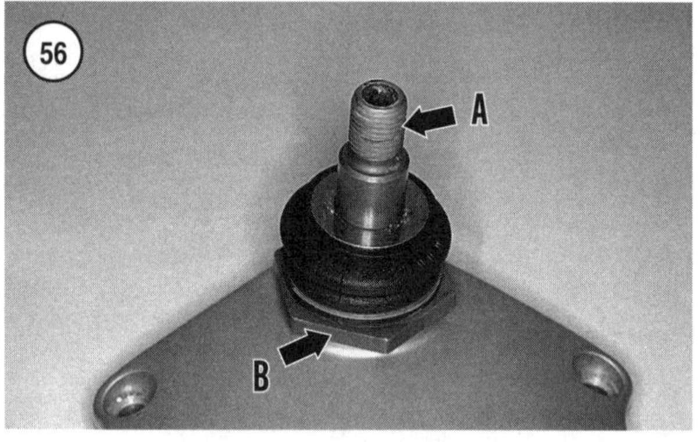

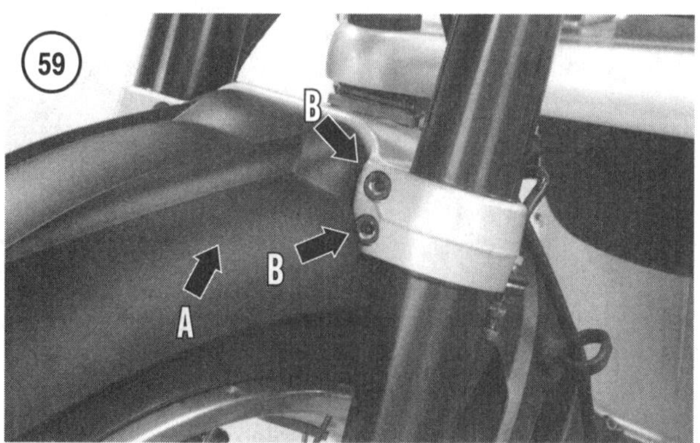

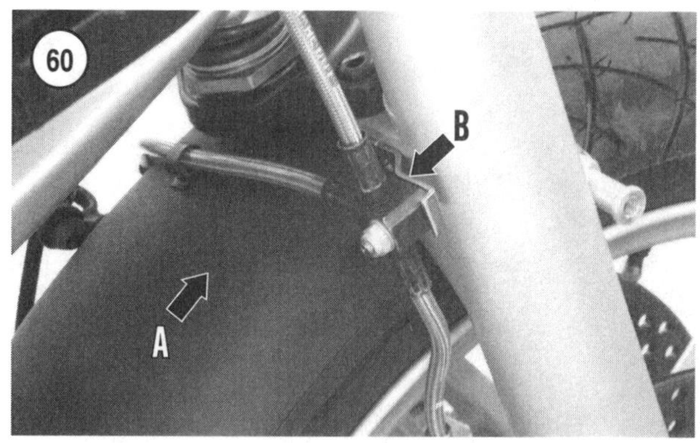

1. Inspect the lower fork bridge for wear, cracks or mounting hole elongation. Refer to **Figure 54** and **Figure 55**. Replace if necessary.
2. Inspect the threads (A, **Figure 56**) for the hex nut. If damaged, repair the threads with the appropriate size metric die.
3. Inspect the ball joint for wear or damage. Make sure the rubber boot (**Figure 57**) is not torn or damaged. Check for hardness or deterioration and replace if necessary.
4. Clean all threadlocking compound from the ball joint threads using cleaning solvent and a wire brush.
5. Inspect the hex nut threads for damage.

Ball Joint Replacement

1. Place the lower fork bridge in a vise with soft jaws.
2. Use a 46 mm 6-point socket wrench and loosen the hex fitting (B, **Figure 56**) portion of the ball joint.
3. Remove the ball joint from the lower fork bridge and install a new one.
4. Apply a light coat of waterproof grease to the threads and tighten the ball joint to 230 N•m (170 ft.-lb.).

FRONT FORK (R, GS, RS AND RT)

Removal

1. Remove the front wheel (A, **Figure 58**) as described in this chapter.
2. Remove both front brake calipers (B, **Figure 58**) as described in Chapter Fourteen.
3. On R, RS and RT models, remove the fairing side panels as described in Chapter Fifteen.
4. Remove the front fender (A, **Figure 59**), and on some models, the rear portion of the fender (A, **Figure 60**) as described in Chapter Fifteen.
5. On GS models, remove the fuel tank as described in Chapter Nine.
6. On R, RS and RT models, remove the handlebars as described in this chapter.
7. On R1100 models, remove the bolt (A, **Figure 49**) securing the front brake line distribution block (B) and move the block out of the way.
8. Remove the fasteners securing the front brake line assembly (B, **Figure 60**) to the right side fork slider.
9. On ABS equipped models, perform the following:
   a. Detach the ABS sensor line from the lower fork bridge.
   b. Unhook the sensor electrical lead from the clips on the fork (**Figure 61**).

c. Remove the T-25 Torx screws securing the front wheel ABS sensor (C, **Figure 58**) to the left fork tube. Remove the ABS sensor and shim. Move the sensor and electrical lead out of the way to avoid damage.

10. On R1150 GS models, loosen the clamping bolts (B, **Figure 59**) on the lower fork bridge.

11. Remove the Allen bolts securing the fork tubes to the lower fork bridge. Refer to **Figure 62** or B, **Figure 59**.

CAUTION
When the fork tube assembly is removed from the frame, hold the fork tube and slider together since they will separate. They are not mechanically attached to each other. Also keep the fork tubes upright to avoid the loss of fork oil.

12. On RS models, perform the following:
  a. Loosen the clamping bolt (**Figure 63**) on the upper fork bridge.
  b. Lower the fork assembly (**Figure 64**) straight down and out of the upper fork bridge. It may be necessary to slightly rotate the fork tubes while pulling them down and out of the upper fork bridge.

13. On R, GS and RT models, perform the following:
  a. Carefully pry off the top trim cap (**Figure 65**).
  b. Hold the hex fitting (**Figure 66**) on the upper end of the fork tube assembly (A, **Figure 67**) with an open-end wrench while loosening the nut on the upper threaded connection.
  c. Loosen the nut (B, **Figure 67**), then remove it.
  d. On R, RT and R850GS and R1100GS models, carefully lower the fork assembly straight down and out of the upper fork bridge pot-type joint. Do not damage the threads on the upper connection while lowering the fork assembly.
  e. On R1150GS, carefully lower the fork assembly straight down and out of the upper and lower fork bridges.

Installation

1. Clean any corrosion or dirt from the upper (and lower on R1150 GS) fork bridge bores.

NOTE
The fork tubes must be reinstalled on the correct side of the motorcycle so the brake caliper mounting brackets will be in the correct location. On models so equipped, the front brake ABS sensor mounting

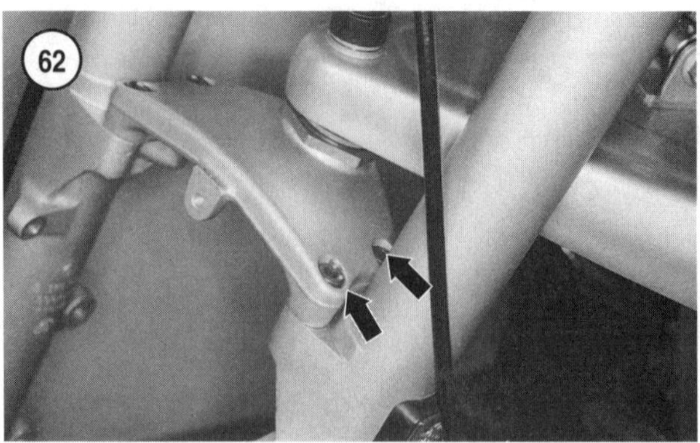
62

63

64

65

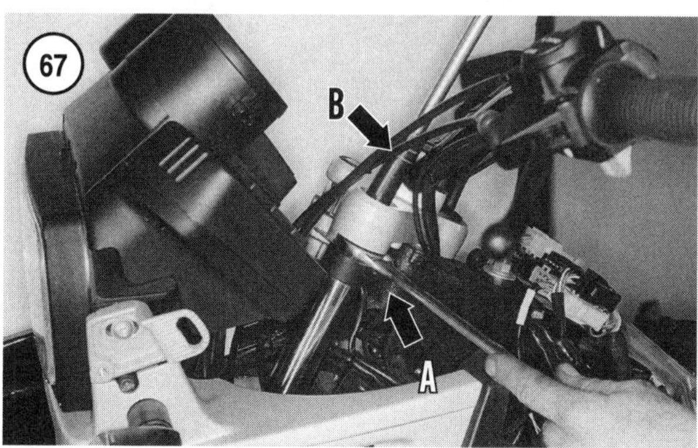

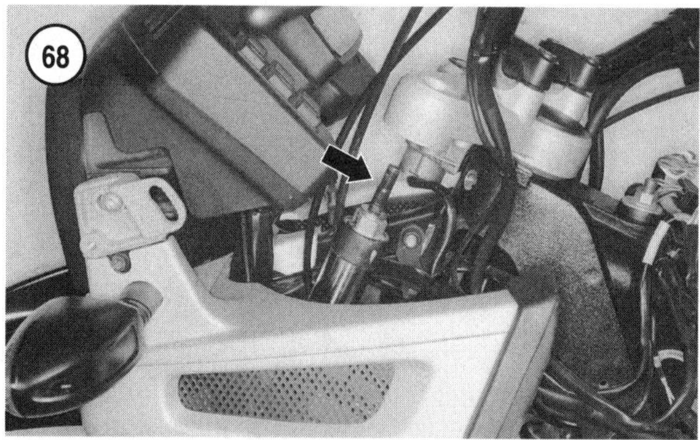

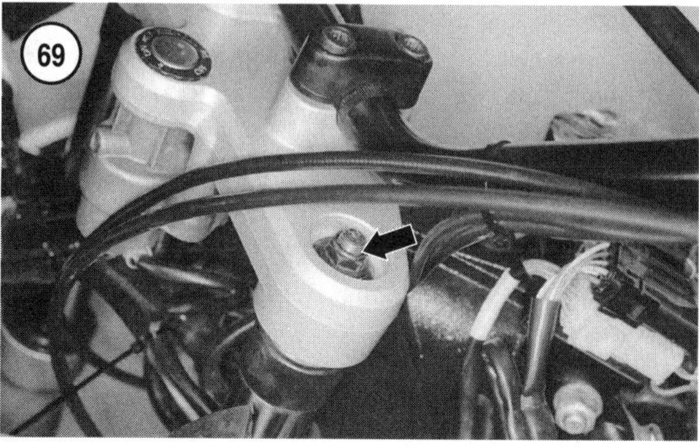

bracket is located on the left side of the motorcycle.

2A. On RS models, perform the following:

a. Raise the fork assembly (**Figure 64**) up and into the upper fork bridge. It may be necessary to slightly rotate the fork tubes while pushing them into the upper fork bridge.

b. Correctly align the lower fork bridge mounting bolt holes, then install the Allen bolts finger-tight. Refer to **Figure 62** or B, **Figure 59**.

c. On R1100RS models, position the fork assembly so the top surface of the fork tubes are 4.5-5.5 mm (0.18-0.22 in.) above the top surface of the upper fork bridge, then tighten the upper fork bridge clamping bolt to 22 N•m (16 ft.-lb.).

d. On R1150RS models, position the fork assembly so the top surface of the fork tubes are 5 mm (0.20 in.) above the top surface of the upper fork bridge, then tighten the upper fork bridge clamping bolt (**Figure 63**) to 22 N•m (16 ft.-lb.).

2B. On R, RT and R850GS and R1100GS models, perform the following:

a. On R1150 GS models, raise the fork assembly up through the lower fork bridge and into the upper fork bridge. Be careful not to damage the upper threaded connection while pushing it into the pot joints in the upper fork bridge.

b. On all models except R1150GS, raise the fork assembly up and into the upper fork bridge. Be careful not to damage the upper threaded connection (**Figure 68**) while pushing it into the pot-type joints in the upper fork bridge.

c. Correctly align the lower fork bridge mounting bolt holes, then install the Allen bolts (**Figure 62**, typical) finger-tight.

d. Install the upper nut (**Figure 69**) finger-tight.

e. Hold the hex fitting (**Figure 66**) on the upper end of the fork tube assembly (A, **Figure 67**) to secure it while tightening the upper threaded connection nut.

f. Tighten the nut on the upper connection (B, **Figure 67**) to 45 N•m (33 ft.-lb.).

NOTE

Step 3 is required to ensure proper alignment between both fork tubes.

3. Install the front axle into the fork tubes (**Figure 70**) and install the front axle bolt. Tighten the bolt securely, then tighten the axle clamp bolts securely.

4. On R1150GS models, tighten the Allen bolts on the lower fork bridge to 45 N•m (33 ft.-lb.).

12

5. On R, GS and RT models, install the top trim cap (**Figure 65**) and make sure it seats properly.
6. On ABS equipped models, perform the following:
   a. On models so equipped, install the shim (A, **Figure 71**) onto the ABS sensor (B).
   b. Install the sensor onto the front fork slider. Install the screws (**Figure 72**) and tighten them securely.
   c. Hook the sensor electrical lead onto the clips on the fork (**Figure 61**). Ensure the lead is secured in place to avoid contacting the rotating front wheel.
   d. On R1100 models, attach the ABS sensor line (C, **Figure 49**) onto the lower fork bridge.
7. On R1100 models, move the front brake line distribution block (B, **Figure 49**) into position on the lower fork bridge and install the bolt (A). Tighten the bolt securely.
8. Secure the front brake line assembly to the right side fork slider and tighten the screw securely.
9. On GS models, install the fuel tank as described in Chapter Nine.
10. On R, RS and RT models, install the handlebars as described in this chapter.
11. Remove the front axle installed in Step 3.
12. Install the front wheel as described in Chapter Eleven.
13. Install the front fender as described in Chapter Fifteen.
14. On R, RS and RT models, install the fairing side panels as described in Chapter Fifteen.
15. On ABS equipped models, check the rotor to sensor clearance and adjust if necessary. Refer to Chapter Fourteen.

FRONT FORK (R1100S)

Removal

1. Remove the front wheel as described in Chapter Eleven.
2. Remove both front brake calipers as described in Chapter Fourteen.
3. Remove the fairing side panels as described in Chapter Fifteen.
4. Remove the front fender (**Figure 73**) as described in Chapter Fifteen.
5. Remove the fuel tank as described in Chapter Nine.
6. On ABS equipped models, perform the following:
   a. Detach the ABS sensor line from the lower fork bridge.
   b. Unhook the sensor electrical lead from the clips on the fork.

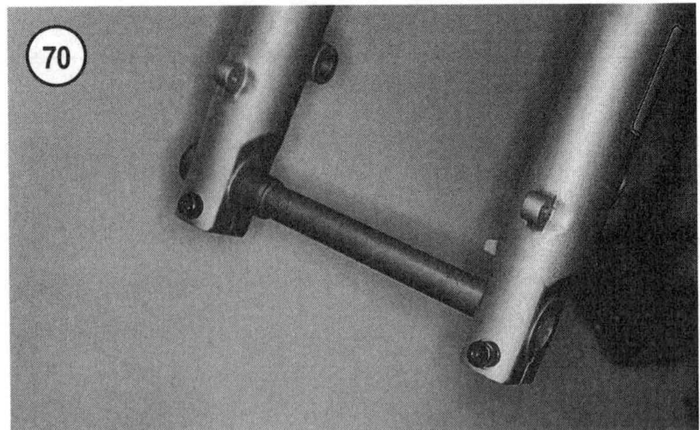

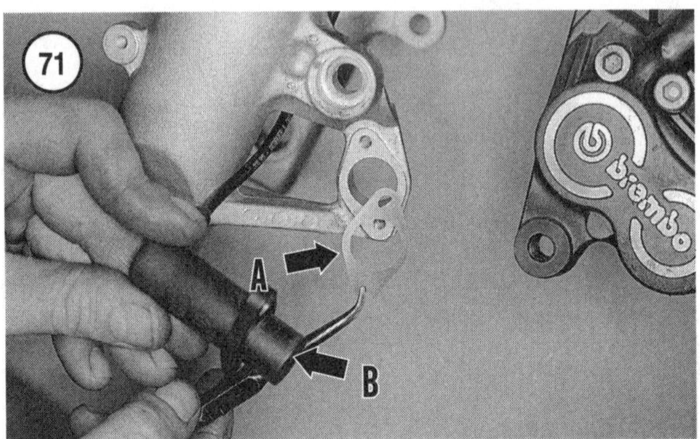

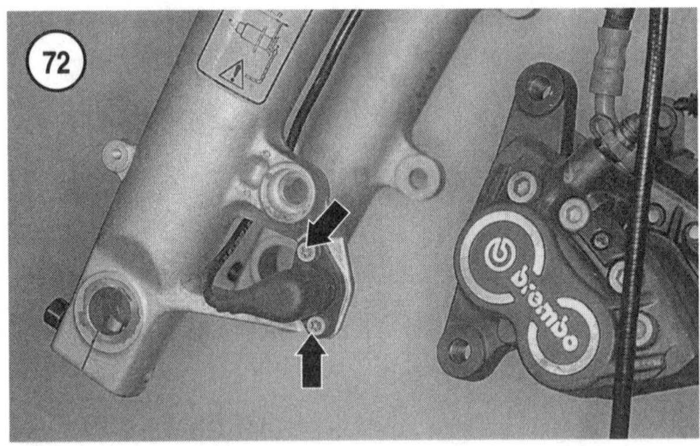

   c. Remove the Torx screws securing the front wheel ABS sensor to the left fork tube. Remove the ABS sensor and shim. Move the sensor and electrical lead out of the way to avoid damage.

7. Loosen the clamp bolt securing the handlebars to the fork tube.

8. Loosen the clamping bolts (B, **Figure 73**) on the lower fork bridge.

9. Remove the retaining clip from the fork tube at the upper fork bridge.

73

74

NOTE
When the fork tubes are removed from the frame, hold the fork tube and slider together as they are not mechanically attached to each other—they will separate easily. Keep the fork tubes upright to avoid the loss of fork oil.

10. Lower the fork assembly straight down and out of the upper and lower fork bridges. It may be necessary to slightly rotate the fork tubes while pulling them down and out of the lower fork bridge.

Installation

1. Clean any corrosion or dirt from the upper and lower fork bridge bores.

NOTE
The fork tubes must be reinstalled on the correct side of the motorcycle so the brake caliper mounting brackets will be in the correct location. On models so equipped, the front brake ABS sensor mounting bracket is located on the left side of the motorcycle.

2. Raise the fork assembly up through the lower fork bridge, the handlebar and the upper fork bridge. It may be necessary to slightly rotate the fork tube while pushing them into both upper fork bridges.
3. Install the retaining clip securing the fork tube to the upper fork bridge.
4. Hand tighten the clamping bolts (**Figure 73**) on the lower fork bridge.

NOTE
Step 5 is required to ensure proper alignment between both fork tubes.

5. Install the front axle into the fork tubes and install the front axle bolt. Tighten the bolt securely, then tighten the axle clamp bolts securely.
6. Tighten the Allen bolts on the lower fork bridge to 25 N•m (18 ft.-lb.).
7. Tighten the clamp bolt securing the handlebars to the fork tube to 25 N•m (18 ft.-lb.).
8. On ABS equipped models, perform the following:
   a. Install the shim and the front wheel ABS sensor to the left fork tube. Install the screws and tighten them securely.
   b. Hook the sensor electrical lead onto the clips on the fork. Ensure the lead is secured in place to avoid contacting the rotating front wheel.
   c. Attach the ABS sensor line onto the lower fork bridge.
9. Install the fuel tank as described in Chapter Nine.
10. Install the front fender as described in Chapter Fifteen.
11. Install the fairing side panels as described in Chapter Fifteen.
12. Install both front brake calipers as described in Chapter Fourteen.
13. Remove the front axle installed in Step 5.
14. Install the front wheel as described in Chapter Eleven.
15. Install the front fender as described in Chapter Fifteen.
16. Install the fairing side panels as described in Chapter Fifteen.
17. On ABS models, check the rotor to sensor clearance and adjust if necessary. Refer to Chapter Fourteen.

FRONT FORK (R850C AND R1200C)

Removal

1. Remove the front wheel as described in Chapter Eleven.

2. Remove both front brake calipers (A, **Figure 74**) as described in Chapter Fourteen.
3. Remove the front fender as described in Chapter Fifteen.
4. Remove the fuel tank as described in Chapter Nine.
5. On ABS equipped models, perform the following:
   a. Detach the ABS sensor line from the lower fork bridge.
   b. Unhook the sensor electrical lead from the clips (**Figure 75**) on the fork slider.
   c. Remove the Torx screws securing the front wheel ABS sensor (B, **Figure 74**) to the left fork tube. Remove the ABS sensor and shim. Move the sensor and electrical lead out of the way to avoid damage.
6. Carefully remove the top cap (**Figure 76**) from the top of the fork tube.
7. Hold onto the hex fitting (**Figure 77**) on the upper end of the fork tube assembly with an open-end wrench while loosening the nut on the upper threaded connection.
8. Loosen the nut, then remove it.
9. Remove the Allen bolts (A, **Figure 78**) securing the lower fork bridge to the fork sliders.
10. Remove the front fork assemblies as described in this chapter.
11. Lower the fork assembly straight down and out of the upper fork bridge. It may be necessary to slightly rotate the fork tubes while pulling them down and out of the lower fork bridge.
12. Carefully lower the fork assembly (B, **Figure 78**) straight down and out of the upper fork bridge pot joint. Do not damage the threads on the upper connection while lowering the fork assembly.

Installation

1. Clean any corrosion or dirt from the upper (and lower on R1150GS) fork bridge bores.

NOTE

The fork tubes must be reinstalled on the correct side of the motorcycle so the brake caliper mounting brackets will be in the correct location. On models so equipped, the front brake ABS sensor mounting bracket is located on the left side of the motorcycle.

2. Raise the fork assembly up through the lower fork bridge and into the upper fork bridge. Be careful not to damage the upper threaded connection while pushing it into the pot joints in the upper fork bridge.
3. Correctly align the lower fork bridge mounting bolt holes, then install the Allen bolts (A, **Figure 78**) finger-tight.
4. Install the upper nut finger-tight.

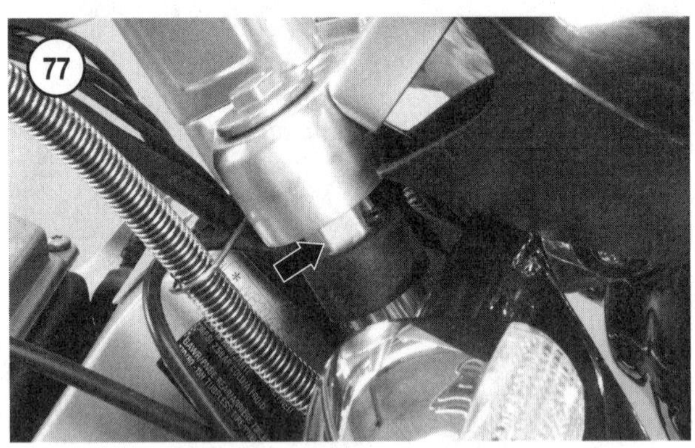

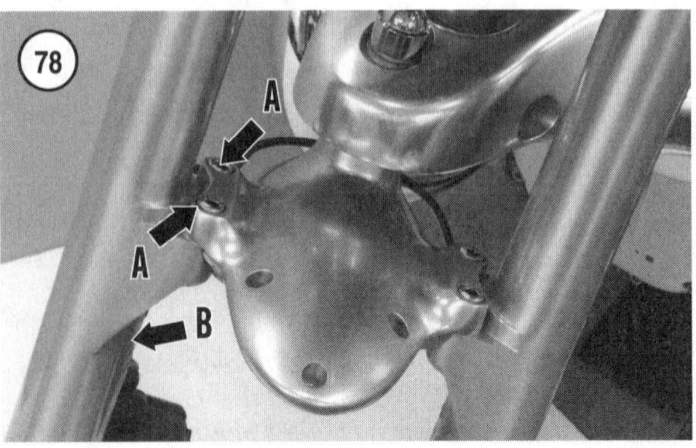

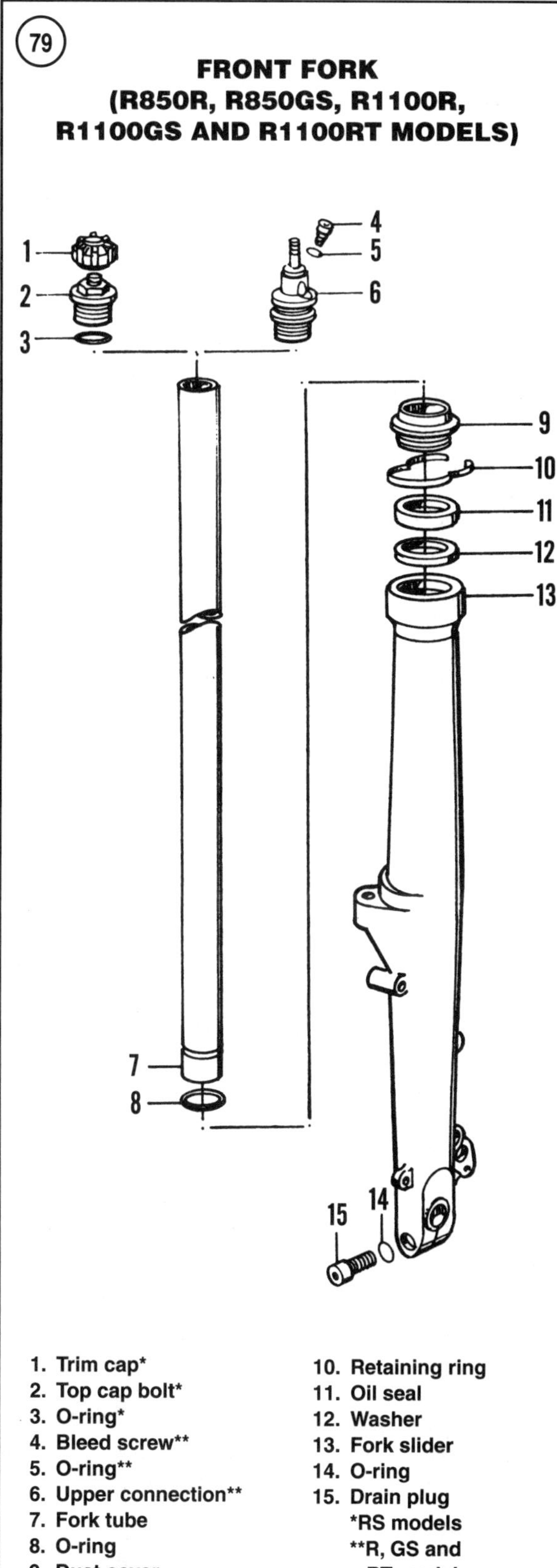

5. Hold the hex fitting (**Figure 77**) on the upper end of the fork tube assembly to secure it while tightening the upper threaded connection nut.

6. Tighten the nut on the upper connection to 35 N•m (26 ft.-lb.).

NOTE
Step 7 is required to ensure proper alignment between both fork tubes.

7. Install the front axle into the fork tubes and install the front axle bolt. Tighten the bolt securely, then tighten the axle clamp bolts securely.

8. Tighten the Allen bolts on the lower fork bridge to 22 N•m (16 ft.-lb.).

9. Install the top cap (**Figure 76**) and make sure it seats properly.

10. On ABS equipped models, perform the following:
   a. Install the shim and the front wheel ABS sensor (B, **Figure 74**) to the left fork tube. Install the screws and tighten them securely.
   b. Hook the sensor electrical lead onto the clips on the fork (**Figure 75**). Ensure the lead is secured in place to avoid contacting the rotating front wheel.

11. Remove the front axle installed in Step 7, then install the front wheel.

12. Install both front brake calipers (A, **Figure 74**) as described in Chapter Fourteen.

13. Install the front fender as described in Chapter Fifteen.

14. Install the fuel tank as described in Chapter Nine.

15. On ABS equipped models, check the rotor to sensor clearance and adjust if necessary. Refer to Chapter Twelve.

12

FRONT FORK OVERHAUL (ALL MODELS)

Disassembly

To simplify fork service and to prevent the mixing of parts, the legs should be disassembled and assembled individually.

Refer to **Figure 79-82**.

1. Remove the dust seal from the slider.

2. Hold the fork assembly vertically and withdraw the fork tube from the slider.

NOTE
In Step 3, the internal nylon bushings slide up and down within the fork assembly. They are not secured to either the fork slider or fork tube.

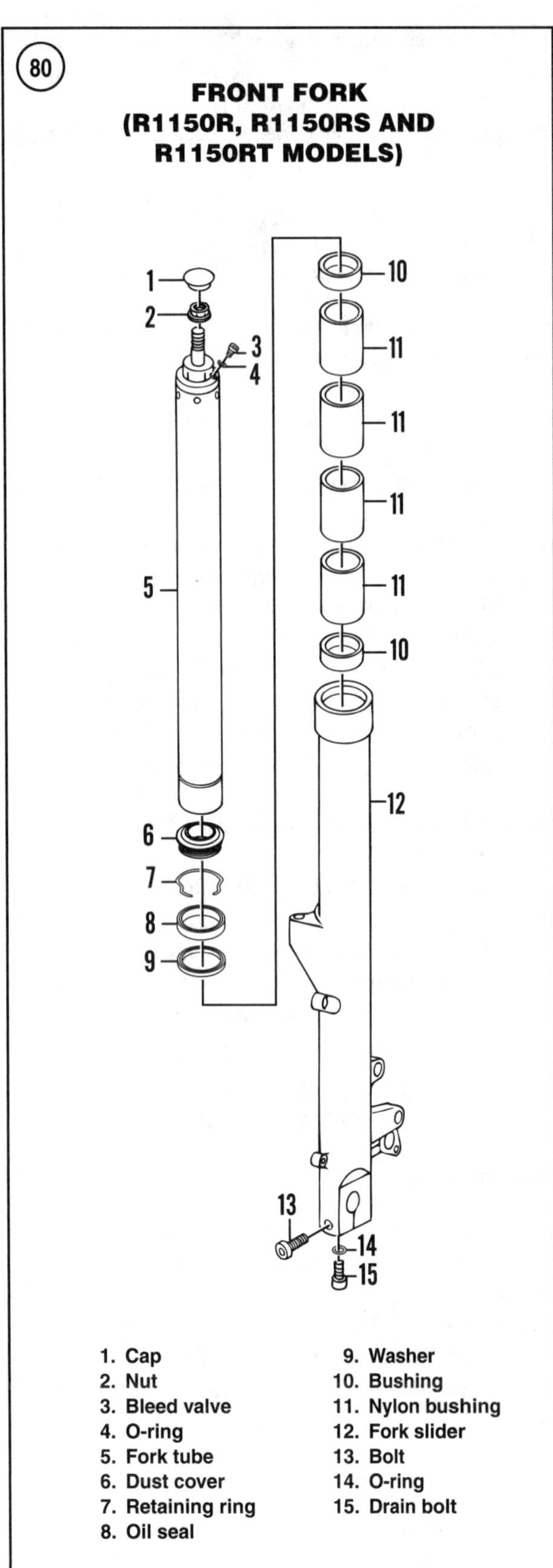

1. Cap
2. Nut
3. Bleed valve
4. O-ring
5. Fork tube
6. Dust cover
7. Retaining ring
8. Oil seal
9. Washer
10. Bushing
11. Nylon bushing
12. Fork slider
13. Bolt
14. O-ring
15. Drain bolt

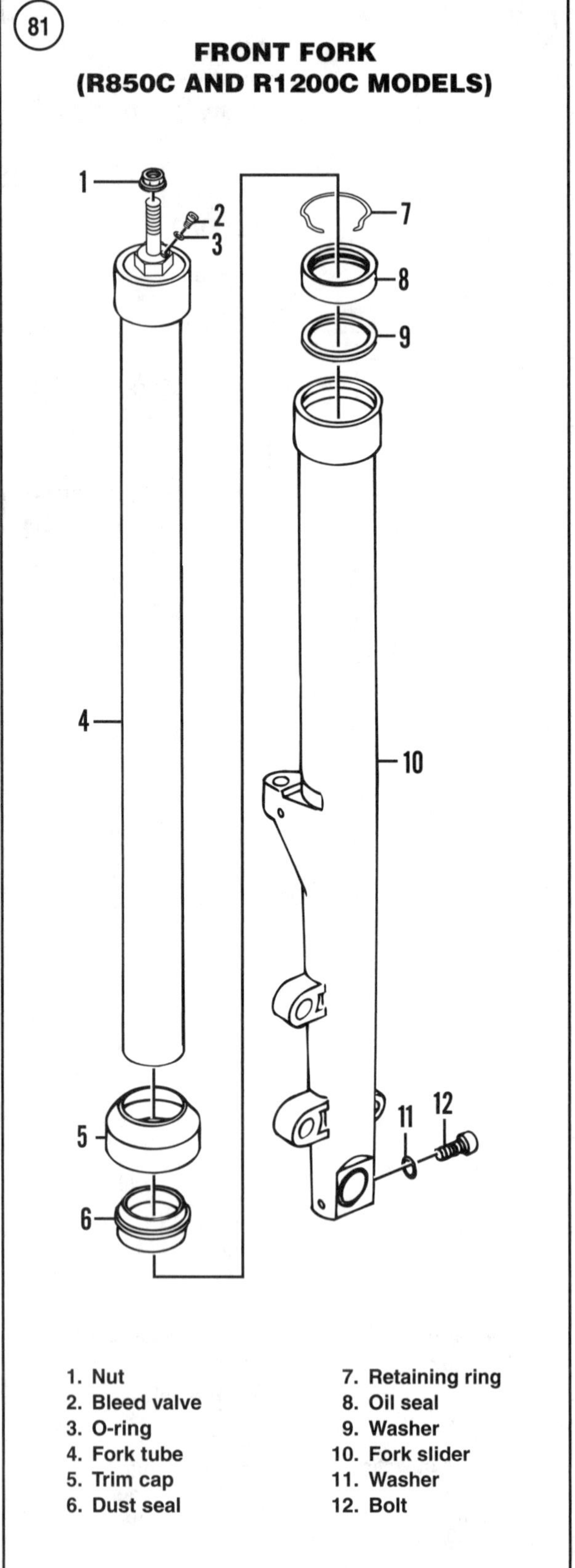

1. Nut
2. Bleed valve
3. O-ring
4. Fork tube
5. Trim cap
6. Dust seal
7. Retaining ring
8. Oil seal
9. Washer
10. Fork slider
11. Washer
12. Bolt

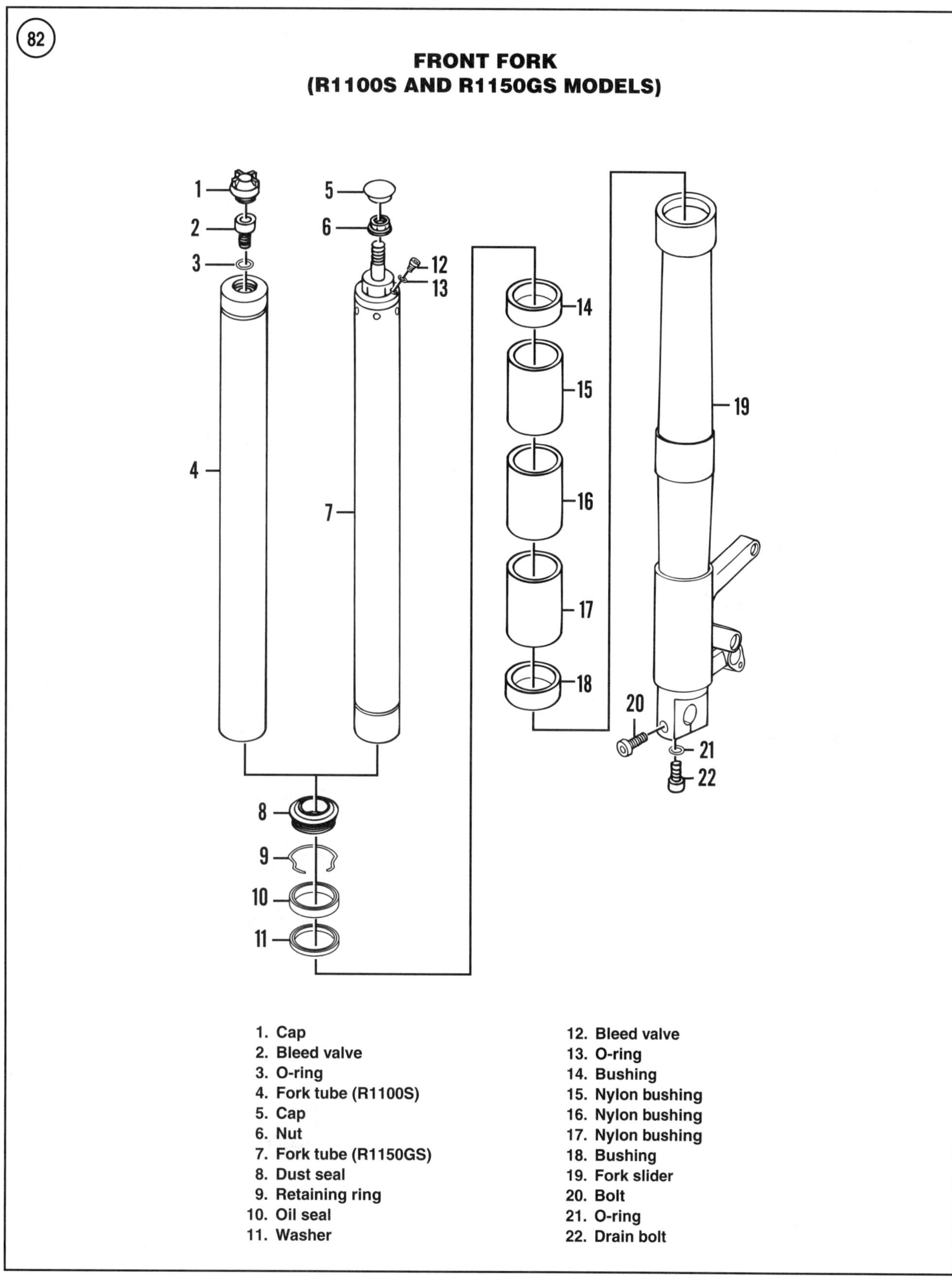

1. Cap
2. Bleed valve
3. O-ring
4. Fork tube (R1100S)
5. Cap
6. Nut
7. Fork tube (R1150GS)
8. Dust seal
9. Retaining ring
10. Oil seal
11. Washer
12. Bleed valve
13. O-ring
14. Bushing
15. Nylon bushing
16. Nylon bushing
17. Nylon bushing
18. Bushing
19. Fork slider
20. Bolt
21. O-ring
22. Drain bolt

3. On R1100S, R1150R, R1150GS, R1150RS and R1150RT models, the nylon bushings will either come off with the fork tube or stay within the slider. To remove any bushings from the slider, turn the slider upside down and the nylon bushings will slide out.

NOTE
The fork oil does not have to be replaced if it is not contaminated. Drain oil into a clean, suitable container and cover it to avoid contamination.

4. Tip the slider over and drain out all fork oil into a clean container. Let it drain for 10-15 minutes.
5. On models so equipped, remove the drain plug and O-ring from the base of the slider.
6. Remove the retaining clip (A, **Figure 83**).
7. Carefully pry the oil seal (B, **Figure 83**) out of the fork slider. Protect the edge of the fork slider with a piece of wood or plastic to keep the tool from contacting the slider while prying out the oil seal.
8. Remove the washer.
9. Clean all parts in solvent and thoroughly dry with compressed air.
10. Inspect all parts as described in this chapter.

Assembly

Refer to **Figure 79-82**.
1. On models so equipped, install the drain plug and new O-ring seal. Tighten securely.
2. If removed, install the nylon bushing (models so equipped).

NOTE
If reusing the existing fork oil, measure it to make sure the fork is being refilled with the correct amount of oil. Add additional oil if necessary.

3. Fill the fork tube with the following quantity of BMW telescopic fork oil:
   a. R1100S: 170 ml (5.75 oz.).
   b. All models except R1100S: 470 ml (15.89 oz.).

4A. On R1150GS and R1200C, unscrew the Allen bolt bleed valve from the top of the fork tube.
4B. On all models except R1150GS and R1200C, open the bleed valve (**Figure 84**).
5. On R1100S, R1150R, R1150GS, R1150RS and R1150RT models, install the nylon bushings onto the slider.
6. Apply a light coat of fork oil to the lower portion of the fork tube (**Figure 85**).

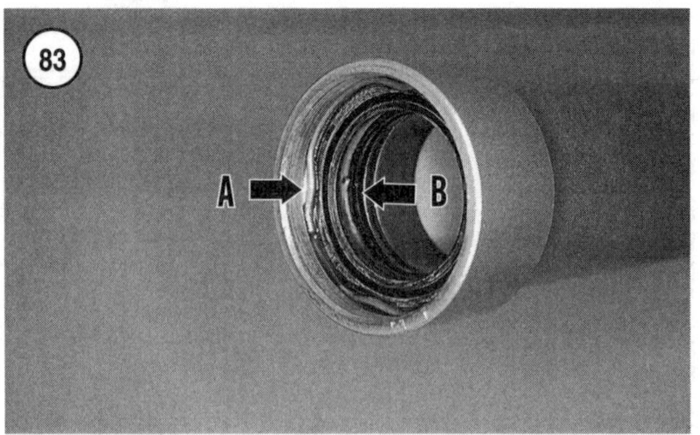

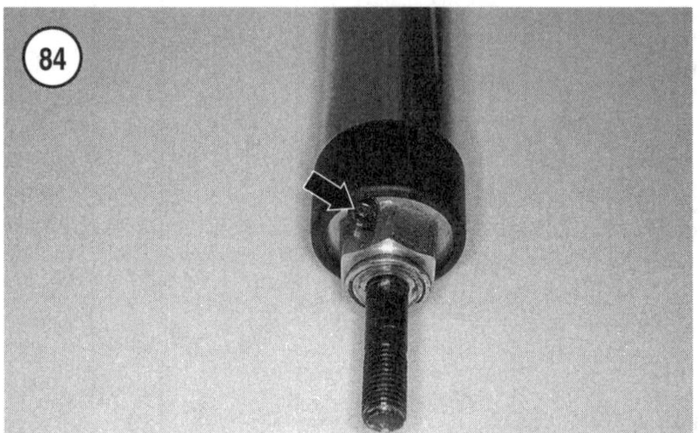

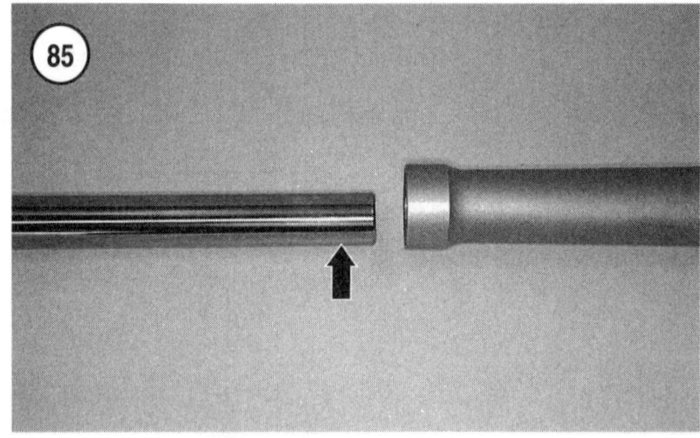

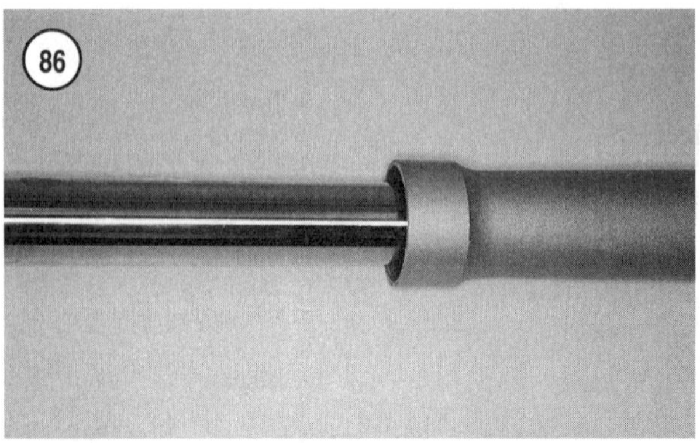

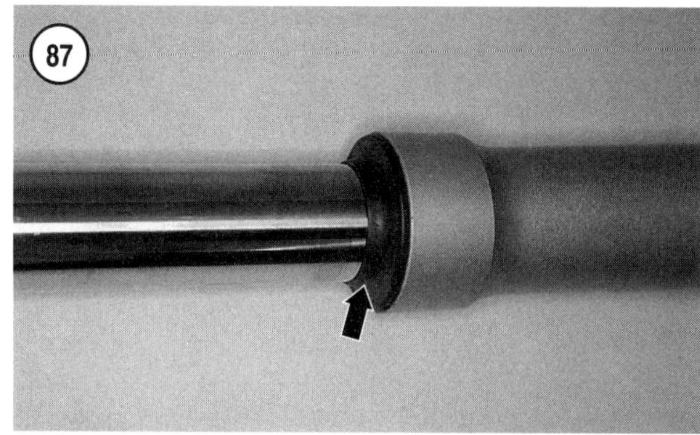

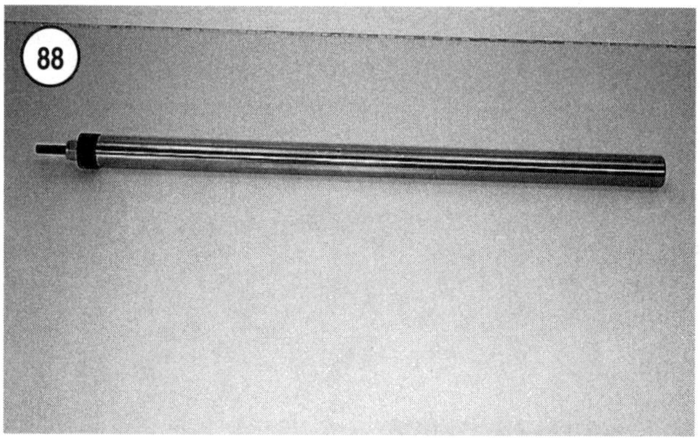

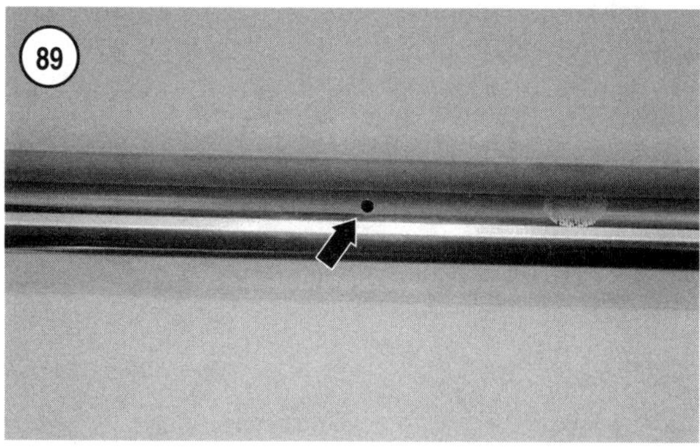

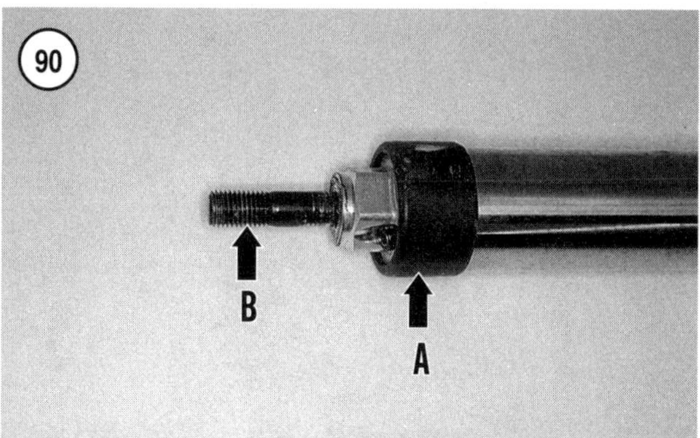

7. Install it into the slider (**Figure 86**). Push the fork tube down until the slider stops.

NOTE
Place plastic wrap over the end of the fork tube and coat it with fork oil. This will prevent damage to the oil seal lips when installing them over the top of the fork tube.

8. Install the washer and side it down the fork tube and into the slider. Make sure it seats squarely in the slider receptacle.
9. Install a new fork seal as follows:
   a. Lubricate the seal lips with fork oil.
   b. Position the seal with the manufacturer's marks facing up.
   c. Slide the seal down the fork tube. Remove the plastic wrap.
10. Carefully tap the seal squarely into the fork slider. Tap it in until it bottoms on the washer.
11. Install the retaining ring and make sure it seats completely in the slider groove.
12. Install the dust seal (**Figure 87**) into the fork slider. Tap it into place until it seats properly.
13. Slowly move the slider up and down to purge air from the fork oil. Tighten the bleed valve securely.

Inspection

1. Thoroughly clean all parts in solvent and dry them.
2. Check the fork tube (**Figure 88**) for straightness, excessive wear or scratches.
3. Check the fork tube for straightness. Place the fork tube on V-blocks and measure the runout with a dial indicator. If the runout is excessive of 0.4 mm (0.016 in.), replace the fork tube.
4. Make sure the oil passage (**Figure 89**) in the fork tube is clear.
5. On R, GS, RT and C models, do not try to remove the upper connection (A, **Figure 90**) from the fork tube. This part is pressed into the top of the fork tube and cannot be replaced separately. Check the threaded portion (B, **Figure 90**) for wear or damage. Clean the threads with an appropriate size metric die if necessary.
6. Check the slider (**Figure 91**, typical) for dents or exterior damage that may cause the fork tube to bind. Replace the slider if necessary.
7. On R1100S, R1150R, R1150GS, R1150RS and R1150RT models, inspect the nylon bushings for wear or deterioration. Replace all as a set even if only one is faulty. Also replace the bushings in both forks at the same time.

8. Inspect the brake caliper mounting bolt bosses (A, **Figure 92**, typical) and the ABS trigger receptacle and threaded holes (B). If there is any damage or indication of cracking, replace the fork slider.
9. Check the front axle clamping bolts (**Figure 93**) for thread damage.
10. Inspect the threaded holes (**Figure 94**, typical) for the lower fork bridge Allen bolts. Clean out with an appropriate size metric tap if necessary.
11. Check the slider, in the area where the fork seal is installed, for wear or damage. Replace if necessary.
12. Inspect the retaining ring groove in the fork slider for wear, corrosion or damage. Clean out the groove if necessary so that the retaining ring can seat correctly.
13. Check the axle bearing surfaces of the slider (**Figure 95**) for wear or gouges. Clean up the surfaces or replace the slider if necessary.
14. On ABS equipped models, make sure the ABS sensor line clips (**Figure 96**) are in place on the slider.

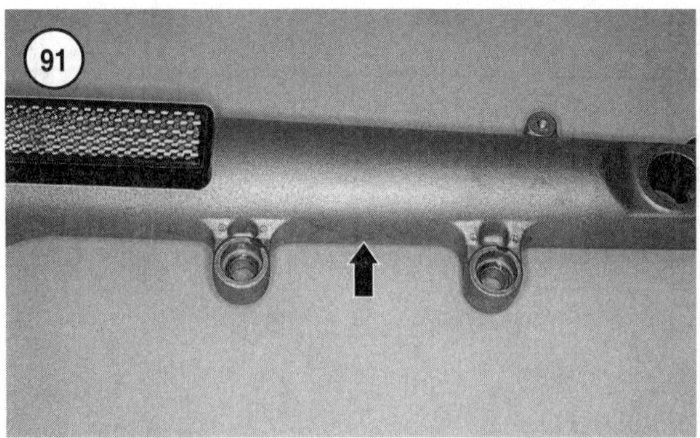

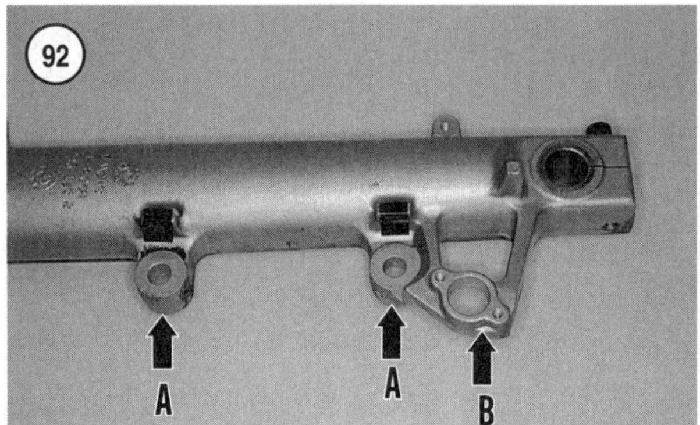

FRONT STRUT ADJUSTMENTS

NOTE
The R1100RT and R1200C models are not equipped with an adjustable front strut.

Spring Preload Adjustment

R1150R and R1150RS

The spring preload can be adjusted to either a hard or soft setting to suit road conditions and riding style.
1. Place the motorcycle on the sidestand.
2. Use a screwdriver provided in the motorcycle tool kit, rotate the adjuster (**Figure 97**) at the base of the spring to the desired position. Rotate the ring *counterclockwise* to achieve the normal or softest setting (S). Rotate the ring *clockwise* to achieve the hardest setting (H).

R1100GS and R1150GS

1. The spring preload can be adjusted to road conditions as follows:
   a. Stage 1 for paved roads.
   b. Stage 3 for loose surface (sand, gravel, or damaged paved surface).
   c. Stage 5 for off road riding.
2. Place the motorcycle on the centerstand with the front wheel off the ground.
3. Use the spanner wrench and extension provided in the motorcycle's tool kit, rotate the adjuster (**Figure 98**) at the base of the spring to the desired position. Rotate the ring

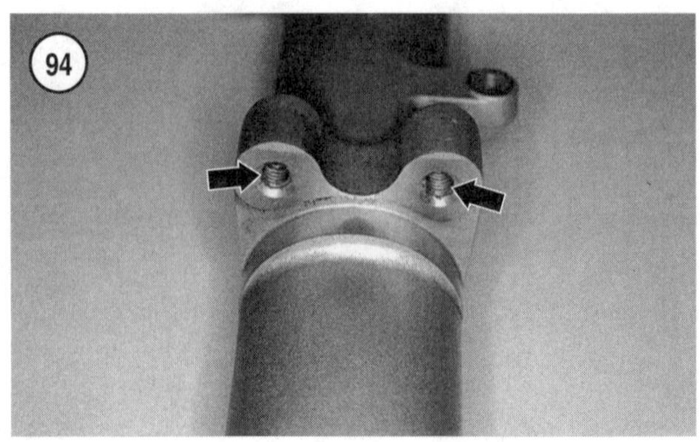

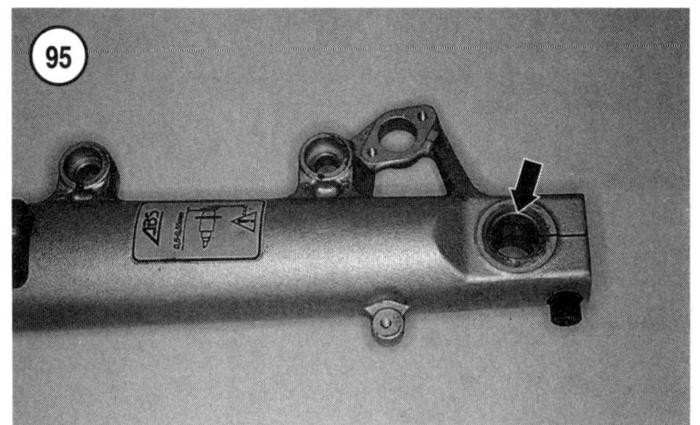

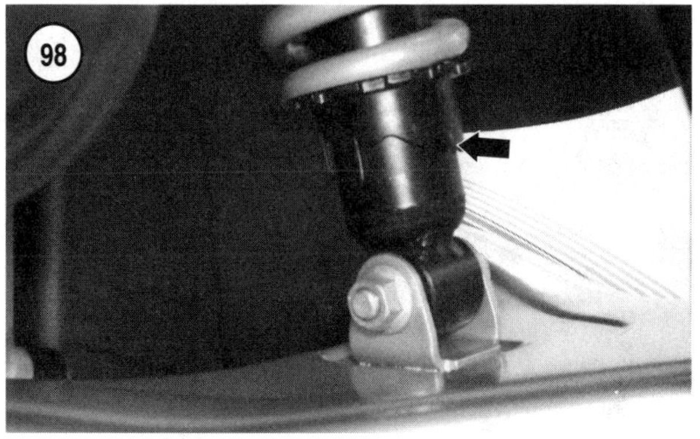

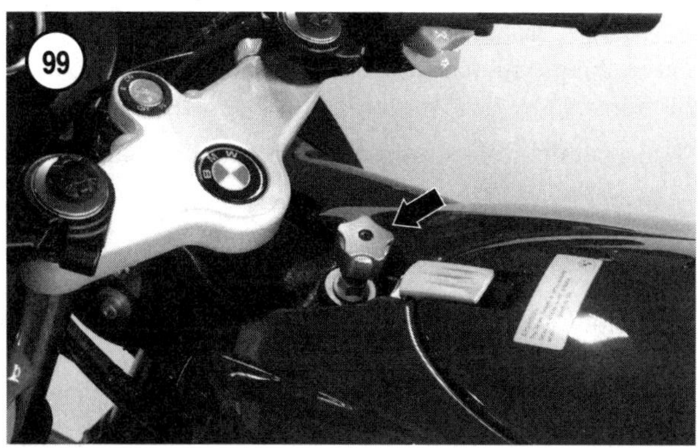

counterclockwise to achieve the normal stage 1 setting. Rotate the ring *clockwise* to achieve progressively stiffer settings.

R1100S

The spring preload can be adjusted to either a hard or soft setting to suit road conditions and riding styles.

1. Place the motorcycle on the sidestand.
2. Rotate the adjust knob (**Figure 99**) located at the front top surface of the fuel tank to the desired position. Rotate the adjust knob *counterclockwise* to achieve the normal or softest setting (S). Rotate the adjust knob *clockwise* to achieve the hardest setting (H).

FRONT STRUT

Removal/Installation

GS, RS, RT and S models

Refer to **Figure 100**, typical.

1A. On GS, RS and S models, remove the front fairing side panels as described in Chapter Fifteen.

1B. On RT models, remove the front fairing as described in Chapter Fifteen.

2. Remove the fuel tank as described in Chapter Nine.
3. Remove the front wheel as described in this chapter.

4A. On R1150R models, remove the bolt and nut securing the front strut to the front suspension A-arm.

4B. On all models except R1150R, remove the bolt, nut and washers (B, **Figure 98**) securing the front strut to the front suspension A-arm.

5. Secure the top mount of the front strut with an Allen wrench (A, **Figure 101**) to keep it from rotating while loosening the hex nut.
6. Remove the hex nut (B, **Figure 101**).

7. Hold the front strut, then remove the hex nut, washer and bushing. Pull the front strut straight down and out of the front frame.

8. Inspect the front strut as described in this chapter.

9. Install by reversing the removal step while noting the following:

   a. Coat the lower strut pivot area on the front suspension A-arm and the pivot bolt with antiseize compound prior to installation.

   b. Tighten the upper hex nut to 47 N•m (35 ft.-lb.).

   c. On GS, R, RT and S models tighten the lower bolt and nut to 50 N•m (37 ft.-lb.).

   d. On R1100RS models tighten the lower 8–mm and 10–mm bolt and nut to 43 N•m (32 ft.-lb.) and 50 N•m (37 ft.-lb.) respectively.

   e. On R1150RS models tighten the lower bolt and nut to 50 N•m (37 ft.-lb.).

R850C and R1200C models

1. Remove the fuel tank as described in Chapter Nine.

2. Remove the front wheel as described in this chapter.

3. On the left side, remove the bolt (A, **Figure 102**) securing the front strut to the front suspension arm.

4. Remove the bolts (A, **Figure 103**) securing the frame cover (B) and remove the cover.

5. Secure the top mount of the front strut (A, **Figure 104**) with an Allen wrench to keep it from rotating while loosening the hex nut.

6. Remove the hex nut (B, **Figure 104**).

CAUTION
Cover the front suspension A-arm to protect the chrome finish.

7. Hold the front strut, then remove the hex nut, washer and bushing. Pull the front strut (B, **Figure 102**) straight down and out of the front frame.

8. Inspect the front strut as described in this chapter.

9. Install by reversing the removal step while noting the following:

   a. Coat the lower strut pivot area on the front suspension A-arm and the pivot bolt with antiseize compound prior to installation.

   b. Tighten the upper hex nut to 47 N•m (35 ft.-lb.).

   c. Tighten the lower bolt and nut to 40 N•m (29 ft.-lb.).

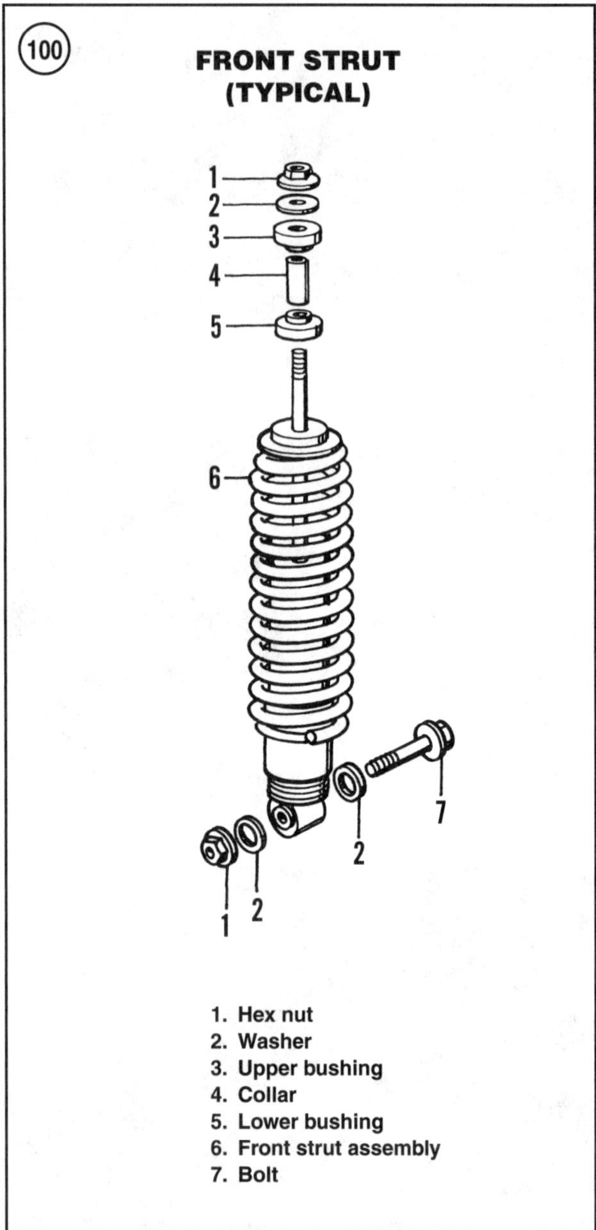

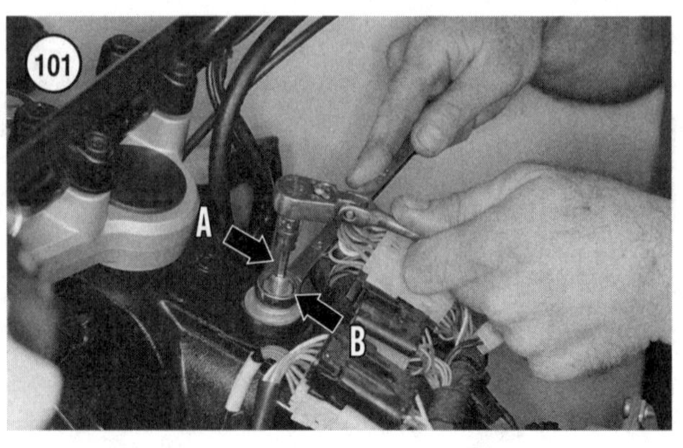

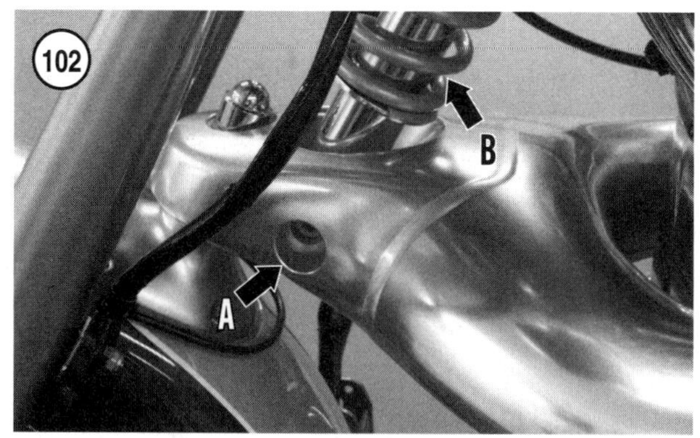

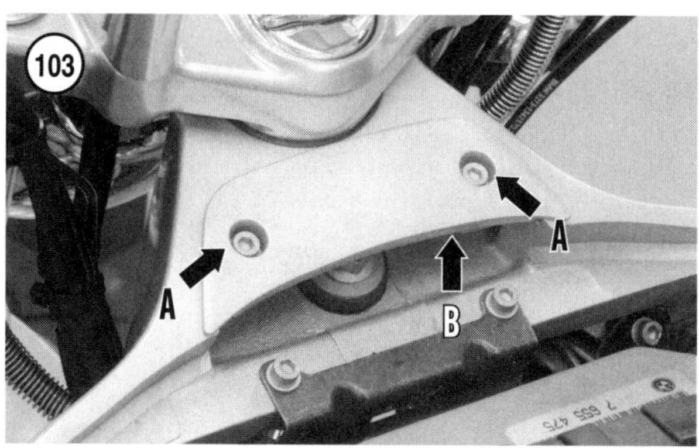

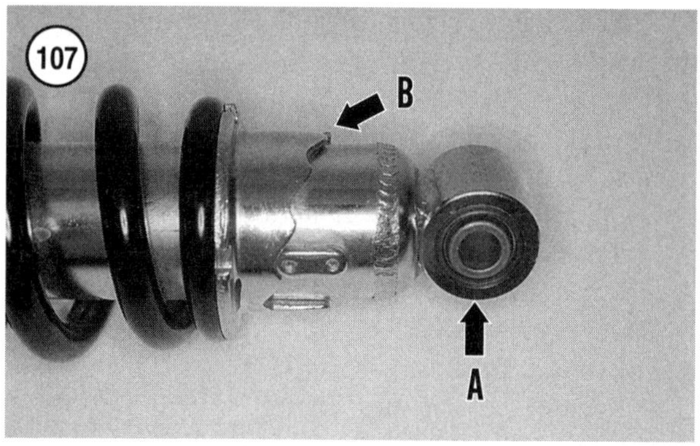

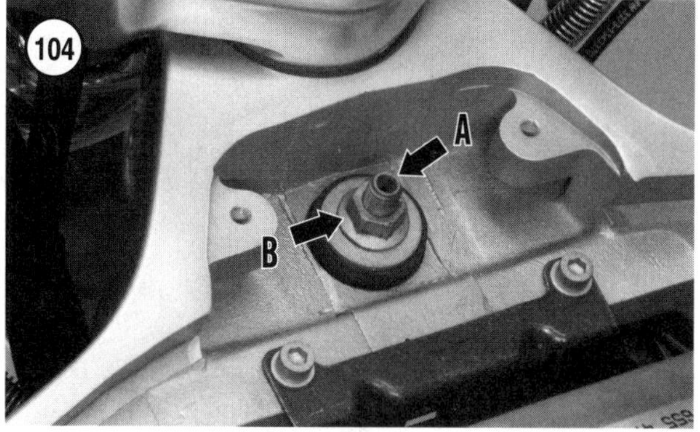

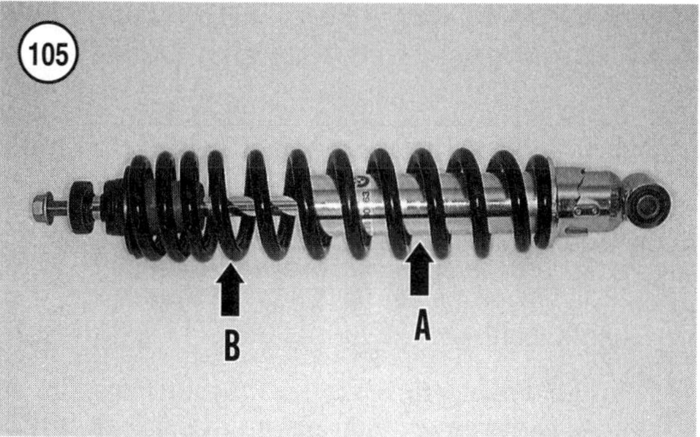

Inspection (All Models)

The only replacement parts available for the front strut are the mounting hardware and bushings. If any other part of the strut is faulty, replace the strut assembly.

1. Inspect the strut (A, **Figure 105**) for oil leakage.
2. Check the spring (B, **Figure 105**) for cracks or other damage.
3. Inspect the rebound cushion (**Figure 106**) for hardness or deterioration.
4. Inspect the lower (A, **Figure 107**) mounting area for wear or damage.
5. On models so equipped, rotate the spring preload adjuster (B, **Figure 107**) from one stop to another to make sure it rotates freely.
6. Inspect the upper mount threads (A, **Figure 108**) for wear or damage. If necessary, clean the threads with an appropriate size metric tap.
7. Check the lower bushing, the upper bushing (B, **Figure 108**), collar, washer and hex nut (**Figure 109**). Replace any parts that are worn or starting to deteriorate.
8. Make sure the spring upper seat (**Figure 110**) is securely in place.
9. If any of these areas are damaged, replace the strut assembly.

FRONT SUSPENSION A-ARM

R850R, R1100S, GS, RS and RT Models

Removal

Refer to **Figure 111**.

1A. On models so equipped, place the motorcycle on the centerstand with the front wheel off of the ground.

1B. On models without a centerstand, place a suitable size jack under the engine to support the motorcycle with the front wheel off the ground.

2. Remove the front wheel as described in Chapter Eleven.
3. Remove the front fork assembly as described in this chapter.
4. Remove the front strut as described in this chapter.
5. Remove the lower fork bridge as described in this chapter.
6. On the left side, perform the following:
   a. Remove the cover (**Figure 112**).
   b. Remove the screw cap (**Figure 113**).
7. On the right side, perform the following:
   a. Remove the cover (**Figure 114**).
   b. Remove the snap ring (**Figure 115**).
   c. Remove the retaining cap (**Figure 116**).
8. On the left side, secure the pivot shaft (**Figure 117**) to keep it from rotating while loosening the bolt in Step 9.
9. On the right side, remove the bolt (**Figure 118**) from the end of the pivot shaft.
10. Carefully tap on the right end of the shaft to partially move the pivot shaft to the left.
11. Withdraw the pivot shaft (**Figure 119**) and remove the front suspension A-arm.
12. Inspect all components as described in this chapter.

Installation

1. Apply a light coat of multipurpose grease to the pivot shaft prior to installation.
2. Align the A-arm pivot points with the mounting bosses on the crankcase.

CAUTION

In Step 3, do not force the pivot shaft through the A-arm and crankcase mounts as the leading edge may become damaged, making bolt installation difficult.

3. Carefully insert the pivot shaft (**Figure 119**) from the left side and tap it through until it bottoms.
4. On the right side, install the bolt (**Figure 118**) into the end of the pivot shaft and hand-tighten.

5. On the left side, secure the pivot shaft (**Figure 117**) to keep it from rotating while tightening the bolt in Step 6.
6. Tighten the pivot shaft bolt (**Figure 118**) to 73 N•m (54 ft.-lb.).
7. On the right side, perform the following:
   a. Install the retaining cap (**Figure 116**) and press it in until it bottoms.
   b. Install the snap ring (**Figure 115**) and make sure it seats correctly in the A-arm groove (**Figure 120**).

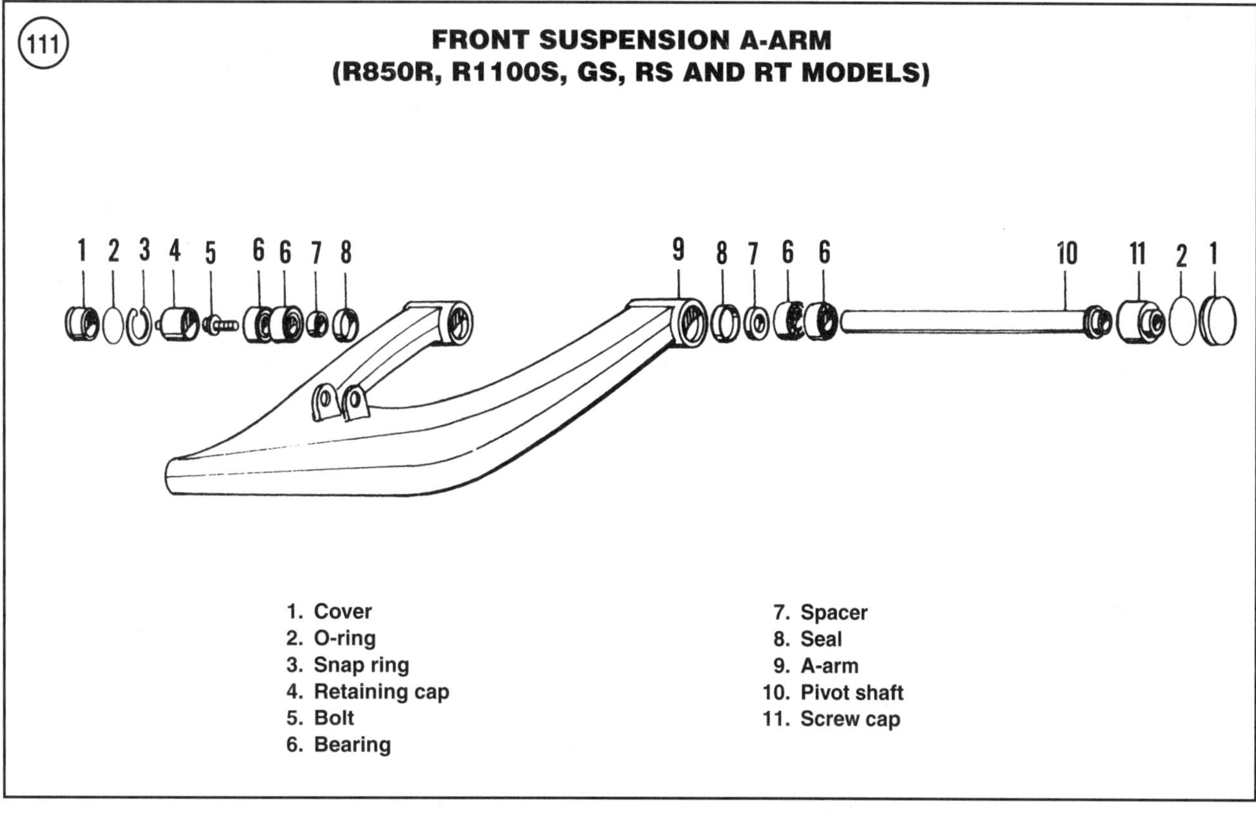
111
FRONT SUSPENSION A-ARM
(R850R, R1100S, GS, RS AND RT MODELS)
1 2 3 4 5 6 6 7 8
9 8 7 6 6
10 11 2 1
1. Cover
2. O-ring
3. Snap ring
4. Retaining cap
5. Bolt
6. Bearing
7. Spacer
8. Seal
9. A-arm
10. Pivot shaft
11. Screw cap

112

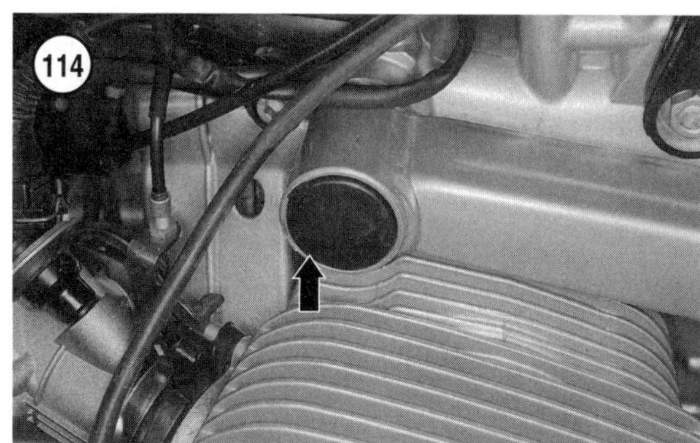
114

113

115

c. Install the cover (**Figure 114**) and make sure it seats properly.
8. On the left side, perform the following:
a. Apply a light coat of antiseize compound to the screw cap threads prior to installation.
b. Install the retaining cap (**Figure 113**) and tighten to 42 N•m (31 ft.-lb.).
c. Install the cover (**Figure 116**).
9. Install the lower fork bridge as described in this chapter.
10. Install the front strut as described in this chapter.
11. Install the front fork assembly as described in this chapter.
12. Install the front wheel as described in Chapter Eleven.

R850C, R1150R and R1200C Models

Removal

Refer to **Figure 121** and **Figure 122**.

1A. On models so equipped, place the motorcycle on the centerstand with the rear wheel off of the ground.

1B. On models without a centerstand, place a suitable size jack under the engine to support the motorcycle with the front wheel off the ground.

2. On R1100S models, remove the side firing panels as described in Chapter Fifteen.
3. Remove the front wheel as described in Chapter Eleven.
4. Remove the front fork assembly (A, **Figure 123**) as described in this chapter.
5. Remove the front strut (B, **Figure 123**) as described in this chapter.
6. Remove the lower fork bridge as described in this chapter.
7. On the left side, perform the following:
a. Remove the cover.
b. On R850C, R1100S, and R1200C models, remove the screw cap.

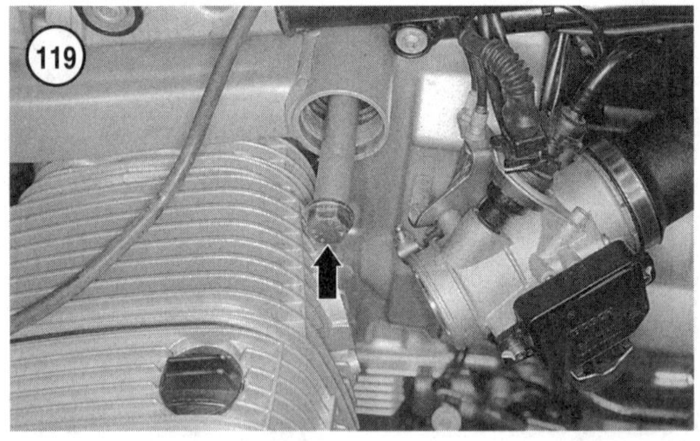

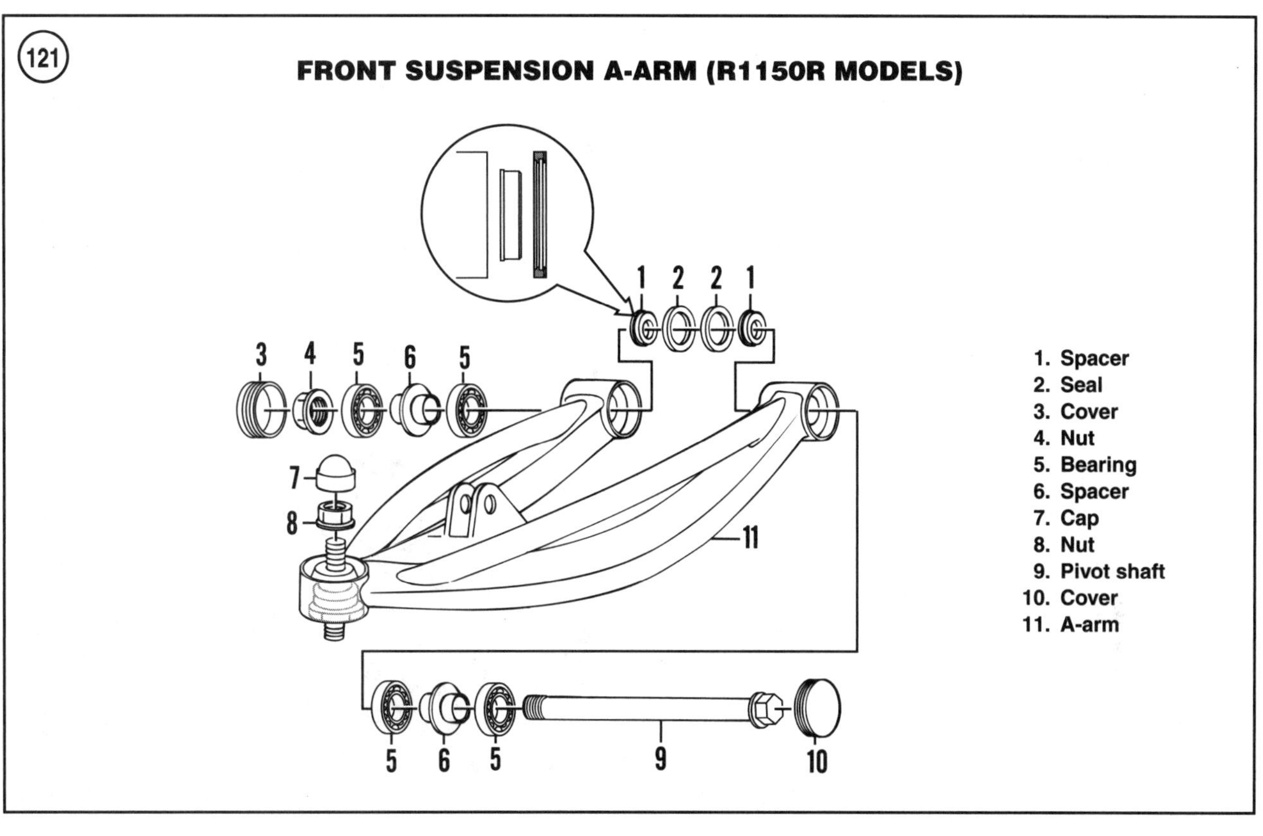
121
FRONT SUSPENSION A-ARM (R1150R MODELS)
1. Spacer
2. Seal
3. Cover
4. Nut
5. Bearing
6. Spacer
7. Cap
8. Nut
9. Pivot shaft
10. Cover
11. A-arm

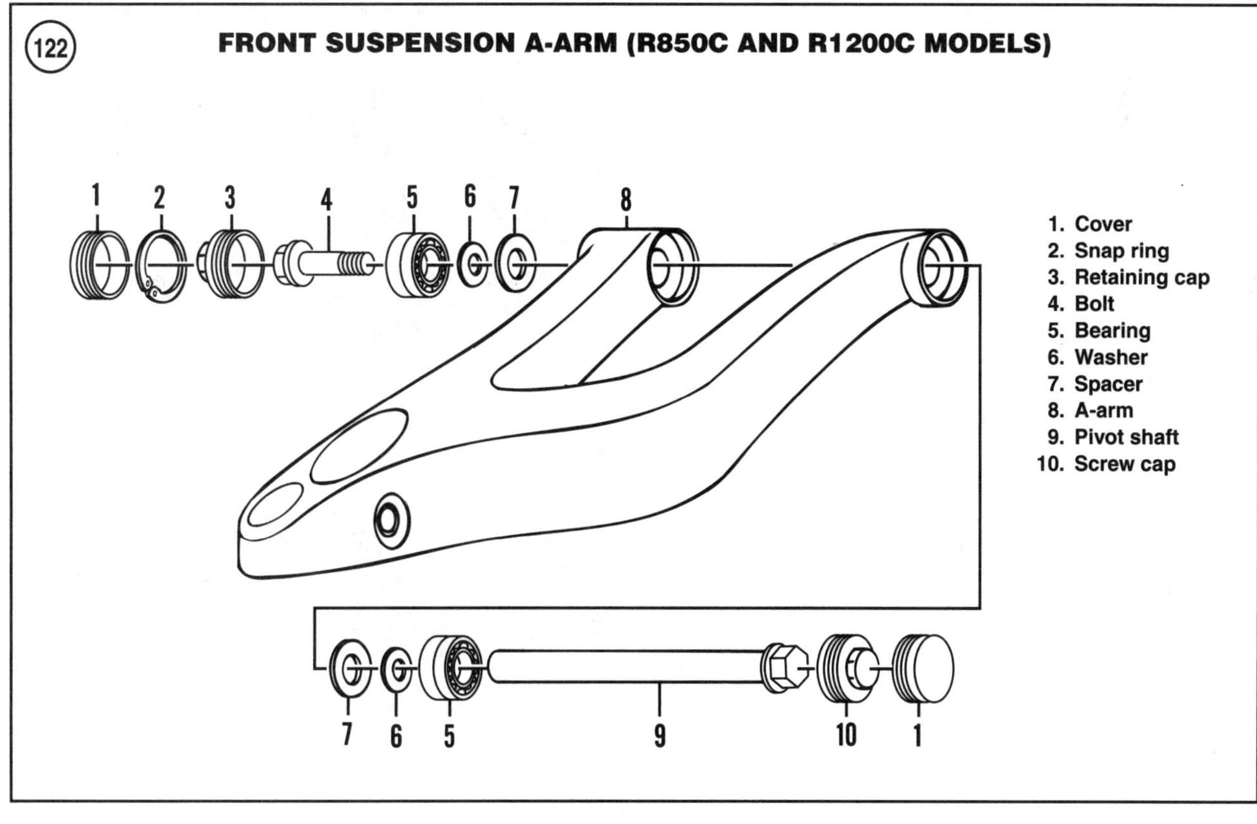
122
FRONT SUSPENSION A-ARM (R850C AND R1200C MODELS)
1. Cover
2. Snap ring
3. Retaining cap
4. Bolt
5. Bearing
6. Washer
7. Spacer
8. A-arm
9. Pivot shaft
10. Screw cap

8A. On R1150R models, on the right side, perform the following:

a. Remove the cover (C, **Figure 123**).
b. Secure the pivot shaft to keep it from rotating while loosening the nut in sub-step c.
c. Loosen and remove the nut (**Figure 124**) from the pivot bolt.

8B. On R850C, R1100S, and R1200C models, on the right side, perform the following:

a. Remove the cover (**Figure 125**).
b. Remove the snap ring.
c. Remove the retaining cap.
d. Secure the pivot shaft to keep it from rotating while loosening the bolt in sub-step e.
e. Loosen and remove the bolt from the pivot bolt.

9. Carefully tap on the right end of the pivot shaft to partially move the pivot shaft to the left.
10. Withdraw the pivot shaft (**Figure 119**) and remove the front suspension A-arm (D, **Figure 123**).
11. Inspect all components as described in this chapter.

Installation

1. Apply a light coat of multipurpose grease to the pivot shaft prior to installation.
2. Align the A-arm pivot points with the mounting bosses on the crankcase.

CAUTION
In Step 3, do not force the pivot shaft through the A-arm and crankcase mounts as the leading edge may become damaged, making bolt installation difficult.

3. Carefully insert the pivot shaft (**Figure 119**) from the left side and tap it through until it bottoms.

4A. On R1150R models, on the right side, perform the following:

a. Install the nut (**Figure 124**) onto the pivot bolt and hand-tighten.
b. Secure the pivot shaft to keep it from rotating while tightening the nut in sub-step c.
c. Tighten the pivot shaft nut to 130 N•m (96 ft.-lb.).
d. Install the cover (C, **Figure 123**) and make sure it seats correctly.

4B. On R850C, R1100S, and R1200C models, on the right side, perform the following:

a. Install the bolt onto the pivot shaft and hand-tighten.
b. Secure the pivot shaft to keep it from rotating while tightening the bolt in sub-step c.
c. Tighten the pivot shaft bolt to 73 N•m (54 ft.-lb.).

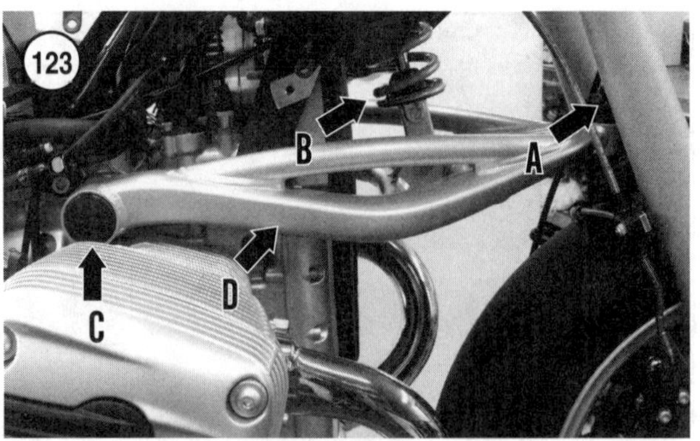

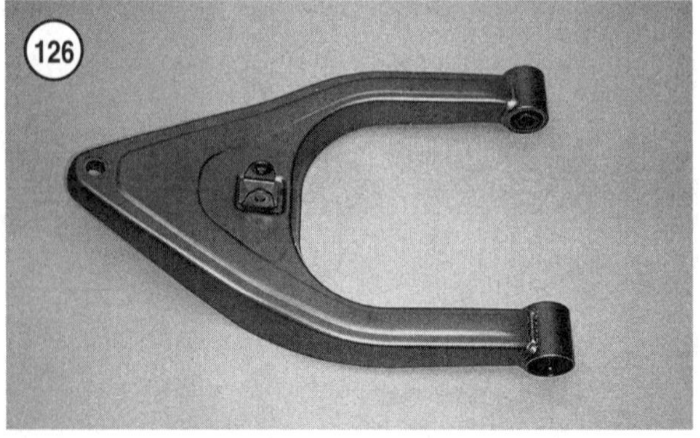

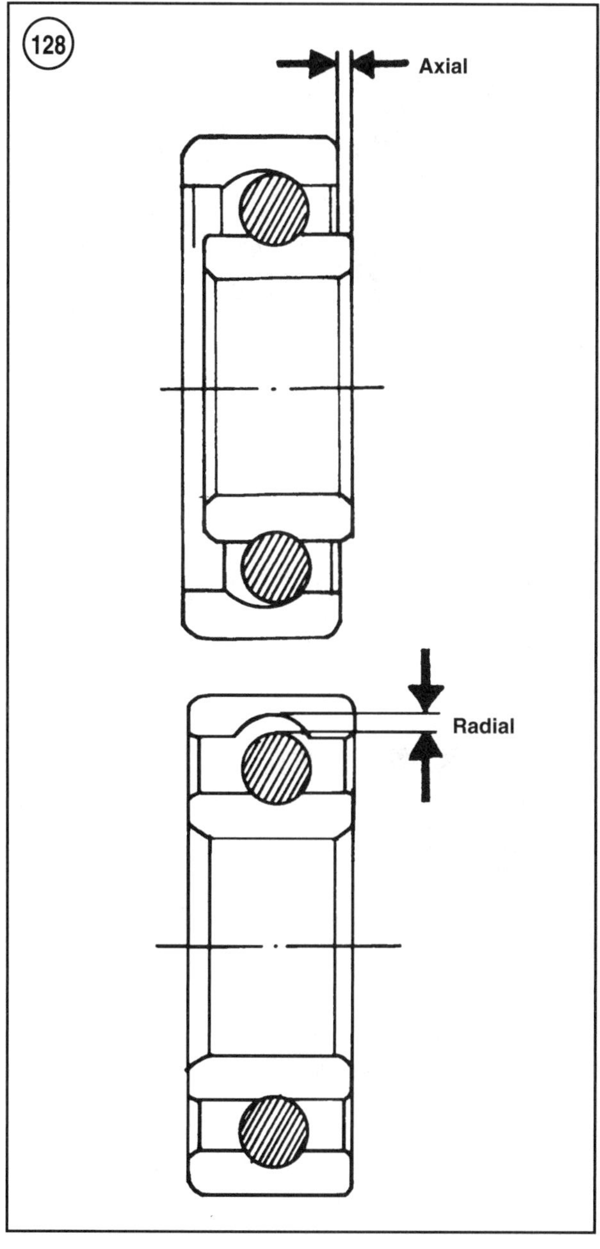

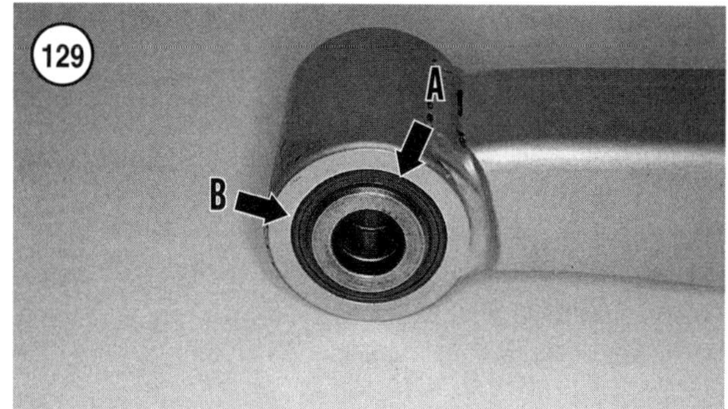

   d. Apply a light coat of antiseize compound to the retaining cap threads prior to installation.
   e. Install the retaining cap and tighten to 42 N•m (31 ft.-lb.).
   f. Install the snap ring and make sure it seats correctly in the A-arm groove.
   g. Install the cover (**Figure 125**) and make sure it seats correctly.
5. On the left side, perform the following:
   a. On R850C, R1100S, and R1200C models, apply a light coat of antiseize compound to the screw cap threads prior to installation. Install the screw cap.
   b. Install the cover.
6. Install the lower fork bridge as described in this chapter.
7. Install the front strut (B, **Figure 123**) as described in this chapter.
8. Install the front fork assembly (A, **Figure 123**) as described in this chapter.
9. Install the front wheel as described in Chapter Eleven.

Inspection (All Models)

WARNING
Do not attempt to repair or straighten an A-arm as this will result in an unsafe riding condition. If any portion of the A-arm is damaged, replace the A-arm.

1. Check the A-arm (**Figure 126**, typical) for cracks or damage.
2. Turn the bearing inner race (**Figure 127**) by hand. The bearing must turn smoothly. Some axial play is normal, but radial play must be negligible. See **Figure 128**. Replace the bearing(s) if necessary.
3. Check the seal (A, **Figure 129**) and spacer (B) for wear or deterioration and replace if necessary.

4. Inspect the front strut lower mounting bracket (**Figure 130**, typical) for cracks, damage and bolt hole elongation.

5. On all models except R1150R, inspect the ball joint mounting hole (**Figure 131**) for damage or hole elongation.

6. Check the pivot shaft and bolt (**Figure 132**) for wear or damage and for thread damage. Repair the threads with a metric tap or die if necessary.

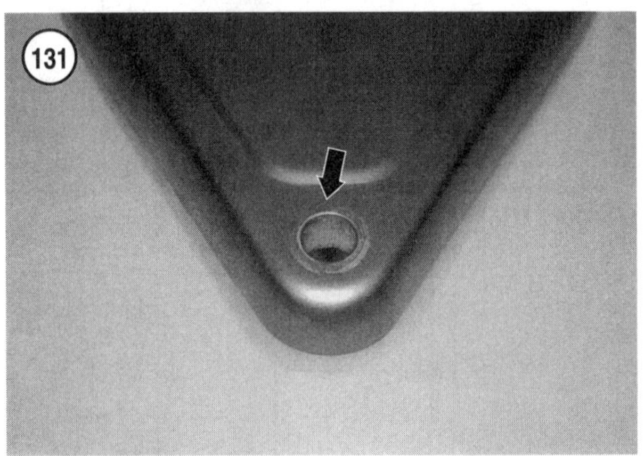

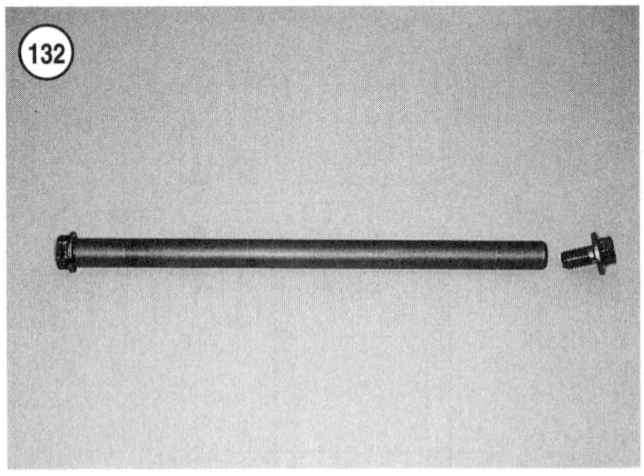

STEERING DAMPER (R1100R MODELS)

Removal/Installation

Refer to **Figure 133**.

NOTE
A heat gun capable of 120° C (248° F) is required to loosen the Allen bolts securing the steering damper to the mounting brackets on the lower fork bridge and front suspension A-arm.

1. Remove the front wheel as described in this chapter.
2. Remove the front fender as described in Chapter Fifteen.
3. Remove the trim cap on the Allen bolt-to-front suspension A-arm mounting bracket.

CAUTION
Do not apply heat to the Allen bolts with any type of propane or welding torch flame.

CAUTION
To protect the painted surface, the front suspension A-arm and the lower fork bridge while heating the Allen bolts, soak several shop rags in water and place them around the A-arm and lower fork bridge.

4. Heat the Allen bolt securing the steering damper to the lower fork bridge. Heat the Allen bolt to 120° C (248° F).

WARNING
The steering damper and lower fork bridge are very hot. Make sure to wear protective gloves when loosening the Allen bolt in the next step.

5. Loosen, then remove the Allen bolt, washers, and ring spacers securing the steering damper to the lower fork bridge.

6. Heat the Allen bolt securing the steering damper to the front suspension A-arm. Heat the Allen bolt to 120° C (248° F).

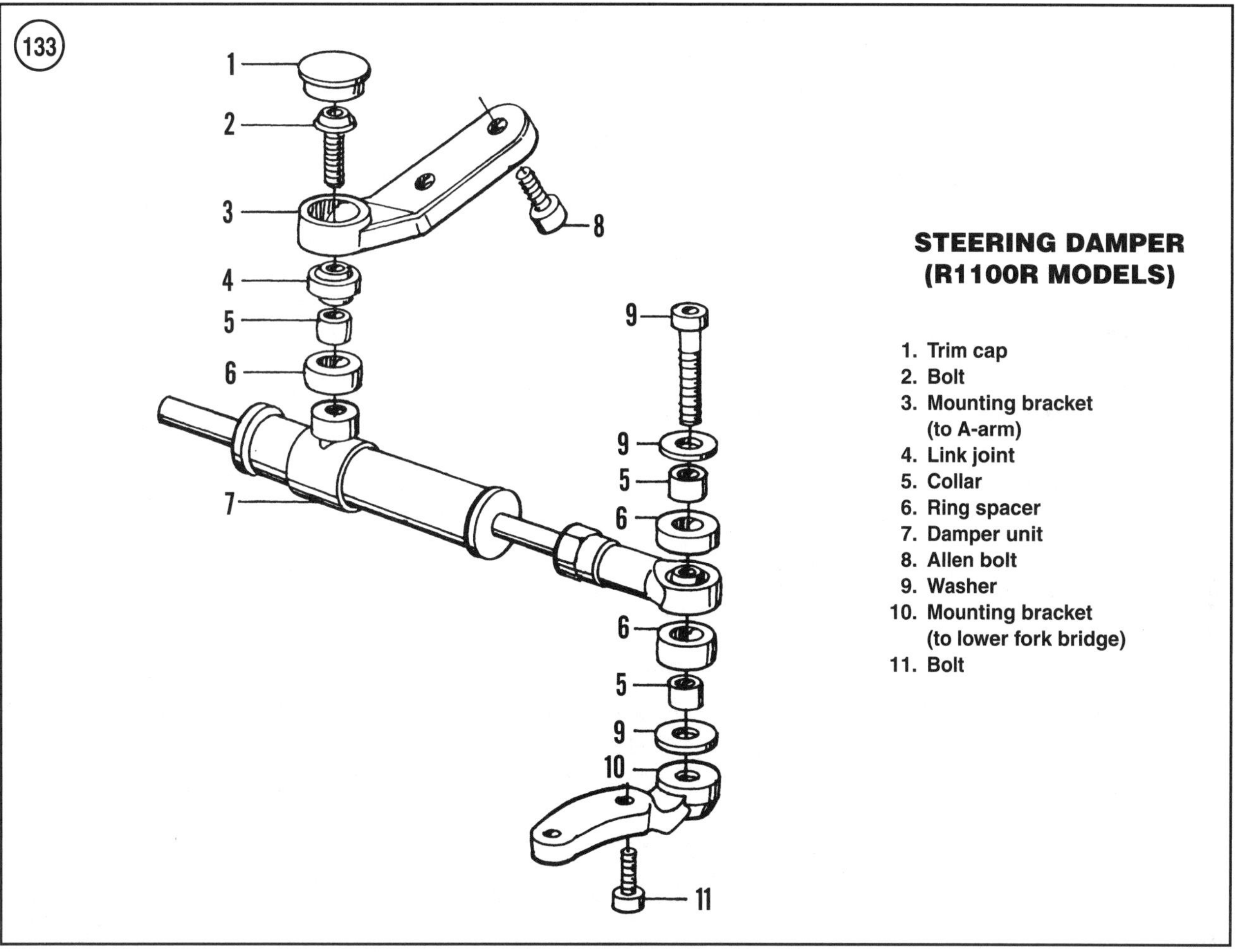

7. Loosen, then remove the Allen bolt and ring spacer securing the steering damper to the front suspension A-arm.

8. Install by reversing the removal steps while noting the following:

a. If the Allen bolts are going to be reused, thoroughly clean all threadlocking compound from the bolt threads using cleaning solvent and a wire brush.

b. Apply Loctite No. 2710, or an equivalent, to the Allen bolt threads prior to installation.

c. Install the Allen bolts and tighten to 20 N•m (15 ft.-lb.).

Inspection

NOTE
The damper unit cannot be repaired; only the attaching hardware and the link joint are replaceable.

1. Check the exterior of the damper unit for oil leakage and damage.

2. Pull slowly on the rod within the damper unit. It should move slowly and smoothly with no hesitation.

3. Inspect the link joint and the ball joint for wear or damage.

Table 1 FRONT SUSPENSION SPECIFICATIONS

Front wheel caster (in normal load)	
R models	127 mm (5 in.)
GS models	115 mm (4.5 in.)
RS models	111 mm (4.4 in.)
RT models	122 mm (4.8 in.)
S models	100 mm (3.9 in.)
C models	86 mm (3.4 in.)
Steering lock angle	
R models	37°
GS models	42°
RS models	32°
RT models	34°
S models	31°
C models	38°
Front suspension travel	
R models	120 mm (4.7 in.)
GS models	120 mm (4.7 in.)
RS and RT models	120 mm (4.7 in.)
S models	110 mm (4.3 in.)
C models	144 mm (5.7 in.)
Fork tube	
Outside diameter	35 mm (1.378 in.)
Maximum amount of runout	0.4 mm (0.0157 in.)
Fork oil	
Type	BMW fork oil 5W or 10W
Quantity	
R1100S	170 ml (5.75 oz.)
All other models	470 ml (15.89 oz.)
Front strut	Coil spring, gas filled shock absorber

Table 2 FRONT SUSPENSION TORQUE SPECIFICATIONS

Item	N•m	in.-lb.	ft.-lb.
Brake master cylinder union bolt	14	124	–
Clutch master cylinder union bolt	14	124	–
Handlebar(s)			
C, R, GS, RT models			
Handlebar-to- upper fork bridge	21	–	15
Handlebars			
RS models			
Handlebar-to-rubber mount	40	–	29
Rubber mount-to-upper fork bridge	40	–	29
Handlebars			
R1100S			
Clamp bolt-to-fork tube	25	–	18
Locating bolt	9	80	–
Handlebar weight mounting bolt	20	–	15
Handlebar lever pivot screw			
R1100S and all R1150 models	11	97	–
Fork upper bridge clamp bolt (RS models)	22	–	16
Front fork			
Upper connection nut			
R, GS, RT models	45	–	33
R850C, R1200C	35	–	26
Fork-to-lower fork bridge bolt			
R1150GS	45	–	33
R1100S	25	–	18
All models except R1150GS, R1100S	22	–	16

(continued)

Table 2 FRONT SUSPENSION TORQUE SPECIFICATIONS (continued)

Item	N•m	in.-lb.	ft.-lb.
Front strut			
Upper hex nut	47	–	35
Lower bolt and nut			
R, GS, RT, S models	50	–	37
R1100RS models			
8–mm	43	–	32
10–mm	50	–	37
R850C, R1200C models	40	–	29
Front suspension arm			
Pivot shaft bolt (right side)	73	–	54
Left side screw cap	42	–	31
Pivot shaft nut (R1150R)	130	–	96
Lower fork bridge			
Ball joint hex nut	130	–	96
Fork bridge-to-fork tube	22	–	16
Ball joint assembly-to-fork bridge	230	–	170
Steering damper-to- suspension A-arm	20	–	15
Upper fork bridge Allen bolt	130	–	96

CHAPTER THIRTEEN

REAR SUSPENSION AND FINAL DRIVE

This chapter covers the rear suspension components and final drive unit.

On all models except the R850C and R1200C, the swing arm is known as the BMW Paralever and it carries the final drive unit and rear wheel on the right side only. The swing arm is made of a high-strength alloy casting that pivots on the transmission case on tapered roller bearings. The drive shaft runs through the hollow swing arm and has a splined universal joint at the front where it attaches to the transmission output shaft and an additional joint at the rear where it attaches to the final drive unit. The universal joint and splines allow for the up and down movement of the swing arm and the slight in and out movement of the drive shaft.

On the R850C and R1200C models, the swing arm is known as the BMW Monolever and it carries the final drive unit and rear wheel on the right side only. The swing arm is made of a high-strength alloy casting that pivots on the transmission case on tapered roller bearings. The drive shaft runs through the hollow swing arm and has a splined universal joint at the front where it attaches to the transmission output shaft and is bolted directly to the final drive unit at the rear. The front universal joint and splines allow for the up and down movement of the swing arm and the slight in and out movement of the drive shaft.

The single shock absorber has a progressively wound coil spring and is hydraulically damped. The spring preload can be adjusted to compensate for additional load (passenger and/or luggage). On some models, the rebound damping can also be adjusted. The shock absorber is matched to the spring and damping rate of the front suspension.

Tire changing, tire repair and wheel balancing are covered in Chapter Eleven.

Some of the components of the rear suspension require heat to loosen and remove. It is therefore necessary to have a heat gun capable of 120° C (248° F). A heat gun is also required for disassembly of some of the front suspension, engine and transmission components.

Table 1 is located at the end of this chapter.

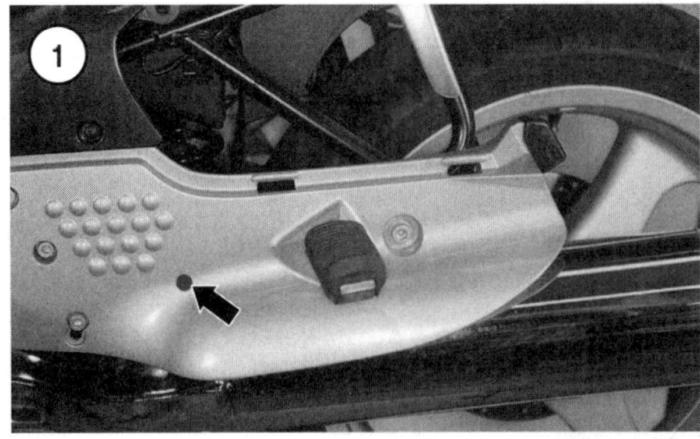

SHOCK ABSORBER

Shock Rebound Adjustment

1. On R850 and R1200 models, the shock absorber rebound adjustment can be adjusted to three settings as follows:
   a. Soft setting (counterclockwise) for solo rider with no luggage.
   b. Normal setting (mid point) for a passenger or heavy luggage.
   c. Firm setting (clockwise) for maximum loads (do not exceed the vehicle's maximum weight limit).

2A. On R1100 and R1150 models, the shock absorber rebound adjustment can be adjusted to two different settings as follows:
   a. Soft setting (counterclockwise) for solo rider with no luggage.
   b. Firm setting (clockwise) for maximum loads (do not exceed the vehicle's maximum weight limit).

2B. On R1100S models, place the motorcycle on the sidestand. On RT models, place the motorcycle on the centerstand with the rear wheel off the ground.

NOTE
*On RT models, insert the screwdriver through the hole (**Figure 1**) in the left side footrest panel to access the adjuster.*

3. Use a slotted screwdriver and rotate the adjuster (**Figure 2**) at the base of the shock absorber. Be sure to place the adjuster in one of the three settings, not between settings. If left in between settings, it will set the shock to the firmer setting.

Spring Preload Adjustment

R850R, R1100R and R1100RS models

1. The spring preload setting can be adjusted to any of three settings as follows:
   a. Stage 1 for solo rider with no luggage.
   b. Stage 4 for a passenger or heavy luggage.
   c. Stage 7 for a passenger and heavy luggage.
2. Place the motorcycle on the centerstand with the rear wheel off of the ground.
3. Using the spanner wrench and extension provided in the factory tool kit, rotate the adjuster at the base of the spring to the desired position.
   a. Rotate the ring *counterclockwise* to achieve the normal or softest setting (No. 1).
   b. Rotate the ring *clockwise* to achieve the hardest setting (No. 7).

R850GS, R1100GS and R1100RT models

1. Place the motorcycle on the centerstand with the rear wheel off the ground.
2. On RT models, remove the right side cover as described in Chapter Fifteen.
3. Rotate the knob (A, **Figure 3**) on the remote adjuster as necessary.

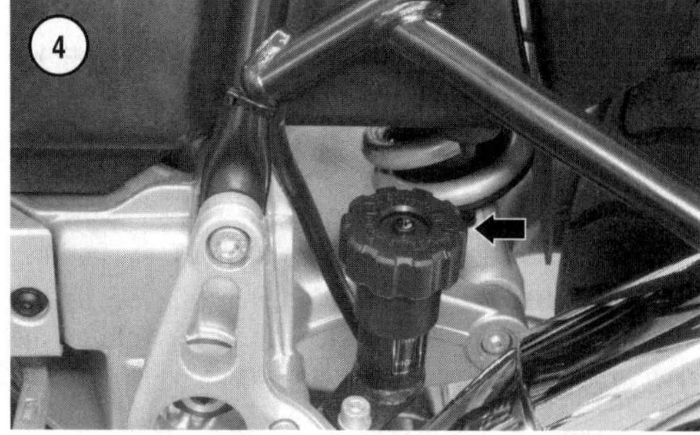

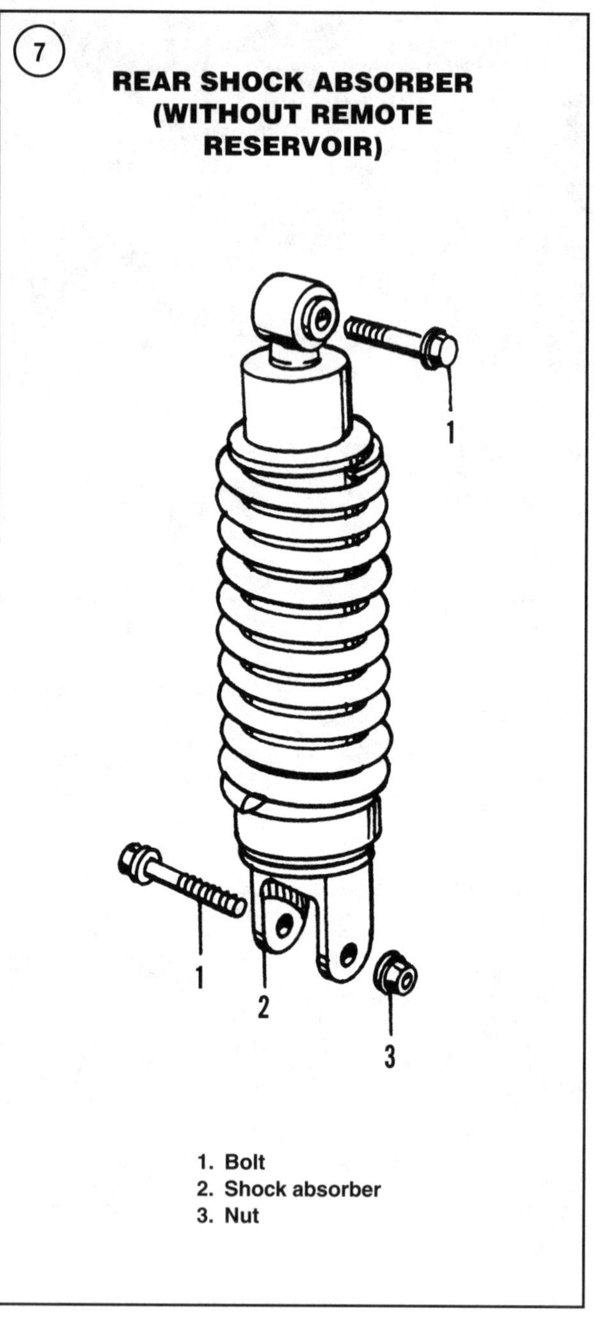

R1150GS, R1150R and R1150RT models

1. Place the motorcycle on the centerstand with the rear wheel off the ground.
2. On RT models, remove the right side cover as described in Chapter Fifteen.
3. Rotate the knob (**Figure 4**) on the remote adjuster to the following:
   a. Rotate the knob *counterclockwise* to achieve the normal or low, setting solo rider with no luggage.
   b. Rotate the knob *clockwise* to achieve the hardest or high setting, with a passenger and heavy luggage.

R1100S models

1. Place the motorcycle on the sidestand.
2. Rotate the knob (**Figure 5**) on the side of the shock absorber adjuster to the following:
   a. Rotate the knob *counterclockwise* to achieve the normal or low setting, solo rider with no luggage.
   b. Rotate the knob *clockwise* to achieve the hardest or high setting, with a passenger and heavy luggage.

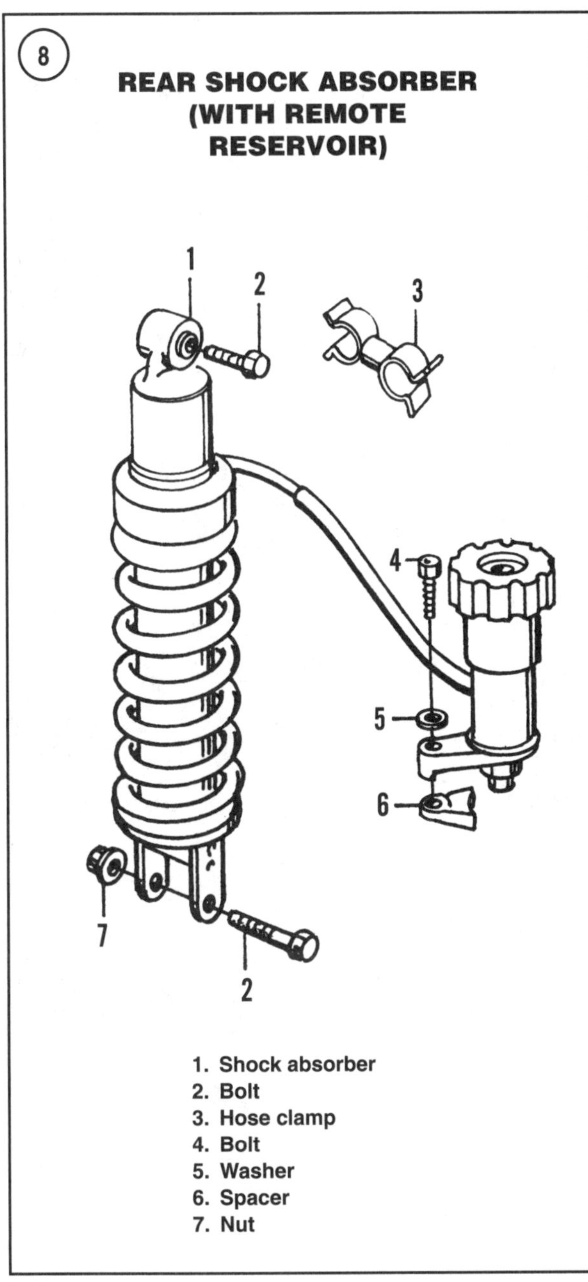

R850C and R1200C models

1. The spring preload setting can be adjusted to any of three settings as follows:
   a. Stage 1 for solo light rider with no luggage.
   b. Stage 3 for solo heavier rider.
   c. Stage 7 for a passenger and/or heavy luggage.
2. Place the motorcycle on the sidestand.
3. Using the spanner wrench and extension provided in the motorcycle's tool kit, rotate the adjuster at the base of the spring (**Figure 6**) to the desired position.

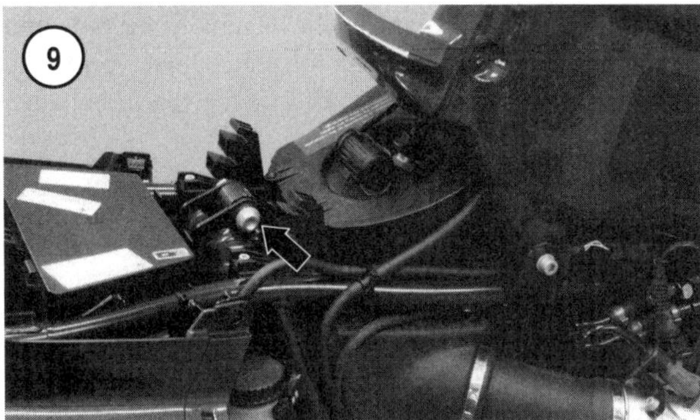

   a. Rotate the ring *counterclockwise* to achieve the normal or softest setting (No. 1).
   b. Rotate the ring *clockwise* to achieve the hardest setting (No. 7).

Removal

Refer to **Figure 7** and **Figure 8**.

1A. On models so equipped, place the motorcycle on the centerstand with the rear wheel off the ground.

1B. On models without a centerstand, place a suitable size jack under the engine to support the motorcycle with the rear wheel off the ground.

2. Remove the seat(s) as described in Chapter Fifteen.
3. On RT models, remove the lower fairing sections as described in Chapter Fifteen.
4. Remove the rear wheel as described in Chapter Eleven.
5. Place wood block(s) under the swing arm to maintain the swing arm in the at-rest position.
6. Remove the upper mounting bolt (**Figure 9**) securing the shock absorber to the frame.

7A. On GS, R and RS models, remove the 6–mm Allen bolt and washer (**Figure 10**) securing the remote reservoir to the front left footpeg bracket.

7B. On RT models, remove the 6 mm Allen bolt and washer (B, **Figure 3**) securing the remote reservoir to the frame mounting bracket. Do not lose the spacer between the reservoir and the frame mount.

8A. On R850C and R1200C models, remove the lower bolt (**Figure 11**) securing the shock absorber to the swing arm.

8B. On all models except R850C and R1200C, remove the lower bolt and nut (**Figure 12**) securing the shock absorber to the mounting boss on the swing arm.

9. Remove the shock absorber from the swing arm mounting boss.

10. Carefully pull the upper end of the shock absorber out of the mounting area in the frame.

11A. On models without a remote reservoir, remove the shock absorber from the frame.

11B. On models with a remote reservoir, carefully remove the shock absorber, remote reservoir and interconnecting hose assembly from the frame.

12. Inspect the shock absorber unit as described in this chapter.

Installation

1. Apply a light coat of molybdenum disulfide paste grease to the upper rubber bushing on the shock absorber.

WARNING

All rear suspension fasteners must be replaced with parts of the same type. ***Do not*** *use non-standard replacement parts as this may affect the performance of the system or result in failure of the part which could lead to loss of motorcycle control. Torque specifications in* ***Table 1*** *must be used during installation to ensure proper retention of these components.*

2A. On models without a remote reservoir, install the shock absorber into the frame.

NOTE

Position the shock absorber so the remote reservoir will be mounted on the left side of the motorcycle .

2B. On models with a remote reservoir, carefully install the shock absorber, remote reservoir and interconnecting hose assembly into the frame.

3. Move the shock absorber into position and align the upper mounting hole with the hole in the frame.

4. Install the upper bolt (**Figure 9**) and tighten to the following:

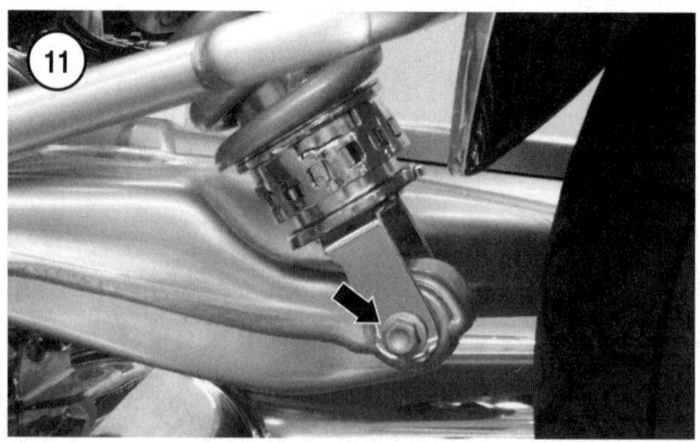
11

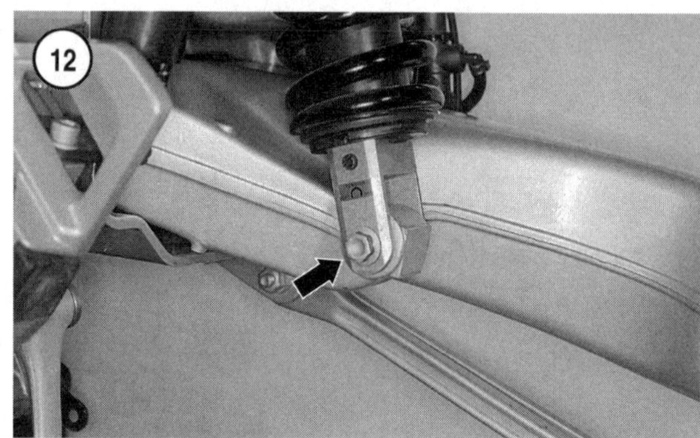
12

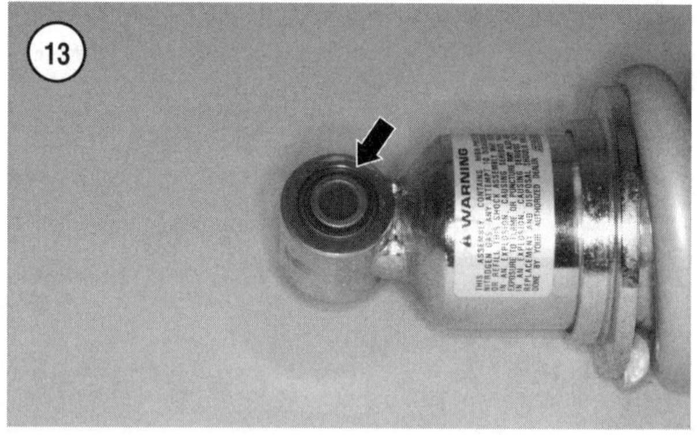

13

14

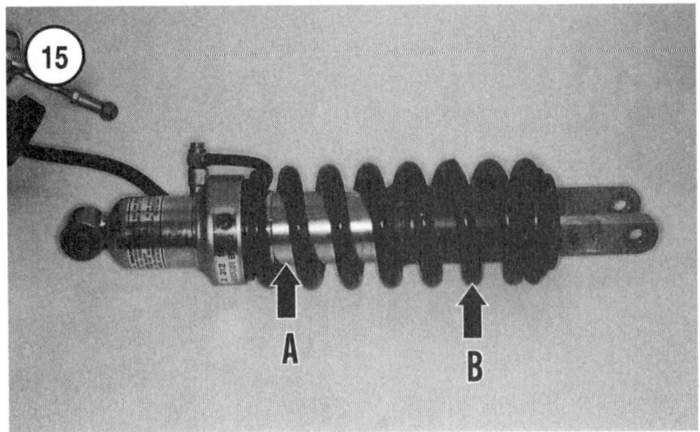

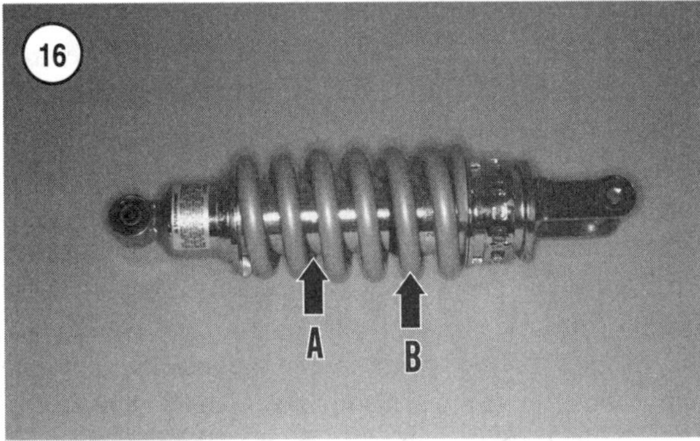

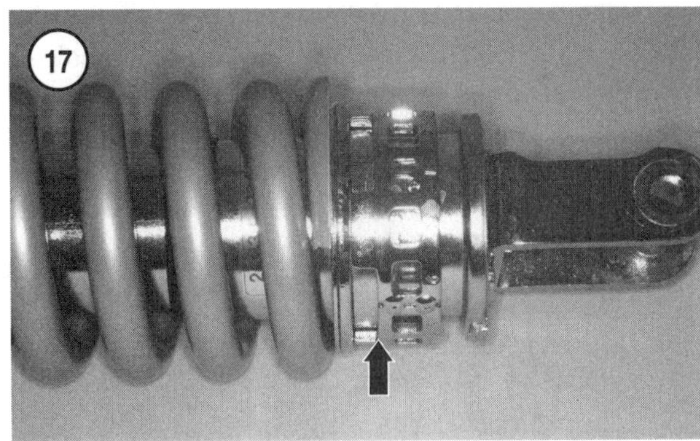

a. On 1995-1998 R850 and all R1100 models: 43 N•m (32 ft.-lb.).

b. On 1999-on R850, all R1100, all R1150 and all R1200 models: 50 N•m (37 ft.-lb.).

5A. On R1200C models, install the lower bolt (**Figure 11**) securing the shock absorber to the mounting boss on the swing arm and tighten to 50 N•m (37 ft.-lb.).

5B. On all models except R1200C, install the lower bolt and nut (**Figure 12**) securing the shock absorber to the mounting boss on the swing arm and tighten to the following:

a. On 1995-1998 R850 and all R1100 models: 50 N•m (37 ft.-lb.).

b. On 1999-on R850, all R1100 and all R1150 models: 58 N•m (43 ft.-lb.).

6A. On GS, R and RS models, install the 6–mm Allen bolt and washer (**Figure 10**) securing the remote reservoir to the front left footpeg bracket. Tighten the Allen bolt to 22 N•m (16 ft.-lb.).

6B. On RT models, position the spacer between the frame bracket and the remote reservoir bracket. Install the 6–mm Allen bolt and washer (**Figure 10**) securing the remote reservoir to the frame mounting bracket. Tighten the Allen bolt to 22 N•m (16 ft.-lb.).

7. Remove the wood block(s) from under the swing arm.
8. Install the seats as described in Chapter Fifteen.
9. On RT models, install the lower fairing sections as described in Chapter Fifteen.
10. Install the rear wheel as described in this chapter.

Inspection

The only replacement part available for the rear shock absorber is the mounting hardware. If any other part of the shock absorber is faulty, it must be replaced.

1. Inspect the upper (**Figure 13**) mounting bushing of the shock absorber where it attaches to the frame. Check for deterioration or damage.
2. Clean the mounting bushing with solvent. Thoroughly dry and apply molybdenum disulfide grease to the mounting bushing.
3. Inspect the lower (**Figure 14**) mounting tabs of the shock absorber where it attaches to the final drive unit. Check for cracks and mounting bolt hole elongation.

4A. On models with a remote reservoir, perform the following:

a. Check the damper unit (A, **Figure 15**) for oil leakage.
b. Make sure the damper rod is straight and that the rubber guide is not damaged or worn.
c. Check the spring (B, **Figure 15**) for cracks or other damage.

4B. On R850C and R1200C and all other models without a remote reservoir, perform the following:

a. Check the damper unit (A, **Figure 16**) for oil leakage.
b. Make sure the damper rod is straight.
c. Check the spring (B, **Figure 16**) for cracks or other damage.

5. On R850C and R1200C models, make sure the spring preload adjuster (**Figure 17**) rotates.

NOTE

***Figure 18** is shown with the left foot peg removed to better illustrate the step.*

6. On models so equipped, inspect the remote reservoir (A, **Figure 18**) and interconnecting hose (B) for damage or deterioration.
7. Replace the shock absorber assembly if any of these areas are damaged.

SWING ARM AND DRIVE SHAFT (PARALEVER MODELS)

In time, the pivot roller bearings will wear and require replacement. The condition of the bearings can greatly affect handling performance, and if worn parts are not replaced, they can produce erratic and dangerous handling. Common symptoms are wheel hop, pulling to one side during acceleration and pulling to the other side during braking.

Refer to **Figure 19-21**.

Removal

NOTE
A heat gun, capable of 120° C (248° F) is required to loosen the right side pivot pin and the left side adjusting pin securing the swing arm to the transmission case.

CAUTION
Do not apply heat to the pivot pins with any type of open propane or welding torch flame.

1A. On models so equipped, place the motorcycle on the centerstand with the rear wheel off of the ground.
1B. On models without a centerstand, place a suitable size jack under the engine to support the motorcycle with the rear wheel off the ground.
2. Remove the muffler as described in Chapter Nine.
3. Remove the rear brake caliper as described in Chapter Fourteen.
4. Remove the rear wheel as described in Chapter Eleven.
5. Remove the shock absorber as described in this chapter.
6. Have an assistant secure the motorcycle, then grasp the rear of the swing arm and try to move it from side to side in a horizontal arc. There should be no noticeable side play. If play is evident and the adjustable pivot pin is tightened correctly, the bearings should be replaced.
7. Remove the final drive unit as described in this chapter.
8. Remove the right (A, **Figure 22**) and left foot pegs as described in Chapter Fifteen.

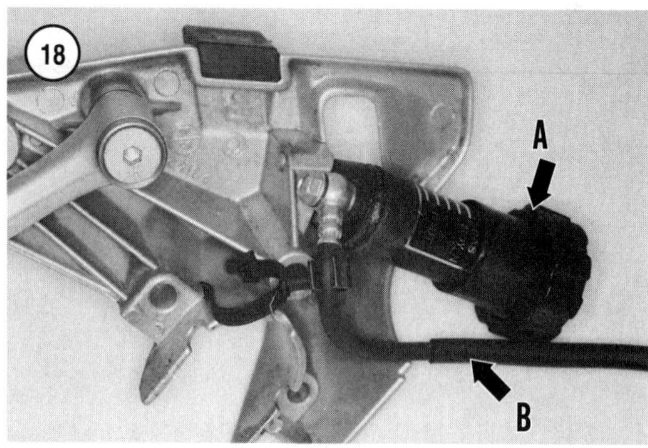

9. If necessary, remove the bolt and nut securing the final drive torque link (**Figure 23**) to the transmission case. Remove the torque link.
10A. On R1100S models, heat the locknut (A, **Figure 24**) and the left side adjust pivot pin (B) to 120° C (248° F).
10B. On all models except the R1100S, heat the locknut (A, **Figure 25**) and the left side adjust pivot pin (B) to 120° C (248° F).
11. At the left pivot point, loosen the locknut, then unscrew and remove the adjusting pivot pin (**Figure 26**).
12A. On R1100S models, perform the following:
  a. Loosen and remove the Allen bolts (A, **Figure 27**) securing the right fixed pivot pin.
  b. Screw a bolt (B, **Figure 27**) into the center hole of the right fixed pivot pin.
  c. Attach a slide hammer to the bolt and withdraw the right fixed pivot pin (C, **Figure 27**) from the rear frame.

WARNING
The swing arm and transmission housing are very hot. Make sure to wear protective gloves when loosening the right pivot pin in the next step.

12B. On all models except the R1100S, perform the following:
  a. Heat the right pivot pin (B, **Figure 22**) to 120° C (248° F).
  b. Unscrew and remove the pivot pin (Figure B, **Figure 22**).
13. Pull the swing arm toward the rear and remove it from the transmission case and drive shaft. The rubber boot will usually stay with the swing arm, but it may stay with the transmission case.
14. Pull the drive shaft (**Figure 28**) and disengage it from the snap ring on the transmission output shaft. Remove the drive shaft assembly.

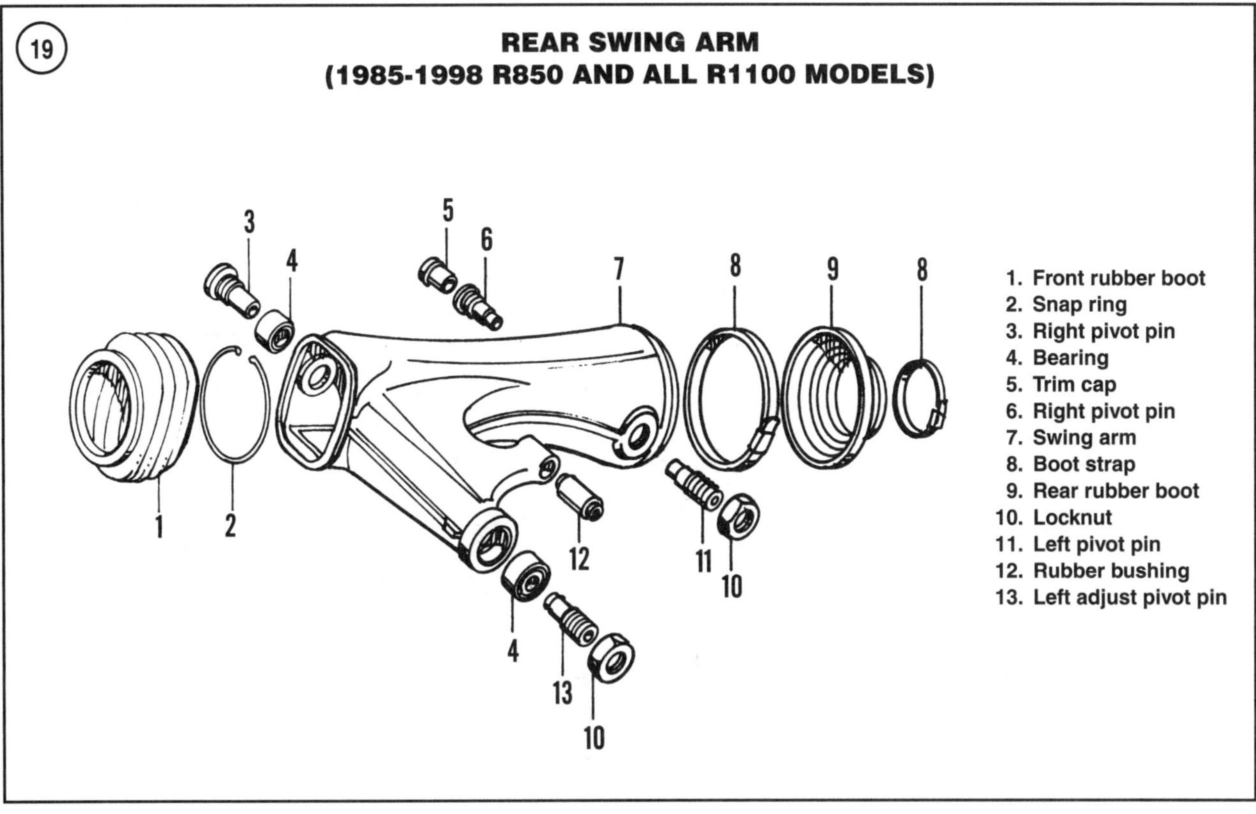
19
REAR SWING ARM
(1985-1998 R850 AND ALL R1100 MODELS)
1. Front rubber boot
2. Snap ring
3. Right pivot pin
4. Bearing
5. Trim cap
6. Right pivot pin
7. Swing arm
8. Boot strap
9. Rear rubber boot
10. Locknut
11. Left pivot pin
12. Rubber bushing
13. Left adjust pivot pin

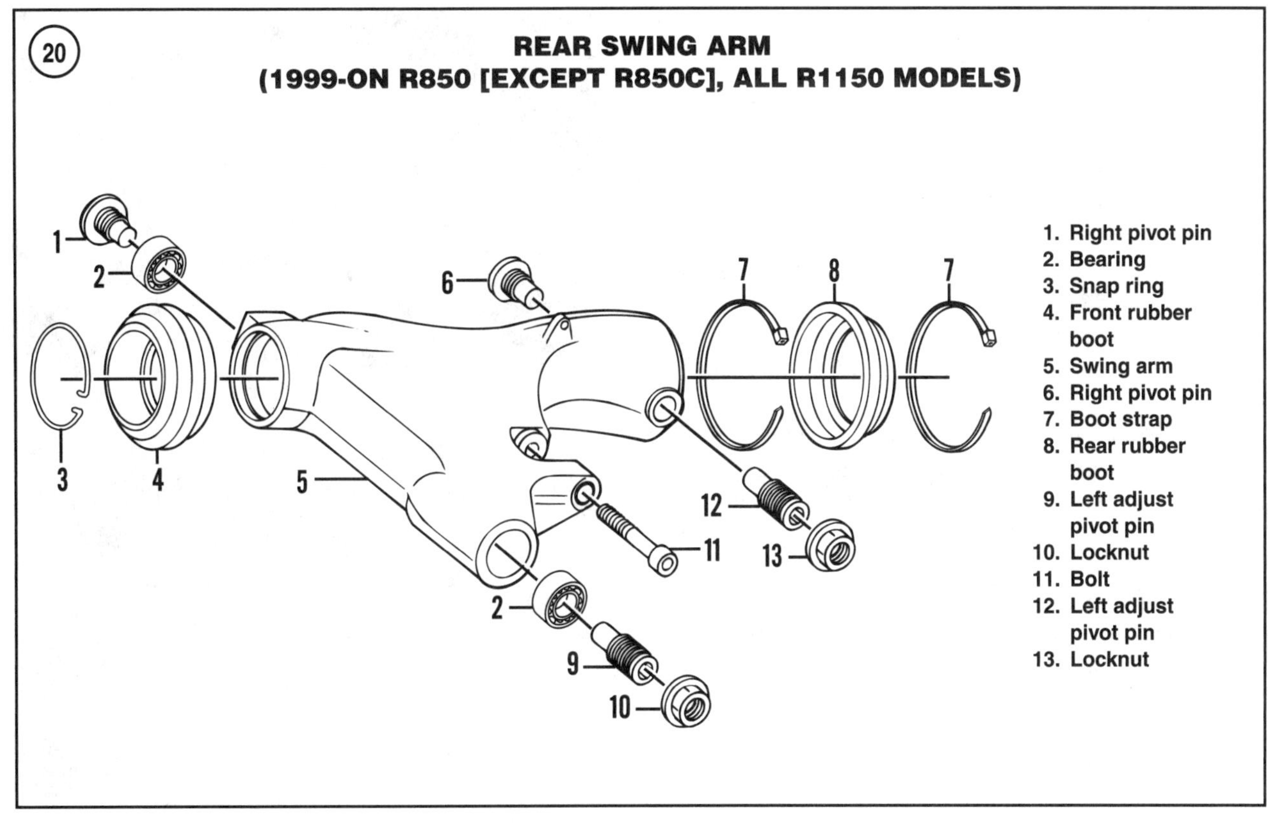
20
REAR SWING ARM
(1999-ON R850 [EXCEPT R850C], ALL R1150 MODELS)
1. Right pivot pin
2. Bearing
3. Snap ring
4. Front rubber boot
5. Swing arm
6. Right pivot pin
7. Boot strap
8. Rear rubber boot
9. Left adjust pivot pin
10. Locknut
11. Bolt
12. Left adjust pivot pin
13. Locknut

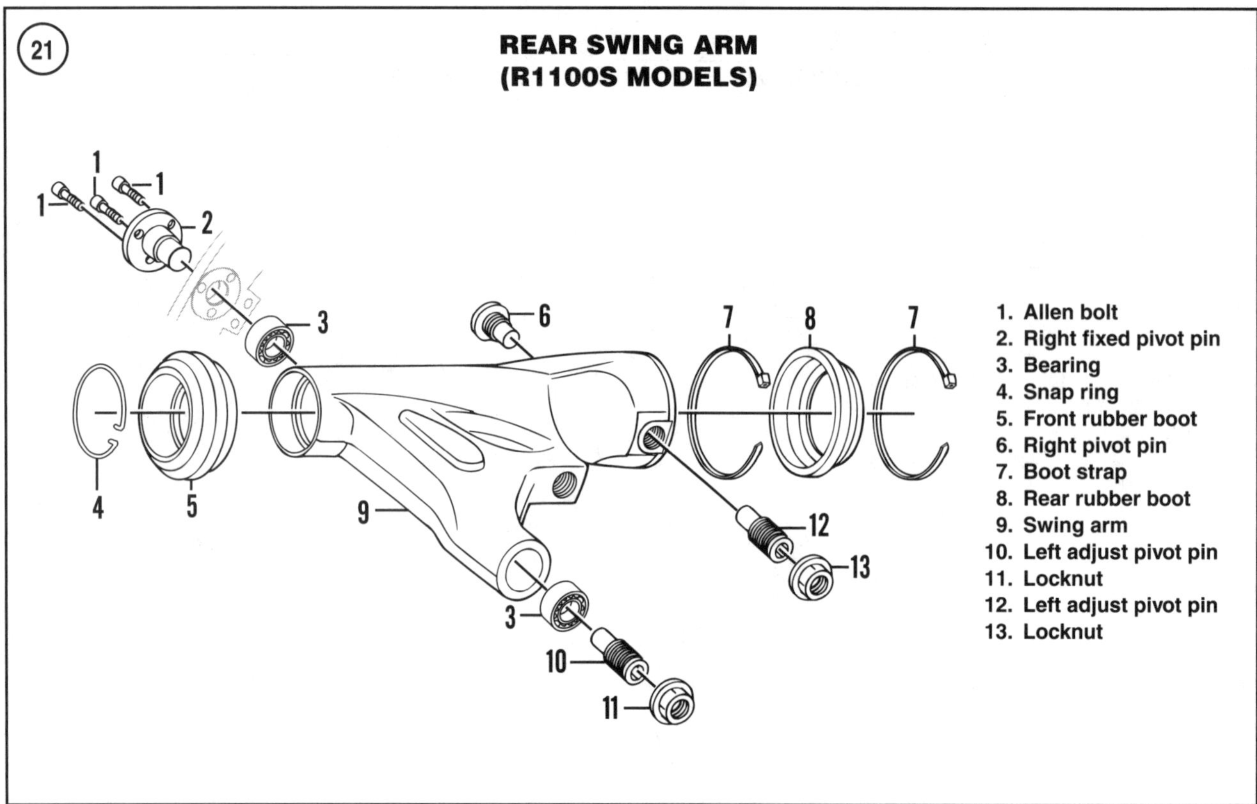

15. Inspect the swing arm as described in this section.

Installation

1. Shift the transmission into top gear.
2. Apply a light coat of BMW Kluberplex BEM 34-132, or Bel Rey Total Performance Lube, to the outer splines of the transmission output shaft and the inner splines of the drive shaft's front universal joint.
3. Position the drive shaft straight out and with the front integral universal joint going in first. Insert the drive shaft onto the transmission shaft (**Figure 29**).
4. Slightly rotate the drive shaft to align the splines of the transmission output shaft and the universal joint. Once the splines are aligned, push the drive shaft forward until the transmission output shaft snap ring is secure in the driveshaft groove.
5. After the snap ring snaps into the groove, pull slightly back on the drive shaft to make sure it seats properly. If the drive shaft moves back off the transmission shaft, it is not properly seated. Repeat Steps 4 and 5 until proper engagement occurs.
6. If removed, install the rubber boot (**Figure 30**) onto the end of the swing arm.

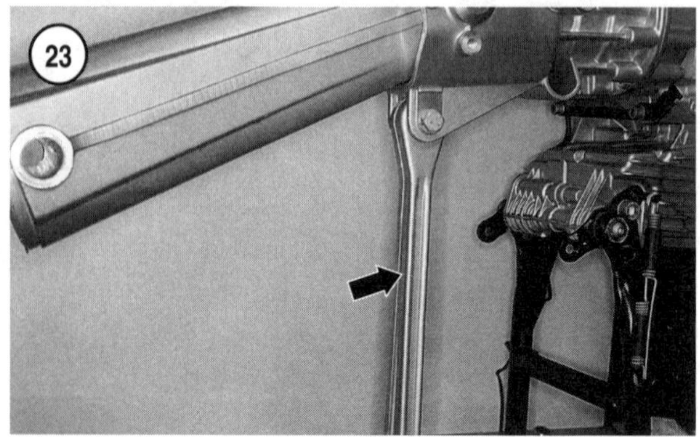

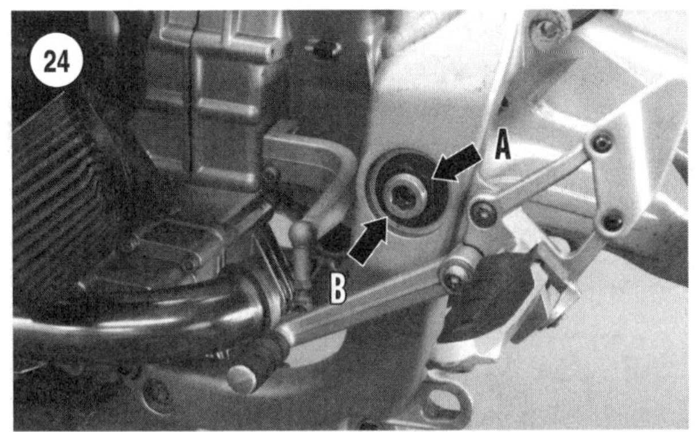

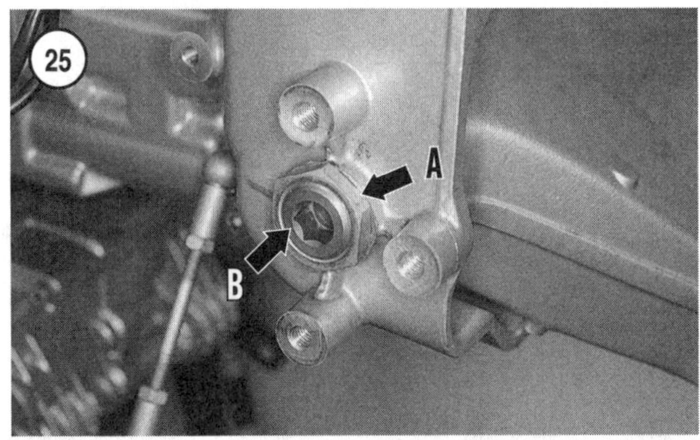

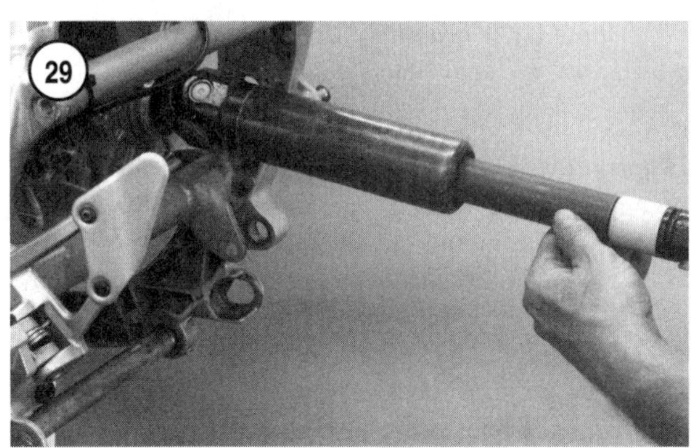

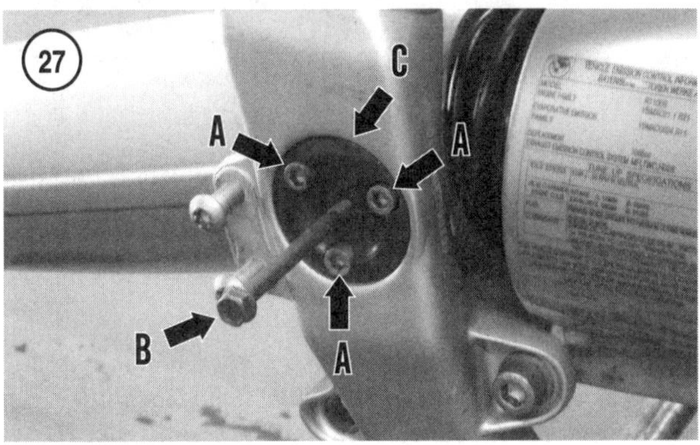

7. Install the snap ring into the inner surface of the rubber boot, securing it to the swing arm.

8. Coat both the inner and outer lips of the rubber boot with BMW Kluberplex BEM 34-132, or Bel Rey Total Performance Lube. Refer to **Figure 31** and **Figure 32**.

CAUTION
The rubber boot must be installed correctly on both the swing arm and the transmission housing flange. This boot protects the universal joint from moisture and debris. If the

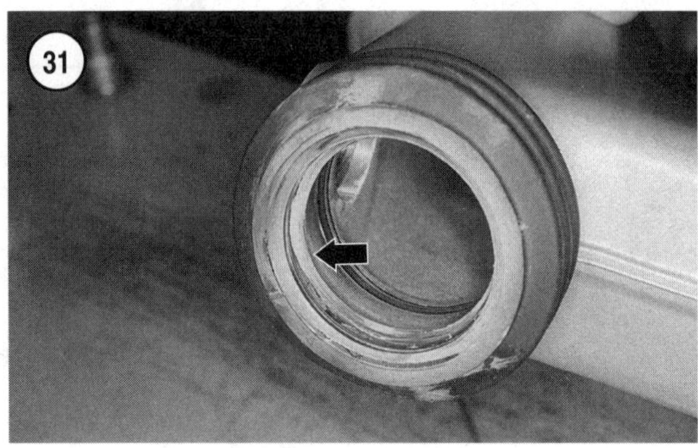

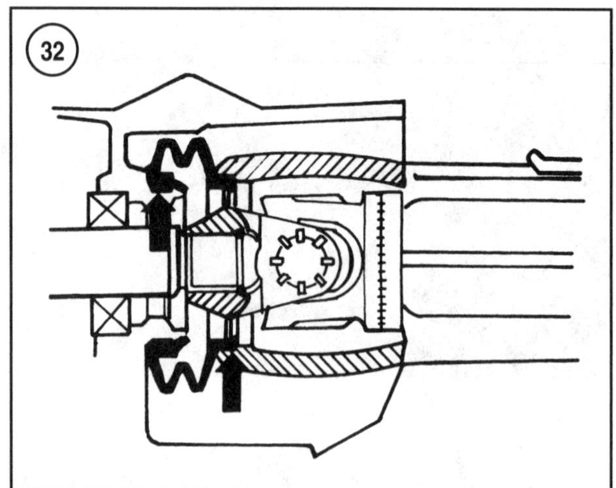

boot is not installed correctly, the universal joint will wear out prematurely.

9. Carefully guide the swing arm over the drive shaft (**Figure 33**), and then position the swing arm into the mounting area of the transmission housing. Slightly move the swing arm in and out until the rubber boot engages correctly on the transmission housing flange. Feel around the circumference of the rubber boot to make sure it seats correctly both on the swing arm and on the transmission housing. Readjust if necessary.
10. After the boot seats on both parts, gently pull the swing arm toward the rear to make sure the boot is properly seated.
11. Place the swing arm on a box to hold it into position.
12A. On all models except the R1100S, perform the following:
   a. Apply Loctite No. 271, or an equivalent, to the entire length of the threads of the right pivot pin and the left adjustable pivot pin prior to installation.
   b. Align the holes in the swing arm with the holes in the transmission housing.
   c. Install the fixed right pivot pin (B, **Figure 22**) to the right side through the transmission housing and into the swing arm. Tighten the right pivot pin to 7 N•m (62 in.-lb.).

12B. On R1100S models, perform the following:
   a. Align the holes in the right fixed pivot with the holes in the transmission housing and install the right fixed pivot.
   b. Tap it into place until it bottoms. Install the Allen bolts (**Figure 34**) and tighten to 9 N•m (80 in.-lb.).

13. Turn the left adjust pivot pin locknut to the outer end of the pivot pin. This will ensure that the pivot pin will travel the required distance into the transmission housing.
14. At the left pivot point, install the adjusting pivot pin (**Figure 26**) through the left side of the swing arm and into transmission housing. Screw the adjusting pivot pin in until it stops, then tighten to 7 N•m (62 in.-lb.).

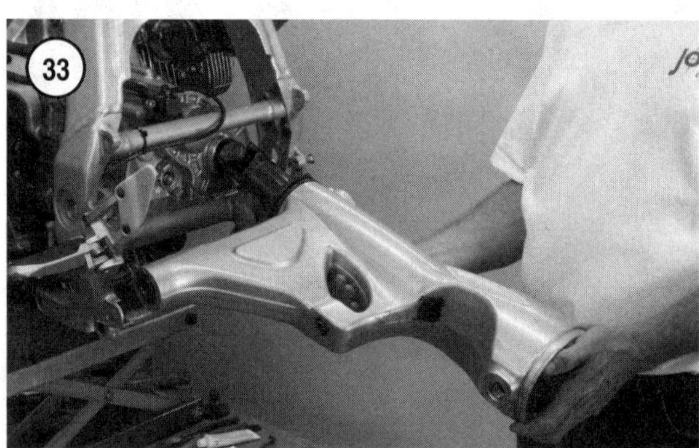

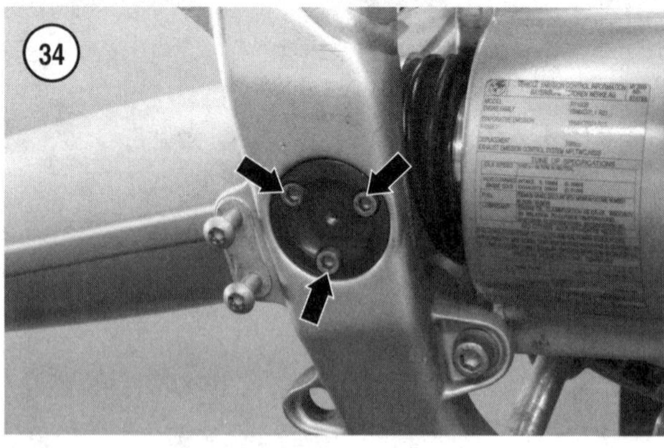

15. Slowly move the swing arm up and down a couple of times to make sure the swing arm seats correctly on the pivot pins.

CAUTION

In Step 16, make sure the left pivot pin does not rotate while tightening the locknut against it.

35

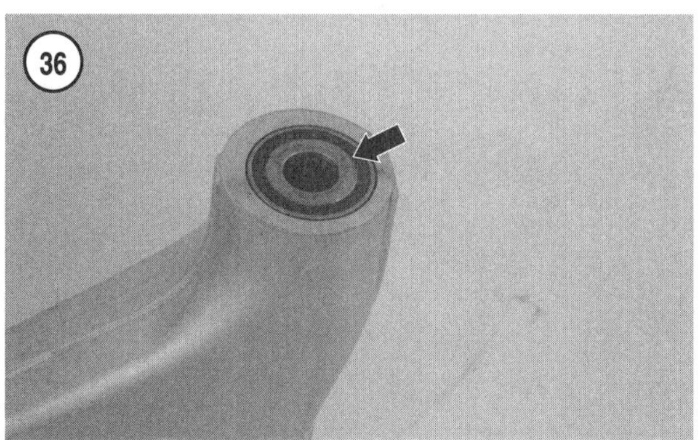

36

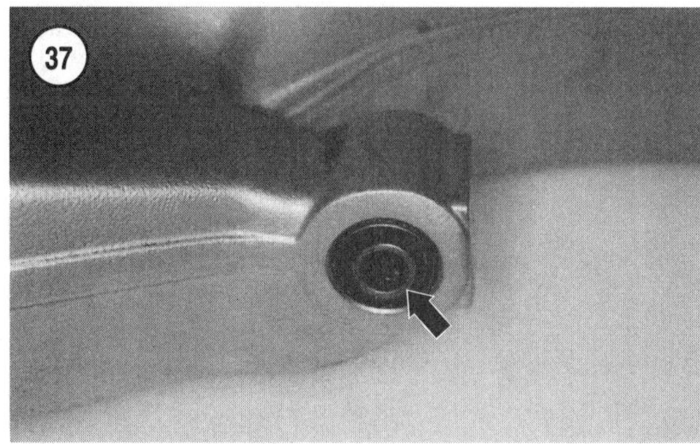

37

38

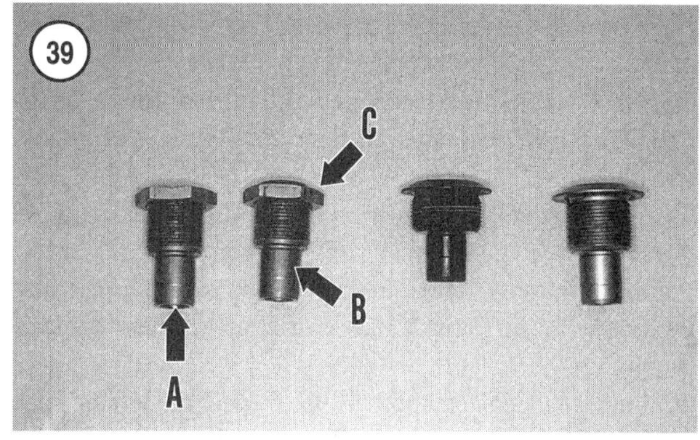

39

16A. On R1100S models, hold the left adjust pivot pin with an Allen wrench and tighten the locknut (A, **Figure 24**) to 160 N•m (118 ft.-lb.).

16B. On all models except the R1100S, hold the left adjust pivot pin with an Allen wrench and tighten the locknut (A, **Figure 25**) to the following:

a. On 1995-1998 R850 and R1100 models: 150 N•m (111 ft.-lb.).
b. On 1999-on R850 and R1150 models: 160 N•m (118 ft.-lb.).

17. If removed, secure the final drive torque link (**Figure 23**) to the transmission case. Tighten the bolt and nut to 43 N•m (32 ft.-lb.).
18. Install the right and left foot pegs as described in Chapter Fifteen.
19. Install the final drive unit and the shock absorber as described in this chapter.
20. Install the rear wheel as described in Chapter Eleven.
21. Install the rear brake caliper assembly as described in Chapter Fourteen.
22. Install the muffler as described in Chapter Nine.

Inspection

1. Inspect the swing arm for wear, cracks or damage.
2. Inspect the pivot bearings for wear or damage. Refer to **Figure 35** for the right side and **Figure 36** for the left side. Turn each bearing inner race by hand. The bearing must turn smoothly. Replace if necessary as described in this chapter.
3. Check the shock absorber lower mounting boss bushing for wear, damage or deterioration. Refer to **Figure 37** or **Figure 38**. Replace if necessary.
4. Thoroughly clean all old threadlocking compound from the pivot pins.

5A. On all models except R1100S, inspect the right side fixed pivot pin (A, **Figure 39**) for wear, cracks or damage.

If the threads are damaged, repair the threads with the correct size metric die or replace the pivot pin.

5B. On R1100S models, inspect the right pivot pin (**Figure 40**) for wear, cranks or damage. Replace as necessary.

6A. On R1100S models, Inspect the left side adjustable pivot pin (A, **Figure 41**) and locknut (B) for wear, cranks or damage. If the threads are damaged, repair the threads with the correct size metric tap or die or replace the pin.

6B. On all models except R1100S, inspect the left side adjustable pivot pin (B, **Figure 39**) and locknut (C) for wear, cranks or damage. If the threads are damaged, repair the threads with the correct size metric tap or die or replace the pin.

7. Inspect the threads at the rear of the swing arm for the final drive unit (**Figure 42**) and at the front for the transmission housing (**Figure 43**). Check for wear, damage or distortion, repair the threads with the correct size metric die if necessary.

8. Inspect the rubber boot (**Figure 30**) for cracks, hardness or damage; replace if necessary.

Bearing Replacement

1. The following BMW tools are available to remove the tapered roller bearing assembly from the swing arm:
   a. Counter support (BMW part No. 00-8-572).
   b. Internal puller 21/2 for the roller bearing (BMW part No. 00-8-571).
   c. Internal puller 21/5 for the outer race (BMW part No. 00-8-563).

NOTE
A heat gun capable of 80° C (176° F) is required to install the bearing into the swing arm pivot area.

CAUTION
Do not apply heat to the swing arm with any type of open propane or welding torch flame.

CAUTION
Do not remove the bearing for inspection purposes. The bearing is damaged during removal. Never reinstall a bearing that has been removed.

2. Remove the swing arm as described in this chapter.
3. Remove the rubber boot from the right side.

4A. To remove the roller bearing and outer race with the BMW tools:

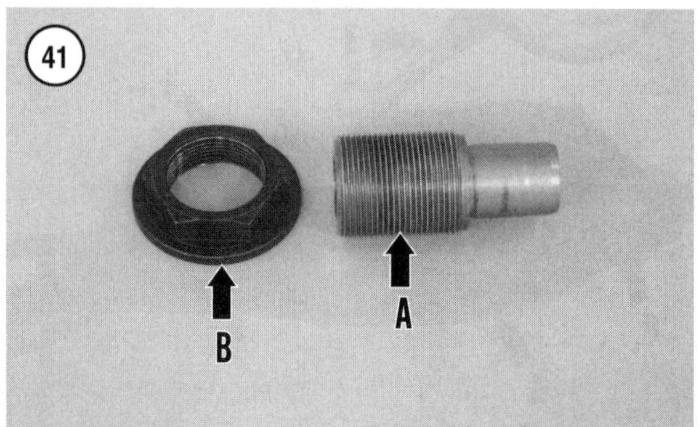

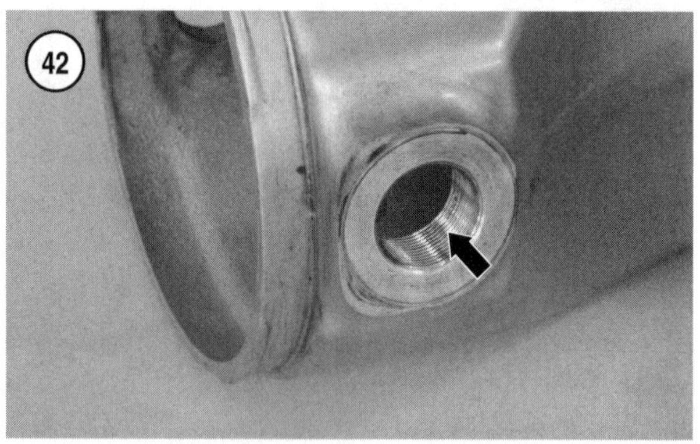

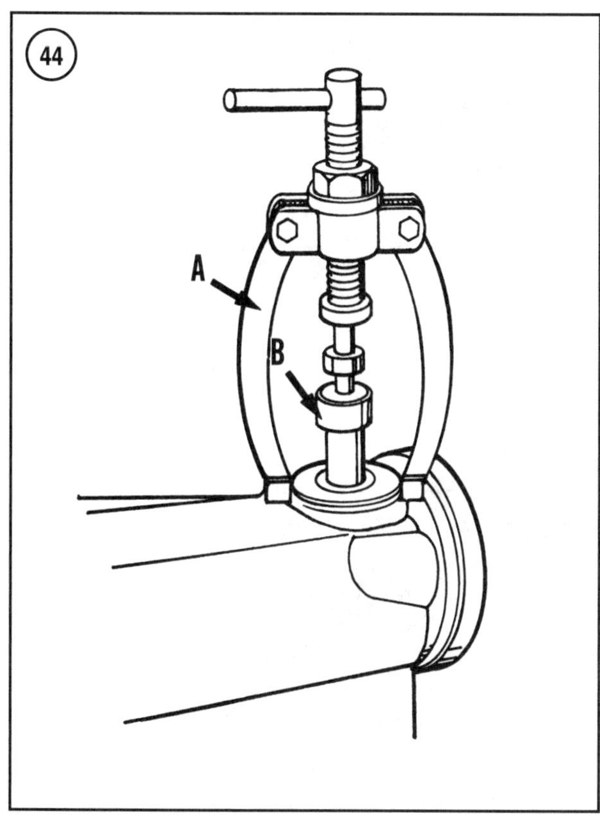

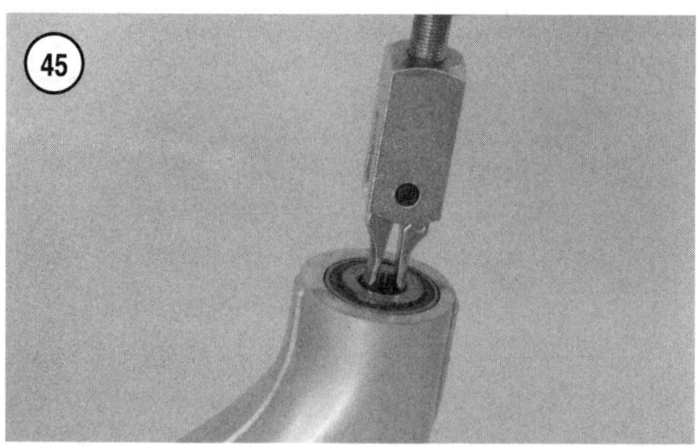

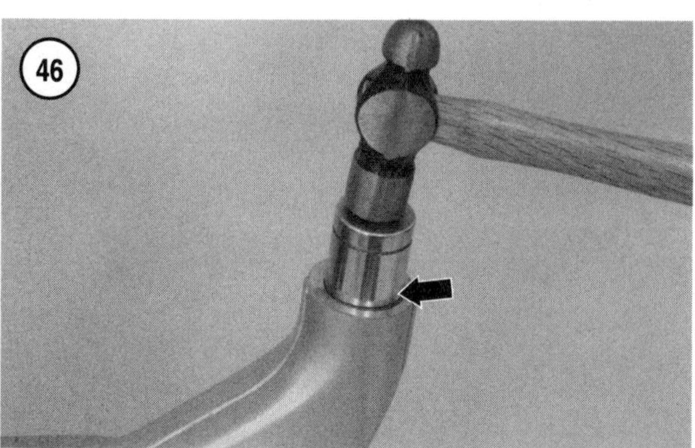

a. To pull the roller bearing, use the counter support (A, **Figure 44**) and internal puller 21/2 (B) and withdraw the roller bearing and seal from the outer race in the pivot point.

b. To pull the roller bearing outer race, use counter support (A, **Figure 44**) and internal puller 21/5 (B) and withdraw the outer race from the pivot point.

4B. To remove the roller bearing and outer race without the special tools:

a. Insert a two jaw bearing puller into the roller bearing and expand the jaws (**Figure 45**).

b. Attach a slide hammer to the bearing puller and withdraw the roller bearing from the pivot point.

c. Repeat sub-steps a and b and withdraw the outer race from the pivot point.

5. On all models except R1100S models, repeat Step 4 for the roller bearing and outer race on the other side.

6. Thoroughly clean out the inside surfaces of the pivot portions of the swing arm with solvent and dry with compressed air.

7. Remove any burrs from the bearing receptacle in the swing arm.

8. Place the new bearing and outer race in a freezer to reduce their overall outer diameter slightly.

CAUTION
To prevent damage to the swing arm, place the opposite end of the swing arm on a piece of soft wood when installing the bearing into the other side.

9. Heat the bearing area of the swing arm to 80° C (176° F).

10. Install the new bearing into the swing arm using a driver that matches the outer race of the bearing (**Figure 46**). Tap the bearing in slowly and squarely until it bottoms (**Figure 36**). Make sure it is properly seated.

11. On all models except R1100S, repeat Step 10 for the bearing on the other side.

12. Install the rubber boot.

13. Install the swing arm as described in this chapter.

Drive Shaft and Universal Joints Inspection

The drive shaft has an integral front universal joint and a removable rear universal joint that joins the drive shaft to the final drive unit. A secondary universal joint is located in the final drive unit.

1. Carefully pry the rear universal joint (**Figure 47**) from the final drive unit.

2. Inspect the drive shaft front universal joint inner splines (**Figure 48**) where they connect to the transmis-

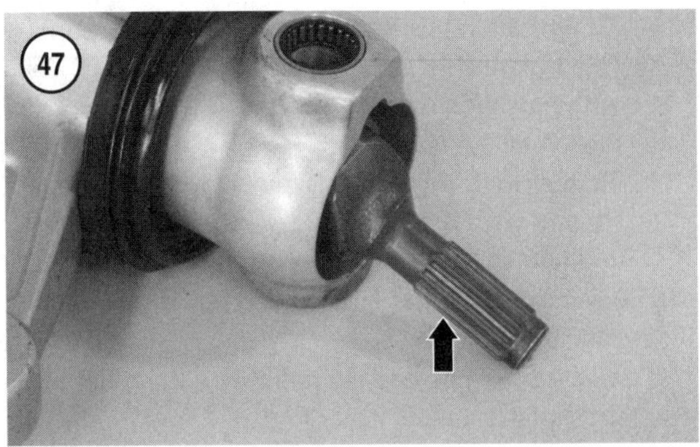
47

48

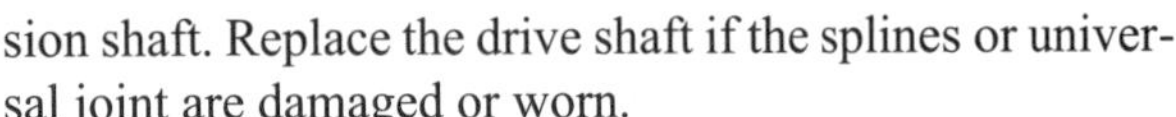
sion shaft. Replace the drive shaft if the splines or universal joint are damaged or worn.

NOTE
If the splines are damaged, also check the splines of the transmission shaft; it may also require replacement.

3. Inspect the drive shaft rear inner splines (**Figure 49**) where they connect to the rear universal joint. Replace the drive shaft if the splines or universal joint are damaged or worn.

4. Inspect the front universal joint pivot points for play (**Figure 50**). Rotate the joint in both directions. Replace the drive shaft if there is noticeable side play.

5. Install the rear universal joint assembly into the rear of the drive shaft (**Figure 51**). Slide the universal joint in and out (**Figure 52**) and check for smooth operation. The universal joint must move without binding. Replace the drive shaft and/or universal joint if movement is not smooth.

6. Inspect the rear universal joint inner splines (**Figure 53**). Also check the outer splines (A, **Figure 54**). If the splines are damaged or worn, replace the rear universal joint.

NOTE
If the splines are damaged, also check the splines of the final drive unit; it may also require replacement.

7. Inspect the rear universal joint pivot points for play (B, **Figure 54**). Rotate the joint in both directions. Replace the universal joint if there is noticeable side play.

49

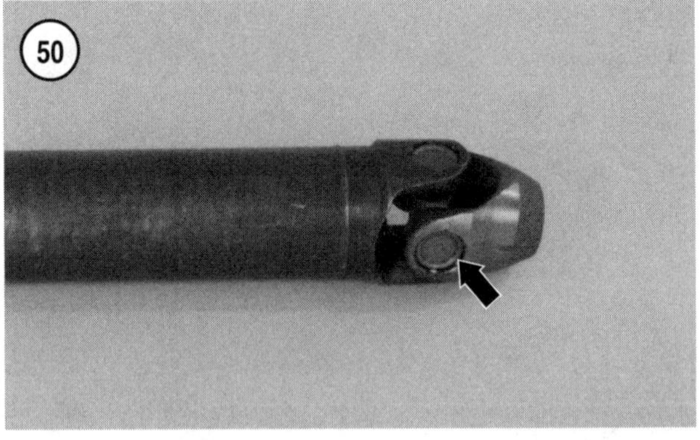
50

51

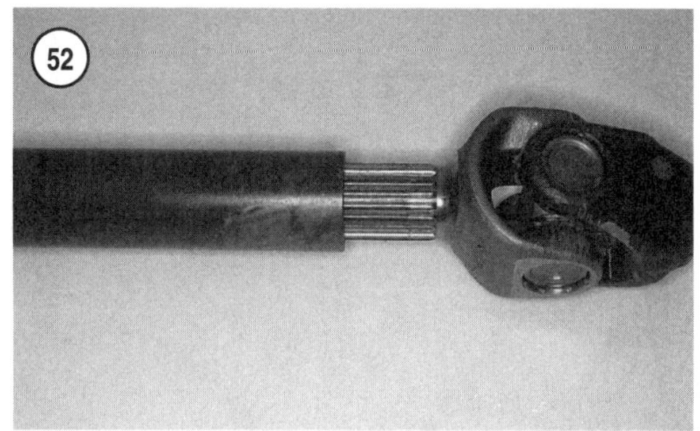

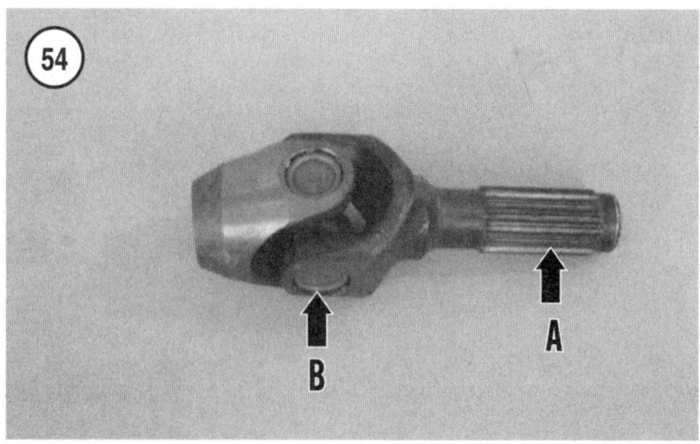

FINAL DRIVE UNIT (PARALEVER MODELS)

Removal

NOTE
A heat gun capable of 120° C (248° F) is required to loosen the right pivot pin and the left adjusting pivot pin securing the final drive unit to the swing arm.

CAUTION
Do not apply heat to the pivot pins with any type of flame (propane or welding torch).

1. Remove the rear brake caliper assembly as described in Chapter Fourteen. Support the caliper with wire and move it out of the way.
2. Remove the rear wheel as described in this chapter.
3. On models where the rear disc brake is not attached to the rear wheel, remove the brake disc (**Figure 55**) from the final drive unit as described in Chapter Fourteen.
4. Place wood block(s) (**Figure 56**) under the swing arm to support it.
5. On models so equipped, disconnect the ABS sensor electrical connector from the wiring harness.
6. For ease of handling the final drive unit, reinstall the rear wheel mounting bolts (**Figure 57**) and tighten securely.

13

7A. On early models, unscrew the front clamping screw on the rubber boot. Remove the front clamp (A, **Figure 58**) from the rubber boot.

7B. On later models, carefully cut and remove the plastic retainer (**Figure 59**).

8. Remove the bolt and nut (B, **Figure 58**) securing the torque link to the final drive unit. Lower the torque link; it is not necessary to completely remove it.

9. Heat the locknut (A, **Figure 60**) and left adjusting pivot pin (B) to 120° C (248° F).

10. At the left pivot point, loosen the locknut (A, **Figure 60**), then unscrew and remove the left adjusting pivot pin (B).

11. Heat the locknut and right adjusting pivot pin (C, **Figure 58**) to 120° C (248° F).

WARNING
The swing arm is very hot. Make sure to wear protective gloves when handling the swing arm and pivot pin in the next step.

12. At the right pivot point, unscrew and remove the locknut and the right adjusting pivot pin (C, **Figure 58**).

NOTE
If the final drive unit still has oil in it, do not place the final drive unit on its side as the oil will drain out the top vent pipe.

13. Pull the final drive unit and rear universal joint to the rear and remove it from the drive shaft.

14. Carefully pry (A, **Figure 61**) the rear portion of the rear universal joint (B) from the pinion gear splines.

15. Inspect all parts as described in this chapter.

Installation

1. Apply a thick coat of BMW Kluberplex BEM 34-132, or Bel Rey Total Performance Lube, to the pinion gear outer splines (**Figure 62**) and to the inner splines on the rear universal joint (**Figure 53**).

2. Install the rear universal joint onto the final drive unit (**Figure 47**). Push it on until it locks into place.

3. Shift the transmission into fifth gear. This will prevent the drive shaft from rotating while aligning the final drive splines to the drive shaft splines.

4. Apply a light coat of BMW Kluberplex BEM 34-132, or Bel Rey Total Performance Lube, to the inner race of the pivot needle bearings (**Figure 63**).

5. If removed, install the rubber boot (A, **Figure 64**) onto the final drive unit.

6A. On early models, tighten clamping screw (B, **Figure 64**) on the rubber boot.

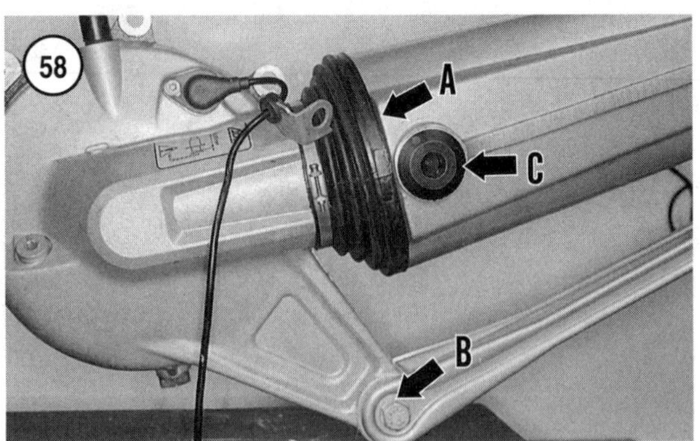

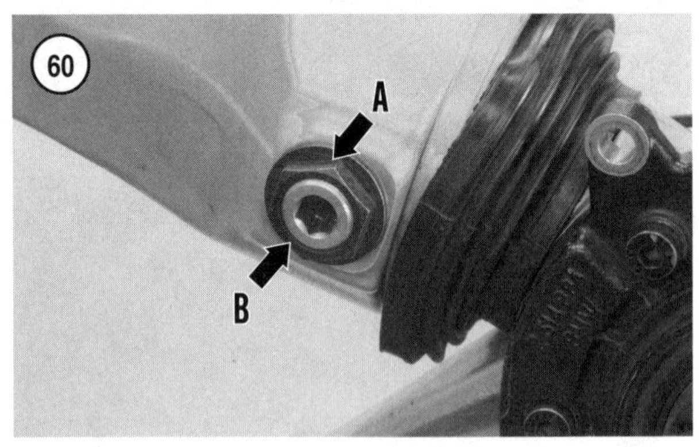

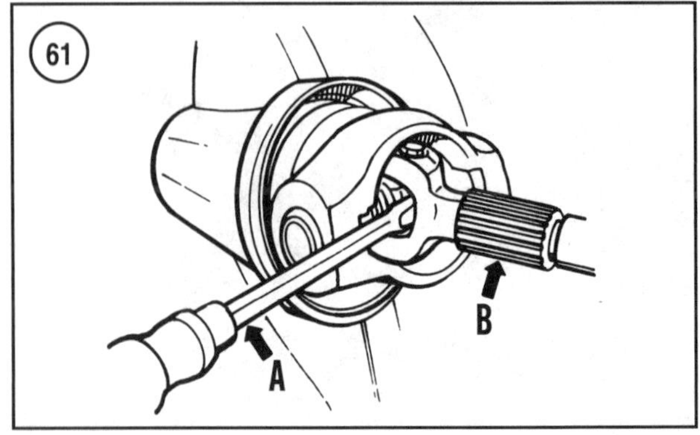

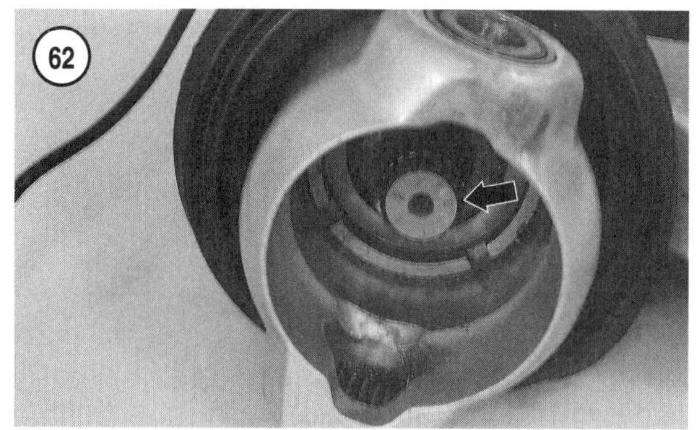

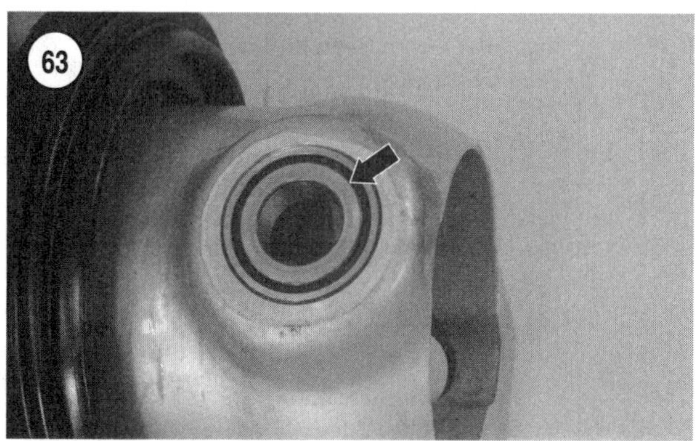

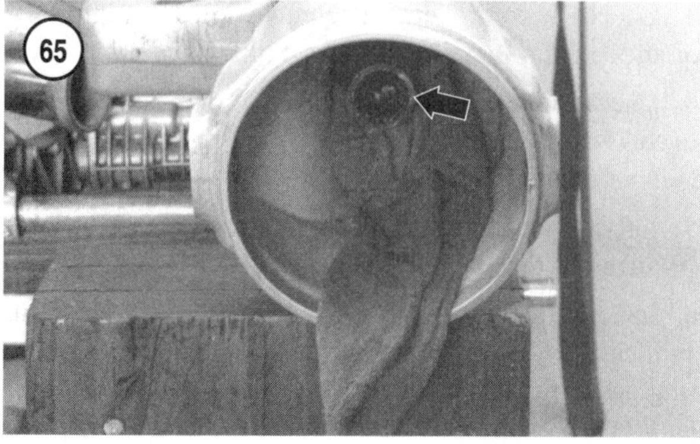

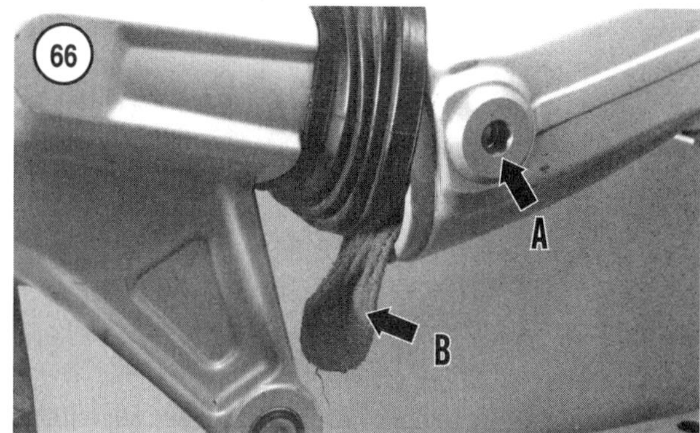

6B. On later models, install a *new* plastic retainer and tighten securely.

7. Make sure the swing arm is in the correct height position.

8. Place a shop cloth into the swing arm and center the drive shaft in the housing (**Figure 65**). Leave a portion of the shop cloth outside of the swing arm as a reminder to remove the cloth after the final drive unit is installed.

9. Install the final drive unit onto the swing arm and drive shaft; slightly rotate the rear wheel flange until the splines of the drive shaft align. Push the final drive unit on until it stops. Support the final drive unit in this position on wood block(s).

10. Align the pivot pin holes of the final drive unit with those in the swing arm.

11. Apply Loctite No. 271, or an equivalent, to the entire length of the threads of the right pivot pin and the left adjust pivot pin prior to installation.

12. Install the fixed right pivot pin (A, **Figure 66**) into the right side through the swing arm and into the final drive unit. Tighten the right pivot pin to 7 N•m (62 in.-lb.).

13. Turn the left pivot pin locknut to the outer end of the pivot pin. This will ensure that the pivot pin will travel the required distance into the final drive unit.

14. Install the left adjust pivot pin (B, **Figure 60**) through the swing arm and into the left side of the final drive unit. Screw the pin in until it stops, then hand tighten.

15. Withdraw the shop cloth (B, **Figure 66**) from the swing arm installed in Step 8.

16. Correctly position the rubber boot on the swing arm.

17. Shift the transmission into neutral. Rotate the rear wheel flange several complete revolutions to make sure the final drive unit is correctly meshed with the drive shaft.

18A. On early models, tighten the front clamping screw (A, **Figure 58**) on the rubber boot.

18B. On later models, install a *new* plastic retainer (**Figure 59**) and tighten securely.

19. Slowly move the swing arm up and down a couple of times to make sure the swing arm seats correctly on the pivot pins.

CAUTION

In Step 20, make sure the left adjust pivot pin does not rotate while tightening the locknut against it.

20. Secure the left adjust pivot pin (B, **Figure 60**) with an Allen wrench and tighten the locknut (A) to the following:
   a. On 1995-1998 R850 and R1100 models: 105 N•m (77 ft.-lb.).
   b. On 1999-on R850 and R1150 models: 160 N•m (118 ft.-lb.).

21. Move the final drive torque link up into position onto the final drive unit and install the bolt, washers and nut (B, **Figure 58**). Tighten the bolt and nut to 43 N•m (32 ft.-lb.).

22. Move the final drive unit, swing arm and control rod up and down to make sure the entire assembly moves freely.

CAUTION

Make sure the rubber boot is installed correctly, otherwise moisture and debris will enter this area and cause damage.

23. If installed, remove the two rear wheel mounting bolts (**Figure 57**) from the final drive unit.

24. Remove the wood block (**Figure 56**) from under the swing arm.

25. On models so equipped, connect the ABS sensor electrical connector onto the wiring harness.

26. On models where the rear disc brake is not attached to the rear wheel, attach the brake disc (**Figure 55**) onto the final drive unit as described in Chapter Fourteen.

27. Install the rear wheel as described in Chapter Eleven.

28. Install the rear brake caliper assembly as described in Chapter Fourteen.

29. Take the motorcycle off of the centerstand and depress the rear suspension to make sure all components work properly.

Inspection

1. Inspect the exterior of the final drive unit housing for cracks or damage.

2. Inspect the rubber bushing (A, **Figure 67**) in the torque link attachment point on the final drive unit. Replace the bushing if worn or damaged.

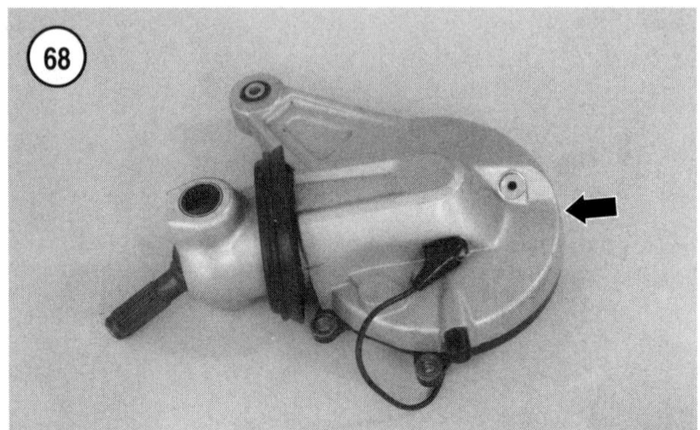

3. Check the control arm attachment boss (B, **Figure 67**) on the final drive unit for cracks or damage.

4. Check the rear brake caliper mounting bosses (C, **Figure 67**) on the final drive unit for cracks, damage or hole elongation.

5. Inspect the exterior of the final drive unit housing (**Figure 68**) for cracks or damage.

6. Inspect the pinion gear splines (**Figure 62**). If the splines are worn or damaged, replace the pinion gear and ring gear assembly as described under *Final Drive Overhaul* in this chapter.

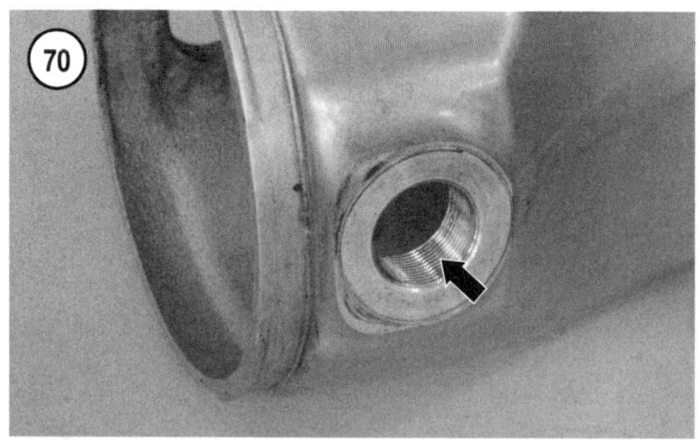

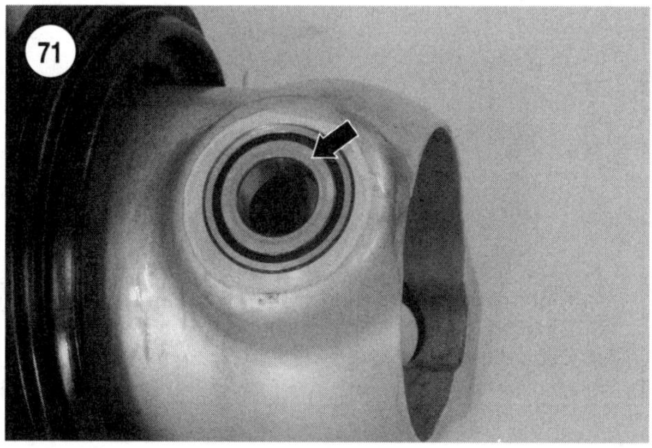

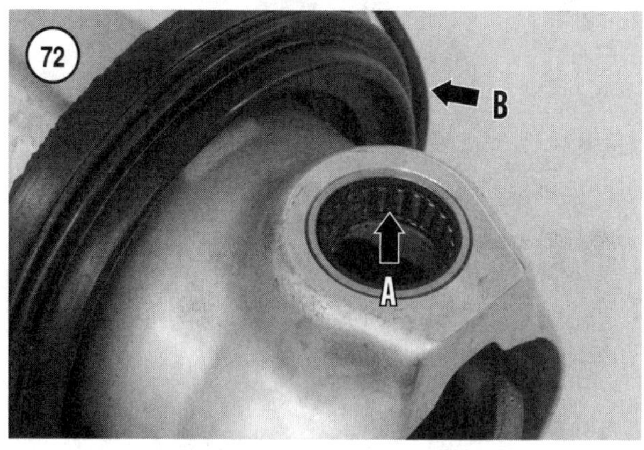

NOTE
If the splines are worn or damaged, also inspect the splines on the rear universal joint for damage as it may also require replacement.

7. Check for oil leakage at the spline portion. If the seal is leaking, replace it as described under *Final Drive Overhaul* in this chapter.
8. Make sure the mounting bolts securing the cover (D, **Figure 67**) are tight. If loose, tighten to 35 N•m (26 ft.-lb.).
9. Thoroughly clean all threadlocking compound from the threads on the right pivot pin (**Figure 69**) and the left pivot pin and lockwasher and from the pivot pin threads (**Figure 70**) in the swing arm.
10. Inspect the threads of both pivot pins for wear or damage. If necessary, clean out the threads with the correct size and pitch die or replace.
11. Inspect the pivot pin bores (**Figure 71**) on each side for wear or burrs. Clean off any burrs that may be present.
12. Inspect the pivot bearings (A, **Figure 72**) for wear or damage. Turn each bearing inner race by hand. The bearing must turn smoothly. Replace if necessary as described in this section.
13. Apply a light coat of BMW Kluberplex BEM 34-132, or Bel Rey Total Performance Lube, to the pivot needle bearings.
14. Inspect the rubber boot (B, **Figure 72**) for wear, tears or deterioration. If its condition is questionable, remove the clamping band and replace it while the final drive unit is removed.

SWING ARM AND DRIVE SHAFT (MONOLEVER MODELS)

In time, the pivot roller bearings will wear and require replacement. The condition of the bearings can greatly affect handling performance, and if worn parts are not replaced, they can produce erratic and dangerous handling. Common symptoms are wheel hop, pulling to one side during acceleration and pulling to the other side during braking.

Refer to **Figure 73**.

Removal

NOTE
A heat gun capable of 120° C (248° F) is required to loosen the right side pivot pin and the left side adjusting pin securing the swing arm to the transmission case.

CAUTION
Do not apply heat to the pivot pins with any type of open propane or welding torch flame.

1. Place a suitable size jack under the engine to support the motorcycle with the rear wheel off the ground.
2. If necessary, remove the muffler assembly as described in Chapter Nine.

3. Remove the rear brake caliper as described in Chapter Fourteen.
4. Remove the rear wheel as described in Chapter Eleven.
5. Remove the rear brake disc (**Figure 74**) from the final drive unit as described in chapter Fourteen.
6. Remove the shock absorber as described in this chapter.
7. Have an assistant secure the motorcycle, then grasp the rear of the swing arm and try to move it from side to side in a horizontal arc. There should be no noticeable side play. If play is evident and the adjustable pivot pin is tightened correctly, the bearings should be replaced.
8. Remove the final drive unit as described in this chapter.
9. Secure the swing arm up to the rear frame with a tie-down (**Figure 75**).
10. Use two screwdrivers and carefully pry the cap (**Figure 76**) covering the left side adjust pivot pin.
11. Loosen and remove the Allen bolts (**Figure 77**) securing the right fixed pivot pin.
12. Screw a bolt into the center hole in the right fixed pivot pin.
13. Attach a slide hammer to the bolt and withdraw the right fixed pivot pin (**Figure 78**) from the frame.
14. At the left pivot point, loosen the locknut (A, **Figure 79**), then unscrew and remove the adjusting pivot pin (B).
15. Pull the swing arm toward the rear and remove it from the transmission case and drive shaft. The rubber boot will usually stay with the swing arm, but it may stay with the transmission case.
16. Pull the drive shaft and disengage it from the small snap ring on the transmission output shaft. Remove the drive shaft assembly.
17. Inspect the swing arm as described in this chapter.

Installation

1. Shift the transmission into top gear.
2. Apply a light coat of BMW Kluberplex BEM 34-132, or Bel Rey Total Performance Lube, to the outer splines of the transmission output shaft and the inner splines of the drive shaft's front universal joint.
3. Position the drive shaft straight out and with the front integral universal joint going in first. Insert the drive shaft onto the transmission shaft.
4. Slightly rotate the drive shaft to align the splines of the transmission output shaft and the universal joint. Once the splines are aligned, push the drive shaft forward until the transmission output shaft snap ring is secure in the driveshaft groove.

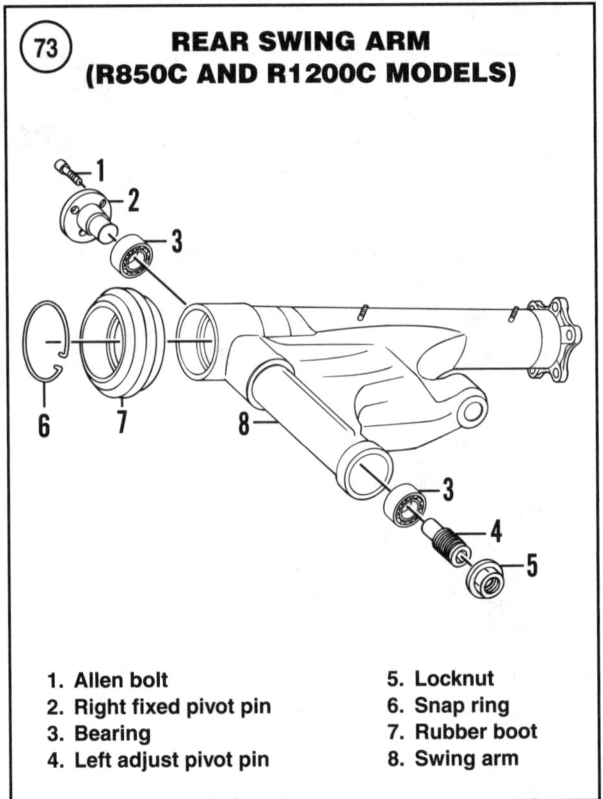

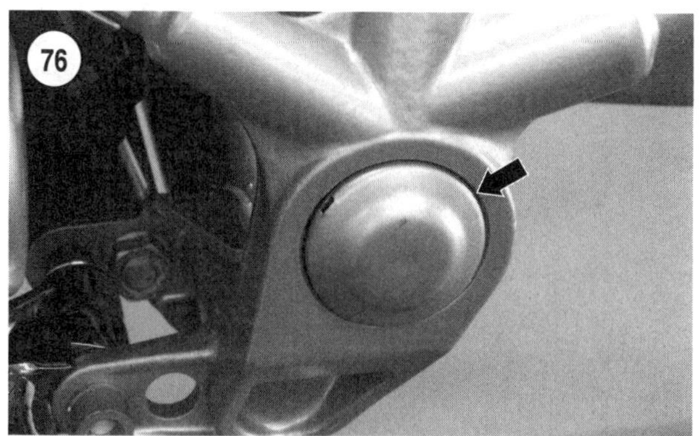

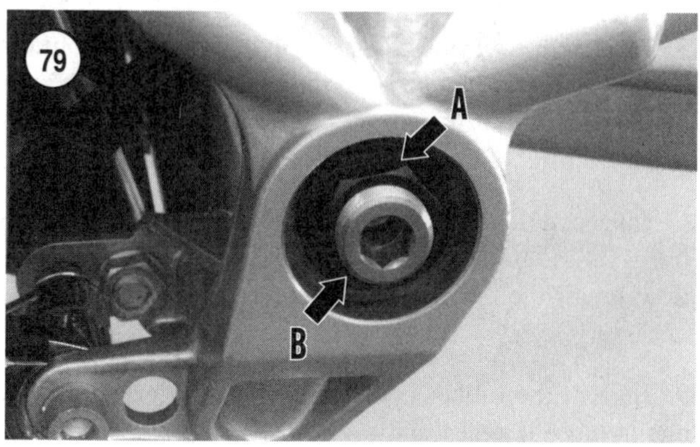

5. After the snap ring snaps into the groove, pull slightly back on the drive shaft to make sure it seats properly. If the drive shaft moves back off the transmission shaft, it is not properly seated. Repeat Steps 4 and 5 until proper engagement occurs.

6. If removed, install the rubber boot onto the end of the swing arm.

7. Install the snap ring into the inner surface of the rubber boot, securing it to the swing arm.

8. Coat both the inner and outer lips of the rubber boot with BMW Kluberplex BEM 34-132, or Bel Rey Total Performance Lube.

CAUTION

The rubber boot must be installed correctly on both the swing arm and the transmission housing flange. This boot protects the universal joint from moisture and debris. If the boot is not installed correctly, the universal joint will wear out prematurely.

9. Carefully guide the swing arm over the drive shaft and then position the swing arm into the mounting area of the transmission housing. Slightly move the swing arm in and out until the rubber boot engages correctly on the transmission housing flange. Use your fingers, and feel around the circumference of the rubber boot to make sure it seats correctly both on the swing arm and on the transmission housing (**Figure 80**). Readjust if necessary.

10. After the boot seats on both parts, gently pull the swing arm toward the rear to make sure the boot is properly seated.

11. Secure the swing arm up to the rear frame with a tie-down (**Figure 75**).

12. Align the holes in the right fixed pivot with the holes in the transmission housing and install the right fixed pivot pin (**Figure 81**).

13. Tap it into place until it bottoms. Install the Allen bolts (**Figure 77**) and tighten to 7 N•m (62 in.-lb.).

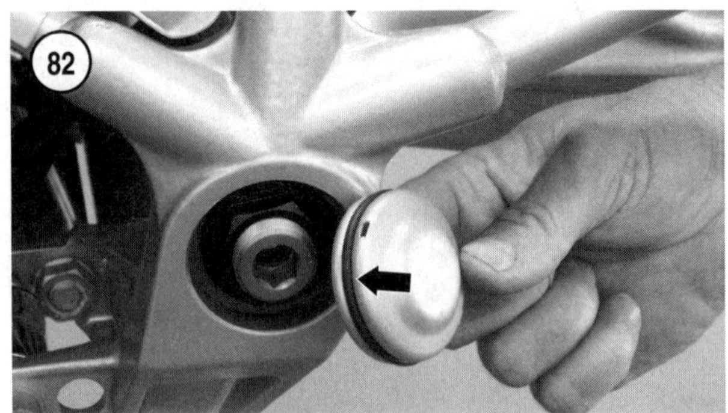

14. Turn the left adjusting pivot pin locknut to the outer end of the pivot pin. This will ensure that the pivot pin will travel the required distance into the transmission housing.
15. At the left pivot point, install the adjust pivot pin (B, **Figure 79**) through the left side of the swing arm and into transmission housing. Screw the adjust pivot pin in until it stops, then tighten to 10 N•m (88 in.-lb.).
16. Slowly move the swing arm up and down a couple of times to make sure the swing arm seats correctly on the pivot pins.

CAUTION
In Step 17, make sure the left pivot pin does not rotate while tightening the locknut against it.

17. Hold the left adjusting pivot pin (B, **Figure 79**) with an Allen wrench and tighten the locknut (A) to 160 N•m (118 ft.-lb.).
18. Make sure the O-ring seal (**Figure 82**) is in place on the cap and install the cap (**Figure 76**). Push it on until it bottoms.
19. Install the final drive unit as described in this chapter.
20. Install the shock absorber as described in this chapter.
21. Install the rear brake disc (**Figure 74**) onto the final drive unit as described in chapter Fourteen.
22. Install the rear wheel as described in Chapter Eleven.
23. Install the rear brake caliper as described in Chapter Fourteen.
24. If removed, install the muffler assembly as described in Chapter Nine.

Inspection

1. Inspect the swing arm for wear, cracks or damage.
2. Inspect the pivot bearings for wear or damage. Turn each bearing inner race by hand. The bearing must turn smoothly. Replace if necessary as described in this chapter.

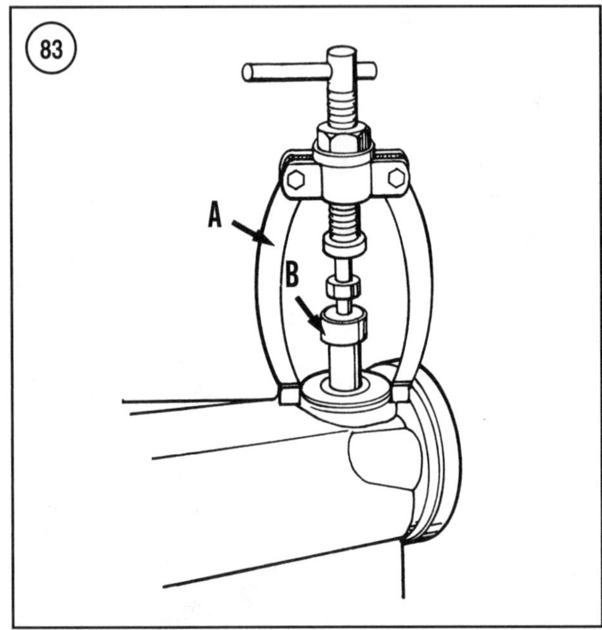

3. Check the shock absorber lower mounting boss bushing for wear, damage or deterioration. Replace if necessary.

4. Inspect the right side fixed pivot pin for wear, cracks or damage. If the threads are damaged, repair the threads with the correct size metric die or replace the pivot pin.

5. Inspect the left side adjusting pivot pin and locknut for wear, cranks or damage. If the threads are damaged, repair the threads with the correct size metric tap or die or replace the pin.

6. Inspect the threads at the front of the swing arm for the transmission housing. Check for wear, damage or distortion; repair the threads with the correct size metric die if necessary.

7. Inspect the rubber boot for cracks, hardness or damage; replace if necessary.

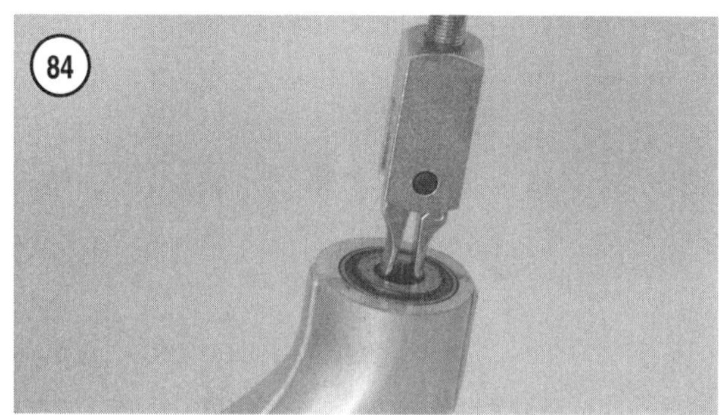

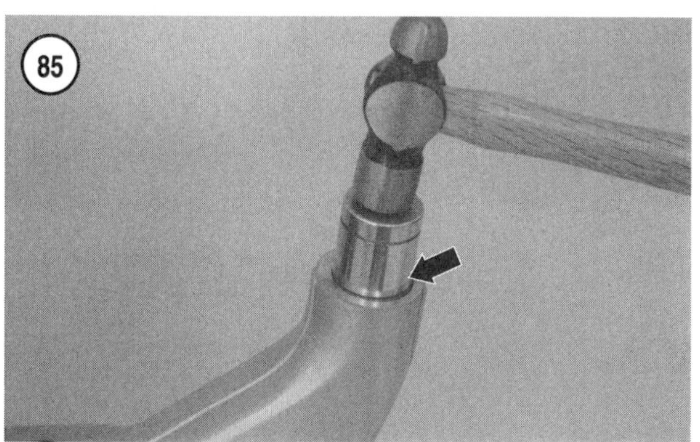

Bearing Replacement

1. The following BMW tools are available to remove the tapered roller bearing assembly from the swing arm:
   a. Counter support (BMW part No. 00-8-572).
   b. Internal puller 21/2 for the roller bearing (BMW part No. 00-8-571).
   c. Internal puller 21/5 for the outer race (BMW part No. 00-8-563).

NOTE
A heat gun capable of producing 80° C (176° F) is required to install the bearing into the swing arm pivot area.

CAUTION
Do not apply heat to the swing arm with any type of open propane or welding torch flame.

CAUTION
Do not remove the bearing for inspection purposes. The bearing is damaged during removal. Never reinstall a bearing that has been removed.

2. Remove the swing arm as described in this chapter.
3. Remove the rubber boot from the right side.

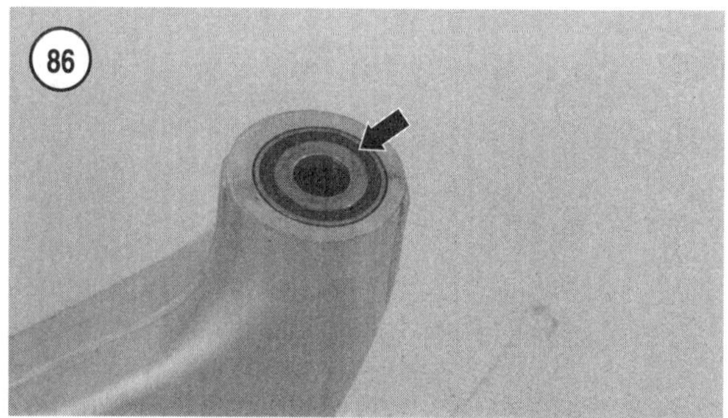

4A. To remove the roller bearing and outer race with the BMW tools:
   a. To pull the roller bearing, use the counter support (A, **Figure 83**) and internal puller 21/2 (B) and withdraw the roller bearing and seal from the outer race in the pivot point.
   b. To pull the roller bearing outer race, use counter support (A, **Figure 83**) and internal puller 21/5 (B) and withdraw the outer race from the pivot point.

4B. To remove the roller bearing and outer race without the special tools:
   a. Insert a two jaw bearing puller into the roller bearing and expand the jaws (**Figure 84**).
   b. Attach a slide hammer to the bearing puller and withdraw roller bearing from the pivot point.
   c. Repeat sub-steps a and b and withdraw the outer race from the pivot point.

5. Repeat Step 4 for the roller bearing and outer race on the other side.
6. Thoroughly clean out the inside surfaces of the pivot portions of the swing arm with solvent and dry with compressed air.
7. Remove any burrs from the bearing receptacle in the swing arm.
8. Place the new bearing and outer race in a freezer to reduce their overall outer diameter slightly.

CAUTION
To prevent damage to the swing arm, place the opposite end of the swing arm on a piece of soft wood when installing the bearing into the other side.

9. Heat the bearing area of the swing arm to 80° C (176° F).
10. Install the new bearing into the swing arm using a driver that matches the outer race of the bearing (**Figure 85**). Tap the bearing in slowly and squarely until it bottoms (**Figure 86**). Make sure it is properly seated.
11. Repeat Step 10 for the bearing on the other side.
12. Install the rubber boot.

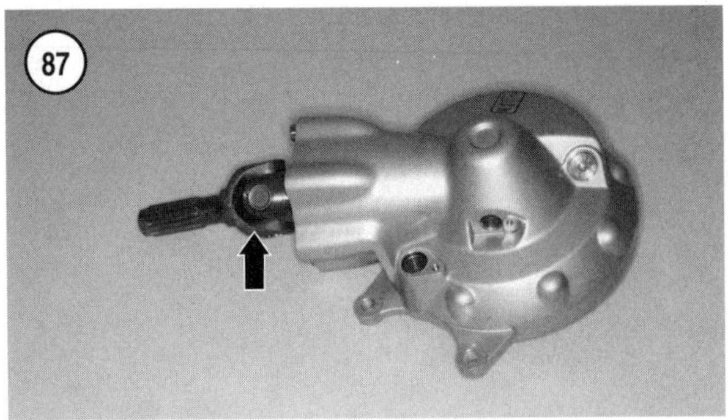
87

88

13. Install the swing arm as described in this section.

Drive Shaft and Universal Joints Inspection

The drive shaft has an integral front universal joint and a removable rear universal joint that joins the drive shaft to the final drive unit. A secondary universal joint is located in the final drive unit.

1. Carefully pry the rear universal joint (**Figure 87**) from the final drive unit.
2. Inspect the drive shaft front universal joint inner splines (**Figure 88**) where it attaches to the transmission shaft. Replace the drive shaft if the splines or universal joint are damaged or worn.

NOTE
If the splines are damaged, also check the splines of the transmission shaft; it may also require replacement.

3. Inspect the drive shaft rear inner splines (**Figure 89**) where they connect to the rear universal joint. Replace the drive shaft if the splines or universal joint are damaged or worn.
4. Inspect the front universal joint pivot points for play (**Figure 90**). Rotate the joint in both directions. Replace the drive shaft if there is noticeable side play.
5. Install the rear universal joint assembly into the rear of the drive shaft (**Figure 91**). Slide the universal joint in and out (**Figure 92**) and check for smooth operation. The universal joint must move without binding. Replace the drive shaft and/or universal joint if movement is not smooth.
6. Inspect the rear universal joint inner splines (**Figure 93**). Also check the outer splines (A, **Figure 94**). If the splines are damaged or worn, replace the rear universal joint.

NOTE
If the splines are damaged, also check the splines of the final drive unit; it may also require replacement.

89

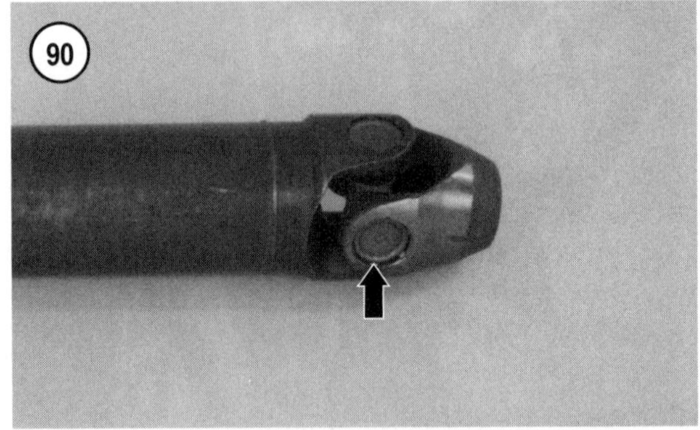
90

91

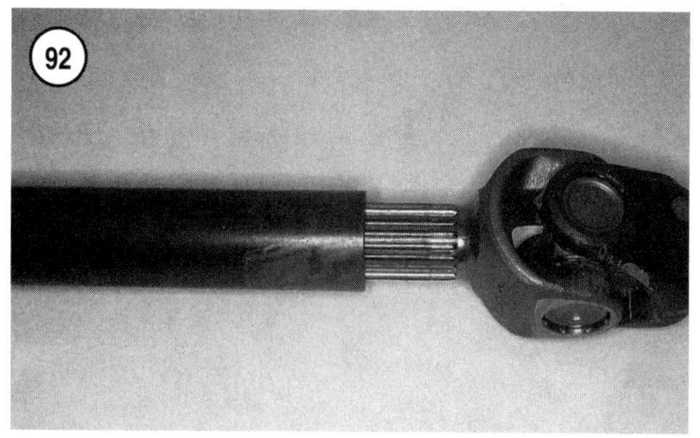

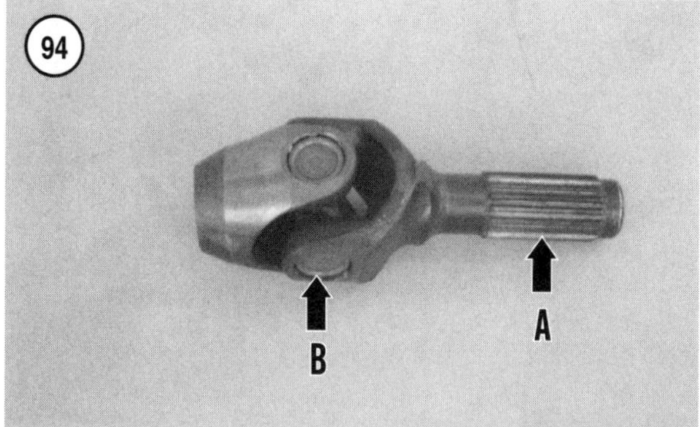

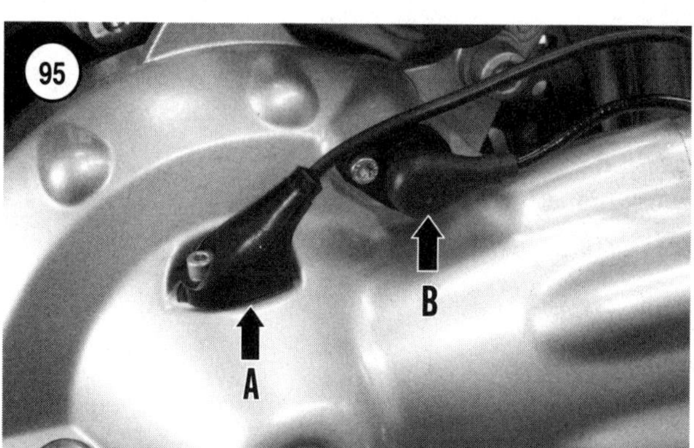

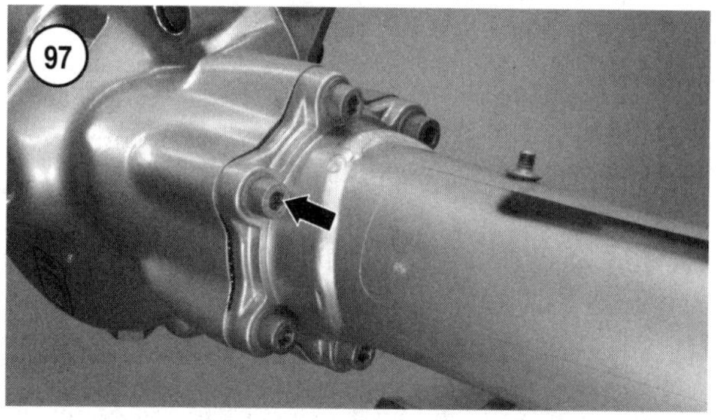

7. Inspect the rear universal joint pivot points for play (B, **Figure 94**). Rotate the joint in both directions. Replace the universal joint if there is noticeable side play.

FINAL DRIVE UNIT (MONOLEVER MODELS)

Removal

1. Remove the mounting bolt and remove the speed sensor (A, **Figure 95**) from the final drive unit.
2. Remove the mounting bolt and remove the ABS sensor and shim (B, **Figure 95**) from the final drive unit.
3. Remove the rear brake caliper assembly and brake line from the swing arm as described in Chapter Fourteen. Support the caliper with wire and move it out of the way.
4. Remove the rear wheel as described in Chapter Eleven.
5. Remove the brake disc (**Figure 96**) from the final drive unit as described in Chapter Fourteen.
6. Using a crisscross pattern, loosen then remove the Allen bolts and washers (**Figure 97**) securing the final drive unit to the swing arm.

NOTE

If the final drive unit still has oil in it, do not place the final drive unit on its side as the oil will drain out the top vent pipe.

7. Pull the final drive unit and rear universal joint to the rear and remove it from the drive shaft and swing arm. Do not lose the two locating dowels on the final drive unit.
8. Secure the swing arm up to the rear frame with a tie-down (**Figure 98**).
9. Carefully pry the rear universal joint (**Figure 87**) from the final drive unit.
10. Inspect all parts as described in this chapter.

Installation

1. Apply a thick coat of BMW Kluberplex BEM 34-132, or Bel Rey Total Performance Lube, to the pinion gear outer splines and to the inner splines on the rear universal joint (**Figure 93**).
2. Install the rear universal joint onto the final drive unit. Push it on until it locks into place.
3. Shift the transmission into top gear. This will prevent the drive shaft from rotating while aligning the final drive splines to the drive shaft splines.
4. Make sure the swing arm is in the correct height position.
5. Place a shop cloth into the swing arm and center the drive shaft in the housing (**Figure 99**). Leave a portion of the shop cloth outside of the swing arm as a reminder to remove the cloth after the final drive unit is installed.
6. If removed, install the two locating dowels (**Figure 100**) into the final drive unit.
7. Install the final drive unit onto the swing arm and drive shaft (A, **Figure 101**); slightly rotate the rear wheel flange until the splines of the drive shaft align.
8. Remove the shop cloth (B, **Figure 101**), then push the final drive unit on until it stops. Support the final drive unit in this position on wood block(s).
9. Align the mounting bolt holes of the final drive unit with those in the swing arm.
10. Install the mounting bolts and washers (**Figure 97**) and tighten hand tight.
11. Shift the transmission into neutral. Rotate the rear wheel flange several complete revolutions to make sure the final drive unit is correctly meshed with the drive shaft.
12. Using a crisscross pattern, tighten the mounting bolts (**Figure 97**) to 21 N•m (15 ft.-lb.).
13. Install the brake disc (**Figure 96**) onto the final drive unit as described in Chapter Fourteen.
14. Install the rear wheel as described in Chapter Eleven.
15. Install the rear brake caliper assembly and brake line onto the swing arm as described in Chapter Fourteen.
16. Install the ABS sensor and shim (B, **Figure 95**) onto the final drive unit as described in Chapter Fourteen.

98

99

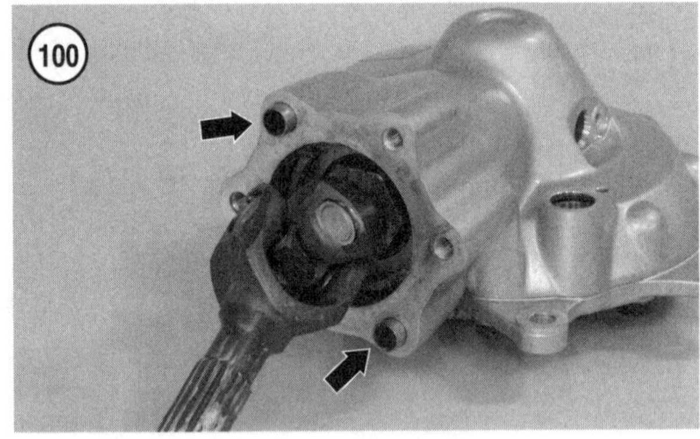
100

17. Install the speed sensor (A, **Figure 95**) onto the final drive unit and tighten the bolt securely.
18. Take the motorcycle off of the centerstand and depress the rear suspension to make sure all components work properly.

Inspection

1. Inspect the exterior of the final drive unit housing for cracks or damage.

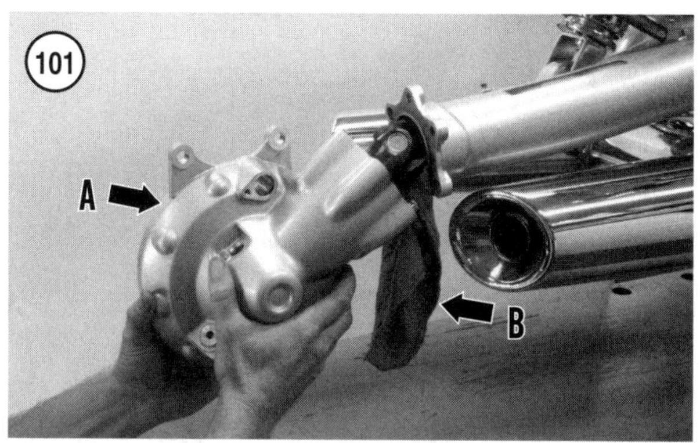

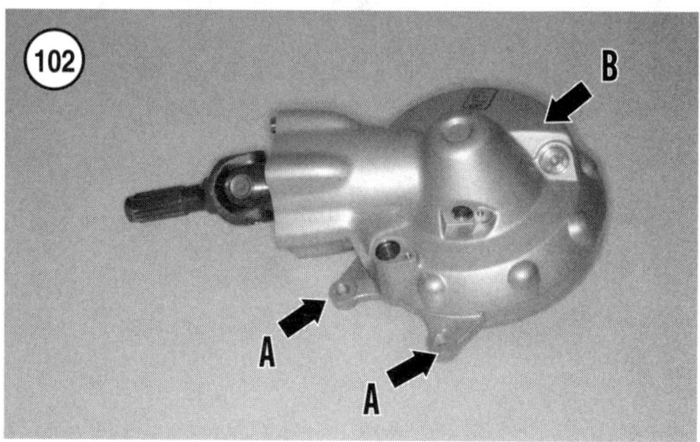

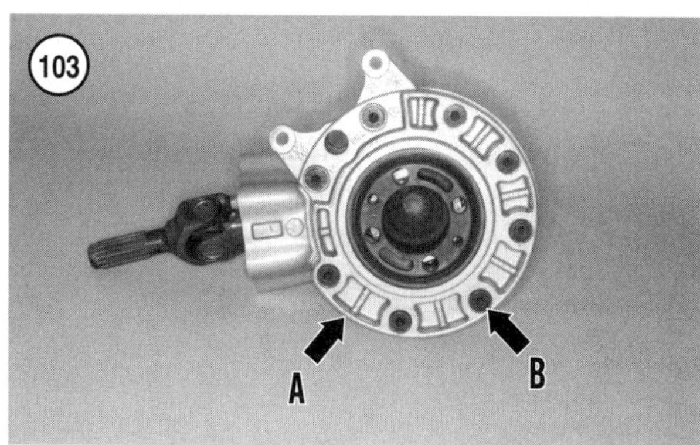

2. Check the rear brake caliper mounting bosses (A, **Figure 102**) on the final drive unit for cracks, damage or hole elongation.

3. Inspect the exterior of the final drive unit housing (B, **Figure 102**) for cracks or damage.

4. Inspect the exterior of the final drive unit housing cover (A, **Figure 103**) for cracks or damage.

5. Inspect the pinion gear splines. If the splines are worn or damaged, replace the pinion gear and ring gear assembly as described under *Final Drive Overhaul* in this chapter.

NOTE
If the splines are worn or damaged, also inspect the splines on the rear universal joint for damage as it may also require replacement.

6. Check for oil leakage at the spline portion. If the seal is leaking, replace it as described under *Final Drive Overhaul* in this chapter.

7. Make sure the mounting bolts (B, **Figure 103**) securing the cover are tight. If loose, tighten to 35 N•m (26 ft.-lb.).

FINAL DRIVE OVERHAUL (ALL MODELS)

The final drive unit is very durable and rarely requires any type of service. To maintain the final drive unit in good condition, change the gear oil at the recommended intervals listed in Chapter Three.

If overhaul is requred, consider having the service performed by a BMW dealership.

Final drive unit overhaul requires the following special tools:

1. Holding fixture (BMW part No. 33-1-500).
2. Special socket wrench (BMW part No. 33-1-720).
3. Pin wrench (BMW part No. 33-1-700).
4. Ball bearing puller (BMW part No. 00-7-500).
5. Bearing inner extractor (BMW part No. 00-8-573).
6. Bearing internal puller (BMW part No. 00-8-572).
7. Bearing inner extractor support (BMW part No. 00-8-570).
8. Special drift (BMW part No. 33-1-760).
9. Special drift retainer (BMW part No. 00-5-550).
10. Special drift (BMW part No. 36-3-700).
11. Bearing puller and insert (BMW part Nos. 33-1-830 and 33-1-307).
12. Internal extractor (BMW part No. 00-8-560).
13. Backlash adjuster (measuring ring) (BMW part No. 33-2-600)
14. Measuring arm (BMW part No. 33-2-604).
15. Measuring ring (BMW part No. 33-2-601).
16. Depth gauge (BMW part No. 00-2-550).
17. Special drift (BMW part No. 33-1-860).
18. Drift retainer (BMW part No. 00-5-500).
19. A heat gun capable of 120° C (248° F).

Disassembly

Refer to **Figure 104**.

(104)

FINAL DRIVE UNIT (ALL MODELS)

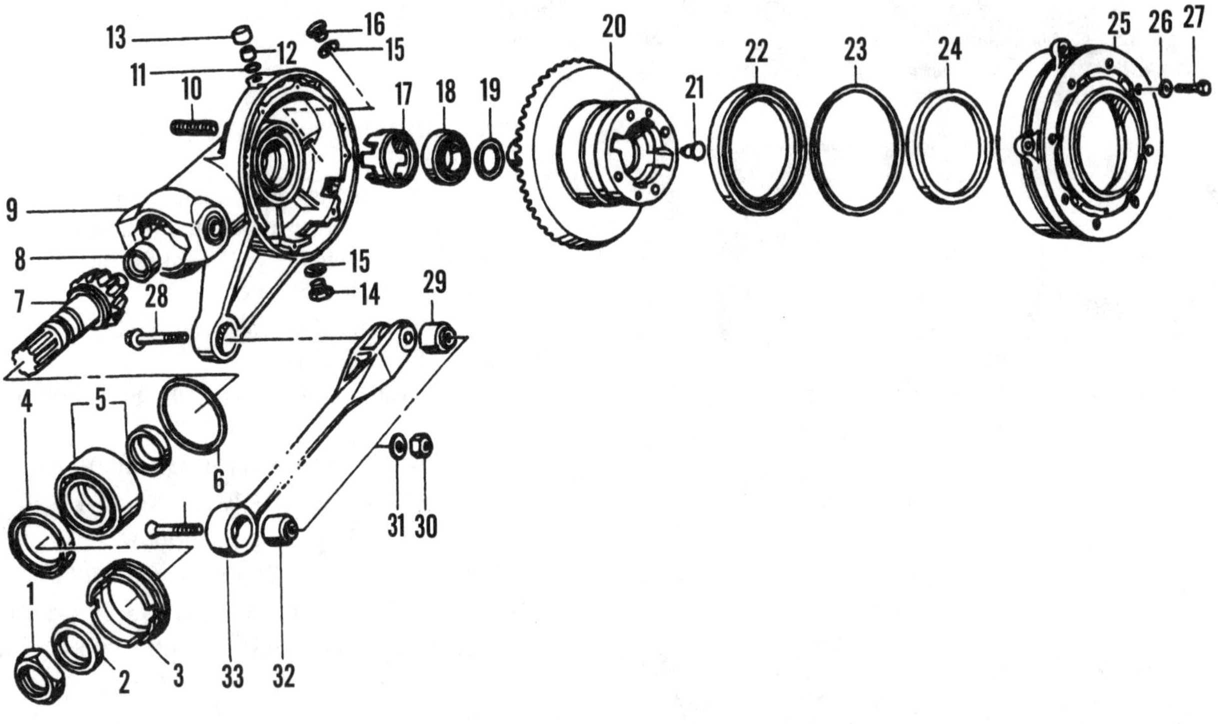

1. Hex nut
2. Thrust ring
3. Threaded ring
4. Oil seal
5. Bearing and inner race
6. Shim
7. Pinion gear
8. Bearing
9. Case
10. Threaded stud
11. O-ring
12. Vent sleeve
13. Cap
14. Drain plug
15. Gasket
16. Fill cap
17. Speedometer sensing ring
18. Tapered roller bearing
19. Shim
20. Ring gear
21. Cover
22. Ball bearing
23. Shim
24. Oil seal
25. Cover and O-ring
26. Washer
27. Bolt
28. Bolt
29. Bushing
30. Nut
31. Washer
32. Bushing
33. Torque link

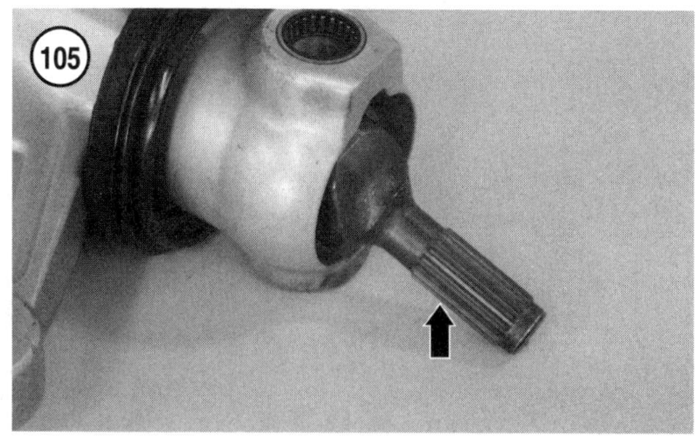

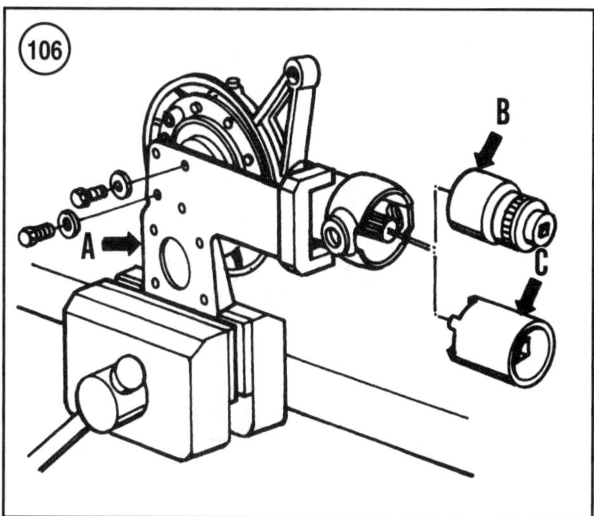

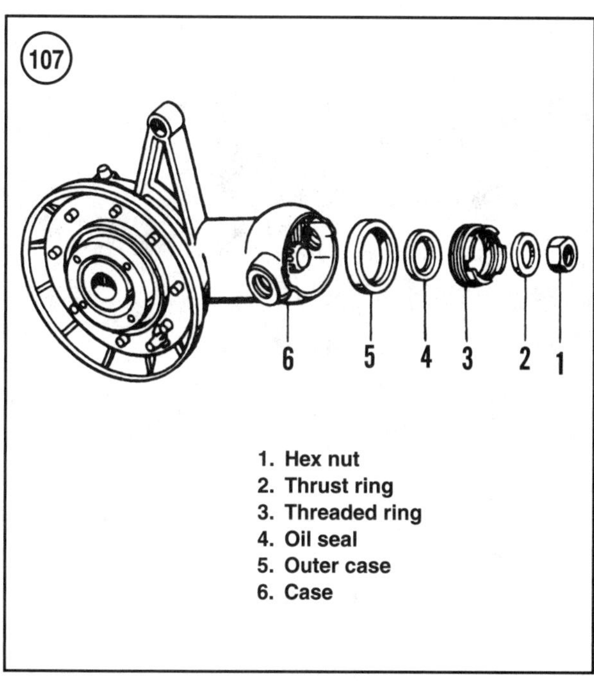

1. Hex nut
2. Thrust ring
3. Threaded ring
4. Oil seal
5. Outer case
6. Case

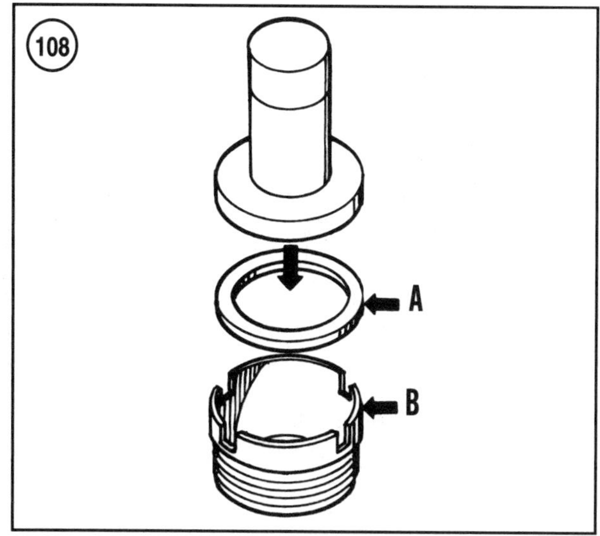

WARNING
During this procedure, many of the components must be heated for removal and will be very hot

1. If still in place, pry the rear portion of the drive shaft (**Figure 105**) from the splines on the pinion gear. Remove the drive shaft.
2. On models so equipped, remove the screws securing the rear brake disc to the final drive unit. Remove the disc from the final drive unit as described in Chapter Fourteen.
3. Remove the drain plug and the fill cap. Drain all of the gear oil, then reinstall the drain plug and fill cap and tighten both securely.
4. Secure the final drive unit in the holding fixture (A, **Figure 106**) and secure the special tool in a vise. Tighten the mounting bolts to 105 N•m (77 ft.-lb.).
5. Heat the pinion gear hex nut to 120° C (248° F).
6. Using the special socket (B, **Figure 106**), completely unscrew and remove the hex nut from the pinion gear.
7. Remove the thrust ring from the pinion gear shaft.
8. Heat the final drive unit neck to 120° C (248° F).
9. Using the pin wrench (C, **Figure 106**), completely unscrew the threaded ring. Remove the threaded ring and the seal (**Figure 107**).
10. To remove the seal from the threaded ring, perform the following:
   a. Using a suitable size driver, press the seal out of the threaded ring.
   b. Position the new seal with the lettering facing toward the outside surface of the threaded ring.
   c. Using the drift and drift retainer, drive the new seal (A, **Figure 108**) into the threaded ring (B).

13

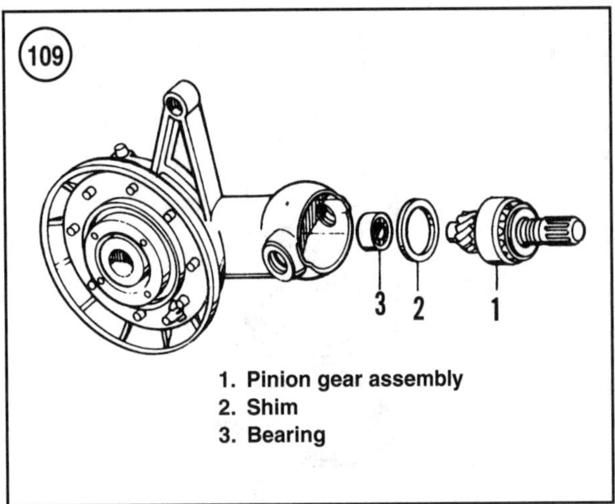

1. Pinion gear assembly
2. Shim
3. Bearing

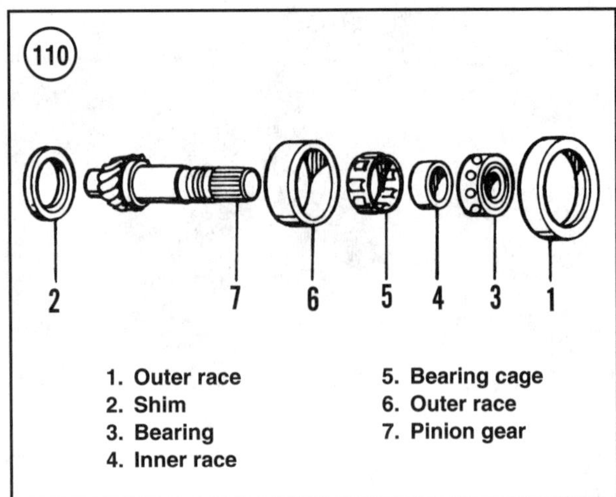

1. Outer race
2. Shim
3. Bearing
4. Inner race
5. Bearing cage
6. Outer race
7. Pinion gear

11. Heat the final drive unit's neck (surrounding the ball bearing outer race) to 120° C (248° F).

CAUTION
Do not damage the splines on the pinion gear while removing the pinion gear and ball bearing from the final drive unit neck.

12. Use a pair of slip joint pliers or locking pliers and carefully withdraw the pinion gear and the ball bearing from the final drive unit's neck. Remove the shim from the shaft (**Figure 109**).

13. To remove the bearing assembly from the pinion gear (**Figure 110**), perform the following:
   a. Secure the pinion gear and ball bearing in a vise with soft jaws to protect the gears.
   b. Install the bearing puller onto the pinion gear and bearing (A, **Figure 111**).

NOTE
Hold a pan under the vise as the bearing assembly may separate during removal and the loose bearing balls may fall out.

   c. Tighten the center bolt on the puller (B, **Figure 111**) and withdraw the bearing from the pinion gear.
   d. Disassemble the bearing and place all parts in a box to keep the small parts together.

14. Make alignment marks (**Figure 112**) on the case and cover to ensure correct alignment of the two parts during assembly.

15. Install the final drive unit in the holding fixture and secure it with the left pivot pin (A, **Figure 113**) and tighten with the locknut (B).

16. Remove the screws securing the cover (**Figure 114**) to the case.

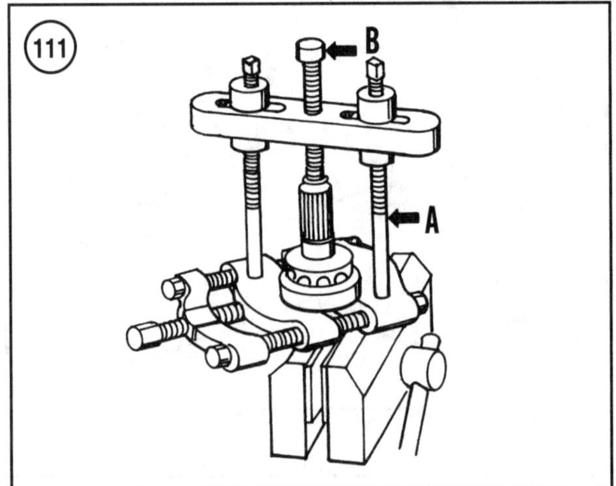

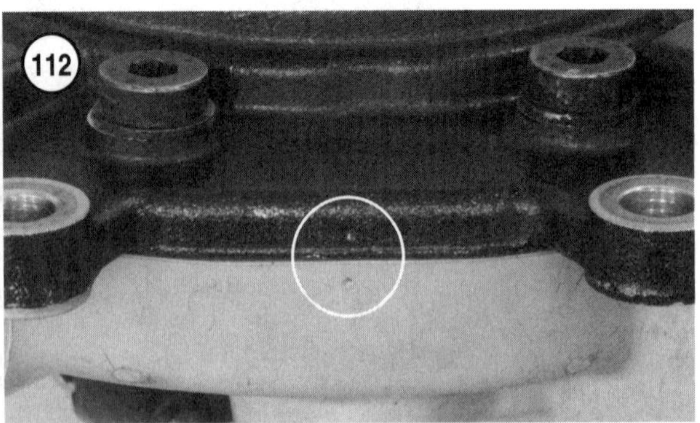

17. Using a plastic hammer or soft-faced mallet, tap around the perimeter of the cover until it is loose.

18. Remove the cover and the ring gear assembly from the case.

19. Heat the final drive cover to about 100° C (212° F).

113

B

A

20. Using thick gloves or heavy pot holders, separate the ring gear (A, **Figure 115**) from the cover (B). Do not lose the shim between the ring gear bearing and the cover. It must be reinstalled.

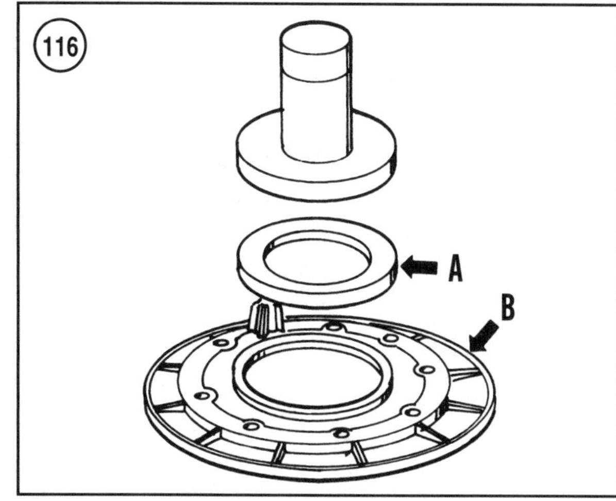

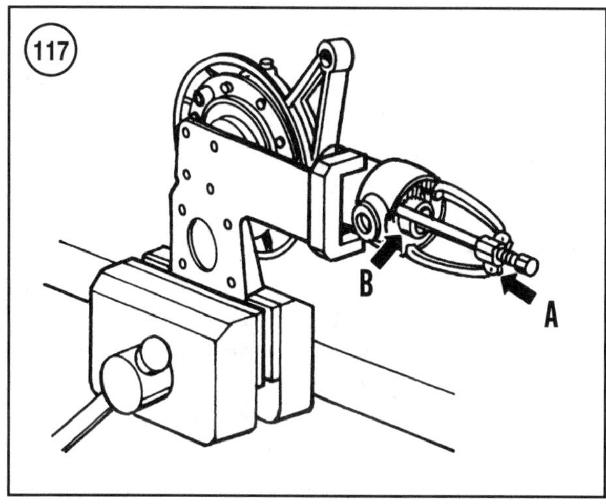

21. To replace the ring gear seal in the cover, perform the following:

   a. Use a hammer and drift and work around the perimeter of the seal and carefully tap the seal out of the cover. Discard the seal. Be careful not to damage the cover in the area of the seal.

   b. Clean out the seal area of the cover with solvent and thoroughly dry.

   c. Apply a light coat of oil to the outer surface of the new seal (A, **Figure 116**).

   d. Using the drift and drift retainer, carefully tap the new seal into the cover (B, **Figure 116**). Be sure to tap the seal in squarely until it bottoms in the cover.

22. To remove the pinion gear needle bearing from the case, perform the following:

   a. Insert the bearing extractor (A, **Figure 117**) and extractor support into the neck of the case and position

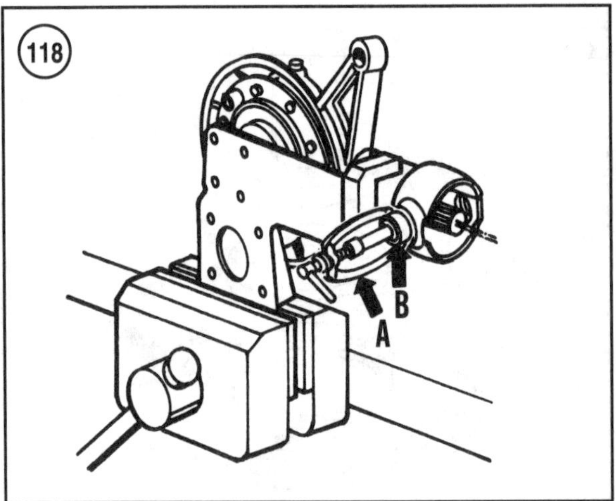

it behind the needle bearing (B). Turn the end of the extractor to expand it behind the needle bearing.

b. Heat the final drive unit neck (surrounding the needle bearing) to 100° C (212° F).

c. Carefully and slowly tighten the bearing extractor and withdraw the needle bearing from the case.

23. To remove the pivot pin needle bearings from the case, perform the following:

a. Insert the bearing extractor (A, **Figure 118**) and bearing puller into the neck of the case and position it behind the needle bearing (B). Turn the end of the extractor to expand it behind the needle bearing.

b. Heat the final drive unit neck (surrounding the needle bearing) to 120° C (248° F).

c. Carefully and slowly tighten the bearing puller and withdraw the needle bearing (**Figure 119**) from the case.

d. Repeat for the other bearing if necessary.

24. To remove the ring gear tapered roller bearing outer race (**Figure 120**) from the case, perform the following:

a. Secure the final drive unit in a vise with soft jaws with the open portion of the case facing up to access the ring gear tapered roller bearing outer race.

b. Install the internal bearing puller onto the outer race (A, **Figure 121**).

c. Carefully and slowly tighten the bearing puller (B, **Figure 121**) and withdraw the outer race from the case.

d. Remove the final drive case from the vise.

25. To remove the ball bearing on the ring gear, perform the following:

a. Secure the ring gear, ball bearing side up, in a vise with soft jaws.

b. Insert the insert onto the center of the ring gear (A, **Figure 122**).

c. Install the bearing puller onto the ball bearing (B, **Figure 122**).

d. Carefully and slowly tighten the bearing puller and withdraw the ball bearing from the ring gear (C, **Figure 122**).

e. Remove the special tools from the ring gear.

26. To remove the tapered roller bearing, inner race and shim from the ring gear (**Figure 123**), perform the following:

a. Secure the ring gear, tapered roller bearing side up, in a vise with soft jaws.

b. Install the bearing puller onto the tapered roller bearing (A, **Figure 124**).

c. Carefully and slowly tighten the bearing puller center bolt (B) and withdraw the tapered roller bearing from the ring gear.

d. Remove the tapered roller bearing, inner race and shim from the ring gear.

Assembly

Refer to **Figure 125** and **Figure 126**.

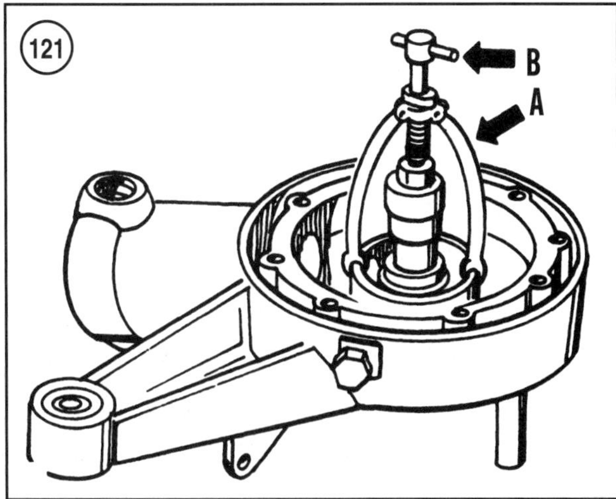

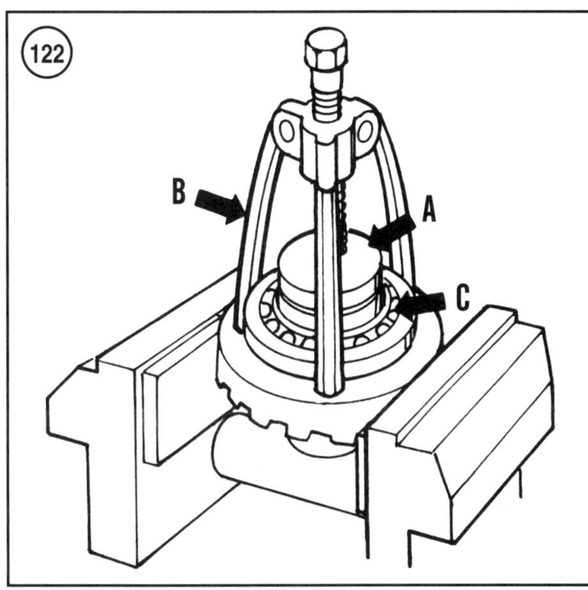

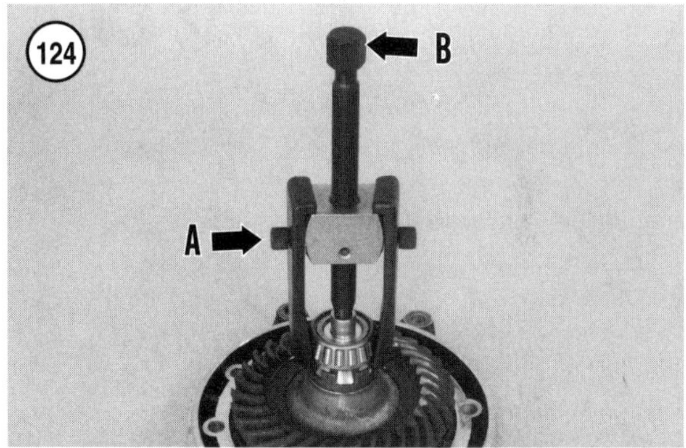

1. To install the tapered roller bearing (**Figure 123**), inner race and shim onto the ring gear, perform the following:
   a. Position the ring gear with the portion where the tapered roller bearing rides facing up.
   b. Secure the ring gear in a vise with soft jaws.
   c. Position the shim of the correct thickness with the inner diameter chamfer facing down toward the ring gear and install the shim (A, **Figure 127**) onto the ring gear.
   d. Heat the bearing and inner race to 80° C (175° F).
   e. Install the bearing (B, **Figure 127**) onto the ring gear and tap it down until it bottoms.
   f. Remove the ring gear from the vise.
2. To install the ball bearing on the ring gear, perform the following:
   a. Position the ring gear with the portion where the ball bearing rides facing up.
   b. Secure the ring gear in a vise with soft jaws.
   c. Install a shim of the correct thickness onto the ring gear.
   d. Using a heat gun or hot plate, heat the bearing to 80° C (175° F).
   e. Install the bearing onto the ring gear and tap it down until it bottoms.
   f. Remove the ring gear from the vise.
3. To install the ring gear tapered roller bearing outer race into the case, perform the following:
   a. Place the tapered roller bearing outer race in a freezer for 10-15 minutes. This will reduce its overall size.
   b. Using a heat gun or hot plate, heat the case to 120° C (248° F).
   c. Set the case on wood blocks with the open portion of the case facing up.
   d. Install the tapered roller bearing outer race (A, **Figure 128**) into the case.
   e. Insert the drift and drift retainer onto the center of the outer race (B, **Figure 128**) and tap it down in un-

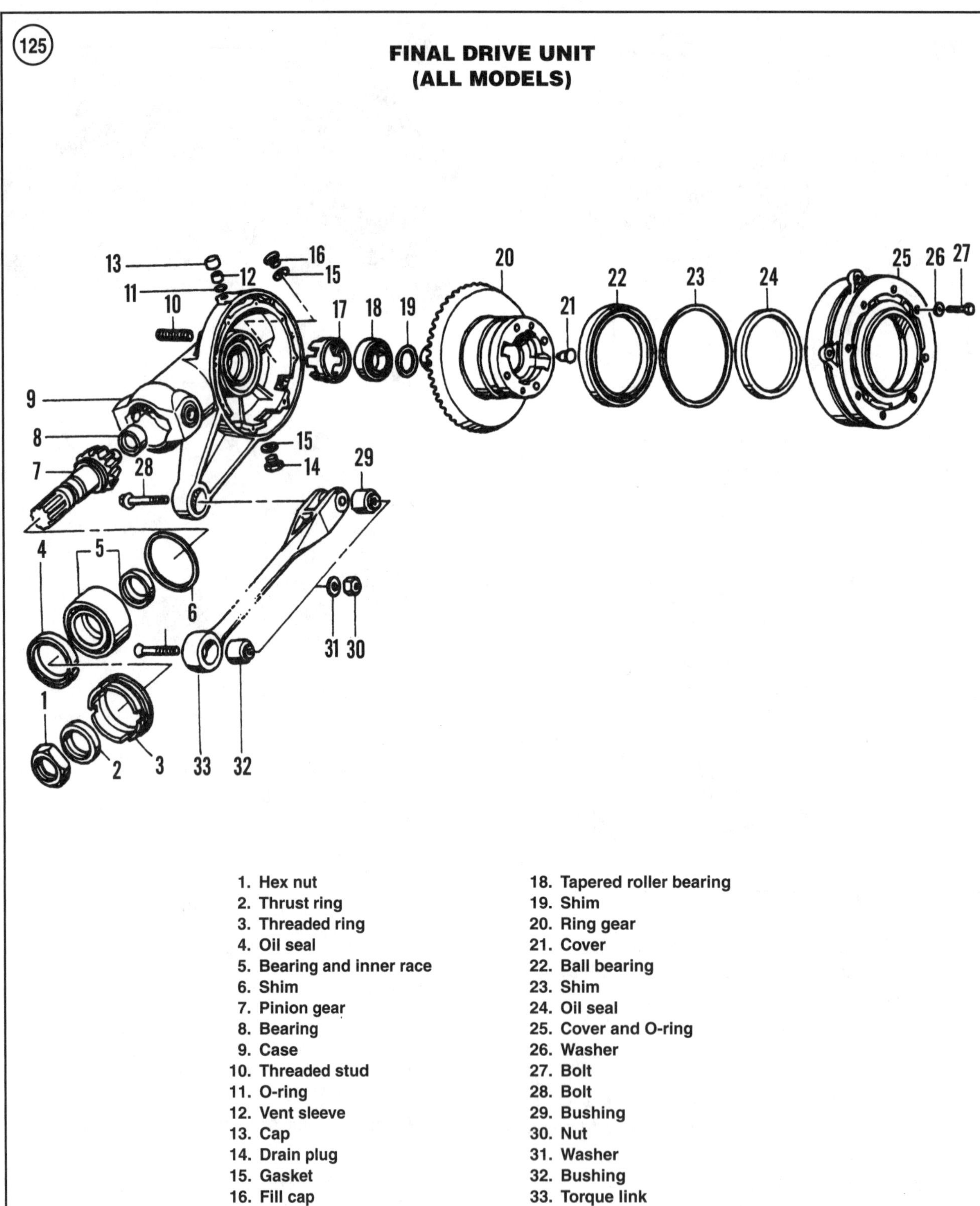

1. Hex nut
2. Thrust ring
3. Threaded ring
4. Oil seal
5. Bearing and inner race
6. Shim
7. Pinion gear
8. Bearing
9. Case
10. Threaded stud
11. O-ring
12. Vent sleeve
13. Cap
14. Drain plug
15. Gasket
16. Fill cap
17. Speedometer sensing ring
18. Tapered roller bearing
19. Shim
20. Ring gear
21. Cover
22. Ball bearing
23. Shim
24. Oil seal
25. Cover and O-ring
26. Washer
27. Bolt
28. Bolt
29. Bushing
30. Nut
31. Washer
32. Bushing
33. Torque link

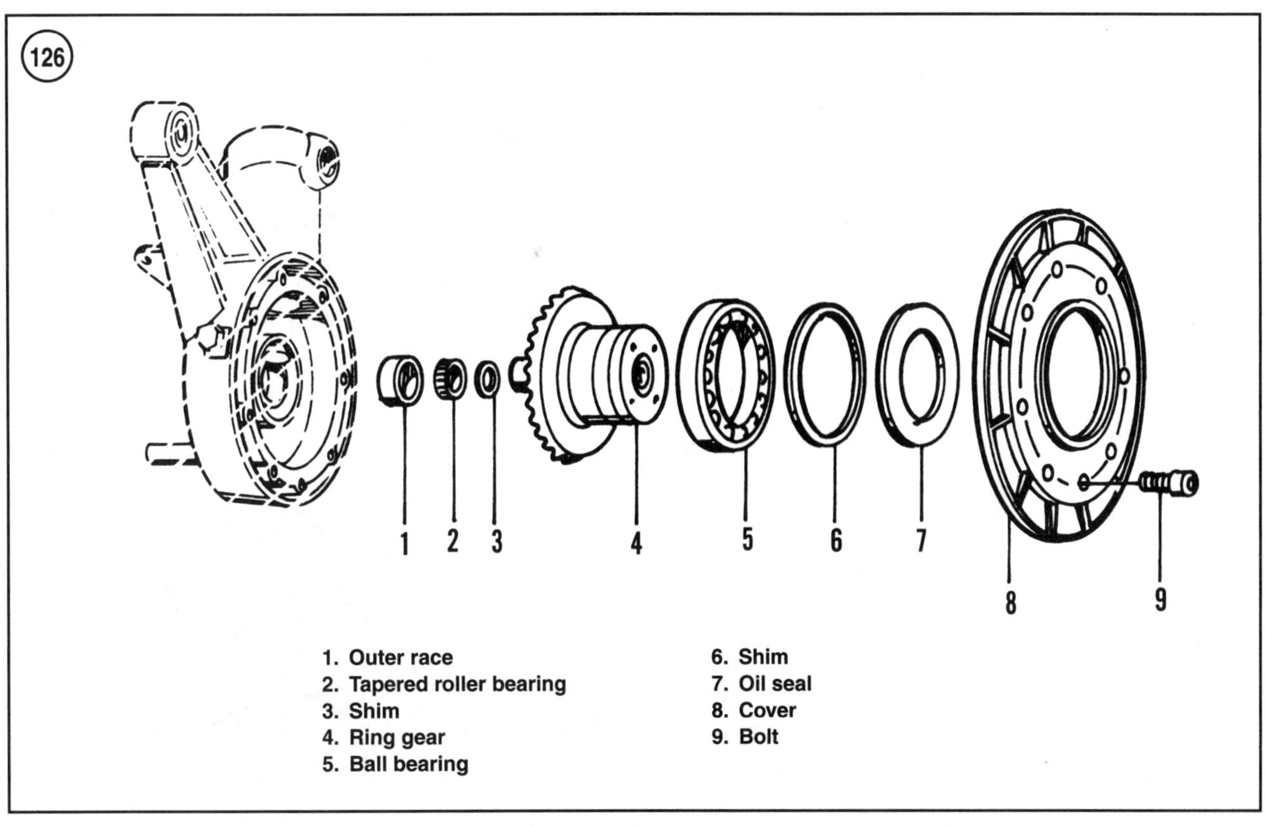

1. Outer race
2. Tapered roller bearing
3. Shim
4. Ring gear
5. Ball bearing
6. Shim
7. Oil seal
8. Cover
9. Bolt

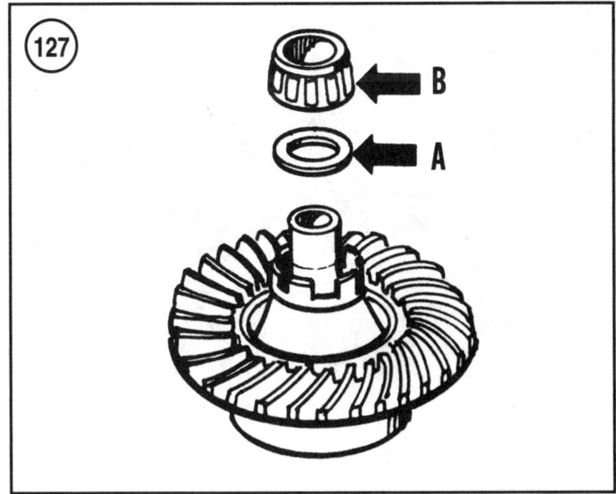

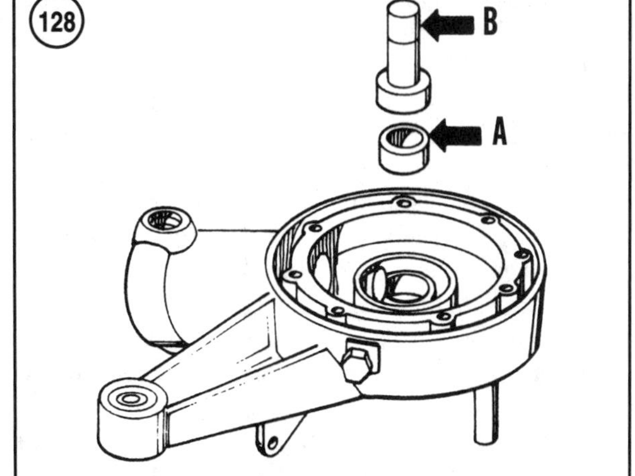

til it bottoms in the case. Make sure the outer race is installed straight.

4. To install the pivot pin needle bearings into the case, perform the following:

a. Clamp the final drive case in the holding fixture.

b. Place the pivot pin needle bearing in a freezer for 10-15 minutes. This will reduce its overall size.

c. Heat the case in the area where the needle bearing is to be located. Heat the case to 100° C (212° F).

d. Position the needle bearing with the identification marks facing out.

e. Install the needle bearing into the case and tap it in with a suitably sized driver or use the pinion gear. Tap it in until it is flush with the outer surface of the case (**Figure 119**). Make sure the needle bearing is installed straight.

5. To install the pinion gear needle bearing into the case, perform the following:
   a. Clamp the final drive case in the holding fixture.
   b. Place the pinion gear needle bearing in a freezer for 10-15 minutes. This will reduce its overall size.
   c. Heat the case in the area where the needle bearing is to be located. Heat the case to 100° C (212° F).
   d. Position the needle bearing with the identification marks facing out.
   e. Install the needle bearing into the case and tap it in with a suitable size driver or use the pinion gear. Tap it in until it bottoms in the case. Make sure the needle bearing is installed straight.
6. Place the ring gear assembly in a freezer for about 15-30 minutes.
7. Install the shim onto the needle bearing in the case.
8. Remove the ring gear assembly from the freezer and install the ring gear onto the case. Using a plastic hammer or soft-faced mallet, tap around the perimeter of the ring gear until it bottoms.
9. If the pinion gear and ring gear were replaced with a new gear set, or if any of the bearings were replaced, perform *Pinion Gear-To-Ring Gear Adjustment* as described in this section, prior to installing the cover.
10. Install the shim on the ring gear bearing.
11. Install a new O-ring seal (**Figure 129**) into the groove in the cover. Make sure it is seated around the perimeter of the cover.
12. Install the cover onto the case, referring to the alignment marks (**Figure 112**) made during *Disassembly* Step 14. Using a plastic hammer or soft faced mallet, tap around the perimeter of the cover until it bottoms.
13. Install the bolts securing the cover (**Figure 114**) to the case. Tighten the bolts to 35 N•m (26 ft.-lb.).
14. To install the bearing assembly onto the pinion gear, refer to **Figure 110** and perform the following:
   a. Place the pinion gear in a freezer for about 30 minutes.
   b. Using a heat gun or hot plate, heat the cylindrical roller bearing inner race to 100° C (212° F) and install the bearing inner race onto the pinion gear shaft.
   c. Carefully tap the cylindrical roller bearing inner race into place until it bottoms.
   d. Install the cylindrical needle bearing outer race and the cylindrical roller bearing cage into place on the inner race.
   e. Using a heat gun or hot plate, heat the ball bearing assembly to 100° C (212° F) and install the bearing inner race onto the pinion gear shaft.

   f. Carefully tap the ball bearing assembly into place until it bottoms.
   g. Heat the final drive unit neck (surrounding the ball bearing outer race) to 120° C (250° F).
   h. Install the pinion gear assembly along with the shim of the correct thickness into the case. Push the assembly in until it bottoms on the ball bearing in the case.
   i. Place the ball bearing outer race in a freezer for about 30 minutes.

j. Install the ball bearing outer race into the final drive unit neck and over the ball bearing. Push it in until it seats on the ball bearing.

NOTE
*Refer to **Figure 106** for Steps 15-19.*

15. Thoroughly clean the threaded ring of all oil and grease.

16. Secure the final drive unit in the holding fixture (A, **Figure 106**) and secure the special tool in a vise. Tighten the mounting bolts to 105 N•m (77 ft.-lb.).

17. Coat the threaded ring with a coat of Hylomar SQ 32 M grease and place it in a freezer for about 15 minutes.

CAUTION
Do not damage the new seal in the threaded ring during installation. After the threaded ring is installed, make sure the seal lip seats correctly around the pinion gear shaft.

18. Start the threaded ring by hand, then using the pin wrench, screw in the threaded ring. Tighten the threaded ring to 118 N•m (87 ft.-lb.).

19. Apply Loctite No. 273 to the gear nut and install the nut.

20. Using a suitable size socket, tighten the pinion gear nut to 200 N•m (147 ft.-lb.).

21. Install the drain plug and new sealing washer. Tighten the drain plug securely.

22. On cast wheel models, install the rear brake disc and mounting screws as described in Chapter Fourteen.

23. Apply a coat of BMW Kluberplex BEM 34-132, or Bel Rey Total Performance Lube, to the pinion shaft splines and install the rear universal joint. Carefully tap the rear universal joint onto the splines until it locks into place.

24. Refill the final drive unit with the recommended type and quantity of oil.

Inspection

1. Wash all parts in solvent and dry with compressed air.

2. Inspect the teeth on the ring (A, **Figure 130**) and pinion gear set (**Figure 131**). If the teeth are worn or damaged on either of the gears, both gears must be replaced as a set.

3. Inspect the case (**Figure 132**) and the cover (B, **Figure 130**) for cracks or other damage. Make sure all ribs and bosses are not damaged or missing. Replace either or both parts.

4. Inspect the threads on the threaded ring for wear or damage. Clean out the threads with the correct size and pitch thread tap or replace them.

5. Inspect the two threaded holes (A, **Figure 133**) for the brake disc mounting screws. Check for wear or damage. If necessary, clean out the threads with the correct size and pitch thread tap or replace them.

6. On all models, inspect the four threaded holes (B, **Figure 133**) for the wheel mounting bolts. Check for wear or damage.

PINION GEAR-TO-RING GEAR ADJUSTMENT (ALL MODELS)

If the ring and pinion gear set is replaced, they must be a matched pair provided by the manufacturer. The gears are run on a test stand and paired up in sets to provide the correct amount of backlash. After testing, both gears are marked with a pair code.

If a *new* ring and pinion gear set is going to be installed into a used case or a *new case* is going to be used with the used ring and pinion set, the tolerance between these parts must be checked. A specified distance that provides the correct relationship of the ring gear to the pinion gear.

CAUTION
If any of the final drive unit bearings have been replaced, all of the following procedures must be followed.

The first section of the procedure is the adjustment of the ring gear backlash to the pinion gear. This adjustment is made to correctly locate the ring gear to the pinion gear. A shim is used to achieve the up and down location of the ring gear so it can be aligned correctly with the pinion gear.

The second section of the procedure is for the pinion gear adjustment. This adjustment is made to correctly locate the pinion gear in relation to the case. A shim is used to achieve the location of the pinion gear in the case and to correctly achieve the correct bearing preload. This also correctly aligns the tooth contact pattern. The gear contact must be centered otherwise there will be abnormal stress placed on the gear teeth, causing premature wear.

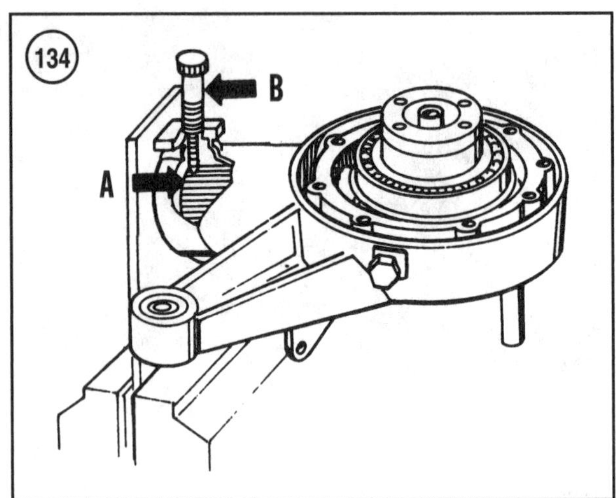

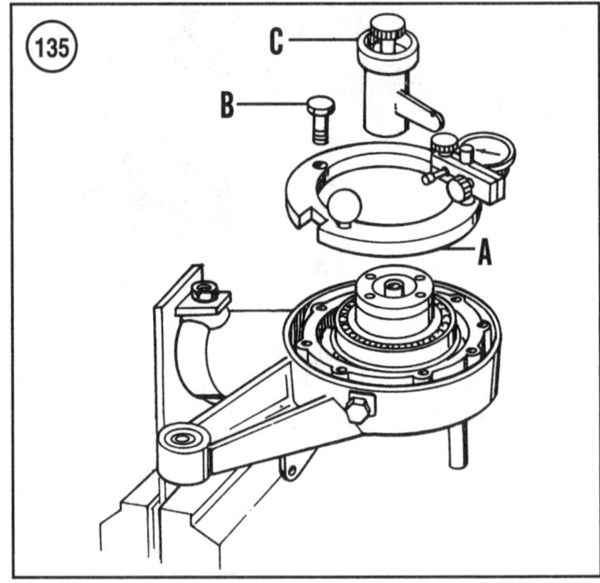

Ring Gear Backlash

1. The check and adjustment of ring gear backlash requires the following special tools:
   a. Holding fixture (BMW part No. 33-1-500).
   b. Measuring ring assembly (BMW part No. 33-2-600).
   c. Measuring arm (BMW part No. 33-2-604).

NOTE
All locking and measuring tools must be secured tightly in place to the case and to the gear assembly. If they are loose, a false reading will be obtained.

2. Mount the gearcase in the holding fixture.
3. Lock the pinion gear in place (A, **Figure 134**) with the knurled screw (B). The pinion gear must not move during this procedure.
4. Install the measuring ring assembly (A, **Figure 135**) onto the case and secure with the bolts (B).
5. Install the measuring arm (C, **Figure 135**) onto the center of the ring gear and tighten securely.
6. Adjust the measuring ring so the dial gauge is positioned at a 90° angle to the rod on the special tool (**Figure 136**). Adjust the dial gauge to zero.
7. Using the palm of your hand, press down on the measuring arm and slightly move the ring gear and measuring arm back and forth and note the dial gauge reading.
8. Reposition the measuring ring and check backlash at 120° from the point tested in Step 6. Note the reading.

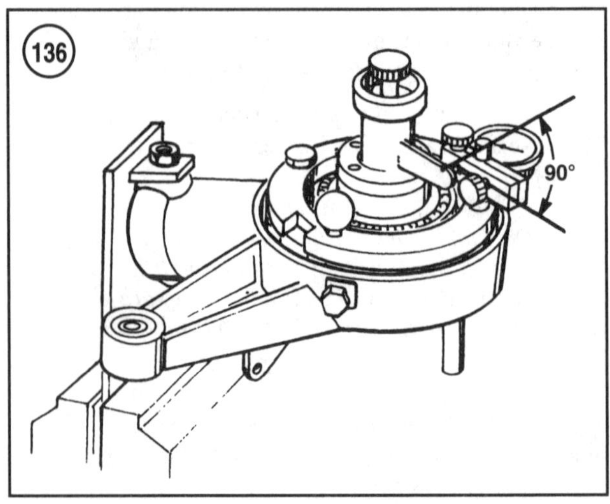

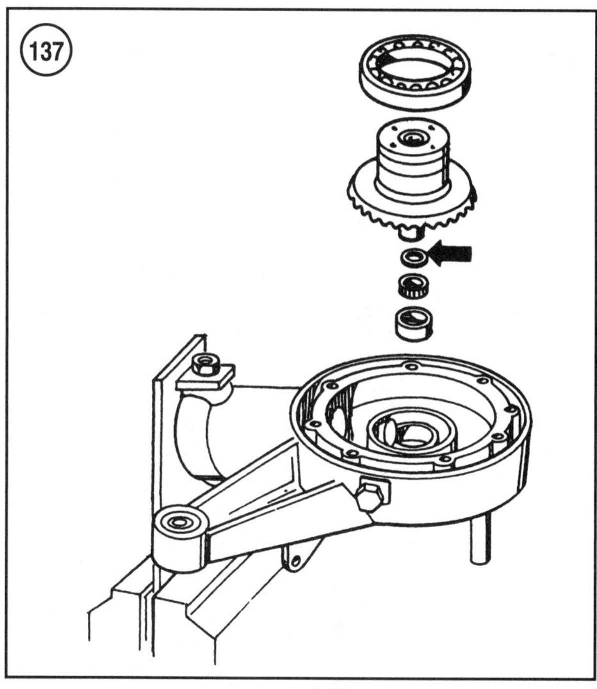

9. Again, reposition the measuring ring and check backlash at 120° from the point tested in Step 7. Note the reading.

10. The specified backlash is 0.07-0.16 mm (0.003-0.007 in.)

11A. If the backlash is within specification, remove the special tools from the ring gear and gearcase.

11B. If the backlash is incorrect, remove the special tool and perform the following:

   a. Remove the ring gear from the final drive unit as described in this section.
   b. Remove the shim (**Figure 137**) and replace it with one of the appropriate size to establish the correct backlash. The shims are available in 0.05 mm thickness increments.

12. Repeat Steps 3-8 until the correct backlash is established.

13. Remove the special tools and the gearcase from the holding fixture.

Tooth Contact Pattern

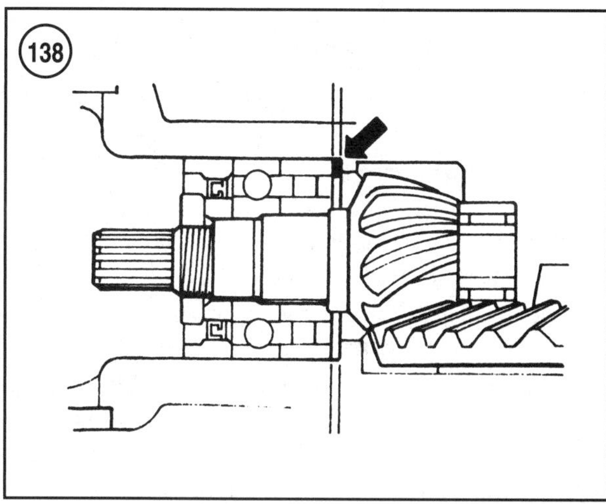

The shim located between the pinion shaft bearing and the gearcase (**Figure 138**) controls the tooth contact pattern between the ring and pinion gears.

1. Remove the ring gear from the final drive case.
2. Thoroughly clean and dry the ring and pinion gear teeth.
3. Apply a light coat of marking compound to the pinion gear teeth.
4. Install the ring gear into the final drive case.
5. Press down firmly on the ring gear and rotate it back and forth as necessary to transfer the marking compound from the pinion gear to the ring gear teeth.
6. Remove the ring gear from the final drive case.
7. Observe the pattern on the pinion gear. If the pattern is similar to **Figure 139**, the tooth contact pattern is correct. If correct clean the marking compound from both gears. 13

NOTE
Perform Steps 8-14 only if the tooth contact pattern is not correct.

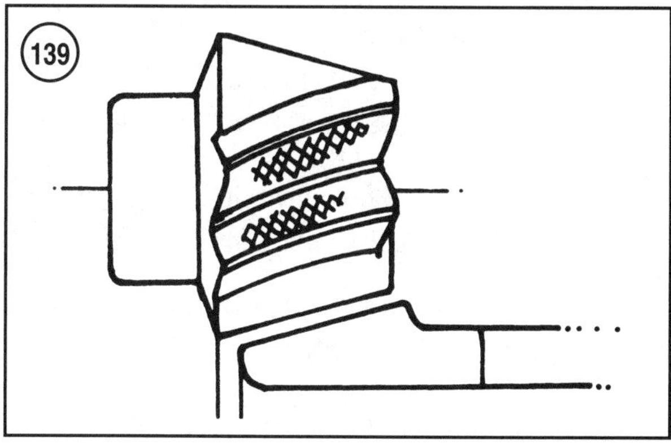

8. If the pattern is not correct as shown in **Figure 139**, compare it to the following illustrations:
   a. **Figure 140**—pinion gear must be moved farther out in the final drive case. Replace the existing shim with a thicker shim between the pinion gear and the final drive case.
   b. **Figure 141**—pinion gear must be moved farther back into the final drive case. Replace with an existing shim with a thinner shim between the pinion gear and the final drive case.
9. Replace the shim (**Figure 138**) between the pinion gear and the final drive case.

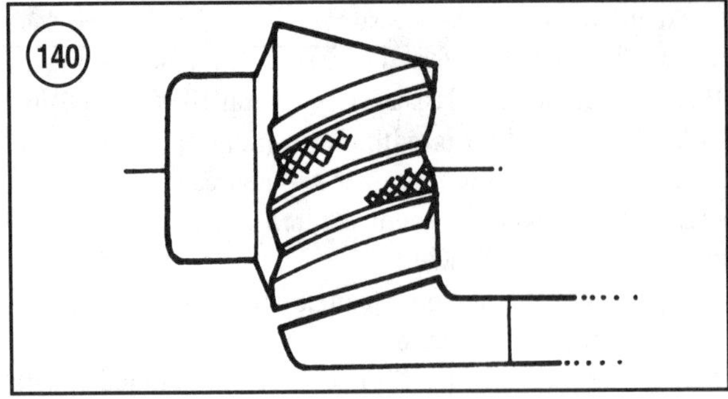

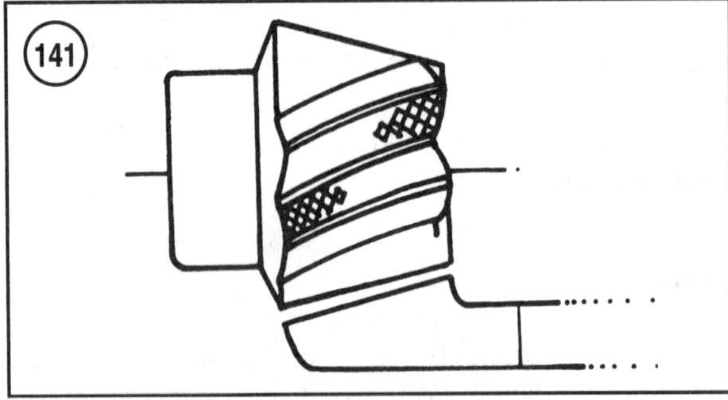

10. Apply another light coat of marking compound to both sides of the teeth on the pinion gear.

11. Install the ring gear into the final drive case and pinion gear.

12. Press down firmly on the ring gear and rotate it back and forth several times to transfer the marking compound to the ring gear teeth.

13. Remove the ring gear from the final drive case.

14. Observe the pattern on the pinion gear. If the pattern is similar to **Figure 139**, the tooth contact pattern is correct. If not, repeat this procedure until the tooth contact pattern is correct.

15. Remove the ring gear from the final drive case. Clean the marking compound from both gears.

TAPERED ROLLER BEARING PRELOAD

The preload on the tapered roller bearing, located on the right side of the ring gear, is controlled by the shim placed between the ball bearing, located on the left side of the ring gear ball bearing and the case cover. The correct spacing of this ball bearing determines the preload on the tapered roller bearing. A specific amount of preload is necessary for the tapered roller bearing to seat and operate properly. The specified preload dimension is 0.05-0.10 mm. The shims are available in thickness from 0.1-1.7 mm in 0.1 mm increments.

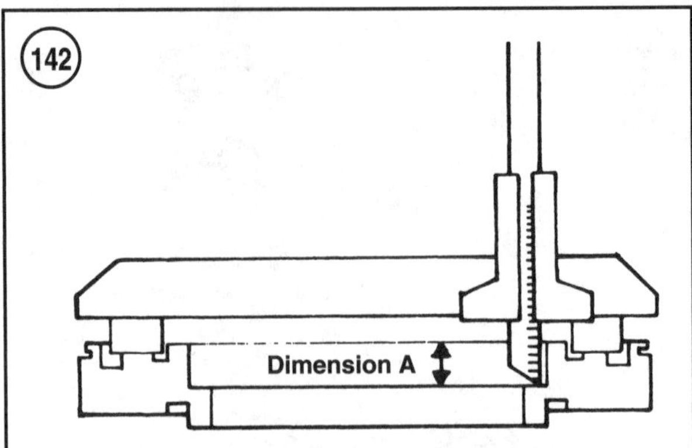

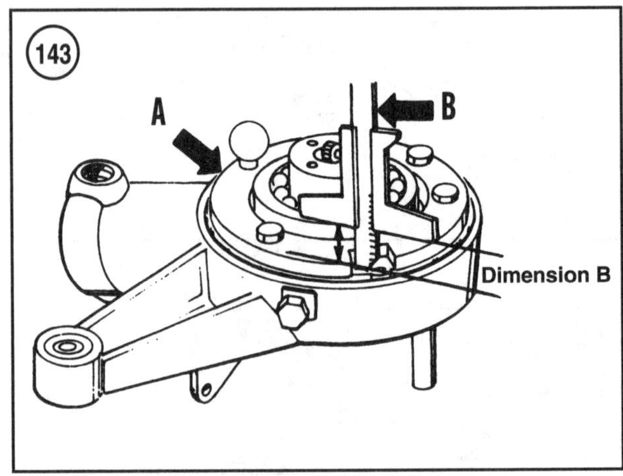

1. Place the case cover on the workbench with the inner surface facing up.

2. Place the depth gauge on the case-to-cover mating surface of the cover (**Figure 142**).

3. Measure the distance from the mating surface down to the ball bearing seating shoulder of the cover. This is dimension A.

4. Install the ring gear and ball bearing assembly into the final drive case and pinion gear.

5. Place the measuring ring (A, **Figure 143**) onto the gearcase and secure it with the bolts.

6. Place the depth gauge (B, **Figure 143**) on the upper surface of the ball bearing on the ring gear. Place the special tool in the opening in the gauge ring.

7. Measure the distance from the ball bearing upper surface to the case-mating surface of the case. This is dimension B.

8. Subtract dimension B from dimension A. This dimension is the shim thickness required to achieve the specified preload.

9. Install a new shim and repeat this procedure.

Table 1 REAR SUSPENSION TORQUE SPECIFICATIONS

Item	N•m	in.-lb.	ft.-lb.
Final drive unit (Paralever models)			
Torque link-to-transmission case	43	–	32
Torque link-to-final drive unit	43	–	32
Threaded ring	118	–	87
Pinion gear nut	200	–	147
Cover mounting bolts	35	–	26
Unit-to-BMW special tool (33-1-500)	105	–	77
Final drive unit (Monolever models)			
Unit-to-swing arm bolt	21	–	15
Threaded ring	118	–	87
Pinion gear nut	200	–	147
Cover mounting bolts	35	–	26
Unit-to-BMW special tool (33-1-500)	105	–	77
Shock absorber			
Upper bolt and nut			
1993-1998 R850 and all R1100 models	43	–	32
1999-on R850, R1100, R1150, all R1200 models	50	–	37
Lower bolt and nut			
R1200C	50	–	37
1993-1998 R850 and R1100 models	50	–	37
1999-on R850, R1100, R1150,	58	–	43
Remote reservoir (GS, R, RS, RT models)	22	–	16
Swing arm-to-final drive unit (Paralever models)			
Right pivot pin	7	62	–
Left adjust pivot pin	7	62	–
Left adjust pivot pin locknut			
1993-1998 R850 and R1100 models	105	–	77
1999-on R850 and R1150 models	160	–	118
Swing arm-to-transmission case (Paralever models)			
R1100S models			
Right pivot pin	9	80	–
Left adjust pivot pin	7	62	–
Left adjust pivot pin locknut	160	–	118
All models except R1100S models			
Right pivot pin	7	62	–
Left adjust pivot pin	7	62	–
Left adjust pivot pin locknut			
1993-1998 R850 and R1100 models	150	–	111
1999-on R850 and R1150 models	160	–	118
Swing arm-to-frame (Monolever models)			
Right fixed pivot Allen bolts	7	62	–
Left adjust pivot pin	10	88	–
Left adjust pivot pin locknut	160	–	118

CHAPTER FOURTEEN

BRAKES

The brake system on all models consists of a dual front caliper and a single rear caliper. This chapter describes repair and replacement procedures for all brake components.

NOTE
On all ABS equipped models, whenever a component is removed, or a brake line loosened, or a brake fluid leak has occurred the system must be bled. The ABS brake system ***must*** *be bled with a power bleeder.*

WARNING
Do not try to bleed the ABS brake system without the power bleeder as it is impossible to manually purge all of the air from the system. Any attempt to manually bleed the system will result in an unsafe brake system.

Table 1 and **Table 2** are located at the end of this chapter.

BRAKE SERVICE

WARNING
Do not intermix DOT 5 (silicone-based) based brake fluid as it will lead to brake component damage and possible brake failure.

WARNING
When working on the brake system, do ***not*** *inhale brake dust. It may contain asbestos, which is a known carcinogen. Do* ***not*** *use compressed air to blow off brake dust. Use an aerosol brake cleaner. Wear a facemask and wash thoroughly after completing the work.*

The disc brake system transmits hydraulic pressure from the master cylinders to the brake calipers. This pressure is transmitted from the caliper(s) to the brake pads, which grip both sides of the brake disc(s) and slow the motorcycle. As the pads wear, the pistons move out of the caliper bores to automatically compensate for wear. As this occurs, the fluid level in the master cylinder reservoir goes down. Compensate for this by occasionally adding fluid.

The proper operation of this system depends on a supply of clean brake fluid (DOT 4) and a clean work environment when any service is being performed. Any

particle of debris entering the system can damage the components and cause poor brake performance.

Brake fluid is hygroscopic (easily absorbs moisture) and moisture in the system reduces brake performance. Purchase brake fluid in small containers and properly discard small quantities that remain. Small quantities of fluid will quickly absorb the moisture in the container. Only use fluid clearly marked DOT 4. If possible, use the same brand of fluid. Do not replace the fluid with a silicone fluid. It is not possible to remove all of the old fluid. Other types are not compatible with DOT 4. Do not reuse drained fluid. Discard old fluid properly. Do not combine brake fluid with fluids for recycling.

When adding fluid, punch a small hole into the edge of the fluid container's seal to help control the fluid flow. This is especially important to prevent spills while adding fluid to the small reservoirs.

Perform service procedures carefully. Do not use sharp tools inside the master cylinders, calipers or on the pistons. Damage to these components could cause a loss in the system's ability to maintain hydraulic pressure. If there is any doubt about the ability to correctly and safely service the brake system, have a professional technician perform the task.

Consider the following when servicing the brake system:

1. The hydraulic components rarely require disassembly. Make sure disassembly is necessary.
2. Keep the reservoir covers in place to prevent the entry of moisture and debris.
3. Clean parts with an aerosol brake parts cleaner or isopropyl alcohol. Never use petroleum-based solvents on internal brake system components. They will cause seals to swell and distort.
4. Do not allow brake fluid to contact plastic, painted or plated parts. It will damage the surface.
5. Dispose of brake fluid properly.
6. If the hydraulic system, not including the reservoir cover, has been opened, bleed the system to remove air from the system. Refer to *Bleeding the System* in this chapter.
7. The manufacturer does not provide service limit specifications for the master cylinder assemblies. Use good judgment when inspecting these components or consult a professional technician for advice.

EVO AND INTEGRAL BRAKES

BMW introduced the EVO (evolution) brake technology along with Partial and Fully Integral brake system in 2002. Both systems are combined and are either standard or optional depending on model and year.

EVO Brakes

The EVO brake system is improved two-fold with weight reduction and increased braking efficiency. It incorporates two larger diameter front rotors along with increased size in two sets of the pistons in the front calipers. The sintered metal brake pads used with the system have a 50% longer operating life and can be replaced without having to remove the caliper from the disc.

The braking effort at the hand lever is reduced by about 15% and the maximum braking force is 15-20% higher depending on model.

EVO models have the BMW logo on the side of the caliper (A, **Figure 1**) and the toothed pulse-generating ring (B) is a light weight stamped part instead of being a heavier cast part.

Partially Integral Brake System

The partially integral brake system links the front and rear brakes together as a single system. This allows the rider to apply the front brake lever and apply both brake simultaneously. The electronic controller in the ABS controller computes the braking force distribution between the front and rear wheels, and applies the brakes accordingly.

This system also allows the rider to operate the rear brake independently with the rear pedal only.

Fully Integral Brake System

The fully integral brake system links the front and rear brakes together as a single system. This allows the rider to apply either the front brake lever and/or the rear brake pedal and apply both brakes simultaneously. The elec-

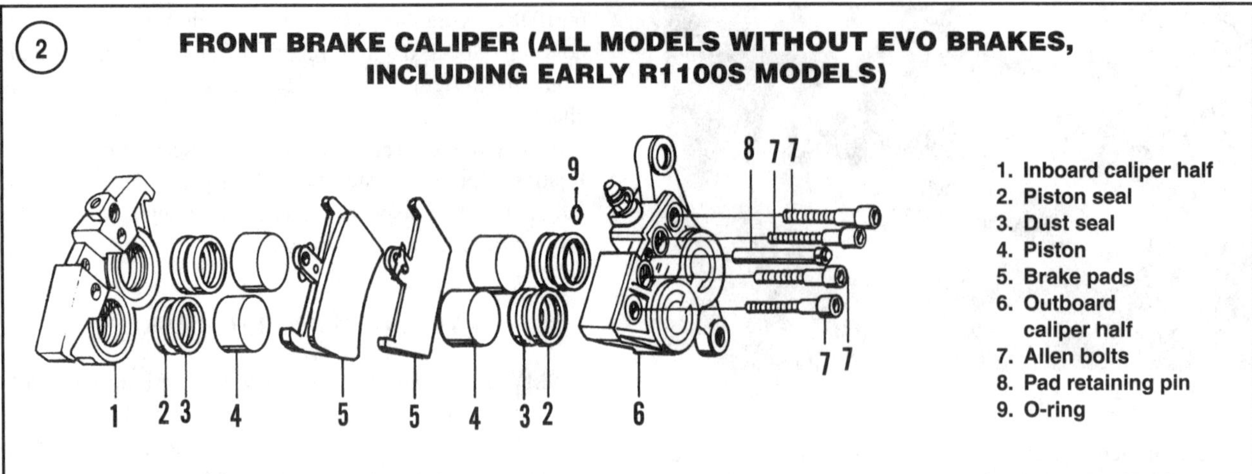

tronic controller in the ABS controller computes the braking force distribution between the front and rear wheels, and applies the brakes accordingly.

BRAKE PAD REPLACEMENT INTERVAL

There is no recommended mileage interval for changing the brake pads. Pad wear depends on riding habits and conditions. Frequently check the brake pads for wear. Increase the inspection interval when the wear indicator reaches the edge of the brake disc. After removal, measure the thickness of each brake pad with a vernier caliper or ruler, and compare the measurements to the dimensions in **Table 1**.

Always replace both pads in the caliper at the same time to maintain even brake pressure on the disc. Do not disconnect the hydraulic brake hose from the brake caliper for brake pad replacement. Only disconnect the hose if the caliper assembly is going to be removed.

CAUTION

Watch the pads more closely when the minimum thickness or wear line approaches the disc. On some pads, the wear line is very close to the metal backing plate. If pad wear happens to be uneven for some reason, the backing plate may come in contact with the disc and cause damage.

FRONT BRAKE PAD REPLACEMENT

All Models Without EVO Brakes Including Early R1100S Models

Refer to **Figure 2**.

NOTE

*Models not equipped with the EVO (evolution) brake system have the BREMBO logo on the side of the caliper (A, **Figure 3**) and the toothed pulse-generating ring (B) is a heavy cast part.*

1. Read *Brake Service* in this chapter.
2. The pistons must be repositioned in the caliper assembly prior to installing the new brake pads. The front mas-

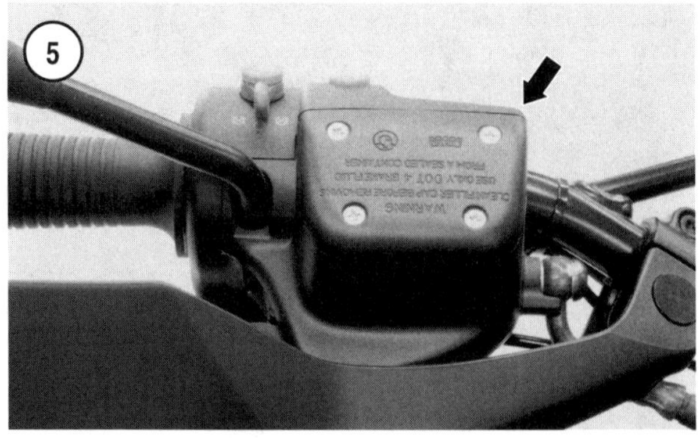

ter cylinder brake fluid level will rise as the caliper pistons are repositioned. Perform the following:

a. Remove the screws securing the cover and remove the cover and the diaphragm from the master cylinder. Refer to **Figure 4** or **Figure 5**.
b. Use a shop syringe and remove about 50% of the brake fluid from the reservoir. Do *not* remove more than 50% of the brake fluid or air will enter the system. Discard the brake fluid properly.

3. Carefully push, then pull, the caliper against the brake disc. This will press the pistons back into the caliper bores. This will allow room for the new brake pads

CAUTION
Do not allow the master cylinder to overflow when performing Step 3. Brake fluid damages most surfaces it contacts.

CAUTION
The pistons should move smoothly when compressing them in Step 3. If not, check the caliper for sticking pistons or damaged caliper bores, pistons and seals. Repair requires the overhaul of the brake caliper assembly.

4. Remove the caliper from the brake disc as described in this chapter. Do not disconnect the hydraulic brake line from the caliper.
5. To prevent the accidental application of the front brake lever, place a spacer between the front brake lever and the throttle grip and secure it in place. If the brake lever is inadvertently squeezed, the pistons well not be forced out of the cylinders.
6. Using needlenose pliers, remove the clip (**Figure 6**) securing the pad retaining pin.
7. Hold the brake pads in place, then use needlenose pliers and withdraw the pad retaining pin (**Figure 7**).

14

NOTE
If the brake pads are going to be reused, mark them so they can be reinstalled into their original locations.

8. Turn the caliper assembly over and remove both brake pads.
9. Clean the pad recess and the end of the pistons (**Figure 8**) with a soft brush. Do not use solvent, a wire brush or any hard tool that would damage the pistons.
10. Carefully remove any rust or corrosion from the disc.
11. Lightly coat the end of the pistons and the backs of the new pads (**Figure 9**) with disc brake lubricant.
12. Check the brake pads (**Figure 10**) for wear or damage. Measure the thickness of the brake pad friction mate-

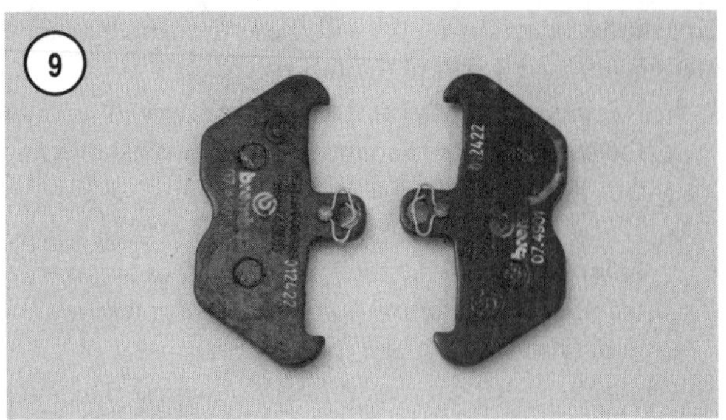

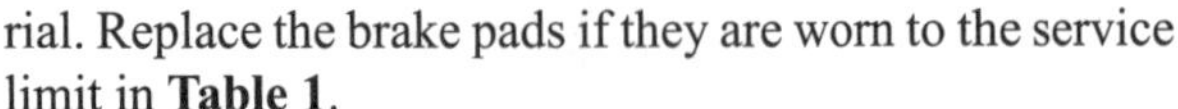

rial. Replace the brake pads if they are worn to the service limit in **Table 1**.

13. Check the friction surface of the new pads for any debris or manufacturing residue. If necessary, clean them off with an aerosol brake cleaner.

NOTE
When purchasing new pads, make sure the friction compound of the new pad is compatible with the disc material. Remove roughness from the backs of the new pads with a fine-cut file, then thoroughly clean them with brake cleaner.

14. Make sure the springs (**Figure 11**) are in place on the retaining pin holes.

15. Install the outboard pad (**Figure 12**), and while holding the pad in place, turn the caliper assembly over.

16. Insert the pad retaining pin (**Figure 13**) through the caliper and into the hole and through the spring in the outboard pad. Push the pin slightly past the outboard pad.

17. Install the inboard pad (**Figure 14**), and while holding the pad in place, turn the caliper assembly over.

18. Press the pad retaining pin through the hole and the spring in the inboard pad (**Figure 15**). Push the pin in until it bottoms in the caliper.

19. Insert a screwdriver into the groove in the end of the pad retaining pin and rotate the pin until the pin clip hole is facing up (**Figure 16**).

20. Use needlenose pliers and install the clip (**Figure 17**) into the pad retaining pin hole. Push the clip down until it seats correctly (**Figure 18**).

21. Repeat Steps 3-20 for the other caliper assembly.

22. Remove the spacer from between the front brake lever and the throttle grip.

23A. On models so equipped, place the motorcycle on the centerstand with the front wheel off the ground.

23B. On models without a centerstand, place a suitable size jack under the engine to support the motorcycle with the front wheel off the ground.

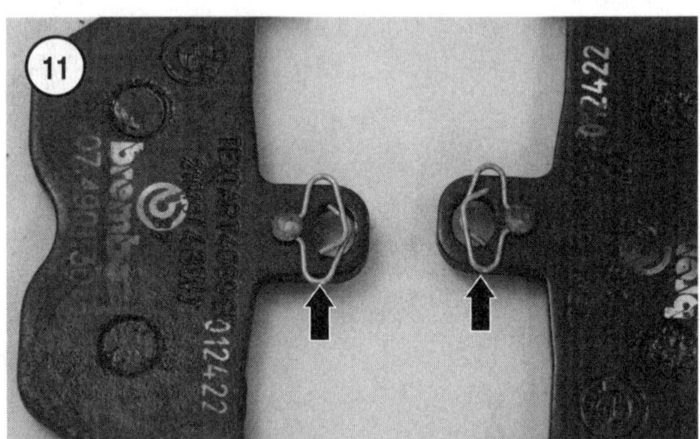

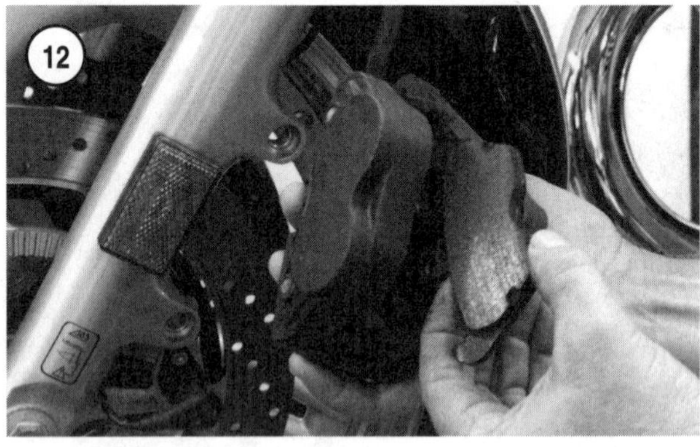

24. Spin the front wheel and activate the front brake lever as many times as it takes to refill the caliper cylinders and locate the brake pads correctly against the disc.

25. Refill the master cylinder reservoir, if necessary, to maintain the correct fluid level as indicated on the side of the reservoir. Install the diaphragm and cover and tighten the cover securely.

WARNING
Do not ride the motorcycle until the front brakes are operating correctly with full hydraulic advantage. If necessary bleed, or have the ABS brake system bled, as described in this chapter.

26. Follow the brake pad manufacturer's instructions regarding break-in of the lining material.

All Models With EVO Brakes Including Late R1100S Models, Except 2004 R1150GS Models

NOTE
Models equipped with the EVO (evolution) brake system have the BMW logo on the side of the caliper (A, ***Figure 19****) and the toothed pulse-generating ring (B) is a*

20

FRONT BRAKE CALIPER (ALL MODELS WITH EVO BRAKES, INCLUDING LATE R1100S MODELS [EXCEPT 2004 R1150GS MODELS])

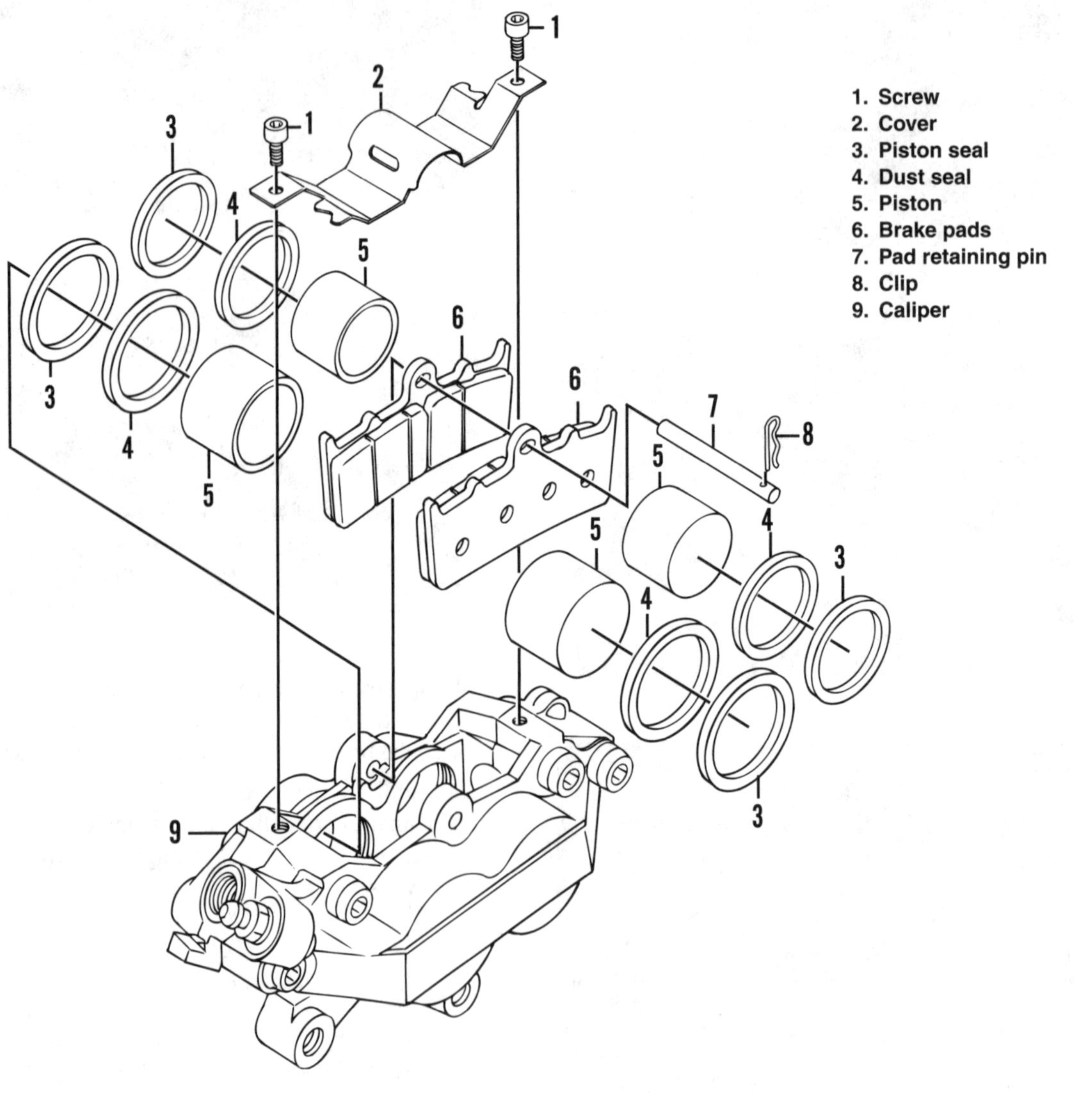

1. Screw
2. Cover
3. Piston seal
4. Dust seal
5. Piston
6. Brake pads
7. Pad retaining pin
8. Clip
9. Caliper

stamped part instead of being a heavier cast part.

Refer to **Figure 20**.

1. Read *Brake Service* in this chapter.
2. The pistons must be repositioned in the caliper assembly prior to installing the new brake pads. The front master cylinder brake fluid level will rise as the caliper pistons are repositioned. Perform the following:
   a. Remove the screws securing the cover and remove the cover (**Figure 21**) and diaphragm from the master cylinder.

21

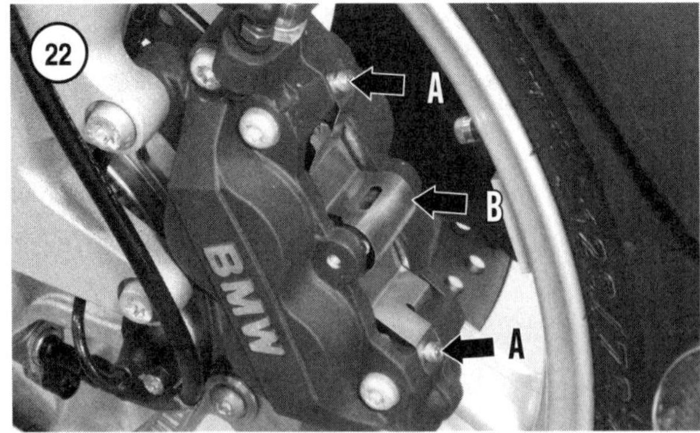

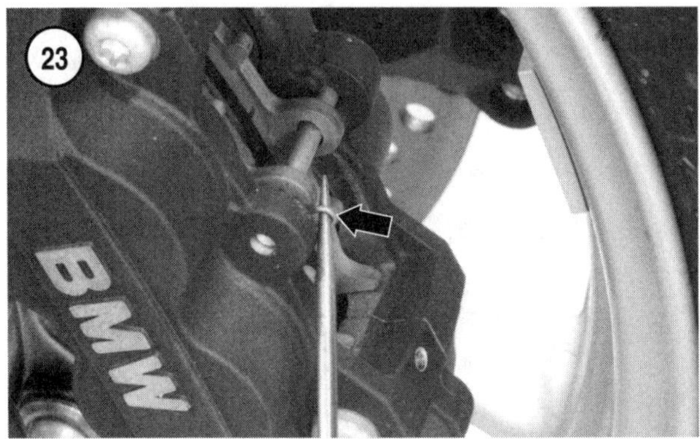

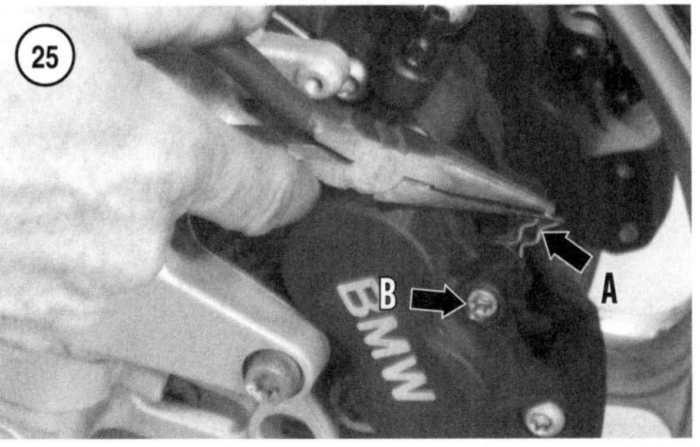

b. Use a shop syringe and remove about 50% of the brake fluid from the reservoir. Do *not* remove more than 50% of the brake fluid or air will enter the system. Discard the brake fluid properly.

3. Carefully push, then pull, the caliper against the brake disc. This will press the pistons back into the caliper bores. This will allow room for the new brake pads

CAUTION

Do not allow the master cylinder to overflow when performing Step 3. Brake fluid damages most surfaces it contacts.

CAUTION

The pistons should move smoothly when compressing them in Step 3. If not, check the caliper for sticking pistons or damaged caliper bores, pistons and seals. Repair requires the overhaul of the brake caliper assembly.

4. To prevent the accidental application of the front brake lever, place a spacer between the front brake lever and the throttle grip and secure it in place. If the brake lever is inadvertently squeezed, the pistons well not get forced out of the cylinders.

5A. On early models, perform the following:

a. Remove the two screws (A, **Figure 22**) securing the cover (B) and remove the cover.
b. Use a pick and withdraw the clip (**Figure 23**) from the pad retaining pin.
c. From the backside of the caliper assembly, push out on the pad retaining pin (**Figure 24**) and withdraw it from the caliper assembly.

5B. On later models, perform the following:

a. Use needlenose pliers and remove the clip (A, **Figure 25**).
b. Unscrew and remove the pad retaining pin (B, **Figure 25**) and withdraw it from the caliper assembly.

NOTE

If the brake pads are going to be reused, mark them so they can be reinstalled into their original locations.

6. Remove both brake pads (**Figure 26**).

7. Clean the pad recess and the end of the pistons with a soft brush. Do not use solvent, a wire brush or any hard tool that would damage the pistons.

8. Carefully remove any rust or corrosion from the disc.

9. Lightly coat the end of the pistons and the backs of the new pads (**Figure 27**) with disc brake lubricant.

10. Check the brake pads for wear or damage. Measure the thickness of the brake pad friction material. Replace the brake pads if they are worn to the service limit in **Table 1**.
11. Check the friction surface of the new pads for any debris or manufacturing residue. If necessary, clean them off with an aerosol brake cleaner.

NOTE
When purchasing new pads, make sure the friction compound of the new pad is compatible with the disc material. Remove roughness from the backs of the new pads with a fine-cut file, then thoroughly clean them with brake cleaner.

12. Install the outboard pad (**Figure 28**) and push it down into place.
13. Insert the pad retaining pin (**Figure 29**) through the caliper and into the hole in the outboard pad. Push the pin slightly past the outboard pad.
14. Install the inboard pad (**Figure 30**) and push it down into place.
15A. On early models, perform the following:
  a. Rotate the pad retaining pin until the pin clip hole is facing up.
  b. Press the pad retaining pin through the hole in the inboard pad (**Figure 24**). Push the pin in until it bottoms in the caliper (A, **Figure 31**).
  c. Use needlenose pliers and install the clip (B, **Figure 31**) into the pad retaining pin hole. Push the clip down until it seats correctly.
15B. On later models, perform the following:
  a. Install the pad retaining pin (B, **Figure 25**) through both brake pads. Screw it into the caliper assembly and tighten securely.
  b. Use needlenose pliers and install the clip (A, **Figure 25**). Make sure it seats correctly in the pad pin retainer groove.
16. Install the cover (B, **Figure 22**) and screws (A). Tighten the screws securely.
17. Repeat Steps 3-16 for the other caliper assembly.
18. Remove the spacer from between the front brake lever and the throttle grip.
19. Place the motorcycle on the centerstand with the front wheel off the ground.
20. Spin the front wheel and activate the front brake lever as many times as it takes to refill the caliper cylinders and locate the brake pads correctly against the disc.
21. Refill the master cylinder reservoir, if necessary, to maintain the correct fluid level as indicated on the side of the reservoir. Install the diaphragm and cover and tighten the cover securely.

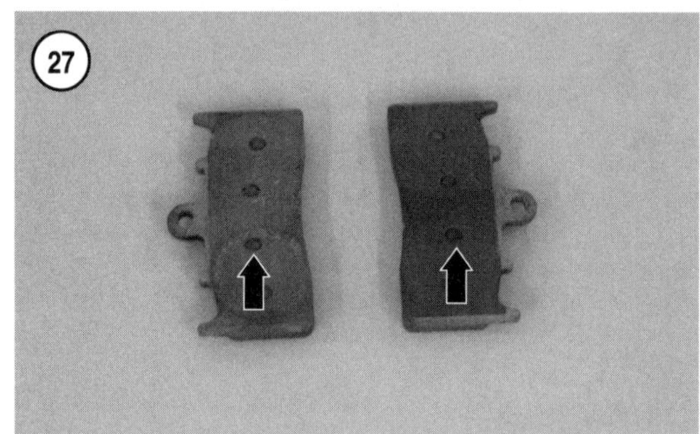

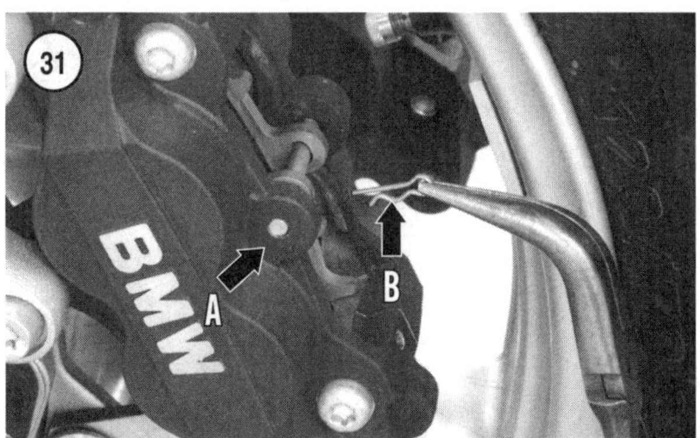

22. On non-ABS equipped models, if necessary, refill and bleed the system as described in this chapter.

23. On ABS equipped models, if necessary, have the brake system filled and bled by a BMW dealership.

WARNING
Do not ride the motorcycle until the front brakes are operating correctly with full hydraulic advantage.

24. Follow the brake pad manufacturer's instructions regarding break-in of the lining material.

2004 R1150GS Models

1. Read *Brake Service* in this chapter.
2. The pistons must be repositioned in the caliper assembly prior to installing the new brake pads. The front master cylinder brake fluid level will rise as the caliper pistons are repositioned. Perform the following:
   a. Remove the screws securing the cover and remove the cover **Figure 32** and the diaphragm from the master cylinder.
   b. Use a shop syringe and remove about 50% of the brake fluid from the reservoir. Do *not* remove more than 50% of the brake fluid or air will enter the system. Discard the brake fluid properly.
3. Carefully push, then pull, the caliper against the brake disc. This will press the pistons back into the caliper bores. This will allow room for the new brake pads

CAUTION
Do not allow the master cylinder to overflow when performing Step 3. Brake fluid damages most surfaces it contacts.

CAUTION
The pistons should move smoothly when compressing them in Step 3. If not, check the caliper for sticking pistons or damaged caliper bores, pistons and seals. Repair requires the overhaul of the brake caliper assembly.

4. To prevent the accidental application of the front brake lever, place a spacer between the front brake lever and the throttle grip and secure it in place. If the brake lever is inadvertently squeezed, the pistons will not get forced out of the cylinders.
5. Use needlenose pliers and remove the clip (**Figure 33**).
6. Unscrew and remove the pad retaining pin and withdraw it from the caliper assembly (A, **Figure 34**).

7. Unhook and remove the pad spring (A, **Figure 35**).

NOTE
If the brake pads are going to be reused, mark them so they can be reinstalled into their original locations.

8. Remove both brake pads.
9. Clean the pad recess and the end of the pistons with a soft brush. Do not use solvent, a wire brush or any hard tool that would damage the pistons.
10. Carefully remove any rust or corrosion from the disc.
11. Lightly coat the end of the pistons and the backs of the *new* brake pads disc brake lubricant.
12. Check the brake pads for wear or damage. Measure the thickness of the brake pad friction material. Replace the brake pads if they are worn to the service limit in **Table 1**.
13. Check the friction surface of the *new* pads (**Figure 36**) for any debris or manufacturing residue. If necessary, clean them off with an aerosol brake cleaner.

NOTE
When purchasing new pads, make sure the friction compound of the new pad is compatible with the disc material. Remove roughness from the backs of the new pads with a fine-cut file, then thoroughly clean them with brake cleaner.

14. Install the outboard pad (**Figure 37**) and push it down into place.
15. Install the inboard pad (**Figure 38**) and push it down into place.
16. Hook the lower end of the pad spring (B, **Figure 35**) into the caliper, then push it down against both brake pads. Make sure the lower end is secured in place.
17. Insert the pad retaining pin (A, **Figure 34**) through the caliper and over the pad spring (B). Push the pin in, then screw it into the other side of the caliper and tighten securely.
18. Use needlenose pliers and install the clip (**Figure 33**). Make sure it seats correctly in the pad pin retainer groove.
19. Repeat Steps 3-18 for the other caliper assembly.
20. Remove the spacer from between the front brake lever and the throttle grip.
21. Place the motorcycle on the centerstand with the front wheel off of the ground.
22. Spin the front wheel and activate the front brake lever as many times as it takes to refill the caliper cylinders and locate the brake pads correctly against the disc.
23. Refill the master cylinder reservoir, if necessary, to maintain the correct fluid level as indicated on the side of

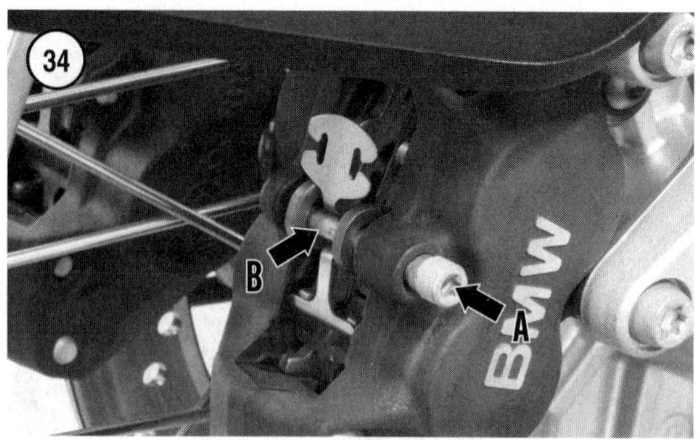

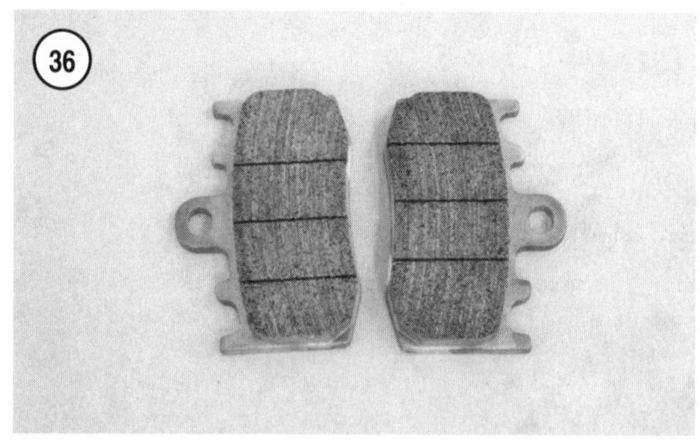

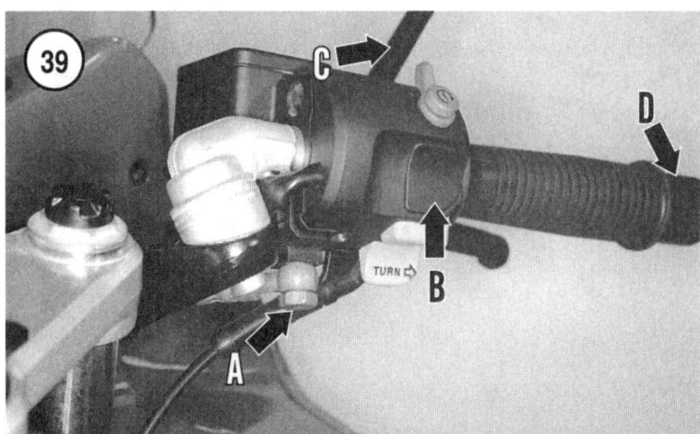

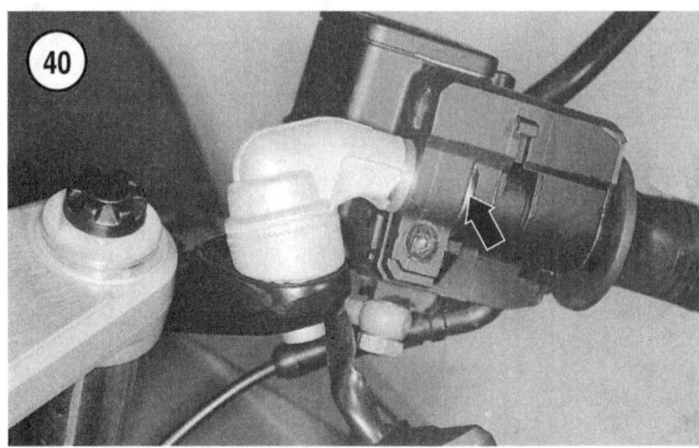

the reservoir. Install the diaphragm and cover and tighten the cover securely.

24. On non-ABS equipped models, if necessary, refill and bleed the system as described in this chapter.

25. On ABS equipped models, if necessary, have the brake system filled and bled by a BMW dealership.

WARNING
Do not ride the motorcycle until the front brakes are operating correctly with full hydraulic advantage.

26. Follow the brake pad manufacturer's instructions regarding break-in of the lining material.

FRONT MASTER CYLINDER

All Models Except R850C, R1100S, All R1150 and R1200C

Removal/installation

1. Read *Brake Service* in this chapter.
2. Place a couple of shop cloths under the union bolt and remove the union bolt and sealing washer (A, **Figure 39**) securing the brake hose to the master cylinder. Remove the brake hose. Tie the brake hose up and cover the end with a reclosable plastic bag to prevent leakage and contamination.
3. Disconnect the negative battery cable as described in Chapter Three.
4. Remove the screw securing the switch assembly (B, **Figure 39**) to the handlebar grip. Move the switch assembly out of the way.
5. Remove the throttle cable cover (**Figure 40**) and disconnect the throttle cable (**Figure 41**) from the throttle grip.
6. Remove the mounting screws and remove the front brake light switch from the master cylinder assembly.
7. On all models except RT models, unscrew and remove the rear view mirror (C, **Figure 39**).
8. Remove the screw and withdraw the handlebar weight (D, **Figure 39**).

9A. For models without heated grips, cut along the length of the hand grip and remove it from the handlebar.

9B. For models with heated grips, perform the following:
   a. Fold back the rubber grip at the end fitting.
   b. Remove the hand grip mounting screws.
   c. Disconnect the electrical cable connector and unfasten the cable shoes.
   d. Pull the electrical cable through the handlebar and remove the heated grip assembly.

14

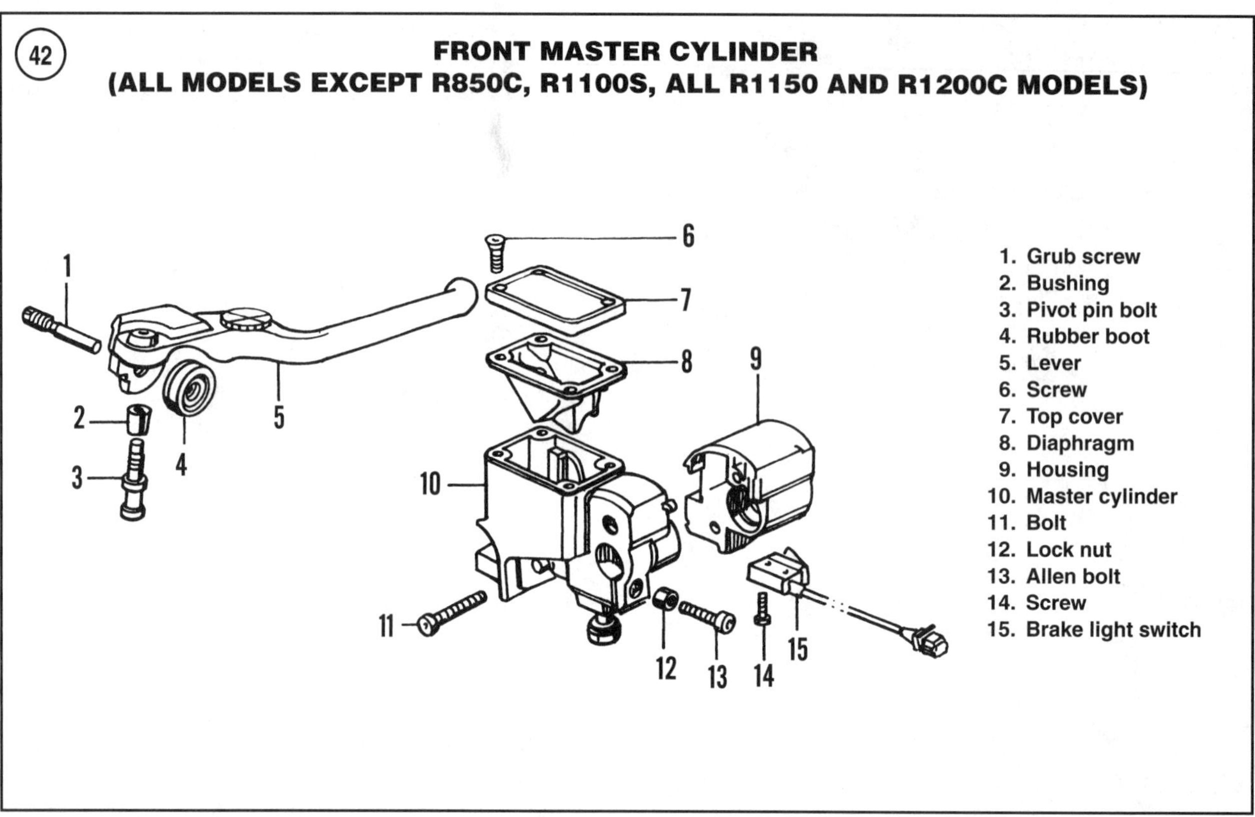

10. Loosen the clamping screw and slide the grip and master cylinder assembly off the end of the handlebar.

11. Install by reversing the removal steps while noting the following:

a. Install the grip assembly onto the handlebar and align the grip slot with the punch mark on the handlebar. Tighten the clamping screw securely.

b. Make sure the throttle cable routes properly in the throttle housing and attaches to the throttle wheel receptacle.

c. Install the brake hose onto the master cylinder. Be sure to place a new sealing washer on each side of the fitting and install the union bolt. Tighten the union bolt to 15 N•m (128 in.-lb.).

d. Check the fluid level in the front master cylinder and top it off if necessary.

e. On non-ABS equipped models, if necessary, refill and bleed the system as described in this chapter.

f. On ABS equipped models, if necessary, have the brake system filled and bled by a BMW dealership.

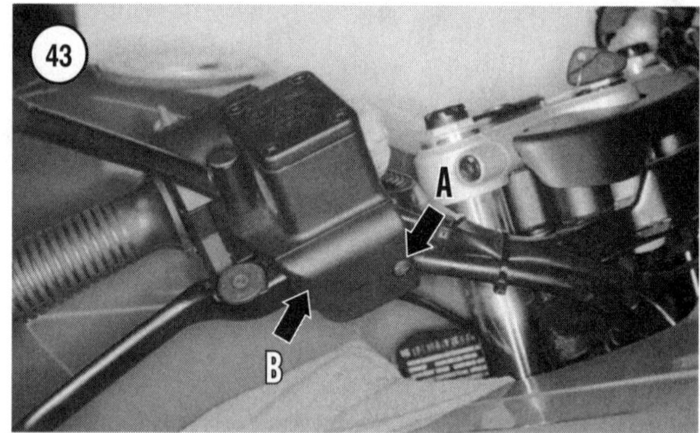

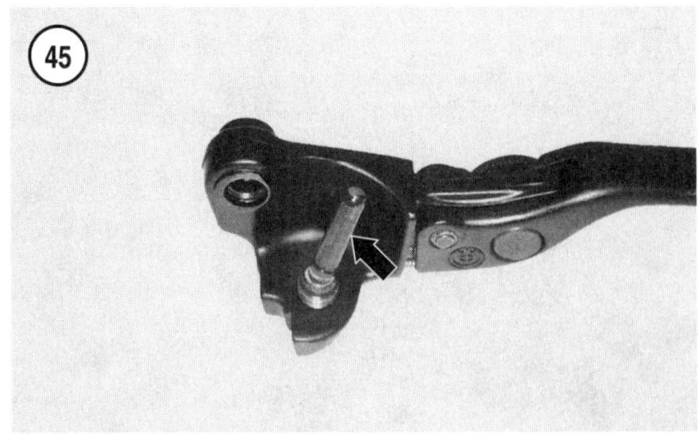

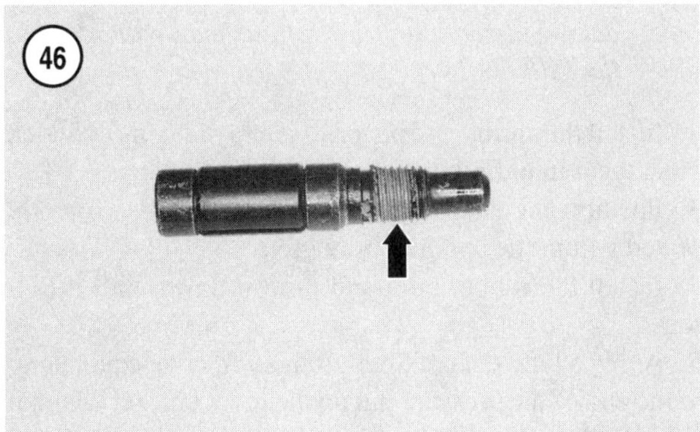

Disassembly/inspection/assembly

It is not necessary to remove the master cylinder from the handlebar to replace the available components.

Refer to **Figure 42**.

NOTE
*The piston assembly is an integral part of the master cylinder body and cannot be replaced separately. The available replacement parts are shown in **Figure 42**.*

1. To service the hand lever, remove the screw (A, **Figure 43**) securing the side cover (B) and remove the cover.
2. Remove the pivot pin bolt securing the hand lever to the master cylinder body.
3. Pull the hand lever straight out and away from the master cylinder body and the rubber boot and remove the lever.
4. Check the rubber boot (**Figure 44**) for wear, hardness or tears. Replace the rubber boot if necessary.
5. Check the tightness of the grub screw (**Figure 45**) on the hand lever. If it is loose, perform the following;
   a. Remove the grub screw and clean off the threadlocking compound from the threads.
   b. Apply a medium strength threadlocking compound to the threads.

WARNING
Never tighten the grub screw more than specified in substep c. If it is tightened further than 1/2 turn, the brakes could fail or be locked on.

   c. Install the grub screw and slowly tighten until there is no play at the hand lever, *then* tighten the screw exactly an additional 1/2 turn.
6. Inspect the hand lever for cracks or damage. Replace the hand lever if necessary.
7. Apply a light coat of Shell Retinax A, or an equivalent, to the grub screw (**Figure 45**).
8. Clean the old threadlocking compound from the threads (**Figure 46**) of the hand lever pivot pin bolt.
9. Apply medium strength threadlocking compound to the threads of the pivot pin bolt.
10. Carefully install the hand lever onto the master cylinder and boot.
11. Install the pivot pin bolt (**Figure 47**) and tighten to 7 N•m (62 in.-lb.).
12. Install the side cover (B, **Figure 43**) and screw (A), tightening the screw securely.
13. To service the master cylinder cover and diaphragm, remove the screws securing the cover (**Figure 48**) and remove the cover.

14. Carefully withdraw the diaphragm (**Figure 49**) from the master cylinder.
15. If necessary, remove the brake fluid from the reservoir and dispose of it properly.
16. Inspect the diaphragm for hardness or damage and replace if necessary.
17. Install the cover and partially tighten the screws.
18A. On non-ABS equipped models, if necessary, refill and bleed the system as described in this chapter.
18B. On ABS equipped models, if necessary, have the brake system filled and bled by a BMW dealership.

R850C, R1100S, All R1150 and R1200C Models

Disassembly

It is not necessary to remove the master cylinder from the handlebar to replace the available components. The available replacement parts are shown in **Figure 50**.

1. Read *Brake Service* in this chapter.
2. Cover the fuel tank and front fairing with a heavy cloth or plastic tarp to protect them from accidental brake fluid spills.
3. Remove the screws securing the cover and remove the cover (**Figure 51**) and the diaphragm from the master cylinder.
4. Drain the brake fluid from the front brake system as described in *Front Brake Caliper Removal* in this chapter.
5. Remove the screw securing the throttle grip cover (**Figure 52**) and remove the cover.
6. Remove the pivot pin bolt securing the hand lever to the master cylinder body.
7. Pull the hand lever assembly straight out and away from the master cylinder body and the rubber boot and remove the lever. Do not lose the two small springs.
8. Carefully push back on the piston and remove the snap ring from the master cylinder bore.
9. Remove the piston assembly and spring from the master cylinder bore.
10. Inspect all parts as described in this section.

Assembly

1. Soak the new cups in clean DOT 4 brake fluid for 15 minutes to make them pliable. Coat the inside of the cylinder bore with clean brake fluid prior to the assembly of parts.

CAUTION
When installing the piston assembly, do not allow the cups to turn inside out as it will be damaged and allow brake fluid leaks within the cylinder bore.

2. Install the spring and piston assembly into the cylinder. Push them in until they bottom in the cylinder.
3. Position the snap ring and make sure it is correctly seated within the cylinder bore groove.
4. Install the rubber boot and push it down until it bottoms.
5. Apply a light coat of Shell Retinax A, or an equivalent, to the end of the pressure pin on the pivot bracket where it rides on the end of the piston.
6. If removed, install the two small springs into the receptacle in the lever.
7. Insert the hand lever assembly straight into the master cylinder body through the rubber boot. Position the brake light switch to make correct contact with the brake lever.
8. Install the pivot pin bolt securing the hand lever to the master cylinder body. Do not tighten.
9. Refill the master cylinder.
10. Turn the ignition switch on and test the brake light operation. Readjust the brake light switch if necessary. Turn the switch off.
11. Tighten the pivot screw to 11 N•m (79 in.-lb.).
12. Install the diaphragm and cover (**Figure 51**) and tighten the screws securely.
13. Have the ABS system bled by a BMW dealership.

Inspection

Replace worn or damage parts as described in this section. It is recommended that a new piston kit assembly be installed every time the master cylinder is disassembled.

1. Clean all parts in isopropyl alcohol or clean DOT 4 brake fluid. Inspect the cylinder bore surface for signs of wear and damage. If it is less than perfect, replace the

50

FRONT MASTER CYLINDER (R850C, R1100S, ALL R1150 AND R1200C MODELS)

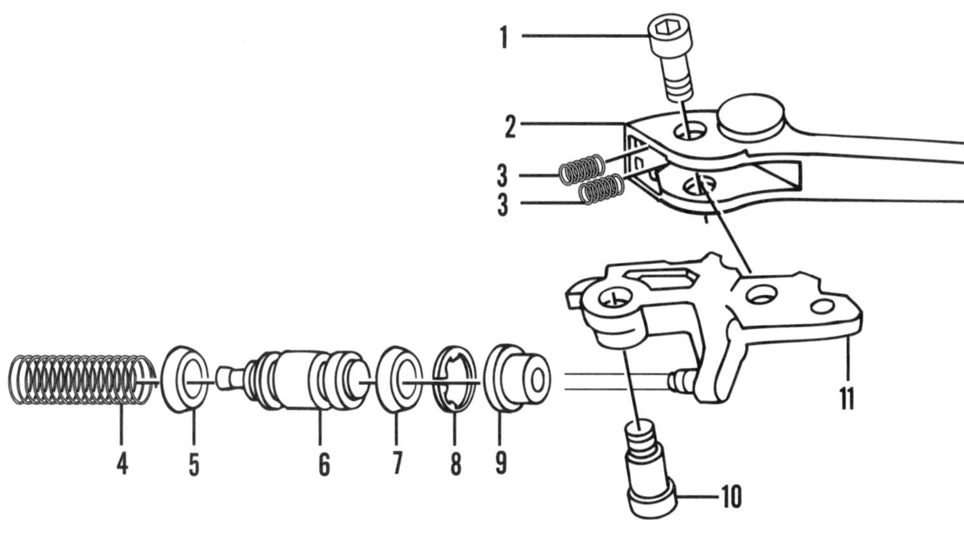

1. Screw
2. Lever
3. Spring
4. Spring
5. Secondary cup
6. Piston
7. Primary cup
8. Snap ring
9. Rubber boot
10. Pivot screw
11. Pivot bracket

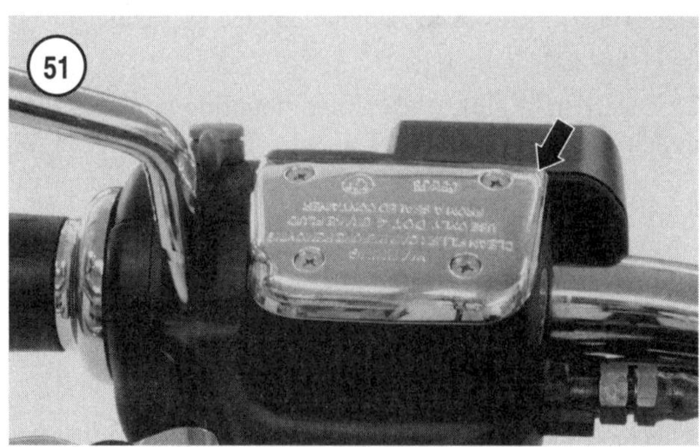

master cylinder assembly. The body cannot be replaced separately.

2. Inspect the piston cups for signs of wear and damage.
3. Inspect the piston contact surface for signs of wear and damage.
4. Check the end of the piston for wear caused by the hand lever pressure pin.
5. Check the hand lever pivot lugs in the master cylinder for cracks or elongation.
6. Inspect the hand lever pivot hole, and the pivot screw for wear, cracks or elongation.
7. Inspect the rubber boot for wear or deterioration.

FRONT CALIPER

All Models Without EVO Brakes Including Early R1100S Models

NOTE

*Models not equipped with the EVO (evolution) brake system have the BREMBO logo on the side of the caliper (A, **Figure 53**) and the toothed pulse-generating ring (B) is a heavy cast part.*

Removal

Refer to **Figure 54**.

1. Read the information under *Brake Service* in this chapter.
2. If the caliper assembly is going to be disassembled for service, perform the following:

NOTE
If the brake pads are going to be reused, mark them so they can be reinstalled into their original locations.

   a. Remove the brake pads as described in this chapter.
   b. Slowly apply the front brake lever to push the pistons part way out of the caliper assembly for ease of removal during caliper service.

3. Drain the hydraulic brake fluid from the front brake system as follows:
   a. Attach a hose to the bleed valve on both caliper assemblies.
   b. Place the loose end of the hose in a container to catch the brake fluid.
   c. Open the bleed valve and continue to apply the front brake lever until the brake fluid is pumped out of the system.
   d. Disconnect the hoses and tighten the bleed valves.
   e. Dispose of this brake fluid properly.
4. On RT models, remove the front fender as described in Chapter Fifteen.

CAUTION
The ABS electronic trigger sensor attaches to the left fork tube. Do not damage the sensor or its electrical cable during caliper removal.

5. On alloy wheels, place a piece of duct tape (**Figure 55**) on the wheel to protect the painted surface during caliper removal.
6. Remove the union bolt and sealing washers (A, **Figure 56**) securing the brake hose to the front caliper. Move the brake hose out of the way and place it in a plastic bag.

NOTE
*If the caliper assembly is going to be disassembled for service, loosen the four Allen bolts (B, **Figure 56**) securing the caliper assembly halves together. The fork slider makes a good holding fixture.*

7. Remove the two mounting bolts (C, **Figure 56**) and remove the front caliper (D).
8. If the caliper is not going to be serviced, place it in a reclosable plastic bag to keep it clean.

9. If necessary, repeat for the other caliper assembly.

Installation

CAUTION
The ABS electronic sensor attaches to the left fork tube assembly. Do not damage the sensor or the electrical cable during caliper installation.

1. Install the brake pads and the caliper assembly onto the disc. Be careful not to damage the leading edge of the pads during installation.
2. Install and tighten the caliper mounting bolts (C, **Figure 56**) to 40 N•m (29 ft.-lb.).

WARNING
*If the distance between the trigger sensor and pulse generating wheel is not maintained correctly, the ABS system will **not** function properly.*

3. After the left brake caliper is installed, inspect the distance between the ABS trigger sensor and the pulse generating wheel as described under *Trigger Sensor* in this chapter.
4. Attach the brake hoses to both calipers. Install a new sealing washer on each side of the hose fitting and tighten the union bolt (A, **Figure 56**) to 15 N•m (132 in.-lb.).
5. On RT models, install the front fender as described in Chapter Fifteen.

6A. On non-ABS equipped models, refill and bleed the system as described in this chapter.

6B. On ABS equipped models, have the brake system filled and bled by a BMW dealership.

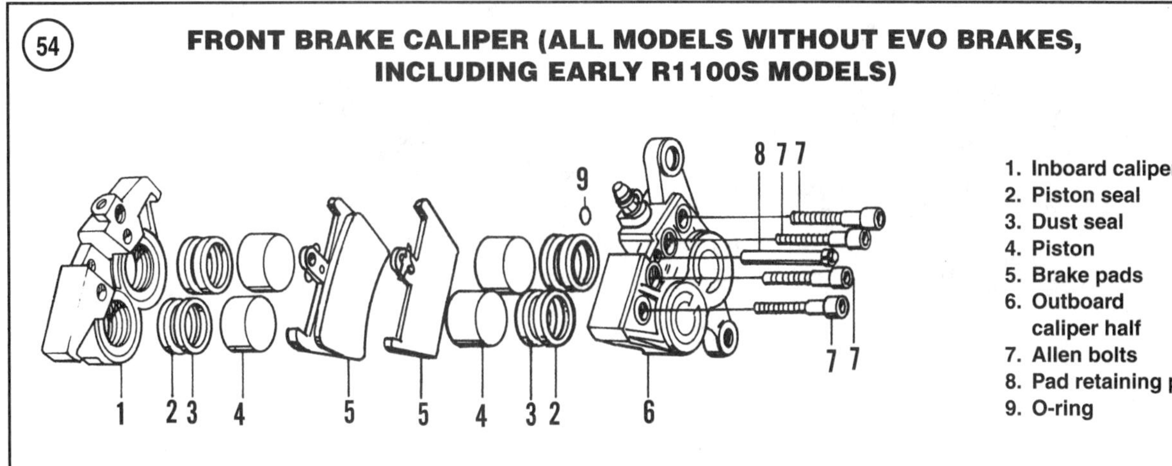

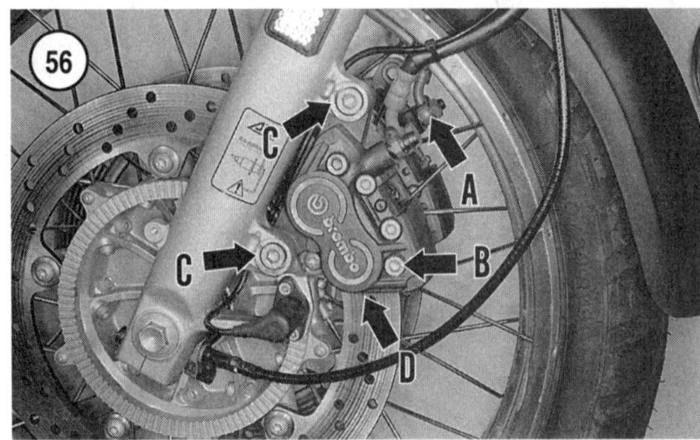

WARNING
Do not ride the motorcycle until the front brakes are operating correctly with full hydraulic advantage.

Disassembly

Refer to **Figure 54**.

NOTE
BMW does not recommend separating the caliper halves for service. However, this procedure is included if you choose to separate the caliper halves to service the caliper assembly.

1. Remove the caliper assembly and the brake pads as described in this chapter.
2. Remove the Allen bolts (**Figure 57**) securing both caliper halves together and separate the caliper halves.
3. Remove the small O-ring seal from the inboard caliper half.
4. Withdraw the pistons from each caliper body half. If the pistons are not easily removed, perform the following:

WARNING
Compressed air forces the pistons out of the caliper under considerable force. Do not cushion the pistons by hand, as injury could result.

a. Two different size pistons are used.
b. Support the caliper on a wooden block with the pistons facing down. Place a thick towel between the pistons and the workbench. Make sure there is enough space beneath the caliper for the pistons to be removed completely.
c. Direct compressed air through the brake line port (**Figure 58**) to remove the pistons.
d. Repeat the procedure for the pistons in the other caliper half.

5. Use a piece of wood or plastic scraper to carefully push the dust seal and piston seal in toward the caliper cylinder and out of their grooves. Remove the piston seals (**Figure 59**) in each caliper body half. Remove all dust seals and piston seals.

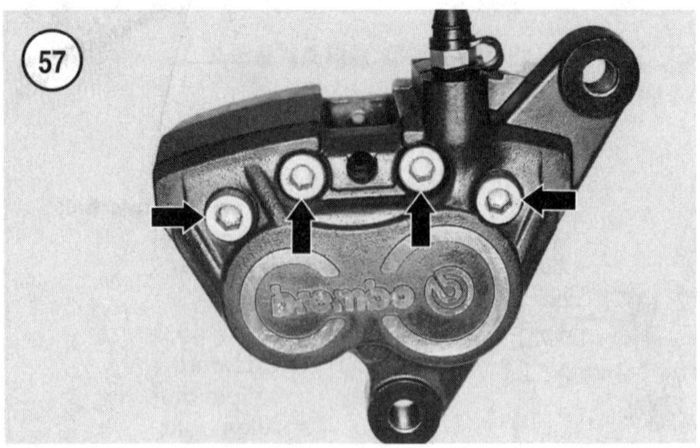

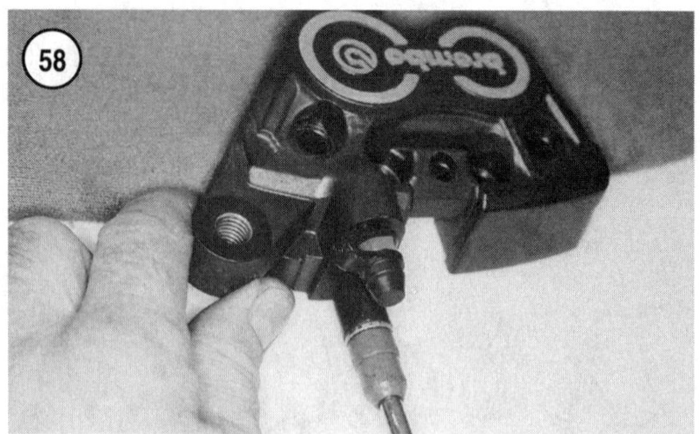

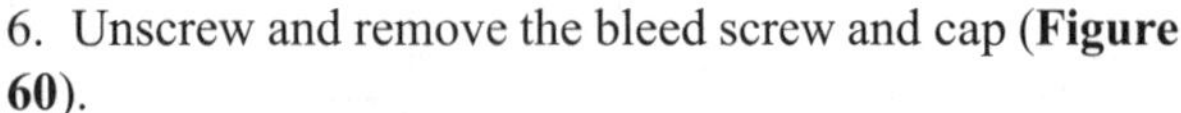
6. Unscrew and remove the bleed screw and cap (**Figure 60**).

Assembly

Use new DOT 4 brake fluid when lubricating the parts in the following steps.

NOTE
Before soaking the new piston and dust seals in brake fluid, compare them to the old parts, determine their sizes and match them to their respective bores. Be sure to install the correct size dust and piston seals into the appropriate cylinders. The seals will be damaged if the larger seals are installed into the smaller cylinders.

1. Soak the new piston and dust seals in DOT 4 brake fluid.
2. Lubricate the pistons and cylinder bores with DOT 4 brake fluid.

NOTE
*The dust seals (A, **Figure 61**) are thinner than the piston seals (B).*

3. Carefully install the new piston seal (**Figure 62**) in the lower groove in both cylinders in each caliper half. Make sure the seals seat properly in the lower grooves (A, **Figure 63**).
4. Carefully install the new dust seal (**Figure 64**) in the upper groove in both cylinders in each caliper half. Make sure the seals seat properly in the upper grooves (B, **Figure 63**).
5. Coat the pistons and the caliper cylinders with fresh DOT 4 brake fluid.
6. Position the pistons with their open ends facing out toward the brake pads and install the pistons (**Figure 65**). Push the pistons (**Figure 66**) in until they bottom.

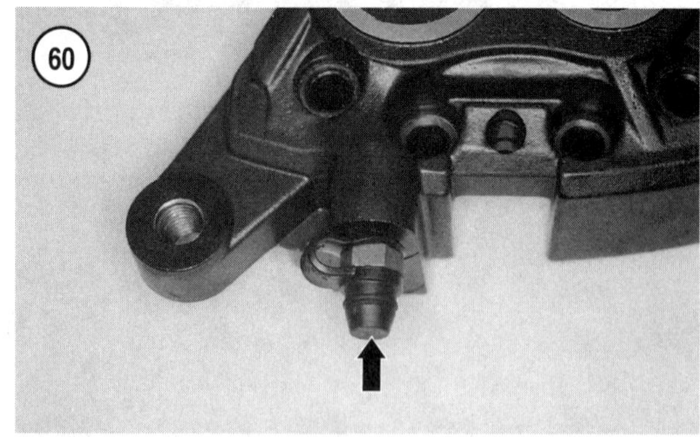

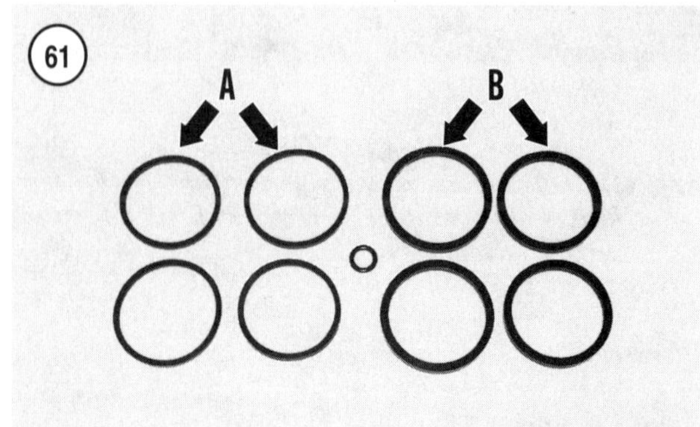

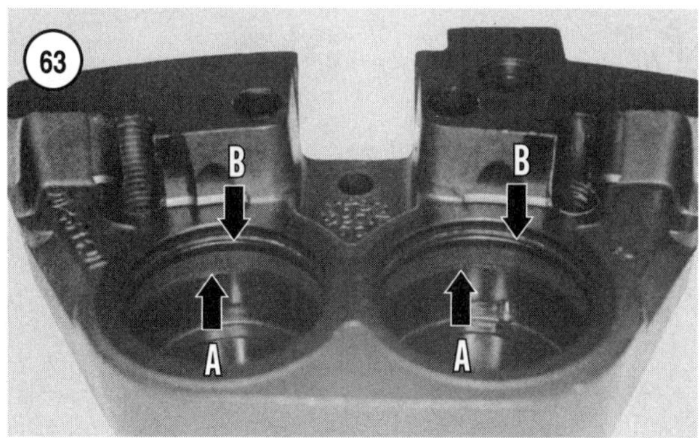

7. Install the bleed valve and cap (**Figure 60**).
8. Coat the O-ring seal with fresh DOT 4 brake fluid. Install a new O-ring seal (**Figure 67**) into the recess in the inboard caliper half.
9. Lay the inboard caliper half down with the pistons facing up and install the outboard half on top of it. This is to prevent the small O-ring seal from falling out during assembly.
10. Install the Allen bolts (**Figure 57**) securing the caliper assembly halves together. Tighten the bolts securely at this time. After the caliper is mounted on the front fork assembly, recheck and tighten securely.
11. Install the brake caliper assembly as described in this chapter.

Inspection

The only specifications available are for a new piston. Refer to **Table 1**. If the caliper assembly exhibits any signs of wear or damage; replace it. Always replace the piston and dust seals whenever the pistons have been removed.

1. Clean both caliper body halves and piston in clean DOT 4 brake fluid or isopropyl alcohol and dry them with compressed air.

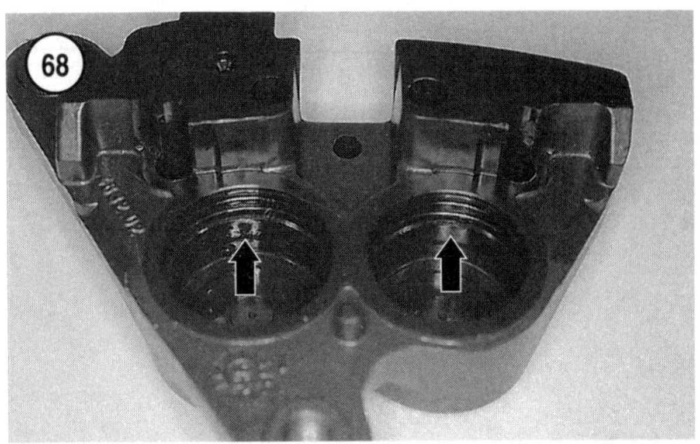

2. Inspect the piston and dust seal grooves (**Figure 68**) in both caliper body half for damage. If they are damaged or corroded, replace the caliper assembly.

3. Make sure the fluid passageways (**Figure 69**) in both caliper body halves are clear. Apply compressed air to the opening and make sure it is clear. Clean them out, if necessary, with clean brake fluid.

4. Inspect the cylinder walls (**Figure 70**) and the pistons (**Figure 71**) for scratches, scoring or other damage. If either is rusty or corroded, replace the caliper assembly. The pistons cannot be replaced separately.

5. Inspect the fluid connecting passageway (**Figure 72**) in each caliper half. Make sure they are clean and open. Apply compressed air to the openings and make sure they are clear.

6. Inspect the union bolt hole threads (**Figure 73**). If it is worn or damage, clean it out with a metric thread tap or replace the caliper assembly.

7. Inspect the bleed screw bolt hole threads. If it is worn or damage, clean it out with a metric thread tap or replace the caliper assembly.

8. Make sure the hole in the bleed screw is clean and open. Apply compressed air to the opening and make sure it is clear.

9. Inspect the caliper body halves for damage. Refer to **Figure 74** and **Figure 75**. If necessary, replace the caliper body.

10. Inspect the caliper half mounting bolt holes. If worn or damage, clean them out with a metric thread tap or replace the caliper assembly.

11. Inspect the caliper assembly mounting bolt holes (**Figure 76**) and bosses. Check for hole elongation or cracks.

12. Check the pad retaining pin and clip (**Figure 77**) for wear or damage.

13. Measure the outside diameter of the two different size pistons (**Figure 78**). Compare the acutal measurements to the specifications in **Table 2**.

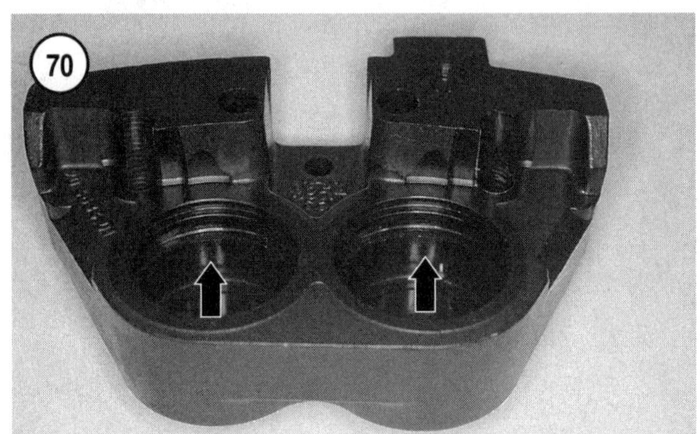

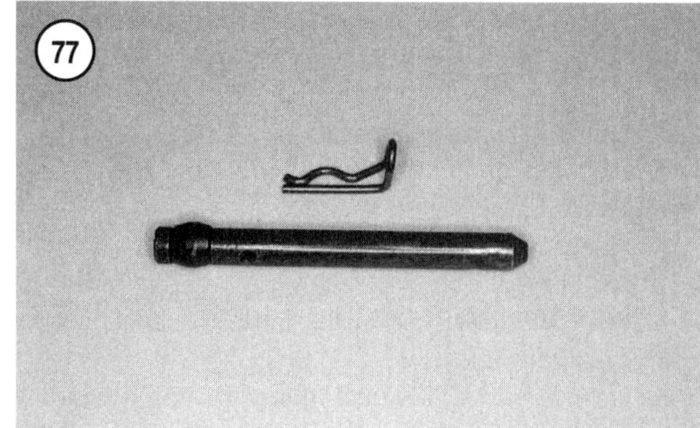

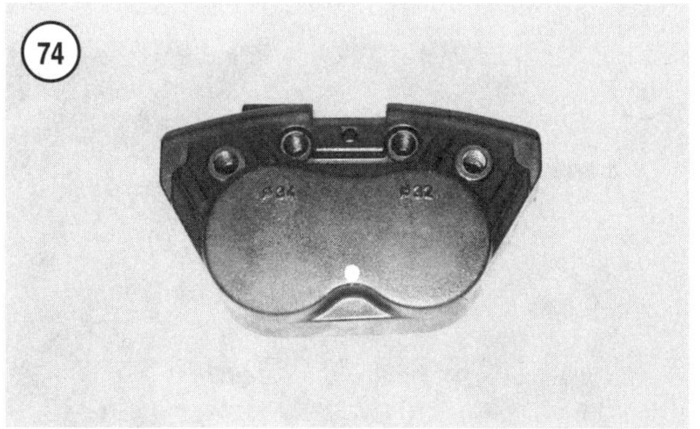

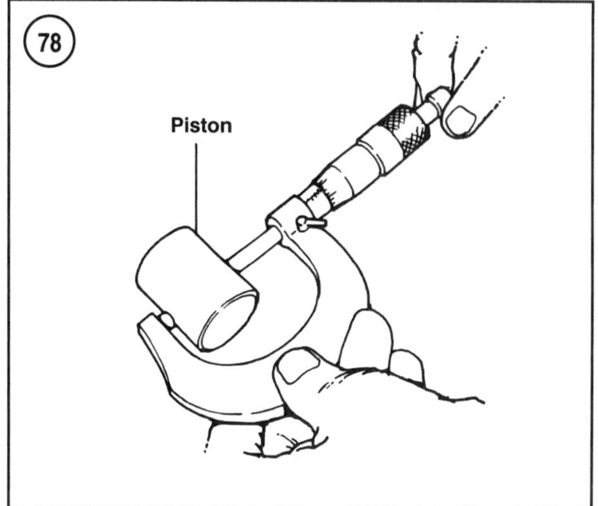

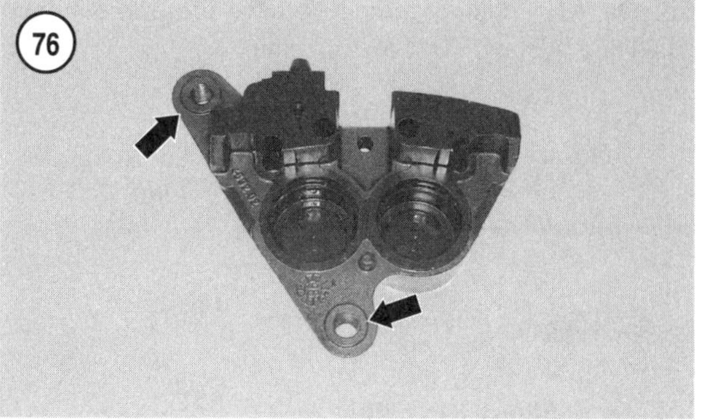

All Models With EVO Brakes Including Late R1100S Models

NOTE
*Models equipped with the EVO (evolution) brake system have the BMW logo on the side of the caliper (A, **Figure 79**) and the toothed pulse-generating ring (B) is a stamped part instead of being a heavier cast part.*

Removal

1. Read the information under *Brake Service* in this chapter.
2. If the caliper assembly is going to be disassembled for service, perform the following:

NOTE
If the brake pads are going to be reused, mark them so they can be reinstalled into their original locations.

a. Remove the brake pads as described in this chapter.
b. Slowly apply the front brake lever to push the pistons part way out of the caliper assembly for ease of removal during caliper service.

3. Drain the hydraulic brake fluid from the front brake system as follows:
a. Attach a hose to the bleed valve on both caliper assemblies.
b. Place the loose end of the hose in a container to catch the brake fluid.
c. Open the bleed valve and continue to apply the front brake lever until the brake fluid is pumped out of the system.
d. Disconnect the hoses and tighten the bleed valves.
e. Dispose of this brake fluid properly.

4. On RT models, remove the front fender as described in Chapter Fifteen.

CAUTION
The ABS electronic trigger sensor attaches to the left fork tube. Do not damage the sensor or its electrical cable during caliper removal.

5. On alloy wheels, place a piece of duct tape on the wheel rim to protect the surface during caliper removal.
6. Remove the union bolt and sealing washers (A, **Figure 80**) securing the brake hose to the front caliper. Move the brake hose out of the way and place it in a plastic bag.
7. Remove the two mounting bolts (B, **Figure 80**) and remove the front caliper (C).
8. If the caliper is not going to be serviced, place it in a reclosable plastic bag to keep it clean.
9. If necessary, repeat for the other caliper assembly.

Installation

CAUTION
The ABS electronic sensor attaches to the left fork tube assembly. Do not damage the sensor or the electrical cable during caliper installation.

1. Install the brake pads and the caliper assembly onto the disc. Be careful not to damage the leading edge of the pads during installation.
2. Install and tighten the caliper mounting bolts (B, **Figure 80**) to 30 N•m (22 ft.-lb.).

WARNING
If the distance between the trigger sensor and pulse generating wheel is not maintained correctly, the ABS system will ***not*** *function properly.*

3. After the left brake caliper is installed, inspect the distance between the ABS trigger sensor and the pulse generating wheel as described under *Trigger Sensor* in this chapter.
4. Attach the brake hoses to both calipers. Install a new sealing washer on each side of the hose fitting and tighten the union bolt (A, **Figure 80**) to 18 N•m (13 ft.-lb.).
5. On RT models, install the front fender as described in Chapter Fifteen.

6A. On non-ABS equipped models, refill and bleed the system as described in this chapter.

6B. On ABS equipped models, have the brake system filled and bled by a BMW dealership.

WARNING
Do not ride the motorcycle until the front brakes are operating correctly with full hydraulic advantage.

Disassembly

Refer to **Figure 81** and **Figure 82**.

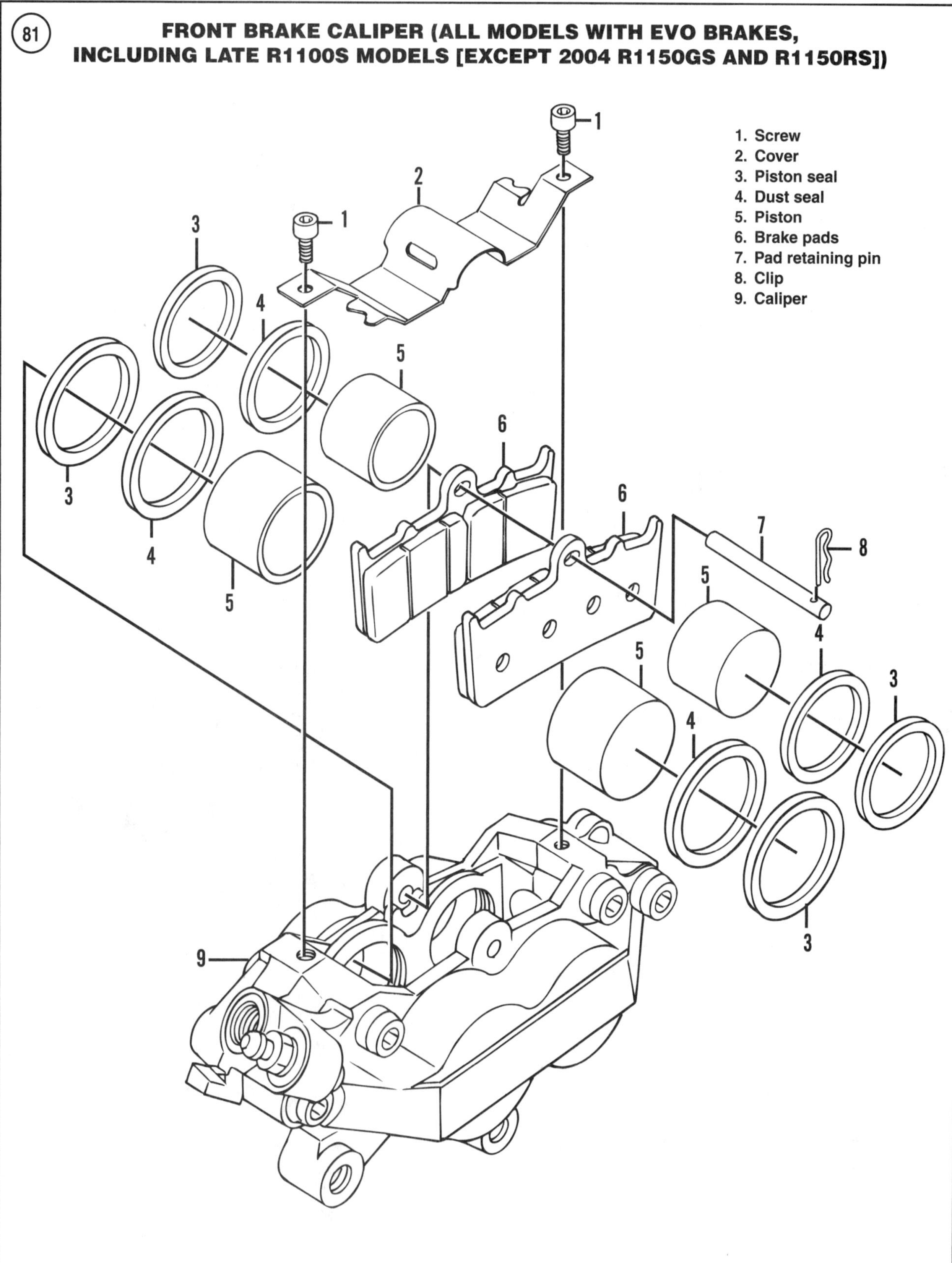
81
FRONT BRAKE CALIPER (ALL MODELS WITH EVO BRAKES, INCLUDING LATE R1100S MODELS [EXCEPT 2004 R1150GS AND R1150RS])
1. Screw
2. Cover
3. Piston seal
4. Dust seal
5. Piston
6. Brake pads
7. Pad retaining pin
8. Clip
9. Caliper
1
2
3
4
5
6
7
8
9

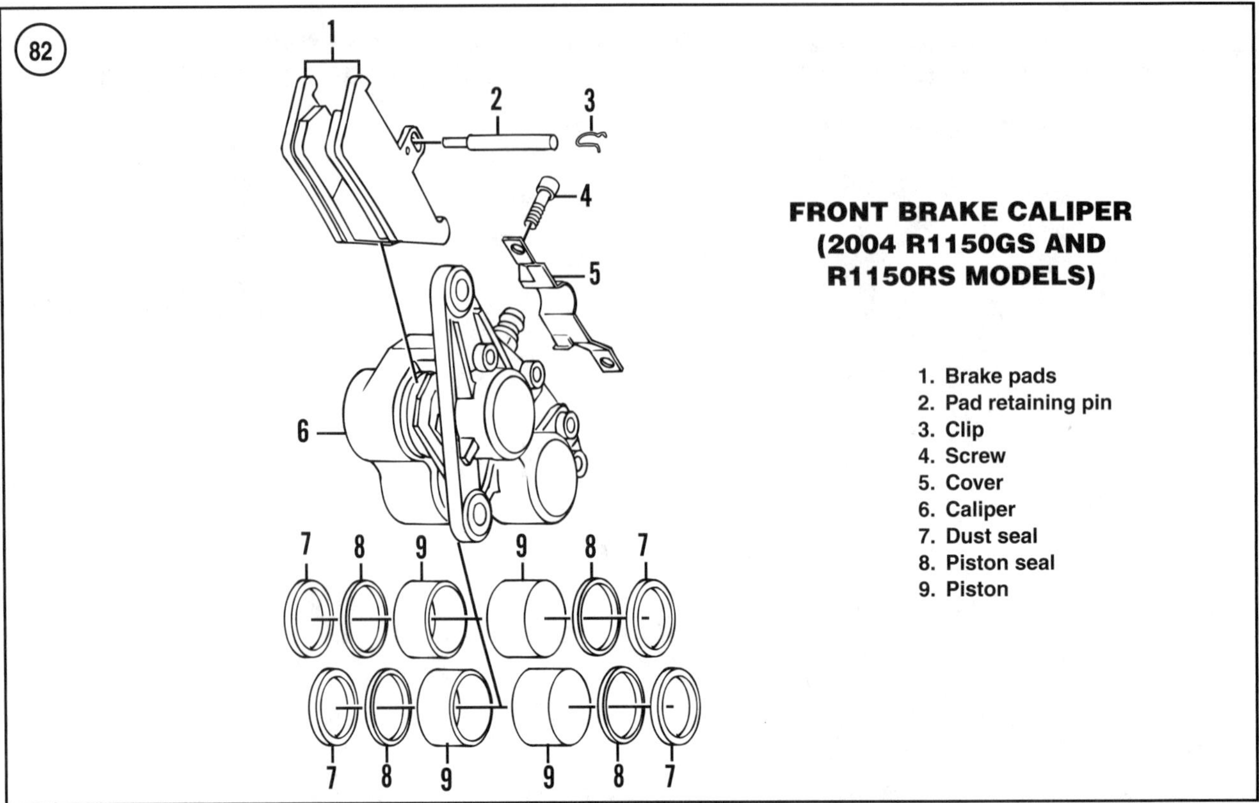

1. Remove the caliper assembly and the brake pads as described in this chapter.
2. Withdraw the pistons from each caliper body half. If the pistons are not easily removed, perform the following:

WARNING
Compressed air forces the pistons out of the caliper under considerable force. Do not cushion the pistons by hand, as injury could result.

   a. Two different size pistons are used.
   b. Place a thick towel between the two sets of pistons. Make sure there is enough space so the pistons can be partially removed from the caliper bores.
   c. Direct compressed air through the union bolt port (A, **Figure 83**) to partially remove the pistons.
   d. Repeat the procedure for the pistons in the other caliper half.
3. Remove the pistons from the caliper halves.
4. Use a piece of wood or plastic scraper to carefully push the dust seal and piston seal in toward the caliper cylinder and out of their grooves. Remove all dust and piston seals.
5. Unscrew and remove the bleed screw (B, **Figure 83**).

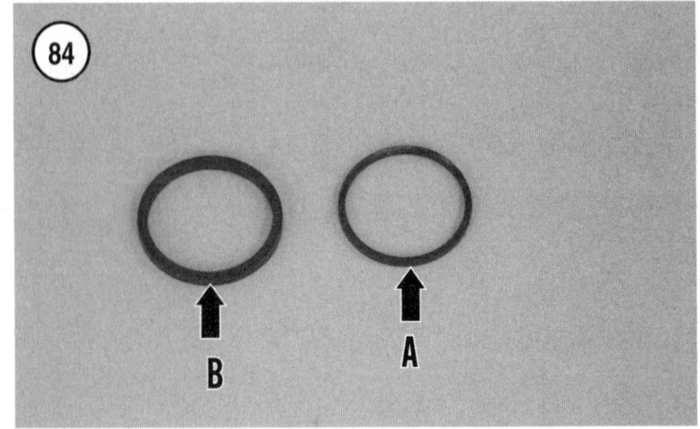

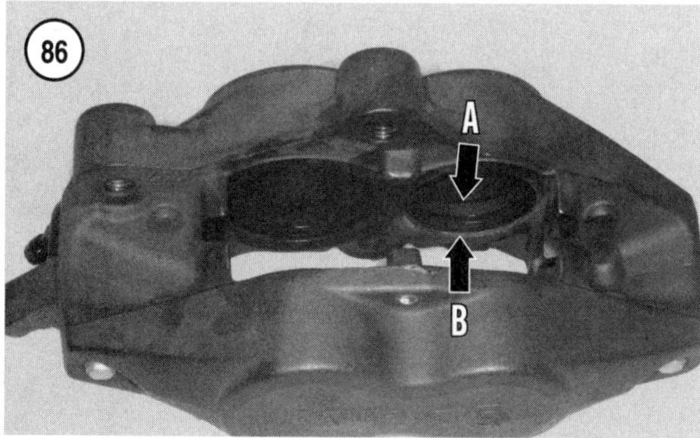

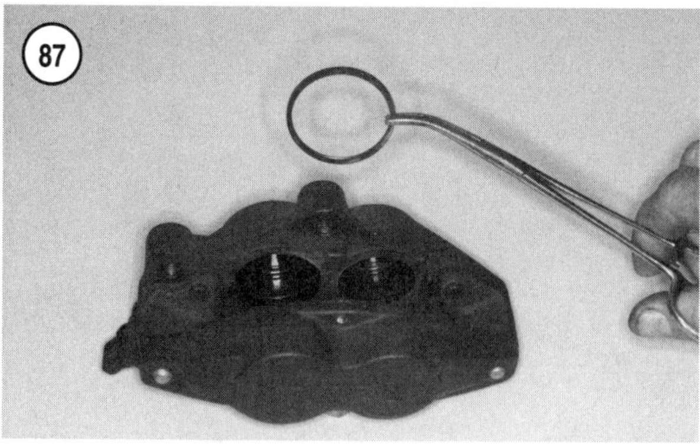

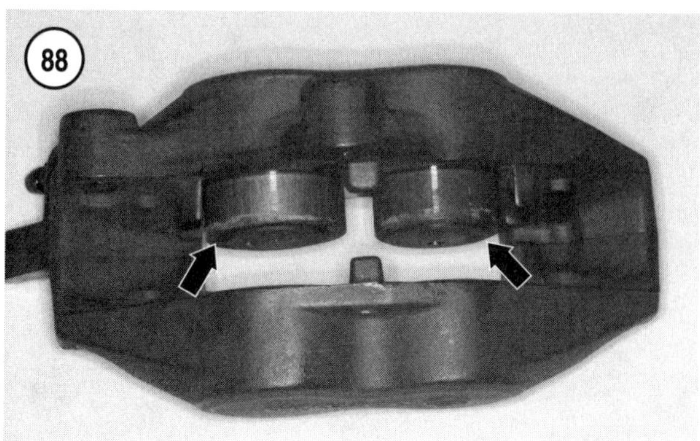

Assembly

Use new DOT 4 brake fluid when lubricating the parts in the following steps.

NOTE
Before soaking the new piston and dust seals in brake fluid, compare them to the old parts, determine their sizes and match them to their respective bores. Be sure to install the correct size dust and piston seals into the appropriate cylinders. The seals will be damaged if the larger seals are installed into the smaller cylinders.

1. Soak the new piston and dust seals in DOT 4 brake fluid.
2. Lubricate the pistons and cylinder bores with DOT 4 brake fluid.

NOTE
*The dust seals (A, **Figure 84**) are thinner than the piston seals (B).*

3. Carefully install the new piston seal (**Figure 85**) in the lower groove in both cylinders in each caliper half. Make sure the seals seat properly in the lower grooves (A, **Figure 86**).
4. Carefully install the new dust seal (**Figure 87**) in the upper groove in both cylinders in each caliper half. Make sure the seals seat properly in the upper grooves (B, **Figure 86**).
5. Coat the pistons and the caliper cylinders with fresh DOT 4 brake fluid.
6. Position the pistons with their open ends facing out toward the brake pads and install the pistons (**Figure 88**). Push the pistons in until they bottom.
7. Install the bleed valve (B, **Figure 83**).
8. Install the brake caliper assembly as described in this chapter.

Inspection

The only specification available is for new pistons. Refer to **Table 1**. If the caliper assembly exhibits any signs of wear or damage; replace it. Always replace the piston and dust seals whenever the pistons have been removed.

1. Clean the caliper body and pistons in clean DOT 4 brake fluid or isopropyl alcohol and dry them with compressed air.
2. Inspect the piston and dust seal grooves (A, **Figure 89**) in the caliper body for damage. If they are damaged or corroded, replace the caliper assembly.

3. Make sure the fluid passageways in both sides of caliper body are clear. Apply compressed air to the opening and make sure it is clear. Clean them out, if necessary, with clean brake fluid.
4. Inspect the cylinder walls (B, **Figure 89**) and the pistons (**Figure 90**) for scratches, scoring or other damage. If either is rusty or corroded, replace the caliper assembly. The pistons cannot be replaced separately.
5. Inspect the union bolt hole threads (A, **Figure 83**). If it is worn or damaged, clean it out with a metric thread tap or replace the caliper assembly.
6. Inspect the bleed screw bolt hole threads. If it is worn or damage, clean it out with a metric thread tap or replace the caliper assembly.
7. Make sure the hole in the bleed screw is clean and open. Apply compressed air to the opening and make sure it is clear.
8. Inspect the caliper body for damage. If necessary, replace the caliper body.
9. Inspect the caliper assembly mounting bolt holes (A, **Figure 91**) and bosses. Check for hole elongation or cracks.
10. Even though the caliper halves were not disassembled, check the tightness of the four bolts (B, **Figure 91**) securing the halves together. If loose, tighten them securely.
11. Check the pad retaining pin and clip (**Figure 92**) for wear or damage.
12. Measure the outside diameter of the two different size pistons (**Figure 93**). Compare the actual measurements to the specifications in **Table 1**.

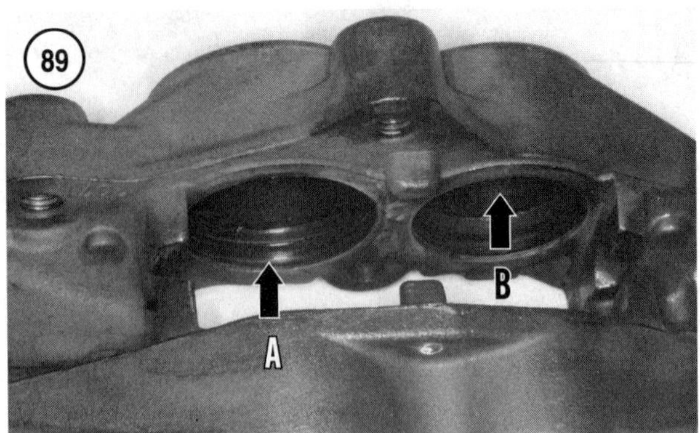

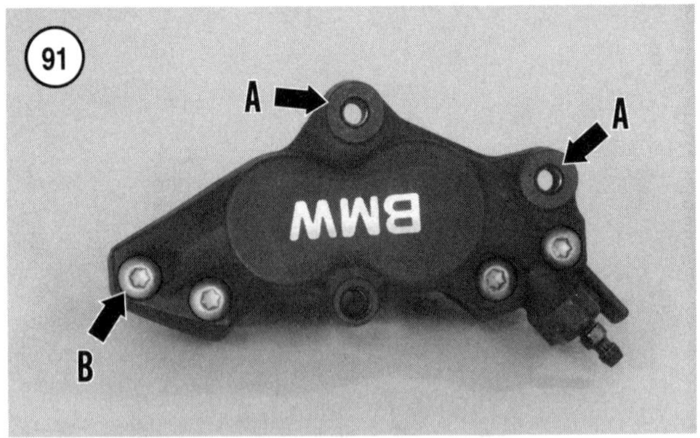

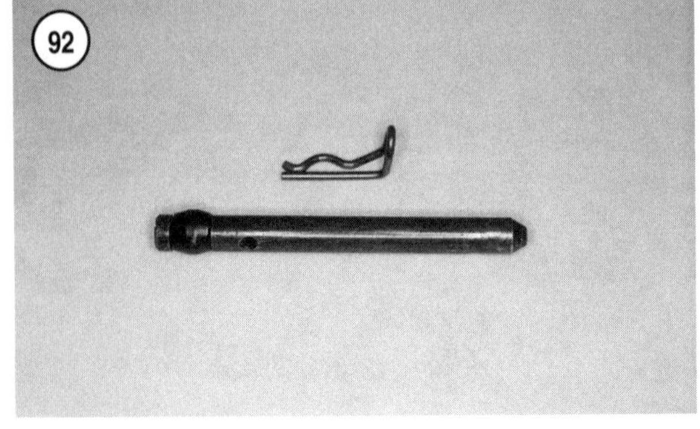

REAR BRAKE PAD REPLACEMENT

R1100RS Models

1. Read the information under *Brake Service* in this chapter.
2. Remove seat as described in Chapter Fifteen.
3. Remove the rear right side panels as described in Chapter Fifteen.
4. The pistons must be repositioned in the caliper assembly prior to installing the new brake pads. The rear master cylinder brake fluid level will rise as the caliper pistons are repositioned. Perform the following:
   a. Unscrew the cover and remove the cover and the diaphragm from the master cylinder remote reservoir (**Figure 94**).
   b. Use a shop syringe and remove about 50% of the brake fluid from the reservoir. Do not remove more than 50% of the brake fluid or air will enter the system. Discard the brake fluid properly.

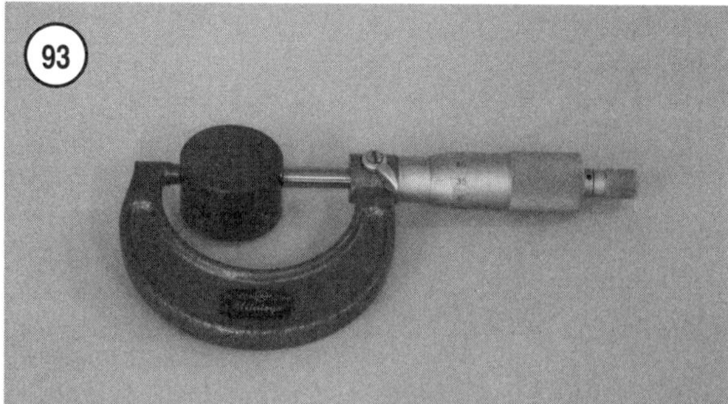

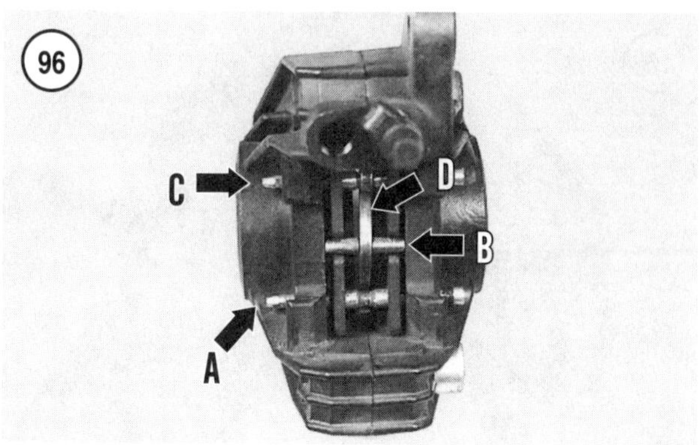

5. Carefully push, then pull, the caliper against the brake disc. This will press the pistons back into the caliper bores. This will allow room for the new brake pads

CAUTION
Do not allow the master cylinder to overflow when performing Step 5. Brake fluid damages most surfaces it contacts.

CAUTION
The pistons should move smoothly when compressing them in Step 5. If not, check the caliper for sticking pistons or damaged caliper bores, pistons and seals. Repair requires the overhaul of the brake caliper assembly.

6. Remove the caliper from the brake disc as described in this chapter. Do not disconnect the hydraulic brake line from the caliper.

7. To prevent the accidental application of the rear brake pedal, secure the pedal to the frame so it cannot be depressed. The pistons will get forced out of the cylinders, if the brake pedal is inadvertenly depressed.

8. Using a large screwdriver, carefully remove the brake caliper cover.

9. Remove the right rear footpeg assembly (A, **Figure 95**) as described in Chapter Fifteen.

10. Remove the mounting bolts securing the caliper (B, **Figure 95**) and remove the rear caliper from the disc. Do not disconnect the hydraulic brake line from the caliper assembly.

NOTE
The following procedure is shown with the caliper completely removed to better illustrate the steps. It is not necessary to completely remove the caliper assembly for this procedure.

11. Using a drift and small hammer, carefully tap out one of the lockpins (A, **Figure 96**) from the backside of the caliper.

12. Hold a finger over the center pin and retaining spring and remove that lockpin.

13. Remove the center pin (B, **Figure 96**).

14. Using a drift and small hammer, carefully tap the other lockpin (C, **Figure 96**) part way out of the caliper and remove the retaining spring (D, **Figure 96**).

15. Remove the inboard brake pad.

16. Remove the lockpin (C, **Figure 96**) from the caliper.

17. Remove the outboard brake pad.

18. Clean the pad recess and the end of the pistons with a soft brush. Do not use a solvent, wire brush or hard tool that would damage the pistons.
19. Carefully remove any rust or corrosion from the disc.
20. Lightly coat the end of the pistons and the backs of the new pads with disc brake lubricant.
21. Check the brake pads (**Figure 97**) for wear or damage. Measure the thickness of the brake pad friction material (**Figure 98**). Replace the brake pads if they are worn to the service limit in **Table 1**.
22. Check the friction surface of the new pads for any debris or manufacturing residue. If necessary, clean them off with an aerosol brake cleaner.

NOTE
When purchasing new pads, make sure the friction compound of the new pad is compatible with the disc material. Remove roughness from the backs of the new pads with a fine-cut file, then thoroughly clean them with brake cleaner.

23. Install the inboard pad and then the outboard pad. If the caliper is still in place on the brake disc, the brake pads may slip down in the caliper assembly since there is no stop to prevent them from doing so.
24. If necessary, pull the brake pads up until the holes align with the caliper assembly.
25. Install one lockpin and retaining spring through the holes in the caliper and both brake pads. Tap it in until it stops and locks in place.
26. Install the center pin into the notch in both brake pads.
27. Partially install the other lockpin through the outer hole in the caliper and outboard brake pad.
28. Press the retaining spring down and push the lockpin over the retaining spring end (**Figure 99**) and through the inboard brake pad and caliper. Tap it in until it stops and locks in place. Make sure the retaining spring hooks under both lockpins correctly and locates within the lockpin recess (**Figure 100**).
29. Install the brake caliper cover.
30. If removed, install the caliper (B, **Figure 95**) and tighten the mounting bolts to 40 N•m (29 ft.-lb.).
31. Install the right rear footpeg (A, **Figure 95**) as described in Chapter Fifteen.
32. Carefully roll the motorcycle back and forth and activate the brake pedal as many times as it takes to refill the cylinders in the caliper and correctly locate both brake pads.
33A. On non-ABS equipped models, refill and bleed the system as described in this chapter.

97

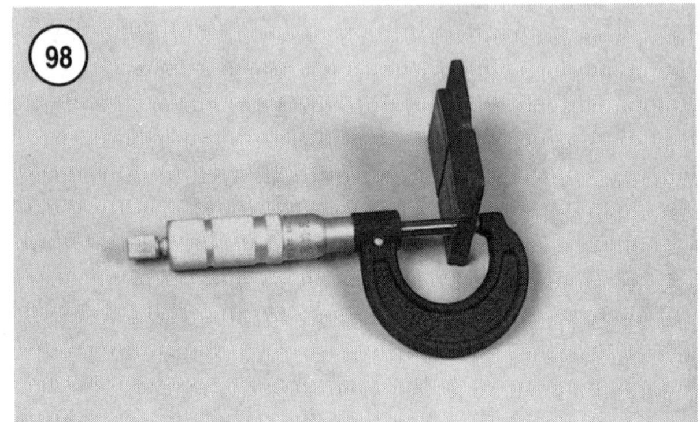
98

99

100

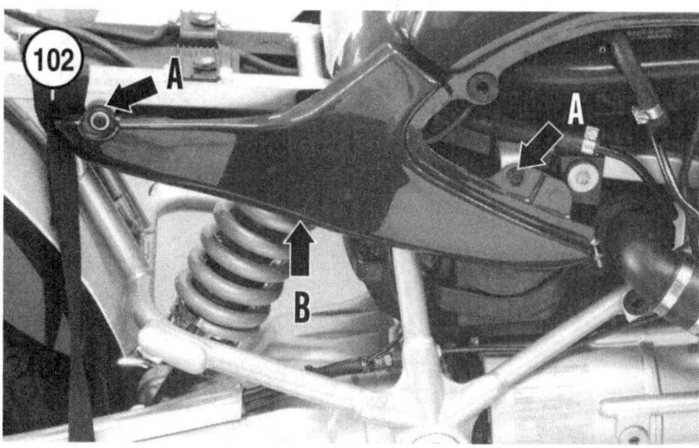

33B. On ABS equipped models, have the brake system filled and bled by a BMW dealership.

34. Install the diaphragm and cover.

WARNING
Do not ride the motorcycle until the front brakes are operating correctly with full hydraulic advantage.

35. Follow the brake pad manufacturer's instructions regarding break-in of the lining material.

All Models Except R1100RS

CAUTION
When changing brake pads, install the correct brake pads designed to work with that specific brake caliper. Do not install sintered-metal brake pads into a brake caliper designed to work with organic brake pads as it will result in an overheating problem leading to rear brake failure. Organic brake pads are black in color and sintered-metal are copper color.

NOTE
When purchasing new brake pads, order them by the motorcycle VIN number. Also check to make sure that the brake pads match the ones being replaced prior to installing them.

1. Read *Brake Service* in this chapter.
2. Remove seat as described in Chapter Fifteen.

3A. On R850C and R1200C models, perform the following:
   a. On the right side, pull straight out and release the posts on the chrome trim panel (**Figure 101**) from the rubber grommets on the fuel tank. Remove the chrome trim panel.
   b. Remove screws (A, **Figure 102**) securing the lower trim panel (B) and remove the trim panel.

3B. On all models except R850C and R1200C, remove the rear right side panels as described in Chapter Fifteen.

4. The pistons must be repositioned in the caliper assembly prior to installing the new brake pads. The rear master cylinder brake fluid level will rise as the caliper pistons are repositioned. Perform the following:
   a. Unscrew the cover and remove the cover and the diaphragm from the master cylinder remote reservoir. Refer to **Figure 103** and **Figure 104**.
   b. Use a shop syringe and remove about 50% of the brake fluid from the reservoir. Do not remove more

105

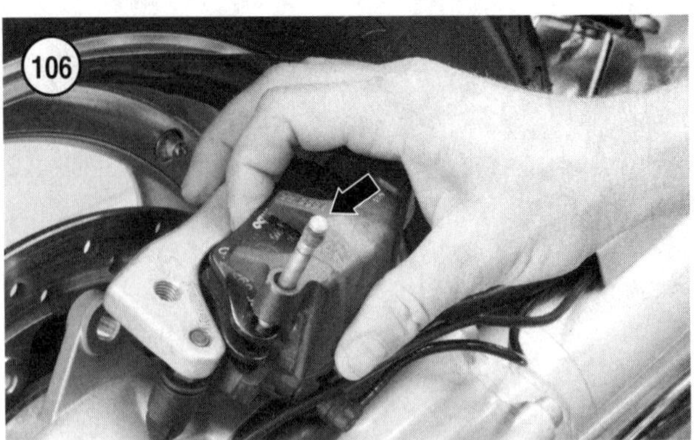

106

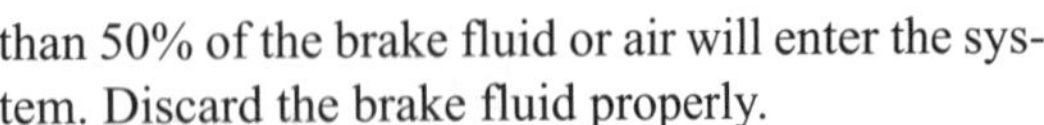

than 50% of the brake fluid or air will enter the system. Discard the brake fluid properly.

5. Carefully push, then pull, the caliper against the brake disc. This will press the pistons back into the caliper bores. This will allow room for the new brake pads.

CAUTION

Do not allow the master cylinder to overflow when performing Step 5. Brake fluid damages most surfaces it contacts.

CAUTION

The pistons should move smoothly when compressing them in Step 5. If not, check the caliper for sticking pistons or damaged caliper bores, pistons and seals. Repair requires the overhaul of the brake caliper assembly.

6. Remove the E-clip (**Figure 105**) from the outer end of the pad retaining pin.
7. Remove the caliper from the brake disc as described in this chapter. Do not disconnect the hydraulic brake line from the caliper.
8. To prevent the accidental application of the rear brake pedal, secure the pedal to the frame so it cannot be depressed. Then if the brake pedal is inadvertently depressed, the pistons well not get forced out of the cylinders.
9. Turn the caliper assembly upside down to gain access to the lower portion of the caliper.
10. Withdraw the pad retaining pin (**Figure 106**) from the caliper and both brake pads.
11. Remove both brake pads. Do not lose the anti-rattle spring (**Figure 107**).
12. Clean the pad recess and the end of the pistons (**Figure 108**) with a soft brush. Do not use a solvent, wire brush or hard tool that would damage the pistons.
13. Carefully remove any rust or corrosion from the disc.

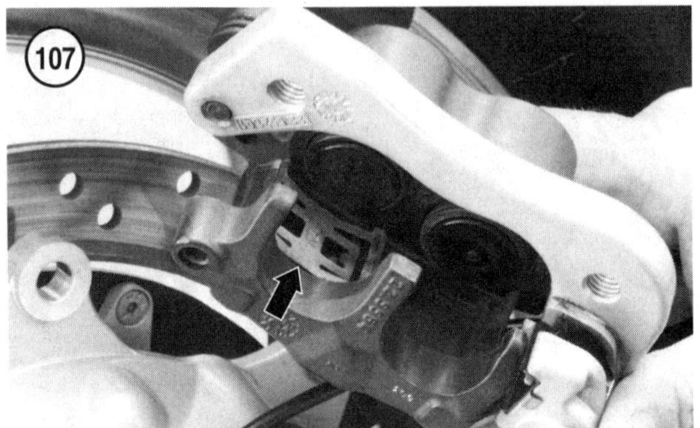

107

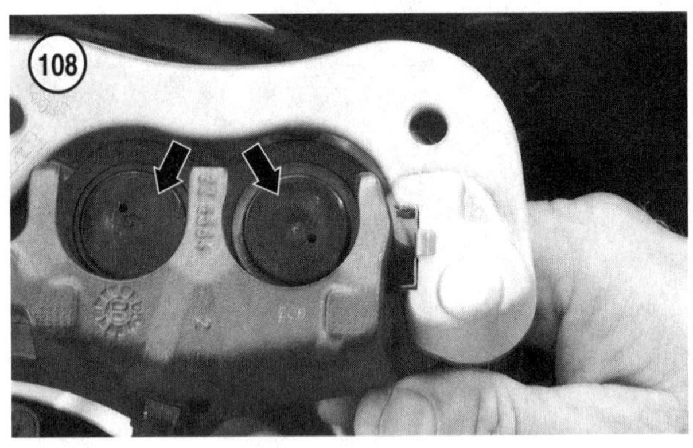

108

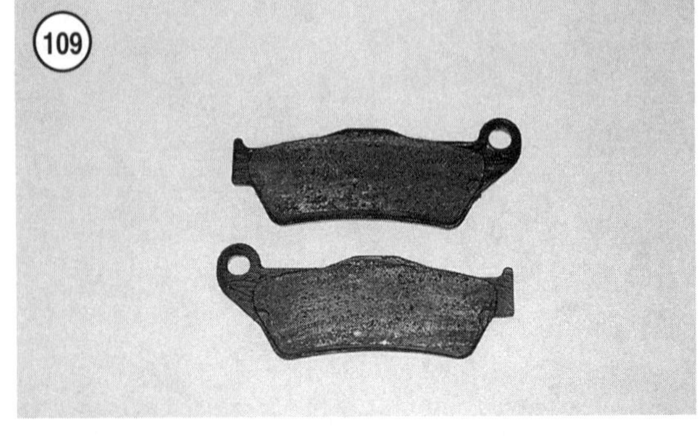

109

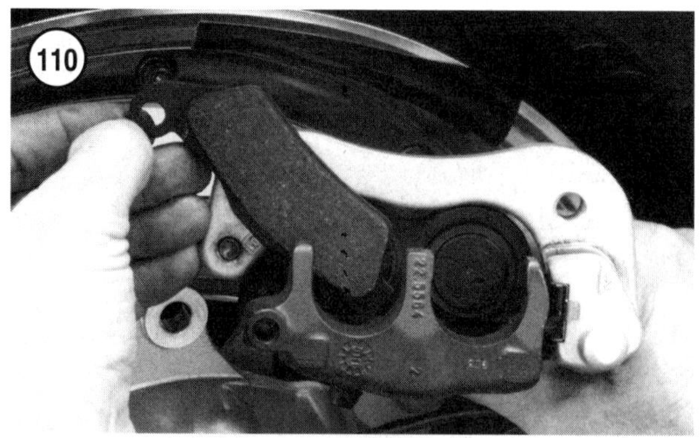

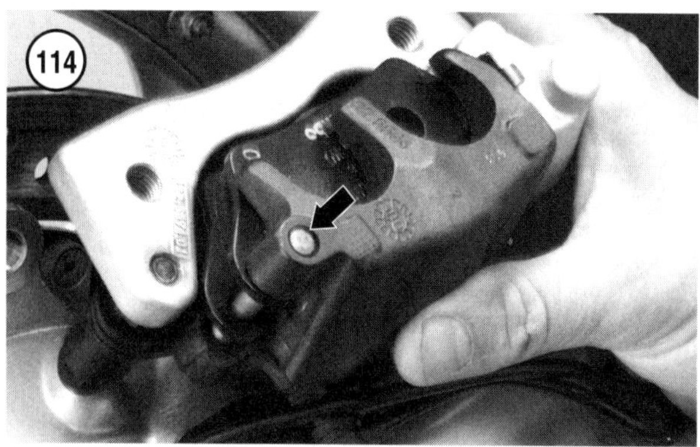

14. Lightly coat the end of the pistons and the backs of the new pads with disc brake lubricant.

15. Check the brake pads (**Figure 109**) for wear or damage. Measure the thickness of the brake pad friction material. Replace the brake pads if they are worn to the service limit in **Table 1**.

16. Check the friction surface of the new pads for any debris or manufacturing residue. If necessary, clean them off with an aerosol brake cleaner.

NOTE
When purchasing new pads, check with the dealership to make sure the friction compound of the new pad is compatible with the disc material. Remove roughness from the backs of the new pads with a fine-cut file, then thoroughly clean them off with brake cleaner.

17. Ensure the anti-rattle spring (**Figure 107**) is still in place.

18. Install the inboard pad (**Figure 110**) and lock it into place (**Figure 111**).

19. Install the outboard pad (**Figure 112**) and lock it into place.

20. Align the holes in both pads with the hole (**Figure 113**) in the caliper assembly and install the pad retaining pin (**Figure 106**) through the caliper and both brake pads.

21. Tap the pad retaining pin in until it stops and locks into place (**Figure 114**).

22. Install the brake caliper as described in this chapter.

23. Install the E-clip (**Figure 115**) onto the outer end of the pad retaining pin. Make sure it seats correctly in the pad retaining pin (**Figure 105**).

24. Untie the rear brake pedal from the frame.

25. Carefully roll the motorcycle back and forth and activate the brake pedal as many times as it takes to refill the

cylinders in the caliper and correctly locate both brake pads.

26A. On non-ABS equipped models, refill and bleed the system as described in this chapter.

26B. On ABS equipped models, have the brake system filled and bled by a BMW dealership.

27. Install the diaphragm and cover.

WARNING
Do not ride the motorcycle until the front brakes are operating correctly with full hydraulic advantage.

28. Follow the brake pad manufacturer's instructions regarding break-in of the lining material.

REAR MASTER CYLINDER AND REMOTE RESERVOIR

The rear master cylinder is a sealed unit and cannot be serviced. If defective, it must be replaced. The remote reservoir diaphragm is replaceable.

Removal/Installation

CAUTION
Cover the surrounding area of the frame, footpeg assembly and the wheel with a heavy cloth or plastic tarp to protect them from accidental brake fluid spills. Wash brake fluid off any painted or plated surfaces immediately, as it will damage the finish. Wash the area with soapy water and rinse completely.

1. Read *Brake Service* in this chapter.
2. Remove seat as described in Chapter Fifteen.

3A. On R850C and R1200C models, perform the following:

a. On the right side, pull straight out and release the posts on the chrome trim panel (**Figure 101**) from the rubber grommets on the fuel tank. Remove the chrome trim panel.
b. Remove screws (A, **Figure 102**) securing the lower trim panel (B) and remove the trim panel.
c. Unscrew the cover and remove the cover and the diaphragm (**Figure 104**) from the master cylinder remote reservoir.

3B. On all models except R850C and R1200C, perform the following:

a. Remove the rear right side panels as described in Chapter Fifteen.

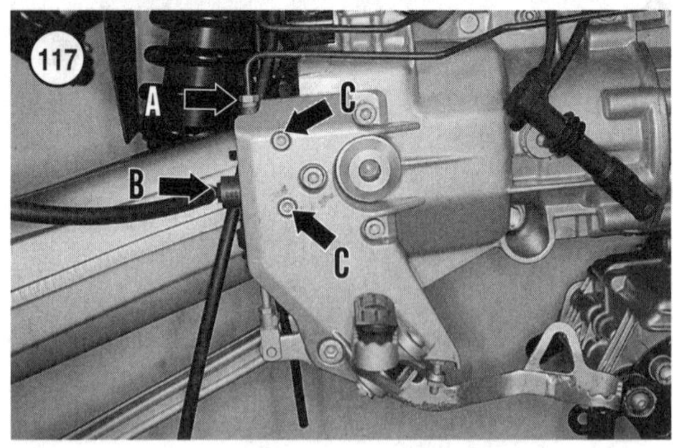

b. Unscrew the cover and remove the cover and the diaphragm (**Figure 103**) from the master cylinder remote reservoir.

4. Use a shop syringe and remove the brake fluid from the reservoir. Discard the brake fluid properly.

5. Drain the hydraulic brake fluid from the rear brake system as follows:

a. Attach a hose to the bleed valve (**Figure 116**, typical) on the caliper assembly.

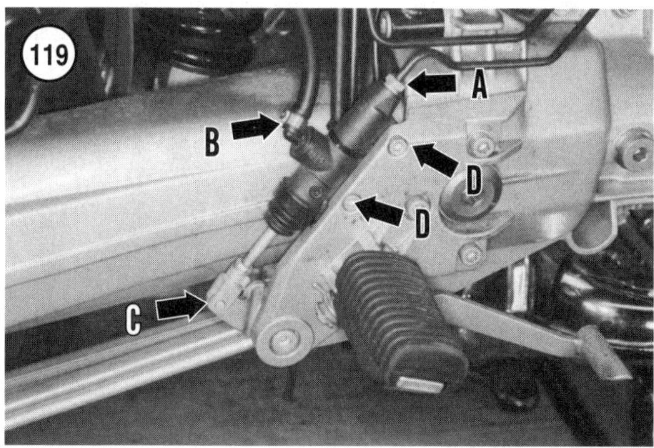

b. Place the loose end of the hose in a container to catch the brake fluid.

c. Open the bleed valve and apply the rear brake pedal until the brake fluid is pumped out of the system.

d. Disconnect the hose and tighten the bleed valve.

e. Dispose of this brake fluid properly.

6. On RT models, remove the right lower fairing section as described in Chapter Fifteen.

7A. On R850R, R1100GS and R1100R models, perform the following:

a. Disconnect the brake hose or line (A, **Figure 117**) from the top of the master cylinder.

b. Disconnect the remote reservoir flexible brake hose (B, **Figure 117**) from the side of the master cylinder. Place the end in a reclosable plastic bag.

c. Remove the pin from the clevis attaching the brake pedal to the master cylinder pushrod.

d. Remove the bolts (C, **Figure 117**) securing the master cylinder to the backside of the right front footpeg bracket.

e. Remove the master cylinder.

7B. On R1150R models, perform the following:

a. Disconnect the brake line (A, **Figure 118**) from the top of the master cylinder. Place the end in a reclosable plastic bag.

b. Disconnect the remote reservoir brake hose (B, **Figure 118**) from the top of the master cylinder. Place the end in a reclosable plastic bag.

c. Remove the spring clip/pin (C, **Figure 118**) attaching the brake pedal to the master cylinder pushrod.

d. Remove the Allen bolts (D, **Figure 118**) securing the master cylinder and foot guard (E) to the right front footpeg bracket. Remove the foot guard and the master cylinder.

7C. On R1150GS models, perform the following:

a. Disconnect the brake line from the top of the master cylinder. Place the end in a reclosable plastic bag.

b. Disconnect the remote reservoir brake hose from the top of the master cylinder. Place the end in a reclosable plastic bag.

c. Remove the spring clip/pin attaching the brake pedal to the master cylinder pushrod.

d. Remove the Allen bolts securing the master cylinder and foot guard (E, **Figure 118**) to the right front footpeg bracket. Remove the foot guard and the master cylinder.

7D. On R1100RS models, perform the following:

a. Disconnect the brake hose or line (A, **Figure 119**) from the top of the master cylinder. Place the end in a reclosable plastic bag.

b. Disconnect the remote reservoir brake hose (B, **Figure 119**) from the side of the master cylinder. Place the end of the hose in a reclosable plastic bag.

c. Remove the pin from the clevis (C, **Figure 119**) attaching the brake pedal to the master cylinder pushrod.

d. Remove the bolts (D, **Figure 119**) securing the master cylinder to the backside of the right front footpeg.

e. Remove the master cylinder.

7E. On R1150RS models, perform the following:

a. Disconnect the brake line (A, **Figure 120**) from the top of the master cylinder. Place the end in reclosable plastic bag.

b. Disconnect the remote reservoir brake hose (B, **Figure 120**) from the top of the master cylinder. Place the end in reclosable plastic bag.

c. Remove the spring clip/pin (C, **Figure 120**) attaching the brake pedal to the master cylinder pushrod.

d. Remove the Allen bolts (D, **Figure 120**) securing the master cylinder and foot guard (E) to the right front footpeg bracket. Remove the foot guard and the master cylinder.

7F. On RT models, perform the following:

a. Disconnect the brake hose or line (A, **Figure 121**) from the top of the master cylinder.
b. Remove the pin from the clevis (B, **Figure 121**) attaching the brake pedal to the master cylinder pushrod.
c. Remove the bolts (C, **Figure 121**) securing the master cylinder to the backside of the right front footpeg.
d. Carefully move the master cylinder out from behind the right front footpeg, then disconnect the remote reservoir hose (D, **Figure 121**) from the side of the master cylinder. Place the hose in a reclosable plastic bag.
e. Remove the master cylinder

7G. On R1100S models, perform the following:

a. Disconnect the brake line (A, **Figure 122**) from the top of the master cylinder.
b. Disconnect the remote reservoir brake hose (B, **Figure 122**) from the top of the master cylinder. Place the end in reclosable plastic bag.
c. Remove the spring clip pin from the ball socket linkage (C, **Figure 122**) attaching the brake pedal to the master cylinder pushrod.
d. Remove the Allen bolts (D, **Figure 122**) securing the master cylinder and foot guard (E) to the right front footpeg bracket. Remove the foot guard and the master cylinder.

7H. On R850C and R1200C models, perform the following:

a. Disconnect the brake line (A, **Figure 123**) from the top of the master cylinder.
b. Disconnect the remote reservoir brake hose (B, **Figure 123**) from the top of the master cylinder. Place the end in reclosable plastic bag.
c. Remove the pin from the clevis (C, **Figure 123**) attaching the brake pedal to the master cylinder pushrod.
d. Remove the Allen bolts (D, **Figure 123**) securing the master cylinder to the right front footpeg. Remove the master cylinder.

8A. On R850C and R1200C models, perform the following:

a. Loosen the hose clamp and disconnect the brake hose (A, **Figure 124**) from the reservoir.
b. Carefully pull out the remote reservoir and disengage it from the frame mounted retainer (B, **Figure 124**).
c. Remove the reservoir from the frame.

8B. On all models except R850C and R1200C, perform the following:

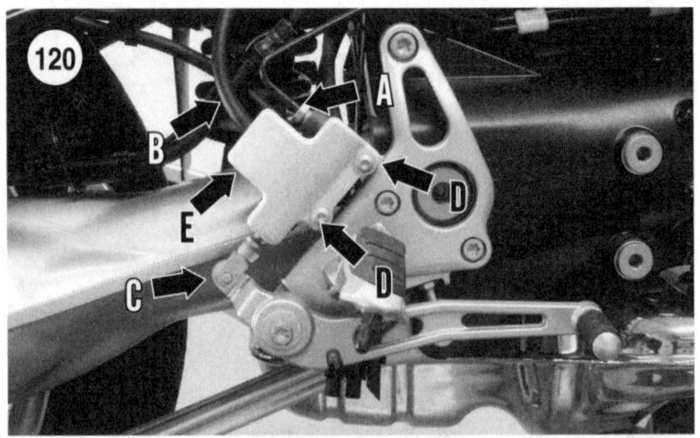

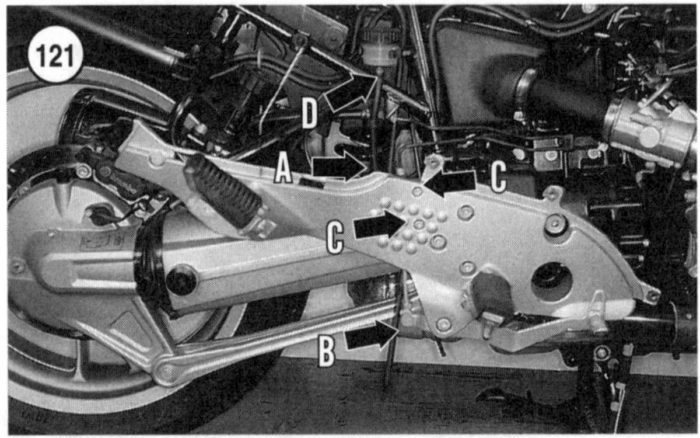

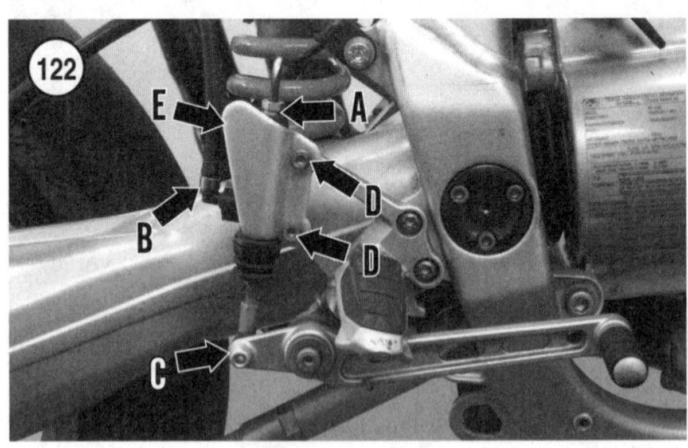

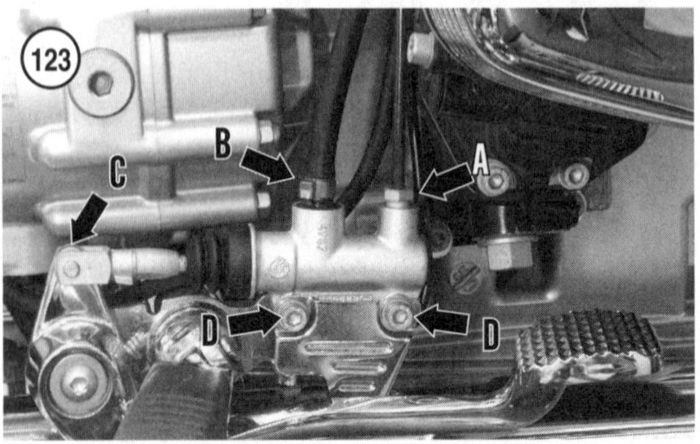

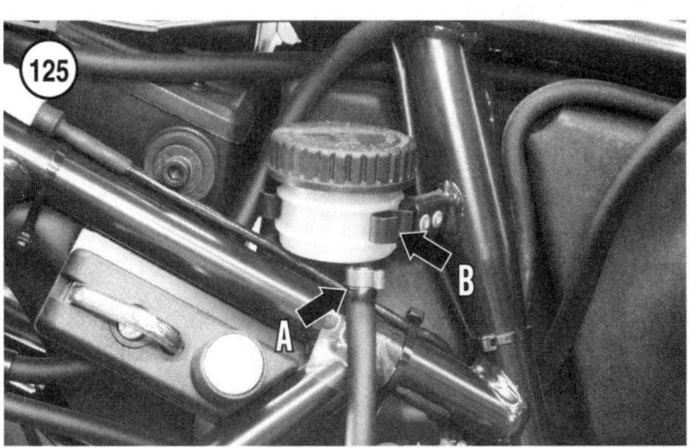

a. Loosen the hose clamp and disconnect the brake hose (A, **Figure 125**) from the reservoir.

b. Carefully pull out the remote reservoir and disengage it from the frame mounted retainer (B, **Figure 125**).

c. Remove the reservoir from the frame.

9. Install by reversing the removal steps while noting the following:

a. Tighten the master cylinder mounting bolts to 9 N•m (79 in.-lb.).

b. Securely tighten the master cylinder brake line fitting.

c. On non-ABS equipped models, refill and bleed the system as described in this chapter.

d. On ABS equipped models, have the brake system filled and bled by a BMW dealership.

WARNING
Do not ride the motorcycle until the rear brakes are operating correctly with full hydraulic advantage.

REAR CALIPER

R1100RS Models

Removal

CAUTION
Do not spill any brake fluid on the painted portion of the rear wheel. Wash away any spilled brake fluid immediately, using soapy water, and rinse completely.

1. Remove the right rear footpeg assembly (**Figure 126**) as described in Chapter Fifteen.

2. On ABS equipped models, remove the Torx bolts and shim securing the rear ABS trigger sensor to the bracket attached to the rear caliper. Move the sensor out of the way. It is not necessary to disconnect it from the main wiring harness.

3. Drain the hydraulic brake fluid from the rear brake system as follows:

a. Attach a hose to the bleed valve on the caliper assembly.

b. Place the loose end of the hose in a container to catch the brake fluid.

c. Open the bleed valve and apply the rear brake pedal until the brake fluid is pumped out of the system.

d. Disconnect the hose and tighten the bleed valve.

e. Dispose of this brake fluid properly.

4. Remove the union bolt and sealing washers securing the brake hose to the rear caliper.

5. Place the loose end in a plastic reclosable bag.

6. On models equipped with ABS, open the clamp and move the rear ABS trigger sensor cable out of the way.

7. Remove the caliper mounting bolts securing the caliper assembly to the final drive unit.

8. Carefully pull the caliper assembly up and off of the brake disc.

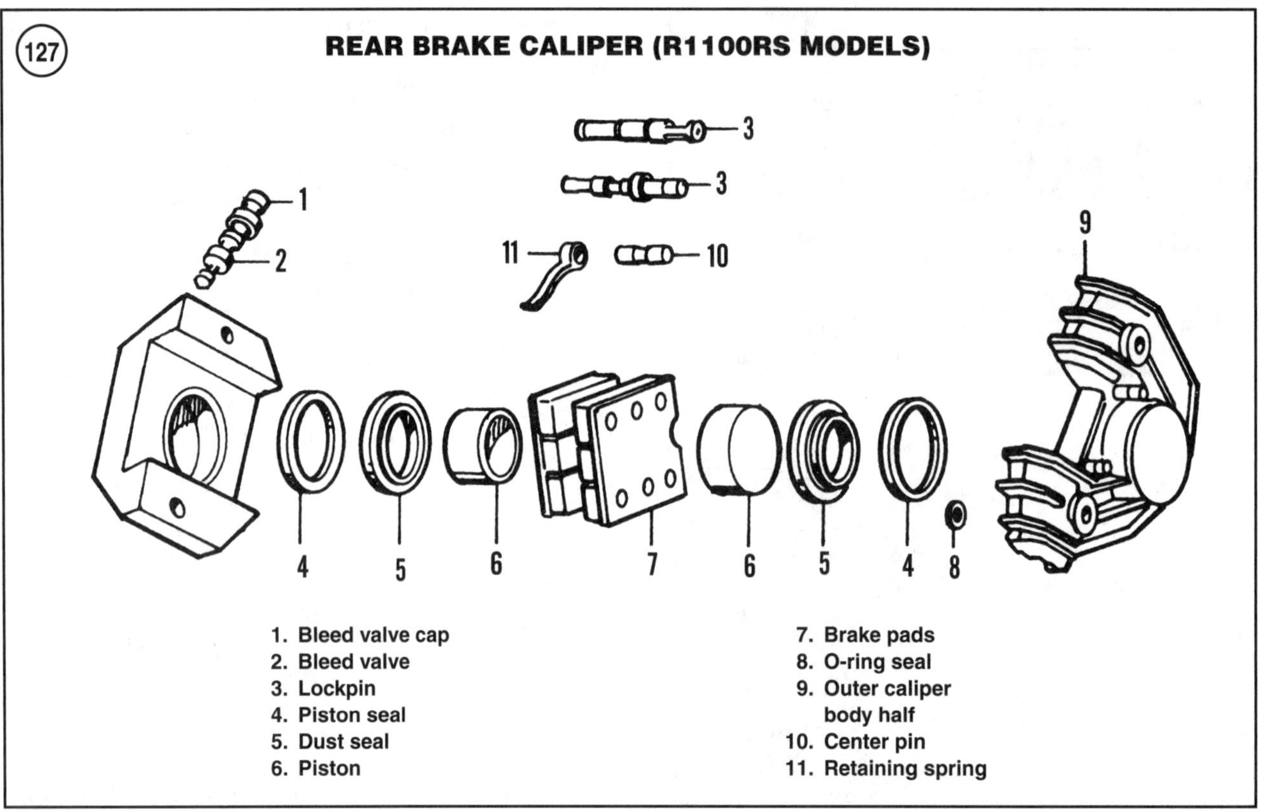

Installation

1. Carefully install the caliper assembly down onto the brake disc. Be careful not to damage the leading edge of the pads during installation.
2. Install the caliper mounting bolts and tighten to 40 N•m (29 ft.-lb.).
3. Install a new sealing washer on each side of the fitting and install the brake hose onto the caliper. Install the union bolt and tighten it to 15 N•m (132 in.-lb.).
4. On models equipped with ABS, move the rear ABS trigger sensor cable into position and close the clamp.
5. On ABS equipped models, move the rear ABS trigger sensor and shim onto the bracket attached to the rear caliper. Tighten the Torx bolts securely.
6. Inspect the distance between the ABS trigger sensor and the pulse generating wheel as described under *Trigger Sensor* in this chapter.
7. Install the right rear footpeg (**Figure 126**) as described in Chapter Fifteen.
8. On non-ABS equipped models, refill and bleed the system as described in this chapter.
9. On ABS equipped models, have the brake system filled and bled by a BMW dealership.

130

131

132

WARNING
Do not ride the motorcycle until the rear brakes are operating correctly with full hydraulic advantage.

Disassembly

Refer to **Figure 127**.

BMW does not provide specifications for any of the rear caliper components. Replace any worn parts.

1. Remove the caliper assembly as described in this chapter.
2. Remove the brake pads as described in this chapter.
3. Remove the two Allen bolts (**Figure 128**) securing the caliper assembly halves together.
4. Separate the caliper halves.
5. Remove and discard the small O-ring seal from the inboard caliper half.

CAUTION
In the following step, do not use a sharp tool to remove the dust seals from the caliper body. Do not damage the cylinder surfaces.

6. Remove the large dust seal from each caliper half. Discard the dust seals.
7. Withdraw the piston (**Figure 129**) from each caliper body half. If the pistons cannot be removed easily, perform the following:

WARNING
Compressed air forces the pistons out of the caliper under considerable force. Do not cushion the pistons by hand, as injury could result.

   a. Either wrap the caliper half and piston with a heavy cloth or place a shop cloth or piece of soft wood over the end of the piston.
   b. Hold the caliper body with the piston facing down toward the workbench.
   c. Direct compressed air through the fluid passageway to partially remove the piston.
   d. Repeat the procedure for the piston in the other half of the caliper.

8. Use a piece of wood or plastic scraper to carefully push the piston seal in toward the caliper cylinder and out of their groove. Remove the piston seal from each caliper body half. Discard the piston seals.

Assembly

1. Coat the new dust seals (**Figure 130**) and piston seals (**Figure 131**) with fresh DOT 4 brake fluid.
2. Carefully install the new piston seal in the groove in each caliper cylinder. Make sure the seal seats properly in the groove.
3. Coat the pistons and the caliper cylinders with fresh DOT 4 brake fluid.
4. Position the pistons with their open end (**Figure 132**) facing toward the brake pads and install the piston into each caliper cylinder. Push the pistons (**Figure 129**) in until they stop.

5. Carefully install the new dust seal in the groove in each caliper cylinder. Make sure the seal seats properly in the caliper half.
6. Install the bleed screw and cap (**Figure 133**).
7. Apply fresh DOT 4 brake fluid and install a new O-ring seal into the recess in the inboard caliper half.
8. Lay the inboard caliper half down on the workbench and install the outboard half on top of it. This is to prevent the small O-ring seal from falling out during assembly.

NOTE
*There are two different length Allen bolts of the same diameter. The longer bolts (A, **Figure 134**) are used to assemble the two caliper halves and the shorter ones (B) are used as mounting bolts to hold the caliper assembly onto the final drive unit.*

9. Install the Allen bolts, securing the caliper halves together and tighten securely.
10. Install the brake pads as described in this chapter.
11. Install the brake caliper cover.
12. Install the brake caliper assembly as described in this chapter.

Inspection

1. Inspect the seal groove in each caliper body half for damage. If damaged or corroded, replace the caliper assembly.
2. Unscrew and remove the bleed valve and cap (**Figure 133**).
3. Inspect the caliper body halves for damage and replace the caliper body if necessary.
4. Inspect the fluid passageway in the base of each cylinder bore. Make sure it is clean and open.
5. Inspect the cylinder walls and the pistons (**Figure 135**) for scratches, scoring or other damage. If either is rusty or corroded, replace the caliper assembly. The pistons cannot be replaced separately.
6. Inspect the caliper mounting bolt hole threads. If it is worn or damage, clean it out with a metric thread tap or replace the caliper assembly.
7. Inspect the caliper halves assembly bolt hole threads. If it is worn or damage, clean it out with a metric thread tap or replace the caliper assembly.
8. Inspect the union bolt hole threads (**Figure 136**). If it is worn or damage, clean it out with a metric thread tap or replace the caliper assembly.
9. Make sure the hole in the bleed valve is clean and open. Apply compressed air to the opening and make sure it is clear.

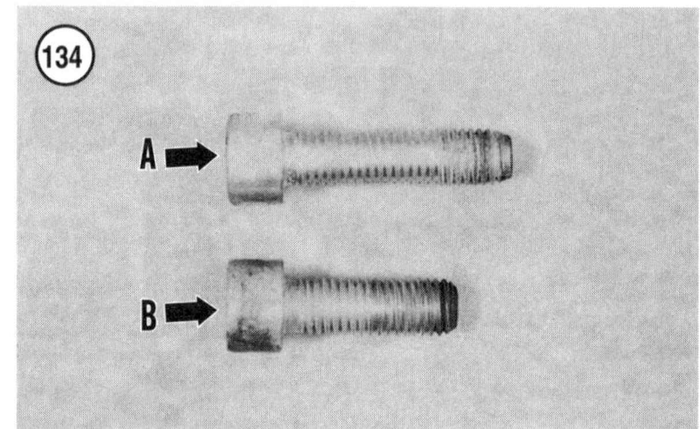

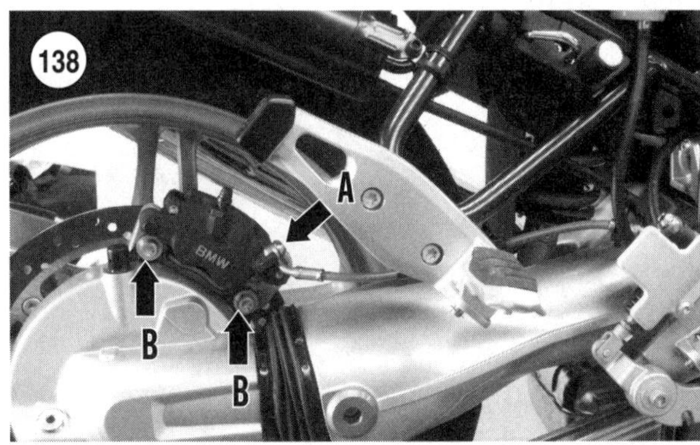

10. If serviceable, clean the caliper body halves with rubbing alcohol and rinse them with clean brake fluid.

All Models Except R1100RS

Removal

CAUTION
Do not spill any brake fluid on the painted portion of the rear wheel. Wash away any spilled brake fluid immediately, using soapy water, and rinse completely.

1. Drain the hydraulic brake fluid from the rear brake system as follows:
   a. Attach a hose to the bleed valve on the caliper assembly.
   b. Place the loose end of the hose in a container to catch the brake fluid.
   c. Open the bleed valve and apply the rear brake pedal until the brake fluid is pumped out of the system.
   d. Disconnect the hose and tighten the bleed valve.
   e. Dispose of this brake fluid properly.
2. On models equipped with ABS, perform the following:
   a. Remove the Allen bolt (A, **Figure 137**) securing the sensor to the final drive unit.
   b. Remove the sensor (B, **Figure 137**) and shim from the final drive unit.
3. Remove the union bolt and sealing washers (A, **Figure 138**) securing the brake hose to the rear caliper.
4. Disconnect the hose and place the end in a reclosable plastic bag.
5. Remove the caliper mounting bolts (B, **Figure 138**) securing the caliper assembly to the final drive unit.

6A. On R850C and R1200C models, perform the following:
   a. Apply several layers of duct tape (**Figure 139**) onto the wheel to protect the finish.
   b. Very carefully pull the caliper assembly up and off of the brake disc. The caliper will brush up against the rim during removal and installation.

6B. On all models except R850C and R1200C, carefully pull the caliper assembly up and off of the brake disc.

Installation

1A. On R850C and R1200C models, perform the following:
   a. If removed, apply several layers of duct tape (**Figure 139**) onto the rim to protect the finish.
   b. Very carefully install pull the caliper assembly onto the brake disc. Be careful not to damage the leading edge of the pads during installation.

1B. On all models except R850C and R1200C, carefully install the caliper assembly down onto the disc and final drive unit.

2. Install the caliper mounting bolts (B, **Figure 138**) and tighten to 40 N•m (29 ft.-lb.).
3. Install a new sealing washer on each side of the fitting and install the brake hose onto the caliper. Install the union bolt and tighten it to 15 N•m (132 in.-lb.).
4. On models equipped with ABS, perform the following:

14

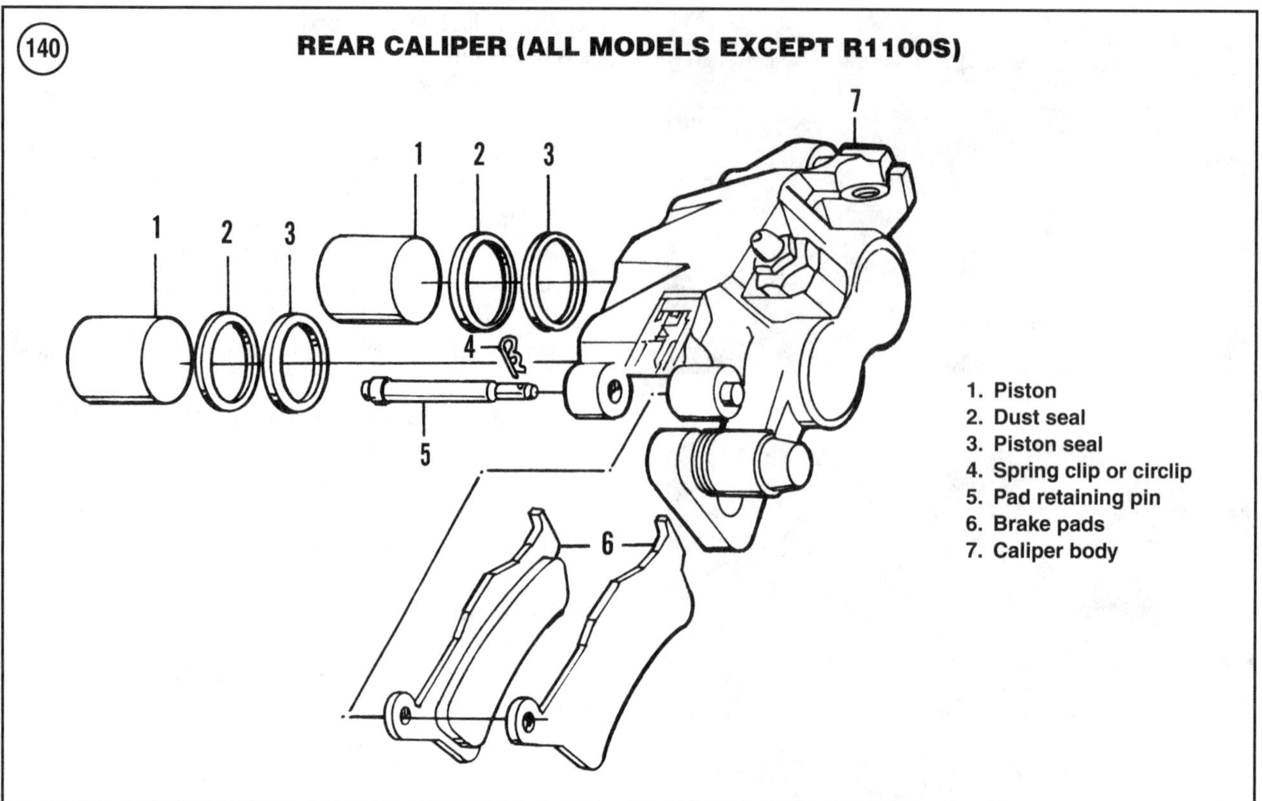

a. Install the sensor (B, **Figure 137**) and shim onto the final drive unit.
b. Install the Allen bolt (A, **Figure 137**) securing the sensor and tighten securely.
c. Inspect the distance between the ABS trigger sensor and the pulse generating wheel as described under *Trigger Sensor* in this chapter.

5. On non-ABS equipped models, refill and bleed the system as described in this chapter.
6. On ABS equipped models, have the brake system filled and bled by a BMW dealership.

WARNING
Do not ride the motorcycle until the rear brakes are operating correctly with full hydraulic advantage.

Disassembly

Refer to **Figure 140**.

There are no specifications for the rear caliper components. Replace any damaged or worn parts.

1. Remove the caliper assembly as described in this chapter.
2. Remove the brake pads as described in this chapter.

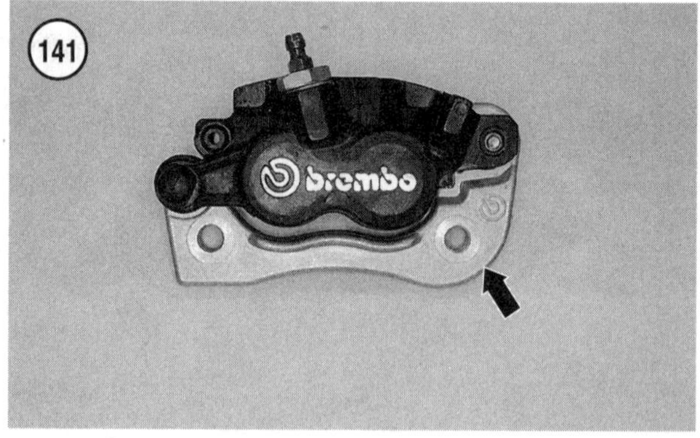

3. Slide off and remove the caliper carrier (**Figure 141**) from the caliper assembly.
4. Withdraw the pistons from caliper body. If the pistons are not easily removed, perform the following:

WARNING
Compressed air forces the pistons out of the caliper under considerable force. Do not cushion the pistons by hand, as injury could result.

a. Two different size pistons are used.

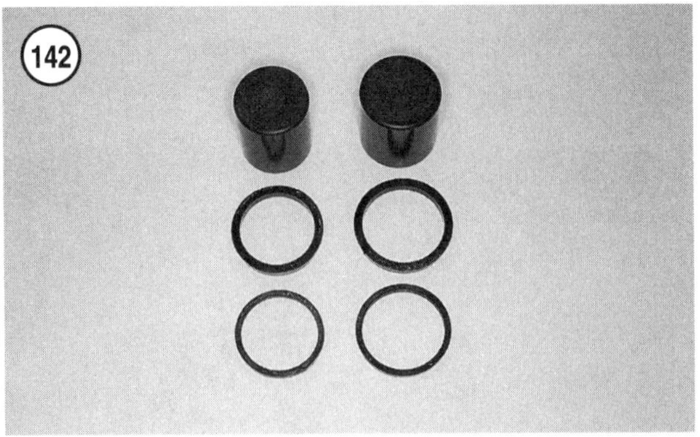
142

143

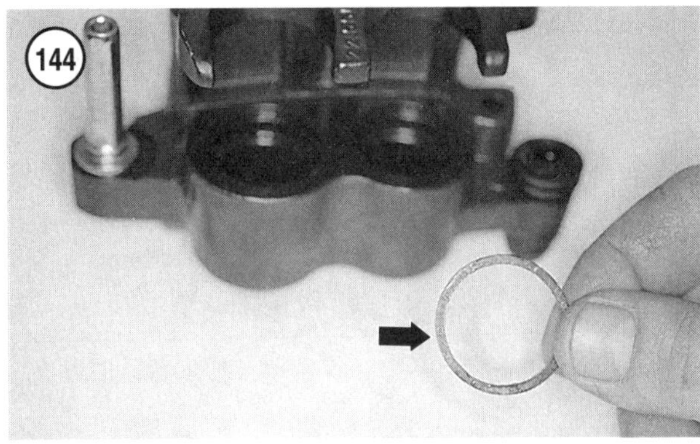
144

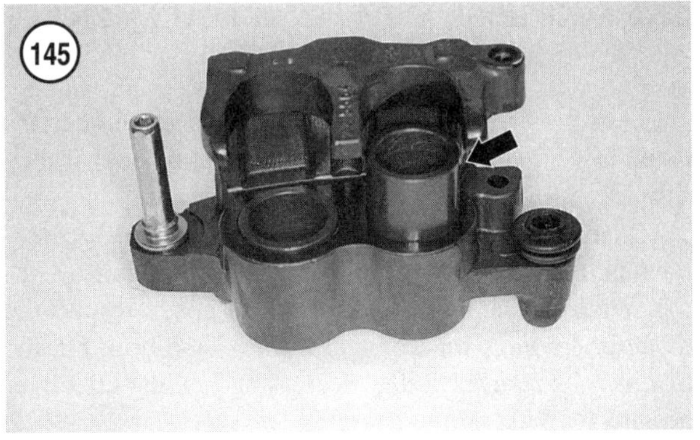
145

b. Support the caliper on a wooden block with the pistons facing down. Place a thick towel between the pistons and the workbench. Make sure there is enough space beneath the caliper for the pistons to be removed completely.

c. Direct compressed air through the brake line port to remove the pistons.

5. Use a piece of wood or plastic scraper to carefully push the dust seal and piston seal in toward the caliper cylinder and out of their grooves. Remove all dust and piston seals.

6. Unscrew and remove the bleed screw.

Assembly

1. Coat the new dust and piston seals and both pistons (**Figure 142**) with fresh DOT 4 brake fluid.

NOTE

The pistons and cylinders are different outer diameters. Make sure to install the correct size dust and piston seals into the appropriate cylinders. The seals will be damaged if the larger seals are installed into the smaller cylinders.

2. Carefully install the new piston seal (**Figure 143**) in each caliper cylinder. Make sure both seals seat properly in the grooves.

3. Carefully install the new dust seal (**Figure 144**) in each caliper cylinder. Make sure the seals seat properly in the grooves.

4. Position the pistons with their open ends facing toward the brake pads and install the pistons into the caliper cylinders (**Figure 145**). Push the pistons in until they bottom.

5. Install the bleed valve and cap and tighten securely.

6. Apply a light coat of disc brake lubricant to the post on the caliper and caliper carrier. Install the carrier through the rubber boots and onto the caliper. Push the carrier on until it bottoms.

7. Install the brake pads as described in this chapter.

8. Install the brake caliper cover.

9. Install the brake caliper assembly as described in this chapter.

Inspection

The only specification available is for new pistons. Refer to **Table 1**. If the caliper assembly exhibits any signs of wear or damage; replace it. Always replace the piston and dust seals whenever the pistons have been removed.

1. Clean the caliper body and pistons in clean DOT 4 brake fluid or isopropyl alcohol and dry them with compressed air.

2. Inspect the piston and dust seal grooves (A, **Figure 146**) in the caliper body for damage. If they are damaged or corroded, replace the caliper assembly.

3. Make sure the fluid passageways (B, **Figure 146**) in both sides of caliper body are clear. Apply compressed air to the opening and make sure it i s clear. Clean them out, if necessary, with clean brake fluid.

4. Inspect the cylinder walls and the pistons for scratches, scoring or other damage. If either is rusty or corroded, replace the caliper assembly. The pistons cannot be replaced separately.

5. Measure the outside diameter of the two different size pistons (**Figure 147**). Compare the actual measurements to the specifications in **Table 1**.

6. Inspect the union bolt hole threads. If it is worn or damage, clean it out with a metric thread tap or replace the caliper assembly.

7. Inspect the bleed screw bolt hole threads. If it is worn or damage, clean it out with a metric thread tap or replace the caliper assembly.

8. Make sure the hole in the bleed screw is clean and open. Apply compressed air to the opening and make sure it is clear.

9. Inspect the caliper body assembly (A, **Figure 148**) for damage; replace the caliper assembly if necessary.

10. Check the caliper post (B, **Figure 148**) for straightness and corrosion. Clean off any corrosion. If the post is bent, replace the caliper assembly.

11. Check the rubber boot (**Figure 149**) for wear, deterioration and tears. Replace as necessary.

12. Check the caliper carrier post (A, **Figure 150**) for straightness and corrosion. Clean off any corrosion. Replace the caliper assembly if the post is bent.

13. Check the rubber boot (B, **Figure 150**) for wear, deterioration and tears. Replace as necessary.

14. Inspect the caliper mounting bolt holes in the caliper carrier. Check for hole elongation or cracks. If the caliper carrier is damaged, it must be replaced along with the caliper assembly. It cannot be replaced separately.

15. Check the pad retaining pin and anti-rattle spring (**Figure 151**) for wear or damage.

16. If serviceable, clean the caliper body halves with rubbing alcohol and rinse with clean brake fluid.

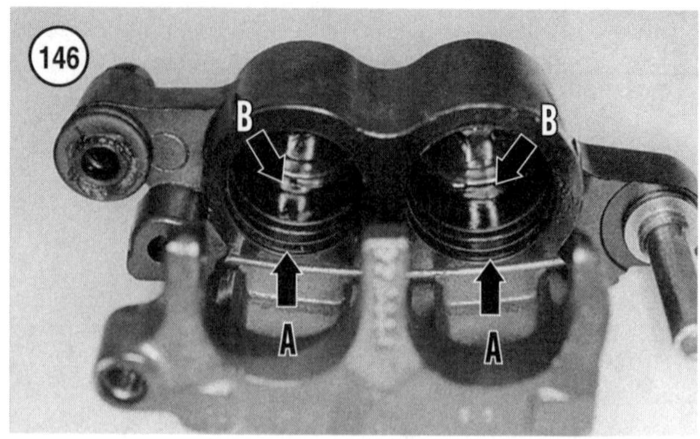

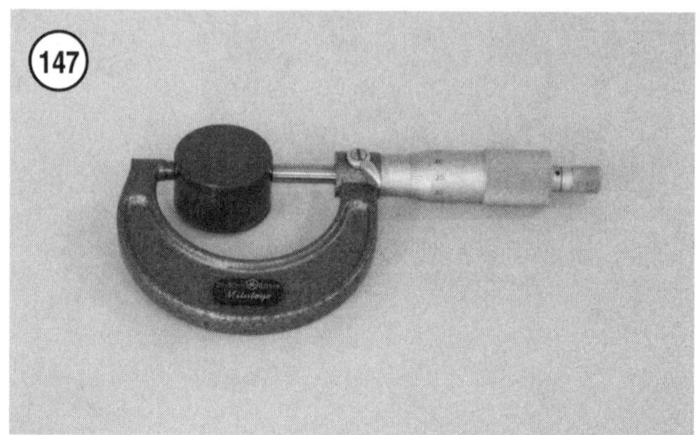

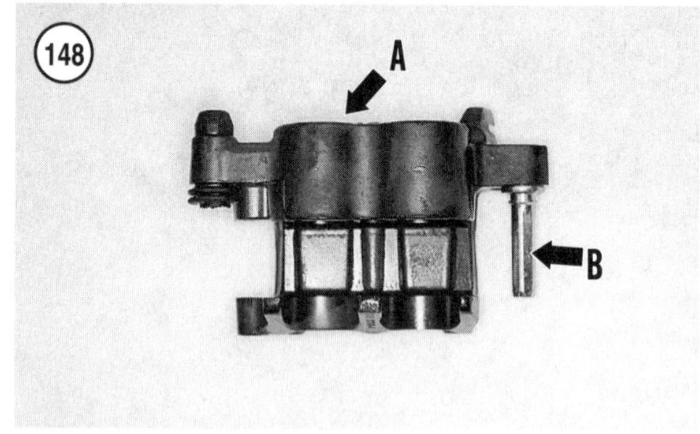

BRAKE HOSE AND LINE REPLACEMENT (NON-ABS MODELS)

Check the brake hoses at the brake inspection intervals listed in Chapter Three. Replace the brake hoses if they show signs of wear or damage.

The metal brake lines do not require routine replacement unless they are damaged or the end fittings are leaking. While replacing the flexible brake hoses, inspect the metal brake lines for damage. If they have been hit, the line may be restricted, thus decreasing braking effectiveness.

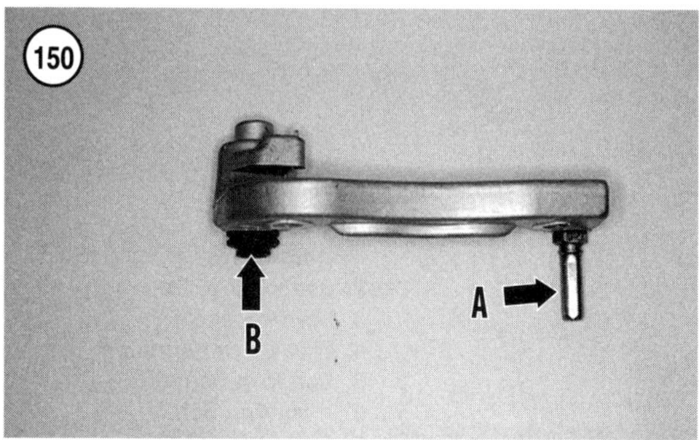

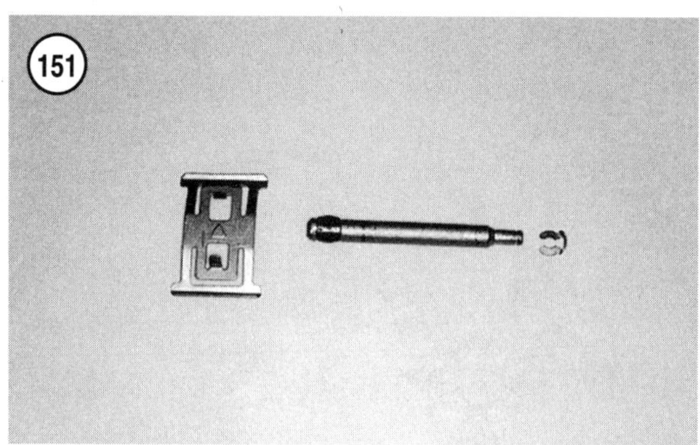

To replace a brake hose, perform the following:

1. Use a plastic drop cloth to cover areas that could be damaged by spilled brake fluid.

2. When removing a brake hose or brake line, note the following:

   a. Record the hose or line routing on a piece of paper.

   b. Remove any bolts or brackets securing the brake hose to the frame or suspension component.

   c. Before removing the union bolts, note how the end of the brake hose is installed or indexed against the part it is threaded into. The hoses must be installed facing in their original position.

3. Replace union bolts with damaged hex-heads.

4. Always install new washers with the union bolts.

5. Reverse these steps to install the new brake hoses, while noting the following:

   a. Compare the new and old hoses to make sure they are the same.

   b. Clean the new washers, union bolts and hose ends to remove any contamination.

   c. Referring to the notes made during removal, route the brake hose along its original path.

   d. Install a new union bolt washer on each side of the brake hose.

   e. Tighten the banjo bolts to the torque specified in **Table 2**.

   f. After replacing a front brake hose, turn the handlebars from side to side to make sure the hose does not rub against any part or pull away from its brake unit.

   g. Refill the master cylinders and bleed the brakes as described in this chapter.

WARNING

Do not ride the motorcycle until the front and rear brakes operate correctly with full hydraulic advantage and the brake light works properly.

Front Brake Hoses Removal/Installation (1993-1998 R1100GS and R1100RS Models)

This procedure covers removal and installation of the front hoses. If replacing only one hose, refer to the steps relating to that specific hose.

Refer to **Figure 152**.

1. On RS models, remove the side sections on the front fairing as described in Chapter Fifteen.

2. Remove the front fender as described in Chapter Fifteen.

NOTE

To prevent the entry of moisture and dirt, cap the end of the brake hoses and lines that are not going to be replaced. Place the loose end in a reclosable plastic bag.

3. Drain the hydraulic brake fluid from the front brake system as follows:

   a. Attach a hose to the bleed valve on each front caliper.

   b. Place the loose end of the hose in a container.

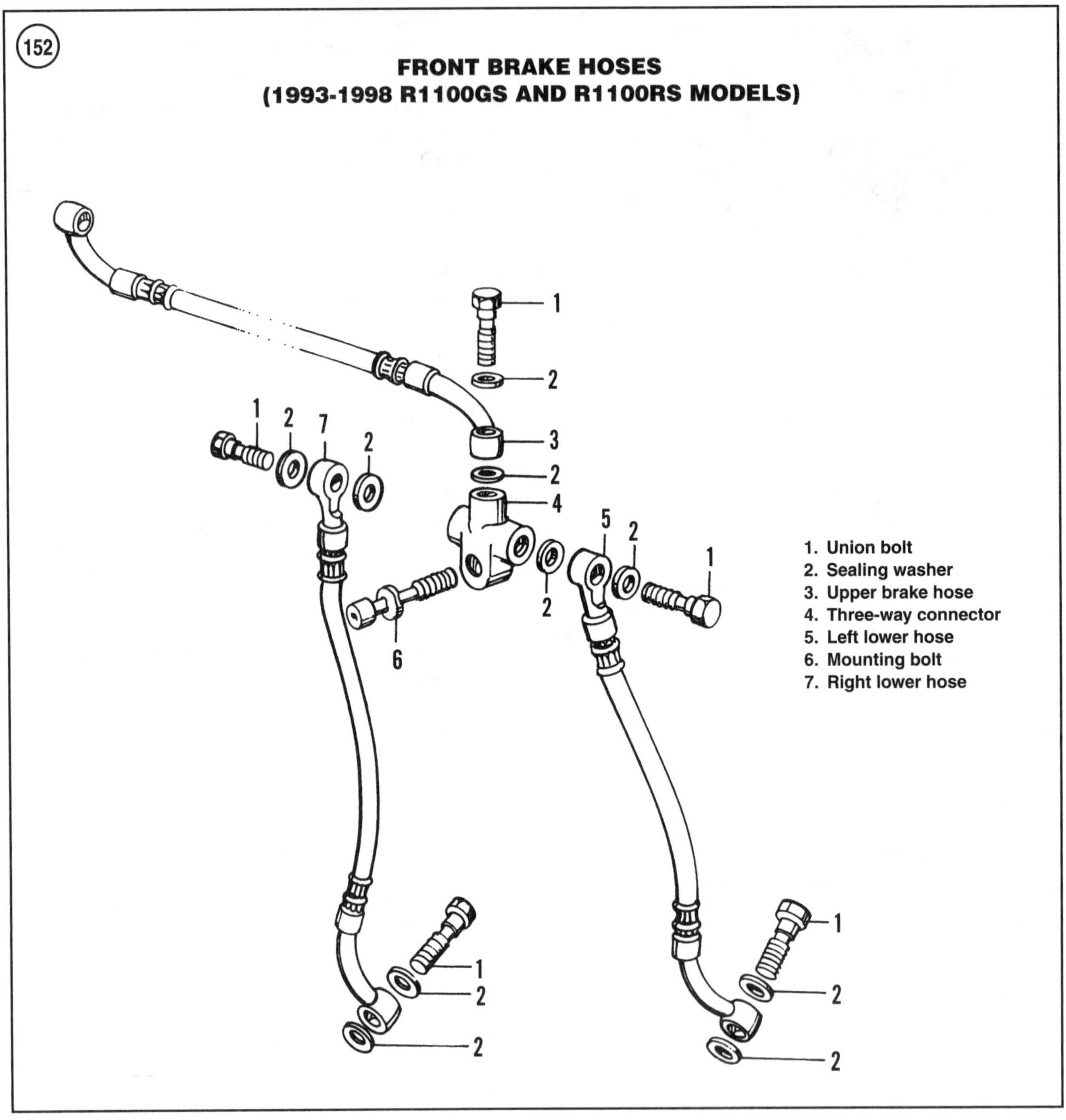

c. Open the bleed valve on each caliper and apply the front brake lever until the brake fluid is pumped out of the system.

d. Disconnect the hoses and tighten the bleed valves.

e. Dispose of this brake fluid properly.

4. To remove the upper hose, perform the following:

a. Place a couple of shop cloths under the union bolt and remove the union bolt and sealing washers (**Figure 154**) securing the upper brake hose to the master cylinder. Disconnect the brake hose from the master cylinder.

b. Remove the union bolt and sealing washers (A, **Figure 155**) securing the upper brake hose to three-way connector. Disconnect the brake hose from the three-way connector.

c. Remove the upper hose from any clamps or tie wraps and remove the upper hose (B, **Figure 155**) from the frame.

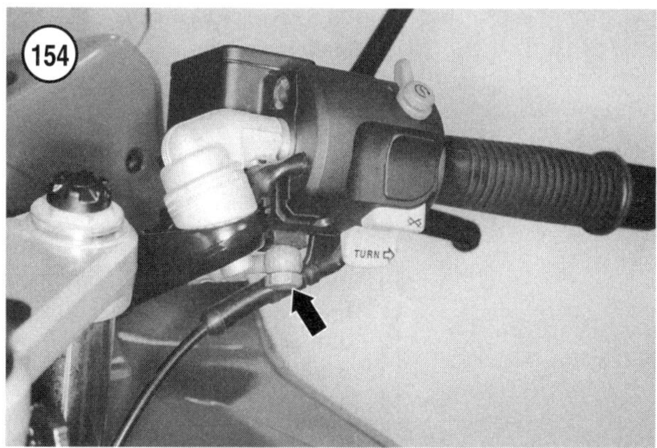

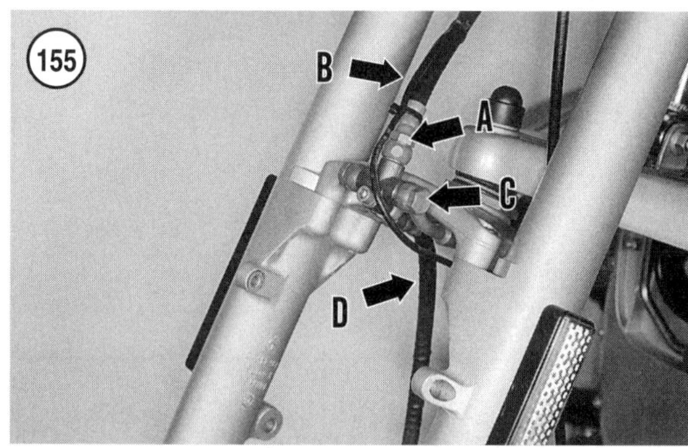

5. To remove the lower hose, perform the following:

   a. Remove the union bolt and sealing washers (**Figure 153**) securing the lower brake hose to the front caliper. Disconnect the brake hose from the front caliper.

   b. Place a couple of shop cloths under the union bolt and remove the union bolt and sealing washers (C, **Figure 155**) securing the lower brake hose to the three-way connector. Disconnect the brake hose from the three-way connector.

   c. Remove the lower hose from any clamps or tie wraps and remove the lower hose (D, **Figure 155**) from the fork area.

6. If necessary, repeat Step 5 for the lower hose on the opposite caliper.
7. Install new hoses, sealing washers and union bolts in the reverse order of removal. Make sure to install new sealing washers in the correct positions.
8. Tighten all union bolts to 15 N•m (132 in.-lb.).
9. Refill and bleed the system as described in this chapter.

WARNING
Do not ride the motorcycle until the rear brakes are operating correctly with full hydraulic advantage.

10. Install the front fender as described in Chapter Fifteen.
11. On RS models, install the side sections on the front fairing as described in Chapter Fifteen.

Front Brake Hoses and Lines Removal/Installation (1993-1998 R1100R and R1100RT Models)

This procedure covers removal and installation of all of the front brake hoses and lines. If replacing only one hose, refer to the steps relating to that specific hose, or line.

Refer to **Figure 156** for this procedure:

1. On RT models, remove the side sections on the front fairing as described in Chapter Fifteen.
2. Remove the front fender as described in Chapter Fifteen.

NOTE
To prevent the entry of moisture and dirt, cap the end of the brake hoses and lines that are not going to be replaced. Place the loose end in a plastic reclosable bag and zip it closed around the hose or line.

3. Drain the brake fluid from the front brake system as follows:
   a. Attach a hose to the bleed valve on each front caliper assembly.
   b. Place the loose end of the hose in a container.
   c. Open the bleed valve on each caliper and apply the front brake lever until the brake fluid is pumped out of the system.
   d. Disconnect the hoses and tighten the bleed valves.

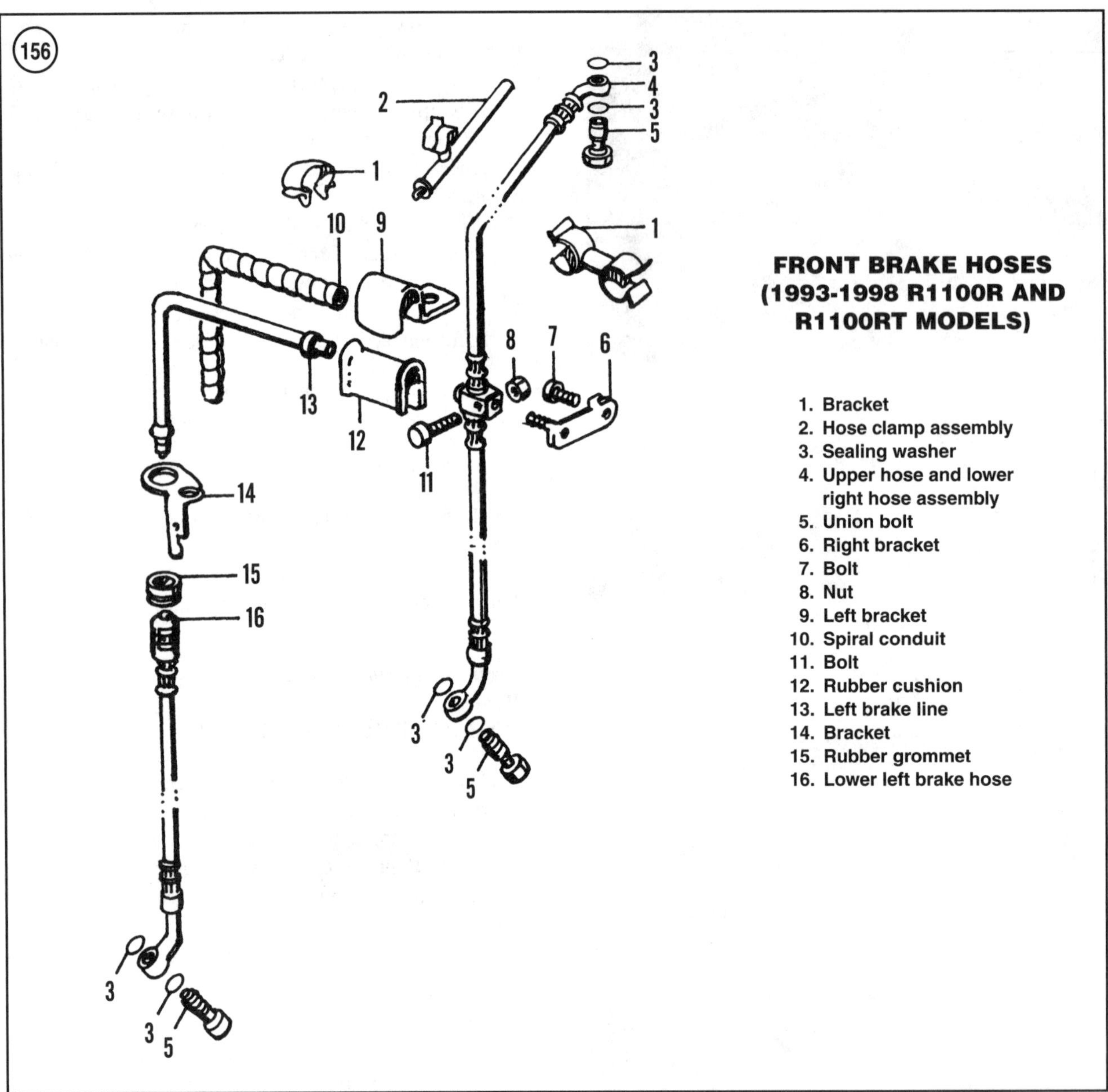

FRONT BRAKE HOSES (1993-1998 R1100R AND R1100RT MODELS)

e. Dispose of this brake fluid properly.

NOTE

The upper brake hose, from the master cylinder, is an integral part of the lower right brake hose that is attached to the right caliper. Also included in this assembly is the connector block where the left brake line attaches.

4. To remove the upper hose and lower right hose, perform the following:

a. Place a couple of shop cloths under the union bolt and remove the union bolt and sealing washers (**Figure 154**) securing the upper brake hose to the master cylinder. Disconnect the brake hose from the master cylinder.
b. Remove the union bolt and sealing washers securing the lower brake hose to left caliper. Disconnect the brake hose from the left caliper.
c. Remove the bolt securing the rubber cushion and bracket to the lower fork bridge. Remove the cushion and bracket to gain access to the following fitting.

d. On the right side, hold the fitting on the connector with a wrench and unscrew the flare nut securing the right brake line to the connector. Disconnect the left brake line from the connector.

e. Remove the bolt and nut securing the connector to the bracket.

f. Remove the upper brake hose and lower right brake hose from any clamps or tie wraps and carefully remove the brake hose from the frame and front fork area.

5. To remove the lower left brake hose, perform the following:

a. Remove the union bolt and sealing washers securing the lower brake hose to the left caliper. Disconnect the brake hose from the left caliper.

b. Hold the fitting on the lower brake hose with a wrench and unscrew the flare nut securing the lower brake hose to the left brake line.

c. Carefully remove the lower brake hose from the bracket and grommet on the left fork leg and remove the lower brake hose.

6. To remove the left brake line, perform the following:

a. Hold the fitting on the lower brake hose with a wrench and unscrew the flare nut securing the lower brake hose to the right brake line.

b. On the right side, hold the fitting on the connector with a wrench and unscrew the flare nut securing the right brake line to the connector. Disconnect the left brake line from the connector and remove the brake line from the bracket and grommet on the left fork leg and remove the left brake line.

7. Inspect the brake line as follows:

a. Check the brake line for any dents, cracks or fractures.

b. Check the threads at each end of the line.

8. Install new hoses, sealing washers and union bolts in the reverse order of removal. Be sure to install new sealing washers in the correct positions.

9. Tighten all union bolts and flare nut fittings to 15 N•m (132 in.-lb.).

10. Refill the master cylinder with fresh brake fluid clearly marked DOT 4. Bleed the front brake system as described in this chapter.

11. Install the front fender as described in Chapter Fifteen.

12. On RT models, install the side sections on the front fairing as described in Chapter Fifteen.

WARNING
Do not ride the motorcycle until the rear brakes are operating correctly with full hydraulic advantage.

Front Brake Hoses Removal/Installation (1999-2000 R1100R, 2002-on R1150R and 1999-2002 R1100S Models)

NOTE
ABS is optional on the R1150R and R1100S models.

This procedure covers removal and installation of both front hoses. If replacing only one hose, refer to the steps relating to that specific hose.

1. Remove the seat as described in Chapter Fifteen.

2. Remove the fuel tank as described in Chapter Nine.

3. On R1100S models, remove the front fairing inner panel (A, **Figure 157**) as described in Chapter Fifteen.

NOTE
To prevent the entry of moisture and dirt, cap the end of the brake hoses and lines that are not going to be replaced. Place the loose end in a reclosable plastic bag.

4. Drain the hydraulic brake fluid from the front brake system as follows:

a. Attach a hose to the bleed valve on each front caliper.

b. Place the loose end of the hose in a container.

c. Open the bleed valve on each caliper and apply the front brake lever until the brake fluid is pumped out of the system.

d. Disconnect the hoses and tighten the bleed valves.

e. Dispose of this brake fluid properly.

5. To remove the upper hose, perform the following:

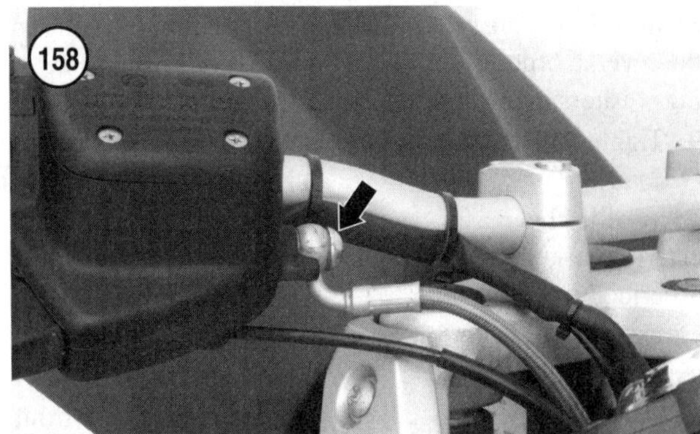

a. On models so equipped, remove the rubber cap (B, **Figure 157**) from the union bolt on the master cylinder upper hose.
b. Place a couple of shop cloths under the union bolt and remove the union bolt and sealing washers (**Figure 158**) securing the upper brake hose to the master cylinder. Disconnect the brake hose from the master cylinder.
c. Remove the rubber cap (A, **Figure 159**) from the union bolt. Remove the union bolt and sealing washer (B, **Figure 159**) and disconnect the upper brake hose from the two-way connector.
d. Remove the upper hose from any clamps or tie wraps and remove the upper brake hose from the frame.

6. To remove the lower hose assembly, perform the following:
a. Place a couple of shop cloths under the union bolt and remove the union bolt and sealing washers (C, **Figure 159**) securing the upper portion of the lower brake hose assembly to the two-way connector. Disconnect the brake hose (D, **Figure 159**) from the two-way connector.
b. On the left side caliper, remove the union bolt and sealing washers (**Figure 160**) securing the lower brake hose to the left front caliper. Disconnect the brake hose from the left front caliper. Place the brake hose in a reclosable plastic bag.
c. On the right side caliper, remove the union bolt and sealing washers (**Figure 161**) securing the lower brake hose to the right front caliper. Disconnect the brake hose from the right front caliper. Place the brake hose in a reclosable plastic bag.
d. Remove the bolt (A, **Figure 162**) securing the lower brake hose assembly to the right fork slider.
e. Unhook the crossover hose from the front fender guide (B, **Figure 162**) and remove the lower hose assembly (C) from the front wheel and frame.

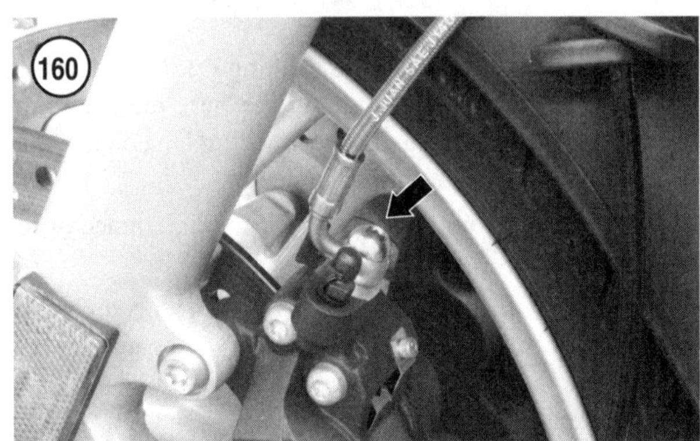

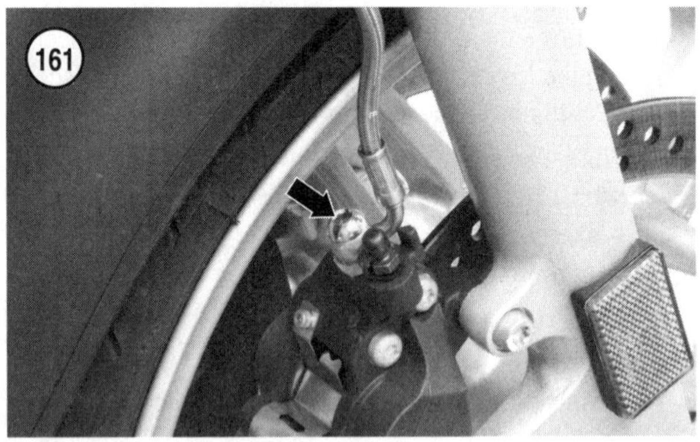

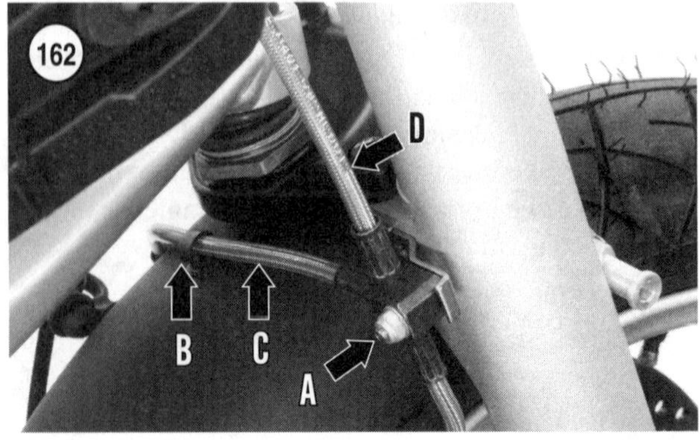

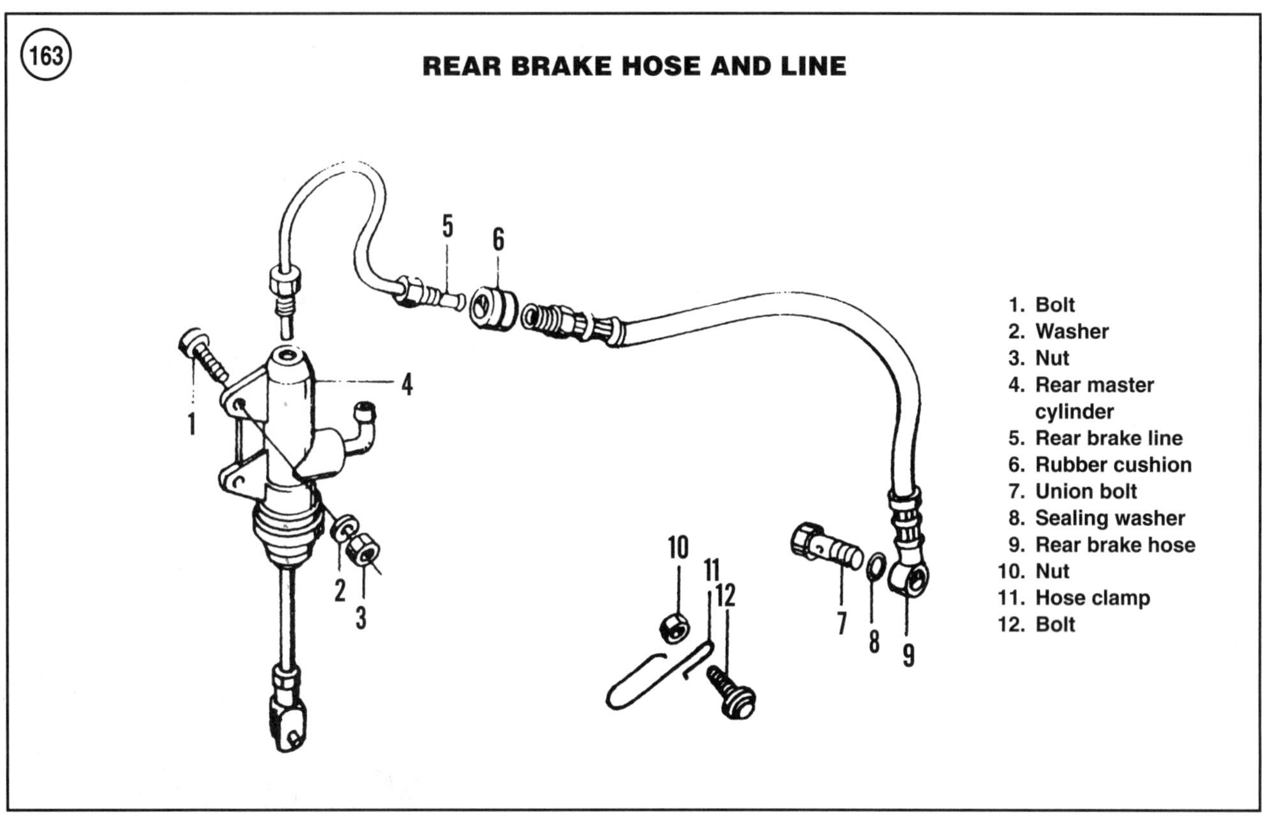

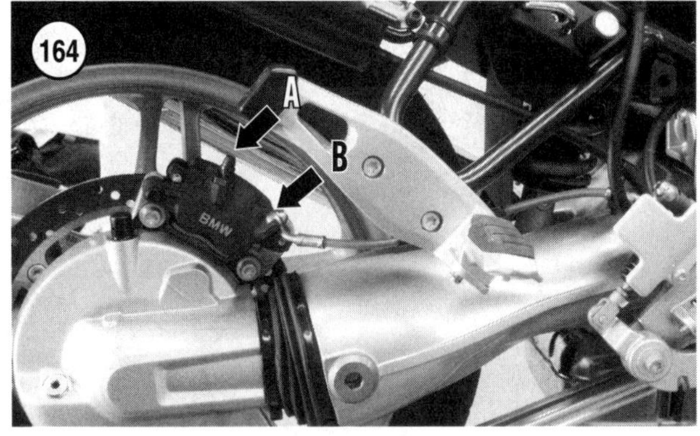

7. Install new hoses, sealing washers and union bolts in the reverse order of removal. Be sure to install new sealing washers in the correct positions.

8. Tighten all union bolts to 15 N•m (132 in.-lb.). Install the rubber caps onto the union bolts where applicable.

9. Refill and bleed the system as described in this chapter.

WARNING
Do not ride the motorcycle until the rear brakes are operating correctly with full hydraulic advantage.

10. On R1100S models, install the front fairing inner panel as described in Chapter Fifteen.
11. Install the fuel tank as described in Chapter Nine.
12. Install the seat as described in Chapter Fifteen.

Rear Brake Hose and Line Removal/Installation (All Models)

Refer to **Figure 163**.

NOTE
This procedure is shown on a motorcycle equipped with ABS. The fittings are the same on all models.

1. Drain the hydraulic brake fluid from the rear brake system as follows:
   a. Attach a hose to the bleed valve (A, **Figure 164**) on the caliper assembly.
   b. Place the loose end of the hose in a container.
   c. Open the bleed valve and apply the rear brake pedal until the brake fluid is pumped out of the system.
   d. Disconnect the hose and tighten the bleed valve.
   e. Dispose of this brake fluid properly.

2. On RT models, remove the right lower fairing section as described in Chapter Fifteen.

3A. On R and GS models, disconnect the brake line (**Figure 165**, typical) from the top of the master cylinder.

3B. On RS models, disconnect the brake line (**Figure 166**, typical) from the top of the master cylinder.

3C. On RT models, disconnect the brake hose or line (**Figure 167**, typical) from the top of the master cylinder.

4. Remove the union bolt and sealing washers (B, **Figure 164**) securing the brake hose to the rear caliper.

5A. On early models, on the right side of the swing arm, perform the following:

   a. Hold the fitting on the rear brake hose with a wrench and unscrew the flare nut securing the rear brake hose to the rear brake line.
   b. Remove the rear brake hose from the clamps and tie wraps on the swing arm.
   c. Carefully remove the rear brake hose and/or rear brake line from the bracket and grommet on the swing arm.

5B. On later models, perform the following:

   a. Remove the union bolt and sealing washers (A, **Figure 168**) securing the brake hose to the master cylinder.
   b. Remove the rear brake hose from the clamps (B, **Figure 168**) and tie wraps on the swing arm.

6. Install a new hose, new sealing washers and a new union bolt in the reverse order of removal. Be sure to install new sealing washers in the correct positions.

7. Tighten all union bolts to 15 N•m (132 in.-lb.).

8. Tighten the flare nut fitting to 15 N•m (132 in.-lb.)

9. Refill the master cylinder with fresh brake fluid clearly marked DOT 4.

10. Bleed the front brake system as described in this chapter.

11. On RT models, install the right lower fairing section as described in Chapter Fifteen.

BRAKE DISC

The brake discs are separate from the wheel hubs and can be removed once the wheel is removed from the motorcycle.

Inspection

It is not necessary to rcmovc the disc from the wheel to inspect it. Small nicks and marks on the disc are not important, but radial scratches deep enough to snag a fingernail (**Figure 169**) reduce braking effectiveness and

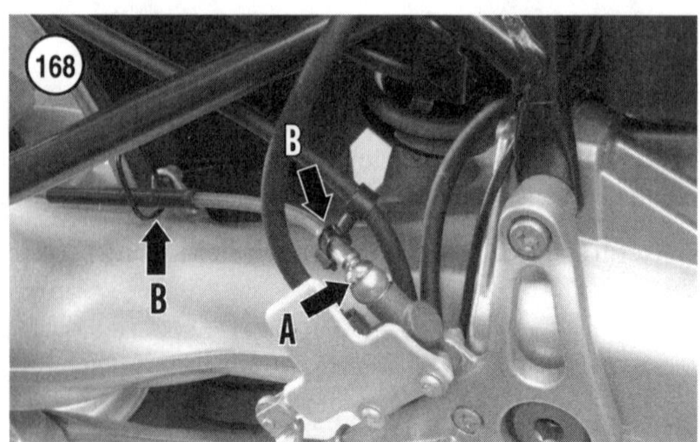

increase brake pad wear. If these grooves are present, and the brake pads are wearing rapidly, replace the disc.

Specifications are in **Table 1**. Each disc is also marked with the minimum (MIN) thickness. If the specification marked on the disc differs from the one in **Table 1**, use the specification on the disc.

When servicing the brake discs, do not have the discs machined to compensate for warp. The discs are thin, and

resurfacing them will reduce their thickness, causing them to warp rapidly. A warped disc may be caused by the brake pads dragging on the disc, due to a faulty caliper, and overheating the disc. Overheating can also be caused by unequal pad pressure on the disc.

NOTE
It is not necessary to remove the wheel to measure the disc thickness. The measurement can be performed with the wheel installed or removed from the motorcycle.

1. Measure the thickness of the disc at several locations with a vernier caliper or a micrometer (**Figure 170**). Replace the disc if the thickness in any area is less than that specified in **Table 1**, or the marked MIN dimension on the disc.
2. Make sure the disc mounting bolts are tight prior to running this check. Check the disc runout with a dial indicator as shown in **Figure 171**.

NOTE
When checking the front discs, turn the handlebar all the way to one side, then to the other side.

3. Slowly rotate the wheel and watch the dial indicator. If the runout exceeds the specification in **Table 1**, replace the disc(s).
4. Clean the disc of any rust or corrosion and wipe it clean with brake cleaner. Never use an oil-based solvent that may leave an oil residue on the disc.

Removal/Installation

1. Remove the front or rear wheel as described in Chapter Eleven.

2A. On a wire front wheel, remove the Torx bolts and washers (**Figure 172**) securing the disc to the wheel hub, and remove the disc.

2B. On an alloy front wheel, remove the Torx bolts and washers (**Figure 173**) securing the disc to the wheel hub, and remove the disc.

3A. On a wire rear wheel, remove the bolts (**Figure 174**) securing the disc to the wheel hub, and remove the disc.

3B. On an alloy rear wheel with the rear disc mounted to the rear wheel, remove the Allen bolts (**Figure 175**) securing the disc to the rear wheel. Remove the disc.

3C. On an alloy rear wheel with the rear disc mounted to the final drive unit, perform the following:

  a. Shift the transmission into fifth gear.
  b. Remove the two special countersunk Allen bolts (A, **Figure 176**) securing the rear disc brake assembly to the final drive unit.
  c. Remove the rear disc brake assembly (B, **Figure 176**) from the final drive unit.

4. Check the brake disc bolts for thread damage. Replace worn or damaged fasteners.

5. Check the threaded bolt holes for the brake disc in the wheel hub for thread damage. True them with a tap if necessary.

6. Clean the disc and the disc mounting surface thoroughly with brake cleaner. Allow the surfaces to dry before installation.

7. Position the disc onto the wheel, or final drive unit, so the disc is rotating in the correct direction. The lower holes (**Figure 177**), closest to the center of the wheel, must be the leading holes, not the trailing holes.

8. Install the disc onto the wheel hub.

9. Apply a drop of medium strength thread locking compound to the threads of new Torx bolts prior to installation.

10. On an alloy rear wheel with the rear disc mounted to the final drive unit, be sure to use the special countersunk Allen bolts (**Figure 178**) to secure the disc to the final drive unit.

11. Install the bolts and tighten to the following:

  a. Front wire wheel: 24 N•m (18 ft.-lb.).
  b. Front alloy wheel: 21 N•m (15 ft.-lb.).
  c. Rear wire wheel: 21 N•m (15 ft.-lb.).
  d. Rear alloy wheel: 24 N•m (18 ft.-lb.).

12. Install the front or rear wheel as described in Chapter Eleven.

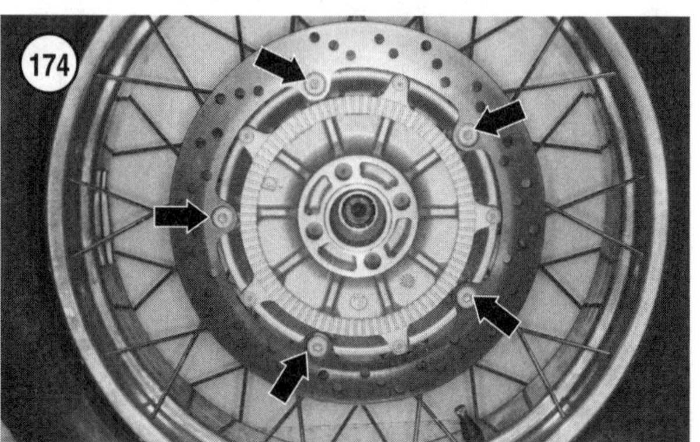

ABS BRAKE SYSTEM

The Anti-lock Braking System (ABS) is designed to prevent wheel locking under heavy braking when the motorcycle is traveling in a straight line. The basic layout of the ABS components is shown in **Figure 179**.

The system consists of the ABS unit, or ABS pressure modulator, that controls the sensing and control functions of the entire system. The ABS unit (A, **Figure 180**), or ABS Pressure Modulator, is located under the fuel tank adjacent to the Motronic control unit (B) and the battery (C). The ABS unit receives information from the pulse generating inductive sensor (A, **Figure 181**) that is located at each wheel. Each inductive sensor relays information regarding wheel rotation speed from the toothed pulse-generating ring (B, **Figure 181**) that is attached to the wheel or the brake disc.

The ABS unit, or pressure modulator, contains the two-channel pressure regulator, an electric motor and sev-

eral microcomputers. This unit interprets the signals from the wheel sensors and sends this information to the pressure modulators to control wheel lockup. When the master cylinder lever or pedal is applied, the hydraulic fluid exits the master cylinder, travels to and goes through the ABS unit's pressure modulator and then travels to the caliper assembly for braking action.

The majority of the brake system plumbing uses metal brake lines with a minimal use of flexible brake hoses. Since brake pressure is critical in an ABS system, the BMW flexible brake hoses are designed to have the same minimal flexing characteristics as the steel lines. When replacing the flexible brake hoses, install only authorized BMW replacement hoses specifically designed for use with the specific ABS system. Using a flexible brake hose of an alternate design will drastically change the characteristics of the brake system.

1993-3002 models are equipped with ABSII. 2002-on models are equipped with the BMW Integral ABS system. There are two versions of this system: Fully Integral System (R1150RT models only) and the Partially Integral System (standard or optional equipment).

If the ABS system malfunctions, the regular brake system will still operate—but without ABS assist. If the warning lights are flashing, immediately take the motorcycle to a BMW dealership for service. If there is a fault within the system, the test procedure and system repairs must be performed by an authorized BMW dealership.

ABSII System

The ABS system has a self-diagnosis feature that activates after the motorcycle reaches a speed of 3 mph (5 km/h).

1. Turn the ignition switch on.
2. Both ABS warning lights (A, **Figure 182**) located on the instrument panel will flash simultaneously.
3. Start the motorcycle and ride slowly. As soon as the motorcycle reaches 3 mph (5 km/h) and after the brakes have been applied for the first time, the ABS warning lights will stop flashing. This indicates that the ABS system is operating correctly. If there is a problem or fault within the system, the red warning lights will operate as follows:
    a. If the warning lights remain on, or flash alternately, there is a fault and the ABS system has been deactivated.
    b. Stop the motorcycle. Turn the ignition switch off, then back on. If the warning lights return to flashing simultaneously, the ABS system was temporarily deactivated and has then returned to normal operation.
    c. If the warning lights continue to flash alternately, the ABS system is still deactivated and the system must be serviced immediately by a BMW dealership.
4. This ABS system is designed to be interactive with the rider. If the system malfunctions, the rider can confirm the fault by pressing the ABS Alert Confirmation button (B, **Figure 182**). When the button is pressed, the upper ABS warning light will no longer be illuminated while the lower warning light remains on constantly. After 4.5 min-

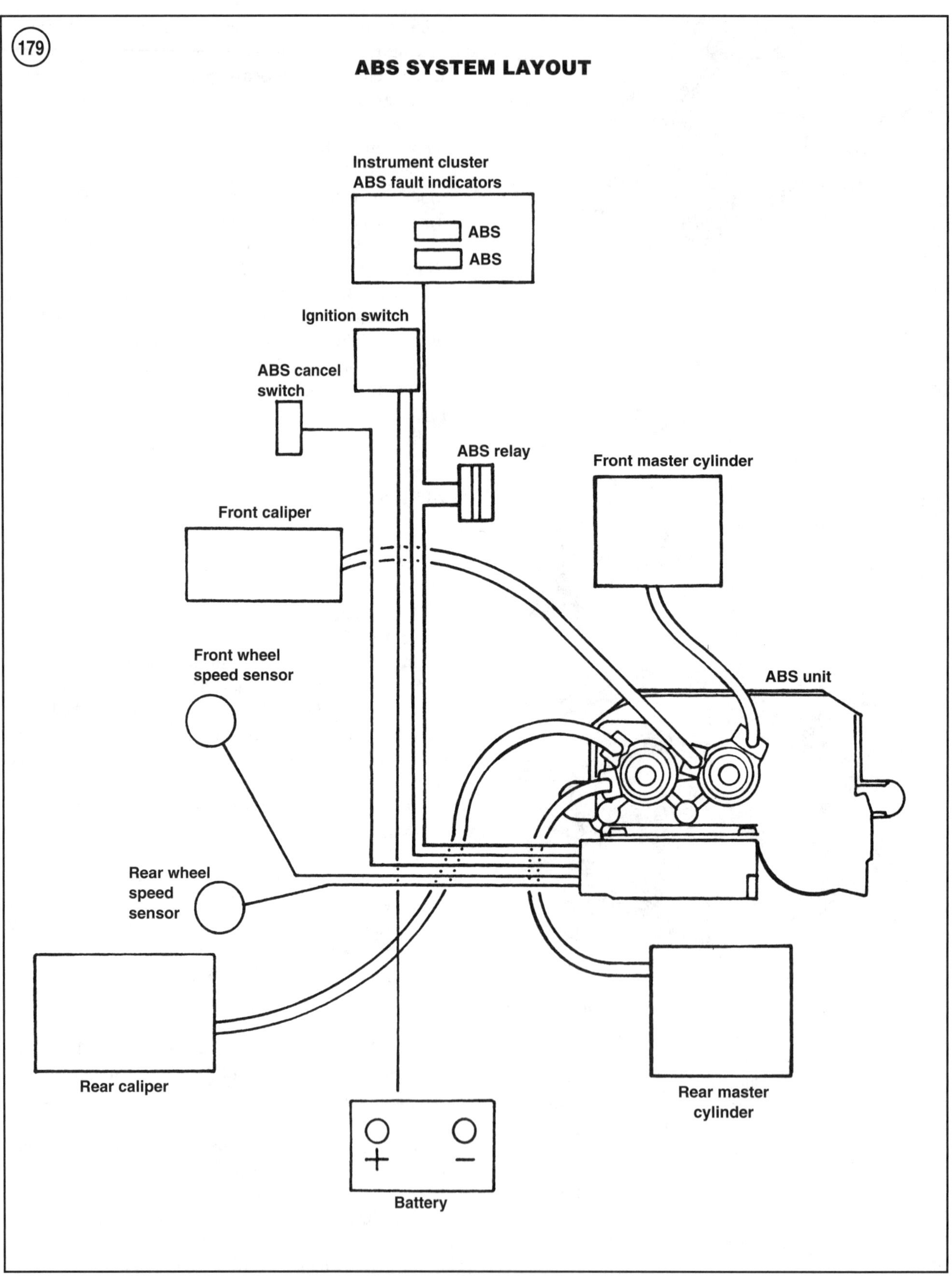
179
ABS SYSTEM LAYOUT
Instrument cluster
ABS fault indicators
ABS
ABS
Ignition switch
ABS cancel
switch
ABS relay
Front master cylinder
Front caliper
Front wheel
speed sensor
ABS unit
Rear wheel
speed
sensor
Rear caliper
Rear master
cylinder
+
−
Battery

utes, both warning lights will once again start flashing alternately reminding the rider that the ABS system still is not *operating.*

Integral ABS System

NOTE
This test is for both the partial integral and full integral brake systems.

This self-diagnosis and pull-away test must be performed prior to the first ride of the day otherwise the ABS will not function.

Self-diagnosis test

1. If parked on a grade, shift the transmission into gear. Keep the clutch lever in the released position. This is necessary to ensure the self-diagnosis is performed correctly. After the self-diagnosis is completed, apply the brakes, disengage the clutch and start the engine.
2. Both the handlebar brake lever and foot lever must be in the released position.
3. Turn the ignition switch on.
4. The ABS warning light (**Figure 183**) will illuminate and flash at 4 flashes per seconds.
5. The general warning light, below the ABS warning light, will now illuminate.
6. The self-diagnosis process is not in progress.
7. The ABS warning light will now flash at 1 flash per second.
8. The general warning light will go off.
9. The self-diagnosis is now complete now perform the *Pull-away test* described in this section.

14

Pull-away test

1. Perform the self-diagnosis test.
2. Start the engine and ride slowly.
3. The ABS warning light (**Figure 183**) will illuminate and flash at 4 flashes per seconds.
4. As soon as the motorcycle reaches 3 mph (5 km/h), the ABS warning lights will stop flashing. This indicates that the ABS system is operating correctly.
5. The pull-away test is successfully completed and integral ABS is available.
6. If there is a problem or fault within the system, both warning lights will once again start flashing alternately reminding the rider that the ABS system still is *not* operating.

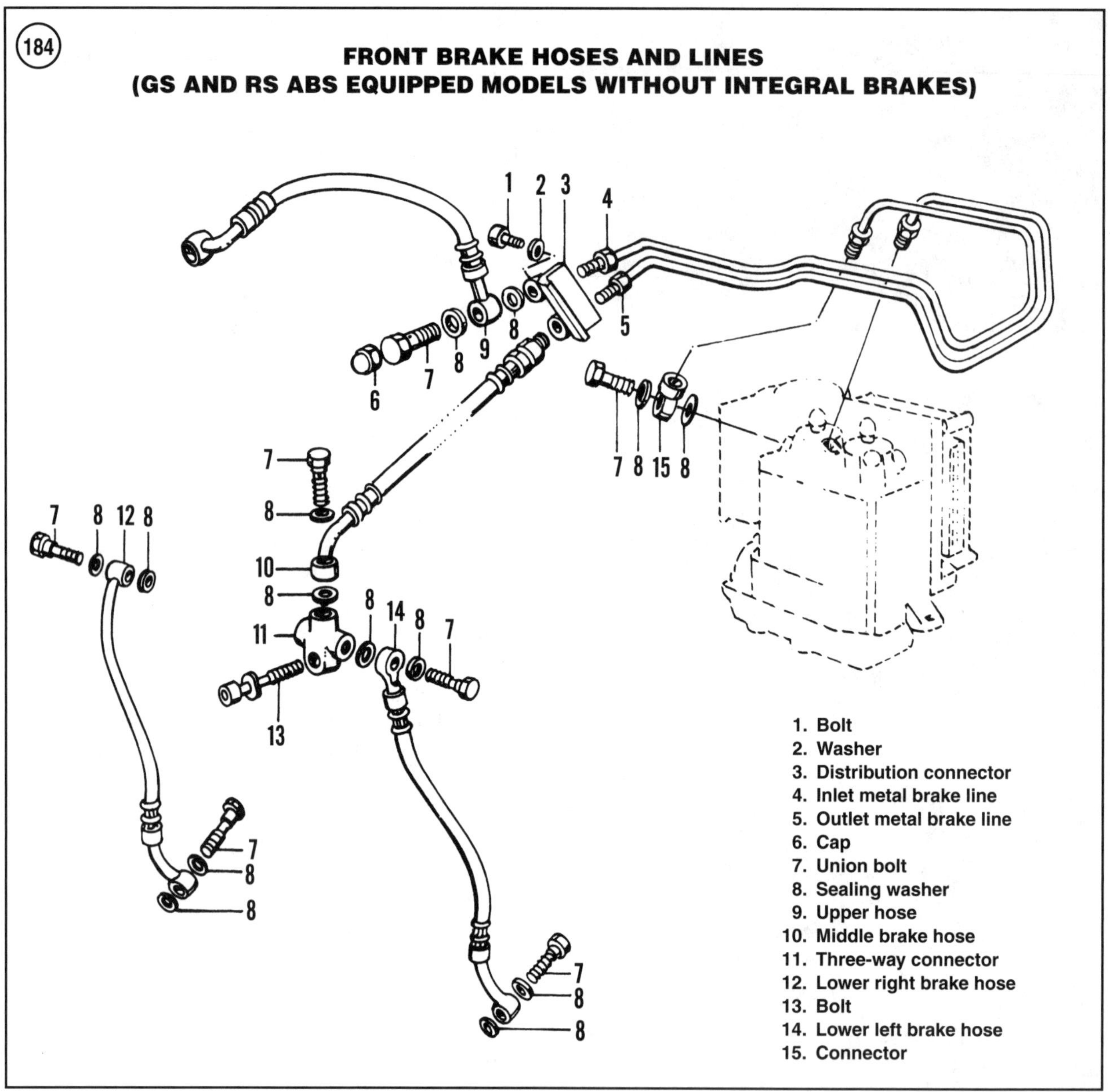

BRAKE HOSE AND LINE REPLACEMENT (ABS EQUIPPED MODELS WITHOUT INTEGRAL BRAKES)

Check the brake hoses at the brake inspection intervals listed in Chapter Three. Replace the brake hoses if they show signs of wear or damage.

The metal brake lines do not require routine replacement unless they are damaged or the end fittings are leaking. While replacing the flexible brake hoses, inspect the metal brake lines for damage. If they have been hit, the line may be restricted, thus decreasing braking effectiveness.

WARNING
Whenever a hydraulic ABS component is disconnected the system must be bled with a power bleeder by a BMW dealership.

WARNING
Always install authorized BMW replacement hoses specifically designed for use with the ABS system. Using a flexible brake hose of an alternate design will drastically

185

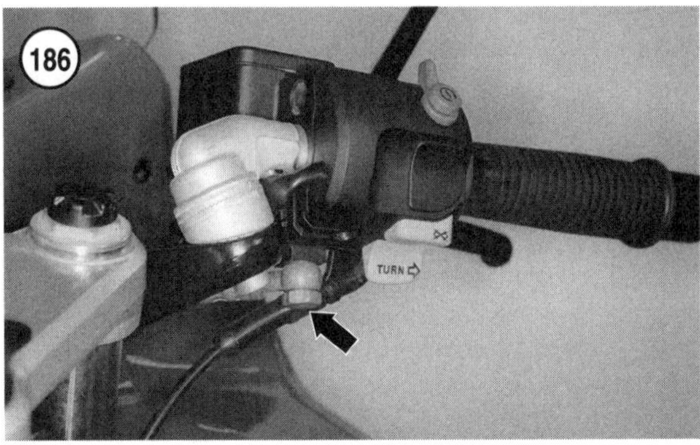

186

change the characteristics of the brake system.

To replace a brake hose, perform the following:

1. Use a plastic drop cloth to cover areas that could be damaged by spilled brake fluid.
2. When removing a brake hose or brake line, note the following:
   a. Record the hose or line routing on a piece of paper.
   b. Remove any bolts or brackets securing the brake hose to the frame or suspension component.
   c. Before removing the union bolts, note how the end of the brake hose is installed or indexed against the part it is threaded into. The hoses must be installed facing in their original position.
3. Replace union bolts with damaged hex-heads.
4. Always install *new* washers with the union bolts.
5. Reverse these steps to install the new brake hoses, while noting the following:
   a. Compare the new and old hoses to make sure they are the same.
   b. Clean the new washers, union bolts and hose ends to remove any contamination.
   c. Referring to the notes made during removal, route the brake hose along its original path.
   d. Install a *new* union bolt washer on each side of the brake hose.
   e. Tighten the union bolts to 15 N•m (132 in.-lb.).
   f. Tighten the flare nuts to 15 N•m (132 in.-lb.).
   g. After replacing a front brake hose, turn the handlebars from side to side to make sure the hose does not rub against any part or pull away from its brake unit.
   h. Refill the master cylinders and bleed the brakes as described in this chapter.

WARNING
Do not ride the motorcycle until the front and rear brakes operate correctly with full hydraulic advantage and the brake light works properly.

Front Brake Hoses and Lines Removal/Installation (GS, RS and S Models)

This procedure covers removal and installation of all of the front brake hoses and lines. Refer to **Figure 184**. If replacing only one hose, refer to the steps relating to that specific hose, or if replacing all hoses, perform all steps.

1. On RS models, remove the side sections on the front fairing as described in Chapter Fifteen.
2. Remove the front fender (A, **Figure 185**) as described in Chapter Fifteen.

NOTE
To prevent the entry of moisture and dirt, cap the end of the brake hoses and lines that are not going to be replaced. Place the loose end in a reclosable plastic bag.

3. Drain the hydraulic brake fluid from the front brake system as follows:
   a. Attach a hose to the bleed valve (**Figure 185**) on each front caliper assembly.
   b. Place the loose end of the hose in a container.
   c. Open the bleed valve on each caliper and apply the front brake lever until the brake fluid is pumped out of the system.
   d. Disconnect the hoses and tighten the bleed valves.
   e. Dispose of this brake fluid properly.
4. To remove the upper hose, perform the following:
   a. Place a couple of shop cloths under the union bolt and remove the union bolt and sealing washers (**Figure 186**) securing the upper brake hose to the master cylinder. Disconnect the brake hose from the master cylinder.

b. Remove the union bolt and sealing washers (A, **Figure 187**) securing the upper brake hose to distribution connector. Disconnect the brake hose from the distribution connector.
c. Remove the upper hose from any clamps or tie wraps, and remove the upper hose (B, **Figure 187**) from the frame.

5. To remove the middle hose, perform the following:
   a. Remove the union bolt and sealing washers (C, **Figure 187**) securing the middle brake hose to the distribution connector. Disconnect the brake hose from the distribution connector.
   b. Remove the union bolt and sealing washers (A, **Figure 188**) securing the middle brake hose to the three-way connector. Disconnect the brake hose from the three-way connector.
   c. Remove the middle hose (B, **Figure 188**) from any clamps or tie wraps and from the frame and fork area.
6. To remove the lower hose, perform the following:
   a. Remove the union bolt and sealing washers securing the lower brake hose to the front caliper. Disconnect the brake hose from the front caliper.
   b. Remove the union bolt and sealing washers (C, **Figure 188**) securing the lower brake hose to the three-way connector. Disconnect the brake hose from the three-way connector.
   c. Remove the lower hose from any clamps or tie wraps and remove the lower hose (D, **Figure 188**) from the fork area.
7. If necessary, repeat Step 6 for the lower hose on the opposite caliper.
8. If necessary, remove the metal brake lines as follows:
   a. On the right side, hold the fitting on the distribution connector with a wrench and unscrew the flare nut(s) (**Figure 189**) securing the front metal brake line(s) to the distribution connector. Disconnect the right brake line from the connector.
   b. Unscrew the flare nut(s) (**Figure 190**) securing the front metal brake line(s) to the ABS unit. Disconnect the front metal brake line(s) from the ABS unit.
   c. Very carefully remove the front metal brake line(s) (**Figure 191**) from any clamps or tie wraps and out from the frame and around the Motronic control unit (**Figure 192**).
9. Install new hoses, sealing washers and union bolts in the reverse order of removal while noting the following:
   a. Install *new* sealing washers in the correct positions.
   b. Tighten the union bolts to 15 N•m (132 in.-lb.).
   c. Tighten the flare nuts to 15 N•m (132 in.-lb.).

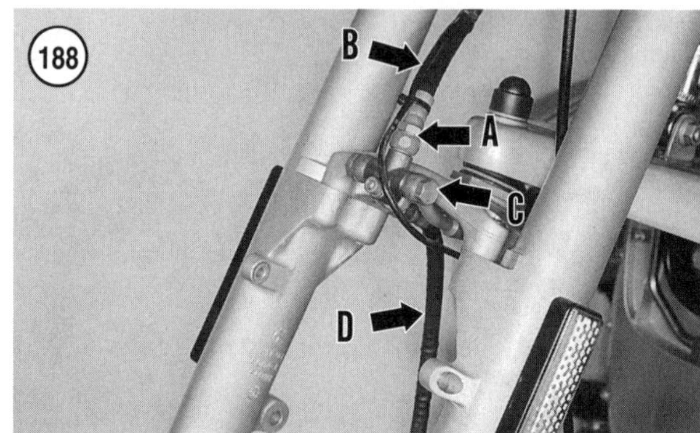

   d. Install the front fender as described in Chapter Fifteen.
   e. On RS models, install the side sections on the front fairing as described in Chapter Fifteen.
   f. Have the brake system filled and bled by a BMW dealership.

WARNING

Do not ride the motorcycle until the front and rear brakes operate correctly with full hydraulic advantage and the brake light works properly.

190

191

192

Front Brake Hoses and Lines Removal/Installation (R and RT Models)

This procedure covers removal and installation of all of the front brake hoses and lines. If replacing only one hose, refer to the steps relating to that specific hose, or line, or if replacing all hoses and lines, perform all steps.

Refer to **Figure 193**.

1. On RT models, remove the side sections on the front fairing as described in Chapter Fifteen.

2. Remove the front fender as described in Chapter Fifteen.

NOTE
To prevent the entry of moisture and dirt, cap the end of the brake hoses and lines that are not going to be replaced. Place the loose end in a plastic reclosable bag.

3. Drain the hydraulic brake fluid from the front brake system as follows:
   a. Attach a hose to the bleed valve on each front caliper assembly.
   b. Place the loose end of the hose in a container to catch the brake fluid.
   c. Open the bleed valve on each caliper and apply the front brake lever until the brake fluid is pumped out of the system.
   d. Disconnect the hoses and tighten the bleed valves.
   e. Dispose of this brake fluid properly.

NOTE
The middle brake hose is an integral part of the lower left brake hose that attaches to the left caliper. Also included in this assembly is the connector block to which the right brake line attaches.

4. To remove the upper hose, perform the following:
   a. Place a couple of shop cloths under the union bolt and remove the union bolt and sealing washers (**Figure 186**) securing the upper brake hose to the master cylinder. Disconnect the brake hose from the master cylinder.
   b. Remove the union bolt and sealing washers (A, **Figure 187**) securing the upper brake hose to the connector block. Disconnect the brake hose from the connector block.
   c. Remove the upper hose (B, **Figure 187**) from any clamps or tie wraps and carefully remove the assembly from the frame and front fork area.
5. To remove the middle and lower left hose assembly, perform the following:
   a. Remove the union bolt and sealing washers (C, **Figure 187**) securing the middle and lower left brake hose to the connector block. Disconnect the brake hose from the connector block.
   b. Remove the union bolt and sealing washers securing the lower brake hose to the left caliper. Disconnect the brake hose from the left caliper.
   c. On the right side, hold the fitting on the connector with a wrench and unscrew the flare nut securing the right brake line to the connector. Disconnect the right brake line from the connector.

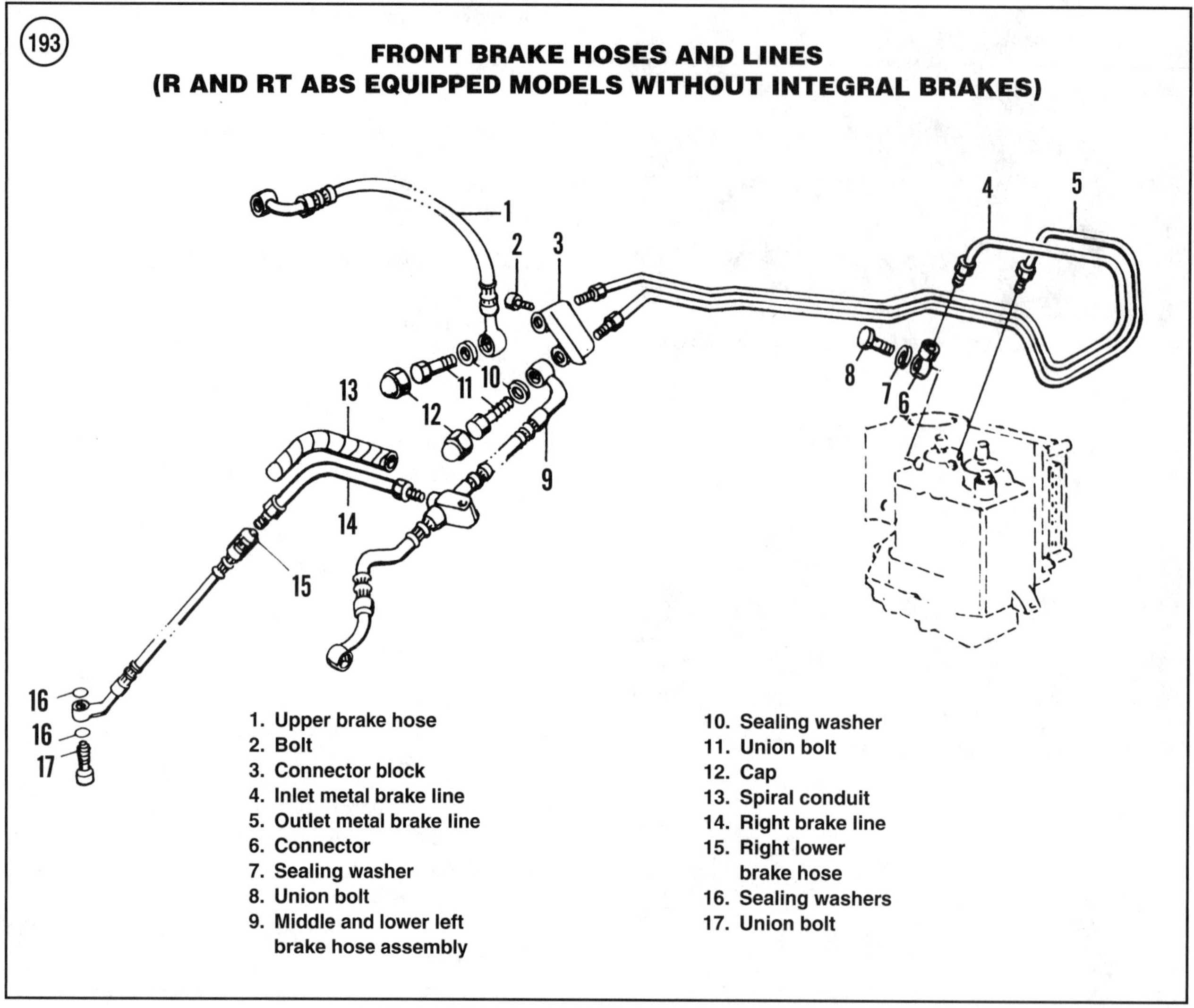

d. Remove the bolt and nut securing the connector to the bracket.

e. Remove the middle and lower left hose assembly from any clamps or tie wraps, then carefully remove the assembly from the frame and front fork area.

6. To remove the lower right brake hose, perform the following:

a. Remove the union bolt and sealing washers securing the lower brake hose to the right caliper. Disconnect the brake hose from the right caliper.

b. Hold the fitting on the lower brake hose with a wrench and unscrew the flare nut securing the lower brake hose to the right brake line.

c. Carefully remove the lower brake hose from the bracket and grommet on the right fork leg and remove the lower brake hose.

7. To remove the right brake line, perform the following:

a. Hold the fitting on the lower brake hose with a wrench and unscrew the flare nut securing the lower brake hose to the right brake line.

b. On the right side, hold the fitting on the connector with a wrench and unscrew the flare nut securing the right brake line to the connector. Disconnect the right brake line from the connector and remove the brake line from the bracket and grommet on the left fork leg and remove the right brake line.

8. If necessary, remove the metal brake lines as follows:

a. On the right side, hold the fitting on the distribution connector with a wrench and unscrew the flare nut(s) (**Figure 189**) securing the front metal brake line(s) to the distribution connector. Disconnect the right brake line from the connector.

b. Unscrew the flare nut(s) (**Figure 190**) securing the front metal brake line(s) to the ABS unit. Discon-

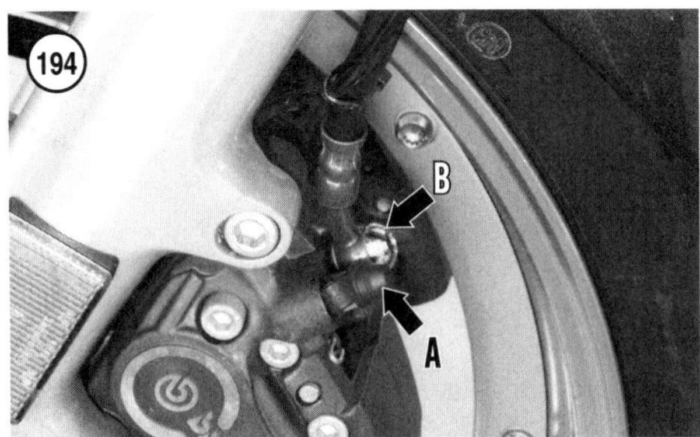

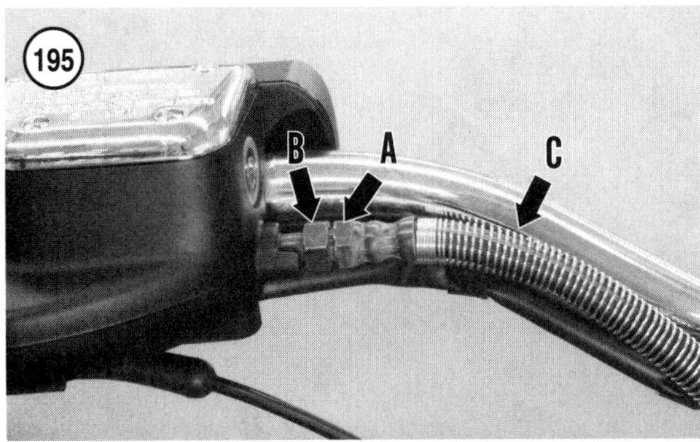

nect the front metal brake line(s) from the ABS unit.

c. Very carefully remove the front metal brake line(s) (**Figure 191**) from any clamps or tie wraps and move it out from the frame and around the Motronic control unit (**Figure 192**). Remove the line(s).

9. Inspect the brake line as follows:
   a. Check the brake line for any dents, cracks or fractures.
   b. Check the threads at each end of the line. Replace the line if the threads are damaged.

10. Install new hoses, sealing washers and union bolts in the reverse order of removal while noting the following:
   a. Install *new* sealing washers in the correct positions.
   b. Tighten the union bolts to 15 N•m (132 in.-lb.).
   c. Tighten the flare nuts to 15 N•m (132 in.-lb.).
   d. Install the front fender as described in Chapter Fifteen.
   e. On RT models, install the side sections on the front fairing as described in Chapter Fifteen.
   f. Have the brake system filled and bled by a BMW dealership.

WARNING
Do not ride the motorcycle until the front and rear brakes operate correctly with full hydraulic advantage and the brake light works properly.

Front Brake Hoses and Lines Removal/Installation (R850C and R1200C Models)

This procedure covers removal and installation of all of the front brake hoses and lines. If replacing only one hose, refer to the steps relating to that specific hose, or line, or if replacing all hoses and lines, perform all steps.

1. Remove the seat as described in Chapter Fifteen.
2. Remove the fuel tank as described in Chapter Nine.

NOTE
To prevent the entry of moisture and dirt, cap the end of the brake hoses and lines that are not going to be replaced. Place the loose end in a reclosable plastic bag.

3. Drain the hydraulic brake fluid from the front brake system as follows:
   a. Attach a hose to the bleed valve (A, **Figure 194**) on each front caliper assembly.
   b. Place the loose end of the hose in a container.
   c. Open the bleed valve on each caliper and apply the front brake lever until the brake fluid is pumped out of the system.
   d. Disconnect the hoses and tighten the bleed valves.
   e. Dispose of this brake fluid properly.
4. To remove the upper hose, perform the following:
   a. Place a couple of shop cloths under the master cylinder hose fittings.
   b. Hold the hose fitting (A, **Figure 195**) with a wrench and loosen the fitting (B) securing the upper brake hose to the master cylinder.
   c. Disconnect the brake hose from the master cylinder.
   d. At the under side of the front frame, unscrew and remove the union bolt and sealing washers securing the upper hose to the upper distribution connector.
   e. Remove the upper hose from any clamps or tie wraps, and remove the upper hose (C, **Figure 195**) from the frame.
5. To remove the lower right side short hose, perform the following:
   a. Unscrew and remove the union bolt and sealing washers (**Figure 196**) securing the lower hose to the brake caliper.

b. Disconnect the brake hose from the caliper.

c. Unscrew the fitting (A, **Figure 197**) securing the cross-over brake line to the right side short hose fitting on the fork slider.

d. Withdraw the brake short hose from the rubber grommet (B, **Figure 197**) on the mounting bracket.

e. Remove the lower right side short hose (C, **Figure 197**) from the mounting bracket.

6. To remove the lower left side hose and middle brake line assembly, perform the following:

a. Unscrew and remove the union bolt and sealing washers (B, **Figure 194**) securing the lower hose to the brake caliper.

b. Remove the tie wraps (A, **Figure 198**) securing the ABS sensor wires to the brake hose fittings.

c. Remove the fastener (B, **Figure 198**) securing the lower distribution connector to the left side fork slider.

d. Unscrew the upper and lower fittings securing the metal brake lines to the upper distribution connector.

e. Carefully lower the upper portion of the middle brake line assembly (C, **Figure 198**) down through the frame and fork sliders and remove it.

7. To remove the metal brake lines from the ABS unit, perform the following:

a. Unscrew the flare nut (**Figure 199**) securing the front metal brake lines to the ABS unit. Disconnect the front metal brake line(s) from the ABS unit.

b. Very carefully remove the front metal brake lines from any clamps or tie wraps and out from the front frame.

8. Install new hoses, sealing washers and union bolts in the reverse order of removal while noting the following:

a. Install *new* sealing washers in the correct positions.

b. Tighten the union bolts to 15 N•m (132 in.-lb.).

c. Tighten the flare nuts to 15 N•m (132 in.-lb.).

d. Tighten the lower distribution connector to the left side fork slider fastener to 9 N•m (80 in.-lb.).

e. Have the brake system filled and bled at a BMW dealership.

WARNING

Do not ride the motorcycle until the front and rear brakes operate correctly with full hydraulic advantage and the brake light works properly.

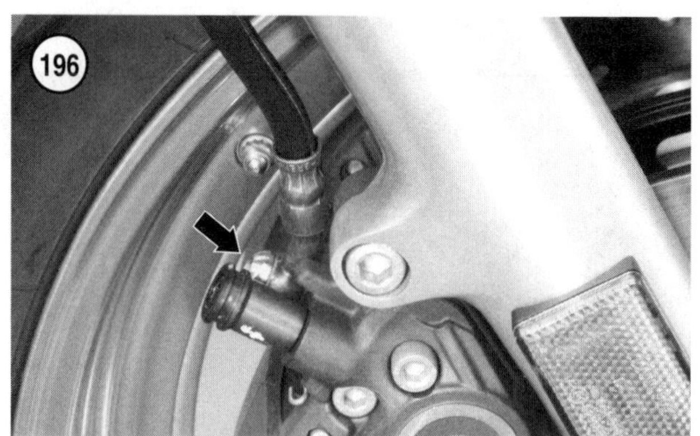

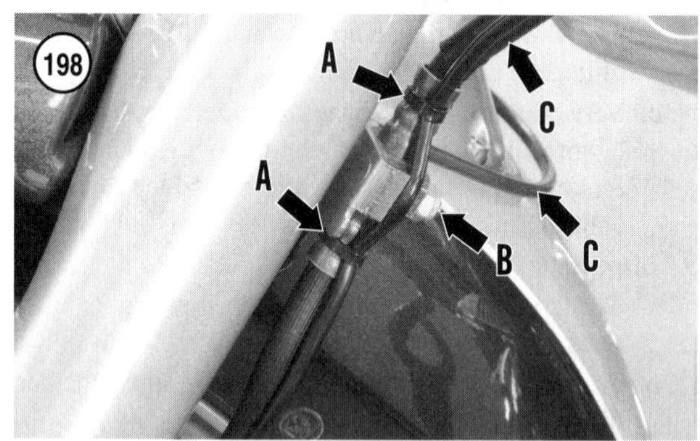

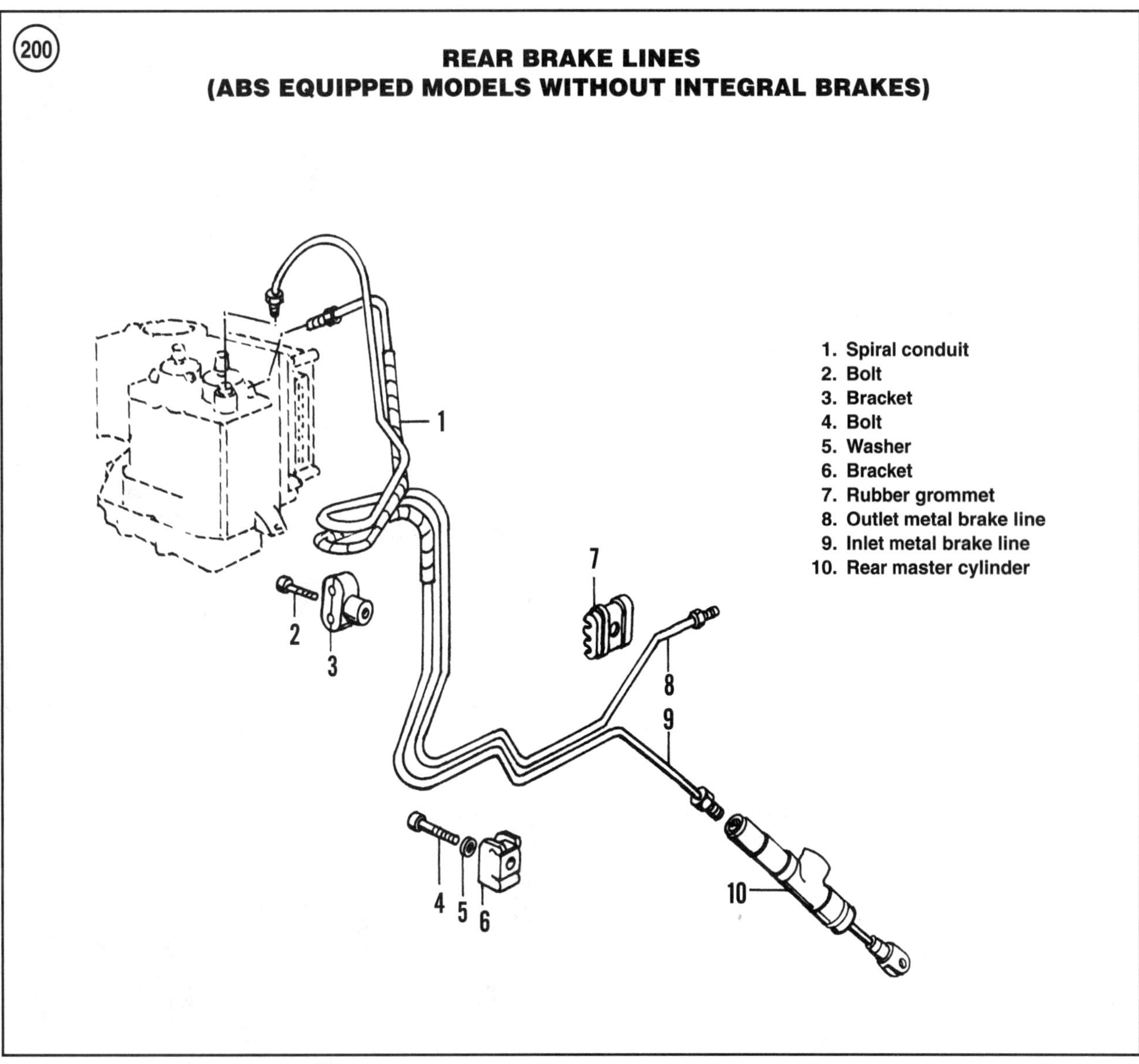

Rear Brake Hose and Lines Removal/Installation (All Models Except R850C and R1200C)

This procedure covers removal and installation of all of the rear brake hoses and lines. If replacing only one hose, refer to the steps relating to that specific hose, or line, or if replacing all hoses and lines, perform all steps.

Refer to **Figure 200**.

NOTE
To prevent the entry of moisture and dirt, cap the end of the brake hoses and lines that are not going to be replaced. Place the loose end in a plastic reclosable bag.

1. Drain the hydraulic brake fluid from the rear brake system as follows:
   a. Attach a hose to the bleed valve (A, **Figure 201**) on the caliper assembly.
   b. Place the loose end of the hose in a container to catch the brake fluid.
   c. Open the bleed valve and apply the rear brake pedal until the brake fluid is pumped out of the system.
   d. Disconnect the hose and tighten the bleed valve.
   e. Dispose of this brake fluid properly.
2. On RT and S models, remove the right lower fairing section as described in Chapter Fifteen.

3A. On R and GS models, disconnect the brake line (A, **Figure 202**) from the top of the master cylinder.

3B. On RS models, disconnect the brake line from the top of the master cylinder.
3C. On RT models, disconnect the brake line from the top of the master cylinder.
4. Remove the union bolt and sealing washers (B, **Figure 201**) securing the brake hose to the rear caliper.
5. On the right side of the swing arm, perform the following:
   a. Hold the fitting on the rear brake hose with a wrench and unscrew the flare nut securing the rear brake hose to the rear brake line (B, **Figure 202**).
   b. Remove the rear brake hose from the clamps and tie wraps on the swing arm.
   c. Carefully remove the rear brake hose and/or rear brake line from the bracket and grommet on the swing arm.
6. If necessary, remove the metal brake lines as follows:
   a. Remove the battery as described in Chapter Three.
   b. Hold the fitting on the rear brake hose with a wrench and unscrew the flare nut securing the rear brake hose to the rear brake line (B, **Figure 202**).
   c. Remove the bolt securing the bracket and rubber grommet (C, **Figure 202**) and brake lines to the transmission housing.
   d. Unscrew the flare nut(s) (**Figure 203**) securing the rear metal brake line(s) to the ABS unit. Disconnect the rear metal brake line(s) from the ABS unit.
   e. Very carefully remove the rear metal brake line(s) (**Figure 204**) from any clamps or tie wraps and out from the frame and around the battery case. Remove the line(s) from the frame and engine.
7. Install new hoses, sealing washers and union bolts in the reverse order of removal while noting the following:
   a. Install *new* sealing washers in the correct positions.
   b. Tighten the union bolts to 15 N•m (132 in.-lb.).
   c. Tighten the flare nuts to 15 N•m (132 in.-lb.).
   d. On RT models, install the right lower fairing section as described in Chapter Fifteen.
   e. Have the brake system filled and bled by a BMW dealership.

Rear Brake Hose and Lines Removal/Installation (R850C and R1200C Models)

This procedure covers removal and installation of all of the rear brake hoses and lines. If replacing only one hose, refer to the steps relating to that specific hose, or line, or if replacing all hoses and lines, perform all steps.

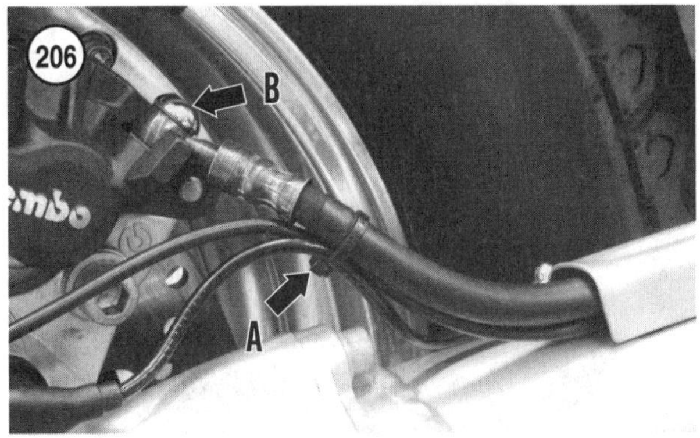

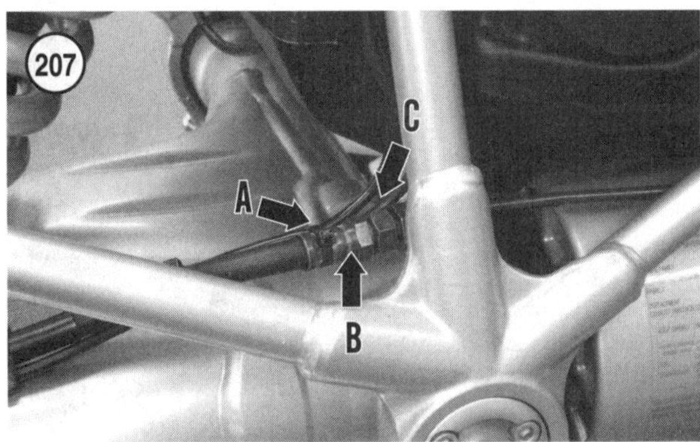

1. Remove the seat as described in Chapter Fifteen.
2. Remove the fuel tank as described in Chapter Nine.

NOTE

To prevent the entry of moisture and dirt, cap the end of the brake hoses and lines that are not going to be replaced. Place the loose end in a reclosable plastic bag.

3. Drain the hydraulic brake fluid from the front brake system as follows:
   a. Attach a hose to the bleed valve (**Figure 205**) on the rear caliper assembly.
   b. Place the loose end of the hose in a container.
   c. Open the bleed valve on each caliper and apply the rear brake pedal until the brake fluid is pumped out of the system.
   d. Disconnect the hose and tighten the bleed valves.
   e. Dispose of this brake fluid properly.
4. Remove the tie wrap (A, **Figure 206**) securing the ABS rear sensor and speed sensor wires to the rear portion of the brake hose.
5. Unscrew and remove the union bolt and sealing washers (B, **Figure 206**) securing the brake hose to the brake caliper.
6. Remove the tie wrap (A, **Figure 207**) securing the ABS rear sensor and speed sensor wires to the front portion of the brake hose.
7. Hold the hose fitting (B, **Figure 207**) with a wrench and loosen the fitting (C) securing the brake hose to the metal brake line.
8. Remove the screws securing the brake hose shield (**Figure 208**) to the swing arm and remove the shield.
9. Unscrew the flare nut (**Figure 209**) securing the metal brake line to the rear master cylinder.
10. To remove the metal brake lines from the ABS unit, perform the following:

   a. Unscrew the flare nuts (A, **Figure 210**) securing the front metal brake lines to the ABS unit. Disconnect the front metal brake lines from the ABS unit.
   b. Very carefully remove the front metal brake lines (B, **Figure 210**) from any clamps or tie wraps and out from the front frame.

11. Install new hoses, sealing washers and union bolts in the reverse order of removal while noting the following:
   a. Install *new* sealing washers in the correct positions.
   b. Tighten the union bolts to 15 N•m (132 in.-lb.).
   c. Tighten the flare nuts to 15 N•m (132 in.-lb.).
   d. Have the brake system filled and bled at a BMW dealership.

WARNING
Do not ride the motorcycle until the front and rear brakes operate correctly with full hydraulic advantage and the brake light works properly.

BRAKE HOSE AND LINE REPLACEMENT (ABS EQUIPPED MODELS WITH INTEGRAL BRAKES)

Check the brake hoses at the brake inspection intervals listed in Chapter Three. Replace the brake hoses if they show signs of wear or damage.

The metal brake lines do not require routine replacement unless they are damaged or the end fittings are leaking. While replacing the flexible brake hoses, inspect the metal brake lines for damage. If they have been hit, the line may be restricted, thus decreasing braking effectiveness.

WARNING
Whenever a hydraulic ABS component is disconnected, the system must be bled by a BMW dealership and then verified with the MoDiTec diagnostic equipment.

WARNING
Always install authorized BMW replacement hoses specifically designed for use with the ABS system. Using a flexible brake hose of an alternate design will drastically change the characteristics of the brake system.

CAUTION
The metal lines are attached to the ABS pressure modulator. All service of the modulator should be performed by a BMW dealership. Any applicable BMW warranty will be void if service is performed by unauthorized service personnel. This procedure is provided if you choose to remove the pressure modulator.

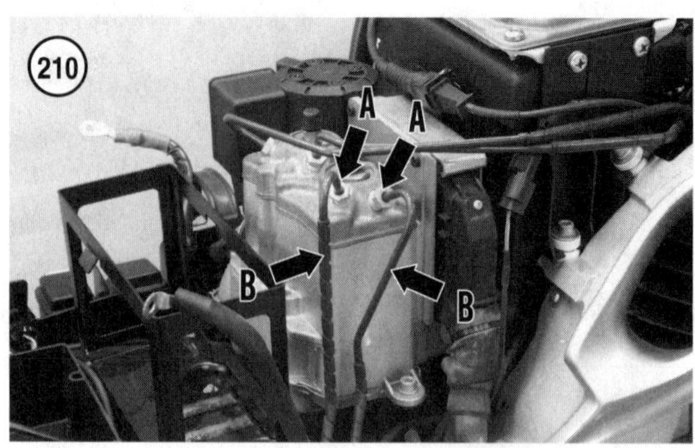

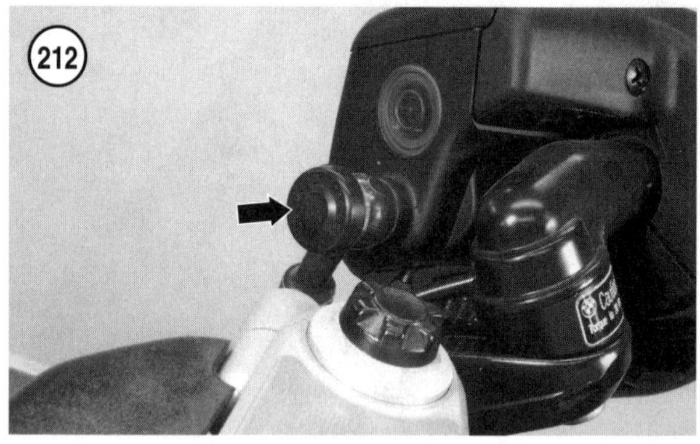

To replace a brake hose, perform the following:

1. Use a plastic drop cloth to cover areas that could be damaged by spilled brake fluid.
2. When removing a brake hose or brake line, note the following:
   a. Record the hose or line routing on a piece of paper.
   b. Remove any bolts or brackets securing the brake hose to the frame or suspension component.

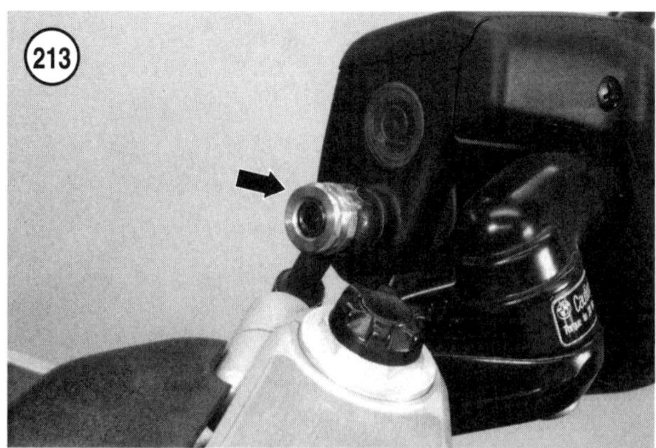

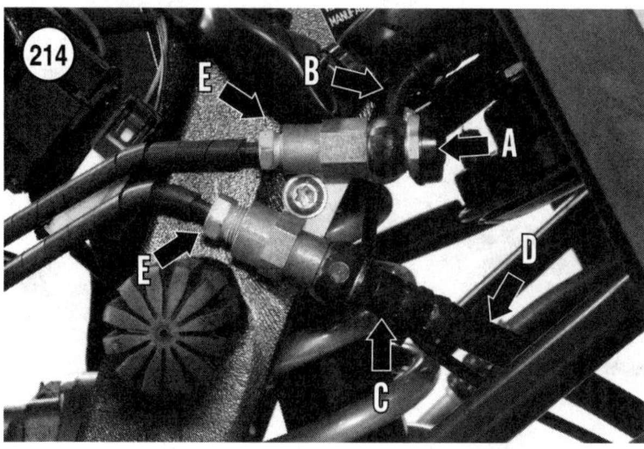

c. Before removing the union bolts, note how the end of the brake hose is installed or indexed against the part it is threaded into. The hoses must be installed facing in their original position.

3. Replace union bolts with damaged hex-heads.
4. Always install *new* washers with the union bolts.
5. Reverse these steps to install the new brake hoses, while noting the following:
   a. Compare the new and old hoses to make sure they are the same.
   b. Clean the new washers, union bolts and hose ends to remove any contamination.
   c. Referring to the notes made during removal, route the brake hose along its original path.
   d. Install a *new* union bolt washer on each side of the brake hose.
   e. Tighten the union bolts to 18 N•m (159 in.-lb.).
   f. Tighten the flare nuts to 18 N•m (159 in.-lb.).
   g. After replacing a front brake hose, turn the handlebars from side to side to make sure the hose does not rub against any part or pull away from its brake unit.
   h. Refill the master cylinders and bleed the brakes as described in this chapter.

WARNING
Do not ride the motorcycle until the front and rear brakes operate correctly with full hydraulic advantage and the brake light works properly.

Front Brake Hoses and Lines

This procedure covers removal and installation of all of the front brake hoses and lines. If replacing only one hose, refer to the steps relating to that specific hose, or if replacing all hoses, perform all steps.

1. Remove the seat as described in Chapter Fifteen.
2. Remove the fuel tank as described in Chapter Nine.
3. On RS, RT and S models, remove the side sections on the front fairing as described in Chapter Fifteen.
4. Drain the hydraulic brake fluid from the front brake system as follows:
   a. Attach a hose to the bleed valve (A, **Figure 211**) on each front caliper assembly.
   b. Place the loose end of the hose in a container.
   c. Open the bleed valve on each caliper and apply the front brake lever until the brake fluid is pumped out of the system.
   d. Disconnect the hoses and tighten the bleed valves.
   e. Dispose of this brake fluid properly.
4. To remove the upper hose, perform the following:
   a. Place a couple of shop cloths under the master cylinder hose fittings.
   b. Remove the rubber cap (**Figure 212**) from the union bolt.
   c. Unscrew and remove the union bolt and sealing washers (**Figure 213**) securing the brake hose to the master cylinder.
   d. Disconnect the brake hose from the master cylinder.
   e. Remove the rubber cap (A, **Figure 214**) from the union bolt.
   f. Unscrew and remove the union bolt and sealing washers securing the brake hose (B, **Figure 214**) at the two-way connector.
   g. Remove the upper hose from any clamps or tie wraps, and remove the upper hose from the frame.
5. To remove the lower left side short hose, perform the following:
   a. Unscrew and remove the union bolt and sealing washers (B, **Figure 211**) securing the lower hose to the brake caliper.
   b. Disconnect the brake hose from the caliper.

c. Unscrew the fitting (A, **Figure 215**) securing the cross-over brake line to the left side short hose fitting on the fork slider.

d. Withdraw the short brake hose from the rubber grommet (B, **Figure 215**) on the mounting bracket.

e. Remove the lower left side short hose (C, **Figure 215**) from the mounting bracket.

6. To remove the lower right side hose and middle brake line assembly, perform the following:

a. Unscrew and remove the union bolt and sealing washers securing the lower hose to the /brake caliper.

b. Remove the tie wraps (A, **Figure 216**) securing the ABS sensor wires to the brake hose fittings.

c. Remove the fastener (B, **Figure 216**) securing the lower distribution connector to the right side fork slider.

d. Unscrew and remove the union bolt and sealing washers (C, **Figure 214**) securing the upper portion of the middle hose to the two-way connector.

e. Carefully lower the upper portion of the middle brake line assembly (D, **Figure 214**) down through the frame and fork sliders and remove it.

7. To remove the metal brake lines from the ABS pressure modulator, perform the following:

a. Unscrew the flare nuts (E, **Figure 214**) securing the front metal brake lines to the two-way connector.

b. Refer to *ABS Pressure Modulator* in this chapter and disconnect the two front brake lines (**Figure 217**) from the pressure modulator.

c. Very carefully remove the front metal brake lines from any clamps or tie wraps and out from the front frame.

8. Install new hoses, sealing washers and union bolts in the reverse order of removal while noting the following:

a. Install *new* sealing washers in the correct positions.

b. Tighten the union bolts to 18 N•m (159 in.-lb.).

c. Tighten the flare nuts to 18 N•m (159 in.-lb.).

d. Tighten the lower distribution connector to the left side fork slider fastener to 9 N•m (80 in.-lb.).

e. Have the brake system filled and bled at a BMW dealership.

WARNING

Do not ride the motorcycle until the front and rear brakes operate correctly with full hydraulic advantage and the brake light works properly.

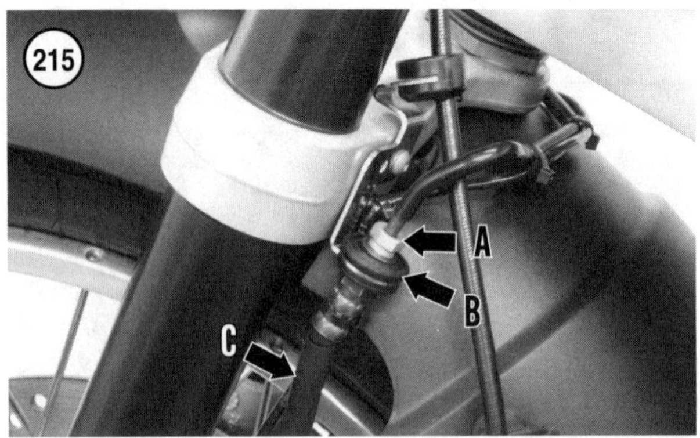

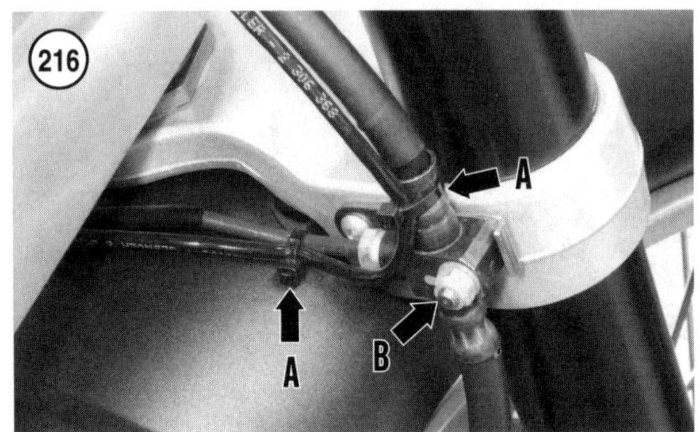

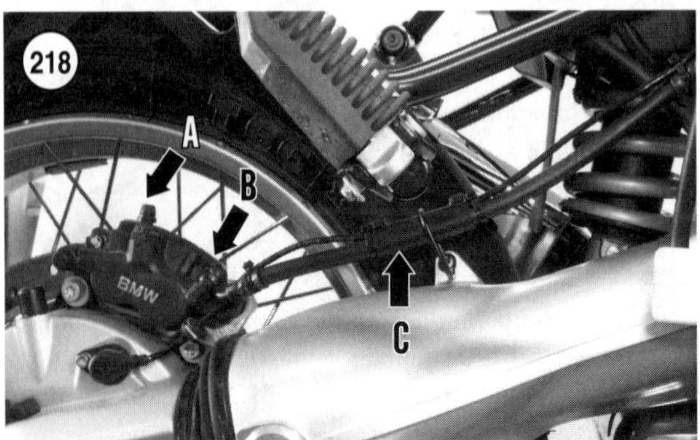

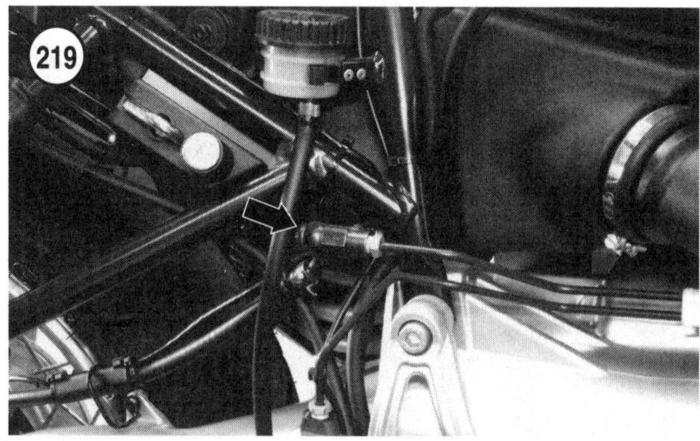

Rear Brake Hose and Lines

This procedure covers removal and installation of all of the rear brake hoses and lines. If replacing only one hose, refer to the steps relating to that specific hose, or line, or if replacing all hoses and lines, perform all steps.

1. Remove the seat as described in Chapter Fifteen.
2. Remove the fuel tank as described in Chapter Nine.

NOTE

To prevent the entry of moisture and dirt, cap the end of the brake hoses and lines that are not going to be replaced. Place the loose end in a reclosable plastic bag.

3. Drain the hydraulic brake fluid from the front brake system as follows:
   a. Attach a hose to the bleed valve (A, **Figure 218**) on the rear caliper assembly.
   b. Place the loose end of the hose in a container.
   c. Open the bleed valve on each caliper and apply the rear brake pedal until the brake fluid is pumped out of the system.
   d. Disconnect the hose and tighten the bleed valves.
   e. Dispose of this brake fluid properly.
4. To remove the rear brake hose, perform the following:
   a. Remove the tie wraps securing the ABS rear sensor wire to the rear brake hose.
   b. Unscrew and remove the union bolt and sealing washers (B, **Figure 218**) securing the brake hose to the brake caliper.
   c. Unscrew and remove the union bolt and sealing washers (**Figure 219**) securing the rear brake hose to the coupler on the rear frame.
   d. Carefully pull the rear brake hose forward and through the guide (C, **Figure 218**) on the swing arm. Remove the rear brake hose.
5. Unscrew the flare nut (A, **Figure 220**) securing the metal brake line to the coupler on the rear frame.
6. Unscrew the flare nut (B, **Figure 220**) securing the metal brake line to the rear master cylinder.
7. To remove the metal brake lines from the ABS pressure modulator, perform the following:
   a. Refer to *ABS Pressure Modulator Removal/Installation* in this chapter and disconnect the two rear brake lines (**Figure 221**) from the pressure modulator.
   b. Carefully remove the rear metal brake lines (C, **Figure 220**) from any clamps or tie wraps and out from the front frame.
8. Install new hoses, sealing washers and union bolts in the reverse order of removal while noting the following:
   a. Install *new* sealing washers in the correct positions.
   b. Tighten the union bolts to 18 N•m (159 in.-lb.).
   c. Tighten the flare nuts to 18 N•m (159 in.-lb.).
   d. Have the brake system filled and bled at a BMW dealership.

WARNING

Do not ride the motorcycle until the front and rear brakes operate correctly with full hydraulic advantage and the brake light works properly.

ABS UNIT (WITHOUT INTEGRAL BRAKES)

The ABS unit is a sealed unit and cannot be serviced.

CAUTION
Whenever a hydrualic ABS component is disconnected the system must be bled with a power bleeder by a BMW dealership.

Removal/Installation

1. Remove the seat as described in Chapter Fifteen.
2. Remove the fuel tank as described in Chapter Nine.
3. Drain the hydraulic brake fluid from the front and rear brake systems as follows:
   a. Attach a hose to the bleed valve on each caliper assembly.
   b. Place the loose end of the hose in a container to catch the brake fluid.
   c. Open the bleed valve on each caliper and apply the front brake lever and then depress the rear brake pedal until the brake fluid is completely pumped out of both systems.
   d. Disconnect the hoses and tighten the bleed valves.
   e. Dispose of this brake fluid properly.
4. On RS, RT and S models, remove the front fairing side panels as described in Chapter Fifteen.
5. Disconnect the ground cable (**Figure 222**). Move it out of the way and insulate it to eliminate the possibility of it making contact with any portion of the engine and/or frame.
6. On the right side, disconnect the wires from the ABS unit as follows:
   a. Insert a thin screwdriver, or scribe, into the hole in the cover (**Figure 223**) and release the catch. Slide the cover up and remove it. Discard the cover as a new one must be installed.
   b. Remove the locknuts and washers (A, **Figure 224**) and disconnect the individual electrical connectors from the terminal block. Discard the locknuts as they cannot be reused.
   c. Disconnect the 2-pin electrical connector (B, **Figure 224**).
   d. Move the individual wires and multi-pin connector and wires out of the way.
7. Remove the battery as described in Chapter Three.
8. Carefully disconnect the large multi-pin electrical connector (**Figure 225**) from the left side of the ABS unit.
9. Disconnect the metal brake lines from the ABS unit as follows:

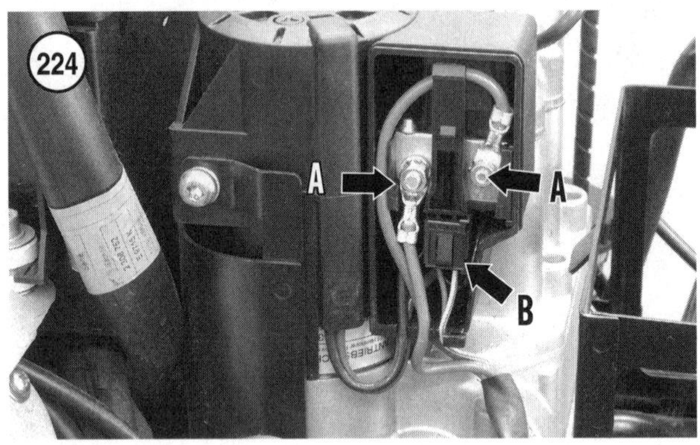

a. On the right side, hold the fitting on the distribution connector with a wrench and unscrew the flare nut(s) (**Figure 226**) securing the front metal brake line(s) to the distribution connector. Disconnect the right brake line(s) from the connector.

b. Unscrew the flare nut(s) (**Figure 227**) securing the rear metal brake line(s) to the ABS unit. Disconnect the rear metal brake line(s) from the ABS unit.

c. Carefully move the metal brake line(s) away from the top of the ABS unit.

10. On the right side, perform the following:

a. Remove the Torx bolt (A, **Figure 228**) securing the ABS unit to the battery case.

b. Remove the Allen bolt and washer (B, **Figure 228**) securing the ABS unit to the mounting bracket.

11. On the left side, remove the Allen bolt and washer (**Figure 229**) securing the ABS unit to the mounting bracket.

12. Remove the ABS unit from the frame. Hold the unit in the upright position so the remaining brake fluid will not drain out.

13. Install by reversing these removal steps while noting the following:

a. Tighten the 6–mm Allen mounting bolts to 9 N•m (79 in.-lb.).

b. Tighten the 6–mm Torx mounting bolts to 5 N•m (44 in.-lb.).

c. Connect the individual electrical connectors onto the posts on the terminal block. Install *new* locknuts and washers (A, **Figure 224**) and tighten securely.

d. Ensure that the electrical wires are positioned correctly then slide the *new* cover down into place. Push it down until it locks into place.

e. Remove the insulating material from the ground strap. Make sure it is clean and free of corrosion. Connect the ground cable (**Figure 222**) to the engine and tighten securely.

f. Tighten the union bolts to 15 N•m (132 in.-lb.).

g. Tighten the flare nuts to 15 N•m (132 in.-lb.).

h. Have the brake system filled and bled at a BMW dealership.

WARNING
Do not ride the motorcycle until the front and rear brakes operate correctly with full hydraulic advantage and the brake light works properly.

ABS PRESSURE MODULATOR (WITH INTEGRAL BRAKES)

WARNING
Whenever a hydraulic ABS component is disconnected the system must be bled at a BMW dealership and then verified with the MoDiTec diagnostic equipment.

NOTE
All ABS pressure modulator service should be performed at a BMW dealership. Any applicable BMW warranty will be void if any type of service is performed unauthorized personnel.

Removal/Installation

1. Remove the seat as described in Chapter Fifteen.
2. Disconnect the negative battery cable (A, **Figure 230**) as described in Chapter Ten.
3. Remove the fuel tank as described in Chapter Nine.
4. Drain the hydraulic brake fluid from the front and rear brake systems as follows:
   a. Attach a hose to the bleed valve on each caliper assembly.
   b. Place the loose end of the hose in a container to catch the brake fluid.
   c. Open the bleed valve on each caliper and apply the front brake lever and then depress the rear brake pedal until the brake fluid is completely pumped out of both systems.
   d. Disconnect the hoses and tighten the bleed valves.
   e. Dispose of this brake fluid properly.
5. On RS, RT and S models, remove the front fairing side panels as described in Chapter Fifteen.
6. Slide out the drawer (A, **Figure 231**) to unlock the pressure modulator electrical connector.
7. On the right side, remove the two bolts and washers (**Figure 232**) securing the pressure modulator to the mounting bracket.
8. Disconnect the hoses from the two bleed valve caps (A, **Figure 233**). Move the hoses out of the way.

CAUTION
Use extreme care to keep any debris falling into the openings once the brake lines have been removed from the pressure modulator

NOTE
Mark each brake line and the fitting to ensure the correct location during installation.

9. At each of the four brake fluid lines, perform the following:
   a. Pull the rubber protective cap (B, **Figure 230**) up on the brake line.
   b. Remove the spring clip securing the brake line into the pressure modulator fitting.
   c. Pull the brake line (C, **Figure 230**) straight up and out of the pressure modulator fitting opening.

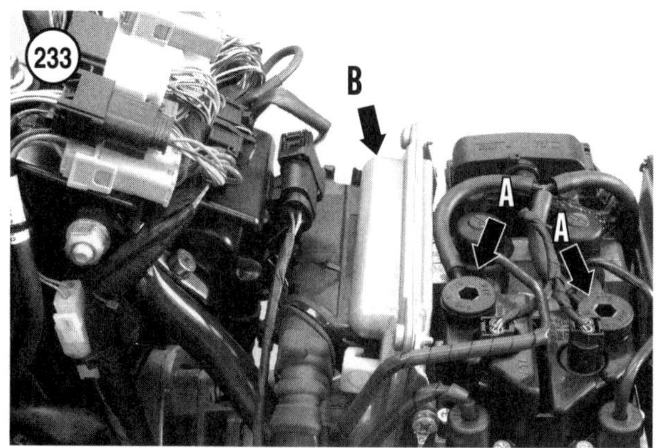

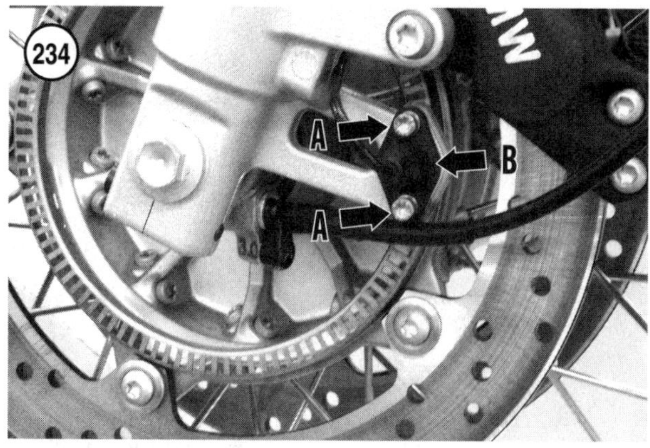

d. Cover the fitting openings with tape to prevent the entry of debris.

CAUTION
Do not allow any brake fluid to enter either of the wheel circuit plug receptacles.

10. Disconnect the front and rear wheel circuit reservoir plugs (D, **Figure 230**) from the pressure modulator receptacles.
11. On the left side, perform the following:
  a. Remove the bolt and washer (E, **Figure 230**) securing the pressure modulator to the mounting bracket.
  b. Loosen the screw (F, **Figure 230**) and move the stabilizer out of the way. It is not necessary to remove it.
12. Pull straight up and disconnect the multi-pin electrical connector (B, **Figure 231**) from the pressure modulator.
13. Remove the Motronic control unit (B, **Figure 233**) as described in Chapter Ten.
14. Carefully pull the pressure modulator straight up and out of the mounting bracket.
15. Keep the pressure modulator in the upright position and take it to the workbench.
16. Place the pressure modulator in a heavy reclosable plastic bag to protect it from debris.

NOTE
New seals and spring clips must be installed to ensure correct positioning of the brake lines within the pressure modulator. Do not install them at this time since the unit must be filled and bled at a BMW dealership. If the new parts are installed at this time, they will have to be replaced again at the dealership.

17. Install by reversing these removal steps while noting the following:
  a. Tighten the mounting bolts to 8 N•m (71 in.-lb.).
  b. Connect the multi-pin connector and slide the drawer back to lock the connector into place.
  c. Do not try to add brake fluid at this time. This must be performed at a BMW dealership.
  d. Install the brake lines, bleed hoses and the front and rear wheel circuit reservoir plugs in their correct locations.
18. Transport the motorcycle to a BMW dealership and have the system filled and bled with a power bleeder and then thoroughly inspected.

TRIGGER SENSORS

Front Trigger Sensor Removal/Installation

NOTE
Models equipped with integral brakes are not equipped with a trigger sensor shim.

1. Remove the fuel tank as described in Chapter Nine.
2. On RS, RT and S models, remove the front fairing side panels as described in Chapter Fifteen.
3. On RS and RT models, remove the front fender as described in Chapter Fifteen.
4. Remove the T-25 Torx screws (A, **Figure 234**) securing the front wheel ABS trigger sensor to the left fork tube. Remove the trigger sensor (B, **Figure 234**) and shim from the receptacle in the left fork slider assembly.
5. Remove the front wheel as described in Chapter Eleven.
6. Unhook the sensor's electrical lead from the clips on the fork (**Figure 235**).
7. Detach the trigger sensor line from the lower fork bridge (**Figure 236**, typical) or over the front fender (**Figure 237**).

8A. On R, GS, S and C models, follow the electrical lead up through the right side of the front frame to where it attaches to the wiring harness and disconnect the electrical connector.

8B. On RS and RT models, follow the electrical lead up through the right side of the front fairing mounting bracket to where it attaches to the wiring harness and disconnect the electrical connector.

9. Disconnect the electrical lead from any clamps or tie-wraps securing the lead to the frame.

10. Install by reversing these removal steps while noting the following:

   a. Install the shim (A, **Figure 238**) onto the front trigger sensor (B).
   b. Install the front sensor and shim into the receptacle in the left fork tube and tighten the Torx bolts securely (**Figure 239**).

WARNING

The distance between the trigger sensor and pulse generating wheel must be maintained correctly, otherwise the ABS system will not function properly.

   c. Inspect the trigger sensor-to-pulse generating wheel clearance as described in this section.

Rear Trigger Sensor Removal/Installation

NOTE

Models equipped with integral brakes are not equipped with a trigger sensor shim.

1. On RS, RT and S models, remove the front fairing side panels as described in Chapter Fifteen.

2A. On R1100RS models, perform the following:

   a. Remove the right rear footpeg (**Figure 240**) as described in Chapter Fifteen.
   b. Remove the Torx bolts and washers securing the rear trigger sensor to the bracket attached to the rear caliper.
   c. Remove the trigger sensor and shim from the receptacle in the final drive unit.

2B. On all models except R1100RS, perform the following:

   a. Remove the T-25 Torx bolt (A, **Figure 241**) securing the rear trigger sensor to the final drive unit.
   b. Remove the trigger sensor (B, **Figure 241**) and shim from the receptacle in the final drive unit.

3. Follow the electrical lead forward along the top of the swing arm and to the rear frame to where it attaches to the wiring harness and disconnect the electrical connector.

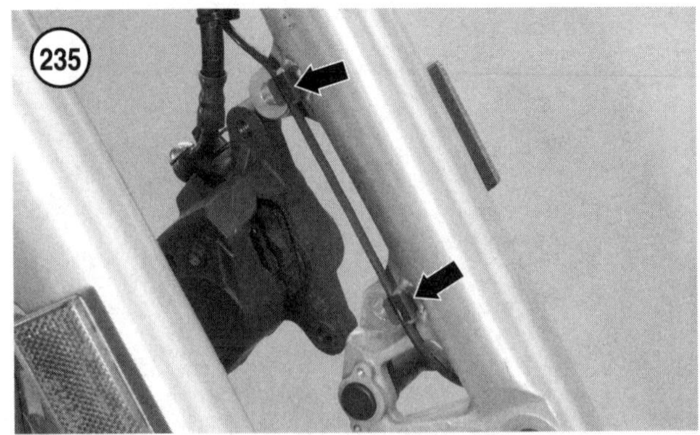

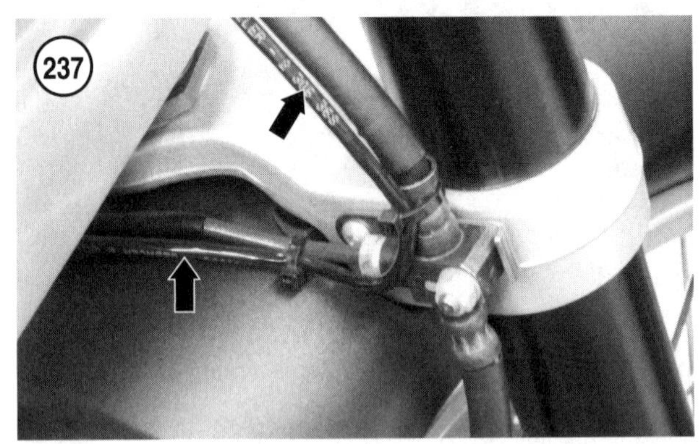

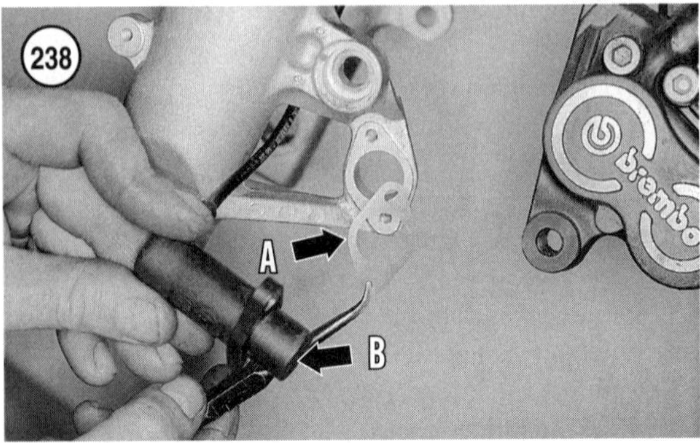

239

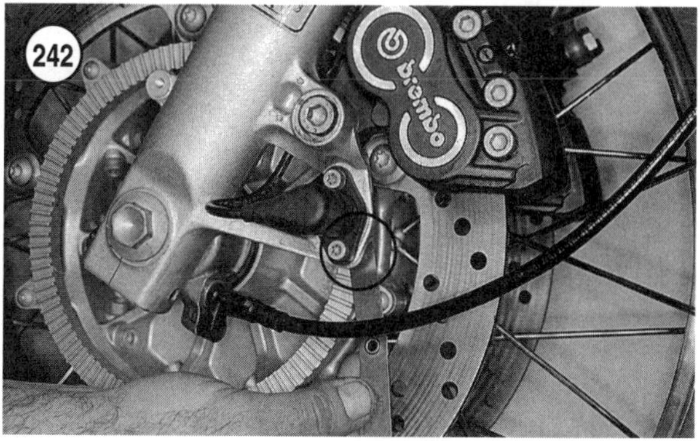

4. Disconnect the electrical lead from any clamps or tie-wraps securing the lead to the swing arm and frame.
5. Install by reversing these removal steps while noting the following:
   a. Install the shim onto the rear trigger sensor.
   b. Install the rear sensor and shim and tighten the Torx bolt securely.

WARNING
The distance between the trigger sensor and pulse generating wheel must be maintained correctly, otherwise the ABS system will not function properly.

   c. Inspect the trigger sensor-to-pulse generating wheel clearance as described in this section.

Trigger Sensor Inspection (Non-Integral Brake System Models)

NOTE
BMW does not provide a service procedure for the integral brake system

Front trigger sensor

WARNING
The distance between the trigger sensor and pulse generating wheel must be maintained correctly, otherwise the ABS system will not function properly.

1. Install the front wheel as described in Chapter Eleven.
2. Insert a flat feeler gauge between the trigger sensor assembly and the pulse generating wheel (**Figure 242**). Perform this step at six different locations 60° apart around the pulse generating wheel. The clearance is listed in **Table 1**.
3. Remove the T-25 Torx screws (A, **Figure 234**) securing the front wheel ABS trigger sensor to the left fork tube. Remove the trigger sensor and shim (B, **Figure 234**) from the receptacle in the left fork slider assembly.
4. Install a new shim of a different thickness if the clearance is not within specification. Shims are available at BMW dealerships.
5. Install the trigger sensor assembly and screws. Tighten the Torx screws securely.
6. Repeat Step 2 and recheck the clearance. Repeat this procedure if the clearance is still not within specification.

Rear trigger sensor—R1100RS models

1. The following special tools are required to measure the clearance of the pulse generating wheel:

a. Measuring adapter (BMW part No. 36-4-600).
b. Dial gauge holder (BMW part No. 00-2-500).
c. Dial gauge (BMW part No. 00-2-510).

WARNING
Substitutions for these special tools may be made, but the measurements must be accurate to ensure that the ABS system will function properly.

WARNING
*The distance between the trigger sensor and pulse generating wheel must be maintained correctly, otherwise the ABS system will **not** function properly.*

2. Remove the rear brake caliper and trigger sensor assembly as described in this chapter.
3. Remove the rear wheel as described in Chapter Eleven.
4. Attach the measuring adapter to the rear caliper mount with a M8 × 60 mm bolt.
5. Attach the dial gauge holder (A, **Figure 243**) to the measuring adapter.
6. Reinstall the rear wheel.
7. Attach the dial gauge (B, **Figure 243**) and measuring shoe (C) to the holder.
8. Zero the dial gauge and slowly rotate the rear wheel.
9. Slowly rotate the rear wheel and note the dial indicator reading.
10. Note where the pulse generating wheel is the farthest distance in, or toward the center of the wheel, and away from the dial indicator pointer. At this point, make a mark (D, **Figure 243**) on the pulse generating wheel.
11. Remove all of the special tools.
12. Install the rear brake caliper and trigger sensor assembly as described in this chapter.
13. Rotate the rear wheel so the mark (D, **Figure 243**) made in Step 10 is opposite the trigger sensor.
14. Insert a flat feeler gauge between the trigger sensor assembly and the mark (D, **Figure 243**) made in Step 10. The correct distance is listed in **Table 1**.
15. There are six shims of various thickness available from a BMW dealership.
16. Remove the rear brake caliper and trigger sensor assembly as described in this chapter.
17. Install a new shim of a of a different thickness if the clearance is not within specification. Shims are available at BMW dealerships.
18. Install the rear brake caliper and trigger sensor assembly as described in this chapter.
19. Repeat Steps 1-14 and recheck the clearance. Repeat this procedure if the clearance is still not within specification.

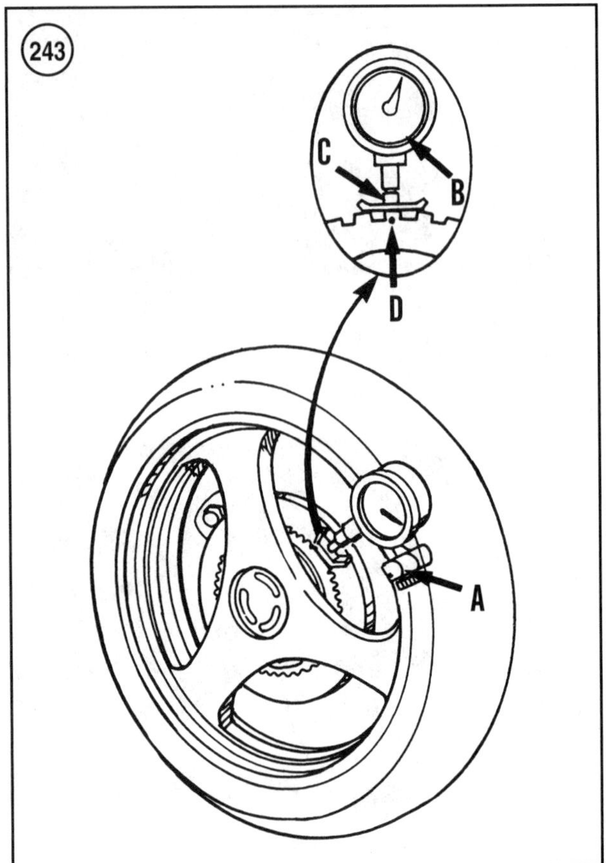

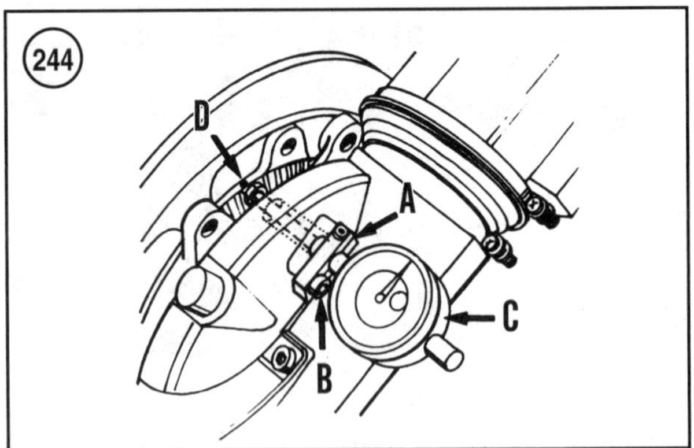

Rear trigger sensor—all models except R1100RS

1. The following special tools are required to measure the clearance of the pulse generating wheel:
a. Measuring shoe extension (BMW part No. 34-2-520).
b. Dial gauge (BMW part No. 00-2-510).

WARNING
Substitutions for these special tools may be made, but the measurements must be accu-

rate to ensure that the ABS system will function properly.

WARNING
If the distance between the trigger sensor and pulse generating wheel is not maintained correctly, the ABS system will not function properly.

2. Remove the rear brake caliper and trigger sensor assembly as described in this chapter.
3. Attach the dial gauge holder with the measuring shoe extension (A, **Figure 244**) to the trigger sensor receptacle in the final drive unit. Tighten the mounting bolt securely (B, **Figure 244**).
4. Attach the dial gauge (C, **Figure 244**) to the shoe extension.
5. Zero the dial gauge and slowly rotate the rear wheel.
6. Note where the pulse generating wheel is the farthest distance in, or toward the center of the wheel, and away from the dial indicator pointer. At this point, make a mark (D, **Figure 244**) on the pulse generating wheel.
7. Remove all of the special tools.
8. Install the rear trigger sensor assembly as described in this chapter.
9. Rotate the rear wheel so the mark is opposite the trigger sensor. Refer to D, **Figure 244** and to **Figure 245**.
10. Inspect the distance between the trigger sensor and the pulse generating wheel with a flat feeler gauge (**Figure 246**). **Table 1** lists the specified distance.
11. There are six shims of various thickness available from a BMW dealership.
12. Remove the sensor from the rear trigger sensor assembly as described in this chapter.
13. Remove the existing shim (**Figure 247**) and replace with one of the appropriate thickness to achieve the correct clearance.
14. Install the trigger sensor assembly and the rear brake caliper as described in this chapter.
15. Repeat Steps 1-14 and recheck the clearance. Repeat this procedure if the clearance is still not within specification.

BLEEDING THE SYSTEM (ALL MODELS WITHOUT ABS)

If air enters the brake system, the brake will feel soft or spongy and braking pressure will be reduced. Bleed the system to remove the air. Air can enter the system if there is a leak in the system, the brake fluid level in a master cylinder runs low, a brake hose and/or line is opened or the brake fluid is replaced.

The brakes can be bled with a brake bleeder or manually. This section includes procedures for both.

Before bleeding the brake system:

1. Check the brake hoses and lines to make sure all fittings are tight.
2. Make sure the caliper pistons do not stick or bind in the bores.
3. Check piston movement in each master cylinder. Operate the lever or brake pedal, making sure there is no binding or other abnormal conditions.

Brake Bleeder Process

This procedure uses the Mityvac hydraulic brake bleeding kit (**Figure 248**) available from motorcycle or automotive supply stores.

NOTE
This procedure is shown on the front wheel and relates to the front wheel as well.

1. Remove the dust cap (**Figure 249**) from the caliper bleed valve.
2. Place a clean shop cloth over the caliper to protect it from accidental brake fluid spills.
3. Open the bleed screw approximately a half turn.
4. Assemble the brake bleeder according to its manufacturer's instructions. Secure it to the caliper bleed valve.
5. Clean the top of the master cylinder of all dirt and debris.

6A. On the front brakes, remove the screws securing the master cylinder top cover, and remove the cover and rubber diaphragm. Refer to **Figure 250** or **Figure 251**.

6B. On the rear brake, unscrew the rear master cylinder reservoir cover (**Figure 252**), and remove the cover and diaphragm.

7. Fill the reservoir almost to the top with DOT 4 brake fluid, and reinstall the diaphragm and cover. Leave the cover in place during this procedure to prevent the entry of dirt.

WARNING
Use brake fluid from a sealed container marked DOT 4 only (specified for disc brakes). Do not intermix different brands or types as they may not be compatible. Do not intermix a silicone based (DOT 5) brake fluid as it can cause brake system failure.

8. Operate the pump (**Figure 253**, typical) several times to create a vacuum in the line. Brake fluid will quickly flow from the caliper into the pump's reservoir. Tighten the caliper bleed valve before the fluid stops flowing through the hose. To prevent air from being drawn through the master cylinder, add fluid to maintain the level at the top of the reservoir.

NOTE
Do not allow the master cylinder reservoir to empty during the bleeding operation or more air will enter the system. If this occurs, the procedure must be repeated.

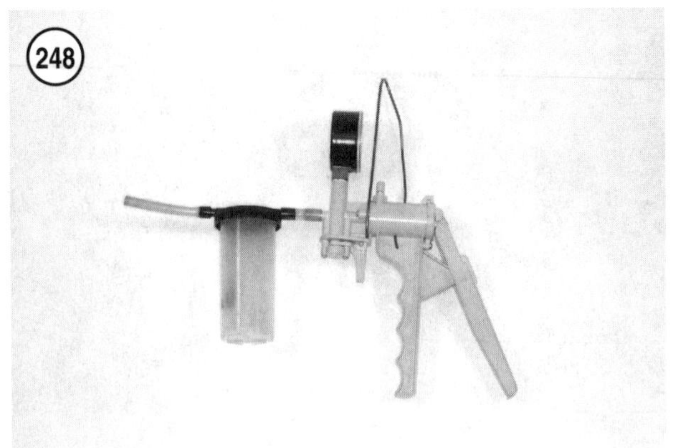

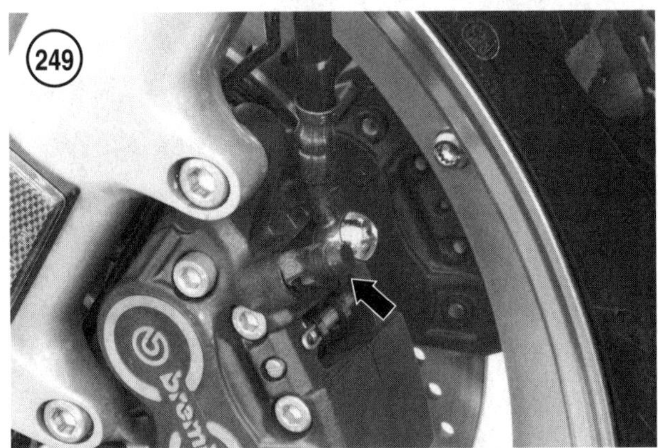

9. Continue the bleeding process until the fluid drawn from the caliper is bubble free. If bubbles are in the brake fluid, more air is trapped in the line. Repeat Step 8, making sure to refill the master cylinder to prevent air from being drawn into the system.

10. When the brake fluid is free of bubbles, tighten the bleed valve and remove the brake bleeder assembly. Reinstall the bleed valve dust cap.

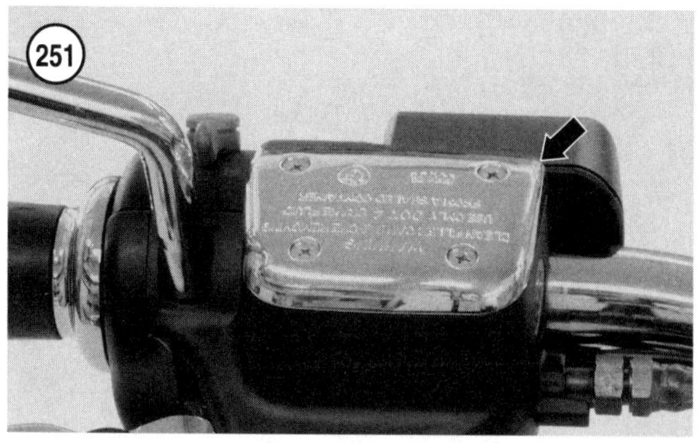

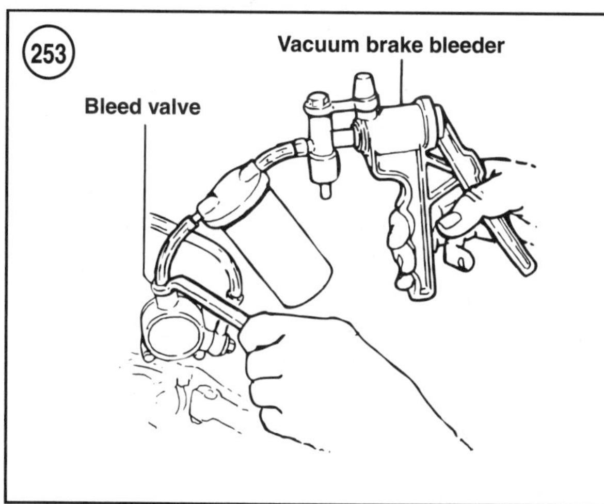

NOTE
Dispose of the brake fluid expelled during the bleeding process. Do not reuse the brake fluid.

11. If necessary, add fluid to correct the level in the master cylinder reservoir. When topping off the front master cylinder, turn the handlebar until the reservoir is level. Add fluid until it is level with the reservoir gasket surface. The fluid level in the rear master cylinder must be slightly below the upper gasket surface.
12. Reinstall the reservoir diaphragm and cover. Install the screws and tighten securely.
13. Test the feel of the brake lever or pedal. It should be firm and offer the same resistance each time it is operated. If it feels spongy, there is probably still air in the system. Bleed the system again. After bleeding the system, check for leaks and tighten all fittings and connections as necessary.

WARNING
Do not ride the motorcycle until the front and/or rear brakes are operating correctly with full hydraulic advantage.

14. Test ride the motorcycle slowly at first to make sure the brakes are operating properly.

Without a Brake Bleeder

NOTE
Before bleeding the brakes, make sure all brake hoses and lines are tight.

1. Remove the dust cap (**Figure 249**) from the caliper bleed valve.
2. Connect a length of clear tubing to the bleed valve on the caliper. Place the other end of the tube into a clean container. Fill the container with enough clean DOT 4 brake fluid to keep the end of the tube submerged. The tube must be long enough so a loop can be made higher than the bleeder valve to prevent air from being drawn into the caliper during bleeding.
3. Clean the top of the master cylinder of all debris.
4A. On the front brakes, remove the screws securing the master cylinder top cover, and remove the cover and rubber diaphragm. Refer to **Figure 250** or **Figure 241**.
4B. On the rear brake, unscrew the rear master cylinder reservoir cover (**Figure 252**), and remove the cover and diaphragm.
5. Fill the reservoir almost to the top with DOT 4 brake fluid, and reinstall the diaphragm and cover. Leave the cover in place during this procedure to prevent the entry of dirt.

WARNING
Use brake fluid from a sealed container marked DOT 4 only (specified for disc brakes). Do not intermix different brands or types as they may not be compatible. Do not intermix a silicone based (DOT 5)

14

brake fluid as it can cause brake system failure.

NOTE
During this procedure, check the fluid level in the master cylinder reservoir often. If the reservoir runs dry, air will enter the system.

6. Slowly apply the brake lever several times. Hold the lever in the applied position and open the bleed valve about a half turn (**Figure 254**). Allow the lever to travel to its limit. When the limit is reached, tighten the bleed valve, then release the brake lever. As the brake fluid enters the system, the level will drop in the master cylinder reservoir. Maintain the level at the top of the reservoir to prevent air from being drawn into the system.
7. Continue the bleeding process until the fluid emerging from the hose is completely free of air bubbles. If the fluid is being replaced, continue until the fluid emerging from the hose is clean.

NOTE
If bleeding is difficult, allow the fluid to stabilize for a few hours. Repeat the bleeding procedure when the bubbles in the system dissipate.

8. Hold the lever in the applied position and tighten the bleed valve. Remove the bleed tube and install the bleed valve dust cap.

NOTE
Dispose of the brake fluid expelled during the bleeding process. Do not reuse the brake fluid.

9. If necessary, add fluid to correct the level in the master cylinder reservoir. When topping off the front master cylinder, turn the handlebar until the reservoir is level. Add fluid until it is level with the reservoir gasket surface. The fluid level in the rear master cylinder must be slightly below the upper gasket surface.
10. Install the diaphragm and top cover, and tighten the screws securely.
11. Test the feel of the brake lever or pedal. It should be firm and offer the same resistance each time it is operated. If it feels spongy, there is probably still air in the system and it must be bled again. After bleeding the system, check for leaks and tighten all fittings and connections as necessary.

WARNING
Do not ride the motorcycle until the front and/or rear brakes are operating correctly with full hydraulic advantage.

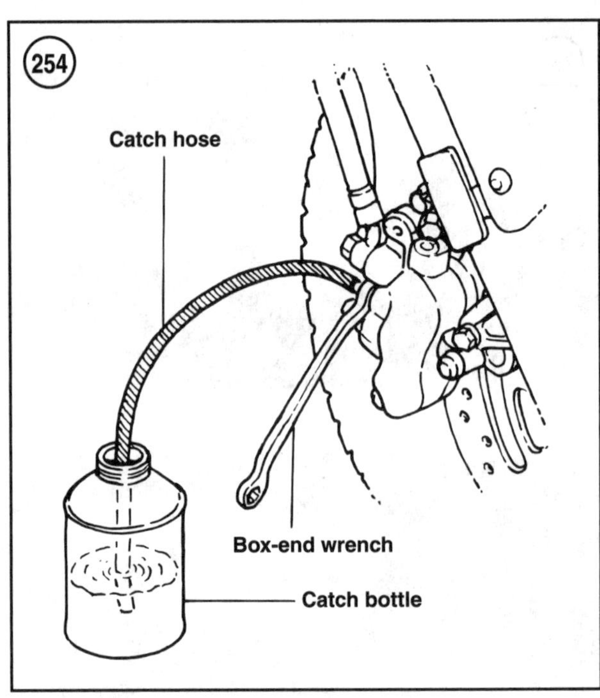

12. Test ride the motorcycle slowly at first to make sure the brakes are operating properly.

BRAKE BLEEDING (ABS MODELS)

Motorcycles equipped with the ABS system *must* have the system bled at a BMW dealership. Due to the number of hydraulic lines and hoses in the ABS system, it is necessary to use the power brake bleeder unit in order to remove the all of the air from the system. It is impossible to remove all of the air from the system without using the power brake bleeder.

On ABS models equipped with the Integral Brake System a special filling funnel tool is required to fill the circuit reservoirs in the ABS modulator with brake fluid. If any portion of the hydraulic system, is leaking, or has been opened, transport the motorcycle to a BMW dealership and have the brake system bled.

REAR BRAKE PEDAL

Removal/Installation

R1100GS

Refer to **Figure 255**.

1. Remove the pivot pin (A, **Figure 256**) securing the brake pedal to the rear master cylinder pushrod.

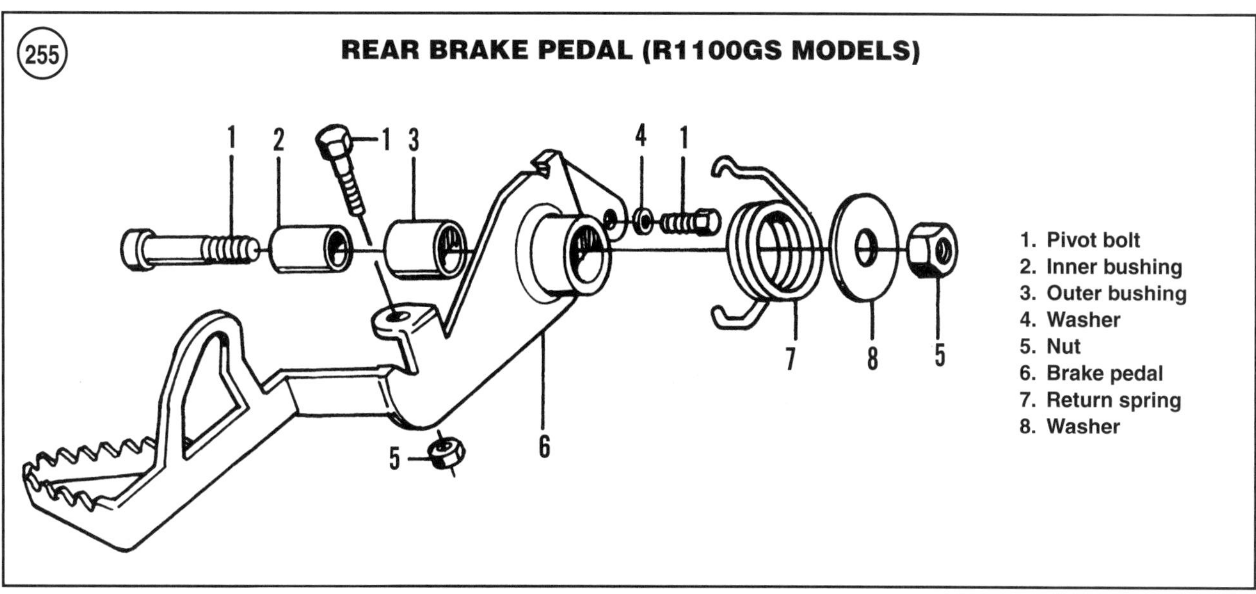

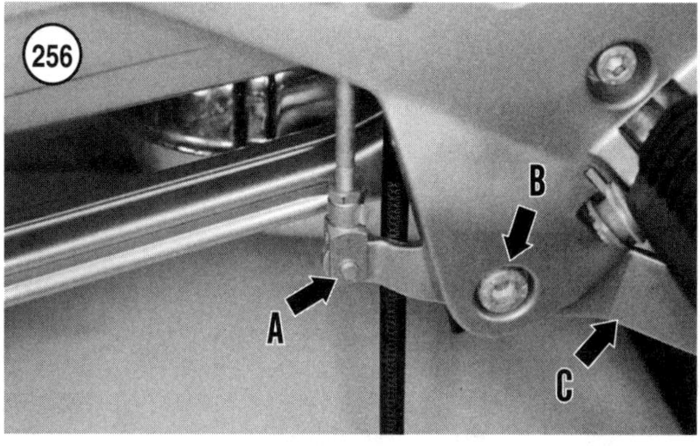

2. Working behind the brake pedal, secure the hex nut with a wrench.
3. Loosen the pivot bolt (B, **Figure 256**) securing the brake pedal to the footpeg assembly. Remove the hex nut and washer on the backside of the pivot bolt.
4. Remove the pivot bolt (B, **Figure 256**).
5. Remove the brake pedal (C, **Figure 256**) and return spring from the footpeg assembly.
6. Remove the bushings from the brake pedal.
7. Inspect the components as described in this section.
8. Install by reversing these removal steps while noting the following:
   a. Apply a light coat of multi-purpose grease to all pivot areas prior to installing any components.
   b. Clean off all grease from the pivot bolt and nut.
   c. Apply a medium strength thread locking compound to the bolt, then tighten the pivot bolt and nut to 37 N•m (27 ft.-lb.).
   d. Adjust the rear brake pedal height as described in Chapter Three.

R1150R and R1150RS models

Refer to **Figure 257**.
1. Remove the cotter pin and washer from the backside of the pivot pin.
2. Remove the pivot pin (A, **Figure 258**) securing the brake pedal to the rear master cylinder pushrod.
3. Loosen, then remove the pivot bolt (B, **Figure 258**) securing the brake pedal to the footpeg assembly.
4. Unhook the return spring (C, **Figure 258**) and remove the brake pedal (D) and return spring from the footpeg assembly.
5. Remove the bushing from the brake pedal.
6. Inspect the components as described in this section.
7. Install by reversing these removal steps while noting the following:
   a. Apply a light coat of multi-purpose grease to all pivot areas prior to installing any components.
   b. Clean off all grease from the pivot bolt.
   c. Apply a medium strength thread locking compound to the bolt, then tighten the pivot bolt to 21 N•m (15 ft.-lb.).
   d. Adjust the rear brake pedal height as described in Chapter Three.

R1150GS models

Refer to **Figure 259**.

14

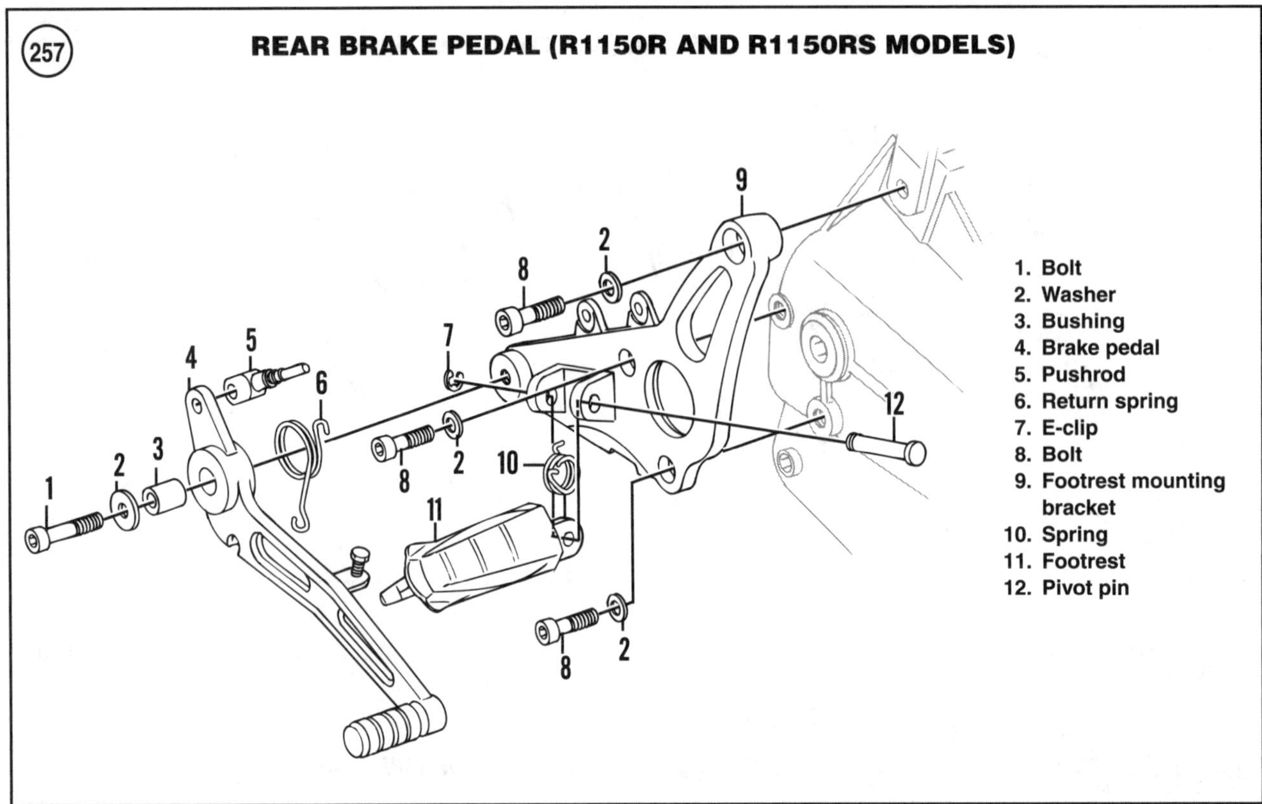

1. Remove the cotter pin and washer from the backside of the pivot pin.
2. Remove the pivot pin (A, **Figure 260**) securing the brake pedal to the rear master cylinder pushrod.
3. Working behind the brake pedal, secure the hex nut with a wrench.
4. Loosen the pivot bolt (B, **Figure 260**) securing the brake pedal to the footpeg assembly. Remove the hex nut and washer on the backside of the pivot bolt.
5. Remove the pivot bolt (B, **Figure 260**).
6. Unhook the return spring and remove the brake pedal (C, **Figure 260**) and return spring from the backside of the footpeg assembly.
7. Remove the bushings from the brake pedal.
8. Inspect the components as described in this section.
9. Install by reversing these removal steps while noting the following:
   a. Apply a light coat of multi-purpose grease to all pivot areas prior to installing any components.
   b. Clean off all grease from the pivot bolt and nut.
   c. Apply a medium strength thread locking compound to the bolt, then tighten the pivot bolt and nut to 37 N•m (27 ft.-lb.).
   d. Adjust the rear brake pedal height as described in Chapter Three.

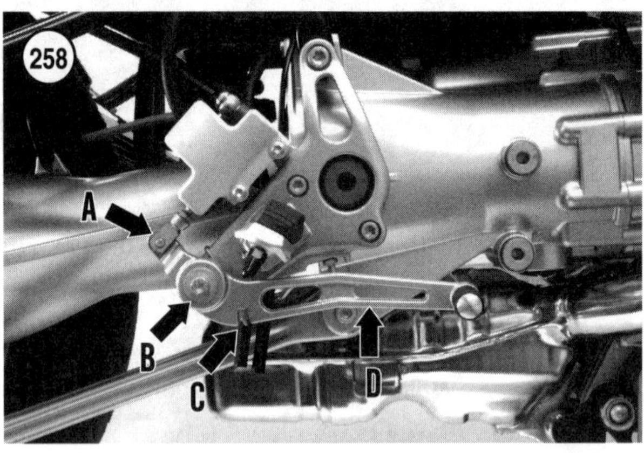

R1100RT and R1150RT models

Refer to **Figure 261**.

1. Unhook the pivot pin clip securing the brake pedal adjust rod to the rear master cylinder.
2. Working behind the brake pedal, secure the hex nut with a wrench.
3. Loosen the pivot bolt securing the brake pedal to the footpeg assembly.
4. Remove the hex nut and washer on the backside of the pivot bolt.

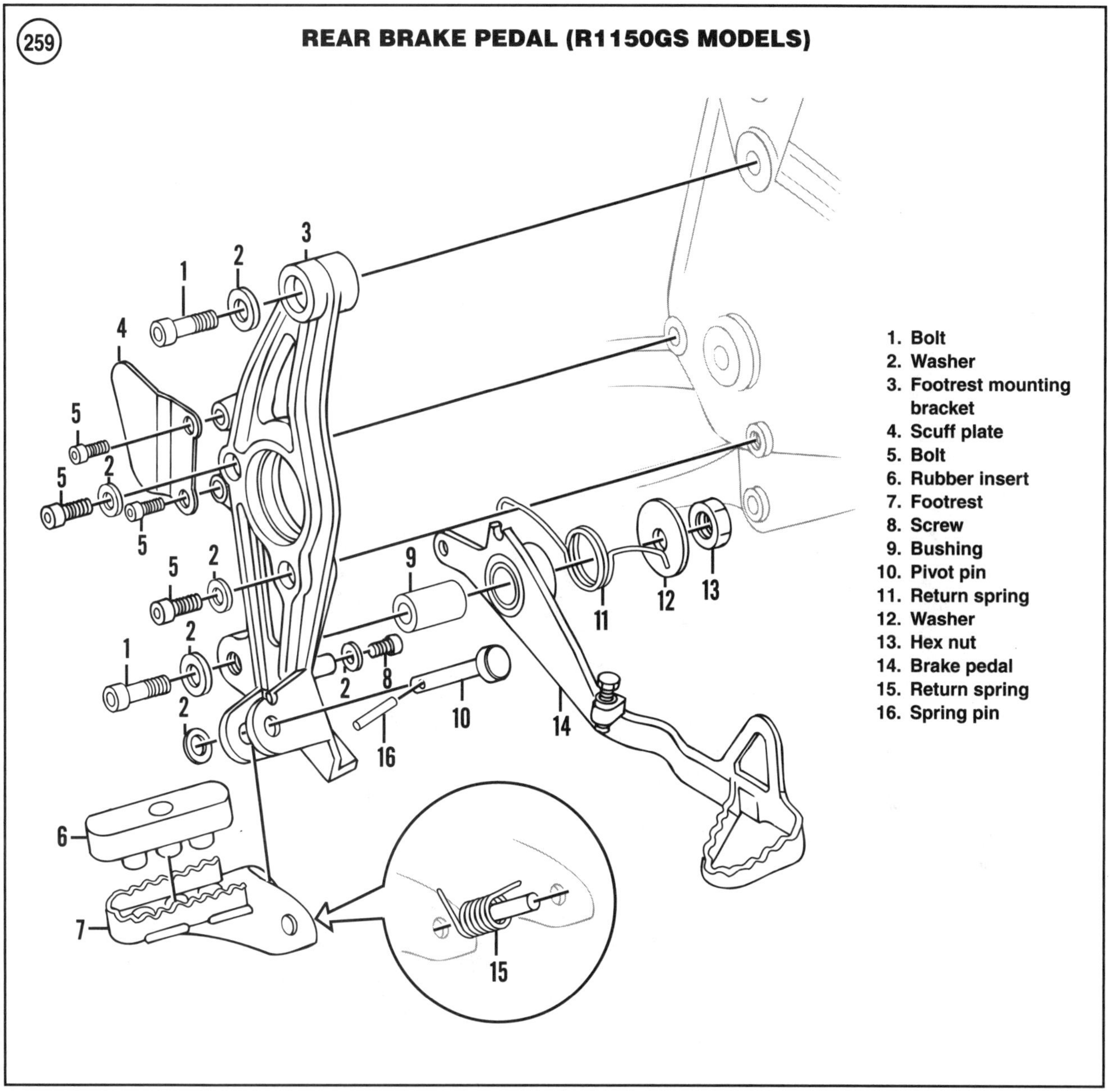

259
REAR BRAKE PEDAL (R1150GS MODELS)
1
2
3
4
5
5
2
5
5
2
9
1
2
2
8
2
10
16
14
11
12
13
6
7
15
1. Bolt
2. Washer
3. Footrest mounting bracket
4. Scuff plate
5. Bolt
6. Rubber insert
7. Footrest
8. Screw
9. Bushing
10. Pivot pin
11. Return spring
12. Washer
13. Hex nut
14. Brake pedal
15. Return spring
16. Spring pin

260
A
B
C

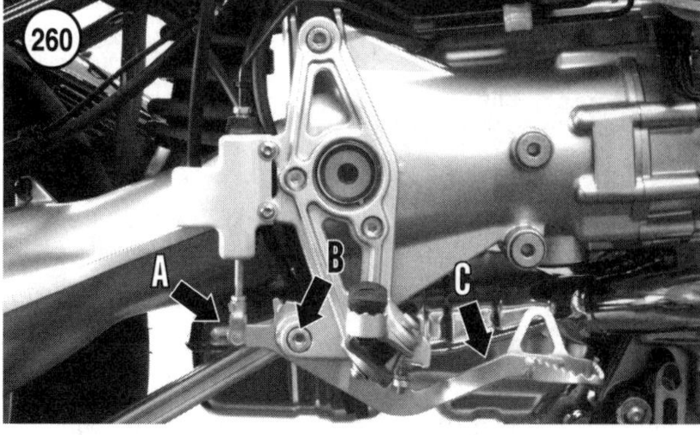

5. Remove the pivot bolt.
6. Unhook the return spring and remove the brake pedal and return spring from the backside of the footrest assembly.
7. Remove the bushing from the brake pedal.
8. Inspect the components as described in this section.
9. Install by reversing these removal steps while noting the following:
   a. Apply a light coat of multi-purpose grease to all pivot areas prior to installing any components.
   b. Clean off all grease from the pivot bolt and nut.

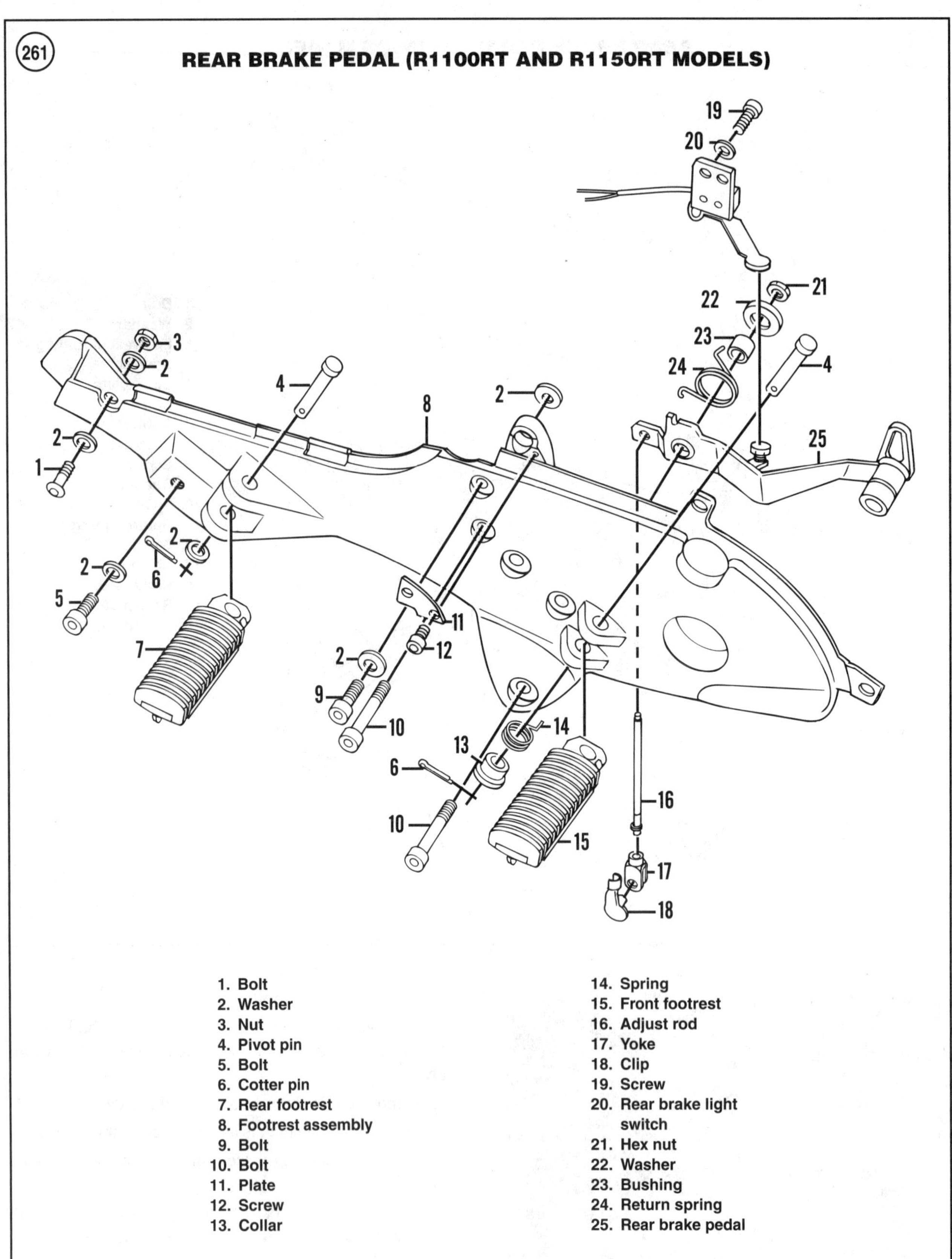

1. Bolt
2. Washer
3. Nut
4. Pivot pin
5. Bolt
6. Cotter pin
7. Rear footrest
8. Footrest assembly
9. Bolt
10. Bolt
11. Plate
12. Screw
13. Collar
14. Spring
15. Front footrest
16. Adjust rod
17. Yoke
18. Clip
19. Screw
20. Rear brake light switch
21. Hex nut
22. Washer
23. Bushing
24. Return spring
25. Rear brake pedal

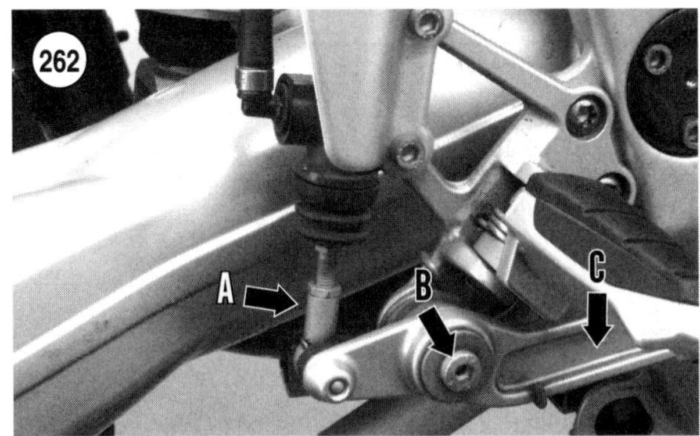

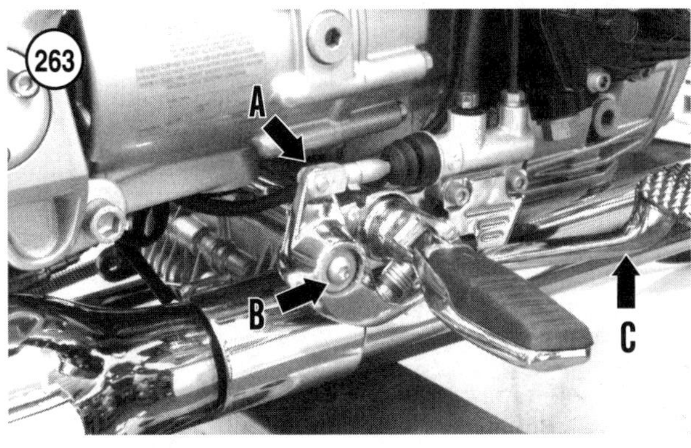

c. Apply a medium strength thread locking compound to the bolt, then tighten the pivot bolt and nut to 37 N•m (27 ft.-lb.).

d. Adjust the rear brake pedal height as described in Chapter Three.

R1100S models

1. Unhook the spring clip securing the brake pedal pivot ball socket to the master cylinder pushrod.
2. Move the master cylinder pushrod back and disconnect the ball socket (A, **Figure 262**) from the brake pedal.
3. Loosen, then remove the pivot bolt (B, **Figure 262**) securing the brake pedal to the footpeg assembly.
4. Unhook the return spring and remove the brake pedal (C, **Figure 262**) and return spring from the footpeg assembly.
5. Do not lose the washer between the rear brake pedal and the pivot post on the footpeg assembly.
6. Remove the bushing from the brake pedal.
7. Inspect the components as described in this section.
8. Install by reversing these removal steps while noting the following:
   a. Apply a light coat of multi-purpose grease to all pivot areas prior to installing any components.
   b. Clean off all grease from the pivot bolt.
   c. Apply a medium strength thread locking compound to the bolt, then tighten the pivot bolt to 21 N•m (15 ft.-lb.).
   d. Adjust the rear brake pedal height as described in Chapter Three.

R850C and R1200C models

1. Unhook the pivot pin clip securing the brake pedal adjust rod (A, **Figure 263**) to the rear master cylinder.
2. Loosen, then remove the pivot bolt and washer (B, **Figure 263**) securing the brake pedal to the footpeg assembly.
3. Remove the brake pedal (C, **Figure 263**) and spring from the backside of the footrest assembly.
4. Remove the bushing from the brake pedal.
5. Inspect the components as described in this section.
6. Install by reversing these removal steps while noting the following:
   a. Apply a light coat of multi-purpose grease to all pivot areas prior to installing any components.
   b. Clean off all grease from the pivot bolt and nut.
   c. Apply a medium strength thread locking compound to the bolt, then tighten the pivot bolt to 37 N•m (27 ft.-lb.).
   d. Adjust the rear brake pedal height as described in Chapter Three.

Inspection (All Models)

1. Inspect the bushing(s) for wear or damage; replace if necessary.
2. Inspect the adjusting bolt and locknut for wear or damage. Replace if necessary.
3. Inspect the return spring for sagging, wear or damage. Replace if necessary.

Table 1 BRAKE SYSTEM SPECIFICATIONS

Item	Specification mm (in.)
Brake pad minimum thickness	
R850C, R1100RS, R1200C	1.5 (0.06)
R1100GS, R1100R, R1100RT	Wear indicator
R1100S, all R1150 models	1.0 (0.04)
Front brake disc (1993-1998) R850R, all R1100, R1150GS, R1200C models	
Outer diameter	305 (12.00)
Thickness	
Standard	4.9-5.1 (0.193-0.201)
Service limit	4.5 (0.177)
Runout limit	0.12-0.15 (0.0047-0.0059)
Front brake disc (1999-on [except R850C, R1200C models]), R850R, R1150R, R850GS, R1150RS, R1150RT models[2]	
Outer diameter[1]	320 (12.598)
Thickness	
Standard	5.0 (0.1969)
Service limit	4.5 (0.177)
Runout limit	0.12-0.15 (0.0047-0.0059)
Front brake disc R850C, R1200C models	
Outer diameter	305 (12.00)
Thickness	
Standard	4.9-5.1 (0.193-0.201)
Service limit	4.5 (0.177)
Front caliper piston outside diameter[2]	
Large piston	34 (1.34)
Small piston	32 (1.26)
Rear brake disc (1993-1998) all R850, all R1100, R1150GS models	
Outer diameter	
R, GS, RT models	276 (10.86)
RS models	285 (11.22)
Thickness (R, GS, RT models)	
Standard	5.0 (0.197)
Service limit	4.5 (0.177)
Thickness (RS models)	
Standard	5.0 (0.197)
Service limit	4.6 (0.181)
Rear brake disc (1999-on [except R850C, R1200C]) R850GS, R850R, R1150R, R1150GS, R1150RS, R1150RT models	
Outer diameter	278 (10.945)
Thickness	
Standard	5.0 (0.197)
Service limit	4.5 (0.177)
Rear brake disc R850C, R1200C models	
Outer diameter	285 (11.22)
Thickness	
Standard	5.0 (0.197)
Service limit	4.5 (0.177)
Rear caliper piston outside diameter R850R, R1100R, R1150R, R1100S models (insulated piston)	
Small piston	26 (1.0236)
Large piston	28 (1.10236)
Rear caliper piston outside diameter R850C, R850GS, R1100GS, R1150GS, R1200C models	
Small piston	26 (1.0236)
Large piston	28 (1.10236)

(continued)

Table 1 BRAKE SYSTEM SPECIFICATIONS (continued)

Item	Specification mm (in.)
Rear caliper piston outside diameter	
R1100RS models (single piston)	26 (1.0236)
R1150RS models	
Small piston	26 (1.0236)
Large piston	28 (1.10236)
Rear caliper piston outside diameter	
R1100RT models (insulated piston)	26 (1.0236)
R1150RT models (insulated piston)	
Small piston	26 (1.0236)
Large piston	28 (1.10236)
Trigger sensor-to-pulse generating wheel clearance	
1995-1998 R850, R1100 models	
Front and rear	0.50-0.55 (0.020-0.022)
1999-on R850C, R1100, R1150GS, R1200C models	
Front and rear	0.45-0.55 (0.0177-0.02165)
R1150R, R1150RS, R1150RT models	
Front and rear	0.2-1.7 (0.0079-0.0670)

1. Effective Sept. 2003 OE rear brake pads changed from organic to sintered metallic.
2. EVO brake specifications for front brake disc and piston outer diameter not available.

Table 2 BRAKE SYSTEM TORQUE SPECIFICATIONS

Item	N•m	in.-lb.	ft.-lb.
ABS brake line fitting flare nuts			
Integral brakes	18	159	–
Non-integral brakes	15	132	–
ABS lower front distribution connector	9	80	–
ABS unit			
Mounting bolts			
6 mm Allen bolts	9	79	–
6 mm Torx bolts	5	44	–
Brake line fitting flare nut	15	132	–
ABS pressure modulator mounting bolt	8	71	–
Brake disc mounting bolt			
Front wire wheel	24	–	18
Front alloy wheel	21	–	15
Rear wire wheel	21	–	15
Rear alloy wheel	24	–	18
Caliper bleed screw	7	62	–
Front caliper mounting bolts			
EVO brakes	30	–	22
Standard brakes	40	–	29
Front master cylinder hand lever pivot pin bolt	7	62	–
Pivot screw	11	97	–
Rear brake pedal			
Pivot bolt and nut	37	–	27
Pivot bolt	21	–	15
Rear caliper mounting bolt	40	–	29
Rear master cylinder-to-footrest bolt	9	79	–
Union bolt			
EVO and late R1100S	18	159	–
All other models	15	132	–

CHAPTER FIFTEEN

BODY AND FRAME

This chapter contains removal and installation procedures for the fairing components.

It is suggested that as soon as a body part is removed from the frame, all mounting hardware be reinstalled onto the removed part. BMW makes frequent changes, so the part and the way it is attached to the frame may differ slightly from the described service procedure in this chapter. Also, if working on a used machine, some of the fasteners may be missing, incorrectly installed or different from the original equipment.

The fairing and frame side cover parts are expensive. After each part is removed from the frame, wrap it in a towel or blanket and store it in a safe area where it will not be damaged.

Quick release plastic fasteners are used in some locations. Carefully release these fasteners to avoid breaking them. Also take care during installation. Align the mounting holes prior to inserting the fastener; do not rely on the fastener to align these parts, as they may distort or break.

Table 1 is at the end of this chapter.

SEAT

Removal/Installation

R1100R models

Refer to **Figure 1**.

1. On the left side, insert the ignition key into the lock and turn it clockwise. Hold the key in this position and lift up and remove the rider's seat.
2. Unhook the pillion seat and remove it.
3. If necessary, remove the bolts securing the adjust mechanism and remove the assemblies.
4. Inspect the components as described in this section.
5. Install by reversing the removal steps while noting the following:
   a. If removed, tighten all bolts securely. If they work loose and fall out, the seat will become loose and unstable.
   b. Push the seat into the locking bar, or adjuster, then push it down to engage the latch properly.

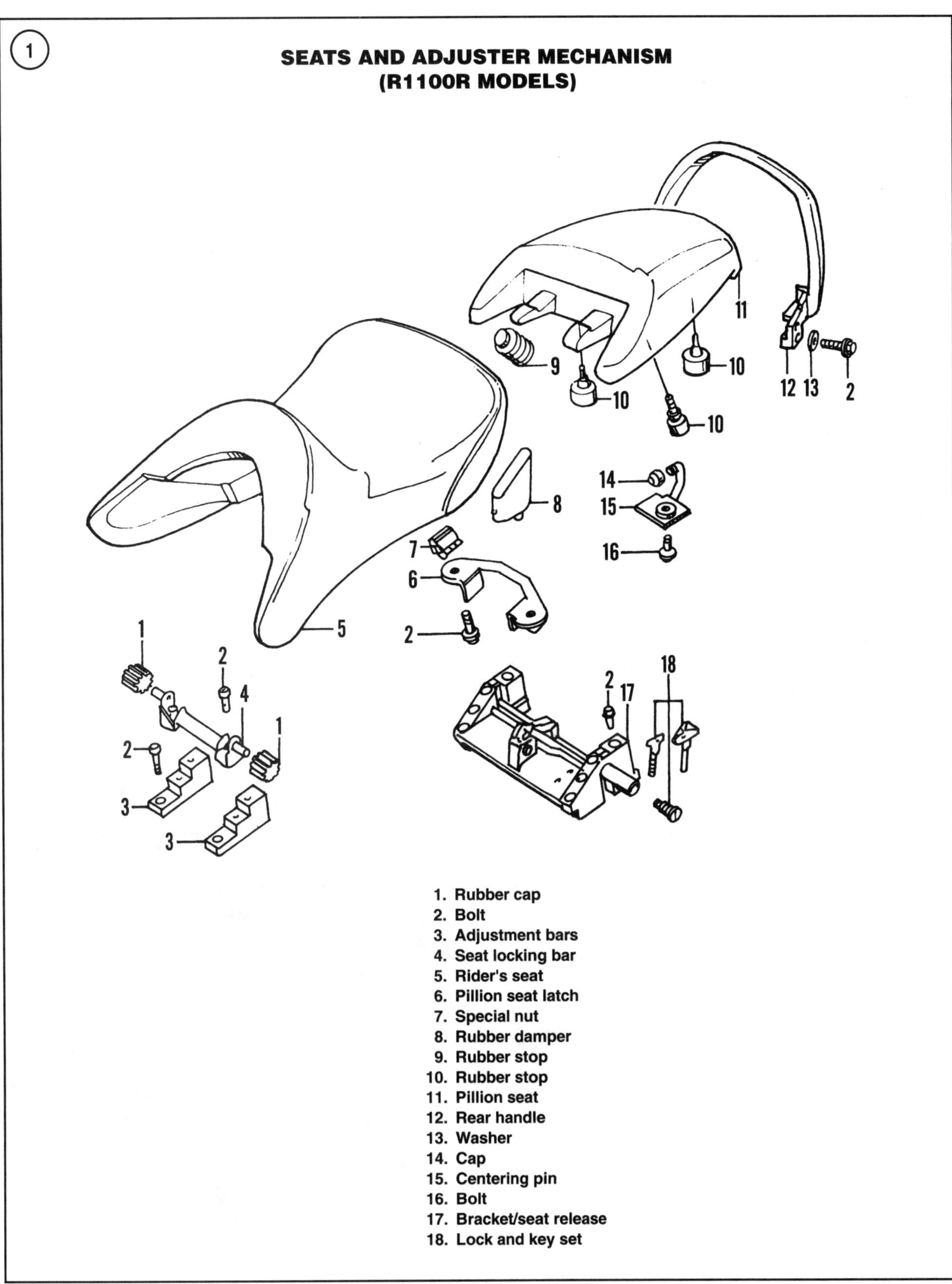

1. Rubber cap
2. Bolt
3. Adjustment bars
4. Seat locking bar
5. Rider's seat
6. Pillion seat latch
7. Special nut
8. Rubber damper
9. Rubber stop
10. Rubber stop
11. Pillion seat
12. Rear handle
13. Washer
14. Cap
15. Centering pin
16. Bolt
17. Bracket/seat release
18. Lock and key set

R1150R models

Refer to **Figure 2**.

1. On the right side, insert the ignition key into the lock and turn it clockwise. Hold the key in this position and lift up toward the rear and remove the pillion seat.
2. Turn the ignition key clockwise, hold the key in this position and lift up toward the rear and remove the rider's seat.
3. Insert the front of the rider's seat (A, **Figure 3**) into the frame mounts, then push down on the rear of the seat (B) to lock it into place. Lift up on the seat to make sure it is locked into place.
4. On models so equipped, make sure the storage compartment lid is in place, and secure, prior to installing the pillion seat.
5. Insert the pillion seat locking tab (**Figure 4**) onto the rear portion of the frame, then push down on the front of the seat to lock it into place. Lift up on the seat to make sure it is locked into place.
6. Inspect all components as described in this section.

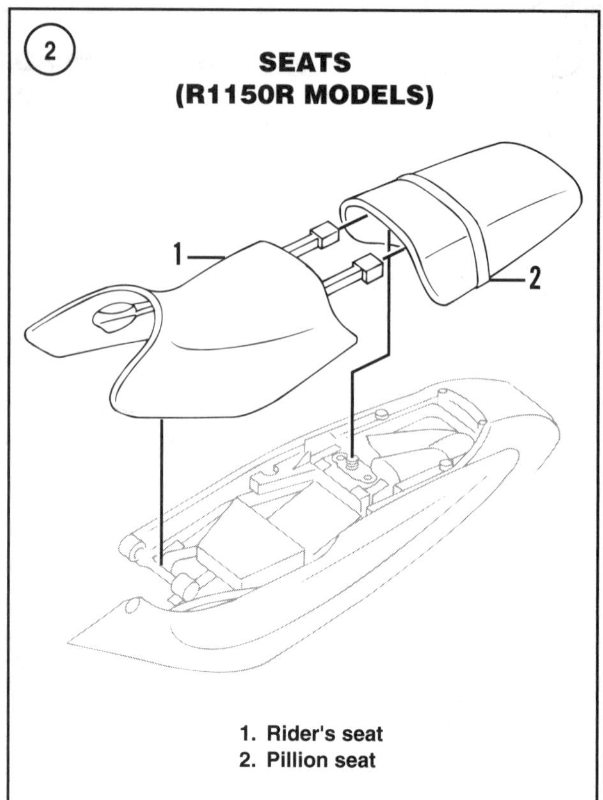

GS models

Refer to **Figure 5**.

1. On the left side, insert the ignition key into the lock and turn it clockwise. Hold the key in this position and lift up and remove the pillion seat followed by the rider's seat.
2. If the pillion seat has been removed, make sure all tools are properly stored and that the cover (**Figure 6**) is in place.
3. Push the front of the rider's seat (A, **Figure 7**) into the locking bar, or adjuster, then push it down on the rear (B) to engage the latch properly. Lift up on the seat to make sure it is locked into place.
4. Insert the front of the pillion seat under the rider's seat (A, **Figure 8**), then push down on the rear of the seat (B) to lock it into place. Lift up on the seat to make sure it is locked into place.
5. Inspect all components as described in this section.

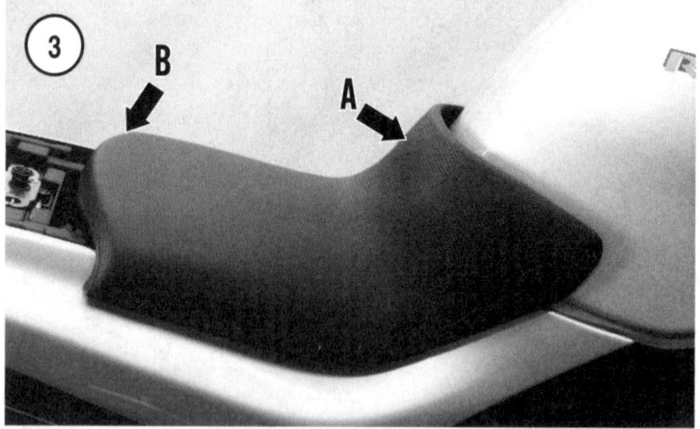

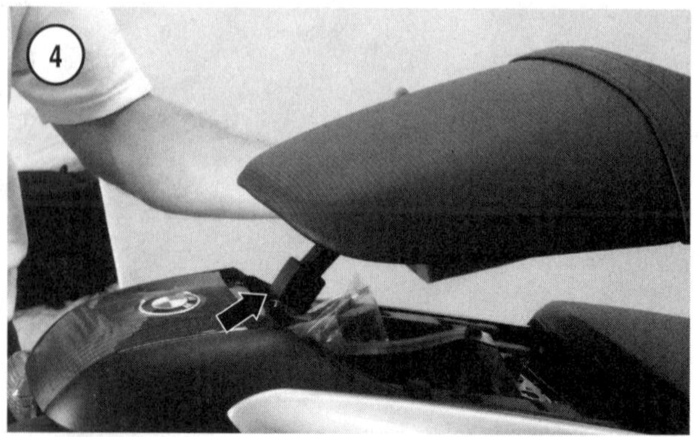

RS models

Refer to **Figure 9** and **Figure 10**.

1A. On a single seat, insert the ignition key into the lock (**Figure 11**) directly below the taillight/brake light and turn it clockwise. Hold the key in this position and lift up and remove the seat assembly.

1B. On dual seats, insert the ignition key into the lock (**Figure 11**) directly below the taillight/brake light and turn it clockwise. Hold the key in this position, lift up and remove the pillion seat followed by the rider's seat.

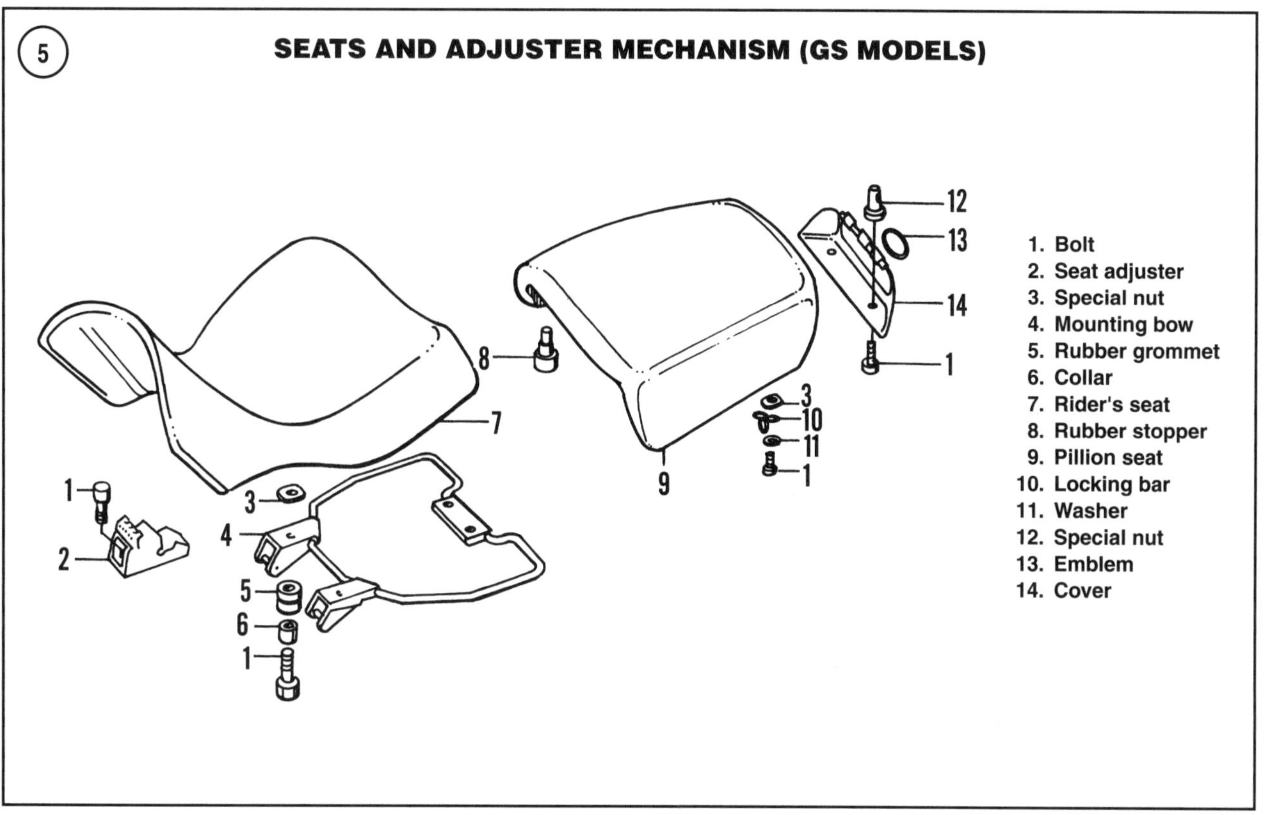

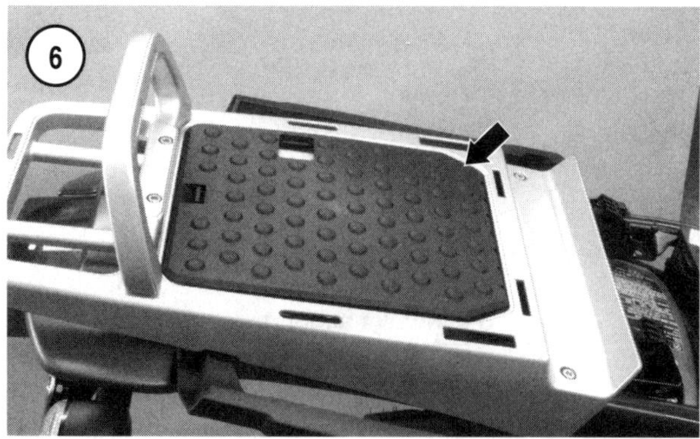

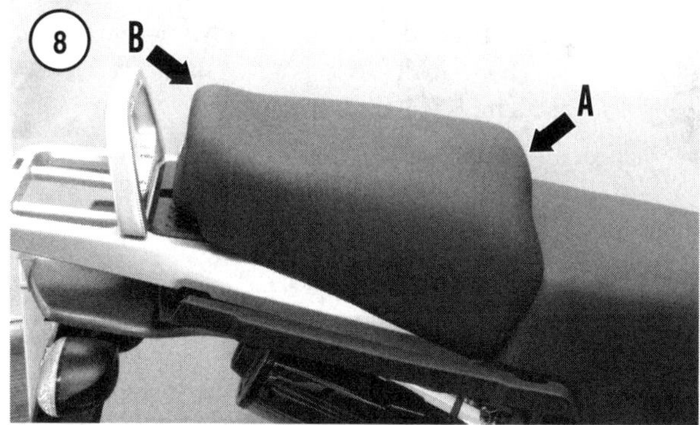

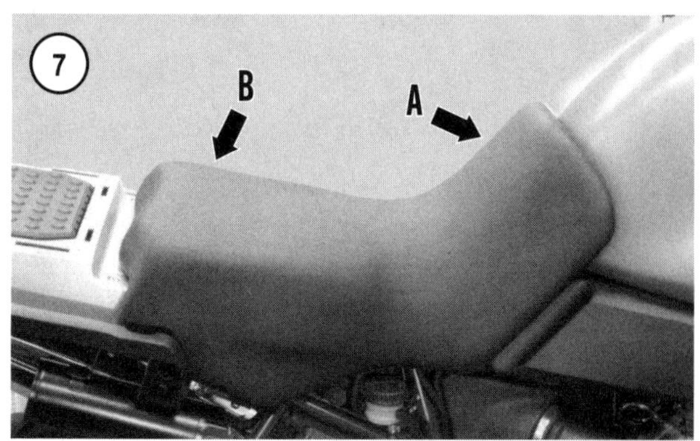

2. On dual seats, if necessary, remove the bolts securing both adjusters and remove them.

3A. On a single seat insert the front of the seat under the frame tab, then push down on the rear of the seat to lock it into place.

3B. On dual seats, perform the following:

a. Install the front of the rider's seat into the locking bar or adjusters (A, **Figure 12**), then push down on the rear of the seat (B). Lift up on the seat to make sure it is locked into place.

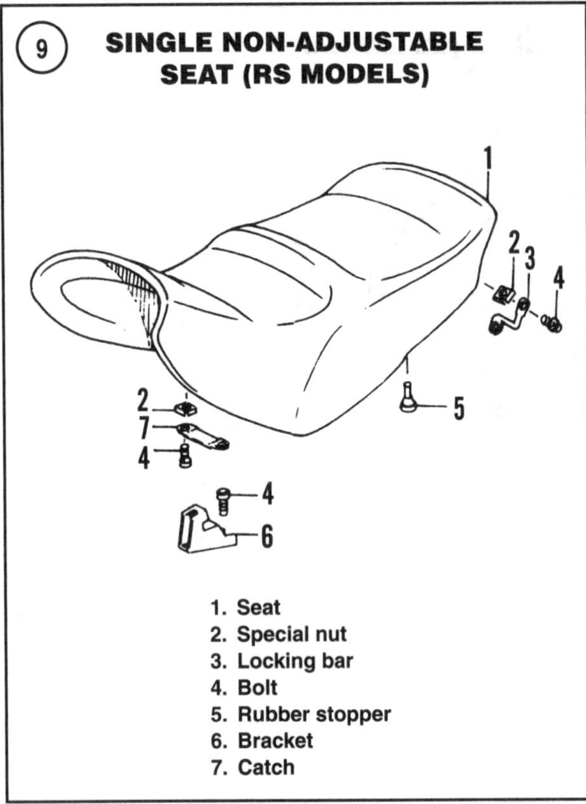

9 SINGLE NON-ADJUSTABLE SEAT (RS MODELS)

1. Seat
2. Special nut
3. Locking bar
4. Bolt
5. Rubber stopper
6. Bracket
7. Catch

b. Insert the front of the pillion seat under the rider's seat (A, **Figure 13**), then push down on the rear of the seat (B) to lock it into place. Lift up on the seat to make sure it is locked into place.

4. Inspect all components as described in this section.

RT models

Refer to **Figure 14**.

1. Directly below the taillight/brake light, insert the ignition key into the lock and turn it clockwise. Hold the key in this position and lift up and remove the pillion seat followed by the rider's seat.
2. If necessary, remove the bolts securing both adjusters.
3. Push the front of the rider's seat (A, **Figure 15**) into the locking bar, or adjuster, then push it down on the rear (B) to engage the latch properly. Lift up on the seat to make sure it is locked into place.
4. Insert the front of the pillion seat under the rider's seat (A, **Figure 16**), then push down on the rear of the seat (B) to lock it into place. Lift up on the seat to make sure it is locked into place.
5. Inspect all components as described in this section.

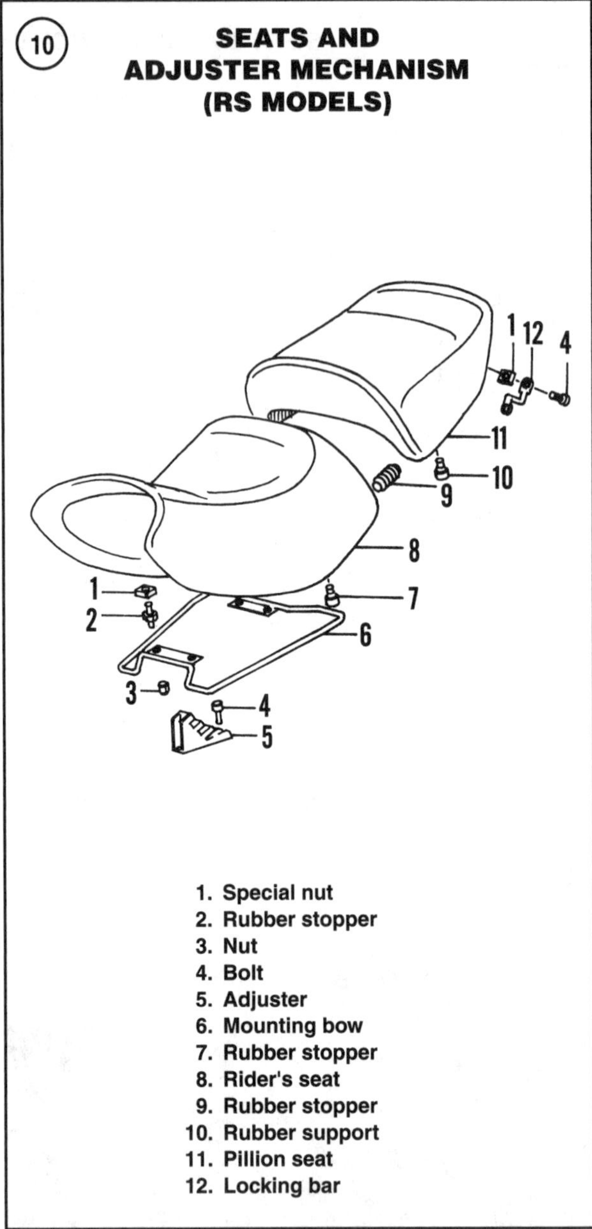

10 SEATS AND ADJUSTER MECHANISM (RS MODELS)

1. Special nut
2. Rubber stopper
3. Nut
4. Bolt
5. Adjuster
6. Mounting bow
7. Rubber stopper
8. Rider's seat
9. Rubber stopper
10. Rubber support
11. Pillion seat
12. Locking bar

11

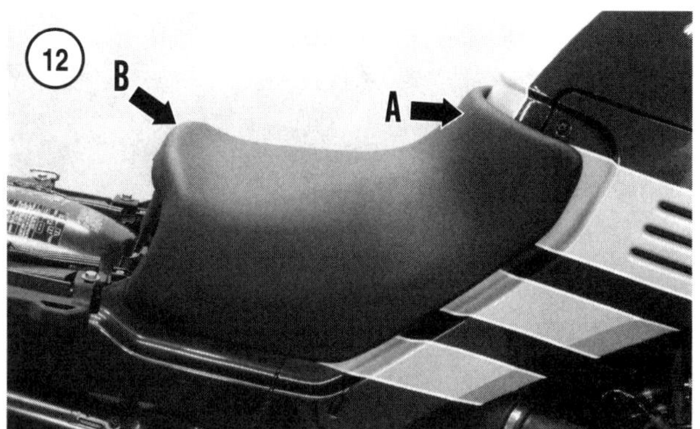

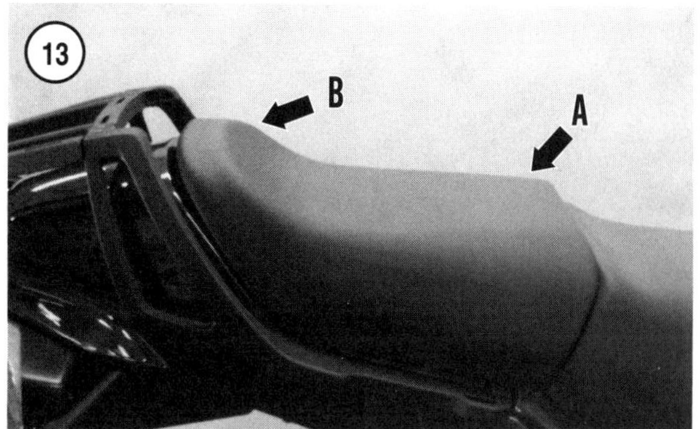

14

SEATS AND ADJUSTER MECHANISM (RT MODELS)

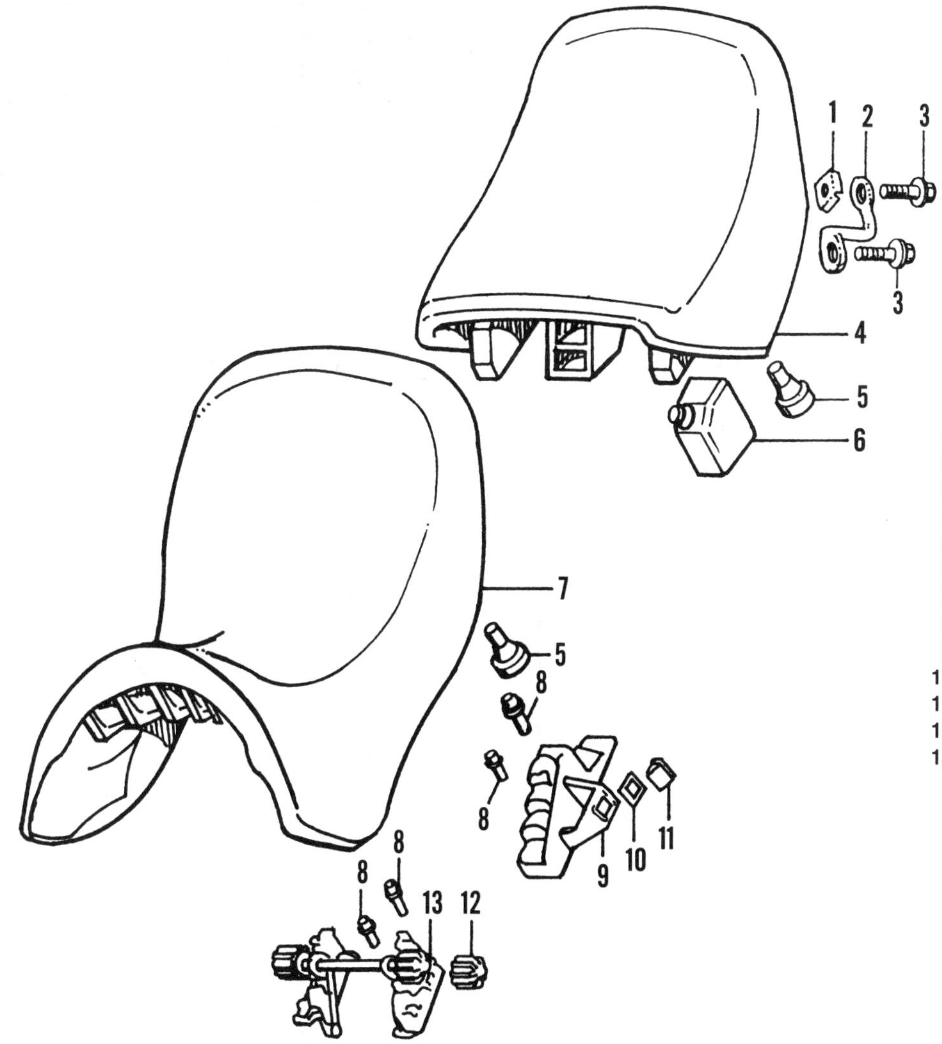

1. Special nut
2. Locking bar
3. Bolt
4. Pillion seat
5. Rubber stopper
6. Bump stop
7. Rider's seat
8. Bolt
9. Adjuster
10. Insert
11. Clip
12. Rubber cap
13. Seat locking bar

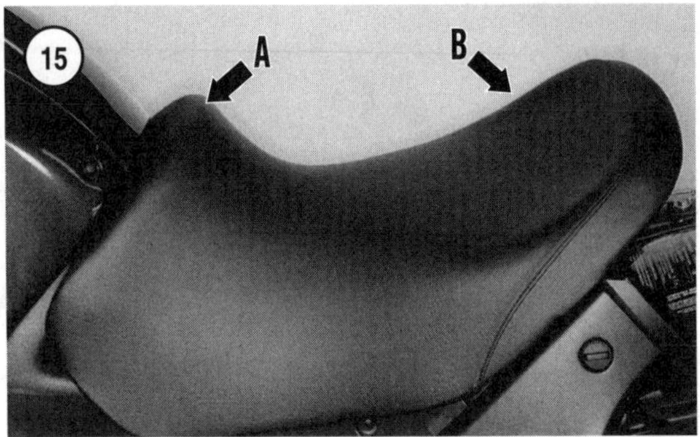

R1100S models

1. To remove the dual seat cover, perform the following:
   a. Turn the quick disconnect fastener (A, **Figure 17**) *counterclockwise* on each side and release them from the seat cover.
   b. Carefully move the seat cover toward the rear and release the cover from the locating tabs at the rear.
2. Remove the seat cover (B, **Figure 17**).
3. Insert the ignition key into the lock (C, **Figure 17**) and turn it clockwise. Hold the key in this position and lift up and remove the seat.
4. Insert the front of the seat into the frame retainers, then push down on the rear of the seat to lock it into place. Lift up on the seat to make sure it is locked into place.
5. To install the dual seat cover, perform the following:
   a. Carefully move the seat cover toward the rear and insert the cover onto the locating slots at the rear. Push the cover on until it is locked into place.
   b. Push the quick disconnect fastener (A, **Figure 17**) down, and then *clockwise* on each side and lock the seat cover into place.
6. Inspect all components as described in this section.

R850C and R1200C models

Refer to **Figure 18**.

1. Remove the screw and washer (**Figure 19**) securing the rear of the seat to the frame.
2. Lift up on the rear of the seat, then pull it back and release if from the front frame crossmember. Remove the seat. Do not lose the collar on each mounting tab.
3. Push the front of the seat (A, **Figure 20**) forward and hook the locking bars under the front frame member. Push

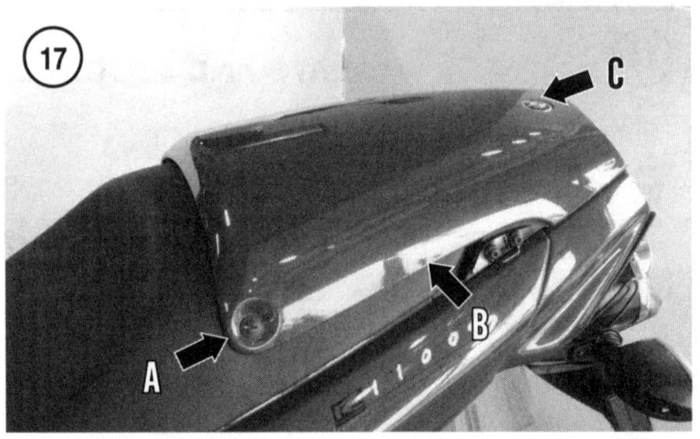

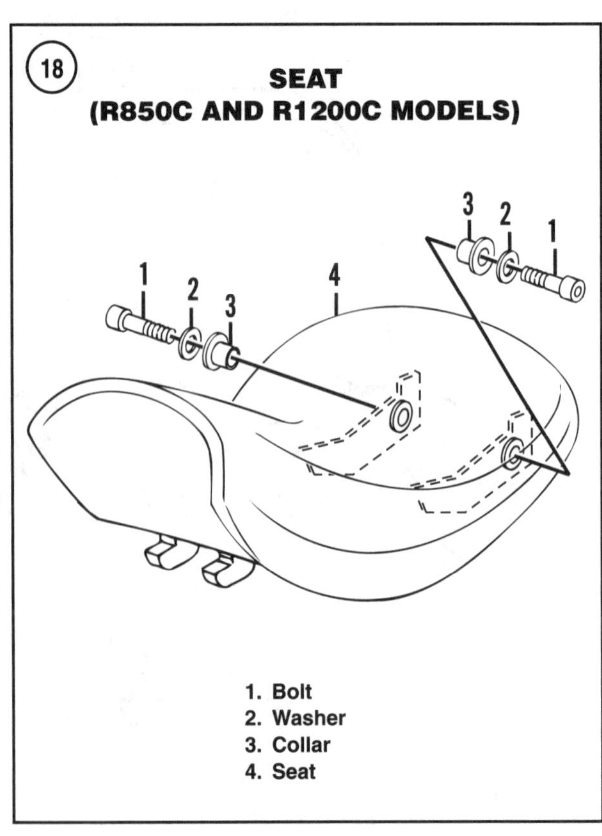

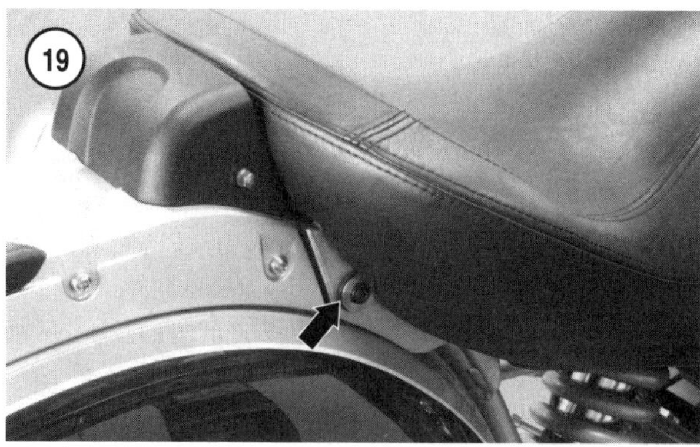

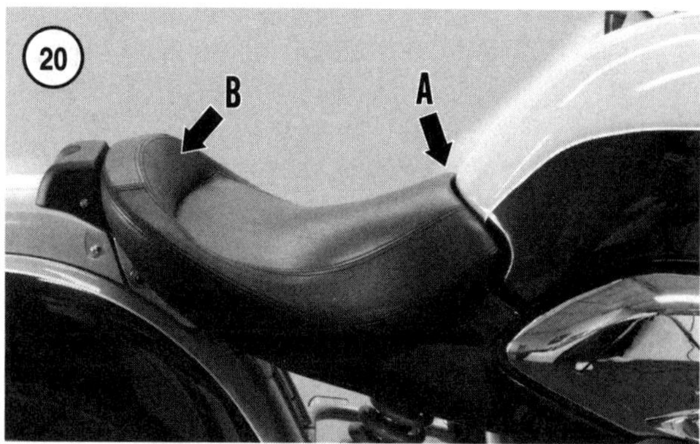

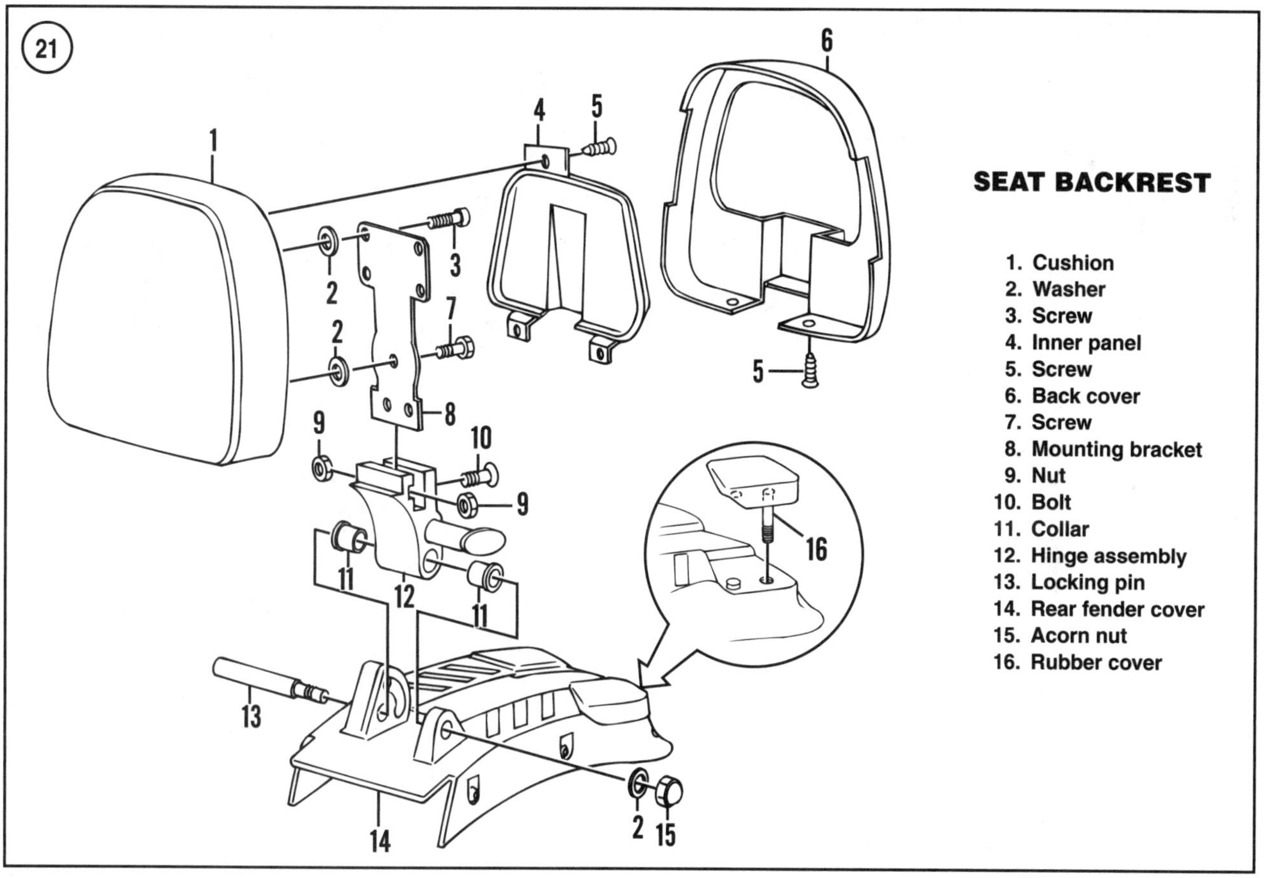

19

20
B
A

21
1
2
2
3
4
5
5
6
7
8
9
9
10
11
11
12
13
14
2
15
16
SEAT BACKREST
1. Cushion
2. Washer
3. Screw
4. Inner panel
5. Screw
6. Back cover
7. Screw
8. Mounting bracket
9. Nut
10. Bolt
11. Collar
12. Hinge assembly
13. Locking pin
14. Rear fender cover
15. Acorn nut
16. Rubber cover

the seat forward until it bottoms, then push it down on the rear (B) to engage the latch properly.

4. Make sure the collar is in place on the seat mounting tab on each side.

5. Install the screw and washer (**Figure 19**) securing the rear of the seat to the frame. Tighten the screws securely. Lift up on the seat to make sure it is locked into place.

6. Inspect all components as described in this section.

SEAT BACKREST (R850C AND R1200C MODELS)

Removal/Installation

Refer to **Figure 21**.

1. Remove the seat as described in this section.

2. Remove the acorn nut and washer from the locking pin.

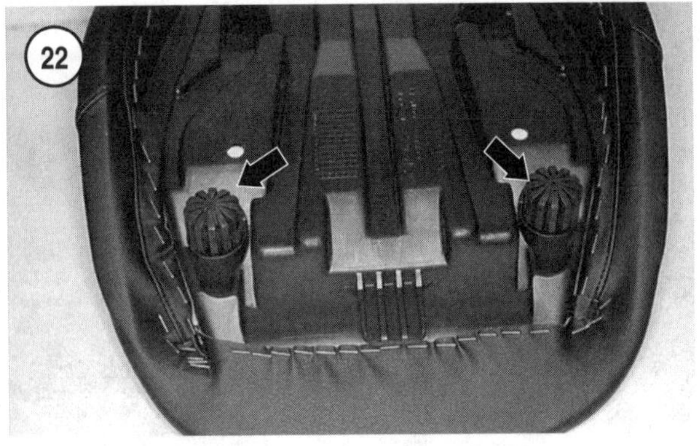

3. Withdraw the locking pin from the right side and remove the seat backrest assembly from the rear fender cover. Do not lose the collar on each side of the hinge assembly.

4. Install by reversing these removal steps. Tighten the acorn nut securely.

Disassembly/assembly

Refer to **Figure 21**.

1. Remove the seat backrest as described in this section.
2. Remove the two screws securing the back cover and remove the cover.
3. Remove the three screws securing the inner panel support to the cushion and remove the inner panel.
4. Remove the screws and washers securing the cushion to the mounting bracket and remove cushion.
5. Remove the screws securing the mounting bracket to the hinge assembly. Remove the mounting bracket, then remove the nuts from within the groove in the mounting bracket.
6. Install by reversing these removal steps. Tighten all screws securely.

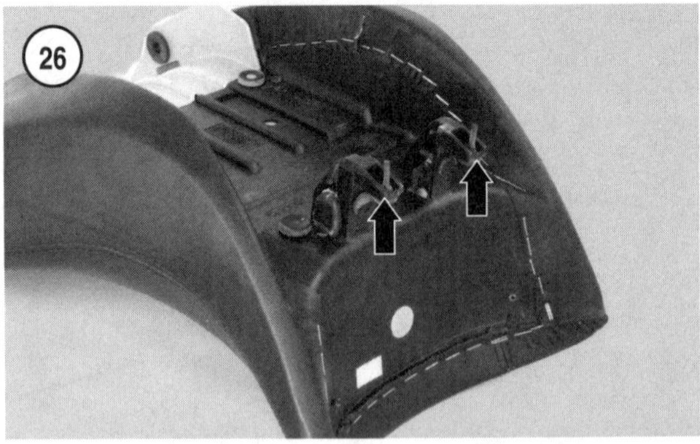

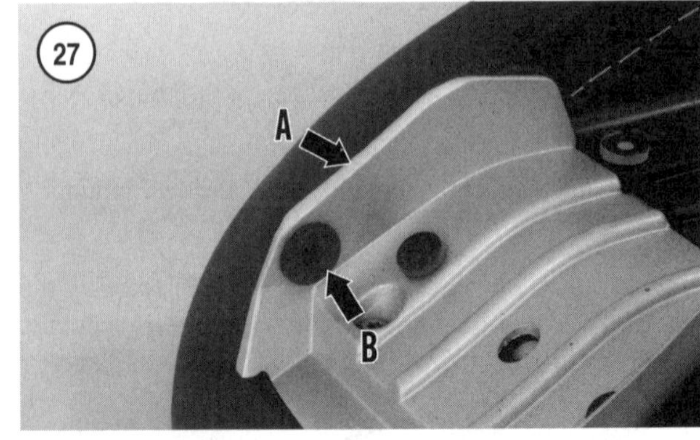

28

MUD GUARD (GS MODELS)

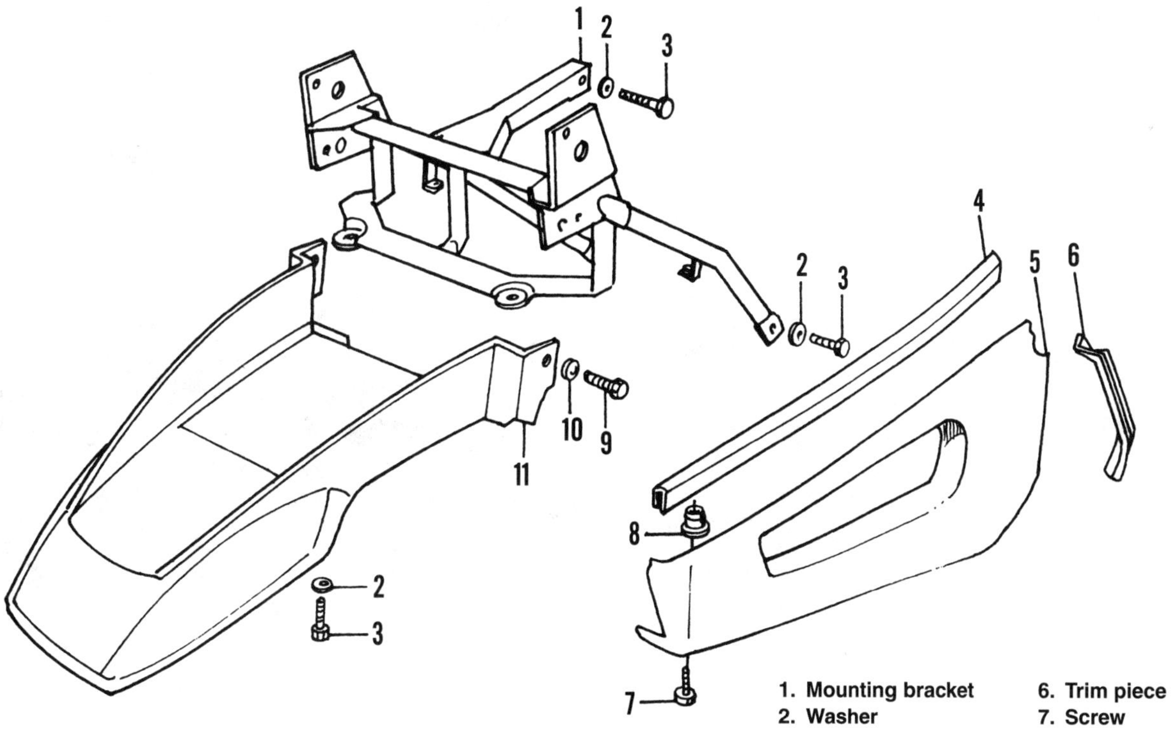

1. Mounting bracket
2. Washer
3. Bolt
4. Trim strip
5. Mud guard side trim
6. Trim piece
7. Screw
8. Nut
9. Bolt
10. Washer
11. Mud guard

Inspection (All Models)

1. Remove the seat(s) as described in this chapter.
2. Inspect the rubber bumpers (**Figure 22**, typical) on the seat for wear or damage; replace if necessary.
3. Inspect the seat catch (**Figure 23**, typical) for wear or damage. If it is damaged, perform the following:
   a. Remove the screws securing the catch to the seat and remove the catch.
   b. Install a new catch and securely tighten the screws and nuts.
4. Inspect the seat locking receptacles (**Figure 24**, typical) for wear or damage. If damaged, replace the seat.
5. Inspect the rubber bumpers (**Figure 25**, typical) on the frame for wear or damage. Replace if necessary.
6. On models so equipped, inspect the adjusters on the frame for wear or damage. If necessary, remove the screws and washers and install a new adjuster. Tighten the screws securely.
7. On R850C and R1200C models, inspect the front locking bars (**Figure 26**) for fatigue and cracks. Also check the mounting bracket (A, **Figure 27**) and rubber grommets (B) for wear or damage.

FRONT FENDER AND MUD GUARD

Removal/Installation

R1100R and R1100GS models

Refer to **Figure 28** (GS model only).

1. Place the motorcycle on the centerstand with the front wheel off the ground.
2. Remove the front wheel as described in Chapter Ten.

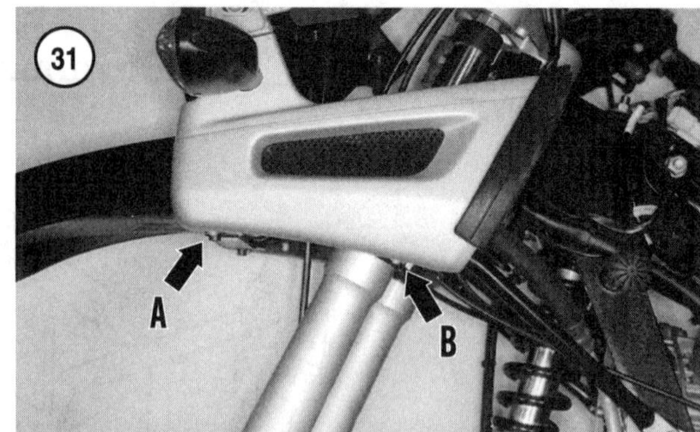

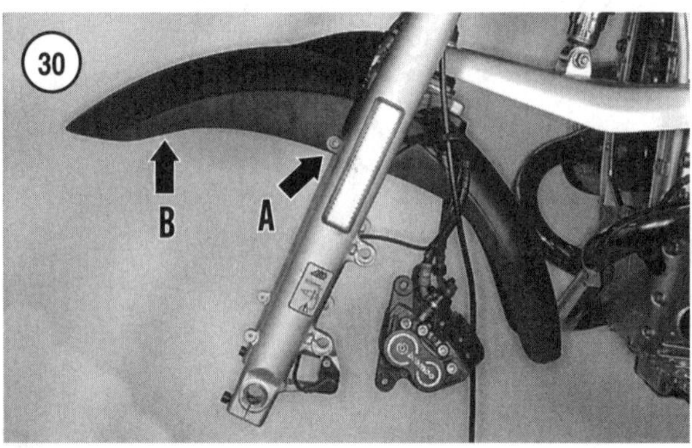

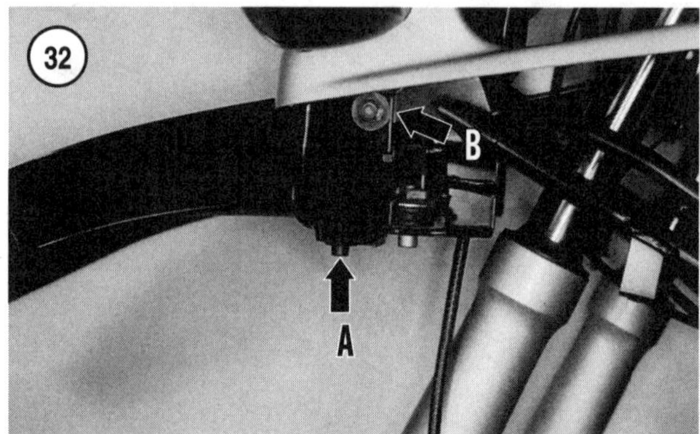

3. To remove the front fender on R1100R models, perform the following:
   a. Carefully remove the brake hoses and speedometer cable retainer (**Figure 29**) from the front fender.
   b. Remove the center bolt and washer from the lower fork bridge.
   c. Remove the bolts, washers and nuts (A, **Figure 30**) securing the fender to the fork slider on each side.
   d. Carefully move the front fender (B, **Figure 30**) forward and out from the fork sliders.
4. To remove the mud guard on R1100GS models, perform the following:
   a. Remove the screw and nut (A, **Figure 31**) securing the mud guard side trim to the mounting bracket. Pull the side trim (B, **Figure 31**) forward and remove it.
   b. Remove the lower bolts and washers (A, **Figure 32**) and the side bolts and washers (B) securing the mudguard to the mounting bracket.
   c. Remove the mudguard (**Figure 33**).
5. Inspect the bolt mounting holes (A, **Figure 34**) and retainer holes (B) for damage and elongation. Replace the fender, if necessary.
6. Install by reversing the removal steps. Tighten the bolts and nuts securely.

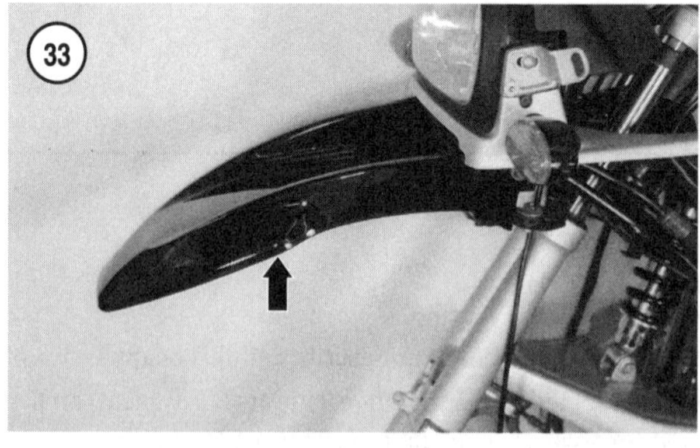

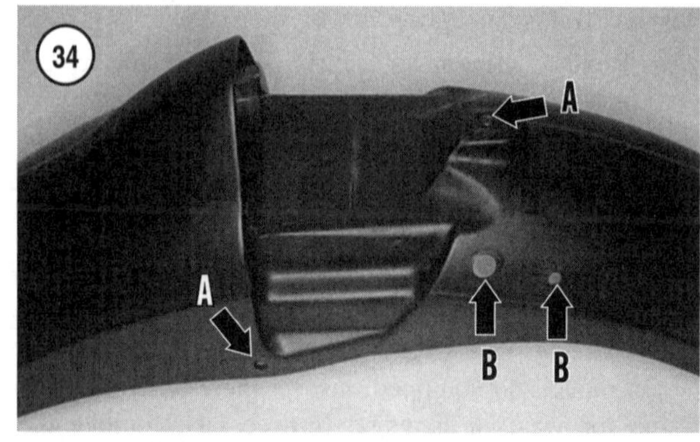

35

FRONT FENDER (R1150R MODELS)

1. Front fender section
2. Screw
3. Screw
4. Rear fender section
5. Cable guide
6. Bolt

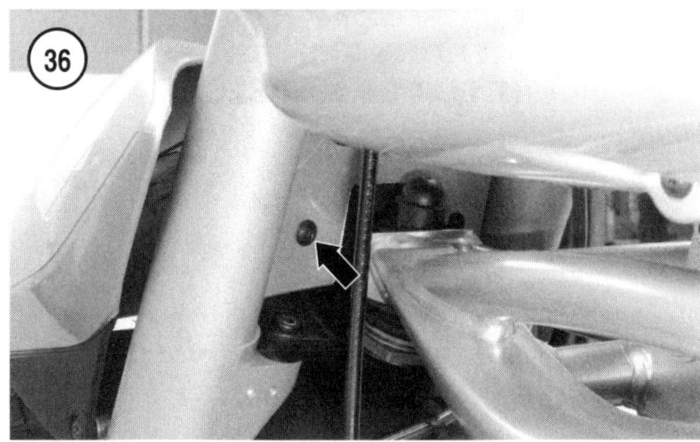
36

37

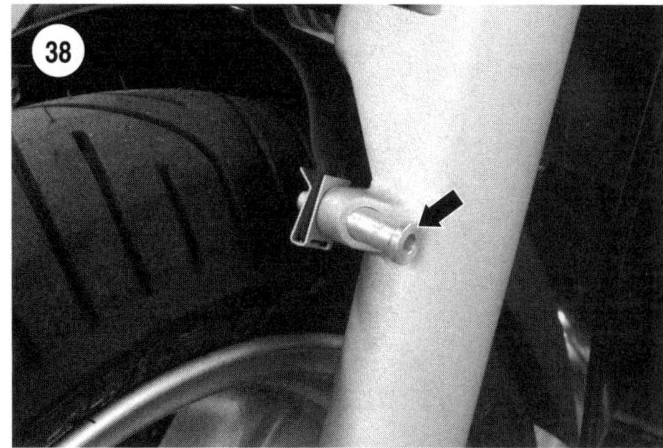
38

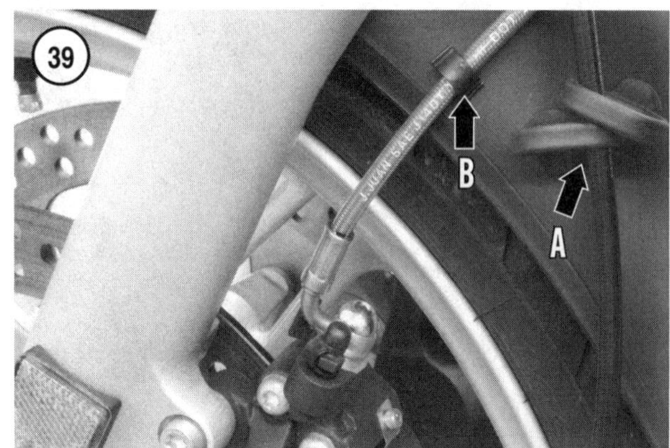

39

R1150R models

Refer to **Figure 35**.

1. Place the motorcycle on the centerstand with the front wheel off of the ground.
2. Remove the screw (**Figure 36**) on each side, securing the backside of the front portion of the front fender to the mounting bracket.
3. Remove the long screw (**Figure 37**) on each side, securing the front portion of the front fender to the rear portion of the front fender.
4. Remove the front portion of the front fender from the fork sliders. Do not lose the long collar (**Figure 38**) on each fork slider.
5. Carefully remove the speedometer cable retainer (A, **Figure 39**) and the brake hose retainer (B) from the rear portion of the front fender.
6. Remove the screw (**Figure 40**) securing the rear portion of the front fender to the base of the mounting bracket.
7. Remove the rear portion of the front fender from the fork sliders.
8. Install by reversing these removal steps while noting the following:

a. Make sure the special nuts (**Figure 41**) are in place on the mounting bracket to accept the screws (**Figure 36**).
b. Be sure to install the long collar (**Figure 38**) onto each fork slider.
c. Tighten the screws securely.

R1150GS models

1. To remove the upper portion, place the motorcycle on the centerstand with the front wheel off of the ground.
2. Remove the large nut (**Figure 42**) securing the front run signals to the fender. Disconnect the turn signal electrical connector and remove both turn signals (A, **Figure 43**) from the fender.
3. Remove the two screws securing the front fender to the bottom surface of the instrument panel mounting bracket (B, **Figure 43**).
4. Slide off the rubber trim piece (C, **Figure 43**) off the front fender.
5. Remove the two screws securing the front fender to the mounting bracket (D, **Figure 43**).
6. Install by reversing these removal steps while noting the following:

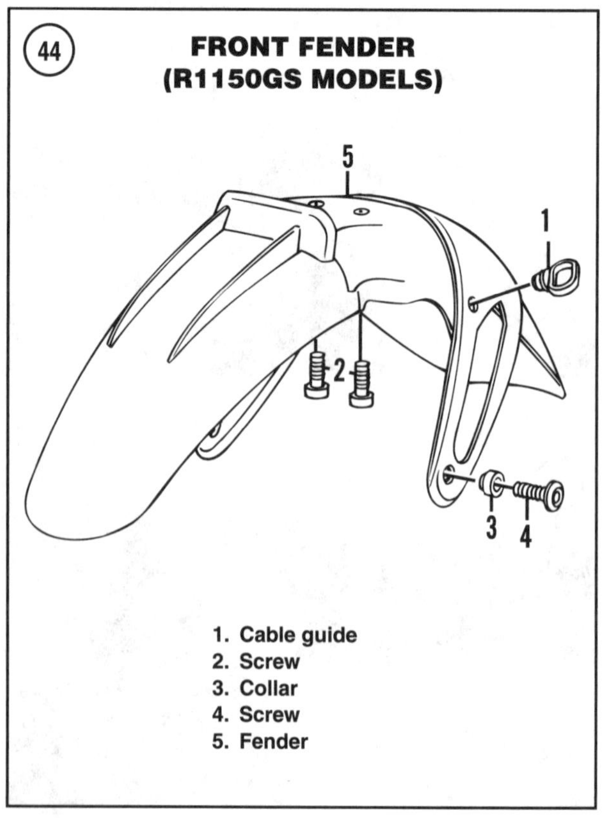

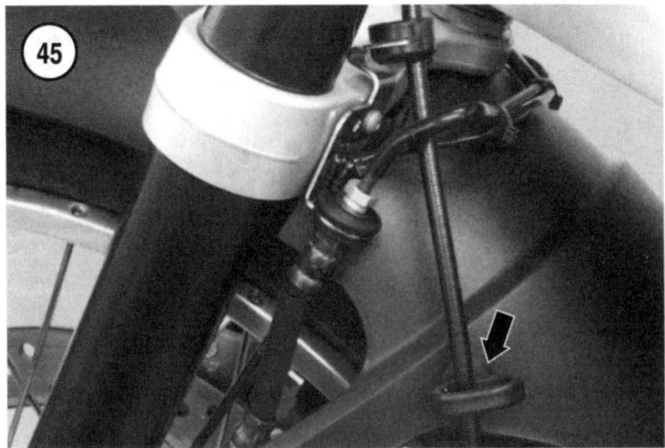

a. Be sure to install the rubber trim piece (C, **Figure 43**).

b. Tighten the screws securely.

7. To remove the lower portion (**Figure 44**), carefully remove the speedometer cable retainer (**Figure 45**) from the front fender.

8. Carefully remove the front brake hose and ABS sensor wire retainer (**Figure 46**) from the front fender.

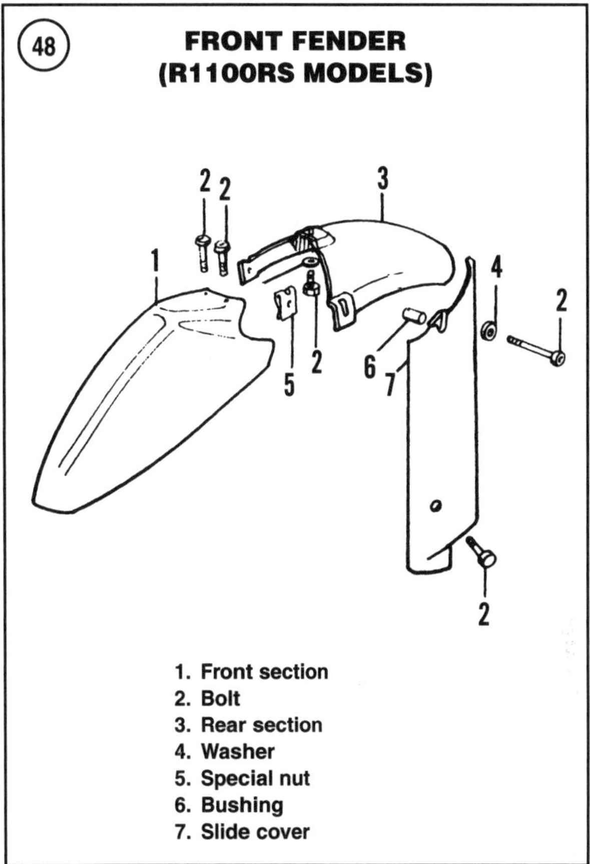

9. Remove the front wheel as described in Chapter Eleven.

10. Remove the screw (A, **Figure 47**) on each side, securing the front fender to the mounting boss on the slider.

11. Working up under the fender, remove the two screws securing the front fender to the lower fork bridge (B, **Figure 47**).

12. Carefully lower the front fender down and away from the lower fork bridge and remove it from the fork sliders.

13. Install by reversing these removal steps while noting the following:

a. Be sure to install the screw and collar (A, **Figure 47**).

b. Tighten the screws securely.

R1100RS and R1100RT models

Refer to **Figure 48** and **Figure 49**.

1. Place the motorcycle on the centerstand with the front wheel off the ground.

2. On RS models, perform the following:

a. Remove the upper two bolts securing the front section to the lower fork bridge.

15

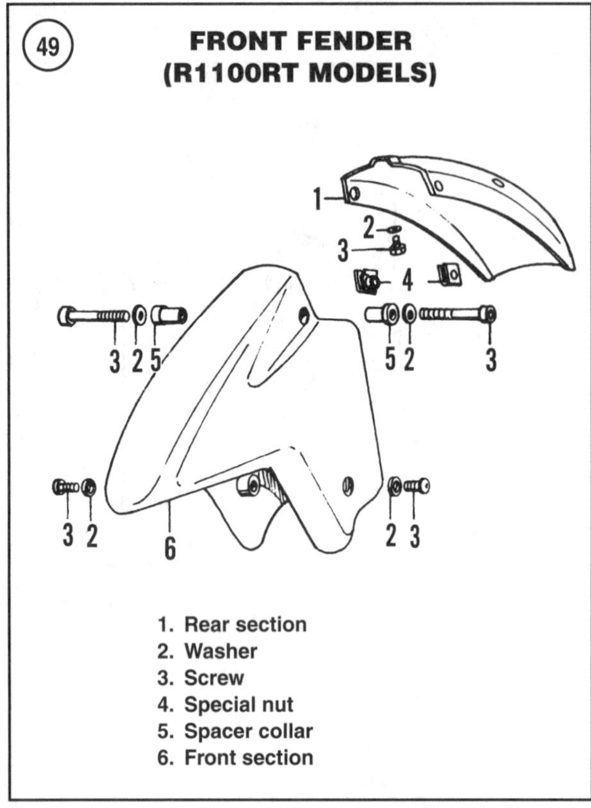

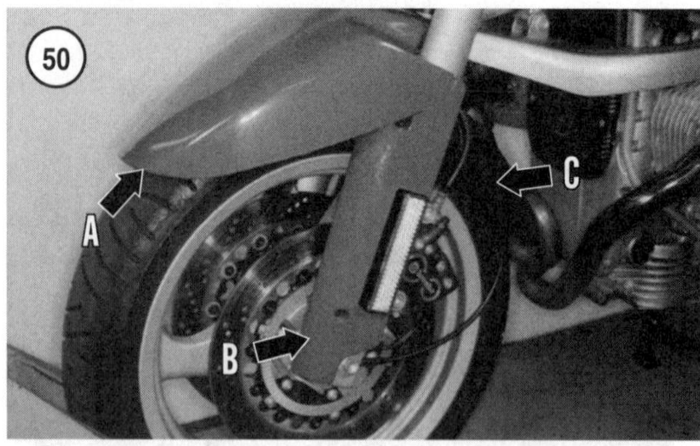

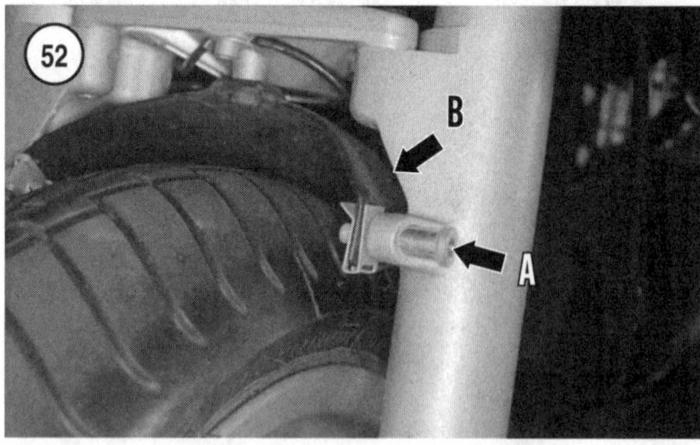

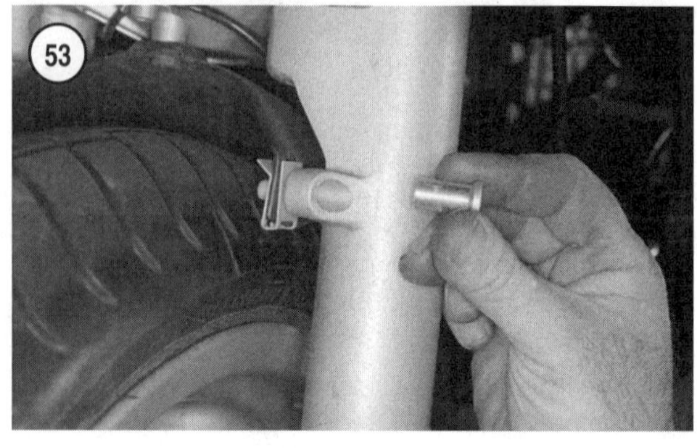

b. Remove the front section (A, **Figure 50**).

c. Remove the lower bolt and the upper bolt washer and bushing securing the slider cover to the fork slider. Remove the cover (B, **Figure 50**). Repeat for the other side.

d. Remove the bolts and washers securing the rear section and remove the rear section (C, **Figure 50**).

3. On RT models, perform the following:

a. Remove the lower bolt and washer (A, **Figure 51**) securing the front section to the fork slider on each side.

b. Remove the upper bolt and washer (B, **Figure 51**) securing the front section to the fork slider on each side. Remove the spacer collar (A, **Figure 52**) located in the fork slider mounting boss on each side.

c. Remove the center bolt and washer securing the rear section to the lower fork bridge. Remove the rear section (B, **Figure 52**).

4. Install by reversing the removal steps while noting the following:

a. Be sure to install the spacer collar (**Figure 53**) into the fork slider mounting boss on each side.

b. Tighten the bolts securely.

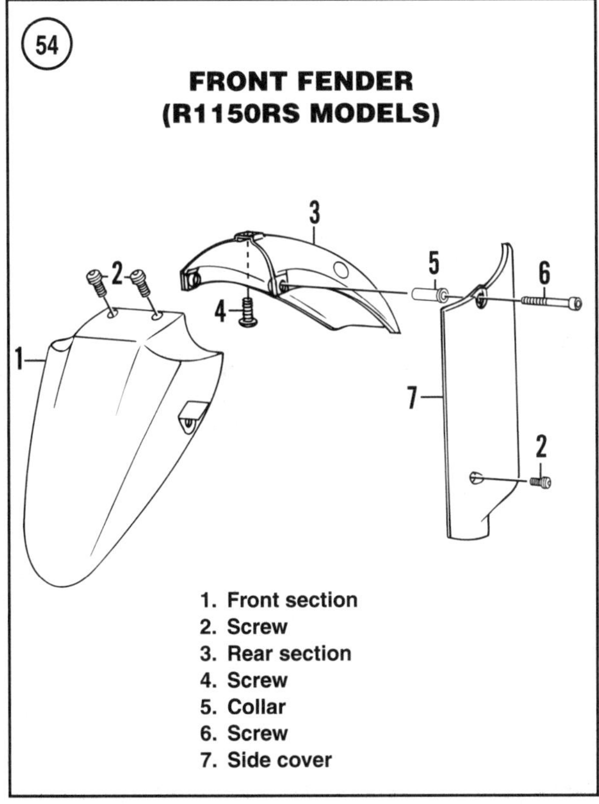

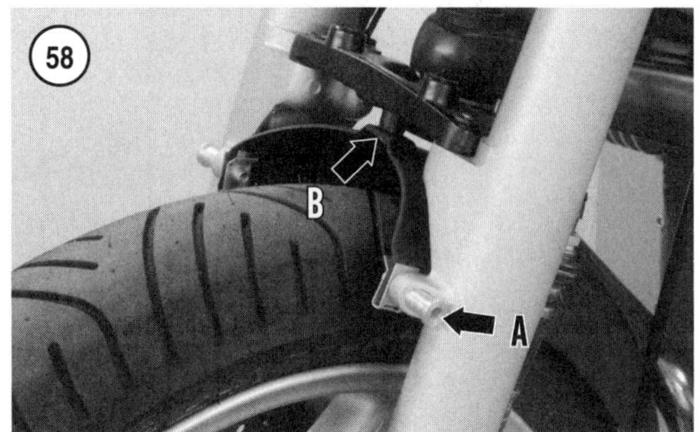

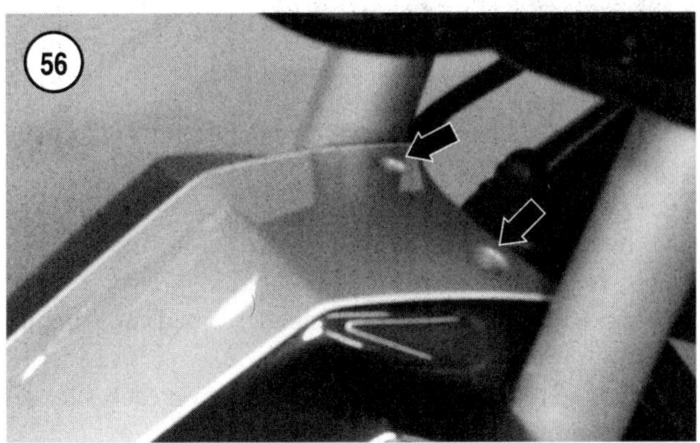

R1150RS models

Refer to **Figure 54**.

1. Place the motorcycle on the centerstand with the front wheel off of the ground.
2. Remove the lower short bolt (A, **Figure 55**) and the upper long bolt (B) and bushing securing the slider cover to the fork slider. Remove the side cover (C, **Figure 55**). Repeat for the other side.
3. Remove the two screws (**Figure 56**) securing the front portion of the front fender to the mounting bracket on the lower fork bridge.
4. Remove the front portion of the front fender (**Figure 57**) from the fork sliders. Do not lose the long collar (A, **Figure 58**) on each fork slider.
5. Remove the screw (B, **Figure 58**) securing the rear portion of the front fender to the base of the mounting bracket.
6. Remove the rear portion of the front fender from the fork sliders.
7. Install by reversing these removal steps while noting the following:
   a. Be sure to install the long collar (A, **Figure 58**) onto each fork slider.
   b. Tighten the screws securely.

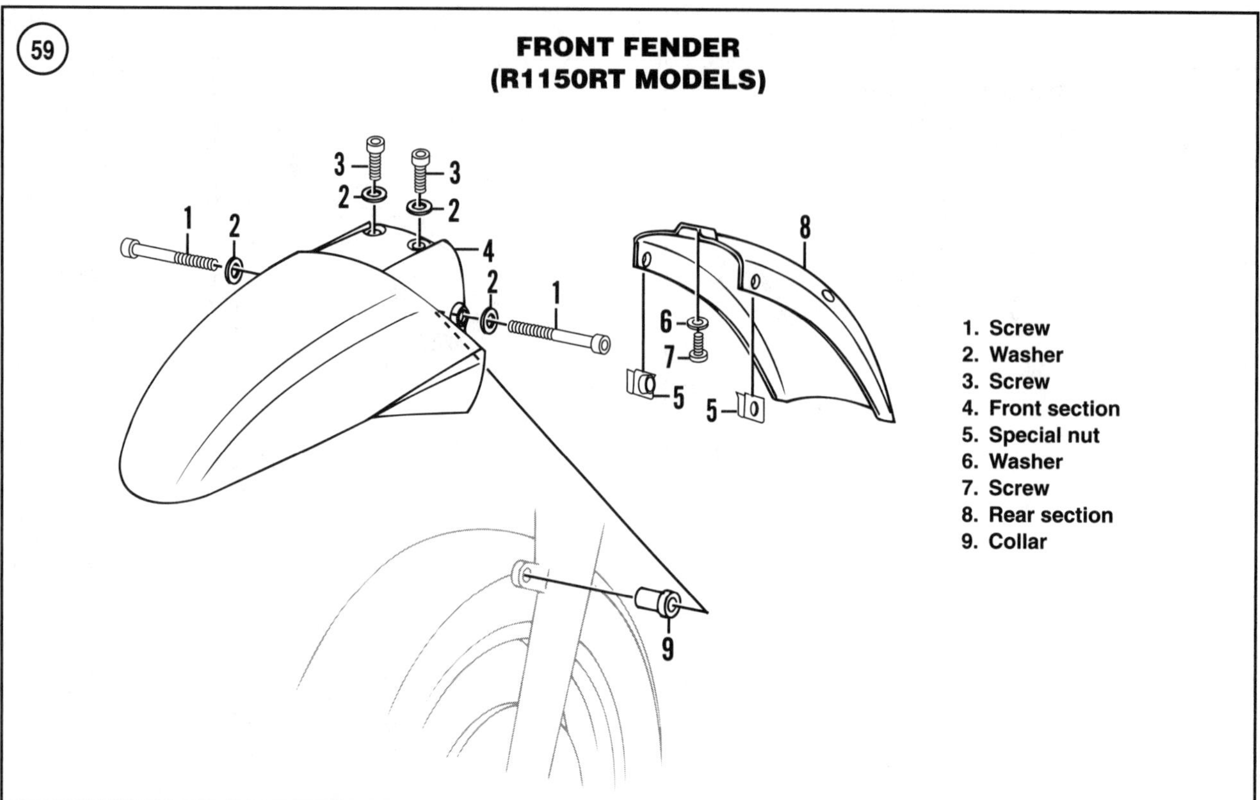

R1150RT models

Refer to **Figure 59**.

1. Place the motorcycle on the centerstand with the front wheel off of the ground.

2. Remove the long screw and washer securing the front portion of the front fender to the fork slider on each side.

3. Remove the two screws and washers securing the top of the front portion of the front fender to the mounting bracket on the lower fork bridge.

4. Remove the front portion of the front fender. Do not lose the long collar on each fork slider.

5. Remove the screw securing the rear portion of the rear fender to the base of the mounting bracket.

6. Remove the rear portion of the front fender from the fork sliders.

7. Install by reversing these removal steps while noting the following:

   a. Be sure to install the long collar onto each fork slider.

   b. Tighten the screws securely.

R1100S models

1A. On models so equipped, place the motorcycle on the centerstand with the front wheel off of the ground.
1B. On models without a centerstand, place a suitable size jack under the engine to support the motorcycle with the front wheel off the ground.
2. Remove the front wheel as described in Chapter Eleven.
3. Remove the two screws and washers on each side securing the front fender to the fork sliders.

61

REAR FENDER AND MUD GUARD (R1100R MODELS)

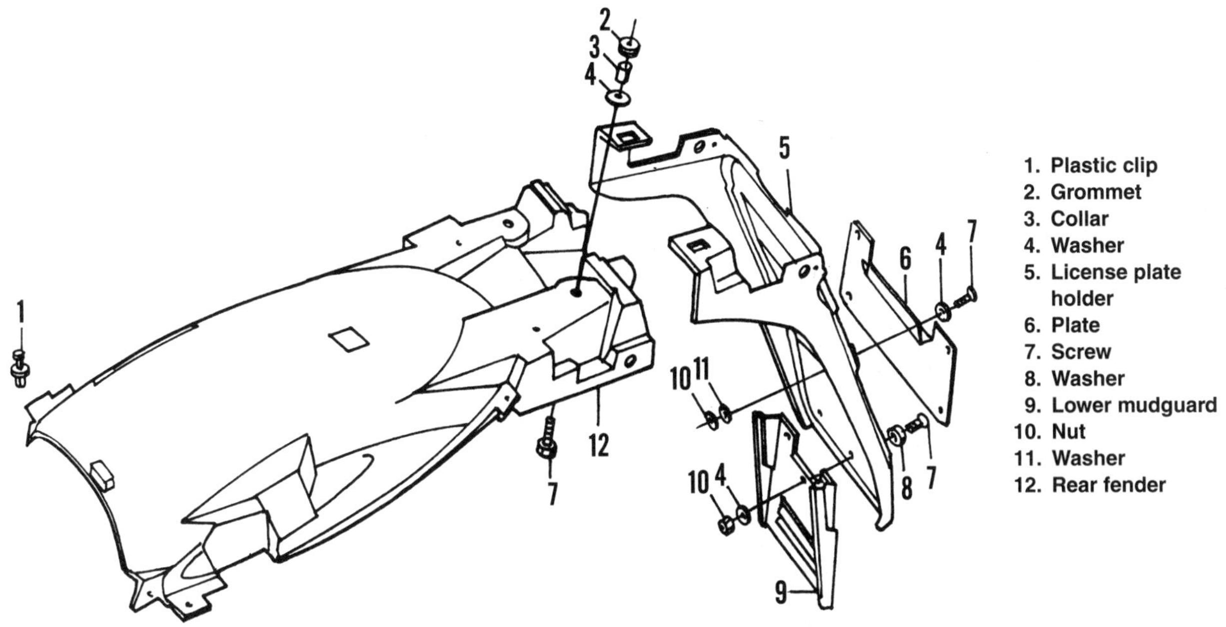

4. Working up under the fender, remove the two screw securing the front fender to the lower fork bridge.
5. Carefully move the front fender forward and away from the lower fork bridge and remove it from the fork sliders.
6. Install by reversing these removal steps. Tighten the screws securely.

R850C and R1200C models

1. Place a suitable size jack under the engine to support the motorcycle with the front wheel off the ground.
2. Remove the front wheel as described in Chapter Eleven.
3. Remove the five screws securing the front fender to the lower fork bridge (A, **Figure 60**).
4. Carefully tip the front fender (B, **Figure 60**) sideways to clear the fork sliders, then remove it from the lower fork bridge and the fork sliders.
5. Install by reversing these removal steps. Tighten the screws securely.

REAR FENDER AND MUD GUARD

The rear fender on these models is not visible since it is covered by body panels and the seat. It is used mainly to direct dirt and moisture away from under the seating area and surrounding body panels. Rarely is it necessary to remove the large rear fender, but the license plate holder and lower extension may require replacement.

Removal/Installation

R1100GS, R1100R and R1150GS models

Refer to **Figure 61-63**.
1. Place the motorcycle on the centerstand with the rear wheel off the ground.
2. Remove the seats as described in this chapter.
3. On models so equipped, remove the luggage and mounting brackets as described in this chapter.
4. On GS models, remove the tool box.
5. On R models, remove the rear side panel as described in this chapter.

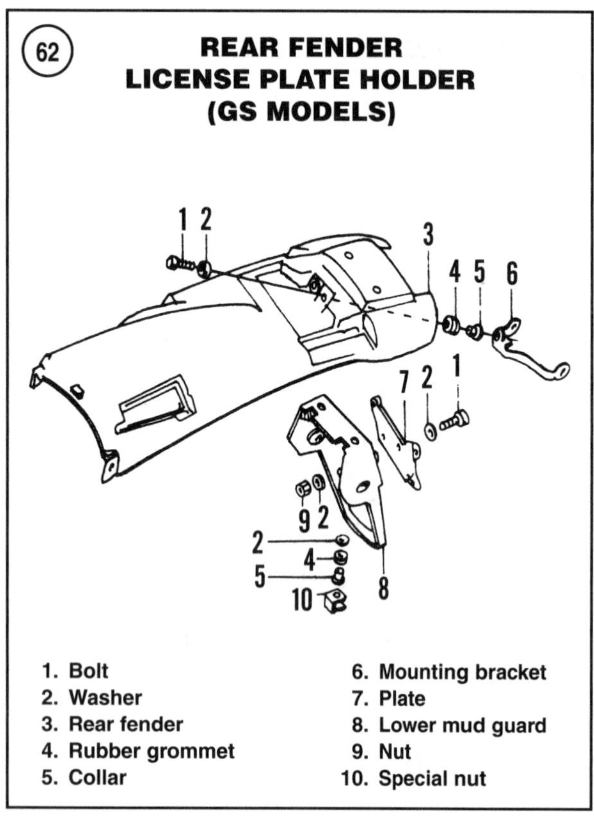

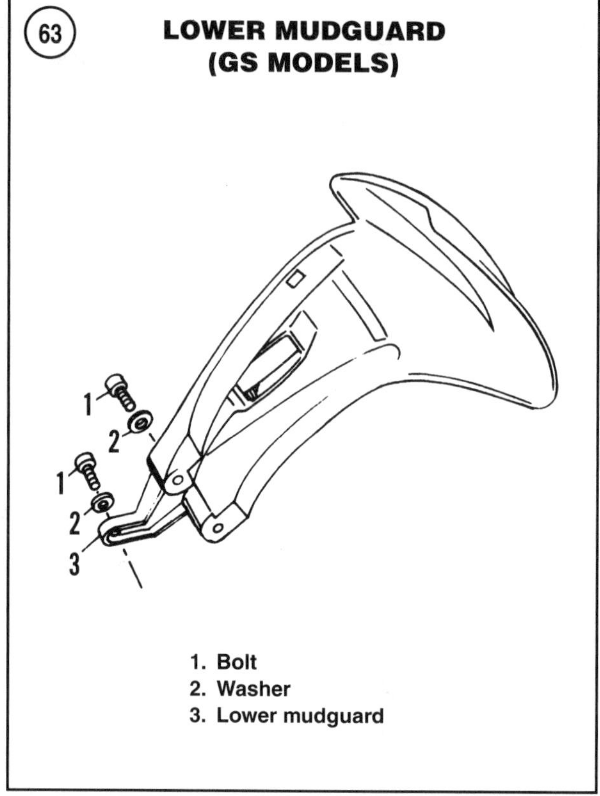

6. Disconnect the electrical connectors for the rear turn signals, brake light and license plate light.

7. Remove the bolts, washer and nuts securing the license plate holder to the rear fender. Remove the license plate holder.

8. Release the front special fasteners and the rear bolt and washer securing the rear fender to the rear frame assembly.

9. Carefully remove the wiring harness from the rear fender.

10. Pull the fender up and out of the receptacles at the front where it is indexed into the rear frame assembly. Remove the rear fender.

11. On GS models, remove the bolts and washers (A, **Figure 64**) securing the lower mudguard to the final drive unit. Remove the mudguard (B, **Figure 64**).

12. Install by reversing the removal steps. Tighten the bolts and nuts securing the fender securely.

R1150R models

Refer to **Figure 65**.

1. Place the motorcycle on the centerstand with the rear wheel off of the ground.

2. Remove the rear wheel as described in Chapter Eleven.

3. Remove the seats as described in this chapter.

4. On models so equipped, remove the luggage and mounting brackets as described in this chapter.

5. Remove the rear side panels as described in this chapter.

6. Remove the taillight/brake light lens assembly as described in Chapter Ten.

7. Remove the two screws securing the mounting bracket at the rear. Remove the mounting bracket.

(65)

REAR FENDER AND MUD GUARD (R1150R MODELS)

1. Screw
2. Taillight/brake light assembly
3. Mounting bracket
4. Tail section and license plate holder
5. Special nut
6. Extension
7. Rear carrier
8. Seat latch
9. Rear fender
10. Nut

8. Working under the tail section and license plate holder assembly, remove the screw on each side securing the tail section and license plate holder assembly to the rear fender.
9. Remove the screw on each side, securing the tail section and license plate holder assembly to the rear fender.
10. Carefully pull the tail section and license plate holder assembly part way toward the rear.
11. Disconnect the multi-pin electrical connector for the taillight/brake light and rear turn signals.
12. Remove the tail section and license plate holder assembly from the frame.
13. Remove the screws securing the seat lock and disengage the control cable. Remove the seat lock.
14. Remove the screws and nuts securing the rear carrier to the rear fender.
15. Remove the screw on each side securing the rear carrier to the rear fender. Remove the rear carrier.
16. Carefully remove any wiring harness from the rear fender.
17. Secure the rear fender to the frame with a bungee cord or it will fall out after the screws are loosened in Step 18.
18. Release the front special fasteners and tab nut on each side securing the rear fender to the rear frame assembly. Lower the rear fender and remove it from the frame.
19. Install by reversing the removal steps. Tighten the bolts and nuts securely.

RS and RT models

Refer to **Figure 66-68**.
1. Place the motorcycle on the centerstand with the front wheel off the ground.
2. Remove the seats as described in this chapter.
3. On models so equipped, remove the luggage and mounting brackets as described in this chapter.
4A. On RS models, remove the rear turn signal assemblies and the taillight/brake light assembly from the rear fender.
4B. On RT models, remove the taillight/brake light assembly from the rear fender.
5. On RS models, perform the following:
   a. Remove the bolts and washers securing the rear grab handle (A, **Figure 69**) and remove the grab handle.
   b. Remove the bolts securing the tail piece (B, **Figure 69**) and remove the tail piece.
   c. Remove the screws securing the rear side panel (C, **Figure 69**) and remove the panel from each side.
   d. If necessary, remove the screws and washers securing the license plate holder and lower mudguard assembly (D, **Figure 69**). Remove the assembly.
6. Working under the rear fender, remove the front bolt and washer on each side securing the rear fender to the rear frame assembly.
7. Remove the front screw and washer and the rear bolt and washer on each side securing the rear fender to the rear frame assembly.
8. Carefully remove the wiring harness from the rear fender.
9. Remove the rear fender.
10. Install by reversing the removal steps. Tighten the bolts and nuts securing the fender.

R1100S models

Refer to **Figure 70**.
1A. On models so equipped, place the motorcycle on the centerstand with the rear wheel off of the ground.
1B. On models without a centerstand, place a suitable size jack under the engine to support the motorcycle with the rear wheel off the ground.
2. Remove the seat (A, **Figure 71**) as described in this chapter.
3. Remove the side covers (B, **Figure 71**) as described in this chapter.
4. Remove the license plate carrier (C, **Figure 71**) as described in Chapter Ten.
5. Remove the rear wheel as described in Chapter Eleven.
6. Remove the muffler as described in Chapter Nine.
7. Remove the protective caps at the rear of the rear fender.
8. Disconnect the multi-pin electrical connector for the taillight/brake light and rear turn signals.
9. Remove the screws and washers on each side securing the tail piece assembly and remove the assembly.
10. Carefully remove any wiring harness from the rear fender.
11. Working under the rear fender, remove the screws and washers securing the rear fender to the rear frame. Lower the rear fender and remove it.
12. Install by reversing the removal steps. Tighten the bolts and nuts securing the fender.

R850C and R1200C models

Refer to **Figure 72**.
1. Place a suitable size jack under the engine to support the motorcycle with the rear wheel off the ground.
2. Remove the seat as described in this chapter.
3. Disconnect the electrical connector for the taillight/brake light and rear turn signal assemblies.

REAR FENDER, SIDE PANEL AND TAIL PIECE (RS MODELS)

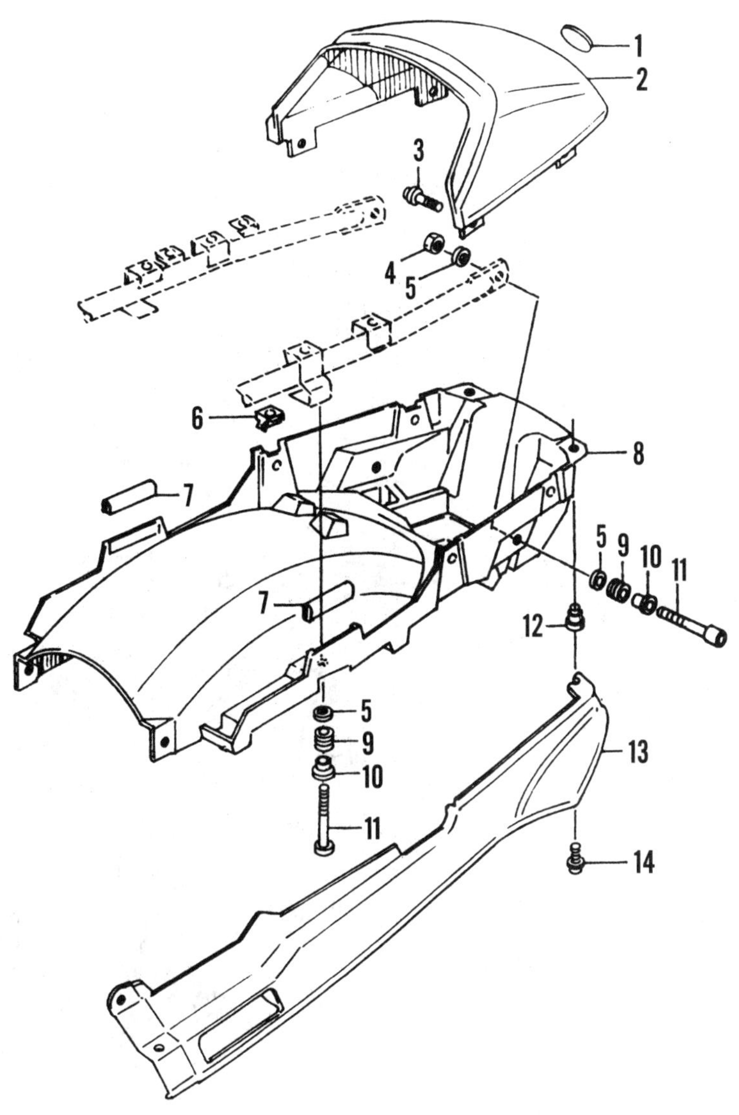

1. Emblem
2. Tail piece
3. Screw
4. Nut
5. Washer
6. Special nut
7. Trim piece
8. Rear fender
9. Rubber grommet
10. Collar
11. Bolt
12. Nut
13. Side panel
14. Screw

(67)

LICENSE PLATE HOLDER AND LOWER MUDGUARD (RS MODELS)

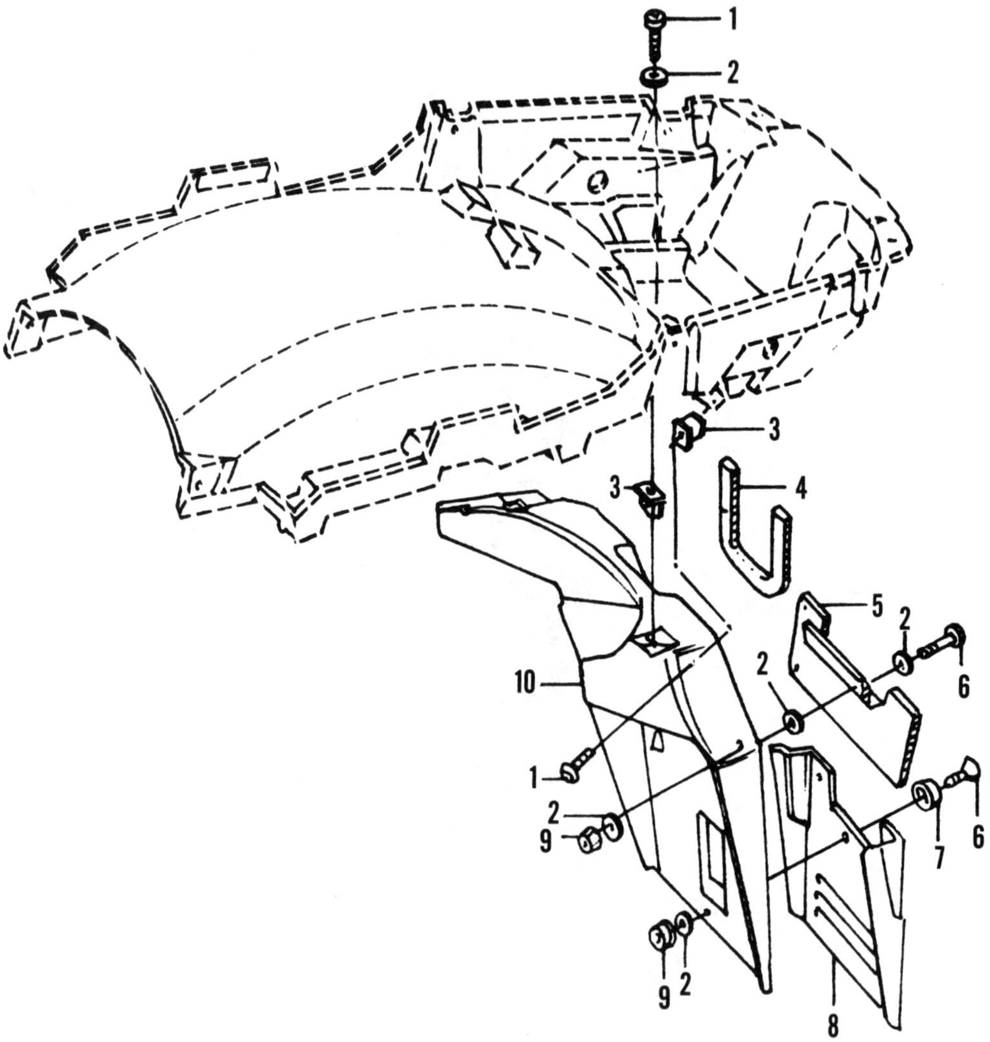

1. Screw
2. Washer
3. Special nut
4. Gasket
5. Plate
6. Screw
7. Washer
8. Lower mudguard
9. Nut
10. License plate holder

(68)

REAR FENDER, LICENSE PLATE HODLER AND LOWER MUDGUARD (RT MODELS)

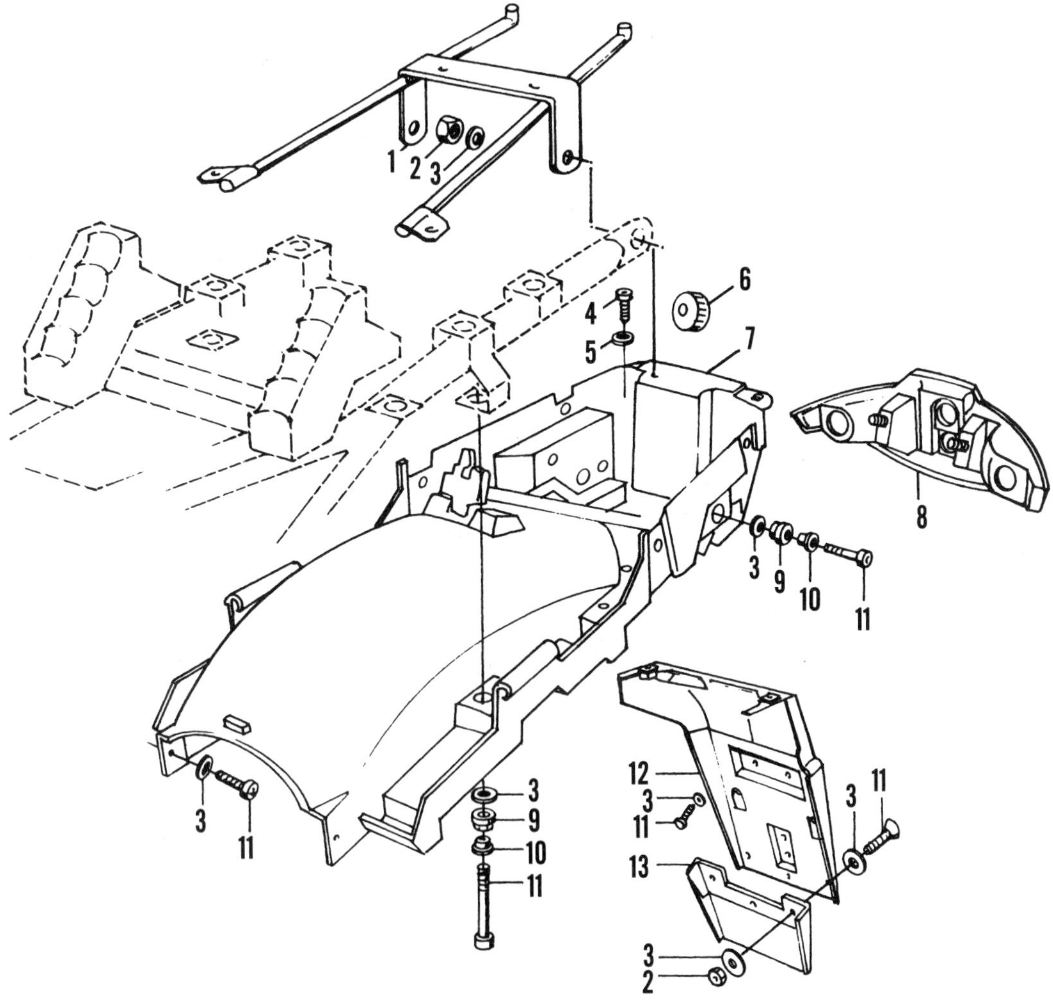

1. Subframe
2. Nut
3. Washer
4. Screw
5. Washer
6. Knurled nut
7. Rear fender
8. Taillight assembly
9. Rubber grommet
10. Collar
11. Bolt
12. License plate holder
13. Lower mudguard

4. Working under the rear fender, remove the nuts securing the rubber cover (A, **Figure 73**) on each side. Remove both rubber covers and reinstall the nuts.
5. Remove the two bolts (**Figure 74**) securing the rear fender to the frame.
6. Carefully pull the rear fender straight up and off the frame.
7. If necessary, remove the screws securing the cover plate (**Figure 75**) and remove the cover plate. Inspect the rubber grommets (**Figure 76**) on the electrical harness for hardness and deterioration. Replace if necessary.
8. Install by reversing the removal steps while noting the following:
   a. Index the receptacle on the under side of the rubber cover with the locating pin on the rear fender. Install the rubber cover and tighten the nuts securely.
   b. Tighten the bolts securing the fender securely.

BODY SIDE PANELS (R MODELS)

Removal/Installation

R1100R models

Refer to **Figure 77**.

1. Place the motorcycle on the centerstand with the front wheel off the ground.
2. Remove the seats as described in this chapter.
3. Release the two quick-release fasteners at the base of the side panel.
4. Remove the rear grab rail upper bolt and loosen the lower one.
5. Carefully pull the front of the side panel away from the frame.
6. Slowly slide the side panel forward and away from the rear grab rail and remove the side panel.
7. If necessary, repeat for the side panel on the other side.
8. Install by reversing the removal steps.

R1150R models

Refer to **Figure 78**.

1. Place the motorcycle on the centerstand with the front wheel off the ground.
2. Remove the seats as described in this chapter.
3. Remove the screw (A, **Figure 79**) securing the side panel to the fuel tank.

NOTE
*B, **Figure** 79 shows the lower screw location only.*

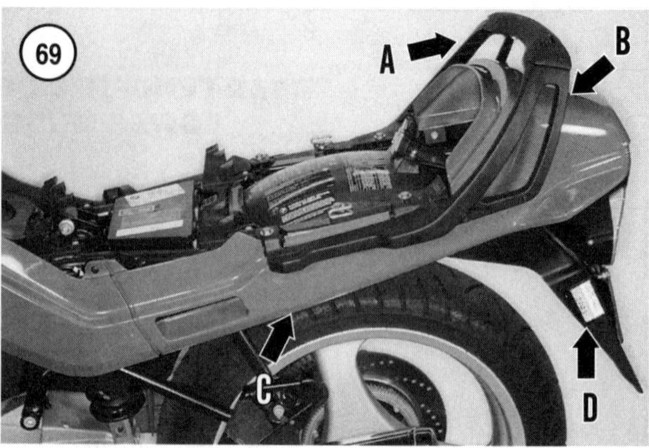

4. On the underside of the side panel, remove the lower screw (B, **Figure 79**) securing the side panel to the rear frame.
5. Remove the two top screws (**Figure 80**) securing the side panel to the frame.
6. Carefully pull the front of the side panel *part way* from the frame releasing the locating tab (**Figure 81**) from the rear frame.
7. Slide the side panel forward to release the locating post from the receptacle in the tail section and license plate holder. Remove the side panel.
8. If necessary, repeat for the other side.
9. Install by reversing the removal steps while noting the following:
   a. Make sure the small washer is in place in the rubber grommet (**Figure 82**) on the fuel tank in order to accept the front screw (A, **Figure 79**).
   b. Index the rear locating post (A, **Figure 83**) on the side panel into the receptacle in the tail section and license plate holder (B).
   c. Carefully push the side panel into place securing the locating tab (**Figure 81**) onto the rear frame. Push the side panel on until this post is fully seated on the frame rail.
   d. Install all screws and tighten securely.

WINDSHIELD (GS MODELS)

Removal/Installation

R1100GS models

Refer to **Figure 84**.

1. Place the motorcycle on the centerstand with the front wheel off the ground.

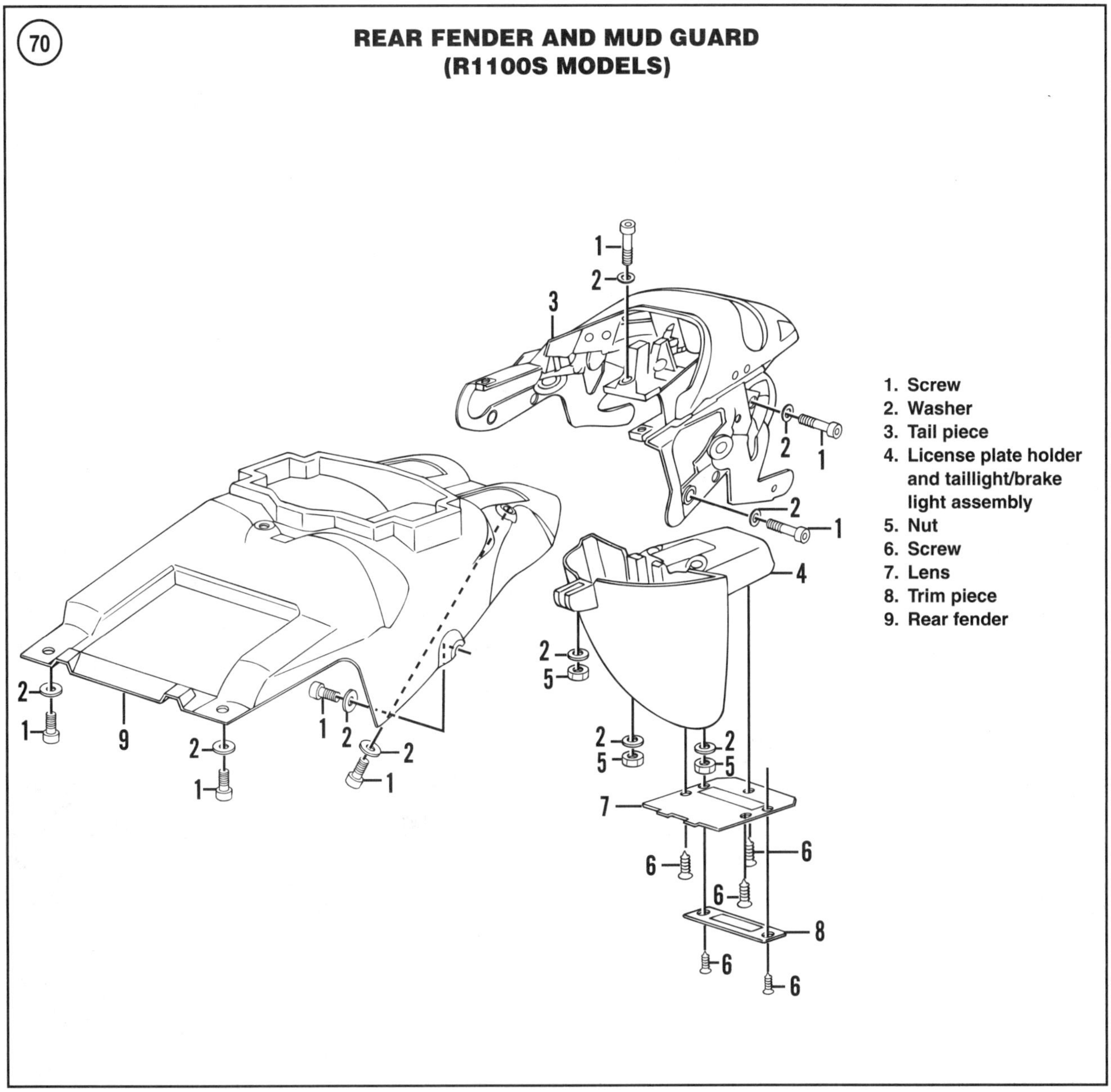

(70)

REAR FENDER AND MUD GUARD (R1100S MODELS)

1. Screw
2. Washer
3. Tail piece
4. License plate holder and taillight/brake light assembly
5. Nut
6. Screw
7. Lens
8. Trim piece
9. Rear fender

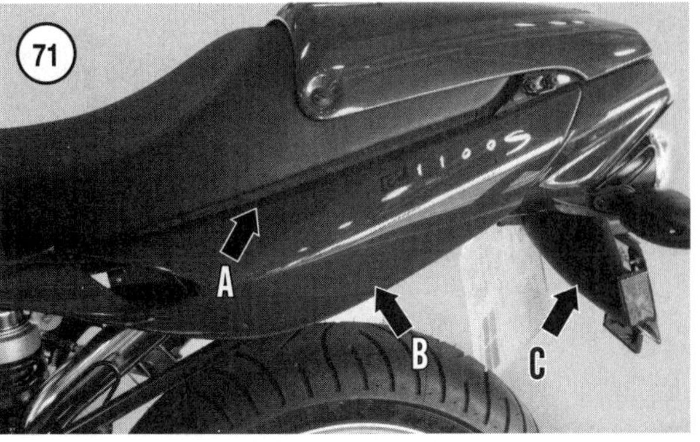

NOTE
Do not loosen, or remove the two upper bolts. These bolts are to remain in place to hold the inner brace to the backside of the windshield.

2. Remove the two upper bolts securing the windshield to the support and remove the windshield.
3. To remove the support, perform the following:
   a. Remove the windshield.
   b. Remove the front fender and mud guard as described in this chapter.

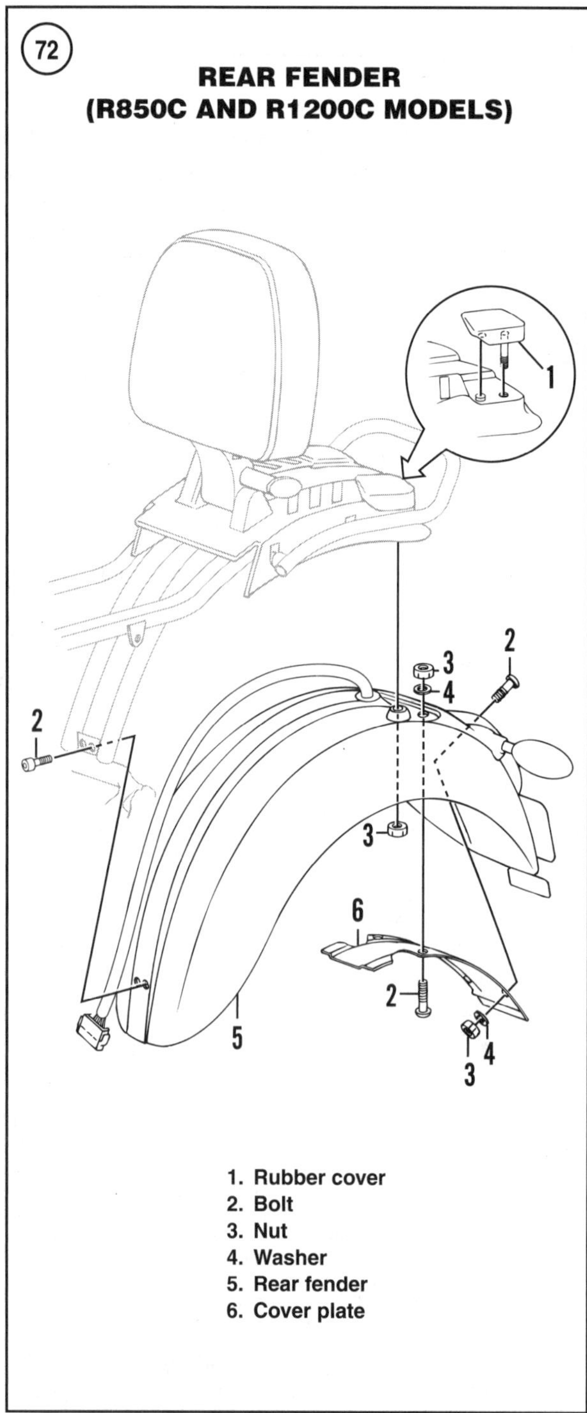

c. Remove the headlight assembly (A, **Figure 85**) as described in Chapter Nine.

d. Remove the front turn signal assemblies (B, **Figure 85**) from the windshield support.

e. Remove the bolts and washer securing the windshield support and cover (C, **Figure 85**).

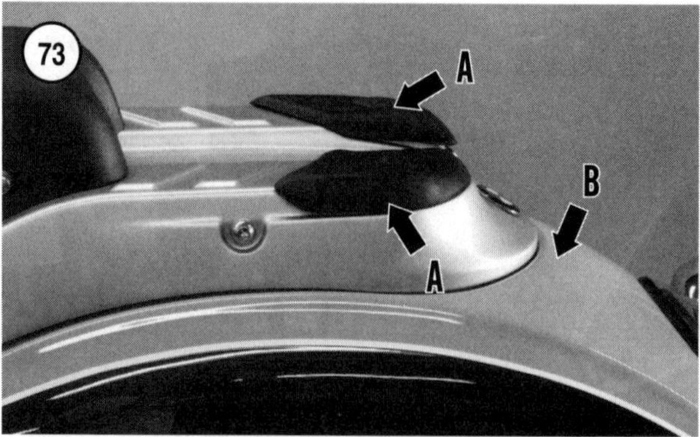

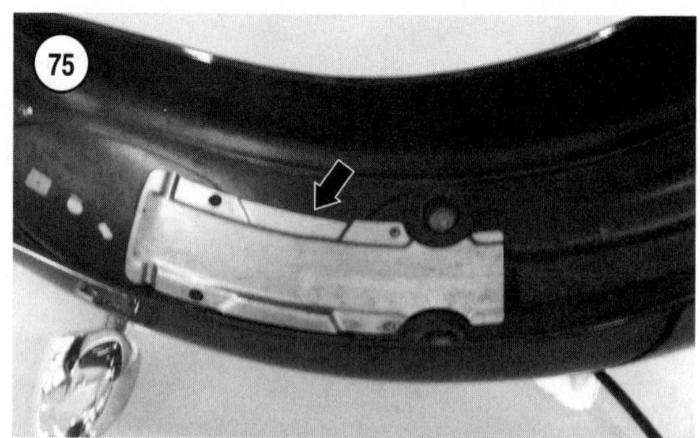

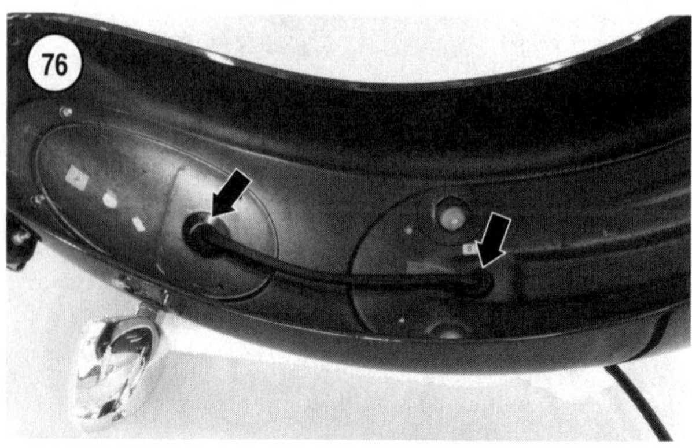

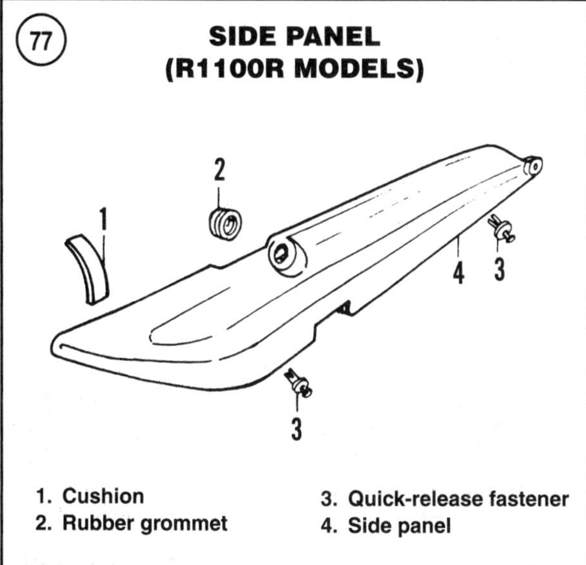
77
SIDE PANEL
(R1100R MODELS)
1
2
4
3
3
1. Cushion
2. Rubber grommet
3. Quick-release fastener
4. Side panel

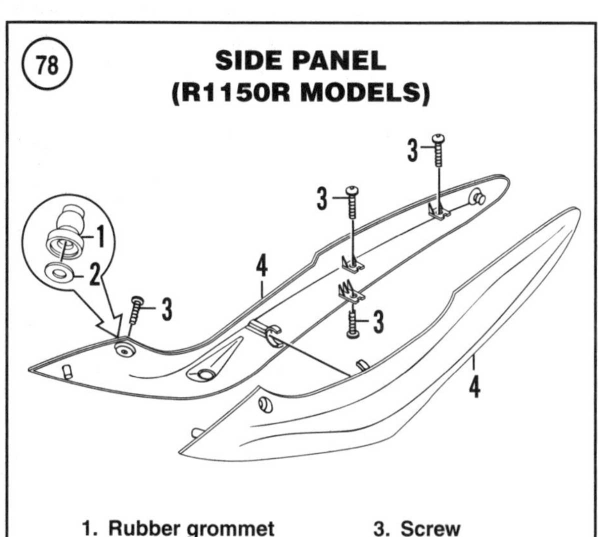
78
SIDE PANEL
(R1150R MODELS)
1
2
3
4
3
3
3
4
1. Rubber grommet
2. Washer
3. Screw
4. Side panel

79
A
B

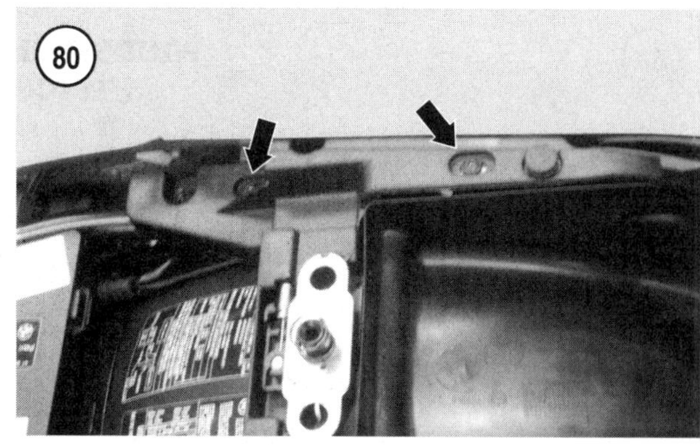
80

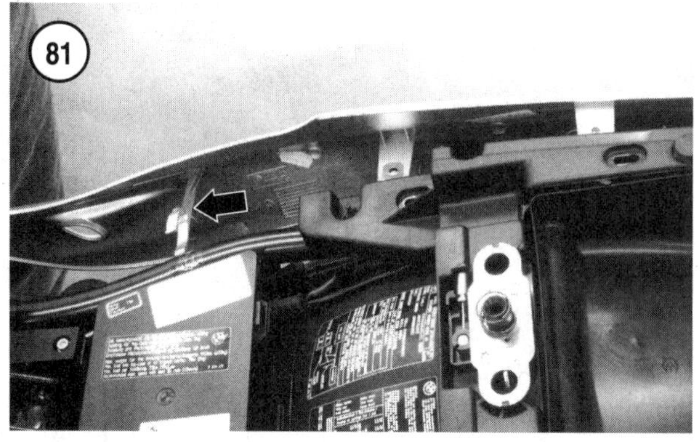
81

82

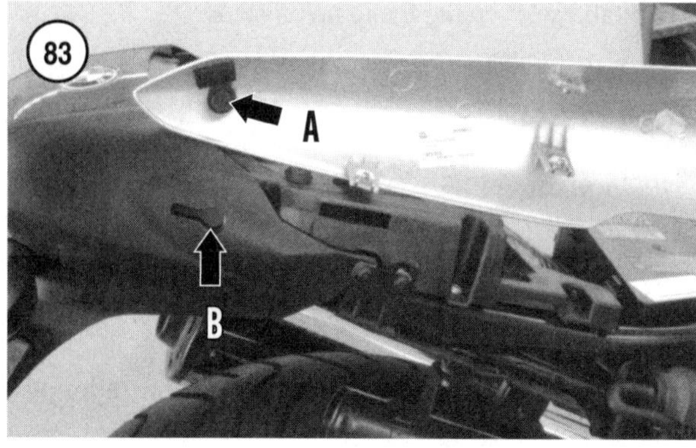
83
A
B

15

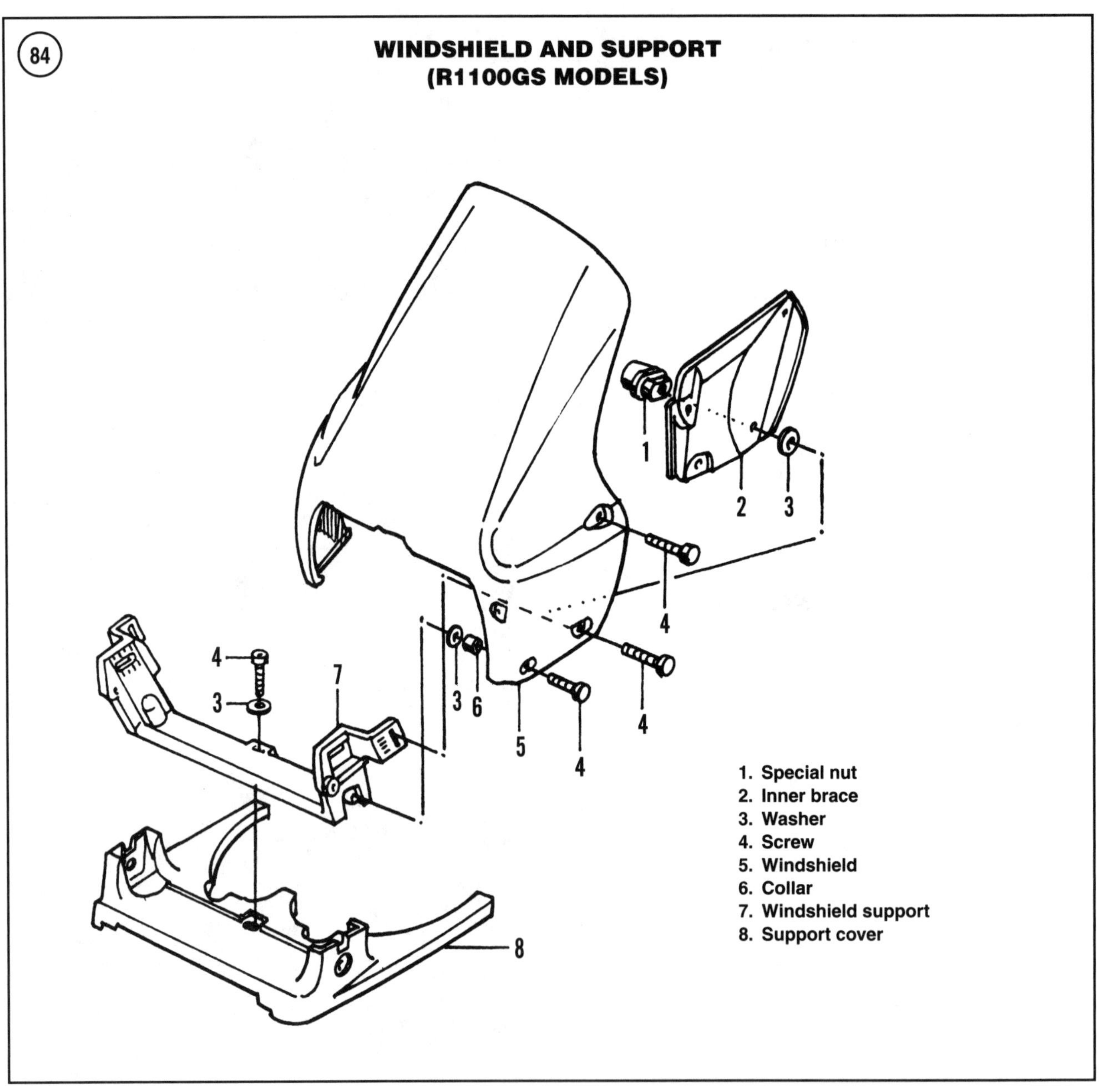

4. Install by reversing the removal steps.

R1150GS models

Refer to **Figure 86**.

1. Place the motorcycle on the centerstand with the front wheel off the ground.
2. Remove the screw (A, **Figure 87**) securing the windscreen on each side.
3. Carefully pull out on the windscreen at the pivot post (B, **Figure 87**) and remove the windshield (C).
4. Install by reversing these removal steps.

BODY PANELS (RS MODELS)

Windshield and Carrier Removal/Installation

R1100RS models

Refer to **Figure 88**.

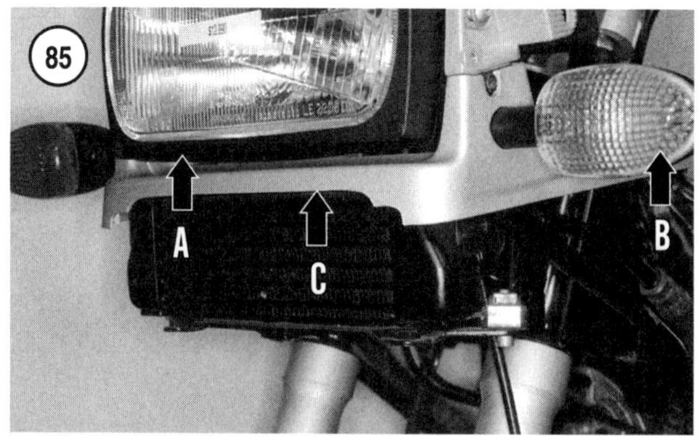

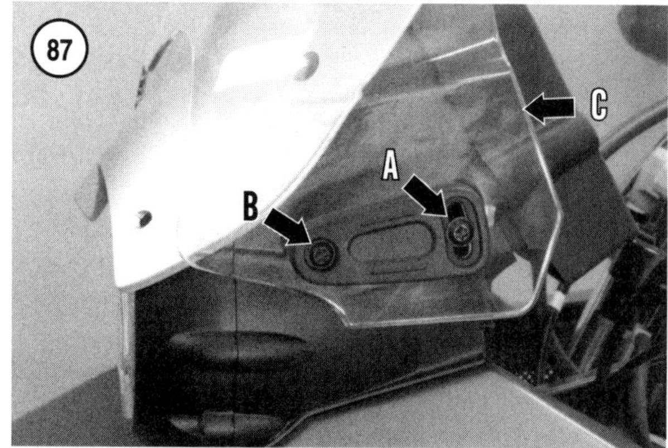

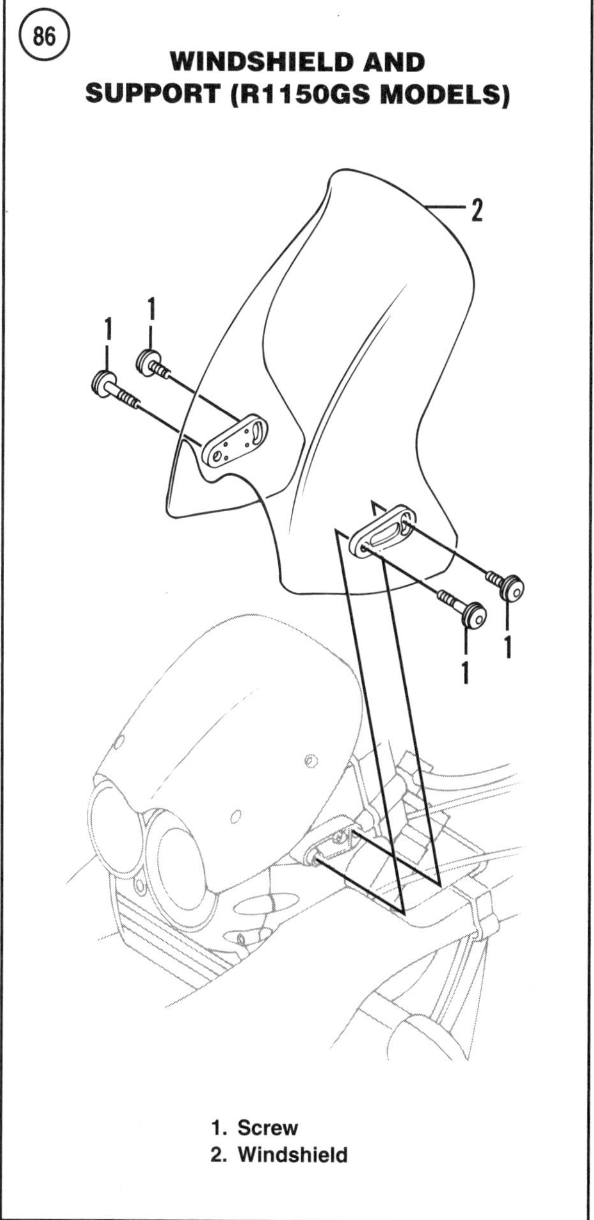

1. Screw
2. Windshield

1. Place the motorcycle on the centerstand with the front wheel off the ground.
2. Remove the screws and washers securing the windshield to the carrier and remove the windshield.
3. To remove the windshield carrier, perform the following:
   a. Remove the screws and washers and remove the windshield (A, **Figure 89**).
   b. Remove the front fairing inner panel and side fairing panel from each side as described in this chapter.
   c. On models so equipped, rotate the windshield adjust knob (B, **Figure 89**) *counterclockwise* and remove it.
   d. Remove the instrument panel (C, **Figure 89**) as described in Chapter Ten.
   e. Remove the headlight case as described in Chapter Ten.
   f. Remove the bolts securing the windshield carrier and support to the front fairing and remove them.
4. Install by reversing the removal steps. Tighten the screws securing the windshield.

R1150RS models

Refer to **Figure 90**.

1. Place the motorcycle on the centerstand with the front wheel off the ground.
2. Remove the screws and washers securing the windshield to the carrier and remove the windshield.
3. To remove the windshield carrier, perform the following:
   a. Remove the two top screws, washers and nuts securing the windshield.
   b. Remove the two lower screws and washers, then remove the windshield (A, **Figure 91**). Do not lose

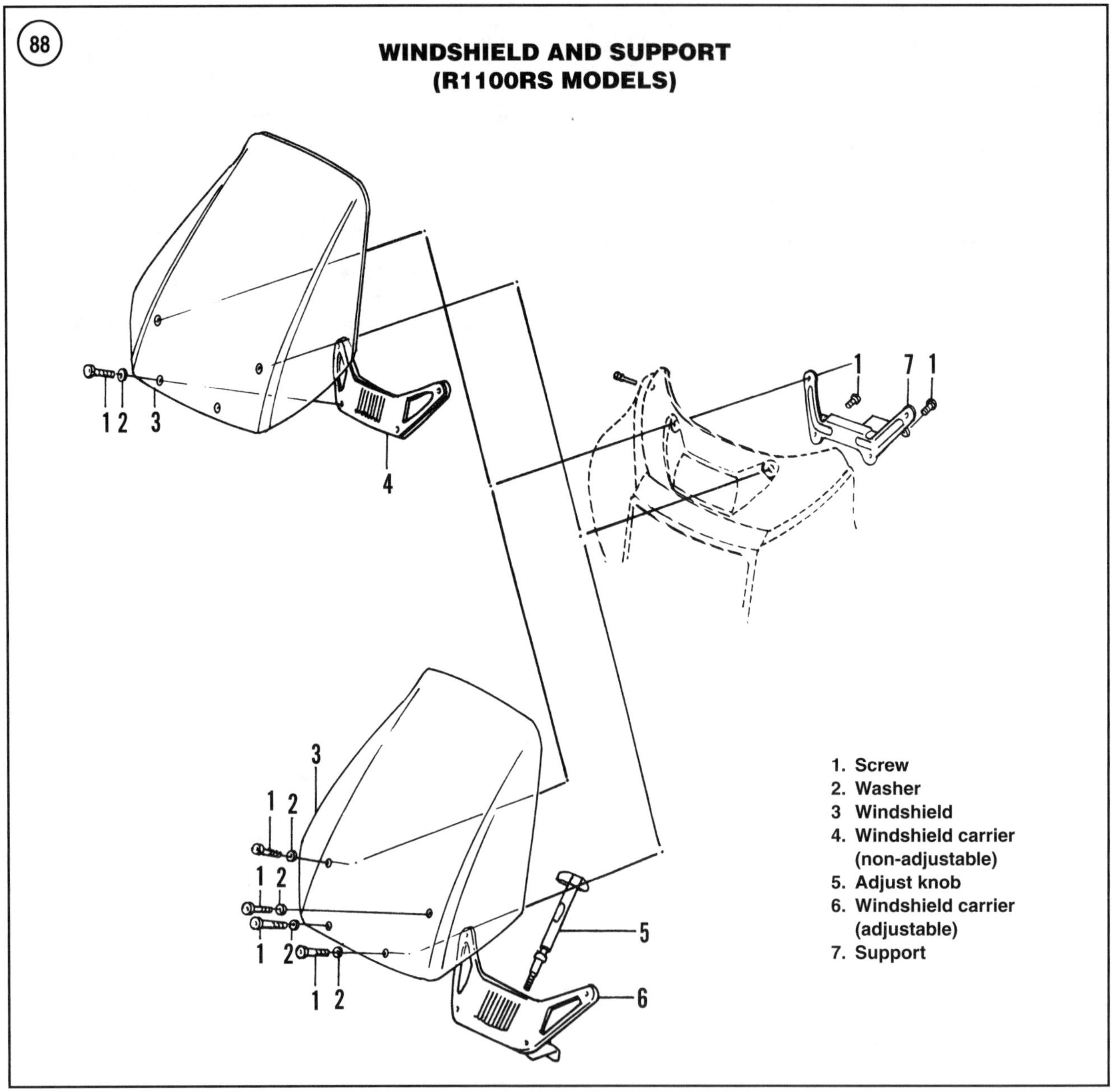

(88)

WINDSHIELD AND SUPPORT (R1100RS MODELS)

1. Screw
2. Washer
3. Windshield
4. Windshield carrier (non-adjustable)
5. Adjust knob
6. Windshield carrier (adjustable)
7. Support

the collar located between the two washers at each screw location.

c. Remove the front fairing inner panel and side fairing panel from each side as described in this chapter.
d. On models so equipped, rotate the windshield adjust knob (B, **Figure 91**) *counterclockwise* and remove it.
e. Remove the instrument panel (C, **Figure 91**) as described in Chapter Ten.
f. Remove the front section of the front fairing as described in this chapter.

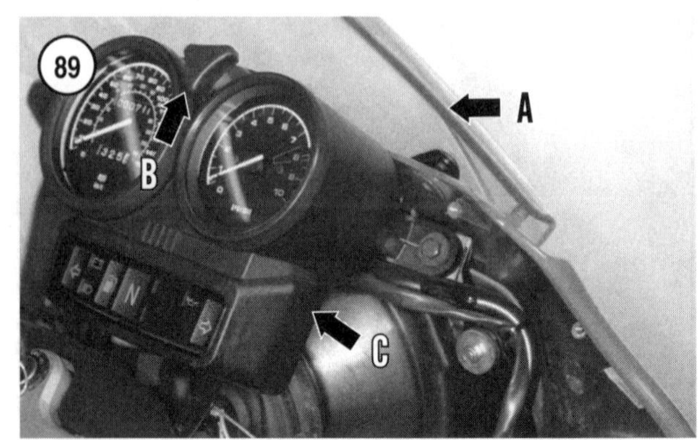

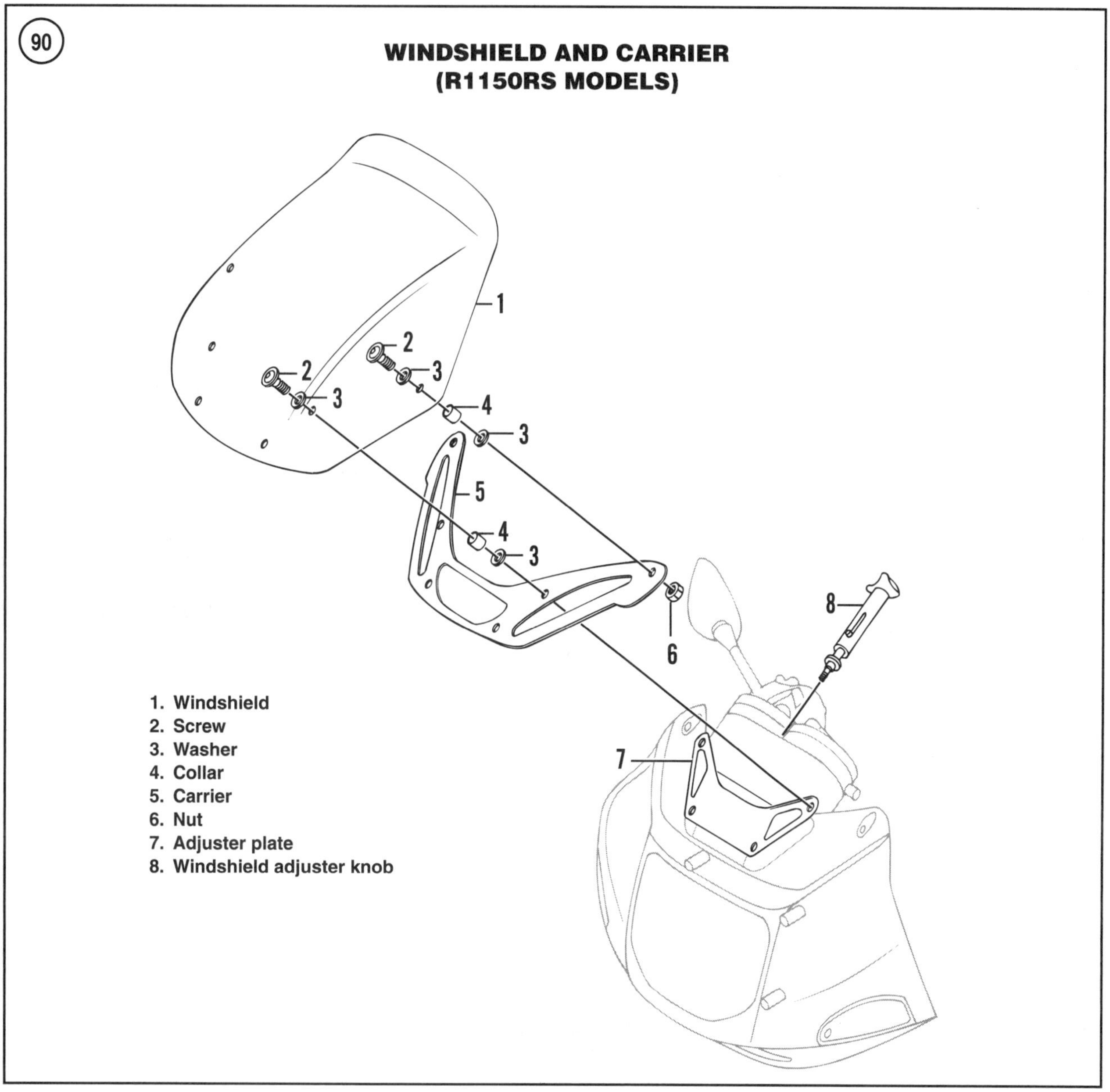

90
WINDSHIELD AND CARRIER
(R1150RS MODELS)
1
2
3
4
5
6
7
8
1. Windshield
2. Screw
3. Washer
4. Collar
5. Carrier
6. Nut
7. Adjuster plate
8. Windshield adjuster knob

91
A
B
C

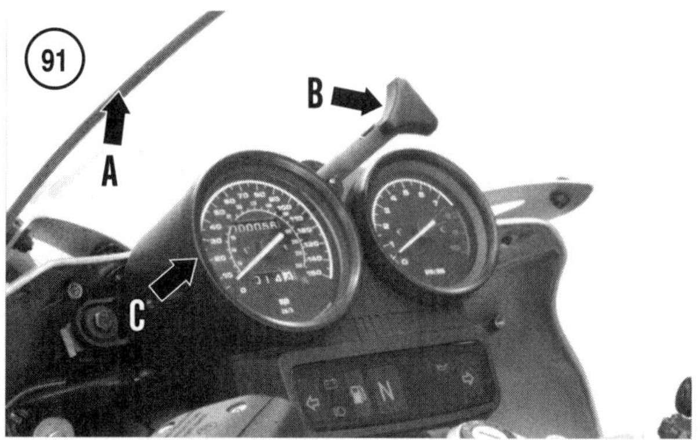

g. Remove the bolts securing the windshield carrier and support to the front fairing and remove them.

4. Install by reversing the removal steps. Tighten the screws securing the windshield.

Fairing Side Panels (RS models) Removal/Installation

Refer to the **Figure 92** and **Figure 93**.

1. Place the motorcycle on the centerstand with the front wheel off the ground.

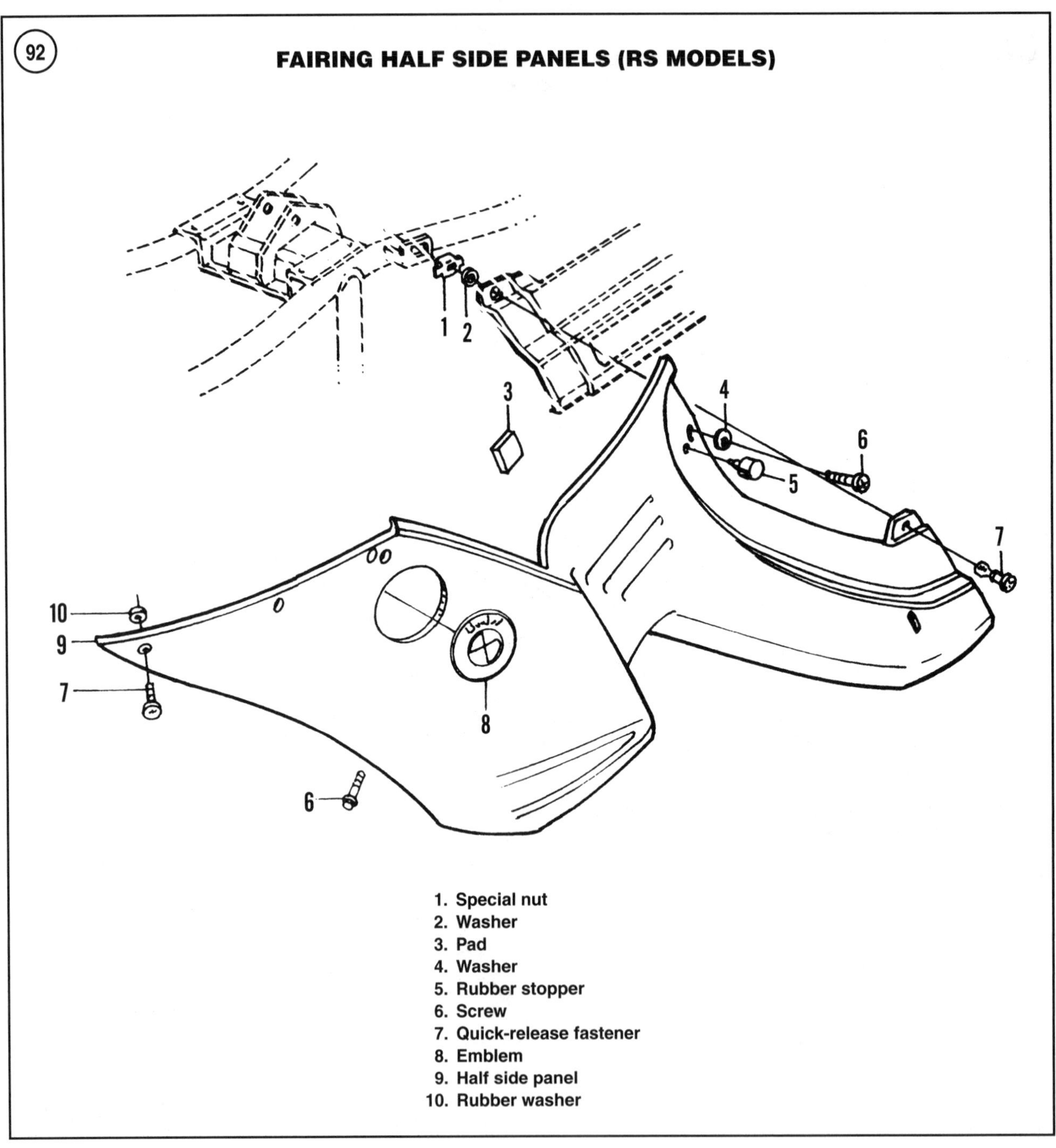

2. Remove both seats as described in this chapter.

3A. On models with a half fairing, perform the following:

a. Remove the front lower screw (**Figure 94**).

b. Remove the upper middle screw (A, **Figure 95**) and rear screw (B).

c. Use a screwdriver and release the single rear quick-release fastener (**Figure 96**).

d. Use a screwdriver and release the four quick-release fasteners (**Figure 97**).

e. Carefully remove the fairing side panel.

3B. On models with a full fairing, perform the following:

a. Perform Step 3A.

b. Remove the additional screws and washers securing the lower portion.

c. Carefully remove the fairing side panel.

93

FAIRING FULL SIDE PANELS (RS MODELS)

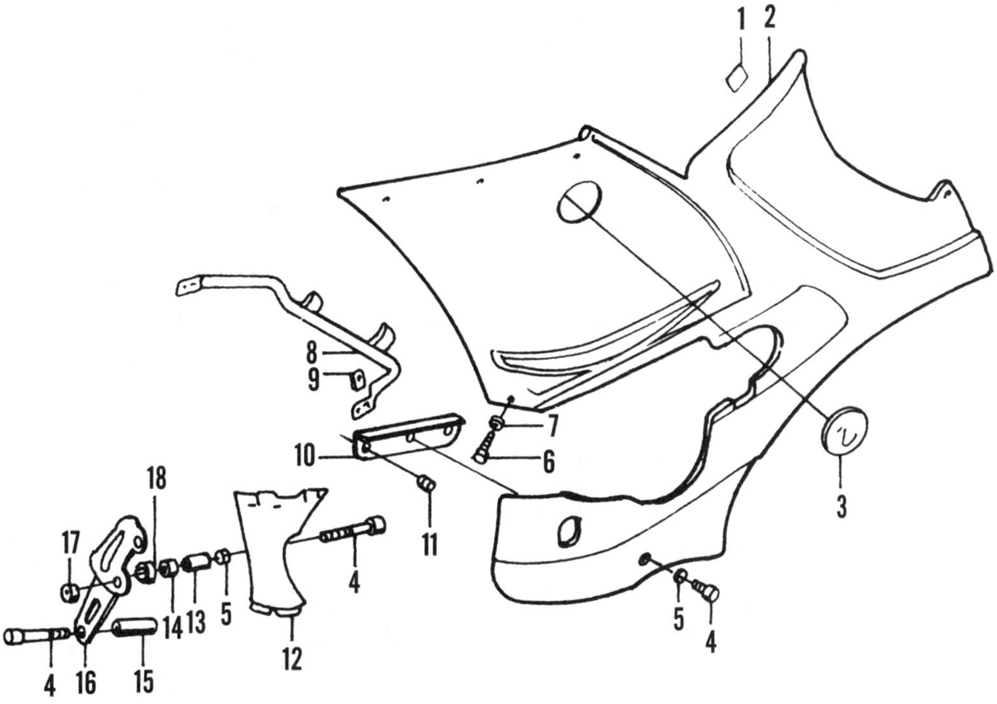

1. Pad
2. Full side panel
3. Emblem
4. Screw
5. Washer
6. Screw
7. Washer
8. Center bracket
9. Special nut
10. Bracket
11. Spacer
12. Front connector piece
13. Collar
14. Spacer
15. Collar
16. Bracket
17. Nut
18. Washer

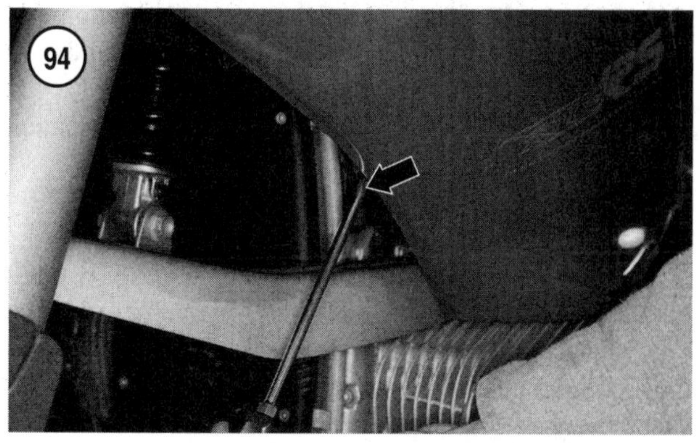

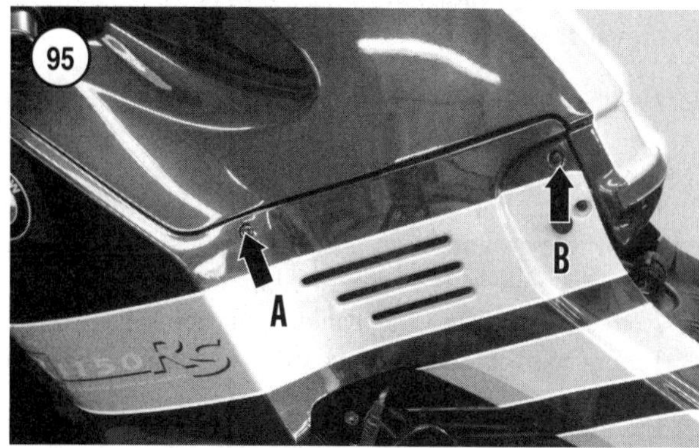

96

97

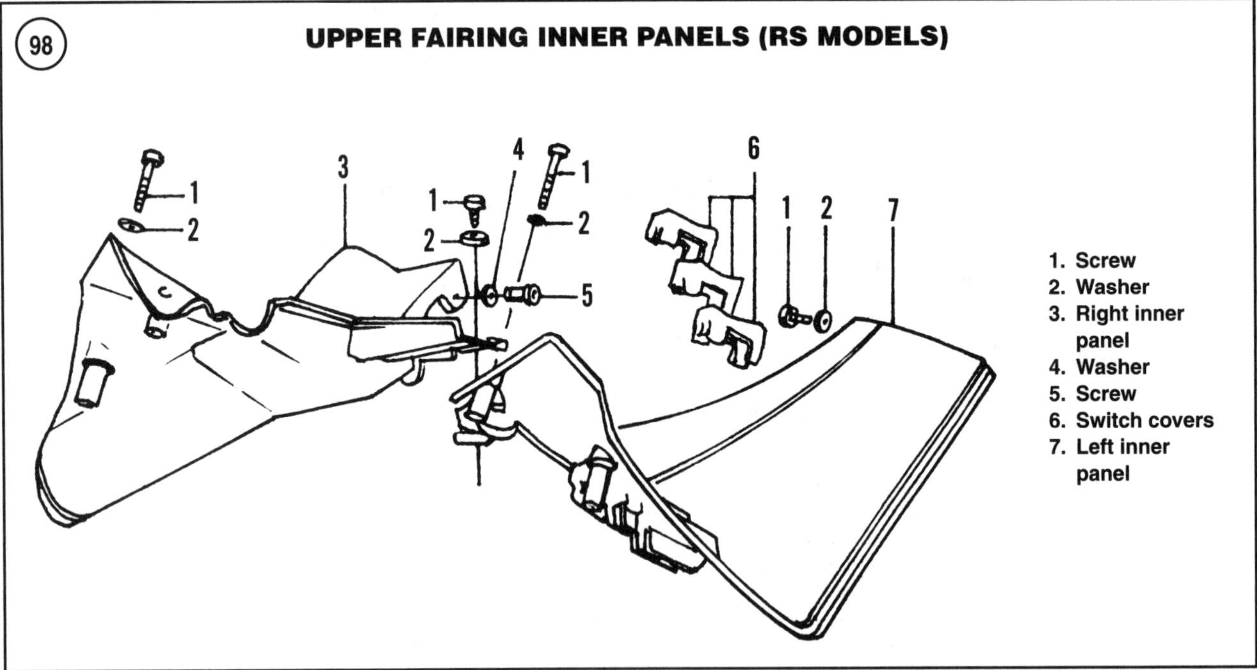

4. Install by reversing the removal steps. Tighten the screws, securing the fairing side panel securely.

Upper Fairing Inner Panels Removal/Installation

R1100RS models

Refer to the **Figure 98** and **Figure 99**.

1. Place the motorcycle on the centerstand with the front wheel off the ground.
2. Remove both seats as described in this chapter.
3. Remove the fairing side panel from each side.
4. Remove the hidden rear screw and washer (**Figure 100**).
5. Remove the front screw and washer (A, **Figure 101**).
6. On the left side, partially pull the inner panel up and out. Then disconnect the electrical connectors (**Figure 102**) for the switches (B, **Figure 101**). Remove the side panel.

7A. On the right side, without the rider information display, perform Step 5A or 5B for this side, then pull the inner panel up and out and remove the side panel.

7B. On the right side, equipped with the rider information display, perform the following:

a. Perform Step 5A or 5B of this side, then partially pull the inner panel up and out.
b. Disconnect the electrical connector (**Figure 103**) from the electrical panel for the rider information display. Remove the side panel.

8. If necessary, on models equipped with the rider information display, remove the two short screws (A, **Figure 104**),

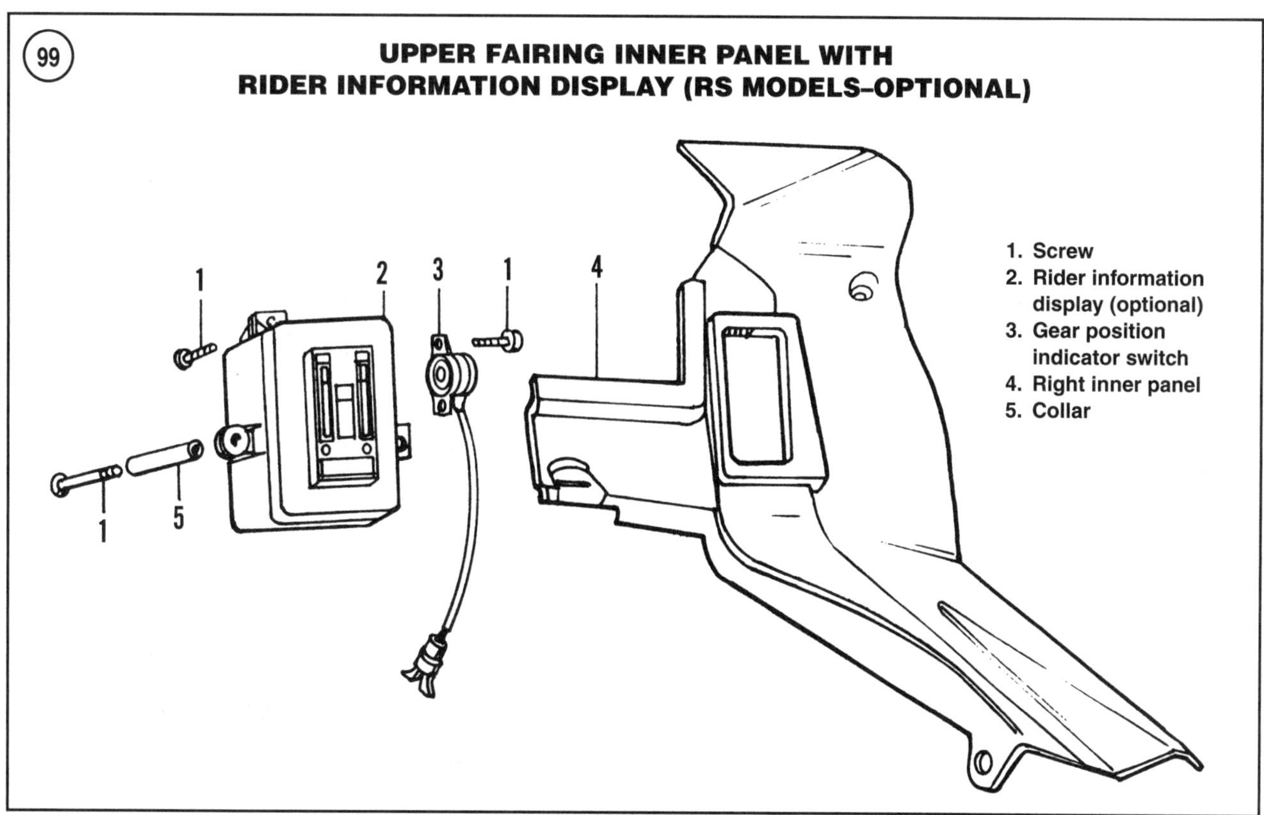
99
UPPER FAIRING INNER PANEL WITH
RIDER INFORMATION DISPLAY (RS MODELS-OPTIONAL)
1
2
3
1
4
1
5
1. Screw
2. Rider information display (optional)
3. Gear position indicator switch
4. Right inner panel
5. Collar

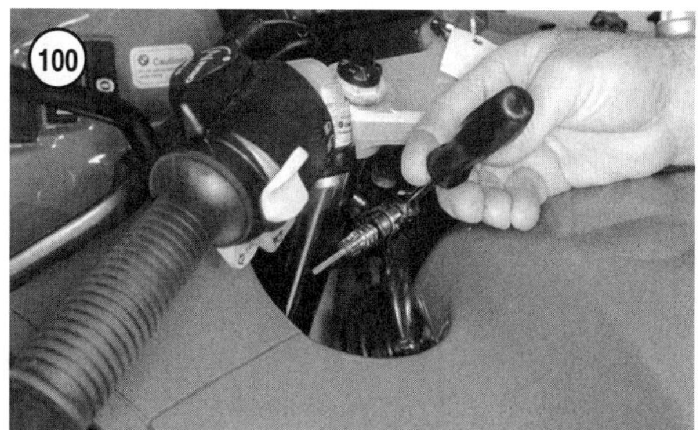
100

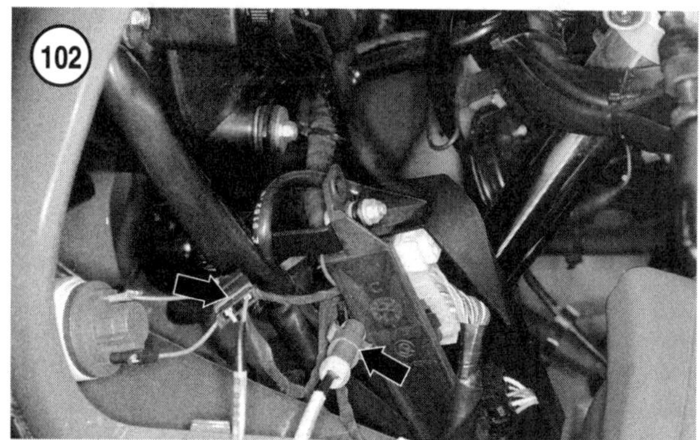
102

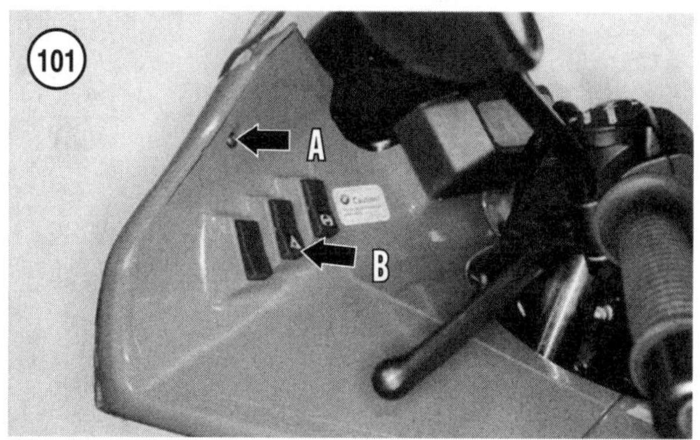
101
A
B

103

the long screw and the collar (B, **Figure 104**). Remove the display unit (C, **Figure 104**).

9. Install by reversing the removal steps. Tighten the screws securing the inner panels securely.

R1150RS models

Refer to the **Figure 98** and **Figure 99**.

1. Place the motorcycle on the centerstand with the front wheel off the ground.
2. Remove both seats as described in this chapter.
3. Remove the fairing side panel from each side.
4. Remove the hidden rear screw and washer (**Figure 105**).
5. On the left side, remove the front screws and washers (**Figure 106**). Remove the side panel.

6A. On the right side, without the rider information display, perform Step 5 for this side, then pull the inner panel up and out and remove the side panel.

6B. On the right side, equipped with the rider information display, perform the following:

a. Perform Step 5 this side, then partially pull the inner panel up and out.
b. Disconnect the electrical connector for the rider information display from the electrical panel. Remove the side panel.

7. If necessary, on models equipped with the rider information display, remove the three screws (A, **Figure 107**) and remove the display unit (B).
8. Install by reversing the removal steps. Tighten the screws securing the inner panels securely.

Upper Fairing Removal/Installation

Refer to **Figure 108**.

1. Place the motorcycle on the centerstand with the front wheel off the ground.
2. Remove the following items as described in this section.
   a. Both seats.
   b. Windshield and carrier.
   c. Both fairing side panels.
   d. Both inner panels.
3. Disconnect the front turn signal electrical connectors (**Figure 109**).
4. Remove the headlight and case mounting nuts (**Figure 110**) on each side. It is not necessary to remove the headlight case assembly, just release it from the upper fairing.
5. Have an assistant hold onto the upper fairing.
6. Remove the front screw and washer (**Figure 111**) and the rear screw and washer (**Figure 112**) securing the upper fairing to the mounting bracket and fuel tank.

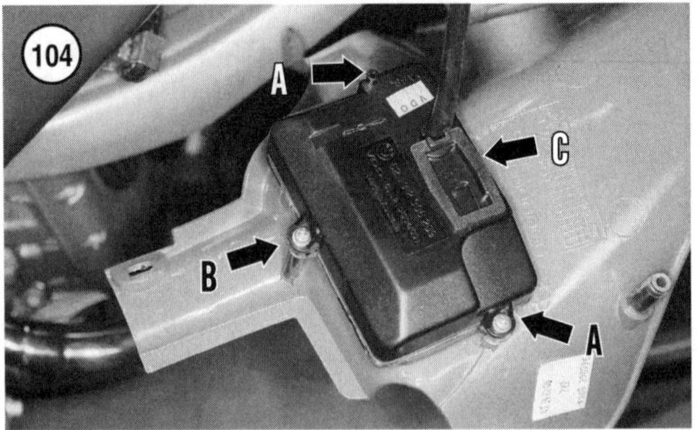

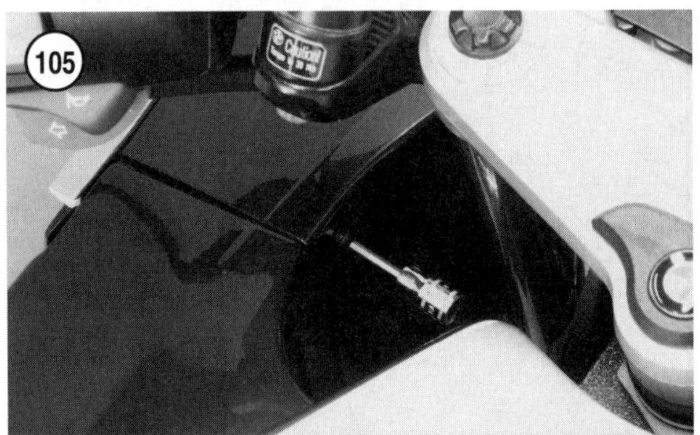

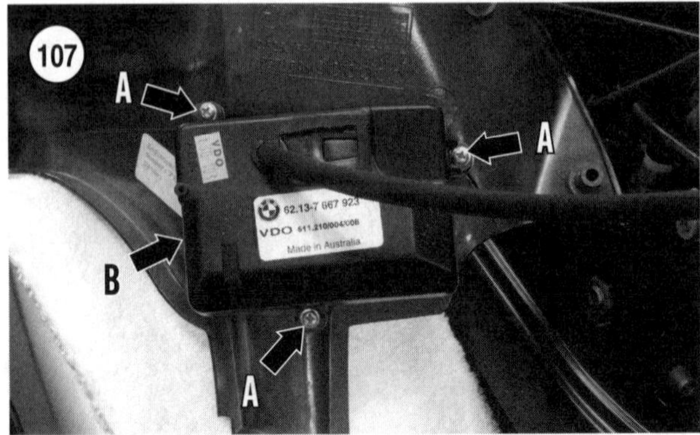

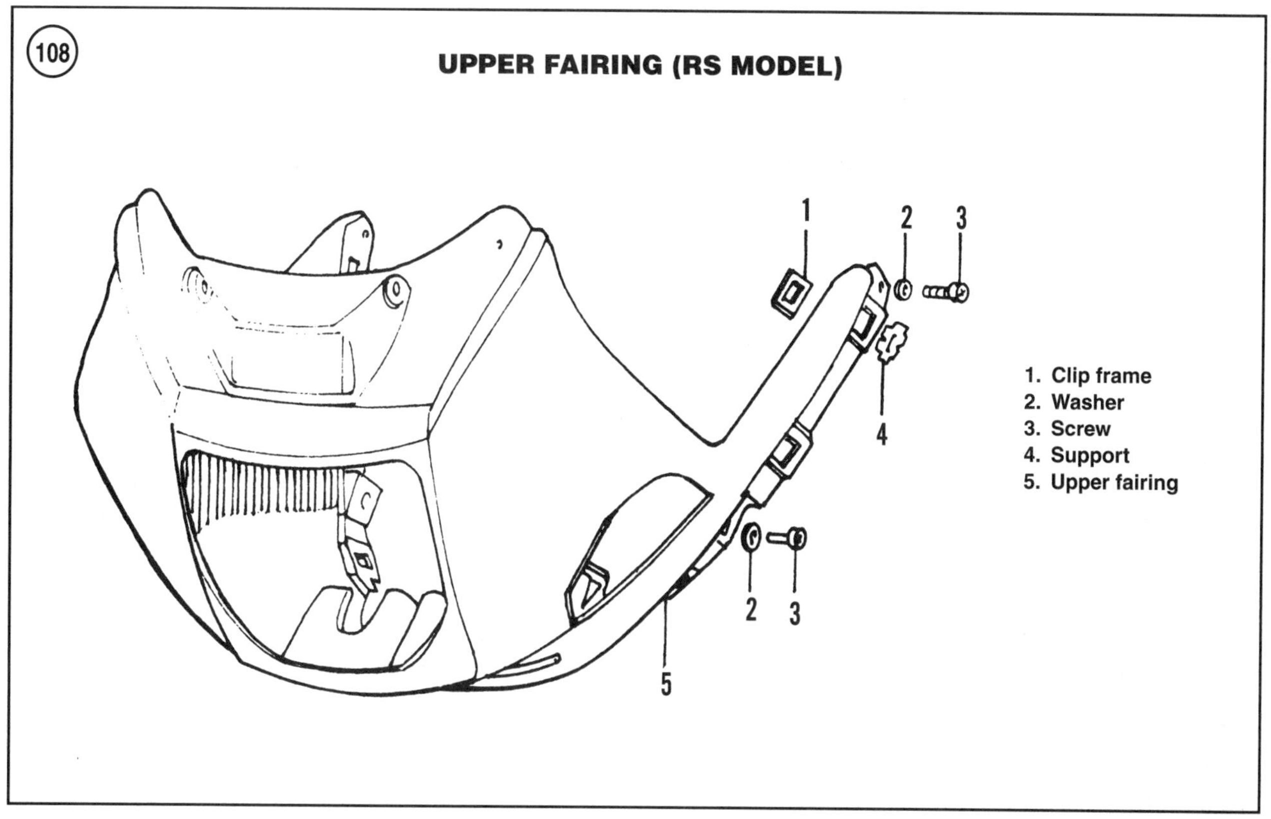
108
UPPER FAIRING (RS MODEL)
1
2
3
4
2
3
5
1. Clip frame
2. Washer
3. Screw
4. Support
5. Upper fairing

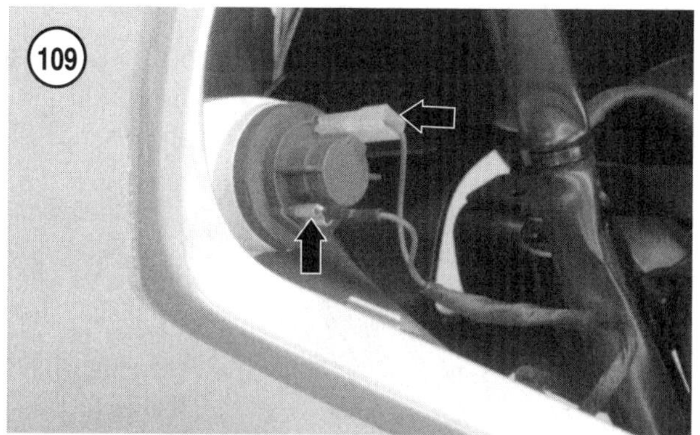
109

111

110

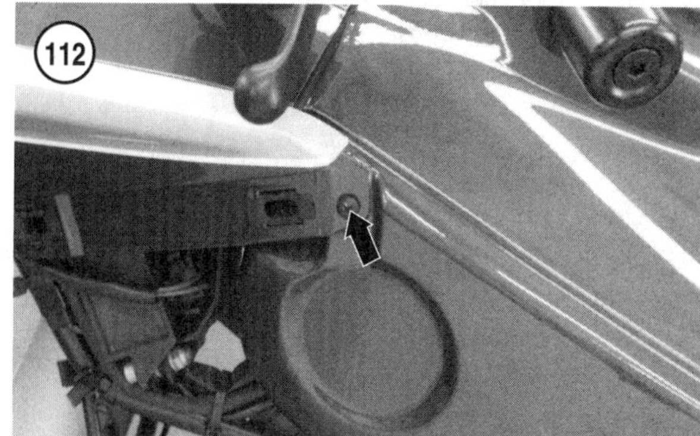
112

7. Carefully pull the upper fairing (**Figure 113**) forward and remove it from the mounting bracket.
8. Install by reversing the removal steps. Tighten the screws securing the upper fairing.

Upper Fairing Mounting Bracket Removal/Installation

Refer to **Figure 114**.
1. Remove all upper fairing components as previously described in this section.
2. Remove the bolts and washers securing the mounting bracket to the front frame assembly and remove the mounting bracket.
3. Install by reversing the removal steps. Tighten the mounting bolts securely.

BODY PANELS (RT MODELS)

Side Cover Removal/Installation

Refer to **Figure 115**.
1. Place the motorcycle on the centerstand with the front wheel off the ground.
2. Remove both seats as described in this chapter.
3. Rotate the quick release fastener (A, **Figure 116**) and release it from the clip on the frame.

NOTE
*On the left side, pull out on the handle (**Figure 117**) and guide the side cover off and onto the handle (B, **Figure 116**) during removal and installation.*

4. Carefully pull the side cover (C, **Figure 116**) up and unhook it from the clips (**Figure 118**) in the foot rest assembly.

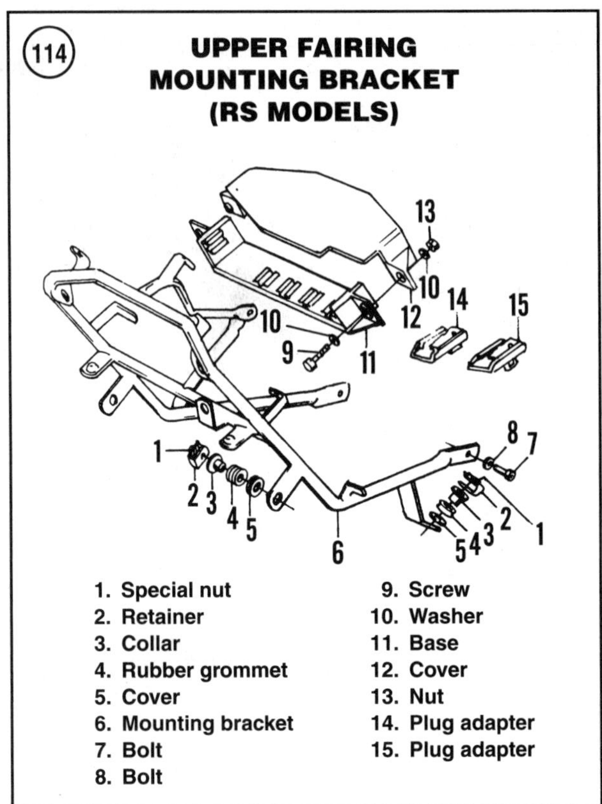

1. Special nut
2. Retainer
3. Collar
4. Rubber grommet
5. Cover
6. Mounting bracket
7. Bolt
8. Bolt
9. Screw
10. Washer
11. Base
12. Cover
13. Nut
14. Plug adapter
15. Plug adapter

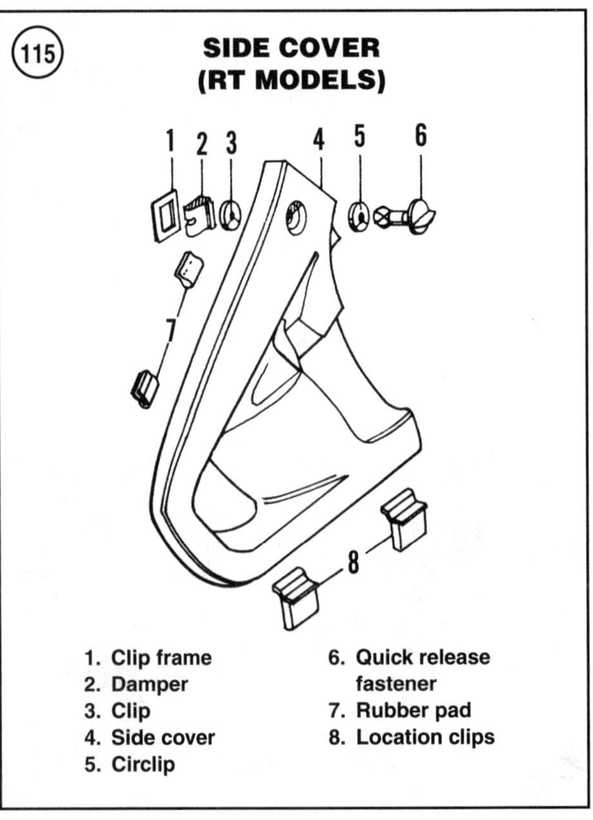

1. Clip frame
2. Damper
3. Clip
4. Side cover
5. Circlip
6. Quick release fastener
7. Rubber pad
8. Location clips

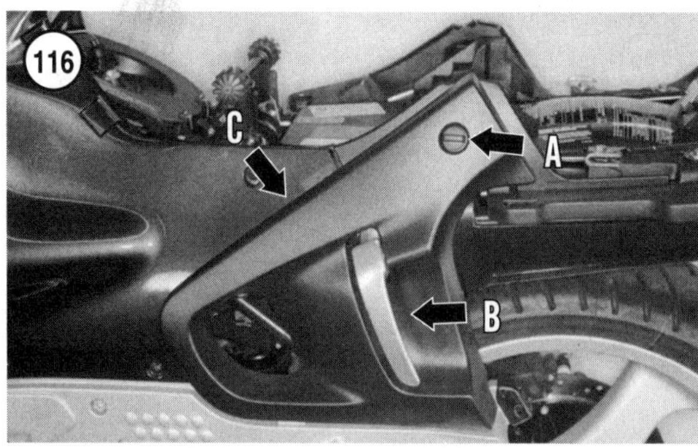

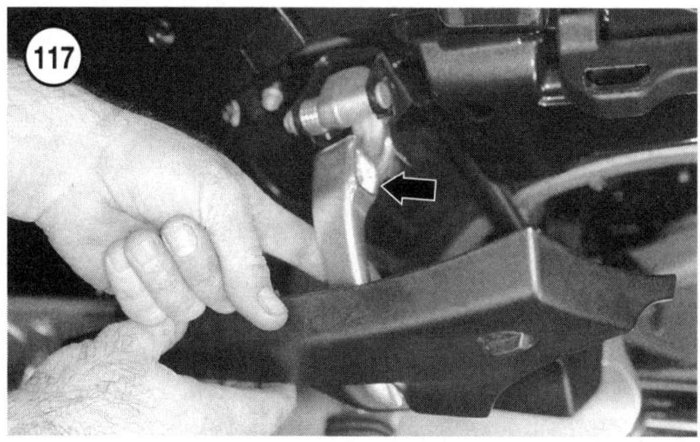

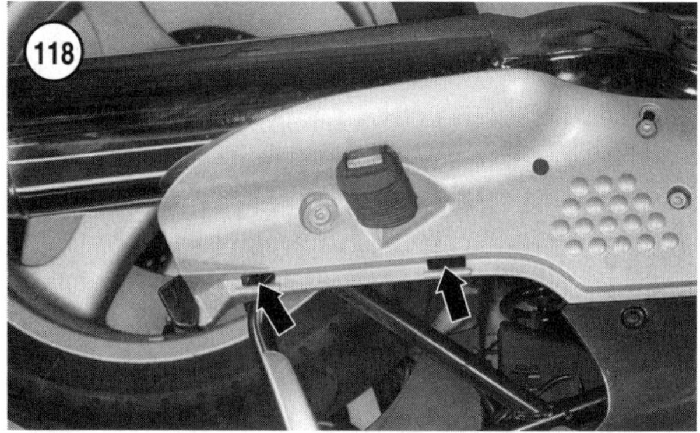

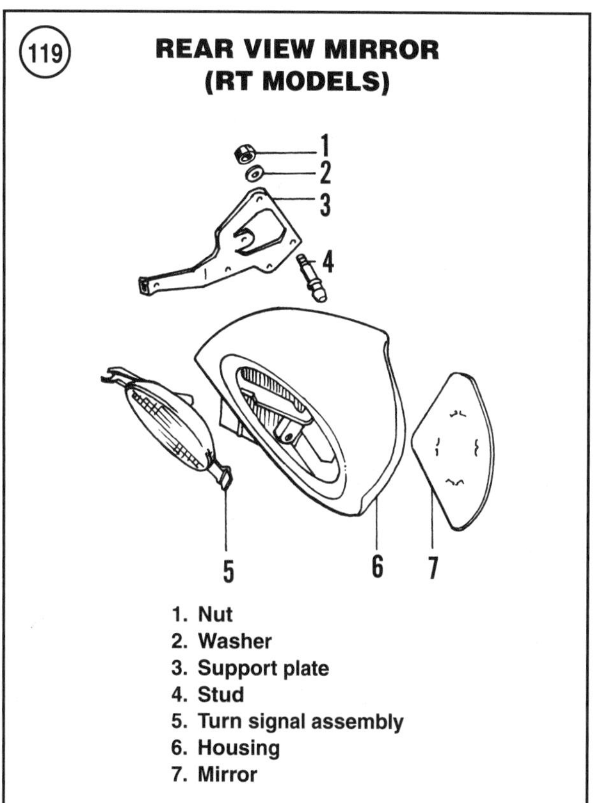

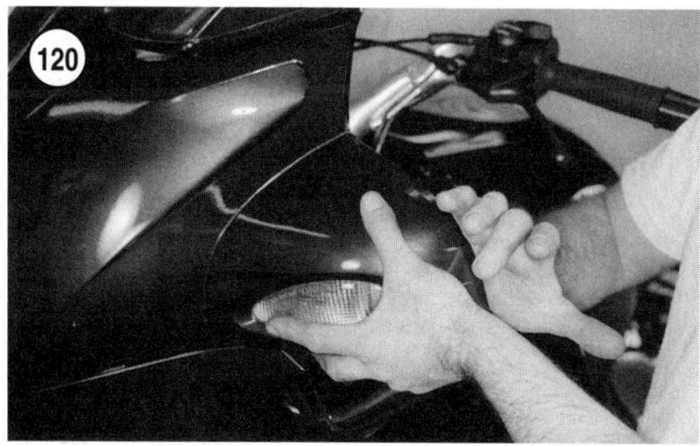

5. Install by reversing the removal steps. Be sure to insert the hooks into the foot rest clips.

Rear View Mirror Removal/Installation

Refer to **Figure 119**.

NOTE
The mirrors are not attached mechanically to the upper fairing. They are designed to break away if hit hard.

1. Place one hand over the mirror assembly to catch it during the following step.

CAUTION
*In the next step, do **not** use any type of tool like a rubber mallet or plastic hammer as it will not only damage the painted finish but could fracture the plastic housing—**use only a hand**.*

2. Apply small forward hits, or knocks, to the outer edge of the mirror housing with the palm of a hand (**Figure 120**)

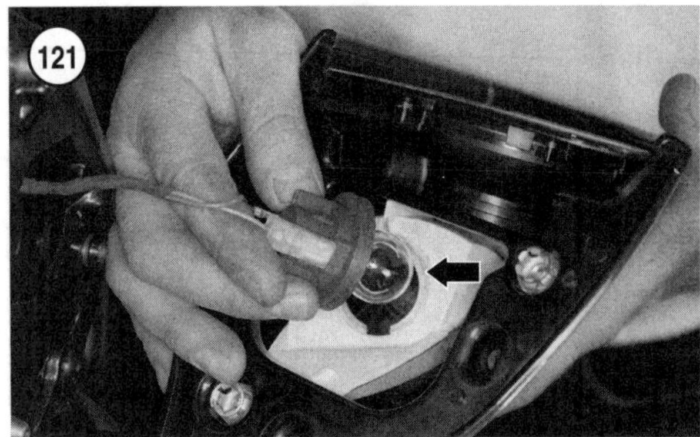

and break the mirror housing away from the support plate on the upper fairing. Continue to hit the mirror until all studs are free from the housing mounting clips.

3. Carefully pull the mirror assembly away from the front fairing. Rotate the turn signal socket/bulb assembly (**Figure 121**) and remove it from the mirror assembly.
4. Remove the rear view mirror assembly.
5. To remove the mirror portion from the assembly, perform the following:

WARNING
Apply masking, or duct, tape to the mirror surface. This will lessen the chance of glass popping out during the removal and installation steps. Also wear eye protection and heavy gloves. Protect yourself accordingly while working with glass.

a. Place several shop cloths on the workbench to protect the pained finish.
b. Turn the mirror upside down on the cloths.
c. Using a flat pry bar, *carefully* pry out the bottom surface of the mirror until the locating posts (A, **Figure 122**) are free from the ball and socket. Remove the mirror (B, **Figure 122**) from the housing.
d. Do not apply any type of lubricant to the ball or socket joint as this may make the joint too loose to maintain the mirror in a fixed position.
e. Position the new mirror into the housing. Align the posts to the ball and socket.
f. *Carefully* press on the center of the new mirror and push it into place in the housing. You will hear a pop when the ball and socket snap into place.

6. Inspect the sockets (**Figure 123**) into which the studs fit. If the sockets are damaged in any way, they will not hold the mirror assembly steady. Replace the mirror assembly if necessary.
7. If necessary, repeat for the rear view mirror on the other side.

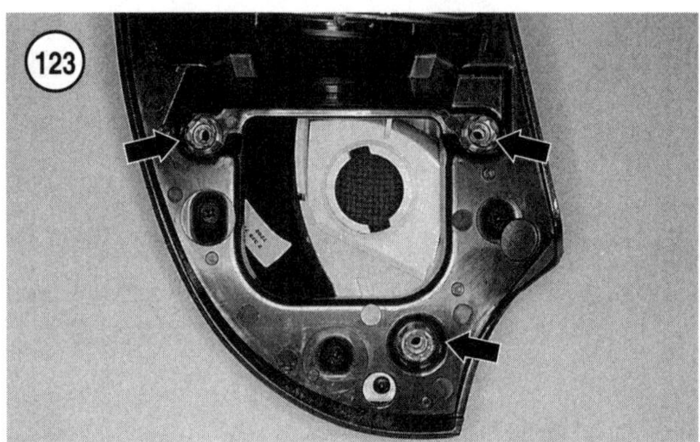

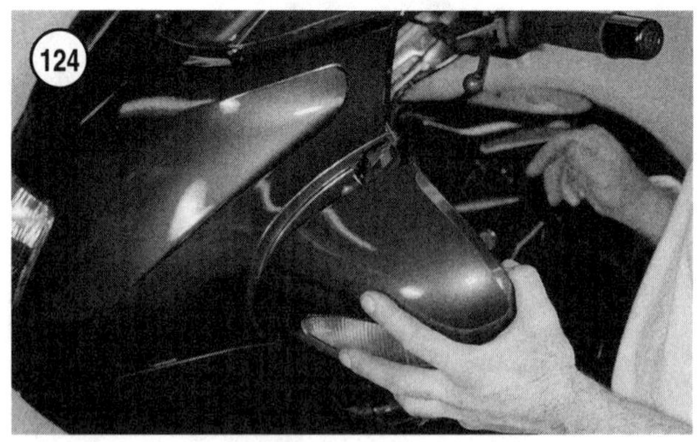

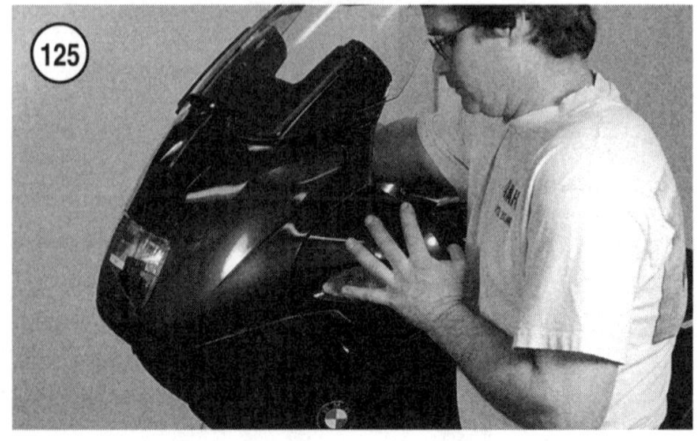

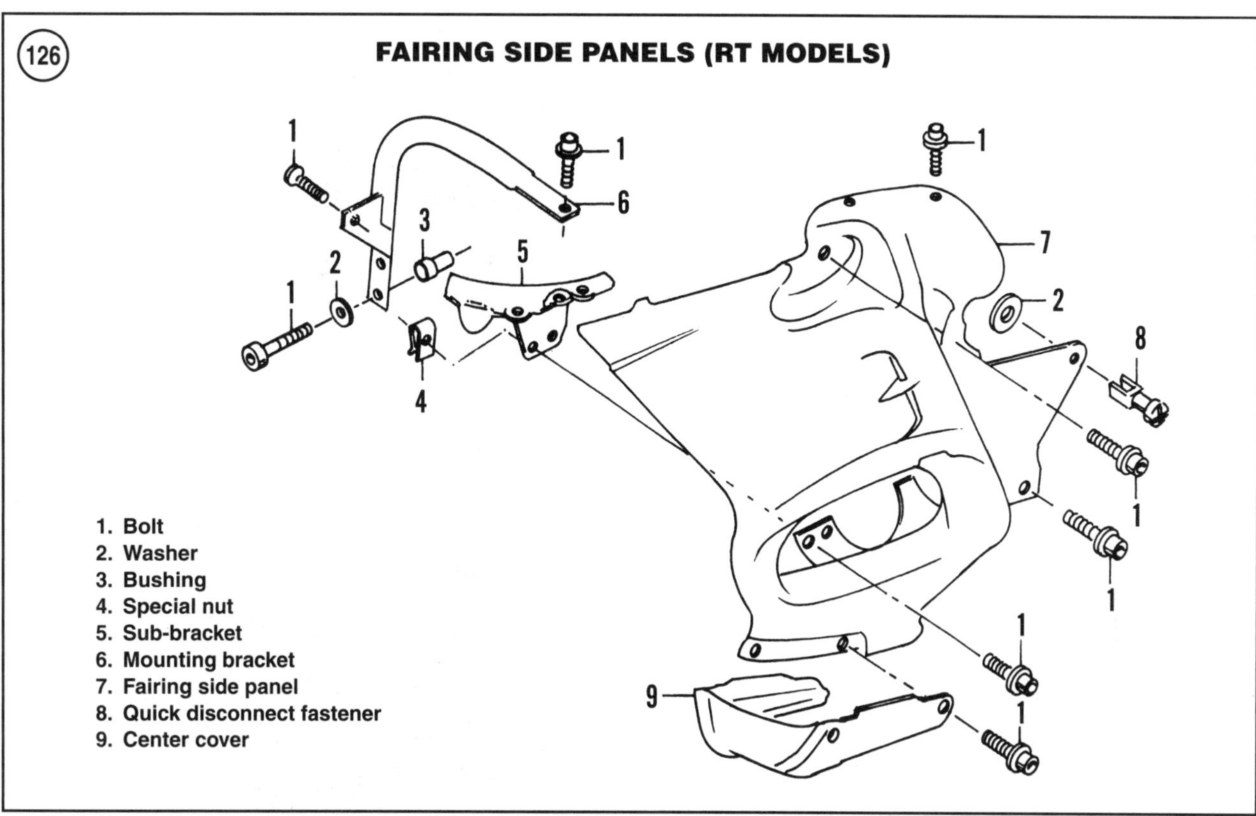

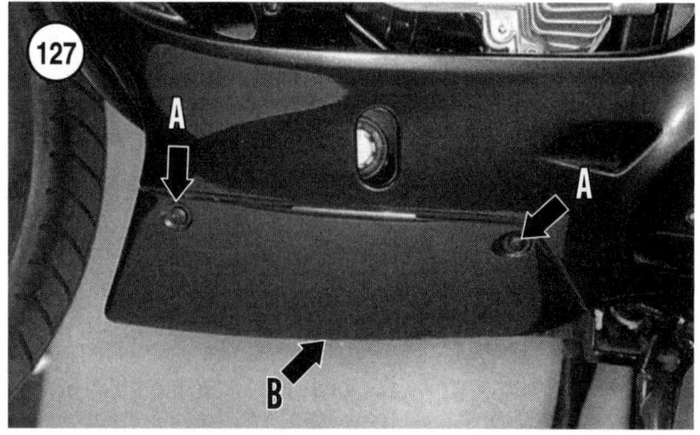

8. To install the mirror, perform the following.
   a. Install the turn signal socket/bulb assembly (**Figure 121**) and rotate it to lock it into the mirror assembly.
   b. Position the mirror assembly onto the mounting bracket assembly on the front fairing. Align the mounting studs with the mirror sockets (**Figure 124**).
   c. Support the backside of the upper fairing with one hand, and again, using the palm of your hand, tap the mirror housing into position (**Figure 125**). Make sure all studs completely lock into the sockets in the mirror. When installed correctly, there should be no gap around the perimeter of the mirror housing.

Fairing Side Panels Removal/Installation

Refer to **Figure 126**.

1. Place the motorcycle on the centerstand with the front wheel off the ground.
2. Remove both seats as described in this chapter.
3. Remove the side cover as described in this chapter.
4. Remove the rear view mirror as described in this chapter.
5. Remove the screws (A, **Figure 127**) securing the center cover (B). Lower the front of the cover to release the top and rear locating tabs.

CAUTION
Have an assistant hold the side panel as the last remaining upper screws are removed. If the side cover is not supported, the locating tabs may fracture if the side panel starts to slip out of place.

6. Remove the following mounting screws and fasteners:

a. Front screw (**Figure 128**) below the headlight assembly.
b. Upper screws (**Figure 129**) and lower screws (**Figure 130**) in the cylinder head recess area.
c. Lower screws (**Figure 131**) above the foot rest assembly.
d. Upper screw (**Figure 132**) next to fuel tank cover.
e. Upper rear quick release fastener (**Figure 133**), rotating and releasing it from the clip on the frame.

7. Slowly lower the side panel and release the locating tab (A, **Figure 134**) from the slot (B) in the upper fairing. Remove the side panel.
8. If necessary, remove the bolts and nuts (A, **Figure 135**) securing the mounting bracket to the sub-brace. Remove the mounting bracket (B, **Figure 135**).
9. Install by reversing the removal steps. Tighten the screws securing the fairing side panels securely.

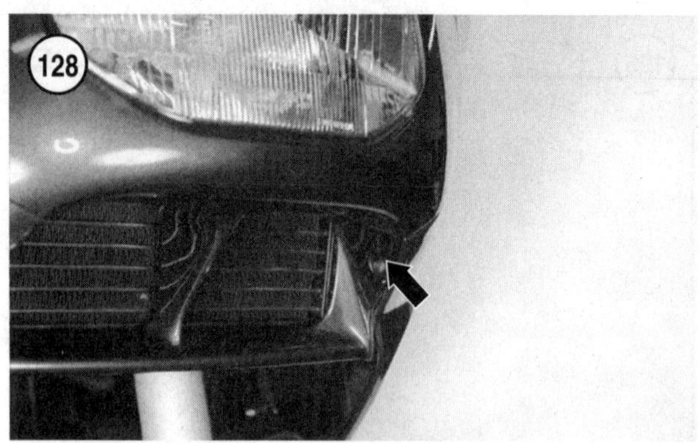
128

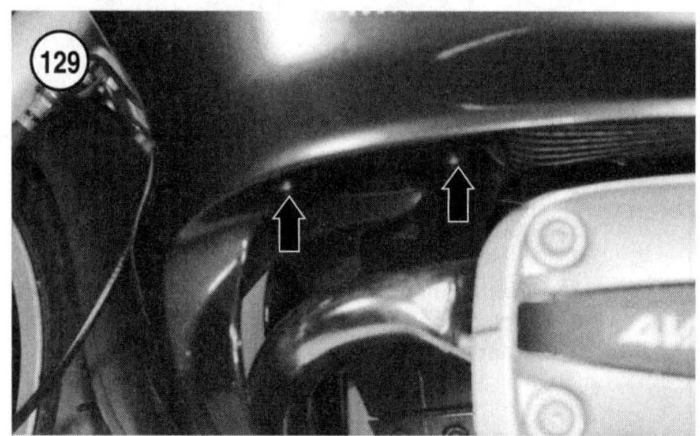
129

Windshield and Lift Mechanism Removal/Installation

Refer to **Figure 136** and **Figure 137**.

1. Place the motorcycle on the centerstand with the front wheel off the ground.
2. To remove only the windshield, perform the following:
   a. Remove the screws (A, **Figure 138**) securing the windshield to the upper fairing and lift mechanism.
   b. Remove the windshield and spacer (B, **Figure 138**). Do not lose the gasket under the spacer.
3. To remove the windshield lift mechanism, perform the following:
   a. Remove the upper fairing as described in this chapter.
   b. Remove the bolts, washers and nuts securing the windshield lift mechanism to the upper fairing, and then remove the lift mechanism assembly.
4. Install by reversing the removal steps. Tighten the screws, securing the windshield securely.

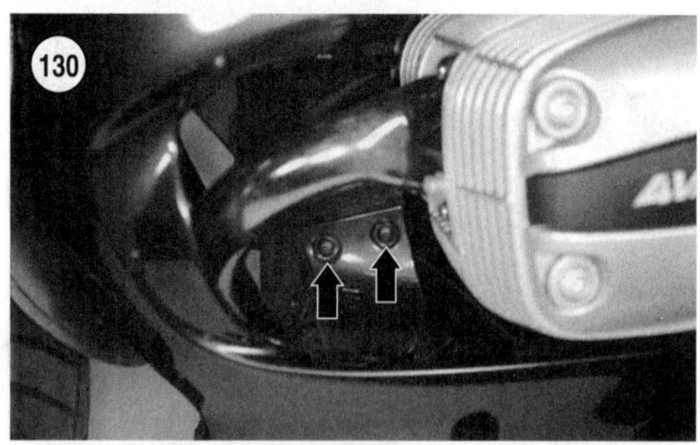
130

Upper Fairing Inner Panel Removal/Installation

Refer to **Figure 139**.

1. Place the motorcycle on the centerstand with the front wheel off the ground.
2. Remove both fairing side panels as described in this chapter.
3. Remove the windshield as described in this chapter.
4. Remove the screws around the perimeter of the inner panel (**Figure 140**) securing the inner panel to the upper

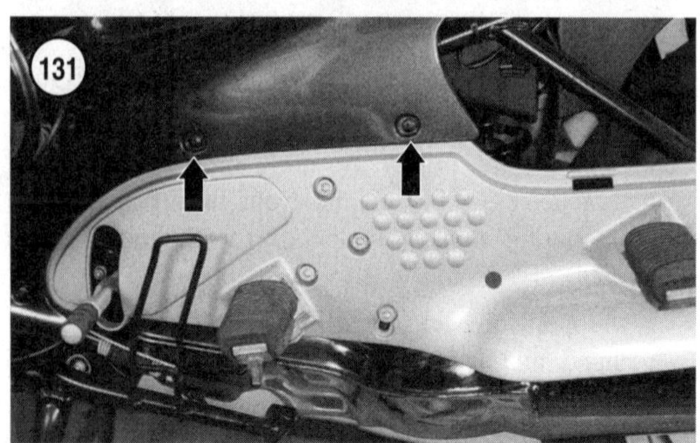
131

132

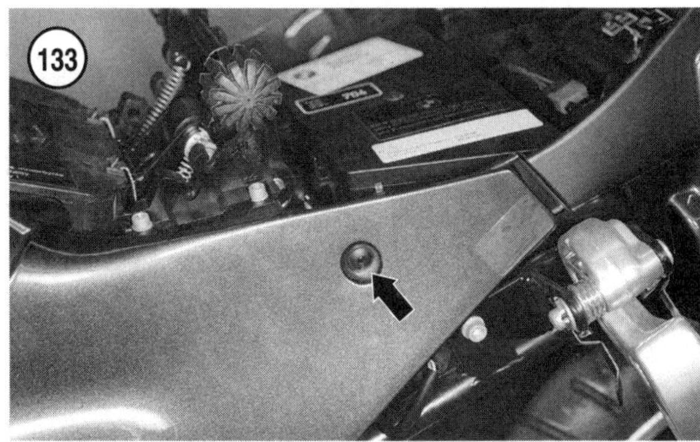
133

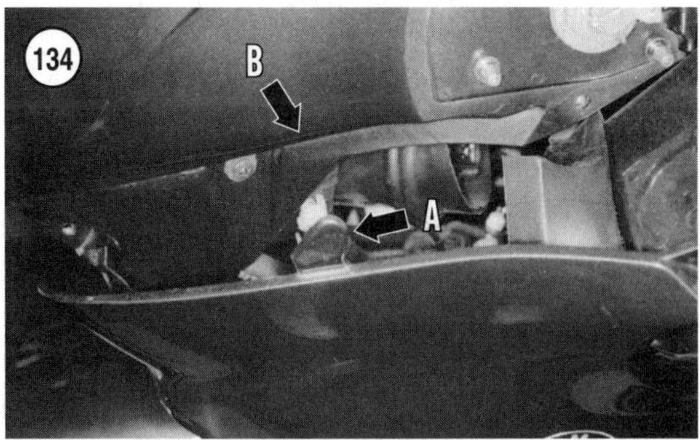

134

135

136

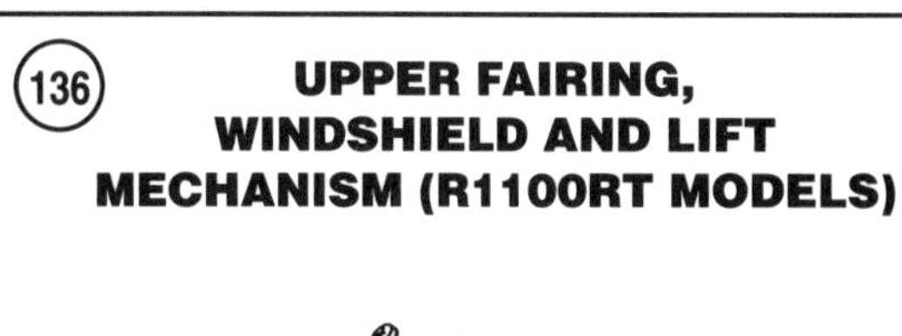
UPPER FAIRING, WINDSHIELD AND LIFT MECHANISM (R1100RT MODELS)

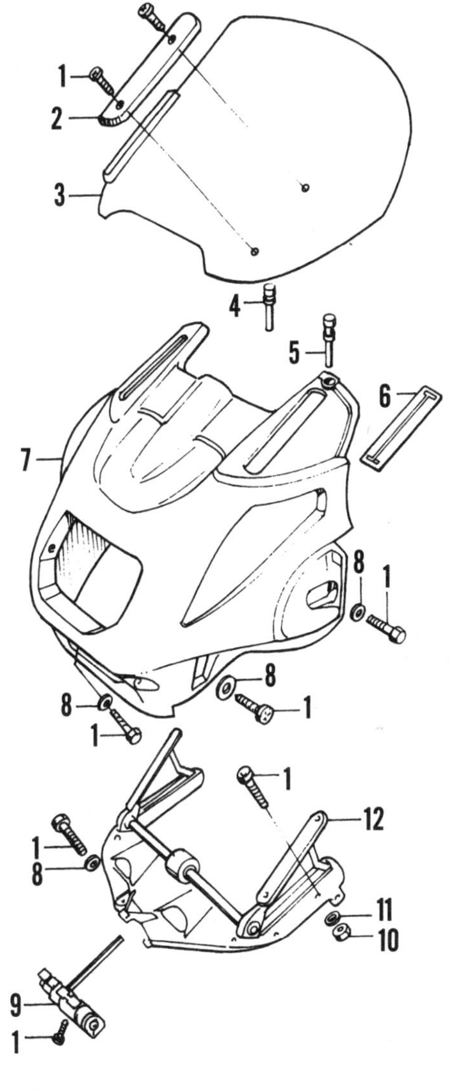

1. Screw
2. Spacer
3. Windshield
4. Rubber stopper
5. Rubber stopper
6. Gasket
7. Upper fairing
8. Washer
9. Motor
10. Nut
11. Washer
12. Lift mechanism

15

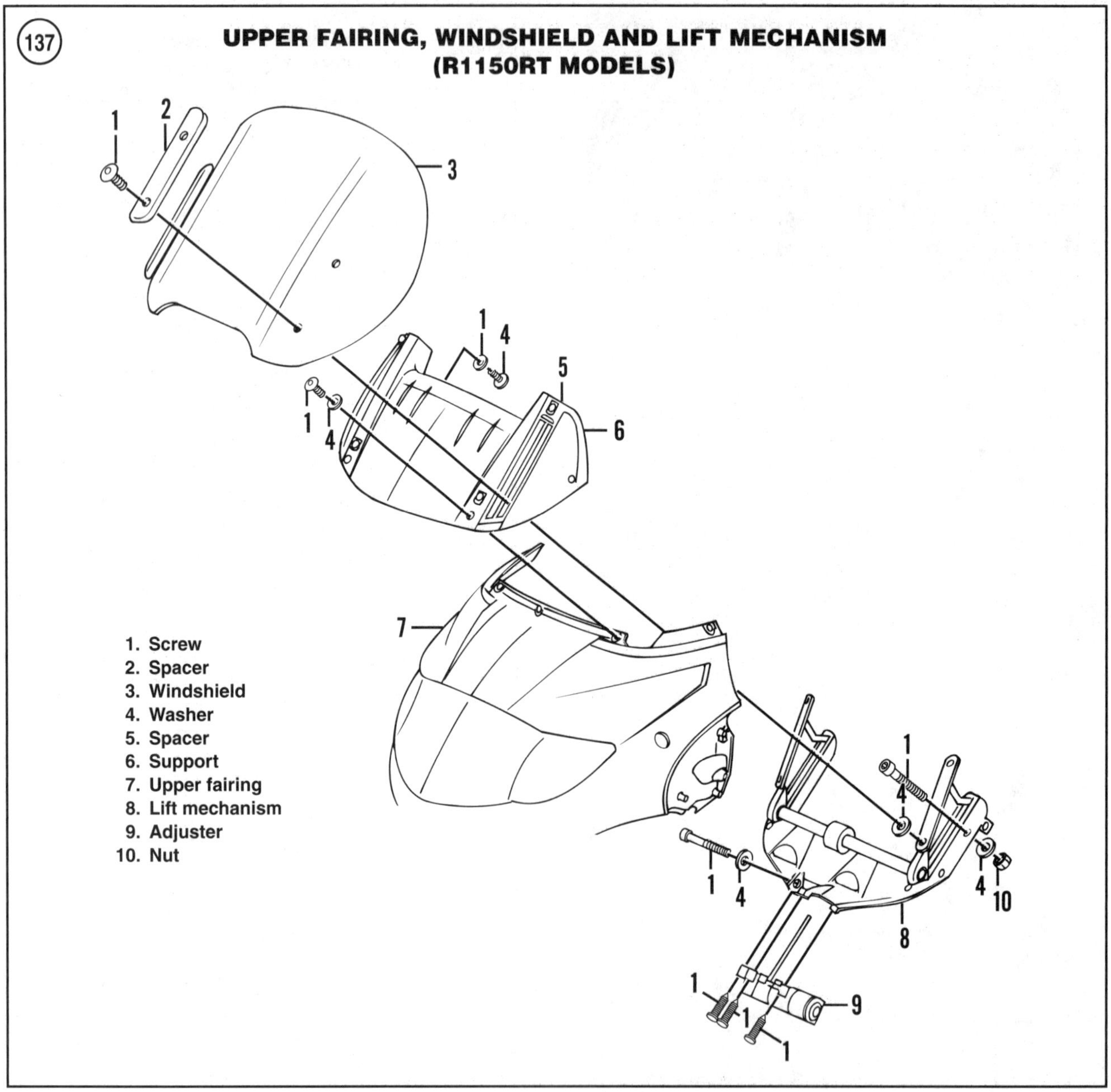

(137)

UPPER FAIRING, WINDSHIELD AND LIFT MECHANISM (R1150RT MODELS)

1. Screw
2. Spacer
3. Windshield
4. Washer
5. Spacer
6. Support
7. Upper fairing
8. Lift mechanism
9. Adjuster
10. Nut

fairing. Do not forget the two center screws (**Figure 141**) above the instrument cluster.

5. Partially pull the inner panel up and out, then disconnect the electrical connectors for the switches and the rider information display.

6. Pull the inner panel up and out and remove the side panel.

7. If necessary on models equipped with the rider information display, remove the mounting screws and remove the display unit.

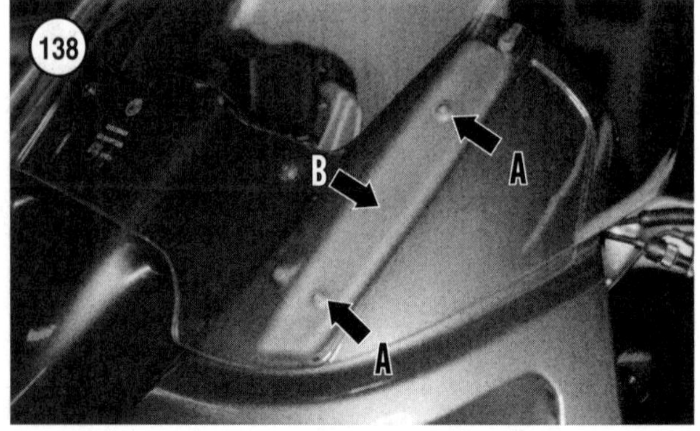

139

UPPER FAIRING INNER PANEL (RT MODELS)

1. Screw
2. Upper fairing inner panel
3. Screw

140

141

8. Install by reversing the removal steps. Tighten the screws, securing the inner panels securely.

Upper Fairing Removal/Installation

Refer to **Figure 136** and **Figure 137**.

1. Place the motorcycle on the centerstand with the front wheel off the ground.
2. Remove the following items as described in this chapter.
    a. Both seats.
    b. Windshield and lift mechanism.
    c. Both fairing side panels.
    d. Both rear view mirrors.
    e. Front fairing inner panel.
3. Remove the headlight and case mounting nuts. It is not necessary to remove the headlight case assembly, just release it from the upper fairing.
4. On models equipped with the radio, unscrew the nut washer and connector securing the radio antenna and remove the antenna.
5. Have an assistant hold the upper fairing. Remove the screws and washers securing the upper fairing to the mounting bracket and fuel tank.
6. Pull the upper fairing straight forward and remove it from the mounting bracket.
7. Install by reversing the removal steps. Tighten the screws securing the upper fairing.

Tail Piece and Frame Covers Removal/Installation

Models without saddle bags

Refer to **Figure 142**.

1. Place the motorcycle on the centerstand with the front wheel off the ground.
2. Remove both seats as described in this chapter.
3. Remove both fairing side panels as described in this chapter.
4. Remove the screws securing the tail piece and remove the tail piece.
5. Remove the bolts and nuts securing the side panel and remove the side panel.
6. Install by reversing the removal steps. Tighten the screws and bolts securing the tail piece and side panels.

Models with saddle bags

Refer to **Figure 143**.

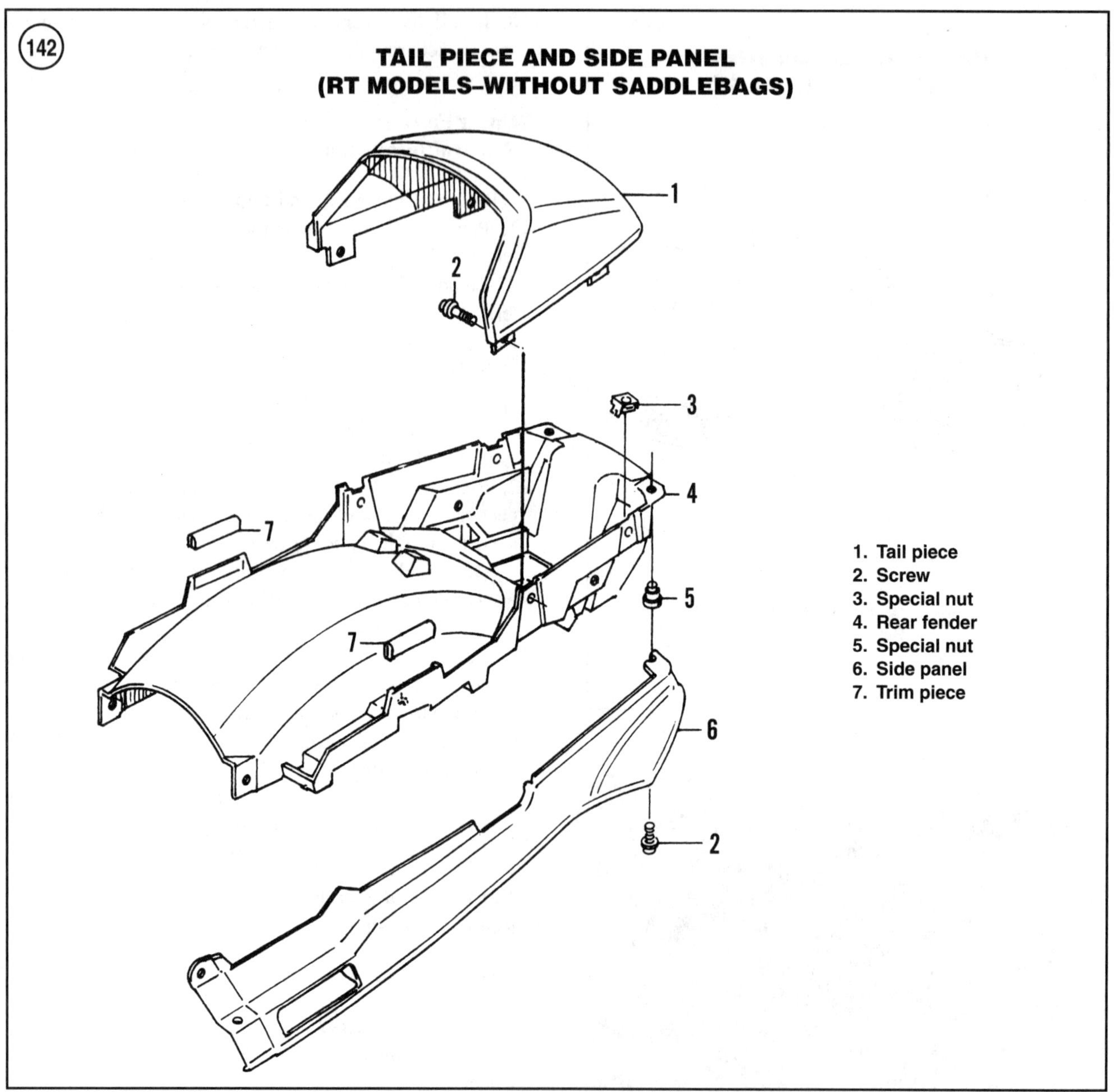

1. Place the motorcycle on the centerstand with the front wheel off the ground.
2. Remove the luggage as described in this chapter.
3. Remove both seats as described in this chapter.
4. Remove the luggage carriers as described in this chapter.
5. Remove both fairing side panels as described in this chapter.
6. Remove the screws securing the tail piece and remove the tail piece.
7. Remove the bolts and washers securing the frame covers and remove the frame covers.
8. Install by reversing the removal steps. Tighten the screws and bolts securing the tail piece and frame covers.

BODY PANELS (R1100S MODELS)

Front Fairing and Windshield Removal/Installation

Refer to **Figure 144**.

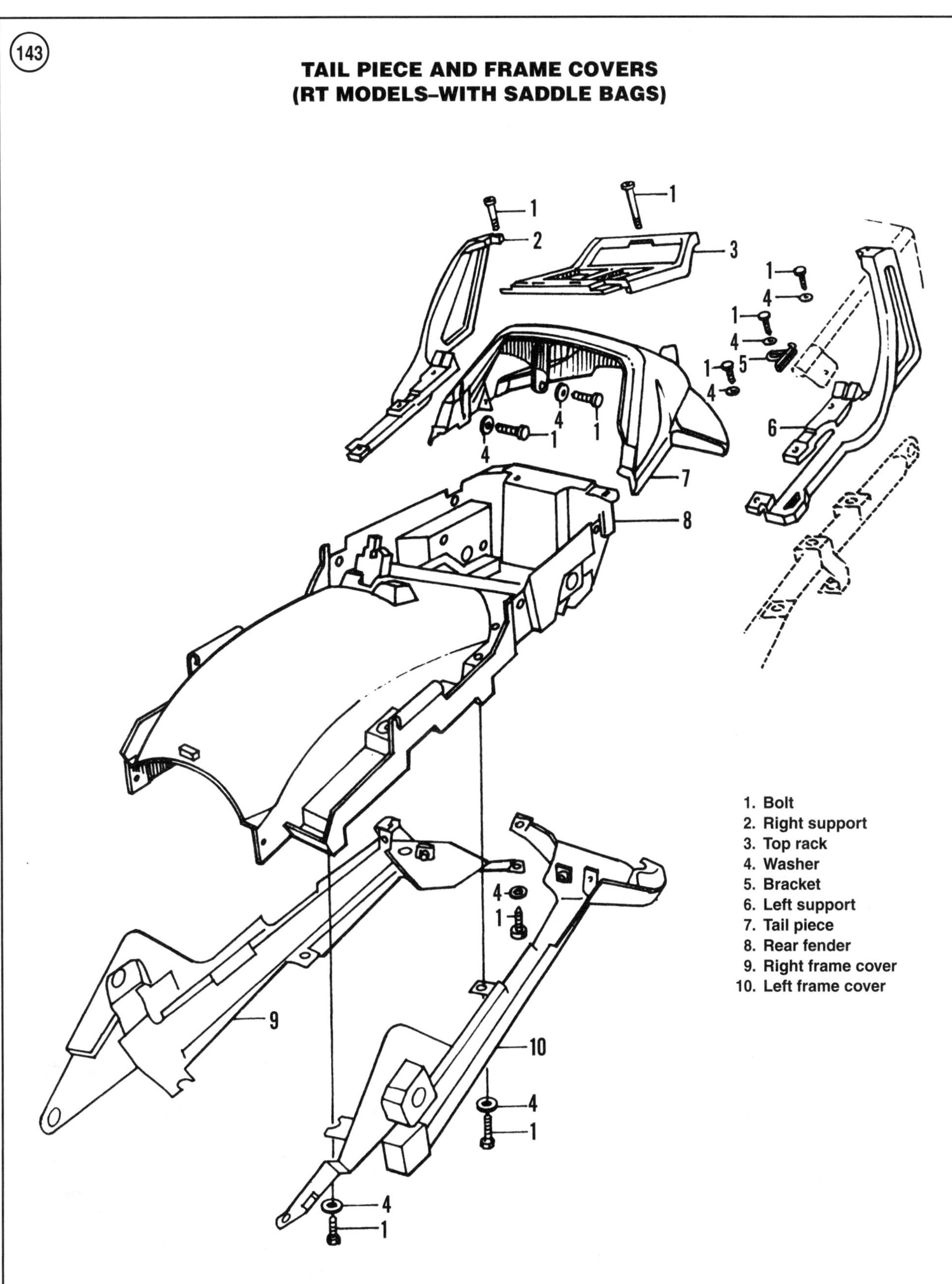
143
TAIL PIECE AND FRAME COVERS
(RT MODELS–WITH SADDLE BAGS)
1. Bolt
2. Right support
3. Top rack
4. Washer
5. Bracket
6. Left support
7. Tail piece
8. Rear fender
9. Right frame cover
10. Left frame cover

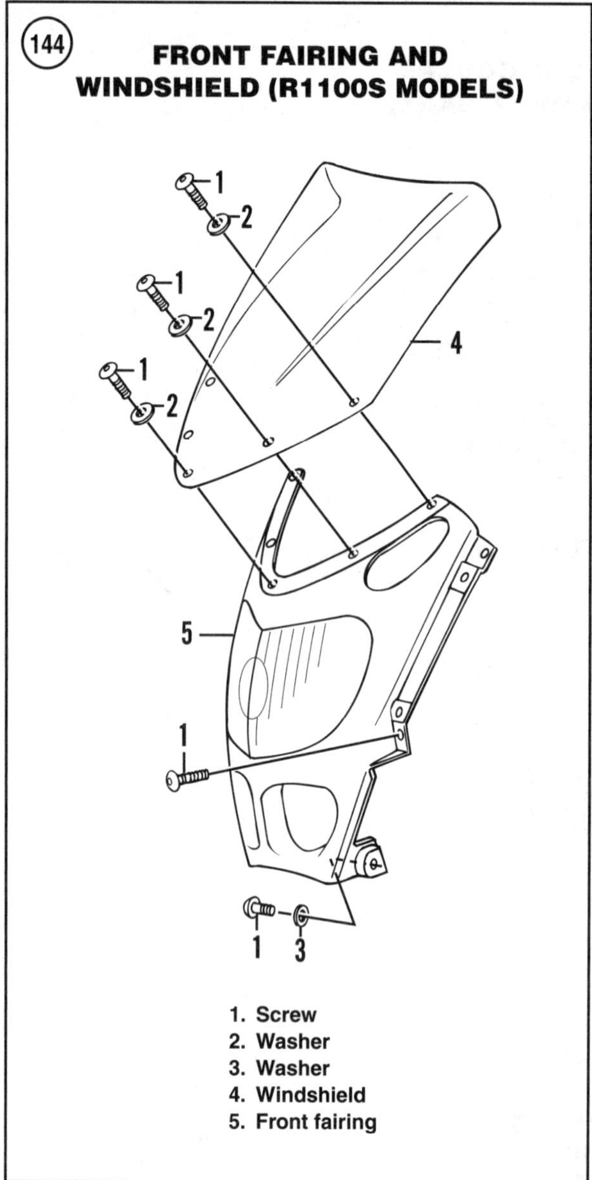

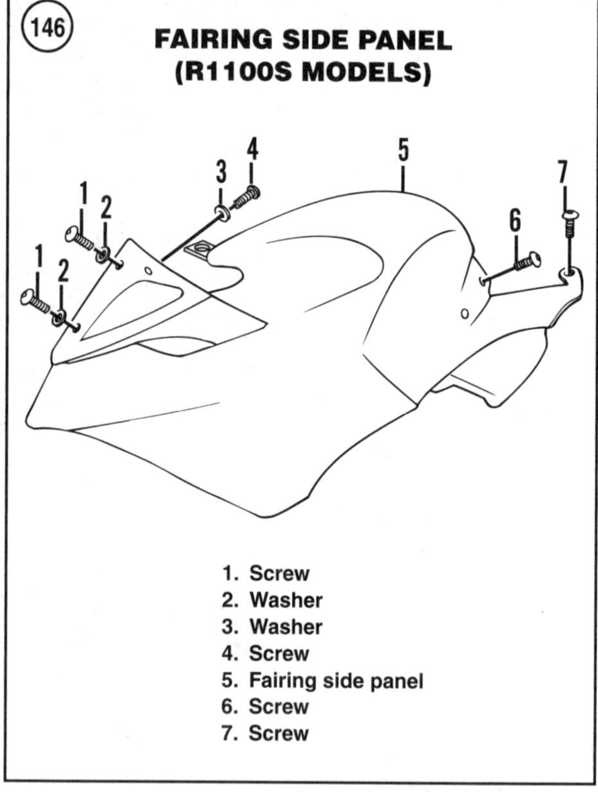

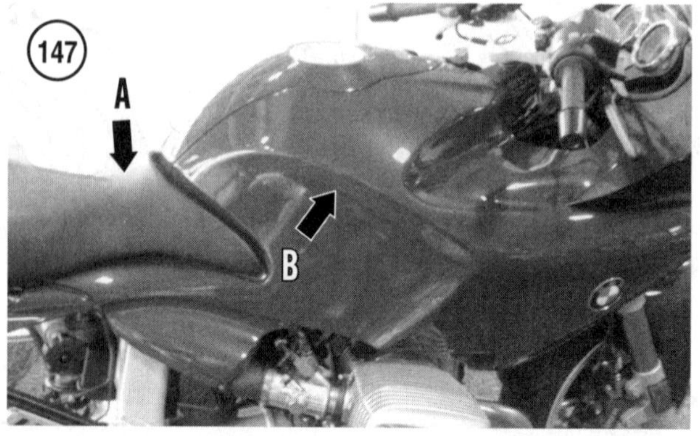

1. Remove the five screws and washers (A, **Figure 145**) at the base of the windshield and carefully remove the windshield (B).

2. Remove the screws and washers securing the mirrors (C, **Figure 145**) and remove both mirrors.

3. Remove the fairing side panels (D, **Figure 145**) as described in this section.

4. Pull the front fairing partially out, then disconnect the headlight electrical multi-pin connector. Remove the front fairing (E, **Figure 145**).

5. Install by reversing the removal steps. Tighten the screws and bolts securely.

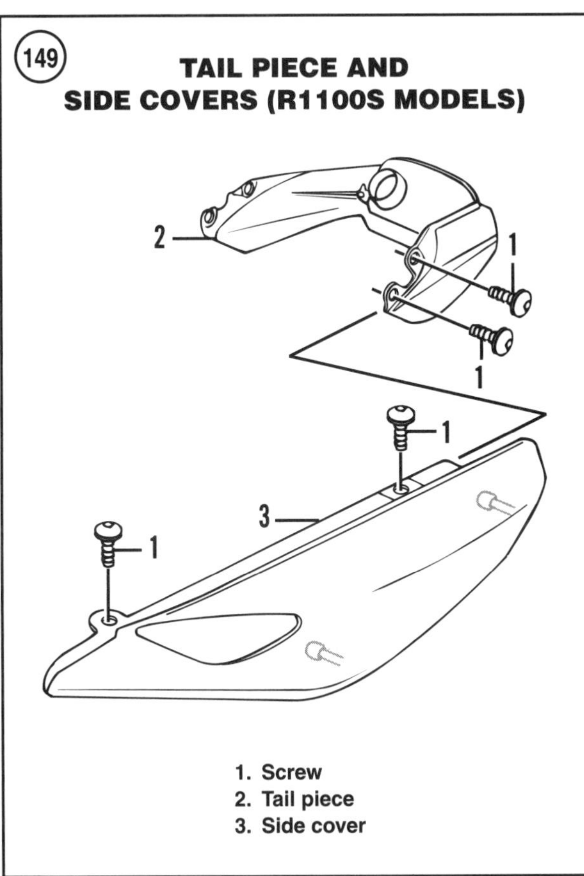

Fairing Side Panels Removal/Installation

Refer to **Figure 146**.

1. Remove the seat (A, **Figure 147**) as described in this chapter.
2. Remove the windshield and mirrors as described in this section.
3. Lift up on the release tab (**Figure 148**) on the fuel tank cover.

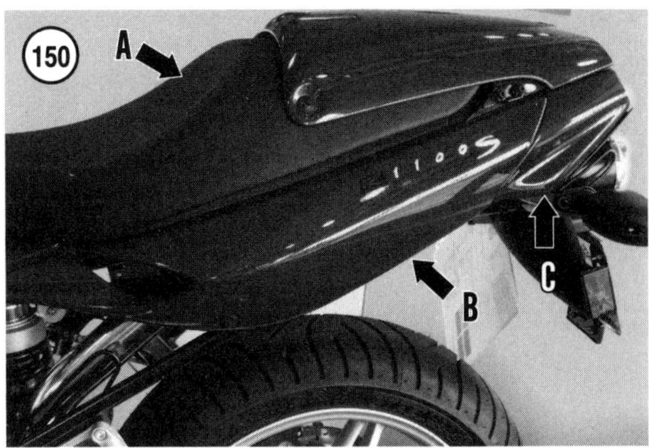

NOTE
The faring left side panel must be removed first to avoid damage to it's locking tabs.

4. To remove the left side panel, perform the following:
   a. Remove the four front screws and the two screws at the rear securing the fairing left side panel.
   b. Carefully lift the left fairing panel and release it from the guide groove on the fuel tank cover.
   c. Rotate the front turn signal socket *clockwise* and remove it from the side panel.
   d. Remove the fairing left side panel.
5. Repeat Step 4 and remove the fairing right side panel (B, **Figure 147**).
6. Install by reversing the removal steps. Tighten the screws securely.

Tail Piece and Side Covers Removal/Installation

Refer to **Figure 149**.

1. Remove the seat (A, **Figure 150**) as described in this chapter.
2. Remove the top two screws securing the side cover, pull straight out on the lower section and release the two mounting posts. Remove the side cover (B, **Figure 150**).
3. To remove the tail piece, perform the following:
   a. Remove the two screws on each side securing the tail piece (C, **Figure 150**) to the frame.
   b. Pull the tail piece part way out and disconnect the taillight/brake light electrical connector.
   c. Remove the tail piece from the frame.
4. Install by reversing the removal steps. Tighten the screws securely.

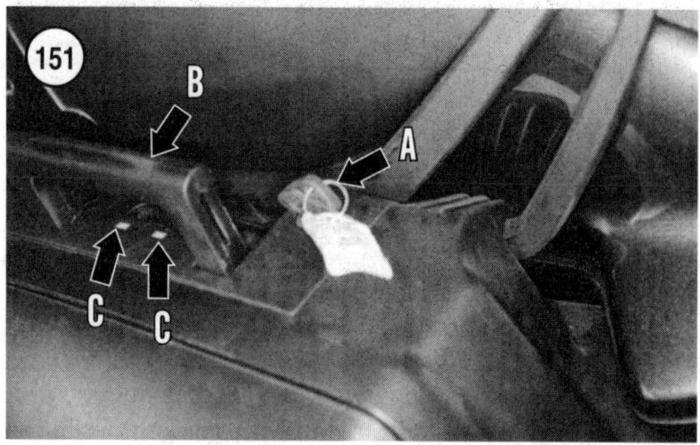

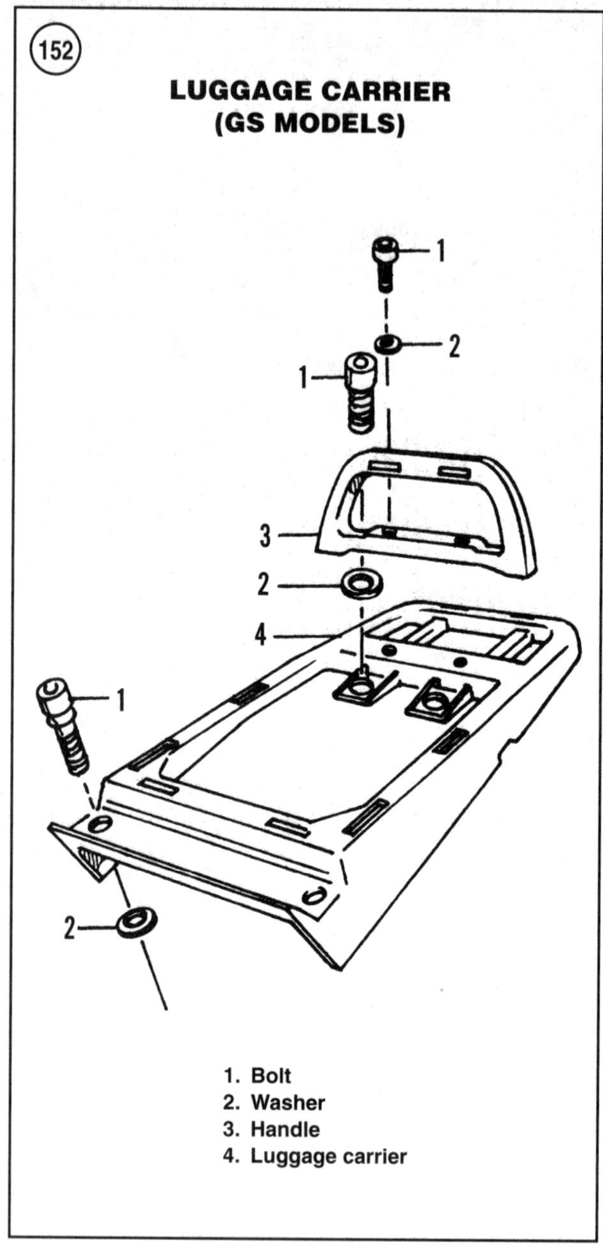

LUGGAGE AND LUGGAGE CARRIER

These items are optional and are not equipped on all models.

Luggage Removal/Installation (All Models)

1. Insert the key into the lock (A, **Figure 151**) and turn it counterclockwise and hold it in this position.
2. Fold up the handle (B, **Figure 151**) and observe the indicator lights. When the two indicator lights are red (C, **Figure 151**), remove the key (A) and lift and remove the luggage case from its mount.

Luggage Carrier Removal/Installation (GS Models)

Refer to **Figure 152**.

1. Place the motorcycle on the centerstand with the rear wheel off the ground.
2. Remove both seats as described in this chapter.
3. On models so equipped, remove the bolts and washers securing the luggage carrier and remove it from the rear frame assembly.
4. Unhook and remove the tool box cover (**Figure 153**).
5. Remove the center bolt (A, **Figure 154**) securing the tools tray. Remove the tool tray and tools (B, **Figure 154**).

NOTE
There are two different length mounting bolts. Install the longer bolts (20 mm) at the front of the carrier and the shorter bolts (16 mm) at the rear.

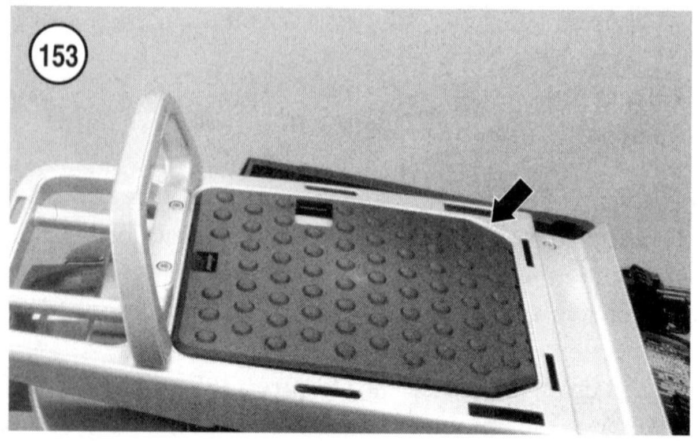

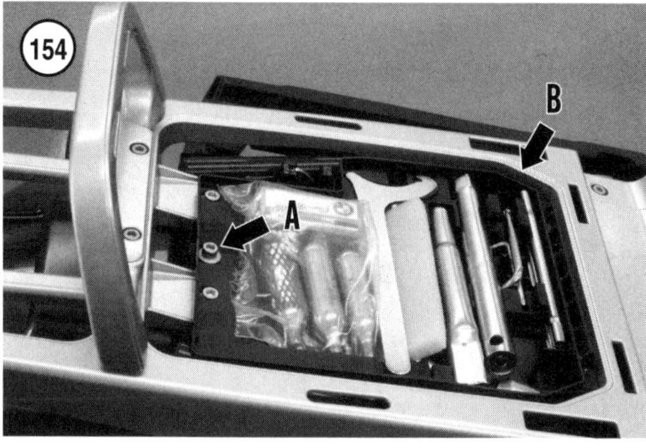

6. Remove the two front bolts (**Figure 155**) and the rear two bolts and washers (**Figure 156**) securing the luggage carrier to the rear frame.

7. Remove the luggage carrier.

8. Install by reversing the removal steps while noting the following:

   a. Make sure the tool tray is secure and snaps into place. It must be correctly seated for the installation of the seat.

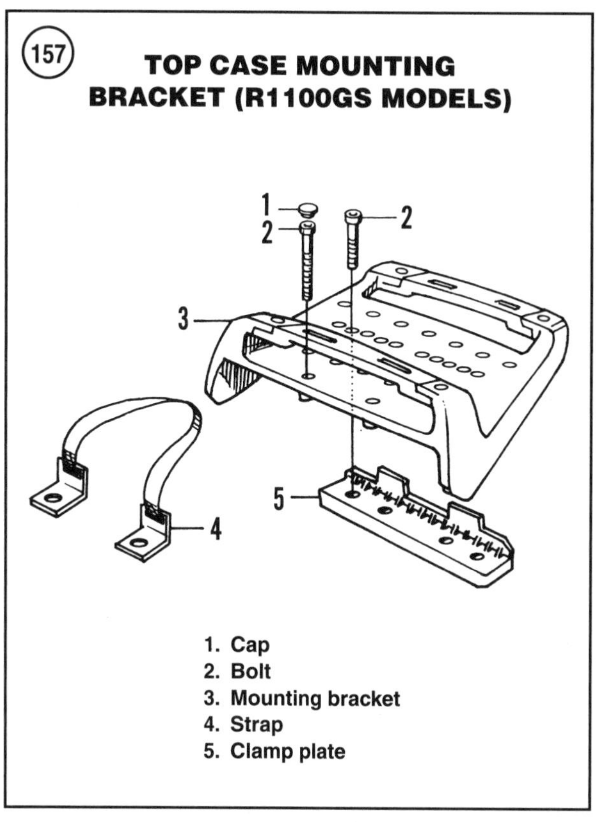

   b. Tighten the bolts securely.

Top Case and Mounting Bracket Removal/Installation (R1100GS Models)

Refer to **Figure 157** and **Figure 158**

1. Place the motorcycle on the centerstand with the rear wheel off the ground.

2. Remove both seats as described in this chapter.

NOTE
There are two different length mounting bolts. Install the longer bolts (60–mm) at the front of the mounting bracket and the shorter bolts (30–mm) at the rear.

3. Remove the bolts and washers securing the mounting bracket to the rear frame assembly.

4. To remove the top case, insert the key into the lock. Turn the key and remove the top case from the mounting bracket.

5. Install by reversing the removal steps. Tighten the bolts securely.

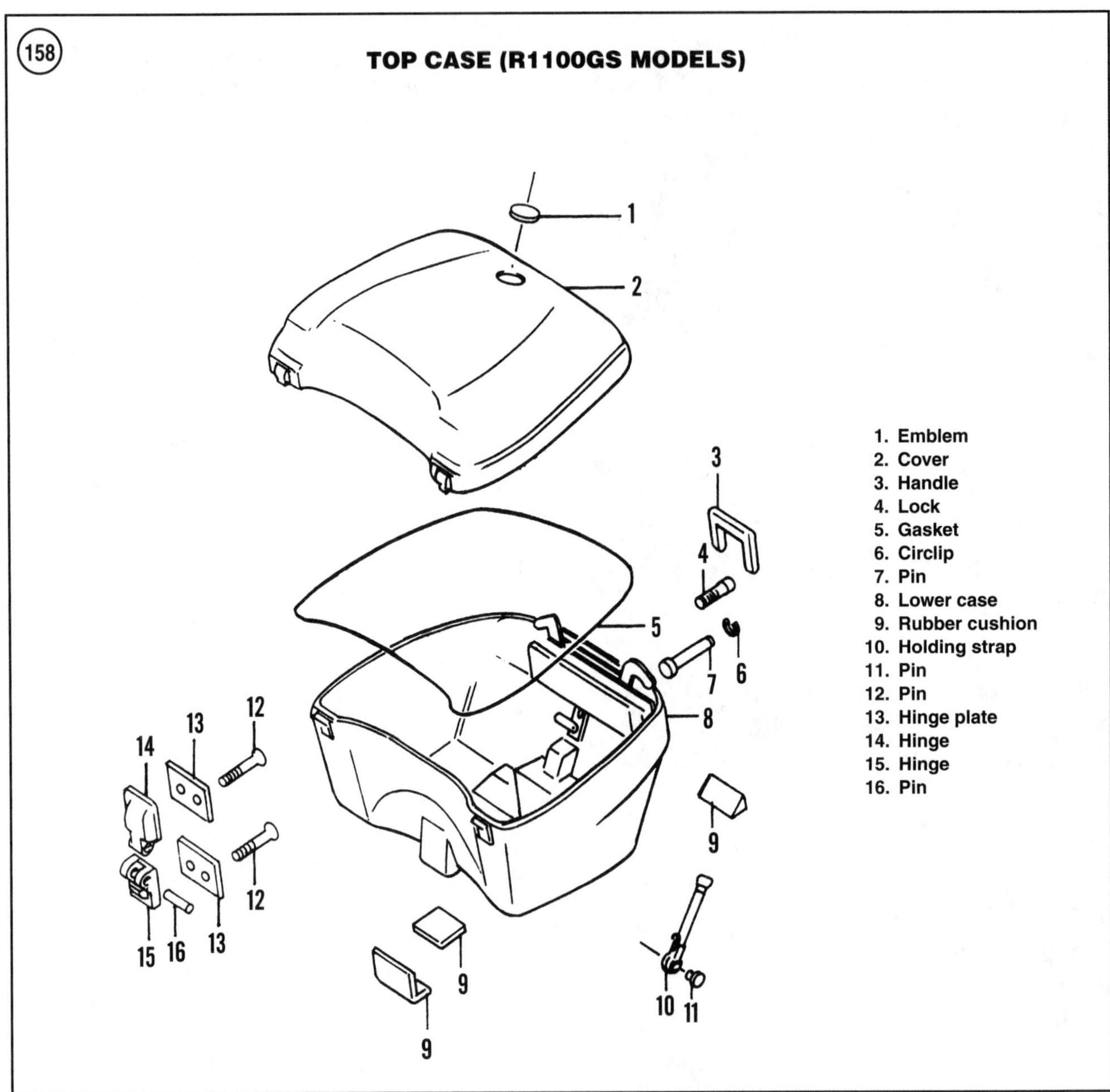

Luggage Rack Removal/Installation

GS models

Refer to **Figure 159**.

1. Place the motorcycle on the centerstand with the front wheel off the ground.
2. Remove the luggage from the rack.
3. Remove the bolts and washers securing the rack to the rear frame assembly.
4. Remove the rack from the frame. On models so equipped, do not lose the spacer at the rear mount.
5. Install by reversing the removal steps. Tighten the bolts securely.

RS and RT models

Refer to **Figure 160**.

1. Remove the luggage from the rack as described in this chapter.
2. Remove seats as described in this chapter.

(159)

LUGGAGE RACK (GS MODELS)

1. Spacer
2. Washer
3. Bolt
4. Luggage rack

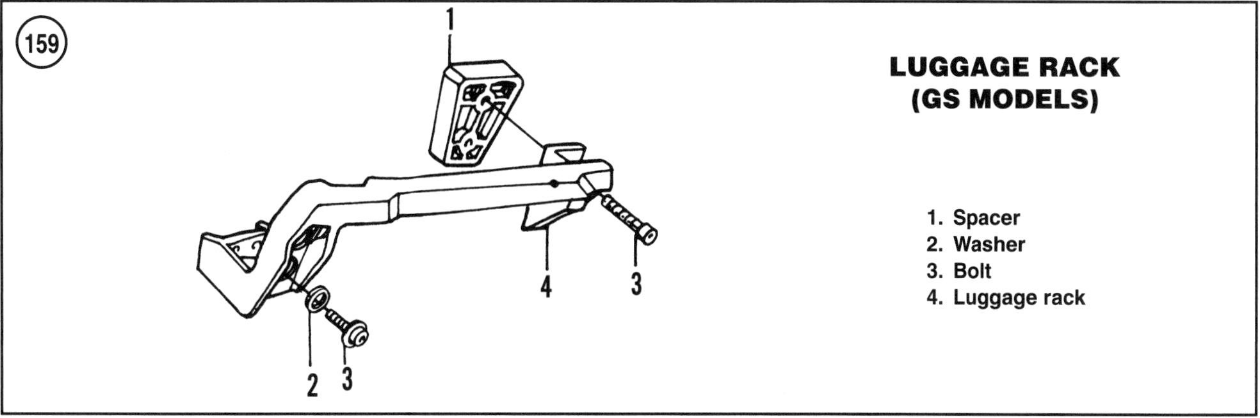

(160)

LUGGAGE RACK (RS AND RT MODELS)

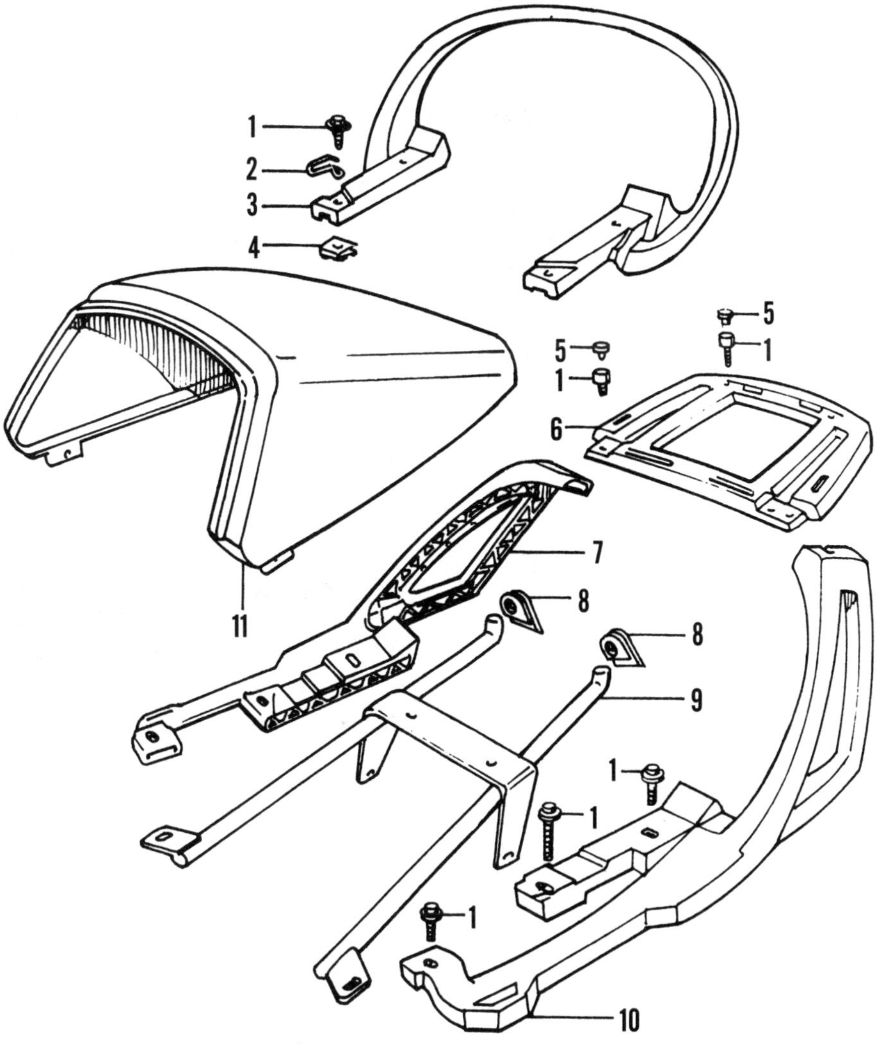

1. Screw
2. Clamp
3. Rear handle
4. Special nut
5. Trim cap
6. Center carrier
7. Right rack
8. Rubber cap
9. Subframe
10. Left rack
11. Tail piece

3. To remove the center carrier, remove the trim caps (A, **Figure 161**), then remove the bolts securing the center carrier (B) and remove it from the luggage rack.
4. Remove the bolts (**Figure 162**) on each side, securing the luggage rack to the rear frame assembly. Remove the luggage rack (**Figure 163**).
5. Install by reversing the removal steps. Tighten the bolts securely.

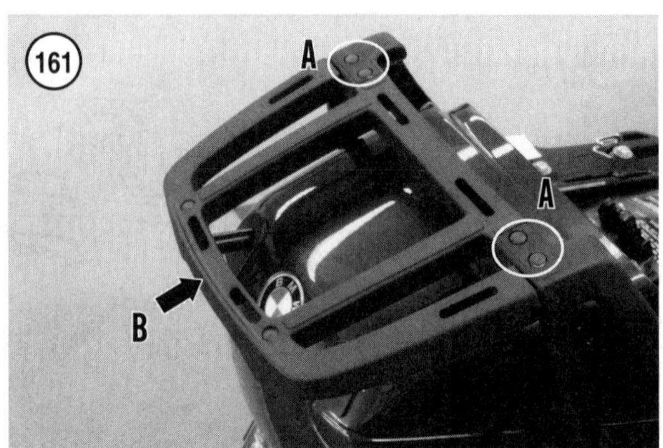

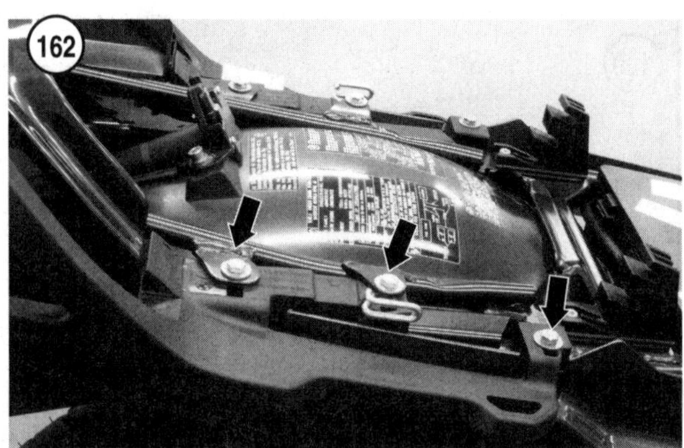

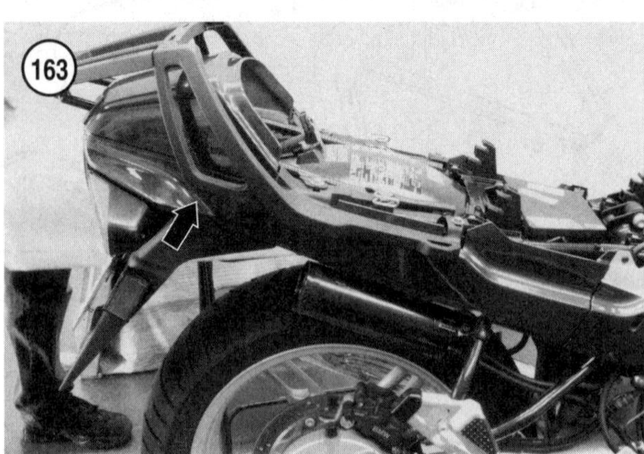

WINDSHIELD CLEANING (ALL MODELS)

Be careful cleaning the windshield as it can be easily scratched or damaged. Do not use a cleaner with an abrasive or a combination cleaner and wax. These products will either scratch or totally destroy the surface of the windshield.

Use a soft cloth or sponge and plenty of soap and water. Rinse with water and dry thoroughly with a soft cloth or chamois—do not press hard.

SIDESTAND

Removal/Installation

All models except R850C, R1100S, R1150GS and R1200C

Refer to **Figure 164** and **Figure 165**.

1A. On GS models, remove the engine lower guard as described in this chapter.

1B. On RT models, remove the front fairing lower side panels as described in this chapter.

2. Place a suitable size jack under the engine to securely support the motorcycle.

NOTE
This procedure is shown with the transmission and centerstand removed for clarity. It is not necessary to remove either of these components for this procedure.

NOTE
This procedure is shown with some of the components removed from the engine for clarity.

3. Raise the sidestand and disconnect the return springs (A, **Figure 166**) from the pin on the frame with locking pliers.
4. Remove the bolt and washer (B, **Figure 166**) securing the sidestand to the mounting bracket.
5. If necessary, remove the bolt and washer (C, **Figure 166**) securing the mounting bracket to the crankcase and remove the bracket.
6. Install by reversing the removal steps while noting the following:

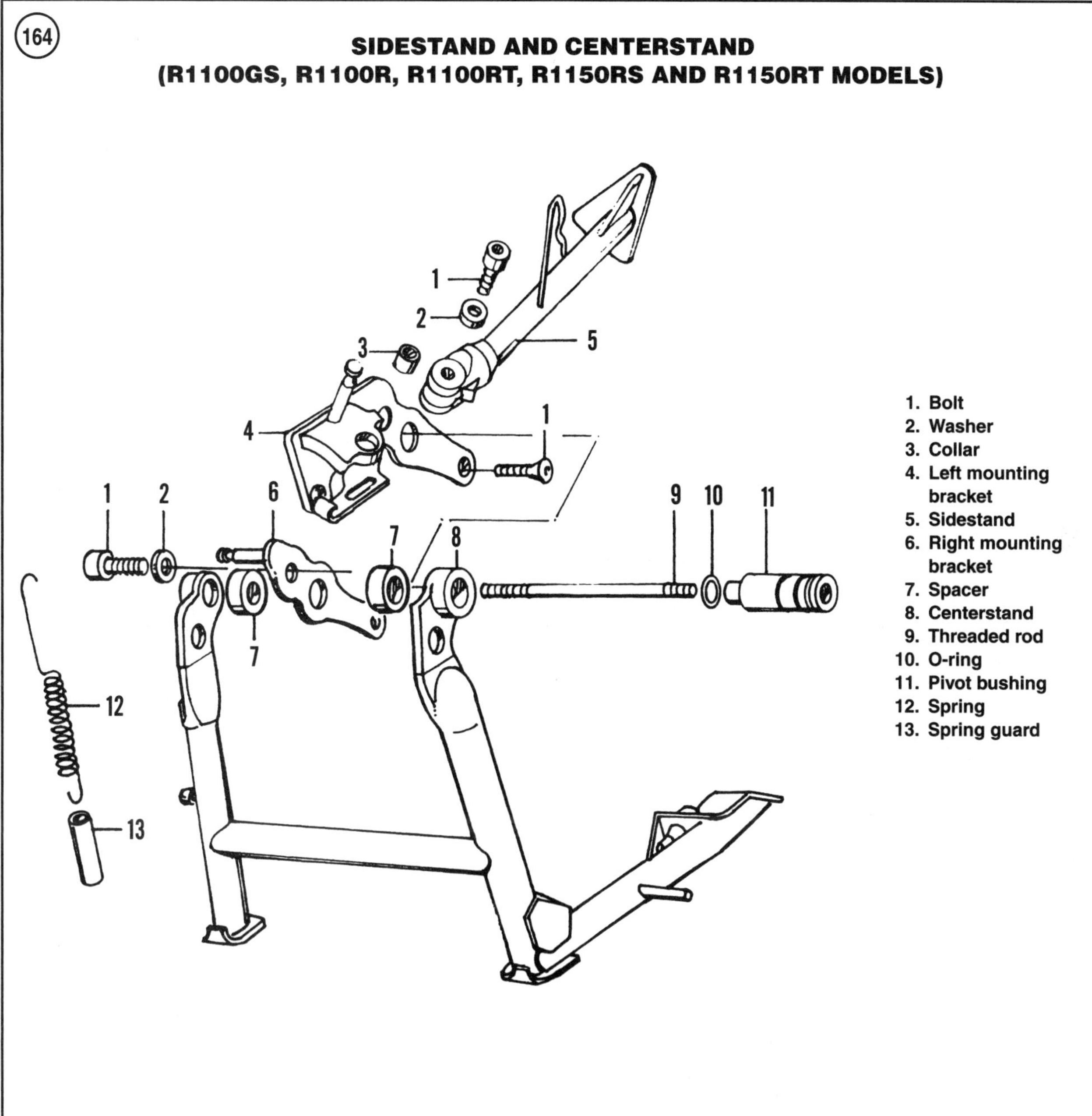

a. Apply a light coat of multipurpose grease to the pivot surfaces prior to installation.
b. Apply a light coat of heavy strength threadlocking compound to threads prior to installation.
c. Tighten the pivot bolt to 42 N•m (31 ft.-lb.).
d. If removed, tighten the mounting bracket bolt to 21 N•m (15 ft.-lb.).
e. If removed, be sure to install the rubber sleeves on the return springs.

R850C, R1100S, R1150GS and R1200C models

Refer to **Figure 167**.

1. Place a suitable size jack under the engine to securely support the motorcycle.
2. Raise the sidestand and disconnect the return springs (A, **Figure 168**) from the spring plate with locking pliers.
3. Remove the side stand switch (B, **Figure 168**) as described in Chapter Ten.

165

SIDESTAND AND CENTERSTAND (R1100RS MODELS)

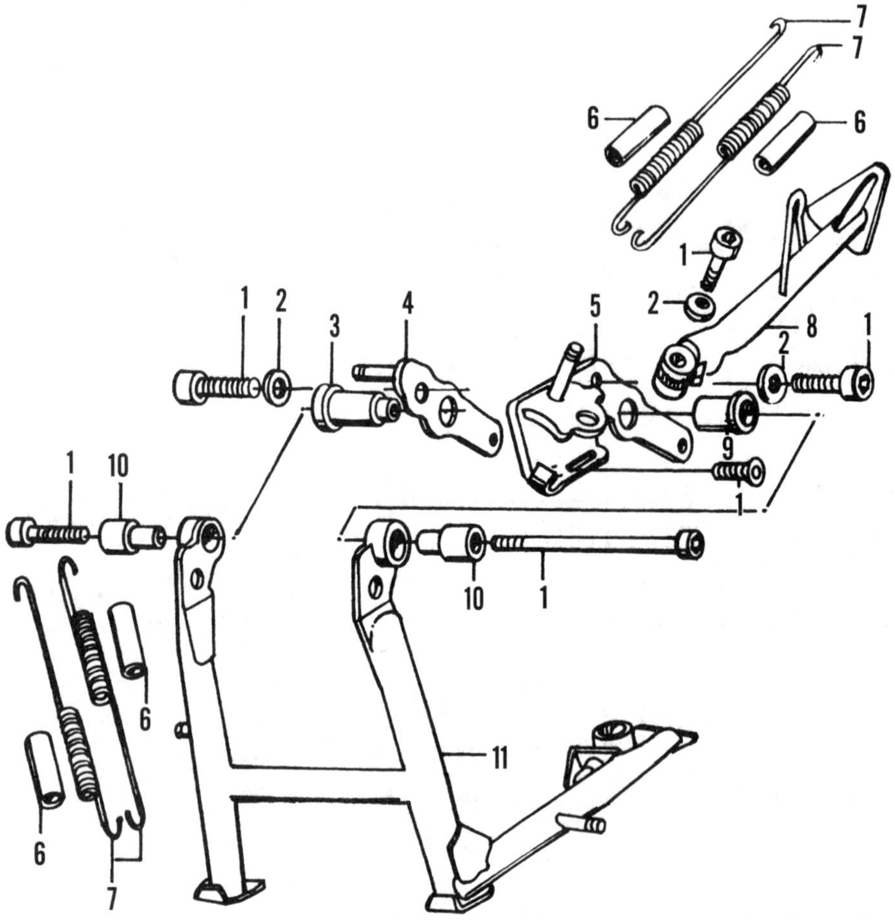

1. Bolt
2. Washer
3. Pivot bushing
4. Right mounting bracket
5. Left mounting bracket
6. Spring guard
7. Springs
8. Sidestand
9. Pivot bushing
10. Pivot bushing
11. Centerstand

4. Remove the snapring securing the pivot bolt to the mounting bracket.

5. Withdraw the pivot bolt, then remove the sidestand and bushing.

6. If necessary, remove the bolt and washer securing the mounting bracket to the crankcase and remove the bracket.

7. Install by reversing the removal steps while noting the following:

   a. Apply a light coat of multipurpose grease to the pivot surfaces prior to installation.

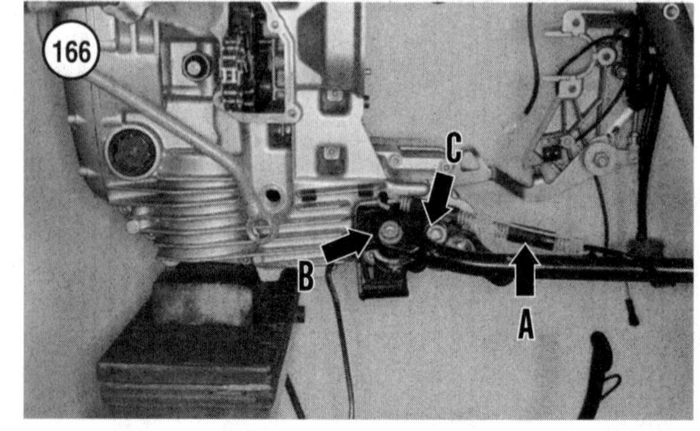

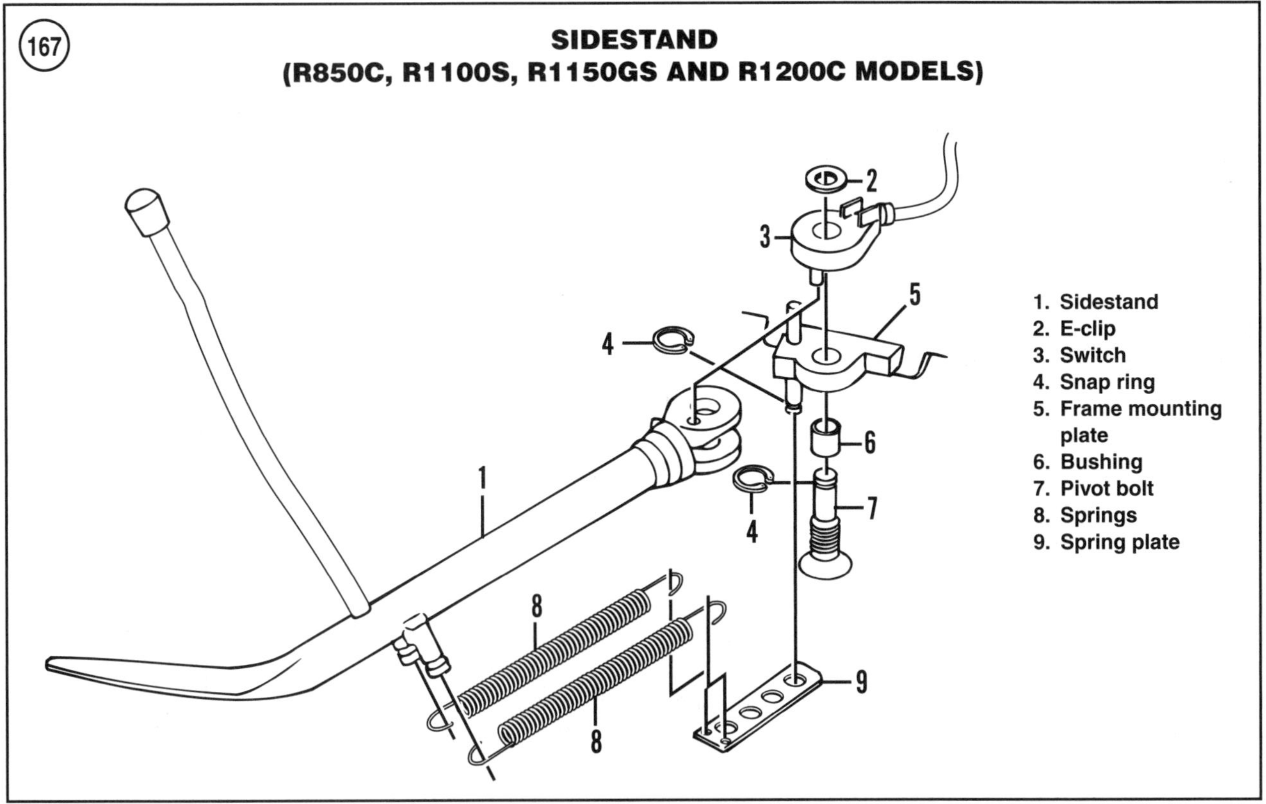

b. Apply a light coat of heavy strength threadlocking compound to threads prior to installation.

c. If removed, tighten the mounting bracket bolt to 58 N•m (43 ft.-lb.).

CENTERSTAND

Removal/Installation

Refer to **Figure 164** and **Figure 165**.

NOTE
This procedure is shown with the transmission and centerstand removed for clarity. It is not necessary to remove either of these components for this procedure.

1A. On GS models, remove the engine lower guard as described in this chapter.

1B. On RT models, remove the front fairing lower side panels as described in this chapter.

2. Place a suitable size jack under the engine to support the motorcycle securely.

3. Raise the centerstand and use locking pliers to unhook the return springs from the stud on the centerstand.

4A. On RS models, perform the following:

a. Remove the bolts and pivot bushings from each side of the centerstand.

b. Remove the centerstand from the mounting brackets and crankcase.

4B. On all models other than RS, perform the following:

a. Unscrew the pivot bushings from each side of the centerstand.

b. Withdraw the long threaded rod (A, **Figure 169**) and remove the centerstand (B) from the mounting brackets and crankcase.

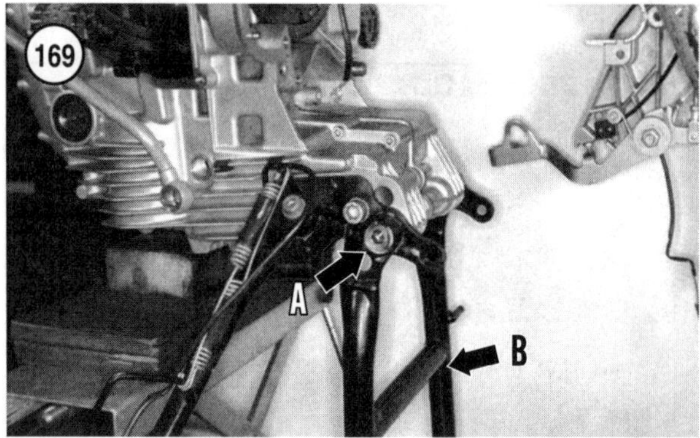

c. Do not lose the bushings on each side. Note the right side bushing is thicker (4.5 mm [0.18 in.]) than the left bushing (2.4 mm [0.10 in.]). Install the bushings in the correct location.

5. If necessary, remove the bolts securing the mounting brackets to each side of the crankcase.

6. Install by reversing the removal steps while noting the following:

a. Apply multipurpose grease to the pivot bolts and bushings.

b. Tighten the bolts and bushings to 21 N•m (15 ft.-lb.).

c. If removed, tighten the 8–mm mounting bracket bolt to 21 N•m (15 ft.-lb.).

d. If removed, tighten the 12–mm mounting bracket bolt to 72 N•m (53 ft.-lb.).

e. If removed, install the rubber sleeves on the return springs.

FOOTRESTS (R1100GS, R1100R and R1100RS MODELS)

Removal/Installation

Front footrest

Refer to **Figure 170**.

1. Place the motorcycle on the centerstand with the front wheel off the ground.

2. To remove the individual footrest, perform the following:

a. Remove the cotter pin (A, **Figure 171**), and sleeve or washer, securing the pivot pin.

b. Remove the pivot pin (B, **Figure 171**) and remove the footrest and spring from the bracket.

c. Make sure the spring is not stretched, cracked or broken. Replace it if necessary.

d. If necessary, slide off the rubber pad and replace it with a new one.

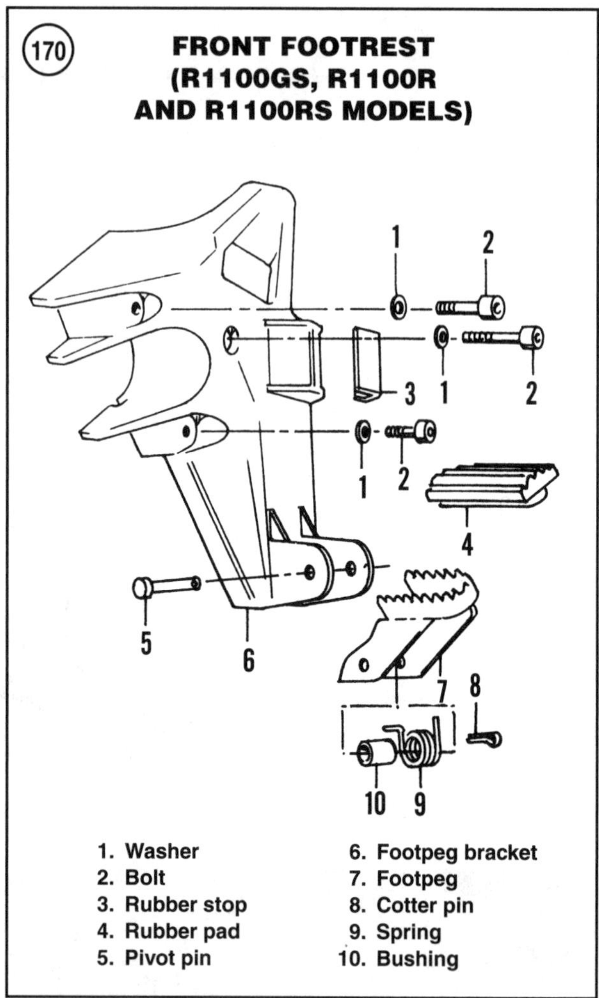

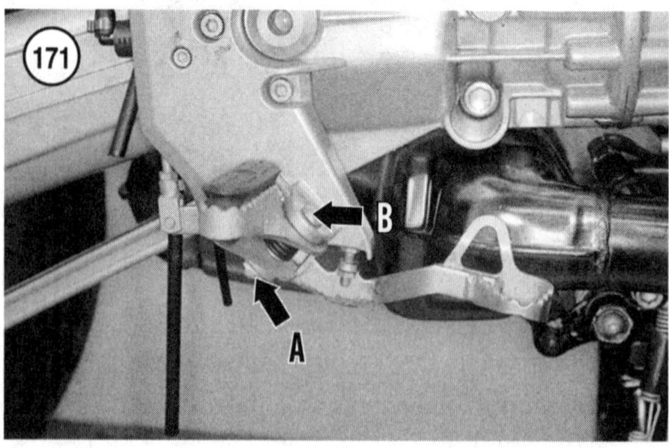

e. Lubricate the pivot point and pivot pin prior to installation. Install a new cotter pin and bend the ends over completely.

3. To remove the entire footrest assembly, perform the following:

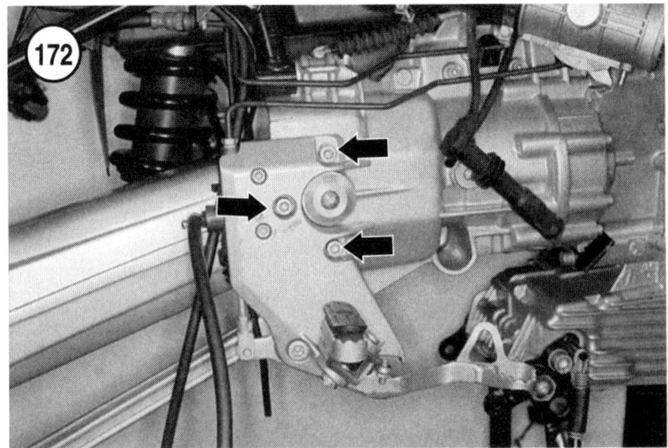

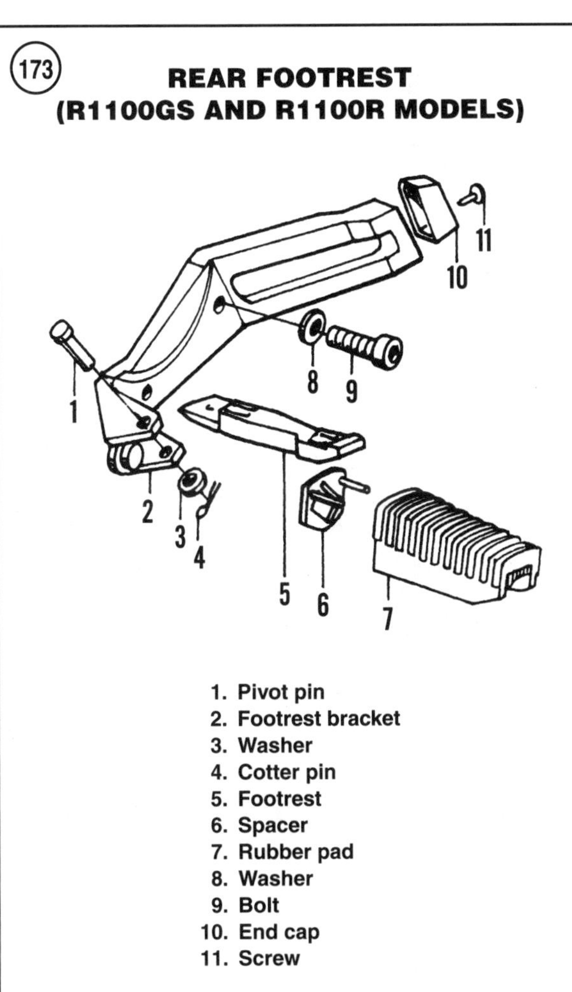

a. Remove the bolts and washers (**Figure 172**) securing the footrest assembly to the transmission case.

b. On the right side, if necessary, remove the rear master cylinder assembly from the backside of the footrest assembly. Refer to Chapter Twelve.

c. Install by reversing the removal steps. Tighten the mounting bolts to 22 N•m (16 ft.-lb.).

Rear footrest

Refer to **Figure 173** and **Figure 174**.

1. Place the motorcycle on the centerstand with the front wheel off the ground.
2. To remove the individual footrest, perform the following:
   a. Remove the cotter pin and sleeve or washer securing the pivot pin.
   b. Remove the pivot pin and remove the footrest and spring from the bracket.
   c. Make sure the spring is in good condition and not broken. Replace as necessary.
   d. If necessary, slide off the rubber pad and replace with a new one.
   e. Lubricate the pivot point and pivot pin prior to installation. Install a new cotter pin and bend the ends completely over.
3. To remove the entire footrest assembly, perform the following:
   a. On RS models, remove the rubber pad (A, **Figure 175**) covering the front mounting bolt.
   b. Remove the bolts and washers (B, **Figure 175**) securing the footrest assembly to the transmission case.
   c. On the right side, if necessary, remove the rear master cylinder assembly from the backside of the footrest assembly. Refer to Chapter Fourteen.
   d. Install by reversing the removal steps. Tighten the mounting bolts to 21 N•m (15 ft.-lb.).

FOOTRESTS (R1150R AND R1150RS MODELS)

Removal/Installation

15

Front footrest

Refer to **Figure 176** and **Figure 177**.

1. Place the motorcycle on the centerstand with the rear wheel off the ground.
2. To remove the individual footrest, perform the followaing:
   a. Remove the E-clip securing the pivot pin.
   b. Remove the pivot pin and remove the footrest and spring from the bracket.
   c. Make sure the spring is not stretched, cracked or broken. Replace it if necessary.

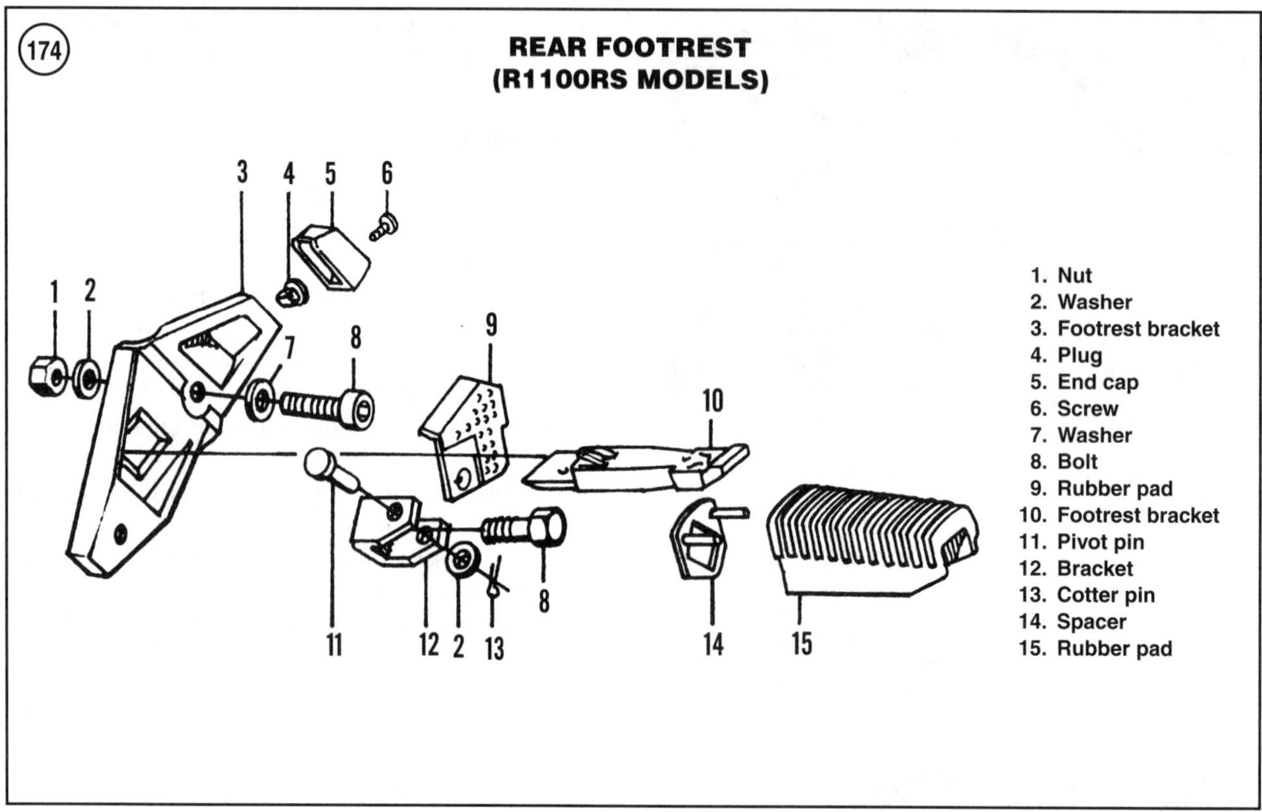

d. Lubricate the pivot point and pivot pin prior to installation. Install a new E-clip onto the pivot pin and make sure it seats correctly in the pivot pin groove.

3. To remove the entire footrest assembly, perform the following:

a. Remove the rear master cylinder assembly (A, **Figure 178**) as described in Chapter Fourteen.

b. Remove the rear brake pedal assembly (B, **Figure 178**) as described in Chapter Fourteen.

c. Remove the bolts and washers (C, **Figure 178**) securing the footrest assembly to the transmission case and to the frame.

d. On the left side, remove the bolt and washer and remove the rear shock absorber damper adjuster.

e. On the left side, if necessary, remove the gearshift lever assembly as described in Chapter Eight.

f. Install by reversing the removal steps.

g. Tighten the footrest-to-transmission bolt to 42 N•m (31 ft.-lb.).

h. Tighten the footrest-to-frame bolts to 21 N•m (15 ft.-lb.).

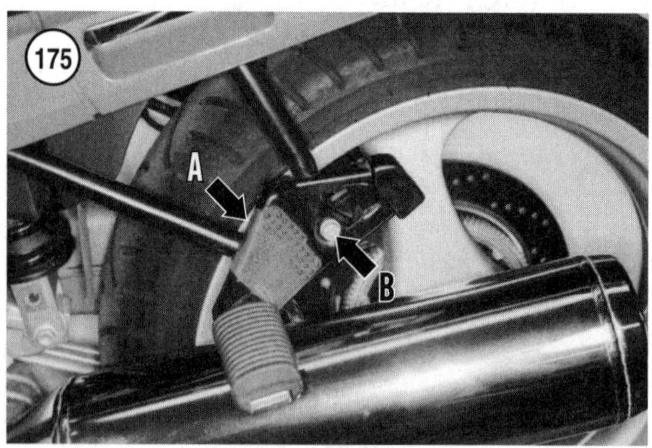

Rear footrest

1. Place the motorcycle on the centerstand with the rear wheel off the ground.

2. To remove the individual footrest, perform the following:

a. Remove the E-clip securing the footrest to the bracket on the footrest bracket.

b. Remove the pivot pin and remove the footrest (A, **Figure 179**) and small springs.

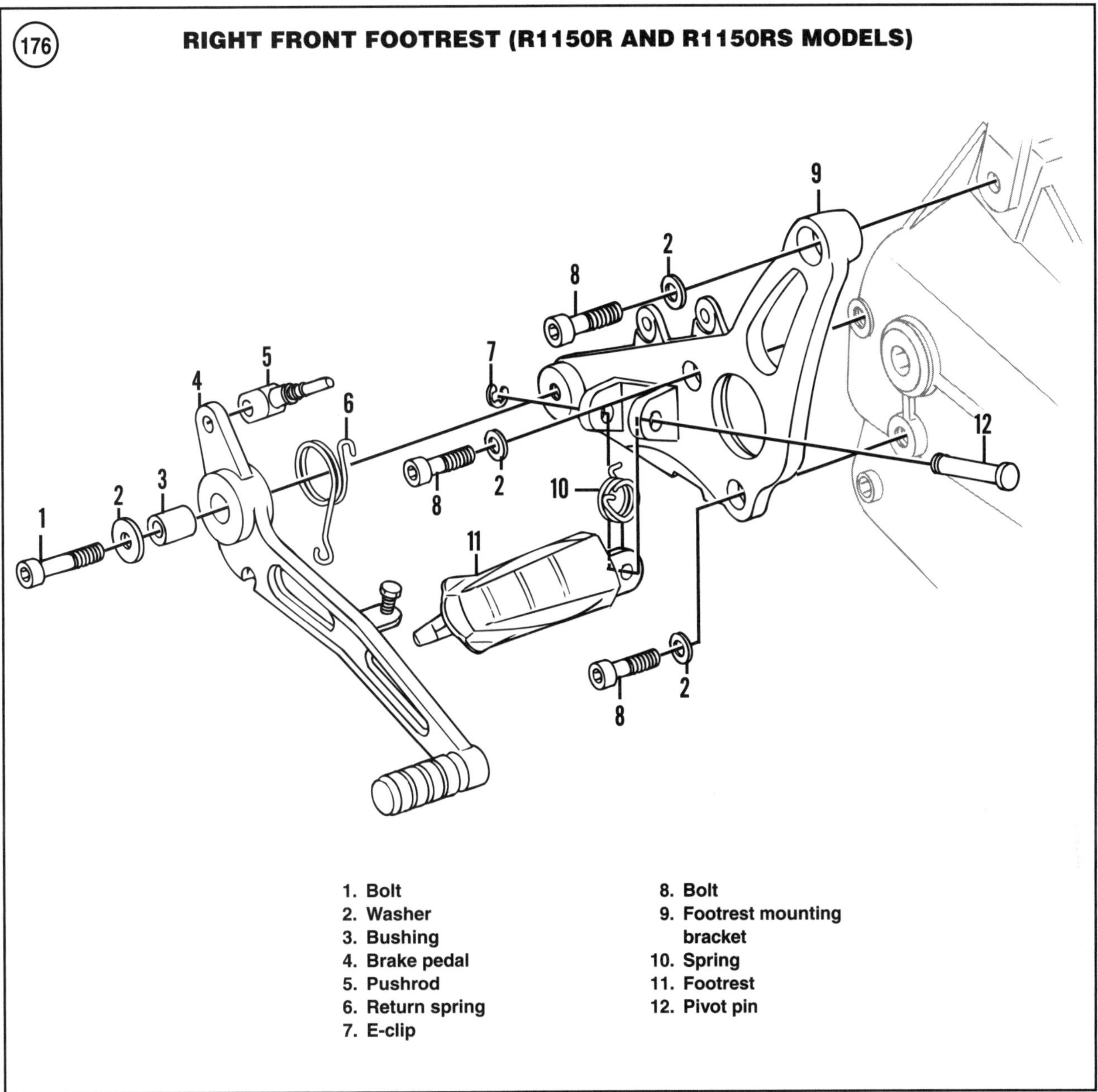

c. Make sure the springs are in good condition and not broken. Replace as necessary.

d. Lubricate the pivot point and pivot pin prior to installation. Install a new E-clip onto the pivot pin and make sure it seats correctly in the pivot pin groove.

3. To remove the entire footrest assembly, remove the bolts and washers (B, **Figure 179**) and remove the footrest assembly from the rear frame.

4. Install by reversing the removal steps. Tighten the mounting bolts to 21 N•m (15 ft.-lb.).

FOOTRESTS (R1150GS MODELS)

Removal/Installation

Front footrest

Refer to **Figure 180** and **Figure 181**.

1. Place the motorcycle on the centerstand with the rear wheel off the ground.

2. To remove the individual footrest, perform the following:

177

LEFT FRONT FOOTREST (R1150R AND R1150RS MODELS)

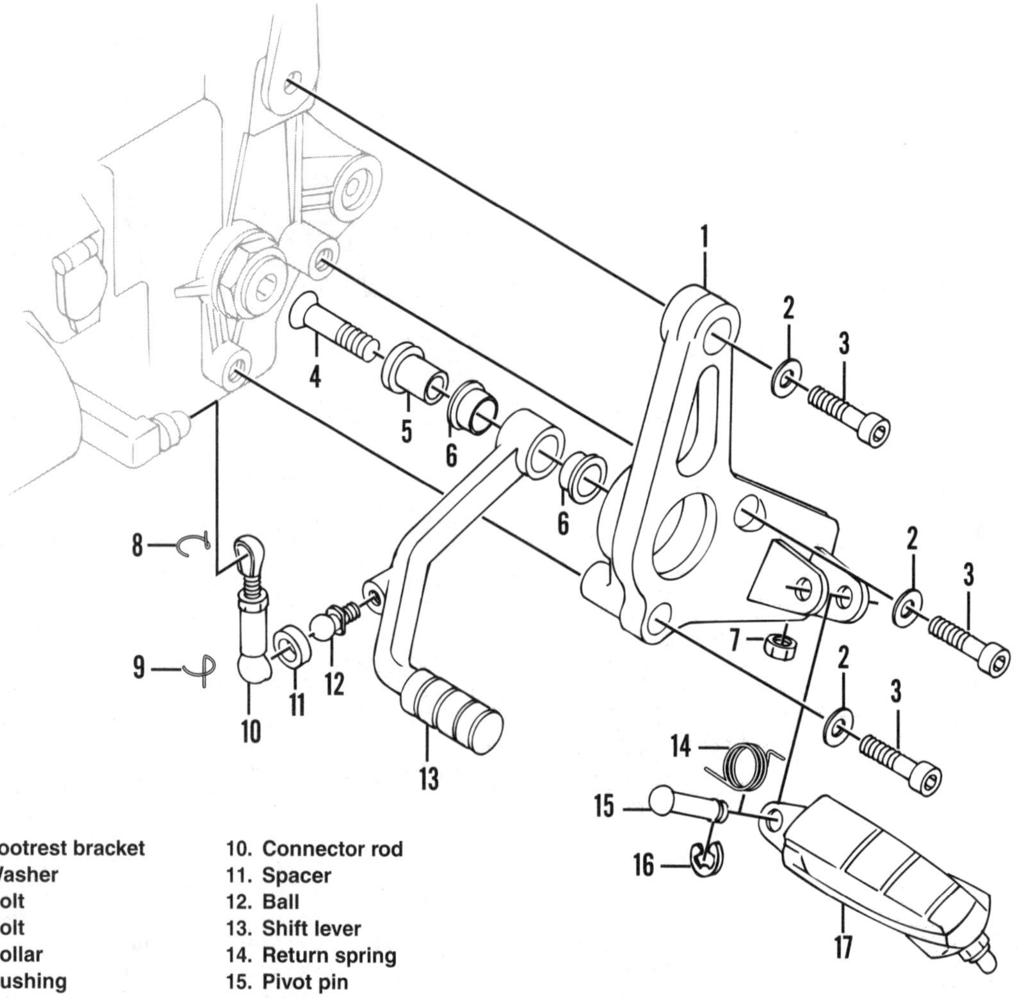

1. Footrest bracket
2. Washer
3. Bolt
4. Bolt
5. Collar
6. Bushing
7. Nut
8. Clip
9. Clip
10. Connector rod
11. Spacer
12. Ball
13. Shift lever
14. Return spring
15. Pivot pin
16. E-clip
17. Foot rest

178

179

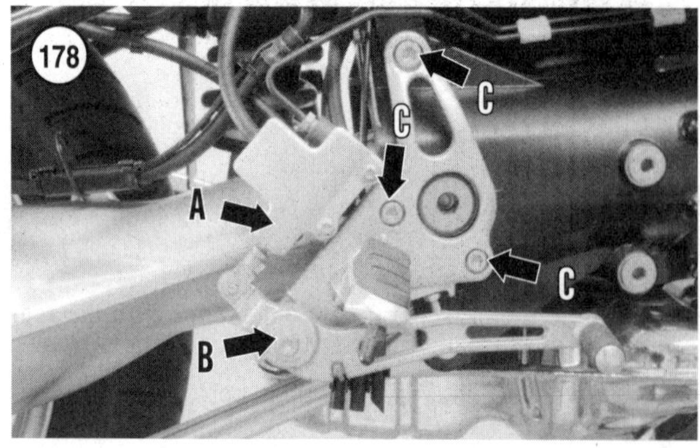

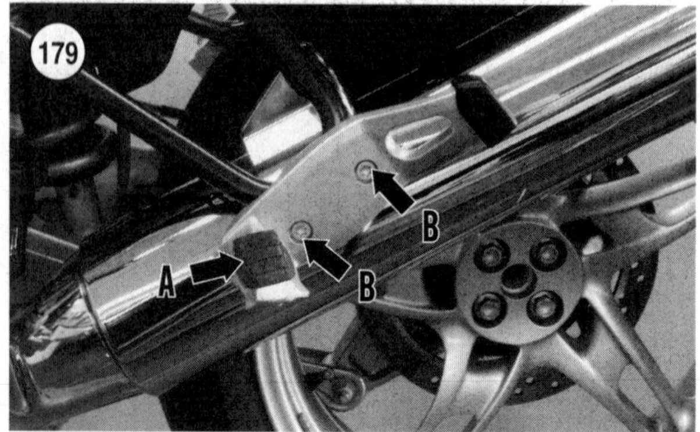

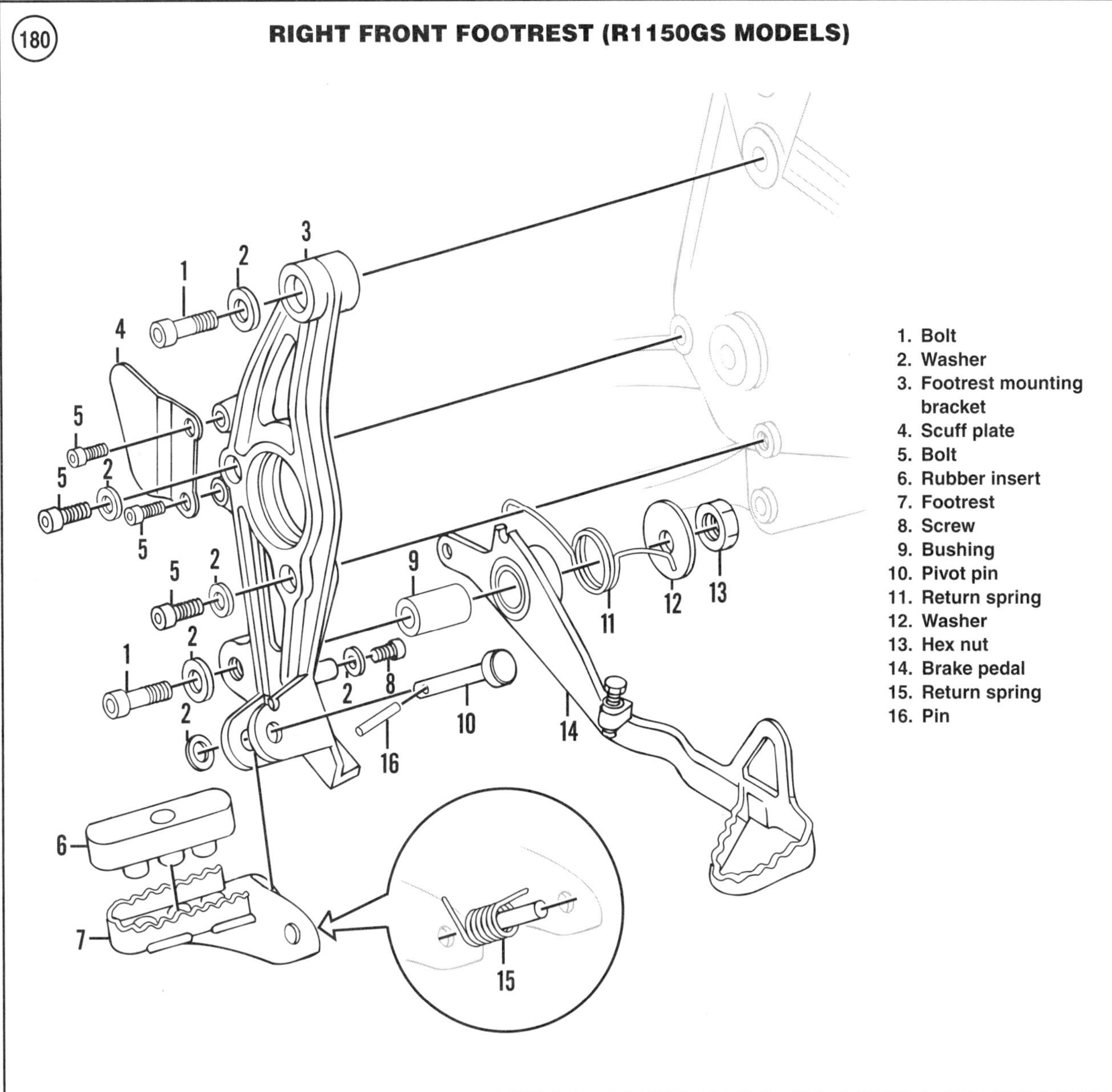

a. Remove the E-clip securing the pivot pin.

b. Remove the pivot pin and remove the footrest and spring (A, **Figure 182**) from the bracket.

c. Make sure the spring is not stretched, cracked or broken. Replace it if necessary.

d. Lubricate the pivot point and pivot pin prior to installation. Install a new E-clip onto the pivot pin and make sure it seats correctly in the pivot pin groove.

3. To remove the entire footrest assembly, perform the following:

a. Remove the rear master cylinder assembly (B, **Figure 182**) as described in Chapter Fourteen.

b. Remove the rear brake pedal assembly (C, **Figure 182**) as described in Chapter Fourteen.

c. Remove the bolts and washers (D, **Figure 182**) securing the footrest assembly to the transmission case and to the frame.

d. On the left side, remove the bolt and washer (**Figure 183**) and remove the rear shock absorber damper adjuster (A, **Figure 184**).

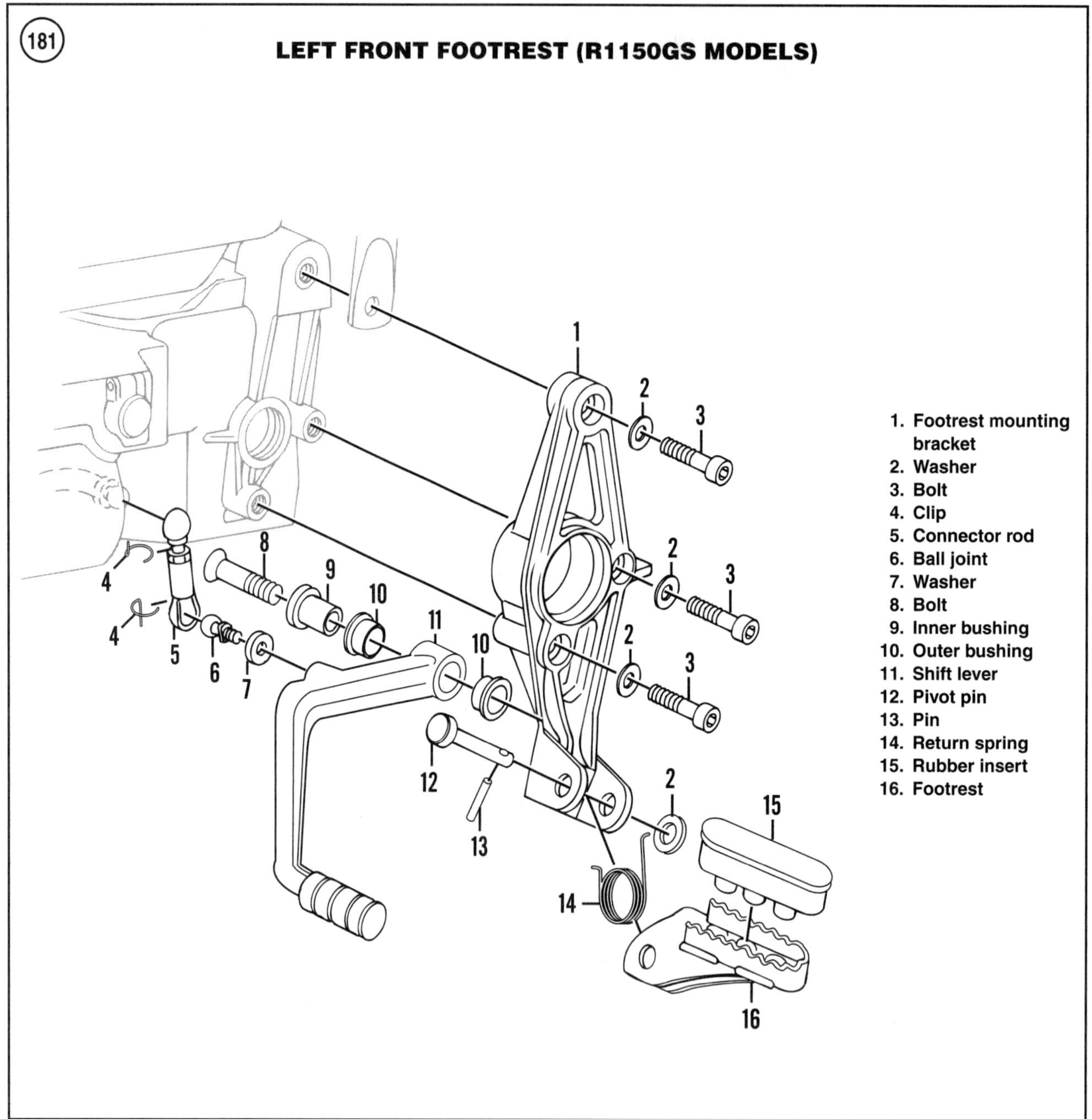

e. On the left side, if necessary, remove the gearshift lever assembly (B, **Figure 184** as described in Chapter Eight.

f. Install by reversing the removal steps.

g. Tighten the footrest-to-transmission bolt to 42 N•m (31 ft.-lb.).

h. Tighten the footrest-to-frame-to-transmission bolts to 21 N•m (15 ft.-lb.).

Rear footrest

1. Place the motorcycle on the centerstand with the rear wheel off the ground.
2. To remove the individual footrest, perform the following:
   a. Remove the E-clip (A, **Figure 185**) securing the pivot.
   b. Remove the pivot pin (B, **Figure 185**) and remove the footrest and spring (C) from the bracket.

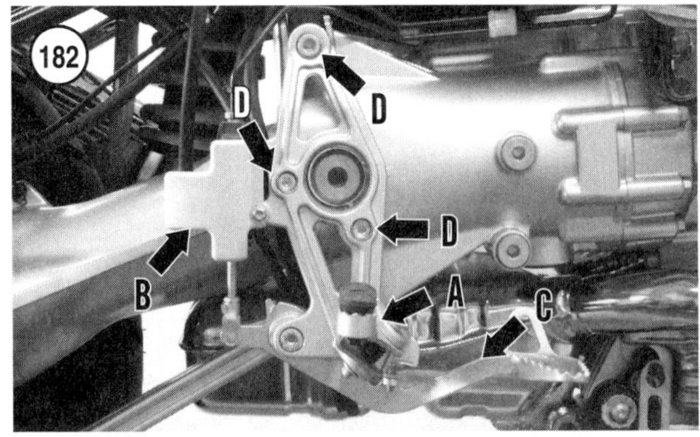

c. Make sure the springs are in good condition and not broken. Replace as necessary.

d. Lubricate the pivot point and pivot pin prior to installation. Install a new E-clip onto the pivot pin and make sure it seats correctly in the pivot pin groove.

3. To remove the entire footrest assembly, remove the bolts and washers and remove the footrest assembly from the rear frame.

4. Install by reversing the removal steps. Tighten the mounting bolts to 21 N•m (15 ft.-lb.).

FOOTREST (RT MODELS)

Removal/Installation

Refer to **Figure 186-189**.

1. Place the motorcycle on the centerstand with the front wheel off the ground.

2. To remove the individual footrest, perform the following:

a. Remove the cotter pin, and sleeve or washer, (A, **Figure 190**) securing the pivot pin.

b. Remove the pivot pin (B, **Figure 190**) and remove the footrest and spring from the bracket.

c. Make sure the spring is in good condition. Replace as necessary.

d. Lubricate the pivot point and pivot pin prior to installation. Install a new cotter pin and bend the ends completely over.

3. To remove the entire left footrest, perform the following:

a. Remove the small side cover above the footrest as described in this chapter.

b. Remove the front fairing side panel (A, **Figure 191**) as described in this chapter.

c. Remove the rear bolt and washer (**Figure 192**) securing the assembly to the rear frame assembly.

d. Remove the bolts and washers (B, **Figure 191**) securing the footrest to the transmission case.

e. Partially pull the footrest away from the engine and frame. Disconnect the gearshift lever from the backside of the assembly.

f. Disconnect the connector from the auxiliary electrical outlet mounted on the backside of the assembly.

g. Remove the left footrest assembly.

4. To remove the entire right footrest, perform the following:

a. Remove the small side cover above the footrest as described in this chapter.

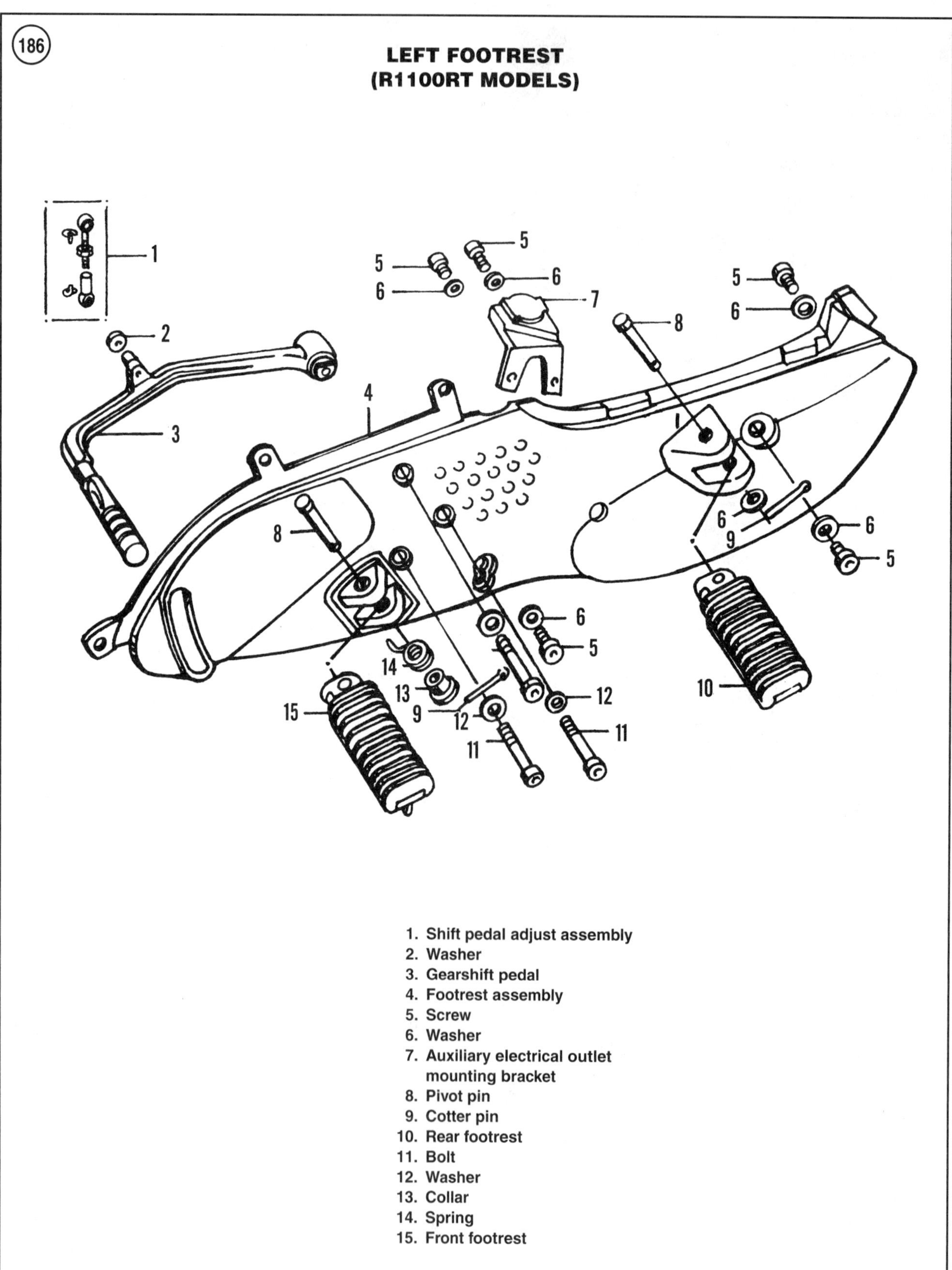
186
LEFT FOOTREST
(R1100RT MODELS)
1. Shift pedal adjust assembly
2. Washer
3. Gearshift pedal
4. Footrest assembly
5. Screw
6. Washer
7. Auxiliary electrical outlet mounting bracket
8. Pivot pin
9. Cotter pin
10. Rear footrest
11. Bolt
12. Washer
13. Collar
14. Spring
15. Front footrest

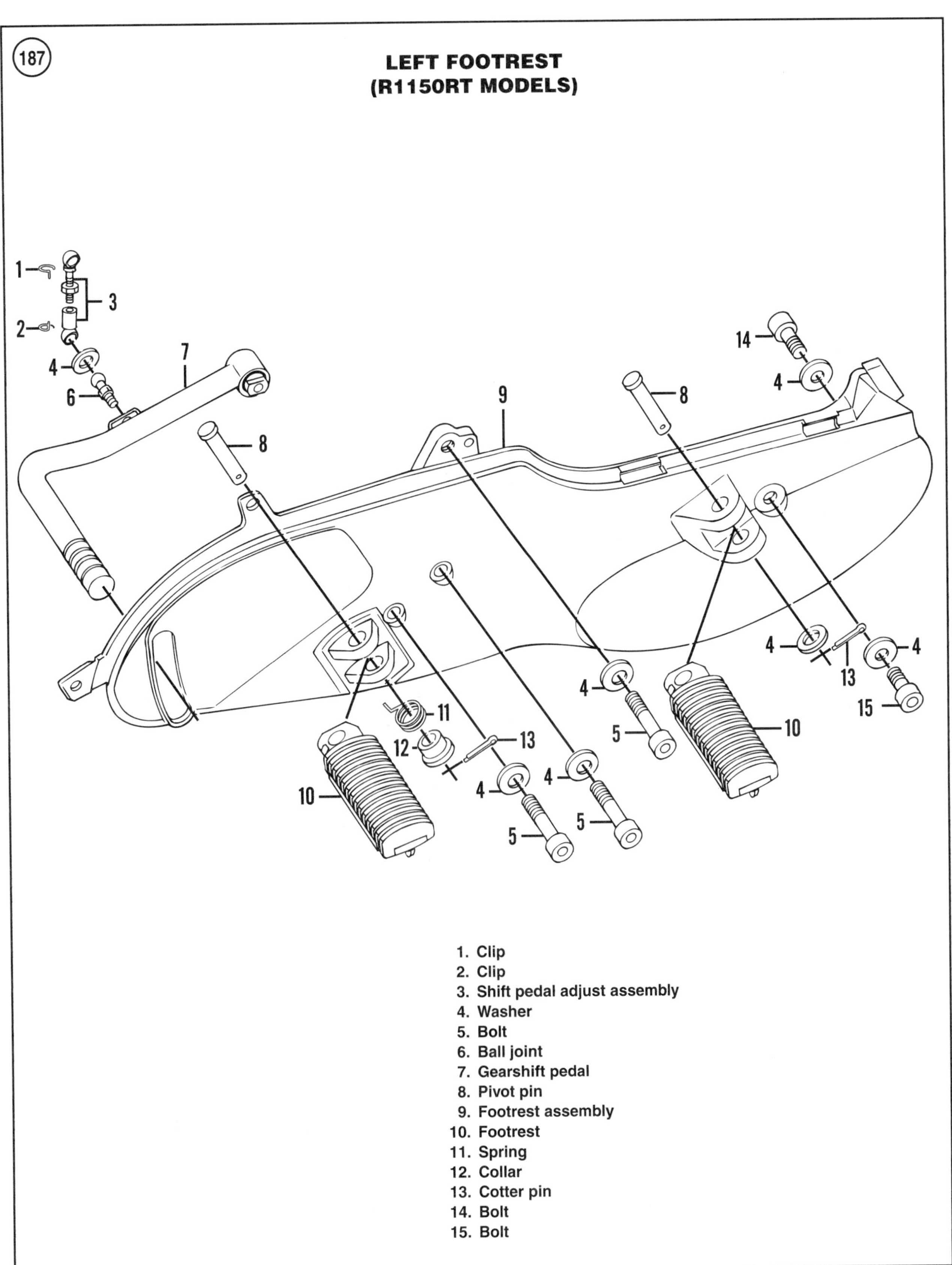

LEFT FOOTREST (R1150RT MODELS)

1. Clip
2. Clip
3. Shift pedal adjust assembly
4. Washer
5. Bolt
6. Ball joint
7. Gearshift pedal
8. Pivot pin
9. Footrest assembly
10. Footrest
11. Spring
12. Collar
13. Cotter pin
14. Bolt
15. Bolt

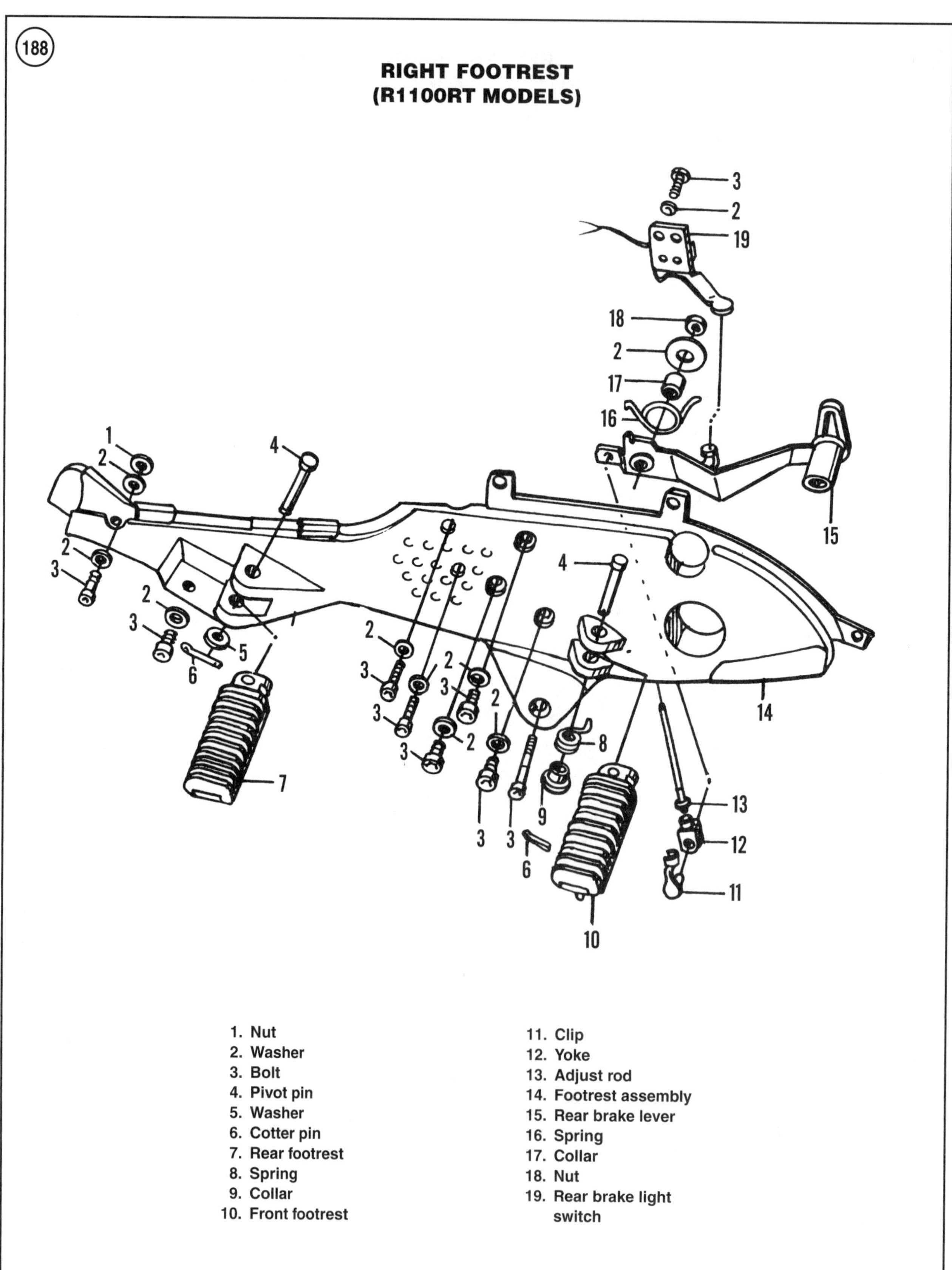

(188)

RIGHT FOOTREST (R1100RT MODELS)

1. Nut
2. Washer
3. Bolt
4. Pivot pin
5. Washer
6. Cotter pin
7. Rear footrest
8. Spring
9. Collar
10. Front footrest
11. Clip
12. Yoke
13. Adjust rod
14. Footrest assembly
15. Rear brake lever
16. Spring
17. Collar
18. Nut
19. Rear brake light switch

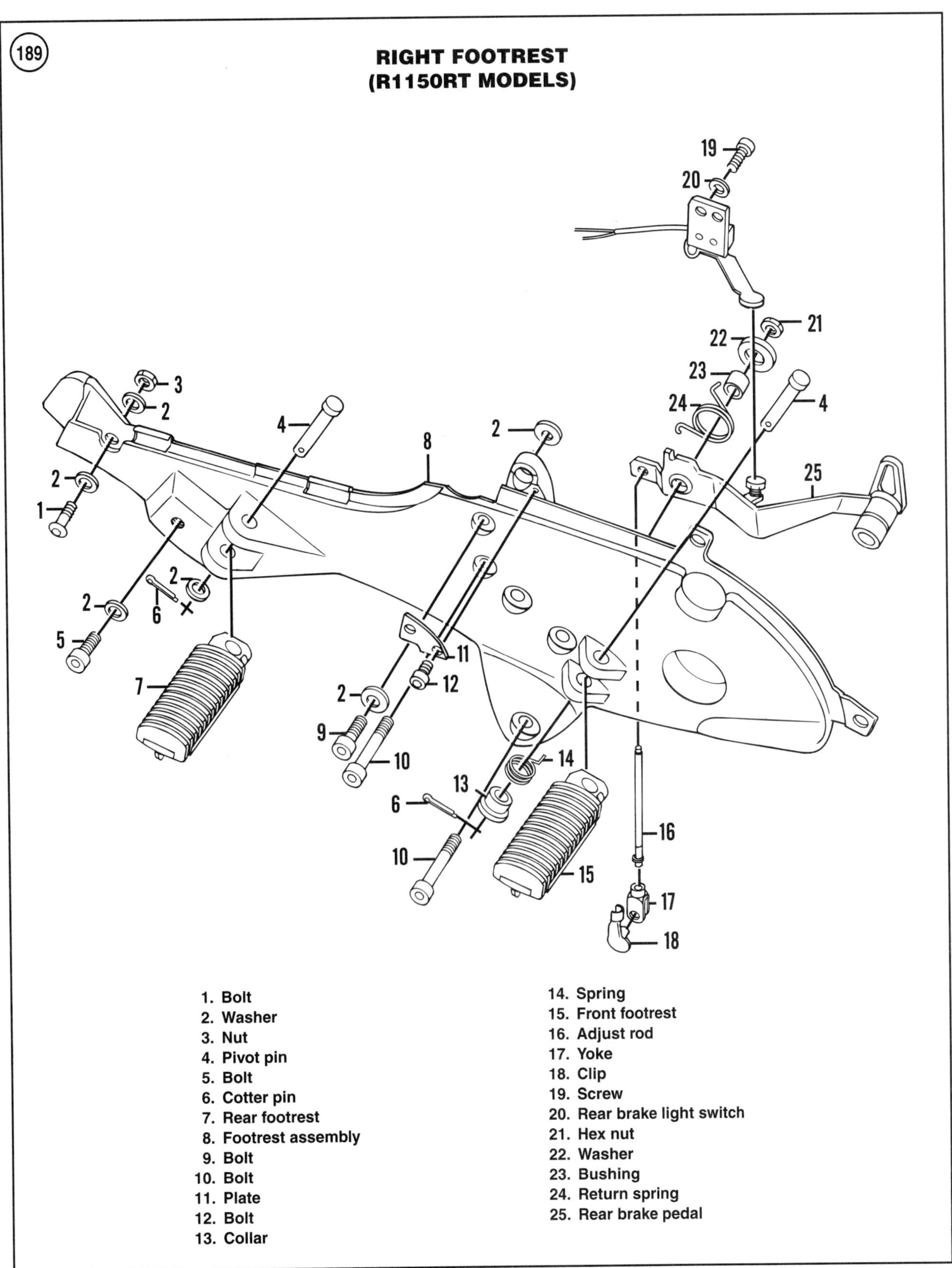

1. Bolt
2. Washer
3. Nut
4. Pivot pin
5. Bolt
6. Cotter pin
7. Rear footrest
8. Footrest assembly
9. Bolt
10. Bolt
11. Plate
12. Bolt
13. Collar
14. Spring
15. Front footrest
16. Adjust rod
17. Yoke
18. Clip
19. Screw
20. Rear brake light switch
21. Hex nut
22. Washer
23. Bushing
24. Return spring
25. Rear brake pedal

b. Remove the front fairing side panel as described in this chapter.

NOTE
*The rear bolt is not visible in **A, Figure 193** as it is hidden behind the rear footrest. Be sure to remove this bolt and washer.*

c. Remove the rear bolt and washer (A, **Figure 193**) securing the footrest to the rear frame assembly.
d. Remove the front bolts and washers (B, **Figure 193**) securing the footrest to the transmission case.
e. Partially pull the footrest away from the engine and frame. If necessary, remove the rear master cylinder assembly from the backside of the footrest assembly. Refer to Chapter Twelve for master cylinder removal and installation instructions.

5. Install by reversing the removal steps. Tighten the mounting bolts to the following:
   a. 6–mm bolts: 6 N•m (53 in.-lb.).
   b. 8–mm bolts: 21 N•m (15 ft.-lb.).
   c. 10–mm bolts: 42 N•m (31 ft.-lb.).

FOOTRESTS (R1100S MODELS)

Removal/Installation

Front footrest

1. Place the motorcycle on the centerstand with the rear wheel off the ground.
2. To remove the individual footrest, perform the following:
   a. Remove the E-clip securing the pivot pin.
   b. Remove the pivot pin and remove the footrest and spring (A, **Figure 194**) from the bracket.
   c. Make sure the spring is not stretched, cracked or broken. Replace it if necessary.
   d. Lubricate the pivot point and pivot pin prior to installation. Install a new E-clip onto the pivot pin and make sure it seats correctly in the pivot pin groove.
3. To remove the entire footrest assembly, perform the following:
   a. Remove the rear master cylinder assembly (B, **Figure 194**) as described in Chapter Fourteen.
   b. Remove the rear brake pedal assembly (C, **Figure 194**) as described in Chapter Fourteen.
   c. Remove the bolts and washers (D, **Figure 194**) securing the footrest assembly to the frame.
   d. On the left side, if necessary, remove the gearshift lever assembly (A, **Figure 195**) as described in Chapter Eight.

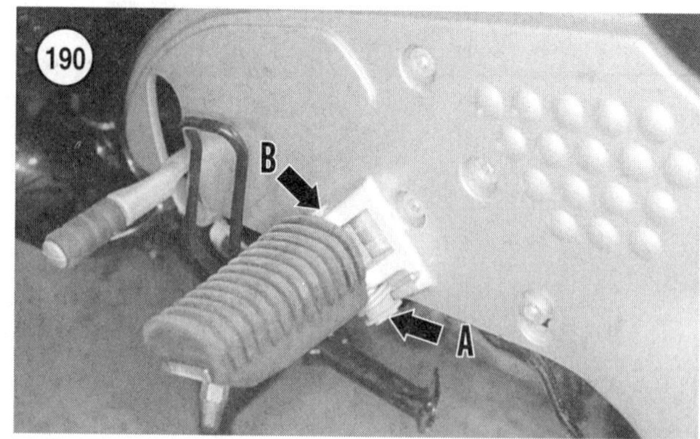

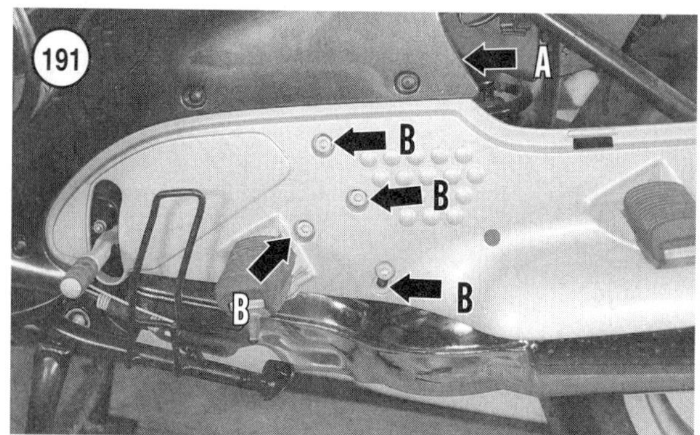

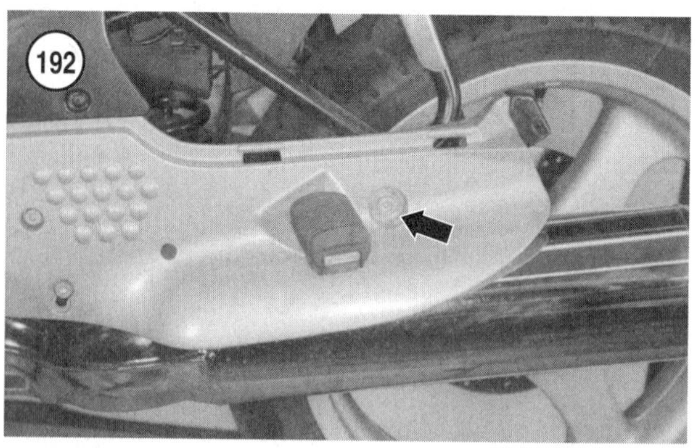

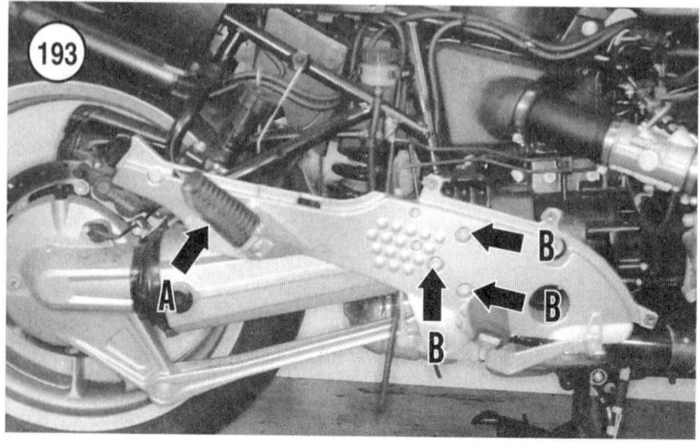

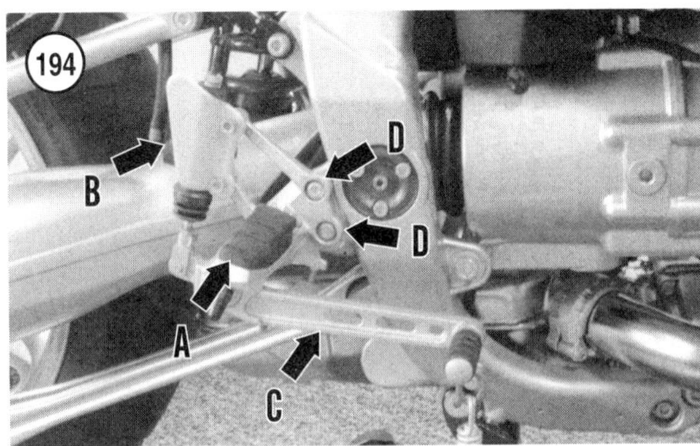

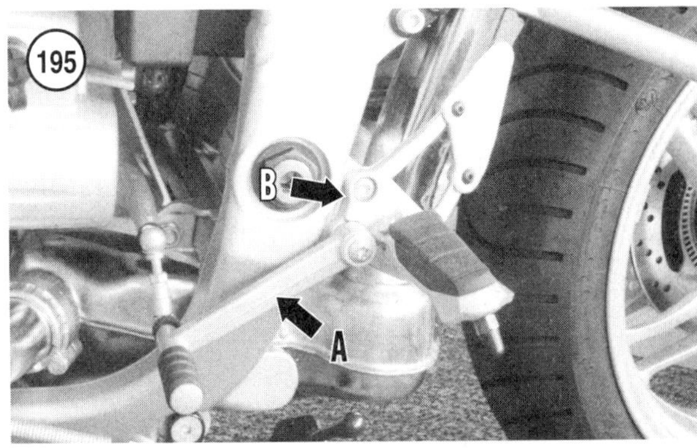

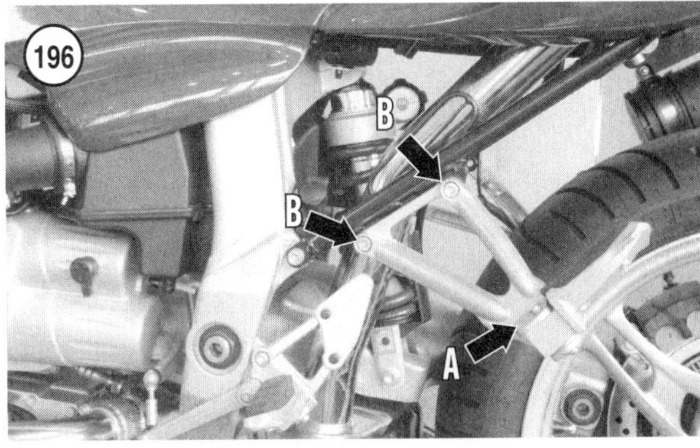

e. Remove the bolts and washers (B, **Figure 195**) securing the footrest assembly to the frame.

f. Install by reversing the removal steps.

g. Tighten the footrest-to-frame bolts to 21 N•m (15 ft.-lb.).

Rear footrest

1. Place the motorcycle on the centerstand with the rear wheel off the ground.

2. To remove the individual footrest, perform the following:

   a. Remove the E-clip securing the pivot pin.
   b. Remove the pivot pin and remove the footrest and spring (A, **Figure 196**) from the bracket.
   c. Make sure the springs are in good condition and not broken. Replace as necessary.
   d. Lubricate the pivot point and pivot pin prior to installation. Install a new E-clip onto the pivot pin and make sure it seats correctly in the pivot pin groove.

3. To remove the entire footrest assembly, remove the bolts and washers (B, **Figure 196**) and remove the footrest assembly from the rear frame.

4. Install by reversing the removal steps. Tighten the mounting bolts to 21 N•m (15 ft.-lb.).

FOOTRESTS (R850C AND R1200C MODELS)

Removal/Installation

Refer to **Figure 197**.

1. Place a suitable size jack under the engine to securely support the motorcycle.

2. Remove the exhaust system (A, **Figure 198**) as described in Chapter Nine.

3. To remove the individual footrest, perform the following:

   a. Remove the cotter pin (B, **Figure 198**) securing the pivot pin.
   b. Remove the pivot pin, washer and spring, then remove the footrest (C, **Figure 198**) from the bracket.
   c. Make sure the spring is not stretched, cracked or broken. Replace it if necessary.
   d. Lubricate the pivot point and pivot pin prior to installation. Install a new E-clip onto the pivot pin and make sure it seats correctly in the pivot pin groove.

3. To remove the entire footrest assembly, perform the following:

   a. Remove the rear master cylinder assembly (D, **Figure 198**) as described in Chapter Fourteen.
   b. Remove the rear brake pedal assembly (E, **Figure 198**) as described in Chapter Fourteen.
   c. Remove the bolts and washers securing the footrest assembly and inner bracket to the frame.
   d. On the left side, if necessary, remove the gearshift lever assembly as described in Chapter Eight.
   e. Remove the bolts and washers securing the footrest assembly to the frame.
   f. Install by reversing the removal steps.
   g. Tighten the footrest-to-frame 8 mm bolts to 21 N•m (15 ft.-lb.).

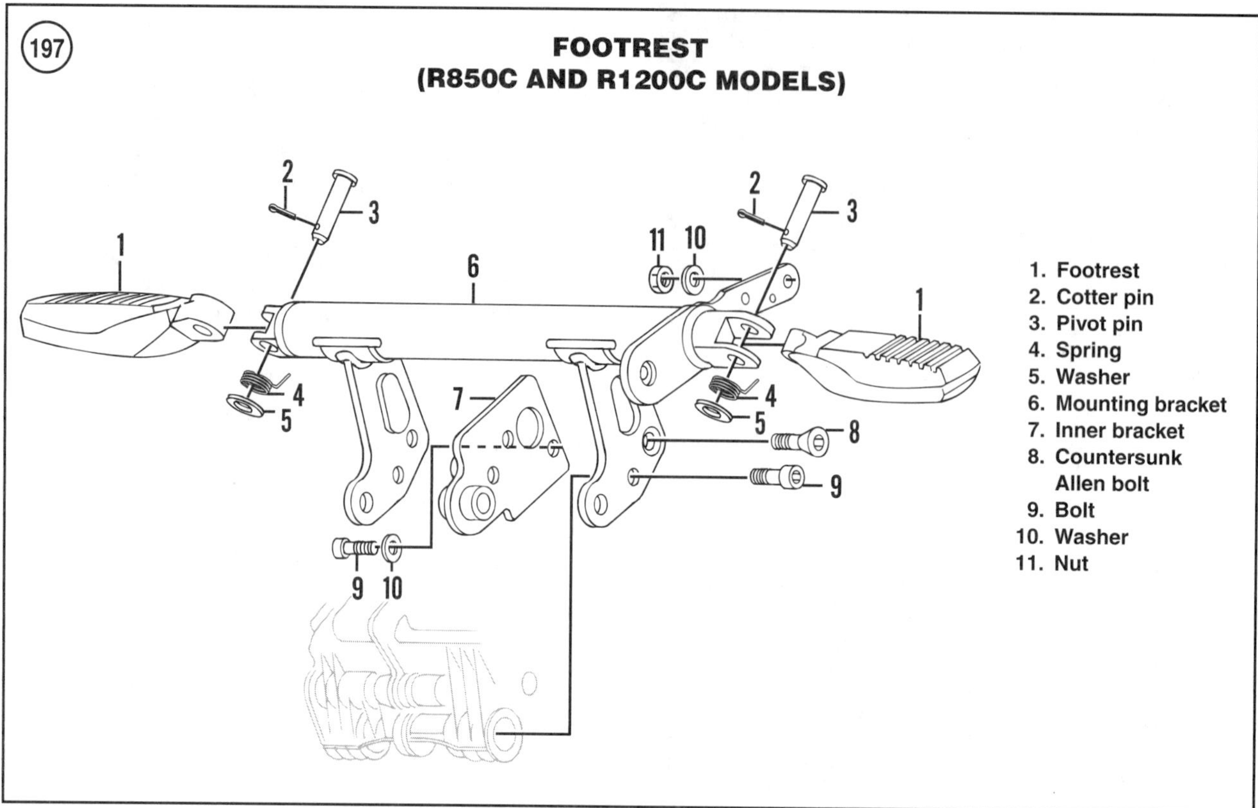

h. Tighten the footrest-to-frame 12–mm bolts to 71 N•m (52 ft.-lb.).

FRONT SAFETY BARS

Removal/Installation

Refer to **Figure 199**.

1. Place the motorcycle on the centerstand with the front wheel off the ground.

2. Remove the bolts, nuts and washers securing the front crossover bar to each side safety bar. Remove the crossover bar.

3. Remove the lower nut and washer securing the lower mounting area to the rubber mount on the crankcase.

4. Remove the upper bolt and washer securing the upper portion of the safety bar to the crankcase.

5. Remove the safety bar from the engine.

6. Repeat for the other side, if necessary.

7. Install by reversing the removal steps. Tighten the mounting bolts and nuts securely.

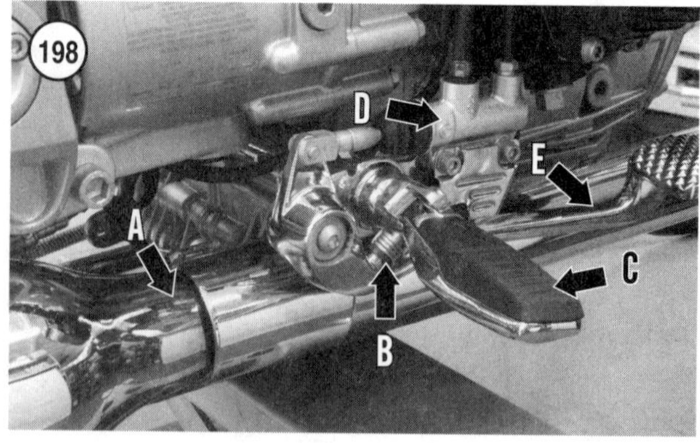

HANDLE (RT MODELS)

Removal/Installation

1. Place the motorcycle on the centerstand with the front wheel off the ground.

2. Remove the seat as described in this chapter.

3. Remove the front fairing left lower side panel as described in this chapter.

4. Remove the cotter pin and washer (A, **Figure 200**) securing the pivot pin.

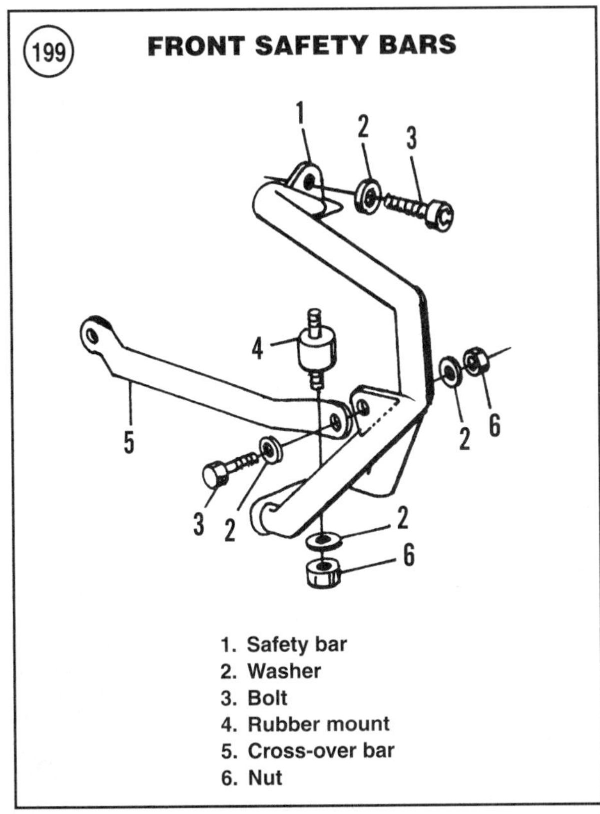

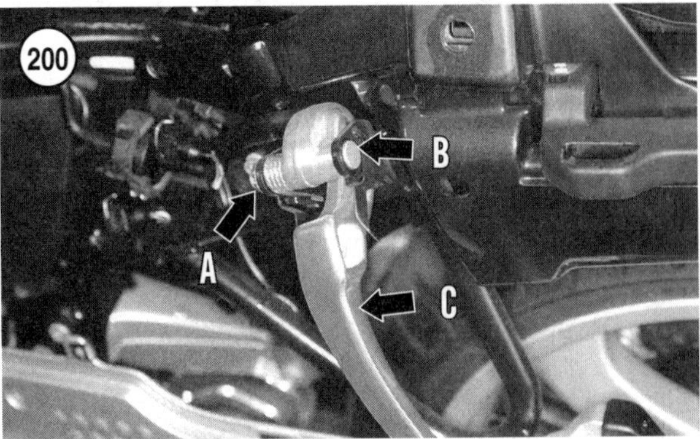

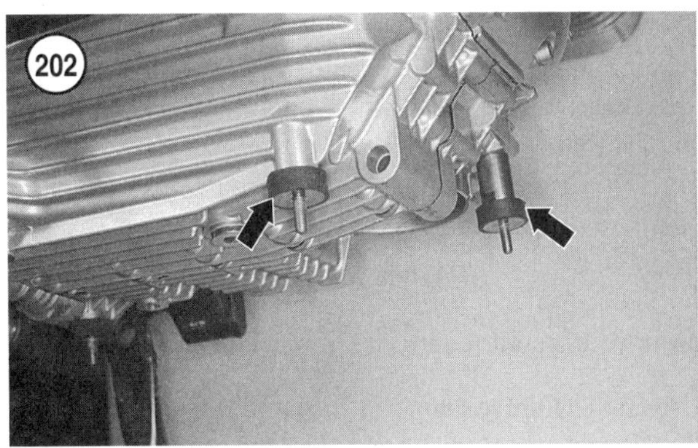

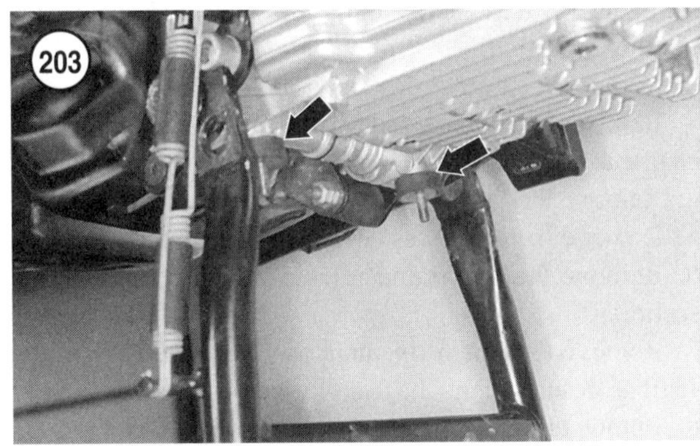

5. Remove the pivot pin (B, **Figure 200**), washer and spring, then remove the handle (C) from the bracket.

6. If necessary, remove both bolts securing the handle and bracket to the rear frame assembly. Remove the handle.

7. Lubricate the pivot point and pivot pin prior to installation. Install a new cotter pin and bend the ends over completely.

8. Install by reversing the removal steps. Tighten the bolts securely.

ENGINE GUARD

Removal/Installation

1. Place the motorcycle on the centerstand with the front wheel off the ground.

2. Remove the nuts and washers securing the engine guard (**Figure 201**) to the crankcase. Lower the engine guard assembly.

3. If necessary, remove the rubber mounts from the crankcase. Refer to **Figure 202** and **Figure 203**.

4. Install the inner plate (**Figure 204**) into the engine guard and align the mounting bolt holes.

5. Protect the starter cover with a shop cloth (**Figure 205**) and install the engine guard onto the rubber mounts on the crankcase. Install the washers and nuts and tighten securely. Remove the shop cloth.

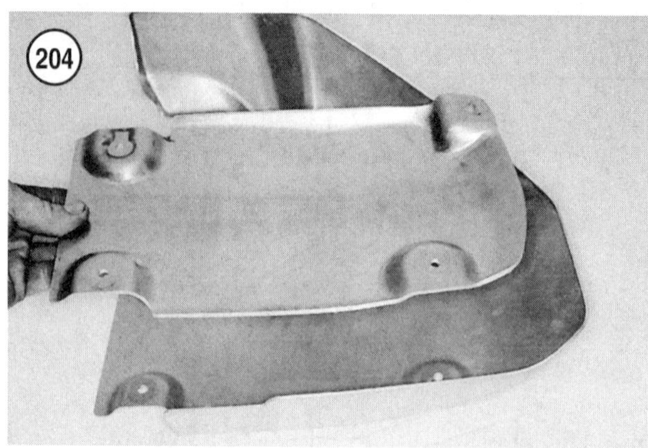

204

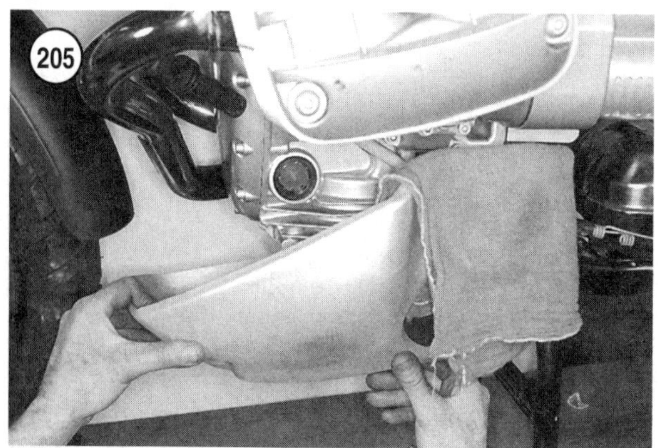

205

MAIN FRAME (R1100S MODELS)

Removal/Installation

Refer to **Figure 206**.

1. Place a suitable size jack under the engine to securely support the motorcycle. Secure the front of the motorcycle in the down as the rear of motorcycle is tail heavy during this procedure.
2. Remove the seat as described in this chapter.
3. Remove the fairing side panels as described in this chapter.
4. Remove the fuel tank as described in Chapter Nine.
5. Remove the battery as described in Chapter Ten.
6. Remove the rear frame assembly as described in this section.
7. Remove the final drive unit, the swing arm and drive shaft as described in Chapter Thirteen.
8. Remove the rear master cylinder assembly and remote reservoir as described in Chapter Fourteen.
9. On models equipped with ABS brakes, refer to Chapter Fourteen and perform the following:
   a. Remove the ABS unit or ABS pressure modulator.
   b. Remove the rear brake lines and hose assembly.
10. Disconnect the shift lever (A, **Figure 207**) from the transmission, then remove the shift lever assembly (B) as described in Chapter Eight.
11. On the left side of the main frame, perform the following:
    a. Remove the lower front Allen bolt and washer (A, **Figure 208**). There is a spacer between the main frame and the crankcase, do not lose it.
    b. Remove the lower front nut and washer (B, **Figure 208**) from the 8–mm bolt.
    c. Remove the lower rear nut and washer (**Figure 209**) from the 10–mm bolt.
12. On the right side of the main frame, perform the following:
    a. Remove the lower front Allen bolt and washer (A, **Figure 210**).
    b. Withdraw the lower front 8–mm bolt and washer (B, **Figure 210**) from the main frame and the crankcase.
    c. Remove the lower rear nut and washer (**Figure 209**) from the 10–mm bolt.
13. On the left side, perform the following:
    a. Remove the bolt and washer (A, **Figure 211**).
    b. Remove the nut and washer (B, **Figure 211**) from the upper 10–mm threaded stud.
14. Make sure all electrical wires and disconnected from the main frame.
15. On the right side, perform the following:
    a. Have an assistant secure the main frame to avoid dropping it.
    b. Remove the bolt and washer (A, **Figure 212**).
    c. Withdraw the upper 10–mm threaded stud (B, **Figure 212**) from the main frame and the crankcase.
16. Remove the main frame (**Figure 213**) from the crankcase.
17. Install by reversing the removal steps. Tighten the bolts and nuts in the following order:
    a. Front upper right 10–mm Allen bolt: initial torque 13 N•m (115 in.-lb.), final 42 N•m (31 ft.-lb.).
    b. Front upper left 10–mm Allen bolt: 42 N•m (31 ft.-lb.).
    c. Upper 10–mm threaded stud nuts: 50 N•m (37 ft.-lb.).
    d. Rear 10–mm bolt and nut: 55 N•m (41 ft.-lb.).
    e. Front lower 12–mm bolts: 80 N•m (59 ft.-lb.).

206

MAIN FRAME (R1100S MODELS)

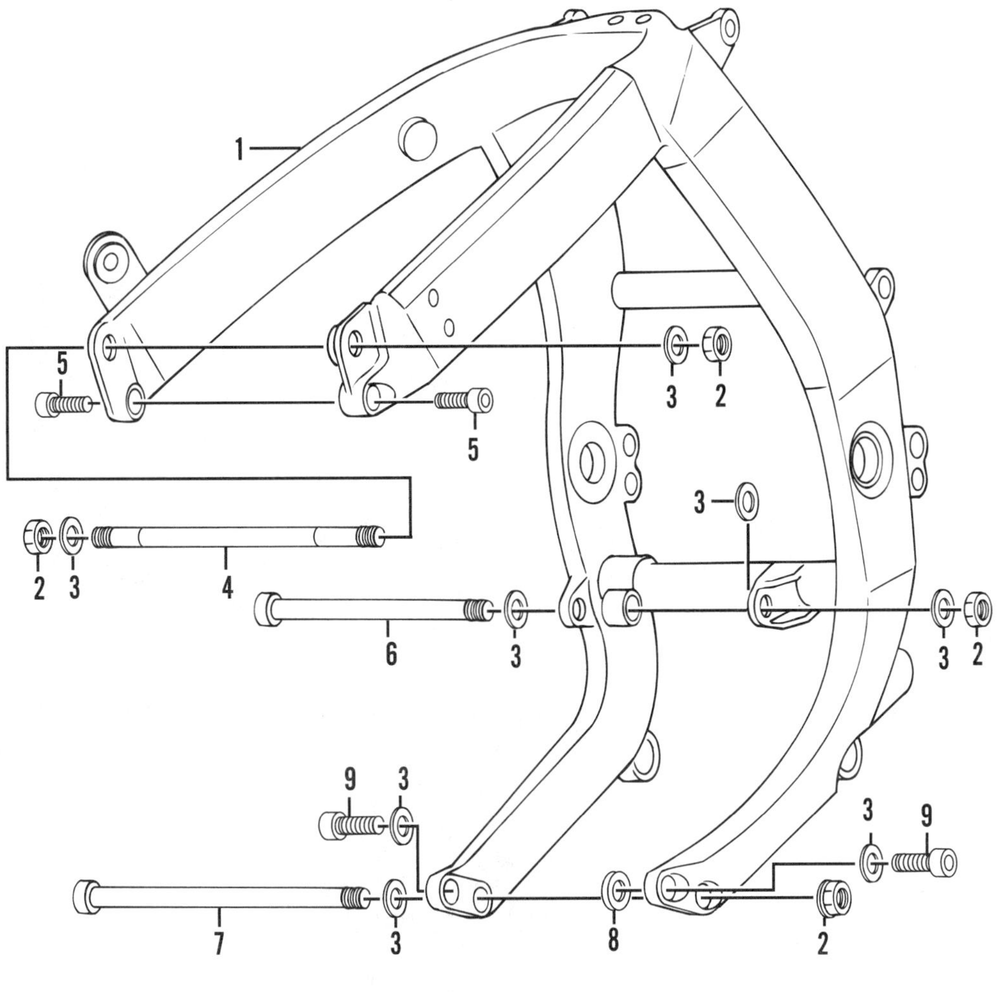

1. Main frame
2. Nut
3. Washer
4. Upper 10–mm threaded stud
5. Bolt
6. Rear 10–mm bolt
7. Lower 8–mm bolt
8. Spacer
9. Bolt

207

208

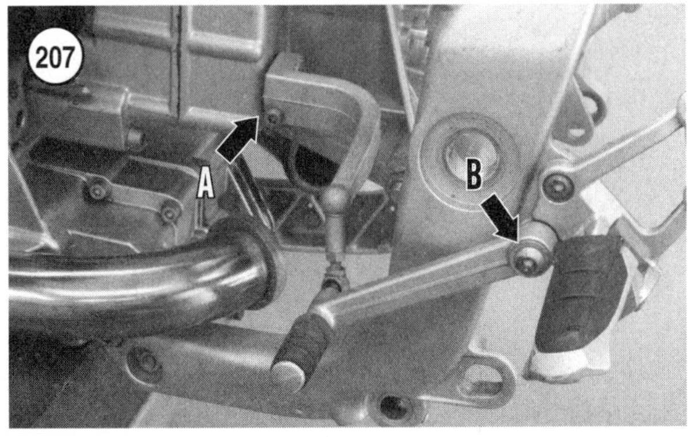

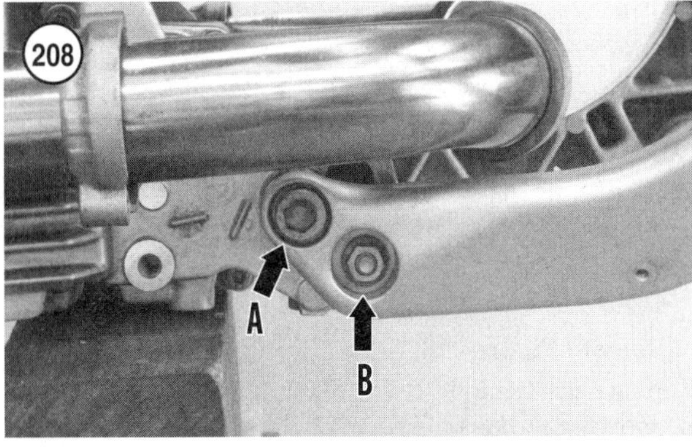

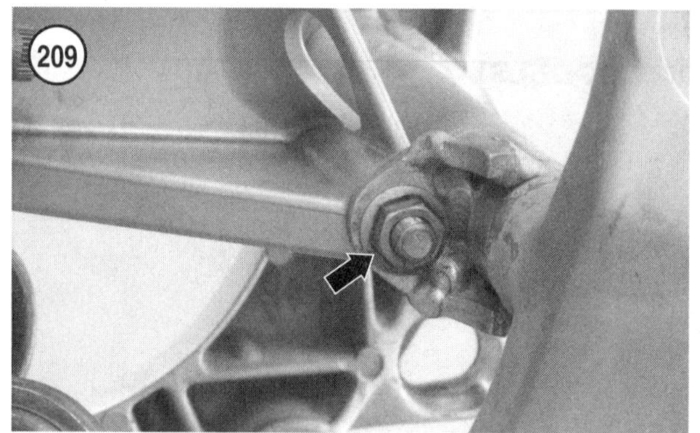

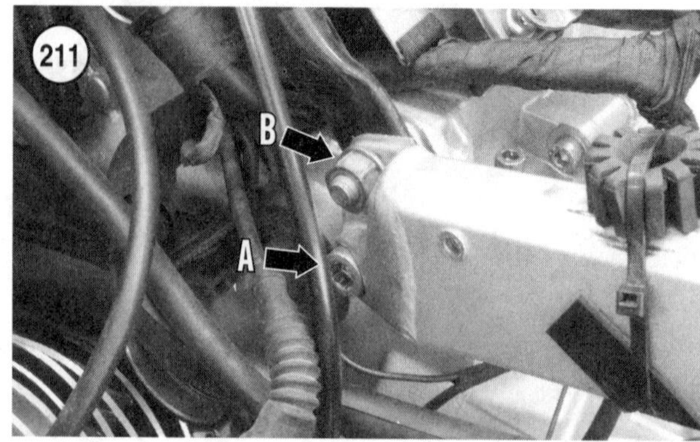

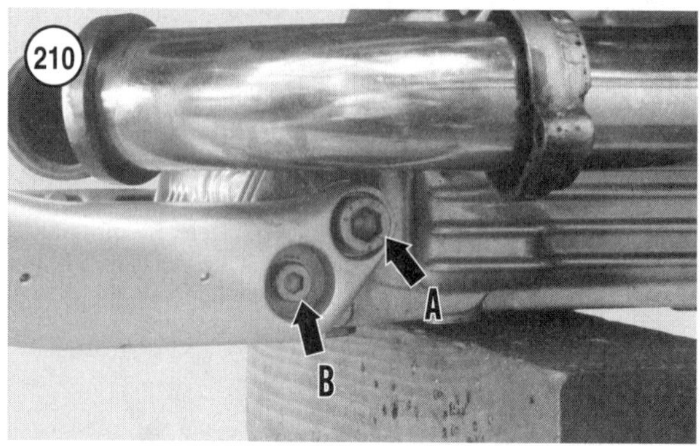

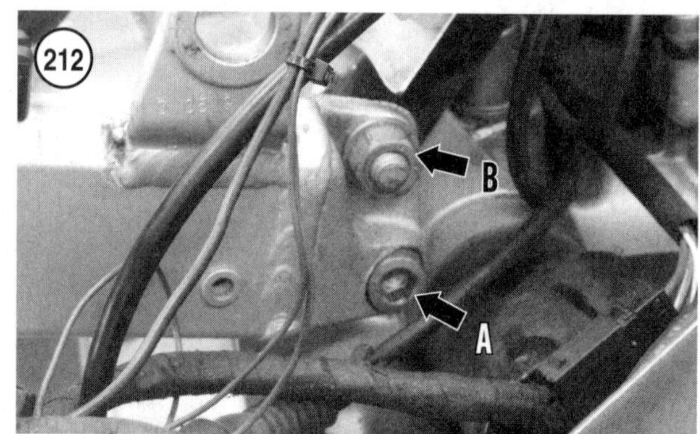

f. Front lower 8–mm bolt and nut: 24 N•m (18 ft.-lb.).
g. Rear frame-to-main frame bolts: 31 N•m (23 ft.-lb.).

Inspection

1. Check the mounting bolt holes for elongation and any cracks. Refer to **Figure 214** and **Figure 215**.
2. Inspect the threads for the swing arm adjusting pivot pin (**Figure 216**) for wear or damage.
3. Inspect the threads for the swing arm right fixed pivot pin (**Figure 217**) for wear or damage.
4. Inspect the frame cross bracing members (**Figure 218**) for wear or damage.
5. Inspect all welded areas (**Figure 219**) for breaks or damage.

FRONT FRAME (R850C AND R1200C MODELS)

Removal/Installation

Refer to **Figure 220**.
1. Place a suitable size jack under the engine to securely support the motorcycle.

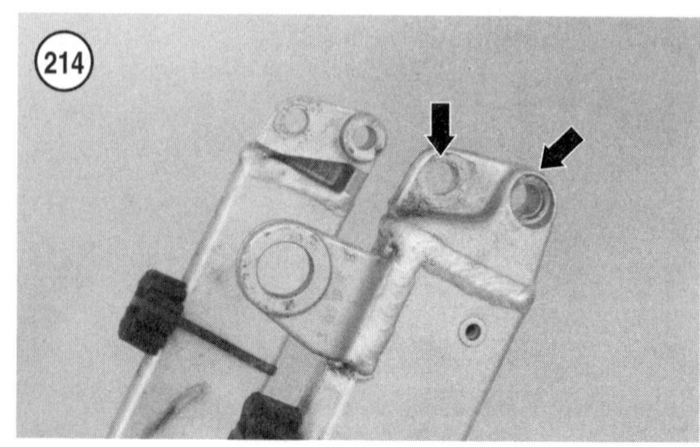

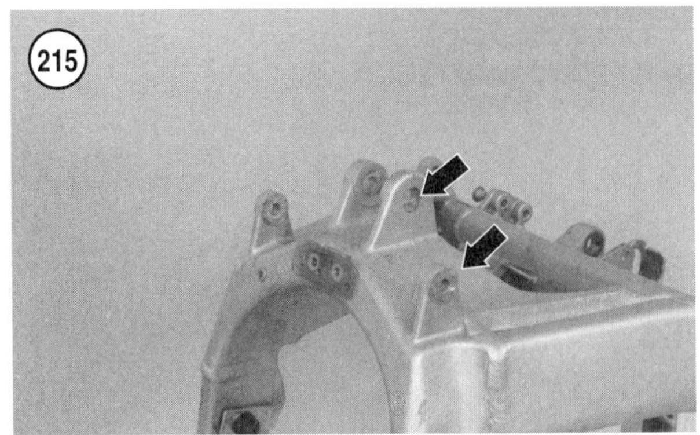

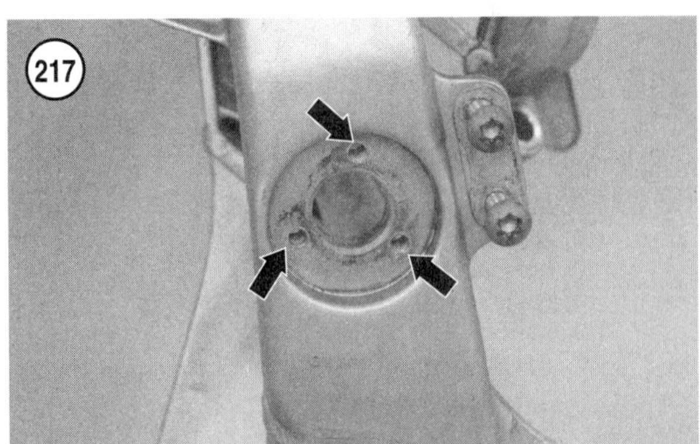

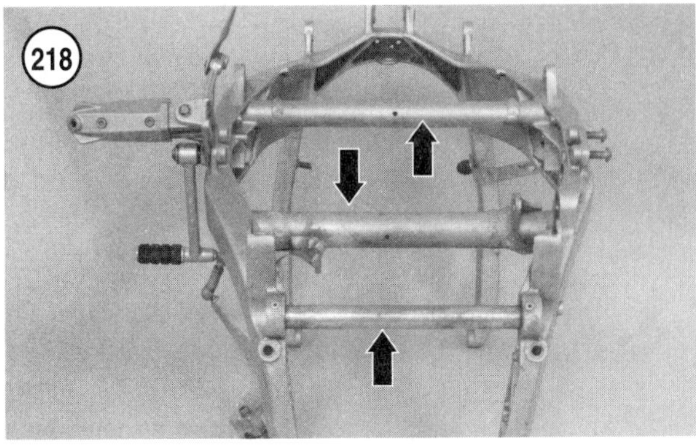

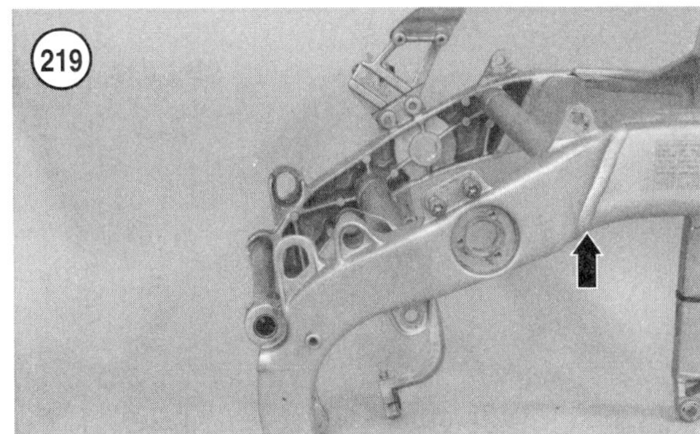

2. Remove the seat as described in this chapter.
3. Remove the fuel tank as described in Chapter Nine.
4. Remove the battery as described in Chapter Ten.
5. Remove the Motronic control unit from the top cover as described in Chapter Nine.
6. Remove the top cover (A, **Figure 221**) from the central electrical equipment box.
7. At the central electrical equipment box (**Figure 222**), disconnect the following electrical connectors:
   a. Instrument panel.
   b. Combination switch for right and left side.
   c. Front brake light switch.
   d. Clutch interlock switch.
   e. Front ABS sensor.
8. Remove the central electrical equipment box as described in Chapter Ten.
9. Remove the ignition coil (A, **Figure 222**) as described in Chapter Ten.
10. Disconnect the throttle cable from the throttle grip as described in Chapter Twelve.
11. Drain the brake fluid from the front brake system as described in Chapter Fourteen.
12. Drain the clutch hydraulic system at the slave cylinder bleed valve.
13. Separate the clutch hose from the clutch line (B, **Figure 222**) adjacent to the central electrical equipment box.
14. Disconnect the brake hoses, the lines at the upper junction block and remove the upper junction block from the main frame.
15. Remove the headlight assembly and front turn signals as described in Chapter Ten.
16. Secure the engine/transmission housing to the jack as the front portion of the motorcycle is going to be removed in the following steps.
17. Refer to Chapter Twelve and perform the following:
   a. Remove the handlebar assembly.
   b. Remove the front wheel.
   c. Remove the front fork assemblies.

220

FRONT FRAME (R850C AND R1200C MODELS)

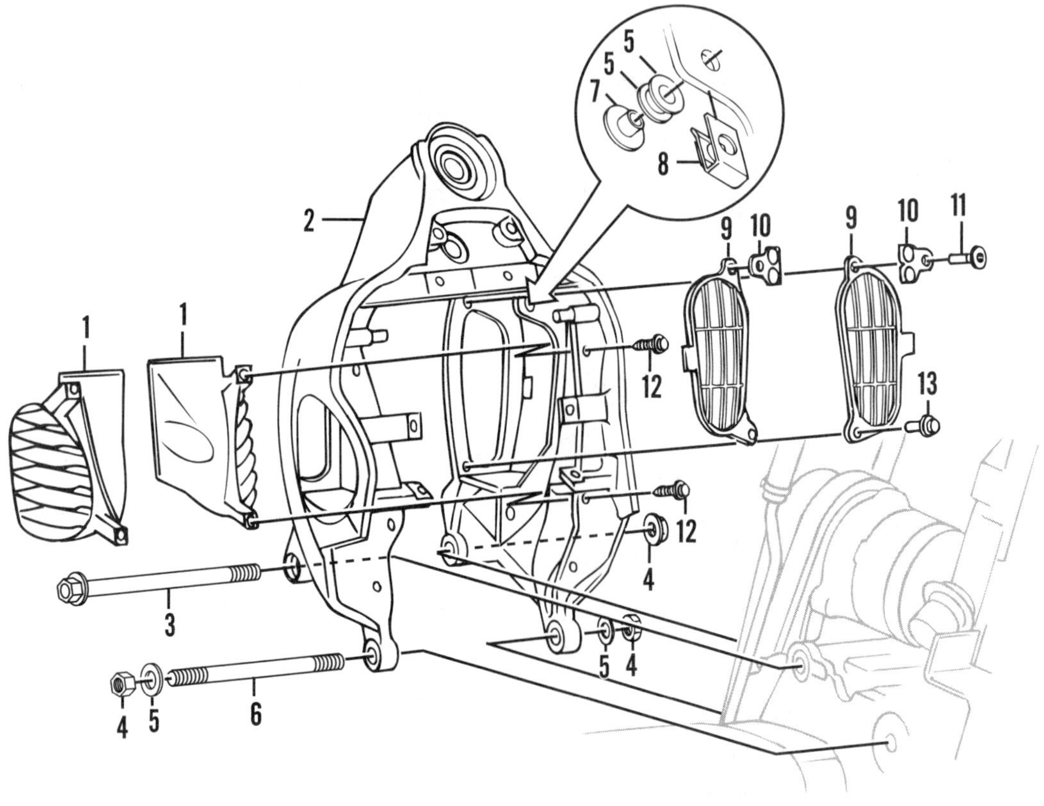

1. Oil cooler
2. Front frame
3. Through bolt
4. Nut
5. Washer
6. Threaded stud
7. Collar
8. Special nut
9. Air guide
10. Special fastener
11. Fastener
12. Screw
13. Screw

221

222

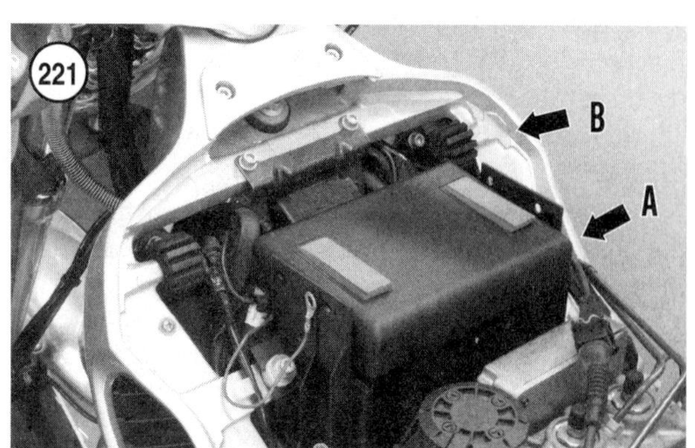

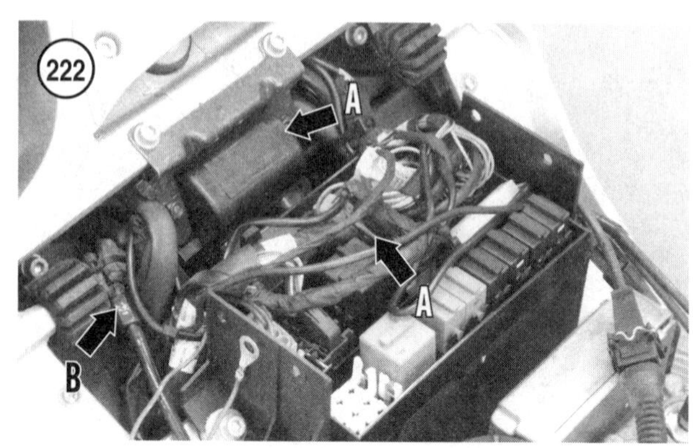

223

REAR FRAME (R1150R AND R1150GS MODELS)

1. Nut
2. Washer
3. Bolt
4. Rear frame
5. Threaded stud

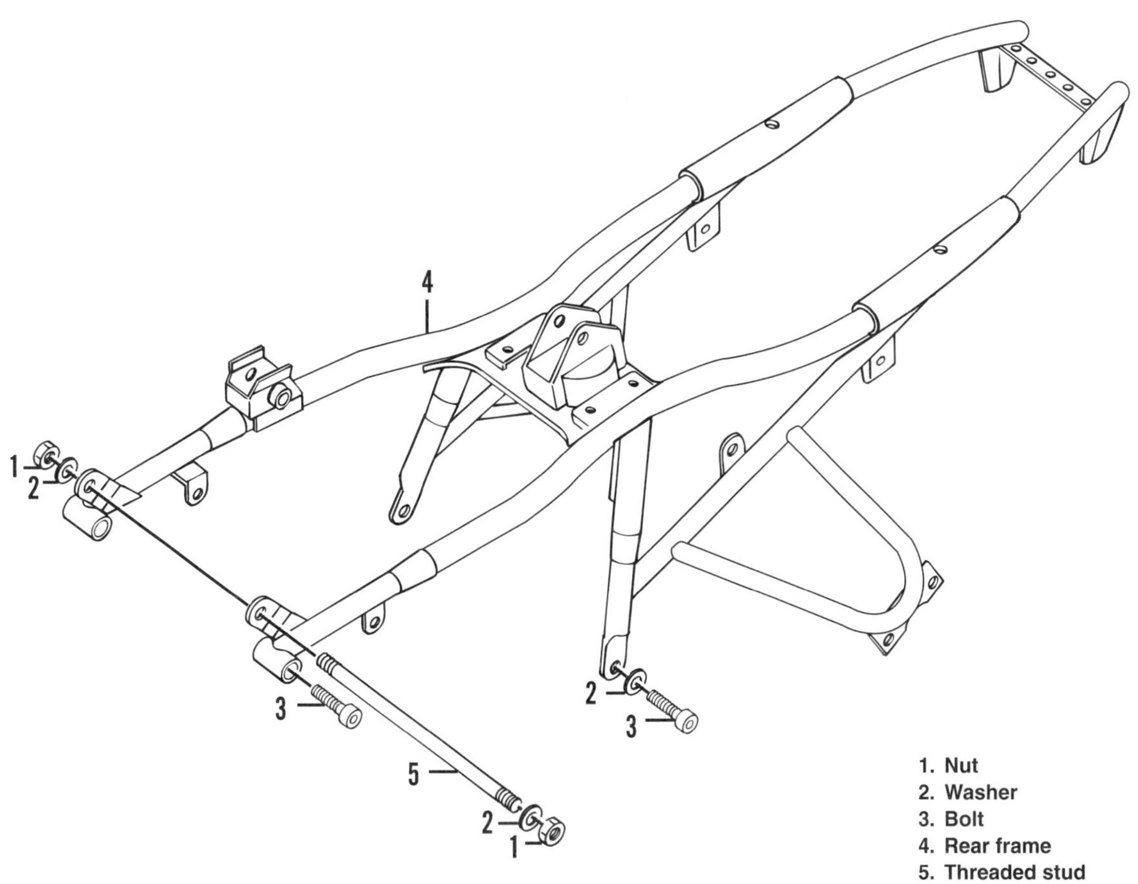

f. Upper fork bridge.

g. Remove the front suspension A-arm.

18. Remove the left air intake pipe as described in Chapter Nine.

19. Remove the horn as described in Chapter Ten.

20. Remove the screws securing the oil cooler air guides and remove both air guides.

21. Disconnect the oil hoses and remove both oil coolers from the front frame.

22. Have an assistant secure the front frame (B, **Figure 221**).

23. On the right side of the front frame, perform the following:

a. Remove the nut from front through bolt.

b. Remove the nut and washer from the rear threaded stud.

24. On the left side of the front frame, perform the following:

a. Withdraw the front through bolt from the front frame and crankcase.

b. Withdraw the rear threaded stud from the front frame and crankcase.

25. Install by reversing the removal steps. Tighten the bolts and nuts:

a. Front through bolt nut: 82 N•m (60 ft.-lb.).

b. Rear threaded stud nuts: 58 N•m (43 ft.-lb.).

REAR FRAME

Removal/Installation

R1150R and R1150GS models

Refer to **Figure 223**.

1. Place a suitable size jack under the engine to securely support the motorcycle. Secure the front of the motorcy-

cle in the down position as the rear of motorcycle is tail heavy.
2. Remove the seat as described in this chapter.
3. Disconnect the negative battery cable as described in Chapter Three.
4. Remove the fuel tank as described in Chapter Nine.
5. On models so equipped, remove the luggage rack as described in this chapter.
6. Remove the rear side panels as described in this chapter.
7. Remove the rear carrier and rear fender as described in this chapter.
8. On the left side, disconnect the electrical connector from the rear brake light switch.
9. On integral brake ABS models, disconnect the rear sensor electrical connector.
10. Remove the tie wrap and release the clutch bleeder line from the rear frame member. Move it out of the way.
11. Remove both rear footrest assemblies (A, **Figure 224**) as described in this chapter. The upper bolt and washer (B, **Figure 224**) also secure the lower rear potion (C) of the rear frame assembly.
12. Disconnect the electrical connector from each fuel injector as described in Chapter Nine.
13. Remove all tie wraps and clamps securing all electrical wiring harness from the rear frame member. It is not necessary to disconnect any connectors, just move the harnesses out of the way.
14. Remove the rear brake master cylinder remote reservoir as described in Chapter Fourteen.
15. On California models, remove the charcoal canister as described in Chapter Nine.
16. Remove the shock absorber as described in Chapter Thirteen.
17. Remove the muffler as described in Chapter Nine.
18. Remove the air filter air box as described in Chapter Nine.
19. Make sure all components, electrical wiring and hoses have been removed or released from the rear frame.

NOTE
Two assistants are required to safely remove the rear frame from the engine.

20. Have an assistant hold the rear frame on each side, then remove the following:
   a. Remove the Allen bolt from each side.
   b. Remove the nut and washer from one side of the threaded stud, then withdraw the threaded stud from the other side of the engine.
21. Slowly lift the rear frame up and off the engine and remove it.

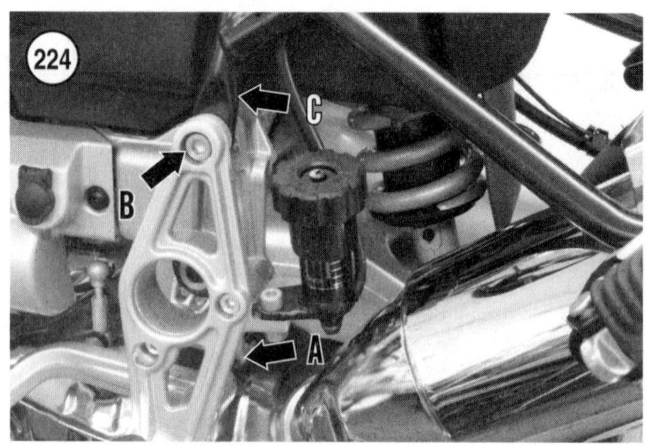

22. Install by reversing the removal steps. Tighten the bolts and nuts to the following:
   a. R1100R and R1100GS models: 47 N•m (35 ft.-lb.).
   b. R1150R and R1150GS models: 42 N•m (31 ft.-lb.).

R1100GS, R1100R, R1100RS, R1100RT, R1150RS and R1150RT models

Refer to **Figure 225**.
1. Place a suitable size jack under the engine to securely support the motorcycle. Secure the front of the motorcycle in the down position as the rear of motorcycle is tail heavy.
2. Remove the seat as described in this chapter.
3. Remove the front fairing and fairing side panels as described in this chapter.
4. Remove the tail piece and rear side panels as described in this chapter.
5. Disconnect the negative battery cable as described in Chapter Three.
6. Remove the fuel tank as described in Chapter Nine.
7. On models so equipped, remove the luggage rack as described in this chapter.
8. Remove the rear carrier and rear fender as described in this chapter.
9. Remove the bolts securing the seat adjusters and remove the seat adjusters.
10. Remove the central electrical equipment box as described in Chapter Ten.
11. On the left side, disconnect the electrical connector from the rear brake light switch.
12. On integral brake ABS models, perform the following:
   a. Disconnect the rear sensor electrical connector.
   b. Disconnect the bleed hoses and wheel circuit reservoirs as described in Chapter Fourteen.
   c. Disconnect the holder for the brake lines, then remove the rear brake lines.

(225)

REAR FRAME (R1100GS, R1100R, R1100RS, R1100RT, R1150RS AND R1150RT MODELS)

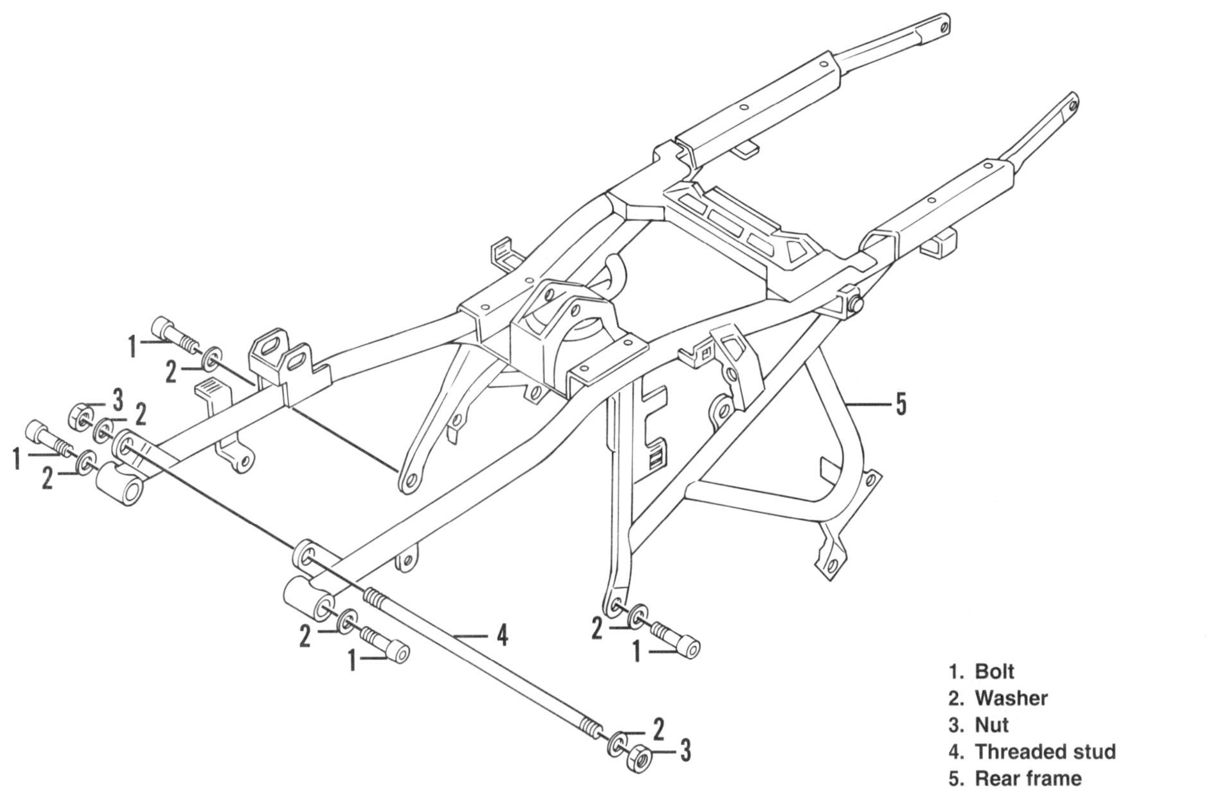

1. Bolt
2. Washer
3. Nut
4. Threaded stud
5. Rear frame

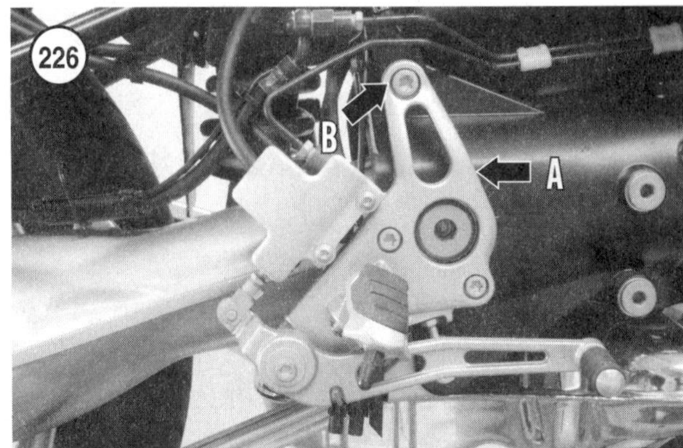

13. Remove the tie wrap and release the clutch bleeder line from the rear frame member. Move it out of the way.

14. Remove both rear footrest assemblies (A, **Figure 226**) as described in this chapter. The upper bolt and washer (B, **Figure 226**) also secure the lower rear potion of the rear frame assembly.

15. Remove the shock absorber as described in Chapter Thirteen.

16. Disconnect the electrical connector from each fuel injector as described in Chapter Nine.

17. Remove all tie wraps and clamps securing all electrical wiring harness from the rear frame member. It is not necessary to disconnect any connectors, just move the harnesses out of the way.

18. Remove the rear brake master cylinder remote reservoir as described in Chapter Fourteen.

19. On California models, remove the charcoal canister as described in Chapter Nine.

20. Remove the muffler as described in Chapter Nine.

21. Remove the air filter air box as described in Chapter Nine.

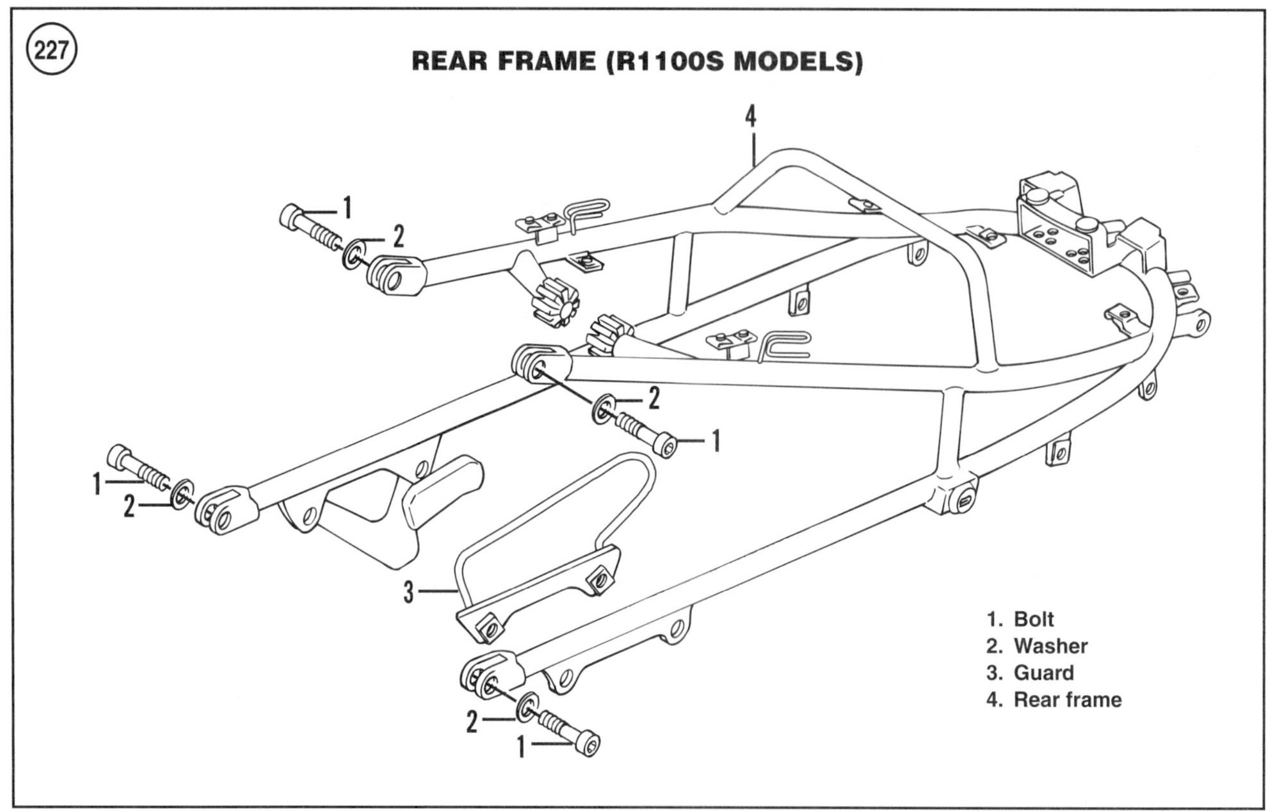

22. Make sure all components, electrical wiring and hoses have been removed or released from the rear frame.

NOTE
Two assistants are required to safely remove the rear frame from the engine.

23. Have an assistant hold the rear frame on each side, then remove the following:
   a. Remove the Allen bolt from each side.
   b. Remove the nut and washer from one side of the threaded stud, then withdraw the threaded stud from the other side of the engine.
24. Slowly lift the rear frame up and off the engine and remove it.
25. Install by reversing the removal steps. Tighten the bolts and nuts to the following:
   a. R1100GS, R1100R, R1100RS and R1100RT models: 47 N•m (35 ft.-lb.).
   b. R1150RS and R1150RT models: 42 N•m (31 ft.-lb.).

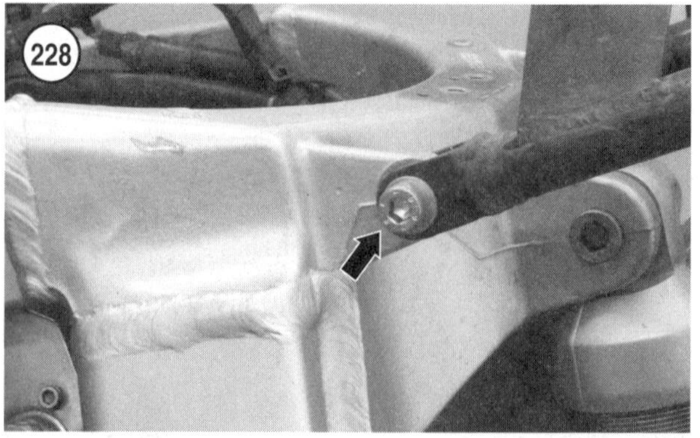

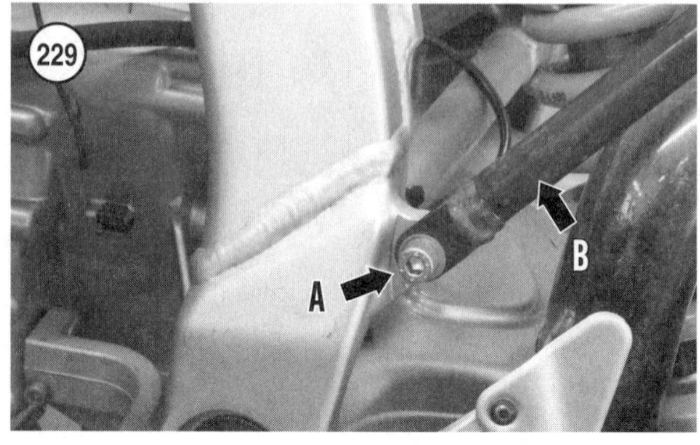

R1100GS, R1100R and R1100S models

Refer to **Figure 227**.

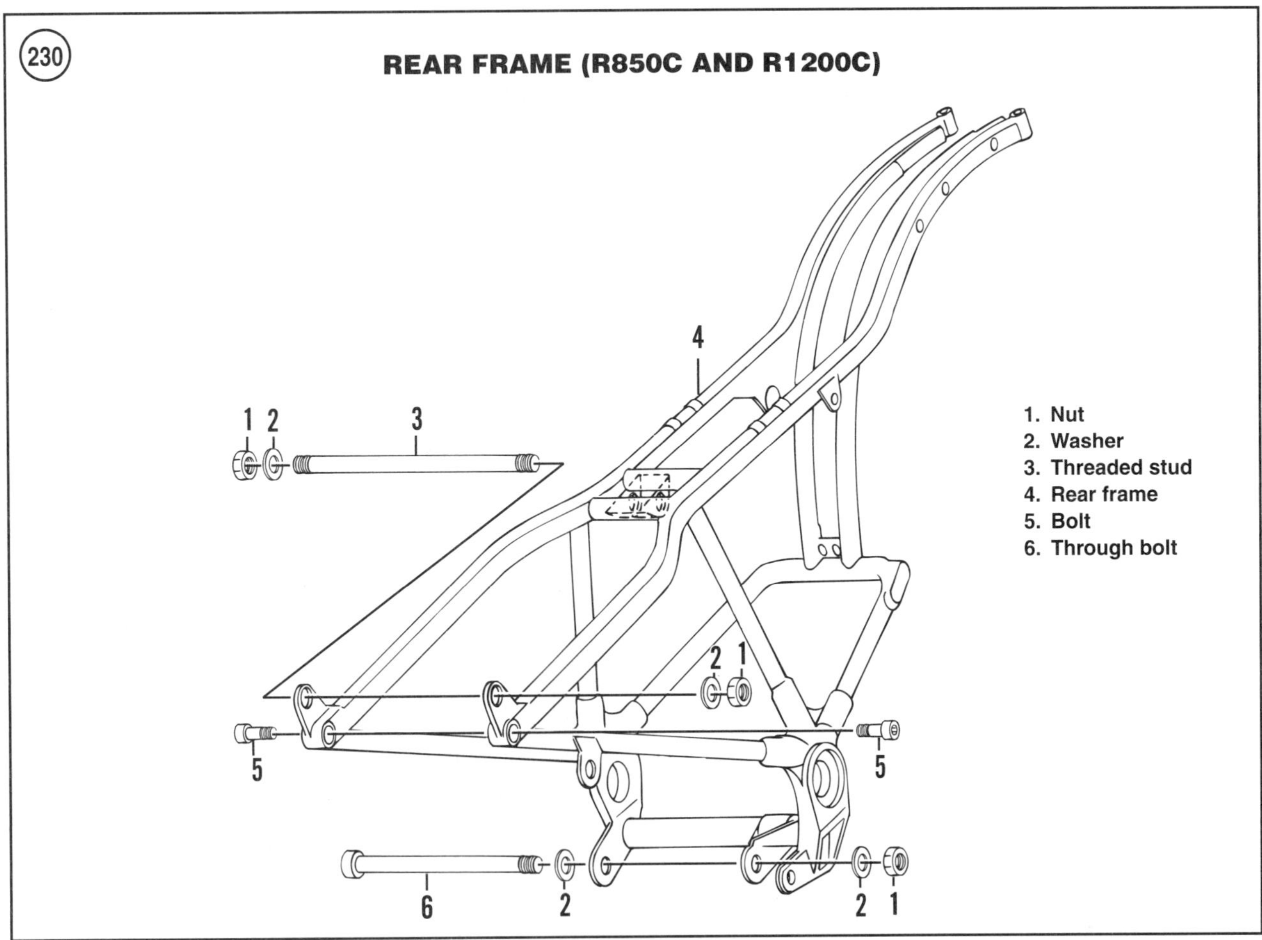

1. Place a suitable size jack under the engine to securely support the motorcycle. Secure the front of the motorcycle in the down position as the rear of motorcycle is tail heavy.
2. Remove the seat as described in this chapter.
3. Remove the fairing side panels as described in this chapter.
4. Remove the rear side panels and tail piece as described in this chapter.
5. Remove the bolts and washers securing the tail piece mounting bracket to the rear frame and remove the bracket assembly.
6. Remove the taillight/brake light assembly as described in Chapter Ten.
7. Remove the rear brake caliper as described in Chapter Fourteen.
8. Remove the rear fender assembly as described in this chapter.
9. Remove the rear wheel as described in Chapter Eleven.
10. Remove the muffler assembly as described in Chapter Nine.
11. Remove the rear master cylinder remote reservoir as described in Chapter Fourteen.
12. Remove the bolt securing the rear brake line and hose connector to the rear frame. Move it out of the way.
13. On California models, remove the charcoal canister as described in Chapter Nine.
14. Disconnect any electrical wiring harness attached to the rear frame and move it out of the way.
15. Remove the bolts and washers securing the rear frame to the main frame. Refer to **Figure 228** and A, **Figure 229**.
16. Remove the rear frame (B, **Figure 229**) from the main frame.
17. Install by reversing the removal steps. Tighten the upper and lower bolts to 31 N•m (23 ft.-lb.).

R850C and R1200C models

Refer to **Figure 230**.

1. Place a suitable size jack under the engine to support the motorcycle with the rear wheel off the ground.

2. Disconnect the negative battery cable as described in Chapter Three.
3. Remove the seat as described in Chapter Fifteen.
4. Remove the fuel tank as described in Chapter Nine.
5. Remove the rear wheel as described in Chapter Eleven.
6. Remove the muffler assembly as described in Chapter Nine.
7. Remove the final drive unit and swing arm as described in Chapter Thirteen.
8. Remove the rear brake master cylinder remote reservoir as described in Chapter Fourteen.
9. Remove the external shift mechanism as described in Chapter Seven.
10. On the left side, disconnect the throttle position electrical connector.
11. Unhook the straps and remove the tool kit from the brackets.
12. Detach both fuse boxes from the bracket and move them out of the way.
13. Disconnect the side stand switch electrical connector.
14. Disconnect the neutral switch electrical connector as the transmission case.
15. Remove the fuel injectors and air intake assembles as described in Chapter Nine.
16. Disconnect the breather hose from the air cleaner air box.
17. Remove the tie wrap and release the clutch bleeder line from the rear frame member. Move it out of the way.
18. Disconnect the rear brake light switch electrical connector.
19. On California models, remove the charcoal canister as described in Chapter Nine.
20. Remove the bolts and washers securing the air filter air box to the rear frame and remove it.
21. Remove all tie wraps and clamps securing all electrical wiring harness from the rear frame member. It is not necessary to disconnect any connectors, just move the harnesses out of the way.
22. Make sure all components, electrical wiring and hoses have been removed or released from the rear frame.

NOTE
Two assistants are required to safely remove the rear frame from the engine.

23. Have an assistant hold the rear frame on each side, then remove the following fasteners.
24. On the left side, perform the following:
   a. Remove the front Allen bolt.
   b. Remove the nut and washer from the threaded stud and the through bolt.
25. On the right side, perform the following:

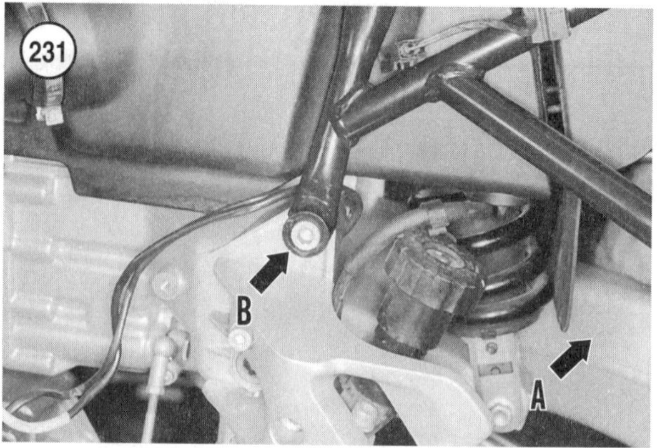

   a. Remove the front Allen bolt.
   b. Withdraw the lower through bolt.
   c. Withdraw the threaded stud.
26. Slowly lift the rear frame up and off the engine and remove it.
27. Install by reversing the removal steps. Tighten the bolts and nuts to the following:
   a. Front Allen bolts: 41 N•m (30 ft.-lb.).
   b. Through bolt and nuts: 71 N•m (52 ft.-lb.).
   c. Threaded stud and nuts: 58 N•m (43 ft.-lb.).

RAISING REAR FRAME

Some of the service procedures require raising the rear frame assembly to gain access to some components. It is not necessary to remove the rear frame assembly, just move it up out of the way.
1. Place the motorcycle on the centerstand.
2. Remove the seats as described in this chapter.
3. Remove the rear portions of the front fairing as described in this chapter.
4. Remove the fuel tank as described in Chapter Nine.
5. Remove the battery as described in Chapter Three.

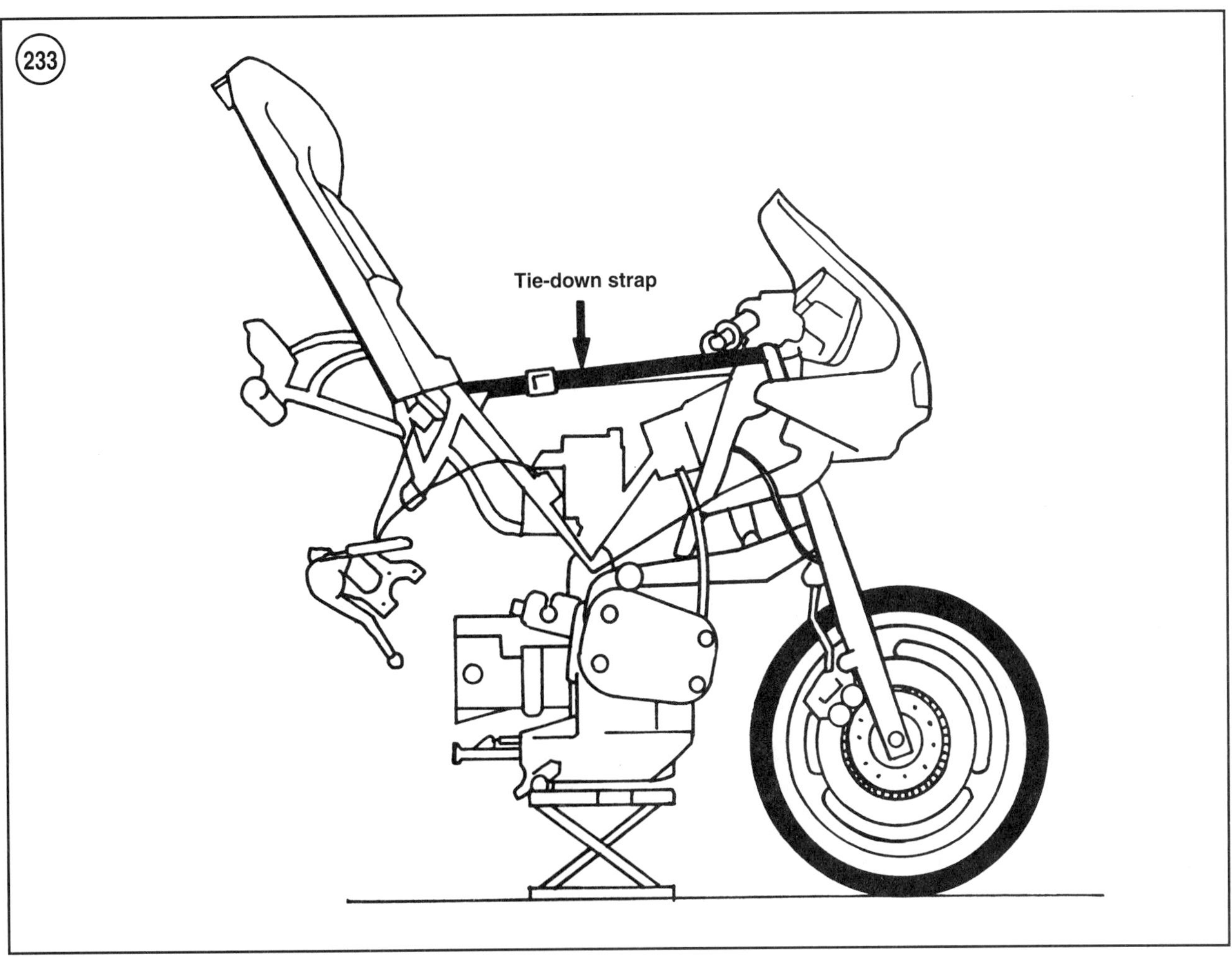

6. Remove the battery case a described in Chapter Ten.
7. Remove the exhaust system as described in Chapter Nine.
8. Remove the front footrests as described in this chapter. It is not necessary to completely remove the footrests; only move them enough to keep them out of the way.
9. Remove the swing arm (A, **Figure 231**) and drive shaft as described in Chapter Thirteen.
10. Remove the bolts securing the rear frame assembly to the crankcase; refer to **Figure 232** and B, **Figure 231**.

CAUTION
Prior to raising the frame, make sure all electrical wiring and cables are disconnected and moved out of the way.

11. Raise the rear end of the frame assembly up and secure it with tie-down straps to the front frame or handlebar assembly (**Figure 233**).
12. Lower the rear frame assembly by reversing these steps. Tighten the mounting bolts securely.

Table 1 FRAME AND BODY TORQUE SPECIFICATIONS

Item	N•m	in.-lb.	ft.-lb.
Centerstand			
Mounting bracket			
8 mm	21	–	15
12 mm	72	–	53
Pivot bushing			
RS, GS, RT models	21	–	15
Footrest assembly (RT models)			
Mounting bolts			
6 mm	6	53	–
8 mm	21	–	15
10 mm	42	–	31
Front footrest			
Peg mounting bolt (GS, R, RT models)	22	–	16
Mounting bolt (R850C, R1200C models)	21	–	15
Front frame (R850C, R1200C models)			
Front through bolt and nut	82	–	60
Rear through bolt and nut	58	–	43
Main frame (R1100S models)			
Upper right 10 mm Allen bolt			
Initial	13	115	–
Final	42	–	31
Upper left 10 mm Allen bolt	42	–	31
Upper 10 mm threaded stud nut	50	–	37
Rear 10 mm bolt and nut	55	–	41
Front lower			
12 mm bolt	80	–	59
8 mm bolt	24	–	18
Rear frame-to-main frame bolt	31	–	23
Rear footrest			
Peg mounting bolt (GS, R, RT models)	21	–	15
Mounting bolt (R850C, R1200C models)			
8 mm	21	–	15
12 mm	71	–	52
Rear frame (R850R, R1100GS, R1100R, R1100RS, R1100RT models)			
Bolt and nut	47	–	35
Rear frame (R850GS, R1150GS, R1150R R1150RS, R1150RT models)			
Bolt and nut	42	–	31
Rear frame (R1100S models)			
Upper and lower bolts	31	–	23
Rear frame (R850C, R1200C models)			
Front Allen bolt	41	–	30
Through bolt and nut	71	–	52
Threaded stud and nut	58	–	43
Sidestand (R850C, R1100S, R1150GS, R1200C models) bolt and nut	58	–	43
Sidestand (all other models)			
Mounting bracket bolt	21	–	15
Pivot bolt	42	–	31

INDEX

A

Air filter 65-67
Alternator 370-380
drive belt, adjustment 96
support cover 159-164

B

Battery 49-57
case. 442-444
charging rates/times. 99
state of charge. 99-100
Body and frame
body panels
R1100S models 690-693
RS models 672-682
RT models 682-690
body side panels (R models) 668
centerstand 701-702
engine guard. 717-718
fender and mud guard
front 653-661
rear. 661-668
footrest
R850C and
R1200C models 715-716
R1100GS, R1100R
and R1100RS models. 702-703
R1100S models 714715
R1150GS models 705-709
R1150R and
R1150RS models 703-705
RT models 709-714
Frame
front
(R850C and
R1200C models) 720-723
main (R1100S models). 718-720
rear 723-726
raising 728-729
front safety bars 716
handle (RT models) 716-717
luggage and
luggage carrier 694-698
seat 644-651
backrest
(R850C and
R1200C models) 651-653
sidestand. 698-701
torque specifications 730
windshield
cleaning. 698
GS models 668-672
Brake. 67-71
ABS brake system 608-611
ABS pressure modulator,
with integral brakes 628-629
ABS unit,
without integral brakes 626-627
bleeding the system
ABS models 636
all models without ABS 633-636
brake disc 606-608
brake hose and line replacement
ABS equipped models
with integral brakes 622-625
without integral brakes. . . 612-622
non-ABS models 598-606
brake pedal, rear 636-641
caliper
front 571-582
rear. 591-598
EVO and integral brakes 557-558

16

Brake (continued)
master cylinder
front . . . 567-571
rear and remote reservoir . . . 588-591
pad replacement
front . . . 558-567
interval . . . 558
rear . . . 582-588
service . . . 556-557
specifications . . . 642-643
torque specifications . . . 643
troubleshooting . . . 45-46
trigger sensors . . . 629-633

C

Charging system, troubleshooting . . . 44
Clutch . . . 71-72, 208-215
cable . . . 218-219
hydraulic system . . . 223-224
master cylinder . . . 219-221
release cylinder . . . 221-222
release mechanism,
cable operated models . . . 215-218
specifications . . . 224
torque specifications . . . 224
troubleshooting . . . 38-39
Connecting rods . . . 194-199
Control cable, service . . . 61-64
Crankcase . . . 174-180
breather, inspection . . . 73
Crankshaft . . . 188-194
Cylinder head . . . 104-115
cover . . . 103-104
fasteners . . . 80
Cylinder, and piston . . . 131-137
leakdown test, troubleshooting . . . 38

D

Drive shaft
auxiliary
camshaft chains and
tensioner assemblies . . . 182-188
mechanism . . . 164-168

E

Electrical system
alternator . . . 370-380
drive belt, adjustment . . . 96
support cover . . . 159-164
battery . . . 49-57
case . . . 442-444
charging rates/times . . . 99
state of charge . . . 99-100
bulbs, replacement . . . 445-446
central electrical equipment
box or modules . . . 439
charging system . . . 369-370
troubleshooting . . . 44
direct ignition coils . . . 389-390
electrical component,
replacement . . . 369
fuses . . . 440-442
fundamentals . . . 18-20
hall sensor unit . . . 381-387
headlight . . . 396-411
horn . . . 444
ignition coil, main . . . 387-389
ignition system . . . 380-381
instrument panel . . . 427-439
lighting system . . . 395-396
relays . . . 440
rider information display
1993-1998 GS, RS
and RT models . . . 426-427
spark plug
primary wires,
dual-plug models . . . 392-393
secondary wires . . . 390-392
specifications . . . 445-
starter . . . 393-395
relay . . . 395
starting system . . . 393
switches . . . 421-426
taillight/brake light
and license plate light . . . 411-415
torque specifications . . . 446
troubleshooting . . . 40-43
turn signals . . . 415-420
wiring diagrams . . . 735-799
Emission control
crankcase breather system,
U.S. models only . . . 356
evaporative emission control
system, California
models only . . . 356-359
motronic control unit . . . 316-318
motronic system . . . 304-306
specifications . . . 368
torque specifications . . . 368
Engine
break-in . . . 204-205
cylinder head . . . 104-115
cover . . . 103-104
cylinder, and piston . . . 131-137
engine compression test . . . 83-84
lower end
alternator, support cover . . . 159-164
auxiliary drive shaft
camshaft chains and
tensioner assemblies . . . 182-188
mechanism . . . 164168
connecting rods . . . 194-199
crankcase . . . 174-180
crankshaft . . . 188-194
engine break-in . . . 204-205
oil coolers and hoses . . . 199-204
oil pump . . . 168-174
rear main seal,
replacement . . . 180-182
service notes . . . 151
removal/installation
R850C and R1200C models 157-159
R1100S models . . . 155-157
R, GS, RS and RT models . . 152-155
servicing in frame . . . 151
specifications . . . 205-207
torque specifications . . . 207
troubleshooting . . . 37-38
noises, troubleshooting . . . 36-37
oil and filter . . . 57-58
performance, troubleshooting . . . 35-36
piston and piston rings . . . 137-142
service notes . . . 102-103
starting, troubleshooting . . . 30-33
top end
cylinder head . . . 104-115
cover . . . 103-104
cylinder and piston . . . 131-137
engine service notes . . . 102-103
general specifications . . . 142-143
piston and piston rings . . . 137-142
specifications . . . 143-150
torque specifications . . . 150
valve gear, holder . . . 115-124
valves, and
valve components . . . 125-131
troubleshooting
lubrication . . . 37-38
noises . . . 36-37
performance . . . 35-36
Evaporative emission control
system . . . 73
Exhaust system . . . 73, 359-367

F

Fastener
cylinder head . . . 80
inspection . . . 79
Final drive . . . 60-61
Monolever models . . . 539-541
overhaul (all models) . . . 541-551
Paralever models . . . 529-533
troubleshooting . . . 39
Front suspension and steering
fork bridge
lower . . . 486-489
upper . . . 479-486

front fork
overhaul 495-500
R850C and R1200C 493-495
R1100S 492-493
front strut 501-503
adjustments 500-501
front suspension
A-arm 504-510
specifications 512
torque specifications 512-513
handlebar 468-472
controls 472-479
lever clearance,
adjustment, R1100S
and all R1150 models 479
inspection 74-77
steering damper,
R1100R models 510-511
troubleshooting 44-45
Fuel
air filter assembly 320-324
fuel filter, replacement 72, 346-352
fuel hose, inspection 73
fuel injection system
components 306-307
fuel injectors 309-313
precautions 308-308
fuel level sending unit 355-356
fuel pump 352-355
pressure test 355
fuel system, depressurizing 307
fuel tank 332-346
increase idle (choke) cable
replacement, (all models except
R850C and R1200C) 330-332
motronic control unit 316-318
motronic system 304-306
pressure regulator 314-316
rollover valve
(all R1150 models) 346
specifications 368
throttle
body 313-314
cables 324-330
position sensor 318-320
torque specifications 368
type 47-48

G

General information
basic service methods 20-25
conversion formulas 27
electrical fundamentals 18-20
fasteners 4-6
manual organization 1-2
metric tap and drill size 28
metric, inch and
fractional equivalents 29
safety 2
serial numbers 3-4
shop supplies 6-8
storage 25-26
technical abbreviations 28
tools
basic 8-13
precision measuring 13-18
torque specifications 26
warnings, cautions, and notes 2

H

Handlebar 74, 468-472
controls 472-479
handlebar grips

I

Ignition system 380-381
coil, main 387-389
ignition timing 83
troubleshooting 44
Inspection
crankcase breather 73
fastener 79
frame, rear 78
fuel hose 73
spark plug 89-91
suspension
front 74-77
Rear 77-78

L

Lighting system, troubleshooting 44
Lubrication
control cable, service 61-64
engine
oil and filter 57-58
evaporative emission control
system 73
final drive 60-61
lubricants, recommended
and capacities 99-100
maintenance schedule 97-98
specifications 100-100
torque specifications 101
transmission 59-60

M

Maintenance
air filter 65-67
alternator drive belt, adjustment 96
battery 49-57
charging rates/times 99
state of charge 99-100
brake
brake system 67-71
rear brake pedal, pivot shaft
bolt and bushing lubrication 64
clutch 71-72
control cable, service 61-64
crankcase breather inspection 73
cylinder head, fasteners 80
exhaust system 73
fastener, inspection 79
final drive 60-61
front suspension, inspection 74-77
fuel
filter, replacement 72
hose, inspection 73
type 47-48
handlebars 74
grips 74
lubricants, recommended
and capacities 99-100
maintenance schedule 97-98
pre-ride check list 48
rear frame, inspection 78
rear suspension, inspection 77-78
sidestand, lubrication 64
shift lever,
cleaning and lubrication 64
spark plug
dual-plug ignition system 86-89
inspection 89-91
single plug ignition systems . . . 84-86
specifications 100-100
throttle and choke cable, adjustment
1993-1995 R850C and
R1200C models 94
all models except R850C
and 1200C models 91-94
throttle body synchronization
and idle speed, adjustment 94-96
tire
and wheels 48-49
inflation, pressure 98
torque specifications 101
transmission 59-60
tune-up, procedures 79
valve clearance 80-82
windshield adjust shaft,
RS models 65

O

Oil
- coolers and hoses 199-204
- pump.................... 168-174

P

Piston, and piston rings 1374-142

R

Rear suspension
- final drive unit
  - Monolever models........ 539-541
  - overhaul (all models)...... 541-551
  - Paralever models 529-533
- pinion gear-to-ring gear adjustment (all models) 551-554
- shock absorber 515-520
- swing arm and drive shaft
  - Monolever models........ 533-539
  - Paralever models 520-528
- tapered roller bearing preload..................... 554
- torque specifications 555

S

Sidestand, lubrication............. 64
Spark plug
- dual-plug ignition system...... 86-89
- inspection.................. 89-91
- single plug ignition systems 84-86

Starting system
- troubleshooting 44
  - Starting difficulties 33-35

Suspension
- front and steering
  - fork bridge
  - lower 486-489
  - upper 479-486
  - front fork
    - overhaul............... 495-500
    - R850C and R1200C...... 493-495
    - R1100S 492-493
  - front strut............... 501-503
  - adjustments 500-501
  - front suspension
    - A-arm 504-510
    - specifications 512
    - torque specifications 512-513
  - handlebar 468-472
    - controls 472-479
  - lever clearance, adjustment, R1100S and all R1150 models 479
  - steering damper, R1100R models 510-511
- rear and final drive
  - final drive unit
    - Monolever models....... 539-541
    - overhaul (all models)..... 541-551
    - Paralever models 529-533
  - pinion gear-to-ring gear adjustment (all models) ... 551-554
  - shock absorber........... 515-520
  - swing arm and drive shaft
    - Monolever models....... 533-539
    - Paralever models 520-528
  - tapered roller bearing preload 554
  - torque specifications 555

T

Throttle and choke cable
- adjustment
  - 1993-1995 R850C and R1200C models.............. 94
  - all models except R850C and 1200C models ... 91-94
- body synchronization and idle speed, adjustment 94-96

Tires
- and wheels 48-49
- inflation, pressure 98

Tools
- basic....................... 8-13
- precision measuring 13-18

Torque specification
- body and frame 730
- clutch....................... 224
- electrical system 446
- engine
  - lower end.................. 207
  - top end 150
- front suspension 512-513
- fuel and exhaust system 368
- general...................... 26
- lubrication, maintenance and tune-up 101
- transmission
  - five speed 260
  - six speed 302
- wheel....................... 467

Transmission................ 59-60
- five speed
  - gearshift mechanism 254-258
  - housing cover........... 230-233
  - neutral switch and gear position switch.......... 229-230
  - specifications 259
  - transmission case......... 225-229
  - torque specifications 260
  - transmission cover and housing bearings and seals 258-259
  - transmission shafts........ 239-254
  - transmission shafts and gearshift mechanism 233-239
- six speed
  - gearshift mechanism 291-298
  - neutral/gear position switch 266
  - torque specifications 302
  - transmission case......... 261-266
  - transmission cover and housing oil seals......... 298-302
  - transmission housing 266-269
    - cover 274-275
  - transmission shafts........ 275-291
    - gearshift mechanism 269-274
  - specifications 302
- troubleshooting 39

Troubleshooting
- brake system................ 45-46
- charging system................ 44
- clutch 38-39
- cylinder leakdown test........... 38
- electrical, testing 40-43
- engine
  - lubrication 37-38
  - noises.................... 36-37
  - performance............... 35-36
- final drive 39
- front suspension and steering ... 44-45
- ignition system................. 44
- lighting system................. 44
- operating requirements 30
- starting system................. 44
  - starting difficulties.......... 33-35
  - starting the engine 30-33
- transmission................... 39

Tune-up
- air filter.................... 65-67
- cylinder head, fasteners 80
- engine
  - compression test 83-84
- fuel
  - filter, replacement 72
  - hose, inspection............... 73
  - type 47-48
- ignition timing................. 83
- spark plug
  - dual-plug ignition system 86-89
  - inspection................. 89-91
  - single plug ignition systems ... 84-86
- specifications 100-100

Tune-up (continued)
throttle body synchronization
and idle speed, adjustment. 94-96
torque specifications 101
tune-up, procedures 79
valve clearance 80-82

V

Valve
clearance. 80-82
components. 125-131
gear, holder. 115-124

W

Wheels, hubs and tires
front hub. 456-462
tire
changing 464-467
repairs 467
wheel
front 447-452
rear. 453-456
service specifications 467
spoke service 464
runout and balance 462-464
torque specifications 467
Windshield adjust shaft, RS models . . 65
Wiring diagrams 736-799

1998 R1200C (U.K.), 1999-2004 R1200C (U.S) 2000-2001 R850C (U.K.) ENGINE

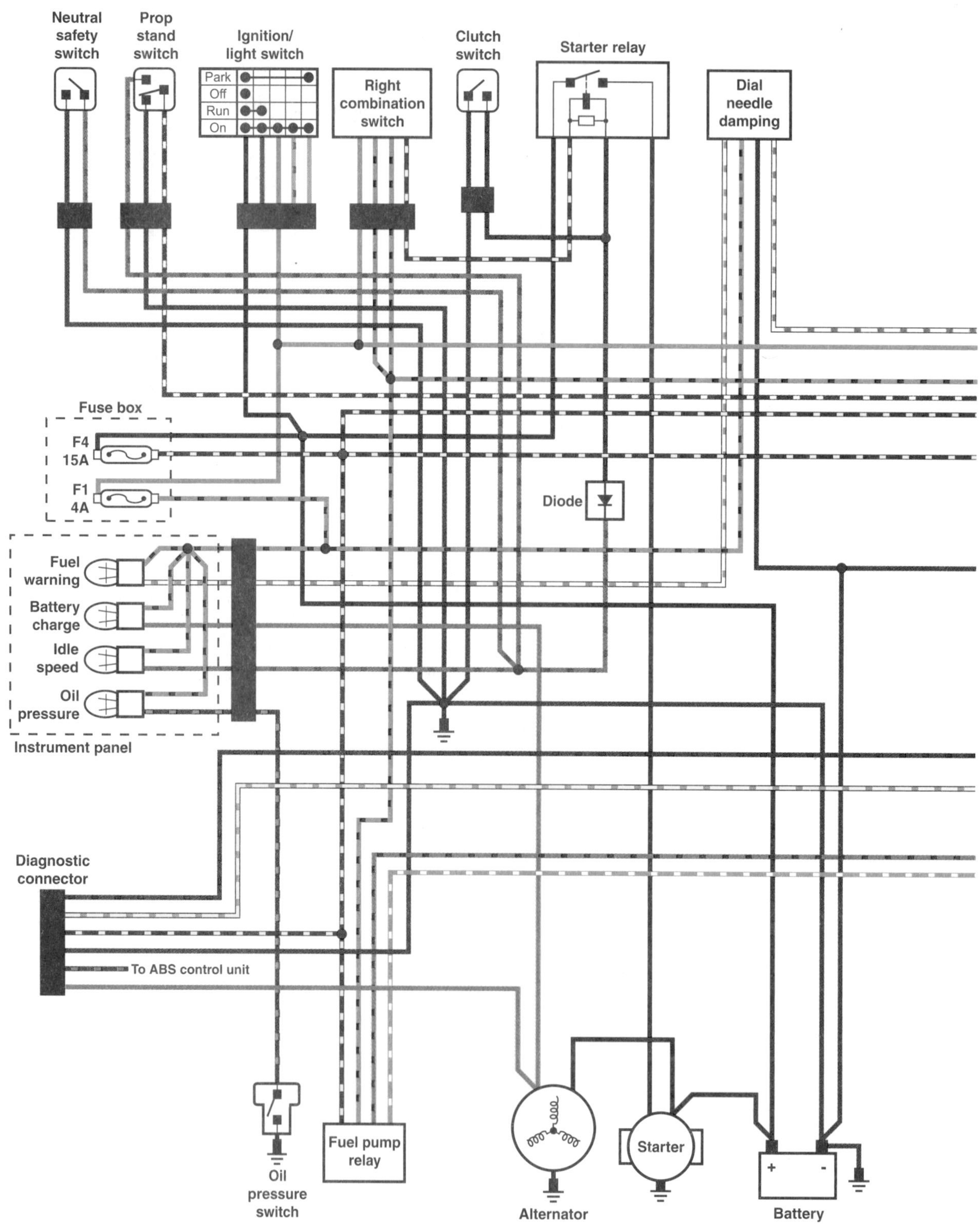

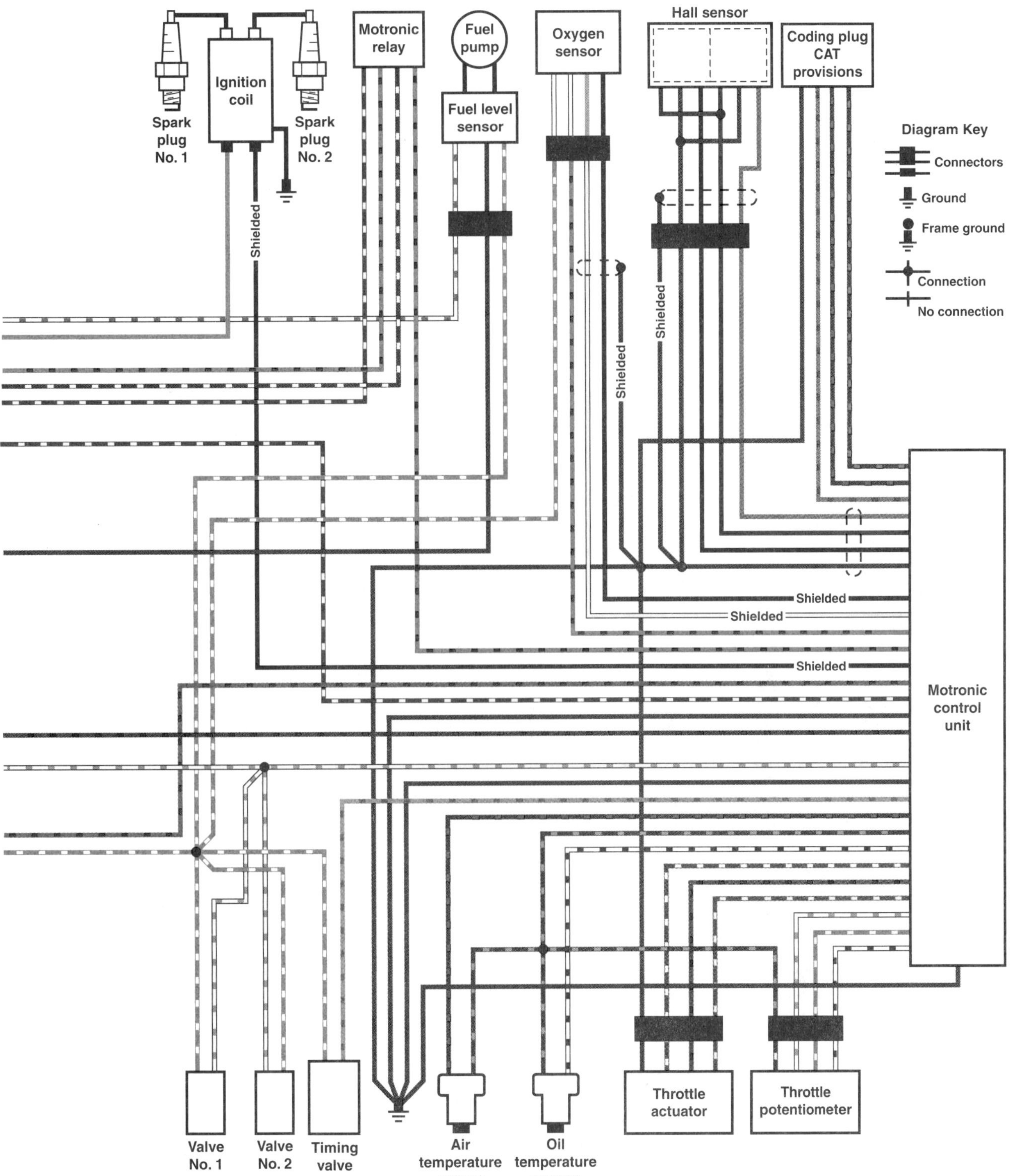
Spark plug No. 1
Ignition coil
Spark plug No. 2
Motronic relay
Fuel pump
Fuel level sensor
Oxygen sensor
Hall sensor
Coding plug CAT provisions
Diagram Key
Connectors
Ground
Frame ground
Connection
No connection
Shielded
Shielded
Shielded
Shielded
Shielded
Shielded
Motronic control unit
Valve No. 1
Valve No. 2
Timing valve
Air temperature sensor
Oil temperature sensor
Throttle actuator
Throttle potentiometer

2000-2001 R850C (U.K.) AND 1999-2004 R1200C (U.S) 1998-2004 R1200C (U.K.) FRAME

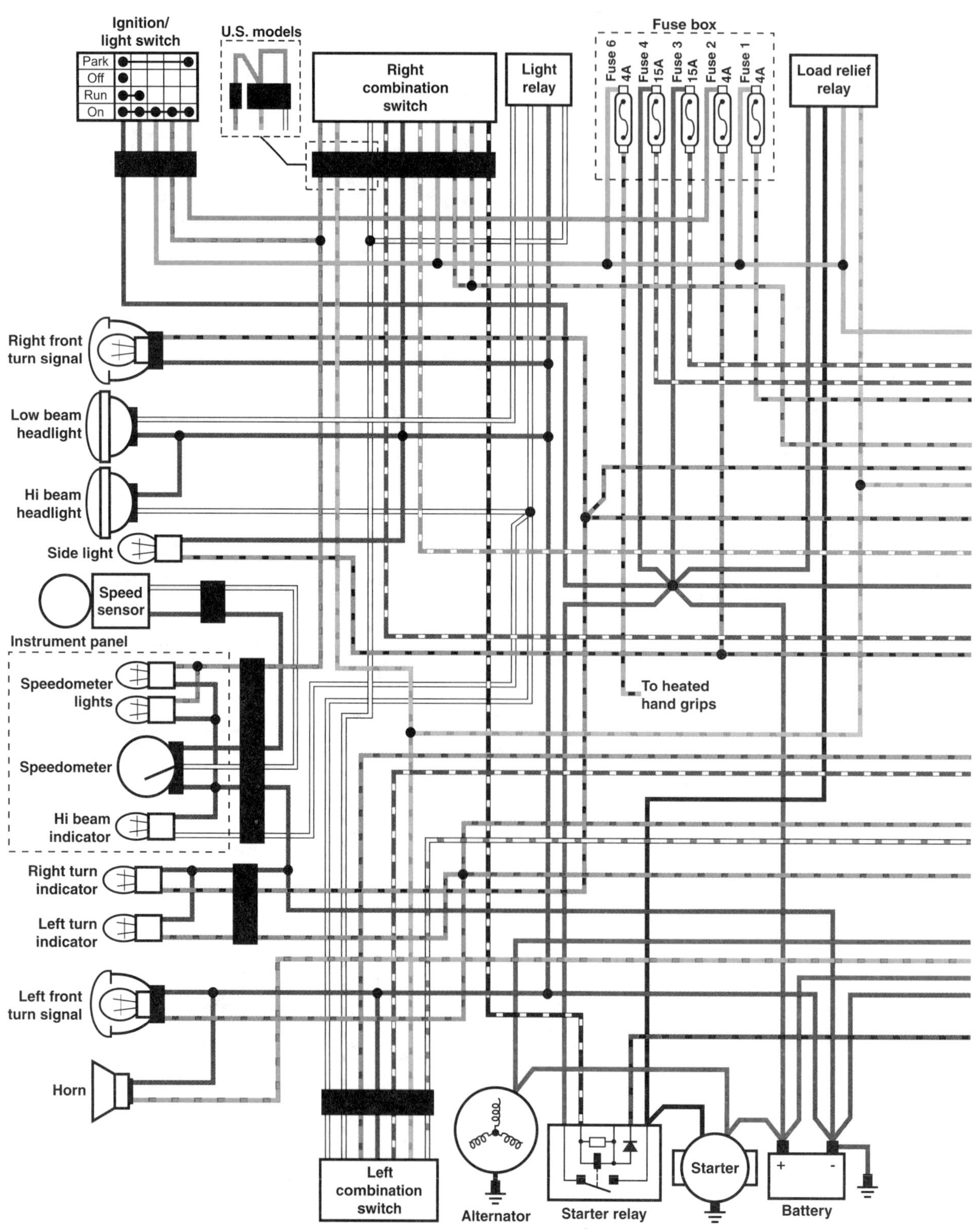

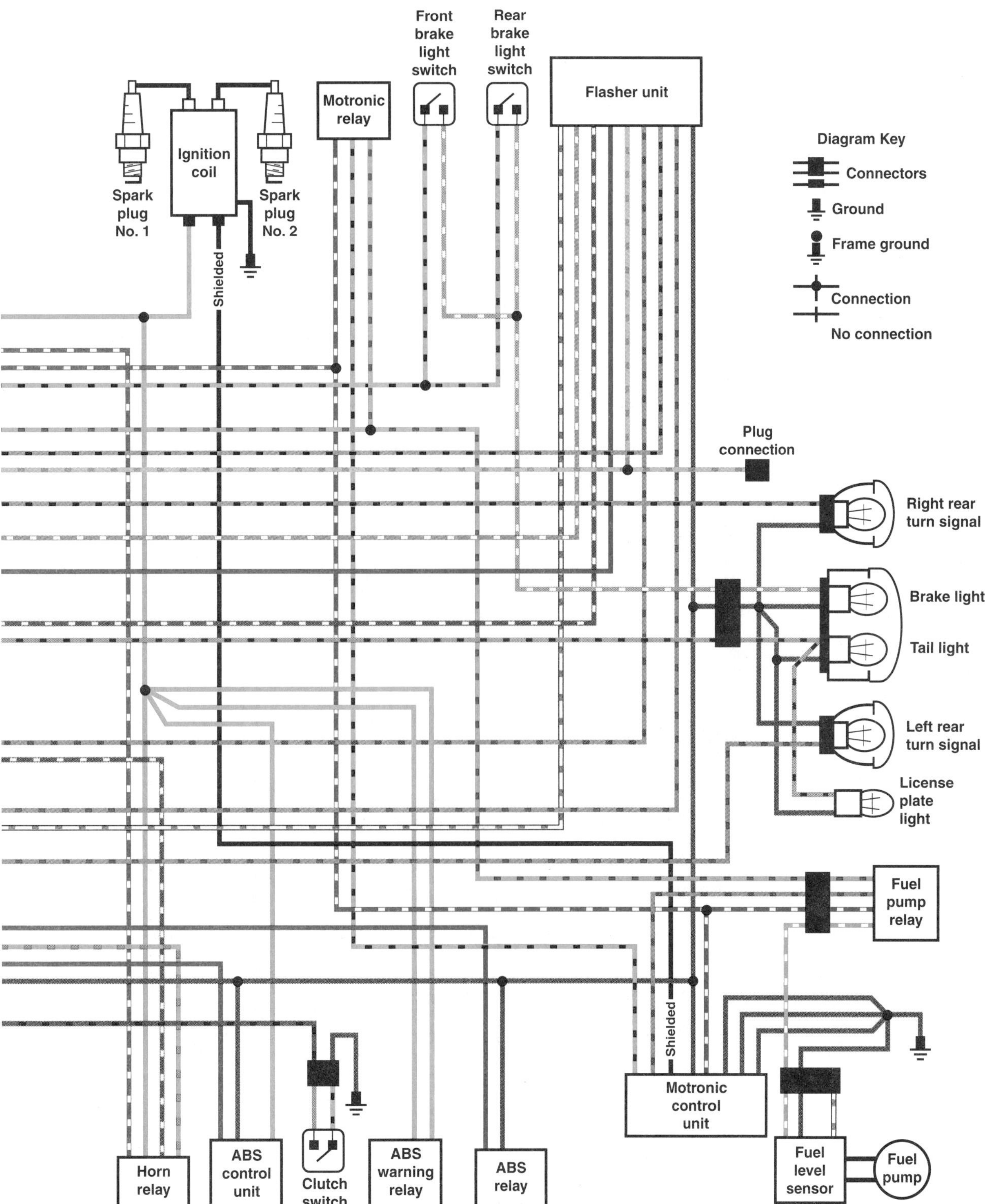
Front brake light switch
Rear brake light switch
Flasher unit
Motronic relay
Ignition coil
Spark plug No. 1
Spark plug No. 2
Shielded
Diagram Key
Connectors
Ground
Frame ground
Connection
No connection
Plug connection
Right rear turn signal
Brake light
Tail light
Left rear turn signal
License plate light
Fuel pump relay
Shielded
Motronic control unit
Fuel level sensor
Fuel pump
Horn relay
ABS control unit
Clutch switch
ABS warning relay
ABS relay

1996-1998 R850R (U.S), 1995-2001 R850R (U.K) 1995-2001 R1100R (U.S. AND U.K.) ENGINE

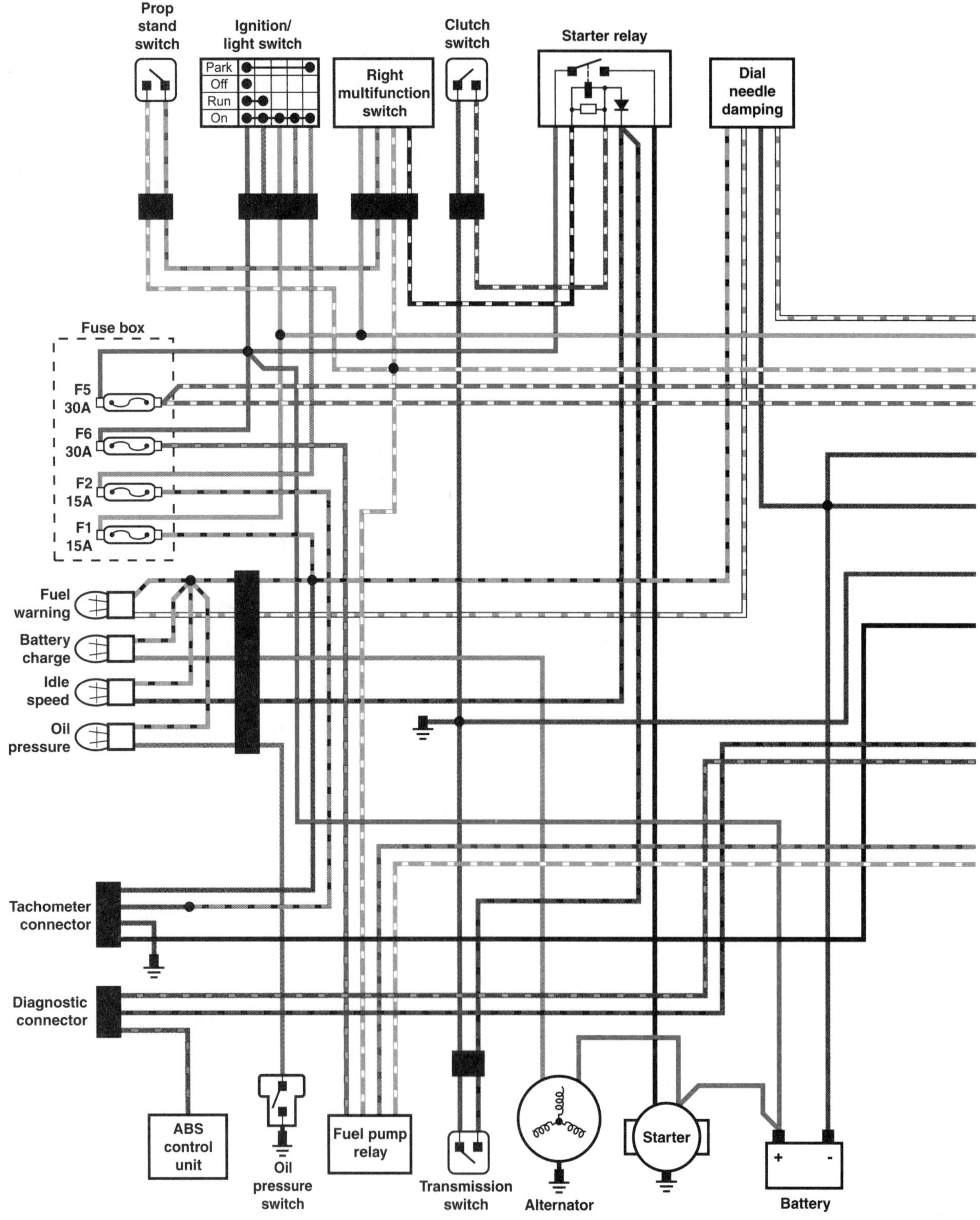

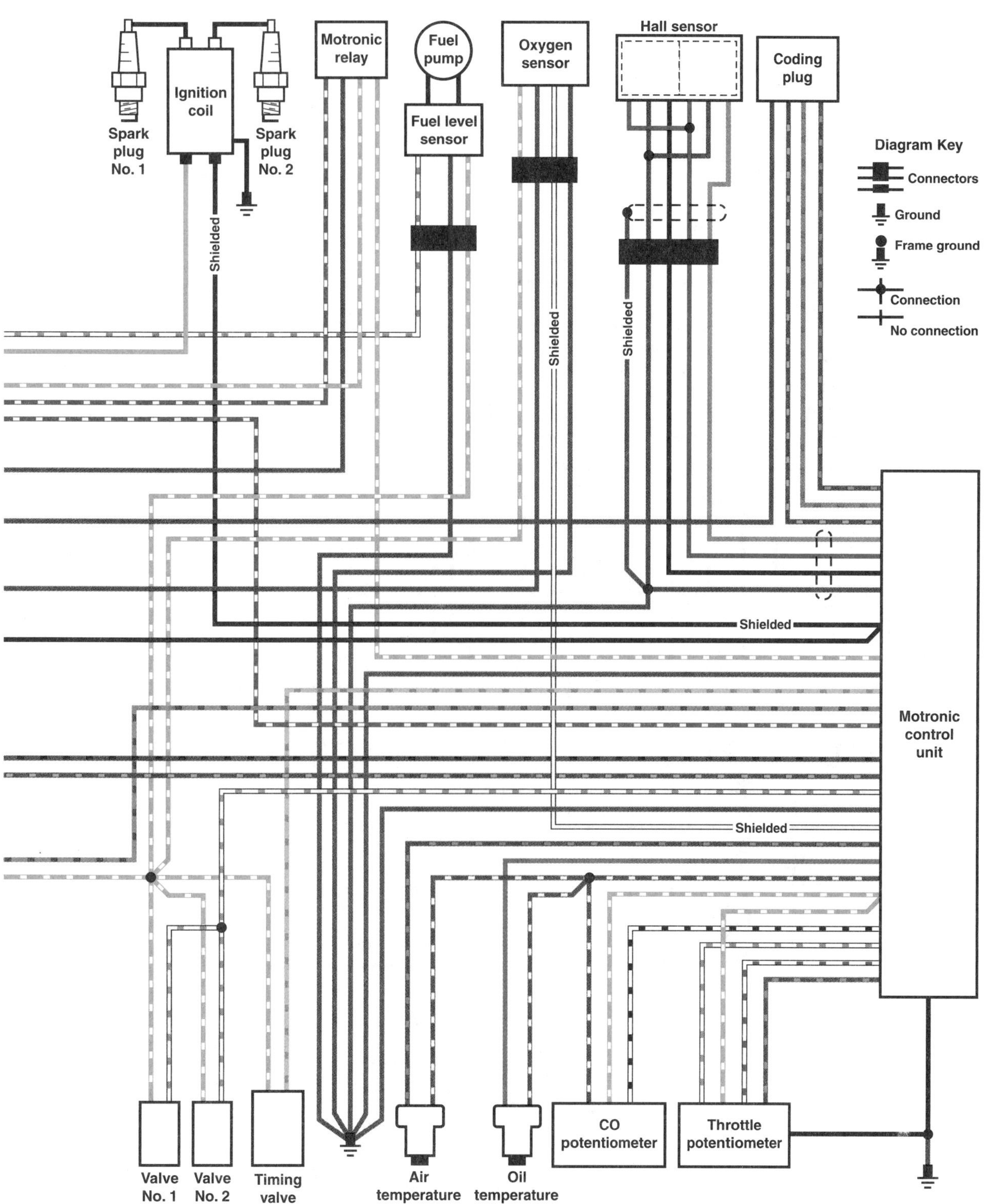

Spark plug No. 1
Ignition coil
Spark plug No. 2
Motronic relay
Fuel pump
Fuel level sensor
Oxygen sensor
Hall sensor
Coding plug
Diagram Key
Connectors
Ground
Frame ground
Connection
No connection
Shielded
Shielded
Shielded
Shielded
Shielded
Motronic control unit
Valve No. 1
Valve No. 2
Timing valve
Air temperature sensor
Oil temperature sensor
CO potentiometer
Throttle potentiometer

1996-1998 R850R (U.S), 1995-2001 R850R (U.K.) 1995-2001 R1100R (U.S. AND U.K) FRAME

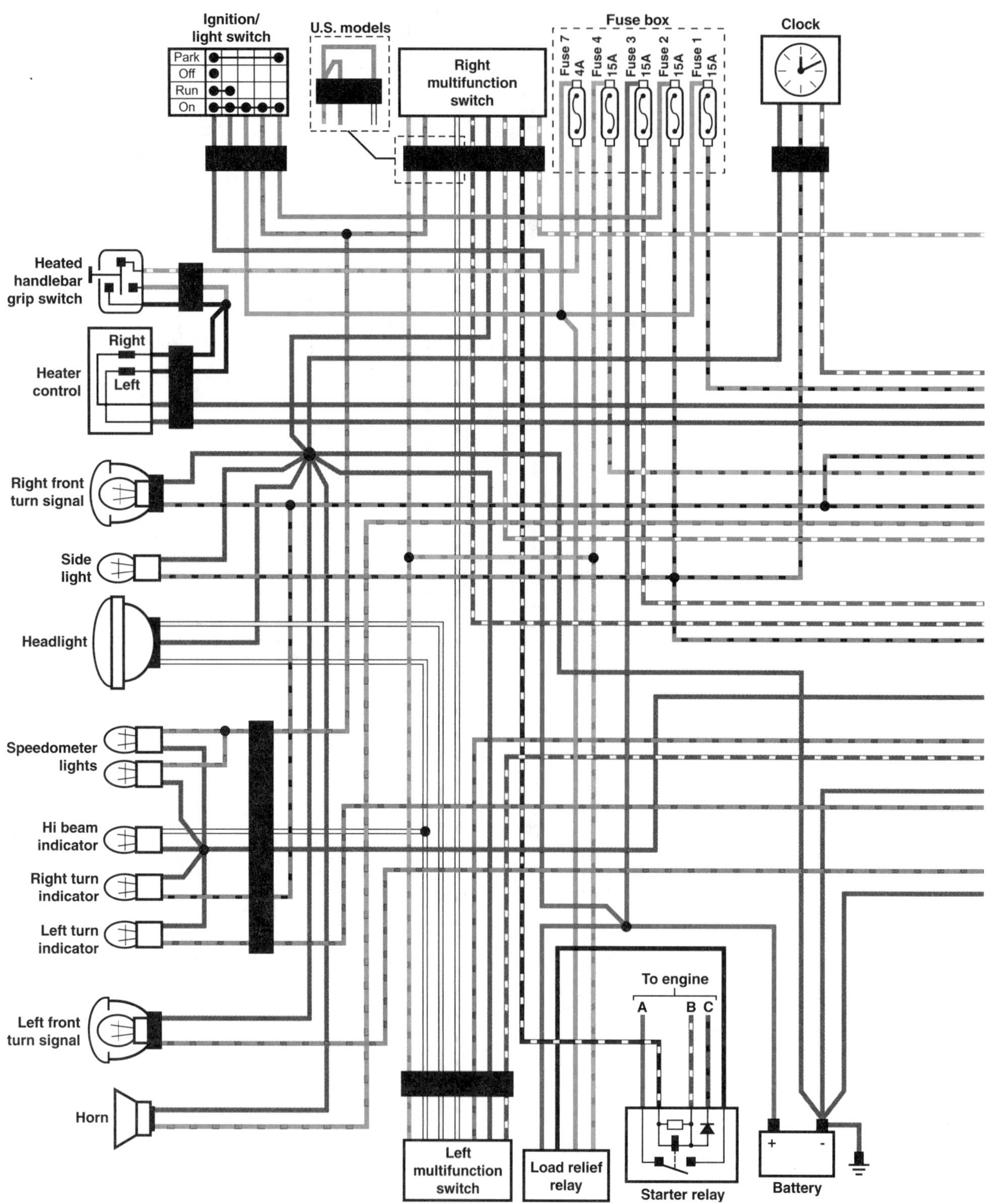

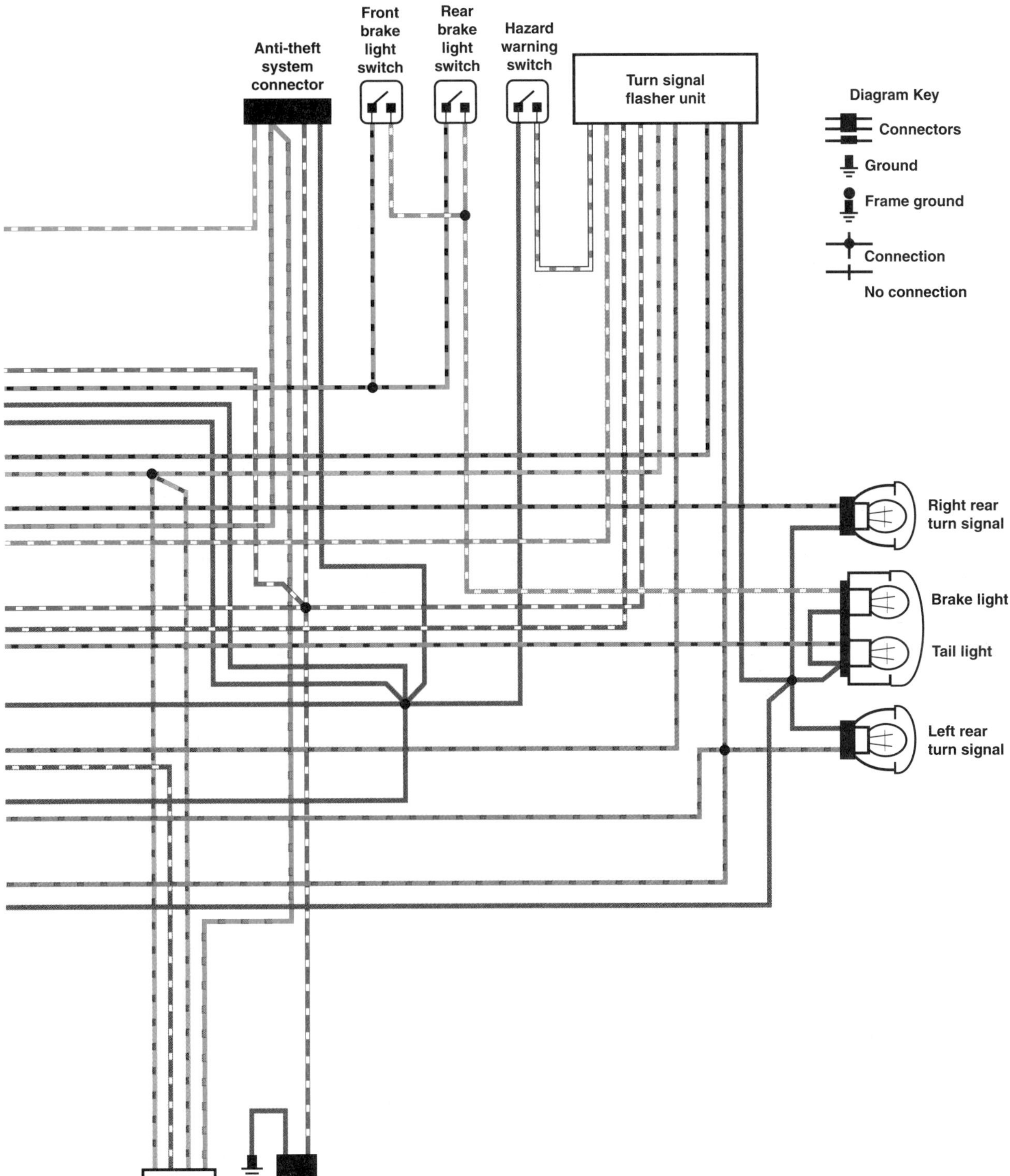
Front brake light switch
Rear brake light switch
Hazard warning switch
Anti-theft system connector
Turn signal flasher unit
Diagram Key
Connectors
Ground
Frame ground
Connection
No connection
Right rear turn signal
Brake light
Tail light
Left rear turn signal
Horn relay
Socket connector

1993-2001 R1100RS AND 1994-1999 R1100GS ENGINE (U.S AND U.K)

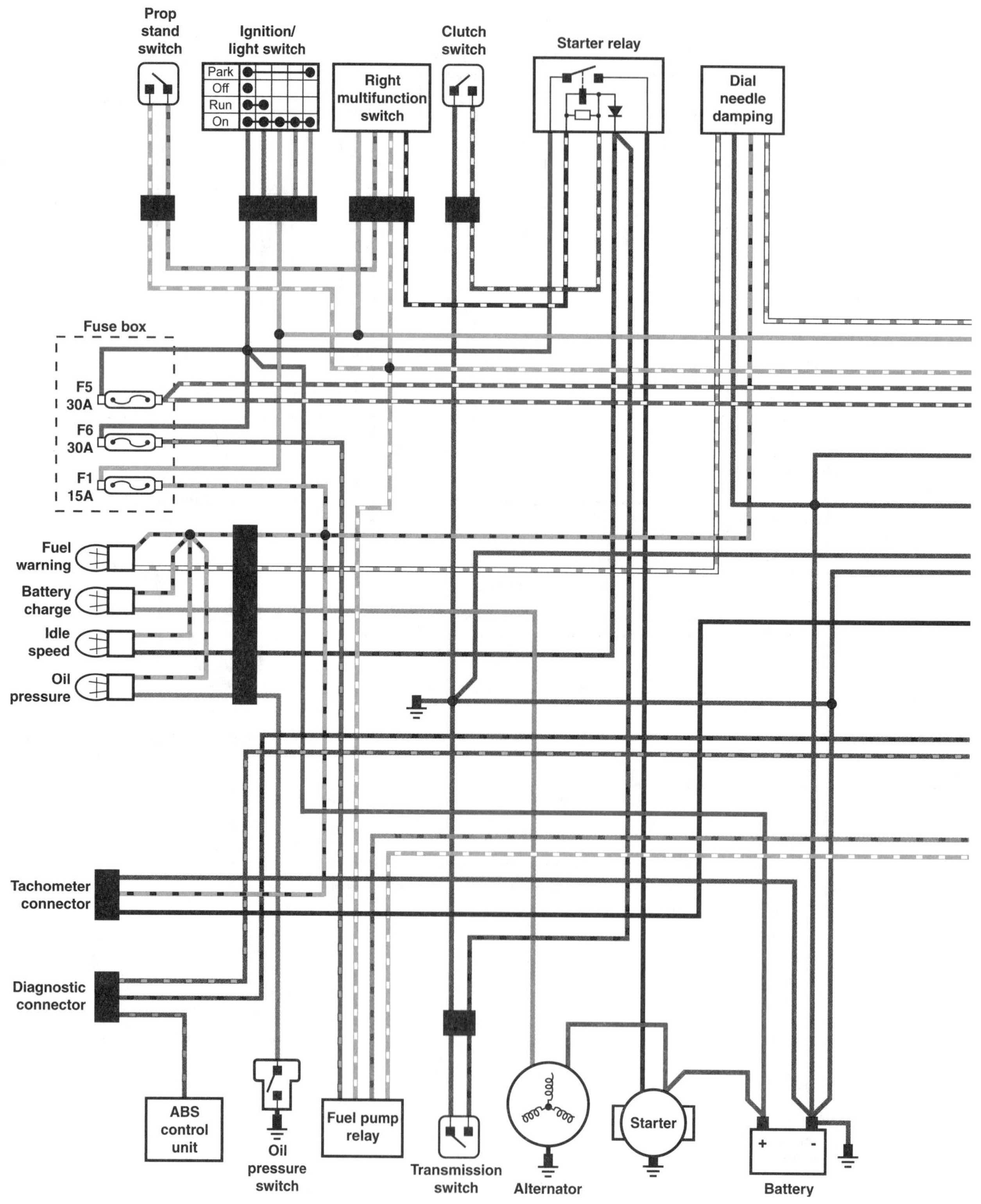

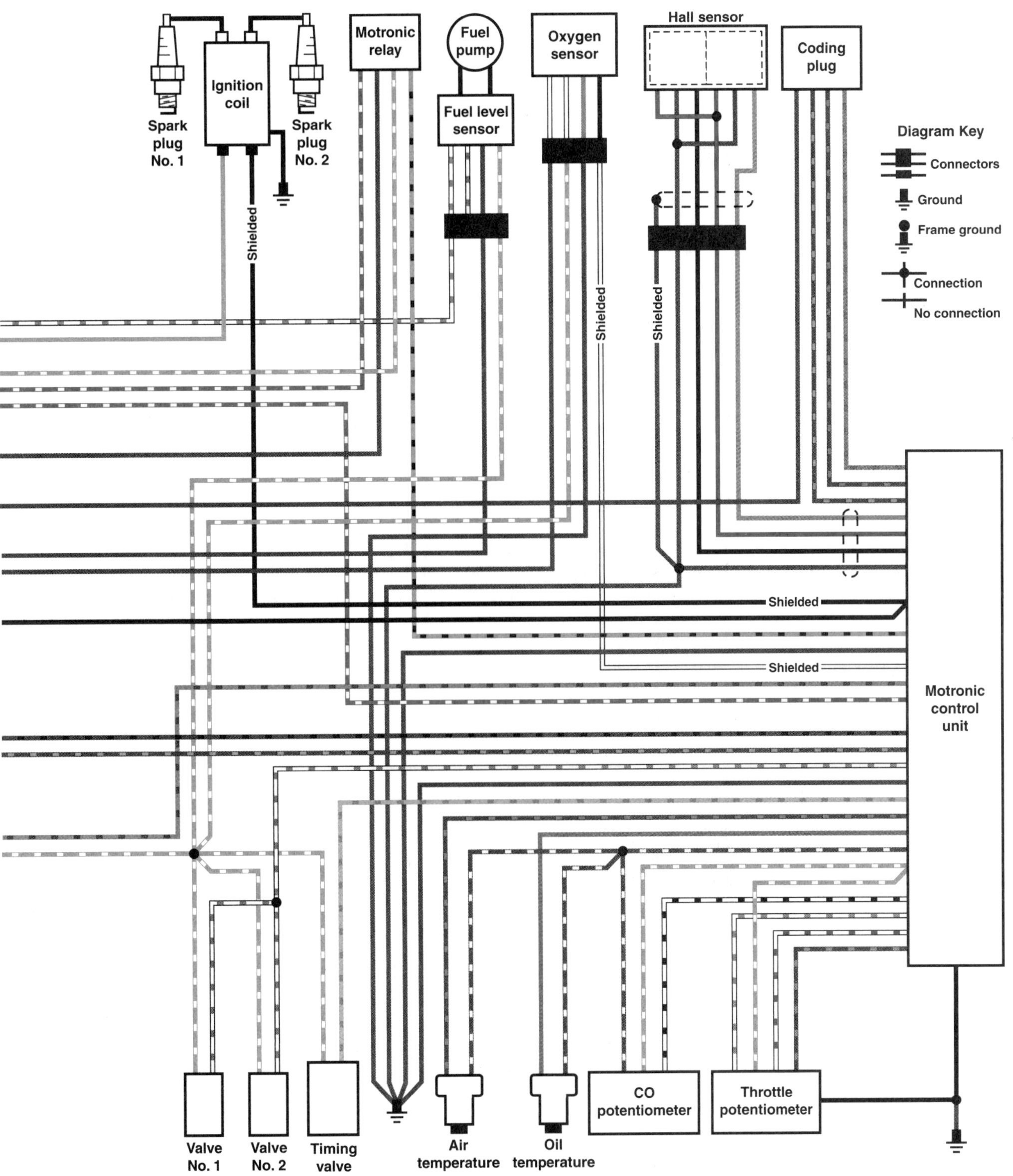
Spark plug No. 1
Ignition coil
Spark plug No. 2
Shielded
Motronic relay
Fuel pump
Fuel level sensor
Oxygen sensor
Shielded
Hall sensor
Shielded
Coding plug
Diagram Key
Connectors
Ground
Frame ground
Connection
No connection
Shielded
Shielded
Motronic control unit
Valve No. 1
Valve No. 2
Timing valve
Air temperature sensor
Oil temperature sensor
CO potentiometer
Throttle potentiometer

1993-2001 R1100RS AND 1994-1999 R1100GS

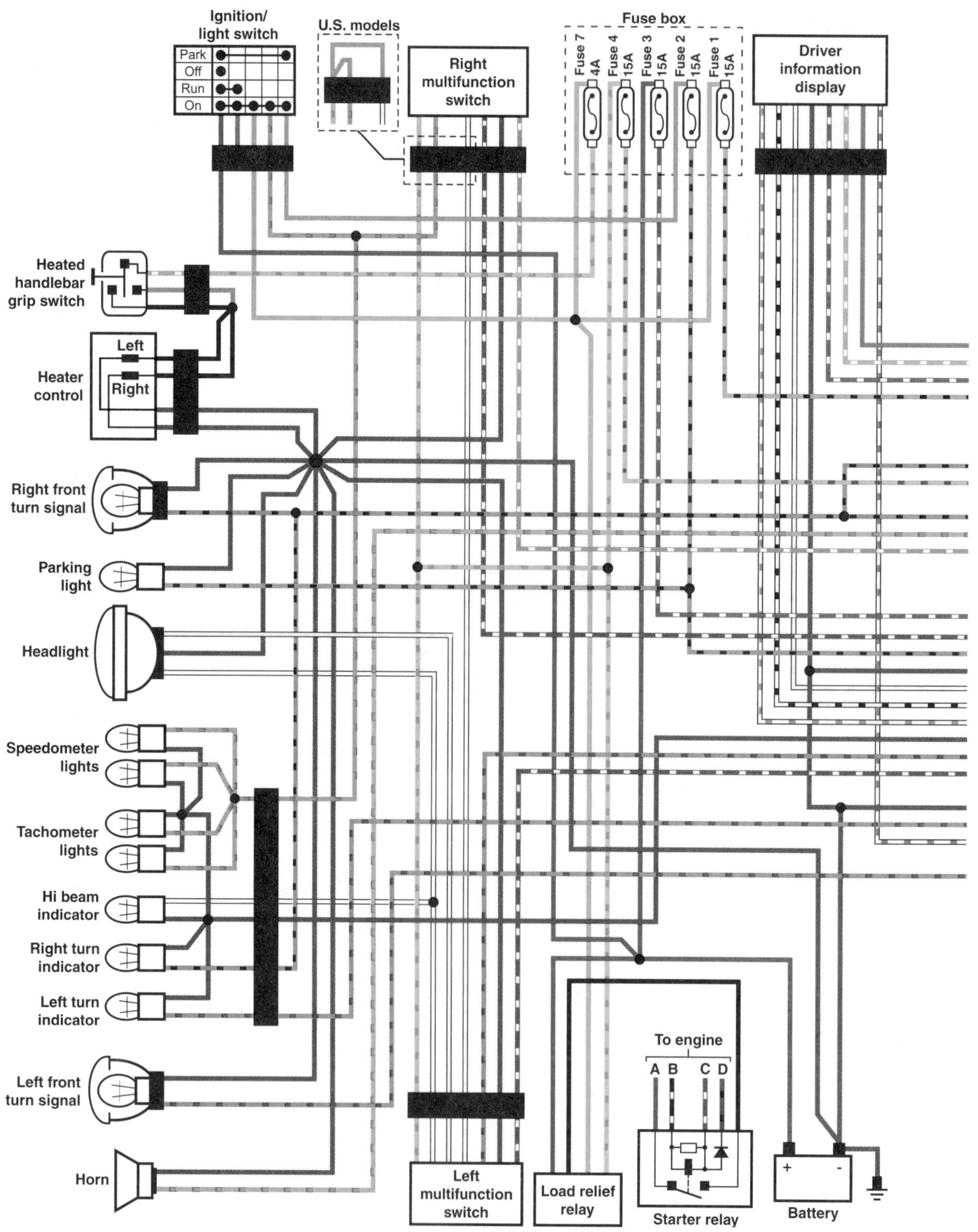

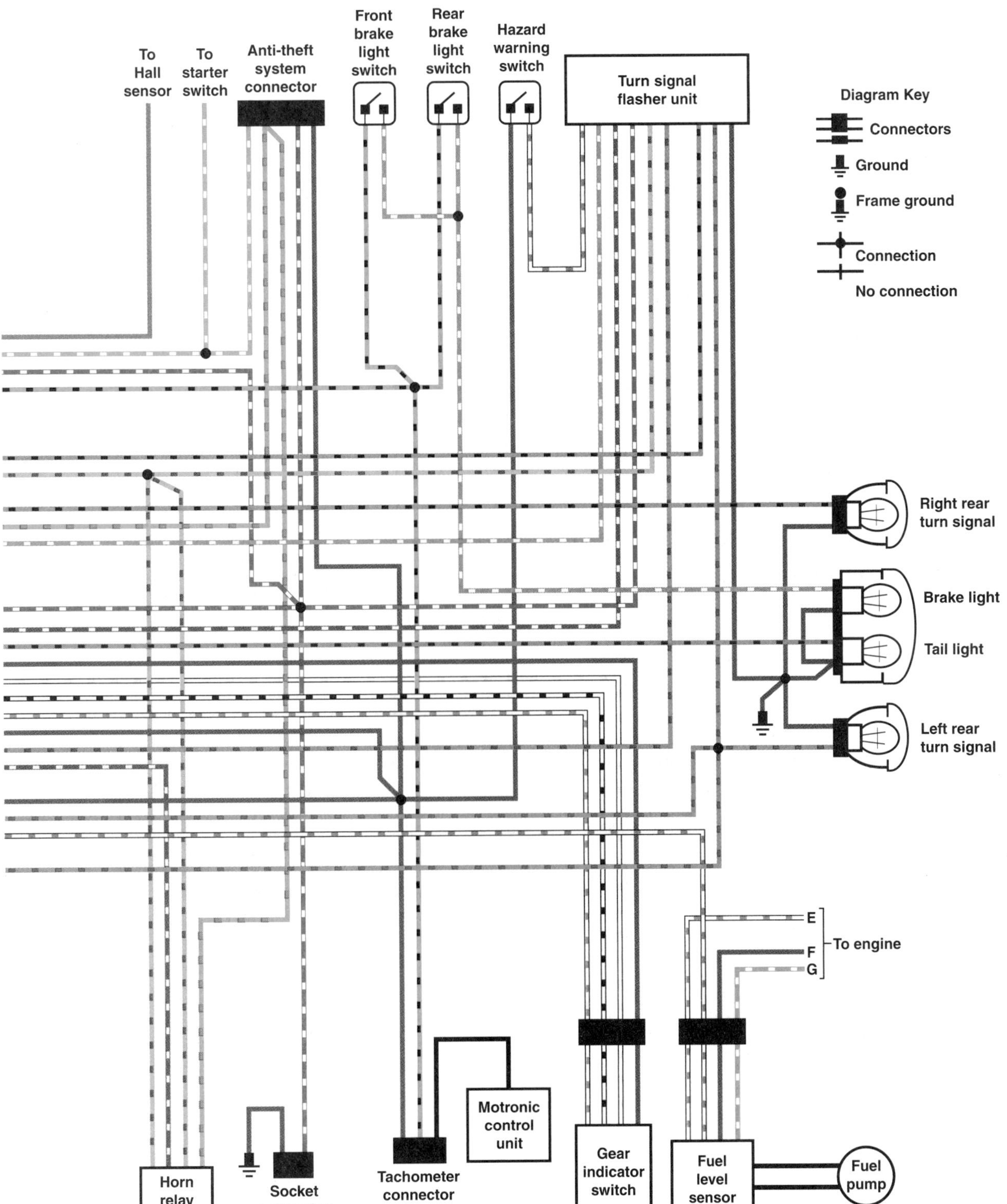
To Hall sensor
To starter switch
Anti-theft system connector
Front brake light switch
Rear brake light switch
Hazard warning switch
Turn signal flasher unit
Diagram Key
Connectors
Ground
Frame ground
Connection
No connection
Right rear turn signal
Brake light
Tail light
Left rear turn signal
E
F
G
To engine
Horn relay
Socket connector
Tachometer connector
Motronic control unit
Gear indicator switch
Fuel level sensor
Fuel pump

1995-2001 R1100RT ENGINE (U.S. AND U.K)

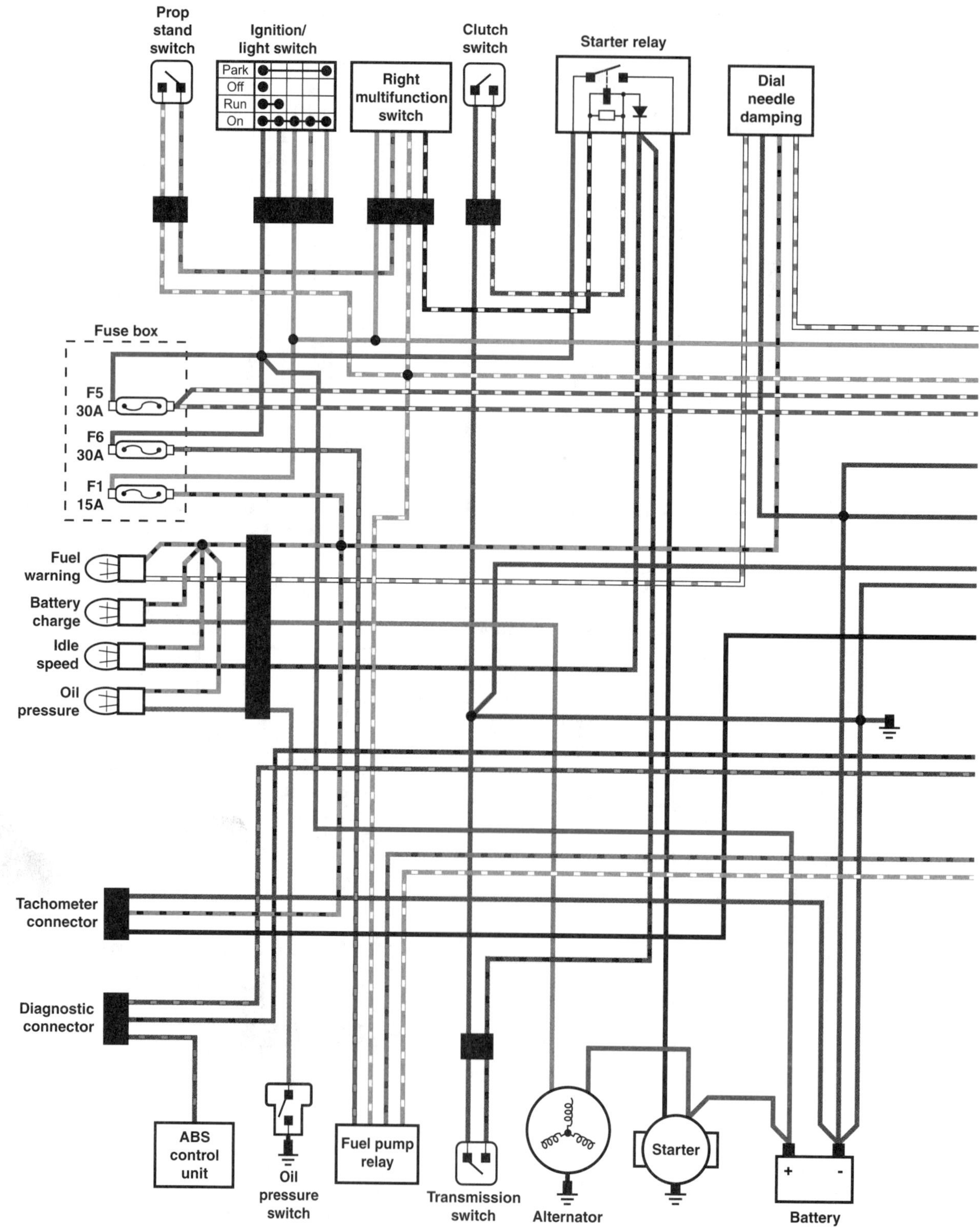

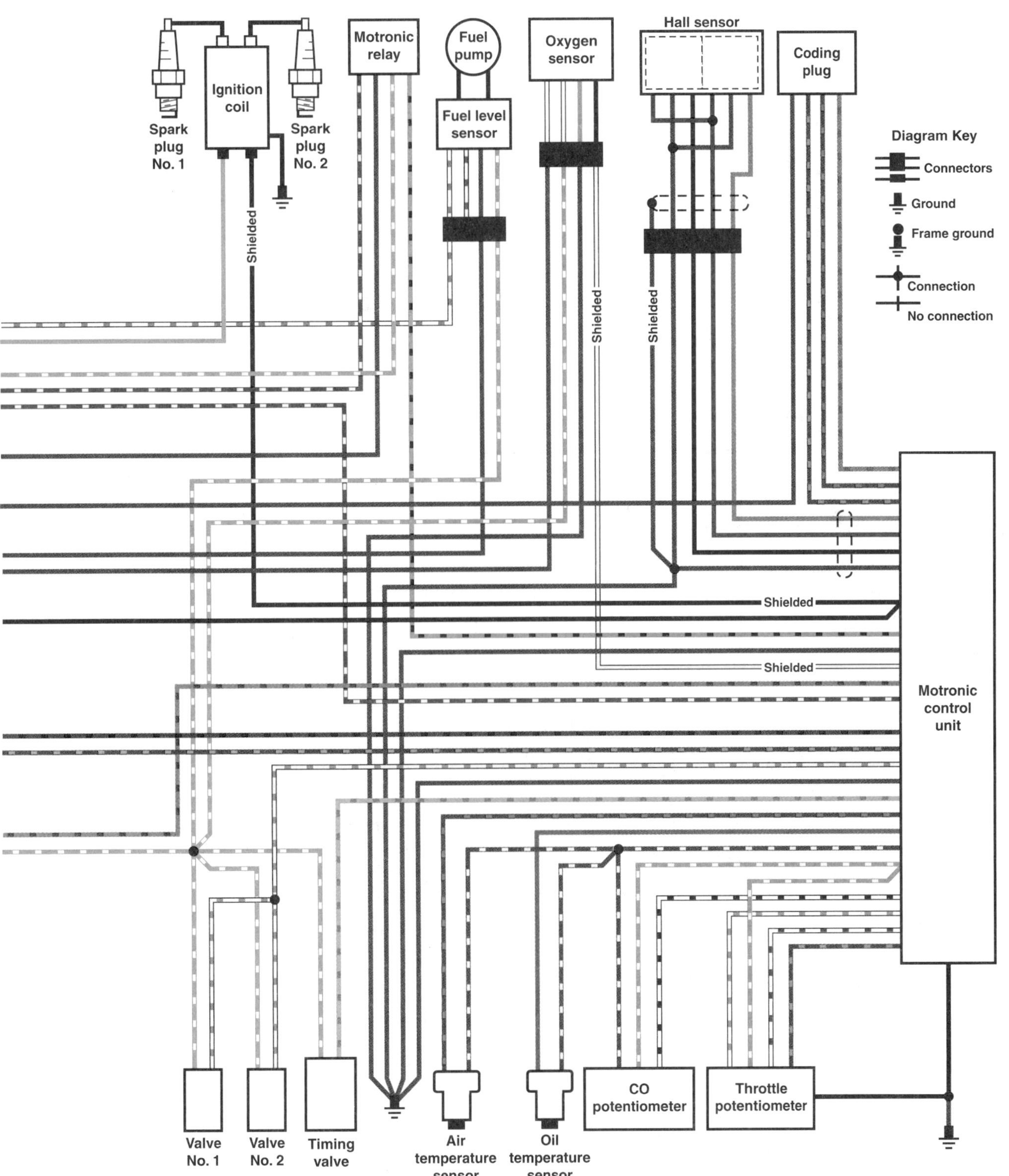

Spark plug No. 1
Ignition coil
Spark plug No. 2
Motronic relay
Fuel pump
Fuel level sensor
Oxygen sensor
Hall sensor
Coding plug
Diagram Key
Connectors
Ground
Frame ground
Connection
No connection
Shielded
Shielded
Shielded
Shielded
Shielded
Motronic control unit
Valve No. 1
Valve No. 2
Timing valve
Air temperature sensor
Oil temperature sensor
CO potentiometer
Throttle potentiometer

17

1995-2001 R1100RT FRAME (U.S. AND U.K.)

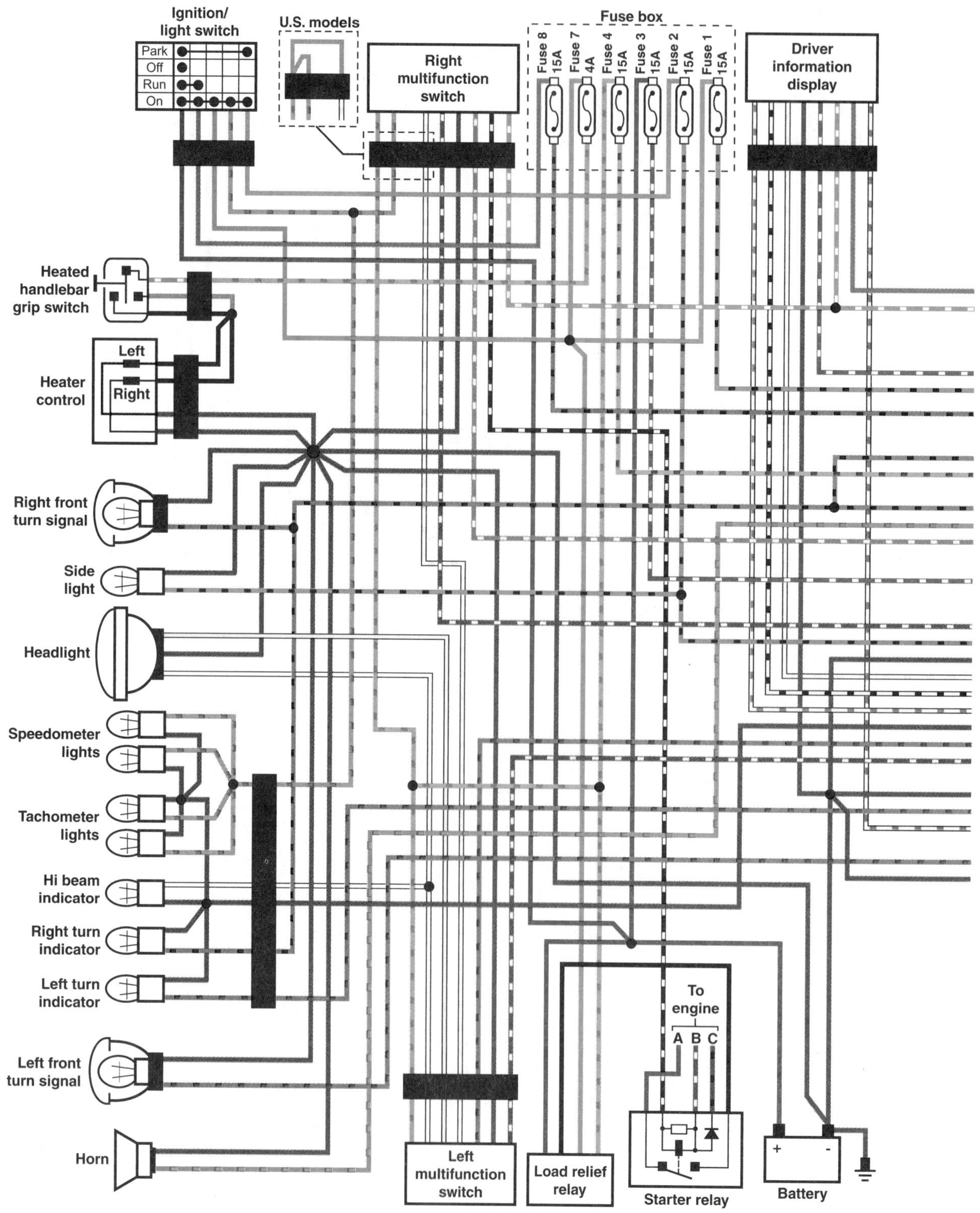

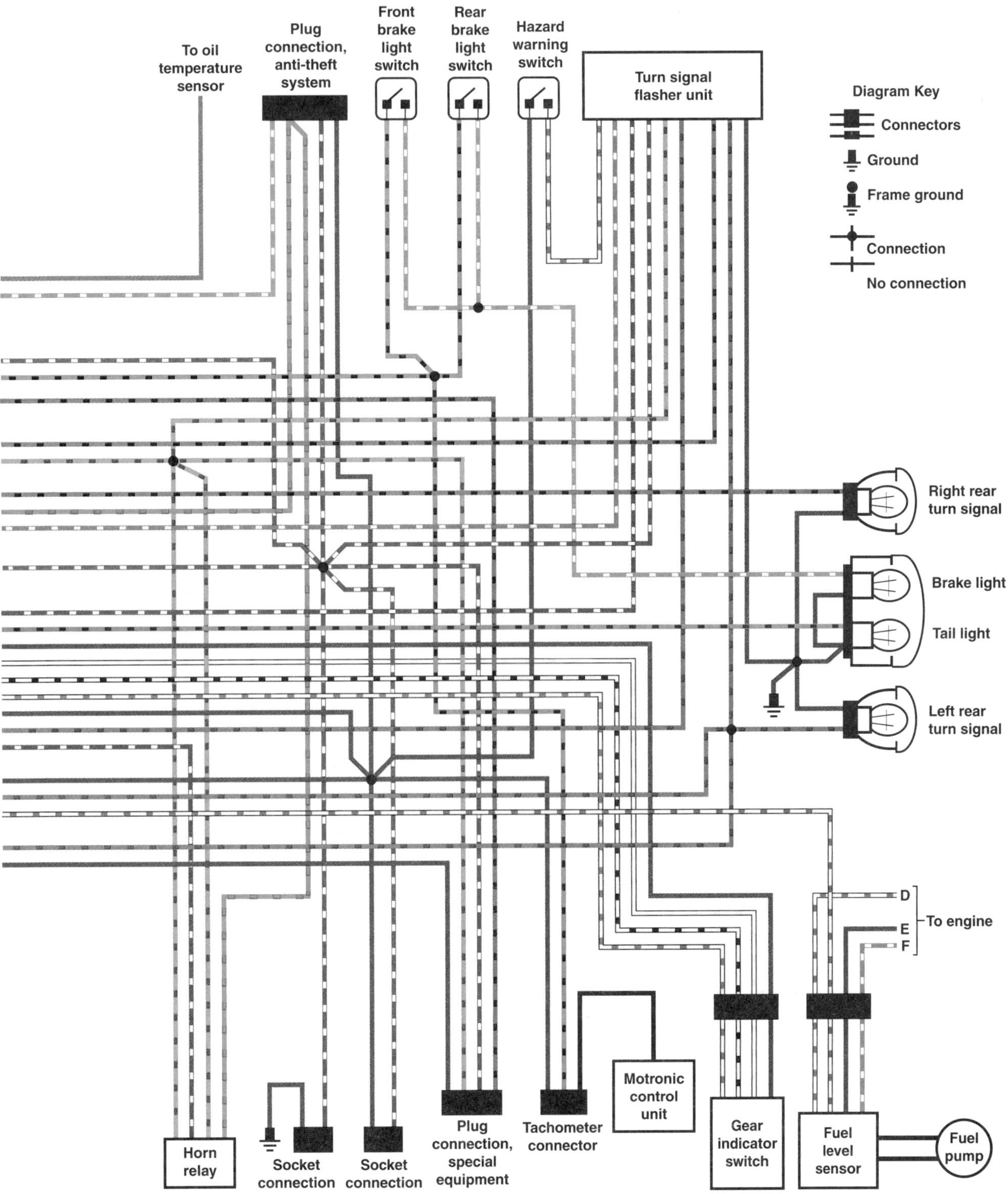
To oil temperature sensor
Plug connection, anti-theft system
Front brake light switch
Rear brake light switch
Hazard warning switch
Turn signal flasher unit
Diagram Key
Connectors
Ground
Frame ground
Connection
No connection
Right rear turn signal
Brake light
Tail light
Left rear turn signal
D
E
F
To engine
Horn relay
Socket connection
Socket connection
Plug connection, special equipment
Tachometer connector
Motronic control unit
Gear indicator switch
Fuel level sensor
Fuel pump

1999-2004 R1100S (U.S) AND 2000-2003 R1100S (U.K.) ENGINE

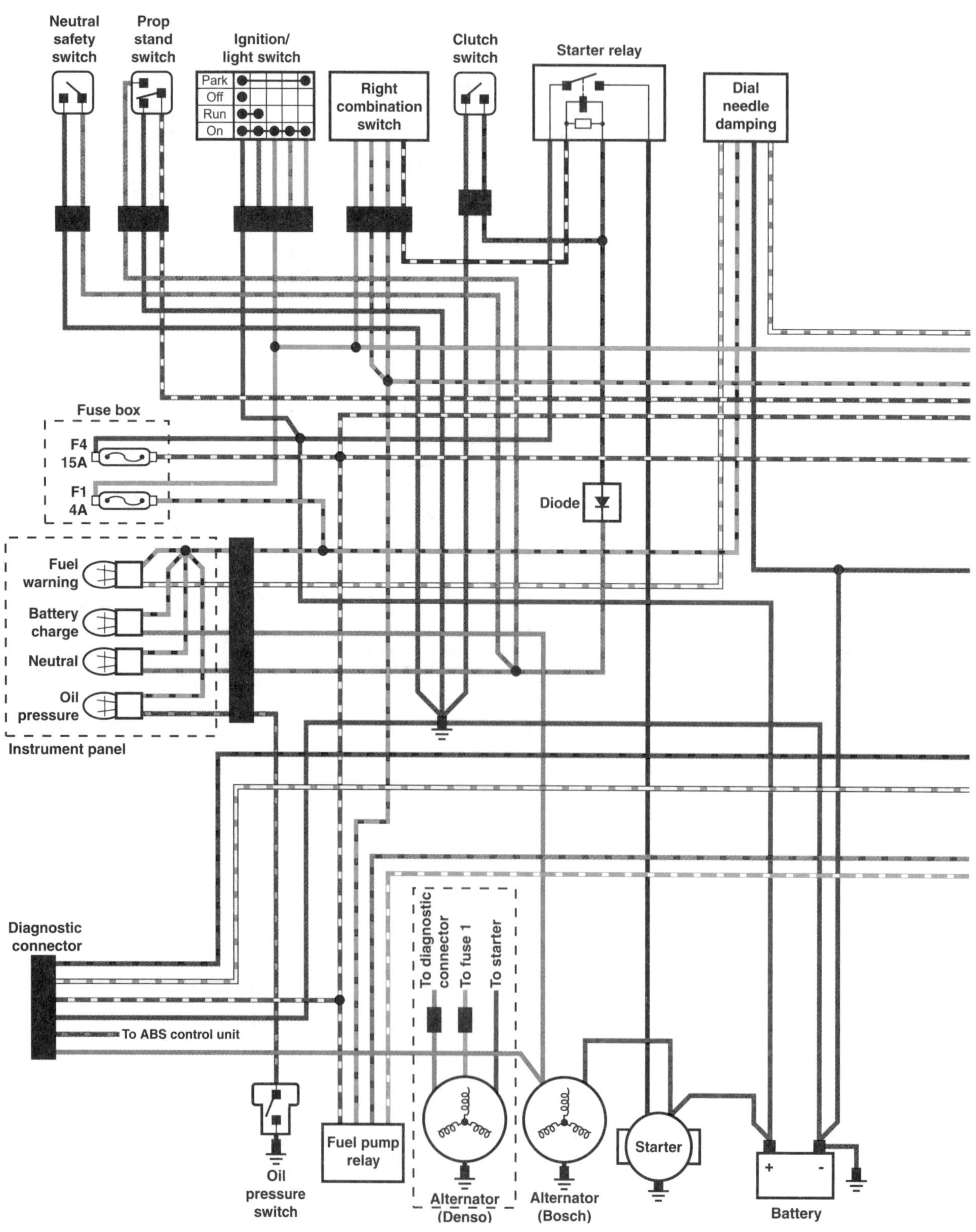

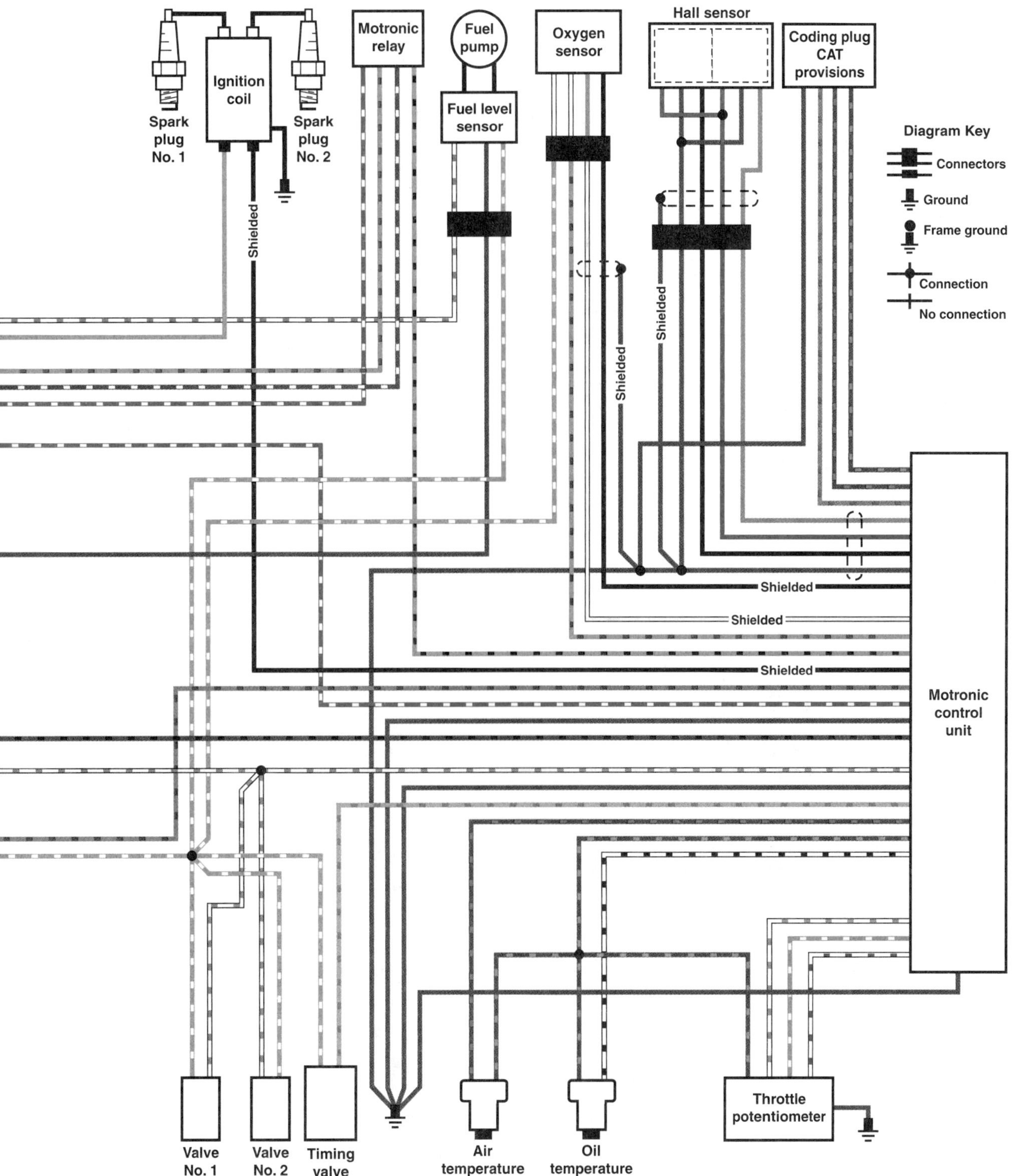
Spark plug No. 1
Ignition coil
Spark plug No. 2
Motronic relay
Fuel pump
Fuel level sensor
Oxygen sensor
Hall sensor
Coding plug CAT provisions
Diagram Key
Connectors
Ground
Frame ground
Connection
No connection
Shielded
Motronic control unit
Valve No. 1
Valve No. 2
Timing valve
Air temperature sensor
Oil temperature sensor
Throttle potentiometer

1999-2004 R1100S (U.S.) AND 2000-2003 R1100S (U.K) FRAME

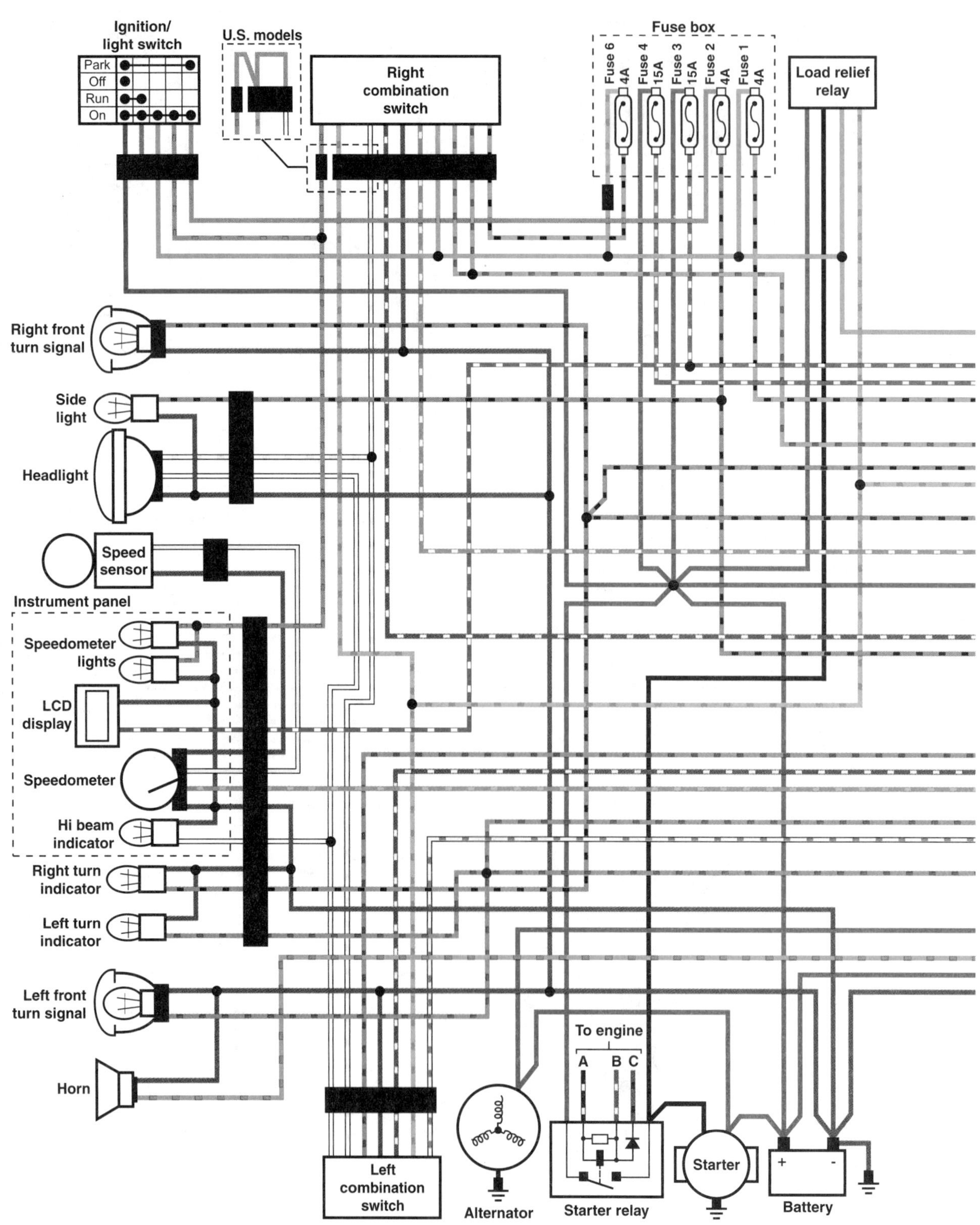

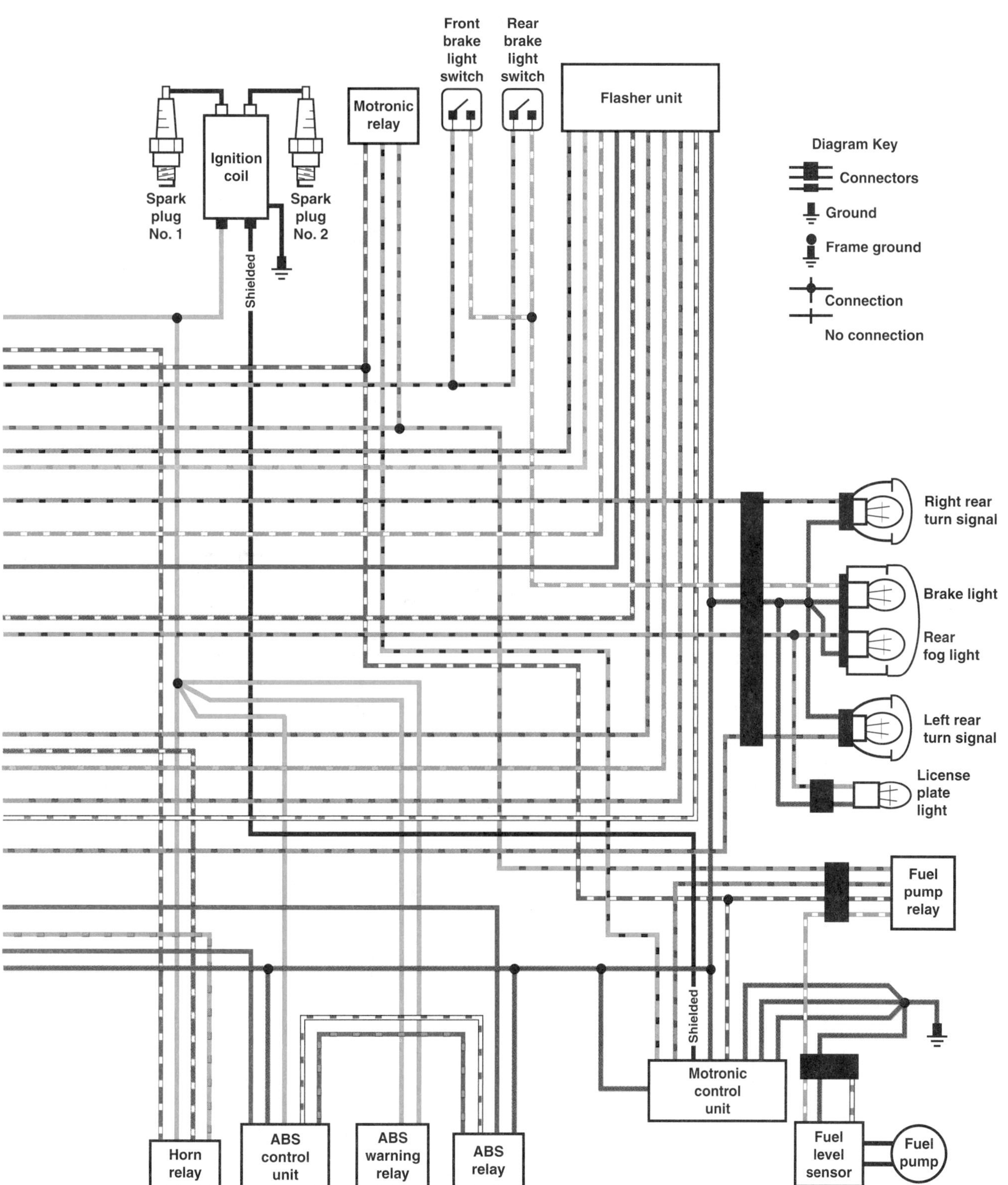
Front brake light switch
Rear brake light switch
Motronic relay
Flasher unit
Ignition coil
Spark plug No. 1
Spark plug No. 2
Shielded
Diagram Key
Connectors
Ground
Frame ground
Connection
No connection
Right rear turn signal
Brake light
Rear fog light
Left rear turn signal
License plate light
Fuel pump relay
Shielded
Motronic control unit
Fuel level sensor
Fuel pump
Horn relay
ABS control unit
ABS warning relay
ABS relay

1999-2003 R1150GS (U.K) AND 2000-2004 R1150GS (U.S) MOTRONIC WITH INPUTS

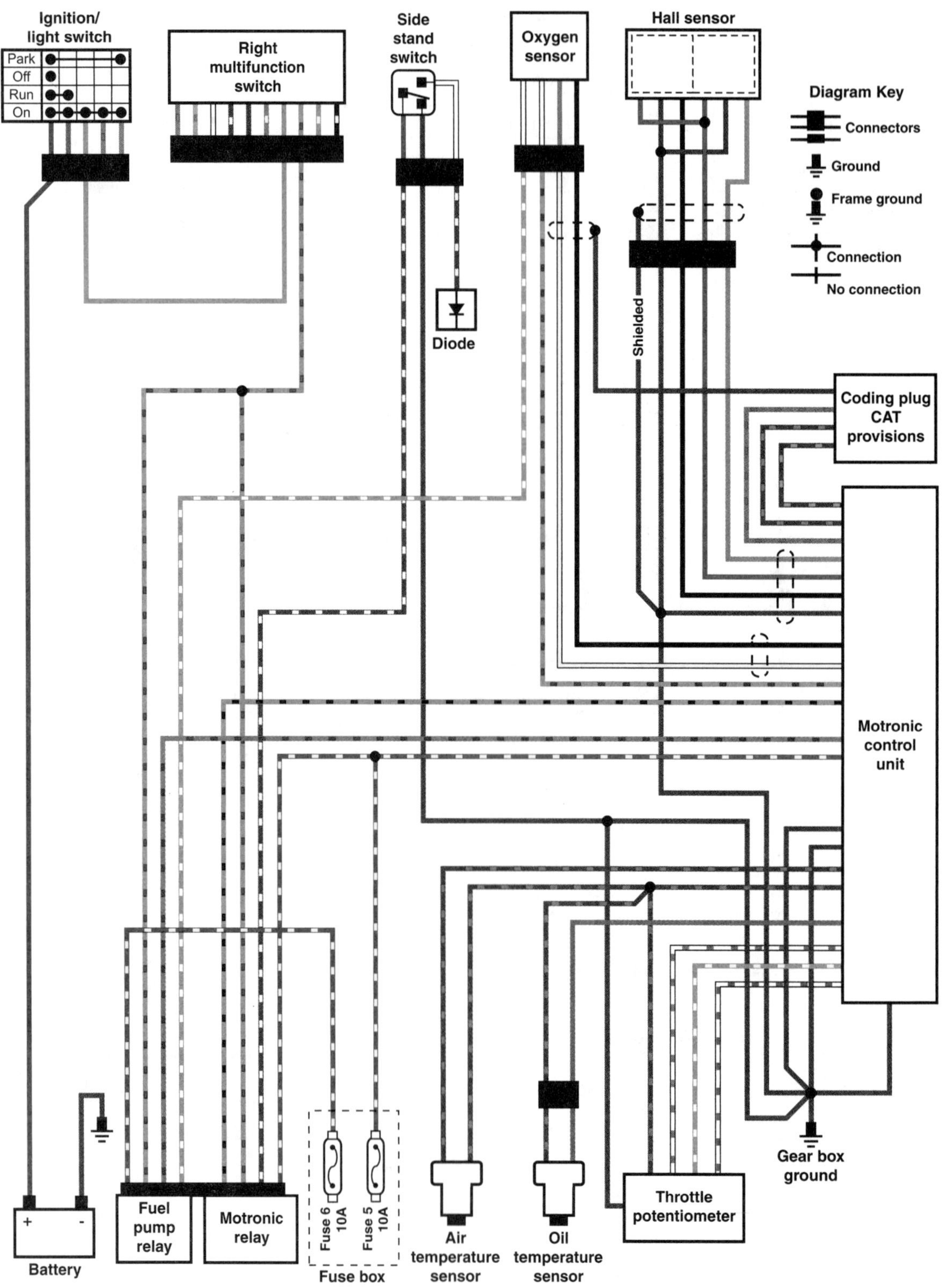

1999-2003 R1150GS (U.K.) AND 2000-2004 R1150GS (U.S.) MOTRONIC WITH OUTPUTS

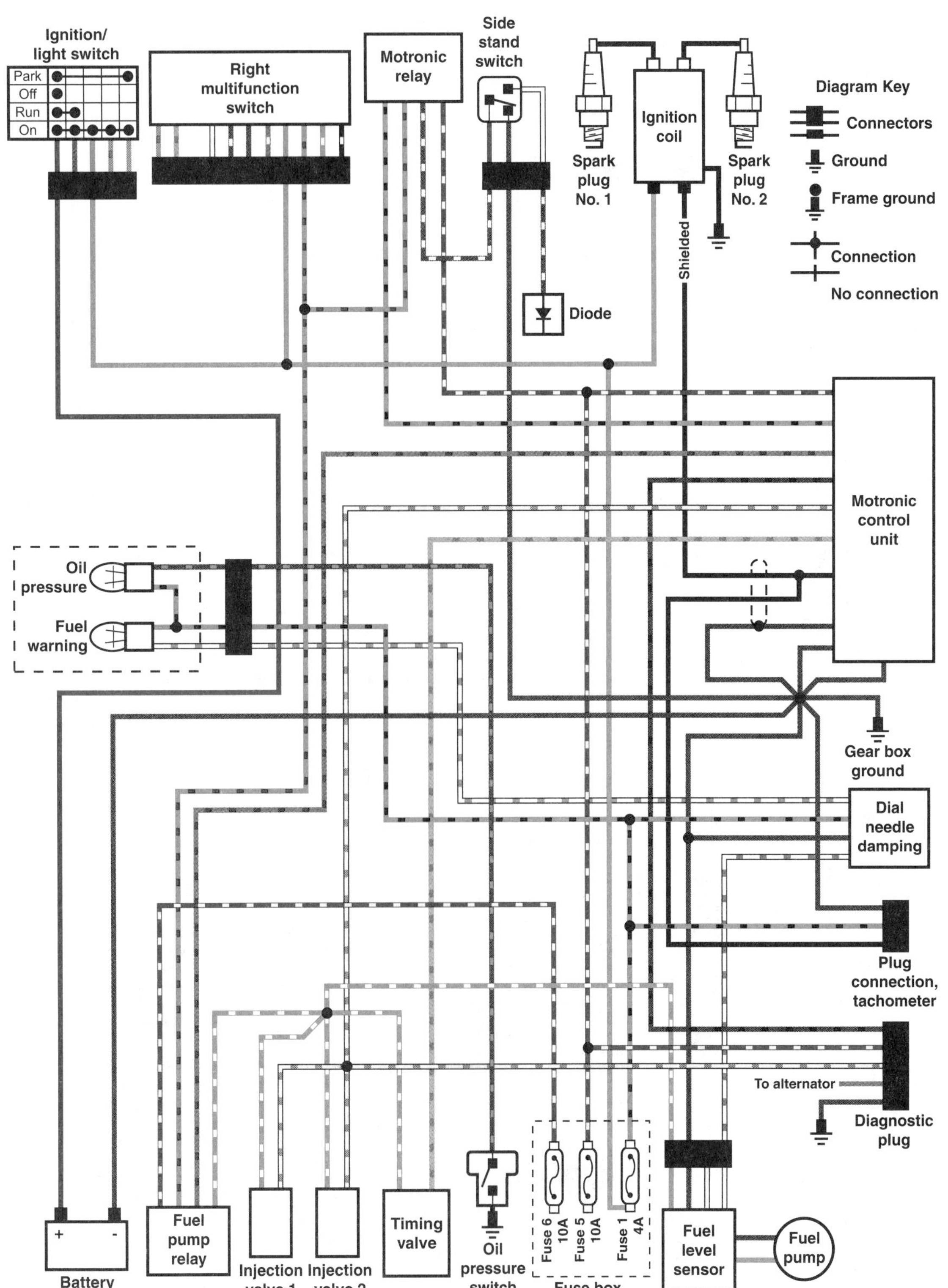

1999-2003 R1150GS (U.K.) AND 2000-2004 R1150GS (U.S.) FRAME

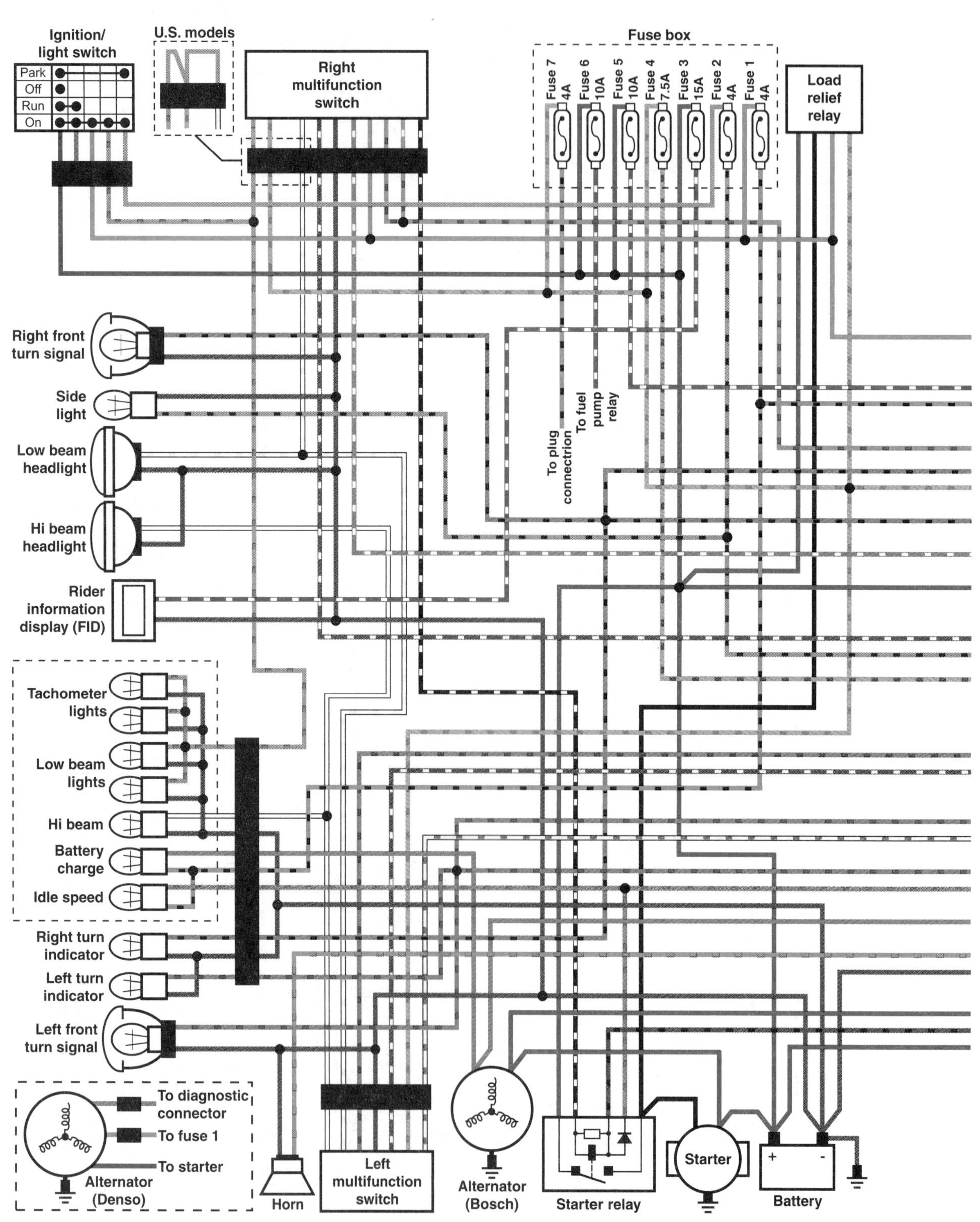

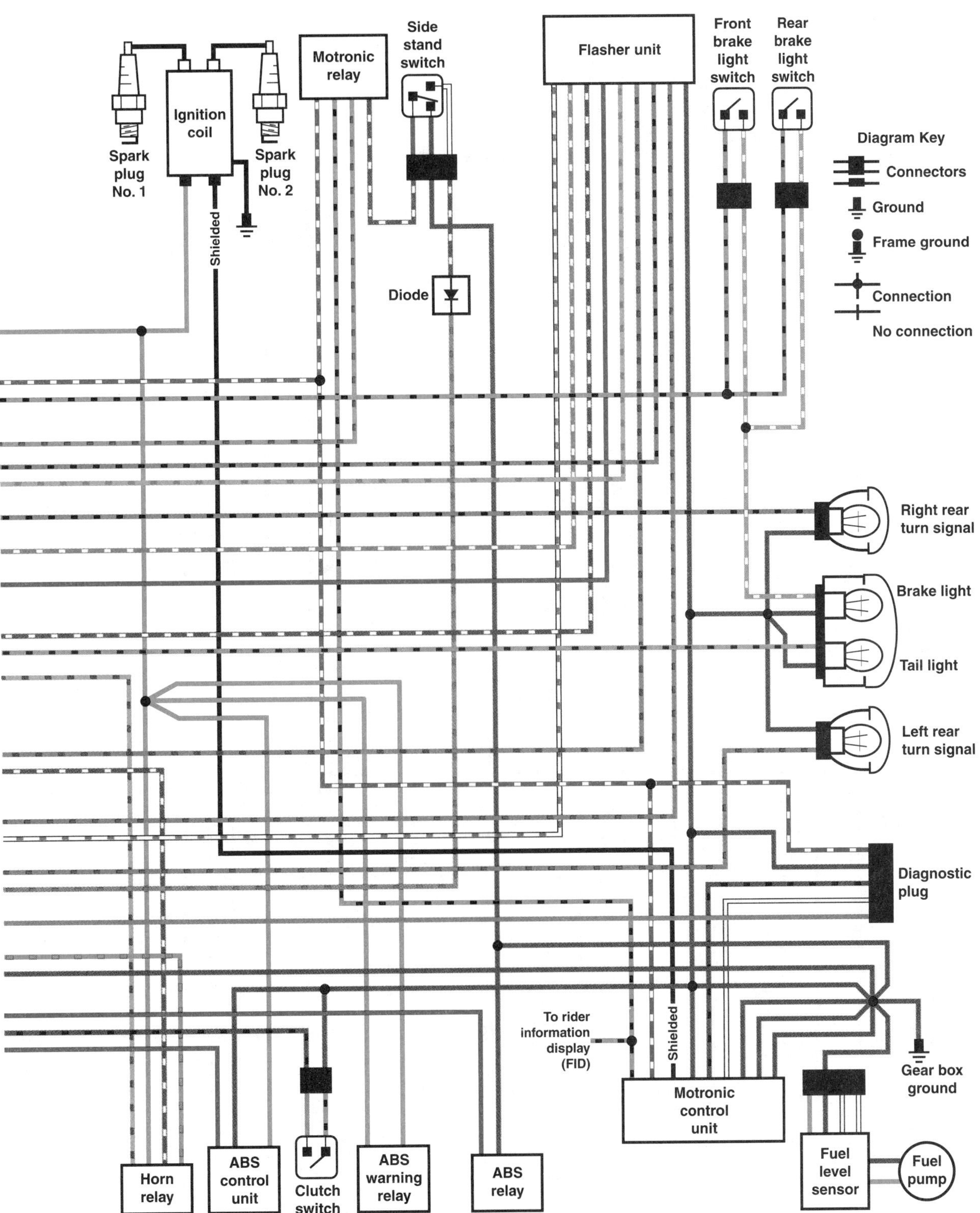
Spark plug No. 1
Ignition coil
Spark plug No. 2
Motronic relay
Side stand switch
Flasher unit
Front brake light switch
Rear brake light switch
Diagram Key
Connectors
Ground
Frame ground
Connection
No connection
Shielded
Diode
Right rear turn signal
Brake light
Tail light
Left rear turn signal
Diagnostic plug
To rider information display (FID)
Shielded
Gear box ground
Motronic control unit
Fuel level sensor
Fuel pump
Horn relay
ABS control unit
Clutch switch
ABS warning relay
ABS relay

2002-2004 R1150R (U.S.) AND 2000-2001 R1150R (U.K) MOTRONIC WITH INPUTS

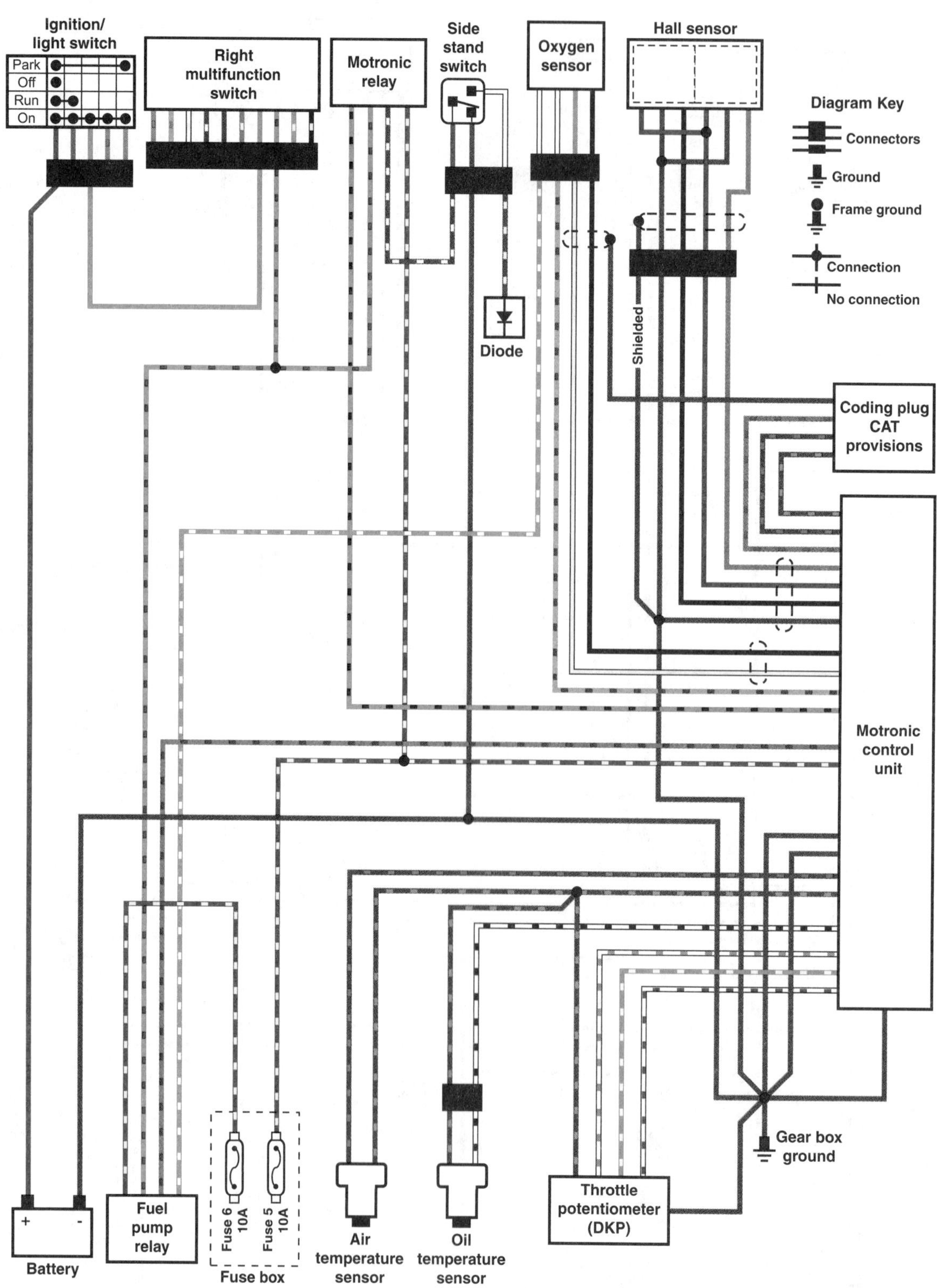

2002-2004 R1150R (U.S.) AND 2000-2001 R1150R (U.K.) MOTRONIC WITH OUTPUTS

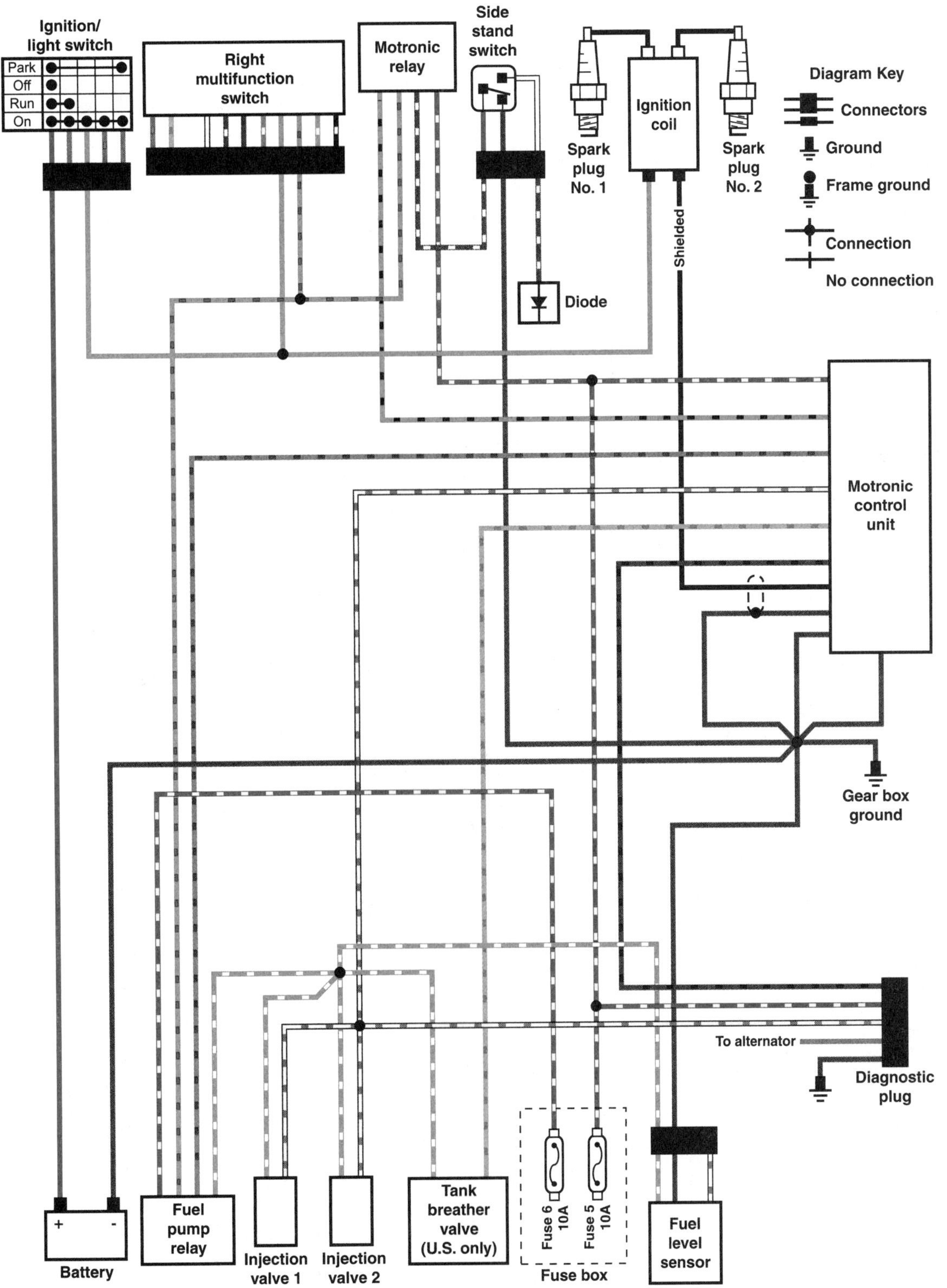

2002-2004 R1150R (U.S.) AND 2000-2001 R1150R (U.K) FRAME

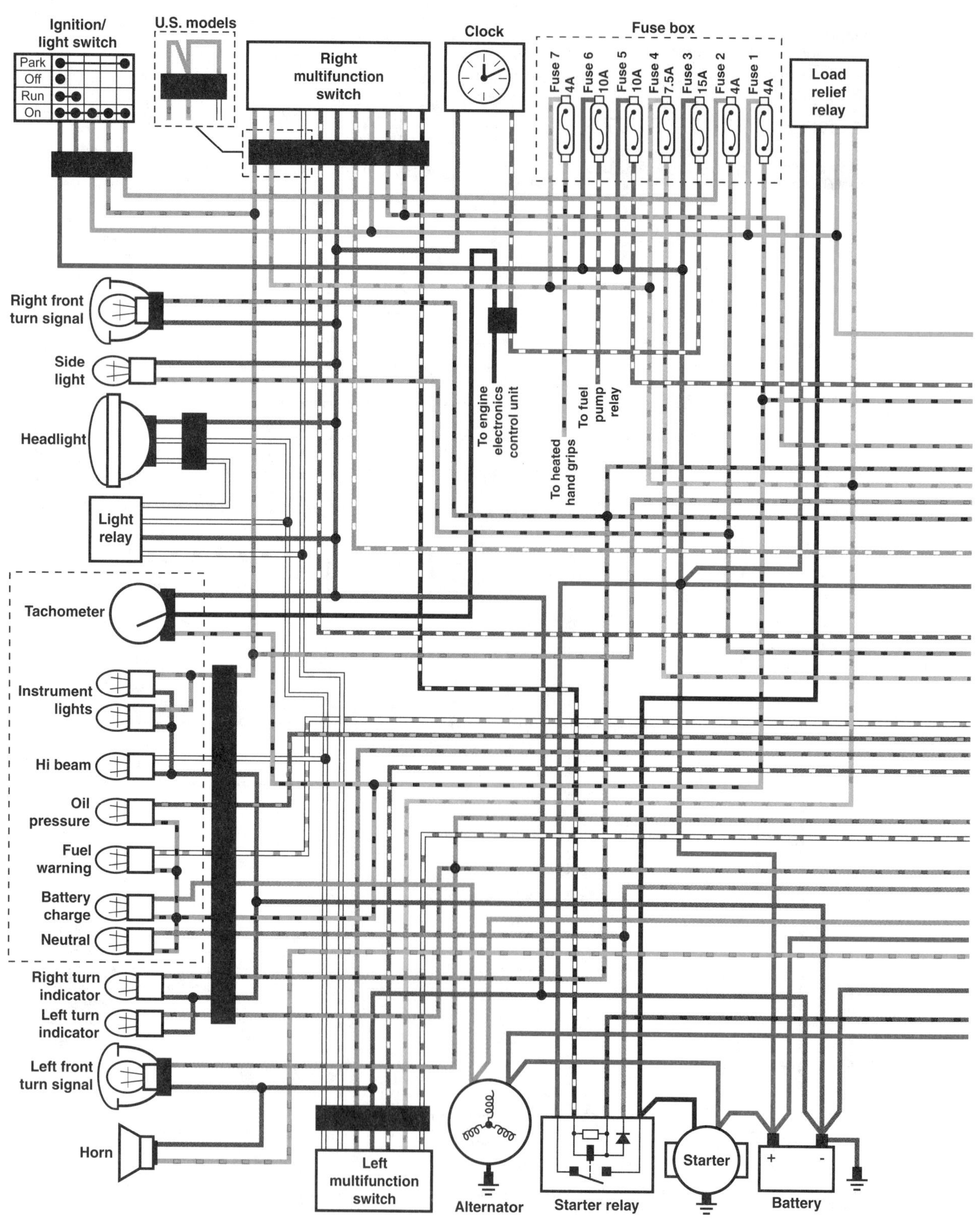

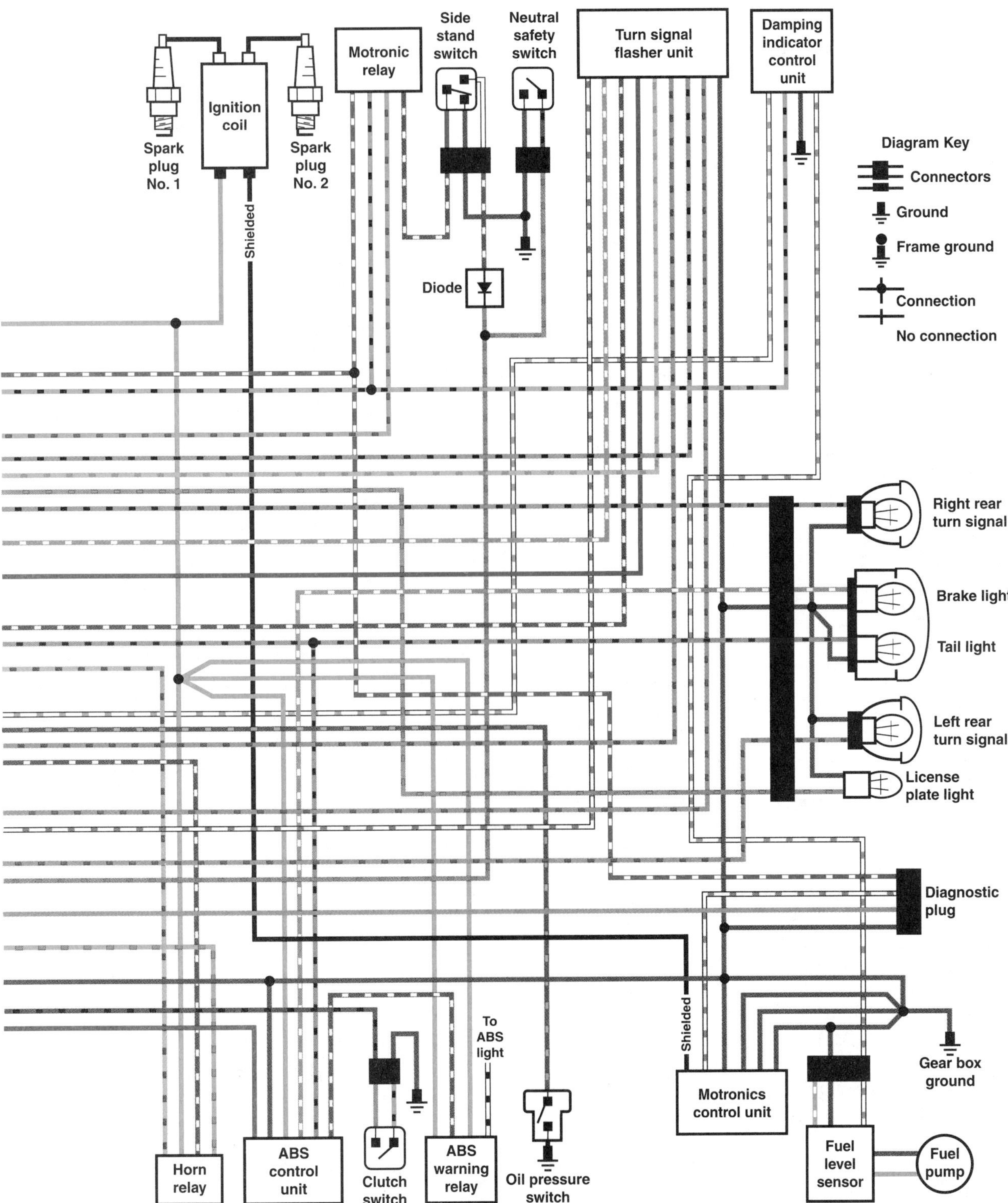
Spark plug No. 1
Ignition coil
Spark plug No. 2
Shielded
Motronic relay
Side stand switch
Neutral safety switch
Diode
Turn signal flasher unit
Damping indicator control unit
Diagram Key
Connectors
Ground
Frame ground
Connection
No connection
Right rear turn signal
Brake light
Tail light
Left rear turn signal
License plate light
Diagnostic plug
Shielded
Gear box ground
Horn relay
ABS control unit
Clutch switch
To ABS light
ABS warning relay
Oil pressure switch
Motronics control unit
Fuel level sensor
Fuel pump

17

2003-2004 ROCKSTER (U.S.)
MOTRONICS WITH LOAD RELIEF RELAY II

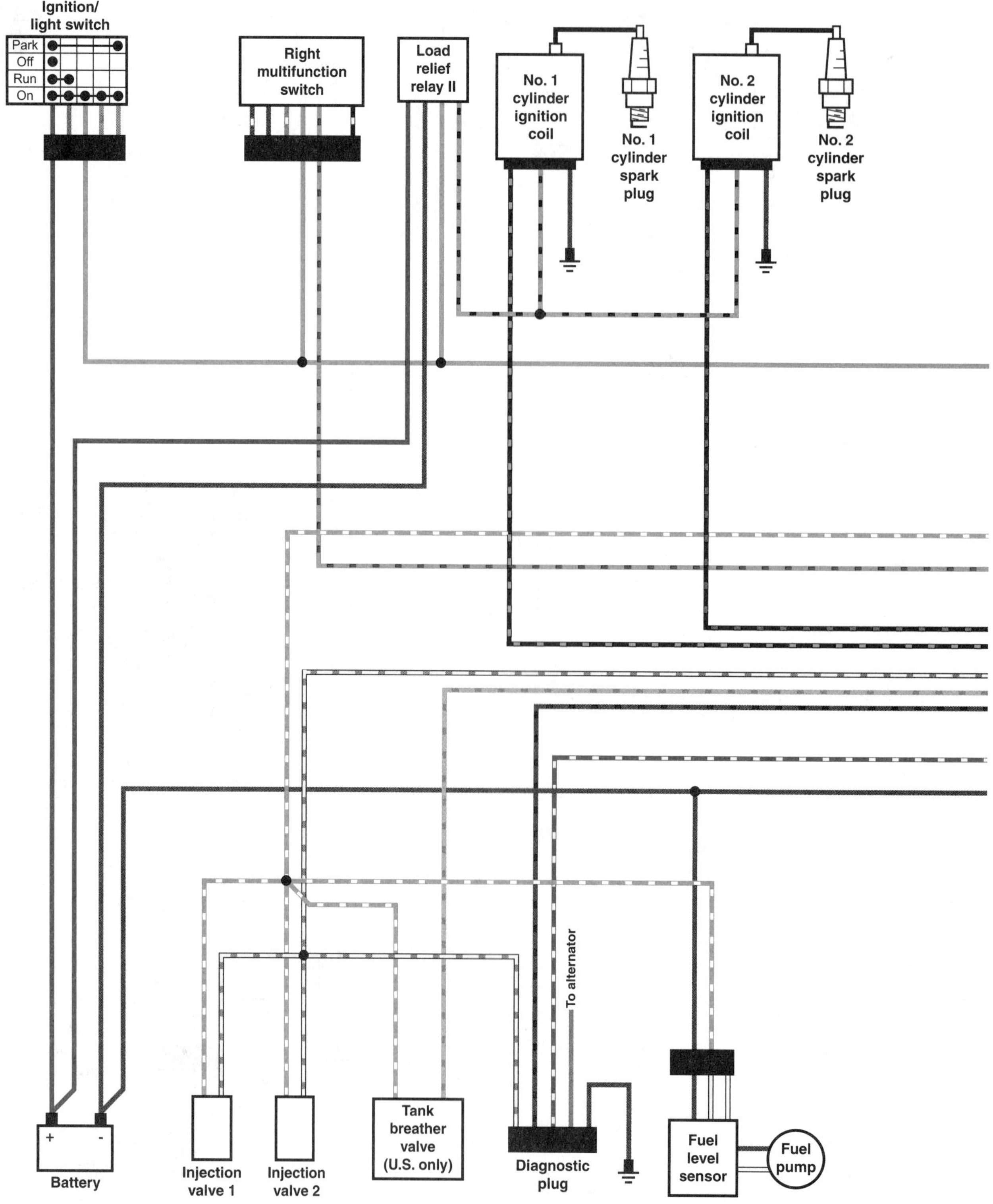

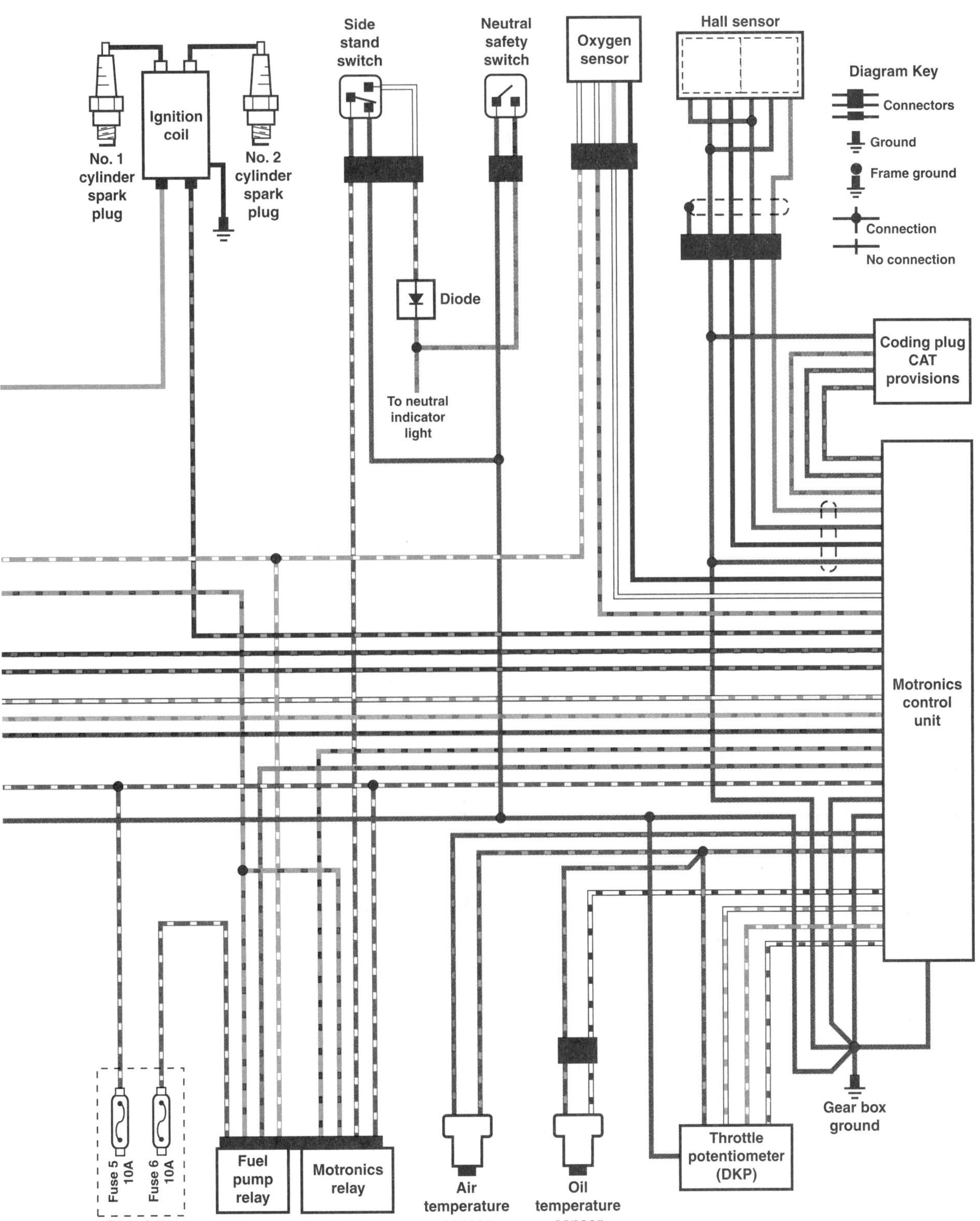

No. 1 cylinder spark plug
Ignition coil
No. 2 cylinder spark plug
Side stand switch
Neutral safety switch
Oxygen sensor
Hall sensor
Diagram Key
Connectors
Ground
Frame ground
Connection
No connection
Diode
To neutral indicator light
Coding plug CAT provisions
Motronics control unit
Fuse 5 10A
Fuse 6 10A
Fuse box
Fuel pump relay
Motronics relay
Air temperature sensor
Oil temperature sensor
Throttle potentiometer (DKP)
Gear box ground

2003-2004 ROCKSTER (U.S.)
MOTRONICS WITHOUT LOAD RELIEF RELAY II

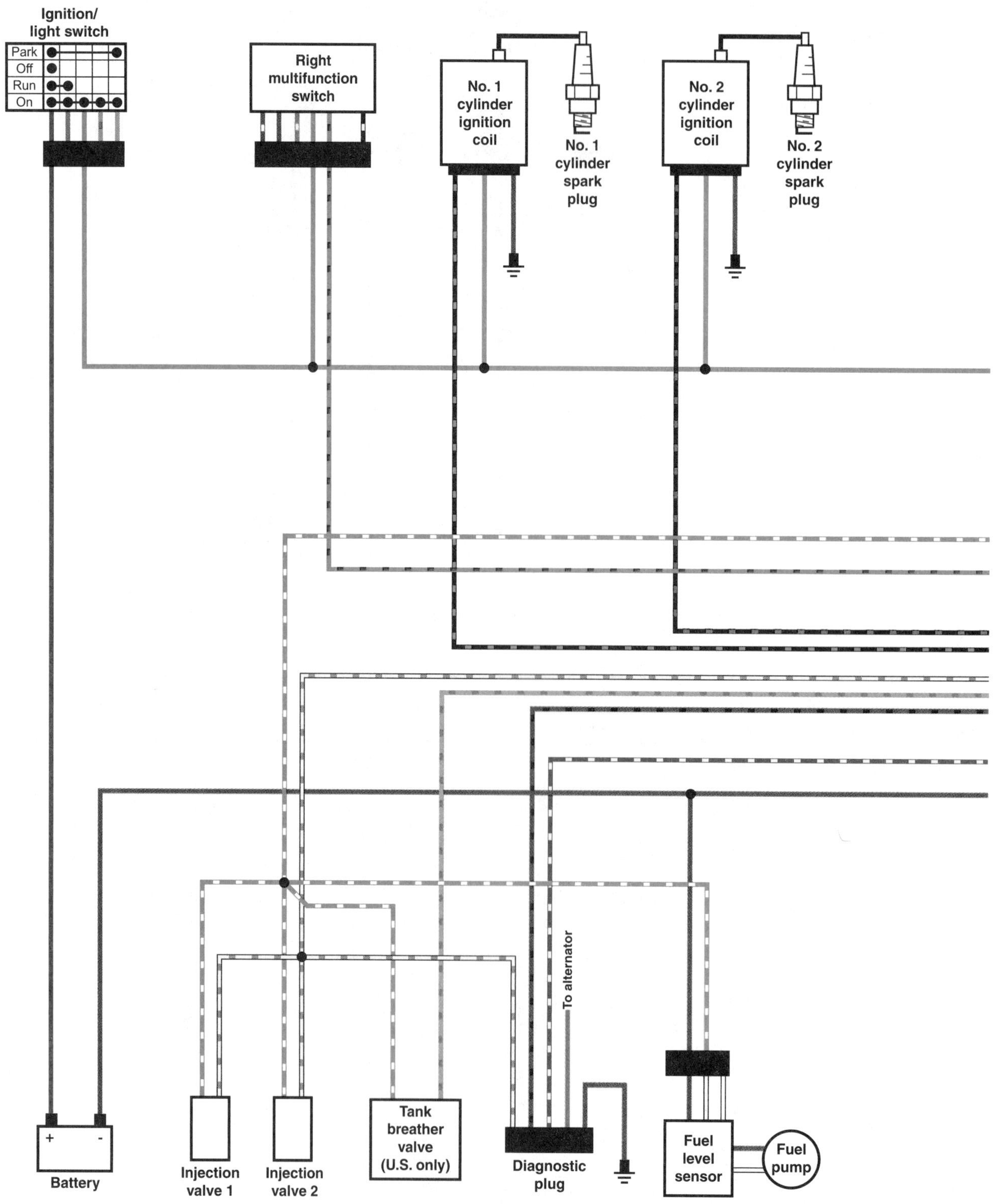

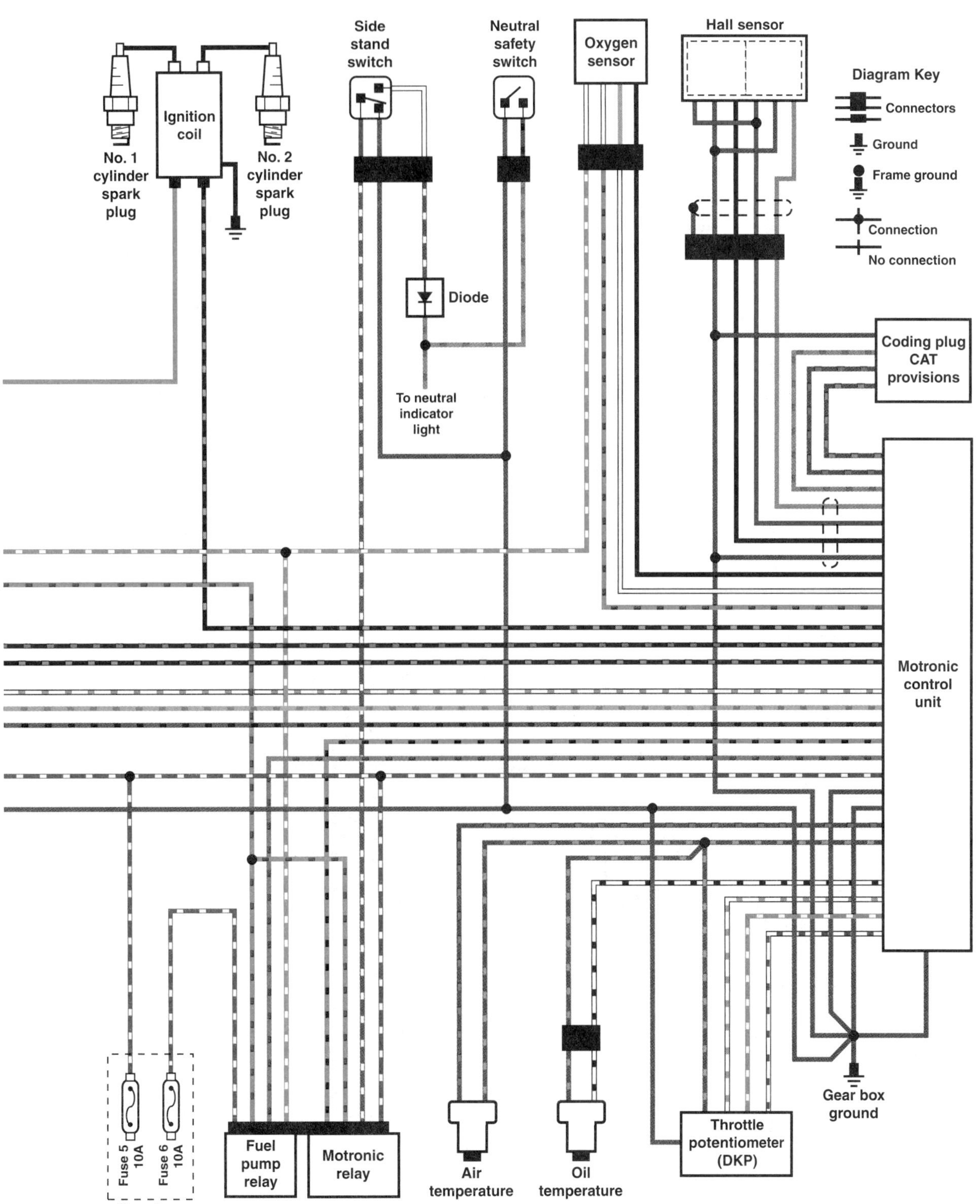

Side stand switch
Neutral safety switch
Oxygen sensor
Hall sensor
Diagram Key
Connectors
Ground
Frame ground
Connection
No connection
Ignition coil
No. 1 cylinder spark plug
No. 2 cylinder spark plug
Diode
To neutral indicator light
Coding plug CAT provisions
Motronic control unit
Fuse 5 10A
Fuse 6 10A
Fuse box
Fuel pump relay
Motronic relay
Air temperature sensor
Oil temperature sensor
Throttle potentiometer (DKP)
Gear box ground

2003-2004 ROCKSTER (U.S) FRAME

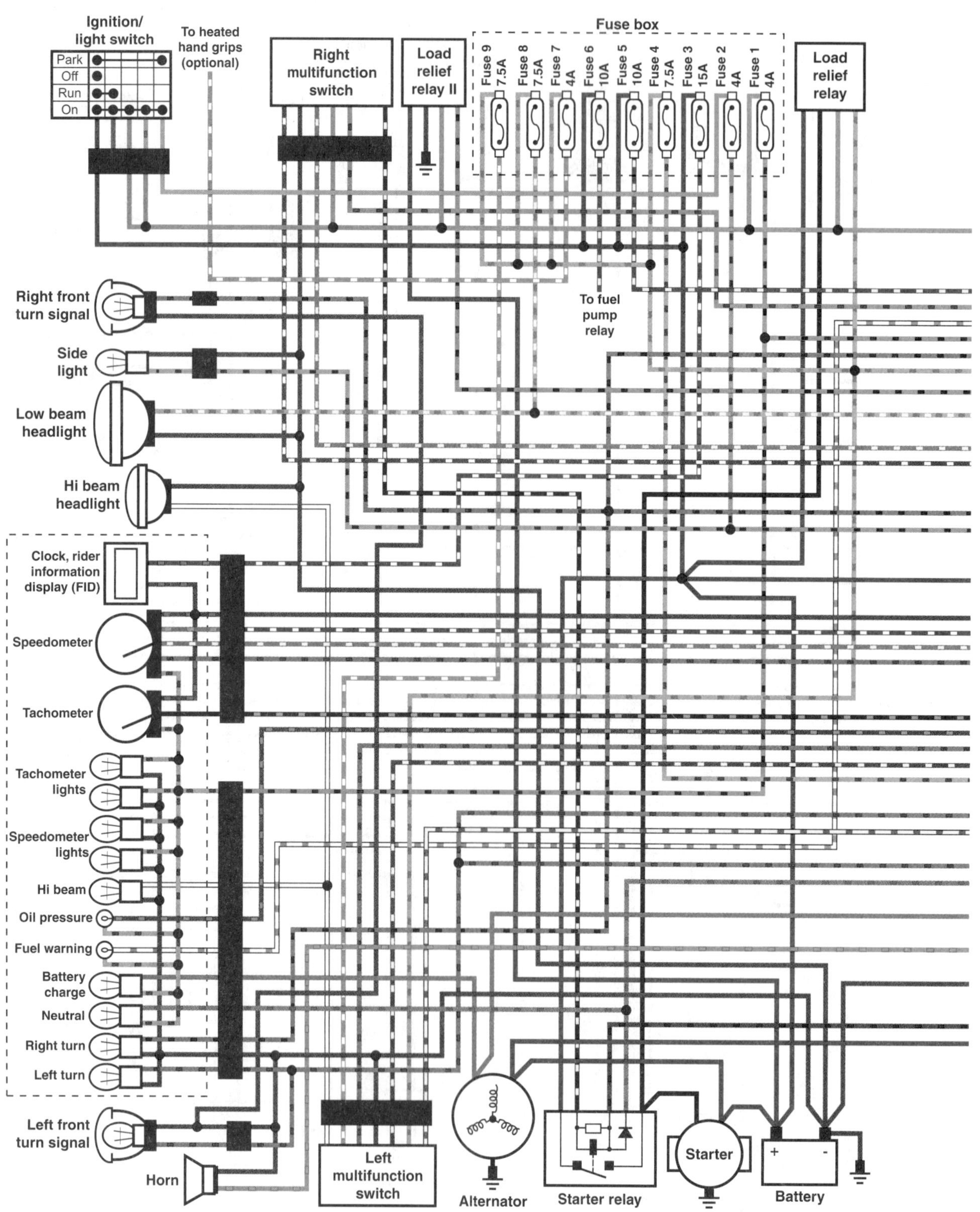

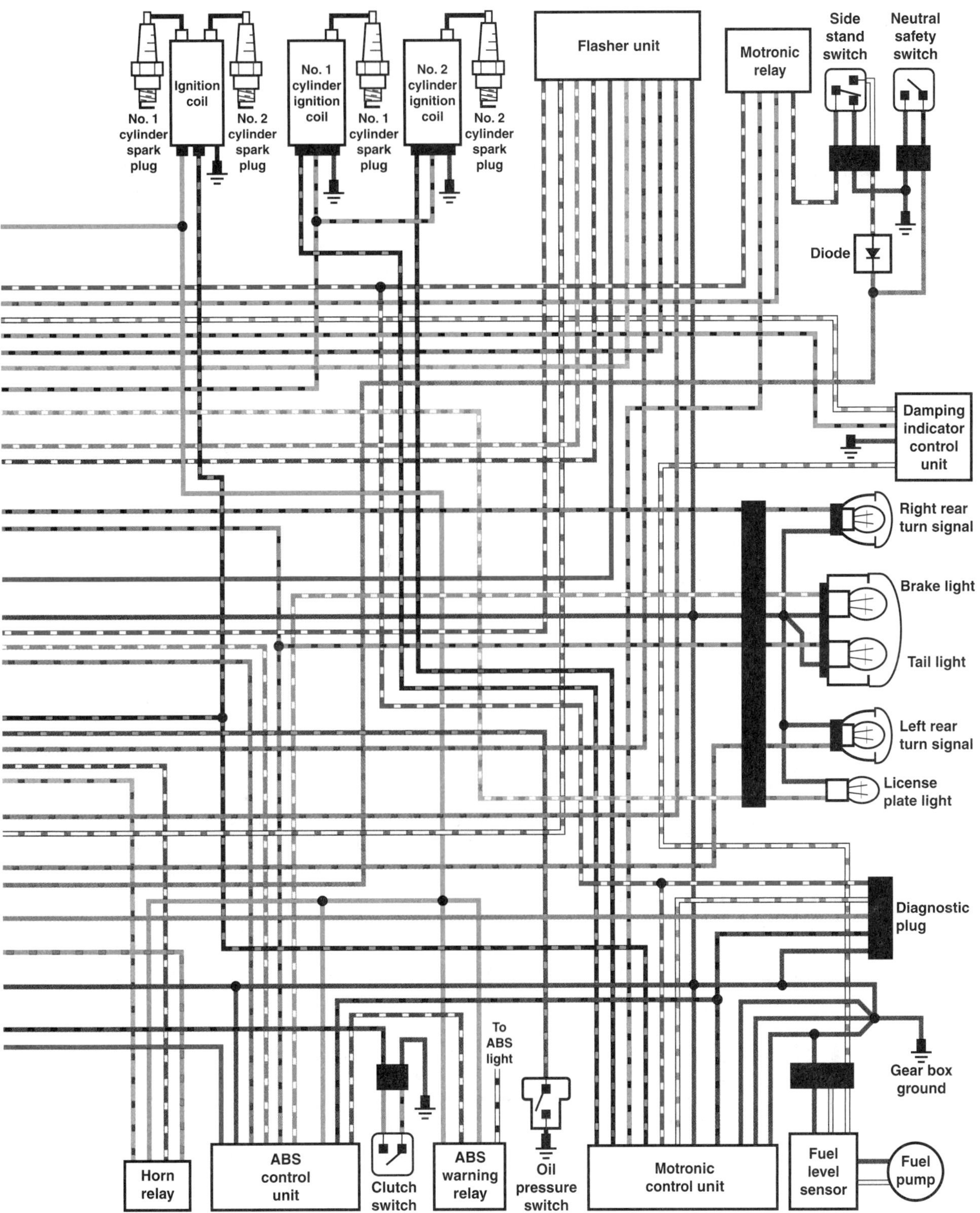
No. 1 cylinder spark plug
Ignition coil
No. 2 cylinder spark plug
No. 1 cylinder ignition coil
No. 1 cylinder spark plug
No. 2 cylinder ignition coil
No. 2 cylinder spark plug
Flasher unit
Motronic relay
Side stand switch
Neutral safety switch
Diode
Damping indicator control unit
Right rear turn signal
Brake light
Tail light
Left rear turn signal
License plate light
Diagnostic plug
Gear box ground
To ABS light
Horn relay
ABS control unit
Clutch switch
ABS warning relay
Oil pressure switch
Motronic control unit
Fuel level sensor
Fuel pump

2001 R1150RS (U.K) AND 2002-2004 R1150RT (U.S.)
ENGINE ELECTRONICS WITH INPUTS

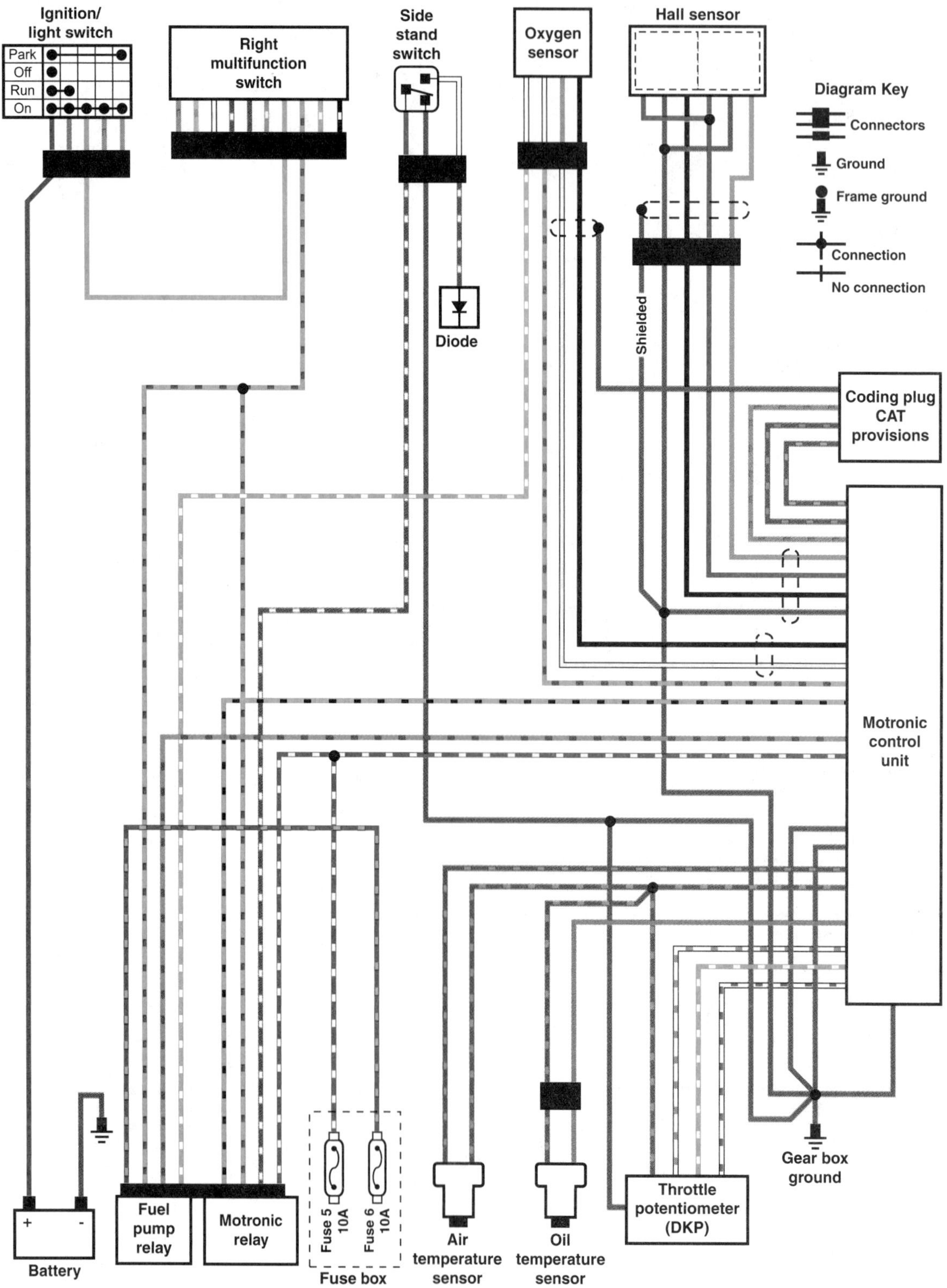

2001 R1150RS (U.K) AND 2002-2004 R1150RS (U.S.) ENGINE ELECTRONICS WITH OUTPUTS

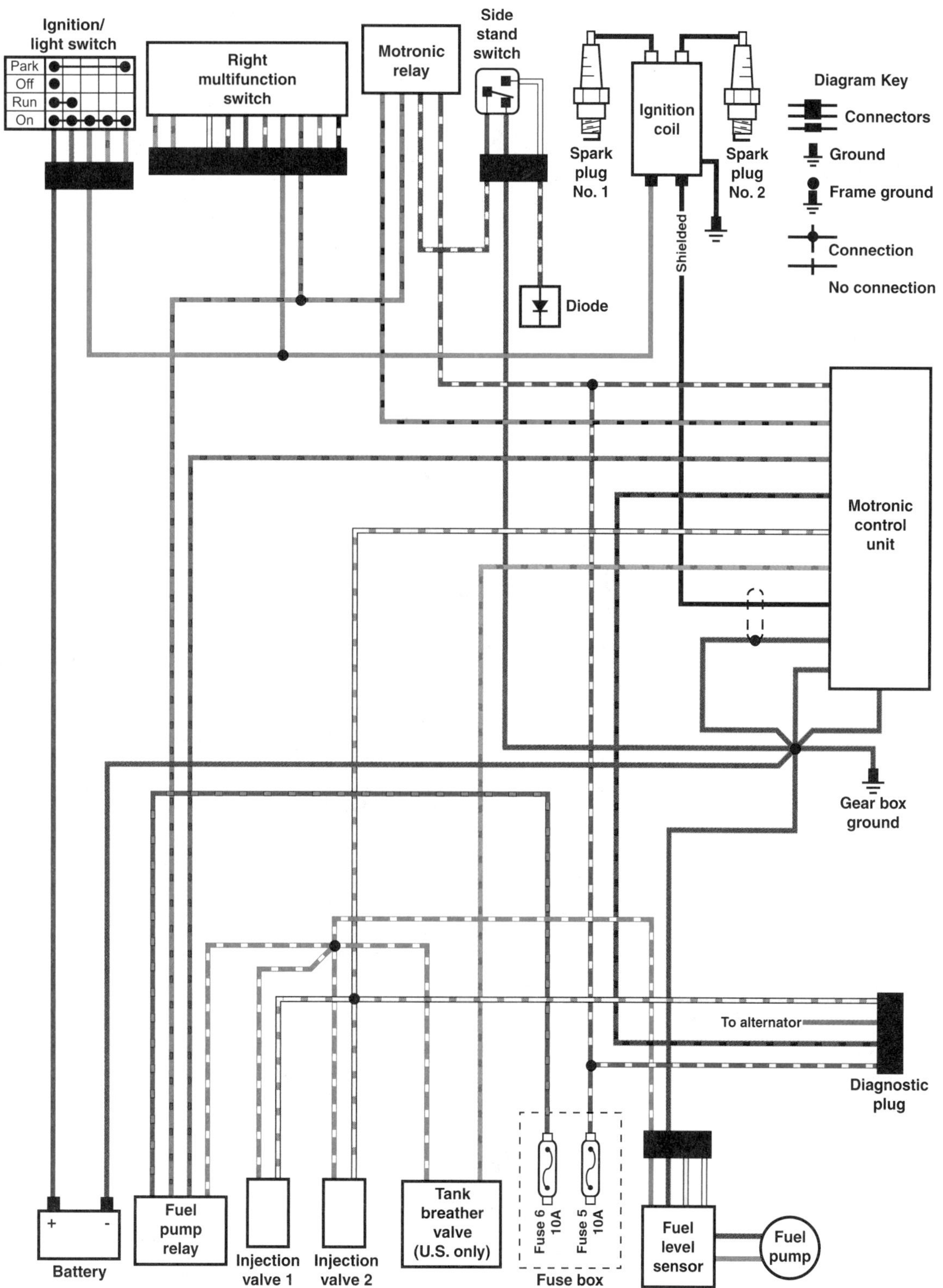

2001 R1150RS (U.K) AND 2002-2003 R1150RS (U.S) FRAME

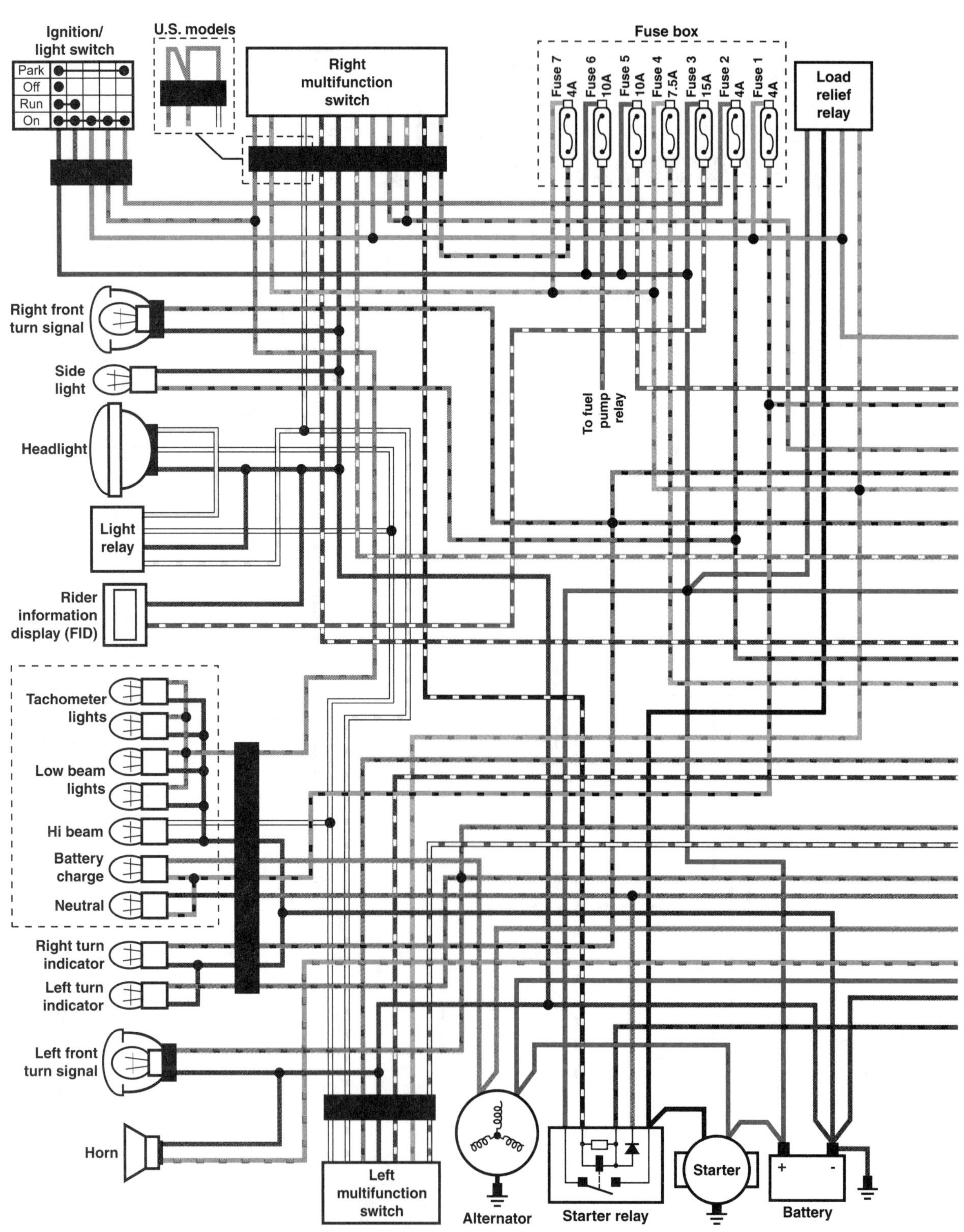

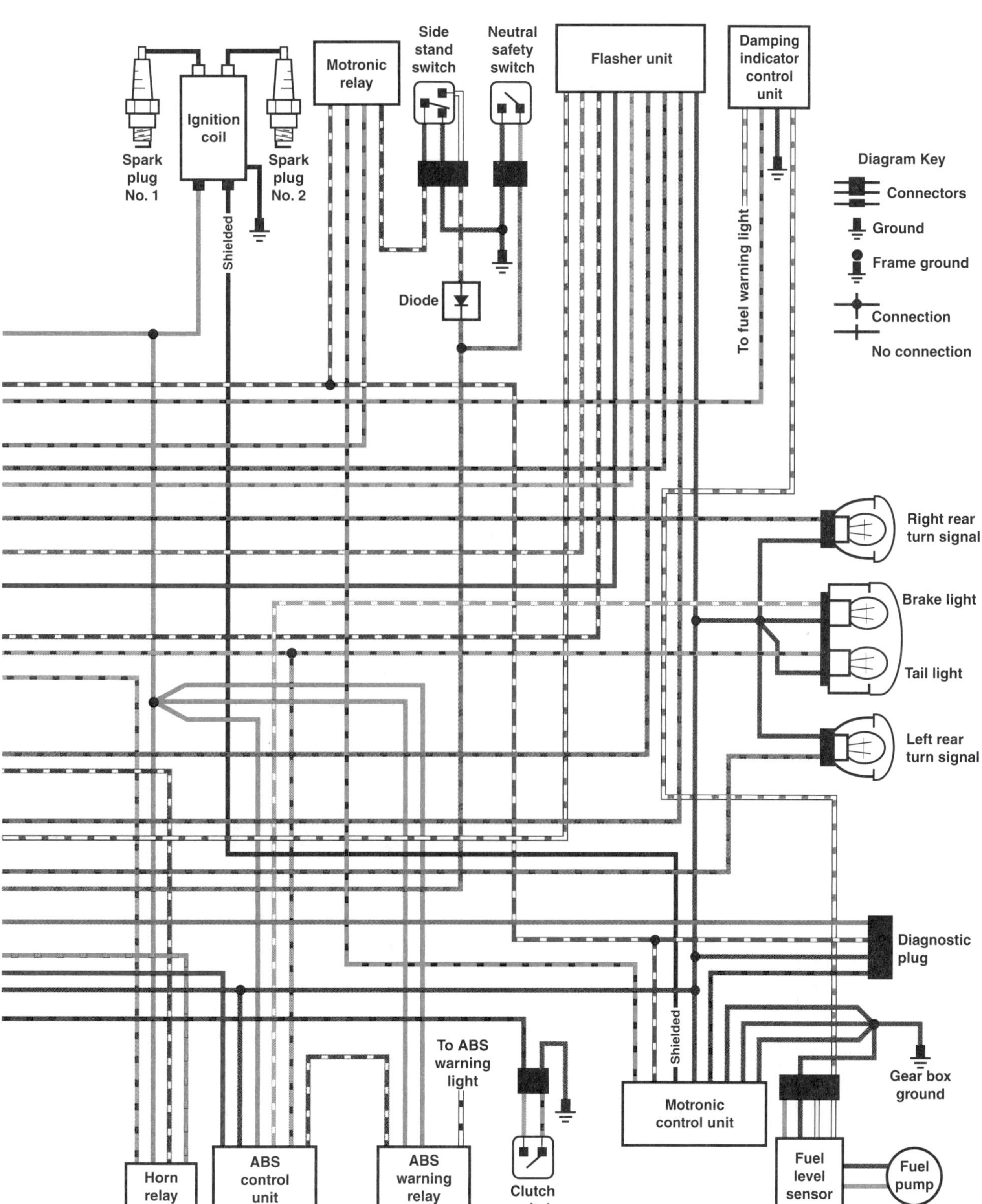
Spark plug No. 1
Ignition coil
Spark plug No. 2
Shielded
Motronic relay
Side stand switch
Neutral safety switch
Diode
Flasher unit
Damping indicator control unit
To fuel warning light
Diagram Key
Connectors
Ground
Frame ground
Connection
No connection
Right rear turn signal
Brake light
Tail light
Left rear turn signal
Diagnostic plug
Gear box ground
Shielded
Horn relay
ABS control unit
To ABS warning light
ABS warning relay
Clutch switch
Motronic control unit
Fuel level sensor
Fuel pump

17

2001-2003 R1150RT (U.K) AND 2002-2004 R1150RT (U.S) MOTRONIC WITH INPUTS

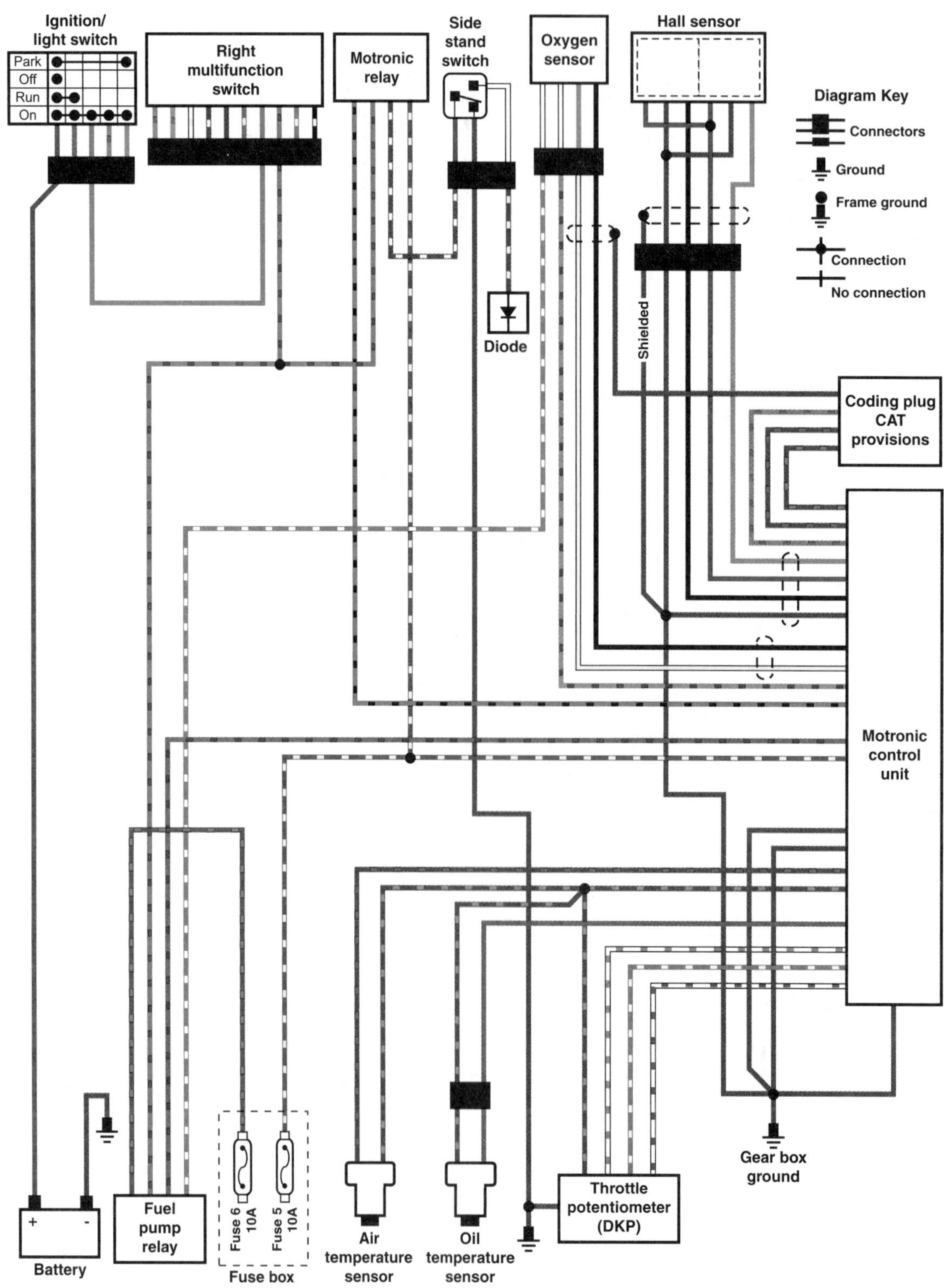

2001-2003 R1150RT (U.K) AND 2002-2004 R1150RT (U.S) MOTRONIC WITH OUTPUTS

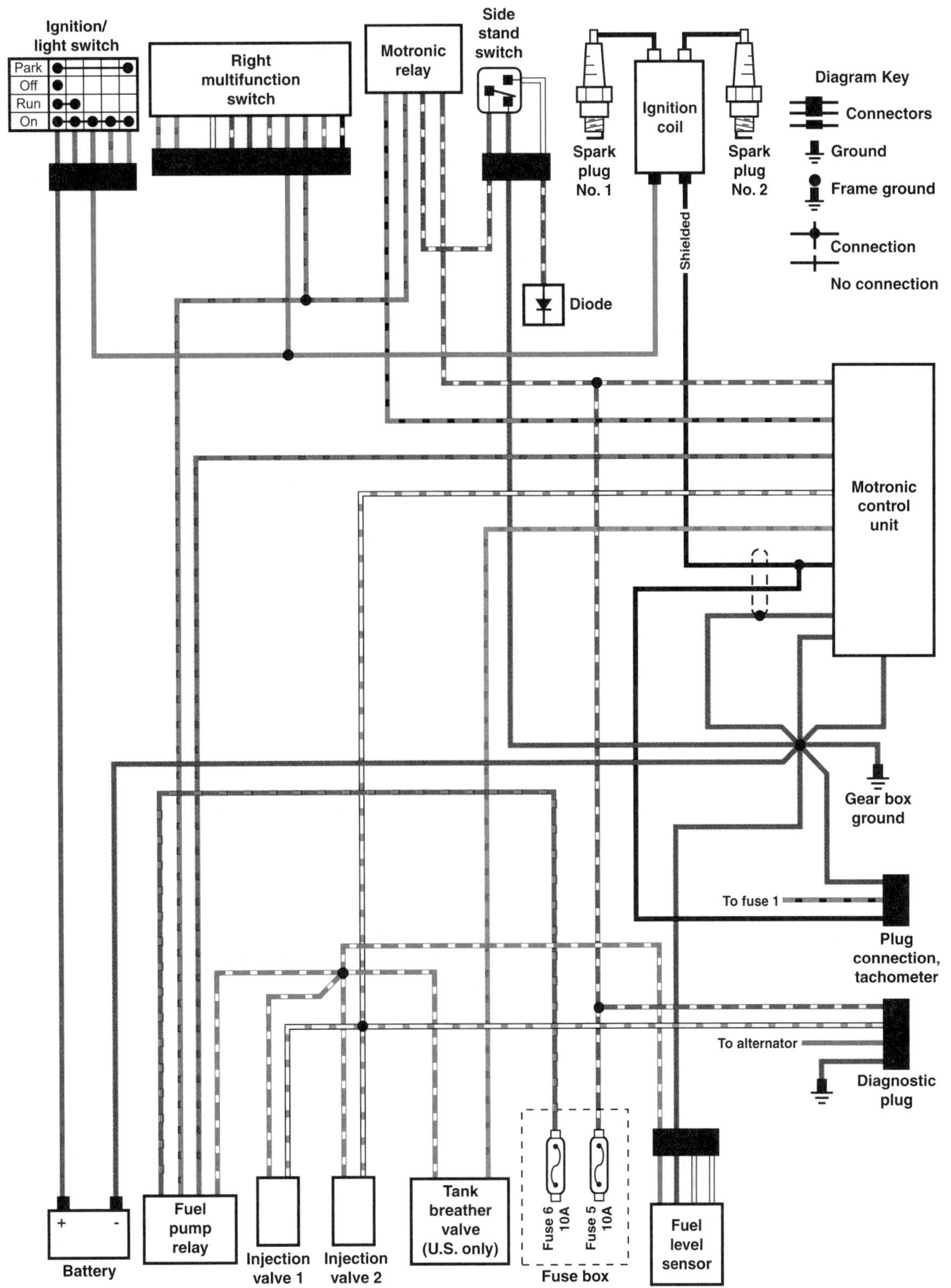

2001-2003 R1150RT (U.K.) AND 2002-2004 R1150RT (U.S.) FRAME

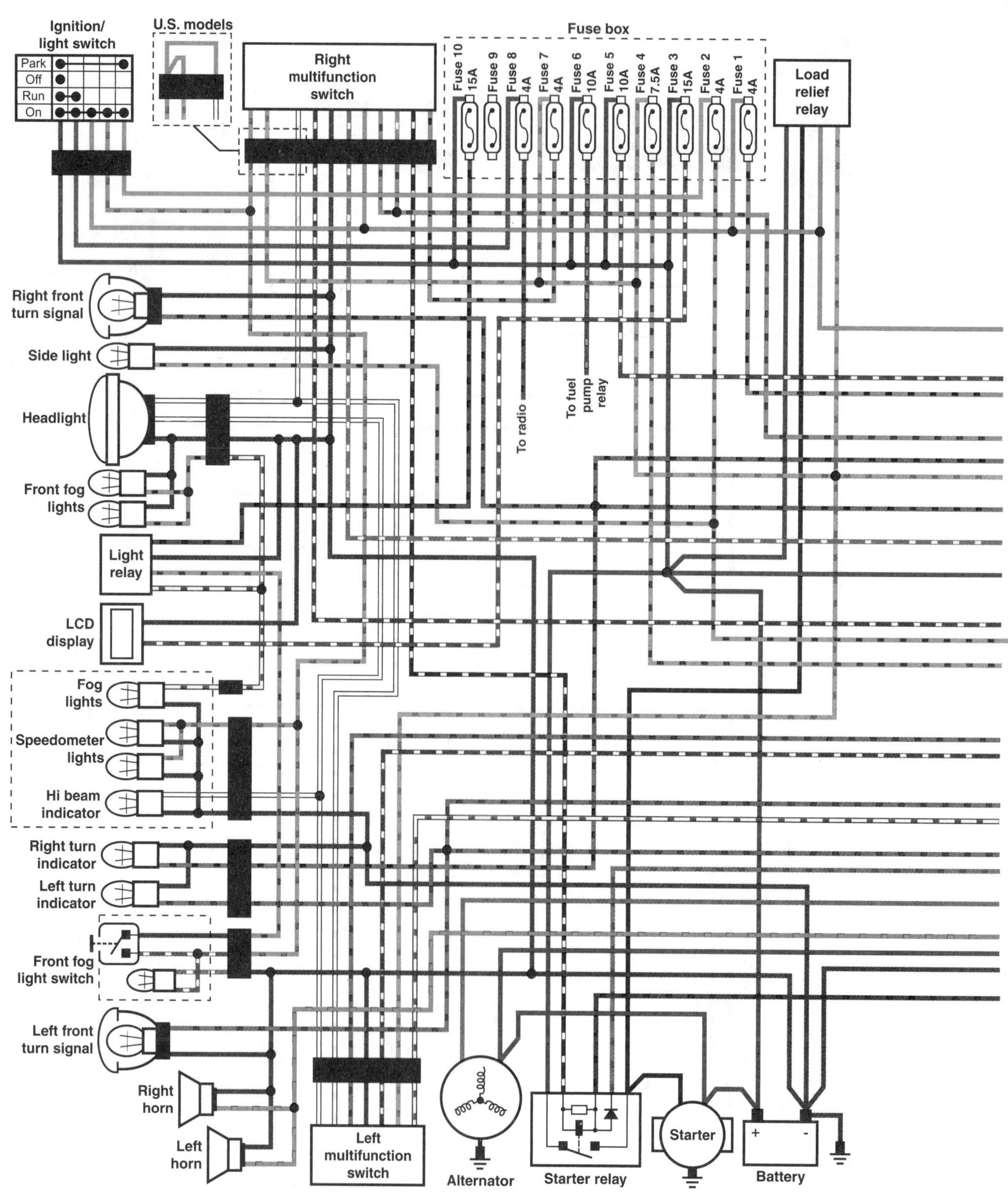

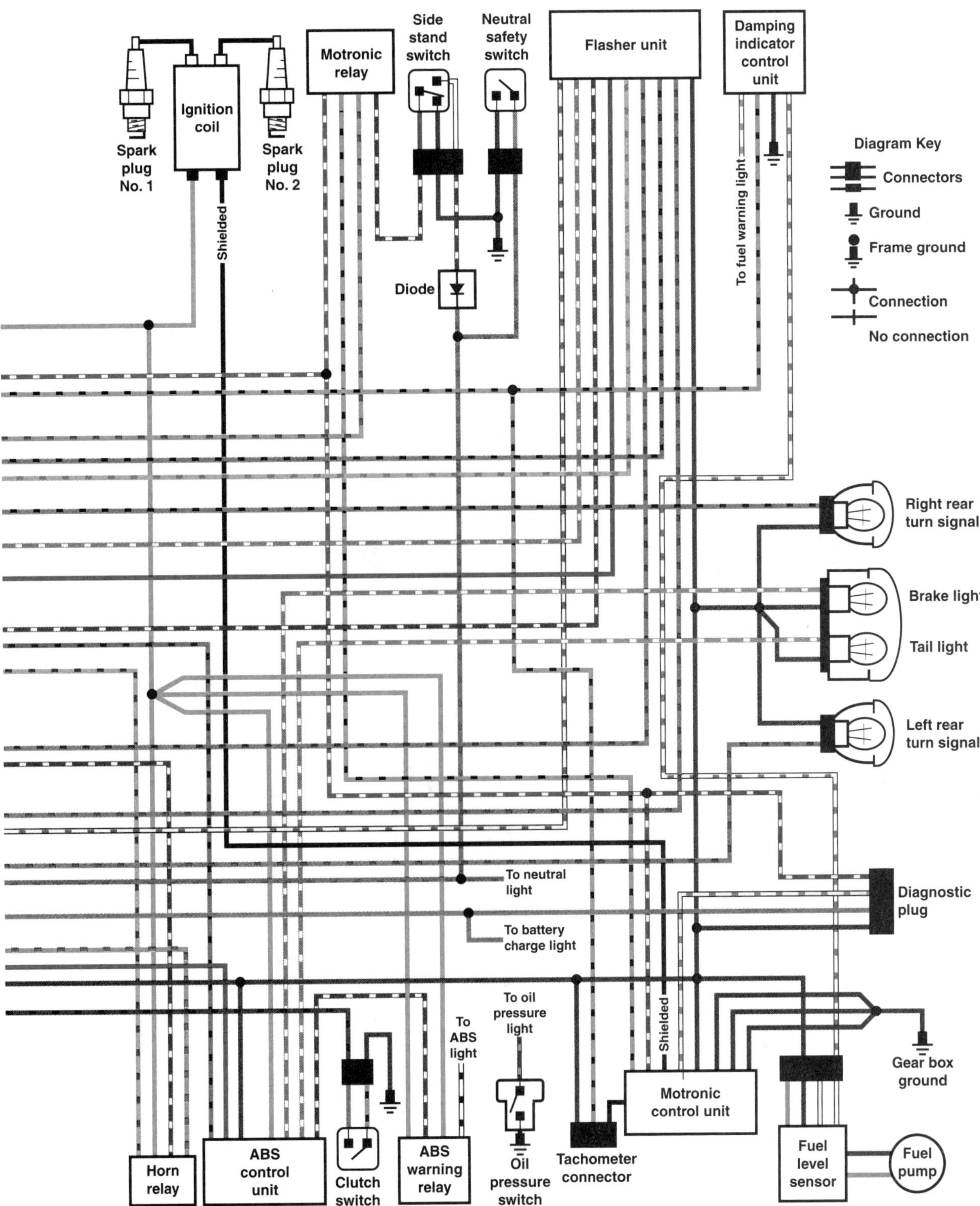
Spark plug No. 1
Ignition coil
Spark plug No. 2
Shielded
Motronic relay
Side stand switch
Neutral safety switch
Diode
Flasher unit
Damping indicator control unit
To fuel warning light
Diagram Key
Connectors
Ground
Frame ground
Connection
No connection
Right rear turn signal
Brake light
Tail light
Left rear turn signal
Diagnostic plug
To neutral light
To battery charge light
To oil pressure light
To ABS light
Shielded
Gear box ground
Horn relay
ABS control unit
Clutch switch
ABS warning relay
Oil pressure switch
Tachometer connector
Motronic control unit
Fuel level sensor
Fuel pump

17

1998-2004 R1200C (U.K.), 1999-2004 R1200C (U.S.) 1999-2001 R850C (U.K.) ABS

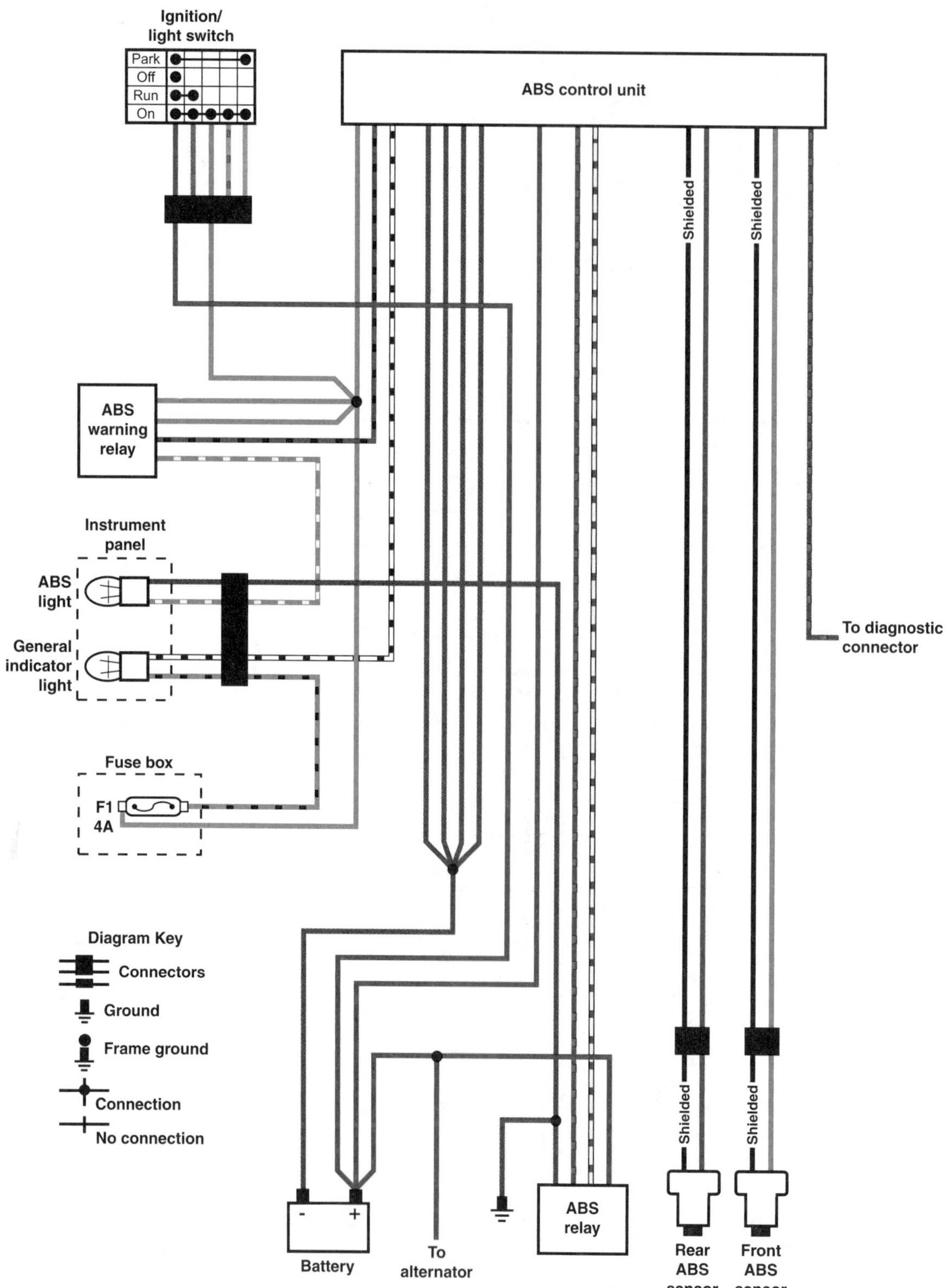

1993-2001 R1100RS (U.S.), 1995-2001R850/R1100R (U.S. AND U.K.) ABS

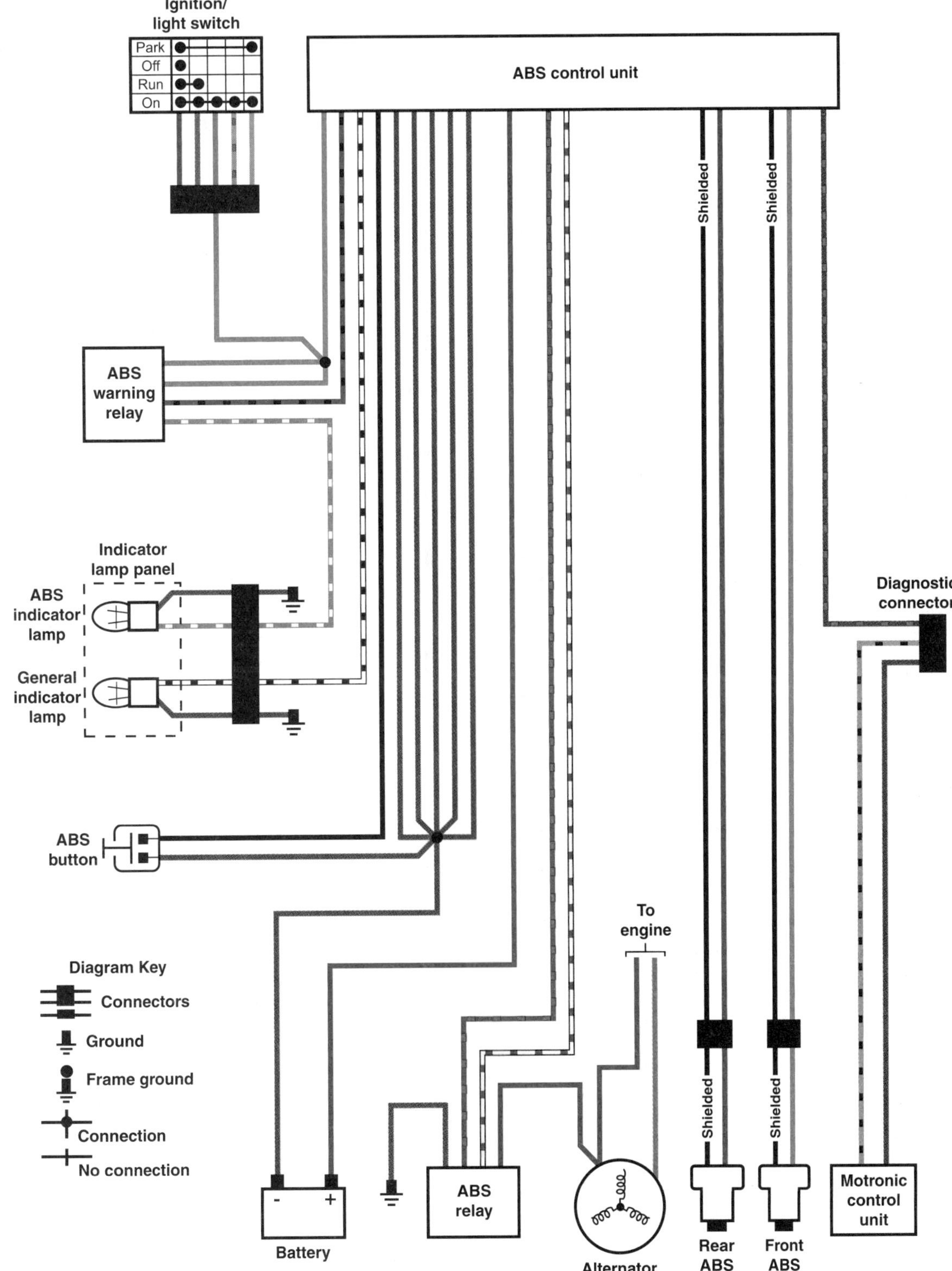

1995-2001 R1100RT ABS (U.S. AND U.K.)

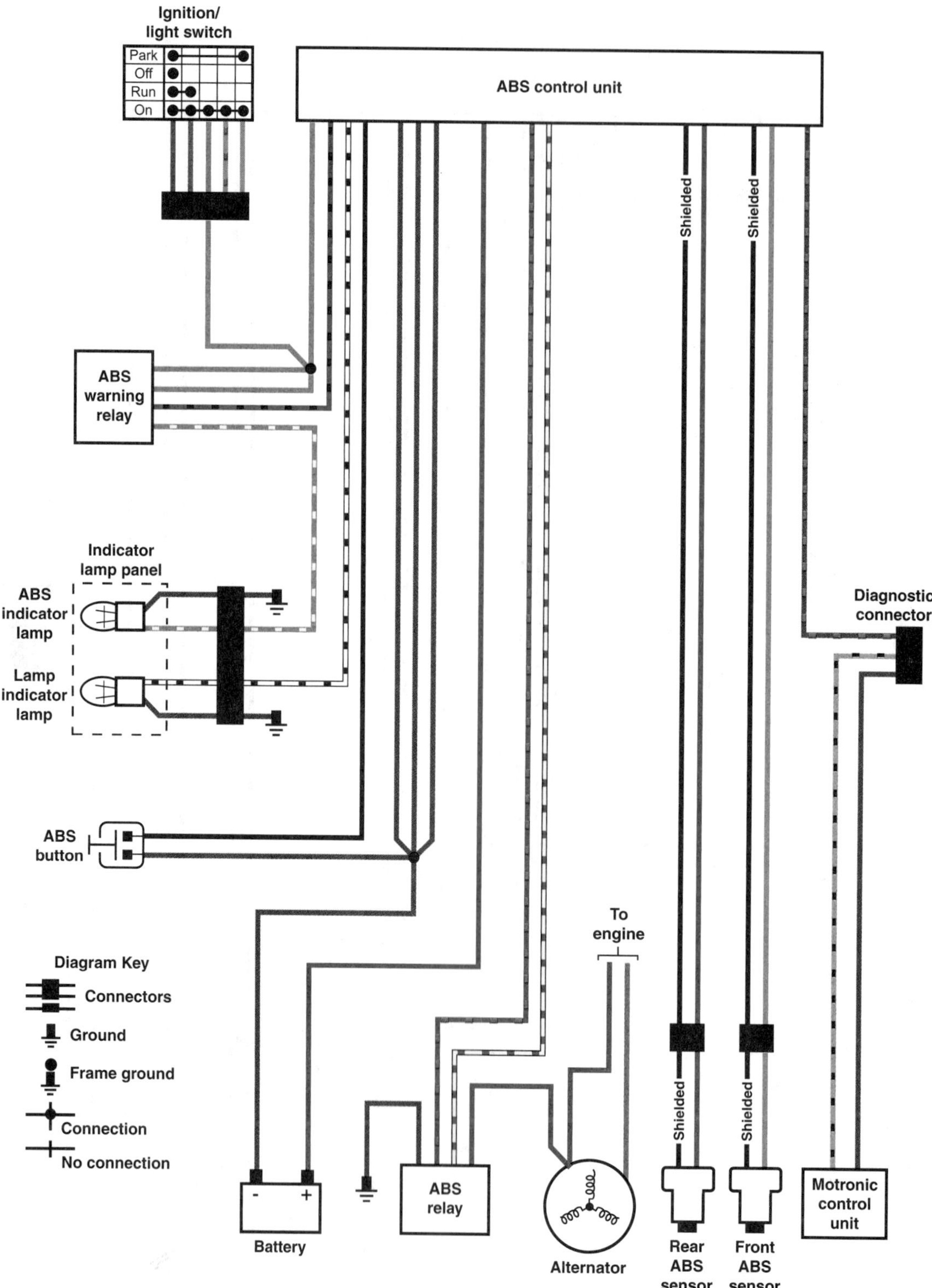

1999-2004 R1100S (U.S.) AND 2000-2003 R1100S (U.K.) ABS

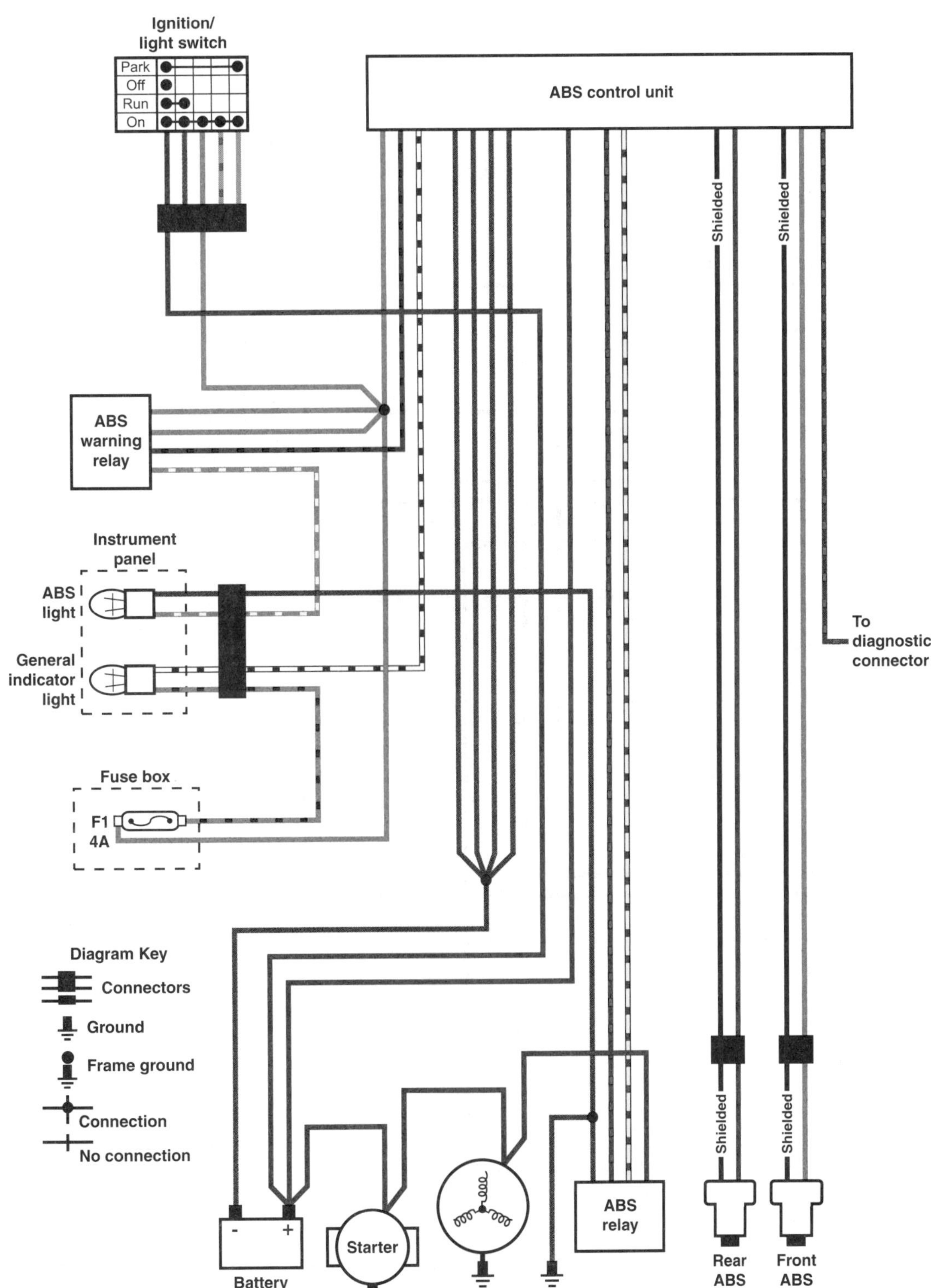

1999-2003 R1150GS (U.K.) AND 2000-2004 R1150GS (U.S.) ABS

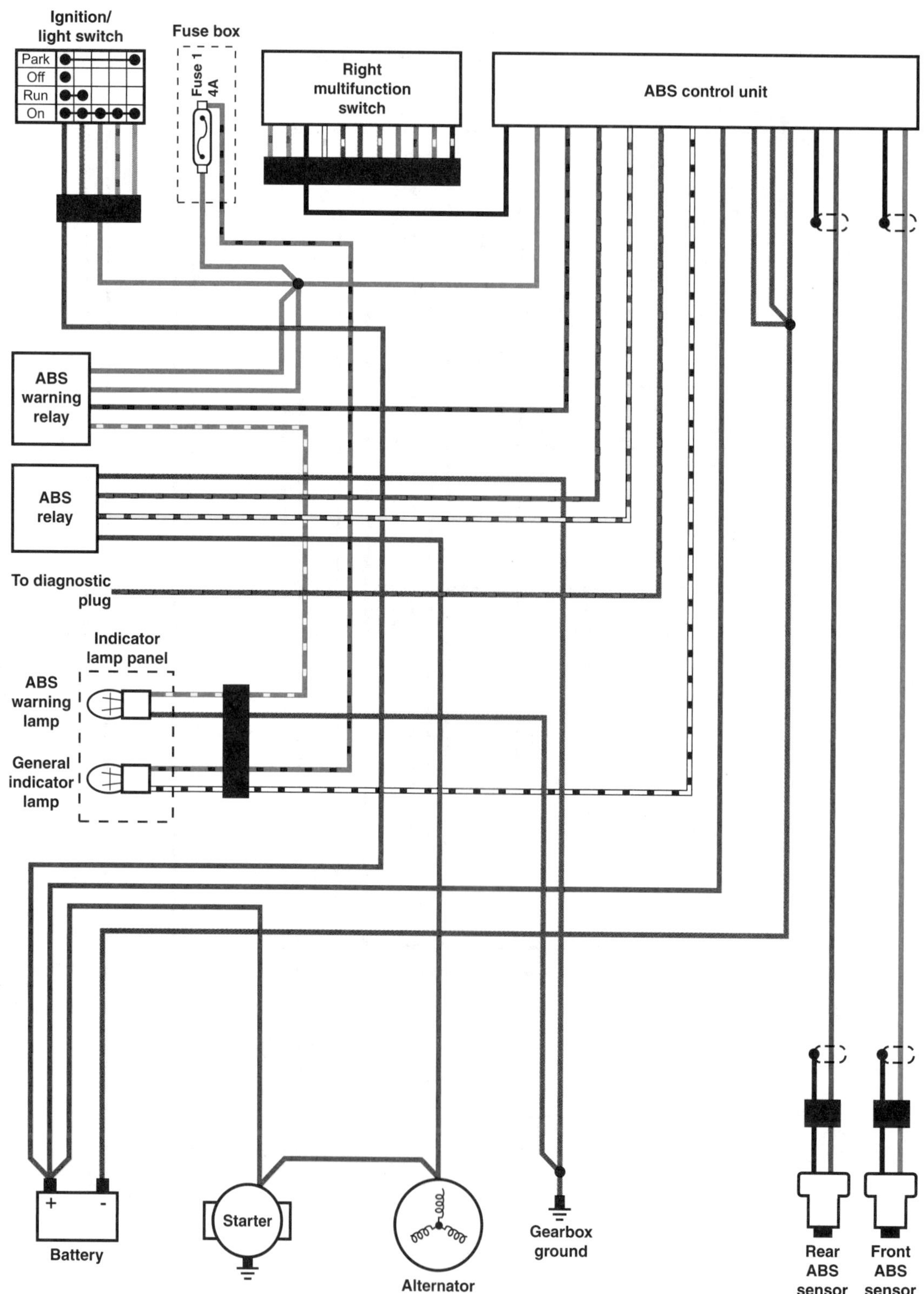

2002-2004 R1150R (U.S) AND 2000-2001 R1150R (U.K.) ABS

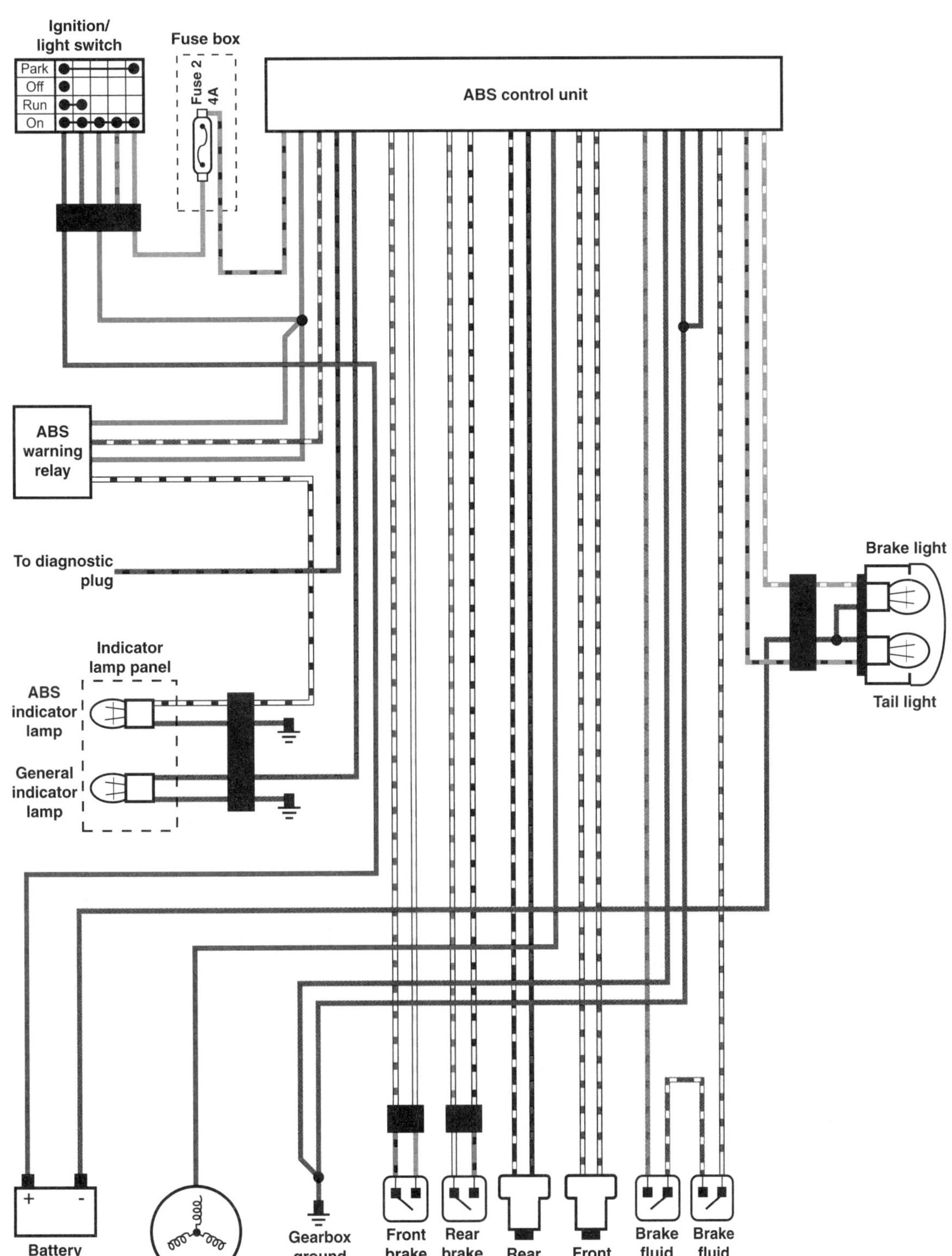

2003-2004 ROCKSTER (U.S.) ABS

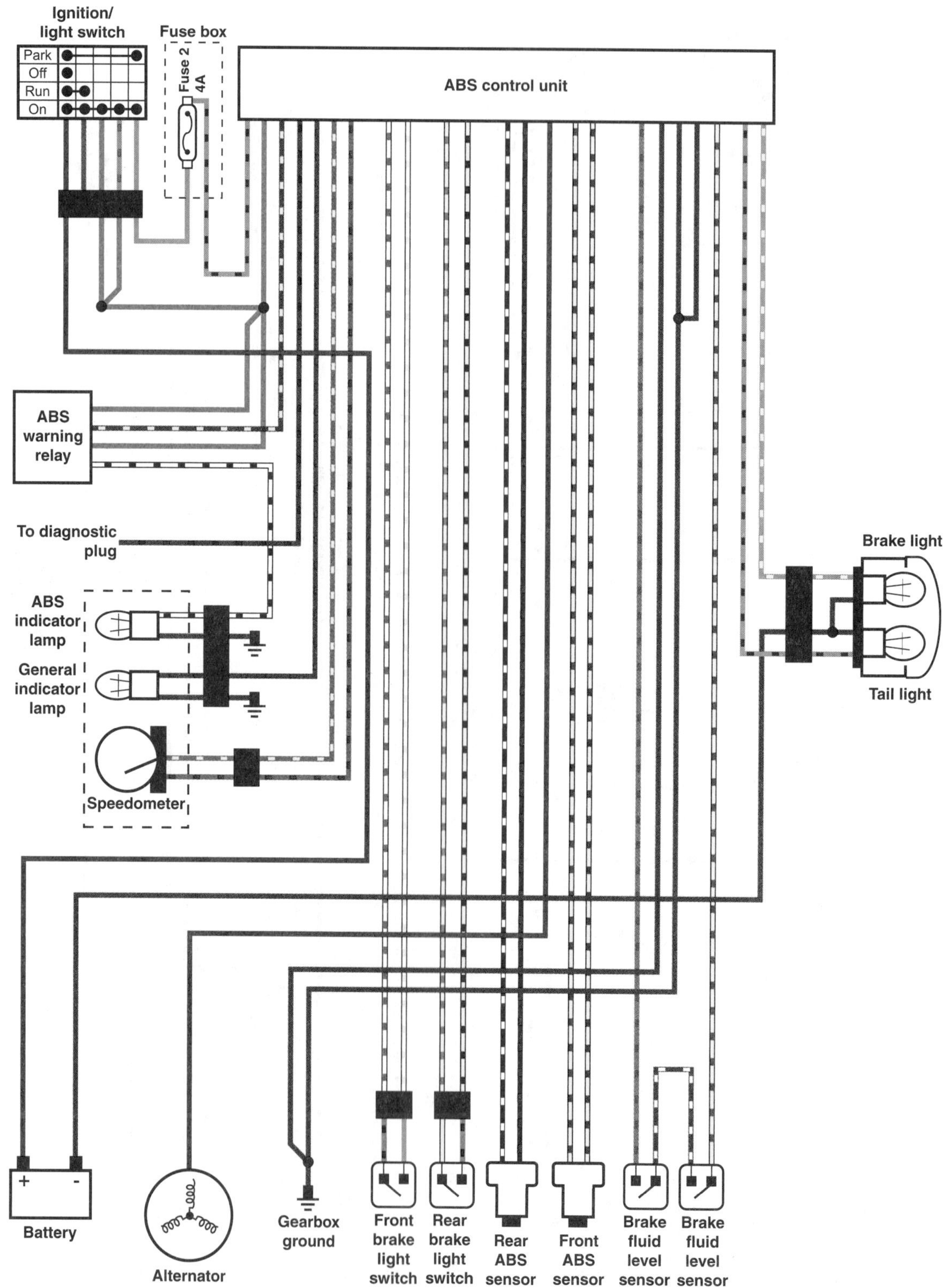

2001 R1150RS (U.K.) AND 2002-2004 R1150RS (U.S.) ABS

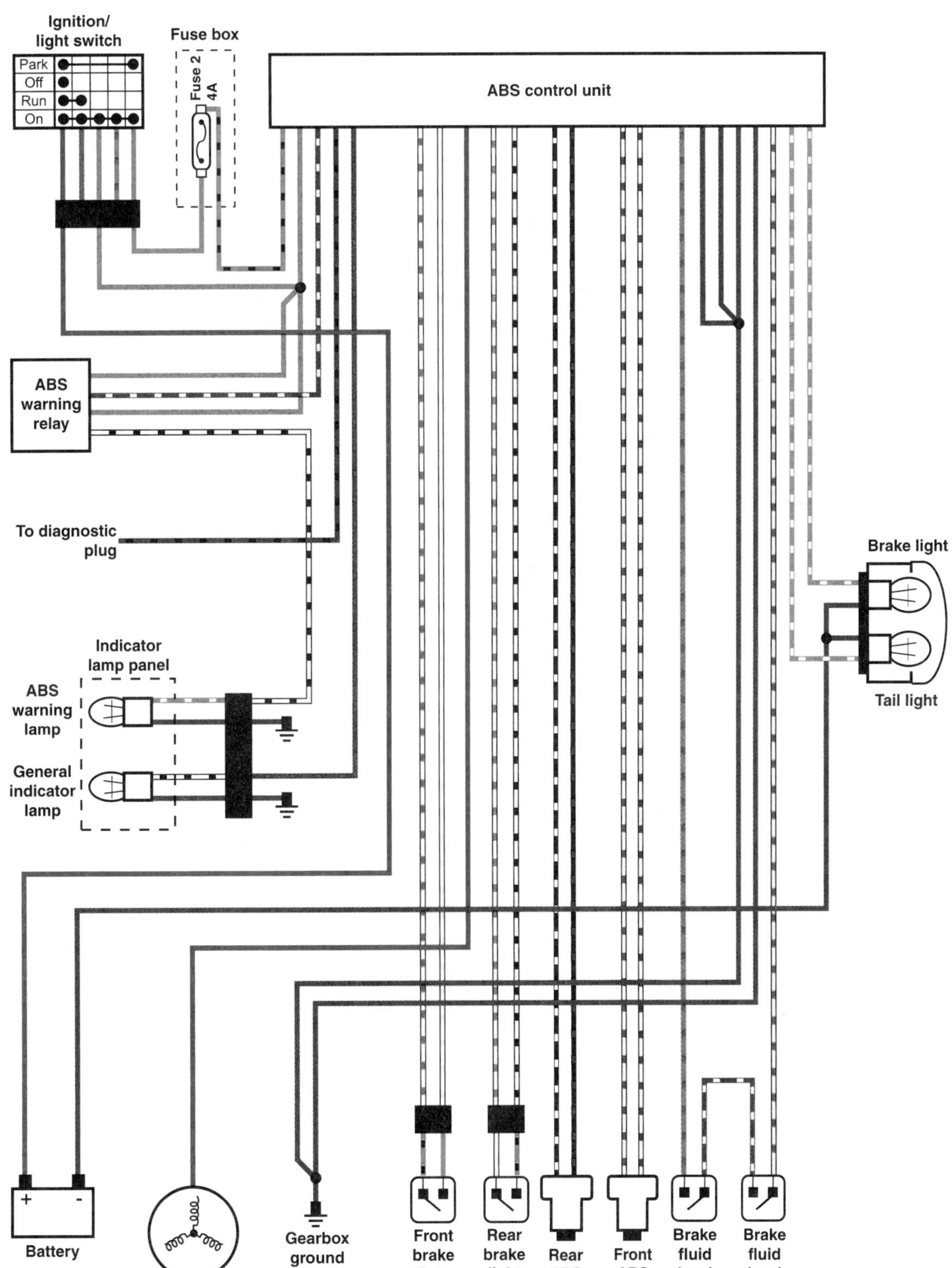

2000-2003 R1150RT (U.K.) AND 2002-2004 R1150RT (U.S) ABS

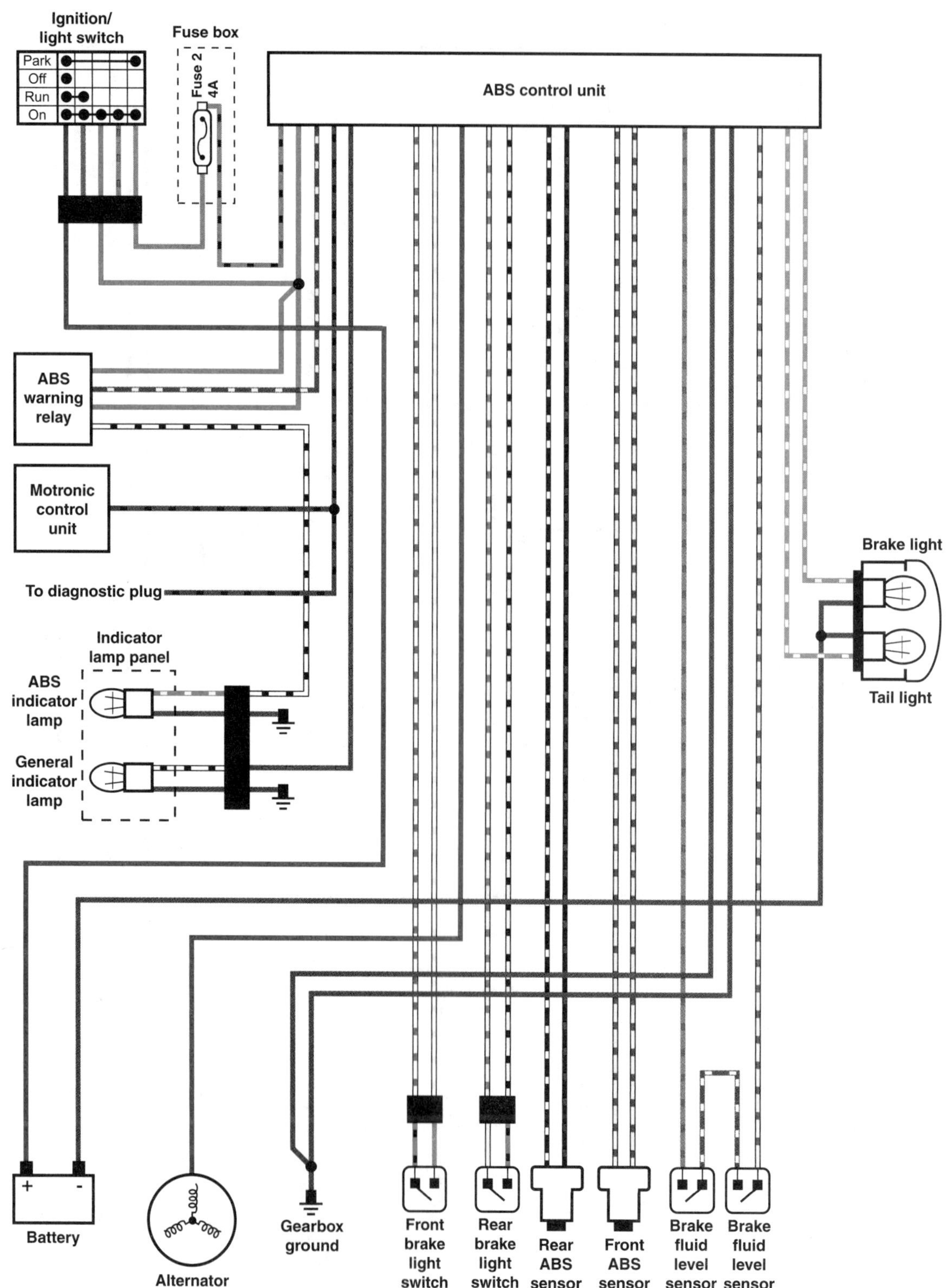

2002-2004 R1150R (U.S.) AND 2000-2001 R1150R (U.K.) BRAKE LIGHT AND TAIL LIGHT WITHOUT ABS ACCESSORIES

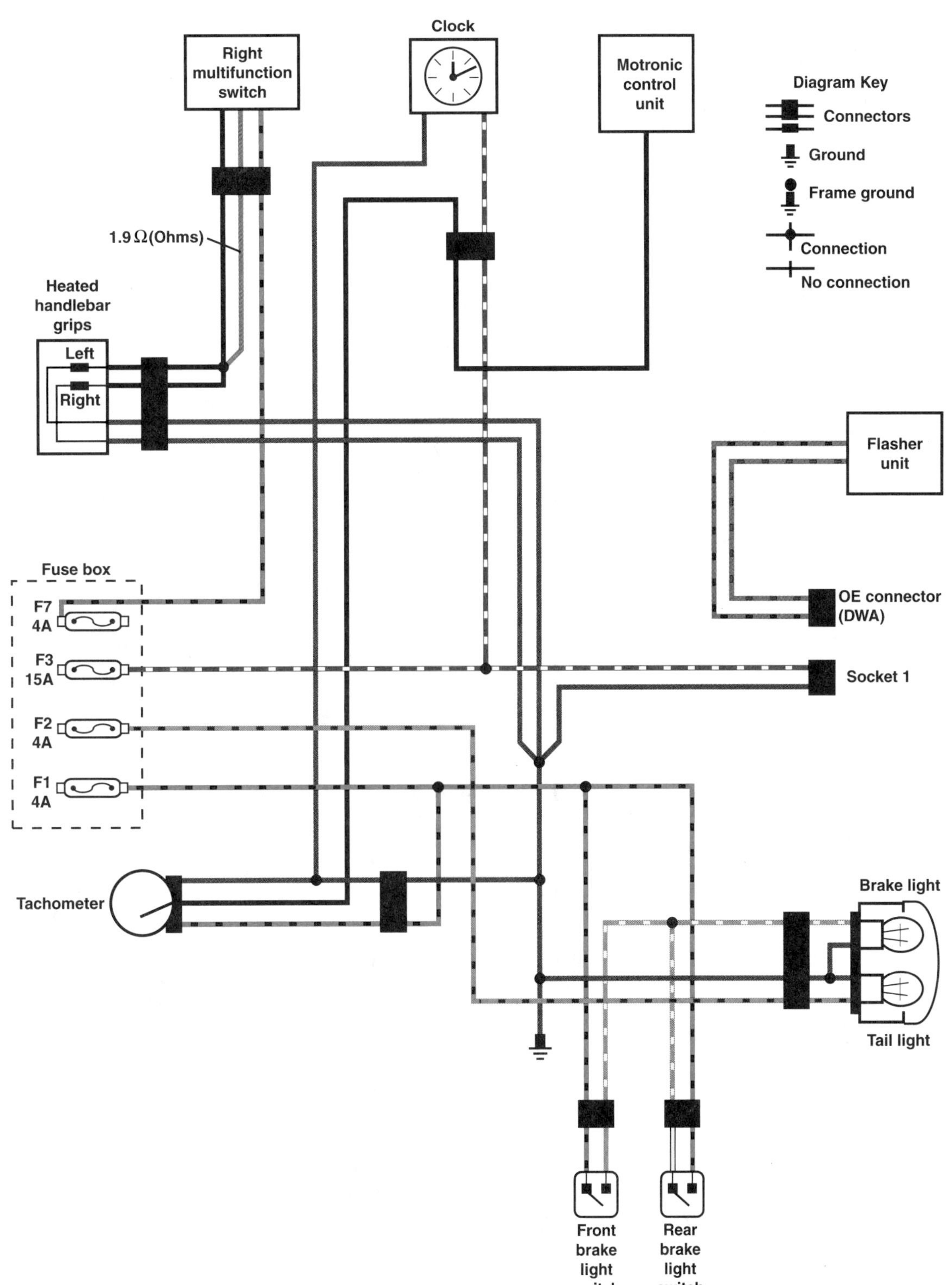

2003-2004 ROCKSTER (U.S)
BRAKE LIGHT AND TAIL LIGHT WITHOUT ABS ACCESSORIES

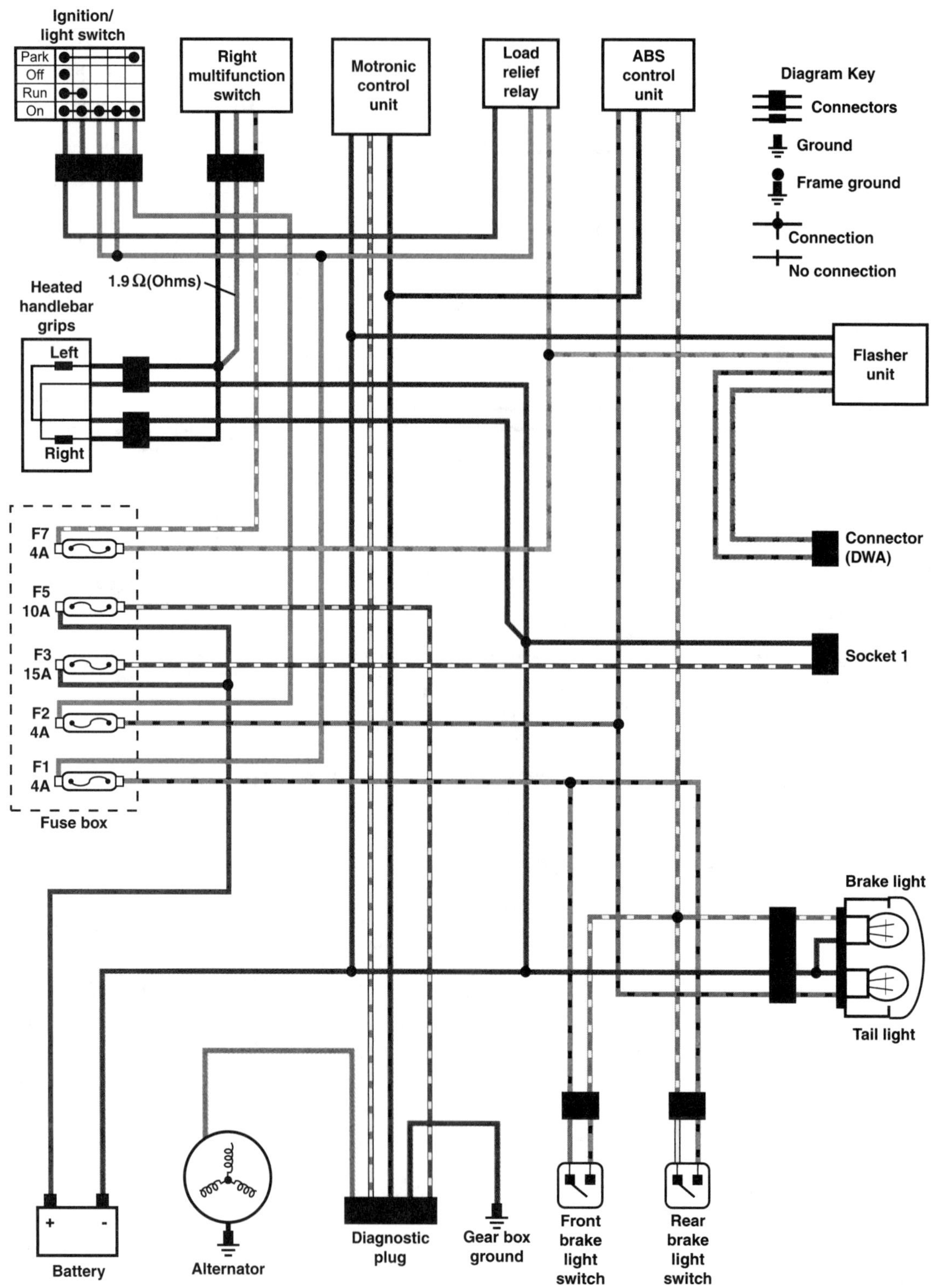

2001 R1150RS (U.K.) AND 2002-2004 R1150RS (U.S.) BRAKE LIGHT AND TAIL LIGHT WITHOUT ABS

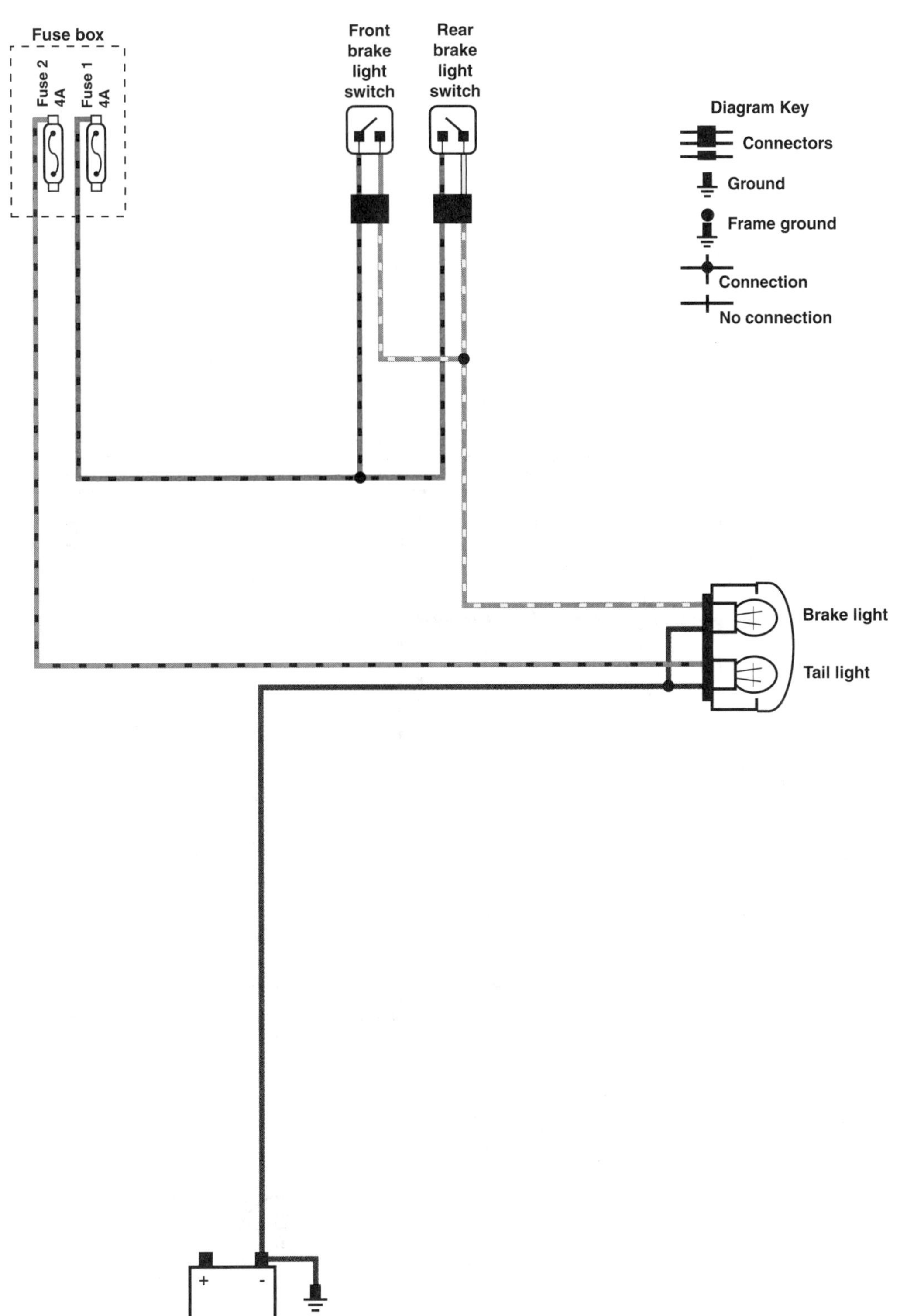

2003-2004 ROCKSTER (U.S.)
INSTRUMENT PANEL WITH ABS

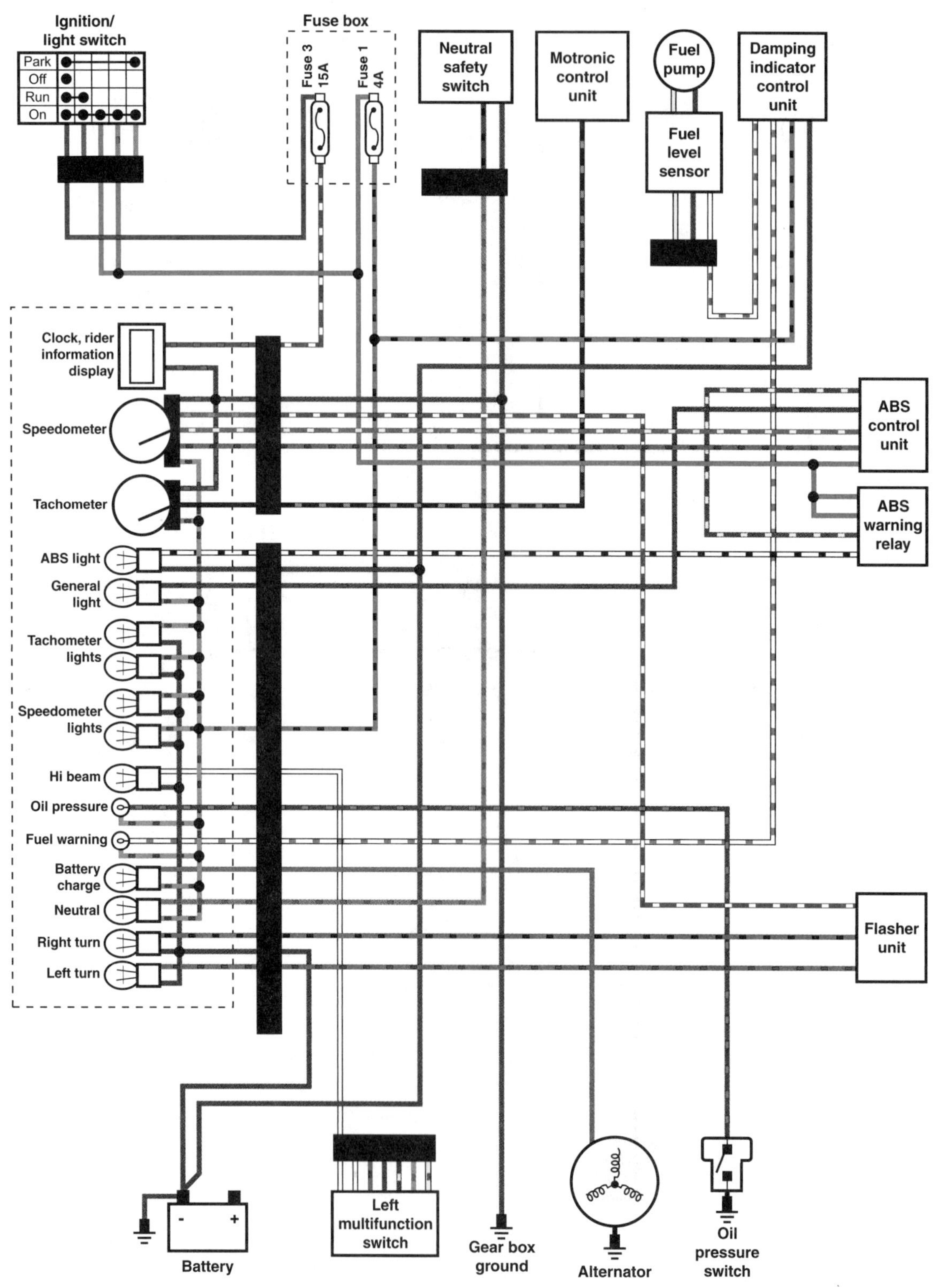

2003-2004 ROCKSTER (U.S.) INSTRUMENT PANEL WITHOUT ABS

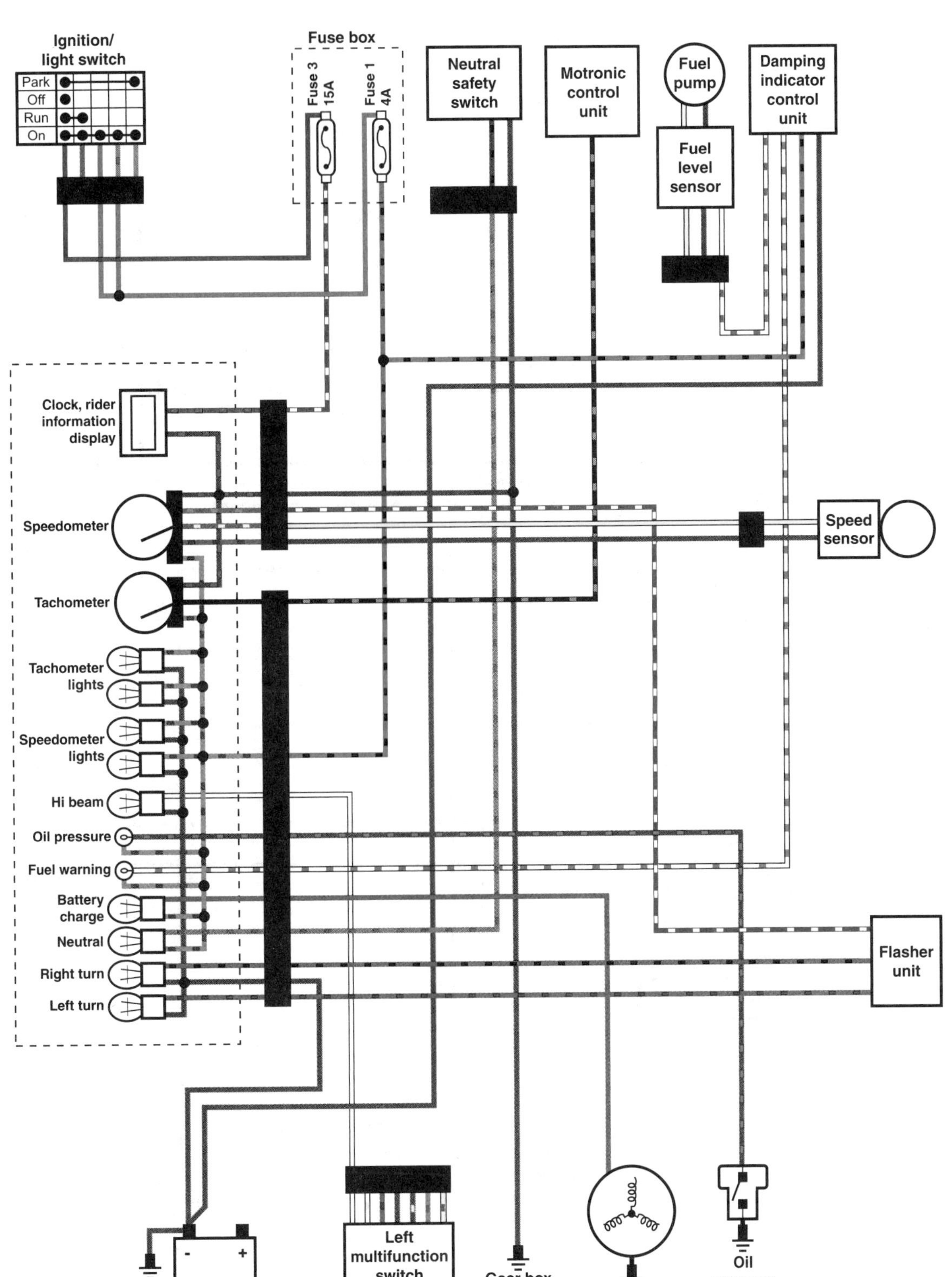

2001 R1150RS (U.K.) AND 2002-2004 R1150RS (U.S.) INSTRUMENT CLUSTER/RIDER INFORMATION DISPLAY

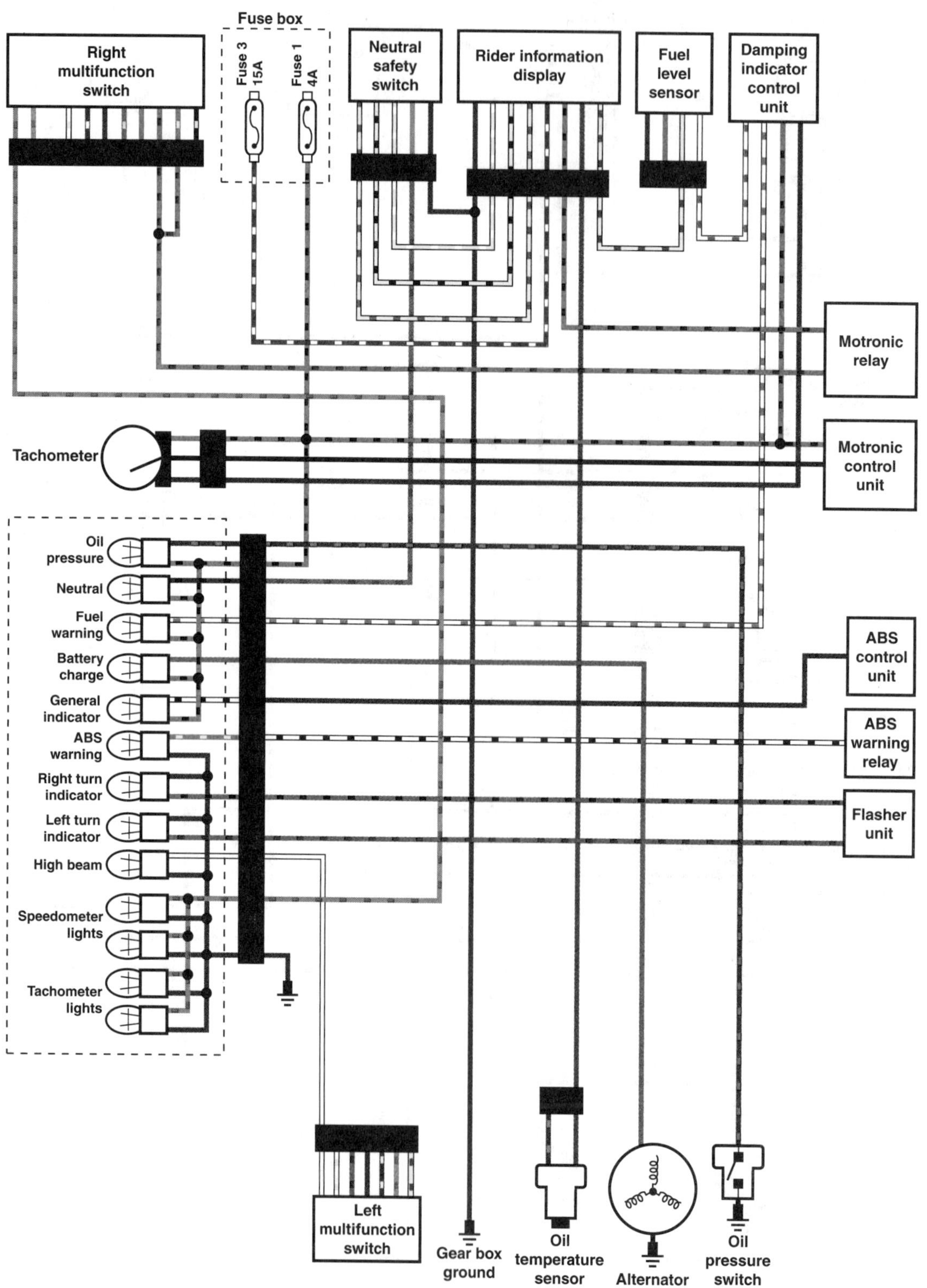

1998 R1200C (U.K.), 1999-2004 R1200C (U.S.), 1999-2001 R850C (U.S. AND U.K.), 1999-2004 R1100S (U.S.) AND 2000-2003 R1100S (U.K.) ACCESSORIES

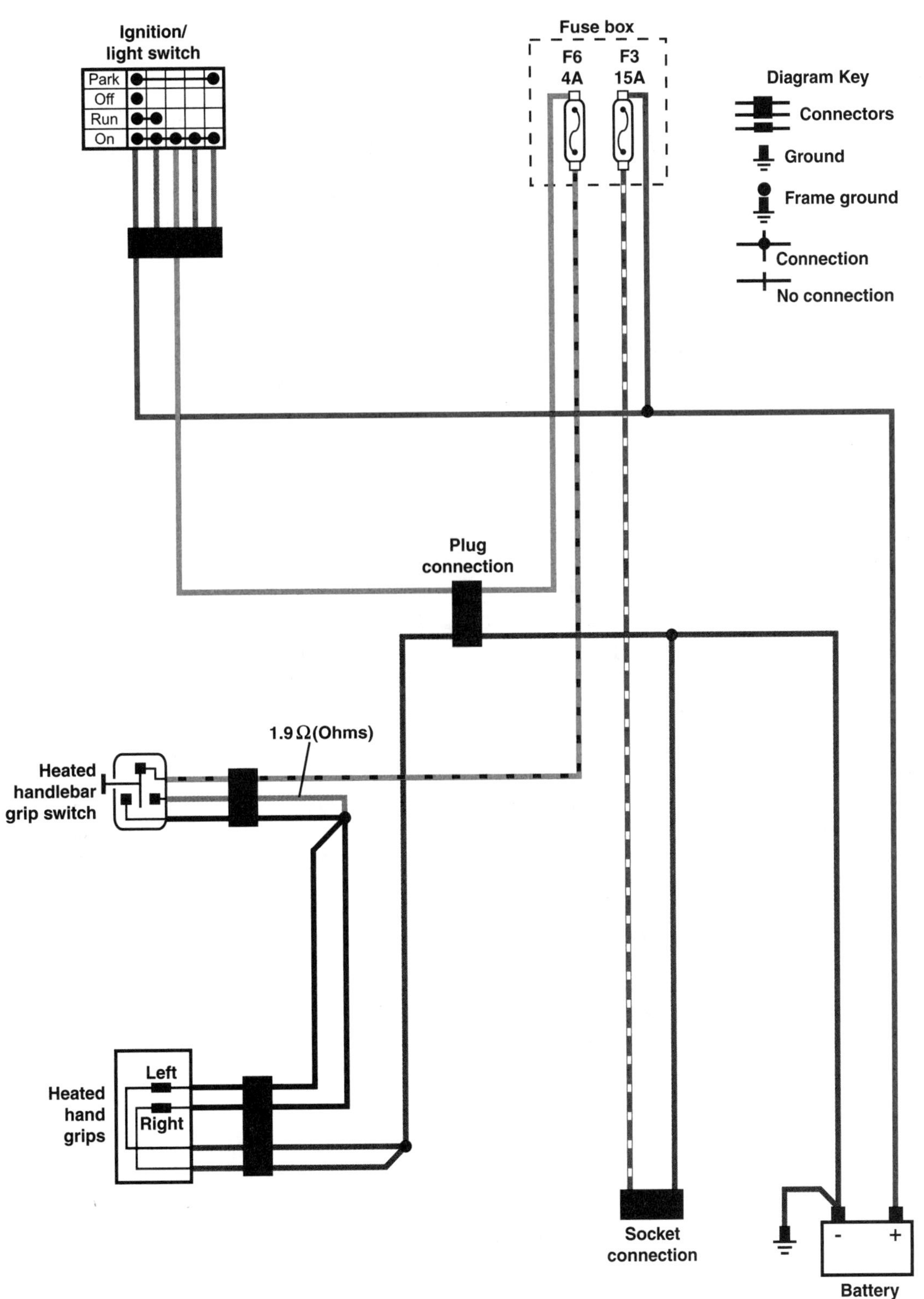

1999-2003 R1150GS (U.K.) AND 2000-2004 R1150GS (U.S.) ACCESSORIES

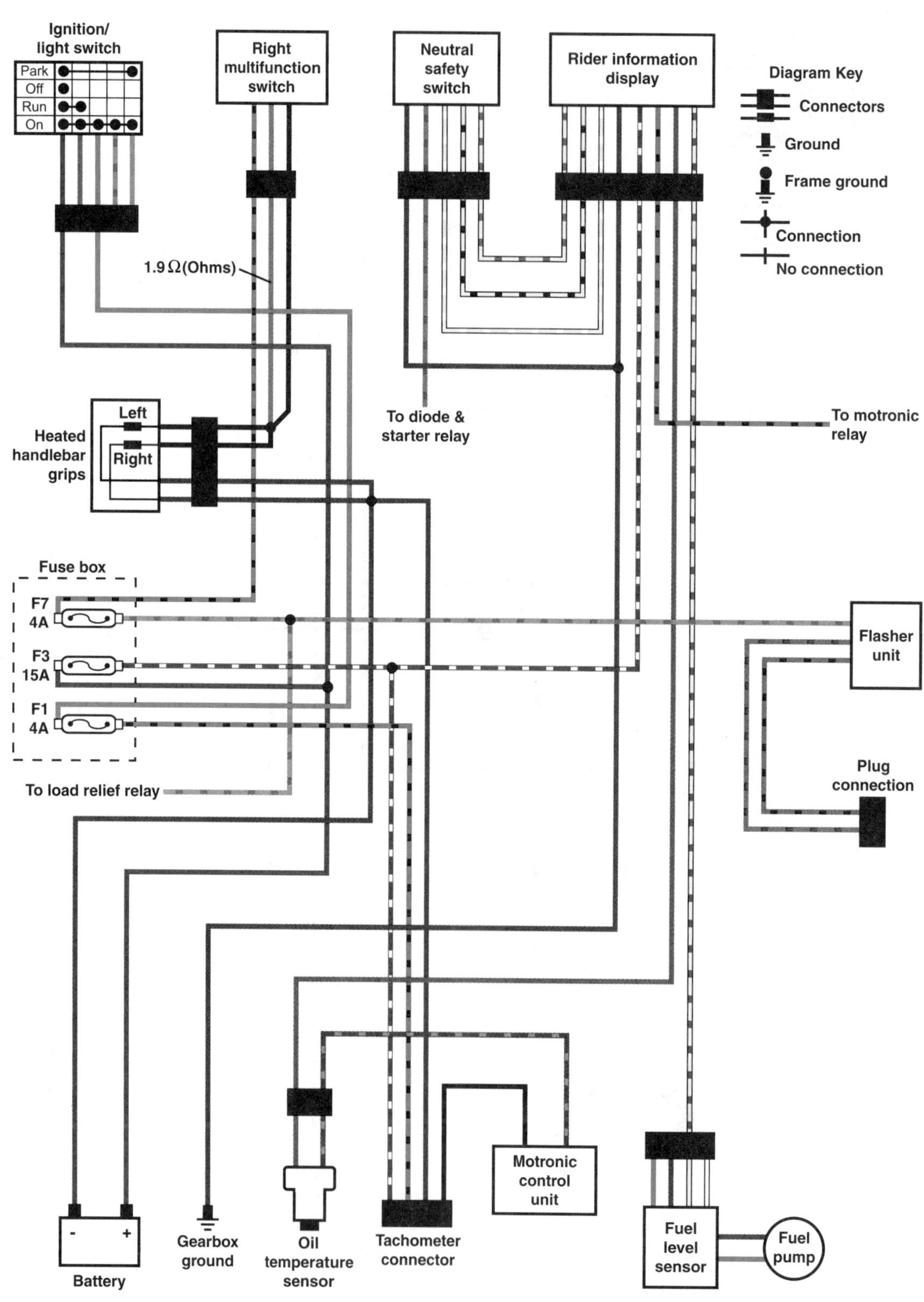

2001 R1150RS (U.K.) AND 2002-2004 R1150RS (U.S.) ACCESSORIES

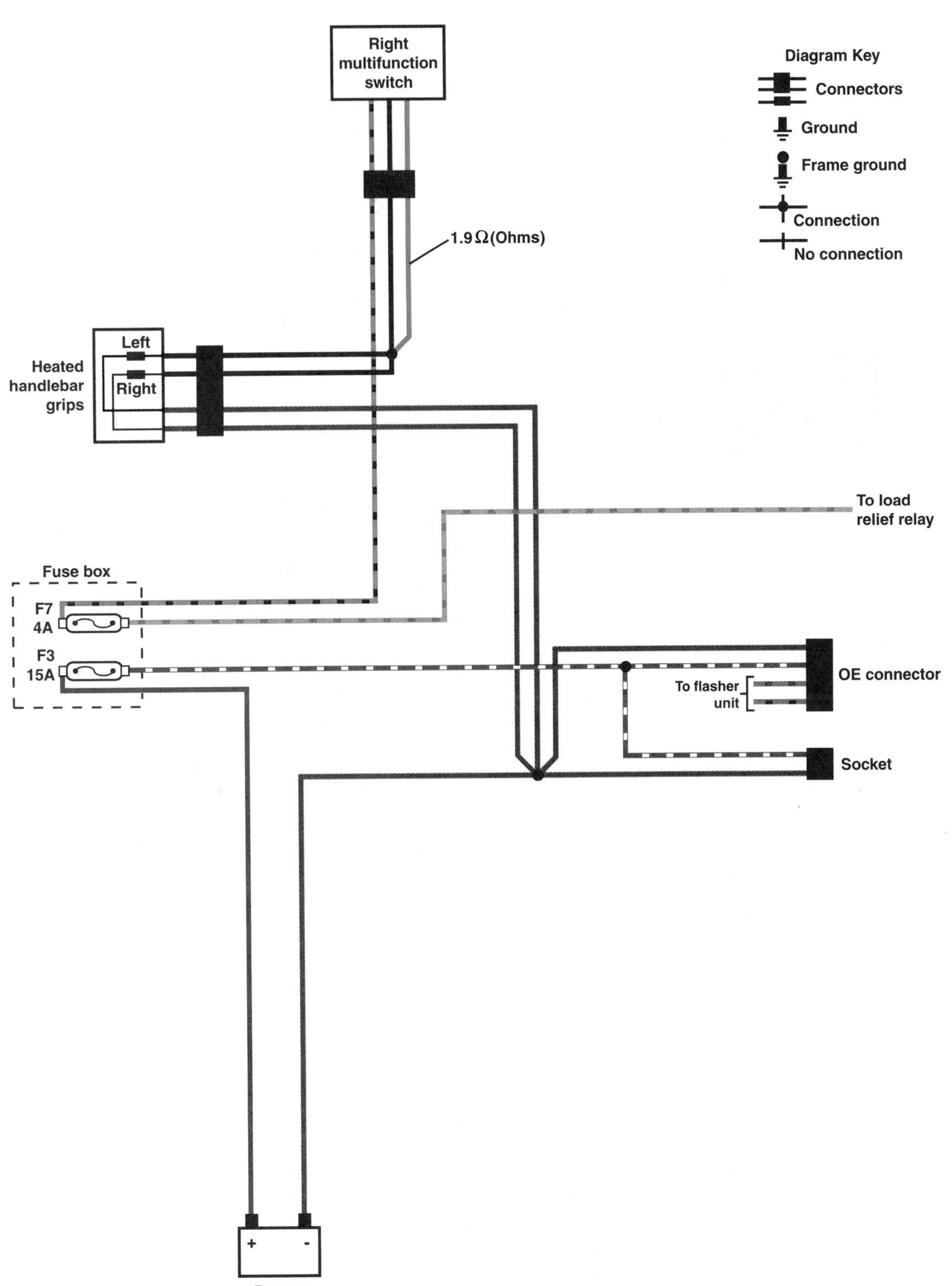

2000-2003 R1150RT (U.K.) AND 2002-2004 R1150RT (U.S.) ACCESSORIES

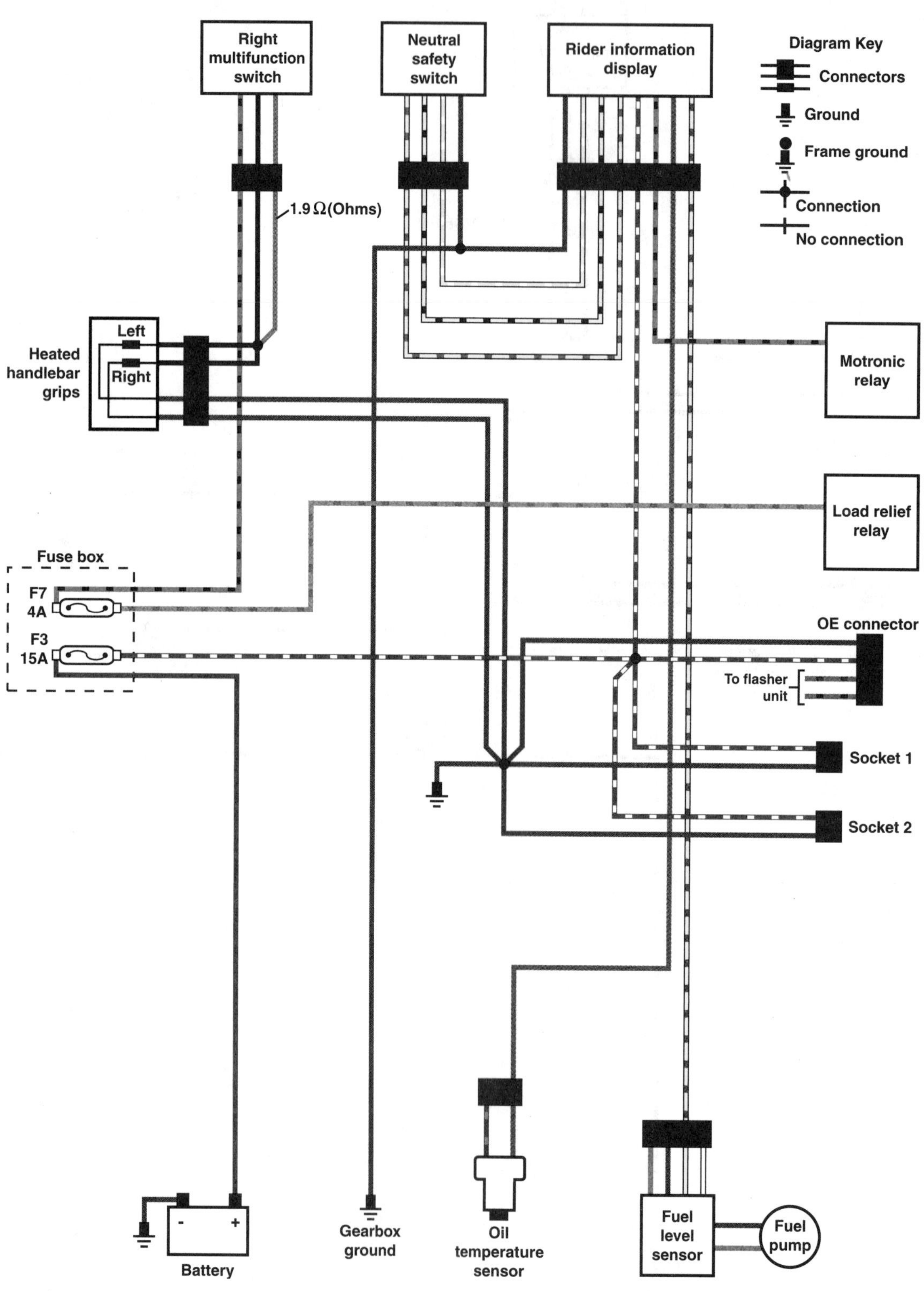

1995-2001 R1100RT RADIO

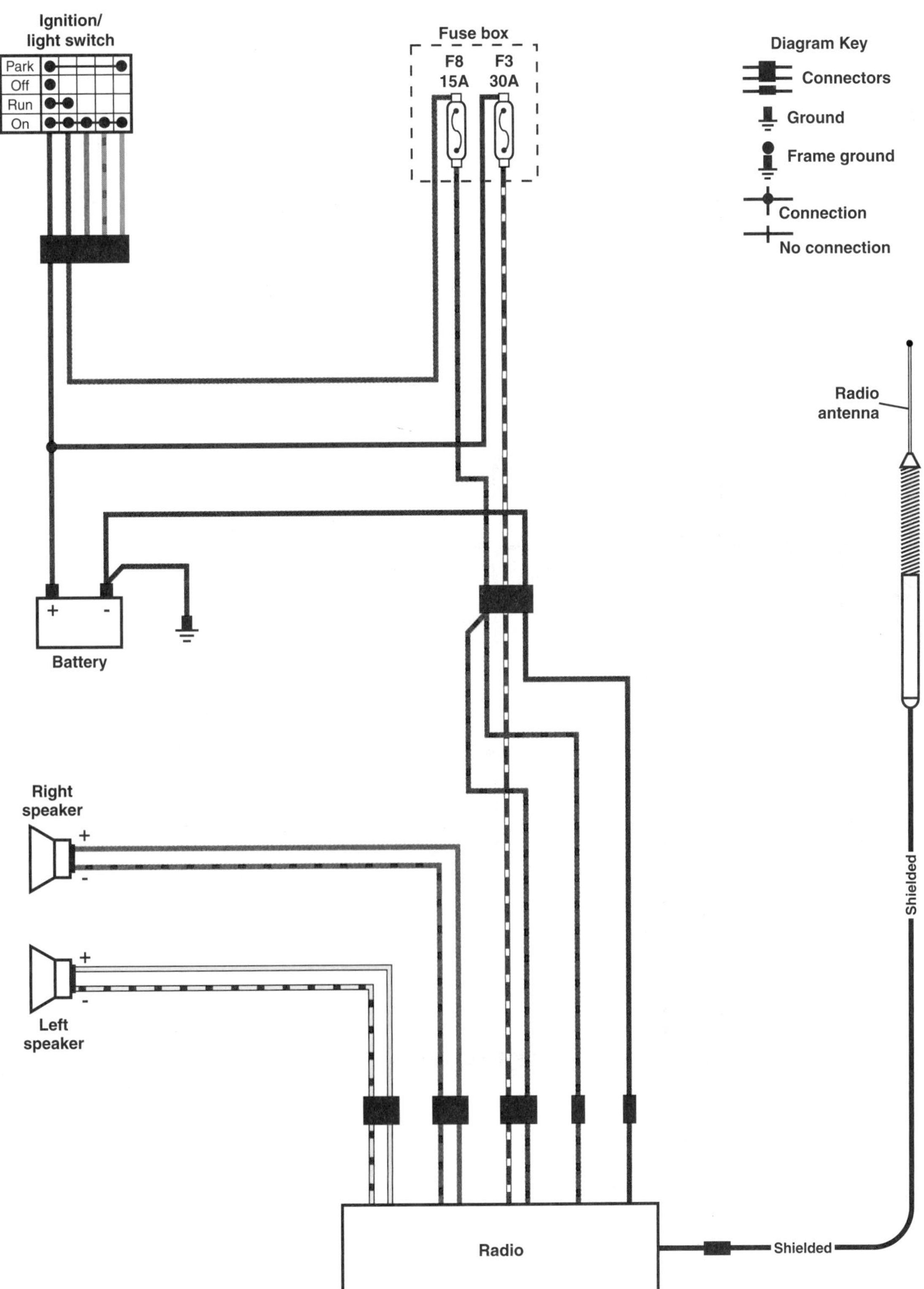

2000-2003 R1150RT (U.K.) AND 2002-2004 R1150RT (U.S.) RADIO

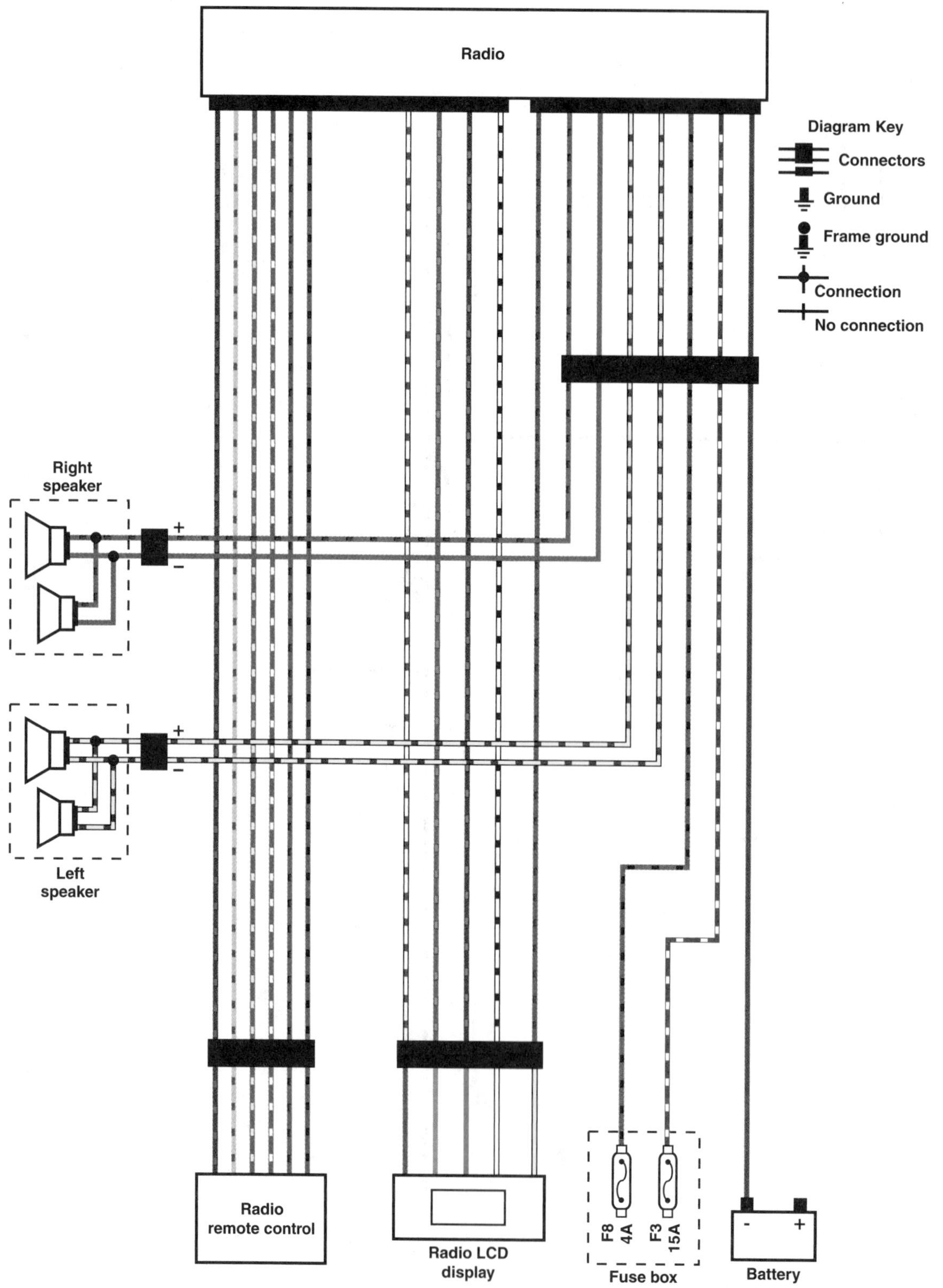

1995-2001 R1100RT (U.S. AND U.K.), 2000-2003 R1150RT (U.K.) AND 2002-2004 R1150RT (U.S.) WINDSHIELD

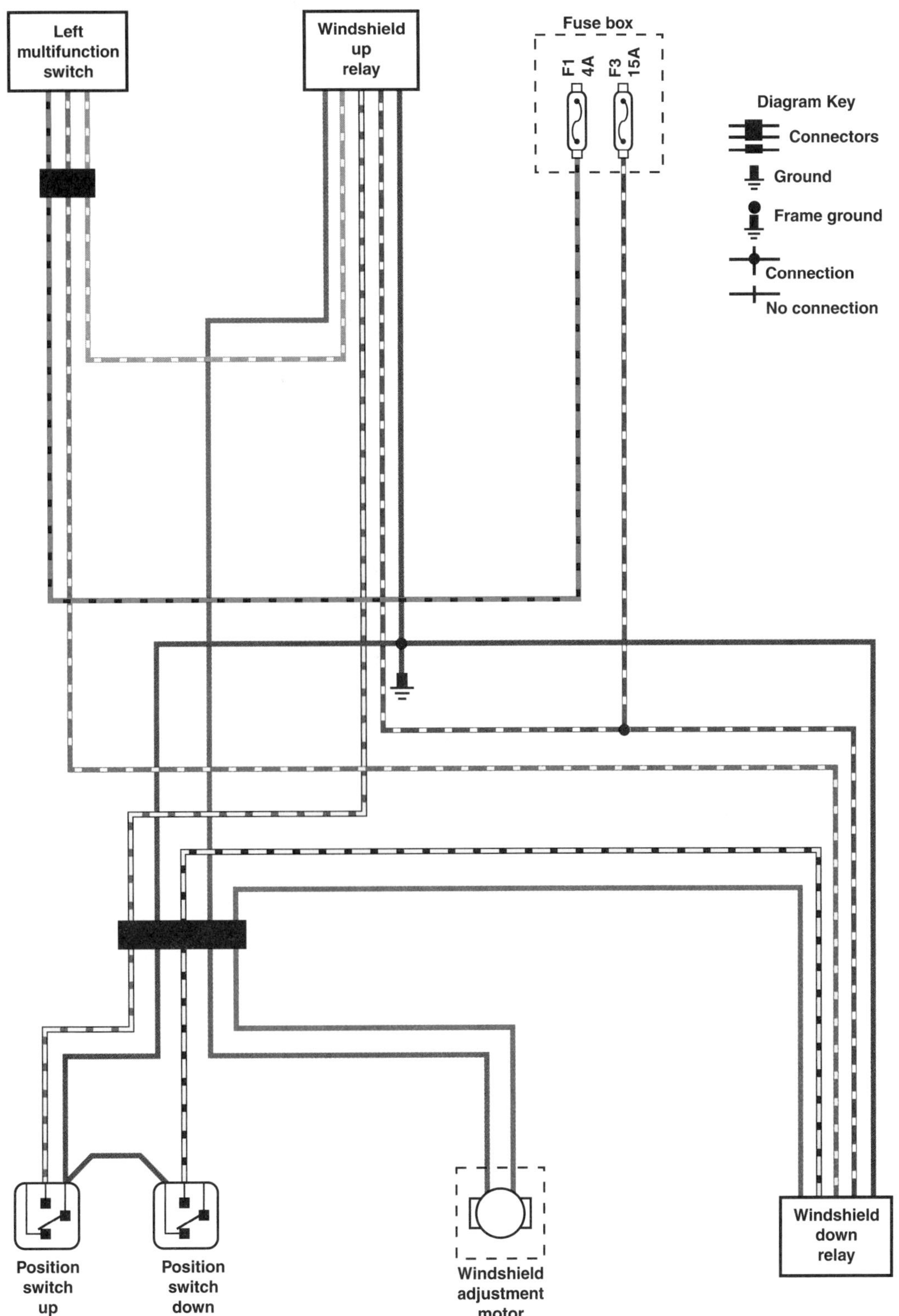

17

NOTES

MAINTENANCE LOG

Date	Miles	Type of Service